THE YALE EDITION

OF

HORACE WALPOLE'S

CORRESPONDENCE

EDITED BY W. S. LEWIS

(1895–1979)

VOLUME FORTY-SEVEN

HORACE WALPOLE'S CORRESPONDENCE

COMPLETE INDEX

COMPILED BY
WARREN HUNTING SMITH
WITH THE ASSISTANCE OF
EDWINE M. MARTZ, RUTH K. McCLURE,
AND WILLIAM T. LA MOY

IV

MOLÉ *TO* SALLIER

NEW HAVEN
YALE UNIVERSITY PRESS
OXFORD · OXFORD UNIVERSITY PRESS

1983

Molé, Édouard (1540–1616):
  Nanteuil's print of, **15.** 100
Molé, Édouard-François-Mathieu (1760–94), Comte de Champlâtreux; Marquis de Méry:
  marriage of, **7.** 109
Molé, François-René (1734–1802), actor:
  acts in: *Britannicus*, **7.** 277; *Fausse Agnès*, **7.** 275; *Hamlet*, **42.** 213n; *Honnête criminel, L'*, **4.** 22; *Phèdre*, **7.** 275
  Clairon, Mlle, gives benefit for, **3.** 201, 230, 234, 237, 240
  Ducis's *Hamlet* could not be saved by, **42.** 213
  Du Deffand, Mme, admires 'Hamlet' of, **4.** 282
  HW sees, in comedies, **7.** 263
  HW's opinion of, **39.** 213
  imprisoned for refusing to act, **38.** 538n
  song for Clairon's performance for, **8.** 129–30
Molé, Mathieu-François (1705–93), président:
  Hénault's social relations with, **7.** 299
  son of, **7.** 109
Mole; moles (maritime):
  at Leghorn, **17.** 303, **18.** 27, **25.** 581
  at Naples, **22.** 6
Molehill:
  African, outshines SH, **42.** 117
Molenist; Molenists:
  Damiens may have been instigated by, **21.** 48
Molesey, Surrey:
  HW to visit Suttons at, **12.** 154
Molesey Hurst:
  Hampton Races held at, **32.** 137n
Molesworth, Vcts. *See* Alleyne, Mary Anne (ca 1730–1819); Lucas, Jane (d. 1742); Usher, Mary Jenney (ca 1723–63)
Molesworth, Hon. Amelia (d. 1758):
  family of, **37.** 356
Molesworth, Hon. Charlotte (b. 1755):
  birth of, **22.** 140
Molesworth, Hon. Coote (ca 1697–1782), M.D.:
  escapes fire at sister-in-law's, **22.** 139, 140, **38.** 201
  sister-in-law persuades her husband to give annuity to, **22.** 140
Molesworth, Mrs Coote. *See* Palmer, Mary
Molesworth, Eleanor (d. 1784):
  in Yorkshire, **39.** 109
Molesworth, Hon. Elizabeth (1751–1835), m. James Stewart:
  escapes fire in Upper Brook St, **22.** 139–40, **38.** 201
  family of, **37.** 356
  refuses to eat, **22.** 146
  sister visited by, **22.** 145
  uncle sees leap of, **22.** 139
Molesworth, Frances (b. 1756–62, d. 1829), m. (1785) Hon. John Jeffreys Pratt, styled Vct Bayham, 1786; 2d E. Camden, 1794; cr. (1812) M. of Camden:
  biographical information on, **43.** 103
  fortune of, nursed by Lucan after Molesworth depleted it, **33.** 506n

HW calls, 'Vice-Queen,' **12.** 152
Lucan entertains, **33.** 254
Lucan family accompanied by, to Florence, **24.** 417
Mann receives sooty drawings from, **24.** 462
—— saw, with her aunt and cousin, **25.** 620
marriage of, **25.** 620, **33.** 506
Shelburne rejected by, **7.** 13, **24.** 317, **33.** 6
Shelburne, Cts of, visited by, **32.** 153
title of husband of, corrected, **43.** 286
Molesworth, Hon. Henrietta (1745–1813) m. (1774) Rt Hon. John Staples:
  escapes fire in Upper Brook St, **22.** 139
  family of, **37.** 356
  Grosvenor, Lady, visited by, **22.** 145–6
  leg of, cut off after fire, **22.** 139, 145, **38.** 201
Molesworth, Hon. Letitia (d. 1787), m. (1753) Lt-Col. James Molesworth:
  family of, **37.** 356
Molesworth, Hon. Louisa (1749–1824), m. 1 (1769) William Brabazon Ponsonby, cr. (1806) Bn Ponsonby; m. 2 (1823) William Fitzwilliam, 4th E. of Fitzwilliam, 1756:
  escapes fire in Upper Brook St, **22.** 140, **38.** 201
  family of, **37.** 356
Molesworth, Hon. Mary (d. after 1774), m. (1736) Robert Rochfort, cr. (1738) Bn and (1751) Vct Belfield, (1756) E. of Belvidere:
  beauty of, **18.** 220
  family of, **37.** *356*
  Rochfort's affair with, **18.** 220
Molesworth, Hon. Mary (b. 1744):
  birth of, **22.** 140
Molesworth, Hon. Mary (1747–63):
  burnt in fire in Upper Brook St, **22.** 138, 145, **38.** 201
  family of, **37.** 356
Molesworth, Hon. Melesina (1746–63):
  burnt in fire in Upper Brook St, **22.** 138, 145, **38.** 201
  family of, **37.** 356
Molesworth, Richard (ca 1680–1758), 3d Vct Molesworth, 1726; M.P.; army officer:
  Conway sees, in Dublin, exhibiting decay, **37.** 356
  daughter of, **18.** 220
  dragoons under, **37.** 31n, 45n
  moribund, but has young wife and large family, **37.** 356
  wife of, **22.** 140
  wife persuades, to give annuity to his brother, **22.** 140
Molesworth, Richard Nassau (1748–93), 4th Vct Molesworth, 1758:
  family of, **37.** 356
  SH visited by, **12.** 221
  Westminster schoolboy, **22.** 140
Molesworth, Robert (1656–1725), cr. (1716) Vct Molesworth, M.P.; writer:
  Shaftesbury's letters to, **16.** 369
Molesworth, Robert (1729–1813), 5th Vct

[Molesworth, Robert (1729–1813), *continued*]
Molesworth, 1793; army officer:
Conway, Hon. Henrietta Seymour, wants HW to ask Conway to get promotion for, in Dragoons, 39. 109–12
Molesworth, Mrs Robert. *See* Alleyne, Mary Anne
Molesworth, William (1763–1815), 6th Vct Molesworth, 1813:
in Yorkshire, 39. 109
Molesworth, Sir William:
Molesworth, Frances, cheated by, 33. 506n
Molesworth family:
George II's and George III's pensions to, 37. 356n
Molette, Jean-François-Charles de (b. 1726), Comte de Morangiès:
sentenced, 5. 364–6, 401
Voltaire defends, 5. 400–1, 419, 28. 279n
Moleyns, Catherine (d. 1465), m. John Howard, D. of Norfolk:
shield of, 16. 86n
Moleyns. *See also* Molyneux
Molière (Jean-Baptiste Poquelin) (1622–73), dramatist:
Amphitryon, HW alludes to Cardinal and D. of York as characters in, 22. 257
Aristophanes inferior to, 41. 155
Avare, L': Du Deffand, Mme, cites, 4. 393; frontispiece to, by Hogarth, 43. 220; HW and Gray see poor performance of, 13. 162; HW quotes, 33. 375; Hogarth's frontispiece to translation of, 16. 173
Bourgeois gentilhomme, Le: 'Mamamouchi' in, compared to D. of Newcastle, 20. 72; *New Ode* alludes to, 18. 52; read by Le Texier, 33. 383
(?) Chamfort eulogizes, 7. 326
Colisée to supersede, 39. 145
comedy had court fools until time of, 41. 153
Comtesse d'Escarbagnas, La, 7. 317
Dépit amoureux, Le, paraphrased, 32. 248
École des femmes, L', Du Deffand, Mme, quotes, 4. 495, 5. 412, 7. 39
École des maris, L', 7. 277
Femmes savantes, Les: Du Deffand, Mme, cites, 3. 262; recited by Mme du Deffand's guests, 5. 117, 7. 350
Fourberies de Scapin, Les: 28. 39n; Du Deffand, Mme, paraphrases, 3. 331, 4. 267, 274; HW quotes, 10. 251, 28. 39
French abandon, 31. 43
HW likes, 6. 44
HW mentions, 10. 283
HW praises, 33. 492
housekeeper's judgment trusted by, more than Boileau's, 41. 372
Malade imaginaire, Le, physician in, 19. 256
Médecin malgré lui, Le: 35. 420; HW alludes to, 28. 218; HW mentions, 9. 321; HW quotes, 34. 90
Misanthrope, Le, by: and *George Dandin* are

serious comedies by, 41. 153–4; Du Deffand, Mme, absents self from, 4. 131; Du Deffand, Mme, cites, 3. 126, 4. 18, 422, 6. 339; Du Deffand, Mme, paraphrases song in, 3. 91; HW paraphrases song in, 3. 44; HW sees, 7. 345; (?) HW to see, 6. 217; to be recited by Mme du Deffand's guests, 5. 117
no arrogance in, 33. 537
Parisians are weary of, 13. 162
Pinkerton depreciates, 33. 492
Précieuses ridicules, Les, 7. 272
Sganarelle, Hogarth's frontispiece to translation of, 16. 173
Tartuffe, Le: 4. 222, 7. 265; banned by Abp of Paris, 18. 63; Cibber's *Nonjuror* adapted from, 33. 492; *Don Pilogio* imitates, 18. 41; ladies recite, 6. 466, 7. 350
tragic writers might learn from, 41. 297
Molin, Mme. *See* Lemaure, Catherine-Nicole
Molina, José de (b. 1710) Spanish military gov. of Rio Grande de S. Pedro:
death of, rumoured, 24. 223
Molinari, Marchese —— (b. ca 1724):
Milanese, 18. 138
rich, 18. 29, 138
rich uncle of, vice-legate of Bologna, 18. 138
size of, 18. 29, 138
Suares, Vittoria, wooed by, 18. 29, 138
Molinari, Antonio (1665–1727), painter:
(?) 'Feast of Bacchus' by, in Pierson's sale, 23. 570n
Molinari, Giovanni Carlo (ca 1717–63), Abp of Damascus; legate of Bologna, 1741; nuncio at Brussels:
nephew of, 18. 138
Moline, Pierre-Louis, librettist:
Daphnis and Chloe augmented by, 32. 259n
Molinedo ('Molinero'), Chevalier, secretary to Spanish embassy in London ca 1789–ca 1794:
SH visited by, 12. 232
Molineux, Crisp (1730–92), M.P.:
candidacy of, for King's Lynn, 41. 91
King's Lynn suffers from, 39. 96
Orford, E. of, assists, to become M.P., 39. 96n
reads petition at Cambridge, 2. 207
Wilkes's friend and Chatham's admirer, 39. 96n
Molineux. *See also* Molyneux
Molini, (?) Dr:
Gloucester, D. of, attended by, at Leghorn, 23. 394
Molini, Giuseppe:
(?) printer of *Il Conclave*, 24. 65n, 70
Molini, Polidori, Molini, & Co.:
printers in Haymarket, 35. 436n
Molinos, Miguel da (1640–97), Spanish priest:
quietism the doctrine of, 5. 12n
Moll, Capt.:
Lord Howe commanded by, 32. 387n
Möller, J. G. P. (1729–1807):
Letters on Iceland translated by, 29. 31n
Moll Flanders. See under Defoe, Daniel

Mollineux. *See* Molineux; Molyneux

Mollwitz, battle of:
Frederick II runs away from, 18. 505, 21. 5n

'Moll Volatile Evaporated':
Carter, Mary, signs herself as, 42. 407

'Molly.' *See* Mann, Mary (ca 1718–78); Shadwell, Molly

Moloch:
French Revolution's progress in hands of, 12. 66, 86

Molo di Gaeta:
Orford, Cts of, ill at, 24. 312, 317

Molone [?Maloney *or* Malone], ——, merchant at Cadiz:
ship of, 21. 269

Molowitz; Molwitz. *See* Mollwitz

Molowsky, ——, Russian officer:
Meshcherskiĭ accompanied by, 25. 84n

Molteno, (?) Colnaught, printseller:
SH visited by, 12. 237

Moltke, Anton Hendrik (1734–92), Marshal to Christian VII of Denmark:
HW can tell more of, 35. 329

Molyneux, Lady. *See* Gerard, Frances (d. 1620)

Molyneux, Vcts. *See* Brudenell, Hon. Mary (ca 1680–1766); Stanhope, Lady Isabella (1748–1819)

Molyneux, Misses:
Lobkowitz and Signora Capello accompanied by, 37. 289

Molyneux, Adam de (d. 1450), Bp of Chichester; Keeper of the Privy Seal:
documents witnessed by, 14. 76
murdered by mob, 14. 76

Molyneux, Charles William (1748–95), 8th Vct Molyneux; cr. (1771) E. of Sefton:
death date of, corrected, 43. 353
HW mentions, 5. 75
HW visits, 33. 203
Hobart, Mrs, entertains, at play at Ham Common, 33. 370
mother of, 12. 149n
reports on American affairs, 33. 305, 306
Selwyn sends HW's *Historic Doubts* to Lambert by, for Carlisle, 30. 251–2
wife of, 10. 305n

Molyneux, Sir Francis (before 1737–1812), Kt, 1765; 7th Bt, 1781; gentleman usher of the Black Rod, 1765:
Kingston, Ds of, guarded by, 28. 262
—— threatens, by showing him a pistol-mark, 24. 198

Molyneux, Hon. Mrs Thomas Joseph. *See* Leverly, Maria

Molyneux, William Philip (1772–1838), styled Vct Molyneux; 2d E. of Sefton, 1794:
house of, 12. 169n
SH visited by, 12. 248
Twickenham resident, 42. 481

Molza, Mme (b. ca 1657), Mary of Modena's attendant:
(?) Modena, Ds of, discusses Old Pretender's legitimacy with, 17. 44

Momo (game):
lansquenet resembled by, 17. 194
played, 17. 194, 218

Monaco, P. of. *See* Honoré III (1720–95); Honoré IV (1758–1819)

Monaco, Ps of. *See* Aumont de Mazarin, Louise-Félicité-Victoire d' (1759–1826); Brignole, Marie-Catherine de (1739–1813)

Monaco, 'Prince Joseph of.' *See* Goyon-de-Matignon de Grimaldi, Joseph-Jérôme-Marie-Honoré

Monaco, 'Princess Joseph of.' *See* Choiseul-Stainville, Thérèse-Félicité de

Monaco:
castle at, 4. 455n
Monaco, P. of, at, 6. 212
situation of, awkward, 22. 555
York, D. of, dies at, 7. 321, 365–6, 22. 553–4, 555, 23. 345, 31. 136

Monaco, Hôtel de, Rue de Varenne, Paris:
HW and Mariette visit, 7. 337
Monaco, Ps of, does not return to, 4. 438

Monaghan, Ireland:
Maclaine, Rev. Thomas, Presbyterian minister in, 20. 168n
militia recruiting in, resisted, 39. 323–4

Monaldeschi, Marchese Gian Rinaldo (d. 1657); equerry to Q. Christina:
Christina has, murdered, 9. 272n
Fontainebleau's associations with, 39. 208

Monarca, Spanish ship:
captured, 25. 16n

Monarch, English ship:
La Belle Poule approached by, 24. 395n

Monarch; monarchs:
crimes of, HW's reflections on, 23. 292
HW's reflections on, 22. 254, 25. 336
See also Crown; King; Monarchy; Prince; Royalty

Monarchy:
HW's reflections on, 15. 51

Monarchy or No Monarchy in England. See under Lilly, William

Monarquía eclesiastica, La. See under Pineda, Juan de (d. ca 1593)

Monasteries:
French, to be sold, 42. 286–7
HW interested only in architecture of, 16. 27
See also Convent

Monasticism:
decreased in France before Revolution, 34. 193

Monasticon Anglicanum. See under Dugdale, Sir William

Monasticon Eboracense. See under Burton, John

Monastic orders:
disrepute of, 39. 2
two, reported to have been forbidden by Joseph II to receive new members, 25. 283

Monboddo, Lord. *See* Burnett, James (1714–99)

Moncada, Tommaso; vice-general of Dominican order:
aid for plague victims requested by, 18. 262n

Moncastello. *See* Montcastello; Pavon e Moncastello

Monceaux. *See* Moulceau

Monceaux d'Auxy, Marie-Louise de (ca 1706–83), m. (1720) Jacques-Charles, Marquis de Créqui:
(?) Salm, Ps of, called on by, after duel, 6. 279

Monck, Christopher (?1653–88), 2d D. of Albemarle:
wife of, 10. 109n, 25. 564n

Monck *or* Monk, George (1608–70), cr. (1660) D. of Albemarle:
Dumouriez compared to, 12. 1, 2
French counterpart of, may arise, 31. 324
letter by, sent to HW by Dalrymple, 15. 36–7
monument to, 13. 25n
portrait of, 40. 284
statue of, in Westminster Abbey, 38. 126

Monckton, John (1695–1751), cr. (1727) Vct Galway; M.P.:
brag to be played by, out of town to avoid earthquake, 20. 137

Monckton, Mary (1748–1840), m. (1786) Edmund Boyle, 7th E. of Corke, 1764:
HW visits, and sees her dance, 33. 321

Monckton, Hon. Robert (1726–82); army officer; M.P.:
Beau Séjour captured by, 35. 240
letter of, about Martinique capture: HW compares, with Thucydides and Mlle de Scudéry, 10. 22; *London Gazette* prints, 10. 22
Martinique conquered by, 10. 22, 22. 15–16, 21, 29–30
—— news awaited from, 22. 7n
Pitt receives from, news of Quebec capture, 21. 337n
wounded at Quebec, 21. 338

Monckton, William (?1725–72), 6th Vct Galway, 1751; M.P.:
brother of, 22. 15n

Monclar, Marquis de. *See* Ripert, Jean-Pierre-François de

Monconseil, Marquis de. *See* Guignot, Étienne-Louis-Antoine

Monconseil, Marquise de. *See* Rioult de Douilly, Claire-Cécile-Thérèse-Pauline

Monconseil, Étiennette Guignot de. *See* Guignot de Monconseil

Moncour (Lorraine):
Richecourt buys, 21. 62n

Moncrif. *See* Paradis de Moncrif

Mon dernier mot. See under Clément, Jean-Marie-Bernard

Mondo della luna. See under Galuppi, Baldassare

Mondomaine, ——, Choiseul's servant:
escapes injury, 5. 122

Mondonville. *See* Cassanea de Mondonville

Mondovi (Italy):
Maillebois and Don Philip may march by, 19. 58

Moneta di dieci paoli:
value of, 17. 82n

Money, ——, Maj.:
Orford, E. of, said to entertain, at High Beech, 25. 596n

Money, John (fl. 1734–59), King's messenger:
Chute's letter sent by, 35. 3
Genoa visited by, with dispatches for Rowley, 19. 12
HW reassures Mann about, 17. 152
Mann sends, to Hanover instead of England, 17. 113, 115, 208
—— sends letters to HW by, 17. 115, 144
Turin visited by, 19. 12
Walpole, Bns (Cts of Orford) to receive leases from, 17. *108*, 113, 115
Walpole, Sir Robert, orders, to find HW, 17. 108, 115
Wilkes not arrested by, 38. 197n

Money, John (1752–1817), aeronaut; officer:
Orford, E. of, encourages balloon ascent by, 25. 596

Money:
Conway would not use, as well as HW, 37. 172
Dutch give, to soldiers, 37. 276
HW advises Cole about exchange in, on going to France, 1. 98
HW's advice from Conway about, 37. 39
HW's ignorance of, 36. 96
HW's reflections on folly of worry over, 34. 192
Haarlem mob throws excisemen's into canal, 37. 286
half of, in England, sacrificed to encourage vice, 37. 172
ignorance of Dutch language creates problems about, 37. 134
Mann's reflections about, 22. 353
man-of-war drops, at Minorca for garrison, 37. 313
metallic, proved useless by French Revolution, 31. 377–8
paper: French prefer, to gold and silver, 31. 378; HW's reflections on, 31. 377–8; *see also* Assignats
pleasure does not recognize want of, 25. 243
See also Currency; Riches; Wealth

Money Bill. *See under* Parliament, Irish: acts of

Moneyers. *See* Corporation of Moneyers

Monfaucon. *See* Montfaucon

'Monfort, M. de.' *See* Phélypeaux, Jean-Frédéric

Monfort. *See also* Montfort

Mongewell, Oxon:
Guise of, 11. 288n

Mongez, Antoine (1747–1835):
Histoire de la reine Marguerite de Valois:
Mme du Deffand owns, 8. 34; (?) Mme du Deffand reads, 6. 412

'Mongibel, Baron de':
Mann may receive title of, 18. 484

Monier, Le. *See* Le Monnier

'Monimia':

in Otway's *Orphan*, **40.** 374
nickname of Gen. Harvey's mistress, **11.** 61
'Monimia to Philocles.' *See under* Hervey, John, Bn Hervey
Monimo. *See* Moñino
Monin, ——:
  HW's letter to be sent to Hertford by, **38.** 282, 290, 296, 306, 314, 323, 328, 332, 336
  Hertford, Cts of, receives two letters through, **38.** 314
  Versailles visited by, **38.** 314
Moñino, Don Francisco, Spanish envoy to Tuscany 1782–4:
  brother said to tell state secrets to, **25.** 416–17
  Charles III declared by, to be able to have Gibraltar when he pleases, **25.** 416
  Crillon writes to, **25.** 340
  Gibraltar news from, **25.** 300n
  Mann calls, poor senseless creature, **25.** 416
  —— told by, of French victory, **25.** 393
  Maria Louisa receives letters through, **25.** 334
  receives letters about Gibraltar, **25.** 324, (?) 334
  Spanish gazette published by, in Italian, **25.** 329
  Tuscan Court always attended by, at Pisa, **25.** 334, 548
Moñino y Redondo, José (1728–1808), cr. (1773) Conde de Floridablanca; Spanish ambassador to Rome 1772–6; prime minister 1777–92:
  Almodóvar's dispatches from, **24.** 458n
  brother said to hear state secrets from, **25.** 416–17
  Charles III told by, of Pius VI's intention to release Jesuits, **24.** 115
  Charles IV receives witty retort from, **11.** 54
  Clement XIV expects, **23.** *413*
  —— threatened by, for not expelling Jesuits, **23.** 428, 430
  —— told by, that Jesuits' total suppression alone can satisfy Charles III, **23.** 446
  Cumberland's negotiations with, **25.** 82n
  death date of, corrected, **43.** 284
  Ferdinand of Parma's rift with Charles III proposed by, for Clement XIV's mediation, **23.** 473n
  Fitzherbert's negotiations with, **39.** 478n
  France cannot seduce, against Spanish interests, **24.** 478
  France wanted by, to send ships to Santo Domingo, **24.** 300n
  French negotiations by, for invasion of England, **24.** 478n
  friends who knew, at Rome, inform Mann of his character, **24.** 478
  Grantham notified by, of Almodóvar's leaving Madrid, **24.** 366n
  Grimaldi succeeded by, as Spanish prime minister, **24.** 263n
  Jesuits' suppression aided by, **23.** 473n
  Pairet stabs, **11.** 76

Spain prevented by, from joining English-French naval pact, **24.** 300n
Tanucci blames, for rumours of Clement XIV's poisoning, **24.** 42n
Vergennes plans attack on England with, **24.** 437n
Moniteur universel, Le:
  Dupont's speech printed in, **31.** 381n
Monitor (periodical):
  Russians will not waste time writing, **22.** 60
  Shebbeare the author of, **21.** 39
Monk (surname). *See* Monck
Monk; monks:
  Carthusian, HW to become, **13.** 181
  Chute and HW to be buried by, **35.** 131
  Cole's partiality for, **1.** 129
  doom of religion reflected by, in France, **35.** 127
  dress of, **13.** 210
  fifteenth-century, Chatterton's poetry not in the language of, **16.** 340–1
  Franciscan: account of journey of, to Jerusalem, **14.** 174–5; Gray's, HW wants dates of, **14.** 178
  Franciscan and Olivetan in Bologna, **13.** 193
  HW on, **1.** 330
  HW on historical writings of, **1.** 129
  of Somersetshire would not use same dialect as Scottish bishop, **16.** 351–2
  only learned people of their time, **16.** 352
  sensible in building good mansions, **35.** 305
  superstition disclaimed by, **13.** 170
  topographers praise, **16.** 26
  See also Convent; Friar; Monastery; Monasticism, *and under names of orders*
Monkey; monkeys:
  Conway to be followed by, in green and orange cockades, **37.** 371
  element of: in human composition, **23.** 192, 194, 201; suggested by Voltaire's *Candide*, **43.** 283
  English resemble, **35.** 364
  fowls plucked by, in kitchen, **33.** 515–16
  HW calls himself, **31.** 114
  HW compares D. of Newcastle to an old, **31.** 68-9
  HW plays with, **41.** 5
  heraldic supporters of Fitzgerald family are, **34.** 177
  in Clermont's paintings, **35.** 79n
  in Haymarket, **42.** 506
  in portrait of Lord Rochester, **32.** 353
  jerboa resembles, **9.** 142
  La Fontaine stresses characteristics of, **41.** 29
  Mathews's crew hang crucifix on neck of, **18.** 79n
  parrot destroyed by, **33.** 515–16
  pertness of, **16.** 271
  Richmond, D. of, compared to, **36.** 222
  Temple, Cts, mentions, in verses, **10.** 115
  to be sent to London, **37.** 24
  worship of, on banks of Thames, **33.** 399
  See also 'Jackoo, General'; 'Pug'

Monkey Island, in the Thames:
Marlborough, D. of, has, as fishing preserve, **9.** 20n
Montagu visits, **9.** 20
Monkhouse, Thomas:
Clarendon's *State Papers* edited by, **33.** 549n
Monluc, Damien de (ca 1587–1612), Seigneur de Balagny:
Herbert mentions men killed by, in duels, **40.** 357
Pinocin mortally wounds, **40.** 357
Monmayeux, Marie-Marthe (d. 1794), m. (1764) Jean-François de la Harpe:
leaves Voltaire, **4.** 42
Monmouth, D. of. *See* Scott, James (1649–85)
Monmouth, E. of. *See* Carey, Henry
Monmouth, English ship:
Foudroyant fired on by, **21.** 193
French ships pursued by, **19.** 411
Gardiner, capt. of, **21.** 193n
Hervey's ship, **21.** 225n
in Mediterranean in Osborne's squadron, **21.** 135n
Monmouth, Monmouthshire:
Cadogan, Lady, accompanies Cooper to jail at, **36.** 329
Monmouth, New Jersey:
battle of: **28.** 409n, 433n; Congress dismisses Lee for misconduct at, **20.** 363n; Mann praises Clinton's conduct at, **24.** 408; Mann to consider, an English victory, **24.** 405–6
Monmouthshire:
Mathews opposes Tories in election at, **19.** 33
Morgan remains lord lieutenant of, **23.** 174
Williams, Sir C. H., erroneously said to resign lord lieutenancy of, **30.** 312
Monmouth's Rebellion:
Scrope participates in, **17.** 457n
Monmouth St, London:
second-hand clothing shops in, **28.** 173n
Selwyn's witticism on, **28.** 173
Monnerat, David (*or* Daniel) (d. 1785):
children of, **30.** 360
death of, **33.** 506
(?) Du Deffand, Mme, sends letter by, **5.** 91, 93
dying of dropsy, **33.** 503, 505
Ellis, Mrs, and, **12.** 140, 141, **33.** 105
fall of, from coach-box, **39.** 209
Gem, Dr, attends, **7.** 410
'grotto' mispronounced by, **12.** 140, 141, **33.** 105
HW employs, in Paris, **5.** (?) 90n, **6.** 214n
HW gives letter to, to post, **33.** 99
HW leaves money with, **7.** 412
HW's appointment of Bedford witnessed by, **34.** 13n
HW saved by, from fall, **33.** 319
(?) HW scolds, **32.** 326
(?) HW sends, for blunderbuss after robbery, **33.** 296–7, 298
HW's 'fever' may be a fiction by, **29.** 249
(?) HW's footman, **1.** 345

HW with, during attempted robbery, **32.** 249
(?) Mary told donor's name by, **35.** 431
not with HW during attempted robbery, **32.** 308
(?) reports on Gordon Riots, **33.** 189
tax for, to be paid to Excise, **41.** 433
wages of, paid, **7.** 410, 413
Württemberg, D. of, sent away by, **28.** 258
Monnerat, John:
HW's bequest to, **15.** 338n, **30.** 360
Monnerat, Mary:
HW's bequest to, **15.** 338n, **30.** 360
See also Mary ——, HW's maid in Arlington St
Monnet, Jean (ca 1710–85), dramatist:
Anthologie françoise edited by, (?) Montagu mentions, **10.** 186
Monnier, Le. *See* Le Monnier
'Monody on the Death of Q. Caroline, A.' *See under* West, Richard
Monomotapa, Africa:
Du Deffand, Mme, mentions, **3.** 163
king of, **28.** 448
Mecklenburg countess worthy of, **38.** 401
monkeys from, **33.** 515
Monophysites:
HW dislikes Gibbon's account of, **42.** 221
Monpellier. *See* Montpellier
Monreale, Abp of. *See* Testa, Francesco Maria (d. 1773)
Monreale (Sicily):
York, Cardinal, may succeed Acquaviva as archbishop of, **19.** 416–17
Monro, James (1680–1752), M.D.:
Bedlam physician, **18.** 224n
English army needs, **18.** 224
epigram by, **17.** *168*, **30.** 30, **35.** 11
'mad doctor,' **19.** 191, 196
Newport under care of, **9.** 148n
son of, **19.** 191, 196
Walpole, Sir Robert, advised by, about change of air and asses' milk, **33.** 254
—— friend of, **19.** 210
Monro, John (1715–91), M.D.:
attendant for E. of Orford sent by, to Eriswell, **36.** 119
Bedlam physician, **25.** 11n
Bouverie accompanied by, at Rome, **19.** *191*, 196
(?) Child, Lady Dorothy, attended by, **37.** 309n
Cony prevents Orford's executors from paying, **42.** 355–6
Ferrers's lunacy attested by, **21.** 397
Florence visited by, on way from Rome to England, **19.** 400
George III should make, groom of the Bedchamber, **25.** 11
HW advised by, to take E. of Orford to London, **36.** 118
HW sends, to Brandon, to treat E. of Orford, **42.** 355

HW tells, to quit E. of Orford when it is safe, 24. 368

Hardinge wants HW to save him from, 35. 571

Old Pretender entertains, after being congratulated by him at St Apostoli, 19. 191, 196

Orford, E. of, attended by, 12. 95, 34. 47, 36. 335, 336, 42. 355–6

—— praises, to Martha Turk, 24. 372

——'s condition diagnosed by, 24. 316

——'s letter to Withers brought by, to HW, 24. 367

——'s recovery reported by, 24. 367

pension of, said to be withdrawn, 19. 400

(?) too old to attend E. of Orford, 34. 129n

travelling physician, 19. 196, 210, 400

Walpole, Sir Robert, has made, travelling physician, 19. 210

Williams, Sir Charles Hanbury, under care of, 33. 78n

Monro, Thomas (1759–1833), M.D.:

Orford, E. of, attended by, 34. 129

Monro. See also Monroe; Munro

Monroe Clan:

Young Pretender to be opposed by, 19. 105

Mons (Flanders):

capture of, 19. 261n, 275

Cobourg at, 12. 3n

Conway and Scott visit, 39. 536

Dumont at, 4. 425

Dumouriez returns to, 12. 2n

English may relieve French siege of, 37. 188

French to besiege, 18. 417

Maria Theresa cedes, to France, 21. 117n

Ostend more important than, 19. 69

Monseme, ——, Capt.:

captured at Velletri, 18. 491

Monsey, Messenger (1693–1788), physician:

print of, 1. 364

'Monsieur.' See Charles X; Louis XVIII

Monsieur le prévôt des marchands:

verses to air of, 5. 232, 6. 406, 407, 7. 98

Monsignore; Monsignori:

Grant sends, to scold Chute, 35. 61

HW's conversation with, at Conclave, 17. 29

Monsigny, Pierre-Alexandre de (1729–1817):

music by, for Sedaine's Rose et Colas, 5. 269n

Monson, Bns. See Capel, Lady Elizabeth

Monson, Lady Anne. See Vane, Lady Anne

Monson, Hon. George (1730–76), army officer; M.P.:

groom of the Bedchamber, 21. 460n

leg rumoured to be lost by, 9. 369

Monson, John (1727–74), 2d Bn Monson, 1748:

brother of, 20. 36

resigns as chief justice in eyre, 22. 471

Rockingham joined by, in voting with Court, 22. 507n

Monson, John (1753–1806), 3d Bn Monson, 1774:

Albemarle St house of, 42. 219n

Broxbournbury sold by to Bosanquet, 42. 219n

HW negotiates with, over pictures at Broxbournbury, 42. 218–19

Keith entertains, with Conway at Vienna, 39. 538

portraits brought by, to his Albemarle St house, 42. 281

Monson, Hon. Lewis. See Watson, Hon. Lewis

'Monster, The.' See Williams, Renwick

Monstrelet, Enguerrand de (d. 1453), chronicler:

Chroniques, Gray quotes from, 14. 76–7

Mont, Du. See Du Mont

Montacute. See Montagu

Montagne. See Montaigne

'Montagne, La' (French revolutionary faction):

assassins of 'Old Man' of, 12. 54, 116

Montagu, Abbot. See Montagu, Walter (ca 1603–77)

Montagu, Bn. See Montagu, Sir Edward (d. 1644); Montagu, Edward (1616–84); Montagu, John (1735–70); Montagu, Ralph (1638–1709)

Montagu, Bns. See Montfort, Elizabeth de (d. 1354)

Montagu, Ds of. See Cavendish, Lady Elizabeth (1654–1734); Churchill, Lady Mary (1689–1751); Gordon, Susan (1774–1828); Montagu, Lady Mary (ca 1711–75)

Montagu, D. of. See Brudenell, George (1712–90); Montagu, John (1690–1749); Montagu, Ralph (1638–1709)

Montagu, E. of. See Montagu, Edward (1602–71)

Montagu, Lady:

Stuart, Lady Louisa, writes to, about HW's memoirs, 43. 371

Montagu, Lady. See also Crouch, Margaret

Montagu, M. of. See Neville, John (ca 1431–71)

Montagu, Vct. See Browne, Sir Anthony (ca 1528–92); Browne, Anthony (1686–1767); Browne, Anthony Joseph (1728–87); Browne, George Samuel (1769–93)

Montagu, Vcts. See Mackworth, Frances (1731–1814)

Montagu, Mr and Mrs:

SH visited by, 12. 240

Montagu, Lady Alice de (ca 1406–62), m. (1424) Sir Richard Nevill, later 5th E. of Salisbury; Cts of Salisbury, s.j., 1428:

biographical information on, corrected, 43. 183

in Margaret of Anjou's escort, 14. 73, 74

Montagu, Anna Maria (d. after 1771):

Halifax accumulates money for, 10. 246

——'s child by Anna Maria Falkner, 38. 57n

jewels of, 10. 204

Montagu, Anne, m. Christopher Wilmot, M.D.:

Blenheim St residence of, 10. 159

genealogy of, 10. 352

Montagu asked by, to procure tickets for SH from HW, 10. 158–9

Montagu, Lady Anne (ca 1715–66), m. (1750) Joseph Jekyll:

[Montagu, Lady Anne (ca 1715–66), *continued*]
Bath visited by, **10.** 169, 173, 178
children of, **10.** 185, 195, 196
Conway gives pension to friend of, **10.** 186
—— would be 'kissed to death' by, **10.** 186
(?) Cumberland, D. of, rumoured to have affair with, **30.** 62
death of, **10.** 220, 221
genealogy of, **10.** 352
Guilford to be visited by, **10.** 169
HW a favourite of, **9.** 355
HW asks, about Halifax's plans, **9.** 353
Halifax reconciled with, **10.** 221
Maintenon, Mme de, imitated by, in retirement, **9.** 201
Montagu, George, asks HW's opinion of, **9.** 355
—— dances with, at Dallington, **10.** 195, 196
—— describes, **10.** 185
—— mourns loss of, **10.** 221
——'s correspondence with, **9.** 353
—— to accompany, to Guilford's, **10.** 169
—— to be visited by, at Greatworth, **10.** 169, 173
—— to visit, at Dallington, **10.** 182, 220, 221
—— unable to attend funeral of, **10.** 220
—— visited by, at Greatworth, **9.** 291, **10.** 126
—— visits, at Dallington, **9.** 201, **10.** 160, 161, 185, 195, 196
Piozzi, Mrs, befriended by, **9.** 353n
(?) portrait of, by Davison, **10.** 334
suite of, **10.** 169
Talbot, Henry, visited by, **9.** 20
Wilkinson, Mrs, a friend of, **10.** 186
Montagu, Lady Anne (1742–61), *see* Montagu Dunk, Lady Anne
Montagu, Arabella (d. 1798), m. (1750) Nathaniel Wettenhall:
brother's death to be announced to, **9.** 12
brother's supposed death distresses, **30.** 106–7
Cholmondeley Castle near home of, **10.** 309
Dacre tells, to get drawing of Holte's house, **9.** 362
genealogy of, **10.** 352
HW asks, to seek chairs, **9.** 384
HW declines Montagu's invitation to visit, **10.** 312
HW entertains, at SH, **9.** 233
HW expects visit from, **9.** 87
HW not to be blamed by, for Montagu's illness, **9.** 96
HW's anecdote not to be shown to, **9.** 91, (?) 236
HW's 'cheeses' inquired after by, **9.** 170
HW sends compliments to, **9.** 17, 39, 45, 51, 87, 95, 103, 112, 136, 161, 178, 203, 204, 227
HW sends condolences to, **9.** 13
HW's letter to Montagu forwarded by, **9.** 404
HW to entertain, at SH, **9.** 231
HW to frank letter for, **9.** 396, 402, 404, **10.** 31

HW to receive compliments of, **9.** 101, 291, **10.** 228
(?) hamper of, **9.** 46
health of, **10.** 123, 261, 268, 299
horse of, not well, **9.** 286, 287
Malpas, Vcts, her friend, visited by, **10.** 96–7
marriage of, **9.** 111n, **43.** 116
Montagu, George, corresponds with, **9.** 286, 287
—— seeks design for church window for, **10.** 11
—— to be visited by, at Greatworth, **9.** 286, 287, **10.** 123, 173, 246, 248
—— to send horses to meet, **10.** 173
—— to transact business with, **10.** 286
—— to visit, **9.** 194, 290, 383, **10.** 24, 286
—— urges HW to visit, **10.** 309
—— visited by, at Greatworth, **9.** 174, **10.** 126
—— visits, **9.** 161, **10.** 25, 227, 299
'purge' and 'prayer' may interrupt, **9.** 231
rose window for church of, **10.** 11, 18
stout, **10.** 268
Vernons not joined by, on excursion to SH, **10.** 123
Wetenhall estate recovered by lawsuit of, **9.** 174
Montagu, Augusta (d. 1849), m. (1789) Francesco Giuseppe Maria Enrico di Viry, Conte di Viry:
Sandwich's child by Martha Ray, **24.** 459, **33.** 101
Montagu, Lady Barbara (d. 1765):
Bath to have been visited by, **10.** 173
death of: **10.** *165*–6; affects Montagu deeply, **10.** 168–9, 173; keeps Miss Jeffreys from ball, **10.** 166
genealogy of, **10.** 352
health of, **10.** 169
house of, at Batheaston, **10.** 234
Jeffreys, Miss, does not know, **10.** 166
Montagu, George, describes, **10.** 169
—— had hoped to see, at Bath, **10.** 173
—— has not seen, for a long time, **10.** 165
—— loves, **10.** 169
(?) portrait of, by Davison, **10.** 334
Ravant, Miss, friend and neighbour of, **10.** 234
Riggs family, friends and neighbours of, **10.** 234
Montagu, Basil (1770–1851), legal writer:
Sandwich's child by Martha Ray, **24.** 459, **33.** 101
Montagu, Lady Caroline (1736–1818), m. (1775) Capt. Charles Herbert:
Charlotte, Q., has as bridesmaid, **21.** 529
Du Deffand, Mme, has social relations with, **5.** 283
HW entertained by, at tea, **10.** 77
marriage of, correction about, **43.** 94
SH visited by, **12.** 223
walks at Kimbolton, **10.** 77
Montagu, Sir Charles (fl. ca 1600):
genealogy of, **10.** 351

Montagu, Charles (1661–1715), cr. (1700); Bn
Halifax, (1714) E. of Halifax; statesman;
M.P.; (?) 'Quu of Habiculeo':
contribution by, to Dryden's monument, 21.
140
daughter of, 10. 165n
genealogy of, 10. 351, 352
miniature of, at Wandesford's, 10. 12
Montagu hopes grandnephew will resemble,
10. 121
poem by, on Battle of the Boyne, 18. 266
Pope satirizes, as 'Bufo,' 15. 26, 21. 140
portrait of, in Cosby collection, 10. 103
(?) secretary from California not acceptable
to, 9. 45
wife of, 10. 338
Montagu, Charles (ca 1662–1722), 4th E. of
Manchester; cr. (1719) D. of Manchester:
genealogy of, 10. 351
Montagu, Charles (d. 1759) of Papplewick;
M.P.:
death of, 9. 238
genealogy of, 10. 352
son succeeds, in Parliament, 9. 238
Montagu, Charles (d. 1777), army officer;
George Montagu's brother:
Anecdotes of Painting said to be borrowed by,
from Montagu, 10. 66
army posts of, 43. 112, 119
army promotion of, requested by HW, 43.
314–15
Beaumont Lodge, home of, 10. 268, 322
Bedford would not have favoured recommendation of, from HW, 9. 210, 215
brothers of, 36. 11, 37. 298n
chaplain to regiment of, 35. 265, 40. 90–1
Chute entertained by, 10. 199
—— frequents house of, 10. 206
—— may be visiting, 10. 264
—— sends game to, 10. 179
—— to receive compliments of, 10. 136
death of: 32. 369; falsely reported, 30. 106–8
departure of, from Dublin, expected, 10. 2, 3
Ditton Park visited by, 10. 100
drinks wine and water, 9. 391
Dublin riot reported by, 9. 266
—— to be left by, 9. 332
—— to be visited by, 10. 66, 215
—— visited by, 10. 149, 217, 39. 73
(?) estate to be inherited by, 9. 207
father-in-law's wealth to be inherited by, 10.
215, 217
Fox, Henry, does not mention, 9. 145
—— to be called on by, 9. 136
Frogmore residence of, 10. 74–5, 83, 97–9, 102,
124, 132, 134, 135, 173, 179, 210, 246
—— visited by, 10. 42
genealogy of, 10. 352
George III not to be offended by, 36. 76
'Good,' the, not to be pursued by, 9. 31
Grosvenor Sq. house of, 32. 369n
Guildford visited by, 9. 174

HW accompanies, from the Vyne to SH, 38.
27
HW asks, to retain Galfridus Mann's heirs
as regimental clothiers, 9. 204–5
(?) HW entertains, at SH, 9. 233
HW exchanges calls with, 9. 174, 221, (?) 229,
10. 43, 118
HW hopes, will not go to Germany, 9. 221
HW invites Montagu to bring, to SH, 9. (?)
52, 293, 10. 34
HW jokingly congratulates, 10. 40
HW not to be visited by, 9. 300
(?) HW offered services of, for errands, 9. 204
HW's activities not known to, 10. 149
HW sends compliments to, 1. (?) 51, 136, (?)
161, (?) 195, 203, 215, 406
HW's errand to be performed by, 10. 121
HW's health not discussed by, 10. 214
HW's opinion of, 9. 182–3
HW's servant to deliver letter to, 10. 51
HW to entertain, at SH, 9. (?) 231, 10. 99–
101
HW to frank letters for, 9. 258, 319, 328, 352,
357, 371, 405, 10. 144, 145
HW to receive compliments of, 9. 291, 386,
394, 399, 403, 415, 10. 13, 43, 100, 103, 131,
135, 136
HW to send pedigree to Montagu by, 9. 221
HW treated with deference by, 9. 182
HW visited by, at SH before going to the
Vyne, 37. 388
HW wishes Irish annals from, 9. 263
Halifax may have favoured, through Board of
Trade, 9. 258–9
—— recommends, to Bedford and Rigby, 9.
208
—— treats, well in Dublin, 9. 393, 395–6, 415
——visited by, at Horton, 9. 164
Hamilton, William Gerard, ill-treats, 10. 37–8
Hankelow to be visited by, 9. 293
health of: gout, 10. 268; 'out of order,' 10.
135; recovering, 10. 204
house of: at St Stephen's Green, Dublin, 9.
357; in London, 10. 132; sought in London,
10. 43; see also Beaumont Lodge; Frogmore
Ireland to be destination of, 9. 196, 201, 300,
10. 75
Irish embroidery commended by, 9. 355
Irish rioters to be suppressed by, 10. 24
London house to have been taken by, 9. 257
—— visited by, 10. 194
made Knight of the Bath, 23. 272
Mann, Galfridus, to supply clothing for regiment of, 9. 182
marriage of, arranged, 10. 51
Miller to visit, 9. 383
Montagu, George, asks HW about payment
by, for muff, 10. 151
—— asks HW to intercede for, 9. 136
—— assisted by, in Ireland, 10. 47
—— entertained by, 10. 199
—— informed by, of HW's World, 9. 166–7
—— may live with, 9. 175–6

[Montagu, Charles (d. 1777), *continued*]
(?) —— mortified by, **10.** 173
——'s correspondence with, 9. 208, 266, 357, 370, **10.** 213, 214, 217
——'s Irish bill to be paid by, **10.** 126
—— sups with, every night, in Dublin, 9. 391, 400
—— to be visited by, at Greatworth, 9. 370, **10.** 33, 83
—— to occupy house of, in Dublin, 9. 357, 383
—— to visit, 9. 286, **10.** 75, 97, 134
—— visited by, 9. 215, **10.** 37, 131, 132
—— visits, at Frogmore, **10.** 134
—— well treated by, 9. 385
Montagu, Henrietta, to be left by, 9. 165
—— would be distressed by presence of, in her illness, 9. 174
Montagu, John, to visit, at Beaumont Lodge, **10.** 320
murders himself by trying to be in the *bon ton* at 63, 36. 134
Oxford visited by, **10.** 41–2
parents-in-law to be visited by, **10.** 66
(?) Pitt, William Augustus, a friend of, 9. 314
Plymouth visited by, 9. 194
portrait of, by Eccardt, Grandison, Vcts, asks Montagu for, promising him a copy, **10.** 132
promotion of: 9. 180; to Irish staff, 9. 257–9
regiment assigned to: 9. 332, **14.** 88; giving chaplaincy to brother's parson and clothing contract to Galfridus Mann, 35. 265
regiment of: 9. 208n; ordered to Bristol, 9. 190; ordered to Dublin, 9. 208; rumoured to be going on secret trip, 9. 196; summoned abroad, 9. 31
Rigby favours, 9. 257, 266
SH and the Vyne visited by, 35. 184–5
SH to be visited by, with brother, 35. 177
(?) technically a prisoner, after Roucour battle, 43. 113–14
Villiers's inoculation to be supervised by, **10.** 234
—— to visit, **10.** 81
Waldershare to be visited by, 9. 164
Welsh inscriptions to be corrected by, 9. 218
Welsh unintelligible to, 9. 221
wife of, 1. 236, **10.** 51n
wife's peerage not extended to, **10.** 240
wounded at Fontenoy, 37. 192, 43. 110–11
Montagu, Mrs Charles (d. 1780). *See* Calladon, Anne
Montagu, Lord Charles Greville (1741–84), M.P.:
appointed governor of South Carolina, **10.** 152n
Christ Church, Oxon, attended by, 9. 303
Montagu invites Beauchamp to accompany, to Greatworth, 9. 303
Montagu, Lady Charlotte (d. 1762), m. Gen. James Johnston:
child of, still-born, **10.** 25
death of, **10.** 25
family of, 34. 260

genealogy of, **10.** 352
health of, fever, **10.** 25
husband of, 9. 245n
(?) portrait of, by Davison, **10.** 334
Montagu, Christopher (d. ?1735), (George Montagu's great-uncle):
genealogy of, **10.** 352
Montagu, George, inherits Roel from, **10.** 352
Montagu, Rev. Christopher (ca 1717–45), army chaplain; George Montagu's brother:
Cole friend of, **10.** 333
death of, **10.** 333, 43. 110
genealogy of, **10.** 352
killed at Fontenoy, 36. 11
ordination of, **10.** 333
Trinity College, Cambridge attended by, **10.** 333
Montagu, Sir Edward (d. 1557), chief justice of Court of Common Pleas:
common ancestor of Montagus, 9. 394n
genealogy of, **10.** 351
lord chief justice, **10.** 341
portrait of, at Boughton House, **10.** 341
Montagu, Edward (d. 1602) of Boughton:
genealogy of, **10.** 351
Montagu, Sir Edward (ca 1562–1644), cr. (1621) Bn Montagu; M.P.:
genealogy of, **10.** 351
Montagu, Edward (1602–71), 2d E. of Manchester; M.P.:
genealogy of, **10.** 351
Warwick's widow marries, **10.** 76n
wife of, **10.** 78n
Montagu, Edward (1616–84), 2d Bn Montagu; M.P.:
genealogy of, **10.** 351
Montagu, Edward (1625–72), cr. (1660) E. of Sandwich; 'the Admiral'; M.P.:
Barba translated by, 16. 6
bed of, 40. 283
Bentley's designs of life and death of, 9. 267
death date of, corrected by HW, 16. 6
death of, portrayed at Hinchingbrooke, 40. 283
diary of, gives campaign conditions on Spanish-Portuguese border, 40. 240
genealogy of, **10.** 351
heart of, embalmed, formerly at Hinchingbrooke, **10.** 80
Hinchingbrooke appropriate to, **10.** 79
MS diary of, quoted by HW about bee-keeping, 40. 256n
memoirs of, **15.** 132
portrait of, by Lely, at Hinchingbrooke, **10.** 79
portraits of, at Hinchingbrooke, 40. 283, 284
son of, 9. 255n
Montagu, Edward (b. 1649):
genealogy of, **10.** 351, 352
Montagu, Edward (1648–88), 2d E. of Sandwich; M.P.:
genealogy of, **10.** 351
HW confuses, with father, 16. 6

portrait of, **40**. 284

Montagu, Edward (ca 1670–1729), 3d E. of Sandwich:
genealogy of, **10**. 351
marriage of, **1**. 89n

Montagu, Edward (d. 1722), styled Vct Hinchingbrooke; M.P.:
genealogy of, **10**. 351

Montagu, Edward (d. 1738), George Montagu's father; army officer:
army officer, **10**. 333
genealogy of, **10**. 351, 352
monument to, at Horton, **10**. 333
son of, **1**. 36n, **2**. 211

Montagu, Edward (1692–1775):
large estate left by, to wife, **28**. 203
Sandwich's obligations to, **19**. 413n
wife of, **6**. 337n, **9**. 258, **11**. 275n, **28**. 35n

Montagu, Lt-Col. Edward (d. 1745), George Montagu's brother:
death of, at Fontenoy battle, **9**. 11, 12, **19**. 43, **36**. 11, **37**. 192
genealogy of, **10**. 352

Montagu, Mrs Edward. *See* Pelham, Elizabeth (d. 1723); Robinson, Elizabeth (1720–1800); Trevor, Arabella, (d. 1734); Winwood, Anne (d. 1642)

Montagu, Sir Edward Hussey. *See* Hussey, Sir Edward

Montagu, Edward Wortley (1678–1761), M.P.; ambassador to Turkey 1716–18:
ambassadorship of, corrected, **43**. 268
avarice of, **21**. 472n
daughter of, **12**. 42n, **28**. 164n
daughter to inherit fortune of, **9**. 338
death of: **21**. 472, 527; benefits Bute, **21**. 473, 527
health and money the only objects of, **35**. 268
inoculation introduced by, **13**. 3n
HW calls, 'old Avidien,' **21**. 472
lodge of, at Wantley, Wharncliffe, **43**. 176
Montagu, William, sponsored by, for election, **19**. 450n
Palmer executor to, **33**. 521n
Pierrepont, Lady Mary, agrees to marry, **14**. 244
Pope satirizes, **21**. 472n, **35**. 268–9
son gets small allowance from, **20**. 226
son of, has to leave Paris because of promise to avoid, **20**. 226n
wealth and bequests of, **9**. 338, **21**. 472–3, 483
wealth of, compared with Clive's, **31**. 21
Wharncliffe Lodge home of, **35**. 268–9
wife cruel to, **14**. 243
wife of, **6**. 282n, **9**. 106n, 119n, **14**. 38n, 242n

Montagu, Edward Wortley (1713–76). *See* Wortley Montagu, Edward

Montagu, Mrs Elizabeth. *See* Robinson, Elizabeth

Montagu, Elizabeth (d. 1731), m. (1683) Sir Christopher Wandesford, 2d Bt; cr. (1707) Vct Castlecomer:
genealogy of, **10**. 352

grandson of, **10**. 12

Montagu, Elizabeth (b. 1680), m. Richard Thoresby:
genealogy of, **10**. 352

Montagu, Lady Elizabeth (d. 1789), m. Henry Archer:
genealogy of, **10**. 352
Guilford and Montagu to visit, at Hale, **10**. 280
party entertained by, **10**. 210n
(?) portrait of, by Davison, **10**. 334

Montagu (formerly Brudenell), Lady Elizabeth (1743–1827), m. (1767) Henry Scott, 3d D. of Buccleuch:
Adderbury may be left by, temporarily, **10**. 262
at Mrs Boyle Walsingham's ball, **42**. 222n
Banbury visited by, to see play, **10**. 266
Bath to be visited by, **10**. 266
Bedford, Ds of, mentions, **38**. 400
cards to be played by, with Montagu, **10**. 268
Christmas to be spent by, at Adderbury, **10**. 284
dowry of daughter of, **11**. 121
genealogy of, **10**. 351
Guines's ball attended by, **32**. 96n
HW's opinion of, **10**. 259
Holland visited by, **33**. 562
loo played by, **10**. 302
Montagu accompanies, to Banbury, **10**. 266
——'s neighbour at Adderbury, **10**. 259
——'s opinion of, **10**. 268
——'s relations with, **10**. 266, 268, 302
mother's bequest to, **24**. 99
mother's guests mostly friends of, **38**. 358
pregnancy of, **10**. 281
Scotland visited by, **10**. 284
Tavistock said to be marrying, **38**. 358
visited by Fitzwilliam and Ladies Frances and Jane Scott, **10**. 302

Montagu, Lady Elizabeth (1745–68). *See* Montagu Dunk, Lady Elizabeth

Montagu, Lady Frances (d. 1788), m. (1739) Sir Roger Burgoyne, 6th Bt:
Brown, Lt-Gen. John, makes, executrix, **10**. 169
genealogy of, **10**. 352
Jackson, Richard, to be paid legacy by, **10**. 169
Montagu, George, asked by, for copy of *Life of Edward Lord Herbert of Cherbury*, **10**. 143
—— asked by, to ask HW about whereabouts of Richard Jackson, **10**. 169
—— at house of, hears of Lady Barbara Montagu's death, **10**. 169
(?) —— avoids cabals of, **9**. 360
—— visits, **10**. 263
(?) portrait of, by Davison, **10**. 334
son of, **10**. 295n

Montagu, Lady Frances (1743–64). *See* Montagu Dunk, Lady Frances

Montagu, Frederick (1733–1800), M.P.; George
Montagu's heir:
Anecdotes of Painting liked by, **10**. 20
Anstey said by, to be author of *Heroic Epistle*,
28. 75
Barré's pension signed by, **29**. 264
Bath visited by, **9**. 247
Burton knows, **10**. 13
Cavendish, Lords John and Frederick, friends
of, **9**. 303
Chatsworth visited by, **9**. 303
father succeeded by, in Parliament, **9**. 238
franking privilege of, to be used for letters
by Montagu, **10**. 261
genealogy of, **10**. 352
Gray described by, **9**. 303
HW and Mrs Delany called on by, **29**. 91
HW entertains, at SH, **10**. 306
HW hears of Montagu pedigree from, **9**. 259
HW hears Parliamentary news from, **29**. 109
HW may be visited by, **9**. 229
HW mentions, **29**. 337
HW returns George Montagu's letters to, **9**. 1
HW's correspondence with, **9**. 1
HW's letter too late to be carried by, **28**. 313
HW's MSS transmitted by, **36**. 310–11
HW's opinion of, **9**. 308
HW to be told by, about Sulgrave enclosure
bill, **9**. 336–7
Halifax urges Grenville to put, in Board of
Trade, **10**. 194n
Hanover Sq. residence of, **10**. 13
health of: gout, **9**. 247, 248; prevents his
being Speaker, **36**. 183; recovers, **29**. 91
lord of the Treasury, **25**. 392
Mason does not find, at home, **29**. 321n
——'s correspondence with, **28**. 312
—— to accompany, to London, **28**. 272
Montagu, George, to receive from, through
HW, a book about Montagu family, **9**. 257
—— visited by, at Greatworth, **9**. 303
Nivernais's *Jardins modernes* given to, **12**. 260
Northampton re-election to be lost by, **10**. 194
North family to get reversion from George
Montagu after death of, **2**. 211n
Norton may be succeeded by, as Speaker,
29. 28
offers to carry letter to Mason, **28**. 488
Williams, Sir William, makes, his heir, **9**.
369
Montagu, Lord Frederick (1774–1827):
godson and heir to George Montagu, **9**. 361n
Montagu, George (ca 1622–81) of Horton:
daughter of, **10**. 12n
genealogy of, **10**. 351, 352
Montagu, George (ca 1684–1739), 2d Bn Halifax; cr. (1715) E. of Halifax, n.c., M.P.:
daughter of, **9**. 201n
genealogy of, **10**. 351–2
nephew of, **37**. 298n
part of Horton built by, **10**. 334
portrait of, at Horton, **10**. 335
portrait of, by Jervas, in crayon, **10**. 335

spaniels, black, scarce after death of, **18**. 293
Warburton quotes Bentley's remark to, **13**.
39n
wife of, **9**. 17n
Montagu, George (1712–90). *See* Brudenell,
George
Montagu, George (ca 1713–80), HW's correspondent; M.P.:
See Vols 9–10 passim
age of, **9**. 333, 402, 409, **10**. 143, 195
appearance of, **9**. 339, 354–5, 370, **10**. 75, 97,
136, 187, 190, 191, 259
Barrett Lennard to receive compliments of,
20. 87
Barrett Lennards knew HW through, **20**. 78
Berry, Mary, quotes remark by, on rich relations, **12**. 114
Bentley asked about by, **35**. 261
——'s correspondence with, **35**. 177, 205
——'s designs owned by, **35**. 644
biography of, corrected, **43**. 109
birthday of, **10**. 143–5
brother of, **1**. 236n
brother's supposed death distresses, **30**. 106–7
calls himself, 'poor woman, old and blind,'
10. 134, 159, 283
cards enjoyed by, **35**. 185
ceremonious behaviour of, **9**. 309
children disliked by, **10**. 81
Chute meets at SH, **38**. 453
Cole invited to visit, **2**. 212n
——'s acquaintance with, **2**. 212
Conway's correspondence with, **37**. 6–7, 266
—— to receive compliments of, **37**. 433
—— to write to, **37**. 23
costume of, for Ireland, **9**. 354–5, 357, 358,
360, **10**. 1, 9–10
'country squirehood' to envelop, **35**. 161
'cried and roared,' **35**. 70
crosses himself, **35**. 161
dances: at Dallington, **10**. 195, 196; at Reims,
9. 303
death of, **2**. 211
departure of, on Grand Tour, **40**. 21
diet of, **9**. 300, 391 (*see also* habits of: drinking)
disinterestedness of, **9**. 77–8
Du Deffand, Mme, considers, HW's intimate
friend, **3**. 403, **4**. 6
—— eager to know, **3**. 392
—— glad of appointment of, **33**. 352
—— offers lodgings to, **5**. 65n
—— sends messages to, **3**. 113, 354, 357, 394,
4. 345
effeminate and witty, **35**. 648
embarrassments of, **10**. 48
finances and financial habits of, **9**. 257, 258,
10. 47, 66, 126, 179, 223, 256, 267, 284,
286, 296
fish named 'Speckle-belly' by, **35**. 205
former servant of, awaits HW at Paris, **37**. 41
France visited by, **37**. 6–7, 23, 41
genealogy of, **10**. 351, 352

Gray and HW expect visit from, **13.** 177, 180
Gray mentions bereavement of, **14.** 86
Guilford's correspondence with, **43.** 137
HW accompanied by chatter of, **37.** 433
HW accompanies, from the Vyne to SH, **38.** 27
HW asks about, **35.** 102
HW delivers Chute's excuse to, **35.** 69–70
HW expects to see, in London, **35.** 265
HW forwards letter of, to Bentley, **35.** 177, 205
HW loses friendship of, **5.** 345n
HW mentions, **37.** 488
HW quotes, **37.** 298
HW requests favour for, from Henry Fox, **30.** 110
HW's correspondence with, **7.** 376, 377, 379–81, 385, 389, Vols 9–10, **36.** 310–11, **37.** 6–7, 344, **38.** 167
HW's description of masquerade intercepted by, **35.** 206
HW sends compliments of, to Mme du Deffand, **4.** 366
HW's opinion of, **2.** 211
HW's 'quondam friend,' **29.** 37
HW's relations with, **9.** 77, 174–5, **10.** 4, 7–8, 13, 51, 85–6, 140–1, 143, 164–6, 184, 195, 268–9, 277–8, 290, 305, 306, 318
HW taken by, to Warkworth, **35.** 77
HW tells, to explain delay to Chute, **35.** 97
HW to inform, of Chute's inheritance, **35.** 85
HW to visit, **39.** 107, **40.** 288
HW visited by: **3.** 113; at SH, **4.** 345, **35.** 161, 184, **38.** 453; at SH before going to the Vyne, **37.** 388
HW visits, **1.** 36, 37, 41, 42
HW writes regularly to, **38.** 94
habits of: at Dublin, **9.** 393, 399, 400; card-playing, **10.** 144, 268; drinking, **9.** 293, 375, 390, 393, **10.** 61, 68, 97, 101, 258; reading, **9.** 328, **10.** 111, 114; riding, **9.** 175, 275, 293, 309, 328, **10.** 67, 151, 229, 234, 261, 321; walking, **10.** 179
handwriting of, **10.** 165
health of: **9.** 96, 174, 175, 243–5, 247, 248, 375, 378, **10.** 33, 34, 67, 75, 85, 120, 121, 126, 128, 134, 146, 151, 158, 162, 164, 170, 189, 194, 217, 227, 234, 236, 238, 258, 261, 276, 296, 310, 319; better in the country, **9.** 343, **10.** 215, 243, 256, 266, 302, 303; bruised in carriage accident, **10.** 135; cold, **10.** 30; cold avoided, **10.** 120; cough, **10.** 275; eyes, **9.** 227, **10.** 144, 207, 223; fever, **10.** 31; gout, 9, 293, 300, 334, 370, 371, 399–400, 403, 404, **10.** 27, 100, 101, 220, 221, 248, 251, 275; gout avoided, **10.** 29; influenza, **10.** (?) 30, 31; lame leg, **10.** 195, 196; palsy, **10.** 275; paralytic symptoms, **10.** 164; rheumatism, **9.** 370–1, **10.** 195, 214, 275; scurvy, **10.** 61; speech impaired, **10.** 275, 276; stroke dreaded, **10.** 164; tooth lost, **10.** 275, 276; vapourish, **10.** 284; weight lost, **10.** 196

impatient, **10.** 84, 129
in Cheshire, but comes to town for winter, **35.** 261
income of, **9.** 361n
lawsuit of, lost, **9.** 345, 346, (?) 385
letters of, to be burnt by HW, **9.** 2
London finds, a recluse, but neighbours beset him in country, **35.** 70
memoirs appeal to, **9.** 14
Miller, parson of, **35.** 265, **40.** 90
Montagu, Frederick, receives bequest from, **29.** 37
musical tastes of, **10.** 20
North allows, to do the honours at Wroxton, **35.** 72
Northampton election sought by, **9.** 141
not dead, **32.** 369
Parliamentary vote by, on privately-raised regiments, **26.** 19
Pelham gets information from, about Nicholas Hardinge, **35.** 605
philosophical but not silent, **37.** 258
philosophy of, **10.** 141, 142, 144, 164–5, 173, 177–8
politics disliked by, **10.** 170
punctuation of, **10.** 165
Reims lady attracts, **37.** 7
returns to Greatworth from London, **35.** 161
Selwyn travels with, **15.** 8n
sisters of, **30.** 106
SH to be visited by, with brother, **35.** 177
Vyne, the, visited by, **35.** 185
Whiggism of, **10.** 217
Windsor house of, **30.** 106, **37.** 258
witticism by, on earthquake, **33.** 93, **35.** 373, 414, **38.** 486–7
Montagu (after 1741, Montagu Dunk), George (1716–71), 2d E. of Halifax, 1739; 'Great Cu of Haticuleo':
additional salary of, turned over to D. of Leeds, **21.** 489
Africans under care of, **9.** 81n
agrees with rest of Cabinet Council, **22.** 295
American plunder may be missed by, **10.** 202
appoints Osborn gov. of New York, **9.** 149n
Bedford, D. of, and Fox oppose Northampton and, on Turnpike Bill, **20.** 112n
Bedford, D. of, entertains, at dinner, **22.** 298n
—— may be succeeded by, in Trade and Plantations, **20.** 259
—— opposes, in debate on Address, **37.** 416
—— presents ultimatum of, to George III, **22.** 307
—— recommends, as first lord of Trade, **20.** 121n
Bedfords entertain, **9.** 363
Bentley 'licks shoes of,' **10.** 125
—— may visit, **9.** 134
—— mentions, in *Patriotism*, **10.** 154
—— praises, **10.** 128n, **14.** 134n
——'s *Epistle to Lord Melcombe* compliments, **9.** 408–9
——'s *Philodamus* admired by, **9.** 414

[Montagu, George (1716–71), *continued*]
—'s *Wishes* attended by, 9. 382
—— witnesses 'Gartering' of, 10. 125
brother of, 2. 211n
Bubb Dodington rails at, for double-dealing, 39. 412
—— tells, he is eventually to be treasurer of the Navy, 21. 74n
Buckhounds mastership of, given to his predecessor, 9. 33
Buckinghamshire's marriage to exonerate, from charge of mistreating Miss Drury, 9. 357
Bushey Park residence of, 9. (?) 213, 371, 10. 203, 207, 335
Bute affronted by opposition of, to Regency Bill, 22. 299–300
—— hinted by, to have fomented riot, 30. 182
—— may be asked by, for office, 10. 238
—'s removal demanded by, 10. 99n, 22. 168
chaplain of, 9. 399, 10. 8, 22n
Chatham administration not to include, 10. 222
Chatham (Pitt) disclaims responsibility for disappointment of, 30. 135
—— proscribes, 22. 161
—— refuses to make new secretaryship of state for, 9. 212, 21. 104
—'s conversation with, 10. 237
—'s resignation to be known by, 9. 392
Cole describes, 10. 335
Conway opposed by, 22. 507
—'s dismissal perhaps opposed by, 38. 240
—— succeeds, as secretary of state, 22. 310
Cosby, Mrs, describes Montagu's appointment by, 9. 355
—— told by, of Hertford's Irish appointment, 38. 474–5, 483
cousin of, 10. 210n
Crane accompanies, in Ireland, 9. 399
—— chief chaplain to, 9. 399n
—— vainly urged by, to accept bishopric of Elphin, 10. 8
daughter of, 9. 20n
daughter's fortune to be shared by, 38. 536
daughter's marriage arranged by, 10. 195, 203
death of: 23. 310, 313; rumoured, 10. 296
dismissals of anti-Court voters not blamed on, 38. 264
dismissed, 22. 310
dispatches from Egremont's office signed by, during vacancy, 22. 159n
Drury, Mary Anne, possible wife for, 9. 278, 300, 357, 10. (?) 244, 335
—'s match with, broken off, though he keeps Drury Lane actress, 35. 302
Dupplin does not yet succeed, as lord of Trade, 21. 104, 111
Duras resembles, 39. 16
Egremont may be succeeded by, 10. 29
election expenses beggar, 10. 256n
English diplomatists in Italy ordered by, to welcome Vorontsov, 22. 173
English Privy Council warned by, of Irish money bills, 43. 125–6

entertains at Horton, 10. 162
Éon arrested for misbehaviour at house of, 22. 190, 217
—— forced by, to promise not to fight Vergy, 38. 244n
—— shows madness at house of, 38. 244
estate of, 9. 105n
Eton attended by, 10. 334
Falkner, Anna Maria, cause of ruptured marriage negotiations of, 10. 335, 35. 302
—— expensive to, 10. 287
—— has children by, 38. 57
—— left by, at Hampton Court Green, 10. 186
—— not to be taken to Ireland by, 9. 355
—— taken by, to Horton, 10. 162
family portraits neglected by, 9. 309, 10. 334
finances of, 9. 213, 10. 209, 287, 335
first lord of the Admiralty, 22. 42, 91
Fox's acceptance from, dependent on Robinson's taking Seals, 39. 412n
—'s dismissal not to be assigned to, 30. 183
Frederick, P. of Wales, dismisses, 18. 551
—— makes, lord of the Bedchamber, 18. 159
game to be shot by, in Rockingham Forest, 10. 209
Garter granted to, 10. 121, 125, 22. 227, 38. 377
genealogy of, 10. 351, 352
gentry ignore, at Northampton races, 10. 179
George II attended by, at St James's Palace, 17. 338
George III advised by, to commission Granby, Richmond, and Waldegrave to suppress riot, 30. 181
—— and D. of Cumberland unite in hating, 22. 364
George III arrogantly treated by, 22. 309
—— defends Hertford against, 38. 440n
—— dismisses, but has to recall him, 22. 302
—— forced by, at Q. Charlotte's house, to propose omitting Ps of Wales from Regency Bill, 22. 297n
—— orders, to move a Regency Bill similar to Richmond's, 22. 297
—— to get resignation of, 38. 558
—— treats, coldly, 22. 307
Granby told by, that he prefers Cabinet membership to Garter, 21. 111n
Grattan welcomes, at Dublin, 9. 393
Grenville and Bedford faction adhered to by, 38. 534
Grenville, George, cannot be succeeded by, as manager of House of Commons, 22. 91
—— replaced by, as secretary of state, 22. 91, 38. 184
—'s ministry dissatisfies, 38. 286
—— succeeds, as first lord of Admiralty, 10. 45, 22. 91
—— to be succeeded by, as secretary of state, 10. 45
Guilford predicts 3 years' stay in Ireland for, 9. 355

HW approves of behaviour of, in Ireland, **10**. 20

HW hopes Bentley will receive benefit from, **10**. 69

HW identifies, **28**. 187n

HW meets, **9**. 170

HW mentions, **9**. 211, **20**. 292, **37**. 317

HW pleased by Montagu's reconciliation with, **10**. 205

HW's opinion of, **9**. 214, 396–7

HW sups with, **9**. 163

habits of, in Ireland, **9**. 393, 399

Halifax, Nova Scotia, named for, **20**. 40n

Hamilton no longer reports to, in state department, **40**. 384

Hamilton welcomes, at Dublin, **9**. 393

health of: jaundice, **10**. 152; illness keeps, from Poor Bill voting, **38**. 529; recovering from great crisis, **23**. 304

heirs not produced by, **9**. 310

Hertford gets letter from, about Conway's dismissal, **38**. 387

——'s correspondence with: about allowance for expenses, **38**. 269n; diplomatic, **38**. 219; formal, **38**. 329

—— to write to, **38**. 351–2

—— wanted Irish lord lieutenancy when obtained by, **38**. 491

Hillsborough, Cts of, entertains, **9**. 344

Hinchingbrooke, Vct, aide de-camp to, **10**. 9

—— to marry daughter of, **10**. 195–6

Holdernesse not to be superior to, **20**. 249

—— to be replaced by, in secretary's office, **9**. 145, **20**. 346

Horton residence of, **9**. 164, (?) 213, **10**. 81–2, 162, 186, 194, 287, 333–5

houses built by, **9**. 213, **10**. 334

Irish lords justices expected by, to obstruct Septennial Bill, **38**. 149

Irish lord lieutenancy of, **9**. 340, 347, 351–3, 355, 369–71, 379–81, 386, **21**. 485, 489, **22**. 42, **30**. 162

Irish Parliament's relations with, **9**. 399, **10**. 18–21

——'s resolution provokes, to scold lords justices, **38**. 148

Irish popularity of, **9**. 403, 409, 415, **10**. 11, 18, 20, 24, 335

Irish post may be retained by, **38**. 184

Irish residence of, may be prolonged by his reappointment or ended by his return to England, **9**. 355, **10**. 18, 25, (?)28, 29, 31, 32, 45, 47

Irish salary augmentation offered to, and rejected, **10**. 18–21

Irish welcome, on his arrival at Dublin, **9**. 393

James II's robe worn by, at opening of Irish Parliament, **9**. 399

Jekyll, Lady Anne, reconciled with, **10**. 221

Jenison succeeded by, as Master of the Buckhounds, **18**. 551

lords justices left by, in Ireland, **38**. 147

Lucan dedicated to, **29**. 11n, **35**. 644

Mann encloses to, D. of York's letter to brother, **22**. 235n

——'s report to, about Damer's and Gascoigne's escapade, **22**. 287

——writes to, asking for promotion, **22**. 318–21

marriage of, rumoured, **9**. 278

(?) match of, off, **10**. 244

may be chief justice in eyre, **9**. 33

ministry does not include, **9**. 203

Montagu, Charles, may have been favoured by, through Board of Trade, **9**. 258–9

—— recommended by, to Bedford and Rigby, **9**. 208

—— visits, at Horton, **9**. 164

—— well treated by, at Dublin, **9**. 393, 395–6, 415

Montagu, George, asks HW about plans of, **9**. 352

—— asks HW for news of English promotion of, **10**. 28

—— avoids cabals of, **9**. 360

—— called on by, **10**. 204

—— courted by, **10**. 206

—— defends, to (?)Abp of Armagh, **9**. 409–10

—— disturbed by rumour that Irish reappointment may not go to, **10**. 37

—— does not congratulate, on Garter, **10**. 121

—— favourably mentioned by, **9**. 163

—— frequently called on by, **10**. 209

—— hopes, will resemble great-uncle, **10**. 121

—— hopes not to be made to drink at parties of, **9**. 390

—— ill-treated by, **9**. 159

—— jokingly congratulates, **10**. 40

(?) —— kept awake by triumphs of, **10**. 119

—— may obtain Irish position through, **9**. 347, 351, 352, 355

—— never writes to, **9**. 170

—— not given family portraits by, **9**. 310

——'s correspondence with, **9**. 267, 345, 346, 356, 357, **10**. 246

——'s relations with, **9**. 159, 163, 170, 213–14, 310, 393, 395–7, 402, 415, **10**. 24, 40, 121, 196, 204–6, 209, 246

—— to accompany, to Powerscourt, **10**. 12

—— to arrange pictures for, **9**. 267

—— to be visited by, at Greatworth, **10**. 229

—— to take oaths to, at Bushey Park, **9**. 371

—— well treated because of, **9**. 385

—— well treated by, in Dublin, **9**. 393, 395–7, 402, 415, **10**. 24

motto of, **9**. 402

name of, changed, **10**. 335

Newcastle, D. of, breaks promise to, of secretaryship of state, **30**. 135n

—— negotiates with Pitt to regain, for Board of Trade, **21**. 111n

—— proposes, for secretary of state, **21**. 86n

Northampton election expensive to, **10**. 287

—— races attended by, **9**. 300, **10**. 178–9

—— seat controlled by, **10**. 194n

[Montagu, George (1716–71), *continued*]
North rumoured to succeed, at Board of Trade, **9**. 340
Northumberland reports to, about Irish Parliament, **43**. 131
—— reverses anti-Stone Irish policy of, **38**. 251n
notice posted by, in White's coffee-room, **35**. 313
Nova Scotia to be colonized by, **20**. 40
opposes inclusion of Ps of Wales in Regency Bill, **10**. 152n
Opposition joined by, **18**. 159
Osborn acts by advice of, **10**. 235n
Osborn, Hon. Mrs, accompanies, to Bushey Park, **10**. 207
—— gives news of, **9**. 370
Osborn, Sir George, well treated by, at Northampton races, **10**. 178–9
Paolists drink to health of, **23**. 31n
Parliamentary activity of, on Regency Bill, **38**. 543–5, 552–3
Parliamentary motion against Hanover troops advocated by, **18**. 159, 356
Parliamentary motion on Regency Bill proposed by, in House of Lords, **22**. 297n
Parliamentary speeches by: **9**. 229, 393, 399, **10**. 19–21; answered by Raymond, **17**. 230, 263
Parliament's adjournment opposed by, **30**. 181n
Pelham favours, for secretary of state, **20**. 202n
Pitt, Harriot, might be taken by, **38**. 58
plantations to be taken from, and put under Board of Trade, **20**. 259
popular with merchants, **22**. 43
portraits of, at Horton, **10**. 334, 335
Powerscourt to be visited by, **10**. 12
privately-raised regiments defended by, **19**. 154
prompts, at play, **9**. 382
Ranger of Bushey Park, **10**. 335
regent, **10**. 153
regiment raised by, **19**. 128, **30**. 98
relatives ill-treated by, **10**. 152, 287
'Repeal, The,' caricatures, **22**. 400
resignation of: **9**. 212, 213, **30**. 135; predicted, **9**. 179
retires early, after daughter's wedding, **10**. 207
ribbon of, to go to Bp of Osnabrück, **23**. 313
Robinson opposed by, for archbishopric, **22**. 276n
Salusbury accompanies, to Wales and Dublin, **9**. 340n
Sandwich opposes, over Turnpike Bill, **20**. 121
—— 's relations with, **10**. 195
—— succeeded by, as secretary of state, **23**. 268
Sandys succeeds, in Board of Trade, **21**. 489
secretary of state, **10**. 335, **23**. 263n

secretaryship of state lost by, **9**. 161, 162, 165, 178
secretaryship of state may be given to, **9**. 159, 200
secretaryship of state rejected by, **22**. 38n
sister and cousin of, **10**. 234n
sister of, **9**. 360n
sisters of, **9**. 353n, **10**. 221, 334
Stanley, Hans, entertained by, at Horton, **10**. 194
Stanstead the seat of, **12**. 206n
successor to, as lord lieutenant, not named, **10**. 45
Suffolk may succeed, as secretary of state, **23**. 304, 310
Talbot family know intentions of, **9**. 351
Talbot to succeed, in Board of Trade, **21**. 486
Temple might support, on General Warrants, **38**. 563
—— rebuked by, for reference to Spanish ministry, **38**. 233
—— reconciled with, **22**. 304
—— refuses dinner invitation of, for King's Birthday, **30**. 187
Tongs residence of, **9**. 105, 118
trade entered by, **10**. 335
Trinity College, Dublin, attended by, **10**. 334
uncle's estate to be shared by, **10**. 204, 209
University of Dublin welcomes, **9**. 393
Wales visited by, **9**. 340n
Walpole, Sir Robert, 'cut' by, at House of Lords, **17**. 338
West Indian department disjoined to accommodate, **21**. 488
West Indies secretaryship of state demanded by, **9**. 212
wife of, **10**. 335
Wilkes arrested by warrant of, **38**. 197
—— complains to, **22**. 138
—— 's successful suit against, **4**. 323n
witticism by, to Clevland, on overtures to Henry Fox, **22**. 93n
wrangling by, over *Essay on Woman*, in House of Lords, **38**. 229, 230n
Montagu, George (1737–88), styled Vct Mandeville; 4th D. of Manchester, 1762; M.P.:
accounts for Customs place ordered by, **42**. 47
at Mrs Boyle Walsingham's ball, **42**. 222n
barbarisms in speech of, **33**. 399
Boughton House in litigation between Cts of Cardigan and, **10**. 340
Cambridge petitioners patronized by, **2**. 207
Canadian news distortions resented by, in House of Lords, **32**. 284n
Cardigan's proposal told by, to George Montagu, **10**. 200
(?) Carmarthen's dinner attended by, **33**. 554n
Court ball attended by, **9**. 406
Cumberland, D. of, offered support of, **30**. 187
Drawing-Room enjoyed by, **33**. 336
Du Deffand, Mme, mentions, **7**. 111

——'s social relations with, **5.** 283, 288, 311, 315, 320

—— to send letter by, **5.** 324, 328

—— to send parcels by, **5.** 322, 324–5

family portraits unknown to, **10.** 78

genealogy of, **10.** 351

George III appoints, to Bedchamber, **10.** 46

Greatworth pleases, **10.** 41

HW entertains, at SH, **9.** 233

HW escapes invitation of, to spend night at Kimbolton, **10.** 77

HW mentions, 9. 402, 403, 38. 555

HW promises that George Montagu will identify paintings of, **10.** 78

HW receives Mme du Deffand's letter through, **5.** 335

HW reluctantly visits, **10.** 77–8

Kimbolton the seat of, **14.** 177n

may continue in office, **35.** 518

member of committee, **2.** 208n

Monaco, P. of, entertains, in Paris, **5.** 292

Montagu, George, considers, too young, **10.** 85

—— not to visit, **10.** 85

——'s patrimony devised to, **9.** 361n

—— thinks Sandwich a better liar than, **10.** 186

—— visited by, **10.** 41

Paris post to be assumed by, **25.** 398

Parliamentary motion by, for American dispatches, **24.** 205n

peace news from, **25.** 428n, 432n

resigns as Bedchamber lord, **39.** 122

Rous's roll of Earls of Warwick, with drawing of Richard III, lent by, to HW, **1.** 133, 138, 147, **14.** 173, 177, 182, **15.** 124, **41.** 134–5, 144, 225, **42.** 285

Rubens's 'Prometheus' attributed by, to Titian, **10.** 78

Sandwich attacked by, in newspapers, **10.** 180

sister of, **10.** 77n

unmarried, **10.** 29

weepers for Ds of Marlborough pulled off by, at private Court ball, **38.** 143–4

Montagu, George (d. 1767):

death of, **10.** 246n

Halifax's child by Anna Maria Falkner, **38.** 57n

Montagu, Hon. Mrs George. *See* Irby, Elizabeth

Montagu, Grace (ca 1687–1767), m. Brig.-Gen. William Cosby:

backgammon played by, **10.** 166

bill of lading signed by, for portraits, **10.** 103

biographical information on, corrected, **43.** 118

(?) carriage exercise recommended for, **9.** 253

family portraits given by, to George Montagu, **10.** 67, 81, 85, 102

furniture of, to be moved from Hampton Court, **10.** 67, 81, 85

genealogy of, **10.** 352

(?) Grafton, D. of, to send venison to, **10.** 240

HW entertains, at SH, 9. *134*

HW to frank letter for, **10.** 48

HW to send venison to, for Montagu, **10.** 238

Halifax tells, of Hertford's Irish appointment, **38.** 474–5, 483

Hampton Court (?) residence of, **9.** 134

—— to be left by, **10.** 102

health of, **9.** 253

Jeffreys, Miss, forbidden by, to go to ball, **10.** 166

Montagu, George, has received only one picture from, **10.** 87

—— hears of appointment from, **9.** 355

—— may visit, **9.** 191

—— not to send venison to, **10.** 240

Montagu portraits not given by, to HW. **10.** 103

Thomas, Lady Sophia, talks with, **10.** 166

'whimsical,' **10.** 103

Montagu, Henrietta (Harriet) (d. 1755); 'Hounsibella'; George Montagu's sister:

brother's death to be announced to, **9.** 12

brother's supposed death distresses, **30.** 106–7

brothers to leave, for three weeks, **9.** 165

Buxton visited by, **9.** *106*

Chute invites, to the Vyne, **9.** 165

death of, **9.** 174–5, **14.** 86n, **35.** 255

genealogy of, **10.** 352

HW expects visit from, **9.** 87, 91

HW invites, to SH, **9.** 165

HW not to be blamed by, for Montagu's illness, **9.** 96

HW's anecdote not to be shown to, **9.** 91

HW's apologies to, **9.** 151

HW sends compliments to, **9.** 17, 39, 45, 51, 87, 95, 103, 112, 117, 136, 144, 154, 155, 158, 161, 164, 167, 168, 170

HW sends condolences to, **9.** 13

HW to receive compliments of, **9.** 101, 164

(?) hamper of, **9.** 46

health of: **9.** 106, 114, 165, 166, 170–4; HW asks about, **9.** 132; Montagu compares, with Lady Barbara Montagu's, **10.** 169

Montagu, Charles, would aggravate illness of, by his presence, **9.** 174

solitaire played by, **9.** 49

SH visited by, **9.** 167

tomb of, ordered under HW's supervision, **9.** 187, 200, **10.** 333

waters taken by, **9.** 106

Windsor visited by, **30.** 106

Montagu, Lady Henrietta ('Harriot') Brudenell (ca 1748–66):

death of, **7.** 397

Montagu, Sir Henry (ca 1563–1642), cr. (1620) Vct Mandeville, (1626) E. of Manchester; M.P.:

brother of, **10.** 233n

genealogy of, **10.** 351

Montagu's ancestor, **9.** 122n

(?) portrait of, **9.** 233, 234, 257, 261

portraits of, at Horton, **10.** 335

[Montagu, Sir Henry, *continued*]
son of, **10.** 229n
Montagu, Irby:
genealogy of, **10.** 352
Montagu, Lady Isabella (d. 1786), m. 1 (1723)
William Montagu, 2d D. of Manchester; m.
2 (1743) Edward Hussey, cr. (1762) Bn Beau-
lieu and (1784) E. of Beaulieu:
Albemarle, Cts of, thought by, to mourn too
long, **33.** 299
attempted murder by former servant of, **37.**
8–9
ballad mentions, **31.** 415
Bateman, Richard, admires, **30.** 317
Boughton House in litigation between sister
and, **10.** 89, 340
Cardigan's dukedom hard on, **10.** 233
Churchill, Gen., admires, **30.** 317
Coke admires, **17.** 247n
Conway pursues, **37.** 2–3
death of, **33.** 551
Dover St house of, **30.** 58, **33.** 551n
Englefield Green home of, **9.** 20–1, 36
father's bequest to, **20.** 80
father's will not to be contested by, **9.** 94
Fox, Henry, refused by, **30.** 313
genealogy of, **10.** 351
Grandison, Vcts, would have been told by,
about seeing Williams's portrait, **10.** 107
HW inquired after by, **10.** 204
HW invites, to breakfast at SH, **10.** 100, 101
HW's opinion of, **10.** 191
HW visited by, at SH, **10.** 106, 107
Hervey intimate with, **30.** 313
—— persuaded Fox to make love to, **30.** 313
husband tells, about non-wakefulness, **38.** 379
Hussey encouraged by, to challenge C. H.
Williams, **30.** 312
——'s match with, would be impeded by new
laws, **37.** 361
Lovel admirer of, **30.** 317
—— dines with, **30.** 42
masquerades frequented by, **37.** 9
marriage of, **9.** 27n, 36, 127n
Montagu, D. of, and, **33.** 299
Montagu, George, entertained by, **10.** 200
—— invited, to visit at Ditton, **10.** 178
—— may be given post as deputy-ranger of
Rockingham Forest by, **10.** 188, 189, 191,
192, 194, 200
—— receives flowers from, **10.** 204
—— scolded by, for hurrying SH visit, **10.**
107
——'s relations with, **10.** 178, 188, 194, 199
—— thinks, did not notice Williams's portrait at SH, **10.** 107
—— to accompany, to SH, **10.** 107
—— visits, **9.** 20–1
Montagu title pursued by, **10.** 27
Nivernais's *Jardins modernes* given to, **12.** 260
O'Brien pursues, **9.** 110
rebus mentions, **30.** 42
relations of, with parents, **9.** 94, 95

Robinson, Sir George, corresponds with,
about deputy ranger's post, **10.** 188
Scarbrough was to marry, **30.** 313
sister deprives, of use of Montagu title, **10.** 27
Stanhope, Charles, admirer of, **30.** 317
(?) Townshend, Vcts, intimate with, **30.** 313
Williams, Sir C. H., writes ode on wedding
of, **30.** 312
—— satirizes, **30.** 312, 313, 317
Montagu, James (ca 1568–1618), Bp of Bath
and Wells, 1608, of Winchester, 1616:
Bath Abbey restored by, **10.** 233
genealogy of, **10.** 351
portrait of, at Horton, **10.** 334
Montagu, Hon. James (ca 1602–63) of Lack-
ham, Wilts:
genealogy of, **10.** 351
(?) Montagu asks HW to visit seat of, **10.**
229
Montagu, James (1666–1723), Chief Baron of
the Exchequer; M.P.:
genealogy of, **10.** 352
Montagu, James (d. 1790):
(?) Montagu asks HW to visit seat of, **10.**
229
Montagu, Jean de. *See* Montaigu, Jean de
Montagu, Jemima (d. 1759), m. Sir Sidney
Meadows:
will of, **9.** 255, 258
Montagu, John de (ca 1350–1400), 3d E. of
Salisbury, 1397:
HW identifies, **42.** 138
lover of Christine de Pisan, **2.** 195, **34.** 7
not a noble author, **33.** 575
Orléans, Duc d', not to be included with,
34. 7
poem said to be written by, **33.** 552, 559
Montagu, Hon. John. *See* Hussey Montagu,
Hon. John
Montagu, John (1690–1749) 2d D. of Montagu,
1708; 'head of the "Cues"':
animals protected by, **9.** 94
armorial bearings of, at Boughton House may
be a pun, **10.** 89, 340
Banks, Margaret, loved by, **30.** 101n
—— praised by, in addition to HW's *Beauties*,
30. 329n
birth date of, corrected, **43.** 115
Cardigan, Cts of, lends no money to, **9.** 95
—— resembles, **10.** 341
co-heiresses of, **10.** 188n, 233n
daughter of, **10.** 259n, **24.** 99n, **37.** 297n
death of, **9.** 94, 95, **20.** 79
dinner of, at Bath, for stutterers, **33.** 554
Edgcumbe sure of getting Bath installation
tickets from, **30.** 79
estate and will of, **20.** 80
fireworks for the peace in charge of, **19.** 511n
Fox, Henry, attacks raising of regiments by,
19. 153–4
Frederick, P. of Wales, offends, **17.** *391*
genealogy of, **10.** 351
Grand Mastership of the Bath vacated by

death of, coveted by D. of Cumberland, **20**. 120n
health of, 'violent fever,' **20**. 79n
house of, in Privy Gardens, **20**. 79n
letter owned by, **14**. 107
lines by, protesting absence of Margaret Banks from HW's *Beauties*, **9**. 38n
Manchester, Ds of, likes, **9**. 94
mother-in-law's will bound by, with *Old Woman's Will*, **18**. 566
officers of, listed, **20**. 79n
opera announced by, **18**. 104
Ordnance vacated by death of, **20**. 120n
pensions paid by, **20**. 79
portrait of, at Horton, **10**. 335
Ragman's Castle, Twickenham, occupied by, **42**. 483
regent, **18**. 209n
regiment of, to be headed by Sandwich, **19**. 176
regiments raised by, **19**. 128, **26**. 13, 16
Rockingham Forest neglected by, **10**. 214
troop of horse raised by, **19**. 110
Walpole, Sir Robert, wants to make, generalissimo, **20**. 79
wife of, **9**. 94n
will of, **9**. 94, **20**. 80
witticism by, on opera bass, **18**. 342
Montagu, John (?midshipman), George Montagu's brother:
Bushey Park to be visited by, **9**. 371
cribbage played by, with Montagu, **10**. 111
Dacre to entertain, **10**. 4
genealogy of, **10**. 352
Guilford visited by, at Wroxton, **10**. 312
HW calls, 'little John,' **10**. 191, 193
(?) HW entertains, at SH, **9**. 233
HW inquires about, **10**. 238
(?) HW invites Montagu to bring, to SH, **9**. 52, **10**. 34, 304
HW may be called on by, **9**. (?) 229
HW offers spectator's place to, for Coronation, **9**. 384, 390, 392, 404
HW praises, **10**. 145
HW regrets having missed, **9**. 215
(?) HW sends box to, **7**. 404
HW sends compliments to, **9**. (?)51, (?)161, (?)195, (?)203, 204, **10**. 109, 181, 227, 267, 301, 304, 312
HW's ill health regretted by, **10**. 268
HW to entertain, at SH, **9**. (?)231, **10**. 99, 100, 101, 135, 224, 225, 304
HW to receive compliments of, **9**. 202, 213, 291, **10**. 43, 100, 110, 183, 225, 226, 228, 230, 239, 261, 266, 271, 303, 320
Halifax's speech refusing augmentation to be shown to, by HW. **10**. 19
health of: deaf, **10**. 275; fever, **9**. 376, **10**. 31, 158; ill, **10**. 238; (?) influenza, **10**. 31; not well, **9**. 378; (?) recovered, **9**. 221
London visited by, **9**. 371, **10**. 3–4, 267, 320
Montagu, Charles, to be visited by, at Beaumont Lodge, **10**. 320

Montagu, George, embarrassed by, **10**. 48
—— lives with, in mutual boredom, **10**. 178
—— plays cards with, **10**. 144
——'s birthday celebrated by, **10**. 143–4, 145
—— sends enclosures for, to HW, **10**. 7–8
——'s letters to be called for by, at HW's, **10**. 3
—— spends evenings with, **10**. 144
—— wishes place for, at George III's Coronation, **9**. 381, 383, 390
'old woman' lost by, **10**. 178
Montagu, John (1718–92), 4th E. of Sandwich, 1729; 'Jemmy Twitcher':
'able, but obstinate, peevish and intractable,' **25**. 276
Admiralty abilities of, **23**. 263, 350
—— lord, **18**. 550, 561, **19**. 176, 388
—— post of, corrected, **43**. 368
—— resignation by, rumoured, **7**. 112
——'s first lord, **19**. 464, **23**. 263, **24**. 435n, 438n, **32**. 317
——'s Jersey news told by, to Hertford, **39**. 349
agrees with rest of Cabinet Council, **22**. 295
Aix peace conference attended by, **19**. 422n
—— preliminary treaties signed by, **19**. 479n
ambassador to Holland, **19**. 289, 294, 341, 351, 422
American colonists called cowardly by, **28**. 211n
American news not received by, **33**. 30
American plunder may be missed by, **10**. 202
announcement not made by, about fleet, **33**. 30
'Anti-Sejanus' letters attributed to, **31**. 57
attacked both by Opposition and Court, **25**. 221
ball and concert given by, **9**. 258
ball given by, for D. of Cumberland, **20**. 121
barely escapes official inquiry, **29**. 187
Barré attacks, in Parliamentary speech, **22**. 283–4, 286, **38**. 513
Beauclerk resigns from pique against, **20**. 135
Bedford, D. of, and, most unpopular people in England, **20**. 202n
Bedford, D. of, and D. of Cumberland seek support of, **20**. 113
Bedford, D. of, entertains, at dinner, **22**. 298n
—— governed by, through the Duchess, **20**. 120
—— hunts and gambles with, **20**. 113
—— may be abandoned by, **20**. 305
—— may be succeeded by, as secretary of state, **20**. 217, 235
—— presents ultimatum of, to George III, **22**. 307
—— 'protector' of, **20**. 144
—— would have become Master of the Horse if reversion had gone to, **20**. 217n
Beefsteak Club expels, for blasphemy, **10**. 110, 111
behaviour of, to Miller the printer, forgotten, **28**. 141, 142

[Montagu, John (1718–92), *continued*]

Berlin post wanted by, **19.** 456n

bishops 'coquet' with, **35.** 587

blamed for attacking Wilkes, **38.** 232–3

Breda visited by, **19.** 289n, 351

Bushey Park visited by, **10.** 207

Bute affronted by opposition of, to Regency Bill, **22.** 299–300

—— hinted by, to have fomented mob, **30.** 182

——'s removal credited to, **22.** 168n

Cambridge high stewardship sought by, **10.** 142n, **14.** 131, **22.** 219, **38.** 248, 341n, 355, 360, 362–3, **43.** 186

—— students enraged at electioneering of, **38.** 363

Chatham administration not to include, **10.** 222

Chesterfield may be succeeded by, as secretary of state, **19.** 413

chief justice in eyre may be post of, **9.** 181, **35.** 263

Churchill satirizes, **22.** 261, **38.** 290

coffee-girl's affair with, **22.** 284

colonelcy of regiment added by, to his posts as Admiralty lord, lt-col. to Bedford, and aide-de-camp to Richmond, **19.** 176

'conjurer's tricks' of, **38.** 407

contention enjoyed by, **38.** 362–3

Conway less accurate than, in counting Parliament numbers, **39.** 79

——'s attack on, in Parliament, **35.** 616

——'s speech on, **35.** 616

Cornwallis and Allen vilify, to Rigby, **38.** 247

Courtenay's brother-in-law, **19.** 413n

Cradock asked by, to aid Cassiobury theatricals, **32.** 180n

cricket played by, **10.** 235

Cumberland, D. of, anxious not to displease, **20.** 120n

—— intimate with, **20.** 207n

—— might secure navy through Bedford and, **20.** 222n

—— no longer friendly with, **10.** 79

—— reported safe, in letter withheld by, **9.** 50–1

—— supports, **20.** 113, 201

—— takes house of, **9.** 341

—— visited by, before returning to The Hague, **37.** 265

cunning preferred by, to prudence, **24.** 435

daughter-in-law's fortune to be shared by, **38.** 536

Dayrolles resident at The Hague under, **19.** 403, 422

defeat of, over Parliamentary report, **35.** 215

dismissal borne well by, **30.** 192

dismissals of anti-Court voters blamed on, **38.** 264

dismissed: as secretary of state, **20.** 258, 266, **22.** 310; from Admiralty post, **9.** 115

docks visited by, with Anson and Beauclerk, **20.** 80

Dunn said to be employed by, to attack Wilkes, **38.** 265

Dutch embassy to be given to, **9.** 39, 40

Dutch ships' searching advocated by, **33.** 156n

Eliott's and Murray's dispatches to, **25.** 136n

Essay on Woman hurts, more than it hurts Wilkes, **38.** 243

—— laid by, before House of Lords, **38.** 229–30

——'s reprints obtained by, **22.** 195n

Essex election lost through interference of, **38.** 263

Fair Quaker's preface praises, **28.** 110, 119, 120

Fane gives annuity to, **20.** 258, 266

first lord of the Admiralty, **24.** 435n, 438n, **32.** 317

fleet said to be detained by, at Portsmouth, to divert George III and Charlotte, **24.** 377

foes of, numerous, but friends not lacking, **25.** 238

Foote's retort to, **5.** 192

Fox, C. J., attacks, in Parliament, **25.** 244

—— demands investigation of, **33.** 248n

—— demands removal of, **24.** 460

—— makes motion against, **33.** 328n, **35.** 616n

Fox, Henry, appoints, to make tie with D. of Cumberland, **22.** 103n

——'s dismissal not to be assigned to, **30.** 183

Frederick, P. of Wales, hates, for slurs on Hanover, **20.** 217

French capture of fleet enrages City against, **36.** 198–9

French confuse, with Wilkes, **31.** 68

Garter rumoured for, **38.** 463

genealogy of, **10.** 351

George II dislikes Bedford because of his attachment to, **20.** 235n

—— expects, to support Treaty of Dresden, **20.** 300n

—— keeps, in government, **10.** 152n

—— refuses to sign credentials of, **19.** 422n

George III and D. of Cumberland unite in hating, **22.** 364

George III arrogantly treated by, **22.** 309

—— considers shifting, to secretary of state from Admiralty, **24.** 445n

—— dismisses, but has to recall him, **22.** 302

—— may still support, **24.** 449

—— persuaded by, to give St Eustatius's captors all private property there, **36.** 199n

—— possibly forced by, at Q. Charlotte's house, to propose omission of Ps of Wales's name from Regency Bill, **22.** 297n

——'s desire for conquest roused by, **28.** 94

—— tells, to reduce number of ships, **23.** 475n

—— to get resignation of, **38.** 558

Germain angers, by blaming Yorktown on navy, **25.** 241n

gold muslins carried by, to Q. Charlotte, **29.** 123

good humour and industry of, **38.** 231

Gordon rioters attack, **29.** 62, **33.** 184

Gower resents conduct of, 9. 115
——'s daughter given, by, to Col. Waldegrave, 20. 258
—— seeks support of, 20. 113
——'s quarrel with, 20. 258
Grafton called to order by, 17. 231–2, 263
—— succeeds, as secretary of state, 22. 310
grandmother's heir, 1. 89
Gray's verses on, 28. 166, 169–70
Grenville-Bedford faction adhered to, by, 38.
534
Griffin disobliged by Conyers's support from,
in Essex election, 38. 263
Guastalla conceded by, at Aix, 19. 481n
Guilford entertains, 10. 209–10
HW advises C. J. Fox to attack North instead
of, 33. 326n
HW brings Noble's Memoirs of the Cromwells
to, 42. 140
HW calls: 'Lord High Admiral,' 33. 30;
'roguish lad,' 32. 317
HW describes character of, 19. 361, 24. 435
HW expects, has gone off, 38. 316
HW fears his letters are opened by, 38. 282
HW forbidden by physician to see, 42. 134
HW given Lenclos portrait by, because 'dead
mistress' not 'living one,' 40. 94–5
HW gives Gramont's Mémoires to, 41. 237–8
HW identifies 'Twitcher' as, 16. 346
HW informed by, of drawing of Richard III,
41. 134–5
HW jokes about asking, to defend Tuscany,
18. 561
HW jokes about future grandson of, 10. 209
HW jokes about possible conversion of, to
Methodism, 31. 62
HW mentions, 20. 292, 29. 76, 128
HW receives Ninon de Lenclos's portrait
from, 10. 54n, 35. 99–100, 40. 94–5, 41.
237–8
HW's attentions from, keep him from repeat-
ing anecdotes, 38. 231, 260
HW's attitude towards, 38. 231, 232–3
HW's correspondence with, 31. 6, 40. 94–5,
41. 134–5, 237–8, 42. 127–8, 134, 140
HW's letter might be intercepted by, 38. 316,
39. 102
HW's opinion of, 10. 111
HW tells D. of Richmond not to put, in min-
istry, 41. 86
HW tells Hertford not to believe, 38. 285
HW terms conduct of, 'out-Sandwiching him-
self,' 10. 111
HW undertakes to carry election for, at Cam-
bridge, 32. 165
HW wearies of political activities of, 10. 167
Hague convention signed by, 19. 455n
Hague, The, visited by, 19. 301n, 37. 265
Halifax opposed by, over Turnpike Bill, 20.
121
——'s relations with, 10. 195
Hardwicke's contest with, over Cambridge

high stewardship, 10. 142n, 14. 131, 22. 219,
38. 248, 341n, 355, 360, 362–3
Harrington's and Newcastle's instructions to,
at Breda, 19. 289n
Hawke succeeded by, as first lord of Admiralty, 23. 263
Hertford has no connection with, 38. 329
—— hears news of Jersey from, 39. 349
—— invites, with Almodóvar, 24. 438n
—— told by, to tell waterman to petition Admiralty for release from impressment, 39.
290–1
—— wants anecdotes about, 38. 245
—— would be disgraced by any connection
with, 38. 283
Hertfordshire and Huntingdonshire protests
produced by, 25. 11n
Hervey compensated by, for loss of command,
22. 175n
Historic Doubts praised by, 14. 173
hooted off the stage with Scott, 22. 410
House of Commons correctly counted by, 39.
79
—— whitewashes, 33. 326, 328
Huntingdon festivities of, 10. 151n
Huntingdonshire boroughs of, 19. 413, 43. 133
impiety of, equal to Wilkes's, 38. 233
(?) informer, 28. 286
Jacobite healths proposed by, 19. 388
'Jemmy Twitcher,' 14. 133, 28. 81n, 38. 363;
see also 'Twitcher'
Johnstone does not trust, 29. 110
joint vice-treasurer, 10. 9
Jones a tool of, 22. 495n
Keene repairs omissions of, in Spanish treaty
at Aix, 20. 198
Keith, Robert, secretary to, 9. 45, 19. 403n
Kempenfelt dispatched by, with only 14 ships,
25. 221
—— pleases, by victory, 33. 313
Keppel refuses to take orders from, 24. 262n
——'s court martial will be regretted by, 24.
435
——'s enemy, 24. 438n
——'s messenger fails to find, 28. 408
——'s persecution by, disgraces the Court,
24. 447
Legge's intimacy with, a reason for getting
Berlin post, 19. 458n
Lely painting given by, to Blackwood, 10. 79
letter by, on mistress's death, 2. 156n
Leveson Gower, Lady Elizabeth, aided in marriage by, 9. 115, 20. 258
libels written by, 22. 323
lies are expected from, 38. 328
Liotard's portrait of, 40. 283
loaves distributed by, at Huntingdon, 10.
151–2
London magistracy attacked by, 38. 258
Macanaz has conference with, at Breda, 19.
393n
Manchester, D. of, attacked by, in newspapers, 10. 186

[Montagu, John (1718–92), *continued*]
—— reconciled with, 9. 257–8
—— visits, 9. 258
Mann facilitates marriage of, 19. 351
—— neglected by, 19. 351, 361
—— once knew, well, 24. 435
——'s correspondence with, 17. (?)382, (?)
    396, 19. 12, 351, 363, 373, 375, 22. 318–19,
    321–2
——'s friendship with, 17. 230–1, 18. 561, 19.
    294, 373, 21. 77, 22. 103, 112, 159, 23. 350
——'s protector, 24. 160
Mansfield, E. of, likes to mortify, 38. 258
MS list sent to HW by, 14. 177
Marlborough and Pembroke declare against,
    24. 435
Mason does not expect, to be converted to
    Christianity, 28. 256
——'s *Heroic Postscript* mentions, 28. 113
—— sneers at, 29. 51
Mastership of the Horse may go to, 20. 217
merchants planned to ask George III to re-
    move, 33. 27
'Methodism' of, 10. 110
Mirepoix's promotion may depend on, 20. 29
mistress of: dies, 2. 156n, 7. 131; married to
    Dr Dodd, 32. 185; *see also* Ray, Martha
money lost by, at cricket, 10. 235
Montagu, Edward Wortley, has election in-
    terests secured by, 19. 450n
——'s bequest to, 21. 473
(?) Montagu, George, kept awake by tri-
    umphs of, 10. 119
(?) —— refers to, 10. 142
——'s opinion of, 10. 112, 186
——'s relations with, 10. 196, 209
Montagu regiment to be headed by, 19. 176
naval disaster may cause downfall of, 25. 221
Navy Bill proposed by, 20. 33
nephew of, 9. 405n
Newcastle, D. of, asked by, for Paris embassy,
    20. 29n
—— cannot forgive conduct of, at Aix, 20.
    120n
—— disagrees with Harrington over orders to
    be sent to, 19. 326n
—— hates, 20. 120
—— negotiates with Granville to strengthen
    himself against, 20. 72n
—— refuses to be thoroughly reconciled to,
    20. 120n
——'s instructions to, regarding Aix, 19. 448n
—— to meet with, and Bentinck, 19. 485n
Newcastle House meeting attended by, 22.
    541n
Niccolini a friend of, 20. 217
—— correctly describes unpopularity of, 20.
    225
Noble brought by, to breakfast with HW, 33.
    468
——'s patron, 33. 468, 42. 133n
not a seaman, 28. 120

Nugent attacks, in Parliament over West-
    minster scrutiny, 20. 123
officiates at Handel jubilee, 33. 468
Old Pretender has connection with, 17. 231n
Opposition's lost opportunities known to, 38.
    355
Orange, P. of, urged by, to carry on war
    against France, 19. 403n
Orford, 3d E. of, temporarily succeeded by,
    in parks rangership, 25. 266n
Osborn, Hon. Mrs, accompanies, to Bushey
    Park, 10. 207
Osborn, Sir George, beats, at cricket, 10. 235
—— visited by, 10. 235
out of town at arrival of Ushant news, 33. 49n
Palliser resuscitated by, 29. 47
——'s clearance sought by, 7. 116n
—— warned by, of court martial, 24. 444n
Parliamentary activity of, on Regency Bill,
    38. 552
Parliamentary attacks upon, 20. 123, 22. 283–
    4, 24. 445, 25. 244
Parliamentary inquiry into conduct of, killed
    by vote of approbation, 25. 243
Parliamentary motions advocated by: against
    Hanover troops, 18. 356; against Wilkes,
    14. 130n
Parliamentary motion for removal of, de-
    feated, 24. 464
Parliamentary vote of, with minority, 38. 529
Parliament's adjournment opposed by, 30.
    181n
Parry's cause to be Eton fellow deserted by,
    20. 121
'Patriot,' 20. 198
Pecquigny injured by, in horse play, 38. 295
Pitt (Chatham) hates, 20. 38
—— jealous of, 20. 38, 138
—— proscribes, 22. 161
——'s speech ridiculed by, as nonsense, 23.
    167
—— supports Newcastle against, 20. 222
Poor Bill supported by, 38. 529
postmaster, 22. 569, 571
precedence disputed by ladies at ball given
    by, 20. 121, 144
profane conversation of, drives harlequins
    from club in Drury Lane theatre, 22. 185
prosecution of, in House of Commons, will
    probably lead to nothing, 25. 241
Puisieux and, decide on congress at Aix, 19.
    430n, 446n
Ray, Martha, lost by, 33. 99, 100–1
—— mistress of, 24. 459
recall of, from Holland, rumoured, 19. 303
refuses to retire, despite attacks, 28. 402
regent, 10. 153
removal of, planned, 24. 439n
'Repeal, The,' caricatures, 22. 400
reprieved by Parliamentary recess, 25. 222
resignation of: expected, 25. 236n; suggested,
    24. 447n

retires early, after son's wedding, **10**. 207

Robinson opposed by, for archbishopric, **22**. 276n

Rockingham answered by, **25**. 222n

—— attacks, in House of Lords, **25**. 221

Rous's roll of Earls of Warwick borrowed by, for HW, **1**. 133n, **15**. 124n

Sackville's principal enemy, **25**. 238

St-Séverin tells, that French are ready to sign Aix treaty, **19**. 482

Scott, James, patronized by, **28**. 466, **32**. 20n

——'s attitude towards Pitt depends on status of, **22**. 410n

secretary of state, **10**. 110, **22**. 159, 167

secretary of state's post lost by, **10**. 161, 162, 165, 178

secretary of state's post to be resigned by, **23**. 263

Selwyn's witticism on, at tennis game, **20**. 155

sent to the devil, **22**. 312

Seymour, Francis, married widowed mother of, **20**. 216n

Seymour, Henry, half-brother of, **20**. 217

Skrine, Mrs, bestowed by, on the public, **22**. 402

son of, **10**. 9

son recommended by, at dismissal, **30**. 192n

son's marriage arranged by, **10**. 195–6

Spanish post rumoured for, **22**. 103, 112, **38**. 534

Spanish war expected by, **39**. 324

Stanhope, John, succeeds, in Admiralty post, **19**. 464n

subscription masquerade promoted by, **9**. 113

Suffolk may be succeeded by, as secretary of state, **24**. 450

talents of, fit him to be head of the marine, **23**. 350

Temple reconciled with, **22**. 304

—— refuses dinner invitation of, for King's Birthday, **30**. 187

Thespian activities of, **14**. 31

threats against, **9**. 48

tie wig worn by, **18**. 561

Townshend, Vct, does caricature of, **21**. 77

Townshend, Capt. George, court-martialled because of, **19**. 332, 361, 373

Townshend, Thomas, attacks, and Rigby makes no defence, **38**. 499

travels of, qualify him for Breda post, **19**. 289n

treaty with Saxony defended by, in Parliament, **20**. 300

tricky, **22**. 382

'Twitcher,' **10**. 153, 186, **33**. 116

universally hated, **20**. 201

unpopular, **20**. 138, **33**. 328

valet of, **1**. 363

Waldegrave's marriage arranged by, **20**. 258

Waldegrave's wager on head being lost by, **38**. 274–5, 281

Warburton to reinstate Pitt's name in place of, in sermon dedications, **38**. 316

Weymouth succeeded by, as secretary of state, but in northern province, **23**. 255

Wheate's account of combined fleets not believed by, **28**. 461

wife separated from, because of her insanity, **22**. 312n

wife's fortune and insanity will be useful to, **22**. 396

wife's treatment from, **20**. 258

Wilkes accused by, of writing *Essay on Woman*, **38**. 230

—— attacked by, in House of Lords, over *Essay on Woman*, **38**. 293–4

—— demands examination of, **4**. 173n

—— does not hate, **10**. 180

—— forgets, **38**. 362

—— frightens, with demand for examination in House of Commons, **10**. 272

—— reads *Essay on Woman* to, **22**. 185

——'s *Essay on Woman* denounced by, in House of Lords, **22**. 184

——'s impeachment instigated by, because of *Essay on Woman*, **10**. 111

Williams, Sir C. H., opposed by, for Aix commission, **19**. 456n

will return, even if he has to marry wife, **22**. 312

Wiseman addressed at place of, **21**. 380n

Wortley Montagu's bequest to, **21**. 473

Wright's murder seen by, at Florence, **37**. 34

Yonge succeeded by, as vice-treasurer of Ireland, **20**. 518

Montagu (before 1749, Brudenell), John (1735–70), styled Bn Montagu 1735–62, M. of Monthermer 1766–70; cr. (1762) Bn Montagu; M.P.:

art objects imported by, from Italy, **38**. 358

genealogy of, **10**. 351

mother's guests mostly friends of, **38**. 358

peerage granted to, **10**. 27, **22**. 31

Queensberry, Ds of, invites to ball under wrong title, **38**. 342

Montagu, John (b. and d. 1742):

birth of, **18**. 130

Montagu, John (1743–1814), styled Vct Hinchingbrooke; 5th E. of Sandwich, 1792; M.P.:

Bushey Park given to, by father-in-law, **10**. 203

—— to be scene of wedding of, **10**. 203

coming of age of, **10**. 151n

cricket played by, **10**. 235

father recommends, to George III, **30**. 192n

genealogy of, **10**. 351

Guilford entertains, **10**. 209–10

Halifax's aide-de-camp in Ireland, **10**. 9

joke about, **10**. 234

marriage of, **10**. 195–7, 203, 207, **38**. 536

mother's inheritance settled on, **10**. 203

Osborn visited by, **10**. 235

unwell, **10**. 210n

[Montagu, John (1743–1814), *continued*]
wife of, 9. 396n

Montagu, John (b. ca 1771), naval Capt.:
Sandwich's son by Martha Ray, 24. 459, 33. 101

Montagu, Lucy (1679–1720), m. (1702) John Morley Trevor:
genealogy of, 10. 352
Newcastle and Pelham cousins of, 17. 366n
(?) Rice, George, inherits money from, 9. 134

Montagu, Lucy (ca 1709–34), m. (1728) Francis North, 7th Bn North; cr. (1752) E. of Guilford:
genealogy of, 10. 352

Montagu, Lady Mary (d. 1743), m. (1740) Sir Danvers Osborn, 3d Bt:
genealogy of, 10. 352
husband of, 9. 149n
inscription to, on columbarium, 10. 170
marriage of, at Chicksands, 10. 169
(?) portrait of, by Davison, 10. 334
son of, 9. 248n

Montagu, Lady Mary (ca 1711–75), m. (1730) George Brudenell, 4th E. of Cardigan, cr. (1766) D. of Montagu:
animals protected by, 9. 94
appearance of, 10. 341
art treasures of, 38. 357–8
ball given by, 36. 41, 38. 357–8
Beaulieu's agent to consult with, about ranger's post, 10. 189
bequests of, to daughter and husband, 24. 99
Blackheath visited by, 31. 57
Boughton House in litigation between sister (or sister's husband) and, 10. 89, 340
—— visited by, 10. 89, 340
capriciousness of, 10. 89
children of, to bear Montagu name, 10. 341
cold dinner brought by, 10. 89
crayon pictures by, at Boughton House, 10. 340
death of: 24. 98–9; afflicts Anne Pitt, 24. 105; reported, 9. 405
Deene Park to be visited by, 10. 89
equipage of, 10. 89
father resembled by, 10. 341
father's bequests to, 9. 94, 20. 80
father's financial relationships with, 9. 95
genealogy of, 10. 351
HW asked by, to buy commodes in Paris, 31. 98, 106, 110
HW avoids, 10. 89, 340
HW calls: 'Tisiphone,' 33. 299; 'vixen turtle,' 32. 315
HW in love with, but not for her person, 37. 298
HW invited by, though her enemy, while Ds of Bedford is excluded, 38. 358
HW mentions, 37. 337
HW praises, 31. 4
HW's opinion of, 10. 191
HW's pun about, 10. 191
HW's treatment of her grandfather in *Royal*

and Noble Authors might be resented by, 9. 219, 10. 340, 11. 105
HW to meet, at Lady Sophia Thomas's at Hampton Court, 37. 297
HW visits, at Blackheath, 35. 234
house of: at Richmond, 31. 2; in Privy Gardens, 38. 357–8
husband mourns for, 32. 315–16
husband said by, to be unfit for state office, 32. 315n
husband's treatment of, 10. 341
Montagu, George, may be given post of deputy ranger of Rockingham Forest by, 10. 188, 189, 191, 192, 194
——'s opinion of, 10. 188, 189
Monthermer title wished by, for husband, 10. 27
Pitt, Anne, hears from, of HW's inquiries, 31. 4
Queensberry, Ds of, invites, to ball, 38. 342
sister's wish for Montagu title thwarted by, 10. 27
tavern visited by, after opera, 37. 54
Violette, Mlle, entertained by, 9. 28
wealth of, 10. 341
yacht awaits at Calais, the return of, from Spa, 17. 141

Montagu, Lady Mary (1748–61):
Meadows, Lady, leaves legacy to, 9. 255, 258

Montagu, Lady Mary Wortley (1689–1762). *See* Pierrepont, Lady Mary

Montagu, Mary Wortley (1718–94). *See* Wortley Montagu, Mary

Montagu, Matthew (formerly Robinson) (1762–1831), 4th Bn Rokeby, 1829:
HW sends letter to Hannah More under cover to, 31. 327

Montagu, Mrs Matthew. *See* Charlton, Elizabeth (d. 1817)

Montagu, Ralph (1638–1709), 3d Bn Montagu; cr. (1705) D. of Montagu; M.P.:
death of, 25. 564n
genealogy of, 10. 351
mother of, 10. 341
portraits of: at Boughton House, 10. 341; at Hinchingbrooke, 40. 283
St-Évrémond intimate with, 10. 34n
wife married by, as Emperor of China, 25. 564
wife of, 10. 109n
wife produced by, in Westminster Hall, 25. 564n

Montagu *or* Mountague, Richard (1577–1641), Bp of Chichester, 1628, of Norwich, 1638; controversialist:
De originibus ecclesiasticis commentationum by, quoted by Lort, 16. 146–7

Montagu, Robert (ca 1634–83), 3d E. of Manchester; M.P.:
genealogy of, 10. 351

Montagu, Robert (ca 1710–62) 3d D. of Manchester, M.P.:
Bishop Auckland visited by, 9. 310

chamberlain, lord, to Q. Charlotte, **9.** 377, **21.** 517, **32.** 7, **38.** 96
daughter of, **21.** 530
death of, **10.** 29
Durham, Bp of, talks with, **9.** 310
genealogy of, **10.** 351
George III does not retain, in Bedchamber, **9.** 324, **21.** 460
men presented by, to Q. Charlotte, **21.** 531
Montagu, George, hopes, will hear of Sandwich's distributing loaves, **10.** 152
—— receives letter from, **9.** 257
Sandwich reconciled with, **9.** 257-8
—— visited by, **9.** 258
son of, **9.** 303n
Montagu, Robert (1763-1830); Adm., 1810:
Sandwich's child by Martha Ray, **24.** 459, **33.** 101
Montagu, Sir Sidney (d. 1644):
genealogy of, **10.** 351
Montagu, Thomas de (d. 1428), 4th E. of Salisbury:
marriage of, **9.** 68
Montagu, Sir Walter:
genealogy of, **10.** 351
Montagu, Walter (ca 1603-77), Abbot of St Martin's:
HW to think of, at Pontoise, **10.** 190
miniature of, at Wandesford's, **10.** 12
Montagu, George, has epitaph of, **10.** 190
Montagu, William de (ca 1302-44), cr. (1337) E. of Salisbury:
Bisham founded by, **9.** 100n
Drayton mentions, **11.** 71n
Montagu, William (1700-39), 2d D. of Manchester:
death of, **37.** 44
genealogy of, **10.** 351
masquerades hated by, **37.** 9
wife of, **9.** 20n
Montagu, Capt. William (ca 1720-57), M.P.; naval officer:
election of, **19.** 450n
Montagu, William:
Sandwich's child by Martha Ray, **24.** 459, **33.** 101
Montagu, William (1771-1843), 5th D. of Manchester, 1788:
marriage of, **34.** 216
Montagu, Hon. William Augustus (1752-76), M.P.:
cricket played by, **10.** 235
father calls, 'William Rufus,' **10.** 209
Guilford entertains, **10.** 209-10
Montagu's opinion of, **10.** 210
Osborn, Sir George, visited by, **10.** 235
Montagu, English ship:
midshipman in, **17.** 36n
Rodney detaches, **25.** 24n
Montagu Dunk, Lady Anne (1742-61):
genealogy of, **10.** 352
Montagu Dunk, Lady Elizabeth (1745-68),

m. (1766) John Montagu, styled Vct Hinchingbrooke, 5th E. of Sandwich, 1792:
Allen, Lady, to entertain, at Christmas Ale, **9.** 415
Bedford, Ds of, to present, at Court, **10.** 210
Bushey Park given to, by father, **10.** 203
—— to be scene of wedding of, **10.** 203
death of, expected, **10.** 263
genealogy of, **10.** 351, 352
health of, **10.** 261
jewels of, pretty, **10.** 204
marriage of, **10.** 195-7, 203, 207, **38.** 536
(?) Melvill, Margaret, and Hon. Mrs Osborn discuss, **10.** 234
Montagu's opinion of, **10.** 195-6
noblemen from University of Dublin call on, **9.** 396
Montagu Dunk, Lady Frances (1743-64):
Allen, Lady, to entertain, at Christmas Ale, **9.** 415
genealogy of, **10.** 352
noblemen from University of Dublin call on, **9.** 396
Montagu Dunk, George. *See* Montagu, George (1716-71), E. of Halifax
Montague. *See* Montagu
Montagu family:
armorial bearings of: at Boughton House, **10.** 89; to be on Henrietta Montagu's tomb, in colour, **9.** 200
descent of, from Earls of Warwick, **35.** 606
HW good to, **10.** 261
HW jokes with George Montagu about, **9.** 256
HW's letters to be preserved by, **9.** 275
Halifax neglects portraits of, **9.** 309
——'s relations with, **10.** 152, 287
illegitimate ancestry of, said to be disproved by Oxford tomb, **10.** 42
ladies of, dislike Ds of Bedford's presenting Vct Hinchingbrooke at Court, **10.** 210
livery of, **9.** 275
Montagu dukedom restored to, **10.** 233
Montagu, Frederick, tells HW of pedigree of, **9.** 259
—— to send book about, **9.** 257
Montagu, George, calls, the 'Cu's,' **35.** 184n
—— threatens to desert name of, **10.** 119
pedigree of, prominently displayed at Boughton House, **10.** 340
political successes and failures of, **10.** 152
portraits of: at Horton, **10.** 334-5; by Dobson, **10.** 341; Cosby, Mrs, does not give, to HW, **10.** 103; damaged, **10.** 103; given to Montagu by Mrs Cosby, **10.** 67, 81, 85, 102, 103; HW describes, **10.** 103-4; HW promises to take charge of, **10.** 83, 86, 103-4; HW to send Wicks to pack, **10.** 102; Louis uses Conway papers in packing, **10.** 107; Montagu likes, **10.** 107; not given by Halifax to George Montagu, **9.** 310; route of, to Greatworth, changed, **10.** 104; temporarily

[Montagu family, *continued*]
in cloister, at SH, **10.** 103; to be collected at Greatworth, **9.** 257; Wicks packs, **10.** 104
pride of, **9.** 26
scream, **35.** 161, 184
Montagu House, London:
Albemarle, Ds of, confined at, **25.** 564n
mentioned, **12.** 254
Montagu, Mrs, opens new rooms at, **11.** 290
Montaigne ('Mountain'), George (1569–1628), Bp of London 1621–8:
Cole's print of, **1.** 149
Montaigne, Michel Eyquem de (1533–92), philosopher; essayist:
Du Deffand, Mme, mentions, **3.** 174
Essais of: Du Deffand, Mme, bored by, **3.** 246; Du Deffand, Mme, defends, **3.** 155, 160, 164, 226, 227, 246; Du Deffand, Mme, owns, **8.** 32; HW comments on, **3.** 151
HW corrects misstatement by, **16.** 156
HW disparages, **36.** 249–50
HW paraphrases, **23.** 529
HW tired of reading essays and travels of, **32.** 195
Journal du voyage by: Du Deffand, Mme, dislikes, **6.** 53, 58; Du Deffand, Mme, sends, to HW, **6.** 60, 63; editor of, *see* Meusnier de Querlon; HW's opinion of, **24.** 16–17
mistake about René I made by Powell, not by, **16.** 159
René I's self-portrait seen by, at Bar-le-Duc, **16.** 143
Mont-aigu:
HW's pun about, **10.** 310
Montaigu, ——, Chevalier de Bouzols:
social relations of, in Paris, **7.** 290, 292
Montaigu or Montagu, Jean de (ca 1349–1409), 'Provost':
HW asked by Montagu to find tomb and get copy of epitaph of, in Paris, **10.** 190
Montaigu-Bouzols, Anne-Joachim de (1737–1825), Comte de Bouzols:
after-dinner balls given by, **5.** 322
health of, **7.** 138
social relations of, in Paris, **6.** 100, **7.** 345, 352
Montaigu-Bouzols, Joachim-Charles-Laure de (1734–1818), Vicomte de Beaune; Marquis de Bouzols:
brother of, **7** 138
Du Deffand, Mme, given cup by, **7.** 439
——'s correspondence with, **7.** 431
—— writes to Necker about, **7.** 452
Fitzjames visited by, **7.** 426, 461
Gibbon given almanac by, **7.** 5
leaves Paris, **7.** 426
Paris visited by, **7.** 432
Praslin visited by, **7.** 461
regiments to be reviewed by, **7.** 427
social relations of, in Paris, *see* index entries *ante* **8.** 444
Strasbourg visited by, **7.** 427
SH visited by, **12.** 240
SH visitors sent by, **12.** 243

Montailleur, Bn de. *See* Foncet, Jean-Joseph
Mont Albano (Italy):
garrison at, **19.** 323
See also Monte Albano
Montale (Italy):
Spaniards stationed near, **19.** 30
Montallegre, Duca di. *See* Guzmann, José Joaquín
Montalto (Italy):
Spaniards at, **17.** 265n
Montalto, Villa. *See* Negroni, Villa
Montamy. *See* Arclais de Montamy
Montandre, Marquis de. *See* La Rochefoucauld, François de
Montandre, Marquise de. *See* Spanheim, Mary Anne von
Montaran. *See* Michau de Montaran; Michau de Montaran de Montblin
Montauban, Comtesse de. *See* Vaulserre des Adretz, Marie-Olympe de
Montauban, Prince de. *See* Rohan, Charles de (1693–1766)
Montauban, généralité de:
establishment of, **7.** 424
Montausier, Comte (later Marquis) de. *See* Crussol d'Uzès, Anne-Marie-André de
Montausier, Duc de:
Rambouillet, Mlle de, receives 'Guirlande de Julie' from, **42.** 93n
Montazet, Marquis de. *See* Malvin, Charles de
Montazet, Antoine de Malvin de. *See* Malvin de Montazet, Antoine de
Montbarey, Chevalier de. *See* St-Mauris, Claude-Antoine-François de
Montbarey, Mlle de. *See* St-Mauris, Marie-Françoise-Maximilienne de
Montbarey, Prince de. *See* St-Mauris, Alexandre-Marie-Léonor de
Montbarey, Princesse de. *See* St-Mauris, Marie-Françoise-Maximilienne de
Montbazon, Princesse de. *See* Le Tonnelier de Breteuil, Louise-Gabrielle-Rosalie
Montblin. *See* Michau de Montaran de Montblin
Montboissier, Messrs de:
SH visited by, **12.** 223
Montboissier, Jean de (fl. 1584):
Montmorency obtains Alais from, **14.** 127n
Montboissier-Beaufort, Claude-François de (ca 1693–1761), called Abbé de Canillac, French chargé d'affaires at Rome 1742–5:
Benedict XIV's dislike prompts recall of, **35.** 59
biographical information about, corrected, **43.** 360
Montboissier-Beaufort, Ignace de (1750–1812), Vicomte (later Comte) de Canillac:
marriage of, **5.** 225
Montboissier-Beaufort-Canillac, Louise-Agnès-Élisabeth de (1755–92), m. (1773) Dom Vicente de Souza Coutinho:
marriage of, **5.** 342

Montbruel, Baronne de. *See* Le Maure, Catherine-Nicole

Montcalm de St-Véran, Louis-Joseph (1712–59), Marquis de:
Albany threatened by, **21.** 229n, **30.** 138n
alleged victory by, **21.** 344
Brest sailed from by, **20.** 541n
death of, **21.** 338
English to be driven by, from Louisbourg, **21** 229–30
Ft William Henry surrenders to, **21.** 144n
Oswego captured by, **21.** 12n

Mont Cenis pass:
Charles Emmanuel III retreats through, into Piedmont, **18.** 142n

Mont Castello (Italy):
Spaniards force Charles Emmanuel III to abandon, **19.** 120

Monteagle, Bn. *See* Parker, William (1575–1622)

Monteagle, Bns. *See* Spencer, Anne (d. 1618)

Monte Albano (Italy):
road to, **18.** 532
See also Mont Albano

Monteallegri. *See* Montallegre

Monte Cassino (Italy):
Charles of Naples may visit, **18.** 447

Monte Cavallo (Italy):
Clement XIV and D. of Gloucester talk in garden of, **23.** 389
popes abandon St Peter's for, in summer, **24.** 344
York, D. of, visits, **22.** 228–9

Monte Cavo:
Carter, Mary, digs marble fragment from, **42.** 406

Montecuccoli, (?) Raimondo:
(?) Aix treaty negotiated by, **20.** 400n
HW mentions, **17.** 42
HW sees, at Reggio, **17.** 44–5

Monte del Salo:
Florentine public fund, **20.** 266n

Monte di Pietà:
at Leghorn, Leghorn houses to be repaired with money from, **17.** 304
at Rome: Kingston, Ds of, takes treasure from, **24.** 404; Old Pretender said to deposit jewels at, **19.** 94, 96, **22.** 387n

Monte di Santa Maria (Italy):
Benedict XIV disputes control of, with Francis I, **20.** 428
Del Monte family hold, as imperial fief, **20.** 422, 428, 437

Montefiascone (Italy):
Inquisition officers sent to, to examine the Madonna di Valentano, **24.** 30, 39–40, 42

Monte Guffone, villa in Tuscany:
Mann visits, **20.** 160

Monteil, Castellane-Adhémar de. *See* Castellane-Adhémar de Monteil

Monteil, Charles-François-Just (b. 1718):
may be appointed minister to Parma, **5.** 209

Monteil, François-Louis, Chevalier de:

social relations of, in Paris, **7.** 300, 309, 317

Montel. *See* Vedel-Montel

Montelatici, Antonio Filippo, LL.D.; Florentine notary public:
Lady Orford's will registered by, at the Archivio, **43.** 288–9

Monteleone (Italy):
earthquake account mentions, **25.** 376

Montem (Eton festival):
George III and Q. Charlotte attend, **33.** 49

Montemar, Duque de. *See* Carrillo de Albornoz, Don José

Montenegro:
Dolgorukov's conduct in, disapproved by Catherine II, **23.** 160
—— to mobilize, against Turks, **23.** 160n

Montenero (Italy):
earthquake refugees flee to, **17.** 303

Montenoy. *See* Palissot de Montenoy

Monte Oliveto, Naples, Italy:
Correale, Gabrielle, buried at, **20.** 369n

Montepulciano (Italy):
Bucelli Collection at, **25.** 531n

Monteran. *See* Michau de Montaran

Montero, Don Geronimo:
Nuestra Señora del Cabadonga commanded by, **18.** 463n

Monte Rodimibile:
Florentine public fund, **20.** 266n

Monte Rosi (Italy):
Austrian army at, **18.** 525, 534

Monte Rosso (Italy):
Young Pretender at, **18.** 388

Monte Rotondo (Italy):
Atrisco to attack, **4.** 443
Lobkowitz's troops rendezvous at, **18.** 443
—— to approach Naples through, by Benedict XIV's permission, **18.** 437

Montesan, Mme de *See.* Béraud de la Haie de Riou, Charlotte-Jeanne

Montesinos's cave, in *Don Quixote*:
Roche Abbey resembles, **1.** 275–6

Montespan, Marquise de. *See* Rochechouart, Françoise-Athénaïs de

Montesquieu, Baron de. *See* Secondat, Charles de (1689–1755)

Montesquiou-Fézensac, Anne-Élisabeth-Pierre de (1764–1834), Baron de Montesquiou; cr. (1809) Comte de Montesquiou-Fézensac:
Hampton Court visited by, **33.** 409
SH visited by, **25.** 423, **33.** 408–9

Montesson, Marquise de. *See* Béraud de la Haie de Riou, Charlotte-Jeanne

Montesson, Jean-Baptiste (ca 1676–1769), Marquis de:
widow of, to marry again, **5.** 357

Montessuy, ——:
receipt signed by, **8.** 38

Monte Toro, Minorca:
Augustinian monastery on, **37.** 314

Monteynard, Marquise de. *See* Monteynard, Marie-Françoise de

Monteynard, Louis-François (b. 1716), Marquis de; minister of war:
affairs of, **5.** 402, 436
becomes minister of war, **4.** 380n, **5.** 4–5
Boufflers, Comtesse Amélie de, makes remark on, **6** 11
Choiseul courteously spoken of by, **5.** 15
dismissed, **6.** 10, 12, 15
Fenouilhet, Lady, aided by appeals to, from: Beauvau, **5.** 380; Mme du Deffand, **5.** 371, 373; Maréchale de Mirepoix, **5.** 376, 380, 402, 405
Fenouilhet, Lady, appeals to, **5.** 366, 373
—— has indicated suitable houses to, **5.** 379
—— to be protected by, **5.** 372, 375
French drag out, to fill government, **23.** 264
La Vrillière brings dismissal to, **6.** 10, 12
Louis XV first consents to plea of, then punishes him, **23.** 284
Maillebois aided by, **23.** *283*
Maupeou supported by, **5.** 285
may become member of Ordre du St-Esprit, **6.** 11
mistakenly invited to council, **5.** 53
Montazet recommended by, **5.** 435–6
relatives of, **5.** 377
resignation of, rumoured, **23.** 284
Stormont does not know, **5.** 372, 373, 379
thought to be insecure, **5.** 45
Monteynard, Marie-Françoise de (b. 1734), m. (1753) Louis-François, Marquis de Monteynard:
Monteynard tells, of invitation to council, **5.** 53
Montezuma [Moctezuma] II (1477 *or* 1479–1520), Emperor of Mexico:
alleged descendants of, **43.** 91
birth date of, corrected, **43.** 91
England to take place of, **28.** 293
ghost of, should not complain now, **22.** 49
Q. Elizabeth had more gold and silver plate than, **32.** 323
'Montezuma.' *See* George IV
Montezuma (opera). See *Motezuma*
Montfaucon, Bernard de (1655–1741), writer; priest:
Antiquitas explanatione et schematibus illustrata (*Antiquité expliqueé* . . .) by: Conway buys, **37.** 422; costume for play taken from, **9.** 335
Bayeux tapestries described by, **40.** 221
Gray advises HW not to imitate, **14.** 122
Marguerite de Valois in print by, **7.** 313
Mémoires de littérature by, Dover church tower mistaken in, for pharos, **16.** 211
Monumens de la monarchie françoise, Les, by: **1.** 138–9, 383, **2.** 307, **43.** 49, 183, 216; Gray refers HW to, **14.** 70, 77; HW to imitate, **16.** 27, **40.** 211, 213, 217, 218, 220; pictures in, **14.** 76; Strutt follows plan of, **1.** 351n
Montfort, Bn. *See* Bromley, Henry (1705–55);

Bromley, Henry (1773–1851); Bromley, Thomas (1733–99)
Montfort, Bns. *See* Blake, Mary Anne
Montfort, Elizabeth de (d. 1354) m. (ca 1292) William de Montagu, 2d Bn Montagu:
arms on tomb of, at Oxford, **10.** 42
Chute may know about, **10.** 43
HW knows nothing about, **10.** 43
Montfort, Philogène-Charles de (b. 1733) *or* Jean-Louis de (b. 1763):
(?) Jerninghams bring, to SH, **33.** 406
Montforts:
scene of, reenacted, **22.** 303
Montglas *or* Montglat, —— de, secretary to Comte d'Eu:
Du Deffand, Mme, gives account of, **6.** 23
sends desired permission to Mme du Deffand, **3.** 375
wife of, escapes on way to convent, **6.** 23
Montglas *or* Montglat, Mme ——:
duel fought over, **6.** 23, 30
escapes on way to convent, **6.** 23
Eu's mistress, **3.** 375, **6.** 23
Montgolfier, Jacques-Étienne (1745–99) *and* Jacques-Michel (1740–1810), aeronauts:
balloon ascents by, **25.** 449n, 450n, **39.** 419n
HW imagines, as balloon commanders, **39.** 425
HW puns on name of, **42.** 110
Montgomerie, Alexander (1723–69), 10th E. of Eglintoun, 1729:
(?) at Chesterfield's assembly, **37.** 327
at private Court ball, **38.** 143
Bute's friend, **21.** 460n, 465n
Florence visited by, **18.** 479
George III includes, in Bedchamber, **9.** 324, **21.** 460
Grant hears from, of Jacobite plot, **35.** 61n
HW mentions, **9.** 402, 403
Maclaine robs, **20.** 168
Mann entertains, **20.** 426
Ramsay communicates Jacobite sympathies to, when his tutor, **19.** 112–13
York, D. of, wants, included in royal Household, **9.** 324
Montgomerie, Archibald (1726–96), 11th E. of Eglintoun:
Chaillot visited by, **6.** 357
(?) Conway, Hon. Jane, 'pensions,' **9.** 30
Mrs Montagu's social relations with, **6.** 357
Montgomerie. *See also* Montgomery
Montgomery, Cts of. *See* Clifford, Anne (1590–1676); Vere, Susan de (1587–1629)
Montgomery, E. of. *See* Herbert, George Augustus (1759–1827); Herbert, Philip (1584–1650)
Montgomery, ——, Irish half-pay officer:
Lee, Charles, leaves Bologna with, **20.** 363n
Montgomery, Anne (d. 1819), m. (1773) George Townshend, 4th Vct Townshend, cr. (1787) M. Townshend:
HW offers chaise to, at Houghton, **41.** 261

Orford, E. of, invited by, to recuperate at Raynham, **42.** 334, 336

Montgomery, Augustus Retnuh. *See* Reebkomp, Augustus Retnuh

Montgomery, Nicholas. *See* Archdall, Nicholas

Montgomery, Richard (1738–75), American army officer:
Carleton said to be defeated and St John's captured by, **24.** 156–7, 161
Crown Point left by army of, **24.** 133n
death of, in attack on Quebec, **24.** 185
Irishman, **24.** 158

Montgomery, Sir Thomas (d. 1495), Kt, 1461; K.C., 1476:
Bourchier's commission to, as Edward IV's executor, **41.** 124

Montgomery. *See also* Montgomerie

Montgomery, American privateer:
merchantmen captured by, **24.** 229n

Montgomery, Fort, N.Y.:
Clinton captures, **32.** 400

Montgomeryshire:
election in, **39.** 183, 186–7
sheep and oxen roasted in, at E. of Powis's orders, **32.** 302n
Talbot justice for, **9.** 181n

Monthermer, M. of. *See* Montagu, John (1735–70)

Monthermer, Marquisate of:
Cardigan, Cts of, wishes husband to have, **10.** 27

Monthermer family:
coat of arms of, at Boughton House, **10.** 340
Montagu family's descent through, from Earls of Warwick, **35.** 606

Monthly Magazine:
Bedford, Horace W., contributor to, **42.** 492

Monthly Review:
account in, of Taylor's *Proclus*, **34.** 83
accusation against HW in, **2.** 50, 51
Anecdotes of Painting reviewed in, **2.** 267, 270
Bewley writes for, **16.** 349
HW implied by, to be author of Heathcote's *Letter*, **10.** 241
HW's connection with Chatterton affair mentioned in, **41.** 396
HW's notes on review in, of Milles's edn of Chatterton, **16.** 360
HW's *Royal and Noble Authors* abused in, **13.** 30, **16.** 24, **35.** 107n
Hamilton's *Collection of . . . Antiquities* criticized by, **35.** 444n
Hayley praised in, **29.** 114
Mann wants, **22.** 36, 49
Marcus Flaminius reviewed in, **34.** 170n
(?) Marmontel's *Les Incas* reviewed in, **28.** 299
Melissa and Marcia reviewed in, **34.** 90n
Milles confuted in, **29.** 225
Nash's edition of *Hudibras* reviewed in, **43.** 389n

Remarks on the Speech of M. Dupont criticized by, **31.** 389
(?) reviews in, **35.** 462
Ruffhead's review in, of HW's *Royal and Noble Authors*, **35.** 107n

Monti, Filippo Maria (1675–1754), Cardinal, 1743:
Benedict XIV makes, cardinal, **18.** 302n
Young Pretender's departure from Rome described by, **18.** 418–19

Monti, Del. *See* Del Monte

Monticelli, Angelo Maria (ca 1710–64), opera singer:
admired, **17.** 190, 211
alleged print of, **41.** 452
Burlington, E. of, supports, in action against opera house, **20.** 4n
Calais visited by, **17.** *141*, **30.** 19
Conway, Bns, to have, sing at assembly, **17.** 334
elephant to have been ridden by, **17.** 358
English women in packet boat call, 'the creature,' **30.** 19
Frederick, P. of Wales, sends for, **17.** 279
HW accuses Lady Mary Walpole of loving, **17.** 487
HW has, sing at entertainment, **17.** 274
HW's opinion of, **9.** 157
HW's witticism on Lady Rich's desertion by, **18.** 481
HW travels with, **17.** 141, **30.** 19
Holdernesse entertains, **18.** 131
ill, **17.** 190
London opera retains, **17.** 191, 358, **30.** 5
Middlesex sued by, for salary, **20.** 4
salary of, **17.** 191
sings in the *Olimpiade*, **17.** 401
spelling of name of, corrected, **43.** 239
to sing, at opera, **17.** 185
Townshend, Vcts, to entertain, **17.** 211
Walpole, Sir Robert, often dines with, **17.** 487
—— remarks on hearing, **17.** 274n
women overlook defects of, **35.** 14
yacht visited by, **17.** 141

Monticello. *See* Monticelli

Montigny, Jean-Charles-Philibert Trudaine de. *See* Trudaine de Montigny, Jean-Charles Philibert

Montigny, Mme Jean-Charles-Philibert Trudaine de. *See* Bouvard de Fourqueux, Anne-Marie-Rosalie de

Montigny, Louise-Fidèle-Ste-Eugénie de (1738–1809), m. (1763) Louis-Marie-Anne de Talleyrand-Périgord, Baron de Talleyrand:
Chanteloup visited by, **8.** 202

Montigny, Marie-Anne de (1748–67), m. (1766) Louis-Jean-Baptiste-Antonin Colbert, Marquis de Seignelay:
death of, **3.** 259

Montigny (France):
Trudaine's death at château at, **6.** 466n

Montijo, Count:

[Montijo, Count, *continued*]
Ferdinand VI admits, to ministry, **19.** 278n

Montijon, ——:
Mme du Deffand's social relations with, **7.** 340

Montini, ——:
executed at Naples for treason, **18.** 271

Montlausier, —— de:
number of prisoners in French jails estimated by, **11.** 233n

Montmartel. *See* Paris de Montmartel

Montmartre, Abbess of. *See* Montmorency-Laval, Marie-Louise de

Montmartre, Paris:
Denis, St, martyred on, **3.** 305

Montmartre, Rue, Paris:
Mouchard lives in, **8.** 8, 11
Uzès, Hôtel d', in, **5.** 140n

Mont Merion. *See* Mount Merrion

Montmorency, Baronne de. *See* Charette de Montebert, Marie-Madeleine-Élisabeth

Montmorency, Duc de. *See* Montmorency, Anne de (1492–1567); Montmorency, Anne-Léon de (1731–99); Montmorency, Henri de (1534–1614); Montmorency-Luxembourg, Anne-François de (1735–61)

Montmorency, Duchesse de. *See* Des Ursins, Marie-Félice (1601–66); Diane (1538–1619); Montmorency-Luxembourg, Charlotte-Anne-Françoise de (b. 1757); Montmorency-Luxembourg, Louise-Françoise-Pauline de (1734–1818)

Montmorency, 'Marquis' de. *See* Montmorency, Anne-Léon (II) de

Montmorency, Princesse de. *See* Montmorency-Luxembourg, Louise-Françoise-Pauline de (1734–1818); Wassenaer, Marguerite-Élisabeth-Barbe de (1749–76)

Montmorency, Anne de (1492–1567), Duc de, Constable of France:
portrait of, in enamel, **1.** 103, **7.** 284

Montmorency, Anne-Julie de (1704–78), m. (1724) Emmanuel Rousselet, Marquis de Châteaurenaud:
Choiseuls visited by, in exile, **5.** 169
death of, **7.** 88
Du Deffand, Mme, awaits arrival of, **5.** 88
—— receives nothing through, **5.** 88
Gennevilliers visited by, **7.** 327
HW's correspondence with Voltaire approved by, **4.** 117–18
health of, **4.** 193
scientific affectations of, **7.** 363
sister-in-law of, dies, **7.** 6
social relations of, in Paris, **4.** 117, 272, **5.** 138, **7.** 321, 327–8, 336
York's misunderstanding about, **3.** *333*

Montmorency, Anne-Léon, Comte de:
(?) news of Fort St David's capture brought by, to Versailles, **21.** 279n

Montmorency, Anne-Léon (1705–85), Baron de:
wife of, dies, **7.** 6

Montmorency, Anne-Léon (II) (1731–99), Duc de; formerly Marquis de Fosseux:
social relations of, in Paris, **3.** 345–6, (?) **7.** 284, 286

Montmorency, Henri (1534–1614), Duc de; Constable of France:
Herbert of Chirbury friend of, **30.** 46
statue of, at Chantilly, **7.** 260, **30.** 46, **43.** 105

Montmorency, Louis-Ernest-Gabriel (1735–68), Prince de:
daughter of, marries, **7.** 92

Montmorency, Louise-Auguste-Élisabeth-Marie-Colette de (1763–1831), m. (1778), Marie-Joseph de Lorraine d'Elbeuf; Duc d'Elbeuf, Prince de Vaudemont:
Chanteloup to be visited by, **7.** 150
marriage of: **7.** 92; rumoured, **5.** 147

Montmorency, Louise-Augustine de (b. 1735), m. (1759) Charles-François, Comte de Broglie:
Cholmondeley, Mrs, liked by, **4.** 240
Cossé, Duchesse de, friend of, urges Broglie's recall, **24.** 19n
Du Deffand, Mme, gives opinion of, **3.** 356, 369, 377
——'s relations with, **3.** 369, 377, **6.** 231, **7.** 48, 102
HW finds, witty, **3.** 377
HW liked by, **3.** 354, 356
HW sends compliments to, **36.** 55
HW thanked for sending seeds to, **3.** 363
Holdernesse talks to, **3.** 86–7
Jonzac, Marquise de, visits, **6.** 211
lawsuit lost by, **7.** 425
leaves Paris, **7.** 427
Metz to be visited by, **6.** 272, 281
Noyon, Bp of, visited by, **6.** 231
Rueil visited by, **7.** 335
Ruffec occupied by, **5.** 225, 231, 256, **6.** 211
social relations of, in Paris, *see index entries ante* **8.** 446
Triomphe de l'amitié, Le, read to, **3.** 363–4

Montmorency, Marie-Anne-Philippine-Thérèse de (d. 1797), m. (1747) Charles-Joseph, Duc de Boufflers:
Court position resigned by, **5.** 106
Crécy visited by, **7.** 426
Du Deffand, Mme, and, **6.** 231, **7.** 48, 102
Gatti unsuccessfully inoculates, **7.** 266, **22.** 357–8
health of: **7.** 458; smallpox, **31.** 92
(?) La Harpe's play at Gonesse seen by, **4.** 445
Luxembourg, Duchesse de, succeeds, **5.** 129n
Noyon, Bp of, visited by, **6.** 231
Paris left by, **7.** 423
social relations of, in Paris, *see index entries ante* **8.** 446

Montmorency. *See also* Gand de Mérode de Montmorency; Montmorency-Bouteville; Montmorency-Laval; Montmorency-Logny; Montmorency-Luxembourg

Montmorency:

aucune a more impressive name than, **23**. 435
name of, mentioned by Conway, **11**. 86
Montmorency (France), Mme de Luxembourg's seat:
  Conway meets Conti at, **39**. 231
  Luxembourg, Mme de, occupies, **3**. 334, 338, **4**. 168, 243, 319, 446, **5**. 66, 350, 353, 427, 431, 436, **6**. 49, 116–18, 182, 375, 377–9, 495, 500, **7**. 143
  occupants of, return to Paris, **3**. 10, 11, **6**. 378–9, 499
  Rousseau sheltered at, **3**. 91n
  visitors to: **4**. 168, 319; Ailesbury, Cts of, **6**. 117–19; Boufflers, Comtesse de, **3**. 191, 334, 338, **4**. 243; Boufflers, Marquise de, **4**. 319; Cambis, Mme de, **4**. 319; **5**. 301, **6**. 499; Conti, **3**. 191, 338, 385, 389, **4**. 243, **39**. 231; Conway, **6**. 117–19, **39**. 231; Damer, Mrs, **6**. 117–19; Du Deffand, Mme, **3**. 4, 9, 61, 62, 65, 334, **4**. 84, 168, 245, 319, **5**. 78, 80–1, **7**. 145; Geoffrin, Mme, **4**. 87; Pont-de-Veyle, **5**. 302; Princes of the Blood, **5**. 304; Rousseau, **3**. 91n
Montmorency (Canada):
  Wolfe writes from, to Pitt, **21**. 336n
Montmorency family:
  Boufflers, Comtesse de, connected with, **10**. 71
  Chantilly and Alais belonged to, **14**. 127
  Desormeaux's history of, **3**. 69
  French Revolution swallows up, **39**. 475
  genealogy of, merely proves their long vassalage, **22**. 483
  Walpole, Bns, makes reply worthy of, **33**. 392
Montmorency-Bouteville, François-Henri de (1628–95), Maréchal de Luxembourg:
  misshapen, **41**. 225
Montmorency-Laval, Comtesse de. *See* Tavernier de Boullongne, Catherine-Jeanne
Montmorency-Laval, Anne-Alexandre-Marie-Sulpice-Joseph de (1747–1817), Marquis (later Duc) de Laval:
  Choiseul, Duchesse de, describes, **6**. 303
  Du Deffand, Mme, gives opinion of, **6**. 302–3
  social relations of, in Paris, **6**. 277, 302, 404
  verses on, **6**. 406
Montmorency-Laval, Gui-André-Pierre de (1723–98), Duc de Laval:
  governor of Compiègne, **4**. 441–2
  Provence receives resignation of, **7**. 439
  social relations of, with Rochfords, **4**. 15
Montmorency-Laval, Guyonne-Josèphe-Élisabeth de (1755–1830), m. (1768) Louis-Joseph-Marie-Charles-Amable d'Albert, Duc de Luynes:
  cure of dislocated arm of, **4**. 352–3
Montmorency-Laval, Louis-Joseph de (1724–1808), Bp of Metz 1761–90; cardinal, 1779:
  Du Deffand, Mme, given purse by, **7**. 447
  ——'s correspondence with, **7**. 437
  Louis XVI nominates, for cardinal, **7**. 437
  social relations of, in Paris, **7**. 13, 436, 437, 444, 449, 450

Montmorency-Laval, Marie-Louise de (1723–94), Abbess of Montmartre 1760–92:
  false rumour of death of, **11**. 52
Montmorency-Laval, Mathieu-Paul-Louis de (1748–1809), Vicomte de Laval, later Comte de Montmorency-Laval:
  heir to governorship of Compiègne, **4**. 441–2
  marriage of, **4**. 410n
  Provence receives resignation of, **7**. 439
Montmorency-Logny, Princesse de. *See* Montmorency-Luxembourg, Louise-Françoise-Pauline de
Montmorency-Logny, Louis-François-Joseph (b. 1737), Prince de:
  desires to be attached to Dauphin's service, **4**. 298
  Louis XVI gives grandes entrées to, **8**. 52
  social relations of, in Paris, **7**. (?)292, 306
  wife of, **3**. 346n
Montmorency-Luxembourg, Anne-Charles-Sigismond de (1737–1803), Duc de Luxembourg:
  arrives in London with family, **11**. 39
  (?) Jerninghams bring, to SH, **33**. 406, **35**. 532
  name of, corrected, **43**. 140
  satirized in English print, **11**. 54
  300,000 livres set on head of, **11**. 39
  Versailles lodging given to, **5**. 129
  wife of, **5**. 106n
Montmorency-Luxembourg, Anne-François de (1735–61), Duc de Montmorency:
  Doumenil has portrait of, **7**. 313
  wife of, **3**. 346n
Montmorency-Luxembourg, Anne-Henri-Renier-Sigismond de (b. 1772–d. ca 1793–1803), Duc de Châtillon:
  (?) arrived in London, **11**. 39n
  name of, corrected, **43**. 140
Montmorency-Luxembourg, Anne-Paul-Emmanuel-Sigismond de (b. 1742), called Chevalier de Montmorency-Luxembourg; Duc de Luxembourg, 1781:
  Jersey invasion troops to be reinforced by, **39**. 361
Montmorency-Luxembourg, Bonne-Charlotte-Renée-Adélaïde de (b. 1773), m. (1788) Anne-Pierre-Adrien de Montmorency-Laval, Duc de Laval:
  (?) arrived in London, **11**. 39n
Montmorency-Luxembourg, Bonne-Marie-Félicité de (1739–1823), m. (1754) Armand-Louis, Marquis (later Duc) de Sérent-Kerfily:
  social relations of, with Louis XVI and Marie-Antoinette, **6**. 105
Montmorency-Luxembourg, Charles-Anne-Sigismond de (1721–77), Duc d'Olonne:
  anecdote of, **3**. 43
Montmorency-Luxembourg, Charles-Emmanuel-Sigismond de (1774–1861):
  (?) arrived in London, **11**. 39n
  name of, corrected, **43**. 140

Montmorency-Luxembourg, Charles-François-Christian de (1713–87), Prince de Tingry:
Beauvau replaced by, 6. 50
Choiseuls visited by, after their disgrace, 5. 32, 45, 169
Montmorency-Luxembourg, Charles-François-Frédéric de (d. 1764), Duc de Luxembourg; Maréchal de France:
Coventry rudely thanks, for calling wife's coach, 20. 338
death of sister of, 4. 47
marriage of, 3. 12n
widow of, 8. 83n, 14. 155n
Montmorency-Luxembourg, Charlotte-Anne-Françoise de (b. 1757), m. (1767) Anne-Léon (II), Duc de Montmorency:
Hénault's social relations with, 3. 345–6
Montmorency-Luxembourg, Gillette-Françoise de (1704–68), m. (1722) Louis de Pardaillan de Gondrin, Duc d'Antin:
death of, 4. 47
Montmorency-Luxembourg, Louise-Françoise-Pauline de (1734–1818), m. 1 (1752) Anne-François de Montmorency-Luxembourg, Duc de Montmorency; m. 2 (1764) Louis-François-Joseph, Prince de Montmorency-Logny:
Choisy visited by, 4. 472
Crécy home of, 6. 470
daughter of, may be married, 5. 147
Du Barry, Mme, accompanied by, 4. 298, 472, 5. 30
grandes entrées obtained by, 7. 340
Luxembourg, Mme de, to visit, 6. 470
retires from Court, 5. 285
social relations of, in Paris, see index entries ante 8. 447
Montmorency-Luxembourg, Marie-Madeleine-Charlotte-Henriette-Émilie de (b. 1778), m. (ca 1790) Miguel Cayetano Alvares Pereira de Mello, Duque de Cadaval:
(?) arrives in London, 11. 39n
print satirizes, 11. 54n
Montmorin, Jean-Baptiste-François de (1704–79), Marquis de St-Hérem:
Louis XVI gives grandes entrées to, 6. 52
said to be promoted, 5. 179
Montmorin-St-Hérem, Armand-Marc (ca 1745–92), Comte de; French ambassador to Spain; minister of foreign affairs:
Charles III wishes, recalled, 24. 375n
dismissed, 39. 467n, 43. 140
Eden's negotiations with, 39. 457n, 458n
Simolin gets passports from, for French royal family, 34. 229n
Vergennes's dispatches from, 24. 458n
Montmorin-St-Hérem, Victoire-Marie-Françoise de, m. (1784) César-Guillaume, Comte de la Luzerne:
Clarence, D. of, honours, at ball at Almack's, 39. 465n
Montopoli (Italy):
Barrett Lennards invite Mann to, 20. 194
Goldsworthy's country house probably at, 20. 1n

Mont Orgueil, Jersey. See Mount Orgueil
Montpelier Row. See under Twickenham
Montpellier (France):
Brownlow, Lady Betty, married at, 18. 116–17
'demoiselles' of, see Girard, Mlles
Eu presides over assembly at, 6. 23
Girard, Mlles, of, 4. 74n, 5. 301
Grave writes from, 41. 143
HW visits, 13. 11, 17. 103, 119, 127, 132
Mann, Horace II and Lady Lucy, visit, 24. 246–7
Mirepoix dies at, 21. 141n
Montglas, Mme de, consigned to convent in, 6. 23
Montglas, M. de, formerly president of chambre des comptes at, 6. 23
visitors to: Beauvau, Prince and Princesse de, 3. 186, 4. 310; Clive, 23. 14n; Grave, 4. 310, 8. 139; Mirepoix, Bp of, 6. 255; Moulceau, 5. 424n; Toulouse, Abp of, 4. 310; Trudaine de Montigny, M. and Mme de, 4. 310
Montpellier Row. See under Twickenham
Montpensier, Duc de:
HW dreams of capture of, 21. 212
See also Bourbon d' Orléans, Antoine-Philippe d'
Montpensier, Duchesse ('Mlle') de. See Bourbon d'Orléans, Anne-Marie-Louise de
Montpeyroux. See Dio-Palatin de Montpeyroux
Montpipeau, Marquis de. See Du Cluzel, François-Pierre
Montpipeau, Marquise de. See Deflandre de Brunville, Marie-Françoise
Montrath. See Mountrath
Montreal (Canada):
American capture of, expected, 9. 308
Amherst moves against, 21. 301n
Byron captures ships destined for, 24. 440
English capture of, 9. 308, 21. 416, 421, 437, 440, 445
French proclaimed English repulse at, 22. 21, 89
Jesuits dispersed after capture of, 22. 233n
Johnson, Col. Guy, brings Indians to, 41. 312n
Vaudreuil joined by Indians near, 21. 357n
Montreal, English ship:
Joseph II boards, 23. 108
York's body to go in, to England, 22. 554
Mont Reale. See Monreale
Montreuil (France):
baggage examined at, 37. 39
Cour de France, La, inn at, 1. 102, 7. 333
HW at, 7. 259, 324, 333–4
Hertford writes from, 38. 211–12
Hertfords at, 38. 211–12
how to enter, after gates are shut, 1. 101–2
prettily situated, 37. 41
suitable for over-night stay, 37. 40
Montrevel, Comtesse de. See Choiseul, Élisabeth-Céleste-Adélaïde de
Montrond, Comte de. See Mouret, Claude-Philibert-Hippolyte de

Montrond, Comtesse de. *See* Franquetot de Coigny, Anne-Françoise-Aimée de

Montrose, Ds of. *See* Manners, Lady Lucy (ca 1717–88)

Montrose, D. of. *See* Graham, James (1682–1742); Graham, James (1755–1836); Graham, William (1712–90)

Montrose, M. of. *See* Graham, James (1682–1742)

Montrose (Scotland):
anti-American address from, 39. 270n, 41. 311n
Drummond's army moves towards, 37. 216
Soleil bound towards, 19. 173

Montroth. *See* Mountrath

Montrouge (France):
Champrond, Abbé de, entertains at, 4. 243, 442–3, 445, 446, 451, 7. 337, 422–9, 432, 433, 453–6, 458, 459
—— spends summers at, 4. 228n, 7. 123, 132
Fréron's house near, 6. 284n
visitors to: Aulan, 7. 427, 431; Aulan, Marquise d', 7. 94, 123, 132, 422, 423, 427, 428, 431; Bauffremont, 4. 443; Beauvau, Chevalier de, 4. 443; Boufflers, Marquise de, 4. 442–3; Cholmondeley, Henrietta Maria, 4. 442–3; Cholmondeley, Mrs, 4. 243, 442–3; Du Deffand, Mme, 4. 243, 442–3, 445, 446, 451, 6. 353, 7. 62, 337, 422–9, 432, 433, 453–6, 458, 459; Elliot, Gilbert, jr, 4. 442–3; Elliot, Hugh, 4. 443; HW, 7. 337; Sanadon, Mlle, 4. 443, 7. 337; Sickingen, 4. 442–3; Sigorgne, 4. 443

Montsabert. *See* Goislard de Montsabert

Montserrat, Joaquín, Marqués de Cruillas; viceroy of Mexico 1761–6:
wealth of, disregarded, 22. 89

Montserrat, West Indies:
Blake of, 1. 240n

Montughi (Italy):
Florentine view from Capuchin monastery at, 17. 58n

Montvandermeer, Capt. Davide:
made Baron for bringing rhinoceros, 20. 127–8

Montyon, Baron de. *See* Auget, Antoine-Jean-Baptiste-Robert

Montyon, ——:
Mémoires, 8. 32, 43. 108

Monument; monuments:
brass plates for inscriptions on, 2. 234
for Roger Townshend, designed by HW, 40. 166–7
Girardin's fondness for, 29. 283
in Eton chapel for 5th E. Waldegrave, 36. 285–6, 329
in Westminster Abbey, MS relating to, 28. 166; *see also under* Westminster Abbey
Mason designs: for Dr Dealtry, 28. 97; for Gray, 28. 176
Middleton, Mrs, asks Gray to sketch, for her husband, 15. 314

Winnington's, Williams, Sir C. H. writes epitaph for, 30. 320
See also Tomb; Urn, *and under* Gough, Richard

Monument, the, in London:
Beardmore returns key of, 30. 234
Godolphin, Lord, compared to, 33. 203
HW jokes about balloon picking up passengers from top of, 39. 425
HW wants poplars as tall as, 39. 133
illumination planned at: 3. 108; cancelled on Pitt's earldom, 30. 234; for Opposition victory, 38. 324
Marie-Antoinette's feathers lower than, 32. 254

Monumenta. See Middleton, Conyers: *Germana quædam antiquitatis monumenta*

Monumen[t]s de la monarchie française. See under Montfaucon, Bernard de

Monval, ——:
acquitted, 8. 200
Tort to pay damages to, 8. 200

Monvel. *See* Boutet de Monvel

Monxton, Hants:
Apthorpe rector of, 1. 35n

Monzone, Conte di. *See* Cioia de Forges, Bernardo

Moody, John, Hardinge's servant:
blunder of, delays present to HW. 35. 600

Moon, Francis, clerk to James Hall:
HW's will and codicil witnessed by, 30. 368, 377

Moon, the:
balloon resembles, 39. 419, 424
Europeans would reduce, to a province, 25. 451
Galileo's retort about, 20. 149–50
in Moorfields, 42. 110
London bonfires eclipse, 21. 314
March, Sersale remarks about malignity of, 20. 429
Milton's lines on, 22. 382
Townshend's witticism on Lady Mary Coke and, 37. 557
travellers to, would instantly hunt for gold, 25. 545
West's dream about, 13. 130–2
Wilkins, Bp, invents universal language for want of interpreter on, 39. 425

Moone, William (ca 1725–97), Exchequer clerk; E. of Orford's steward:
biographical information about, corrected, 43. 348, 368
Boone and, see Hertford about Orford's interest in Callington borough, 39. 192
HW accompanied by, to Houghton, 32. 142
HW aided by, in care of E. of Orford, 32. 349
HW confers with, 41. 376
HW sends, to Newmarket, 32. 159
HW's letter to, about Orford's consent, 36. 158
HW summons, to Eriswell, 36. 121

[Moone, William, *continued*]

(?) Orford, E. of, plundered by, **36**. 95–6

(?) ——'s illness concealed from, **34**. 130

—— to be approached by, about getting borough for Hon. Henry Seymour-Conway, **39**. 192

retrenchments in Orford's expenses made by, **36**. 97

Serpentine River cottage of, has tree and plant collection, **32**. 135n

takes letter to Lord Ossory, **32**. 135

Walpole, Hon. Thomas, corresponds with, on Orford's insanity, **36**. 331

—— gets reports from, from Great Chesterford, Essex, **23**. 460n, 461n, 463n

Moonlight:

Hervey, G. W., walks about only in, at Stowe, **30**. 51

Mann and Horace Mann II walk in garden by, before supper, **24**. 157

Waldegrave girls awestruck by, **36**. 154

Moor (surname). *See* Moore; Mor; More

Moor; Moors:

England should send, to invade Spain, **22**. 100

fortress of, on Minorca, **37**. 315

Francis I's ships to intercept ships of, **20**. 102n

Gothic architecture not invented by, **42**. 305

HW admires, **2**. 149

Minorca a refuge of, **25**. 189n

princes of, attend Richmond's fireworks, **9**. 81

Moore, Col., of Twickenham:

SH visited by, **12**. 232

Moore, Misses:

(?) Beaufort's social relations with, **7**. 271

Moore, Mr, of Whittlesy:

Cole's conversation with, **1**. 198n

Moore, Mrs. *See* Lennard, Anne

Moore, Mrs, of Twickenham:

SH visited by, **12**. 242

Moore, Rev. Mr:

involved with Cock Lane Ghost, **10**. 5n

Moore, A. (fl. 1722–48), bookseller:

Campbell writes pamphlet for, **13**. 21

Moore, Arthur (ca 1666–1730), economist and politician:

coffin of, chained to whore's in St Giles's vault, **20**. 181

Craggs's remark to, on entering coach, **20**. 181

footman's livery formerly worn by, **20**. 181

Leatherhead or Fetcham, Surrey, may be burial place of, **20**. 181n

Moore, Charles (1712–64), 2d Bn Moore of Tullamore, 1725; cr. (1758) E. of Charleville:

Pulteney, Mrs, punished by, for her insult at whist, **40**. 28

Moore, Charles (1730–1822), 6th E. of Drogheda, 1758; cr (1791) M. of Drogheda:

dragoons of: **5**. 57n; move against Whiteboys, **22**. 24n

Hamilton succeeded by, as Irish chief secretary, **38**. 393

Hertford notified by, of daughter's death, **39**. 452

marriage of, arranged, **39**. 51–2

Northumberland House dinner attended by, **38**. 529–30

ruined health and fortune of, **33**. 448

sisters visited by, **39**. 59

wife of, **10**. 107n

Moore, Edward (1712–57), writer; editor; dramatist:

editor of *The World*, **3**. 93n, **13**. 24

Fielding tries to place, as deputy licenser of stage, **35**. 176n

financial difficulties of, **9**. 195

Foundling, The, by, **19**. 465, 469

Gamester, The, by, **4**. 44, **11**. 237, **29**. 324

Gil Blas by, **14**. 47

HW reconciles Lyttelton with, **35**. 176

Lyttelton angers, by giving place to Bower, **35**. 176

Trial of Selim the Persian by, **35**. 176n

World contributions by, **20**. 400n, **35**. 176n, **38**. 89

Moore, Capt. Edward:

Fame privateer commanded by, **25**. 120n

Moore, Edward (1770–1837), 2d M. of Drogheda:

mother sends, to England for education, **33**. 448

Moore, Francis:

print of, **40**. 237

Moore, Helen, m. Sir John Webb, 3d Bt:

(?) social relations of, in Paris, **7**. 270, 271

Moore, Lady Isabella (1766–87):

death of, **39**. 452–3

Moore, Sir John (1718–79), cr. (1766) Bt; naval officer:

George III's remonstrance from, for Keppel trial, **24**. 332n

HW expects treachery from, **35**. 109–10

Hazard reports to, at the Downs, **22**. 70n

Hughes reinforces, in West Indies, **21**. 279n

member of Byng court martial, **21**. 63, 64, 65

men-of-war dispatched by, to intercept Dutch convoy, **22**. 71

release from oath of secrecy said to be wanted by, **35**. 97

squadron of, to fight Bompart's at Martinique, **21**. 297

Townshend and Tyrell bring dispatches of, to Pitt, **21**. 277n

Moore, Sir John (d. 1790), 5th Bt:

Devonshire, D. of, visited by, at Chatsworth, **38**. 19

Moore, John (1730–1805), D.D.; Bp of Bangor 1775–83; Abp of Canterbury 1783–1805:

Beauclerk, Lady Diana, corresponds with, about Pinkerton, **16**. 286, 291, 311–12

—— to ask, to let Pinkerton see books, **16**. 280–2

Derry, Bp of, condemned by, **25**. 530n

Lort not chaplain to, **16**. 280

Marlborough family's recommendation will be honoured by, **16**. 326

moderate and not a persecutor, **16**. 328

Pinkerton's application for British Museum post unlikely to be accepted by, **16**. 327

—— wants HW to get permission for him from, to see Lambeth books, **16**. 280

Planta's foreign trip might be permitted by, **16**. 295

votes against Fox's East India bill, **29**. 350

Moore, Mrs John. *See* Eden, Catherine

Moore, Joseph:

Ordinary of Newgate's Account, The, by, describes Wesket's death, **38**. 490n

Moore, Lady Lucy (b. 1739):

half-brother and his wife to visit, **39**. 59

Moore, Hon. Robert (1688–1762), M.P.:

Teynham, Bns, marries, **9**. 170n, **13**. 179

Moore, Lady Sarah (d. 1778), m. (1748) William Pole:

brother and sister-in-law to visit, **39**. 59

Moore, Stephen (ca 1695–1766), cr. (1764) Bn Kilworth, (1766) Vct Mountcashell; M.P.:

(?) Hertford's daughter rumoured to be engaged to, **10**. 194

peerage suggested for, **38**. 377n

son of, **39**. 51–2

(?) wealth of, **10**. 194

Moore, Stephen (1730–90), 2d Vct Mountcashell, 1766; cr. (1781) E. Mountcashell:

Seymour-Conway, Lady Frances, might be married by, **10**. 194, **39**. 51–2

(?) wealth of, **10**. 194

Moore, William, publisher, of Fleet St:

Whisperer, The, published by, **23**. 196n, 219n

Moore Abbey, Ireland:

Drogheda, Cts of, dies at, **39**. 426n

Moorfields, London:

anecdote about Ds of Queensberry's ball almost worthy of, **38**. 343

balloon to stop at, **42**. 110

bookselling in, **1**. 305, 353

catalogue of Charles I's collection found in, **42**. 354n

Cole's purchases in, **2**. 326

Gordon, Lord George, appropriate to, **25**. 23

list of Charles I's collection found in, **16**. 290n

madmen go to Tower instead of, **36**. 187

sane minority should be confined for safety in Bedlam Hospital in, **35**. 386–7

trees in, uprooted by hurricane, **24**. 431n

Wesley preaches in, **25**. 23n

Whitefield preaches in, **13**. 250n, **20**. 52n, **25**. 23n

Moor Fields, Minorca:

public ball in, **37**. 311

Moorish architecture. *See under* Architecture

Moorish mosaics. *See under* Mosaic

'Moorish princes.' *See* Sessaracoa, William Ansah

Moor Park, Herts, Anson's seat:

Brown landscapes, **9**. 285

visitors to: (?) Conway, **37**. 301; HW, **9**. 285, 30. 62, (?)**37**. 301; Rigby, **30**. 62

Moose-deer:

Orford's, offered to Dr Hunter by HW, **41**. 264–5

Mor (*or* Moore *or* More), Anthonis (1519–75), painter:

painting attributed to, **1**. 305n, **9**. 124n, **16**. 51n, **42**. 247–8

portrait by, **9**. 98n

Sheffield's portrait by, bought by HW, **41**. 352

Mora, Marqués de. *See* Pignatelli y Gonzaga, José

Mora, Marquésa de. *See* Pilar, María Ignacía del

Moral and Political Dialogues. See under Hurd, Richard

Moral Essays. See under Pope, Alexander

Morality:

expunged by French philosophers, **34**. 192

Moralizing:

HW's reflections on, **30**. 272

or thinking, not the road to felicity, **34**. 206

Morande. *See* Thévenot de Morande

Morangiès, Comte de. *See* Molette, Jean-François-Charles de

Morant, Edward:

(?) Churchill living near, in Essex, **7**. 374

(?) ——'s history told by, **7**. 374

(?) social relations of, with HW in Paris, **7**. 350, 352

Morant, Mrs Edward. *See* Goddard, ——

Morant, Philip (1700–70), writer and antiquary:

Biographia Britannica has articles by, **14**. 62n

Conyers tells, of painting, **40**. 248

Ducarel's correspondence with, **40**. 247–8

Knapton receives transcribed notes from, **40**. 248

Tapestry Hangings in the House of Lords by, **18**. 127

Moranville, Comte de:

Boufflers, Mmes de, bring, from Richmond to see SH, **39**. 473

SH visited by, **12**. 236, **39**. 473

Morar, Laird of. *See* Macdonald, Allan (d. 1756)

Morar, Scotland:

Young Pretender at, **37**. 253

Moras. *See* Peirenc de Moras

Morat. *See* Maratti, Carlo

Moratt, Jeffrey (d. 1737), former negro servant to Ds of Manchester:

housemaid wounded by, **37**. 8–9

Moravia:

Austrian victory in, **17**. 372

Braitwitz may be sent to, **17**. 407

Broglie to be driven from, by Austrian army, **17**. 401n

Daun retires into, **21**. 95

France cannot send troops to, **20**. 589n

Frederick II calls outposts from, **22**. 63

—— plans diversion in, **17**. 315n

——'s invasion of, may be a feint, **21**. 204n

Khevenhüller's corps to enter, **17**. 372n

[Moravia, *continued*]

Lobkowitz's corps to enter, **17.** 372n

Piccolomini commands Austrian troops in, **21.** 5n

priests said to be ill-treated in, **17.** 445

visitors to, Conway and David Scott, **39.** 537–8

Moravian; Moravians:

chief of, *see* Latrobe, Benjamin

Christ's wounded side arouses passions of, **35.** 156

colony of, in London, **20.** 359

religious freedom demanded by, in Bohemia, **24.** 95n

Reus is, **20.** 359

success of, due to nonsense, **34.** 83

Zinzendorf buys Lindsey House for, **20.** 359n

Moravian baron:

creditors release, to cheat Chesterfield at picquet, **35.** 258

Moravian ode:

Anstey writes, in *New Bath Guide*, **10.** 218

Morawitzky, ——, Bavarian army officer:

regiment of, **17.** 289n

Morawska, Countess. *See* Radziwill, Teofila Konstancia

Moray, E. of. *See* Stewart, James (ca 1531–70); Stuart, James (ca 1708–67)

Morbihan (France):

Conflans may convoy fleet of, **21.** 358n

Mordaunt, Mr:

Northampton, Cts of, attended by, to Naples, **22.** 142n

Mordaunt, Mr:

SH visited by, **12.** 238

Mordaunt, Anna Maria (d. 1771), m. (1733) Stephen Poyntz:

Croxall writes *The Fair Circassian* for, **20.** 208n, **22.** 163n

Devonshire's deterioration reported by, **38.** 447

French royal family kiss, **22.** 164

husband ruined by, in marrying off her poor cousins, **20.** 208

maid of honour to Q. Caroline, **20.** 208n, **22.** 163n

Spa to be visited by, **22.** 164

Victoire, Mme, cured by, in Paris, with Mrs Stephens's medicine, **22.** 163–4

Mordaunt, Anna Maria (d. 1803), m. (ca 1743) Jonathan Shipley, Bp of St Asaph 1769–88:

social relations of with Hannah More and Mrs Garrick, **31.** 213

Mordaunt, Charles (ca 1658–1735), 3d E. of Peterborough, 1697:

army hunted by, in Spain, **18.** 180, **24.** 482

Bevismount: associated with Pope and, **33.** 42–3; seat of, **35.** 250

campaign of, **13.** 146n

HW's article on, in *Royal and Noble Authors*, **14.** 167

oration by Demosthenes allegedly translated by, **16.** 370

poem by, on Cts of Suffolk, **42.** 87

Pope celebrates, **24.** 112n

Swift's letter from, **12.** 256

verses attributed to, **14.** 243n

witticism by, on being shown the Sainte Ampoulle at Reims, **24.** 112–13

Mordaunt, Sir Charles (?1697–1778), 6th Bt, 1721; M.P.:

Philipps opposed by, in Horn Tavern conclave, **35.** 216n

voted for, as commissioner, **17.** 438

Mordaunt, Henry (1621–97), 2d E. of Peterborough:

daughter of: **9.** 287n; his sole heir, **10.** 341–2

Succinct Genealogies of the . . . Houses of Mordaunt, **10.** 343

Mordaunt, Sir John (1697–1780), K.B., 1749; army officer; M.P.:

acquittal of: **21.** 165, 174, 177; HW hopes for, **35.** 285

appointed to staff for South Britain, **20.** 73n

arrest of, **21.** 163

at Perth, **37.** 249n

Bevismount occupied by, **35.** 251

biographical information about, corrected, **43.** 270, 274

clamour against, for failure of Rochefort expedition, **21.** 143, **30.** 142

Conway and Hawke confer with, about returning to England, **37.** 507n, 509n

Conway's colleague, **9.** 217n

—— visits, at Bevismount, **37.** 514–16, 519

court martial on, **21.** 143n

Cumberland, D. of, gives Pretender's coach to, **9.** 35

death of, **36.** 184

George II accuses, of cowardice, **30.** 142

—— joins, to Conway for Rochefort expedition, **9.** 217n, **21.** 118n, **37.** 493n

—— receives, badly, **21.** 143–4, **37.** 519

——'s instructions to, copied for Conway, **21.** 119n

—— strikes: from generals proposed for Flanders, **37.** 542n; from staff for America, **21.** 165n

HW advises Conway not to blame, **37.** 517–18

Hardwicke probably intends execution of, **30.** 140, 141

Hawke testifies at court martial of, **21.** 145n

inquiry demanded by, **21.** 145, 154–5

Kingston's lieutenant-colonel, **26.** 14

Knight of the Bath, **20.** 71n, **29.** 87

naval officers prefer Conway's conduct to that of, in Rochefort affair, **37.** 517

Parliamentary debates by: against Scotch Bill, **20.** 311, **26.** 31, 32, 33; on privately-raised regiments, **21.** 14, 18

Pitt's instructions for, approved, **21.** 119n

——'s letter to: on army embarkation, resented, **37.** 504; on George II's impatience, **37.** 503n

regiment of, **18.** 449n

Rochefort attempt of, said to be restrained to protect Hanover, **30.** 143, **37.** 518–19

Rochefort expedition fills, with apprehension, **21**. 118n

Rochefort inquest attended by, **21**. 155n

summoned to London, **30**. 141

Wolfe witness against, at Rochefort inquiry and court martial, **21**. 267n

Mordaunt, Hon. John (?1709–67), Lt–Col.: Pembroke, Cts of, marries, **17**. 495n

Mordaunt, Lady Mary (ca 1659–1705), Bns Mordaunt, s. j., 1697; m. 1 (1677) Henry Howard, styled E. of Arundel, 7th D. of Norfolk, 1684 (divorced, 1700); m. 2 (1701) Sir John Germain, Bt:

Cole describes career of, **10**. 341–2

D. of Norfolk plundered by, **15**. 114

Fermor, Sir William, buys statues from, **20**. 470n

husband of, **9**. 287n

Mordaunt, Lady Mary Anastasia Grace (1738–1819), Bns Mordaunt, s. j., 1814:

HW thanked by, for epitaph on Lady Dysart, **36**. 256

HW to entertain, at dinner at SH, **35**. 521

HW visited by, at SH, **12**. 21

Johnston, Lady Cecilia, visited by, at Petersham, **35**. 521

Mordaunt family:

Dee's 'black stone' belonged to, **43**. 389n

Drayton seat of, **10**. 341

Germain plunders, **9**. 287

Morden, William. *See* Harbord, Sir William

'Mordington, Lady.' *See* Douglas, Mary (1718–91)

Moré, Comtesse de. *See* Jourda de Vaux, Adélaïde-Françoise-Jeanne-Marie-Louise

More, ——:

Edgcumbe thought, should pay for 'Kitten's' burial, **30**. 90

More, ——, capt. of English merchant ship:

Estaing's probable loss conjectured by, **24**. 545

Experiment merchant ship commanded by, **24**. 545n

More, Mr, from Ireland:

Florence visited by, after meeting HW at Reims, **37**. 71

ships said by, to be England's bastions, ravelins, and hornworks, **37**. 71, 72

untimely visit of, to Reims, **13**. 179–80

More, Mr:

SH visited by, **12**. 246

More, Mrs:

Vauxhall gatekeeper, **9**. 87

More, Sir Antonio. *See* Mor, Anthonis

More, Gertrude. *See* More, Helen

More, Hannah (1745–1833), religious writer; HW's correspondent:

Amherst, Lady, visited by, **11**. 260

antagonists of: HW denounces, **31**. 392; HW discusses, with Harcourt, **31**. 396

at Adelphi, **31**. 211, 259, 291, 293

at Cowslip Green, **31**. 248–50, 264–6, 279–81, 289–90, 300, 307–8, 310–12, 315–18, 333–41, 347, 358, 369–71

at Hampton, **31**. 336

aversions of, to: anarchy, atheism, despotism, and popery, **31**. 329; Christian VII of Denmark, **31**. 274; large dinner parties, **31**. 228; metaphysical jargon, **31**. 370; religious sectarianism and bigotry, **31**. 335; war, **31**. 388

Bas Bleu, The, by, **31**. 212, 222, 226, 271, 330, 333, **33**. 512

Bath visited by, **31**. 364, 374

benevolence of, **11**. 213–14, 253

Berry, Mary, corresponds with, **12**. 209

Bishop Bonner's Ghost by: **43**. 342; authorship of, will not be secret, **31**. 306; author's name not to appear in, **31**. 306, 308; Boscawen, Mrs, receives, in MS, **31**. 301; brown paper copies of, **31**. 313, 316, 318; Cambridge's 'Progress of Liberty' compared with, **34**. 87; Carter, Elizabeth, praises, **31**. 318; Coke, Lady Mary, does not admire, **31**. 314; composition of, rapid, **31**. 303; delayed by trouble with rolling press, **34**. 53; Gardiner mentioned in, **31**. 301; Gloucester, Ds of, thanks HW for, **36**. 254; Gloucester, Ds of, would like to have written, **31**. 318; HW hopes Lady Ossory admires, **34**. 56; HW praises, **11**. 34–5, **31**. 301–2; HW rereads, **31**. 330; HW's edition of, to be given only as presents, **31**. 306; HW's emendations to, **31**. 301–2, 303, 309; HW sends, to Lady Ossory, **34**. 52; HW sends, to Mary Berry, **11**. 33, 37, 38; HW sends, to Mrs Carter, **42**. 250; HW thinks Darwin's *Botanic Garden* influenced, **31**. 302; HW to print 200 copies of, **31**. 302, 306; HW to send, to Conway, **39**. 469; inspired by bench at Fulham Palace, **11**. 33; Jerningham writes poetic tribute to, to HW, **42**. 256; London edition of, urged unsuccessfully, **31**. 306, 308–9, 319; magazines will reprint, **31**. 306, 309; More, Hannah, consents to HW's printing of, **31**. 303–4; More, Hannah, praises SH edition of, **31**. 315–16; More, Hannah, receives 64 copies of, **31**. 304, 313; notes to, **31**. 306; Porteus, Bp of London, receives 30 copies of, **11**. 41, **31**. 304, 306, 313, **34**. 54; printed at SH Press, **11**. 34, 35; printed by Kirgate, **42**. 252–3; printing of, begun, **31**. 309; recipients of copies of, **31**. 304, 306, 309, 310, 311, 313, 314, 318; signature of, **31**. 306, 313, 342; slave trade's abolition discussed in, **31**. 314; universal praise of, **31**. 318; vignette of SH on title-page of, **31**. 316

Boscawen, Mrs, invites, to stay with her at Rosedale, **31**. 347–9

Bristol, birth-place of, **31**. 277

——'s credit redeemed by, **31**. 277

characteristics of: anti-slavery sentiments, **31**. 296, 297, 342, 362, 372; charitable, **31**. 348; criticism except from friends does not disturb, **31**. 389; 'duplicity,' **31**. 311–12; first thoughts often best, **31**. 303; has little of virtu and antiquarianism, **31**. 211; modest,

[More, Hannah, *continued*]
31. 360; no philosopher, 31. 322; novels not read without recommendation, 31. 274; obstinate, 31. 348; praise from the great demoralizes, 31. 320; 'puritanism,' 31. 260–1, 296; sabbatarianism, 31. 260–1, 271, 300, 314, 348, 359, 363, 365, 393–4, 396, 399; sweet piety, 31. 333; varied talents, 31. 226; 'walking hospital,' 31. 338; *see also under* virtues of

Cheap Repository Tracts by: Gloucester, Ds of, to subscribe to, 31. 396; HW receives packet of, 31. 398; HW subscribes to, 31. 396–7; prospectus for, distributed by HW, 31. 396; prospectus for, sent to HW, 31. 395

Cheddar reforms of, 31. 328, 334

Christmas spent by, with Mrs Boyle Walsingham and Mrs Garrick, 42. 205

classical learning of, 11. 38

Coke, Lady Mary, admires many writings of, 31. 314

correspondence of, with: Berry, Mary, 31. 401–2; Boscawen, Mrs, 31. 251, 328, 339, 358; Carter, Elizabeth, 31. 252; Cremorne, Vcts, 31. 357; Gloucester, Ds of, 31. 398; HW, 31. 210–12, 218–27, 230–1, 239–56, 259–60, 264–84, 289–96, 300–51, 357–65, 369–98, 401–3, 412; Hamilton, Mary, 31. 273, 276, 296; Porteus, Bp, 31. 303, 311, 314, 358, 387; Waldegrave, Cts, 31. 395

Dogberry favourite character of, 31. 358

Dryden disliked by, 31. 213

Estimate of the Religion of the Fashionable World, An, by, 11. 214, 361. 365

Fatal Falsehood by: HW cannot attend, 33. 101; ignored by HW, 31. 226n

Florio by: advertised, 33. 512; dedication of, to HW, 31. 239–40; HW praises, 31. 240–1, 243; HW quotes, 31. 241; HW rereads, 31. 330

HW and Mary Berry prayed for by, 31. 390n

HW asks, to write sermon vindicating Providence for permitting French Revolution, 36. 285–6

HW calls: 'Miss Anti-Lactilla,' 42. 205; 'my imprimée,' 11. 288; 'the best of our numerous Calliopes,' 33. 533

HW compares: with Alma Mater, 31. 338; with Bonner's ghost, 31. 323; with Charles I, 31. 341; with Christine de Pisan, 31. 244; with Marlborough, Ds of, 31. 342; with Sappho, 31. 309; with Vesey, Mrs, 31. 247; with weeping willow, 31. 347

HW forgiven by, for teasing about religion, 31. 399

HW gives publications to, 31. 242, 243–4

HW hopes to see, 31. 368, 386, 412

HW invites: to Berkeley Sq., 31. 241–2, 393; to SH, 31. 211

HW lends books to, 31. 245, 296, 412

HW more admired by, for humanity than for wit, 31. 249

HW promises to write to, 12. 209

HW puns on name of, 31. 219

HW rebuked by, for ridiculing religion, 31. 404

HW regrets teasing, about religion, 31. 399

HW scolds, for giving *Castle of Otranto* to Mrs Yearsley, 31. 221

HW's correspondence with: 31. 210–11, 218–27, 230–1, 239–56, 264–75, 276–84, 289–96, 300–51, 357–65, 369–98, 401–3, 412; MSS of, 36. 313; over *Bishop Bonner's Ghost*, 42. 250

HW's couplet to, 31. 250

HW's death, commented on by, 31. 403–4

HW sends 'morsels of criticism' to, 31. 281

HW sends prints to, 31. 265, 272–3

HW sends Stratford's *Fontenoy* to, through Mrs Garrick, 42. 40

HW's finding fault with, considered a mark of favour, 31. 252

HW's friendship with: early years of, 31. 210; unclouded during 20 years, 31. 403–4

HW's inscription to, in Bible, 31. 399

HW's names for: 'Anti-Lactilla, Miss,' 42. 205; 'bishop *in partibus infidelium*,' 31. 365; 'classic author,' 31. 271; 'female saint,' 31. 394; 'nymph of the dale,' 31. 251; muse, 31. 267; saint, 31. 401; 'Saint Hannah,' 31. 374, 398

HW's relations with, 31. 210–11, 213, 227–9, 258, 260–1, 296–7, 399

HW's society rarely enjoyed by, for 3 years, 31. 387

HW styles himself 'slave' of, 31. 260

HW suspects, would be glad to break winter union with Mrs Garrick, 31. 348

HW teases, 31. 213, 399

HW to be prayed for by, 31. 399

HW to rebuke, at Mrs Montagu's dinner, for silence, 42. 205

HW urges, to write sermon vindicating divine providence, 31. 395, 397

HW urges composition by, 31. 247, 271, 330–1

HW visited by, at SH, 36. 285–6

HW visits: 11. 249; at the Adelphi, 31. 351

HW would aid Louisa to please, 31. 208

health of: 31. 259, 267, 276, 291, 346, 375, 387; cough, 31. 339, 376; fever, 31. 272; HW's concern for, 31. 379–80, 386, 392; headaches, 31. 248–9, 339, 369, 371; improving, 31. 364, 381; jaundice, 31. 364; rheumatism, 31. 279

'hermitage' of, in garden at Cowslip Green, 31. 249

imagination of, disordered by Wye valley scenery, 31. 320

James's powders cure fever of, 31. 272

Johnson, Dr, quoted by, 31. 320, 399

lives with Mrs Garrick, 31. 211 and *passim*

London diversions avoided by, 31. 266

'Louisa' and Mrs Yearsley befriended by, 33. 490

Monboddo said to have proposed to, **29**. 271n

name of, revered by all who have religion or principles, **31**. 392

Nivernais's *Jardins modernes* given to, **12**. 260

occupations of: gardening, **31**. 250, 264; 'printing work,' **31**. 258

pamphlets attack, **31**. 388–9

pen of, should be preserved in shrine, **31**. 398

Percy by: HW admires Mrs Siddons in, **34**. 2; HW sees and comments on, **32**. 404–5; HW sees performed, and scolds Hannah More for not going to it, **31**. 258; HW wishes Hannah More would write another, **31**. 226; Lewis acts in, **41**. 456; Siddons, Mrs, acts in, **31**. 226

Perry, Mrs, case of, occupies, **11**. 253

politics written intelligibly by, **31**. 401

Pope preferred by, to Dryden, **31**. 213

Porteus, Bp, entertains, at dinner, **11**. 288, 291

—— friend of, **11**. 42n

—— visited by, **42**. 250

—— would please, as Abp of Canterbury, **31**. 342–3

portrait of, by Opie: Boscawen, Mrs, hangs, **31**. 258; HW's copy of, by Roberts, **31**. 279; HW wants copy of, **31**. 258

Priestly reported to have married, **31**. 328, 332–3

protégés of, **31**. 337–8; *see also* Cromartie, Ann; Louisa

reflections by, on: criticism, **31**. 389–90; egotism, **31**. 390; evil, **31**. 321–2, 349–50; forgiveness of offences, **31**. 350; managing and accomplished wives, **31**. 316; position of women, **31**. 370

Remarks on the Speech of M. Dupont by: answers to, **31**. 388–9, 391; Cadell publisher of, **31**. 381; HW anxious to see, **31**. 386; object of, **31**. 381–2; Porteus forces Hannah More to sign, **31**. 382–3; price of, **31**. 382

resembles dissipated fine lady rather than hermit, **31**. 321

saints' days may have to be celebrated by, at night now that daytime is unfashionable, **12**. 121

satires readily published by, **31**. 301

Slavery by, **31**. 260, 268

social relations of, with: Amherst, Bns, **31**. 351; Barrington, **31**. 258; Boyle, Charlotte, **31**. 228; Burney, Charles and Frances, **31**. 213; Carter, Elizabeth, **31**. 228; Hamilton, Mary, **31**. 228–9; Herries, Lady, **31**. 229; Jenyns, Mr and Mrs, **31**. 213; Montagu, Mrs, **31**. 228, 258; Mount Edgcumbe, Vct, **31**. 258; Ord, Mrs, **31**. 213; Pepys, Mrs, **31**. 213; Pepys, W. W., **31**. 213, 228, 260; Porteus, Bp, **11**. 288, 291, **31**. 258, 351, **42**. 250; Rothes, Cts of, **31**. 213; Shipley, Bp, **31**. 210–11, 213; Shipley, Mrs, **31**. 213; Smelt, Mr and Mrs, **31**. 228; Vesey, Mrs, **31**. 210, 213, 214, 228, 242–3, 244; Waldegrave, Cts, **34**. 203; Walsingham, Mrs, **31**. 213, 228

'Specimen of the English Language, A,' by, **31**. 224–7

Strictures on Female Education by, disliked by Mary Berry, **31**. 390n

SH may be visited by, **31**. 295

SH to be visited by, **31**. 262

SH visited by, **12**. 229, 235, **31**. 211, 395

Thoughts on the Importance of the Manners of the Great by, **31**. 260–1, 301

urged to go abroad for health, **31**. 376

verses by, Mrs Yearsley's witticism on, **31**. 274

Vesey, Mrs, parties of, organized by HW, Mrs Carter and, **31**. 227

Village Politics by: HW not informed of, by Hannah More, **31**. 380, 382–3; HW praises, **31**. 380; virtues of, **31**. 220, 247, 254–5, 271, 312, 314, 323, 338, 341, 342, 346, 358–9, 371, 380, 391, 392, 395, 401

visitors to, at Cowslip Green: De Vesci, Vcts, **31**. 252; Garrick, Mrs, **31**. 321; Montagu, Mrs, **31**. 321; Warton, Joseph, **31**. 281; Wilberforce, **31**. 321

visits by, to: Beaufort, Ds of, **31**. 281, 320; Montagu, Mrs, **31**. 321; Porteus, Bp, **31**. 303, 388, 399

visits planned by, to: Beaufort, Ds of, **31**. 335; Bouverie, Mrs, **31**. 294; Montagu, Mrs, **31**. 281; Porteus, Bp, **31**. 295

Waldegrave, Cts, relations of, with, **31**. 394, 395, 398

—— sends to, HW's letter, **36**. 288

water believed by, to have great curative powers, **31**. 364

Williams, Helen Maria, has, as subscriber to her *Poems*, **33**. 533n

writings of: increasing editions of, **31**. 271; promote virtue, **31**. 271, 283; *see also under individual titles above*

Yearsley, Mrs, quarrels with, **31**. 242, 244, 247, 253–4, **33**. 490, 537–8, **36**. 251

More, Helen ('Gertrude') (1603–33):
Bretherton copies print of, **1**. 313, 316

life of, **1**. 353

print of, **1**. 289, 291, 292, 296, 297, 313, 316, 353–5, 360, 365

More, Rev. Henry (1614–87), Cambridge Platonist:
Hurd's dialogues the 'offspring' of, **16**. 34

print of, by Faithorne, **1**. 155

More, Margaret (1505–44), m. (ca 1525) William Roper:
HW compares himself to, **9**. 349

More, Martha:
Mendip Annals by, **31**. 334n

More, Robert (1703–80), M.P.:
(?) HW mentions, **17**. 123

More, Sir Thomas (1478–1535); lord chancellor; writer; saint:

[More, Sir Thomas, *continued*]
  Chesterfield puts Hardwicke in company of, **28.** 303
  daughter of, 9. 349
  Dialogue . . . of Images by, **15.** 177n
  Edward V's death as treated by, **1.** 308n
  family of, **35.** 155
  great-granddaughter of, **1.** 289n
  HW considers, unreliable, **1.** 308–9n
  HW's query about, **2.** 3n
  HW's unfavourable remarks on, **14.** 166n
  HW thought of writing tragedy about, but was deterred by More's mirth and bigotry, **41.** 289–90
  History of King Richard the Thirde by: **43.** 199; HW calls, unreliable authority, **15.** 170, 173, 177, 184; HW cites, **14.** 182; *Historic Doubts* disparages, **41.** 126; should be corrected, **35.** 609
  Masters accuses HW of stigmatizing, **2.** 240n
  More, Hannah, might be descended from, **31.** 389n
  Morton boasts of policy to, **15.** 172
  Shore, Jane, known by, when she was old, **41.** 112
  Utopia by, Lort has first edition of, with Holbein's illustrations, **16.** 160
  Zouch knows descendants of, **16.** 49
More, Thomas (1722–95), Jesuit:
  descendant of Sir Thomas More, **16.** 49n
More. *See also* Moore
More family:
  Holbein's painting of: at Burford, **35.** 155; copies of, **16.** 48; stolen and sent abroad, **16.** 49
Morea (Peloponnesus), Greece:
  France said to have seized, **36.** 220
  Greek inhabitants of, support Russian invasion, **23.** 204
  Greeks in, **23.** 235
  Russian fleet reaches coast of, **23.** 204–5
  Russians abandon, for lack of Greek assistance, **23.** 226, 235
  Russians to distribute arms to people of, **23.** 202
  Russian victory repairs disgrace of leaving, **23.** 235
  Turks and Russians haggle over villages in, **23.** 224
Moreau, Jean-Michel (1741–1814), engraver:
  print by Macret and, **29.** 275n
Moreau de Beaumont, Jean-Louis (1715–85):
  finance committee member, **6.** 457
  signing to be done by, **6.** 457
Moreau de Champlois, Marie-Madeleine de, m. (1760) Joseph-Gabriel de Maury de la Peyrousse:
  (?) La Marche, Comtesse de, employs, **7.** 293
  (?) social relations of, in Paris, **7.** 293, 298, 299
Moreau de Maupertuis, Pierre-Louis (1698–1759), mathematician and astronomer:

astronomical studies continued by, in Paris after service with Frederick II, **18.** 52n
Catalogue of French Books, A, satirizes, **18.** 52
Moreau de Séchelles, Jean (1690–1760), controller general of finances:
  French finances and navy to be rehabilitated by, **20.** 500
Morefields. *See* Moorfields
Morehead, Mrs:
  Florence to be visited by, **19.** 477
  Hunt accompanies, to Paris, **19.** 477
  —— leaves estate to, **19.** 477
  Mann entertains, **19.** 489
  —— talks to, at Mrs Strode's, **19.** 477
  passes in France and Lorraine for a lady of condition, **19.** 489
  weeds worn by, for Hunt, **19.** 477
Moreira, ——, confessor to K. of Portugal:
  dismissal of, **21.** 217n
Morel, André:
  spelling of name of, corrected, **43.** 194
Morel, Jean-Marie (1738–1810), landscape architect:
  ideas borrowed by, from Whately, **16.** 190
  Théorie des jardins by, bought by Lort at Paris, **16.** 190
Morel, Mme Marie-Josèphe:
  (?) Wiart receives letter from, **6.** 39
Morel, Thomas (1703–84), D.D. *See* Morell
Morel; morels:
  Elizabeth, Q., shrivelled like, **34.** 118
Moreland, ——, George Montagu's agent:
  army joined by, **9.** 192
  (?) HW to be given Lovell's address by, **9.** 183
  HW to get Montagu's wardrobe from, **9.** 156
  journals to give employment to, **9.** 52
  keys to Freeman's house fetched by, **9.** 133
Moreland, Mr:
  SH visited by, **12.** 225
Moreland. *See also* Morland
Morel du Faux, Mme:
  HW's correspondence with, **7.** 389
Morell, Rev. Thomas (1703–84), D.D.; F.S.A.; classicist and librettist:
  Cole's friend, **1.** 8
  'Hymn to Liberty' might seem to imitate, **16.** 376
  mangled odes for Handel, **28.** 55
  (?) print of, **14.** 120, **43.** 184
  'See the Conquering Hero' by, **16.** 376n
Morelle, Mrs, governess to Molesworth family:
  death of, in fire, **22.** 138, 140, **38.** 201
Morellet, André (1727–1819), abbé; encyclopedist:
  admires violinist's execution, **4.** 257
  Geoffrin, Mme, leaves annuity to, **6.** 484
  Mémoire sur la situation actuelle de la Compagnie des Indes by, **5.** 400
  Portrait de Mme Geoffrin by, **6.** 496, 497
  (?) sings, **7.** 299
  social relations of, in Paris, **4.** 257, **7.** 289, (?) 299, 338

translates treatise, 3. 173n

Morelli, Signora, called 'La Corilla':
improvisation by, 23. 64n

Morelli, Giovanni (fl. 1787–1812), basso:
in Paisiello's *Il Re Teodoro*, 33. 587

Morelli, Jacopo:
Bibliotheca Maphæi Pinelliana by, 42. 240n

Morelli Adimari, Signora. *See* Franchini, Agnese

Morello cherries. *See under* Cherry

More Park. *See* Moor Park

Moréri, Louis (1643–80), abbé:
Dictionnaire historique by, 1. 291n, 5. 276, 7. 97, 8. 32

Moret (France):
barley sugar from, 7. 426
Louis XVI's aunts stop at, 11. 208n

Moreton, Antoine-Apollinaire Guigues de (1708–93), Bailli de Chabrillan; Conti's capt. of the guard and head of stables:
Boucault, Mme, wedding of, attended by, 5. 349
Desmond, Cts of, subject of joke by, 7. 370
Du Deffand, Mme, asks, about Conti, 3. 344
(?) HW mentions, 3. 342
social relations of, in Paris, 5. 349, 7. 299, 325

Moreton, Jacques-Aimar-Henri de, Comte de Chabrillan; army officer:
Aiguillon, Mme d', fond of, 3. 295
Boucault, Mme de, wedding of, attended by, 5. 349
Du Deffand, Mme, gives opinion of, 4. 256
—— hears about SH and House of Commons from, 3. 306
—— sends letter by, 3. 278, 280
—— told by, that she is to know of couriers' departures, 4. 94
—— to send toy by, 3. 272
goes to England, 3. 274n
HW entertains, at SH, 43. 85
HW likes, 3. 295, 43. 86
(?) HW's correspondence with, 42. 473n
HW sends books by, 3. 297
London visited by, 3. 237, 278
social relations of, with Mme de Forcalquier, 5. 349
SH dinner to be attended by, 30. 244
to return to Paris, 4. 256
Véret visited by, 4. 146

Moreton, Joseph-Dominique de Guigues de (b. 1744), Marquis de Chabrillan:
Boucault, Mme, wedding of, attended by, 5. 349
(?) Du Deffand, Mme, gives opinion of, 4. 340
gambling losses of, 4. 54
Holdernesse compared to, 3. 77
marriage of, 3. 130, 183
Rueil visited by, 7. 320, 329, 335
social relations of, in Paris, *see under* entries *ante* 8. 448

Moreton, Matthew Ducie (before 1700–70), 2d Bn Ducie:
HW hopes to visit house of, 30. 150

Moreton, Sir William (?1696–1763), Kt, 1755; M.P.:
George III's report from, about prisoners in Newgate, 40. 194n
jury directed by, in Canning case, 35. 175

Moreton, Dorset:
Frampton of, 13. 166n

Moreton de Chabrillan, Hippolyte-César de Guigues de (1767–1835), later Marquis de Chabrillan:
birth of, 3. 382

Moreton de Chabrillan, Jeanne-Marie-Thérèse-Tècle de (d. 1812), m. 1—— Boucault; m. 2 (1773) François-Louis-Antoine de Bourbon, Comte de Bourbon-Busset:
Aiguillon, Duchesse d', friend of, 4. 143
Artois, Comtesse d', includes, in household, 5. 342, 357
—— to be met by, 5. 412
Boulogne-sur-Seine visited by, 7. 331
Bourbon-Busset marries, 5. 344, 347, 349
Canisy, Mme de, visited by, 4. 242
Du Deffand, Mme, gives opinion of, 4. 242, 246, 256, 305
Forcalquier, Mme de, friend of, 4. 242, 246, 305
husband sought for, 5. 342
Irwin devoted to, 4. 232–3, 242
—— picked by Mme du Deffand to marry, 4. 142–3, 146
marital relations of, 5. 350
Rueil visited by, 4. 130, 7. 320
social relations of, in Paris, *see index entries ante* 8. 448
to return to Paris, 4. 256
Véret visited by, 4. 146, 270
Versailles visited by, 5. 357

Moretti, Gasparo:
Albani recommends, to Mann, 20. 37, 46
England to be visited by, on business, 20. 37
London address of, 20. 37n
Mann recommends, to Whithed, 20. 46
—— writes letter of introduction for, to HW, 20. 37, 46
Roman merchant, 20. 46

Morfontaine. *See* Le Peletier de Morfontaine

Morgan, ——, of Glantyrnam, Wales:
Herbert's letter to, 40. 358–9

Morgan, Mr:
HW sends letters from Paris to England by, 7. 396

Morgan, Anne (d. 1607), m. (1545) Henry Carey, Bn Hunsdon:
Vertue's engraving of, 9. 101

Morgan, Sir Charles Gould (1726–1806), 1st Bt; M.P.:
Gideon, Sir Sampson, nominated by, 2. 219

Morgan, Daniel (1736–1802), American Gen.:
Tarleton defeated by, 29. 124n

Morgan, David *or* Thomas David (d. 1746), barrister:
called 'the Pretender's councillor,' 19. 287n
'Country Bard' by, 19. 287n

[Morgan, David, *continued*]
execution of, 19. 287, 30. 319
Williams, Sir C. H., wrote and published 'speech' of, 30. 319
'Morgan, Sir James':
Conway might be threatened by, with petition, 39. 222
Morgan, Marcia (ca 1735–1819), m. (1753) John Pitt:
effect of Lord Cholmondeley's marriage on, 11. 241
Morgan, Mrs Mary, Cts of Strathmore's maid:
Strathmore, Cts of, elopes with, 33. 460
Morgan, Thomas (1727–71) of Tredegar; M.P.:
Beaufort tries to wrest lieutenancy of Wales counties from, 23. 174
Whig enemy of Beaufort family, 23. 174
Morgan, Thomas (fl. 1751–85), china merchant:
HW to send Montagu's letter to, 10. 271
lodgings of, at corner of Arlington St, Montagu asks HW to look at, 10. 270–1
Montagu's correspondence with, 10. 271
Morgan, Thomas David. *See* Morgan, David
Morgason. *See* Morgueson
Morgueson, wood at the Vyne:
Chute cuts walks in, 35. 640, 642
origin of name of, 35. 641
Morguesson (France):
battle near, 35. 641
Chute's wood named after, 35. 641
Morice, —— (d. 1777), sister of Humphry Morice:
death of, 32. 392
Morice, Rev. Francis (1721–78):
Atterbury's grandson, 15. 110
HW attributes story of Atterbury and Wynne to, 13. 33
Morice, Humphry (?1723–85), M.P.:
Aix-la-Chapelle visited by, 7. 239
Amelia, Ps, entertains, 32. 307, 33. 104
Bath visited by, for gout, 25. 191, 195, 202, 213, 216, 220, 235, 33. 300
biographical information about, corrected, 43. 118, 276
Brown, Lady, leaves estate to, 25. 246
cameo sent through, by Mann to HW, 25. 51, 56, 65, 88, 89, 94
Chiswick Grove bought by, from Grantham, 25. 298n
Chiswick visited by, 25. 266
Chute's friend, 21. *389*, 442
—— to be approached by, about Sophia Lucchi, 22. 266
—— visits, in Cornwall, 9. 164
Clerk of the Green Cloth, 21. 389
comes to town, and can attend to business, 25. 266
comptroller of the Household, 22. 103, 113
confined in the country, 25. 97
crutches used by, 25. 435
death of, 33. 506
death of, mistakenly reported, 33. 404, 407–8
dines with HW, 32. 365

disapproves of delaying tactics of lawyers, 25. 202
Duane recommended by, to take his place in Mozzi affair, 25. 298, 303, 33. 362, 372
Du Deffand, Mme, sends letter by, 5. 266
—— to send parcel by, 5. 265
——'s social relations with, in Paris, 7. 234, (?) 425
England revisited by, 25. 51, 56, 87, 33. 252
Florence to be visited by, on way to Naples for health, 21. 389
—— visited by, 21. 389, 442, 22. 28, 29, 36, 23. 113, 25. 51
France left by, 23. 147
German mud-baths to be visited by, 25. 307, 33. 352
going abroad for health, 25. 297–8, 303
HW agrees with, in Mozzi-Orford affair, 25. 164
HW agrees with advice of, about choosing Handel oratorios, 22. 41–2
HW and, to take care of Mozzi's affairs, 25. 162, 230
HW dines with, at Chiswick, 25. 298
HW encloses letter to, to Mann, 25. 432, 434
HW has not seen, 25. 97, 176
HW insists he had written to Mann about, 21. 450
HW meets, on way to Paris, 35. 120
HW mentions, in postscript, 21. 457
HW receives copy of paper sent by Sharpe to, 25. 186
HW receives report from, on Mozzi's affairs, 25. 191
HW recommends, to Mann, 21. 389
HW's collaborator in Mozzi's business, 25. 172
HW's correspondence with, 25. 286, 289, 297–8, 432, 434, 435, 33. 288
HW will advise, to consult Duane, 20. 217
HW willing to deal with, if permitted to act like gentleman, 25. 158
HW will meet, at The Grove, 33. 281
health of: bad, 7. 234, 25. 265; better, 25. 435, 31. 204, 33. 407–8, 452; gout, 25. 51, 97, 184, 202, 213, 33. 252, 288; gout confines, at Paris, 7. 234, 25. 74; looks dreadfully ill, 33. 104, 252–3; loses use of legs, and feet, 25. 298; melancholy account of, 25. 202; not better, 33. 562; not in danger but weakened by overbathing, 25. 220; not likely to recover, 25. 216; not so bad as Lucas reported, 25. 217; poor, 40. 468; recovers use of legs, 33. 357; relapse, 25. 289; unable to come to town, 25. 246; worse, 25. 297–8
heavy luggage left by, at Margate, 25. 88
Ischia visited by, 33. 452
Launceston elects, to fill vacancy, 20. 113n
Lausanne visited by, 25. 432, 33. 408
lives near SH, 25. 159
Lucas replies to scolding by, about his delay, 25. 286

Mann advises Mozzi to write to, about intended gift to Duane, 25. 524
—— asks to be remembered to, 25. 182
—— discusses Chute and HW with, 21. 442, 22. 39
—— entertains, at dinners, 25. 435
—— sends compliments to, 25. 171
—— sends letter through, to HW, 23. 140–1, 146, 147
—— thinks Mozzi should not write to, 25. 171
—— told by, to ask HW to get advice in seeking oratorios, 22. 36
—— wants to congratulate, on being Comptroller of the Household, 22. 113
Mozzi advised by: to name Duane as referee, 25. 298; to sell his rights, 25. 286
—— begs HW and, to conclude affairs, 25. 190
—— cannot be aided by, 25. 247
—— commissions, to handle affairs in England, 25. 157–8
—— confers with, 25. 434–5
—— hopes to see, at Cambrai, 25. 303
—— names, as moderator in dispute with Orford, 36. 202
—— pleased to have aid from HW and, 25. 181
——'s affairs delayed by illness of, 25. 216–17
—— says that division of money held by Hoare was opposed by, 25. 426
——'s correspondence with, 25. 168, 230, 304
—— should have younger assistants than HW and, 25. 344
—— to accept decision of HW and, 25. 162, 169
—— told by, not to come to England, 25. 435
Naples to be visited by, 21. 389, 25. 289, 432, 435, 33. 408
—— visited by, when ill with gout, 25. 51
Newcastle gives George II the request of, to go abroad, 21. 389n
Orford, E. of, thinks HW and, will differ, 25. 164
Paris visited by, 7. 234, 23. 140–1, 146, 25. 74
Petraia palm tree praised by, 22. 29
privateer avoided by, 25. 89
referee in E. of Orford's suit, 33. 274
Rome to be visited by, 25. 435
Sharpe advises, to call for papers, 25. 289
—— sends papers to, 25. 184
sister of, dead, 32. 392
Tissot regulates motions of, 25. 435
travels of, 31. 204
Turton, Dr, treats illness of, 33. 300
will and codicil of, 25. 289n
withdrawal of, causes Mozzi to decide on English trip, 25. 303
writing-box of, 25. 94
Morice, Sir William (?1707–50), 3d Bt, 1726; M.P.:
heir of, 21. 389

Launceston vacancy caused by death of, 20. 113n
Morice, William, High Bailiff of Westminster 1719–31:
Atterbury's son-in-law, 15. 110
son of, 13. 33n
Morice family:
Launceston a borough of, 20. 113
Morigi, ——, singer:
in burletta company, 22. 474n
Morin, ——:
HW's social relations with, 7. 329
Morin, Catherine-Zélie, m. (1758) Cosme de Picquet de Juillac de Vignolles:
(?) HW's social relations with, 10. 156, 31. 62, 43. 133
(?) Pyrenees, home of, 10. 156
(?) Schaub, Lady, resembles, 10. 156
(?) SH visited by, 10. 156, 31. 36
Morin-Dumesnil, Anne-Louise (1729–83), m. Jean-Baptiste-Jacques Élie de Beaumont; writer:
Anecdotes de la cour . . . d'Édouard II finished by, 6. 284, 294
Cholmondeley, Mrs, urges, to send HW details about Voisins, 41. 173
Du Deffand, Mme, seldom seen by, 41. 173
—— to read unpublished novel by, 3. 114
(?) HW mentions, 3. 341
HW's account of Hume-Rousseau quarrel to be read by, 3. 99–100
HW's correspondence with, 7. 382, 383, 41. 173–5
Historic Doubts praised by, 4. 72
law suit won by, 7. 323
Lettres du Marquis de Roselle by: HW quotes 'Legnor' in, 38. 553; recommended by HW, 22. 271, 28. 7
name of, corrected, 43. 82, 279, 293, 376
social relations of, in Paris, see index entries ante 8. 443
Morison, Col.:
guards alerted by, against riot, 23. 7n
Morison, Robert (1620–83), M.D., botanist:
print of, 40. 237
Morison, William (d. 1772):
(?) HW talks to, 18. 294
Morison. See also Morrison; Moryson
Morlaix. See Morellet
Morland, Mrs:
Montagu sends message to, about lodging, 9. 333–4
—— to receive parcels through, 9. 213, 214
Morland, George (1763–1804), painter:
SH ticket not used by, 12. 246
Morland, William:
(?) brother of, 10. 215
(?) HW to be asked by, for SH ticket, 10. 215
(?) Montagu requests SH ticket for, 10. 215
Morland, Westmorland:
Brown, vicar of, 14. 37n
Morland. See also Moreland
Morley, Bn. See Parker, William (1575–1622)

Morley, J.:
Rawdon promised money by, for Wallingford election, **17**. 400
Morley, William (d. 1679):
genealogy of, **10**. 352
wife of, **9**. 191n, 252
Morley, Mrs William. *See* Clark, Elizabeth
Morlière. *See* La Morlière; Rochette de la Morlière
Mormorai, Antonio (ca 1712–84), Florentine senator:
(?) Mann seeks maps for, **23**. 411, 413, 418, 427, 431
Morning Chronicle, The:
cited by HW, **33**. 202
Cunningham's *History* advertised in, **43**. 202
cutting from, of verses on Rowley poems, **16**. 351
locusts in Queen Square reported by, **39**. 418n
Morning dress:
Walpole, Sir Robert, wears nightgown and nightcap for, in portrait, **30**. 370
Morning Herald:
Bate starts, **32**. 331n
HW called 'veteran of SH' by, **42**. 170
HW praised in, **33**. 516
HW's *Mysterious Mother* mentioned in, **39**. 372n
McMahon's anti-French articles in, **25**. 557n
Pope parody in, **34**. 55, 60
Morning Post:
Bate publishes, **29**. 25n
——'s abuse in, of D. of Richmond, **33**. 171n
——'s editorship of, corrected, **43**. 300
Bell, publisher of, **32**. 332n
Gordon, Hon. Cosmo, writes scandal for, **33**. 117n
HW praised in, **33**. 219
HW's name for Bns Greenwich, **39**. 197–8
HW's visitors read, **28**. 305
lies in, **33**. 8–9
Mason attacked in, **28**. 368, 370, 375
——'s *English Garden* ridiculed by correspondent in, **28**. 310
new, scandal in, **32**. 332
old, protests against *New Morning Post*, **32**. 331–2
Ossory, Lady, attacked by, **33**. 80
reports rumour that 5 American colonies seek peace, **28**. 440
Richmond attacked in, **28**. 379, **33**. 171n
scandal in, **33**. 354
tittle-tattle would not be printed by, after Agincourt or Naseby, **35**. 364
Mornington, Cts of. *See* Hill, Anne (1742–1831)
Mornington, E. of. *See* Wellesley, Richard
Moro, Dr Bartolommeo, Lady Mary Wortley Montagu's secretary:
Montagu, Lady Mary Wortley, accompanied by, **22**. 3
Morocco, K. of. *See* Abd el Malech (d. 1578)
Morocco, Emperor of. *See* Mohammed (ca 1710–90) ben Abdallah; Muley Ismail (1646–1727)

Morocco:
ambassador from, fashionable, **9**. 185
ambassadors from and to, *see under* Ambassador
slaves of, **24**. 469
Morocco leather:
Bible bound in, **31**. 399
Morogues. *See* Bigot de Morogues
Moroni, Gianbattista (1525–78), painter:
Surrey's portrait at Knole attributed to, **35**. 134n
Moroni, Pietro Celestino, Col. in Spanish service:
Riva, Maria da, marries, **18**. 86
Morosini, Cavaliere Francesco (fl. 1744–85), Venetian ambassador to England:
Hammersmith house taken by, **22**. 76n
Venice sends, to England, **21**. 508
Morpeth, Vcts. *See* Cavendish, Lady Georgiana Dorothy
Morpheus:
gesso of: at Leghorn awaiting shipment, **18**. 329; HW receives, preferring it in plaster to black marble original, **18**. 561; Mann may not send, to HW, **18**. 303; to be sent to England, **18**. 178
HW receives sleep from, **11**. 182
Mann has, copied in gesso for HW, **18**. 153
'Morpheus.' *See* Morpheus
Morphy, Marie-Louise (ca 1738–1815), m. 1 (1755) Jacques de Beaufranchet d'Ayat; m. 2 (ca 1759) François-Nicolas Le Normant, cr. (1765) Comte de Flaghac; m. 3 (before 1798) Louis-Philippe Dumont (divorced, 1798); Louis XV's mistress:
Irish must drink health of, in whisky, **37**. 364
lodges at Versailles and has child, **35**. 173
Louis XV's Irish mistress, **35**. 173n
(?) Pompadour, Mme de, provides, as Louis XV's mistress, **21**. 542
Morray. *See* Moray
Morres, Hervey Redmond (ca 1743–97), 2d Vct Mountmorres, 1766:
candidate for Westminster, **28**. 174
defeated as Wilkes's candidate for Westminster, **24**. 52
social relations of, in Paris, **5**. 320, **7**. 353
SH visited by, **12**. 236, 241
Morrice. *See* Morice
Morris, Mr:
SH visited by, **12**. 232, 237
Morris, Mrs Charles. *See* Delaval, Anne
Morris, Corbyn (d. 1779), commissioner of Customs:
commissioner of customs, **41**. 327
Essay towards Fixing the True Standards of Wit by, **18**. 464
Treasury's letter from, **24**. 175n
Morris, John (ca 1730–88):
(?) HW hoped to visit house of, **30**. 150
Morris, John (d. 1776), naval Capt.:
killed in Charleston attempt, **24**. 236, **32**. 318
Morris, John:

Schomberg's house injured by, **33**. 189n

Morris, Margaret (1734–1803), m. (1766) Peter Shakerley:
HW writes to Mary Berry about Twickenham house of, **11**. 47
SH visited by, **12**. 241

Morris, Mary (d. 1742):
death of, **17**. 504

Morris, Robert, secretary of Supporters of the Bill of Rights:
Miller's counsel, **23**. 279n
Wheble advised by, **23**. 279n

Morris, Sarah (ca 1673–1731), m. 1 Robert Drake; m. 2 (ca 1710) Conyers Middleton:
Cole's account of, **15**. 305
death of, **15**. 305
HW calls, mistakenly, 'Mrs Robinson,' **15**. *291*
Middleton receives fortune from, **15**. 291–2, 314
oddness of, **15**. 308

Morris, Staats Long (ca 1730–1800), M.P.; army officer:
second husband of Ds of Gordon, **15**. 154

Morris, Thomas (d. 1717) of Mt Morris:
Middleton marries daughter of, **15**. 305

Morris, Thomas (fl. 1750–ca 1800), engraver:
HW employs, for *Description of SH*, **25**. 532n
(?) prints by, at SH, **2**. 274n

Morris. *See also* Morice; Morres

Morris dancers:
at Park Place, **31**. 146
go to open houses at Christmas, **32**. 408

Morrison, ——:
Richmond's secretary at Paris, **22**. 405n

Morrison, George (ca 1704–99), army officer:
ball, masked, attended by, **7**. 300
HW's correspondence with, **9**. 306
Rochfords entertain, **9**. 269
York, D. of, accompanied by, to SH, **9**. 304
——'s body accompanied by, **7**. 366, **22**. 554
——'s equerry, **37**. 479
—— taken by, to Monaco, **22**. 553

Morrison, William (d. ?1772), secretary to the opera:
HW talks to, of expenses, **18**. 294

Morrison. *See also* Morison; Moryson

Morrow. *See* Morvo

Morsels of Criticism. See under King, Edward

Morsztyn, Countess. *See* Gordon, Lady Catherine (living 1687)

Mortanges, —— de:
French fleet to be countermanded upon return of, **23**. 475n

Mortar (for masonry):
Boyle, Miss, may carry hod of, **42**. 205

Mortar; mortars:
batteries of, surrounding St Philip's, **25**. 233
Schulenburg obtains, to subdue Genoa, **19**. 367
Spaniards to receive, from Naples by Adriatic, **19**. 30
Wade demands, for Ostend, **19**. 69

Mortcloth:

HW mentions, **37**. 397

Mortellari, Michele (1750–1807), composer:
Armida by, **25**. 646n

Mortemart, Duc de:
Élisabeth, Mme, dances with, **7**. 343n

Mortemart, Duchesse de. *See* Cossé-Brissac, Adélaïde-Pauline Rosalie de (d. 1808); Harcourt de Lillebonne, Anne-Catherine-Gabrielle d' (1750–78)

Mortgage, mortgages:
German, George II's money in, **21**. 450, **38**. 79
HW has to lower interest on, **39**. 494
HW ignorant of, **36**. 96
HW involved with, for E. of Orford, **32**. 121, 141
HW jokingly proposes, for SH, **10**. 278
Houghton estate overwhelmed by, **23**. 510, 515, **34**. 134n, 145n
on Linton, falsely imposed by Edward Louisa Mann's will, **24**. 176, 181, 187, 258
(?) on Twickenham Manor, **42**. 418

Mortification; mortifications:
never single, **35**. 495

Mortification in the legs:
occurrence of, **25**. 394

Mortification of the bowels:
HW has, **34**. 211

Mortimer, ——, painter:
(?) Bellotto's views of Verona copied by, **23**. 299n

Mortimer, John Hamilton (1741–79), historical painter:
Barry praises, excessively, **29**. 301

Mortimer, Martha *and* Paul:
heirs to SH, **13**. 17n

Mortimer, Roger de (1287–1330), 8th Bn, cr. (1328), E. of March:
Bute compared with, **22**. 53
site of capture of, **35**. 278
story of, **10**. 52n

'Mortimer's Hole,' Nottingham:
HW does not see, **35**. 278

Mortimer St, London:
Lovel, statuary in, **21**. 128n, **35**. 644
Rich of, **12**. 102n

Mortlake, Surrey:
tapestries from, **1**. 5n, **16**. 159n, **43**. 38

Mortlock, Mr (d. 1775) of Cambridge:
death of, **1**. 371

Morton, Cts of. *See* Heathcote, Bridget (ca 1723–1805); Villiers, Anne (d. 1654)

Morton, E. of. *See* Douglas, George (1761–1827); Douglas, James (ca 1702–68); Douglas, Sholto Charles (1732–74)

Morton, Mrs:
house of, visible from Park Place, **39**. 550

Morton, Rev. Dr:
Gloucester, D. and Ds of, married by, **36**. 63n, 92
Walpole, Sir Edward, mistakes Baddeley for, **36**. 62–3

Morton, Charles (1716–99), M.D., 1748; librarian of British Museum:
Cavendish, Lord Charles, and George Onslow know, 31. 427
HW's acquaintance, 15. 92
SH visitors sent by, 12. 225, 227
Suffolk, Cts of, solicits Newcastle's vote for, as master of Charterhouse, 31. 427
Twickenham resident, 42. 486, 490
wife of, 31. 427
Morton, Mrs Charles. See Berkeley, Mary
Morton, John (ca 1420–1500), Bp of Ely 1479–86; Abp of Canterbury 1486–1500:
boasts of, 15. 172
Bourchier's commission to, as Edward IV's executor, 41. 124
—— succeeded by, 14. 79
Cole's life of, 1. 136, 144
conspirator against Richard III, 15. 184
Ely bishopric of, 43. 49
HW finds fault with, 14. 166n
HW on, 1. 136, 144
Masters accuses HW of taking liberties with, 2. 240n
painting of, in Pomfret's collection, 20. 390
Register Book of, at Lambeth, 41. 124
Morton, John (?1671–1726), naturalist:
Natural History of Northamptonshire, The, by, 2. 277
Morton, John (?1714–80), chief justice of Chester; M.P.:
Parliamentary activity of, on Regency Bill, 22. 299n, 38. 549
Morton, Thomas (1564–1659), Bp of Chester 1615–18, of Lichfield 1618–32, of Durham 1632–59:
monument to, at Easton Maudit, 10. 339
relations of, with Yelverton family, 10. 339
Morton, Thomas (ca 1764–1838), dramatist:
Children in the Wood, The, by, 12. 78, 34. 194, 43. 153
Morval, Cornwall:
Buller of, 11. 352n
Morville, Hugh de (d. 1204):
Becket's murderer and Barrett Lennard's ancestor, 35. 184
Morvo or Morrow, John, master mason; 'Murdo':
Hearne mentions work of, at Scottish cathedrals, 42. 69
inscriptions by, at Melrose Abbey, 42. 69
Moryson, Fynes (1566–1630), traveller:
HW's mistaken reference to, 15. 93
Itinerary by, mentions Cts of Desmond, 40. 111n
Moryson. See also Morison; Morrison
Mosaic:
at Malvern Priory, 35. 151
Gothic Saracen, on table from Salerno church, sent by Hamilton to HW, 35. 408–9
HW's Florentine box inlaid with, 24. 15n
HW's table of, 26. 7
in churches, sought by Agincourt, 42. 104

Moorish, at the Alhambra, 42. 53
painting in, in gilded frame, 22. 234n
paper, by Mrs Delany, 42. 179
picture in: given to D. of Cumberland at Rome, 23. 566; given to D. of York at Rome, 22. 229, 232
plate ornamented with, 16. 84
Roman: at Cirencester, 12. 59; at Woodchester, excavated by S. Lysons, 15. 251, 334; workmanship of, compared to French, 5. 176
shrine of, Hamilton sends, to HW, 35. 406–7, 409
See also Scagliola
Mosaic creation:
Pownall's system of, 32. 94–5
Mosca, Agapeto (1678–1760), cardinal, 1732:
Albani faction tries to elect, 21. 207
Moscovy. See Russia
Moscow, Metropolitan of. See Levshin, Petr Georgievich
Moscow (Russia):
Joseph II to visit, 25. 72
Pugachev marching to, 32. 184
riots at, 22. 205n
Royal Library at, alleged Homer poem found in, 16. 179
Moseley, Richard (ca 1698–1754), M.A.; 'Philo Christus':
(?) Impartial Inquiry by, 43. 212
Letter to the Rev. Mr John Jortin, A, by, 15. 304
Mosely, Capt.:
rioters apprehended by, 33. 189n
Mosely. See also Moseley; Mosley
Moses:
animals preserved and distinguished by, 20. 71
Bolingbroke writes Craftsman against, 20. 454
HW refers to rods of, 10. 138
HW's 'moral fable' on vision of, of Promised Land, 33. 450
'legation' of, 16. 38
Middleton alludes to, 15. 18
—— and Warburton write on, 15. 302
——'s pamphlet on, 15. 292
Nanteuil's print of, 15. 100
'Rowley' ranked with, 33. 317
Warburton's proof of inspiration of, 16. 352
—— writes about, 10. 278
See also under Warburton, William
Moses, Isaac:
jewels stolen by, 11. 206n
Moses, Solomon. See Porter, Solomon
Moslem:
HW asks if Wilkes becomes, 22. 290
Mosley, Charles (d. 1770):
engraving by, 14. 34n
Mosley, Sarah (?1725–83), m. Sir Thomas Frankland, 3d Bt:
Cromwell miniature might be sold by, to Ds of Kingston, 42. 125
Cromwell miniatures owned by, 41. 263

sale of, does not include Cromwell miniature, **42**. 125
Mosley. *See also* Moseley; Mosely
Mosque; mosques:
Stowe temple influenced by, **35**. 77
Turks refuse to cede places containing, **23**. 469–70
Mosquito; mosquitoes:
warm weather does not bring, **39**. 498
Mosquito Coast *or* Shore, Central America:
English capture fort on, **24**. 543–4
triumphs on, **33**. 150
Moss, Mrs:
Conway, Hon. Henrietta Seymour, lodges with, near Oxford Chapel, London, **38**. 24
Moss, Charles (1711–1802), Bp of St David's, 1766, of Bath and Wells, 1774:
Roman Catholics said by, to be dwindling, **25**. 66n
Sophia Matilda, Ps, baptized by, **32**. 129n
Moss, James (d. 1758), King's Messenger:
(?) Giberne sends letter through, **17**. 454
Mann receives instructions by, **17**. 405
—— sends letter by, **17**. 408, 412
Moss, William, Fanny Burney's servant:
Burney, Fanny, sends, to HW, **42**. 296
former servant to Mrs Schwellenberg, **42**. 296n
Mossop, Henry (?1729–74), actor:
performs in Smock Alley Theatre, Dublin, **37**. 412n
'Most Noble She-Witch,' by HW:
advertisement for, **17**. 313n
text of, **26**. 9
Mostyn, Ann (d. 1759) *or* Elizabeth (d. 1785), housekeepers at Hampton Court:
(?) 'crooked,' **35**. 244
Mostyn, John (1709–79), M.P.; Gen., 1772:
birth date of, corrected, **43**. 237
Conway's possible rival, **38**. 84n
Fabrigas sues, for assault, **23**. 551n
garrulity of, **20**. 4
Granby thanks, for cavalry's success at Warburg, **38**. 74
military candidate, **37**. 577n
Pomfret challenges, in bed for having laughed at him in Court, **25**. 96
Rich, Lady, and, **17**. *139*
Rigby told by, that Vernon called him a bruiser, **30**. 331n
wounded at Fontenoy, **36**. 12
Mostyn, Savage (?1713–57), naval officer; M.P.:
Admiralty post for, **21**. 73
Motezuma (opera). *See under* Bottarelli, Giovan Gualberto; Sacchini, Antonio
Moth; moths:
'disturbed from parchment groves,' **30**. 288
killing of, **30**. 289
Mothe, La. *See* La Mothe
Mothe-Fénelon, La. *See* La Mothe-Fénelon
'Mother' (of brothel):
Chudleigh, Elizabeth, can never lack, **37**. 447
Mother Bank:

ship arrives at, **11**. 201n
Mother Bunch's Closet Nearly Broke Open:
Nicoll, Miss, buys, **14**. 225
Mother Bunch's Tales:
(?) harmless, **43**. 189
Mother Goose's Tales:
canonization of, **33**. 319
curiosities, if printed at SH, **2**. 248
HW jokes about seven-league boots in, **31**. 160
HW leaves theological questions to, **4**. 220
HW prefers, to gravity of 17th century, **33**. 550
Richard III's alleged crimes are, **35**. 562
Mother Midnight's Oratory. See Smart, Christopher: *Old Woman's Oratory*
Mother Shipton, pantomime:
performed at Covent Garden, **31**. 152
scenery in, **31**. 152
Motier. *See* Du Motier
'Motion, The,' satiric print:
Gravelot's print of, **18**. 21
HW asks origin of, **37**. 96
Motte, De la. *See* La Motte
Motte, La. *See* La Motte
Motteux, John:
East India Co., director, **25**. 490n
Motteville, Mme de. *See* Bertaut, Françoise
Mottley, John (1692–1750), dramatist:
Devil of a Wife adapted by, **13**. 167n
Devil to Pay by, 'Lady Loverule in, **12**. 150
Joe Miller's Jests by, **9**. 35, **35**. 565
Motto; mottoes:
Appleby Castle portraits have, **10**. 185
Damer, Mrs, may not use, on coat-of-arms, **35**. 495
for pictures, Uguccioni provides, for Cts of Pomfret, **18**. 545
HW's: **33**. 274–5; for ruby ring, **35**. 215
Hanoverian soldiers', **35**. 94
Holland's, **19**. 397, 411
in fireworks, **18**. 242
Mann seeks, **20**. 475, 480, 482, 487
religious, at Hinchingbrooke, **40**. 283
Scottish, **42**. 12
seal and mourning ring for Robert Child inscribed with, **32**. 361
seldom suit two generations of a family, **35**. 427
Surrey's, **35**. 134
tickets for Huntingdon chapel have, **10**. 179
Wall's, **35**. 94
Walpole, Horatio (1678–1757) seeks, **35**. 93
Walpole family's, **21**. 167
wrapped in sugar, **33**. 213
Mottraye. *See* La Mottraye
Mouchard, Mlle:
Mme du Deffand's social relations with, **7**. 460
Mouchard, François-Abraham-Marie:
Armet brought by, to Mme du Deffand, **7**. 461
custodian of Mme du Deffand's cash, **8**. 31
daughter of, **6**. 428n
Du Deffand, Mme, leaves snuff-box and set of Voltaire to, **4**. 131n, **7**. 130n, **8**. 8, 26, 32

[Mouchard, François, *continued*]
—— names, as her executor, **8.** 8, 11, 47
social relations of, in Paris, **7.** 428, 432, 434–7, 441, 448, 458, 460–1
Mouchard, Marie-Anne-Françoise (1737–1813); m. (1753) Claude de Beauharnais, Comte de Roches-Baritaud:
Du Deffand, Mme, mentions, **6.** 428
Mouchy, Duc de. *See* Noailles, Artus-Charles-Jean-Tristan-Languedoc de (1771–1834); Noailles, Philippe de (1715–94)
Mouchy, Duchesse de. *See* Arpajon, Anne-Claudine-Louise d'
Mouchy, Maréchal de. *See* Noailles, Philippe de
Mouchy, Maréchale de. *See* Arpajon, Anne-Claudine Louise d'
Mouchy, Marquis de. *See* Noailles, Philippe de
Mouchy, Hôtel de, Paris:
Mme du Deffand's apartment faces, **8.** 15
Mouin, ——:
HW's social relations with, **7.** 306
Moulceau, ——, president of the chambre des comptes at Montpellier:
Corbinelli's letters to, **5.** 420n
Girard, Mlles, granddaughters of, **4.** 74n
HW thinks, was not good company, **32.** 172
Sévigné, Mme de, corresponds with, **4.** 74n, **5.** 373n, 423–4
—— writes witticism to, **35.** 466
Mould; moulds:
for artificial stone, **41.** 229
for casting type, Baskerville makes, **40.** 276
Mouldings:
carved, **31.** 88
Moulin-Joli, Le, Watelet's isle, Paris:
HW's description of, **28.** 220–1, 224, 228
Mason asks HW to visit and describe, **28.** 215
visitors to: Bingham, Lady, **6.** 333, 349; Gibbon, **6.** 459; HW, **7.** 346; Marie-Antoinette, **6.** 349; Neckers, **7.** 346; Thomas, **6.** 459
Moulins (France):
Barthélemy praises bridge at, **8.** 201
Choiseul-Stainville, Abp, dies at, **6.** 94n
Moulsey, Surrey:
cricket match at, **36.** 251
Windham and Sadler make balloon ascent from, **25.** 579
Mounds:
HW wants to know, whether Danish, British, or Saxon, **28.** 37
Mount; mounts:
for fan, *see under* Fan
temple on, at Ranelagh, **20.** 47
Mt Agatha, Minorca:
cavern and Moorish fortress on, **37.** 315
Mountagu. *See* Montagu
'Mountain, lady of.' *See* Farrington, Mary, Mrs Selwyn
'Mountain, old man of the,' *See* Hasan-ibn-al-Sabbah
Mountain. *See* Montagne, La; Montaigne
Mountain; mountains:
at Bath, **10.** 231–3

Hamilton writes on formation of, from volcanic explosions, **35.** 412
Lady Gertrude Hotham's and Lady Huntingdon's faith to move, in Wales, **24.** 91
Mountain ash. *See under* Ash
Mt Anna, Armagh:
Mee of, **11.** 133n
Mt Ararat, Richmond:
Wray, Mrs, dies at, **12.** 100n
Mt Athos, Greece:
Polish subscription unlikely to remove, **15.** 225
storms reach, **32.** 364
Mount Cashell, Vct. *See* Maccarty, Hon. Justin (d. 1694)
Mount Cashell, Vct and E. *See* Moore, Stephen (1695–1766); Moore, Stephen (1730–90)
Mounteagle. *See* Monteagle
Mountebank; mountebanks:
Dodd and Whaley mistaken for, **40.** 3
Mt Edgcumbe, Cts of. *See* Gilbert, Emma (1729–1807); Hobart, Lady Sophia (1768–1806)
Mt Edgcumbe, E. of. *See* Edgcumbe, Ernest Augustus (1797–1861); Edgcumbe, George (1720–95); Edgcumbe, Richard (1764–1839)
Mt Edgcumbe, Vct. *See* Edgcumbe, George (1720–95)
Mt Edgcumbe, Vcts. *See* Gilbert, Emma (1729–1807)
Mt Edgcumbe, Cornwall, Edgcumbe's seat:
beauty of, **33.** 211
Conway considers going to, **39.** 281, 456
—— spoiled for Park Place by visit to, **39.** 294
Edgcumbe to be addressed at, **30.** 67
—— writes from, **40.** 54
HW and Rigby may visit, **30.** 92
HW mentions, **12.** 41, 164, 203
HW prefers, to Hagley, **35.** 148
oak trees at, destroyed, **33.** 212
old view of, **40.** 283
visitors to: Ailesbury, Cts of, **32.** 375; Chatham, **23.** 387n; Conway, **32.** 375, **39.** 294; Damer, Mrs, **32.** 375; George III and Q. Charlotte, **11.** 31–2; HW, **19.** 92, 101, **30.** 94, **35.** 148, **37.** 202, 205, 206, 208, 217; Ossory, Lady, **33.** 211–12
Mountenay. *See* Mounteney
Mounteney, Richard (1707–68), Bn of the Irish Exchequer:
play by Sir Edward Walpole seen by, **10.** 11
Mt Ephraim, Sussex:
Hertfords to go to their temporary villa at, **39.** 305
Mountfort, William:
King Edward the Third by: **43.** 128; Wilkes's dedication in Hutchett's adaptation of, **10.** 52
Mountfort. *See also* Montfort
Mount Helicon:
HW averse to 'nurses of,' **41.** 63
Mounting tiger (game):

old people ridiculous when playing, 24. 194

Mountjoy, Bn. *See* Blount, William (ca 1478–1534); Gardiner, Luke (d. 1798)

Mountjoy, Vct. *See* Gardiner, Luke

Mountjoy, Vcts. *See* Boyle, Anne

Mt Lebanon, Twickenham:
Conolly, Lady Anne, builds, on site of brother's house, 35. 279n

Mt Merrion, Dublin, Fitzwilliam's seat:
landscape effects at, 9. 400
Montagu visits, 9. 400
stables at, 9. 400

Mountmorres, Vct. *See* Morres, Hervey Redmond

Mt Morris, Kent:
Morris of, 15. 305

Mountnorris, E. of. *See* Annesley, Arthur (1744–1816); Annesley, George (1771–1844)

Mt Orgeuil, Jersey:
Bentley's painting of, 35. 243, 644

Mt Palatine, Rome:
Sion House resembles, 38. 429

Mt Parnassus:
HW would not take long trip to see, 39. 456

Mount Pleasant. See under Roscoe, William

Mountrath, Cts of. *See* Newport, Lady Diana

Mountrath, E. of. *See* Coote, Algernon (1689–1744); Coote, Charles Henry (ca 1725–1802)

Mt Stewart; Mountstewart. *See* Mount Stuart

Mt Stewart of Wortley, Bns. *See* Wortley Montagu, Mary (1718–94)

Mount St, Grosvenor Sq.:
Theodore of Corsica resident in, 40. 192

Mt Stuart, Vct. *See* Stuart, John (1744–1814)

Mt Stuart, Vcts. *See* Windsor, Hon. Charlotte Jane (1746–1800)

Mouret, Claude-Philibert-Hippolyte de, Comte de Montrond:
lover of Duchesse de Fleury, 12. 30n
wife of, 11. 181n

Mouret, Jean-Joseph (1682–1738):
Femme, La, by, 7. 260

Mourning:
Ancaster, Ds of, tells Lady Anna Horatia Waldegrave to wear, 24. 494, 33. 114
attendance at Court omitted during, 4. 193, 197
attendance at other than Court functions permitted by, 4. 195
black coat a sign of, 20. 175
black satin worn for, 25. 123n
black wax used on letters during, 17. 164
close, by 132 people, for Cts Gower, 36. 233
condolence letters during, 6. 352, 355
Conway to wear, for D. of Devonshire, 38. 452–3
Court: dress for, 32. 101–2; regulated by lord chamberlain, 39. 222; servants' costumes magnificent during period of, 10. 204
Craon, Princesse de, finds, painful to her eyes, 18. 228
—— gets, 22. 536
cuffs for, 6. 359

draping of royal carriages for, 32. 255
Ds of Kingston's, 28. 225
Florence has gala in spite of, 22. 532
Florentine theatres closed during, 18. 559, 22. 340
for: Archduchess of Brussels, 17. 193, 433; Brandenburg-Bayreuth, Margrave of, 38. 204; Chabot, Comtesse de, 4. 265; Conti, 6. 346; Conti, Princesse de, 6. 194; Eleonora, Ps, 17. 433; Empress Dowager, 20. 211; Francis I, 22. 337, 340, 347, 354; Frederick William I, 37. 63; Frederick William, P., 10. 204n, 39. 49; George II, 21. 462; Louis XV, 6. 50, 51; Madame Royale, 18. 558–9, 19. 1, 8, 14, 20. 211; Marie Leszczyńska, 4. 80–1, 169, 23. 78; Orange, Ps of, 38. 8; Prussia, Q. of, to be postponed till after Birthday, 35. 189; Queensberry, Ds of, 32. 366; Sens, Mlle de, 38. 537
for father-in-law, six months, 4. 406
Guerchy, Comtesse de, sees no one during, 3. 362, 4. 63, 75
HW orders, for Cts of Orford, 25. 123, 29. 106
HW's waistcoat cannot be worn by Mann because of, 17. 433
HW to get, for Q. of Denmark, 24. 104
Hertford wears, for Malpas, 38. 353
London may assume, for Pitt's resignation, 21. 540
Louis XV and Marie Leszczyńska do not go into, for Dauphin, 7. 290
mourning-ring sent to Robert Child, 32. 361
observances during, 10. 166, 204, 310, 311, 339, 17. 122–3
on Electress's death, 18. 175, 190–1, 206
Orford, Cts of, may wear, 19. 37, 42, 47, 49, 53
possibility of, for Gloucester, 6. 483
rings for, out of fashion among people of rank, 25. 124
rouge forbidden to Viennese ladies during, 22. 354
servants want to wear, 21. 165
Strafford to wear, for D. of Devonshire on getting legacy, 38. 452–3
suit of, ordered to be ready in 8 hours, 35. 159
Tarente, Princesse de, usually wears, 35. 193
Vienna to regulate, for Tuscan Court, 22. 337, 340, 354
Waldegrave, Cts, puts servants into, for Louis XVI, 36. 285n
white instead of black may have denoted, in medieval dress, 42. 38
White's Club to put up escutcheon of, for deaths of gambling and Mrs Winnington, 37. 201–2
See also Weepers

Mourning Bride, The. See under Congreve, William

Mourning ring. *See under* Ring

Mouse; mice:

[Mouse; mice, *continued*]
God compared to, **18.** 79
Mason electrifies, **28.** 200
Ossory, Lady, will be deserting, **32.** 208
owl bites feet off, to keep them quiet to fatten, **39.** 9
time's womb will not bring forth, **24.** 356
Mousehold, Cornwall:
Pentraeth, Dolly, 'old woman of,' **2.** 164
Mousquetaire; mousquetaires:
étourderie of, **38.** 203
Parliamentary registers demanded by, **39.** 65–6
See also Musketeer
'Mousseline la sérieuse.' *See* Bulkeley, Anne; *see also under* Hamilton, Anthony, *Quatre facardins*
'Moustache' (? HW's dog):
Conway regrets, **37.** 137
'Moustache' (fairy). *See* Crébillon, Claude-Prosper Jolyot de: *Écumoire, L'*
Moustier, Éléonore-François-Élie (1751–1817), Comte (Marquis, 1801) de; army officer; minister to England, 1783:
English mission of, **25.** 363
Mouton, Rue du, in Paris:
Tissot lives near, **7.** 72n
Moutray, ——, Capt. of the *Warwick*:
Carleton sends, from Quebec, with news of Burgoyne's surrender, **24.** 339n
Moutray, John (d. 1785), Capt. of the *Thetis*:
Cadiz news brought by, **22.** 12n, 19n
Moving picture:
ships appear in, **34.** 40
sun and moon resemble, **33.** 104
Mowat, Francis Ritchie (d. 1788), naval Capt.:
orders to burn American seaports reported by, at Falmouth, **24.** 161n
Mowbray, Bn. *See* Howard, Henry Frederick (1608–52)
Mowbray, Anne (1472–81), Cts of Norfolk; m. (1478) Richard (Plantagenet), D. of York, cr. (1477) D. of Norfolk:
alliance of, **42.** 422
death of, **32.** 504–5
marriage of, **2.** 364, **16.** 4, **32.** 504–5
Mowbray, Eleanor, Ds of Norfolk. *See* Bourchier, Eleanor
Mowbray, John de (1444–76), 6th D. of Norfolk:
widow of, **2.** 364
Mowbray family:
arms of, on monument, **16.** 88
HW does not forget, **42.** 422
Howards and Fitzalans connected with, **12.** 209
Moyle, ——:
Edgcumbe about to visit, **40.** 54
Moyle, Joseph (d. 1742), M.P.:
(?) son of, **40.** 55n
Moyne, Le. *See* Le Moyne
Moyser ('Moyzer'), Col. [John (b. ca 1660)]:
Bethell accompanies, **43.** 244, 247

Mann receives, at Galfridus Mann's recommendation, **17.** 408
Moysey, Dr. Abel (1715–80), physician:
daughter implored by, not to marry Hervey, **23.** 93
Moysey, Mary, m. Rev. John Richards of Long Bredy House, Dorset:
Hervey in love with, **23.** 193
Moyston (?Mostyn), Mr:
(?) groom to Edward, D. of York, **37.** 479
Moyston. *See also* Mostyn
Mozart, Wolfgang Amadeus (1756–91):
composes concerto for Duc de Guines and daughter, **7.** 363n, **43.** 98
Mozzi (*or* Mozzi del Garbo), Signora. *See* Barbolani da Montauto, Isabella; Bartolini Salimbeni, Maria Luisa (1766–1813)
Mozzi, Giulio Giuseppe (1730–1813), cavaliere; poet; mathematician:
affair of, over E. of Orford's claims against Cts of Orford's estate: **25.** 167, 439–41, 444–7, 448, 504, 509–11, **36.** 202; adjusted, **33.** 452; claims and counter-claims in, **25.** 169, 335; compromise suggested in, **25.** 335, 471–3, 478–9; delayed, **25.** 150, 168, 191, 215–17, 397, **33.** 288 300, 302; Duane accepts arbitration in, **25.** 330; Duane allows some of Lucas's claims in, **25.** 414; Duane and Lucas dispute about, **25.** 397–8; Duane writes to HW about, **25.** 447; HW and Morice joint referees in, **25.** 161–2, 181, 230; HW attemps to conclude, **25.** 505–6; HW confers with Duane, Lucas, and Sharpe about, **25.** 419, 429, 439–41, 444–7, 471–2; HW declines acting as sole arbiter for, **25.** 216, 265–6, 304; HW disagrees about harm to Orford from delay in, **25.** 265–6; HW's delay in, caused by Lucas, **25.** 172, 200; HW's note from Lucas about concluding, **25.** 516; HW's tenderness to Mozzi prevents his dropping, **25.** 328; HW wants Camden as referee in, **25.** 216; less involved than Chancery suit would be, **25.** 397; Morice wants HW to write to Florence about, **25.** 432; Mozzi impatient to conclude, **25.** 190, 200, 202, 345, 421; Mozzi wants to end HW's vexation in, **25.** 345; must rest until he goes to England, **25.** 304; Orford thanks HW for concluding, **25.** 516; Sharpe and Duane too much for Lucas in, **25.** 410
age of, past 50, **25.** 535
ancestral town house of, partly purchased by Cts of Orford, **24.** 260
appearance of, fallen off, **23.** 237
beauty of, is his attraction for Cts of Orford, **25.** 130
bride not taken home by, till two days after wedding, **25.** 535, 539
Carder, Mrs, persuades, not to accept compromise, **25.** 419
—— sends letter to, **25.** 168

—— to be paid by, **25**. 512

—— urges, to come to England, **25**. 435

caveat's removal demanded by, **25**. 504, 509

claim of, against Cts of Orford's landed estate explained by Mann, **25**. 168–9

Corsini and Strozzi matches available to, **25**. 130, 498

could foil Lucas only by another like him, **25**. 298

courier perhaps sent by, **25**. 121

decency and civility will be of no use to, **25**. 328

desires only what Cts of Orford's will entitles him to, **25**. 162

disinterestedness of, communicated to HW by Mann, **25**. 324

Duane approved by, as referee, **25**. 229–30

—— gets *carte blanche* from, **25**. 412

—— is sent Guercino painting and Florentine prints by, **25**. 524, 568, 571–2

—— neglects, **25**. 371, 390

——, Orford, and Sharpe to be paid by, through Hoare, **25**. 492

Duane recommended to, by Morice, **25**. 298, 303

—— replaces Morice as representative for, **33**. 362, 372

——'s correspondence with, **25**. 304, 315, 328, 333, 390, 391, 514–15, 524

——'s decision approved by, **25**. 478

—— should be employed by, **25**. 216–17

English journey contemplated by, **25**. 144, 217, 220, 230–1, 235, 265, 289, 298, 300, 307, 315, 319, 320, 322, 328, 330, 341, 390, 391, 396, 404, 431, 496, 516

English might dislike, for getting old lady's inheritance away from her son, **25**. 396, 404

family of, ancient, **25**. 130

family to be protected by, from future claims, **25**. 466

fears of: of irritating Sharpe, **25**. 341; that Sharpe may not produce papers favouring him, **25**. 333

finances of, not poor for Florence, **25**. 130

Florence admires, for devotion to Cts of Orford, **25**. 396

(?) Gem, Dr, reports about, **23**. 158

Geoffrin, Mme, called on by, at Paris, **23**. 141–2

glad to escape from Lucas and Sharpe, **25**. 161

HW advises: not to be sanguine, **25**. 266; to come to England, **25**. 217, 220, 235, 265, 289, 298, 320, 328, 330; to offer or accept compromise, **25**. 320; to put himself in Duane's hands, **25**. 320; to sell claim to rich lawyer, **25**. 328

HW agrees with Morice in affairs of, **25**. 164

HW and Morice authorized by, to employ chamber counsel, **25**. 232

HW asked by, to conceal doubts of Sharpe, **25**. 341

HW asks Mann to inform, of E. of Orford's inherited wealth, **25**. 126

HW, as E. of Orford's nominee, cannot altogether favour, **25**. 462

HW as referee favoured, **25**. 516

HW asserts he is not partial to, **25**. 445

HW condemns Sharpe and Lucas for forcing, to come to England, **25**. 315

HW dares not write letters to, for fear of being put in his power, **25**. 265

HW declines to tell Morice how to advise, **25**. 298

HW desires list from, of demands Cts of Orford might have had on her son, **25**. 158

HW does not wish to favour, **25**. 216

HW earns gratitude of, by trouble with Lucas, **25**. 404

HW expects Orford to accommodate, **25**. 184

HW has saved, from Chancery suit, **25**. 448

HW hopes Duane will be accepted by, as referee, **25**. 216

HW hopes Duane will prevent injustice to, **25**. 350

HW meets, when calling on Hollands at Holland House, **23**. 229–30

HW not an enemy of, **25**. 158

HW proposes to obey commands of, **25**. 350

HW's and Duane's letters from, will end their arbitrage, **25**. 462

HW's conferences with Lucas please, **25**. 156

HW's connection with, might jeopardize claim to impartiality, **25**. 235

HW's correspondence with, **25**. 417, 421, 426, 470, 477, 519

HW's letter raised hopes of, **25**. 417

HW's relations with Duane over affairs of, **25**. 320, 330, 333–5, 344, 371, 391, 404, 419, 421–2, 439–41, 444–8, 465–6, 471–3, 477–8, 495, 516, 519

HW's relations with Lucas over affair of, **25**. 124, 126, 131, 143, 147–8, 154–8, 166, 167, 172, 176, 184, 186, 195, 213, 215–17, 235, 266, 286, 315, 331, 404, 419, 421–2, 427, 439–41, 444–7, 448, 471–3, 477–8, 495, 505–6, 509, 515, 516, 519

HW thanked by, **25**. 190, 229, 230, 341, 345, 431, 521

HW to act as counsel for, though not partial to him, **25**. 158

HW to favour, as much as equity will allow, **25**. 166

HW to tell Duane and Sharpe of resolution of, **25**. 466

HW unable to make a report to, **25**. 347

HW unable to tell, what Orford's demands are, **25**. 176

health of: fever, **25**. 322; nervous disorder, **23**. 155, 237; 'out of order,' **25**. 300; spits blood, **25**. 322

[Mozzi, Giulio Giuseppe, *continued*]

Hoare authorized by, to pay E. of Orford, 25. 498, 504, 509, 511, 521, 540

——'s bank informs, of balance due to Lady Orford, 25. 130

house of, 24. 260, 322, 330

houses of pleasure frequented by, 23. 158

Huntingdon knows, 21. 70

indolent and peaceable, averse to going to law, 25. 341

lawyer consulted by, about interest on jointure arrears, 25. 456

lawyers probably suggested E. of Orford's claims on, 25. 186

less than £4,000 to be received by, 25. 515n

London lawyers complicate case of, 25. 397–8

Lucas and Sharpe suspected by, of wishing him to go to law, 25. 322

Lucas complains of being blamed by, for delay, 25. 213–14

—— demands back interest from, 25. 637

—— expects to get five or six thousand pounds from, 25. 286

—— gives gout as excuse for delaying business of, 25. 195

——'s negotiations with Sharpe displease, 25. 492

—— suspicious of reasonableness of, 25. 298

—— wishes to get something from, 25. 143

Mann alarms, by threat that HW may quit arbitrage, 25. 469

—— always visited by, after arrival of post, 25. 404, 465

—— asks HW not to forget, 25. 283

—— calls, 'Gloria in Excelsis,' 21. 70

—— communicates HW's news to, 25. 319, 396, 426, 456, 469, 478

—— declines invitation to wedding banquet of, 25. 535

—— dissuades: from bribing Lucas, 25. 200; from setting out for England, 25. 200; from writing to HW or Morice, 25. 171

—— gets letters from, on Cts of Orford's illness, 24. 312, 25. 112, 113

—— has conference with, 25. 229–30

—— not to alarm, by account of HW's dissatisfaction with Lucas, 25. 509

—— receives letter from, and sends it to HW, 25. 231–2, 235

—— shown Cts of Orford's writing-box by, 25. 114

—— to inquire of, about Orford deeds, 25. 160

—— told by, of Cts of Orford's heart palpitation, 25. 102

marriage of: prevented by affair with Cts of Orford, 25. 130; takes place, 25. 535; to girl of 17, to take place, 25. 498, 512, 527; unhappy, 25. 568, 571

mathematician, 23. 155, 237, 25. 130

money left in London by Cts of Orford should be divided by, with E. of Orford, Sharpe thinks, 25. 154–5

money wanted by, to invest in French funds, 25. 477

Morice advises: to name Duane referee, 25. 298; to sell his rights, 25. 286

—— cannot assist, 25. 247

—— commissioned by, to handle affairs in England, 25. 157–8

—— confers with, 25. 434–5

—— informs, of intention of going abroad, 25. 303

—— is HW's fellow-labourer in affairs of, 25. 171, 172

—— may be informed by, of intended gift to Duane, 25. 524

—— perhaps to be seen by, at Cambrai, 25. 303

——'s and HW's decision to be accepted by, 25. 162

——'s correspondence with, 25. 168, 230, 304

——'s withdrawal causes determination of, to come to England, 25. 303

—— tells, not to come to England, 25. 435

mother of, wants him to marry, 25. 130

oath to be administered to, by Mann and Palombo, 25. 167

obliged but not consoled by HW's news, 25. 292

Orford, Cts of, accompanied by: at Calais, 23. 158; at Naples, 23. 155; to London, 23. 113n, 229–30; to Paris, 23. 141–2, 155, 158

—— attended by, while pleading bad health, 23. 158

—— buys house next to that of, 24. 260, 322, 330

—— did not confide English affairs to, 25. 129

—— enriches, 23. 158

—— leaves everything to, 25. 114, 122n, 168–9

—— leaves paintings to, 25. 524

—— left by, because of his family affairs, 25. 145

—— lives with, 2. 171n

—— may be abandoned by, unless she forsakes Naples, 23. 559, 24. 305

—— nearly discards, for lack of sexual prowess, 21. 70

—— not expected by, to die, 25. 129

—— said to have deposited sums in French funds in name of, 25. 113

——'s effects expected by, from Naples, 25. 160

—— sends, as messenger to Mann, 23. 464

——'s furniture listed by, 25. 163, 169

——'s papers received by, from Naples, 25. 162

—— the obstacle to marriage of, 25. 130

—— to recombine next-door house with that of, 24. 330

—— turned back by, at Calais, to keep her from meeting her son, 23. 158

—— will probably leave Italian property to, 25. 113

Orford, E. of, answers offer of, 25. 495

—— approves mother's disposition in favour of, **25**. 168, 181

—— offers to assist, in tossing Lucas in a blanket, **25**. 322, 328

—— pleased by conduct of, **25**. 156

—— presented by, with Clinton portrait, **25**. 298n

——'s correspondence with, **25**. 176, 186, 300, 301–2, 306–7, 319, 322, 328, 330

——'s creditors should get money returned by, **25**. 440, 441, 446

——'s creditor told by Lucas that money would come from, **25**. 286, 439

——'s demands on: **33**. 274, 281, **36**. 202; at last received, **25**. 333; awaited impatiently, **25**. 161; counter-claims against, **25**. 166, 333; delayed in transmission, **25**. 172, 191; should be moderate, **25**. 147; to be met, **25**. 144, 161, 163

—— sent list by, of things taken to Italy by Cts of Orford, **25**. 151, 156

—— should not give mother's portrait to, **25**. 501–2

——'s lawyers irritated by, **25**. 216

——'s lawyers may be quickened by, **25**. 307

——'s opinion of, improved by Mrs Carder, **25**. 168

——'s proceeding against, called by HW 'unjust, nugatory, and insulting,' **25**. 328

——'s release to, **25**. 466, 498, 521, 527

—— to be paid by, through Hoare, **25**. 492

Orford deeds unknown to, **25**. 160

Orford papers sent to England by, **25**. 161

Pisa baths visited by, **25**. 421

'poor emaciated low-spirited knight of St Stephen who is said to be a *savant*,' **23**. 141

Pratolino cannot be night lodging of, **24**. 23

Richecourt compared with, **25**. 122, 130

safer in HW's hands than in Sharpe's, **25**. 158

sculptor does hideous bust of Cts of Orford for, **25**. 504–5

Sharpe advises, to divide sum equally with E. of Orford, **25**. 419

—— assures, that E. of Orford will act honourably, **25**. 144

—— employed by, **25**. 160

—— informs, of Duane's death, **25**. 568

—— is surprised at being employed by, because of connection with Orford, **25**. 320, 333

—— less zealous for, **25**. 200

—— mistakenly trusted by, and is his enemy, **25**. 172

—— must be retained by, despite bad conduct, **25**. 181

—— neglects, **25**. 390

—— not a friend to, **25**. 320

—— not answered by, **25**. 419, 459

—— notifies, of Hoare's acceptance of order to pay E. of Orford and withdrawal of caveat, **25**. 511

—— offers to collect rents for, at salary, **25**. 492–3

—— reports to, on Cts of Orford's affairs, **25**. 144–5

——'s correspondence with, **25**. 137, 156, 166, 168–9, 216, 289, 315, 324, 333, 412, 465, 471, 478, 479, 492, 500, 504, 524

——'s duplicity angers, **25**. 333

—— thinks, should divide Cts of Orford's money (in Hoare's bank) with E. of Orford, **25**. 157, 160, 217, 335, 426

—— thinks Cts of Orford should not have left so much to, **25**. 161–2

—— to receive from, copy of paper signed by Yorke, **25**. 169

—— urges, to come to England, **25**. 435

—— wishes to evade claim of, against deficiencies in Cts of Orford's jointure, **25**. 172

should have younger assistants than Morice and HW. **25**. 344

Skrine wanted by E. of Orford to aid in affair of, **25**. 158, 162, 163–4, 166

submissions of, have worked against him, **25**. 298

trunks unpacked by, **25**. 435

verses by, on Buondelmonte's death, **21**. 70–1, 79

Zincke's portrait of Cts of Orford may be sent to, or copied in oils, **25**. 501

Mozzi, Piazza de', at Florence:

Mozzi's house in, **24**. 260n

Mozzi family:

Mozzi the only male of, **25**. 130

—— wants to protect, from claims by Cts of Orford's estate, **25**. 466

Mr Burke's Speech. See under Burke, Edmund

Mr Hervey's Letter to the Rev. Sir William Bunbury, Bart. See under Hervey, Hon. Thomas

'Mr Pope's Welcome from Greece.' *See under* Gay, John

'Mr Robinson's Address':

Mann, Sir Horace II, opposed in, **25**. 290n, 291n

Mubashshir ibn Fātik:

Dictes and Sayings of the Philosophers, translated by Rivers, **40**. 119, 120

Much Ado About Nothing. See under Shakespeare, William

Muchausen. *See* Münchhausen

Muckender. *See* Handkerchief

Mud-baths:

Morice to visit, in Germany, **25**. 307, **33**. 352

Mudge, Thomas (1717–94), watchmaker:

print of, **1**. 282

Mud Island, in Delaware River:

captured, **33**. 3

capture of, rumoured, **32**. 411

See also Fort Mifflin

Muette, La. *See* La Muette

'Muff,' Berrys' dog:

['Muff,' continued]
HW orders clipped and dipped for mange, 12. 163

Muff; muffs:
Ailesbury, Cts of, gives, to Mme du Deffand, 6. 133
Du Deffand, Mme, sends, to Miss Lloyd, 4. 330, 333, 365
fox-skin, Hannah More puns about, 31. 213
French army does not have, 21. 435
grey, Nugent has, 17. 165
HW and Gray wear, in crossing Alps, 13. 189
HW sends, to Pandolfini, 17. 42, 45, 47, 52
marrow-bones in, 35. 21
Montagu's, bought by HW, 10. 144–6, 151, 182
Scott, Lady Caroline, wears, 32. 338
spy hanged in, 19. 201
Walpole, Hon. Robert, sends, to his niece, 4. 335, 365

Muffeteens:
velvet, worn by Lady Mary Wortley Montagu, 22. 3

Muffetts, Herts:
Walpole, Lady Mary, to visit Hon. Mary Townshend at, 37. 202

Muffin:
buttered, verses on, 39. 241

Muffits. See Muffetts

Mufti, Muftis:
of Algiers, 24. 122
of Turkey, see Durrisade Mustafa Efendi

'Mufti,' HW's pet:
HW can not abandon, 9. 306
Montagu to kiss, for HW. 10. 205
(?) ossuarium not to be made for, till dead, 10. 155

Mugello, the, in Tuscany:
San Marino fortress at, 19. 11

'Mug-house':
Birmingham's term for ale-house, 35. 147

Muhammad 'Alī Khān (1717–95), Nawab of Arcot and the Carnatic; Wālājāh, 1765:
Benfield said to be agent for, 25. 117
——'s loans to, 29. 102n
biographical information about, corrected, 43. 125
godfather to Rumbold's son, 29. 35
HW jokes about, 9. 379
members of Parliament said to be in pay of, 29. 123, 33. 244
Pigot and Madras council dispute over sums paid by, from Tanjore, 24. 288n
Smith's agreement with, to prevent pillage, 23. 561n
Tuljajī refuses tribute to, 23. 561n

Muhammed-ben-Othman (ca 1710–91), Dey of Algiers:
O'Reilly's attack awaited by, 25. 416
reward offered by, for Spanish heads, 24. 122

Muhammed Shah (d. 1748), Mogul emperor ('Great Mogul') 1719–48:

Francis I's designs on treasure of, foiled by Mann, 20. 101, 22. 547
HW may be with, at Agra, 37. 278

Muhemed Ben Milas (b. ca 1721), Moroccan ambassador to Tuscany:
medal of Leopold's reception of, 24. 469, 478, 500

Muhsinzade Mehmet Pasha (1707–74), Grand Vizir 1771–4 of Turkey:
Rumiantsev concludes treaty with, 24. 33n
—— cuts off retreat of, 24. 33
—— to attack, at Schuma, 24. 29
treaty signed by, 24. 33, 40

Muir. See Mure

Mulberries:
forks for, 4. 262, 263

Mulberry tree; mulberry trees:
HW to sit in shade of, 9. 46
Minorca not planted with, 7. 284

Mule; mules:
Beauchamp may get, for lack of horses, 22. 336
caravan of, turned back by Nonsuch, 19. 51
convoy of, 18. 460
Cumberland rides, 29. 146
HW and Spence count, on road to Genoa, 17. 91, 30. 17
races for, at Port Mahon, 37. 311
Richecourt procures, 19. 11
——'s letter carried by, 21. 80
Three Princes of Serendip mentions, 20. 408

Muleteers:
in Spanish travel-books, 15. 137

'Muley.' See Russell, John, 4th D. of Bedford

Muley Ismail (1646–1727), Sultan of Morocco 1672–1727:
butchery of, 34. 162
tyranny of, 11. 207

Muley Moloch. See Abd el Malek (d. 1578)

Mulgrave, Bn. See Phipps, Constantine (1722–75); Phipps, Constantine John (1744–92); Phipps, Hon. Henry (1755–1831)

Mulgrave, Bns. See Hervey, Hon. Lepell

Mulgrave, E. of. See Phipps, Hon. Henry (1755–1831); Sheffield, Edmund (1564–1646); Sheffield, John (1647–1721)

Mulinari. See Molinari

Mull, Scottish:
HW receives, from Colquhoun, 42. 322

Müller, Gerard Friedrich (1705–83):
Catherine II encourages, 3. 300n

Müller, Johannes von (1752–1809), Swiss historian:
Boone's, Kinloch's, and Nicholls's correspondence with, 41. 353n
HW's correspondence with, 41. 353–6
HW's Historic Doubts and his love of liberty recommend him to, 41. 353–4
HW will refer queries of, to antiquarian friends, 41. 355

Müller, John Sebastian (1715–ca 1785), engraver:

Gray's head engraved by, **14.** 63n

plates engraved by, for *Designs by Mr R. Bentley for Six Poems by Mr T. Gray*, **20.** 368n, **43.** 191

Mulloy, Terence, sergeant:

rebels repelled by, **19.** 105

Mulso, Hester (1727–1801), m. (1760) John Chapone; writer:

Letters on the Improvement of the Mind by, very popular, **28.** 197n

Miscellanies in Prose and Verse by, **28.** 197n

writings of, admired by Mrs Delany but HW cannot read them, **28.** 197

Multiplication table:

HW never understood, **39.** 494

Mum, Brunswick:

Mason recommends, **29.** 170

Mummius, Lucius (fl. 154–42 B.C.); consul; Roman general:

sailors told by, to replace any lost statues, **19.** 264, **37.** 102

Mummy; mummies:

Cambridge receives gift of, **15.** 17–18, 19

Egyptian, of a crane, HW compares himself to, **32.** 43

HW calls Mirepoix a walking, **38.** 203

Mumps:

occurrences of, **39.** 52

Mun, Comtesse de. *See* Helvétius, Élisabeth-Charlotte

Mun, Alexandre-François (d. 1816), Comte de:

(?) Beauvau, Princesse de, takes, to theatre, **7.** 344

social relations of, with Mme de Luxembourg, **6.** 404

verses on, **6.** 407

Muncaster, Bn. *See* Pennington, John (1737–1813); Pennington, Lowther (1745–1818)

Muncey. *See* Monsey

Münchhausen, Freiherrin von. *See* Wangenheim, Wilhelmina Sophia von

Münchhausen, Gerlach Adolf (1688–1770), Freiherr von; Hanoverian statesman:

Cumberland, D. of, rebukes, **21.** 145

dinner given by, **20.** 125

George III's marriage arranged through, **43.** 277

looks like a judge, **37.** 360

Mann forwards letter through, **19.** 99

Offley's affected distress for, **30.** 266

Williams's distich translated by, into German, **37.** 354, 360

Mundell & Son, R. Bank Close, Edinburgh:

Scotland's Skaith published by, **42.** 432n

'Mun Gulph's Head':

balloon to stop at, **42.** 110

Muniain, Juan Gregorio (b. ca 1700):

Squillace succeeded by, as minister of war, **39.** 64n

Munib. *See* Ibrahim Minnib

Munich (Germany):

A.A., Mr, visits Paris en route to Court of, **30.** 215

Austrian army threatens, **17.** 289

Cologne, Elector of, possibly goes to, **42.** 495

Court of, may be sought by Suares family, **17.** 161

Cowper's installation notice from, **25.** 568

Grevilles in, **3.** 124

Niccolini may be at, **20.** 2, 7

Walpole, Thomas jr, addressed at, **36.** 227, 231, 235, 250

Munich, von. *See* Münnich

Munichausen. *See* Münchhausen

Münnich, Gräfin von. *See* Mengden, Dorothea von

Münnich, Burchard Christoph (1693–1767), Graf von; field marshal:

banished, **22.** 11

Biron sent by, to Siberia, **10.** 39n

Catalogue of New French Books, A, satirizes, **18.** 53

HW curious about fate of, **22.** 59

Münnich, Ernst, Graf von; head steward of Catherine II's household:

banished, **22.** 11

Münnich, Ernst Gustav (d. 1812), Maj.-Gen.; or Johann Gottlieb:

Elizabeth of Russia banishes family of, **22.** 11

Florence visited by, **22.** 11

Munpferdt, J. P. E. C. L.:

alleged centaur, **35.** 643

Munro, ——:

Mann writes to, at Birmingham about double-silver-plated dish-covers, **24.** 32

Munro, Elizabeth (?ca 1730–97), m. (?) —— Neale; 'Betty'; fruit vendor:

bons mots of, not wanted by HW. **30.** 208

Mason's *Heroic Epistle* immortalizes, **28.** 81

news adulterated by, **33.** 168

officers guard fruit-shop of, **38.** 109

Petersham, Lady Caroline, hires, to serve at party, **9.** 109

remark of, on Frederick II's supposed death, **30.** 156

Sackville's disgrace publicly discussed by, **38.** 20

Selwyn to visit SH when tired of, **30.** 150

Ticonderoga cannot be spelled by, **30.** 148

weather too good to be sauntered away with, **37.** 533

Munro, Sir Harry (ca 1720–81), 7th Bt; M.P.:

troops led by, **37.** 236

Munro, Sir Hector (ca 1726–1805), K.B., 1779; army officer; M.P.:

army of, perhaps defeated by Mahrattas, **25.** 141n

glory of, in East Indies, **25.** 282

Pondicherry's surrender reported by, **24.** 455n

Munro, Sir Robert (1684–1746), 6th Bt; M.P.; army officer:

biographical information about, corrected, **43.** 250

[Munro, Sir Robert, *continued*]
former regiment of, at Culloden, **37.** 239
Highland regiment commanded by, **18.** 237
killed at Falkirk, **19.** 204
Munro. *See also* Monro
Munster, Bns de. *See* Pratt, Caroline (d. 1805)
Münster, Bp of. *See* Klemens August (1700–61); Maximilian Franz (1756–1801); Maximilian Friedrich (1708–84)
Münster, Ds of. *See* Schulenburg, Ermengarde Melusina von der
Münster (Germany):
Abreu congratulates Alt on capture of, **21.** 315–16
Frederick II tells chapter of, not to admit Maximilian as canon, **25.** 80
Munster, Ireland:
plantation of, left by Herbert (one of its undertakers), to his daughter, **40.** 356n
Munter, Mme. *See* Poll, Margarethe Cornelia van de
Müntz, Johann Heinrich (1727–98), painter:
alleged affair of, with SH servant, whom he may have married, **40.** 169n
Bateman's house remodelled from drawings by, **10.** 42n
Bentley finds, in Jersey, **21.** 239
—— had recommended, to HW, **9.** 259
—— receives abusive letter from, **9.** 259
——'s directions from, enclosed by HW, **35.** 352
——'s painting finished by, **35.** 644
—— to be fetched to SH by, **9.** 216
brother of, **40.** 92
Buckingham to be visited by, **9.** 193
(?) card-matches made up by, at siege of Genoa, **9.** 259
chimney-boards painted by, at SH, **35.** 100
Chute pleased with, **35.** 232
——'s design for SH Cloister praised by, **35.** 110
—— to send, to SH, **35.** 89
—— visited by, at the Vyne, **35.** 241
cloths ordered by, for Bentley, **35.** 263
copies picture for HW, **9.** 223n
copper plates by, for prints to *Fugitive Pieces,* **37.** 552n
Court aspirations of, joked about by HW, **9.** 260, 345
drawing by: of HW at SH, presented to Conway, **37.** 475; of Radnor House, **9.** 53n; of the Vyne by, **14.** 83
drawings at Buckingham House traced by, on oil paper, **41.** 320n
drum's progress to be watched by, **9.** 192
earnings of, **9.** 259
Encaustic: or Count Caylus's Method of Painting in the Manner of the Ancients by, **9.** 282, **13.** 34, **16.** 168n, 170, **21.** 239n
encaustic painting practised by, **28.** 301, **29.** 137
England may be left by, **9.** 161

engraving by, **2.** 105n
Farmer's agreement witnessed by, **40.** 165
foreign gazettes preferred by, to palette, **35.** 265
(?) Fox's portrait by, **43.** 312
HW asks Lort to write to Madrid about, **16.** 170
HW attributes painting of Elizabeth Castle to, **35.** 243
HW awaits drawing by, of the Vyne, **35.** 89
HW dismisses, for impertinence, **13.** 34
HW employs, as painter, **40.** 93
HW gives Montagu's messages to, **9.** 239
HW ill-treated by, **9.** 259, 260
HW keeps, in house, **20.** 554, **21.** 120, 239, **35.** 226, 232, 265
HW mentions, **37.** 465
HW pleased by paintings and behaviour of, **35.** 242
HW presents landscapes by, to Montagu, **9.** 259, 265, 266
HW's Arlington St house may not have room for works of, **35.** 228
HW's benefactions to, **9.** 259, 260
HW scolds Bentley for advancing money to, **35.** 226–7
HW's correspondence with, **40.** 169–70
HW's protection renounced by, **40.** 169–70
HW's tales not believed by, **35.** 236, 238
HW suggests employing, at SH and the Vyne, **35.** 185–6
HW to be enlightened by, on military events, **35.** 103
HW wants to know more of history of, **35.** 242
health of, fever, **35.** 256
idleness of, **9.** 212n
Kingston to be visited by, **9.** 192
landscape genius of, **21.** 239
landscapes by, **9.** 239, 247, 250, 253, 259, 261, 265, 266
miniature by, of Comtesse de Grignan, **10.** 12
mistress of, **9.** 250, 259
Montagu asks HW to pay, **9.** 194
—— asks prices of, **9.** 261
—— offended by insolence of, **9.** 260
—— orders landscapes from, **9.** 239, 247, 250, 253, 261
—— sends compliments to, **9.** 197, 245, 250, 253, 261
——'s picture finished by, **9.** 192
——'s snuff-box not started by, **9.** 250
——'s visit from, deferred, **9.** 194
—— takes, to Lovell's shop, **9.** 191
—— to be accompanied by, to SH, **9.** 190
—— to be visited by, at Greatworth, **9.** 193
—— waits for painting to be executed by, **9.** 187
—— wishes prints by, of Isleworth, **9.** 401
Poland, K. of, employs, **12.** 263
Protestant, **40.** 93
returns to England, **12.** 263
Rigby does not promote, **9.** 259

(?) Scott inspires, to be landscape painter, 9. 261

SH visited by, 9. 187, 20. 554, 21. 120, 239

Swiss engineer in French service, 21. 239, 35. 185n

Twickenham's coaches said by, to outnumber all France's, 35. 234

(?) Twickenham views by, 9. 404

'Vasen en Urnen,' MS by, mentions HW, 40. 170n

views by: in Jersey, 30. 370; of SH, 30. 370, 35. 232

Vyne, the, visited by, 14. 93, 35. 232, 241, 243, 252, 256

Waddilove has not heard of, 16. 168

Wanstead price not to be told to, 35. 238

warlike spirit of, must not interfere with work at SH and the Vyne, 35. 91

Welsh transcribed by, 9. 218

works only to pay mistress's bills, 9. 250

Müntz, Theobald, 'ministre du régiment suisse de Brocard in the French service in Corsica': HW seeks passport for, 40. 92–3

Protestant, 40. 93

Munzell. See Muzell

Murad, Sultan of Turkey: Christian VII treated as, by courtier, 35. 328

Murard, ——: attends sessions of parliament of Paris, 8. 172

Murat, Charlotte (living 1834), m. (1776) Alexandre-Frédéric-Jacques de Masson, Marquis de Pezay: husband of, dies, 6. 499

marriage of, 6. 381

social relations of, with Mme du Deffand, 7. 439

Muratori, Lodovico Antonio (1672–1750), historian: Annals of Italy by, 25. 491

Della pubblica felicità by, disappoints Florentines, 20. 117

Francis III of Modena's librarian, 17. 324, 20. 117

——'s rights to Ferrara investigated by, 17. 324

Scotland lacks, 16. 379

Murcott, John (d. 1763), Dacre's butler: Blake murders, 38. 193

Murder: Conway's era carries art of, to perfection, 37. 422

English law for immediate execution after conviction for, 20. 317

Murderer; murderers: bodies of, delivered to surgeons, 21. 388

property of, goes to county sheriff, 21. 398

Murdo, John. See Morow or Morvo, John

Murdoch, John: John Paul Jones's raid reported by, 24. 378n

Mure, Mr: SH visited by, 12. 243

Mure, Hutchinson (ca 1711–94), trader:

Mason satirizes, 28. 437

Mure, son, and Atkinson: provisions to be sent by, to English army in Boston, 41. 312n

Muri, Ab1, (?) Mann's physician: (?) Cocchi recommends, 25. 270

(?) Mann kept in bed by, 25. 555, 556

(?) —— permitted by, to see Hollands, 22. 467

(?) ——'s ailment called gout by, 24 479

——'s legacy to, 25. 667n

(?) Mann told by, that chalkstones are painful, 25. 656

(?) Mann, Horace II, reassured by, 25. 607

Muriccioli, the, at Florence: Bosville, Mrs, misbehaves upon, 18. 286

Murillo (Bartolomé Esteban) (1617–82), painter: Julienne has paintings by, 7. 286

Presle has paintings by, 7. 346

Murphy, Arthur (1727–1805), dramatist: All in the Wrong by: acted at Mrs Hobart's, 33. 368–9; announced at Drury Lane, 38. 276; at Drury Lane, 38. 87

Alzuma by, 28. 80, 32. 100–1

Clive, Mrs, entertains, 9. 269

Garrick flatters, 35. 568

Grecian Daughter, The, by, 35. 568

HW's opinion of, 9. 269–70

Hentzner's Journey speeded to printer by, 40. 112

No One's Enemy but His Own by: 22. 199; seen at Covent Garden by royal family, 38. 288

Pitt, Elizabeth, offers letters to, for The Test, 21. 46

prologue by, to Braganza, 28. 177

Test, The, written by Francis and, 9. 203n

Three Weeks After Marriage by, 33. 428

Way to Keep Him, The, by: acted at Richmond House, 33. 563, 580; Conway's prologue to, 39. 546–8; HW attends, at Richmond House, 39. 448; not to be acted at Richmond House, 33. 560

Murphy, James Cavanah (1760–1814), architect; antiquary: Travels in Portugal by: 43. 156; Sanskrit inscription quoted from, 12. 178

Murphy. See also Morphy

Murrain: cold weather may hamper, 19. 174

English cattle struck by, 19. 174

physicians call, infectious disease from abroad, not caused by poisoned pools, 19. 174

Murray, Lady. See Baillie, Grizel (ca 1691–1759)

'Murray': Bute's pseudonym, 23. 91, 96

Murray, ——, British agent in Corsica: Paoli tells, of his needs, 23. 46

Murray, ——, printer. See Sands, Donaldson, Murray, and Cochran

Murray, ——, Major:

[Murray, Major, *continued*]
memorandum mentions, **12**. 270n
Murray, Mr:
HW mentions, **37**. 489
Murray, Hon. Alexander (1712–78) cr. (1759)
titular E. of Westminster:
brother of, **16**. 293, **20**. 223
brother tries to put, in custody of serjeant-at-arms, **20**. 249
counsel desired by, at bar of House of Commons, **20**. 224–5
flees to France, **20**. 286
House of Commons sentences, to Newgate, **16**. 293, **20**. 225, 227, 234, **38**. 315
Philipps moves King's Bench to produce, **20**. 249
sentences resumed against, by House of Commons, **20**. 286
Westminster high bailiff names, **20**. 224
Westminster petition instigated by, **20**. 223
Wilkes's letter to, **22**. 174n
Murray, Alexander, army officer:
Allen's death blamed on, **23**. 20
Murray, Alexander (1736–95) solicitor-general of Scotland:
counsel in House of Lords's appellant jurisdiction, **35**. 622
Murray, Mrs Alexander. *See* Baillie, Grizel
Murray, Lady Anne. *See* Mackenzie, Lady Anne
Murray, Lady Anne (ca 1731–1817):
Berry, Mary, identifies, **12**. 58n
HW likes to visit, **12**. 58
HW mentions, **12**. 203
HW visited by, **12**. 20
neat, **12**. 20
quiet, **12**. 146
Radnor House occupied by, **42**. 480
SH visited by, **12**. 250
Murray, Lady Augusta:
Sussex, D. of, marries, at Rome, **35**. 442n
Murray, Lady Catherine. *See* Stewart, Lady Catherine
Murray, Charles, actor:
Earl Goodwin to be acted by, **31**. 331n
Murray, Christina Theresa Josepha (ca 1755–1813), m. (1779) James Ogilvy, 7th E. of Findlater:
marriage of, **32**. 55n
SH visited by, **12**. 233
Murray, Cordelia (b. 1781), m. (1803) Rev. Henry Hodges:
escapes from Minorca to Leghorn, **25**. 179, 180
father recommends, to Mann, **25**. 349
father seeks pension for sake of, **25**. 364
Murray, David (ca 1689–1748), 6th Vct. Stormont:
brother of, **17**. 250n
Murray, David (1727–96), 7th Vct Stormont, 1748; 2d E. of Mansfield, 1793:
absences from Paris expected of, **6**. 301
Aiguillon confers with, **5**. 345
——'s correspondence with Guines altered at desire of, **41**. 299n

Aiguillon, Duchesse d', admires, **4**. 342–3
—— brings, to Mme du Deffand, **4**. 357
—— courted by, **4**. 348
Ailesbury, Cts of, corresponds with, **6**. 291
—— knows, **37**. 395
—— notified by, of Conway's summons to Jersey, **39**. 359
—— sends messages by, **6**. 457
—— talks of Mme du Deffand with, **6**. 250
allowance denied to, for journey to diplomatic post, **38**. 269n
ambassador to France, **5**. 258
Barrymore, Cts of, borrows house of, **6**. 265
—— paid attentions by, **6**. 282
Beaumarchais's mémoires said by, to be current in London, **6**. 20, 26
Beauvau does errand through, **6**. 173
Boulogne visited by, on way to England, **24**. 365
Brühl entertains, at Dresden, **37**. 473
Calais to be visited by, **6**. 171
Carmarthen's dinner attended by, **33**. 554n
character of, will be forgotten because he is a Scot and Mansfield's nephew, **24**. 526
Chesterfield's letters may be obtained through, **6**. 38, 41
Conway accompanied by, at Florence and Rome, **37**. 324
—— and party to be escorted from Paris by, **6**. 156
—— can be introduced by, to Maurepas, **39**. 198
—— lives with, at Rome, **20**. 296, 298
—— longs to see, **38**. 33
—— 's correspondence with, **6**. 82, 90, 96, 388, **37**. 473, **38**. 32–3
—— sends messages by, **6**. 457
—— 's friend, **7**. 28, **23**. 18, **24**. 526
—— 's good opinion of, **37**. 324, **38**. 32–3
—— to receive current writings from, **6**. 160
courier from, leaves Paris before horses are stopped at Louix XV's death, **24**. 1
Czartoryski's country house visited by in Poland, **38**. 33
daughters of, **12**. 20n
Deane, Silas, said to be interviewed by, **32**. 339
dirge by, on P. of Wales's death, **20**. 261
disobliging, **6**. 18
Du Deffand, Mme, a royalist from politeness to, **6**. 492
—— asks if HW has seen, **5**. 386
—— discusses Conway with, **6**. 273
—— given information by, **6**. 283
—— hears Conway party's impressions of Paris from, **6**. 170
—— hopes HW will repeat her compliments to, **5**. 324
—— inquires about, **6**. 177, 315, **7**. 34
—— may not see, before his departure, **5**. 371
—— may receive goods through, **5**. 307, 331, 334, **6**. 226
—— promises not to write about, **6**. 321

—— receives letter through, **6.** 63
——'s correspondence with, **6.** 312, **7.** 32
—— seeks book from, **6.** 423, 427
—— sends HW's suit through, **6.** 41
—— sends letter by, **7.** 36, 37
—— sends letter through, **6.** 190, 304–5
—— sends message to, **6.** 171
—— sends parcels by, **7.** 14, 16, 36–9
——'s opinion of: **5.** 320, 323, 363, 380, **6.** 18, 60, 68, 96, 179, 238, 260, 288, 459–60; Stormont indifferent to, **5.** 334
——'s relations with, **4.** 348, **5.** 323, **6.** 238, **7.** 28, 185, 237
—— to appeal to, for Lady Fenouilhet, **5.** 371
—— to send letter by, **5.** 375, **6.** 169, 171, **7.** 4
—— to send parcels by, **6.** 292, 295, 296, **7.** 8, 18, 32, 33
—— to send volume of Sévigné letters through, **5.** 373, 395
embargo detains at Boulogne, **28.** 376
English-French naval disarmament pact signed by, **24.** 299n
Florence left by, **23.** 24
Foote at dinner with, **28.** 189
Forbach, Comtesse de, disputes with, **7.** 34
Forcalquier, Mme de, courted by, **4.** 348
Francis I's decision about converted Tuscan girls to be contested by, **22.** 250
Franklin triumphs over, **28.** 374
French and English Courts to be reconciled by, **28.** 78
French embargo delays, **24.** 365, **28.** 376
French ministry notifies, of fleet being prepared, **23.** 474n
Fullarton lately secretary to, at Paris, **25.** 31
Germain differs with, over Carleton, **25.** 241n
——'s resignation throws burden on, **33.** 326
German politics scarce entered by, **37.** 472–3
Gordon examined before, **25.** 71n
Gordon rioters attack, **7.** 231, **25.** 53, **29.** 62, **33.** 175, 184
Gower dislikes secretary of state's position of, **39.** 343
HW and Mme du Deffand may settle accounts through, **6.** 196
HW expects, to sign shameful treaty with France, **29.** 65
HW may not know, **37.** 309
HW's danger alarms, **23.** 15
HW sends compliments to, **31.** 154
HW sends parcels by, **6.** 335
HW's health reported on by, **6.** 7
HW's opinion of, **5.** 379, 380
HW thanks, for messages, **23.** 22
HW to ask, about Sévigné letters, **5.** 376
HW to be visited by, **31.** 368
HW to get Guines's mémoire from, **6.** 188
HW to receive compliments of, **23.** 15
HW to see, **6.** 172
HW to send letter through, **6.** 388, 389
HW wants Mann to describe, **20.** 291
Hamilton sees at Rome, **23.** 2n
Hamiltons not to visit, **31.** 217

Harcourt brings, to Mme du Deffand, **4.** 342
Holland may have to be route of, home to England, **24.** 366
Hôtel des Deux Ponts taken by, **6.** 282, 291
Huntingdon's friend, **20.** 457, **22.** 113
Italian translation of *Elfrida* dedicated to, **28.** 172
itinerary of, from Florence to Vienna, **23.** 18, 24–5
Langlois secretary to, **25.** 246
Laurens examined by, **25.** 91n
London to be visited by, **5.** 307, **6.** 166, 169, 284, 291, 292
—— visited by, **6.** 172
lord president of the Council would not swear in, **33.** 131
Louis XV's illness said to have caused a request to, to fetch Sutton, **24.** 2
Louis XVI's consecration not to be attended by, **6.** 195
made secretary of state, **28.** 469n
Mann and Lorenzi entertained by, **20.** 285
Mann notified by, of order to quit Paris, **24.** 373
—— praises, **20.** 285, 291, 297, 457, **22.** 113
—— recommends, to Albani, **20.** 298
—— sends to, copy of letter to Albani, **22.** 384n
——'s MS account of Tuscany praised by, **23.** 27–8
—— suspects, to be author of letters on Poland, **23.** 502–3
—— talks with, about HW and Conway, **23.** 18
—— told by: about Ferdinand of Naples, **23.** 17; that Americans are much reduced, **24.** 306
—— visited by, **23.** 2, 11, 15, 18, 22, 24
marriage of, **6.** 305, 306–8, 312, **38.** 32, 35–6
Maty chaplain to, **16.** 171
Maurepas and Vergennes get protests from, about aid to America, **24.** 316n
melancholy of, impairs his health, **23.** 18
Minorca's relief proposed by, to George III, **25.** 187n
misdeed of, **6.** 4, 18
Monteynard does not know, **5.** 372, 373, 379
Necker, Mme, corresponds with, **6.** 203
Necker, M., gives book to, **6.** 183
Neckers friends of, **6.** 192
—— may be accompanied by, **6.** 288
Orléans, Duc d', said to have quarrelled with, **24.** 50
Paris left by, to avoid meeting Pretender, **6.** 160n
—— said to be visited by, **5.** 345, 433, 436
—— to be visited by, **8.** 214
—— visited by, **6.** 7, **37.** 309, 324
Paul secretary to, **9.** 113n
peerage of, corrected, **43.** 151
Petersham, Lady Caroline, entertains, **9.** 158
plaque of, stolen, **6.** 203
popularity of, **9.** 158

[Murray, David (1727–96), *continued*]
portrait of, by Reynolds, 9. 158n
president of the Council, 12. 117, 25. 391
Radnor's Regency amendment questioned by, in Lords, 25. 684n
recalled, from Paris embassy, 7. 31, 24. 364, 373, 28. 373, 29. 76
recall of, rumoured, 6. 445
resignation of, expected, 25. 236n
return of, rumoured, 7. 41
Rockingham answered by, 25. 222n
Rome visited by, 20. 298, 23. 2
Russian dispatches to, 25. 118n
Russian war plans revealed by, 23. 438–9
Scotland to be visited by, 6. 203
Scottish post for, 24. 179
secretary of state for the North, 7. 185, 435, 24. 455n, 33. 131
sisters of, 12. 20n
social relations of, in Paris, *see index entries ante* 8. 450
Spanish neutrality expected by, in House of Lords speech, 24. 463n
Stanhope, Lady Harriet, liked by, 6. 134, 147, 160, 170, 175, (?) 265
—— said to have rejected, 6. 179, 186, 197, 200, 203, 240
SH visited by, 12. 247
sublime nonsense of, 33. 273
Suffolk, E. of, succeeded by, as secretary of state, 24. 525–6, 39. 342
Trudaine de Montigny, Mme, said to attract, 6. 82
uncle's letter possibly written by, 33. 364
valet-de-chambre of, reports that Frederick II approaches Dresden, 21. 2
Vergennes's audience with, 24. 306n
Viennese post to go to, 22. 130
virtu absorbs, 22. 298
Viry, Mme de, suspected of being bribed by, 6. 474n
war parley attended by, 6. 459
Yorke may replace, at Paris, 24. 179
Murray, David William (1777–1840), 3d E. of Mansfield:
birth of, 6. 415
Murray, *or* Murry, Edward, page to D. of York:
(?) illness of, 22. 225n
Murray, Lady Elizabeth (ca 1628–98), Cts of Dysart, s.j., m. 1 (ca 1647) Lionel Tollemache, 3d Bt; m. 2 (1672) John Maitland, cr. (1672) D. of Lauderdale:
first husband of, 16. 285
HW jokes about seeing ghost of, at Ham House, 10. 306
Murray, Hon. (later Lady) Elizabeth Mary (1760–1825), m. (1785) George Finch Hatton:
birth of, 38. 60–1
HW hopes, will not love drinking like a Pole, 38. 61
Murray, Elizabeth Mary (1783–5):
birth of, expected, 25. 364

'Murray, Fanny' (Fanny Rudman) (ca 1729–78), m. (1757) David Ross; courtesan:
Atkins gives money to, 9. 80
HW's 'Beauties' claimed by Rigby to allude to, 30. 101
marriage of, uncertain, 9. 80
possible allusion to, 30. 44–5
twenty-pound note eaten by, 9. 80
Wilkes's *Essay on Woman* dedicated to, 22. 184
Murray, Frances Cairnes (ca 1734–1820), m. (1752) William Henry Fortescue, cr. (1770) Bn, (1776) Vct, and (1777) E. of Clermont:
Amelia, Ps, entertains, at Gunnersbury, 33. 416n, 517, 39. 441, 533
—— rebukes, for passing snuff-box across her, 35. 533
(?) Cholmondeley, Mrs, acquaintance of, 4. 271
'conversation' of, attended by HW and Dashkov family, 33. 172
Du Deffand, Mme, not called on by, 6. 395
dinner given by, for Duc de Chartres, 29. 302
Farnham, Lord, and, 32. 283
French players at Lady William Gordon's to be heard by, 39. 441
French rumour received by, 32. 387
Hôtel d'Entragues occupied by, 6. 383
Joseph II's attentions to, 33. 290
Marie-Antoinette notices, at Paris, 6. 282, 25. 357n
(?) Paris visited by, 4. 271
social relations of, in Paris, 7. 260, 262, 282, 329, 352–3
SH visited by, 12. 236
SH visitors sent by, 12. 247
success of, 6. 282
Murray, Lord George (1694–1760):
Old Pretender and Venice visited by, 19. 379
Young Pretender joined by, 19. 104
Murray, George (d. 1761), sculptor and carver:
(?) HW hurries, at SH, 35. 173
Murray, George (1741–97), naval officer; M.P.:
Mann presents, at Tuscan Court, 22. 350
Murray, James (1690–1764), 2d D. of Atholl, 1724:
brother of, 19. 104, 106n, 254n
London visited by, 19. 102
troops cannot be raised by, 19. 102
wife of, 13. 173n
wife separated from, 19. 106
Young Pretender at house of, 19. 106
Murray, Hon. James (ca 1690–1770), cr. (1721) titular E. of Dunbar:
about to leave Rome for Avignon, 19. 378
Acquaviva will not give passports to English without recommendation from, 19. 15
Avignon may be visited by, 19. 376, 378
brother of, 17. 250n, 19. 283
Chute and Whithed maligned by, 19. 136
Chute rebuked by, for neglect, 35. 61
Del Monti's account of Young Pretender's departure distributed by, at Rome, 18. 418

English Jacobite visitors at Rome court, **19.** 136

HW asks about rôle of, in Old Pretender's quarrel with sons, **20.** 345

Johnson, Murray, and Stone accused of toasting, **20.** 361

lies told by, about Young Pretender's prospects, **19.** 311

lives with Old Pretender's family, **13.** 217–18

Mansfield might have enjoyed Old Pretender's confidence through, **23.** 248n

Old Pretender said by, to be offended at Chute and Whithed, **19.** 136

——'s intrigues with, **17.** *18*

——'s prime minister, **17.** 250n

Petroni assembly harangued by, **19.** 218

probably no longer a Jacobite, **23.** 328

Rivera persuaded by, that Charles Emmanuel III should support Young Pretender, **19.** 142

Rome probably left by, **19.** 143

sensible, agreeable, and well-bred, **13.** 218

Spanish naval operations reported by, to HW, **17.** 20

Young Pretender's absence from Scotland admitted by, **19.** 145

—— said to have left Rome with, **17.** 113

——'s escape from Rome facilitated by, **18.** 377

——'s invasion asserted by, **19.** 93–4

Murray, Hon. James (ca 1719–94), army officer; gov. of Canada; gov. of Minorca:

arrested, **25.** 361

capitulation of, criticized by army people, **25.** 269

cheerfulness of, based on vain hope of reinforcement, **25.** 233

Collet informs, of enemy's approach, **25.** 349

conduct at Minorca given favourable construction by, at home, **25.** 200

Conway procures mitigation of apology by, to Draper, **25.** 364

Corsicans at Leghorn cannot aid, **25.** 196

court martial of, **25.** 308–9, 327, 342, 348, 355, 358, 360, 361, 373

Crillon attempts to bribe, **25.** 207–8, 213, 229, 263n

—— lends apartment to, **25.** 269

—— praises, **25.** 189, 263–4

——'s attack surprises, **25.** 198

——'s relations with, **25.** 229, 263–4, 269

Draper accuses, of losing Minorca, **22.** 383n

—— has more partisans than, among officers, **25.** 269

—— provoked by bad treatment by, **25.** 360

——'s complaint against, rejected by Judge Advocate, **25.** 308–9

——'s harsh expressions to, during Minorca siege, **25.** 361

——'s quarrel with, **25.** 269, 271, 327, 342

enemy preparations to attack St Philip's described by, **25.** 233–4

England the destination of, **25.** 269

Florentine communication with, cut off, **25.** 59

French defeat, in Canada, **21.** 416, 421, 422

—— feared by, to cut Minorca-Leghorn communications, **24.** 443

—— strongly resisted by, **25.** 207

George III excuses, from reprimand, **25.** 364

Greeks (independent) do not aid, **25.** 196–7

grieved by reports in gazettes, **25.** 269

HW never saw, **20.** 354

health of, much indisposed, **25.** 269

Hillsborough's dispatches from, **25.** 136, 207, 233

Jesuits forbidden by, to accept recruits in Canada, **22.** 233n

Leghorn visited by, **25.** 269

letters reach Florence from, **25.** 196

Mann can send communications of, by cipher, **24.** 469, **25.** 42

—— does not wish to accuse, of neglect, **25.** 200

—— has no news from, **25.** 192, 196

—— ordered to supply Udny with everything required by, **25.** 429

——'s apology to, to be conveyed by Horace Mann II, **25.** 358, 370–1

——'s correspondence with, **24.** *380*, **25.** 348–9

—— sends communications of, to England, **24.** 380, 437, 443, 457

——'s letter criticizing, produced by Draper, **25.** 354n

—— unsure of guilt of, **25.** 360

—— visited by, **25.** 268–9

—— wishes, could be informed (by nephew) of his sympathy, **25.** 349

Minorca defended by, **22.** 290

—— to be defended by, to last extremity, **25.** 174, 179, 190

Minorcan attempt by French feared by, **24.** 380, 437, 468, **25.** 59

Minorcan castle's siege expected by, to last long, **25.** 229

more men needed by, to defend Minorca, **25.** 174

no aid can come to, except from England, **25.** 197

pension asked by, for children's sake, **25.** 364

privateers of, successful, **24.** 437

Quebec's siege raised by, **15.** 71n

sails with family from Leghorn to Antibes, **25.** 271

Sturt dispatched by, as courier, **25.** 42

Sutherland's rift with, **25.** 81

Udny forwards dispatches of, **25.** 233

—— unable to aid, **25.** 197

Weymouth tells, to send his secrets to Mann to be ciphered and forwarded by post, **25.** 42

wife and children of: escape from Minorca to Leghorn, **25.** 179, 180, 290; pension for, **25.** 364; recommended to Mann, **25.** 349

Murray, James (1727–99) of Broughton; M.P.:

Johnston, Grace, elopes with, **33.** 489

Murray, James (1734–94), of Strowan, army officer; M.P.:
Gordon, Lord George, denounced by, **25.** 55, 29. 53, **33.** 177
Parliamentary membership of, corrected, **43.** 306
Murray (- Pulteney after 1794), Sir James (ca 1755–1811), 7th Bt, 1771; army officer:
London reached by, from army, **39.** 502–3
marriage of, **11.** 238n
Menin's recapture reported by, **39.** 505n
Murray, Mrs James. *See* Whitham, Anne
Murray, James Patrick (1782–1834), army officer:
father seeks pension for sake of, **25.** 364
Murray, John (ca 1670–1748), of Sacombe; antiquary:
Russell attended by, on scaffold, **16.** 50
Zouch bought medal from, **16.** 50
Murray, John (1685–1752), 2d E. of Dunmore, 1710; army officer:
brother of, **19.** 104
Cumberland, D. of, served by, **19.** 20
Fontenoy battle missed by, **36.** 12
Newcastle recommends Hon. George Townshend to, **36.** 7n
Plymouth position granted to, **19.** 62
Townshend, George, serves under, **36.** 6
Murray, Lord John (1711–87), M.P.; army officer:
in Damas St, Dublin, **37.** 332
(?) regiment of, due in Boston, **24.** 197n
Townshend accompanies, to Flanders, **37.** 196n
Murray, John, Lt-Col.:
(?) Guise advised by, to retire, **17.** 485
Murray, John (ca 1714–75), English Resident at Venice; ambassador to Turkey:
Coronation probably not to be celebrated by, **21.** 542
courier from India sent on by, to England, **21.** 523
death of, **7.** 398
Grenville may be succeeded by, at Constantinople, **22.** 356
HW knew, in England, **21.** 562
HW might be helped by, to get Zanetti's tiger gem, **21.** 562, **22.** 14, 116
Halifax's orders to, about D. of York, **22.** 173n
Lind chaplain to, at Constantinople, **23.** 565
——'s quarrel with, **23.** 565
Mann corresponds with, **22.** 14, 116
of Isle of Man, **21.** 562n
Paduan opera attended by company of English in uniform from Venice led by **21.** 512–13
Sultan might lock up, **23.** 479
Murray, Sir John (1715–77), of Broughton; titular 7th Bt 1770; secretary to Young Pretender:
capture of, **19.** 274
confessions by, **19.** 288

HW sees, at Tower, **9.** 46
has evidence concerning proposed invasion of 1743–4, **15.** 134n
King's evidence turned by, **9.** 40
Mann anxious to hear disclosures of, **19.** 303
—— astonished at silencing of, **19.** 391
name of, corrected, **43.** 258
testimony of, at Lovat's trial, **19.** 381
Murray, John (1729–74), 3d D. of Atholl, 1764; M.P.:
brother of, **22.** 350, **29.** 53n
suicide of, after 'apoplectic fit,' **23.** 56, **32.** 214, 214n
Murray, John (1730–1809), styled Vct Fincastle 1752–6; 4th E. of Dunmore, 1756; colonial gov.:
Congressman and old cannon captured by, in fight with Americans, **24.** 157
Du Deffand, Mme, at Opéra-Comique with, **4.** 276
——'s social relations with, **4.** 276–7, 283
expects to return to Virginia, **29.** 184
government of, on shipboard, **28.** 237, 355
HW mentions, **6.** 297
HW wishes him 'his dose' on going to America, **33.** 298
not yet beyond the Delaware valley, **39.** 321
pensioned, **29.** 156
protest by, **22.** 7
troops of, desert, **24.** 88
Virginians involved by, in war with Indians, **41.** 312
Murray, John (1745–93), bookseller:
Gray's poems published by, **28.** 149n
HW receives Dalrymple's *Annals* from, **15.** 140
Mason's quarrel and law suit with, **28.** 310–11, 313, 322, 326, 452, **29.** 141
Murray, John (1755–1830), 4th D. of Atholl, 1774, cr. (1786) E. Strange:
Highlanders would have killed, **33.** 384n
Ossory leases house from, in Grosvenor Place, **32.** 223n
uncle of, **29.** 53
Murray, Joseph Jacob (1718–1802), Graf Murray de Melgum; Austrian army officer:
Joseph II sends mandate to Austrian Netherlands through, **33.** 570
Murray, Maria, m. Thomas Pitt, sr:
jointure of, **21.** 517
Murray, Hon. Marjory (d. before 1770), m. (1715) Hon. John Hay, cr. (1718) titular E. and (1727) titular D. of Inverness; Old Pretender's mistress:
Albano visited by, **17.** 28
Murray, Lady Marjory (d. 1799), dau. of 6th Vct Stormont:
Berry, Mary identifies, **12.** 58n
HW likes to visit, **12.** 58
HW mentions, **12.** 203
SH visited by, **12.** 20
neat, **12.** 20
quiet, **12.** 146

Radnor House, Twickenham, occupied by, **42**. 480
SH visited by, **12**. 250
Murray, Lady Mary (1720–95), m. (1749) James Ogilvy, 6th E. of Findlater, 1764:
Northumberland House dinner attended by, though never before out of Scotland, **38**. 529–30
Murray, Patrick (1703–78), 5th Bn Elibank, 1736; lawyer; army officer:
brother of, **20**. 223
brother repulses effort of, to put him in custody of serjeant-at-arms, **20**. 249
Considerations on the Present State of the Peerage of Scotland by, **16**. 292
Cromarty's financial relations with, **19**. 284
Cumberland to sue, **19**. 284
HW asks Pinkerton to bring account of publications of, for revised *Royal and Noble Authors*, **42**. 197
HW's cutting of obituary of, **16**. 293
Inquiry into the Original and Consequences of the Public Debt by, **16**. 292
Jacobite, **19**. 284
Lyttelton's *Correspondents* may have been answered by, **16**. 293
Pinkerton asked by HW for list of writings of, **16**. 292
supplemental matter for *Royal and Noble Authors* finished except for article on, **16**. 294
Thoughts on Money, Circulation and Paper Currency by, **16**. 292
Westminster petition instigated by, **20**. 223
Murray, Thomas, coal-heaver:
trial of, **23**. 39n
Murray, William (ca 1600–ca 1653), cr. (1643) E. of Dysart:
Charles I's tutor and secretary, **40**. 285n
Jamesone leaves medals to, **40**. 285
Murray, William (1689–1746), styled M. of Tullibardine 1708–46; cr. (1717) Jacobite D. of Rannoch:
brother receives word from, **19**. *106*
brother's house prepared by, for Young Pretender, **19**. 106
brought to London, **19**. 272
capture of, **19**. 254, **37**. 245
dies in Tower after being captured after Culloden battle, **19**. 106n
foreign reinforcements necessary to success of, **19**. 131
outlawed, **19**. 106n
Murray, Hon. William (1696–1756), 3d E. of Dunmore, 1752:
Townshend serves under, in Flanders, **37**. 196n
Young Pretender joined by, **19**. 104
Murray, Hon. William (1705–93), cr. (1756) Bn Mansfield, (1776) E. of Mansfield; lord chief justice; M.P.:
acrostic makes mention of, **12**. 261
Adam a 'vent' for discontents of, **28**. 481n

attorney-general, **17**. 344n, **20**. 453
attorney-general rebuked by, for not taking out *capias utlegatum* for Wilkes, **23**. 12
Balmerinoch's conversation with, **19**. 283, 303
Beauclerk's house taken by, **33**. 184n, 255n
Bedford, D. of, defeated by, in defence of London magistracy, **38**. 257–8
begotten by Bolingbroke and begot Markham, **28**. 72
Bembridge's trial before, **25**. 408n
brother of, **13**. 218, **17**. 250n, **19**. 283, **23**. 328n
Bute outlines peace plans to, **22**. 30n
Byng's investigation opposed by, in House of Lords, **21**. 64–5
Caen Wood, house of, **33**. 255
Camden blames, for Boston, Quebec, and Restraining Bills, **41**. 304n
——'s debate with **41**. 10
Chief Justice, **20**. 557, **21**. 64, 99, **24**. 134, **32**. 90
court procedures on Wilkes explained by, in House of Lords, **38**. 293
cowardice of, **28**. 265, 303, **29**. 135
cowed, **20**. 453
Dividend Bill discussed by, **22**. 534
Du Deffand, Mme, gives opinion of, **6**. 96
——'s social relations with, **6**. 90, 93, 96
Duke of Newcastle's Letter . . . to Monsieur Michell by, **21**. 281, 286
Dunning annoys, by *Inquiry*, **22**. 274n, **38**. 474
elections held invalid by, if soldiers are called in, **17**. 252
England's defeat by France would be welcomed by, **29**. 65
Éon's affair and, **22**. 248n, **38**. 356, 507n
Exchequer seal to be carried by, **21**. 99
faculties of, unimpaired, **33**. 516n
Fitzpatrick intimidated by, for rioting, **22**. 121n
footman questioned by, at Prescott's trial, **33**. 425
France visited by, **6**. 90, 93, 96, **28**. 172, 174, 189, 227, 415
Frederick P. of Wales, thinks, is a Jacobite, **20**. 364
—— trusts, **20**. 364
(?) French mission of, **33**. 331
frightened out of Speaker's chair, **23**. 247
Gascoyne mis-cites Levinz to, **35**. 563
George II sends word to Pitt and Newcastle through, **37**. 487n
George III confers with Gower and, **25**. 379n
—— trusts, more than Elliot, **32**. 99n
Gloucester, D. and Ds of, may have been proscribed by order of, **36**. 77
Glyn, Oliver, and Camden attack, **23**. 256n
Gordon, Lord George, tried before, **25**. 122n, **29**. 103
Gordon rioters break coach glasses of, **33**. 174, 175

[Murray, Hon. William (1705–93), *continued*]
Gordon rioters burn house of, **7.** 232, **25.** 57, 29. 57, 60, 62, 67n, **33.** 184, 185
HW asks Mann for Roman gossip about, **20.** 360
HW blames, for Quebec Act, **41.** 312n
HW calls, 'casuist,' **28.** 295
HW identifies, as 'our great chief justice,' **16.** 348
HW indifferent to, **10.** 263
HW mentions, **29.** 147, 314, 317
HW owns print of, **15.** 192
HW sarcastically calls, 'Whig,' **9.** 329
HW's correspondence with, **37.** (?) 465
HW's MS 'portrait' of, **43.** 241
HW's prerogative in acting for E. of Orford would be supported by, **32.** 159
HW would protect, from Duc de Broglie, **33.** 25
Harcourt's appointment regarded by, as cipher, **9.** 145, **20.** 345
Hayter's conversation with, **9.** 145
—— urged by, to promote Stone, **20.** 345
Hervey, Bns, a friend of, **31.** 416
House of Hanover's destruction would be welcomed by, **28.** 378, 441
Hume told by, of Charles Townshend's treachery, **39.** 94
Hurd a friend of, **32.** 168
(?) incognito of, satirized, **35.** 471
innocence asserted by, in fine speech, **20.** 361
Inquiry into the Doctrine attacks, **22.** 274n
Jacobite sympathies of, **28.** 352–3, **30.** 91, **33.** 334
Johnson and Stone contemporary with, **20.** 345
judge of appellant division of House of Lords, **35.** 622
Junius paper will discourage, **23.** 247
Kingston, Ds of, championed and then deserted by, **28.** 204n, 237, 263, 265
—— wished by, to have private hearing in chamber of Parliament, **24.** 150
Letters to, by Andrew Stuart, **32.** 89–90
Limon's letter from, **33.** 363–4
Lloyd debates with, on Westminster election, **17.** 250
London house of: attacked in Gordon riots, **33.** 184, 185, 195; burnt, **7.** 232, **33.** 184; in Great Russell St, **33.** 255
London leaders saved by, from Bedford's and Sandwich's threats in House of Lords, **38.** 257–8
lord chancellor's post declined by, **23.** 174, **28.** 78
lord chief justice, **20.** 557, **21.** 64, 99, **24.** 134, **32.** 90
Lovat's trial conducted by, as solicitor-general, **19.** 379–80
Luxembourg, Mme de, pleased by, **6.** 96
'Macscurvy, Chief Justice,' **36.** 85
Mason hopes translation of *Caractacus* will be dedicated to, **28.** 172

—— satirizes, **28.** 436, 440
Massachusetts Bay assembly's act rejected by, **22.** 520
Maupeou's counterpart, is now England's chief justice, **24.** 134
may be lord chief justice, **20.** 557
meeting not attended by, **29.** 58n
Melcombe entertains, **9.** 373
method of, never equalled, **35.** 550–1
Morning Herald compliments, **42.** 170n
nephew of, **9.** 158, **20.** 261, 411n, **24.** 526, **28.** 172
Newcastle, D. of, advised by, about retiring, **22.** 37n
—— cannot spare, from House of Commons, **20.** 557
——'s scheme considered hopeless by, **21.** 99
Newton, Bp, makes, his hero, **35.** 514–15
Newton's life perhaps revised by, **29.** 254
niece of, marries, **33.** 307
nieces of, **12.** 58n
North Briton's printers persecuted by, at trials, **38.** 433
North Briton threatens, for persecuting Wilkes, **23.** 28
Opposition joined by, **29.** 322
Paris might be visited by, to arrange treaty, **24.** 44n
—— said to be visited by, **7.** 7, 9
Parliamentary address debated by, **37.** 415, 416
Parliamentary activity of, on Regency Bill, **38.** 542, 543
Parliamentary brilliance of, at expense of law practice, **18.** 383–4
Parliamentary speeches by: **28.** 203n; against prerogative, **22.** 464; at Wilkes's trial, **23.** 29; on Denbighshire election, **17.** 344; on Dresden treaty, **42.** 495–6; on *Essay on Woman*, **38.** 230; on Habeas Corpus, **37.** 529; on Massachusetts Bay Act, **22.** 520; on Scottish jurisdictions, **37.** 268; on Westminster election, **17.** 250; reduces opposition, **38.** 248; 'Rubicon speech,' **28.** 415, 459, **29.** 60, 187
Parliamentary voting by, with minority, **38.** 529
Parliament avoided by, to keep from discussing Ps of Wales as possible regent, **22.** 297
Parliament may prosecute, **23.** 256, 268, 282
Pelham may be succeeded by, as prime minister, **20.** 411–12, 419, **35.** 165
——'s protégé, **18.** 384
Pitt (E. of Chatham) answers, **18.** 123
—— attacks, **39.** 246
—— opposed by, over Wilkes, **23.** 209n
——'s American bill frightens, from House of Lords, **32.** 235
——'s Spanish war proposal opposed by, **38.** 131n
——'s speech answered by, **23.** 167
——'s speech opposes, **32.** 228n

——'s veiled attack on, in speech, **35.** 194n

—— terrifies, **37.** 416

Pope's friend, **17.** 250n, 344n

Poor Bill supported by, **38.** 529

Pratt and Henley handle, roughly, **22.** 520

Pratt's rift with, over habeas corpus, **21.** 205

preceptor to George III, **28.** 72n

press violently opposed by, at printers' trials, **38.** 433

proclamation drawn up by, about seizure of prize ships, **21.** 281

pronouncement by, on venue for events occurring overseas, **23.** 551n

Prussian memorial answered by, **20.** 362, 365

Prussian subsidy opposed by, **22.** 32n

quibbles in Parliament on taxes, **37.** 445

Ravensworth accuses, of toasting Old Pretender and Dunbar, **20.** 360, 364, 367

rebel lords tried by, **19.** 283

'Repeal, The,' caricatures, **22.** 400

reverses decision on question of literary property, **28.** 137–8, 142

Royal Marriage Bill written by, **23.** 390, **36.** 85

royal prerogative revered by, **28.** 227

Ryder succeeded by, as attorney-general, **20.** 453n

Sackville, Elizabeth, not related to, **33.** 307

Scottish origins of, a disadvantage, **20.** 412

Sewell, master of the Rolls, mistaken for, **22.** 464

Shippen enraged by apostasy of, **18.** 123

solicitor-general, **9.** 144–5, **17.** 250n, 344n, 494, **18.** 118, **19.** 283, 379, **20.** 345, 411n

speaks for first time in House of Commons, **18.** 123

Stone and Scott countenanced by, in dispute over George III's tutorship, **20.** 323

Strange succeeded by, as solicitor-general, **17.** 494, **18.** 118

Stuart's *Letters* to, *see under* Stuart, Andrew

subsidy treaties defended by, **35.** 253

Suffolk, Cts of, asks, to make Morton master of Charterhouse, **31.** 427

Townshend tried by, **23.** 346n

Townshend's treachery betrayed by, **22.** 552, **39.** 94

unpopularity of, **23.** 256

'vomits martial law,' **29.** 62, 65

Warburton refuses invitation from, to dine with Helvétius, **38.** 365

Watson Wentworth, Lady Henrietta, ties up fortune by deed deposited with, **38.** 456–7

Whigs disown, **20.** 345

wife of, **28.** 249n

Wilkes abuses, in speech, **24.** 13

——'s hearing adjourned by, **23.** 19

Worsley trial before, **25.** 245n

writ of certiorari by, in Ds of Kingston's case, **24.** 142n

York, Abp of, rescues, **33.** 181

Young Pretender would probably be entertained by, **30.** 91

Murray, Lord William (1762–96), army Col.: (?) Highlanders would have killed, **33.** 384n

Murray. *See also* Moray

Murry. *See* Murray

Murshidabad, Bengal: nabobs at, better known than poets in England, **28.** 45

Murville. *See* André, Pierre-Nicolas

Musæ Anglicanæ. See Musarum Anglicanarum analecta

Musæ juveniles. See under Cooke, William

'Musæ puerilis': Chute's, **35.** 21

Musæus. See under Mason, William

Musarum Anglicanarum analecta: HW consults, **15.** 111, **16.** 15

Musarum deliciæ. See under Mennes, Sir John; Smith, James

'Muscovita,' opera singer: Clive, Mrs, mimics, **17.** 435

Conway praises, **37.** 50

HW dislikes, **37.** 57

Middlesex's mistress, **17.** 191n

opera directors retain, to please Middlesex, **17.** 358

salary of, **17.** 191

'Muscovy, Mrs.' *See* Trevor, Anne

Muscovy. *See* Russia

Muse; Muses: ancients called, 'daughters of memory,' **41.** 178

comic, stoops in *She Stoops to Conquer*, **32.** 108

HW jokes about: More, Hannah, and, **31.** 244; More, Hannah, as, **31.** 267; Yearsley, Mrs, as spurious issue of, **31.** 244

HW's, Fox jokes about, **30.** 102

HW's verses mention, **10.** 316

mentioned, **30.** 258

Newton, Richard, thinks that ale obstructs, when available in morning, **30.** 89

statues of, at Stowe, **10.** 315, **31.** 146

'Muse de l'Encyclopédie, la.' *See* Lespinasse, Julie-Jeanne-Éléonore de

Muse Recalled, The. See under Jones, Sir William

Muses rivales, Les. See under La Harpe, Jean-François de

Museum, The: HW's contributions to, **13.** 15–16

Museum; museums: HW plans to add Gothic, to SH, **30.** 176–7

See also British Museum

Museum Florentinum: Antinori, Buondelmonte, and Pini concerned in, **18.** 390–1

Buondelmonte gives, to Kaunitz, **17.** 49

directors of, send commission through HW to English bookseller, **18.** 390

Dodsley answers publishers of, **18.** 417

Granger obtains, from Gulston, **41.** 219

HW receives, **18.** 560

price of, **18.** 330

[*Museum Florentinum*, continued]
Walpole, Sir Robert, to receive three last volumes of, **18.** 329–30
Museum Mazzuchelianum. See under Gaetani, Pier Antonio; Mazzuchelli, Conte Giovanni Maria
Museum Minervæ:
grant of coat of arms for, **16.** 151
House of Lords committee may have given rise to, **16.** 152
Kynaston the first regent of, **16.** 151
Musgrave, Elizabeth (d. 1820), m. (1768) Heneage Legge:
Berry, Mary, kindly treated by, **11.** 325
Berrys accompanied by, to Bologna, **11.** 359–60, 365n
Florence visited by, **11.** 359–60
(?) SH visited by, **12.** 229 *bis*
Musgrave, George (?1740–1824), M.P.:
(?) Chute asks HW to recommend, to Mann, **23.** 375
(?) Graves to accompany, to Florence, **23.** 375
(?) HW knows, slightly, **23.** 375
Musgrave, George (1769–1861) of Shillington Manor, Beds:
(?) SH visited by, **12.** 242 *bis*
Musgrave, Mrs George. *See* Kennedy, Margaret
Musgrave, Dr Samuel (1732–80):
address by, **7.** 367
Musgrave, William (fl. 1738), writer:
Brief and True History of Sir Robert Walpole [*Genuine Memoirs*] by, **1.** 59, 60, 63, **43.** 46
Musgrave, Sir William (1735–1800), 6th Bt, 1755; antiquary:
Carlisle, Cts of, falsifies age of, when about to marry him, **9.** 260
Carlisle, E. of, under guardianship of, **39.** 96n
collection of, **9.** 109n
commissioner of Customs, **41.** 327
disbelieves in Ireland's MSS, **15.** 321
Granger arranged collection of, **40.** 313n
—— hears praises from, of HW's *Historic Doubts*, **41.** 133–4
HW out of town during presence of, **41.** 376
HW receives from, a specimen of Granger's book, **40.** 312
HW's aid to Granger's *Biographical History* obtained through, **41.** 133n
HW's correspondence with, **40.** 312, **41.** 376, **42.** 124, 264
HW serves tea to, at SH, after Hampton Court visit, **39.** 104
Nivernais's *Jardins modernes* given to, **12.** 260
Northampton, Cts of, said to have married, **10.** 337
SH visited by, **1.** 56n, **39.** 104
tells HW of Granger's *Biographical History*, **1.** 57
wife of, **2.** 187n, **7.** 50n, **9.** 219n
Mushroom; mushrooms:
beds of, destroyed at Claremont, **31.** 10–11
Kensington Palace floor produces crop of, **20.** 88

Shaw poisoned by, **31.** 10
Music:
Addenbrooke's Hospital to have benefit from performance of, **1.** 267, **2.** 94, 95, 97, 331
ancient, HW reads Pliny on, **35.** 419
and the 'savage beast,' **40.** 347
at Bath, **40.** 10
at Dublin, surpasses Bath's, **37.** 412
at Goodwood, **32.** 204
at Ranelagh: ends at 10 P.M., **24.** 310; not heard by late arrivals, **24.** 310, **25.** 317
at Twickenham church, **34.** 115
at Villa Patrizi, **17.** 25
bad, in new opera at Florence, **17.** 79
bands of: at Northumberland House, **38.** 401n; Kingston, Ds of, said to take, with her, **24.** 556, 564, 567; Mann to have been serenaded by, **17.** 104
Bayreuth, Margravine of, composes, **20.** 478
Bingham daughters study, **24.** 462
books on: left by Ussé to Pont-de-Veyle and Argental, **5.** 276; wanted by HW for Hawkins, and sought by Mann, **21.** 466–7, 477, 482, 491, 492
Boyle, Charlotte, mistress of, **31.** 251n
Broadie, Miss, sings, at Mrs Sutton's, **12.** 157
Burney's, to drive away Saul's evil spirit, **42.** 202
Carlisle, Cts of, gives concert of, **2.** 187
Chatterton's father fond of, **16.** 332
church, used by opera performers for dance music, **19.** 369
Du Deffand, Mme, on, **6.** 413, **7.** 16, 66
English dislike, in opera, **17.** 190
expense of, for *Don Pilogio*, **18.** 41
festival of three choirs (Gloucester, Worcester, and Hereford) for, **11.** 109, **20.** 338
firecrackers to be set to, **37.** 297
footmen's gallery in King's Chapel filled with musicians for, **38.** 87
French: HW calls, shocking, **10.** 175; HW can bear, **31.** 103
French taste for, declines, **38.** 483
gallery for, in Cross Bath at Bath, **31.** 130n
Gluck to play, on drinking-glasses, **19.** 234
Grafton, Ds of, studies, **22.** 29
Gray describes that of *King Arthur*, **13.** 97–8
——'s books of, **43.** 61
——'s knowledge of, **13.** 233
Greeks perhaps set standards for, **33.** 479
—— probably graceful in, **16.** 270
HW develops taste for, **33.** 41–2
HW dislikes, **30.** 100
HW has little knowledge of, **22.** 42
HW has no ear for, **29.** 174, 312, 316
HW interested in old instruments for, **35.** 419
HW's performance of, **43.** 176
HW's reflections on, **32.** 182
HW tries to learn, **37.** 4
HW wants 'ancient harmony' restored to, **29.** 7
HW wishes Mann to get, for Elizabeth Rich, **17.** 166, 301–2

Hamilton, Lady (1st), proficient in, **26**. 46

Hamilton, Lady (2d), studies, **35**. 441

Hawkins writes history of, **21**. 466–7

hazard and racing eclipse, **23**. 570–1

Hertford has band of, on George III's birthday, **38**. 398

history of, *see under* Hawkins, Sir John

Italian, kept alive in England by politics only, **38**. 2

Ligniville's collection of, **23**. 96n

Mann discusses, with Margravine of Bayreuth, **20**. 478

—— has, performed in his garden, **17**. 112, 483, **18**. 1, **19**. 277

—— orders, from HW, for Mme Branchi, on Ds of Grafton's account, **22**. 35–6, 42, 50, 73

—— to procure, from England, for Accademia, **18**. 13, 31

—— to send: to D. of York, **22**. 390; to HW, **17**. 240, 263, **18**. 13

Martini's book on, **21**. 492, 495–6

Middleton and 3d wife skilled in, **15**. 293, 310

'mi' no longer a note in, **22**. 234

Nicholls and Misses Abrams sing glees at Mrs Udny's, **11**. 109

Norfolk heiress displays 'talents' for, **18**. 316–17

opera-goers more interested in rival singers than in, **16**. 280

Oxford meeting for, **12**. 258

Pandolfini promoter of, **18**. 150

Pomfret, Cts of, poses ridiculously when hearing, **20**. 584

Purcell's: **33**. 42; for Dryden's *King Arthur*, squalled, **31**. 152

Richecourt has concert of, after dinner, **20**. 478

rustic, at Ranelagh jubilee-masquerade, **20**. 47

St-Germain's talent for, **26**. 20

tarantula bites said to be cured by, **35**. 425

the food of love, **35**. 649

Walpole, Sir Edward, makes witticism about modern miracles in, **25**. 577

water: concert of, at D. of Richmond's fireworks, **20**. 56; gondola for, at Ranelagh, **20**. 47

See also Accademia; Æolian harp; Airs; Andante; Bagpipe; Ballad; Band; Barcaroles; Bassoon; Bass viol; Cantata; Castrato; Catch; Celestinette; Cembali; Clarinet; Clarionets; Clavecin; Concert; Concerto; Contralto; Cymbals; Double-bass; Drums; Dulcimer; Farces; Fiddle; Fiddler; Fife; Flageolet; Flute; French horns; 'God Save the King'; Guitars; Hand-organ; Harp; Harpsichord; Hautboy; Horns, Horns, French; Hurdy-gurdy; Hymn; Jew's harp; Jigs; Kettle-drum; 'Long Live George the King'; Lute; Lyre; Madrigal; *Miserere*; Musical instruments; 'Old Sir Simon the King'; Opera; Opera singer; Oratorio; Orchestra; Organ; Overture; Pentachord; Pianoforte; Pipe; **Pipera**; Prick-song; Psaltery; Quintettos; Sackbut; Saltbox; Serenade; Serpent; Singer; Singers, French; Singing; Sistrum; Sonata; Songs; Tabor; Thorough-bass; Tibia; Trumpets; Tympani; Vaudeville; Violin; *See also under names of composers*

Musical clock. *See under* Clock

Musical contests:

in France, described in *Gazette littéraire*, **28**. 374

Musical instruments:

Abyssinian and Theban described by Bruce, **28**. 249–50

Musica vaga ed artificiosa. See under Micheli, Romano

Music booths:

at Southwark Fair, **32**. 108n

Musician; musicians:

at Florence, mostly illiterate, **21**. 482

Lucca may import, from Genoa, **22**. 222

Walpole, Sir Robert, despises, **17**. 487

Musicians, Decayed:

fund for, **25**. 647n

Music stand:

Ussé leaves, to Aumont, **5**. 276

Musin Pushkin, Alexei Semenovich (1732–1817), Russian ambassador to England 1766–73:

Chesterfield compliments Catherine II through, **23**. 376

Christie's interview with, **43**. 286

Cony consults, about sale of Houghton pictures, **26**. 55

Houghton pictures viewed, by, for Catherine II, **24**. 502n

Muskerry, Bn. *See* Deane, Robert Tilson

Muskerry, Vcts. *See* Burgh, Lady Margaret de (d. 1698)

Musket; muskets:

ammunition for, **17**. 66

Birmingham hopes to make, for American war, **24**. 77

discharges 8–10 bullets at once, **33**. 439n

Francis III orders, **17**. 324

French might load invasion boats with rods instead of, **38**. 34

Hertford and sons charge, in Gordon riots, **33**. 187

soldier must shoulder, when presenting message, **19**. 439

Young Pretender tries to take, to Scotland, **19**. 87

Musket balls:

lead coffins melted for, **20**. 428

Musketeers:

abolished, **6**. 251

See also Mousquetaires

Muslin; muslins:

Ailesbury, Cts of, has errands about, **38**. 124

Burney, Frances, occupied in folding, **31**. 271

gold, presented by Hastingses, folded by Fanny Burney for Q. Charlotte, **31**. 272n

[Muslin; muslins, *continued*]
  jacket trimmed with, **32.** 154
  masquerade costumes of, **10.** 80
  Ossory, Lady, needs, **33.** 63
  Raynal discusses, **39.** 168
  ruffles of, **31.** 89
Musquito. *See* Mosquito
Musselburgh:
  Pinkie in, **16.** 51n
Mussell, Ebenezer:
  classical and Egyptian antiquities of, sold, **31.** 36n
Musselman. *See* Mohammedan
Mussenden, Mrs:
  Hervey, Bp, said to have affair with, **25.** 455n
Mustafa III (1717–74), Sultan of Turkey 1757–74:
  acquisition or loss of acres by, inconsequential, **23.** 420
  campaign must be attempted by, **23.** 310–11
  Erekle II's advance said to drive, to Adrianople, **22.** 420n
  France arms, against Catherine II, **23.** 338
  HW inquires about probable defeat of, **31.** 152
  HW jokes about Lady Mary Coke's visiting, **31.** 149
  HW mentions, **32.** 5
  HW prefers, to Catherine II, **23.** 195
  ignorant of weak army, and rejects peace offers, **23.** 173
  might lock up Murray, **23.** 479
  Polish Catholics invited by, to turn Mohammedan, **23.** 81
  Russians will probably give a good account of, **23.** *81*
  undisturbed by impending Russian invasion, **23.** 205
  wants peace, **23.** 470
Mustafā Aġa, Tartar emissary to Berlin:
  Williams, Sir C. H., exposes Frederick II's misrepresentation of mission of, **30.** 321
Mustapha et Zéangir. See under Chamfort, Sébastien-Roch-Nicolas
Mustard, Rev. David (ca 1684–1775), rector of Mistley:
  HW's skill in heraldry praised by, **9.** 93
  Rigby entertains, **9.** 93
Mustard:
  Du Deffand, Mme, receives, from Fitzroys, **6.** 96
Mustard-bowl; mustard-bowls:
  Chatham's, **39.** 239
  North 'rumbles about,' **38.** 309
  thunder reproduced by, in stage productions, **38.** 309n
Mustard pot; mustard pots:
  served as hors d'œuvres, **19.** 357
  Sèvres, sent to HW by Hertford, **38.** 278
Musters. *See* Commissary-General of the Musters
Muswell Hill, Middlesex, seat of Topham Beauclerk:

Beauclerk, Lady Diana, at, **43.** 299
Beauclerk writes from, **41.** 308
HW dines at, **32.** 122, 241
Mute; mutes:
  Conway to play part of, in changing world, **37.** 86
Muti, Palazzo. *See* Santi Apostoli, Palazzo
Mutineer; mutineers:
  saying by, in Tacitus, **20.** 125
Mutiny; mutinies:
  in regiment at Boston, alleged, **39.** 240
  of French troops, **21.** 336
  of Scottish regiment, **25.** 362
Mutiny Act; Bill. *See under* Parliament: acts of
Mutton:
  Boufflers's witticism on chewing, **39.** 219
  Clement XIII might allow, in Lent, if fish is scarce, **22.** 101
  cold, Henry Fielding dines on, **9.** 84
  from Vernon, **7.** 436
  HW compares eloquence to, **39.** 408
  Hardinge cannot yet invite HW to eat, **35.** 625
  More, Hannah, depends on, for food, **31.** 364
  roast leg of, HW aspires no higher than, **13.** 172
  shoulder of, dog gnaws, in stained glass window, **16.** 47
  Sussex, **38.** 256
Muxaduvad. *See* Murshidabad
Muy, Baron du. *See* Félix d'Ollières, Jean-Baptiste-Louis-Philippe de
Muy, Comte du. *See* Félix, Louis-Nicolas-Victor de (1711–75); Félix d'Ollières, Jean-Baptiste-Louis-Philippe de (1751–1820)
Muy. *See also* Du Muy
Muzaffar Jang, Subahdar of the Deccan, 1750–1:
  Dupleix establishes, **22.** 212n
Muzell, Heinrich Wilhelm (1723–82), called Baron Stosch, 1757:
  Bath visited by, **21.** 461
  Berlin's capture would have distressed, **21.** 446
  burgundy sent by, to Mann, **21.** 424, 427, 491
  cameos sent by, to France, **21.** 201, 434
  England probably to be left by, because of expense, **21.** 503
  —— to be visited by, to sell collection, **21.** 380, 427
  English address of, unknown to Mann, **21.** 415
  English to be learnt by, at Yorkshire clergyman's, **21.** 427
  Florence reached by, **21.** 557
  France too poor to buy collection of, **21.** 434
  Frederick II gives annuity to, **25.** 651
  Frederick Augustus of Poland might buy collection of, **21.** 434
  Gordon, D. of, does not have, as travelling companion, **21.** 503, 512
  Guise to entertain, at dinner, **21.** 429
  HW buys medals from, **15.** 278
  HW calls, 'Stoschino,' **21.** 384

HW comes to London to see, **21.** 426–7, 433
HW dines with, at SH, **21.** 427, 433
HW has not yet heard of, **21.** 418, 420, 473
HW may buy medals from, **21.** 186, 192, 201–2, 215, 384
HW may get, to identify Castiglione painting, **21.** 522
HW pays, for Mann's burgundy, **21.** 427, 491
HW promises to receive, well, **21.** 384
HW's correspondence with, **21.** 440, 461, 527
HW's letters to Mann to be taken back by, to England, **21.** 413, 427, **26.** 36
HW to receive respects of, **21.** 557
health of: fever, **21.** 433; ill, **21.** 459
Italy to be visited by, **21.** 527
Knyphausen says, is expected in London, **21.** 474
letter to, about Zorndorf battle, **21.** 241
London to be visited by, **21.** 461
Mann encloses letter for, **21.** 415, 424, 454, 473, 477, 509, 522
—— praises, **21.** 380
—— promised by, a copy of *Œuvres du philosophe de Sans-Souci*, **21.** 413
——'s correspondence with, **21.** 424, 433, 464, 503, 512, 522, 527
—— will advise, to distribute catalogues of his uncle's collection, **21.** 151
—— writes to, at Lille, **43.** 274
map collection of: Benedict XIV may buy, **21.** 186–7, 192, 434; Ferdinand VI and José Manoel may buy, **21.** 434; Frederick II gives annuity in payment for, **25.** 651
military career of, **21.** 149, 380, 434
Montagu, Lady Mary Wortley, scolds HW through, **21.** 458
Northumberland, D. of, might have, as son's travelling companion, **21.** 512, 514
Paris visited by, **21.** 424
sails for Spain, **21.** 527
Salisbury visited by, **21.** 433, 440, 459
Sardinian Court might buy collection of, **21.** 434
uncle adopts, as his heir, **21.** *149*, 151, 380
uncle recalls, from army, **21.** 149, 434
uncle's collection may be sold by, in England, **21.** 380, 427
uncle's collection of intaglios to be sold by, intact, **21.** 186
uncle's collection unlikely to be sold by, in England, **21.** 512
uncle's obscene prints and drawings may be sold by, to Frederick II, **21.** 202
Wanstead to be visited by, **21.** 427
wants position as travelling companion, **21.** 434, 440, 503, 512
Muzquiz, Miguel de (b. 1719), Conde de Gausa:
Squillace succeeded as Spanish finance minister by, **39.** 64
Myddle, Salop:
Smyth, rector of, **9.** 154n
Myddleton, Althemia, m. —— Bodens *or* Bowden:

family of, **41.** 241
Myddleton *or* Middleton, Mrs Charles. *See* Needham, Jane
Myddleton, Jane (1645–92), Court beauty: family of, **41.** 241n
Myddleton, Jane (1661–1740), m. —— May: (?) family of, **41.** 241
Myddleton, John (1685–1747), M.P.: high sheriff related to, **17.** 344
Parliamentary membership of, **43.** 243
Myddleton, Richard (1726–95), of Chirk Castle; M.P.; Col.:
HW's letter from, desiring painting of Sir Robert Walpole, **42.** 215
Pennant may have been told by, of gift of painting to HW, **42.** 215
Myddleton, William (d. ?1745):
related to M.P., **17.** 344
sentenced to Newgate, **17.** 344
Myddleton family:
painting of P. Arthur and Catherine of Aragon remained with, in Denbighshire, **42.** 215n
Mynde, J. (fl. 1740–70):
plates by, **15.** 20n
Myntz. *See* Müntz
'Myra.' *See* Brudenell, Hon. Frances
'Myra, old.':
HW refers to Pitt as, **21.** 168
Myron (5th cent. B.C.), sculptor:
Ds of Devonshire worthy to be Castalian nymph by, **28.** 386
'Myrtila,' Chute's valet. *See* Martelli, Francesco
Myrtle; myrtles:
Bentley sends, to HW, **35.** 214
Magdalen House chapel decorated with, **9.** 273
Miller, Mrs, crowns successful poets with, **39.** 241
'Myrtle-tree':
at Batheaston, **39.** 240
Mysore, Nawab of. *See* Haidar Shāh
Mysterious Congress, The:
Mann, Galfridus, sends, to Mann, **35.** 50
Mysterious Husband, The. See under Cumberland, Richard
Mysterious Mother, The, by HW:
'Adeliza' least satisfactory in, **41.** 297
Ailesbury, Cts of, to hear reading of, **10.** 260
Beauclerk finds epitaph resembling plot of, **41.** 308–9
Beauclerk, Lady Diana, does drawings illustrative of, for SH, **3.** 392n, **15.** 318, **24.** 524, **31.** 206, 216, 297, **32.** 289, **35.** 385, **41.** 322, **43.** 147
Buckingham, Marchioness of, does picture of, **42.** 256
Burgh transcribed story resembling, **28.** 363, 366
Burney, Frances, dislikes, **31.** 247n
Cambridge college MS has subject similar to, **1.** 186

[*Mysterious Mother, The*, continued]

Charlemont wants new edition of, **42.** 153

—— wants to see, **41.** 191

Choiseul, Duchesse de, not to receive, **5.** 316

Cholmondeley brings to Paris for Nivernais, **42.** 352

Chute likes, **10.** 259

clergyman disapproves of, **10.** 297

Clive, Mrs, to have epilogue in, **10.** 260

Conway and HW to read, to SH guests, **10.** 260

Courtenay objects to subject of, **12.** 94

defective in plan and conduct, **28.** 16

Delany, Mrs, regrets subject of, **28.** 366

Dodsley's new edition of, **42.** 155, 308–10, 312

Dublin bookseller prevented by Charlemont from reprinting, **42.** 309, **43.** 270

Dublin edition of: **42.** 311–12; sent to HW by Walker, **42.** 319; supervised by Walker, **42.** 319, 324–5

Du Deffand, Mme, asks for, **4.** 32, 35, 36, 43, 44, 62, 84, 93–4, **5.** 267, 270

—— inquires about, **4.** 32, 35, 36

—— promises to keep, secret, **5.** 299, 325

—— thanks HW for details of, **4.** 51

—— wishes to have, translated, **5.** 267, 293, **6.** 365

extract from, may be printed, **41.** 427–8

first scene of, printed in *Public Advertiser*, **33.** 429

Francès not to translate, **5.** 320

—— seeks translator for, **5.** 325

—— to translate, **5.** 306

Garrick not to act in, **10.** 259

Gray approves of, **10.** 259

HW asks Woodfall to print no more of, **42.** 85–6

HW averse to performance and publication of, **10.** 259–60, 298, **24.** 524, **28.** 371, **29.** 142, 144, **39.** 372–3

HW blushes at Mann's praises of, **24.** 524

HW derives no prestige from, since it cannot be performed, **41.** 288

HW discusses, **4.** 40, **5.** 336–7

HW disparages, **5.** 270

HW does not want Walker to revise, for the press, **42** 305

HW fears Barthélemy's displeasure for, **5.** 316

HW finishes, **10.** 259, **13.** 43, **43.** 135

HW gives, to Nivernais and Sylvester Douglas, **42.** 351–2

HW has, printed by Dodsley to fend off spurious Irish printing, **2.** 270, 271, **29.** 139–40, 143–4, 148, **33.** 579, **39.** 372, **42.** 155

HW lends: to Bull, **41.** 414, 415; to Mrs Howe, for niece, **34.** 9–10

HW lists number of copies printed of, at SH Press, **43.** 79

HW presents: to Beauclerk, **33.** 578; to Coke, Lady Mary, **31.** 141; to Harcourt, Cts, **35.** 493; to Hardwicke, **41.** 241; to Leroy, **6.** 247; to Mann, **24.** 481, 494; to Parsons, **42.** 275–6

HW prints and gives away copies of, **41.** 427, **42.** 351–2

HW promises, to Mme du Deffand, **5.** 293

HW regrets Montagu's guests reading, **10.** 298

HW 'repeats' scenes from, to Lady Mary Coke, **31.** 139, 141

HW's 'Advertisement' to, **29.** 139

HW said to be printing, **5.** 267

HW's attempts to stifle, are useless, **42.** 308–10, 351–2

HW sends, to Leroy, **6.** 247

HW's gift of, described in *European Magazine*, **33.** 578

HW thought that events in, were in Tillotson's time, **39.** 102–3

Haggitt praises, **35.** 543

Hall's *Resolutions* has subject similar to, **16.** 165

Hamilton, Mary, thinks story of, horrible, **31.** 116

Hamilton, Sir William, has copy of, **24.** 470

Hardinge praises, **35.** 648

incestuous passion of, paralleled in Don Carlos's story, **41.** 291

Irish edition of: advertisement of, embarrassing to HW, **42.** 324–5; HW fails to suppress, **42.** 351–2; HW's corrections to, **42.** 325; rumoured, **29** 148; sent by Walker, **42.** 324; *see also* Dublin edition of

Knight thanks Pinkerton for loan of, **16.** 372

Mann knows Italian incident similar to, **24.** 517

—— praises, **24.** 517

—— wants, **24.** 470

Mann, Horace II, reads, on journey, **24.** 517

—— to bring, to Mann, **24.** 470, 481

Mason cautions HW to lock up, **28.** 54

—— gives HW his copy of, **29.** 142

—— 'improves,' and could write it better, **35.** 493

—— praises observance of 'unities' in, **28.** 181–2

—— sends HW account of play resembling, **28.** 444

——'s alterations to, **28.** 9, 10, 11–16, 16–17, 25, 55–6, 367, 371, 445, **29.** 140–2, 144, 148, **43.** 293

Montagu's guests act, at Adderbury, **10.** 297, 300

—— would not like, **10.** 259

plot of, résumé of, **28.** 10n

postscript to, **43.** 88

Pritchard, Mrs, would be suitable for part in, **10.** 259

Public Advertiser prints bits of, **33.** 429, **35.** 398–9

Rich, Mary, to hear reading of, **10.** 260

SH edition of, exhausted, **33.** 579

subject of: described, **28.** 9, 10n, **29.** 324; disgusting, **24.** 481, **42.** 85, 255, 276, 351; in

Q. of Navarre's *Heptameron*, **4.** 93, 94, **39.**
103; less disgusting than Hayley's, **34.** 37
suspense the only merit of, **41.** 296
Walker and (?) Cts of Moira praise, **42.** 255
Walker too prejudiced in favour of, **42.** 365
Walpole, Sir Edward, praises, **36.** 53
Wiart to supervise translation of, **5.** 299
—— to translate, **4.** 106, **5.** 270
See also under Spencer, Lady Diana: drawings by
Mystery; mysteries:
Methodists', **20.** 271
unskillfulness the source of, in art, **21.** 561
'wisdom of blockheads,' **21.** 466
Mytens, Daniel (ca 1590–before 1648), painter:
James IV's portrait by, **16.** 321
Mandeville, Lady, allegedly painted by, **10.** 78n
Margaret, Q. of Scotland's portrait copied by, **40.** 365n
portraits by, at Knole, **35.** 134n, 135n
portraits of Ds of Richmond ascribed to, **1.** 25–6, 173
Warwick, E. of, supposedly painted by, **10.** 76n
Mythology:
representation of, in classical vases, etc., insipid, **35.** 443
Mytilene:
Turkish ships near, **23.** 235

N

N——, Sir M——:
retains title with followers, **35.** 352
Nabob, The. See under Foote, Samuel
Nabob; nabobs:
at Knightsbridge, **42.** 109
attacked in Parliament, **23.** 483
Bombay governor seeks to install, at Poona, **24.** 509
Choiseul, Mme de, preferable to daughter of, **41.** 108, 110
England dethrones, in India, **23.** 240
English: boroughs contested by, **21.** 484; cannot plunder India's climate, **23.** 305; do not profess religion as an excuse for plundering, **25.** 400; England filled with, **23.** 499; Fox's reform schemes opposed by, **25.** 484; France dreads, **23.** 476; from East Indies, **31.** 22; House of Commons to investigate riches of, **25.** 277; Macheath the begetter of, **23.** 524; ought to be imprisoned like French swindlers, **25.** 604; will not be able to oppress newly-discovered stars, **25.** 614
Francis I seeks to dethrone, **22.** 547
HW calls, 'Regius Professors of plunder,' **35.** 368
HW jokes about depredations of, **33.** 462
HW might save natives from, **16** 132

Lyttelton at disadvantage because he is not, **23.** 511
Rumbold may have to disgorge million acquired as, **25.** 274, 277
St James's St thronged with, **21.** 518
scarce in France, **33.** 343
Nabob of Bengal. *See* Mīr Ja'far 'Alī Khān (1691–1765); Mīr Qāsim 'Alī Khān (d. 1777); Najam-ud-Dowla (ca 1747–66)
Nadaillac, Marquise de. *See* Rancher de la Ferrière, Rosalie-Marguerite-Marie-Thérèse de
Nádasdy, Franz Leopold (1707–83, Graf; army officer:
Hungarians to be commanded by, **21.** 176
Spaniards pursued by, **19.** 244
Nadasti. *See* Nádasdy
Nâdir-Chah, Thamasp Kouli-Khan Vély-Neamen (1688–1747), Persian emperor:
called Thomas Collaghan, **1.** 256
HW compares Clive with, **24.** 60
HW's letter to Lincoln under name of, **18.** 167–8, 188, **30.** 35–6
(?) HW's name for Rumbold, **25.** 545
merchant's wife might claim to be married to, **23.** 550
Mill compared with, **20.** *102*
Nævius, Gnæus (ca 270 B.C.–ca 199 B.C.), Latin poet:
Hector proficiens by, quoted by Bromfield, **40.** 324n
Nag. *See* Horse
Nagel. *See* Nagell van Ampsen
Nagell van Ampsen, Bns van. *See* Du Tour, Anna Catharina Elisabeth
Nagell van Ampsen, Anne Willem Carel (1756–1851), Baron van; Dutch envoy to England 1788–95:
Mirabeau's *Histoire secrète de la cour de Berlin* owned by, **34.** 44
Nail; nails:
Chute might trade in, as holy relics, **35.** 61
cutting of, in hot water, a gout remedy, **35.** 125
iron, shot from pistol, **34.** 175n
price of, rises, **21.** 536
San Donato's, cures hydrophobia, **20.** 509
sold for Coronation constructions, **21.** 536
Nain, Le. *See* Le Nain
Nain jaune, Le. See under Le Jumel de Barneville, Marie-Catherine, Baronne d'Aulnoy
Nairn, Scotland:
English halt at, **37.** 239
rebels ran away at, **37.** 238
Nairn. *See also* Nairne
Nairne ('Nairn'), William Murray (ca 1757–1830), Lord Nairne (restored, 1824):
Scotchman, **25.** 536
Stuart, Charlotte, has, as equerry, **25.** 536
Najam-ud-Dowla (ca 1747–66), Nawab ('Nabob') of Bengal:
Clive makes, nawab of Bengal, **22.** 416
Name; names:

[Name; names, *continued*]
aristocratic, destroyed in French Revolution, **11**. 86
changing of, assigned by Montagu to chief justice's jurisdiction, **10**. 119
Christian, Sir Robert Walpole's low opinion of use of, **30**. 289n
HW's reflections on, **15**. 78
inconsequence of, **11**. 115

Nampont (France):
baggage examined at, **37**. 39

Namptwich. *See* Nantwich

Namur, English ship:
Boscawen commands, **20**. 38n
—— writes from, **21**. 307n
captain of, **18**. 415
Dutch contraband seized by, **25**. 3n
lost in hurricane, **20**. 113n
Mathews arrives at Hyères in, **18**. 370n
—— in, at Vado Bay, **18**. 453n
—— ordered to hoist flag on, **17**. 361n
—— sends letters from, in Villa Franca harbour, **18**. 26n
Sérieux strikes battles with, **20**. 38n

Namur (Flanders):
Artois goes to, **11**. 39n
captured by Louis XIV and later by William III, **28**. 295–6
Conway and Scott visit, **39**. 537
Cutts leads attack on, **9**. 252n
French threaten to explode mines under forts of, **19**. 482
Ostend more important than, **19**. 69

'Nana':
Chute's name for Lady Caroline Petersham, **20**. 140

Nancé, —— de:
anecdote of Duchesse de Berry and, **4**. 22–3

Nancré, Marquis de. *See* Dreux, Louis-Jacques-Aimé-Théodore de

Nancy, Bp of. *See* Sabran, Louis-Hector-Honoré-Maxime de

Nancy. See Ninette à la Cour

Nancy (Lorraine):
Artois obtains capitainerie of, **6**. 397
Boufflers, Marquise de, at, **7**. 241
china figures from, **4**. 338, **7**. 335
Churchill's letter from, **22**. 324
Churchills delighted by sojourn at, **33**. 419
—— settle at, **38**. 464
—— to settle at, **22**. 244, **38**. 410
collegiate church of St-Georges at, **17**. 12n
Conway and Scott visit, **39**. 539
Craon, Princesse de, returns to, **22**. 536
decay of, when no longer the capital, **33**. 419
Filles de Ste-Marie at, **3**. 226
Grenvilles acquainted in, **6**. 254
Guerchy to join his regiment at, **3**. 332
HW will visit, if Princesse de Craon becomes queen, **20**. 132
Hardinge does not use HW's letters of introduction at, **35**. 583

—— wants letter to reputable family of, not nobility, **35**. 581
Maintenon, Mme de, letters of, printed at, **14**. 62n
Marie Leszczyńska visits, **7**. 259
Ossory, Lady, inquires about, **33**. 419
Ossorys may not go to, **33**. 422–4
pastilles of, **6**. 325
Pitt, Anne, to visit, for health, **24**. 131
Stainville, Comtesse de, in convent at, **3**. 217–9, 226
Stanislas I gives apartment at, to Princesse de Craon, **20**. 116
—— visited by daughter at, **39**. 9
supper given at, for D. and Ds of Gloucester, **7**. 347

'Nancy':
subject of HW's poem 'I love and hate Nancy,' **33**. 423–4

Nancy, parliament of:
Nay, Charles-Ignace de, member of, **20**. 197n

'Nancy Dawson.' *See under* Stevens, George Alexander

Nando's coffee-house:
Boehm takes refuge in, in riot, **10**. 273

Nangis, Mlle de. *See* Regnier, Antoinette-Marie de

Nangis, Marquis de. *See* Brichanteau, Louis-Armand de

Nanine. See under Voltaire

Nankeen:
jockeys wear breeches of, **31**. 108
trousers of, **39**. 254

Nannette. *See* Durham, Anne

'Nanny,' Selwyn's servant:
Lyon to be visited by, **21**. 133, 137
Selwyn accompanied by, **21**. 133

Nantes:
American news from, **20**. 366
boutiques de, les, Mme du Barry receives revenues of, **4**. 339, **7**. 370n
carrier sent to, **12**. 162n
edict of, revoked, **4**. 418, **28**. 296
Franklin arrives at, **32**. 357
Hazard at, **4**. 325n
Irish merchant settles at, with black servant, after the '45, **38**. 405n
Jacobite refugees land at, **19**. 270
Joseph II passes through, **22**. 202
Lyttelton probably at, **35**. 251

Nanteuil, Robert (ca 1623–78), painter and engraver:
catalogue of works of, **15**. 72
Dalrymple's interest in, **15**. 72, 92, 95, 106, 107
Evelyn completes etchings under direction of, **16**. 61n
Gilpin does not mention, **15**. 117
HW sends prints by, to Dalrymple, **40**. 320
prints by, listed, **15**. 100
'scripture-piece' by, bad, **15**. 107, 117

Nantucket, Mass.:

letter from, **24**. 361

Nantwich, Cheshire:

Cholmondeley Castle near, **10**. 96n

HW's plants to be left at, for Montagu, **9**. 179

Napier, Bns. *See* Clavering, Maria Margaret (ca 1736–1821)

Napier, ——, Capt. of the *Cygnette*:

Dick sends letters to Adm. Saunders by, **21**. 431

Napier, Frances (d. 1752):

Luton Hoo left by, to Herne, **32**. 91n

Napier (formerly Scott), Francis (ca 1702–73), 6th Bn Napier of Merchistoun, 1706:

collection of papers owned by, **15**. 103

Napier, Hon. George (1751–1804), army officer:

marriage of, **21**. 530n

wife of, **3**. 199n, **9**. 335n, **14**. 120n

Napier, John (1550–1617), 8th Laird of Merchistoun:

Buchan's life of, **16**. 209

Napier, Maj.-Gen. Robert (d. 1766):

regiment of: **9**. 196n; from Yorkshire, **37**. 446n; not arrived in Germany, **37**. 555; suffers, **9**. 246

Napier, Lady Sarah. *See* Lennox, Lady Sarah

Napier, Susan, m. John Highlord of Harrow:

(?) statue of, at Luton Hoo, **32**. 91

Napkin; napkins:

Amelia, Ps, fastens, with pins, **33**. 164

Coventry uses, to wipe off wife's rouge, **20**. 338

Fermor lacks, **19**. 148

George II has, prepared for Flemish trip, **18**. 69

HW does not dare to tuck, under chin, **31**. 67

hot, HW tells Mann to dry his feet with, after using bootikins, **24**. 494

in Pall Mall taverns, adorned with Townshend's caricatures, **37**. 444

Napkin-cap:

Kilmarnock wears, at execution, **19**. 300

Naples, Abp of. *See* Sersali

Naples, K. of. *See* Alfonso V (1416–58); Charles III (1718–88); Ferdinand I (1423–94); Ferdinand IV (1751–1825)

Naples, Q. of. *See* Maria Amalia (1724–60); Maria Carolina (1752–1814)

Naples:

Acquaviva refuses to shut off Roman communications with, **18**. 270

agent from, at Florence, *see* Vernaccini, Francesco

ambassadors from and to, *see under* Ambassador

Ancaster, Ds of, dies at, **12**. 44n

antiquities restored at, **21**. 344

army of: assembled in Garigliano and Pescara, **19**. 345; at Aquila, **18**. 325; at Rome, **18**. 532; called 'Ligur-Napolispani,' **19**. 82; called 'Napolispani,' **17**. 427; England demands withdrawal of, from Lombardy, **18**. 16; Foligno march of, **17**. 265n; French

crossing of the Var would encourage, **19**. 378; Garfagnano may be invaded by, **19**. 65; Genoa may be approached by, **19**. 378; Lobkowitz may be pursued by, **18**. 508; Lobkowitz said to defeat, **37**. 160; Lombardy may be invaded by, **19**. 237, 364, 367, 378, 402; may invade Papal states, **18**. 295–6, 443–4, **19**. 364; Modena threatened by, **19**. 65; near Presidii, **18**. 546; near Rome, **18**. 546; Orbetello the theatre of, **19**. 378; Parma may be the objective of, **19**. 65; 'patrimoine de St-Pierre' reached by, **18**. 546; Pescara the theatre of, **19**. 345; reaches Porta del Popolo at Rome, **19**. 144; reduced, **17**. 464; *Rochester* to blockade, **18**. 453; Romagna to be vacated by, **18**. 43; Ronciglione the theatre of, **18**. 527; San Germano the station of, **19**. 378; Spaniards separated from, **18**. 66; to advance if Don Philip succeeds, **18**. 312; Toulon victory of, **12**. 53, 56; Tuscany may be invaded by, **18**. 295–6, **19**. 364; Tuscany traversed by, to join Gages, **19**. 65; Val Montone the station of, **18**. 447; Velletri fortified by, **18**. 454

Austrian possessions would be endangered if English fleet attacked, **18**. 390

Austrians complain that the English prevented their conquest of, **19**. 423

—— threaten, **18**. 271, 336, 405, 419–20, 434–5, 437, 443–4, 451, 454, 473–6, 502, 508, **19**. 41, 298, 306, 323–4, 423

Austrian threat to, displeases Charles Emmanuel III, **18**. 444

Austria guaranteed her Italian possessions by, **20**. 294n

authorities of, demand secret conference with Charles, **21**. 330

barks from, captured by English, **19**. 56

Benedict XIV may be intimidated by troops of, **19**. 144

Benevento to be seized by, **23**. 24

Boufflers tells the Genoese to expect help from, **19**. 406

Braitwitz accompanied to, by Marchesa Vitelli, **20**. 399

bread shortage at, **22**. 223

Breteuil made ambassador to, **5**. 93n

Brienne ambassador to, **5**. 50n

Byde dies at, **1**. 346n

Byng's conversation with Bucarelli reported to, **20**. 566

Caffarelli-Egizziello feud does not disturb festivities at, **19**. 452

cantata to be given at, **19**. 437–8, 452

Caracciolo's joke to Louis XV on insects and volcanoes at, **5**. 405

Caramanico coming from, **33**. 242

cardinals of, *see under* Cardinal

Castro and Ronciglione to be seized by, **23**. 36

Castropignano leads Neapolitan troops back to, **18**. 3, 7, 16

[Naples, *continued*]

Catalogue of French Books, A, satirizes neutrality of, **18.** 52

cavalry of, **19.** 297

Cavendish dies at, **29.** 161n

Changuion to be chargé d'affaires at, **22.** 112

Charles III (IV of Naples) assembles troops on borders of, to enforce neutrality, **21.** 271

—— behaved better at, than in Spain, **21.** 560

—— does not trust inhabitants of, **18.** 446

—— hates England ever since he was at, **23.** 349–50

—— less likely to be bullied than when at, **22.** 70

—— liked Sir James Gray when at, **21.** 556, 560n

—— must want English approval of his disposal of, **21.** 347

—— notifies, of his intentions about his sons, **21.** 270, 322–3, 324–6, 335

—— not to leave, **19.** 15

—— to return to, **18.** 519

—— unlikely to let France and Vienna seize, **21.** 280

—— will not relinquish, to brother, **21.** 264, 270

—— withdraws troops from confines of, **21.** 275

Charles, P., may get, as reward, **18.** 336

Charles Emmanuel III blames Maria Theresa for wanting to capture, **18.** 461

—— hoped by, to be bribed by Spain, **17.** 145, 291

—— to share invasion of, **18.** 3

Château Neuf at, **42.** 66

Choiseul, Vicomte de, succeeds Durfort as ambassador to, **5.** 141n, **39.** 65

Chute to buy Pergolesi's *Olimpiade* at, **19.** 149

climate of, no longer considered good for consumptives, **20.** 536

Coke, Lady Mary, may have trouble at, **23.** 547

Colonna, Grand Constable of, **17.** 12n

consuls of, impertinent, **19.** 90

convoys of, in Papal ports, should be burnt, **18.** 453

Conway and wife cancel trip to, **39.** 239

Conway may visit, **20.** 293, 296, 304

—— proposes going to, with HW, **39.** 30, 31

corn shortage at, **22.** 224n, 229

Correale buried at Monte Oliveto at, **20.** 369n

Corsican relations with, **18.** 156

couriers from and to, *see under* Courier

Court of: alarmed, **17.** 501, **18.** 3, 13; Albertini tells, of Gray's impending transfer, **21.** 159; assures Sir James Gray of Spain's sincerity, **21.** 551, 555; at Caserta, **20.** 429; complaints of, about stopping Neapolitan ships, **19.** 65n; congratulates Sir James Gray on supposed appointment, **21.** 174; differs from court of Rome on cardinals' costume,

23. 18; disavows Orsini's homage to Young Pretender, **22.** 399; English gardens not appreciated by, **35.** 439; English leave Florence to see, **23.** 18; gives Hamilton a copy of letter to Orsini, **22.** 399; induced by Frescobaldi to banish Marchesa Vitelli, **20.** 399; interested only in shooting, **35.** 433; Masaniello's ghost may alarm, **17.** 501; may flee from plague to Aquila, **18.** 302; may flee to Rome, **18.** 3, 13; Maynard, Vcts, distributes James's powders at, **24.** 451; supplies amusements, **24.** 280–1; to make plans according to Spanish campaign in Savoy, **18.** 302; would reject Sir James Gray if it knew his low birth, **20.** 415–16

Craufurd to winter in, **4.** 140

Damer, Mrs, avoids, **39.** 339

Del Monte said to have fled to, **20.** 437

democratic ideas do not penetrate to, **35.** 442

drought at, **24.** 479

Du Deffand, Mme, acquainted with visitors from, **6.** 395

earthquake damage in, less than was represented, **25.** 391

earthquakes in, **33.** 444, **37.** 104

earthquake victims to be relieved by ships from, **25.** 375

embarkations from, **19.** 55

England gets no ships directly from, **35.** 432

—— said to want attack upon, **18.** 364

——'s commercial treaty with, **20.** 458

English dames at, astonish HW, **21.** 554

English fleet may threaten, to stop Spain's conquest of Portugal, **38.** 186

English fleet should attack, **17.** 291, 306, 311

English fleet should not attack, **18.** 390

English fleet unable to interrupt Genoese commerce with, **19.** 207

English fleet under Martin threatens, **18.** 15, 26, 32, 39, 42–3, 47

English fleet was destined for, **22.** 95

English merchants at, fear retaliation, **18.** 28

English negotiations with, may be upset by Minorca's capture, **20.** 576

English ships are probably forbidden to enter harbour of, **28.** 461

English squadron before, would encourage inhabitants to revolt, **18.** 460

English squadron diverted from, to protect Tuscany, **18.** 37–8

English to crowd to, for Maria Carolina's reception, **23.** 2

English to leave, for Florence, after festivals, **23.** 3

English travellers at, reap no benefits, **35.** 440

English visitors disappointed by lack of shows at, for carnival, **22.** 491–2

English visitors seek passports for, **19.** 15

envoys from and to, *see under* Envoy

Evelyn's journey to, from Rome, **16.** 61, 63

famine in, **22.** 206, 216, 223, 229

Ferdinand and Maria Carolina to sail to, from Leghorn, 25. 594, 600

festivities at: 19. 452, 23. 3; for prince's birth, 43. 263

fishermen of, to be lured to Leghorn, 20. 217

Florentine society surpasses that of, 22. 528n

footmen from, 17. 421, 22. 32

France and Austria give up, to Charles III, 21. 280n

France tries to prevent war between Sardinia and, over reversions, 21. 275n

Francis I guarantees possessions of, 20. 294n

—— may get, instead of Tuscany, 18. 331, 336

—— may invade, 18. 3

French ambassador at Venice sent to, 21. 333n

French-American treaty to be brought to, by extraordinary courier, 24. 369

Frenchmen at, will exclude Guasco, 22. 575

French send courier to, to announce Corsican successes, 19. 437

French-Spanish alliance deemed ill-judged by, 21. 555

friar appeases mob at, 24. 541

Gages advised by, to await Spanish orders after Charles Albert's death, 19. 7–8, 10

—— may be reinforced by troops of, 18. 405, 19. 15

—— prevents Lobkowitz from inciting people of, 18. 471

——'s army covers, 18. 542

Gatti to reach, from Florence, in less than 60 hours, 24. 330

Genoa not accepted by, as an ally, 19. 237

Genoese uprising encouraged by, 19. 364

German dukedom refused by gentleman of, unless his footman was also made a duke, 22. 32

Girifalco dies in prison in, 35. 434

Gray, Sir James, indispensable at, 21. 166

—— to go to, 20. 409

Gray, Thomas, writings done by, when at, 43. 191

HW admires opera plans for, 19. 442

HW and Gray do not expect to visit, 13. 217, 221

HW discourages Mann from trying to go to, 22. 111

HW has friends at, 28. 51

HW hopes Bn Holland's 'caravan' will assemble safely at, 30. 238

HW imagines intrigues of, at Rome, 35. 222

HW's health would not be suited by, 22. 116

HW to procure snuff-box at, for Mann, 17. 26, 29

HW unable to visit Hamiltons at, 35. 414

HW wishes to visit, to avoid heat, 17. 22, 26

HW would like to visit, 10. 48

HW would not go to, if it were on road to New Jerusalem, 39. 30

HW writes from, 13. 222

Haddock's victory reported from, 13. 211, 218

Hamilton, Lady, dies at, 25. 321, 26. 46

Hamilton, Sir William, about to return to, 23. 431, 24. 321

—— brings alleged Correggio painting from, 26. 46

—— in a hurry to reach, 22. 260

—— minister to, 1. 244, 11. 274n, 24. 241n, 25. 459n, 26. 46

—— should not forsake post at, without substitute, 35. 418

—— to return to 'kingdom of cinders' at, 35. 384

—— to succeed Sir James Gray at, 22. 243

—— wants to stay at, 35. 434

—— writes from, 22. 354, 35. 408, 432, 440, 40. 383

Hamiltons about to take a trip from, 35. 427

—— leave, to visit England, 23. 339

—— offer HW an apartment overlooking, 40. 383

—— recommended climate of, to HW, 40. 383

—— return to, 11. 340, 350, 35. 440

—— to go to, 23. 448

Haymarket opera outshines, 11. 218

heats will keep Beauchamp from visiting, 38. 531

Hervey, Bn, tries to quiet creditors at, 25. 652

Holland's maladies unlikely to be cured by, 30. 235

honorary titles of, suggested for Mann, 18. 484

honours profusely distributed at, 22. 32

horses from: for Kaunitz, 17. 49; for Mathews, 18. 453; for Frederick, P. of Wales, 18. 200

inhabitants of, not really eager to revolt, 18. 471, 474, 484

Inquisition's hold upon, to be broken by Maria Theresa, 18. 454

insurrection at, during eruption of Vesuvius, 24. 529

Italy will not be upset by succession at, 21. 280

Jesuits' hoards may be seized by troops of, 23. 36

—— may be banished from, 22. 565

Joseph II to visit, 22. 556

Lavagna minister to, 10. 127n

La Vauguyon reported to be French ambassador to, 6. 87

Leopold and Maria Louisa to escort Ferdinand and Maria Amalia of Parma to, for Carnival, 25. 2

Leopold's possible loss of grand ducal title enrages, 22. 330

letters from: about Ferdinand's cruelty to Florentines, 23. 254; to army, captured with courier, 18. 85–6

library of Greek and Latin authors at, unpublished, 31. 278–9

Liechtenstein, P., to attack, 34. 323–4

Lobkowitz threatens, 18. 271, 405, 419–20, 434–5, 437, 443, 473–6, 512–13

Long sends ships to attack, 18. 470–6

[Naples, *continued*]

Louis XV overcomes opposition of, at Vienna, to Maria Isabella's marriage, 21. 323n

Louis XVI's aunts go to, 11. 208n

Lunardi the secretary from, in London, 25. 528n, 543

Macdonald probably from, 19. 116

Malta to be starved by, 20. 405

Mann has received no account from, of Messina earthquake, 25. 374

—— hears from, of Mrs Garrick's accident, 22. 203

—— hopes that Francis I instead of P. Charles may take, 18. 336

—— might succeed Sir James Gray as minister to, 21. 150, 556, 22. 107, 111, 114–15

—— receives sketch from, of Vesuvius's eruption, 24. 514

—— rumoured to be taking message to, 18. 243

—— said by HW to be agent for conquest of, 18. 466

—— sent to, in ship, with coffin by his side, 24. 180

—— 's presents to Stone from, 18. 115, 330, 445, 496

Mann, Galfridus, might go to, for health, 20. 526, 536

Mann, Horace II, might gallop to Florence from, in a few days, 24. 170

—— urges Mann to accompany him and Lady Lucy to, 24. 129, 131–2

Mann, James II, to visit, 25. 581

Mann, Lady Lucy, may be completely cured by winter at, 24. 136

map of: 35. 435; HW searches, and finds Otranto, 42. 178

Maria Amalia to return to, 18. 519

Maria Carolina's itinerary to, 23. 17–18, 25. 593–4, 600

—— to be accompanied to, by Leopold and Maria Louisa, 23. 2, 11, 17–18

Maria Josefa's entry into, planned, 22. 556

—— 's luggage on way to, 22. 558

Maria Theresa concentrates on conquering, 19. 223n

—— covets, 18. 390

—— does not respect neutrality of, 18. 521

—— 's edict to inhabitants of, 18. 454, 461

Marlow's landscapes of, 23. 211n

Martin may be summoned from, to protect Tuscany, 18. 27

—— 's letter about his ultimatum to, 19. 42–3

Masaniello leads uprising in, 9. 263n

Mass sent from, for Egizziello, 17. 472

Mathews and Maria Theresa differ over war against, 18. 370

Mathews said to prefer prize-taking to capture of, 18. 452–3

Maynard said to have shot himself at, 24. 435

Maynard, Vcts, shunned at, by Countesses of Berkeley and Orford, 24. 451

Medici, Ottaviano de', sends valet to, 17. 238

messenger from: to Turin, 20. 576; travels slowly in chaise, 20. 581

ministers from and to, *see under* Minister

mole of, fortified, 22. 6

Montagu compares Mount Merrion to, 17. 400

Montemar may retire to, 18. 2, 16

—— 's army may be depleted by withdrawal of troops of, 18. 27

Montini's execution at, 18. 271

Morice to write from, to HW, 25. 435

mosaic stars repaired at, 35. 409

Mountrath fails to get passports for, 19. 15

Mozzi procures Cts of Orford's papers from, 25. 160, 162

Neapolitan troops recalled to, from Viterbo, 19. 237

neutrality of: Charles III proclaims, 21. 271; Frederick II must be encouraged by, 21. 271; HW enjoys Mann's accounts of, 18. 68; predicted by Sir James Gray, 22. 5, 12; Tanucci proclaims, 22. 5–6

operas from, 43. 61

Orbetello ruled by governor from, 18. 287

Orford, Cts of, has great effects at, 25. 113, 114

—— has town and country houses at, 23. 2

—— may be abandoned by Mozzi unless she leaves, 23. 559, 24. 305

—— may have bought estate at, 24. 187

—— prefers young men of Aix to those of, 35. 410

—— relinquishes trip to, 24. 70, 83, 25. 107, 112

Otranto in kingdom of, 23. 107

Pallavicini formerly nuncio at, 23. 118

parrot going to, might end in Hungary, 39. 183

people of, demand secret conference with Charles III, 21. 330

Philip, Don, may be promoted to, from Parma, 21. 264, 330

—— may visit, 17. 323, 19. 144

—— should be king of, 35. 14

—— to be escorted by galleys of, 17. 362

Philip Anton's sanity to be judged at, 21. 322–5

Pironi said to have dispersed seditious papers at, 18. 253–4

Pitture antiche di Ercolano expected from, 22. 533

preliminary treaty of Aranjuez guarantees territorial integrity of, 20. 294n

Preston chargé d'affaires at, 23. 342n

prince of, loves Bettina, 17. 421

princess of, born, 18. 478

provisions hoarded in, against plague, 18. 288

public amusements at, bad, 24. 280

public ovens and bread stalls at, 23. 342n

Putello loses voice at, 19. 355

Reggio e Branciforte made member of royal council at, 18. 420n

religious credulity in, 18. 305, 20. 429

revolt might take place in, **18**. 460

Rinuccini's uncle dies in, **20**. 336

riots in, over food shortage, **22**. 206

Roman banker forwards letters to, **17**. 23n

Rome's plea for grain from, refused, **22**. 453n

Royal Gallery at, to contain statue found at Herculaneum, **21**. 364n

royal progeny of, **15**. 188

Russian fleet may be excluded from ports of, **25**. 616n

Salas at, **17**. 215

San Antonio and Santa Barbara, churches in, have paintings, **42**. 66n

San Severino's couriers from and to, **21**. 330, 453, 455, 477

school of, claims invention of oil painting, **42**. 66

secretary of state at, *see* Caracciolo, Domenico

serenade at, **19**. 439

Sersale to go to, **20**. 429

ships of, preyed on by English in Adriatic, **19**. 231

ships sent from, with supplies to Genoa, **19**. 236

Shuttleworth escapes to, **19**. 77

Sicilian rebellion disturbs, **24**. 39

Sicily isolated from, because of plague, **18**. 252

snuff-boxes of, **17**. 26, 29, **18**. 115, 330, 445, 496

soldiers and artillery at, **17**. 154

Spain exchanges couriers with, weekly, **22**. 349

—— not to sing Te Deums for victories in, **18**. 486

—— orders, despite Tanucci's hatred of Tuscany, to grant food to Tuscany, **22**. 448

—— sends troops to, **19**. 367

—— threatens nobles of, with confiscation of *feudi* if they celebrate Francis I's election, **19**. 184

Spaniards may invade Lombardy from, **19**. 367

—— may not be received at, **18**. 413

—— may retire to, **18**. 325, 397–8, 413

—— to receive artillery from, by Adriatic, **19**. 30

Spanish army may be cut off from, **17**. 500

Spanish expedition may join troops from, **17**. 198

Spanish fleet at, for Charles III's departure, **21**. 324, 333

Spanish troops from: reach Aquila, **17**. 265; to join those from Arezzo and Orbetello, **17**. 350

Spanish troops in, may embark, **19**. 410

Spanish troops to go to, **21**. 335

Squillace exiled to, **39**. 64

—— unpopular at, **21**. 330

Stanley puts off visiting, **22**. 326–7

Stephano's inn at, **22**. 292n

Strange copies pictures at, **22**. 108

—— looks in vain for art purchases at, **22**. 115

Tanucci unpopular in, **21**. 330

Thorold dies at, **22**. 380

to make peace with France, **12**. 148n

transports from, escape, **19**. 82

travellers leave, for Rome in Holy Week, **35**. 440

troops march from, to Chieta, **19**. 410n

troops said to advance from, towards Rome, **17**. 110

Tuscan regency gets memorial from, on allodials, **18**. 177

Tuscany imports grain from, **22**. 452n

—— seeks loan from Jews at, **22**. 448

—— stops intercourse with, for fear of plague, **18**. 270

Tylney defers visit to, **24**. 145

——'s house in, **24**. 280–1

——'s possessions at, to be sold for servants' benefit, **25**. 534

—— to give public ball at, **24**. 281

—— to visit, **24**. 251

unnecessary to go to, when England is so hot, **2**. 170

valuables of: at Palazzo Farnese, **18**. 435; stored at Rome and Malta, **18**. 501

Van Dyck threatened with galleys at, **7**. 371

Velletri gate faces, **18**. 488

Vesuvius's eruption at, **24**. 514, 541

viceroy for, **18**. 420

Viennese Court wants to conquer, **18**. 390

visitors to: Adair, **23**. 384n; Allens, **19**. 438; Astrua, **19**. 438; Augustus Frederick, D. of Sussex, **35**. 442–3; Babbi, **19**. 438; Barrett Lennards, **20**. 92, 105; Beaufort, Ds of, **23**. 449; Beauvau, **17**. 11, 16; Berkeley, Cts of, **24**. 451; Binning, Bns, **21**. 301n; Boswell, **22**. 292n; Breteuil, **5**. 209–10; Bridgwater, Ds of, **21**. 550; Bulstrode, **17**. 11; Bute, **23**. 91, 96; Caffarelli, **19**. 438; 439; Caracciolo, **6**. 82; Carlisle, Cts of, **23**. 449; Chartres, Duc de, **25**. 417; Chartres, Duchesse de, **24**. 222; Cholmondeley, E. of, **25**. 324, 346; Chute, **19**. 149, 171; Cock, **23**. 377n; Corsi, **22**. 202; Cumberland, D. and Ds of, **25**. 618, 628; Damer, Mrs, **25**. 184, 645, **35**. 432; Denis, **19**. 439; Dicks, **24**. 251; Doria, **19**. 345; Duclos, **22**. 531; Duncan, Sir William, **24**. 41, 50; Egerton, Miss, **21**. 550; Egizziello, **19**. 438; Eyles Stiles, Mary, **21**. 550; Eyles Stiles, Lady, and Miss, **21**. 550; Ferrers, Cts, **25**. 645; Firmian, **21**. 340; Floyd, **24**. 508; Gascoigne, **24**. 451n; Gatti, **5**. 183, **24**. 330; Gleichen, **5**. 144; Gloucester, D. and Ds of, **25**. 675; Gloucester, D. of, **23**. 336, 342, 370, 374, 375, 377, 384, 405; Grafton, Ds of, **21**. 550; Gray, **13**. 9, 212; HW, **13**. 9, 212, 222, **35**. 11; Hartington, **17**. 16; Hertford's valet-de-chambre, **23**. 56; Hervey, Bn and Bns, **25**. 651; Hervey, Mr and Mrs Frederick, **22**. 398; Hillsborough, **22**, 429; Hills-

[Naples, *continued*]

borough, Cts of, **22**. 398; Hobart, **19**. 408; Holland, Bn, **22**. 492n, 503, **31**. 97; Holland, Bn and Bns, **22**. 503n, **30**. 241; Jebb, **23**. 384n; Karl Wilhelm Ferdinand, **22**. 458; Kingston, Ds of, **24**. 220; La Vaupalière, Marquise de, **5**. 210; Lyttelton, Sir Richard, **21**. 545; Macdonald, **22**. 407; Mann, **21**. 301n, **24**. 180; Mann, Horace II and Lady Lucy, **24**. 115, 118, 129, 131–2, 136, 163, 166, 170, 181, 188, 225, 246; Maria Louisa, **23**. 111; Matignon, Comte and Comtesse de, **5**. 210; Maynard, **24**. 435; Maynard, Vcts, **24**. 451; Montagu, Lady Mary Wortley, **17**. 92; Morice, **21**. 389, **25**. 51, 289, 432, 435, **31**. 204, **33**. 362, 408; Mozzi, **23**. 155; Northampton, Cts of, **22**. 132, 142; Orford, Cts of, **20**. 476, 499, 505, **21**. 550, **23**. 2, 155, 464, 468, 472, 478, 486, 512, 525, 529, 531, 537, 559, **24**. 9, 57, 82, 164, 220, 244, 251, 260, 304, 312, 317, 322, 451, 467, 479; Östergotland, D. of, **24**. 240n; Palmerstons, **12**. 59n; Pars, **35**. 424n; Paul I, **25**. 250; Pelham Clinton, Lord John, **24**. 251n; Pitt, Anne, **24**. 344; Pitt, Mrs George, **23**. 447; Pitt, Thomas, **21**. 545; Pitt, Thomas II, **24**. 486; Pocock, Lady, **30**. 241; Rinuccini, **19**. 8; Robinson, Mrs, **21**. 550; Rohan-Rochefort, P. Camille de, **22**. 556n; Roxburghe, **21**. 550; Rumbold family, **25**. 651; St John, Vct, **29**. 15n; Shelburne, **5**. 144; Smyth, **17**. 16; Spencers, **22**. 180n; Stanhope, Lady, **21**. 550; Stanhope, Sir William, **21**. 550, **22**. 292, 418; Strange, **22**. 108; Strathmore, **21**. 564; Stuart Mackenzies, **24**. 337; Swinburne, **24**. 451n; Tesi, **19**. 438; (?) Vierpyl, **19**. 100–1; Vorontsov, **19**. 184; Warkworth, **21**. 512n; Whithed, **19**. 171; Wilkes, **22**. 281, 292, 305; Worsley, **19**. 476–7

Viviani was mere chargé d'affaires from, **22**. 349

water sold on streets of, during drought, **24**. 479

weather in England hot enough to be named after, **2**. 172

Wortley Montagu may embark from, for Egypt, **22**. 77

Wright hopes for post at, **22**. 500

York, D. of, considers visiting, **22**. 204, 224, 229

Naples, Bay of:

Hamiltons offer HW an apartment overlooking, **40**. 383

Naples biscuit:

small size of, **35**. 378

Napoleon I. *See* Bonaparte, Napoleon

Napoli di Romania (Gulf of Argolis):

Russian fleet in gulf of, **23**. 226

Turks attack Elphinston's squadron in harbour of, **23**. 234

'Napolispani':

new word in Florence for Spanish-Neapolitan troops, **17**. 427

Nappa, Niccola, Neapolitan courier:

news of Tylney's death taken by, to England by way of Florence, **25**. 533

Nappier. *See* Napier

Narbonne, Abp of. *See* Bonzi, Pierre de (1631–1703); Dillon, Arthur Richard (1721–1806)

'Narbonne, Comtesse de':

HW makes, interesting, **42**. 284

Narbonne, Vicomte de. *See* Narbonne-Pelet-Alais-Melguel-Bermond, François-Raymond-Joseph-Hermengilde-Amalric de

Narbonne, Vicomtesse de. *See* Ricard de Bregançon, Marie-Anne-Pauline de

Narbonne (France):

cathedral at, **28**. 472n

Mysterious Mother laid in, **39**. 103

Narbonne-Lara, Louis-Marie-Jacques-Amalric (1755–1813), Comte de:

SH visited by, **12**. 243

Narbonne-Pelet, Comtesse (later Duchesse) de. *See* Du Plessis-Châtillon, Marie-Félicité

Narbonne-Pelet, Blanche-Charlotte-Marie-Félicité de (1760–1840), m. (1780) Augustin-Joseph, Comte de Mailly, Marquis d'Haucourt:

marriage of, **7**. 215, 216, 449

Narbonne-Pelet, M. and Mme Jean-Denis-Hercule de:

(?) provincial glory of, **4**. 104

Narbonne-Pelet, Jean-François (1725–1804), Comte de:

Mme du Deffand's social relations with, **21**. 328, 332, 344, 347

Narbonne-Pelet-Alais-Melguel-Bermond, François-Raymond-Joseph-Hermengilde-Amalric de (1715–ca 1780), Vicomte de Narbonne:

marriage of, **3**. 285n

(?) social relations of, in Paris, **4**. 47, 335, **21**. 338

Narbonne-Pelet-Fritzlar, Comte de. *See* Pelet, Jean-François

Narcissus:

at Little Strawberry Hill, **11**. 300

at SH, **10**. 69

Beaulieu, Cts of, sends, to Montagu, **10**. 204

Nardi (singer):

leg of, broken, **19**. 293n

Middlesex's mistress, **19**. 293

Violette quarrels with, **19**. 293

Nardini, Pietro (1722–93), Leghorn violinist:

Karl Wilhelm Ferdinand invites, to Germany, **22**. 537

Nares, Mrs James. *See* Bacon, Jane

Nares, Rev. Robert (1753–1829):

British Critic edited by Beloe and, **15**. 238n

HW promises dinner to, **15**. 232

HW's correspondence with, **15**. 218, 231, 234, 240, 244, 252

James St the address of, **43**. 204, 205, 208

Man's Best Right by, **15**. 232n

plan of, to disperse cheap essays, **15**. 231–2

Principles of Government by: abridgement of, **15**. 232n; HW thanks Nicol for, **42**. 375; not strong enough, **15**. 220–1

Southgate succeeded by, **16**. 325n

SH visited by, **12**. 236, 242, 243, **15**. 218

See also *British Critic*

Nares, Mrs Robert. *See* Fleetwood, Frances Maria

Nares, William (d. ca 1825), attorney: Nares, Robert, anxious about, **15**. 231, *234*

Narford, Norfolk: pictures at, **1**. 171, *173*

Nargeot, Jean-Denis (1795–ca 1865), engraver: Mme du Deffand's picture engraved by, **8**. 216

Narni, ——: England visited by, **19**. 455

Valenti dances with, in Florentine opera, **19**. 455

See also Nardi

Narrative of the Last Illness of the . . . Earl of Orford. See under Ranby, John

'Narrative of . . . the Quarrel of Mr David Hume and Jean-Jacques Rousseau,' by HW: HW writes, but does not publish it, **13**. 42

Hardinge wants to borrow, **35**. 572

Narrative of What Passed between General Sir Harry Erskine and Philip Thicknesse, Esq.: HW's copy of, **28**. 243n

Naseby, battle of: Charles I at, **2**. 76n

contemporary papers would not have printed tittle-tattle at time of, **35**. 364

Fairfax receives watch from Parliament after, **38**. 340n

HW does not need to write about, **23**. 224

Nash, Elizabeth Rebecca Anne, m. (1779) Henry Venables Vernon Sedley: husband of, **29**. 81n

Sedley leaves estates to, **10**. 190n

Nash, Lt Lewellin, of 14th Dragoons: Maredant's Drops cure, **43**. 58

Nash, Michael (fl. 1793–6), Protestant controversialist: *Gideon's Cake of Barley Meal* by, attacks Hannah More, **31**. 388

Nash, Richard (1674–1761), 'Beau Nash': Bath ballroom built at instigation of, **40**. 10n

bets on Cibber's being survived by, **35**. 258

Nash, Treadway Russell (1725–1811), D.D.; historian: *Archæologia* paper by, on Q. Catherine Parr's corpse, **43**. 385n

Butler's *Hudibras* edited by, **43**. 389, 390n

Collections for the History of Worcestershire by: **2**. 154, 266, **43**. 68, 383; prints from, **43**. 383n, 384n

HW reads notes of, to Butler's *Hudibras*, **42**. 241–2

HW's correspondence with, **42**. 241–2, **43**. 383–4, 385, 388–90

HW to write to, for prints used in his *History*, **42**. 17

HW wants address of, **42**. 17

London visited by, **43**. 385, 390

Pennant's intercession with, for HW, **42**. 19

Pennant travels with, **43**. 384n

Percy's correspondence with, **43**. 390n

Nash, Mrs Treadway Russell, and daughter: Pennant travels with, **43**. 384n

Nash, William (d. ? 1773), lord mayor of London: Hertford's letter to, **7**. 372

Nasmith, James (1740–1808), antiquary: at Norwich, **1**. 290

Catalogus librorum manuscriptorum quos Collegio Corporis Christi by, **1**. 185n, 267n, **2**. 79–80

Cole to receive MSS from, **1**. *185–6*

——'s life of, **2**. 226n

dines: at Emmanuel College, **1**. 193n; with Cole, **1**. 267

Hearne to be emulated by, **28**. 40

Itineraria Simonis Simeonis et Willelmi de Worcestre by, **1**. 267n, **2**. 54, 57, 73–4, 76–7, 79, 82

receipt from, for HW's subscription, **2**. 54, 57, 74

Tanner's *Notitia monastica* edited by, **1**. 268n

to print old historians, **1**. 267

Nassau, P. *See* Clavering Cowper, George Nassau

Nassau, P. of: HW escapes, at Dover, **39**. 7

Nassau, Ann. *See* Labbel, Ann

Nassau, Jan Nicolas Floris (1709–82), Rijks-graaf van; Heer van Ouwerkerk: Cowper not allowed by, to use Auverquerque title, **24**. 370

Nassau, Maria. *See* Harrison, Maria

Nassau, Hon. Richard Savage (1723–80), M.P.: George III does not include, in Bedchamber, **9**. 324, **21**. 460

HW gets, to present petition against Fonnereau, **30**. 331n

Parliamentary memberships of, corrected, **43**. 326

Nassau, Willem Maurits (1679–1753), Graaf van; Heer van Ouwerkerke: Dutch aid to England not known by, **37**. 159

Wade's army slowed by, **37**. 215

Nassau, English ship: African conquest by, **21**. 212

Charles Emmanuel III to be aided by, **19**. 313

expected at Port Mahon, **17**. 285

Nassau d'Auverquerque. *See* Auverquerque

Nassau de Zulestein. *See* Nassau de Zuylestein

Nassau de Zuylestein, George (b. 1756): SH visited by, **12**. 221

Nassau de (*or* van) Zuylestein, William Henry van (1649–1708), cr. (1695) E. of Rochford: William III compels, to call himself Zuylestein not Nassau, **24**. 360

—— does not allow, to use Nassau arms, **24**. 370

Nassau de Zuylestein, William Henry (1717–81), 4th E. of Rochford, 1738:

Albemarle succeeded by, as Groom of the Stole, 35. 203, 213

Allen recommended by, as Mann's proxy, 23. 326–7, 362n, 379

allowance denied to, for journey to Turin, 38. 269n

ambassador at Turin, 20. 58

anti-Pitt, 3. 254

Banti, the, mistress of, 20. 378n

Bedford, D. of, chooses, as envoy to Turin, 20. 58n

Bologna and Venice to be visited by, 20. 376n

Choiseul's reprimand of Fréron known to, 3. 228

Compiègne visited by, 3. 319, 323

Conway may hear from, of Spanish riots, 39. 63

—— receives Lombardy poplar from, from Turin, 39. 133n

courier of: 3. 201, 254, 4. 104; brings news of Townshend's death, 39. 88; Hertford to send notice to HW by, 39. 89

Cumberland, D. of, depicted on buttons ordered by, 9. 49

dances, 35. 213

death of, 25. 191

Dick awaits word from, before accepting Order of St Anne, 24. 85

Du Deffand, Mme, may send parcel by, 4. 82, 85

—— mentions, 4. 107

—— politely treated by, 3. 311

—— receives New Year's gift from, 4. 7

—— sends parcel by, 4. 139

—— sends to, for news, 3. 272

——'s opinion of, 3. 263, 278, 286, 4. 16, 102

enemies of C. H. Williams obtain appointment of, to Turin, 30. 320

Essex left by, for Turin, 20. 420n

expected to go to London, 3. 303, 315, 323, 4. 85

expected to have post in ministry, 3. 313–15

explains English political situation to Mme du Deffand, 3. 261

Florence to be visited by, 20. 376

Forcalquier, Mme de, friend of, 3. 303, 309, 311, 315, 337, 402, 4. 94

former secretary of state, and K.G., 25. 191n

French disarming misrepresented by, in House of Lords, 41. 299

French dislike, 4. 157

French embassy hinted for, 20. 420, 426

gaiety of, 20. 76

Garrick's dinner includes, 35. 244

Garter for, 24. 386n, 32. 381n

George III's household not to include, 9. 316

Gloucester, D. of, applies to, for provision for family, 36. 306

—— makes overtures to George III through, 24. 314

Grimaldi negotiates with, over Honduras logwood, 38. 432n

guitar played by, 9. 269

HW avoids, 9. 88

HW disparages, 28. 49

HW entertains, at SH, 9. 168

HW, Lady Mary Coke, and Caswall occupy box of, at Dauphiness's funeral oration, 31. 134

HW mentions, 10. 7

HW might borrow satire on Conclave from, 24. 65

HW's dealings with, about proxy for Mann's K.B. installation, 23. 341, 350, 362, 371, 408

HW's opinion of, 20. 58

health of, 4. 68, 73, 82, 85

Hertford may be succeeded by, at Paris, 38. 534

hopes of, to get post nearer England, 20. 463

Hume aide to, 4. 213

—— severely criticized by, 3. 253

Irish lord lieutenancy refused by, 24. 263n

Irish lord lieutenancy rumoured for, 3. 246

Irish pension awarded to, 3. 392, 21. 460

letters for, 3. 379

lives near Mme du Deffand, 3. 199

London visited by, 3. 333

Louis XV consults D. of York through, 7. 364

made knight of the Garter, 7. 49

Mann and Hon. Robert Walpole approached by, about Jesuit archives, 23. 533n

Mann asks that proper answer be given to, 23. 358

—— encloses letter to, 24. 44

—— entertains, at Florence, 20. 378

—— not told by, how to treat D. of Gloucester, 24. 129

—— receives circular letter from, 23. 262, 478, 543n

——'s correspondence with, 20. 420, 22. 369, 23. 293, 326–7, 332

—— sends copy of papal bull to, 23. 507

—— sends suppressed satire on the Conclave to, 24. 65

——'s red ribbon may be sent through, 23. 14

——'s relations with, probably good, 23. 255

—— to entertain, at Florence, 20. 370

—— wants to notify, that Cowper's Florentine match is off, 23. 457

marriage of, 3. 172n, 17. 431

name of, corrected, 43. 83, 112, 113

natural daughter of, 3. 325

not HW's kind, 3. 267

'oaf,' 9. 49

Ohio grant approved and Hillsborough opposed by, 23. 424n

Paoli visits, 23. 142n

Paris post expected by, 20. 467

—— post to be accepted by, 22. 420

—— to be visited by, 39. 90

Parliamentary speech by, in House of Lords, 28. 197n

Poulett resigns Bedchamber from pique against, **35**. 223n

Richmond, D. of, attacks, on Falkland Islands issue, **41**. 299n

Rome reached by, from Turin, **20**. 370n

St Osyth seat of, **9**. 88

Sayre's arrest caused by, **24**. 138n, **28**. 227n

secretary of state: **23**. 62, **24**. 138n; for southern province, **23**. 255

social relations of, in Paris, *see index entries ante* **8**. 452

social relations of, with HW; Huntingdon; Maynard, Lady; Morrison; Waldegraves; Walpole, Charlotte; York, D. of, **9**. 269

Spanish declaration received by, **5**. 16n, **23**. 268n, 269n

Spanish disarmament agreement signed by, **23**. 297n

Spanish post desired by, **21**. 166

Strange should have told, of D. of Gloucester's health, **24**. 136

thought not to care about ambassadorship, **3**. 110

to be Groom of the Stole, **20**. 460, 469

to be prosecuted instead of Sayre, **24**. 138–9

Turin returned to by, without increase in rank, **20**. 420n

—— the post of, **11**. 146n, **19**. 465n, **20**. 58, 420, 426

unwilling to take vest to HW, **4**. 143

verification of D. of Gloucester's marriage silly enough to be the work of, **36**. 92n

Villettes to meet, at Paris, **20**. 76

Walpole, Edward, takes attention of, **3**. 253

Weymouth succeeds, as secretary of state for southern province, **24**. 142

wife no longer monopolizes attentions of, **20**. 378

wife of, **9**. 42n, **20**. 58n, **21**. 57n

Nassau de Zuylestein, William Henry (1754–1830), 5th E. of Rochford, 1781:
SH visited by, **12**. 221

Nassau-Dillenberg, Johann (VI) (1535–1606), Graf von, 1559:
(?) portrait of, **34**. 122

Nassau family:
arms of, William III does not let Grantham and Rochford use, **24**. 370
Grantham is of illegitimate branch of, **25**. 78n
illegitimate branches of, **24**. 360
princes of, object to Cowper's bearing their name or arms, **24**. 370

Nassau-Saarbrücken, Ps of. *See* St-Mauris, Marie-Françoise-Maximilienne de

Nassau-Saarbrücken, Heinrich Karl Ludwig (1768–97), P. of:
marriage of, **7**. 180–1

Nassau-Siegen, Karl Heinrich Nicolaus Otto (1745–1808), P. of:
army of, should have been destroyed, **24**. 487
Artois permitted to receive, **7**. 32
Buzançais fights duel with, **5**. 175

Chartres, Duc de, may accompany, to the Levant, **25**. 243n

Eszterházy fights duel with, **6**. 23

Forth's race with, **41**. 6

HW calls, 'roi d'Yvetot,' **24**. 472

HW hopes that attack on Ireland will be led by, **24**. 480

HW's opinion of, **7**. 142

jackboots to be worn by, in horse-race at Paris, **31**. 112

Jersey attack led by, **7**. 135, **24**. 471

—— may again be invaded by, **39**. 321

kingdom of Jersey promised to, **24**. *471*

Wallace's raid cripples force of, **39**. 321

Nassau-Usingen, Friedrich August (1738–1816), P. of; D. of Nassau-Usingen, 1806:
(?) descended from royalty, **22**. 291
(?) Mann attends, in Florence, **22**. 291
title of, corrected, **43**. 280

Nassau-Weilburg, Ps of. *See* Wilhelmina Carolina

Nassau-Weilburg, Karl Christian (1735–88), P. of:
HW's opinion of, **9**. 187–8
HW to entertain, at breakfast at SH, **9**. 189
Richmond, D. of, visited by, **9**. 188
Townshend, Vcts, entertains, at ball, **9**. 188
Wilhelmina Carolina of Orange wooed by, **9**. 187–8

Nassau van Zuylestein. *See* Nassau de Zuylestein

Natalia, Russian frigate:
Houghton collection carried in, **2**. 184n
shipwreck of, alleged, **25**. 2, **43**. 70

Nathan (biblical):
Tyrwhitt compared to, **12**. 150

Nation; nations:
small, more likely to be free, **39**. 488

National Assembly, French:
Berry, Mary, describes, **11**. 128
Berrys visit, **11**. 127
Bonnay president of, **11**. 96n
Bouillé's letter to, **11**. 336–7n
Burke abhors violence, cruelty, and absurdity of, **34**. 118
commissioners named by: **11**. 300n; to arrest Dumouriez, **12**. 1–2
Condorcet recommends to, bust of Anckarström instead of Brutus, **34**. 174–5
contemptible, for destroying archives of old families, **34**. 144
Dauphin to be crowned by, under regent, **11**. 301
debate in, **11**. 233n
debates in, seem ridiculous to Wyndham, **34**. 65–6
Debry proposes assassination corps to, **35**. 446n
disorder in, **34**. 180
Dumouriez condemned in, **12**. 1
English peerage does not need, to lower itself to gutter, **35**. 399
feudal rights abolished by, **39**. 482–3

[National Assembly, French, *continued*]
financial and military reports to, 11. 321
Fitzgerald's remonstrance to, over confiscation of Irish and Scots Colleges at Paris, 42. 286n
France thrown into confusion by, 15. 207
French titles abolished by, 11. 76n
Gordon, Lord George, corresponds with, 31. 332
—— sends petition to, from Newgate, 34. 62n
HW compares members of, to hyenas, 15. 235–6
HW denounces, 31. 324, 332, 386
Jacobins dictate to, 15. 231
Jews petition, 31. 331–2, 34. 76
Lameth a member of, 11. 345n
laws neglected by, in order to abolish nobility and pull king down, 39. 477
left wing of, 11. 136n
Leopold II free to move against, 39. 484
Louis XVI and, 11. 40, 96
——'s capture does not help, 34. 114
——'s declaration to be handed to, 11. 299n
——'s domains taken by, 34. 119
—— suspended by, 31. 371n
Lyon destroyed by, 34. 192
—— to be restored to order by, 11. 104n
Marie-Antoinette investigated by, and its successors, 34. 176
massacres encouraged by, in Paris, 31. 343
may be forgotten in year, 34. 117
members of: receive 18 livres a day, 11. 277, 34. 109, 117, 119, 120; serve beyond time for which they were elected, 34. 119; stipends of, self-bestowed, 15. 207–8; vain and insolent, 34. 173
mentioned, 11. 131, 206, 210, 222, 259, 296, 320, 325, 332, 12. 86
might have provided good government, 34. 111
money issued by, to provinces, 11. 175
'most august Senate of the world,' 34. 178
Necker appears in, 11. 45n
negroes excluded by, from rights of men, 11. 252
new Legislative Assembly succeeds, 39. 485–6
Noailles a hot-head of, 34. 154
oriflamme hung in, 11. 100n
Orléans, Duc d', member of, 11. 99n
—— speaks in, 11. 92n
—— writes to, 11. 85n
Papal property and citizens mistreated by, 34. 120
pedants in, to be succeeded by cobblers and tinkers, 34. 124
Pitt Diamond ordered by, to be sold, 12. 4n
Polish Diet contrasted with, 34. 157
president of, *see* Bonnay, Charles-François
Price's toast to, 11. 135
Priestley proud to be member of, 31. 386
procès-verbal of, records revival of oppression, 34. 162
puerility of, 34. 162

resolution read in, 11. 89n
salaries and armies voted by, 35. 400
seat of Président of, 11. 98n
should not hear of English injustice in Colomb case, 42. 295, 297
size of, reduced in recent vote, 31. 332
Stanhope's speech on, 11. 150
successor to, 34. 114
too weak to form good government, 34. 111
veins of countrymen opened by, 15. 237
violence of, 11. 239
Windham attends, 34. 65n
National Convention, French:
Allier commissioners announce anti-religious measures to, 12. 56n
atheism decreed by, 12. 56, 120
atheism tolerated by, 31. 377
Christianity abolished by, 12. 120n
Condorcet's constitution rejected by, 31. 384–5
decree of, 12. 43n
Fructidor Constitution to perpetuate two-thirds of, 12. 170
HW calls: 'assembly of fiends,' 31. 391; 'Convention of Liars,' 12. 53; 'Pandæmonium,' 12. 23, 71, 86, 120; 'repaire of two-legged hyenas,' 12. 22
HW doubts truth of reports of, 12. 7–8, 66
HW hopes for end of, 12. 37
impudent attempt of, to perpetuate themselves, 15. 269
Jacobins' hostility to, 12. 126, 132
letters to, reported in newspaper, 12. 26
lies told by, 34. 183
Louis XVI accused by, 35. 543–4
Lyon's evacuation announced by, 12. 41, 44
Marie-Antoinette persecuted by, 31. 391
members of, denounced by Hannah More, 31. 375, 388
mentioned, 12. 20, 27, 88, 117, 168
peace made by, with Spain, Portugal, Saxony, and Italy, 12. 148
Prussia, K. of, to be accused by, 12. 86, 90
signs of weakness of, 12. 132–3
Toulon fleet's capture announced by, 12. 8
turns against its own members, 12. 60, 71–2, 86–7
Vendée, La, defeat of royalists in, announced by, 12. 51, 53, 71
National debt. *See under* Debt
Natolia. *See* Anatolia
Natter, Johann Lorenz (1705–63), German medallist and gem-engraver:
catalogue of Stosch's maps printed by, in Holland, 21. 192
England visited by, 19. 243n
Giovanni Gastone de' Medici patron of, 19. 243n
intaglio by, on white cornelian, of Sir Robert Walpole, 16. 69, 40. 89n
medal and seals by, of Sir Robert Walpole, 16. 299
medal by, 19. 364n
Stosch's correspondence with, 19. 243

Walpole, Sir Edward, patronized, **16.** 299
Natural and Civil History of the County of Cork. See under Smith, Charles
Natural children:
HW's reflections on, **24.** 159
Natural history:
HW uninterested in, and wants Hamilton to drop it, **35.** 427
Natural History. See under Pliny the Elder
Natural History and Antiquities of Surrey. See under Aubrey, John
Natural History of Birds. See under Edwards, George
Natural History of Oxfordshire; Natural History of Staffordshire. See under Plot, Robert
Naturalization of the Jews. *See under* Jew; Jews
Natural religion:
Burgh is reproved by Oxford for not stressing, **28.** 199
Nature:
HW's reflections on, **16.** 271
state of, HW makes fun of, **11.** 140
Nature's Pictures Drawn by Fancie's Pencil. See under Lucas, Hon. Margaret, Ds of Newcastle
'Nature Will Prevail,' by HW:
acted at Haymarket, **13.** 50
answers of 'Echo' in, **41.** 243
Colman discovers authorship of, **41** 383n
—— produces, **16.** 253n
HW allows Colman to alter, **41.** 244
HW reserves rôle of 'Current' in, to Woodward, **41.** 243
HW sends, to Colman, **13.** 48, **41.** 242–3, 244, 383
performances of, **43.** 174
Nau, Pierre (d. before 1779):
(?) attends session of parliament of Paris, **8.** 173
Naumachias:
HW does not object to royalty playing at, **25.** 583
Roman, **37.** 297
Naunton, Henry (d. 1599):
stained-glass portrait of, at Letheringham, **35.** 248
Naunton, Mrs Henry. *See* Asheby, Elizabeth
Naunton, Sir Robert (1563–1635), Master of the Court of Wards:
Fragmenta regalia by, has anecdotes of Q. Elizabeth, **35.** 247n
German prince or artist gives bed to, **35.** 247
Letheringham built by, **35.** 247
Naunton, William (d. 1758):
HW grudgingly permitted by, to see house, **35.** 247
Naunton family:
tombs of, at Letheringham, **35.** 248
Nausea:
occurrences of, **10.** 55
Nautilus:
of paper, HW's frame compared with, **34.** 105
Naval stores:

English bounties for, **39.** 354n
Navan, Ireland:
Ponsonbys lose election in, **37.** 422–3
Navarre, Q. of. *See* Marguerite (1492–1549) d'Angoulême
Navarre, Collège de:
Drumgold, professor at, **40.** 302n
Navarro, Juan José (1687–1772), cr. (1744) Marqués de la Victoria; naval officer:
Mathews attacks, **18.** 413
ship of, **18.** 404
Spanish vessels at Toulon under command of, **18.** 371n
Naverete, Battle of:
Calveley and John of Gaunt serve under Chandos at, **41.** 445n
Navestock, Essex, E. Waldegrave's seat:
Chewtons to go to, **36.** 225
Damer visits, **36.** 239
Gloucester, Ds of, writes from, **36.** 329
HW describes, **9.** 243–4
(?) HW to send Walpole portraits to, **9.** 244
HW to visit Waldegraves at, **38.** 74
HW visits, **9.** 243–4
HW wishes that Cts Waldegrave would return to, **43.** 388
Micklethwait, Lady Maria Wilhelmina, dies at, **12.** 50n
news reported from, **33.** 211
Waldegrave, Cts, to rent out, **36.** 273
—— visits, **33.** 495
—— writes from, **36.** 229, 239, 283, 285, 287, 289
Waldegrave, John, buys furniture-pictures at, **10.** 108
Waldegrave, 4th E., writes from, **36.** 233, 247
Waldegraves invite HW to, **36.** 234
Waldegraves spend honeymoon at, **9.** 235
Navette:
Du Deffand, Mme, begins, **7.** 430
Navigation:
improved in Europe, **25.** 141
Raynal discusses, **39.** 168
Naviglio, The (Italy):
Lobkowitz stationed near, **19.** 30
Navy:
Genoa lacks, **37.** 319
Navy, English:
Anson builds up, **20.** 483
commissioner of, Cooper is, **18.** 64n
distant town ineffectually besieged by, instead of aiding home defence, **30.** 96
Dutch prizes taken by, repaid through wreck of Indiaman, **25.** 134
French navy compared with, **21.** 101
French surprised by strength and spirit of, **20.** 483
half-pay bill for, defeated, **32.** 99
half-pay captains of, seek pay increase, **23.** 462
Holmes protests against appointing inexperienced officers in, **37.** 580
House of Commons approves of conduct of, **29.** 180

[Navy, English, *continued*]
—— considers bill to reduce sailors in, **38.** 496
—— should resist corruption in, **26.** 15
impressment exemptions from, **39.** 290–1
impressment for, to overawe France, **39.** 288–9
investigation into: occupies Parliament, **19.** 12, 25, 32–4, 47; proposed in Parliament, **18.** 399, 427
lacking force in England, **37.** 163
Mathews dismissed from, **19.** 321n
Mediterranean fleet of, reported captured by French, **12.** 104
never so formidable, **23.** 156
officer of, known by Charles Emmanuel III to be disloyal, **19.** 147, 150
officers' conduct in, greatly criticized, **21.** 69
officers' court martial in, **19.** 33
officers of, praise Conway, **37.** 517
Pelham proposes reduction of, **20.** 223
Pitt's demand for increase of, defeated by House of Commons, **19.** 168–9
press warrants issued for, **24.** 252
promotion system in, **18.** 507, 509
(?) respited criminal to serve on board of, **38.** 15
Sandwich would give captured property to, **36.** 199n
scurvy might be prevalent in, **38.** 37
shipping embargo to raise sailors for, **37.** 446
strengthened, **24.** 252–3
strength of, at Plymouth, Portsmouth, and Thames estuary, **23.** 40
swinging is the exercise of, **18.** 558
threatened with destruction, **28.** 416
treasurer of: Barré becomes, **25.** 264n; Bubb Dodington regains and loses, **30.** 145n; Bubb Dodington removed as, **21.** 18; Bubb Dodington resigns as, **20.** 39, 54–5; **30.** 319; Bubb Dodington succeeds Grenville as, **20.** 517; Bubb Dodington succeeds Rushout as, **30.** 292n; Bubb Dodington tells Halifax he is to be, **21.** 74n; Bubb Dodington to be, **35.** 263; Clutterbuck becomes, **17.** 391, **30.** 293n; Dundas is, **41.** 321n; Ellis is, **25.** 241n, **32.** 354n; Fox, Henry, covets, **30.** 319; Grenville dismissed as, **20.** 512, 517; Grenville succeeds Bubb Dodington as, **21.** 25, 346n; Grenville to remain as, **21.** 541n; Hardwicke wants Anson to be, **21.** 93; Howe becomes, **22.** 443; Howe will be disgusted by loss of post as, **24.** 309; Legge is, **20.** 39, 417n; Lyttelton covets, **20.** 39; Lyttelton may be, **9.** 72, 159; Newcastle seeks, for protégé, **30.** 196; Onslow resigns as, **17.** 391, **30.** 292n; Rushout to be, **18.** 350, 356; Townshend, Hon. Charles, becomes, **25.** 392; Walpole, Sir Robert, becomes, **22.** 26
unfair promotions in, lead to Admiralty resignations, **39.** 462n
veterans of, Dalrymple's plan to aid, **38.** 205
wind-storm causes damage to, **12.** 179
See also England: fleet of; England: ships of; War

Navy, French. *See* France: navy of
Navy, Papal:
Parker, captain in, **17.** 81n
Navy Bill. *See under* Parliament: acts of
Navy Board. *See* Admiralty
Nawab of Bengal. *See* Mīr Ja'far 'Alī Khān (1691–1765); Mīr Qāsim 'Alī Khān (d. 1777); Najam-ud-Dowla (ca 1747–66)
Naworth Castle:
Pennant to see, by Carlisle's permission, but library is scanty, **41.** 250
Nay, —— de, m. (? 1731) François-Hyacinthe, Comte de la Tour en Voivre de Savonnières:
arrived from Lorraine, **20.** *451*
biographical information about, corrected, **43.** 272
father carries, to Grand Ducal palaces, **20.** 451
(?) father has, in house, **20.** 476
husband of, injured in coach accident, **21.** 442
(?) Mann entertains, at dinner with Cts of Orford, **20.** 480
(?) Orford, Cts of, gives jewels to, **20.** 499, 505, **25.** 144
Nay, Charles de (d. 1789), called Comte de Richecourt:
Constantinople visited by, **20.** 255
death date of, **43.** 266
England visited by, **20.** *90*
father talks with, about Cts of Orford's marriage, **20.** 255
Orford, Cts of, brings up, 'by hand,' **20.** 90
Nay, Charles-Ignace de:
barony conferred on, when member of parliament of Nancy, **20.** 197n
Nay, Emmanuel-François-Joseph-Ignace de (1694–1759), Comte de Richecourt; Marchese di Treschietto:
abbé-secretary of, *see* Niccoli
académie de belles-lettres given for, for Margravine of Bayreuth, **20.** 476–8
Aigle, Comte d', pseudonym of, **17.** 195
Albani does not trust, **19.** 2
—— sends compliments to, **18.** 491
Alberti chosen by, for Tuscan Council, **20.** 220
Algerine-Tuscan treaty negotiated by, **20.** 472
allowance of, increased, **20.** 392
ancestry of, ignoble, **20.** 197, **25.** 130
apartment of, in Palazzo Vecchio, **17.** 224, 283, **19.** 97, 101, 385
appearance of, neither young nor handsome, **25.** 130
appointments of, increased to equal Craon's, **20.** 392n
Archinto entertained by, with story of Wachtendonck and Ps Triulzi, **17.** 489–90
—— often sees, at Florence and Leghorn, **17.** 490
assemblies of, every Thursday night at the Imperialino, **20.** 446
audiences discontinued by, **20.** 192
Austrian successes may make, impertinent, **17.** 477

authority of: confirmed, **20.** 146; greatly increased by presidency of all councils, **20.** 392, 395; re-established, **20.** 355; triumphant, **18.** 122, **20.** 210; unchallenged, **20.** 77
Baden baths may be visited by, **17.** 95
Bagard hoped to supplant, **17.** 368, 406
ball given by, **20.** 432
Bartolommeo accused by, to Francis I, of Spanish leanings, **17.** 406
Bayreuth, Margrave and Margravine of, entertained by, **20.** 476–9
Benedict XIV's prayer to Virgin for, **21.** 6on
Betange the enemy of, **17.** (?) 368, 490
Biglia entertained by, **20.** 446
Borgherini, Mme, told by, about husband's fate, **19.** 473
Botta compared with, **21.** 178
——'s appointment would displease, **19.** 23
Braitwitz attributes orders to, **18.** 120
—— avoids council meeting to escape affronts from, **18.** 66
—— consulted by, about storing jewels, **18.** 285
—— enemy of, **17.** 406, 490
—— to be supplied by, with money, **18.** 66
brother of, **17.** 107, **20.** 9on
brother's correspondence with, **20.** 270, 271n, 277
brother's death afflicts, **20.** 335
Careggi and Imperialino used by, **20.** 116
Careggi the villa of, **19.** 97
—— visited by, for health, **19.** 402
Charles, P., may supplant, **18.** 310
coach of, often waits at Mrs Richmond's door, **19.** 97, 101
Cocchi abandons, **18.** 133
—— conveys Mann's apologies to, **17.** 394
—— might have had ennoblement through, **20.** 204
—— ordered to insert praises of, in book on Pisa baths, **20.** 158
—— receives offer of hospital post through, **17.** 57
——'s defence of HW might offend, **17.** 448
——'s loyalty to Mann offends, **18.** 133
commissary-general 's post coveted by, **20.** 295, 320
Conway and Mann call on, **20.** 295
Corsi christening attended by, **20.** 432
Councils of Finance and War headed by, **20.** 392
courier robbed by Spaniards of money from, **18.** 516
courier sent by, to Vienna, **17.** 314
Craon and Regency asked by, to disavow his enmity to Ginori, **18.** 216
Craon converted by, in Regency Council discussion, **20.** 14
—— discusses, with Mann, **17.** 326
—— employs, despite wife's warning, **20.** 220
—— may be succeeded by, **20.** 29
—— ordered to collaborate with, **17.** 407, 490

—— refuses request of, for certificate about Ginori, **18.** 216
——'s departure opposed by, for fear of getting Stampa, **20.** 24
——'s enemy, **17.** 327, 407
—— superseded by, **21.** 178n
—— to give news of Campo Santo to, **18.** 165
Craon, Princesse de, calls, 'cet homme-la,' **20.** 197
—— may yet triumph over, **20.** 326
—— not yet permitted by, to resume faro, **19.** 501
Craons mortified by, **17.** 189n
customs precedent avoided by, **20.** 537n
daughter lives with, **20.** 476
daughter of, **20.** 499, **21.** 442
daughter of, receives jewels from Cts of Orford, **20.** 499, 505, **25.** 144
daughter's death not yet told to, **21.** 42
daughter taken by, to all the Grand Duke's houses, **20.** 451
departure of, expected, **19.** 48
dinner given by: on Francis I's birthday, **20.** 295, **21.** 9; on Maria Theresa's birthday, **21.** 9
does not retire, despite ill health, **21.** 21
Dumesnil, Alexandre, exchanges couriers with, **17.** 236
—— friend of, **17.** 225, 490
Dumesnil, Joseph, disregards advice of, **19.** 491
economy the object of ministry of, **20.** 472
edict against export of antiquities probably made by, to get Stosch's collection, **20.** 465
Electress blames, for bad relations with Vienna, **20.** 268
—— called on by, **18.** 10–12
——'s estate estimated by, **18.** 176
——'s treatment by, **17.** 225
Eleonora said to be with, **17.** 120
enemies of, dispersed, **17.** 406
England openly hated by, **20.** 581
English at Leghorn claimed by, to be Francis I's subjects, **20.** 266, 275–6
English earthquake known to, **20.** 143
English excluded from dinners of, on holidays, **21.** 9
English fleet enrages, **18.** 325, 328–9
English 'piracies' will be criticized by, to Mann, **20.** 494
English relations with Tuscany may be guided by, through Chesterfield, **17.** 387
English superiority to French fleets denied by, **20.** 472
entertainments forbidden by, **20.** 146
epigrams on, **20.** 268, 272
exposure of, threatened, **17.** 223
Ferreri's case opposed by, in Regency council, **18.** 10, 31
fief obtained by, **19.** 385, 394
finance council's head, **17.** 7n
Florence dull enough to give no pleasure to, **20.** 401

[Nay, Emmanuel de, *continued*]
—— expects, 19. 394
—— left by: 17. 95, 97, 116; secretly, 21. 80–1
Florentine 'chief minister,' 17. 409n
Florentine children call, 'Pilate,' 21. 85
Florentine clocks put on French time by order of, 20. 26
Florentine correspondence of, 17. 120
Florentine money collected by, for deposit at Leghorn, 17. 427–8
Florentines believe that Francis I's order for carnival was countermanded by, 19. 8
Florentines disciplined by, about masks and operas, 19. 8, 14, 20. 216, 219
—— fear return of, 19. 354
Florentine's remark on 'eternal' ministry of, 20. 268
Florentines resent rule of, 18. 352, 19. 8, 20. 77
Florentines terrified of, 18. 145
Florentines to blame for their subservience to, 21. 148
Fogliani tells, to accept Viviani as minister, 20. 350–1
Francis I approves of conduct of, in the case of Leghorn suicide, 20. 14
—— grants fief and title to, 19. 385, 394
—— grants permission to, to visit Vienna when he pleases, 20. 392
—— ignores accusations against, 20. 335
—— impersonated by, at Corsi christening, 20. 432
—— influenced by, against Lucca, 20. 521–2
—— may make, minister to Ratisbon, 19. 49
—— might be persuaded by, to ask Carteret to oust Mann, 18. 362–3
—— orders, to discontinue work on San Lorenzo chapel, 18. 172n
—— receives courier from, 17. 235
—— receives excuses from, 20. 162
—— reinstates, 17. 236n
——'s accountings with, 18. 201
—— said by, to need his aid to become Emperor, 19. 7
——'s favourite minister favours, 17. 189n
——'s plans withheld by, from Mann, 18. 3
——'s prime minister at Florence, 20. 586n, 25. 122n
——'s representative at Electress's death, 18. 171
—— temporarily disgraces, 17. 490
—— to be prejudiced by, against Regency, 17. 282
Frederick II is Mann's retort to insults of, 21. 1–2
French naval superiority over England asserted by, 20. 472
French tax-farmers turned away by, 20. 327
friend of, sees Craon's letters to Francis I, 17. 327
Gages's advance alarms, 19. 11, 40
Gavi friend of, 17. 217, 490
——'s thefts may involve, 17. 217, 224, 239

—— to prepare lodgings for, 18. 309
'gentleman of the old palace,' 20. 465
George II receives complaints from, via Vienna, 18. 328
——'s aid to Maria Theresa disparaged by party of, 17. 371
——'s orders interpreted by, 17. 288
Ginori made governor of Leghorn by, 19. 322
—— opposes, 19. 322–3, 20. 77, 463, 473, 21. 81
—— ordered by, to seize Englishman's effects, 20. 1
——'s funeral forbidden by, 21. 81
——'s plan for Leghorn suburb preferred to that of, 20. 217
——'s Spanish connections hinted by, to Francis I, 17. 395
——'s Vienna mission instigated by, 17. 395, 406, 490, 18. 122
goes into the country, 18. 309
gout thought by, to be cure for headache, 20. 79
Grand Prior of Perugia, 19. 394
HW admires Mann's treatment of, 18. 30–1, 20. 272, 21. 19
HW amazed at subservience of, to Rome, 20. 448
HW distrusts Cts of Orford's influence over, 18. 140
HW mentions, 17. 43
HW pities, in his misery, 21. 55
HW pities the Florentines for enduring, 19. 331
HW prefers, to Richmond as spy on Bns Walpole (Cts of Orford), 18. 31
HW said to have procured downfall of, 17. 97–8
HW's opinion of, 17. 25
HW wishes Mann good riddance of, 20. 342
HW wishes that Mann could triumph over, 21. 347
HW would like to insult, 19. 128
health of: apoplexy, 20. 444, 445; 'attacks,' 20. 476; fever, 19. 402; gout, 19. 402; letters boast of improvement in, 21. 85; stroke of 'palsy,' 21. 15, 21, 27, 29, 42–3; too ill to attend Regency council, 18. 66
hoards of, sought in Bns Walpole's cases, 17. 224
Holy Week devotions of, 19. 31
house of, near Cts of Orford's, 20. 480
house to be taken by, in Padua, 17. 217, 235
Imperialino rented by, 20. 446n
—— used by, 20. 116, 446
insincere, 20. 68
Juvrecourt, Comtesse de, friendly with, 19. 452, 457
Karl Friedrich of Baden-Durlach entertained by, 20. 148
law made by, requiring export licence for art objects, 20. 465, 21. 208

leave of absence probably granted to, when not desired, 17. 134

Lee's correspondence with, about pilots, 17. 455–6

Leghorn visited by, to christen ships, 20. 162

letters opened by, at Florentine post office, 19. 362

levee of, shunned by English colony, 21. 9

Lorenzi disputes with, over citizenship of French at Leghorn, 20. 266–7

—— hears consolatory remarks from, on child's death, 20. 306

—— shows Maillebois's letter to, 19. 89

—— warns Mann against, 18. 362

Lorraine, Primate of, believes, to be banished, 17. 125n

—— steps on toes of, to stop story, 17. 460

Lorraine faction no longer protected by, 21. 125

Lorraine may not be reached by, alive, 21. 85

'Lorraine and chief minister at Florence,' 17. 409n

Lorrainer and Francis I's prime minister at Florence, 25. 122n

Lorraine's recovery expected by, to bring invasion of Tuscany, 18. 285

Lorraine the destination of, 21. 62, 80

'low Lorrainer,' 17. 189n

Lucca persecuted by, 20. 521

—— visited by, 17. 468

Mann complains to, about sbirri, 18. 467

—— consults, about defence of Tuscany by English fleet, 18. 27

—— dines with, 19. 450–1

—— disputes with, over privileges, 20. 146

—— exchanges calls with, 18. 132–3, 364, 19. 80, 20. 68, 295

—— exchanges entertainments with, 19. 501, 20. 273, 446, 476–9

—— explains English affairs to, 18. 4–5, 10–11

—— forces, to submit in dispute over Leghorn factory, 20. 522

—— forgets that HW knew, 25. 140

—— forwards letter to, for Cts of Orford, 19. 51

—— frightens, with story of Zenón's application for passport, 18. 253

—— happy to be rid of, 19. 369

—— hears discussion by, of Hanover-Hessian quarrel and Cts of Orford's letter, 19. 80

—— hears Don Philip's plans from, 17. 323

—— invited by, to dinner, 17. 41

—— loses favour of, by hostility of Cts of Orford, 19. 452

—— misrepresented by, to Francis I, 18. 67

—— mistakenly occupies theatre box of, 17. 394

—— need not fear malice of, 18. 384

—— never discusses the Leghorn suicide with, 20. 14

—— not invited to public dinner of, 20. 295

—— now treated politely by, 18. 67

—— overwhelmed by folly of, 18. 342

—— presents foreign visitors to, 20. 327

—— receives visit of condolence from, on Sir Robert Walpole's death, 19. 37

—— represented by, as hostile to Maria Theresa, 18. 476

—— resorts to snuff to appear nonchalant before, 20. 392

——'s complaints about, to England, 20. 310, 313

——'s correspondence with, 20. 2, 14

——'s curt call, unaccompanied by English visitors, disconcerts, 21. 9

—— sees, but without discussing Cts of Orford, 19. 54

——'s family belittled by, 20. 64n

——'s letters patent submitted to, 17. 7n

——'s memorial to, about citizenship of English at Leghorn, 20. 275–6

——'s Pisa visit ingratiates himself with, 19. 487, 20. 84

——'s privileges disregarded by, 20. 205

——'s quarrel with, over citizenship of English at Leghorn, 20. 266, 275–6

—— supposed by, to be ignorant of ships' prizes, 19. 441

—— talks with, about Cts of Orford's affairs, 19. 50

—— tells, to urge Cts of Orford to sign papers, 18. 487

—— thanked by, for copy of speech, 17. 38–9

—— to be ousted by, 18. 381

—— to denounce 'Onslow' to, 19. 506

—— to give compliments to, on Joseph II's birthday, 20. 129

—— told by: about Leopold of Lorraine's piles, 17. 60; (?) that Frederick II must be punished, 20. 589; that gout will cure pain in breast, 20. 335; that he will be shifted to Genoa, 20. 270, 271n 273, 280, 354

—— translates parts of Ædes Walpolianæ to, 20. 68

Marchese di Treschietto, 19. 385, 394

Maria Theresa's insolence reflected by, 20. 586

——'s treatment from Sir Robert Walpole condemned by, 17. 367

—— tells, in Vienna, that religious devotion is necessary for promotion, 20. 421

Maricone encloses letter to, 17. 309

Mathews disputes with, 18. 309, 328

Mill involves, in his affairs, 19. 427

mob feared by, 21. 80–1

Modena said to be visited by, 17. 195

Modenese news unknown to, 17. 432

Moncour in Lorraine bought by, 21. 62n

money disbursed by, for military camp at San Martino, 18. 76

money-raising occupies, 18. 222

money wanted by, to take to Vienna, 20. 488

Mozzi said to be less creditable than, 25. 122, 130

mules procured by, 19. 11

[Nay, Emmanuel de, *continued*]

mural crown should be flaunted before, by Mann, **21.** 347

Niccoli, Abbé, bribes, to continue salary after dismissal, on orders from Vienna, **20.** 335

—— undersecretary to, **17.** 107, 224, **19.** 42, 49

Niccolini entertained by, **20.** 217

——'s banishment perhaps arranged by, **20.** 2, 7–8, 117

——'s friendship with Frederick, P. of Wales, offends, **19.** 441

——'s relations with, **20.** 77, 146

Nivernais's moving into Palazzo Madama displeases, **20.** 264n

old ladies excluded from party by, **20.** 148

Old Pretender's resignation of pretensions reported by, **17.** 19n

opera box of, Mann changes to, **17.** 240, **18.** 128–9

Orford, Cts of (Bns Walpole), aided by, in journey, **19.** 54

—— appears only at house of, **18.** 122

—— attends, with ptisan, **18.** 67

—— awaited by, to marry him, **20.** 268

—— corresponds with, **19.** 64, 80, 97, **20.** 143

—— encouraged by, to visit England, **17.** 426

—— encouraged by success of, **18.** 122

—— entertains, on Thursdays, **18.** 4

—— given servant by, **19.** 50

—— goes to *festine* to meet, **18.** 439

—— great admirer of, **17.** 360, 367, 409n

—— impelled by departure of, to leave Florence, **17.** 107

—— incites, to oust Mann, **18.** 362–3

—— incites misbehaviour of, **20.** 313

—— influences, against England, **18.** 329

—— intends to visit villa of, **17.** 34n

—— lent money by, **17.** 461

—— lost by, **20.** 272

—— may be followed by, to Venice, **19.** 47

—— may have been entrusted by, with Hanoverian negotiation, **19.** 70

—— may have courted Toussaint through, **18.** 210

—— may receive chariot from, **17.** 53–4

—— may tempt, by her wealth, **20.** 439

—— might be encouraged by, to seek bank credit, **17.** 422

—— more highly regarded by, after gift of jewels, **20.** 505

—— not to accompany, to country, **18.** 314

—— not to be relied upon by, **17.** 409

—— not to follow, to Vienna, **17.** 89, 95

—— not to marry, **20.** 239

—— persuaded by, to sign papers, **18.** 487

—— prejudices, against Mann, **19.** 452

—— prepares lodgings for, **18.** 309

—— probably foresaw departure of, **19.** 49

—— repulsed by, at Imperialino, **17.** 34, 45, 53

—— said to be provided by, with apartments in his country house, **19.** 80

—— soothes fears of, **18.** 520

——'s quarrels avenged by, **18.** 10

—— subject of jokes by, **20.** 444

—— supposed to have had two daughters by, **25.** 122, 130

—— to have access to, by door into palace corridor, **18.** 391

—— to join, at Verona, for return to Florence, **17.** 107

—— told not to interrupt Holy Week devotions of, **19.** 31

—— travels to Padua with, **17.** 419n

—— unlikely to trouble, **20.** 480

—— visits, **18.** 364

—— will await return of, from Vienna, **19.** 144

—— will not please, by her return, **20.** 476

—— would not have left, had he shown more prowess, **20.** 395

Orford, 2d E. of, wants proof of his wife's intrigue with, **19.** 200

Padua visited by, **17.** 217, 224, 235, 419n, **18.** 216

papal court opposed to, **20.** 334

paper by English at Leghorn ridiculed by, to Mann, **20.** 267

Pecci, Cavaliere, ordered by, to examine Tuscan finances, **20.** 327n

Petraia visited by, **20.** 15

pies of fat or meat forbidden by, in theatre, **20.** 219

Pisa baths patronized by, **19.** 487

—— baths visited by, **20.** 162, 252, 480

Plombières baths to be visited by, in litter, **21.** 62

prayer for, to Virgin: Mann sends, to HW, **21.** 60, 79; suppressed, **21.** 60

priest's epigram on, **20.** 268, 272

reasons given for departure of, from Florence, **17.** 97–8

recovers from Cts of Orford's influence, **20.** 68

Regency council blamed by, for publishing Mann's assurances from George II, **17.** 282

Regency council influenced by, against Mann, **20.** 205

Regency council neglected since departure of, **21.** 112

Regency council overborne by, **18.** 328

Regency council's president, **20.** 392

Regency council's writings against, during his Padua visit to be disavowed, **18.** 216

return of, to Florence: **17.** 235–6, 264, 468, **19.** 394, 402, **20.** 392; may re-establish him, **19.** 219; threatened, **17.** 120

Richmond, Mrs, advised by, to quit house, **19.** 238

—— may be kept by, in old palace, **19.** 101

—— not evicted from her house for fear of offending, **19.** 192

—— often called on by, **19.** 80, 97, 101

—— supplies place of Cts of Orford in coach of, **19.** 75, 101

—— suspected of writing to, **19.** 290

—— visits, at Careggi, **19**. 97, 101

Ridolfi disliked by, **18**. 139

Rinuccini ascribes disgrace of, to Sir Robert Walpole, **17**. 108

(?) ——'s attestations against, **17**. 490

Rucellai fears to offend, **18**. 133

St John's Day to have been made festive by, **18**. 462

St-Odile the antagonist of, **20**. 305, 308

Santi Apostoli preferred by, to St James's, **19**. 441

Sardinian treaty pressed by, **19**. 6

Sassi approaches Frederick Augustus II through, **17**. 149

Savoy, D. of, may be preceded by, **20**. 295

secretary of, *see* Niccoli

seditious billets annoy, **20**. 252

Seymour complimented by, on Sandwich's alleged appointments, **20**. 217

Shirley may cause Cts of Orford to forget, **19**. 385

'simplicity' of, **17**. 24–5

son-in-law follows, to Lorraine, **21**. 80

son of, **20**. 90

son talks with, of Cts of Orford's remarriage, **20**. 255

Sortes Virgilianæ for, **17**. 108

Spanish consul's complaints belittled by, **18**. 542

Spanish depredations at Florence feared by, **18**. 295

Stainville may succeed P. of Craon despite efforts of, to remove him, **20**. 45n

——'s appointment feared by, **20**. 45, 84, 162, 192, 197

Stampa disputes with, over chairs and stools, **20**. 320

—— may be succeeded by, as commissary for Italy, **20**. 295, 320

——'s arrival dreaded by, **20**. 24

Stosch's collection may be incorporated by edict of, **20**. 465, 475

Suares, Bp, persecuted by, **18**. 40

—— suspects that his niece is to be married to, **18**. 40

subordinates of, servile to him though enjoying rebuffs to him from Vienna, **20**. 284

Switzerland said to be visited by, **17**. 125, 134

tax farmers upheld by, **19**. 23

Tesi reveals amours of, **17**. 45

—— scolded by Juvrecourt for applying to, **18**. 368–9

Theodore of Corsica aided by, in writing edict, **18**. 51n

Tornaquinci abuses, to Mann, **20**. 267

——'s letter (about English merchants) dictated by, **20**. 267n

—— submits to, **20**. 146

Toussaint may get application from, **18**. 363

—— reconciles, with Francis I, **17**. 490

——'s arrival a surprise to, **20**. 97

——'s creature, **17**. 189n, 490n

treasures of, stored at Venice despite his talk of neutrality, **18**. 513

Turin said to be visited by, **17**. 195

Tuscan discontent muzzled by, **20**. 77

Tuscan disloyalty attributed to dislike of, **19**. 11

Tuscan finances administered by, **19**. 394n

Tuscan government may be taken away from, **18**. 309–10

Tuscan money carried away by, **19**. 115, **20**. 488

Tuscan neutrality may be endangered by Spaniards' interception of letters of, **18**. 516

Tuscan neutrality proclaimed by, **18**. 513

Tuscany kept by, from being ruled by Ps Charlotte, **20**. 355

Uguccioni hopes for preferment through, **18**. 455, **35**. 53

Vaughan would have been sentenced by, for similar insult, **20**. 144

Venice visited by, incognito, **17**. 195

'viceroy of Jerusalem,' **17**. 97, 120

Vienna intrigues of, **19**. 322

—— trip denied to, **20**. 252

—— visited by, **19**. 192, **20**. 327, 334, 335, 421, 488, **21**. 80

Viennese influence of, said to decline, **19**. 219, **20**. 463

Viennese summons to, **17**. 89, 95

villa of, *see* Careggi

Wachtendonck may have procured disgrace of, **17**. 106, 107, 490

—— said to have frightened, from Florence by challenging him to a duel, **17**. 467–8

——'s cousin disgraces, with Francis I, **17**. 490

Walpole, Sir Robert, subject of insulting remarks by, **17**. 406, **18**. 4

Walpole family disparaged by, **17**. 387, 393–4, 406

Wasner instigated by, to plead for Bns Walpole, **18**. 194

witticism about, as 'father of the poor,' **21**. 81

witticisms against, would be punished, **20**. 144

Young Pretender's arrest displeases, **20**. 15, 22

——'s landing in Scotland announced to, **19**. 86, 89

Nay, Louis (*or* Henri)-Hyacinthe de (d. 1752), Comte de Richecourt; Austrian and Tuscan diplomatist:

Berlin visited by, on mission, **18**. *107*

brother probably hears of English earthquake through, **20**. 143

brother told by, that Mann will be shifted to Genoa, **20**. 270, 271n, 277

death of, **20**. 335

England visited by, **20**. 90, 270

English ministers confer with, about Mann and probably about Corsica, **20**. 275, 277

health of, gout, **20**. 335

itinerary of, to England, **20**. 45

[Nay, Louis de, *continued*]
  Maria Theresa's picture carried by, to Lord Hyndford, 18. 107
  marriage of, 20. 45
  minister to England, 20. 271n
  Newcastle negotiates with, at Hanover over Joseph II's election, 20. 178n
  of Turin, 20. 45
  Sherbatov's house in St James's St taken by, 20. 90n

Nay, Louise-Charlotte de (1729–57), m. Conte Francesco di Thurn:
  biographical information about, corrected, 43. 272
  death of, from smallpox after miscarriage, 21. 42–3
  (?) father has, in house, 20. 476
  (?) Mann entertains, at dinner with Cts of Orford, 20. 480
  (?) Orford, Cts of, gives jewels to, 20. 499, 505, 25. 144

Naylor, Bethaia:
  heiress to Hurstmonceaux estate, 18. 62n

Naylor, Francis. *See* Hare Naylor, Francis

Naylor, Mrs Francis. *See* Alston, Carlotta

Naylor, John (1709–61), D.D., 1749; fellow of King's College, Cambridge 1730–47:
  (?) Anstey conveys letter through, 40. 24
  Ashton to send resignation to, at Eton, 40. 40
  Pelham advised by, about Paxton's elimination from King's College competition, 40. 39–40

Nazareth:
  Glasgow compared with, 36. 177
  royal household compared with, 36. 198
  truth coming out of, 32. 179

Neal, Daniel (1678–1743), historian:
  History of the Puritans by, 2. 93, 360

Neale, Mrs Elizabeth. *See* Munro, Elizabeth

Neale, Maria (fl. 1578–1631), m. Everard Digby:
  portrait of, 1. 27n, 10. 333, 43. 45

Neale, James, Fordyce, and Down, bankers in Threadneedle St:
  bank of, fails, 23. 418n
  bankruptcy of, 39. 156n

Neath Abbey, Glamorgan:
  Hoby of, 9. 134n, 41. 117n

Néaulme, ——, Berlin bookseller:
  Frederick II orders, to publish Villiers's *Recueil de quelques lettres* at The Hague, 20. 17n

Neaulme, John, publisher:
  Rymer's *Fœdera* published by, 37. 422n

Neave, Sir Richard (1731–1814), Bt; F.S.A.; F.R.S.:
  HW not acquainted with, 15. 268

Nebuchadnezzar (d. 562 B.C.), K. of Babylon ? 604–562 B.C.:
  George III as, comes to himself, 34. 42
  would enjoy opulence in England, 25. 321

'Nebuchadnezzar':
  character in Pinkerton's play, 16. 253

Necessary woman:
  HW proposes his housekeeper as, 33. 394
  See also under Servant

Neckar, river:
  Broglie reaches, 37. 140
  Charles's army on, 18. 267

Neckcloth; neckcloths:
  plaited and starched, old-fashioned, 35. 124
  Sandys's, 30. 288, 302

Necker, Anne-Louise-Germaine (1766–1817), m. (1786) Eric Magnus, Baron de Staël-Holstein:
  Berry, Mary, admired by, 11. 346n
  husband of, 11. 45n
  parents of, 5. 388n
  return of, to Paris, 11. *346*
  social relations of, with: Mme du Deffand, 7. 430; Voltaire, 7. 36

Necker, Jacques (1732–1804), Swiss banker; French director-general of finances 1777–81, 1788–90:
  ambition of, 11. 209 ,346
  appointment of: as comptroller of finances, 24. 254–5; as director-general of finances, 2. 84, 6. 455
  Assembly of Notables presented by, with controversial questions, 34. 32
  Basle visited by, 11. 45
  Bertin's departments given to, 7. 453
  Broglie threatens, 11. 27
  Burke describes administration of, 7. 216
  Calonne's *Réponse* to, 36. 249n
  controller-general's work given to, 6. 369, 370, 454
  denounced for advancing money to La Fayette, 34. 96
  difficulties of, 7. 221
  dismissed, 11. 36, 39n, 39. 467, 43. 140
  dismissed and reinstated, 34. 50
  Du Deffand, Mme, receives anonymous reply to libel against, 7. 457
  ——'s acquaintance desired by, 5. 388
  ——'s correspondence with, 6. 318, 7. 445, 452, 457, 8. 213–14
  —— sends MS to, 7. 457
  —— sends messages to, 6. 316
  ——'s opinion of, 6. 49, 75, 191, 309–10, 318, 327, 343, 372
  ——'s pension payments to be facilitated by, 6. 372
  ——'s relations with, 6. 370, 391
  —— to receive news of HW from, 6. 307
  —— to receive tea through, 6. 302
  —— to send letter by, 6. 297, 299, 304
  —— to send parcels by, 6. 292, 294, 295, 302, 303
  Éloge de M. Colbert by, 5. 395, 396, 400, 405–7, 409
  England to be visited by, 6. 284, 292, 296, 302
  English war will be averted by, 34. 19
  États généraux called at instance of, 34. 56
  fall of, expected to benefit England, 25. 159

financial plan of, violated, **11**. 26

financial policy of, obstructs war efforts, **39**. 373

financier and politician, but no Richelieu, **34**. 32

Fontainebleau to be visited by, **6**. 372

former Genevan, **24**. 254

Garrick to be seen by, **6**. 292

Geneva said to be destination of, **11**. 36

Gibbon's friendship with, **6**. 436

'great air-balloon,' **34**. 73

Guines's acquittal pleases, **8**. 214

——'s letter to be shown to, **6**. 313, 314

HW dislikes mouthings of, **39**. 258–9

HW exchanges messages with, **6**. 293, 337

HW sends letter by, **6**. 320

HW's opinion of, **6**. 318, 327, **11**. 45, 209

HW visited by, **6**. 307, 309

Historical Review of the Administration of Mr Necker supposedly by, **11**. 331n

insignificant on his return, **39**. 478

Kingston bigamy trial to be attended by, **6**. 292

La Harpe's *Menzikoff* to be given at house of, **6**. 167, 169

Le Texier not esteemed by, **6**. 378

Louis XVI dismisses, **39**. 467

——'s complaints from, about naval expenses, **25**. 159n

——'s permission to let Macartney serve in army given to Mme du Deffand by, **7**. 445

—— to work with, **6**. 369, 372

Macartney's exchange to be facilitated by, **7**. 210, 211

Marchais, Baronne de, at odds with, **6**. 217

Marie-Antoinette consults, about her debts, **33**. 77

Maurepas arranges nomination of, **24**. 255n

——'s support needed by, **6**. 459

—— to be solicited by, for Macartney, **7**. 210

Newmarket not to be visited by, **6**. 292

Paris visited by, **6**. 315, **11**. 48, 259

peace sought by, to prevent new taxes, **7**. 139

Polignac, Duchesse de, courted by, **34**. 67–8

politics may have corrupted the financial skill of, **39**. 468–9

print of, not understood by HW, **34**. 85

Protestant, **24**. 254, **25**. 21, **34**. 19, 56

Protestantism of, devalued by abolition of Catholicism, **39**. 478

Protestant, reformer, and of no birth, **25**. 159

reforms of, **7**. 240–2

regulations of, in 1776, **6**. 385, 386, 392

reinstated in financial post, **34**. 18–19

religion of, prevents his being controller-general, **6**. 454

Réponse au mémoire de . . . Morellet by, **5**. 400

resignation of: **39**. 373; stopped by mob, **11**. 26

retirement of, rumoured, **7**. 11, 16

Richmond contrasts Lord North with, **7**. 95

Roman Catholic Church opposed by, **25**. 21

St-Ouen home of: **5**. 388, **6**. 51, 191, 216, 318, **7**. 346, 348; guests at, *see* St-Ouen: visitors to

Sartine solicited by, for Macartney, **7**. 211

signing not to be done by, **6**. 457

social relations of, in Paris, *see index entries ante* **8**. 452

Stormont friend of, **6**. 192

—— may accompany, **6**. 288

—— receives book from, **6**. 183

SH described by, **8**. 213

SH praised by, **6**. 334

SH to be visited by, **6**. 292, 296

success of, **6**. 459, 471, **7**. 184, 191, 200–1

Sur la législation et le commerce des grains by, **6**. 183, 187, 189, 191, **43**. 98

Thomas influences style of, **5**. 400

to return to Paris, **6**. 238

Turgot's supposed letter to: Mme du Deffand reads, **7**. 450; Necker libelled by, **7**. 225, 227

Turpin recommended by, as lawyer, **36**. 177n

vanity of, **11**. 331, 346

Versailles visited by, **11**. 27

Walpole, Hon. Thomas, aided by, in business trouble, **36**. 177

—— corresponds with, **7**. 228, 229, 231

—— friend of, **7**. 184, 198, 200, 211, 221, 233, 240

Watelet's isle visited by, **7**. 346

Necker, Mme Jacques. *See* Curchod, Suzanne

Necker. *See also* Neckar

Necklace; necklaces:

Charlotte's, of diamonds, **21**. 529

diamond, Cowper gives, to wife, **24**. 232

Henrietta Maria's, on medal, **16**. 50

ladies to wear, for Court mourning, **32**. 101n

Mann distributes among Suares family, **17**. 484

pearl: **18**. 291, **41**. 108, 110; given by Clive to Q. Charlotte, **22**. 540n

Rohan alleged to be buying, for Marie-Antoinette, **25**. 639

Nécrologie des hommes célèbres de la France, Le:

Lort sends vol. of, to HW, **16**. 191

Nectarine; nectarines:

blooms in December, **20**. 16

Cole's, **2**. 113

England imports, from the south, **32**. 359

HW receives, from Mme de Marchais, **39**. 258

HW's, **2**. 111

Née, François-Denis (d. 1817):

Mme du Deffand's portrait engraved by, **8**. 215

Needham, 'Mother' Elizabeth (d. 1731), procuress:

Clement XIII might echo deathbed utterance of, **23**. 32

Hogarth caricatures, **15**. 142n

(?) Pomfret, Cts of, called 'sister' of, **17**. 132–3

Needham, Jane (1645–92), m. (1660) Charles Myddelton *or* Middleton; beauty: daughters of, 41. 241n

Lely's portrait of, in HW's collection: 16. 324, 30. 370; print from, 16. 324

Needham, Father John Turberville (1731–81), scientific writer; F.R.S.: counterpart of, may find that Hindostan was settled by Londoners, 23. 551

'Jesuit,' 23. 551

Needham, Marchamont (1620–78), journalist: Zouch tells HW about, 16. 5

Needham, Thomas (1703–68), 9th Vct Kilmorey: Florence visited by, 20. 271, 278

itinerary of, 43. 269

Nightingale family to separate from, 20. 278

wife mentions *gentil uomo* of, 20. 298

Needle; needles: HW jokes about Lady Ailesbury going through eye of, 39. 174

Pitt, Mrs, threads, by candlelight, 23. 456

Needlework: by Lady Ailesbury, 35. 395

by Mary, Q. of Scots, 42. 314–15

Grey, Lady Susanna, does, 9. 4–5

obsolete, in France, smelly, 35. 123

pictures in: 35. 270; at Burghley House, 10. 345

See also Embroidery; Worsted-work

Negri, Maria Anna Caterina (b. 1701), contralto: sings in *Atalanta*, 13. 102n

Negro; Negroes: 'Angola, P. of,' actually Irish merchant's exservant, 38. 405n

Barbauld, Mrs, sympathizes with, 31. 361

children of, like puppets in HW's indifference to them, 39. 296

children sold by, 32. 242

Codrington's will requires 300 of, always to be employed on his estates, 35. 178

comment by, on Pelew Islands, 34. 29

France wants to keep Senegal or Gorée to provide French West Indies with, 21. 526n

French cooks might be replaced by, as butchers, 24. 21

girl, escapes at Bristol, 31. 340, 350

Gordon rioter, hanged, 33. 214

HW distressed by sale of, 20. 126

HW jokes about treating Hannah More as, 31. 300

HW's sympathy for, 23. 452

Jews greater defaulters than, 31. 331–2

Montesquieu attacks sale of, into slavery, 20. 126

More, Hannah, sympathizes with, 31. 362, 372

mutiny of, in Brazil, 23. 452

persecutions of, 31. 331–2

Porto Bello governor attended by, 37. 54

Portuguese call, 'disaffected,' 23. 452, 462

previously termed barbarians and savages, 34. 177

rights of, denied by French National Assembly, 11. 252

Senegal traffic in, 7. 123

Usher's, suspected of starting fire, 22. 141

See also Gardiner, Charlotte; Moratt, Jeffrey; Sessaracoa, William Ansah; Somerset, James; *and under* Slave; Slavery

Negroni, Andrea (1710–89), cardinal, 1763: exclusion of, revoked by French, Neapolitan, and Spanish ministers, 23. 35–6

Negroni, Giovanni Francesco (1629–1713), cardinal, 1686: Villa Negroni sold to, 20. 69n

Negroni brothers: one of, refuses to sell Villa Negroni, 24. 31

Negroni family: Clement XIV may negotiate with, at Genoa, for villa for Ds of Kingston, 24. 6–7

Kingston, Ds of, sends courier to, about purchase of villa, 23. 567

Negroni villa, at Rome: Clement XIV offers to be Ds of Kingston's agent in procuring, 24. 6–7

hurricane uproots trees at, 20. 69

Kingston, Ds of, may buy, 23. 566–7, 24. 6–7, 14

one of Negroni brothers refuses to sell, 24. 31

Sixtus X builds, when cardinal, 20. 69n

——'s casino at, 24. 7

——'s villa at, 23. 567, 24. 14, 31

Negropont: Russian fleet batters castle at, 23. 331

Negus: Danvers drinks jug of, 35. 70

——'s death attributed to, by HW, 9. 155, 156

for breakfast, 9. 170

Neiberg. *See* Neipperg

Neighbours: HW's reflection on, 29. 307

Neilson, Jacques (1714–88): tapestries made by, 28. 413n

Neipperg, Marie Wilhelmine Josephe (1738–75), Gräfin, m. (1755) Fürst Johann Adam Joseph Auersperg: Guadagni's favour with, 23. 279

Neipperg, Wilhelm Reinhard (1684–1774), Graf; field marshal: army of, joined to Lobkowitz's, 17. 205n

Daun's orders from, 21. 96

Francis I's tutor, 21. 96n

French forces considered inferior by, 18. 250

Hofkriegsrat member, 21. 96n

Königseck visited by, 17. 205

Maria Theresa and, 21. 96n, 28. 454

—— withdraws army of, from Lower Silesia, 17. 205n

Stair's proposals opposed by, 18. 278n

Neisse: Frederick II to relieve, 21. 254, 257

Nekre. *See* Necker

Nelli, ——, senatore, of Casino dei nobili: Leopold's letter to, about ladies' dress, 25. 175n

Nelson, Mr:
HW asks about, 36. 2
Nelson, Mrs Edmund. *See* Suckling, Catherine
Nelson, Horatio (1758–1805), cr. (1798) Bn, (1801) Vct Nelson; naval officer:
grandfather of, 9. 153n
mistress of, 11. 274n
senior naval officer of Dalling's expedition, 29. 91n
uncle of, 24. 178n
Nelthorpe, Sir John (1746–99), 6th Bt, 1746:
SH visited by, 12. 233
Nemi, Duca di. *See* Braschi-Onesti, Luigi
Nemi (Italy):
Austrians at, 18. 454, 473, 488
Benedict XIV entertained at convent at, 19. 416n
letter from camp at, 18. 488
Nemours, Duchesse de. *See* Orléans de Longueville, Marie d'
Nenny, Cornelius, Freiherr von, Austrian cabinet secretary:
toison d'or brought by, from Vienna, 23. 1
Nepean, Evan, undersecretary of state:
Mann receives packet from, for Eliott, 25. 319n
North to deliver seal of secretary of state to, 25. 460n
'Nephew, our.' *See* Frederick II of Prussia
Nephritis:
Choiseul's, 3. 236
Nepos, Cornelius (ca 99–24 B.C.), Roman historian:
Du Deffand, Mme, has works of, 8. 34
Nepotism:
HW's witticism on, 24. 71
Neptune:
Ailesbury, Lady, compared with queen of, 30. 327
classic god of sea-fights, 33. 116
French medals would depict, with Louis XV, 21. 357
George III called, 32. 129, 130
HW's great-nieces might have gone to, if drowned, 39. 311
Jamesone's Edinburgh view includes, 40. 267
Maria Theresa's medal includes, 21. 202
navy referred to as belonging to, 33. 171
Vulcan's dispute with, imagined by HW, 33. 452
'Neptune, our,' *See* Mathews, Thomas (1676–1751); Spencer, George John (1758–1834)
'Neptune.' *See under* King, John (ca 1753–1823): *Letters of Neptune and Gracchus*
Neptune, English man-of-war:
Conway writes from on board, 37. 506–9
expected at Port Mahon, 17. 285
Saunders aboard, at Gibraltar, 22. 12n
Neptune, English merchant ship:
Brown, Thomas, commander of, 18. 354n
Mould, Thomas, commander of, 18. 354n
nearly captured, 18. 354
Neptune, English privateer:

Green, Capt., takes sailors on, contrary to laws of neutrality, 21. 274n
Neptune, Spanish galleon:
in Spanish fleet, 17. 286
Nereid; nereids:
Caroline Matilda called, 32. 130
in Virgil's *Æneid*, 11. 20
Neri, Pompeo (1707–76), Abbé; Florentine scholar and politician:
acting Florentine prime minister, 23. 225n
Botta intimate with, 21. 125n
Craon expects resignation of, 17. 236
(?) Gondi, Mme, courted by, at opera, 18. 86
(?) —— turns off, 17. *136*
Mann's representations to, against Young Pretender, 23. 225n
Milan the station of, in Maria Theresa's service, 21. 125n
new Regency member, 21. 107n, 125
pale, 18. 86
Regency headed by, in Botta's absence, 22. 245n
Néricault, Philippe (1680–1754), called Destouches; dramatist:
Dissipateur, Le, translated by: 33. 244; O'Beirne borrows from, 33. 244n
Fausse Agnès by, 7. 275
Glorieux, Le, by, 6. 279, 8. 196
Philosophe marié, Le, by, quoted by Mme du Deffand, 3. 88
Rucellai translates version by, of Addison's *Drummer*, 20. 118, 151
Voltaire's 'Invitation de souper' to, 6. 279, 8. 196
Nerli, (?) Francesco:
Gabburri, Mme, to make, her cicisbeo, 17. 150
Nero (Nero Claudius Cæsar Drusus Germanicus) (A.D. 37–68), Roman Emperor A.D. 54–68:
Carlisle suggests that HW may vindicate, 30. 252
character of, will seem better on Judgment Day, 32. 146
Dauphin's comment on, 21. 44
defence of, HW inquires about, 15. 62
drowning of mother by, 15. 173
French mob merely a multiplication of, 34. 74
George III compared to, 23. 197n
Labour in Vain mentions, 18. 18
Lucan quoted about, 34. 159
Maupeou would have restored, 24. 35
Pætus and, 32. 230
Rome the soil of, 24. 154
Tacitus's account of, 15. 173, 236
'Nero,' Tower of London's lion:
Harris resembles, 38. 203
Nero, Del. *See* Del Nero
Nerry. *See* Nery
Nerva (Marcus Cocceius Nerva) (A.D. 32–98), Roman Emperor:
HW praises, 15. 50, 33. 479, 35. 127
Nerve; nerves:
agitation of, 20. 377
cold baths for, 17. 452

[Nerve; nerves, *continued*]
English suffer from, **17.** 452
fashionable in England when cured at Bath, **20.** 389
Florence's sunshine and pure cool night air will rehabilitate, **25.** 646
gouty complaints attributed to, **22.** 116, 117
HW jokes about pretending to suffer from, **30.** 86
HW's: **25.** 201, 539; affected by damp, **24.** 289; alarmable, **24.** 272; shattered, **25.** 49, **32.** 186, 192, **33.** 157, 159, 307, **35.** 496; Tunbridge trip considered for, **17.** 452
hot baths too relaxing for, **24.** 280
Mann's: cannot be cured by air or water, **25.** 61; interfere with his writing, **25.** 45–6, 49, 143–4; shattered, **25.** 500; 'wore out' by writing, **20.** 537
Mead and Thompson cure, **20.** 389
Ossory, Lady, suffers from, **32.** 204
Pitt, Anne, suffers from weakness of, **24.** 6
waters supposed to cure, **20.** 389
weakness of, **21.** 281–2, **24.** 6, 430, **25.** 643, 656
Nervous disorder; nervous disorders:
occurrences of, **22.** 74, **23.** 155, **38.** 266
Nervous fever. *See under* Fever
Nervousness:
of no consequence to strong healthy youths, **31.** 354
Nery, ——, carriage maker:
Mme du Deffand's contract with, **8.** 42
Nesbitt, Mr:
HW sends letters by, **7.** 380
Nesbitt, Albert (d. 1753), M.P.:
Courtenay defeats, **19.** 413n
Nesbitt, Dorothy (d. 1779), m. (1757) George Parker, 2d E. of Macclesfield:
(?) Court presentation of, said to suffocate Cottrell Dormer, **31.** 10
Cowper, Cts, forced to walk with, at Coronation, **38.** 122, 126
(?) HW calls, 'common woman,' **31.** 10n
HW sends condolences to, **38.** 358
husband's bequest to, **38.** 349
marriage of, to former paramour, **22.** 211
social relations of, in Paris, **7.** 309–10
Nesbitt, Mrs Mary (d. 1815 or later), mistress of 3d E. of Bristol:
heir of Lord Bristol, **33.** 149
Nesbitt. *See also* Nisbet
Nesi, Francesco Maria (d. after 1800), Mann's surgeon:
(?) Mann informed by, about HW's gout, **25.** 626
(?) Mann's foot treated by, **24.** 79
Mann's legacy to, **25.** 667n
(?) Mann's rheumatism thought by, to be gout, **24.** 479
Nesle, Marquis de. *See* Mailly, Louis de
Nesle, Marquise de. *See* Hautefort, Adélaïde-Julie de
Nesling, Rev. Richard (d. 1724):
chaplain to Robert Walpole, **1.** 51, 75

Nesmond, André, Chevalier de:
commands men-of-war, **13.** 228n
Nestleroi. *See* Nistelrode
Nestor:
HW feels as young as, **32.** 260
HW will not hobble like, to siege of Troy, **25.** 296
not any, in Jamaica, **34.** 218
Nestorians:
HW dislikes Gibbon's account of, **42.** 221
Net; nets:
fish, HW does not use, at SH, **9.** 155
gold, for horse, **18.** 69
Nether Bow, Edinburgh:
Anstruther voted for demolishing, in Porteous affair, **20.** 230n
Netherby, Yorks:
Morris of, **11.** 47n
Netherhall Vaux, manor in East Ruston, Norfolk:
HW's will mentions, **30.** 368
Netherlands. *See* Belgium; Flanders; Holland
Netherlands, Austrian. *See* Belgium; Flanders
Netley Abbey, Hants:
beauties of, **14.** 83
Berry, Mary, does not mention, **11.** 80
Chute visits, **35.** 249, 251
HW calls, 'charming,' **11.** 80
HW suggests Lady Ossory visit, **33.** 42–3
HW visits and describes, **35.** 249, 251
Netscher, Caspar (ca 1639–84), painter:
paintings by, at Julienne's, **7.** 287
Nettancourt, Charles-Jean-François de (1726–1822), Marquis de Vaubecourt:
(?) command given to, **7.** 147
Nettine, Anne-Rose-Josèphe de (ca 1740–1813), m. 1 (1761) Joseph Micault d'Hervelay; m. 2 (1788) Charles-Alexandre de Calonne:
reports desertion of French troops, **11.** 36, **39.** 468
Nettine, Marie-Louise-Josèphe de (d. 1808), m. 1 (1762) Ange-Laurent de la Live de Juilly:
social relations of, with Mme Geoffrin, **7.** 305
Nettine, Rosalie-Claire de, m. (1760) Jean-Joseph, Marquis de la Borde:
husband's fondness for, **31.** 81
pretty, **31.** 80
social relations of, in Paris, **3.** 358, **7.** 280
Nettles:
Houghton overgrown with, **23.** 510, **39.** 172
Nettuno (Italy):
Mann sends ships under Long to , **18.** 460, 475, 476
oats brought to, by ship, **18.** 453
statues to be sent from, **20.** 104n
Neue gelehrte Europa, Das. See under Strodtmann, J. C.
Neufchâteau, Nicolas-Louis-François de (1752–1828):
Mois d'Auguste, Le, by, **6.** 285
Neufchâtel (Switzerland):
balloon voyage to, **25.** 527n
Lentulus governor of, **21.** 4n

Lucan to leave son at, to study, **24.** 462

Neufchâtel (surname). *See* Pinterel de Neuf-châtel

Neufville, Gabriel-Louis-François de (1731–94), Duc de Villeroy:
attends session of parliament of Paris, **8.** 172
marriage of, **3.** 75n
promoted, **5.** *179*
reversion of position of, granted, **7.** 153
(?) social relations of, with Comtesse de Boufflers, **7.** 301
wife of, **3.** 75n

Neufville, John de:
Lee's American-Dutch commercial agreement with, **25.** 91n

Neufville, Louis-François-Anne de (1695–1766), Duc de Villeroy:
Luxembourg, Mme de, sister of, **8.** 83n

Neufville, Madeleine-Angélique de (1707–87), m. 1 (1721) Joseph-Marie, Duc de Boufflers; m. 2 (1750) Charles-François-Frédéric de Montmorency-Luxembourg, Duc de Luxembourg; Maréchal de France:
Académie française to be visited by, **6.** 333
Ailesbury, Cts of, friendly with, but Conway is preferred, **39.** 218
—— liked by, **6.** 101, 104, 115, 117
Antin, Duchesse d', death of, indifferent to, **4.** 47
'Archiduchesse,' **3.** 89
Auteuil expenses of Comtesse de Boufflers shared by, **7.** 218
—— visited by, **6.** 211, 345, 347, 349, **7.** 153, 162, 178, 218, 347
Beauvau, Princesse de, hates and is hated by, **3.** 173, 182n
birthday of, **5.** 203, 225, 382, 394
bled in the foot, **7.** 456
Boufflers, Chevalier de, writes verses to ac-company gifts to, **6.** 3–4, 249, 252, 260
Boufflers, Comtesse de, relations of, with, **3.** 41, 47, 91, 115, 127, 334, **5.** 107, **7.** 153
—— visited by, **7.** 153, 218 (*see also under* Auteuil: visitors to)
Boufflers, Marquise de, visits, at Mont-morency, **4.** 319
Boufflers-des Alleurs wedding party enter-tained by, **4.** 168, 171
bouquet of, **7.** 425
Briges, Marquise de, to be visited by, **6.** 470
Bunbury dislikes, **3.** 229
Cambis, Vicomtesse de, relations of, with, **5.** 206, 226
—— visits, at Montmorency, **4.** 319
cat of, dies, **5.** 180
Chanteloup visited by, **5.** 122, 125, 127, 129, 135, 169, 228, 231, 234, 238, 240–3, 350, 353, 358, 404, 412, 418, 426, **6.** 29, 33, 48, 54, 103, 104, 441, 450, 452, 453
Chantilly to be visited by, **3.** 338
charity of, to Mme du Deffand's embroiderer, **6.** 187, 188, 192

Choiseul, Duc and Duchesse de, predicted by, to return, **6.** 110
—— visited by, in exile, **5.** 122, 125, 127, 129, 135, 169, 228, 231, 234, 238, 240–3
Choiseul, Duchesse de, sends letter by, **5.** 136
conduct of, **3.** 160, 229
contemporary with Mme du Deffand, **7.** 173
Conti given attentions by, **6.** 339
—'s circle necessary to, **3.** 91
Conway liked by, **6.** 104, 117
Craufurd's opinion of, **6.** 485
—'s relations with, **6.** 488
Crécy visited by, **6.** 470, **7.** 454
Croÿ, Duc de, to be given Mme du Deffand's mémoire for Lady Fenouilhet by, **5.** 405, 408
Damer, Mrs, liked by, **6.** 101, 104, 115, 117
daughter of, **5.** 129n
Dauphin's entrée given to, **4.** 444
Des Alleurs, Mlle, receives earrings from, **4.** 168
Du Barry, Comtesse, subject of joke by, **4.** 447–8
Du Châtelet, Comtesse, converses with, **6.** 450
Du Deffand, Mme, always escorted to supper table by, **6.** 26
—— asks HW to send message to, **6.** 227
—— assisted by, **3.** 111
—— attends Opéra-Comique with, **3.** 345
—— attends theatre with, **3.** 133, **6.** 440, 469
—— cites, **6.** 290, 361
—— confides in, about Christmas party, for Duc and Duchesse de Choiseul, **6.** 115
(?) —— does not rely on perseverance of, **5.** 408
—— has, at her chaise longue, **39.** 271
—— hopes not to survive, **7.** 153–4
—— informed by, that d'Alembert attributes HW's letter to Rousseau to her, **41.** 62n
—— leaves girandoles to, **8.** 8, 19
—— mentions, **3.** 267, **4.** 139, 342, **6.** 197
—'s correspondence with, **6.** 129, 360, 450, **7.** 454
—'s gifts from: bouquet, **7.** 459; cup, **6.** 3, 127, **7.** 440; hair in medallion with Pom-pom's miniature, **7.** 97–8, **8.** 9, 26–7; New Year's gifts, blue, with verses, **7.** 197, 200, 203; silverware, **6.** 3; snuff-box with Ton-ton's portrait, **7.** 2, 201n; Voltaire quartos, **4.** 131, **7.** 2
—'s gifts to: bouquet, **5.** 203, **7.** 457; box, **5.** 298; box, red morocco, **7.** 97; chair, **5.** 431, **6.** 3; fan, with verses, **5.** 225, **7.** 413; forks, with L'Isle's verses, **4.** 262–3; gold braid, **5.** 382, 394, **6.** 249, **7.** (?) 1; Pompom the presenter of, **6.** 249, 496–7, **7.** 1; rock crystal goblet, **7.** 439
—'s opinion of, **3.** 77, **4.** 80, 102, 109
—'s 'portraits' of, **8.** 83–4, **43.** 109
—'s relations with, **3.** *11*–12, 16, 59, 87, 91, 109, 117, 132, 191, 214, 385, **4.** 48, 252–3, 335, 446, **5.** 353, 368, 431, **6.** 67, 183, 192, 268, 273, 349, 353, 358, 361, 363, 391, 417,

[Neufville, Madeleine-Angélique de, *continued*]
431, 432, 7. 15, 75, 102, 145, 153, 176, 178,
205, 208, 213
—'s supper for, omitted, 4. 38
—'s verses for, on St Martin, 5. 431
—'s verses to, 5. 225–6, 232, 298, 6. 249,
8. 186
—'s Wednesday supper transferred to, 7.
101
— talks with, about wit, 5. 107
— to establish weekly supper for, 5. 13
enamel of Montmorency owned by, 1. 103
father-in-law of, 4. 283n
Forcalquier, Comtesse de, flattered by, 3. 229
Friday unlucky day for, 5. 122, 129, 180, 216,
7. 97
gambles, 3. 18, 4. 337, 6. 371
Gramont, Duchesse de, relations of, with, 6.
21, 26, 29, 33, 41–2
Gustav III's correspondence with, 5. 135
HW accompanies, to theatre, 7. 285, 33. 543
HW buys fan for Mme du Deffand to give to,
7. 413
HW converses with, 41. 5
HW exchanges compliments with, 3. 26, 6.
234, 7. 174
HW mentions, 3. 342
HW pleases, 3. 385
HW sends regards to, 36. 242
HW's *Gramont* given to, 5. 305
HW's letter to Rousseau disliked by, 7. 294–5
HW's present to, 3. 83, 86, 89, 102, 109, 112,
113, 132, 142
HW's remarks on d'Alembert not shown to,
3. 174
HW sups with, at Hôtel de Luxembourg, 31.
112–13
HW to be welcomed by, 6. 211, 216
hair of, in medallion with Pompom's miniature, 7. 98, 8. 9, 26–7
(?) Harcourt sends vase to, 36. 168, 169
health of, 4. 124, 446, 451, 6. 67, 72, 75, 172,
174, 270, 280, 304, 305, 307, 308, 310, 7.
153, 205, 207, 208, 210, 212, 213, 219, 221,
225, 444, 447
Hôtel de Luxembourg, house of, 3. 22, 7. 284
Hume credited by, with preface to *Exposé
succinct . . .*, 3. 158
— not liked by, 3. 91
Hume-Rousseau quarrel discussed by, 3. 158
in country, 3. 319
L'Isle-Adam visited by, 3. 41, 56, 127–8, 186,
5. 51, 403, 6. 324
joke of, on Conti–La Marche coolness, 4. 12
journeys of, 4. 256, 6. 349, 353, 356, 358, 7. 46
La Harpe's play at Gonesse seen by, 4. 445
— to recite Barmécides at supper of, 5.
322, 338–9
La Marck, Comtesse de, visited by, 6. 232
large supper parties of, 5. 6
La Tuilerie visited by, 6. 339, 7. 345
Lauzun, Duc de, affairs of, not discussed by,
6. 383

— said to be generously treated by, 6. 393
—'s correspondence with, 3. 251
Lauzun, Duchesse de, corresponds with, 7.
183
— sheltered by, 7. 6, 33
La Vallière, Duchesse de, quarrels with, 7.
283
— reconciled to, 6. 431, 436
leaves Paris, 6. 472
Le Val visited by, 6. 232
loss of lovers and beauty has made, agreeable,
14. 155
Mansfield pleases, 6. 96
Marie Leszczyńska's health reported on by,
3. 376
—'s remark to, 30. 218
midnight Mass attended by, 5. 159, 431, 436
Mirepoix, Mme de, hates, 3. 18, 19, 173,
182n
Montauban, Comtesse de, writes verses to,
5. 394
Montesson, Marquise de, visited by, 1. 183
Montmorency, Princesse de, to be visited by,
6. 470
Montmorency, home of, *see* Montmorency
Paris visited by: 3. 127, 354, 356, 365, 4. 446,
6. 331, 348, 453, 466, 473, 493, 495, 500,
7. 66, 68, 235, 456; to see HW, 32. 253
Pompom bearer of gifts to, 6. 249, 496–7, 7. 1
— given watch by, 7. 99
— pet of, 7. 98
Pont-de-Veyle's grief reported by, 4. 471
Port-à l'Anglois, Le, to be visited by, 6. 56
'portraits' of, by Mme du Deffand, 8. 83–4,
43. 109
print satirizes, 11. 54n
Raincy visited by, 6. 224, 228, 229, 7. 425,
428, 459
Rousseau a protégé of, 3. 91, 133
— given money by, 1. 112n
—'s children sought by, 31. 383n
St-Cloud visited by, 6. 304, 441
Ste-Assise visited by, 6. 236, 329, 330, 363,
365, 368, 371, 491, 7. 47, 183, 432, 433, 436
St-Ouen visited by, 6. 224, 229
Ségur, Vicomte de, friend of, 7. 200
— writes verses for, 7. 200
Shuvalov exchanges gifts with, 6. 415, 12.
254
— sends respects to, 8. 206
snuff-boxes of, 36. 237
snuff-boxes to be selected by, 6. 302, 303
social relations of, in Paris, *see index entries
ante* 8. 455–6
son of, 3. 58n
spirits of, 5. 95
Stanhope, Lady Harriet, liked by, 6. 101, 104,
115
suppers of, ended, 7. 443
sups at Mme du Deffand's, 3. 212n
Tonton likes, 6. 447
Tronchin attends, 4. 446, 6. 304, 7. 205, 207,
208, 444

Versailles lodging taken from, **5.** 129
—— visited by, **3.** 376, **6.** 191
verses by: for Shuvalov, **6.** 415; on saints, **5.** 431
verses for dinner given by, **6.** 405–6
Villers-Cotterêts visited by, **5.** 380, 382, 394, **6.** 342, 462, 466
visitors to, *see* Montmorency: visitors to
vow of, to let Duchesse de Gramont precede her, **6.** 26
Neuhof, Élisabeth de:
married Comte de Trevoux, **7.** 364n
Neuhoff, Théodore (1694–1756), Baron de, self-styled K. of Corsica:
act of insolvency benefits, **21.** 45, 140, 148
Aston, Mary, responds to HW's plea for, **40.** 75
Baldanzi's house the retreat of, **18.** 217n
birth date of, corrected, **43.** 84, 172, 188
Braitwitz, Richecourt, and Goldsworthy aid, in writing edict, **18.** 151n
Carteret claimed by, as friend, **18.** 187, 194, 210, 233, **20.** 164, 385
—— discovers deception of, **18.** 216
—— tells, of Bns Walpole's application, **18.** 194
—— urged by, to send Mann a courier, **18.** 190
Charles Emmanuel III cheated by, **20.** 386
coins of, **21.** 45, 140
Corsican coasts skirted by, **18.** 174
Corsicans and English did not want to reinstate, **20.** 386
creditors lure, from privileged place, **20.** 164
Curzay accused of imitating, **20.** 353n
death of, **21.** 39–40, 45
edict of, sent to HW by Mann, **18.** 151, 155–8
England may acquire Corsica by paying debts of, **21.** 59
—— visited by, **18.** 192, **20.** 29n, 40
English fleet neglects, despite alleged orders by George II, Newcastle, and Carteret, **18.** 188
English ministers deceived by, **18.** 222
English newspapers wanted by, in Tuscany, **20.** 378
Folkstone brings, from Corsica, **18.** 187n
Gazette de Berne and *Mercure de Hollande* regularly received by, **20.** 378n
Genoese partisans may assassinate, **18.** 187n, 190n
George II may receive letter from, **19.** 132
—— not to aid, **18.** 210n
German gazette mentions, **18.** 221
Goldsworthy conceals Leghorn visit of, **18.** *145*, 166, 187
—— ill-treats, **18.** 188
HW buys instrument of insolvency of, **21.** 45n
HW erects monument to, in St Anne's churchyard, **8.** 73, **13.** 28, **21.** 140, 148
HW gives Boswell an account of, **14.** 170

HW keeps Corsican electoral capitulations of, in Tribune at SH, **21.** 45n
HW promotes subscription for, **20.** 373–4, 385
HW sees, **41.** 2n
HW's instcription for: **21.** 40n, 140, **43.** 274; Mann asks about translation of, **21.** 197; Mann translates, into Italian, **21.** 148; translation of, pleases HW, **21.** 204
HW to meet, at Lady Schaub's, **20.** 40
handwriting of, illegible, **18.** 205
'history' of, **35.** 49
Hogarth to depict, at HW's request, **20.** 164
imprisoned for debt, **20.** 164, 373
in Voltaire's *Candide* and in *Il re Teodoro*, **33.** 587
kingdom to be occupied by, **18.** 150–1
King's Bench Prison confines, **20.** 164, **21.** 140
King's Bench release of, Reade sends document for, to HW, **40.** 191–2
Leghorn Corsicans expect, **18.** 145
Leghorn near the station of, **19.** 132
life of, *see History of Theodore I*; *Life and History of Theodore I*
Mann accused by, of mishandling his funds, **21.** 378–9
—— consults with, in Florence, **18.** 187, 190, 194
—— less fit to write about, than are Mrs Behn or Mrs Haywood, **18.** 249
—— not a friend of, **20.** 378–9
—— receives frequent communications from, **18.** 187–8, 190, 205, 216
—— refuses to lend money to, **20.** 29
——'s letters mis-used by, in Tuscany, **20.** 378
—— urged by, to find him a villa to hide in, **18.** 217
—— wants Sir Robert Walpole's report on, **18.** 190
Maria Theresa's alleged treaty with, **18.** 208
marriage not immediately contemplated by, **18.** 207–8
Mathews confused about, **18.** 194–5
—— wants to install, **18.** 229
Old Bailey visited by, to benefit by insolvency act, **21.** 45
Pennant's account of, **11.** 93n
Portuguese minister called on by, **21.** 45
release of, from prison, **21.** 45, 140, 148
Rowley not seen by, **19.** 132
rumoured to be on man-of-war at Leghorn, **18.** 145
sails from Leghorn, **18.** 174
secretary of, betrays him to Mann, **20.** 379
silent, when HW saw him, **41.** 2n
Stanhope, Lady Lucy, receives addresses of, **18.** 192, 207, 221, 229
transports of, dispersed, **18.** 174
Trevoux and Louis XV joke about, **7.** 364
Walpole, Sir Robert, claimed by, as friend, **18.** 187, 233
—— denies having had connections with, **18.** 210, 225, 233

[Neuhoff, Théodore, *continued*]
—— knows nothing of Carteret's connections with, 18. 210, 225
wife deserted by, 18. 207n
World, The, prints HW's paper in behalf of, 3. 182–3, 20. 373–4, 385
Yarmouth, Cts of, said to be niece of, 18. 187, 216
Young Pretender's will said to imitate that of, 25. 395
Neuilly (France):
bridge at: Barthélemy praises, 8. 201; medal of, to be sent by Mme du Deffand to HW, 6. 27, 28
Plaine de, cricket match at, 7. 307
Neupergh. *See* Newburgh
Neuremberg. *See* Nuremberg
Neuschattel. *See* Neufchâtel
Neuss (Germany):
Conway visits, 37. 133–5
Neutrality:
American-English-French, proposed by HW, 39. 302
armed, means no good to anybody, 25. 327
Franco-Hanoverian, discontent caused by reported signing of, as contrary to King's speech, 30. 23
of Hanover, angers Luccans, 35. 10
of Tuscany, *see under* Tuscany
Neuville, Père, preacher at French Court:
Jesuits' suppression noted by, 23. 524n
Neuville. *See also* Le Quien de la Neuville
Neve, Cornelius de (fl. 1637–64):
painting by, 1. 363n
Neve, Rev. Timothy (1694–1757):
marriage of, 15. 309
Neve, Mrs Timothy. *See* Green, Christina
Neve. *See also* Le Neve
'Nevers, Duc de.' *See* Mancini-Mazarini, Louis-Jules-Barbon
Nevers (France):
Pitt, Anne, visits, 31. 4n
Pougues near, 3. 59n
Névet, Marie-Thérèse-Corentine de (d. 1778), m. (1729) Jean-Antoine-François de Franquetot, Comte (called Marquis) de Coigny:
social relations of, with Mme de Luxembourg, 7. 308
'Neveu, votre.' *See* Cholmondeley, George James, 4th E. of Cholmondeley; Walpole, Edward; Walpole, George, 3d E. of Orford; William Henry, D. of Gloucester
Nevile, Mrs Christopher. *See* Mann, Mary (d. between 1815 and 1818)
Nevile. *See also* Nevill; Neville
Nevil family:
tombs of, at Mereworth, 35. 144
Nevill, Lady. *See* Montagu, Alice de (ca 1406–62)
Nevill, Anne (1456–85), m. 1 (1470) Edward, P. of Wales; m. 2 (1472) Richard III of England. *See* Anne (Neville) (1456–85)

Nevill, Anne (d. 1480), m. 1 (1424) Sir Humphrey Stafford, cr. D. of Buckingham; m. 2 (1467) Walter Blount, Bn Mountjoy:
Henry VI gives jewel to, 14. 75
received into fraternity of Bury Abbey, 2. 38
Nevill, Arthur Jones (d. ca 1771), surveyor-gen. of Ireland:
dismissed, 12. 256
Irish House of Commons expels, for contempt, 20. 402n
Nevill, Hon. Catherina (1728–? 62):
to be maid of honour, 19. 63
Nevill, Cicely (1415–95), m. (1424) Richard (Plantagenet), 3d D. of York:
descendants of, 2. 364
HW attributes 'old inn' at Fotheringhay to, 10. 91
Hardinge, Mrs, descended from, 35. 610
mother of Edward IV and Richard III, 15. 183–4
not at Henry VII's court, 2. 364, 365
register of births of children of, 1. 319–21
Richard III said to accuse, of whoredom, 41. 115
——'s letter to, 14. 159–60
——'s pre-contracts urged by, 35. 609
Shaw charged, with adultery, 14. 179
tomb of, at Fotheringhay, 10. 91
Nevill, Lady Elizabeth (?1550–1630), m. 1 Sir John Danvers; m. 2 Sir Edmund Carey:
marriages of, 1. 6, 6n
tomb of, 1. 6–7
Nevill, George (1727–85), 15th Bn Abergavenny; cr. (1784) E. of Abergavenny:
Cornbury visited by, with Selwyn and Mrs Frere, 20. 182
costume of, at Ferrers's trial, 9. 281
HW mentions, 37. 337, 425
matriculation of, at Christ Church, Oxon, 19. 387n
mother of, 20. 182
Oxford servant's death attributed to, 19. 387
Westminster Abbey visited by, with Selwyn, 20. 181
wife of, 20. 180n
wife's separation from, due to his affair with nursery-maid, 38. 510–11
Nevill, Henry (after 1527–1587), 6th Bn Abergavenny:
daughter of, 41. 365
Nevill, Lady Isabel (1451–76), m. (1469) George, D. of Clarence:
portrait of, in D. of Manchester's MS, 14. 177
Nevill, John (1493–1543), 3d Bn Latimer, 1530:
Catherine Parr's husband, 42. 114
daughter of, 1. 375n
HW descended from, 12. 165
Nevill, John (? 1520–77), 4th Bn Latimer, 1543:

Camden's *Annals* mentions death of, **37**. 306
daughter of, **1**. 6
Nevill, Margaret (d. before 1426), m. Thomas Beaufort, D. of Exeter:
buried in Bury Abbey, **2**. 39n
marriage of, **2**. 39n
Nevill, Margaret (d. after 1488), m. (ca 1465) John de Vere, 13th E. of Oxford:
at Coronation of Elizabeth of York, **2**. 365
Nevill, Margaret (d. ca 1758), m. Sir Baldwin Conyers, 4th Bt:
auction of ebony furniture of, HW attends, **10**. 76–7
house of, near Kimbolton, **10**. 76
Nevill, Mary (1554–1626), m. (1574) Sir Thomas Fane, Kt; Bns Le Despenser, s.j., 1604:
Le Despenser barony carried by to Fane family, **41**. 365
Nevill, Sir Richard (1400–60), 5th E. of Salisbury:
in Margaret of Anjou's escort, **14**. 72–3
Nevill, Sir Richard (1428–71), cr. (1450) E. of Warwick:
brother of, **9**. 99n
Elizabeth Wydevill said to be in love with, in *Comte de Warwik*, **38**. 276
HW's coat of mail belonged to trooper of, **31**. 26
Lancastrians ruined by party of, **41**. 115
letters of, among Paston letters, **33**. 559
London bribed by, **42**. 192
Louis XI visited by, in exile, **42**. 192
Paston lends money to, **42**. 192
rebellion of, against Edward IV, **15**. 170–1
Nevill, William (d. 1744), 16th Bn Abergavenny, 1724:
damages won by, against Richard Lyddel, **19**. 63n
wife of, **9**. 30n
Nevill. *See also* Nevile; Neville
Nevill family:
genealogy of: brings them no advantages, **20**. 408; mentioned, **15**. 267
Neville, ——, Lt; engineer:
captured by the French, **24**. 477
Neville, Anne. *See* Anne (Neville) (1456–85)
Neville, Cosmus Henry Joseph Migliorucci (b. 1716):
(?) Florence visited by, **23**. 64
Florentine cousin tries to cheat, **20**. 266
(?) Mann escorted by, **23**. 60n
Neville, Edward:
Life of the Lady Warner of Parham by, **43**. 59
Plymouth in an Uproar by, **33**. 135n
Neville, John (ca 1431–71), cr. (1464) E. of Northumberland, (1470) M. of Montagu:
Cowdray said to have been owned by, **9**. 98–9
Neville, Richard Neville Aldworth (1717–93), M.P.:
(?) Florence visited by, **23**. 64
Hertford's predecessor at Paris, **38**. 360
(?) Mann escorted by, **23**. 60n

match of, at Geneva, **20**. 7
Parliamentary minority includes, **42**. 497
Phocias acted by, at Geneva, **37**. 44
Pitt said to abuse, **38**. 360, 368–9
Treaty of Paris brought by, **22**. 118n
Wilkes's treatment at Paris by Hertford based on precedents from, **38**. 279
Neville, Mrs Richard Neville Aldworth. *See* Calendrini, Magdalen
Neville. *See also* Nevile; Nevill
Ne v'là-t-il pas que j'aime:
verses to air of, **7**. 98
New and Complete History of . . . Kingston upon Hull, A. See under Hadley, George
New and Complete History of Norfolk, A:
Gardiner directs, **2**. 120
published by numbers, **2**. 78, 120
New and Easy etc. cioè Nuove e facile grammatica. See under Barker, Edward
Newark, Vct. *See* Medows (later Pierrepont), Charles Pierrepont (1737–1816)
Newark, Notts:
Mellish recorder of, **1**. 305n
Newark Castle:
HW sees ruins of, **35**. 266
New Atlantis, The. See under Manley, Mary de la Rivière
New Bath Guide, The. See under Anstey, Christopher
Newbattle, Lord. *See* Ker, William John (1737–1805)
Newbattle Abbey, Midlothian, M. of Lothian's seat:
portrait of James II of Scotland at, **15**. 208–9
Newbery, John (1713–67):
Midwife published by Smart and, **9**. 131n
New Bond St, London:
Bretherton of, **1**. 313n
Dickinson printseller in, **33**. 401n
Grafton's house in, **22**. 8on, **32**. 8n
Gray, Robert has shop in, **21**. 295n
Robson bookseller in, **1**. 175n, **34**. 36n, **40**. 326n
Shropshire bookseller in, **41**. 271n
Whithed's house in, **14**. 25n
Newborough, Bn. *See* Wynn, Thomas
New Bridewell Prison, London:
burnt by Gordon rioters, **29**. 55, **33**. 187
Newbridge, Co. Dublin:
Cobbe of, **12**. 201n
New Broad St, London:
Walpole and Ellison in, **41**. 226
New Buildings, Charing Cross, London:
Biddulph and Cocks, bankers in, **42**. 453
Newburgh, Bn. *See* Cholmondeley, George Horatio
Newburgh, Cts of. *See* Brudenell, Hon. Frances (ca 1673–1756); Livingstone, Charlotte Maria (1694–1755)
Newburgh, E. of. *See* Radcliffe, James Bartholomew
New Burlington St, London:
blocked by coaches, **11**. 101

Newbury, Berks:
battle of, 29. 179n
Benham near, 11. 100n
Brickenden, Miss, of, 42. 54n
comedy at, 29. 43n
Newby, Yorks:
in Hargrove's book, 15. 267n
Weddell of, 29. 75n, 259n
Newcastle, D. and Ds of. See Newcastle-under-
Line; Newcastle-upon-Tyne
Newcastle, Northumberland. See Newcastle-
upon-Tyne
Newcastle, English ship:
Fox captain of, 18. 152, 182
Legge, George, captain of, cashiered, 21. 296n
Leghorn visited by, 18. 182
Mann sends, to cruise, 18. 460
ordered to England, 19. 12
prize brought by, to Leghorn, 18. 448
Suckling on board, 18. 152, 182
Newcastle estate:
entail of, cut off, 17. 209–10
Newcastle House, London:
Bedford and Rockingham factions meet at,
22. 541–2
Conway visits, 37. 386
Fox, Henry, visits, 35. 199
Karl Wilhelm Ferdinand at, 38. 290–1
meeting at, to reconcile Bedford and Rock-
ingham, 22. 542n
Milbanke and Thomas Pelham lived at, 20.
207
Newcastle, D. of, quits, because 2 servants die
of sore throats, 21. 312–13
Pitt's encounter with C. Townshend at, 30.
136
Rockingham and friends draw paper at,
against Grenville, 22. 566n
Newcastle-under-Line, Ds of. See Stanhope,
Lady Anna Maria (1760–1834)
Newcastle-under-Line (or Lyne), D. of. See
Fiennes Clinton, Henry (1720–94); Pelham
Clinton, Lord Thomas (1752–95); Pelham
Holles, Thomas (1693–1768)
Newcastle-under-Line (or Lyne), duchy of:
Lincoln to inherit, 21. 18, 26
the only dukedom bestowed by George II,
21. 26
Newcastle-upon-Tyne, Ds of. See Godolphin,
Lady Henrietta (d. 1776); Lucas, Margaret
(1617–73)
Newcastle-upon-Tyne, D. of. See Cavendish,
Henry (1630–91); Cavendish, William (1593–
1676); Holles, John (1662–1711); Pelham
Holles, Thomas (1693–1768)
Newcastle-upon-Tyne, Marchioness of. See
Lucas, Margaret (1617–73)
Newcastle-upon-Tyne:
dukes of, as foolish-looking as present one,
35. 271
Newcastle-upon-Tyne, Northumberland:
attacked, 7. 368
Chute and Whithed call, 'Carbonari,' 19. 143

'coals from,' 9. 210, 262, 21. 460, 32. 173
colliers of, said to feed their children with
fire shovels, 20. 450
visitors to: Fitzroy, Lady Georgiana, 22. 8on;
Grafton, D. and Ds of, 22. 8on
Wade and Edinburgh provost meet at, 19.
175–6
Wade marches from, 19. 165
—— stays at, 19. 159
—— to march from, 19. 153
New College, Oxford:
Beauchamp examines paintings in Hall of,
38. 43–4
founder of, see Wykeham, William of
HW mentions crozier, library, and chapel at,
9. 289n
glass at, painted by Price, 1. 201n
HW calls, 'Winchester College,' 38. 43
Jervais's window at, from Reynolds's painting, 2. 170, 33. 417–18, 39. 435, 43. 70
MS in library of, 1. 269
Newcome, Miss:
injured in accident, 2. 316n
Newcome, Anne, m. (1756) Robert Plumptre:
husband of, 2. 154n
Newcome, George William (1763–1833), Cole's
great-nephew:
dines with Cole, 2. 265
Newcome, Dr Henry, schoolmaster at Hackney:
daughter of, 2. 154n
son of, 1. 15n
Newcome, Henry (fl. 1750–80), schoolmaster at
Hackney:
Cole exchanges visits with, 1. 15, 44
injured in accident, 2. 316n
sons of, 2. 265n
SH may be visited by, 1. 44
Newcome, Mrs Henry. See Mawdesley, Mary
Newcome, John (1683–1765), Master of St
John's College, Cambridge:
(?) chair of, sent to Cole, 2. 16
print of wife of, 1. 280, 281, 282, 284, 284n,
285
Newcome, Mrs John. See Squire, —— (d. 1763)
Newcome, Richard (fl. 1779–ca 1800), Cole's
great-nephew:
dines with Cole, 2. 265
Newcome, William (1729–1800), Bp of Dro-
more, 1766, of Ossory, 1775, of Waterford,
1779; Abp of Armagh, 1795:
Irish bishopric sought for, 10. 187
Newcourt, Richard (d. 1716), registrar:
*Repertorium ecclesiasticum parochiale Lon-
dinense* by: cited, 1. 317; HW has not, 1.
319; quoted, 1. 322–24
New Description of Merryland:
Conway likes, 37. 82
Newdigate, Sir Roger (1719–1806), 5th Bt,
1734; M.P.:
Clarendon's *History* boring to, 29. 149
HW and Sir Robert Walpole meet, in Gros-
venor Sq., 18. 25
Orford, Cts of, seen by, at Florence, 24. 488n

Parliamentary memberships of, corrected, **43.** 305–6

Parliamentary seat resigned by, **29.** 35n

Philipps opposed by, at Horn Tavern conclave, **35.** 216n

Pitt answers, in Parliamentary debate, **26.** 10

Rome visited by, **24.** 144

Tories accompany, to Brentford election, **18.** 25

votes with Tories, **29.** 29–30

Young Pretender would formerly have been mourned by, **24.** 144

New England:

Cape Breton said to be taken by troops of, **20.** 474

England may be conquered in, **23.** 551

forces of: may attack Quebec after Burgoyne's defeat, **24.** 342; may join Washington to besiege Clinton, **24.** 342

HW imagines Duke of, **33.** 421

ship from, in Orkneys, **37.** 246

New England Pine. *See* White pine

Newenham, Sir Edward (1732–1814), Kt, 1763; Irish politician:

Franklin introduces, to Vergennes, **25.** 443n

Irish Roman Catholics politically encouraged by, **25.** 529n

Mann's turbulent letter from, sent to Horace Mann II to be shown to C. J. Fox, **25.** 443, 456

New Exchange, the Strand:

Mawhood, druggist and tea-man at, **39.** 250

New Forest, Hants:

Gloucester, D. and Ds of, go to lodge in, **24.** 360

Gloucester, D. of, warden of, **11.** 80n

Park Place's view of, **39.** 550

Paulton Park in, **11.** 41n

Newfoundland:

Biscay and other French provinces have fishing rights off, **38.** 120

capture of, by the French, **22.** 52, 69

England will give fishing rights on, to the French, **21.** 526

English merchants trading at, complain of French encroachments, **38.** 527–8

English recovery of, pleases Leghorn, **22.** 100

Farinelli said to have escaped to, **18.** 119

fisheries at, to be returned to pre-war state, **22.** 76n

fishing in, restricted, **28.** 179n

fishing rights on, **21.** 526n, 536n, 553n

French fisheries at, **32.** 18

French ship with supplies for, captured, **22.** 82

Hertford and D. of Richmond told to enforce treaty regulations concerning, **32.** 18n

Italy gets fish from, **22.** 100–1

peace terms about restitution of, **22.** 55n

ship from, reaches Leghorn, **24.** 246

New Foundling Hospital for Wit:

Almon prints Gray's verses on Lord Holland in, **28.** 118n, 209, **33.** 437n

New Friend on an Old Subject. See under Hervey, Hon. Frederick William

Newgate Prison, London:

Ayliffe committed to, **23.** 74

'Black Bess' sent to, **42.** 503

criminal in, confesses robbery of gentleman's scrutore, **20.** 215

Dance remodels, **15.** 316n

Denbighshire high sheriff sent to, **17.** 344

Dignam sent to, **28.** 289

England's greatest rogues not sent to, **42.** 149

fire at, **38.** 168n

Franklin in, **22.** 188

Gibson and Murray sentenced to, **20.** 225, 227

Gibson receives sacrament at, **1.** 134n

Gordon, Lord George, dies in, **11.** 208n

—— in, **35.** 437

Gordon rioters burn, **33.** 184

Gordon rioters release prisoners from, **29.** 59, 60, **33.** 194

Gregory committed to, **13.** 87n

Grenville ministry ransacks, for writers, **38.** 422

Hogarth's portrait of Sarah Malcolm sitting in, **19.** 460n

Jews committed to, **11.** 206

Maclaine committed to, **20.** 188n

Martin liable to be put into, **38.** 270

Mason fears Yorkshire Association deputies may be put into, **29.** 121

mercer promises to send silk to, for Mrs Rudd, **24.** 153

Mohammedan princess in *Barbarossa* visits lover in, **35.** 198–9

Moratt committed to, **37.** 9n

Moreton reports to George III about prisoners in, **40.** 194n

murderers of turnkey at, executed, **20.** 312

Murray in, denied pen, ink, paper, and visitors, **20.** 225n

Myddleton released from, **17.** 344n

North Briton's printers sent to, **38.** 196

ordinary of, enrolls things, **28.** 440; *see also* Moore, Joseph; Roe, Rev. Stephen

Paxton released from, **17.** 502

—— to be sent to, **17.** 397, 400n

Reynolds and Ward committed to, for borough corruption, **22.** 584n

Rohan, Cardinal de, would not have been sent to, **33.** 495

Russell's levee in, **23.** 82

Sampson committed to, **22.** 588n

Selwyn's joke about, **9.** 256

Stratford's tragedy mentions, **29.** 223, 224

visitors throng to, **20.** 199

Wesket in, **38.** 473

Wilkes dates addresses to constituents from, **23.** 82

—— should have gone to, **22.** 198

Newgate Prison, Dublin:

Fitzgerald dies in, **11.** 326n

Newgate St, London:

Say, printer in, **23.** 231n

[Newgate St, London, *continued*]
Skrine's suicide at tavern in, **25**. 386n, **36**. 210n
White, John, in, **1**. 67

Newhailes, Midlothian, Dalrymple's seat:
Dalrymple, Christian, inherits, **15**. 127n
Dodsley visits, **15**. 37
Pococke describes, **15**. 37n

New Hall, Boreham, Essex, Olmius's seat:
glass from, **9**. 92

New Hall, Wilts:
Batt of, **11**. 17n

New Hampshire, U. S.:
part of, does not rebel against England, **24**. 56n

Newhaven, Bn. *See* Mayne, Sir William (1722–94)

Newhaven, Bns. *See* Allen, Frances (d. 1801); Pierrepont, Gertrude (ca 1663–1732)

New History of Gloucestershire, A. See under Rudder, Samuel

New Holland:
unexploited because it has no wealth, **25**. 545

Newington Green:
Price's sermon at, **11**. 315n

New Inn:
Holme of, **11**. 34n
Lucas lives at, **33**. 281n

New Inn Passage, Clare Market:
Yardley, printseller in, **33**. 512n

'New Interest':
Parliamentary candidates for, **37**. 371

New Jersey:
American army in, estimated, **24**. 339
Americans reoccupy most of, **6**. 415n
Clinton marches through, **28**. 409
Cornwallis is believed to be checked in, **28**. 282
Cosby, governor of, **9**. 134n
Pownall, lt-gov. of, **1**. 293n
Washington said to have retired to, **24**. 338

New Jerusalem:
HW wishes Wilkes were in, **35**. 322

New Lesson for Pope. See Roome, Edward: *Dean Jonathan's Parody*

Newling, John (fl. 1776), mayor:
Cole dines with, **2**. 27

New London, Conn.:
Arnold burns, **29**. 161n
Dalrymple's attack on, **36**. 177n
English defeated at, **33**. 306n

'New Mad Tom.' *See under* Hayden, George

Newman St, London:
Bacon in, **28**. 439n

Newmarket:
Amelia, Ps, tries to keep D. of Cumberland from going to, **38**. 444
bank bill discarded at, **20**. 53
Bever's auction at, **32**. 134n, 159n, **36**. 95n
Bromley prefers, to Holt Castle, **40**. 13
Chartres, Duc de, to visit, **24**. 186
—— will not visit, **6**. 294

Cumberland, D. of, appears in coach at course at, **38**. 456n
—— popular at, for deep gambling and hospitality, **37**. 352
denizens of, disregard monarchs, **23**. 497
dullness of, between meetings, **32**. 389
forests cut down to pay debts contracted at, **28**. 104
Fox, C. J., the first figure at, **25**. 154
French visitors flock to, **25**. 409
Grafton 'ducal apostle from,' **31**. 323
HW at White's prefers, to elections as topic, **35**. 357
HW contrasts houses of, with Modena's and Parma's, **18**. 315
HW does not 'campaign' at, under D. of Cumberland, **37**. 352
HW goes to SH instead of, **37**. 458–9
HW ignorant of affairs from, **36**. 96
HW jokes about: Cts of Northumberland 'sailing' to, **10**. 108; racing rules at, **31**. 107
HW may have to go to, **28**. 92
HW mentions, **11**. 257, 365
HW not interested in races at, **1**. 110
HW preferred to discuss, rather than politics, **25**. 483
HW sells race-horses at, **23**. 497
HW's indifference to, **28**. 173, 197
HW the Anstis of, **32**. 142
HW to have sale of horses at, **31**. 174
HW visits, **13**. 89
HW writes from inn at, **15**. 21n, **31**. 20
hours at, sacred, **31**. 174
inn at, **18**. 315, 332; *see also* Red Lion
jokes about, in Chesterfield's will, **32**. 112
King's Plate run for at, **13**. 89n
language of, unintelligible to HW, **35**. 357
London deserted because of, **25**. 639
Londoners flock to, **23**. 401
matches at, are the only ones that HW knows, **32**. 147
ministers hold 'Wittenagemot' at, **10**. 274
music eclipsed by, **23**. 570–1
Necker, M. and Mme, not to visit, **6**. 292
'never-to-be-violated festival of,' **25**. 264
new Hieroglyphic Tale to be laid at, **32**. 131
Orford, 3d E. of, at inn on road to, **23**. 460
—— frequents, **30**. 167n
—— has farm near, **23**. 495
—— resumes connections with, **6**. 24
——'s bets at, **23**. 503
——'s horses to be on view at, before sale, **31**. 174n
——'s horses to be sold at, **41**. 266
Ossory, Lord, loves, **32**. 154
——'s horses run at, **33**. 502n
Palace, the, in High Street at, **20**. 373n
Panton was horse jockey at, **24**. 499
Parliament adjourns in favour of, **39**. 145
Patriots imbibe principles of honour at, **41**. 344
people will stay in London till it is fashionable to go to, **25**. 105

politics slacken during season of, **25**. 398

Pulteney contributes paper on, to *The World*, **20**. 374

race-horses at, should compete for odes, **16**. 298

races at: **28**. 382, **32**. 131n, 133n; begin, **22**. 174n; forfeits prepaid at, **19**. 318; to begin, **23**. 99, **24**. 20; trial of horses for, **21**. 490

race-week at, **28**. 382

Red Lion inn at: **14**. 166; tapestry in, **1**. 169–70

Rockingham and Orford make wager at, on race between geese and turkeys, **21**. 7n

season at, has for 10 years opened in October, **38**. 272, 273

Selwyn may visit, **30**. 244

——'s witticisms wasted at, **30**. 224

Shafto's winnings, and D. of Cumberland's losses at, predictable, **38**. 272

shooting at, **38**. 29

stables of, thought by French to abound in poisons, **41**. 6

'Timion' in race at, **32**. 131n

Tom Thumb to ride three horses at, **32**. 174

visitors from, expected at Houghton, **18**. 70

visitors to: Bolingbroke, **9**. 307; Boufflers, Comtesse de, **32**. 14; Bunbury, Lady Sarah, **32**. 14n; Chartres, Duc de, **25**. 485n; Cumberland, D. of, **20**. 373, **22**. 288, 297, **37**. 459, **38**. 444, 445, 456, 462, 527, 535, **40**. 361; Devonshire, 4th D. of, **37**. 511; Fox, C. J., **23**. 400; Garrick, **40**. 114; George IV, **25**. 485n; Grafton, **38**. 543; Grosvenor, **21**. 490; HW, **9**. 350, **18**. 315; Hertford, **37**. 385, 511, **38**. 29; March, E. of, **38**. 440; Orford, E. of, **9**. 351; Ossory, Lord, **32**. 113, 134–5; Ponsonby, **21**. 7; Rockingham, **22**. 97n, **38**. 543; Selwyn, **3**. 291, **21**. 7, **38**. 440; Walker, **19**. 511n; Walpole, Horatio (1752–1822), **36**. 121–2

visitors to, pilloried in newspaper letters, **42**. 501

weather bitter in Newmarket week, **33**. 400

younger generation goes to, in England, **24**. 89

'Newmarket,' HW's. *See* Strawberry Hill: HW's Easter party at

Newmarket Heath:

may become airfield, **39**. 425

New Method of Reading Newspapers, A. See under Whitefoord, Caleb

Newminster Abbey, Winchester:

Alfred's will found in register of, **42**. 223n

New Morning Post. See under Morning Post

Newnham, Nathaniel (ca 1741–1809), M.P.; lord mayor of London 1780–90:

Grantham notifies, of peace news, **25**. 356n

Rodney not given banquet by, **25**. 343

Townshend asks, to prevent gambling in the funds on peace news, **33**. 379n

—— notifies, of peace news, **25**. 347n

Newnham. *See also* Newenham; Nuneham

Newnham Paddox, Warwickshire, E. of Denbigh's seat:

HW visits, **10**. 264n

portrait of Catherine Parr at, **33**. 208

New Norfolk St, London:

Hesketh, Lady, lives in, **11**. 235n

Hotham, Lady Gertrude, lives in, **24**. 90n

New North St, Red Lion Sq., London:

Suckling's address, **24**. 209

'New Ode, A.' *See under* Williams, Sir Charles Hanbury

New Ormond St, London:

May dies in, **12**. 96n

New Oxford Guide:

HW proud to appear in, **35**. 462

New Palace Yard, London:

Bedford occupies usher's house in, **42**. 491

covered with grain, **11**. 212–13

HW's Exchequer house in, **40**. 86, 87, **42**. 491

Williams pilloried in, **38**. 512

New Park, Richmond. *See* Richmond: New Park

Newport, Bn. *See* Blount, Mountjoy (ca 1597–1666); Jocelyn, Robert (ca 1688–1756)

Newport, Mr:

SH visited by, **12**. 245

Newport, Lady Diana (d. 1766), m. (1721) Algernon Coote, 6th E. of Mountrath:

Conway to tear HW from, **37**. 301

death and will of, **30**. 222–3, **31**. 123

HW's opinion of, **9**. 135

HW's verses on, **9**. 135n

Hardwicke visits, at Twickenham Park, **9**. 135

intemperance of, **30**. 222

Newcastle, Ds of, inherits Twickenham Park from, **35**. 349n

Twickenham Park House occupied by, **42**. 484

Newport, Francis (1620–1708), cr. (1694) E. of Bradford:

SH built by coachman of, **13**. 17n

Newport, Henry (1683–1735), 3d E. of Bradford:

natural son of, **9**. 148n

Newport, John (ca 1720–83):

Bath, E. of, said to have seized estates of, **9**. 148

Newport, Sir John (1756–1843), cr. (1789) Bt:

SH visited by, **12**. 250

Newport, Lady Katherine (ca 1653–1716), m. (1681) Henry Herbert, 4th Bn Herbert of Chirbury:

(?) miniature of, by Ashfield, at Burghley House, **10**. 346

Newport, Robert, Irish chancellor:

George II has Holdernesse write to, that he expects support for Dorset, **20**. 440n

Newport, Isle of Wight:

Conway writes from, **37**. 495, 499, 501

visitors to: Chudleigh, Elizabeth, **37**. 503; Huntingdon, **37**. 500; Kingston, D. of, **37**. 503; Prideaux, Col. and Mrs, **37**. 503; Richmond, D. and Ds of, **37**. 500

Newport, Rhode Island:

[Newport, Rhode Island, *continued*]
blockade of, 24. 418n
Newport Gat, near Ostend:
Thurot discovered by Capt. Tinker near, 21. 338n
Newport Pagnell, Bucks:
distances from, to Bletchley and Gothurst, 10. 332
Newport St, London:
Eccardt lives in, 9. 371n
Reynolds lives in, 9. 158n
Richter and Bartoli of, 35. 407n
New Prison, London:
HW saw, burning, 35. 354
See also New Bridewell
New Review, A:
Cole reads, 2. 335n
Letters of Literature reviewed in, 16. 274
See also under Maty, Paul Henry (1745–87)
New Road, London:
house destroyed in, 12. 176n
Milbourn in, 11. 113n
thronged, for Q. Charlotte's arrival, 35. 312
Newry (Ireland):
Bedford, D. of, to join army at, 21. 373
News:
paragraphs of, like roasted chestnuts, 33. 213
Newes from Malta . . . Shewing the Desperate Assault:
Bodleian catalogue lists, 1. 249
Newsham, Mrs John. *See* Craggs, Anna
Newsham Craggs, James (1715–69), M.P.:
biographical information about, corrected, 43. 238
(?) mother disinherits, 9. 65
(?) mother of, 17. 165, 254
Newspaper; newspapers:
abound in scurrilities on handsome young women, 24. 267, 25. 364, 584, 41. 404
Adam offended by version in, of Fox's speech, 24. 538
advertisements in: 1. 97, 40. 257; of sexual stimulants, 19. 561; of Sir C. H. Williams's 'Lord Bath to Ambition,' 30. 319
American Declaration of Independence printed in, 24. 230n
American news in, 24. 220
American pacification proposals mentioned in, 39. 374–5
announce patrols in Scotland, 20. 35
anonymous letters in, replace pamphlets, 22. 169n
arrive at noon, 34. 169
at Dover inn, 18. 315
back numbers of, discussed by farmers, 10. 259
Bavaria's neutrality alleged in, 37. 189
Beckford overrated by, 35. 339
Berry, Mary, hurt by notice in, 11. 375–7
Birthday clothes of Lady Walsingham discussed in, 39. 414–15
Bolingbroke, out of the world, has to write from, 37. 354

Bristol's posts announced in, 22. 453
cardinals' creations to be announced in, 18. 302
carried in coaches, 31. 265
Chartres's indecent buttons attacked in, 25. 409
——'s visit to be subject of lies by, 36. 232
Chesterfield's speech in, 19. 52
Child's legacy to fiancée correctly reported in, 30. 172
Choiseul's disgrace reported in, 23. 62
Churchill reads aloud, to wife and HW, 12. 104
circulated over Europe, 25. 146
Cole on lies in, 2. 127, 305n, 330
——'s acquaintance with, 1. 93–4, 97, 112n, 118, 2. 123, 127, 145–6, 305
collect news from coffee-houses, 34. 231
common, lack vivacity but are more useful than HW's correspondence, 37. 548
'common fame' out-lies, 32. 162
contradictory reports in, 33. 156
Conway credited by, with great commissions, 24. 33
—— imagines his obituary in, next to love-sick housemaid's, 37. 189
—— important enough in Ireland to be named in, 37. 375
——'s military progress through Ireland covered by, 37. 399–400
——'s play noticed in, 35. 391
Corsican news in, 21. 140
(?) Craven, Bns, abused in, 36. 210
Cumberland, D. of, called 'royal idiot' by, 23. 230
daily morning, page of political invective always in, 24. 451
'Daily Courants' to inform public what one is *not* doing, 34. 64
Damer, Mrs, sends to Mary Berry at York, 12. 83–4
describe press gangs, 23. 239
detestable for lies, blunders, scandal, and factious letters, 25. 297
Doctors Commons a fit topic for lies of, 24. 427
Dutch war rumoured in, 36. 247
East India Co. denounced in, 23. 457
Egmont's pamphlet much advertised in, 20. 43
Elba affair mentioned in, 18. 47
Elizabeth of Russia's answer in, 21. 368
England's decline chronicled in, 33. 320–1
English: Bergen-op-Zoom mentioned daily in, 19. 448n; Churchills want, in France, 38. 495; France bans, because of scandal about Marie-Antoinette, 25. 557; HW ashamed of, in Paris, 10. 298; in Paris coffee-houses, 28. 356–7
English Court, incite Amsterdam's people to attack Van Berckel, 29. 124
English expedition to Naples mentioned in, 18. 47

English invasion of France reported by, **39.** 526

epigrams in, on Bute and Ps of Wales, **38.** 462

escape of Frenchmen from Prague reported in, **18.** 68–9

evening, Ds of Marlborough's will in, **18.** 528

explanations always given by, though they may be false or incorrect, **25.** 459

false news spread by, to manipulate stock prices, **39.** 512

falsities not a discredit to, **33.** 212–13

follies and scandals in, **25.** 530

foolish, brutal, or scandalous, **25.** 146–7

foreign: copy each other, **18.** 213; Jacobite encouragement reported in, **18.** 426; Repnin's mission to England reported in, **24.** 487; Walpole, Horatio (1678–1757) credited by, with Parliamentary motion, **18.** 427

former pamphleteers now write letters in, **25.** 451

Fox's Martyrs advertised in, **25.** 505

Franklin must comment upon, to French ministers, **24.** 465

French: Conway reads, **39.** 491; French princes do not furnish news items for, **40.** 387; HW horrified by reports in, **12.** 22

French barbarities not exaggerated by, **11.** 91

'French disease' a term used in, **22.** 175

French-hired, might abuse Lord Ossory, **33.** 202

French ridicule of English expeditions cannot be stifled by, **37.** 544

frivolities of, in wartime, **35.** 363–4

full of invasion from France, **21.** 293

full of lies, **2.** 329, **28.** 261, **29.** 207, 273, 307

full of lies and blunders, **31.** 267

full of lies but give main outline of events, **23.** 536

Garrick's prologue on returning to the stage printed in, **31.** 83

——'s Stratford festival in, **10.** 298

George II's trip to Flanders announced in, **18.** 48

George III's Coronation will fill, **21.** 515

German princes abused by, **42.** 496

Gloucester, Ds of, will be abused by, **36.** 67

Gloucester, D. of, called 'D. of Lancaster' in, **22.** 264

—— said by, to be ill, **32.** 123

—— said by, to have died, **25.** 623

Gray's death in, **23.** 319, **35.** 127, **39.** 148

——'s obituary overshadowed by Sir Francis Delaval's in, **28.** 20

HW and Mme de Genlis mentioned by, **33.** 482

HW anticipates account of his arrival in, **32.** 270

HW called 'well-preserved veteran' by, **30.** 279, **33.** 516, **42.** 170

HW calls, drag-nets, **25.** 146

HW can only re-echo, **25.** 212

HW compares, to scavengers, **29.** 146

HW does not correct mistakes in, about himself, **33.** 578

HW does not wish to write more than is in, **25.** 295

HW frightened by war news in, **35.** 308

HW glad that Sundays are free from, **35.** 378

HW has to rely on, for news, **37.** 97, **39.** 196, 411, 508

HW has week of, to read, **33.** 57

HW hears no novelties until they are hashed in, **35.** 360

HW hides accounts of executions in, **33.** 444

HW imagines balloon traffic as written up in, **39.** 425

HW imagines exciting paragraphs from, in Middle Ages, **35.** 222

HW knows only what is told by, **25.** 336

HW lights candle to read, at 11 A.M., **32.** 409

HW mentions, **11.** 30, **12.** 26, 52, 53, 57, 59, 112

HW never hears of events until they are in, **25.** 116

HW never reads, **39.** 108

HW publishes letters in, on political abuse, **13.** 42

HW quotes diction of, **35.** 243

HW reads in: about sweepstakes, **23.** 497; of Gray's death, **35.** 127, **39.** 148; of raising Gibraltar siege, **25.** 331

HW refers to, **32.** 64

HW's activities printed in, **10.** 296

HW said by: to be dying, **28.** 71; to have palsy, **22.** 461

HW's American knowledge limited to reports in, **24.** 38

HW's dependence on, **34.** 196

HW sends paragraph from, to Mary Berry, **12.** 139–40

HW's eyes pained by reading, **16.** 20

HW's 'fellow-labourers,' **28.** 378

HW's information all comes from, **36.** 184, 187

HW's information on lord mayor from, **33.** 199

HW's intelligence no better than, **32.** 167

HW skips over, quickly, **39.** 119

HW's letters can give less news than, **24.** 204

HW's letters often anticipated by, **24.** 370, 385

HW's letters resemble, **30.** 188, **33.** 12

HW's news anticipated by, **35.** 369

HW's news would sound like cross-readings from, **34.** 37

HW's only source of news when at SH, **28.** 53, 210, 348, **29.** 49, 65, 145, 216

HW's opinion of, **10.** 166, **31.** 267

HW's outlines will help Mann understand, **25.** 273, 281

HW's parody of, **9.** 125–30

HW spends morning reading, **12.** 20

HW's reflections on worthlessness of, **22.** 325,

[Newspaper; newspapers, *continued*]
  23. 53, 432, 24. 232, 412, 512, 25. 363–4,
  557, 584, 619, 623
HW's sole source of information, 34. 190, 199
HW's source of material for letters, 12. 33,
  34, 37, 51, 122, 142
HW's unflattering remarks about, 11. 90–1,
  127, 129, 12. 65
HW tired of seeing his name in, 16. 29
HW unable to assess truth in, 33. 132
HW will publish, when he starts inventing
  news, 19. 484
Hall's deposition in, 21. 377
Hanoverian neutrality the topic of, 17. 187
Hanoverian peace with France reported by,
  39. 512
hard pressed for news in a peaceable autumn,
  25. 607
Hardwicke lauded by, 19. 293
Henley's discourses on all subjects in, 30. 56
heralds advertise in, for peeresses' names and
  addresses, 21. 535
heroes and heroines who make war are admired by, 35. 400
Hertford, Cts of, said by, to have died, 22.
  468
Hertford, E. of, said by, to be K.G., 22. 325
——'s embassy abused in, 38. 347
—— should disregard, 38. 366
——'s magnificence at Paris praised by, 38.
  235
horse races and casualties the staple of, 20.
  321
Howe attacked by, 23. 270, 25. 439n
Hyde's death in, 37. 357
inaccuracy of, 15. 329, 42. 424
inventions and lies no longer completely fill,
  36. 251
Irish, *see Universal Advertiser*
Irish rejection of Volunteers in, 35. 382
Irish wonders reported in, 25. 607
Italian, report Irish and Scotch encouragement of French invasion, 18. 415
Italian MS, Mann makes newspapers from,
  17. 156, 158
'Jacobin': Berrys read, only in Yorkshire, 12.
  69, 70, 74; Berrys will not learn truth
  from, 12. 76; *Siege of Berwick* abused in,
  12. 69
Jamaica fleet's arrival in, 25. 302
Jenkinson's death falsely announced in, 10.
  316
——'s promotion rumoured in, 35. 528
Karl Wilhelm Ferdinand said by, to be at
  Florence, 22. 463
Keppel's account criticized by, 24. 402–3
'know everything as well and as soon as anybody,' 28. 479
lack of: in next world, 33. 523–4; on Sunday
  morning, 33. 21, 35. 378
letter might appear in, protesting destruction of Salisbury chapels, 42. 260

letters to, HW's reflections on, 42. 498–501
lie and blunder, 36. 241
lies in, 2. 329
Lincoln's affair in, 23. 368
locusts mentioned in, 39. 418
London Gazette's 'lie' refuted by, 32. 284
London riots in, 23. 305, 24. 117
Luttrells' articles in, 24. 77
Lyttelton, Lady, does not read till it is history, 42. 200
Macklin's letter in, 37. 426
Manchester and Sandwich attack each other
  in, 10. 186
Mann avidly reads about England in, 22. 123
—— can get details from, 25. 79
—— can learn more from, than from HW,
  24. 428
—— credited by, with sending news of Toulon fleet's sailing, 24. 376, 380
—— finds HW's letters more hopeful than,
  24. 388
—— makes, from Italian MS newspapers,
  17. 156, 158
—— reads about Hastings's trial in, 25. 651
—— reads inconclusive accounts in, of new
  administration, 25. 299
—— receives arrears of, 24. 434
——'s death alleged by 'scalping assassins' in,
  33. 533
—— sends, to Anne Pitt, 24. 233
—— sends, to HW, 17. 84
——'s recall from Florence rumoured in, 22.
  315
—— would not trust accounts in, without
  HW's authority, 24. 270
Mann, Horace II, said by, to be ruining himself at cricket, 23. 495
Maria Theresa's treaty with Theodore
  printed in, 18. 208
Mason's squibs in, usually still-born, 28. 254
Maurepas's death reported in, 25. 212
military suppression of Gordon riots attacked in, 25. 77
militia enthusiastically noticed in, 38. 33
Minorca's danger blamed by, on English
  ministry, 24. 468
minute records of events printed in, 25. 363
Montagu sees account of HW's arrival from
  France in, 10. 299
More, Hannah, jokes about, as 'authentic
  sources of information,' 31. 370
—— reported by, to have married Priestley,
  31. 328–9
more communicative, 25. 503
Murray's sentence published in, 25. 361
Newcastle, D. of, thinks, impertinent about
  habeas corpus, 21. 182n
no event escapes notice of, 25. 527
odes on Pulteney frequent in, 18. 90
Orford's arrival noticed in, 20. 251
Oudh too inconsequential to be noticed in,
  25. 13

paragraph in, disturbs Mason, 28. 32

Paris uprisings correctly reported by, 39. 467

Parliamentary debates so fully reported in, that HW could only send extracts, 25. 464

Parliamentary members instructed through, by constituents, 17. 392

Parliamentary proceedings adequately covered by, 32. 231, 235-6

Parliamentary reporting by, injures sale of *Votes*, 22. 406n

Parliamentary speeches incorrectly reported in, 25. 58n

Pembroke's discovery reported in, 22. 19

phrase used in, 18. 277

pistol-firing may be reported in, 35. 526

poem on Pope's death in, 18. 467

political letters in, rarely read by HW, 25. 503

political news in, 10. 153

politicians write letters to, 35. 367

politics abandoned by, 30. 237

politics brought by, to breakfast table, 35. 342

popularity of, 31. 267

Portsmouth mutiny described in, 25. 362

Pozzolini's arrival in England announced in, 25. 344

Prevereau forwards, to Mann, 17. 421-2

Pucci's recall announced by, 21. 108

puffs in, cannot stifle French ridicule of English failures, 37. 544

Regency members listed in, 18. 218

reliability of, in Gordon riots, 35. 355

report in, that combined fleet is at Brest, 25. 186

revolutionary activities inaccurately reported in, 11. 347

revolutionary horrors palliated by, 15. 223-4

Rochefort capture reported in, 30. 144

Roman, *see Diario ordinario*

Roucour reported as Allied victory in, 30. 109

Russian successes reported in, 23. 231, 37. 556

Sandwich said by, to keep fleet at Portsmouth, 24. 377

'scandalous chronicles,' 33. 30

Scots attacked in, 23. 419

severe on Anglo-Spanish peace, 23. 274

Smith probably shows, to HW at Venice, 17. 84

squib in, about possible conquest of England, 19. 129

stocks, horse races, and ship arrivals the staple of, 22. 174

testimonials in, to quacks, 21. 132

Theodore of Corsica wants, 20. 378

Thurot discussed by, 21. 381-2

too vexatious, 34. 217

Tory, satirizes ministry, 18. 33

Townshend's and Wilkes's memorials in, 23. 339

unreliability of, 30. 78, 270, 32. 363, 396, 397, 33. 8-9, 115, 404, 420, 520, 523, 535-6, 578, 34. 208, 226

verses in: 9. 249; on Berkeley and tar-water, 18. 505; on Rollin's death, 30. 24

'vulgar records . . . oracles of the times,' 33. 320

Walpole, Sir Robert, said by, to be recovered from indisposition, 18. 140

—— subject of exaggerated reports in, 17. 165

war council announced in, 21. 163

weekly: abuse Bute, 22. 42; in defence of Sir Robert Walpole, C. H. Williams prepared papers for, but it was dropped, 30. 314

Wilkes's *North Briton* discussed in, 35. 322

Williams, Sir C. H., publishes verses in, 30. 314-15

writers in, purvey rubbish, 25. 146

year 1759 lauded by, 9. 250

York, Cardinal, said by, to have died, 23. 432

Yorke, Sir Joseph, praised by, 29. 114, 118

young Englishmen's follies reported in, 23. 506

See also Gazette; Periodical; Press

Newstead Abbey, Notts, Lord Byron's seat:
Byron sells oaks at, 9. 299
forts built at, 9. 299
HW passes, 35. 279
HW visits and describes, 9. 299, 35. 305
Scotch firs planted at, 9. 299
(?) Venetian windows inserted at, 9. 299

New St, Hanover Sq.:
Darell, Edward, of, 34. 59n
French, Mrs, has house in, 11. 57n

New St, Spring Gardens:
Ravensworth, Bns, dies at house in, 34. 63n

New System, or an Analysis of Ancient Mythology, A. See under Bryant, Jacob

New Testament. *See under* Bible

Newton, Miss:
dances at Robinson's ball, 37. 115

Newton, Mr, of Wimpole St, London:
SH visited by, 12. 249

Newton, Sir Isaac (1642-1727), Kt; natural philosopher:
Analysis pro quantitatum series by, edited by Jones, 40. 357n
bust of: in Hermitage, 14. 39n, 29. 34n, 296; in Mr Chenevix's library at SH, 37. 270
Cambridge's idol, 2. 213
Cooke's sermon discrediting, 2. 213
Du Deffand, Mme, mentions, 7. 202
English summers predicted by, 35. 414
Fontenelle's éloge of, 33. 570n
Frederick II's letters often mention, 34. 33
French have not excelled, 31. 256
gravitation theory of, once fashionable, 20. 154
HW invokes spirit of, 21. 407

[Newton, Sir Isaac, *continued*]
 HW mentions, **28.** 335
 HW quotes, **35.** 265
 HW would swallow a fairy tale by, **16.** 307
 Halley's comet foretold by, **21.** 294
 Kent designs monument to, **35.** 151
 (?) Nivernais to immortalize, **41.** 22
 Orford, Cts of, and Cts of Pomfret should have studied St John Chrysostom instead of, **20.** 555
 Orford, Cts of, discusses, with Andrási, **18.** 555
 Partridge, John, probably envied by, **28.** 277
 Pope's epitaph on, translated by Ashton, **14.** 235
 ——'s lines on, **28.** 408
 prediction by, of alteration in English climate, **20.** 119
 riddle attributed to, **32.** 137, 144
 Roubiliac's statue of, **2.** 330
 Sidney compared with, **40.** 136–7
 unworldly, **33.** 570
 Voltaire introduces, to France, **41.** 153
 white said by, to be offensive to eyesight, **18.** 228
Newton, James (1748–1804), engraver:
 HW employs, for *Description of SH*, **25.** 532n
Newton, Mrs Mary. *See* Chatterton, Mary
Newton, Mary (*alias* Farren) (d. before 1796):
 (?) family of, dependent on HW, **31.** 208
 HW maintained, from infancy, **30.** 360
 HW revokes bequest to, after her death, **30.** 375
 HW's bequest to, **30.** 360–1
 (?) insanity in family of, **31.** 208
Newton, Richard (1676–1753), D.D., 1710; Principal of Hart Hall (after 1740 Hertford College) 1710–53:
 brewing of ale in college criticized by, in *Expense of University Education Reduced*, **30.** 88–9
 Pluralities Indefensible by, **16.** 16n
 Selwyn's principal, **30.** 88
Newton, Rev. Robert (1576–?1635), rector of Gretford, Lincs:
 Countesse of Montgomeries Eusebia by, **16.** 7
Newton, Thomas (1704–82), Bp of Bristol 1761–82; Dean of St Paul's 1768–82:
 Armagh archbishopric declined by, **10.** 145, **22.** 275
 autobiography of, **2.** 321, 323, **29.** 254, 259
 death of, **2** 304, **29.** 186
 'gossiping prelate,' **35.** 569
 HW's opinion of works of, **2.** 323
 New Review lauds, **35.** 514
 Pearce and Bath unable to have Pearce succeeded by, in Rochester see, but get promise of London, **38.** 364–5
Newton. *See also* Newtown
Newton, Cambs:
 Clare rector of, **2.** 256
 Plumptre rector of, **2.** 154n
Newton, Glamorganshire:

 Rice of, **9.** 12n, 134n
Newton College. *See under* Aberdeen
Newton Park:
 Rice, Griffith, of, **41.** 117n
Newtown Butler, Lady. *See* Rochfort, Jane
Newtown Butler, Lord. *See* Butler, Brinsley
Newtown Butler:
 battle of, **41.** 470n
'New Whole Duty of Woman, The,' by HW:
 Cambridge, R. O., wants to see, **32.** 203
 MS of, **13.** 49n, **43.** 173
New Windsor, Berks:
 election for, **31.** 19n, **43.** 329
 Reeve of, **10.** 105n
New Year's Day:
 confectioners' shops at Paris decorated for, **7.** 291
 Conway, Hon. Henrietta Seymour, usually asked HW to frank letters on, **38.** 47
 gallery for Ps Amelia on, **32.** 411, **33.** 2
 gifts on, **3.** 205, 385, 393, 405, 406, **4.** 7, 7–8, 174, 175, 179, 331, **5.** 124, 298, 431, **6.** 3, 127, 249, 496–7, **7.** 1, 2, 97–8, 197, 200, 203, 439, 440, **10.** 114, **32.** 26, 323, **33.** 260, 34. 88, **38.** 278–9, **41.** 197
 HW protests against verses on, **32.** 224
 HW sends greetings to Mrs Boyle Walsingham for, **42.** 205
 HW's wishes for, **34.** 174
 London empty around, **19.** 455
 Mann performs ceremonies of, at Leopold's palace, **24.** 346
 —— sends greetings on, to HW, **20.** 210
 Montagu sends compliments on, to HW, **10.** 191
 Montfort's suicide on, **35.** 202
 Ossory, Lady, sends wishes for, to HW, **33.** 258, 457, **34.** 174
 post delayed around, **5.** 3, 9, 162, 163, 306, **6.** 126, 257, 388
 storm on, considered a bad omen, **24.** 431
 Suffolk, Cts of, entertains on, **10.** 113–14
New Year's Eve:
 HW escorts Ds of Richmond to Palais Marchand on, **31.** 93, **32.** 26
New York (city):
 Americans might recapture, **24.** 347, 348, **25.** 311
 Arbuthnot's fleet at, **33.** 126
 Carleton later commander at, **24.** 215n
 Cathcart marries at, **11.** 60n
 Charleston's surrender rumoured at, **24.** 500
 Clinton at, **28.** 409, **29.** 151
 —— captures fort near, **24.** 500
 —— may have abandoned, **24.** 416
 ——'s army dares not leave, **39.** 333
 ——'s army reaches, **24.** 405, 408
 conflagration in, **24.** 256
 Cornwallis attempting to go to, **25.** 194, **33.** 298
 Dalrymple brings news from, **36.** 177
 defenders of, not numerous, **24.** 342, 347
 dispatch from, **29.** 112

English army finds no plenty in, **24**. 406

English army in: **19**. 69n; estimated, **24**. 347n; lacks provisions, **28**. 294, **33**. 44; small, **24**. 336

English evacuate Philadelphia for, **24**. 393, **28**. 434n

English occupy, **6**. 364n, 368n, **24**. 255–6, 265, 336, **28**. 227, 456

Estaing blockades English fleet at, **24**. 406, 410

—'s fleet might be attracted towards, **24**. 408

Europe may have to take its laws from, **24**. 229

events may be expected in, **24**. 206

French fleet goes to, **33**. 126

gazette from, the only American news in England for a month, **24**. 338

HW expects army at, to surrender, **28**. 434, 473–4

HW thinks Americans at, after Mud Island affair, **33**. 3

Howe, Sir William, and brother to attack, **24**. 242–3, **32**. 321

Howe, Sir William, draws lines between King's Bridge and, **24**. 261

—— lands at Staten Island in face of, **24**. 229, 241

—— leaves Halifax for, **24**. 229

—— might abandon Philadelphia to save, **24**. 342

—— probably will defend, **32**. 400

—— said to have been repulsed at, **24**. 216

—'s provisions at, running short, **28**. 294

—'s victory at, rumoured at Leghorn, **24**. 246

—— takes possession of, **24**. 255, 265

La Fayette said to expect capture of, **25**. 70

letters from, say nothing of colonial revolt, **25**. 321

loyalists driven from, **28**. 206

Loudoun's expedition from, to Halifax, **21**. 130n

mayor of, *see* Mathews, David

mob in, said to have seized cargoes of ships that were to supply Gage, **24**. 111

news does not come from, **24**. 252

news from, on American war, **32**. 387, 396, 397, **33**. 5

news of attack on, expected, **28**. 277

new Xenophon may be produced by, **24**. 62

store ships for Boston seized at, **41**. 303

tea duty resisted by, **24**. 13

Tollemache, Capt., killed in duel at, **32**. 398

Washington's secret correspondence with people at, **33**. 239

Wilson, Sir T., and troops from, join Cornwallis, **33**. 4

New York (colony; state):

better disposed towards England, **24**. 85

Cosby, governor of, **9**. 108n, 134n

Dunmore, governor of, **28**. 237n

Fort Edward covers, **21**. 144n

Fort William Henry's capture exposes, **21**. 144

French fear Pitt might go to, **30**. 216

French threat to, **30**. 138, **37**. 502

Holland, Ilchester, and Upton get grants of land in, **38**. 421n

'opulent and proud colony,' with factions, **21**. 144

New York Gazette:

Howe's alleged victory in, **24**. 334, 338, **32**. 397

report in, on Battle of Brandywine, unconfirmed, **32**. 396

New Zealand:

unexploited because it has no wealth, **25**. 545

Neyret de la Ravoye, Anne (1697–1718), m. (1712) Louis du Plessis, Marquis du Plessis-Châtillon:

death of, regretted by husband and his second wife, **7**. 370

Niagara:

Amherst sends Prideaux to capture, **21**. 301n

English attack on, **20**. 506n

English capture of, **21**. 326, 333, **38**. 27

expedition against, fails, **20**. 495n

'Niagaricus':

Johnson, Sir William, should be called, **35**. 294

Nicaragua:

expedition sent against, ends in disaster, **29**. 90–1

Nicastro (Italy):

earthquake account mentions, **25**. 375

Niccoli, Abbé Raimondo (d. 1780), Tuscan agent and chargé d'affaires at Paris 1767–80; ? Richecourt's undersecretary:

biographical information about, corrected, **43**. 237

clothes of, unsuitable for England, **19**. 49

Franklin knows, **24**. 362

Italian maid brought by, from England, **19**. 290

Leopold told by dispatch from, about high price of food, **24**. *106*

maid seduced by, **19**. 224, 238

Mann told by, of American-French treaty, **24**. 363, 369

misdeed of, discovered in Vienna, **20**. 335

nephew of, acts as his substitute at Paris, **24**. 363

Orford, Cts of, accompanied by, to England, **19**. 42, 46, 49, 224, 238, **20**. 335

—— gives bed to, **17**. 107

—— has cases arranged by, **17**. 224

—— sends news by, **19**. 290

Richecourt bribed by, to continue salary, **20**. 335

(?) —— orders, to give up opera box, **17**. 394

—'s undersecretary, **19**. 42, 49

—— told to dismiss, **20**. 335

(?) Tuscany ruled by, **21**. 62

Niccolina. See Nicolina

Niccolini, Mme ——:

Soderini, Mme, served by, **18**. 251

[Niccolini, Mme ——, *continued*]
Vernacci cicisbeo to, 18. 251
Niccolini, Marchesa. *See* Riccardi, Giulia Maria
Niccolini, Signorita ——:
about to be married, 21. 343
watch from Paris for, 21. 343
Niccolini, Agata (1741–55):
death of, 20. 519
Niccolini, Abbé Antonio (1701–69), Marchese di Ponsacco:
Accademia della Crusca's thanks presented by, for gift of Johnson's *Dictionary*, 25. 643n
Aix-la-Chapelle to be visited by, 19. 485
Albani's letter, about treaty, shown by, 17. 342
Augsburg and Munich may be visited by, 20. 2, 7
ball to be given by, for D. of York, 22. 171
banishment of, revoked, 20. 4n
banishment order fails to reach, 20. 7
Barrett Lennards entertained by, with Mme Capello, Mann, Rinuccini, and Stanhope, 20. 174
Botta told by, of Mann's coming promotion, 22. 318
Bubb Dodington accompanied by, 19. 420
Cambridge visited by, 14. 31
Carlisle and Duncannon told by, about Riccardi's collection, 19. 361
Chute's witticism on banishment of, 20. 3–4
Cunningham tells, of Mann's coming promotion, 22. 317
Delci, Contessa, niece of, 18. 60, 85
England not to be revisited by, now that P. of Wales is dead, 20. 285
—— pleases, 19. 339
—— praised by, 20. 285
—— visited by, 19. 72, 308, 329, 331, 348, 362, 369, 382, 387, 398, 436
English Court unlikely to complain about, to Viennese Court which would not listen, 20. 19
English government subject to lectures by, in Florence, 20. 145–6
English honours proclaimed by, 19. 369
English tour of, 19. 398
Florence dreads return of, 19. 369, 20. 117
Francis I banishes, from Tuscany, 19. 485n, 20. 2, 7
—— permits, to return from Padua to Tuscany, 20. 145n
Frederick, P. of Wales, accompanied by, to Cliveden, 19. 436
—— befriends, 19. 348, 362, 20. 2
—— tells: about Sandwich, 20. 217; that Murray is a Jacobite, 20. 364
freemason lodge in Florence attended by, 19. 364n
George II's death may benefit, 19. 414
Goodwood visited by, 19. 398n
Guasco and Cerati indulge with, in mutual praise, 22. 531
HW entertains, on fast day, 19. 331
HW forwards letter to, 19. 372, 449

HW never sees, 19. 449
HW's inscription for bas relief of Benedict XIV translated by, 21. 126–7
health of, fever, 20. 145–6
Holland visited by, 19. 485n
Kilmorey, Vcts, calls, 'my lord,' 20. 298
knighthood may be acquired by, 19. 414
Lovat's execution attended by, 19. 387
——'s trial shocks, 19. 382
Mann asked by, about George II giving Hanover to D. of Cumberland, 17. 328
—— forwards letter to, through HW, 19. 385, 408, 445, 449
—— gives: copy of HW's inscription for Benedict XIV, 21. 113; copy of HW's inscription for Theodore of Corsica, 21. 148
—— reports to D. of Bedford on affair of, 20. 3n
—— said to have been ordered to complain about, to Regency, 20. 7
—— shows HW's verses to, 18. 372
—— tells Botta and, about insignificance of Carrickfergus raid, 21. 381
—— to be aided by, in getting news of Lady Mary Wortley Montagu, 20. 285
—— to thank, for attentions to D. of York, 22. 179
nephew of, 20. 428, 22. 220
O'Kelly may be accuser of, 20. 2
Orford, Cts of (Bns Walpole), expected by, to return to Florence, 19. 394
—— may see, 19. 353, 362
—— not reliably discussed by, 19. 398
—— to have her jewels sold by, 17. 95, 134–5, 217
Padua may be visited by, 20. 24
Pandolfini's answer from, 20. 24
—— to notify, of banishment, 20. 2
Passionei invites, to Rome, 21. 127
Pomfret, Cts of, corresponds with, 17. 240, 18. 558
—— gives books to, 18. 126–7
—— may introduce, as a genius, 19. 353
—— sees, often, 19. 362
religion alone keeps, from becoming English, 19. 436
Riccardi can arrange sale of gems through, 19. 373
Richecourt angered by friendship of, with P. of Wales, 19. 441
—— announces pardon of, to family, 20. 117
—— hates, 20. 7
—— prepares letter to procure banishment of, 20. 2
——'s relations with, 20. 146
—— still believed to have instigated banishment of, 20. 117
—— told by, that Sandwich is not to be congratulated on his alleged appointments, 20. 217
Sandwich's unpopularity correctly described by, 20. 225
satiric print or drawing of, 22. 531

still in exile, **20.** 77
Tuscan ministry allegedly abused by, **20.** 4
Venice visited by, **20.** 24
Vienna probably visited by, **20.** 7
York, Cardinal, talks with, in Florence, **22.** 256
York, D. of, entertained by, **22.** 215
Niccolini, Lorenzo:
Ferri's altar-piece for villa of, at Bibbiena, **23.** 459n
Niccolini, Luigi (1713–82), Lisbon merchant:
Englishwoman married by, at Lisbon, **20.** 519n
losses of, in earthquake, **20.** 519
Niccolini, Maria Lucrezia (d. 1778), m. (1742) Lodovico Pannocchieschi d'Elci:
crooked, **18.** 85
Dal Borgo entertains, **18.** 85
English riding habit worn by, **18.** 85
marriage of, **18.** 60
Niccolini's niece, **18.** 60
——'s 'sister,' **18.** 85
Niccolini, Teatro. *See* Teatro del Cocomero
Niccols. *See* Nicholls; Nichols
Niccolucci, Stefano, Electress's door-keeper:
(?) Dumesnil asks, for admittance, **17.** 236
Niccotina. *See* Nicolina
Nice (France):
Agincourt's letter to HW shipped from, **42.** 102
Austrians to join Sardinian army at, **19.** 323n
Belle-Isle's and La Mina's headquarters at, **19.** 432n
Butler may go to Genoa or, **25.** 303
Charles Emmanuel III has smallpox at, **19.** 334
—— to attack, **19.** 313
—— to resist Spanish invasion through, **18.** 395
Colonna told not to visit, **7.** 99
Cornish puts in at, **18.** 415
English families at, **34.** 78
English travellers swarm at, **25.** 618
French and Spaniards try to pass through, **18.** 461
Holland, Bn, increases reputation of, **23.** 2
—— to visit, **4.** 327, **22.** 561
Holland, Bns, to visit, **4.** 327
improper place to spend hot months, **24.** 286
letters reach Florence from, **19.** 344
Leutrum to invade, **19.** 432
Macaulay, Mrs, not to visit, **6.** 497
Maillebois may have to retire to, **19.** 237
Mann, Horace II, detained at, **24.** 369, **25.** 404
—— prevented from embarking for, **25.** 203
—— thinks of moving his family to, to break daughter's attachment, **25.** 431
Mathews to forestall Spanish advance on, **18.** 312
one of England's last available foreign ports, **20.** 575
Orford, Cts of, may spend winter at, **23.** 2
Philip, Don, has not started from, **19.** 36
—— makes, his headquarters, **19.** 432

—— may enter, **18.** 271
—— may have to fight his way through, **17.** 408
—— to attack, by land, **18.** 371n
—— to command Spanish army in, **18.** 547
Piacenza ceded by Charles Emmanuel III in exchange for, **19.** 508n
rendezvous for commissioners exchanging territory in Italy, **19.** 508
Sardinians covet, **18.** 448
sea engagement not reported at, **18.** 403
Spanish troops arrive at, **19.** 9
valley of, provides no forage, **19.** 51
Villettes receives letter from, **18.** 413
visitors to: Beauvau, **18.** 448; Bertie family, **2.** 235; Bristol, E. of, **24.** 167, 203; Brown, **19.** 323n; Fleury, Duc de, **11.** 181n; Francis III, **19.** 314n, 432n; Gloucester, Ds of, **33.** 419n; Mann, Horace II, **24.** 369, 381, 530, 551, 569; Mann, Horace II and Lady Lucy, **24.** 64, 77–9, 82, 84, 247, 251, 265, 281, 286, 305–6, 312, 331, 337, 344, 346, 353, 356; Mann, James II, **25.** 580; Philip, Don, **19.** 314n, 432n; Pembroke, E. and Cts of, and family, **25.** 493, 497n; Rivers, Bns, **34.** 81n; York, D. of, **22.** 251n
Nicetas:
Cocchi publishes Greek and Latin versions of Oribasius from collection of, **20.** 34n
Nichol. *See* Nicholl; Nicholls; Nichols; Nicol; Nicoll; Nicolls; Nicols
Nicholas of Apsley (fl. ca 1293), Prior of St Thomas the Martyr:
Maer Manor claimed by, **42.** 146n
Nicholl, Mrs William. *See* Cadogan, Frances
Nicholl. *See also* Nicholls; Nichols; Nicol; Nicoll; Nicols
Nicholls, ——:
(?) acts in play at Holland House, **9.** 335
Nicholls, Rev. Norton (ca 1742–1809), Gray's correspondent:
Berrys hear news of victory from, **12.** 98
'drinks like any fish,' **28.** 418
Florence visited by, **23.** 397, 446
Gray's friend, **23.** 397, 442n
——'s remark to, **28.** 187
HW agrees with Mason about, **28.** 419–20
HW entertains, at dinner, **11.** 17
HW knows and likes, **23.** 403
HW mentions, **12.** 98
HW receives news of Mason from, **28.** 404
HW's letters might be brought back to him by, **23.** 442
HW's letter taken by, to Conway, **39.** 478
HW told news by, **11.** 243–4
HW visits Osterley Park with, **28.** 413, **33.** 26
Hesketh, Lady, visited by, **11.** 236
Huntingdon accompanied by, to Florence, **23.** 397
Mann knows and likes, **23.** 446
—— never mentions, though HW expected them to be congenial, **23.** 442

[Nicholls, Rev. Norton, *continued*]

Mason asks, for Gray's letters to him, **28**. 83, 87

——'s correspondence with, **43**. 295

Müller informed by, about HW, **41**. 353n

reported to have MS of HW's Chatterton narrative, **2**. 132, 133

returns from Italy, **28**. *80*

Richmond to be home of, **11**. 152–3

singing of, **11**. 109, 153

SH visitors sent by, **12**. 226n, 245

Turner, William, leaves money to, **11**. 152

Udny, Mrs, visited by, **11**. 109

Nicholls, Mrs Norton. *See* Floyer, Jane

Nicholls. *See also* Nicholl; Nichols; Nicol; Nicolls; Nicols

Nichols, Mr:

SH visited by family of, **12**. 234

Nichols, Francis:

British Compendium by, **41**. 127

Nichols, John (1745–1826); printer, publisher, and editor:

Abbey of Bec's history translated and published by, **2**. 159n, 166

account of Chatterton's fraud given by, **29**. 182, 186, 206

alien priories subject of account by, **2**. 166, 173, 175, 177, 182

a rapid editor, **2**. 330, 331–2

Atterbury's correspondence published by, **29**. 292–6

Baynes may be informed by, about Wharton's ballad, **42**. 10–11

Bibliotheca topographica Britannica published by, **2**. 272, **12**. 267

Biographical and Literary Anecdotes of William Bowyer by, **2**. 332, 333, **42**. 21, **43**. 76

Biographical Anecdotes of William Hogarth by: **2**. 273, 276, **43**. 73, 124; 2d edn of, **2**. 330, **43**. 73, 124

Cole and HW exchange parcels conveyed by, **2**. 295, 297, 303, 306, 308

Cole fatigued by, with queries, **2**. 276

—— gives seal to, **2**. 295, 308

——'s account of, **2**. 182

—— transcribes funeral oration of Cts of Essex for, **2**. 271–2

—— wanted by, to edit Willis MS, **2**. 336, 338

Collection of all the Wills . . . of the Kings and Queens of England edited by, **43**. 72–3

Gentleman's Magazine's contributions from, **2**. 182, **12**. 22

Gostling's *Account of Hogarth's Tour* printed by, **41**. 435

Gough's printer, **2**. 227

—— to be thanked by, for gift to HW, **42**. 33

HW accuses, of former Jacobitism, **29**. 293

HW allows, to print *Letter to the Editor* in *Gentleman's Magazine*, **42**. 9

HW asks: about Peterborough's poem on Cts of Suffolk, **42**. 87; for impression of Fitz-Othes's seal, **42**. 87

HW corrects attribution in *Miscellaneous Poems* printed by, **42**. 18

HW entertains, at dinner at SH, **2**. 331

HW gets Gough's address from, **42**. 62

HW questions, about reputations of Milles and Bryant, **29**. 183, 186

HW's correspondence with, **41**. 435, 448–52, **42**. 9, 18, 21–2, 28–9, 33, 87

HW sends servant to, **42**. 277

HW's opinion of, **2**. 303

HW thanks: for books and prints, **42**. 33; for Gostling's *Account*, **41**. 435; for prints, **42**. 21

HW to be called on by, at SH, **42**. 28–9

HW visited by, **2**. 303, 308

Hardinge's letter to, **35**. 647n

History and Antiquities of the County of Leicester by, **2**. 243n, **42**. 289

inaccuracies of, **2**. 328–9, 331–2, 333

Johnson's notes to, printed, **12**. 22

King's 'character' by, **32**. 311

——s *Works* edited by, **32**. 310n

Knight delivers HW's *Mysterious Mother* to, **16**. 372

Literary Anecdotes by, calls Warburton the best letter-writer, **35**. 648–9

Nash's edn of *Hudibras* not to be printed by, **43**. 390n

Percy's printed sheets burnt in warehouse of, **41**. 321n

Pinkerton's bookseller, **42**. 277

Reed's and Steevens's *Biographical Anecdotes of William Hogarth* published by, **41**. 448

Select Collection of Poems, A, edited by, **2**. 328–9, **43**. 76

SH to be visited by, **29**. 270

Wilkes's *Theophrastus* printed by, **42**. 263n

Nichols, Rev. Nicholas (d. 1772):

Cole's tutor, **2**. 371

Nichols. *See also* Nicholl; Nicholls; Nicol; Nicoll; Nicolls; Nicols

Nicholson, Mr:

Foire St-Germain attended by, **7**. 309

HW accompanies, to shops, **7**. 308

Nicholson, Margaret ('Margery') (ca 1750–1828), assailant of George III:

(?) allusion to, **12**. 262n

carving on Windsor choir-stall depicts attempt by, **11**. 363, **34**. 11

Fitzherbert, Mrs, coupled with, by Lady Mary Coke, **33**. 528

forgotten, **12**. 117

'Nick, Young.' *See* Johnston, Caroline Georgina

Nickolls. *See* Nicholls

Nickson, Christiana (1732–88), m. (1751) John Hely Hutchinson; cr. (1783) Bns Donoughmore, s.j.:

peerage of, **25**. 433

Nicol, Mr:

Chavigny's social relations with, in Paris, **7**. 317

Nicol, George (ca 1740–1828), bookseller to George III:

biographical information about, corrected, **43.** 143

Farington expects to meet, at SH, **15.** 319

HW entertains at breakfast, **11.** 80–1

HW glad to see, but cannot unlock SH treasures for his friends to visit, **42.** 401

HW invites, to SH, **42.** 283, 315

HW refuses offer of, to publish his works, **16.** 260n, **42.** 371–3

HW's correspondence with, **42.** 283–7, 312–15, 371–6, 401

HW sends obituary notice of Lady Ravensworth to, **34.** 198

HW thanks, for Chamberlaine's *Imitations*, **42.** 375

HW visited by, in Berkeley Sq., **12.** 192, 213

Lodge's *Illustrations* printed for, **11.** 278n

Lodge to receive HW's message from, **42.** 313–15

Martin employed by, to cut type, **42.** 286n

Pall Mall the address of, **42.** 375

Shakespeare edition of, **33.** 546n

SH visited by, **12.** 236, 239, 243

SH visitors sent by, **12.** 245

SH visit pleases, **42.** 284

typography improved by, **42.** 286

Nicol, Mrs George. *See* Boydell, Mary

Nicol. *See also* Nicholl; Nicholls; Nichols; Nicoll; Nicols

Nicolai, Aimar-Charles-François de (1737–94), president:

Beaumarchais mentions, **6.** 35

(?) HW mentions, **6.** 20

Nicolaï, Aimar-François-Chrétien-Michel de (1721–69), Bp of Verdun 1754–69:

Louis XV waited on by, **3.** 263n

Marie-Josèphe will be regretted by, **3.** 257–8

Nicolaï, Aimar-Jean de (1709–85):

(?) attends session of parliament of Paris, **8.** 173

Du Deffand, Mme, gives opinion of, **6.** 35

HW describes, **7.** 276

HW has met, **6.** 35

social relations of, in Paris, **7.** 276, 336

son of, **6.** 35

Nicolaï, Antoine-Chrétien (1712–77), Comte de: gluttonous, **6.** 175

made maréchal de France, **6.** 173

Maillebois favoured by, **6.** 323

Nicole, Pierre (1625–95):

Essais de morale by, **6.** 89

(?) *Logique, La,* by, owned by Mme du Deffand, **8.** 33n

Nicolet (theatre in Paris):

Du Deffand, Mme, praises theatrical troupe of, **8.** 208n

Rousseau compared to shows at, **4.** 434

Siège d'Orléans given at, **7.** 66

visitors to: Aulan, **7.** 66; Boufflers, Marquise de, **7.** 336; Cambis, Vicomtesse de, **7.** 336; Churchills, **7.** 336; Du Deffand, Mme, **7.** 66; Hénin, **7.** 336; Leroy, **7.** 66; Mirepoix,

Mme de, **7.** 66; Tavannes, Comtesse de, **7.** 66

Nicoli. *See* Niccoli

Nicolina *or* Niccotina, Signora, actress. *See* Giordani, Nicolina

Nicolini. *See* Grimaldi, Nicolino; Niccolini

Nicoll, ——:

(?) acts in play at Holland House, **9.** 335

Nicoll, Lady. *See* Blundell, Elizabeth (d. 1743)

Nicoll, Frances Catherine Gunter (ca 1733–1805), m. (1755) William Legge, 2d E. of Dartmouth:

Bath, E. of, said to have discouraged, from marrying son, **9.** 147–8

Magdalen House visited by, **9.** 273–4

Nicoll, Margaret (ca 1735–68), m. (1753) James Brydges, styled M. of Carnarvon; 3d D. of Chandos, 1771:

affair of: **12.** 181n, **30.** 168n, **36.** 315; breaks HW's relations with uncle, **20.** 425; narrative of, **14.** 193–214, **20.** 278, 435; spoiled by lawyers and HW's uncle, **20.** 273; unknown to Mann, **20.** 431

appearance and temper of, HW hopes will improve, **14.** 200

Capper's statement of case of, **14.** 230–3

Chute's attempt to marry, to E. of Orford, **14.** 56n, 57–8, 195, 204, 216–20, 225–32, **20.** 256–7, 262

conduct of, praised by Nuthall, **14.** 227

dental work on, Chute presents bill for, **14.** 229–30

fortune of, **14.** 194, **20.** 238, 256, **21.** 285, **24.** 301, **30.** 168n

fortune-telling ascribed to, by Nuthall, **14.** 224–5

guardianship of, settled, **14.** 229

HW's and Chute's letters to, distress the Cappers, **14.** 226

HW's letter to, forwarded by Chute, **14.** 226

HW's narrative about affair of, **14.** 193–214

HW would have enriched nephew by marrying him to, **21.** 285

husband of, **30.** 168n

inhumanly treated by guardians, **14.** 194

letters referring to affair of, listed by Capper, **14.** 232–3

marriage of, **20.** 238n

Orford, 3d E. of, and, are brought together by Horace Walpole (1678–1757), **14.** 223

Orford gets unfavourable impressions of, **14.** 214–15, 222

—— spurns, **9.** 140n, **20.** 257, 265, **24.** 301, **36.** 298

Rosalba's portrait of, at the Vyne, **43.** 189

Tracys apply for guardianship of, **14.** 95n

unflattering account of, said to have come from HW, **14.** 224

Walpole, Horatio (1678–1757), inquires about HW's zeal for Orford's match with, **14.** 216

—— keeps E. of Orford from marrying, **23.** 367

[Nicoll, Margaret, *continued*]
Walpole family quarrel over, 13. 23
Whithed to have married, 20. 238, 256
Nicoll, Mary (d. 1765), m. Leake Okeover:
Nicoll, Margaret, delivered from, by Chute, 14. 210
—— dislikes living with, 14. 230, 231
—— ill-treated by, 14. 194, 20. 256
Nicoll, W., bookseller:
prosecuted, 23. 29
Nicoll. *See also* Nicholl; Nicholls; Nichols; Nicol; Nicolls; Nicols
Nicolls, Dr Samuel (d. 1763):
Kidgell expects to succeed, 14. 131n
Nicolò, Montagu's servant:
Montagu orders, to get drink for Danvers, 35. 70
Nicols, ——, undersheriff of London:
Ferrers attended by, 21. 399
Nicols, Rev. John (d. 1774):
asks HW to plan window, 1. *163*
urges work on Ely window, 1. 206
Nicols. *See also* Nicholl; Nicholls; Nichols; Nicol; Nicoll; Nicolls
Nicolson, Mr:
HW questions, about Lady George Lennox, 31. 126
SH visited by, 31. 126
Nicolson. *See also* Nicholson
Nicomède. See under Corneille, Pierre
Niddisdale, Scotland:
Morvo directs mason-work at, 42. 69n
Nieberg. *See* Neipperg
Niece (France). *See* Nice
'Nièce, la.' *See* Colbert, Élisabeth-Pauline-Gabrielle, Mme de Jonzac
'Nièce, votre,' or 'vos nièces.' *See* Carolina Augusta Mary; Cholmondeley, Henrietta Maria; Cholmondeley, Hester Frances; Churchill, Mary; Churchill, Sophia; Keppel, Anna Maria; Keppel, Laura; Sophia Matilda; Waldegrave, Lady Anna Horatia; Waldegrave, Lady Charlotte Maria; Waldegrave, Lady Elizabeth Laura; Walpole, Charlotte; Walpole, Laura; Walpole, Maria; Woffington, Mary
Nieukerke. *See* Nieukirchen
Nieukirchen de Nyvenheim, Sophie-Gertrude-Adélaïde-Dorothée-Catherine-Albertine-Frédérique-Élisabeth de (1733–1805), m. 1 (1760) Gerhard Pater; m. 2 (1779) Jean-Louis Quentin de Richebourg, Marquis de Champcenetz:
social relations of, in Paris, 3. *13*, 7. 296, 317, 320
Nieukircke *or* Nieukirke. *See* Nieukirchen
Nieuport (Flanders):
communication with, re-opened, 18. 416
France may use, as Dunkirk's substitute, 21. 527
French besiege, 37. 156
—— capture, 37. 207
—— repulsed at, 12. 49, 51, 53

Maria Theresa gives, to the French, 21. 117
Stair negotiates for English base at, 17. 400n
Nigel (d. 1169), Bp of Ely, 1133:
son of, 35. 565
Nigel, Th.:
print of, 40. 237
Nightcap; nightcaps:
and nightgown, portrait of Sir Robert Walpole in, 30. 370
Balmerinoch dons, for execution, 19. 302
Cromwell's, 37. 440
Egmont, Mme d', attends supper in, 32. 27
French footmen wear, dirty, 31. 55
Geoffrin, Mme, wears, without stays, 31. 59n
HW jokes about wearing, 31. 235
HW repacks his, 32. 84
Herbert, Lady Margaret, wants, pretty in case she is caught by a fire, 35. 210
Kilmarnoch, Cts of, wants, 37. 218
Lyttelton wears, with brocade coat, 15. 331
men wear, at Reggio fair, 22. 148
Sewell said to think better under, than under a judge's wig, 35. 560n
Nightegale, Benedict (fl. 1350), painter:
employed by Edward III, 1. 153
Nightgown; nightgowns:
ancestral statue wears, of plaster and gold, 35. 267
chintz, worn by Conway, 37. 124
Damer, Mrs, wears, English, 31. 142
Gloucester, D. of, wears, when receiving Count Thurn, 23. 352
HW wears: because of rheumatism, 11. 311; linen, worn at Florence, 11. 287; long, worn at Florence, 17. 105; neat white, 13. 179
Lennox, Lady George, attends theatre in, 31. 124n
Lorraine, Primate of, wears, 17. 12, 17
of gold brocade, worn by Bootle at breakfast, 20. 184
Stanislas I's, catches on fire, 22. 402, 403
See also Night-shift
Nightingale, Mr, of Barnes:
SH visited by, 12. 229
Nightingale, Edward (1696–1750), 7th Bt:
family of, 1. 239
violent, 1. 239
Nightingale, Sir Edward (1726–82), 8th Bt:
insanity of, 1. 238–40
(?) Townshend, Vcts, has seen, 40. 47
Nightingale, Mrs Edward. *See* Ethelston, Eleanor
Nightingale, Elizabeth (d. 1755), m. (1754) Wilmot Vaughan, 4th Vct Lisburne, 1766:
chaperon will be needed by, 20. 278
Florence visited by, 20. 271
Mann describes, 20. 271
Methodism familiar to, 20. 271
Rome to be visited by, 20. 278
Nightingale, Sir Gamaliel (1731–91), 9th Bt; naval capt.:
marriage of, 1. 239
Vengeance, ship of, 21. 350n

Nightingale, Mrs Gamaliel. *See* Clossen, Maria

Nightingale, Geoffrey (d. 1771):
death of, **1**. 239

Nightingale, Joseph Gascoigne (d. 1752):
Florence visited by, **20**. 271
Rome to be visited by, **20**. 278

Nightingale, Washington (d. 1754):
Florence visited by, **20**. 271
Rome to be visited by, **20**. 278

Nightingale. *See also* Nightegale

Nightingale, English ship:
Arbuthnot's ship, **43**. 269, 270
Conway expects to go on, from Minorca to Italy, **37**. 313–14

Nightingale; nightingales:
artificial, on music-box, sings 'Nancy Dawson,' **43**. 376
at Park Place, **12**. 97, **39**. 505
at SH, **4**. 77, 239, **9**. 364, **10**. 29, 34, 188, 279, 281, **12**. 98, **28**. 30, 268, **33**. 561, **39**. 3
Du Deffand, Mme, mentions, **3**. 292
HW has heard only one, **32**. 123
HW has heard few, **33**. 8
HW has not yet heard, in May, **23**. 213
HW jokes about, **10**. 279
HW misses, at SH, **42**. 245
Heliogabalus lived on tongues of, **31**. 344
imitated by enamelled bird on snuff-box, **11**. 214
Montagu mentions, **10**. 188
one of HW's spring delights, **33**. 334
Park Place's stucco raised by, **39**. 505
poetesses compared with, **16**. 257
Rich, Lady, as a, **30**. 295
scarlet, at SH, **39**. 3
season for, is over, **10**. 93
sing less than other birds, **39**. 300
thorn pressed by, **9**. 90

Nightingale family:
Kneesworth, seat of, **1**. 238n

Nightmare; nightmares:
Du Deffand, Mme, has, **7**. 117

Nightshift; nightshifts:
Townshend, Lady, takes, to Brompton lodging, **30**. 70

Night-sweat; night-sweats:
occurrences of, **39**. 167

Night Thoughts. See under Young, Edward

Nigon, ——:
attends session of parliament of Paris, **8**. 171

Nigroni, Mme, Mme Grimaldi's sister; Genoese:
Grifoni, Mme, entertains, **17**. 151

Nigroni. *See also* Negroni

'Nikin.' *See* Bosville, Godfrey

Nile River:
Bruce's account of, **11**. 358
Thames contrasted with, **39**. 381
West mentions, **13**. 131

Nimeguen (Holland):
Cuyp's view of, **23**. 569
Tuer, John, at, **1**. 51, 73
York, D. of, retreats towards, **12**. 104n

Nîmes (France):

HW calls, 'forest of wild beasts,' **34**. 181
Maison Carrée at, recommended to HW by Chute, **17**. 121
massacre at, **15**. 237

Nimphidia, the Court of Fayrie. See under Drayton, Michael

'Nina' (? in Paisiello's opera):
sung by Emma Hart, **11**. 340

Nina, ou la folle par amour. See under Marsollier des Vivetières, Benoît-Joseph

Ninepin; ninepins:
Coke, Lady Mary, in earnest about, **37**. 561

Ninepin alley; alleys:
Wentworth Woodhouse bowling-green resembles, **35**. 267
See also under Bowling

Nineteenth century:
HW expects new era in, **25**. 237

Ninette à la cour, pantomime ballet:
at Haymarket theatre, **25**. 134n

Nineveh:
London compared to, **20**. 469, **23**. 133

Ninewells, Berwickshire:
HW addresses Hume at, **41**. 57

Ninnin, ——, French physician:
Wilkes's certificate signed by, **22**. 198

'Niobe, St':
Guido painting to eclipse, **17**. 162
See also under Reni, Guido

Niobe:
children of, 'hatched and fledged,' **11**. 349
(?) Damer, Mrs, begins bust of, **25**. 184
—— models bust of, **12**. 272
Leopold disperses group of, in Uffizi, **25**. 170–1, 530–1
Orford, Cts of, compared with, **32**. 118
passions expressed by, **35**. 445
Reni, Guido, does painting of, **17**. 162, **30**. 370, **35**. 12
sculpture of family of: 'all expression,' **11**. 338; bad placing of, will be described to HW by Mrs Damer, **25**. 203; HW suggests adorning, with rouge, **25**. 178; spoiled by division, **25**. 177–8
statue of, placed in new room at Florence, **33**. 286

Nisbet, Sir Henry (d. 1746), 4th Bt; army officer:
death of, at Roucour, **30**. 108
Townshend, Vcts, abandons, **9**. 47

Nischandschi Mohammed Emin Pasha (ca 1723–69), Turkish Grand Vizir 1768–9:
sacrificed to mob, **23**. 160

Nistelrode (Brabant):
Conway encamped at, **37**. 284–7

Nit; nits:
Temple, Cts, mentions, in verses, **10**. 114

Nitetti. See under Sacchini, Antonio

Nithsdale, Cts of. *See* Beaumont, Elizabeth (d. 1671); Herbert, Lady Winifred (d. 1749)

Nithsdale, E. of. *See* Maxwell, Robert (1586–1646)

Nitre:

[Nitre, *continued*]
Bey's son makes gunpowder of, at Tunis, **20.** 319
Nivelle, ——:
bankruptcy of, **39.** 157
Nivelle de la Chaussée, Pierre-Claude (1692–1754), dramatist:
Mercier's *Indigent* in style of, **6.** 32
Préjugé à la mode by, seen and liked by HW, **6.** 44, **7.** 274
Nivernais, Duc de. *See* Mancini-Mazarini, Louis-Jules-Barbon
Nivernais, Duchesse de. *See* Brancas, Marie-Thérèse de (1716–82); Phélypeaux de Pontchartrain, Hélène-Angélique-Françoise (1715–82)
Nivernais family:
Hertford does justice to, **38.** 243
—— has, to dinner, **38.** 252
Hertfords' good treatment from, compensates for bad impression in England, **38.** 237
Nivernois. *See* Nivernais
Nixon, Adam:
conspiracy by, against Sir Edward Walpole, **43.** 365
Nixon, Andrew (d. 1812), surgeon or apothecary:
(?) appointed apothecary to P. and Ps of Orange, **12.** 143
(?) Tickell's death announced by, **12.** 55
Nixon, Robert (fl. ? 1620), the 'Cheshire prophet':
prediction of, **34.** 43
Nixon, Robert (d. ? 1746), nonjuror:
author of libel, **13.** 105n
Noah (biblical):
animals preserved and distinguished by, **20.** 71
ark of: **32.** 208, **33.** 554; dove and olive branch from, **34.** 199; goat in, eats Adam's breeches and Eve's underpetticoat, **39.** 294
flood of, equalled: at SH, **10.** 215, **35.** 228; in Paris, **11.** 98
HW imitates, in SH flood, **35.** 228
HW might send Ceres to reproach, **35.** 384
HW's grandfather, **34.** 207
HW signs himself as, **35.** 228
peacocks of, croak for rain, **33.** 148
portrait of, in Levis family, **20.** 88n
SH's land would make farm for, **37.** 270
volcanic fires should have boiled, **35.** 383
'Noah, Mrs':
clogs of, **33.** 333
HW jokes about, in storm at SH, **10.** 108
Noailles, Comtesse de. *See* Arpajon, Anne-Claudine-Louise d'
Noailles, Duchesse de. *See* Aubigné, Françoise-Charlotte-Amable d' (d. 1739); Rochechouart, Alice-Elfrède-Victurnienne de (1800–87)
Noailles, Marquise de. *See* Hallencourt de Dromésnil, Charlotte-Françoise de (b. 1745)
Noailles, Vicomtesse de. *See* Noailles, Anne-Jeanne-Baptiste-Pauline-Adrienne-Louise-Catherine-Dominique de
Noailles, Adrien-Maurice (1678–1766), Duc de; Maréchal de France:
Broglie joins, **19.** 267
—— near army of, **37.** 140
death of, **3.** 84
Dettingen called by, an 'engagement' rather than a 'battle,' **18.** 259n
Du Deffand, Mme, gives opinion of, **6.** 433
Du Maine, Duchesse, writes song about, **6.** 432
French reinforcements commanded by, **37.** 160n
HW's opinion of, **6.** 433, 435
Louis XIV entrusts MSS to, **6.** 433
Louis XV accompanied by, to Valenciennes, **18.** 441
Mémoires politiques et militaires pour servir à l'histoire de Louis XIV et de Louis XV by, **6.** 412, 416, 418, 420, 423, 425, 429, 432–5, **15.** 137, **24.** 391, **43.** 101
not wounded, **18.** 265
papers collected by father and, published by son, **28.** 295–7
rashness of, **18.** 224
reported to be wounded at Dettingen, **18.** 260, 265
sister of, **38.** 478
wife of, **10.** 294n
Noailles, Adrienne-Catherine de (1741–1814), m. (1755) René-Mans de Froulay, Comte de Tessé:
acts at Chanteloup, **3.** 382n
Bourbonne to be visited by, **6.** 198
Chaville, home of, **5.** 363
Choiseuls visited by, at Chanteloup, **4.** 469, **5.** 45, 59
Cirey to be visited by, **6.** 198
(?) Du Deffand, Mme, unacquainted with, **4.** 264
Gramont, Duchesse de, to accompany, **6.** 198
—— to visit, **5.** 363 (*see also under* Chaville)
HW has seen, in England, **24.** 353
Italy to be visited by, **6.** 435
Pitt, Anne, recommends, to Mann, **24.** 353
social relations of, in Paris, **4.** 469, **6.** 198, **7.** 443, 451
Noailles, Amable-Gabrielle de (1706–71), m. (1721) Honoré-Armand, Duc de Villars:
Cossé, Duchesse de, replaces, as dame d'atour to Dauphiness, **5.** 106
death of, **5.** 106
Noailles, Anne-Jeanne-Baptiste-Pauline-Adrienne-Louise-Catherine-Dominique de (d. 1794), m. (1773) Louis-Marc-Antoine, Vicomte de Noailles:
Bordeaux visited by, **7.** 428
Chanteloup visited by, **8.** 207
Noailles, Anne-Jules (1650–1708), Duc de; Maréchal de France:
death date of, corrected, **43.** 94

Louis XIV congratulated by, **28**. 295–6

Maintenon, Mme de, corresponds with, **5**. 266, 283

memoirs compiled from papers of, **15**. 137, **43**. 197

Noailles, Antonin - Claude - Dominique - Juste (1777–1846), Comte de, later Prince de Poix: birth of, **6**. 472

Noailles, Artus-Charles-Jean-Tristan-Languedoc (1771–1834), Comte de, later Duc de Mouchy: birth of, **5**. 27

brother of, **6**. 472n

Noailles, Emmanuel-Marie-Louis (1743–1822), Marquis de, ambassador to Holland 1770–6, to England 1776–8, to Austria 1783–92: ambassador to England, **6**. 311, **24**. 179n

ambassador to Holland, **5**. 209

American-French treaty to be avowed by, to England, **24**. 369, **28**. 370, 376

appointment of, as ambassador to England, rumoured, **5**. 143, 146, 169, 209

arrives in England, **24**. 253

Brest attack foreseen by, **24**. 357n

declaration by, **28**. 373n

Du Deffand, Mme, does not know, **6**. 424

English treat, well, despite war prospects, **7**. 36

France's peaceful intentions asserted by, **24**. 262n

HW entertained by, in London, **6**. 427

HW entertains, at dinner at SH, **32**. 357

HW not consoled by appointment of, as ambassador, **24**. 208

Leopold II's rejection of, **11**. 331–2

Nuneham to be visited by, **35**. 475

pas de deux danced by, at Versailles, **32**. 255

Thamas Kouli Can, the subject of vain rescue efforts of, **24**. 366

Weymouth told by, of American-French treaty, **24**. 363–4

wife of, **6**. 461n

wife of, visits England, **28**. 324

Noailles, François de (1519–85), ambassador: *Ambassades de Messieurs de Noailles en Angleterre* by, **1**. 186–8, 192

Noailles, Jean-Gaston de (1669–1720), Bp of Châlons-sur-Marne: preferment sought by, from nephew, **28**. 297–8

Noailles, Jean-Louis-François-Paul de (1739–1824), Comte d'Ayen; Duc d'Ayen, 1766; Duc de Noailles, 1793: acts at Chanteloup, **5**. 382n

Choiseuls to be visited by, in exile, **5**. 45

(?) command given to, **7**. 147

Du Deffand, Mme, unacquainted with, **4**. 264

England likes, on visit, **38**. 402

(?) HW mentions, **22**. 239

HW's social relations with, **7**. 292

Italy to be visited by, **6**. 435

La Fayette forced to await, **6**. 435

——'s departure regretted by, **6**. 427

Maupeou warned by, **8**. 182

Noailles, Louis de (1713–93), Duc d'Ayen, 1737; Duc de Noailles, 1766; Maréchal de France: avaricious, **6**. 175

Dauphin's entrée granted to, **4**. 444

Du Deffand, Mme, requests from, the memoirs of his father, **6**. 412, 420

La Marck, Comtesse de, sister of, **6**. 397–8

made maréchal de France, **6**. 173

Maillebois favoured by, **6**. 323

Mémoires politiques et militaires amassed by father and grandfather of, **28**. 295–8

protests illegal parliament, **5**. 61, 63

St-Germain-en-Laye familiar to, **5**. 337

social relations of, in Paris, **4**. 288, **7**. 440

witticisms by: about father, **28**. 296; to Louis XV on Bernis's recall, **38**. 298

Noailles, Louis-Antoine de (1651–1729), cardinal: Maintenon, Mme de, corresponds with, **5**. 258, 266, 283

Noailles, Louis-Marie de (1756–1804), Chevalier d'Arpajon; Vicomte de Noailles: compared to Malachowski, **34**. 159

Du Deffand, Mme, does not know, **6**. 296

—— to send commissions to HW by, **6**. 290

England to be visited by, **6**. 293

—— twice visited by, **34**. 154

HW refuses to remember, at D. of Queensberry's, **34**. 154

regiment assigned to, **7**. 212

Salm Kyrbourg, P. of, fights duel with, **5**. 175

social relations of, with Comtesse de Boufflers, **7**. 351

Yorktown capitulation arranged by, **25**. 212n

Noailles, Louise-Henriette-Charlotte-Philippine de (1745–1832), m. (1760) Emmanuel-Céleste-Augustin de Durfort, Marquis (later Duc) de Duras: Bordeaux visited by, **7**. 428

dances at ball in honour of Dauphin's marriage, **4**. 410, 411

position of, at Court, **3**. 240

social relations of, with Hénault, **3**. 369, **7**. 270, 329

Noailles, Marie-Adrienne-Françoise de (1759–1807), m. (1774) Marie-Joseph-Paul-Yves-Roch-Gilbert du Motier, Marquis de la Fayette: Chanteloup visited by, **8**. 207

Franklin's letter from, about Charleston, **25**. 69n

husband's departure regretted by, **6**. 427

Noailles, Marie-Anne-Françoise de (1719–93), m. (1744) Louis-Engelbert, Comte de la Marck: Beauvau, Prince and Princesse de, exchange houses with, **6**. 397

brother necessary to, **6**. 397–8

Du Deffand, Mme, corresponds with, about Mrs Ward, **5**. 337, 342, **8**. 192

Le Val, country house of, **6**. 232

—— exchanged by, for Le Boulingrin, **6**. 397

[Noailles, Marie-Anne-Françoise de, *continued*]
Luxembourg, Mme de, to visit, 6. 232
—— visits, 7. 431
Necker accused of giving public money to, 34. 96n
Spa visited by, 7. 239
Noailles, Marie-Louise de (1710–82), m. (1730) Jacques-Nompar, Duc de Caumont:
Marie-Josèphe will be regretted by, 3. 257
Valentinois, Comtesse de, leaves money to, 6. 71
Noailles, Marie-Victoire-Sophie de (1688–1766), m. 1 (1707) Louis de Pardaillan d'Antin, Marquis de Gondrin; m. 2 (1723) Louis-Alexandre de Bourbon, Comte de Toulouse:
children of, 3. 112n
daughter-in-law tends, 41. 34
death of, 3. 146
Forcalquier, Mme de, visits, 3. 92, 99, 102
ill, 3. 112, 114, 118, 124, 136
Louis XV treats, well, despite her un-royal birth, 38. 478
Noailles, Philippe de (1715–94), Marquis d'Arpajon; Comte de Noailles; later Duc de Mouchy and Maréchal de France:
Bordeaux commanded by, 7. 179
Chauvelin temporarily replaced by, at Turin, 20. 497n
Court followed by, 4. 351–2
Dauphin's entrée granted to, 4. 444
illumination for Poix wedding in garden of, 7. 319
made maréchal de France, 6. 173
marriage of, 3. 240n
proud, 6. 175
Ramillon's chamber faces garden of, 8. 13
servant of, finds gout remedy, 6. 197
sons of, 3. 323, 6. 293, 424, 22. 341n
wife of, 3. 240n
Noailles, Philippe-Louis-Marc-Antoine de (1752–1819), Prince de Poix:
acts at Chanteloup, 5. 382n
Beauvau to receive MSS through, 6. 416
Du Deffand, Mme, hardly knows, 6. 424
England now the home of, 5. 27n
—— visited by, with Lafayette, 6. 427n
HW receives from, Beauvau's bequest, 12. 14
HW's civilities to, in England, 41. 357–8
HW's compliments about, to be repeated to his wife and father, 6. 424
Hénin, Princesse d', connected with, 12. 30
London lodging taken by, 12. 30
marriage of, 3. 323, 7. 319, 22. 341n
reversion of Beauvau's position granted to, 6. 59, 61
social relations of, with La Fayette, 7. 113
SH visited by, 12. 243
Noailles, Philippine-Louise-Catherine de (1745–91), m. (1763) Louis-Antoine-Armand de Gramont, Comte de Guiche, later Duc de Lesparre and de Gramont:
(?) Du Deffand, Mme, unacquainted with, 4. 264

resignation of, 7. 455
Noailles, Hôtel de, at Paris:
garden of: Du Deffand, Mme, has freedom of, 4. 351; Ramillon's chamber faces, 8. 13
Nobili:
second rank of Tuscan nobility, 20. 192
society of, acts plays in smallest theatre at Florence, 22. 393
Nobility:
French: Crown supported by, to save mental effort, 7. 360; gens de lettres compared with, 7. 364; haggling of, for rank, 12. 51; in families of, founders have merit, successors the titles and pretensions, 7. 364; polished but ignorant, 7. 354; prefer a royal to a popular yoke, 11. 28; protest honour to house of Lorraine, 4. 408–9, 412; recall of parliament asked by, 5. 47; titles of, abolished, 11. 76, 12. 19n; Weissenburg scene of slaughter of, 12. 51; will be crushed by revolution, 42. 251
Genoa's, decayed, 37. 319
hawk on fist in art a sign of, 34. 146
Horne Tooke calls, 'locusts,' 11. 78
inaccurate genealogies of, 34. 131
in debt to everyone, 32. 391
Irish peeresses' creations ridiculed by HW, 12. 164
levelled by young men's fashions, 11. 273
peers created by George II, 12. 271
thinking is equal to a headache to, 22. 415
See also Peer; Peerage; Peeress
Noble, Rev. Mark (1754–1827), biographer:
Biographical History of England, A, by, 1. 157n, 2. 12n
HW asked by, about newspaper article concerning Lord Hertford, 42. 424, 43. 155
HW called on by, 42. 447
HW invites, to call on him at Berkeley Sq., 42. 189
HW's correspondence with, 42. 133–4, 189, 190–1, 423–5, 446–8
HW tells, to suppress 'celebrated' in describing his audience with the Electress, 42. 190
HW thanks, for 2d edn of Cromwell book, 42. 189
HW to give *Miscellaneous Antiquities* to, 42. 423–4
(?) *History of the Family of Boleyn* by, 42. 423
Italian not known by, 42. 190
Memoirs of the Illustrious House of Medici by: HW praises, 42. 447–8; HW thanks Noble for, 42. 446; lent in MS to HW, 42. 189, 190–1; published, 15. 54n
Memoirs of the Protectorate-House of Cromwell by, 12. 257, 33. 443, 468, 42. 128, 133, 140, 189
Sandwich the patron of, 42. 133n
—— warns, not to publish anecdote by HW written in margin of *Cromwell,* 42. 140n
SH visited by, with Lord Sandwich, 33. 468
(?) *Two Dissertations upon the Mint and*

Coins of Durham by, presented to HW, 42. 189n

'Noble Jeffery,' verses by HW:
enclosed in letter to Lady Ossory, 32. 85–7

Noble Peasant, The. See under Holcroft, Thomas

Noblesse:
riddle concerning, by Mme du Deffand, 31. 75, 83

Noblet de Romery, Louis-Antoine:
(?) attends session of parliament of Paris, 8. 171, 173

Nocera (Italy):
York, Cardinal, arrives from, 20. 332n

Noctes Atticæ. See under Gellius, Aulus

Noddle's Island, Boston harbour:
livestock on, raided, 28. 211n

Noé, Louis Pantaléon (1731–1816), Comte de, French army officer:
SH visited by, 12. 247

Noel, Mrs ——, near relation of Lady Lucy Mann:
HW informed by, of Horace Mann II's movements, 25. 201
HW often sees, at Twickenham Park, 25. 187, 312
HW thinks, would have given him news of Horace Mann II. 25. 319
HW told by: about lover of Lucy Mann, 25. 423; of Lucy Mann's ruptured match, 25. 448
HW to write to, about Horace Mann II, 25. 208
knows nothing of Horace Mann II, 25. 319
Mann, Horace II, expected by, 25. 210
—— not seen by, 25. 187, 312
Mann, Lady Lucy, closely related to, 25. 187
'no-news' of, 31. 288
Northesk tells his tales of voyages to, 35. 373
Twickenham Park to be visited by, 25. 319
SH visitors sent by, 12. 227
uneasy at not seeing Horace Mann II, 25. 208

Noel, Lady Anne (b. 1737):
Amelia, Ps, leaves legacy to, 33. 534

Noel, Sir Edward (1715–74), 6th Bt, 1733; 9th Bn Wentworth, 1745; cr. (1762) Vct Wentworth:
biographical information about, corrected, 43. 278
death of, 39. 206
HW sees, at Oxford, 40. 20
viscounty granted to, 10. 26, 22. 31

Noel, Elizabeth (ca 1688–1737), m. (1704) Henry Bentinck, cr. (1716) D. of Portland:
acquires half interest in Place House, 10. 102n

Noel, Henry (1743–98), 6th E. of Gainsborough, 1759:
Mann, Edward Louisa, to advise, to curb brother-in-law's expenses, 22. 305

Noel, Mrs, in constant correspondence with family of, 25. 187
sister of, 22. 196, 23. 101n, 24. 60n

Noel, Mrs John-Perrot. *See* Amphlett, Margaret

Noel, Juliana (1672–1750), m. (1688) Charles Boyle, 2d E. of Burlington:
husband's gift to Mrs Bracegirdle referred by her to, 25. 74

Noel, Katherine (1657–1733), m. (1674) John Manners, 9th E. of Rutland; cr. (1703) D. of Rutland:
match rumoured for, 34. 259

Noel, Lady Lucy (d. 1778), m. (1765) Sir Horace Mann II, Kt., 1772; 2d Bt, 1786:
Abano baths to be visited by, in hot months, 24. 108
Barcelona-Perpignan-Montpellier trip survived by, 24. 246–7
Barcelona visited by, 24. 239
body of: may reach Linton as husband carouses with electors, 24. 363, 381, 398; on board ship at Gibraltar, 24. 398
burletta attended by, at Florence, 24. 105
child-bearing by, unlikely to resume, 24. 131, 257, 304, 331, 349, 353
children of, 23. 408
daughter absorbs attention of, 24. 97, 105
death of: 24. 356; HW gets Mann's announcement of, 24. 364; on shipboard, would make husband sail to Leghorn, 24. 238; reported in England, 24. 357
diet of, very meagre, 24. 322
family of, demands attention, 24. 60
Florentine visits of, 24. 60, 78, 79, 96–7, 115, 136, 145, 181, 247, 251, 257 286, 289, 298, 312, 337
gay and lively, 24. 298
HW glad that Mann will entertain, 24. 71
HW hopes that son will be born to, 24. 144, 317
HW sorry that Mann is losing, 24. 342
HW to receive compliments of, 24. 313
health of: accounts of, hopeful, 24. 281; accounts of, very bad, 24. 206, 220, 222; allows her to associate with ladies and attend burletta, 24. 105; amusements prevented by, 24. 97; bad, 24. 73, 77; better, 24. 108, 115, 129, 131, 136, 140, 144, 260; better, according to husband but not to others, 24. 275; better than expected, 24. 251, 298; cold, 24. 145; cold weather's onset affects, 24. 337; consumption no longer the diagnosis for, 24. 214, 220; cough, revealed by maid and child, 24. 346; dropsy in the breast, 24. 214, 220; feeble and languorous, 24. 330–1; fever, inflammation, and cough, 24. 190; Florentine air may improve, 24. 84, 101; Gloucester, Ds of, writes of, to HW, 24. 191; great amendment in, 24. 306; HW considers, hopeful, since she has survived so long, 24. 242, 255; HW hopes, is not in danger, 24. 196, 205, 227; HW hopes that journey will benefit, 24. 350;

[Noel, Lady Lucy, *continued*]

HW pleased by Mann's account of, **24**. 144, 261, 282, 300, 311, 317; heat impairs, more than cold, **24**. 305; hectic fever and cough, **24**. 199; husband despairs over, **24**. 203, 353; husband thinks, has gained much at Nice, **24**. 286; illness delays her departure for Rome, **24**. 146; improving but still weak, **24**. 304; laudanum prescribed by physician to make her sleep, **24**. 199; lungs may be affected, **24**. 199; Mediterranean cruise recommended for, **24**. 203; miscarries frequently, **24**. 101; much out of order, **24**. 346; much worse, **24**. 265; Naples rehabilitates, **24**. 181; neither better nor worse than when she left Naples, **24**. 246; not worse, **24**. 239; pleuritic inflammatory fever, **24**. 188; Porto Ferrajo water does not improve, **24**. 318, 322; Puzzuolo and Portici do not benefit, **24**. 190, 203; sea voyage may not help, **24**. 220, 233; tolerable and unaffected by heat, **24**. 318; tolerably well, **24**. 292, 344; Valdagno waters agree with, **24**. 122–3; visible decay, **24**. 353; winter at Naples may completely restore, **24**. 136; worse, **24**. 220

husband feels loss of, as guardian to his daughter, **25**. 405

husband's conduct to, admired by HW, **24**. 282

husband's devotion to, **24**. 97

husband's political rashness condemned by, **24**. 457

husband still mourns, though never mentioning her name, **24**. 523

husband to bring, to dine with HW at SH, **23**. 408

husband to overtake, at Marseille and bring her to Nice, **24**. 265

impatient to leave Nice for Florence, **24**. 353

itinerary of: may have been upset by health and weather, **24**. 225; on Mediterranean cruise, **24**. 222, 225, 233, 239

Leghorn reached by, **24**. 292

Malta visited by, **24**. 233

Mann had better lodge, in Florence, **24**. 60

—— lives with, on easy footing, **24**. 146

—— not sorry to have known, **24**. 369

—— pleased with, **24**. 97, 155

—— prepares his house to receive, **24**. 72

——'s liking for, should bring him to England, **24**. 155

—— to be visited by: in spring, **24**. 78, 79; until cold weather drives her to Nice, **24**. 312

—— to disguise his unwillingness to entertain, **24**. 68

—— urged to accompany, to Naples, **24**. 129, 131–2

—— will be glad to see, **24**. 32

Mann, Edward Louisa, to advise, to curb husband's expenses, **24**. 305

marriage of: **22**. 300; planned, **22**. *196*

Marseille to be visited by, **24**. 265

Mediterranean cruise of, **24**. 203, 214, 220, 222, 225, 233, 239

Montpellier visited by, **24**. 246–7

Montrose, Ds of, related to, **24**. 463n

Naples improves health of, **24**. 181

—— may have to be summer home of, **24**. 188

—— to be winter home of, **24**. 115, 131, 136

Neapolitan dances and amusements shared by, **24**. 181

Nice visited by, **24**. 73, 77–9, 82, 247, 251, 265, 281, 286, 305, 312, 331, 337, 344, 346, 353

Noel, Mrs, near relation of, **25**. 187

Portici visited by, **24**. 203

pregnant, **23**. 408

Puzzuolo visited by, **24**. 190, 203

Rome visited by, **24**. 129, 131, 140, 146, 181

Schio visited by, **24**. 122

southern France visited by, **24**. 60

Toulouse visited by, **24**. 239, 251

Valdagno waters may benefit, **24**. 115, 118, 122–3

Whitham aids, at Majorca, **24**. 353n

Noel, Thomas (? 1705–88), M.P.:

Address may be opposed by, **20**. 510n

Noel, Thomas (d. 1756), naval Capt.:

Edgcumbe sends, to Villefranche and Toulon to spy on French, **20**. 536

Greyhound commanded by, **37**. 246

Princess Louisa commanded by, **20**. 536n

Severn commanded by, **20**. 27

Noel, Hon. William (1695–1762), M.P.; justice:

named in Secret Committee lists, **17**. 385

owns Langton window, **1**. 176

West Looe vacancy created by, when appointed justice of Common Pleas, **21**. 89n

Noel; noels (carols):

Rouette plays, **7**. 317

Nogaret, Jean-Louis de (1554–1642), Duc d'Épernon:

portrait of, at Knole, **35**. 133

Nogent-sur-Seine, Comte de. *See* Boullongne, Jean-Nicolas de

Nogues, ——:

rumour about government obligations reported by, **8**. 161

Noia, Duca di. *See* Carafa, Pompeio

Nointel, Marquis de. *See* Bechameil, Louis de

'Noir-et-tout-noir,' race horse:

HW mentions, **31**. 112

Noirmoutiers, Duc de. *See* La Trémoïlle, Antoine-François de

Noizette de St-Paul, Antoine-Gaspard de (ca 1699–1775):

(?) social relations of, with Comte and Comtesse de Maurepas, **7**. 285

Nolcken, Gustaf Adam von (1733–1812), Swedish envoy to England:

Du Deffand, Mme, sends parcel by, **6**. 281–2, 283

—— to send letter by, 6. 276

'Nolkejumskoi.' See William Augustus, D. of Cumberland

Nollekens, Joseph, sculptor:
sarcophagus by, 12. 204n

Nolle prosequi:
Guerchy fails to get, 38. 523n
Kingston, Ds of, asks George III for, 24. 151, 162

Nolli, Carlo (d. after 1770), engraver:
Hamilton employs, 35. 429n

Nolestein. See Hunolstein

Nomis, Marchesa. See Bothmar, Sofia Eleonora Dorotea

Nomis, Giorgio Luigi (1719–89), Abate, Cavaliere, and Marchese:
Franchini challenges, 18. 110–11
Franchini, Agnese, jilted by, 18. 110
HW shocked by story of, 18. 136
Harrington asks Mann to help, 18. 110
mother asks Mann to recommend, to Prince Craon, 18. 110n

Nonjuror; nonjurors:
Cartwright belongs to, 13. 32
Holdsworth is, 19. 139n

Nonjuror, The. See under Cibber, Colley

Nonpareils:
Cole's, 2. 113

Nonsense:
carries its own mortality, 32. 240
Charles II's witticism about, 22. 57, 24. 52
each generation has its brand of, 32. 348, 34. 38–9
HW has more talent for, than for sense, 33. 430
HW has regard for, 12. 38
HW hopes Lady Ossory prefers, 32. 374
HW likes both sense and, 22. 271
HW prefers his own, to other people's, 30. 194–5
HW prefers Jesuits', to that of philosophers, 30. 208
HW renounces, 12. 39, 45
HW's partiality for, 32. 330, 374, 33. 467, 476, 545, 549, 34. 170
HW's reflections on, among old men and old women, 41. 277
HW will not read, when determined to be diverted, 32. 224
HW writes, 32. 58, 243, 376, 33. 425, 430, 34. 46
Holland, Lord, loves, 34. 38
old-fashioned, more suitable to HW than modern, 32. 348
one, as good as another, 22. 73
perfect, HW likes next to perfect wit, 33. 467
sense acquired by, 100 miles from London, 30. 144

Nonsuch, English ship:
Hodsol, Capt., commands, 19. 235n
involved in Mediterranean war, 19. 207, 235, 269

mule caravan turned back by, 19. 51

Nonsuch Palace, Surrey:
account of, in Archæologia, 2. 164
Antiquarian Society's print of, better than Speed's, 40. 254
archaeological excavation of, 43. 69
HW dates letter from his 'castle' of, 28. 167
Holbein chimney-piece might have been designed for, 2. 150
print depicts, 16. 73–5, 40. 254

No One's Enemy But His Own. See under Murphy, Arthur

Noot, Hendrik van der:
Patriotic Committee in Belgium led by, 39. 456n

Nootka Sound:
England's controversy with Spain over ships taken at, 39. 479n
natives at, 11. 75n
Spanish action at, 11. 125n

Norbiton Place, Lady Philipps's estate at Kingston:
sale of, 34. 29n

Norborne, John (fl. 1788–91), dealer in pictures and toys:
medal brought by, to Lort, 16. 210

Norbury, Surrey:
Lock, William, from, 11. 111n, 139n

Norcliffe, Sir James (1736–1823), 5th D. of Roxburghe, 1805:
delegate from Yorks, 29. 140n

Norden, Frederik Ludwig (1708–42), explorer:
(?) Mémoires of, owned by Mme du Deffand, 8. 34
Voyage d'Égypte et de Nubie by: Baskerville excelled by, 9. 414; Charlemont has, in collection, 9. 414

Norden, John (1548–?1625):
Speculum Britanniæ by, describes Q. Elizabeth's palaces, 42. 216n

Nore, The:
George III and P. of Wales thank Parker and fleet at, 25. 177n
George III sails to, 29. 150

Norfolk, Cts of. See Mowbray, Anne (1472–81); Talbot, Lady Alathea (d. 1654)

Norfolk, Ds of:
Masters's supposed mistake about, 1. 268n; see also Bickerton, Jane (1644–93); Blount, Mary (ca 1702–73); Bourchier, Eleanor (d. 1474); Chedworth, Margaret (d. 1494); Fitzroy Scudamore, Frances (1750–1820); Mordaunt, Lady Mary (ca 1659–1705); Mowbray, Anne (1472–81); Talbot, Lady Alathea (d. 1654); Talbot, Elizabeth (d. 1507)

Norfolk, D. of. See Howard, Bernard Edward (1765–1842); Howard, Charles (1720–86); Howard, Charles (1746–1815); Howard, Edward (1686–1777); Howard, Henry (1628–84); Howard, Henry (1655–1701); Howard, John (ca 1430–85); Howard, Thomas (1443–

[Norfolk, D. of, *continued*]
1524); Howard, Thomas (1473–1554); Howard, Thomas (1538–72); Mowbray, John de (1444–76)
Norfolk, E. of. *See* Bigod, Hugh (d. ca 1177); Howard, Thomas (1585–1646); Thomas (1300–38) of Brotherton
Norfolk, Susanna (1742–92), m. (1783) Michael Lort:
　marriage of, **2**. 335n, **16**. 201n
Norfolk (county):
　Albemarle to visit, **23**. 433n
　'barren land,' **18**. 24
　Bedingfield 'a most bigoted Papist' in, **20**. 532
　Blomefield's *History* of, **1**. 75, 375
　Broome in, **41**. 98
　Chesterfield's 'witticism' on his projected visit to, **30**. 70–1
　Coke, Edward, visits, **30**. 64
　Coke, Thomas William, encounters opposition in, **12**. 185
　—— of, **33**. 105
　Conway and Lady Ailesbury give up trip to, **39**. 282
　coronets of, not rich, **34**. 190
　country gentlemen of, beefy, **35**. 42–3, 46
　custom of vails abolished in, **20**. 89n
　Dashwood wants to hunt on HW's estates in, **42**. 282
　Davis lacks dialect of, **19**. 348
　dialect of, **19**. 348, **30**. 33, 34, 73, 80
　draining of fens in, **1**. 132
　Fenn invites HW to, **16**. 248
　—— probably returned to, **16**. 247
　Gardiner family from, **37**. 183
　gentlemen of, oppose quartering of militia in Norwich, **39**. 297–8
　'getting a say' a colloquialism in, **43**. 64
　Great Massingham in, **16**. 349
　HW anxious to promote Leicester's interest in, **42**. 436–7
　HW compares, to Siberia, **17**. 495, **18**. 68, **30**. 63, 73
　HW does not visit, for many years, **15**. 216
　HW dreads express from, about nephew, **39**. 176
　HW expects bad news from, **33**. 33
　HW in, **1**. 324, **2**. 45
　HW likes, **40**. 21
　HW no longer obliged to spend summers in, **37**. 202
　HW prefers St James's Palace to, **18**. 218
　HW receives entire Walpole estate in, **34**. 134
　HW's election in, **15**. 71
　HW's estates in: **42**. 282, 377; bequeathed to Cholmondeley, **15**. 336–7
　HW's relatives in, too numerous to draw his love from the Conways, **37**. 110
　HW's unexpected inheritance in, clutters the end of his life, **39**. 494
　HW tired of hearing about, **18**. 236, 237–8
　HW to think no more of, **33**. 86

　HW to visit, **17**. 495, **18**. 237, 496, **30**. 62, 66; *see also under* Houghton
　hawking in, **34**. 146
　heiress of, displays musical talents at Houghton, **18**. 316–17
　Hertford may be shooting in, with E. of Orford, **36**. 87
　Hobart from, **19**. 63
　Howard family estate in, **32**. 384
　husbands in, have difficult wives, **37**. 333–4
　Jerningham from, **11**. 67n
　Knight in, sees HW's letter to Bewley, **2**. 132
　Leicester's son not to introduce a third heiress into, **19**. 27
　Leneve family ancient in, **21**. 353n
　Militia Bill opposed by, **21**. 138
　militia of: **9**. 241; at Hull, **25**. 355; at Portsmouth, **21**. 300; HW tries to dissuade E. of Orford from taking command of, **28**. 380; Windham lt-col. of, under Orford, **25**. 11n; Windham resigns from, because of trouble from E. of Orford, **25**. 11n; Wodehouse tries to prevent quartering of, at Norwich, **39**. 297–8
　Mount Edgcumbe, Cts of, visits, **12**. 164
　natives of, visit Houghton in swarms, **30**. 33
　New and Complete History of, A, **2**. 78, 120
　Oldershaw, archdeacon of, **2**. 281n
　Orford, E. of, at inn on road to, **23**. 460
　—— lord lieutenant of, **23**. 482n
　——'s farms in, HW writes letters about, **35**. 464
　——'s fishery in, **36**. 97
　'Patapan' a foreign curiosity to, **18**. 299
　periwigs thought in, to be fashionable, **18**. 318
　poor men from, eligible for Trinity Hospital, **16**. 90
　post from, brings business letters to HW, **34**. 135
　Sayers a lawyer from, **33**. 401
　Storer comes from, **28**. 329, **29**. 372
　Townshend, Vct, dies on arriving in, **38**. 346
　Townshend, Vcts, hates, **9**. 32, 34
　Townshend family of, **10**. 344
　turnip-growing in, **43**. 247
　Walpole, Bn, absent from, **40**. 48
　Walpole, Sir Robert, to retire to, **18**. 458
　Walpole estates in: annuities charged on, **30**. 348–9, 372, 373; entail of, **30**. 344–8, 368–9; mortgages on, **30**. 345, 347; *see also under* Houghton
　Whigs of, mostly avoid petitions, **33**. 166
　Wickes to shoot in, **11**. 72
　Windham a gentleman of, **24**. 521, 524
　Wodehouse, Sir John, opposed in, **12**. 185
　women's costume in, diverts HW, **30**. 34
　women's head-dress in, **30**. 34
　young gentleman of, lost at sea, **21**. 206
Norfolk, Virginia:
　English burn, **29**. 90
Norfolk, duchy of:
　descent of, **22**. 483–4, 485, **30**. 259

Norfolk, Dukes of:
  act of 1824 permits, to act as Earls Marshal though Roman Catholics, 21. 535n
  jewels belonging to, 15. 114
  mansions of, 1. 137
Norfolk College. *See under* Greenwich: Trinity Hospital
Norfolk House, London:
  Brettingham remodels, 37. 438n
  chapel of, to have Anglican and Roman services, in HW's newspaper parody, 9. 128–9
  Norfolks entertain at, 9. 331, 337–8
  select nature of parties at, 9. 331
  Wales, P. of, lives in, 12. 43n
'Norfolk monster.' *See* Bell, Francis
Norfolk St, London:
  Birch in, 40. 134
  Clarke, Anna Maria, no longer lives in, 31. 336
  Ireland's house in, 12. 174n
  Patch, James, lives in, 23. 276
  Stevens, Dr Sacheverel, lives in, 21. 138n
  (?) Tyson lives in, 2. 212
Norford, ——, jr:
  (?) HW tells his housekeeper to admit, at SH, 43. 165
  SH visited by, 12. 240
Norford, William (ca 1721–93), surgeon:
  birth date of, corrected, 43. 230
  Bristol, Cts of, praises, to HW, 42. 342–3
  HW confers with, about nephew, 16. 314
  Orford, E. of, protected by, from removal to Houghton, 42. 342
  unpaid, after treating E. of Orford, 42. 355
  Willis displeased with treatment by, of E. of Orford, 42. 332–3
Norgate, Edward (d. 1650), art connoisseur; herald:
  Felton portrait attributed to, 1. 19
Norman, ——, surgeon of Yatton:
  exorcism ridiculed by, 31. 276n
Norman; Normans:
  Chatterton accuses, of destroying Saxons' art, 16. 114, 115
  English a mixture of, 35. 392
  Pownall thinks Torries are heirs to, 42. 78n
  Saxon liberty corrupted by, 42. 78
  Saxons' art compared with that of, 16. 108
Normanby, Marchioness of. *See* Darnley, Lady Catherine
Normanby, M. of. *See* Sheffield, John
Norman Conquest:
  history of English artistic records might start with, 40. 213
  Kentish men carry boughs at, 9. 198
Norman Court, Hants:
  Whithed of, 14. 18n
Normand; Normant, Le. *See* Le Normand; Le Normant
Normandie, Capt. James de:
  Vanneck's friendship with, 9. 112

Normandy, D. of. *See* Richard I (939–96); Robert (ca 1054–1134)
Normandy:
  Bayeux in, 7. 72n
  Belle-Isle plans invasion of British Isles from, 20. 535n
  Boufflers, Comtesses de, to visit, 6. 462
  Broglie, Maréchal de, commands troops of, 7. 45, 47
  Canada's loss less vital to HW than that of, 38. 56
  Canisy, Mme de, lives in, 4. 242, 245
  England should not want, back, 12. 4
  English invasion skirts, 21. 220
  flat-bottomed boats in dockyards of, 21. 296n
  French forces in, estimated, 37. 531
  French prepare invasion in ports of, 21. 293n
  Gramont, Comtesse de, from, 4. 441
  HW lacks book on, 1. 143–4
  hunt of the Grand Sénéchal of, 33. 385
  Joseph II travels through, 8. 201–2
  Margaret of Anjou's journey through, 14. 72
  St-Lazare said to be in, 19. 86–7
  tiles from, 36. 39
  troops in, sent to Brest, 24. 357n
  unrest in, 11. 215n
  Young Pretender said to stay at Butler's house in, 20. 508n
Normant, Le. *See* Le Normant
Normanton, Cts of. *See* Benson, Jane
Normanton:
  Heathcote may get peerage of, 20. 81
Norogna, Don Diego di, Portuguese minister to Rome:
  Mann entertains, 25. 435n
'No rouge you wear,' by HW:
  HW's verses for Lady Mary Coke, 43. 330
Norris, Anna (ca 1734–1816), m. (1756) Anthony Aufrere:
  Crostwick, living of, solicited by, 12. 196, 42. 441
  HW asked by, for living for son, 42. 441
  HW's correspondence with, 42. 441–2
  twelve children of, 42. 441
Norris, Charlotte Laura (d. 1845), m. (1796) Hon. John Wodehouse, 2d Bn Wodehouse, 1834:
  cousin receives livings of, 42. 441
Norris, Harry (d. 1764), naval officer:
  member of Byng court martial, 21. 63, *64*
  release from oath of secrecy said to be sought by, 35. 97
Norris, Sir John (ca 1670–1749), Kt, 1705; Adm.; M.P.:
  Admiralty disappointment of, makes him resign all positions, 17. 364
  Brest and Toulon squadrons to be prevented by, from joining Spaniards, 17. 146n
  Brest fleet escapes from, 18. 407
  Brest fleet may be pursued by, 18. 400
  Charles of Naples guards against, 17. 145–6
  Dunkirk transports to be burnt by, 18. 402
  fleet of: at Portsmouth, 18. 393; dispersed

[Norris, Sir John (ca 1670–1749), *continued*]
to ports, **17.** 194n; fails to sail, **13.** 229–30;
Lisbon reached by, **40.** 8n
French fleet said to be defeated by, **18.** 420
George II's letter from, about sons, **43.** 257
Haddock to be aided by, **17.** 146n, 194n
Mann inquires about, **17.** 194
men-of-war from Plymouth to join, **18.** 393
news of victory of, expected, **13.** 226
nicknamed 'Foul-Weather Jack,' **18.** 423n
petition against Navy Bill presented by, to
House of Commons, **20.** 33n
returns from cruising off Finisterre, **17.** 194n
return to England requested by, **18.** 423
sailors of, condemn ingratitude of Lisbon
people, **17.** 456
Stewart, Vice-Adm., second in command to,
40. 8n
Norris, John (1734–77), founder of Norrisian
Professorship of Divinity at Cambridge:
(?) Bacton living disposed of by, **42.** 441
family of, **12.** 196n
Norris, John, attorney in Essex St, the Strand:
Blakes, partners of, **12.** 180n
legal firm of, **42.** 348n
Norris, Mrs John. *See* Fisher, Catherine Maria
Norris, Richard (fl. 1735–44), naval Capt.:
absconds after battle of Toulon, **17.** 471n
court martial of, on board the *Torbay*, **19.**
55n
England may be visited by, to stand trial,
19. 55
father writes about, to George II, **43.** 257
investigation of, **19.** 25n
Spanish galleys attacked by, **17.** *471*
tartans captured by, **18.** 455
Norris, William (1719–91), secretary to Society
of Antiquaries:
HW's letters to, **13.** 47
HW's withdrawal regretted by, **32.** 84
Norris Castle, Isle of Wight:
Seymour Conway, Hon. Henry, of, **9.** 225n
Norsa, Miss —— (sister of Hannah Norsa):
marriage of, expected, **19.** 419
Norsa, Hannah (d. 1785), mistress of 2d E. of
Orford:
biographical information about, corrected,
43. 116
father of, **19.** 284
Jewess, **18.** 249n
Orford, E. of, entertains, **9.** 109
——'s mistress, **13.** 13n, **18.** *249*, **19.** 284, 419
Rich intimate with, **19.** 419
singer, **18.** 249n
Walpole, Lady Maria, not to be contaminated
by, **18.** 249
Norsa, 'Isaachar':
HW sees, at trial of rebel lords, **19.** 284–5
tavern-keeper, **19.** 284
North, Bns. *See* Furnese, Katherine (d. 1766);
Hobart, Maria Frances Mary (ca 1760–94);
Montagu, Lucy (ca 1709–34); Speke, Anne
(ca 1740–97)

North, Miss:
SH visited by, **12.** 229
North, Hon. (after 1790, Lady) Anne (1764–
1832), m. (1798) John Baker Holroyd, **cr.**
(1781) Bn and (1816) E. of Sheffield:
cribbage not enjoyed by, **12.** 167
HW dines with, at Bushey House, **11.** 114
HW entertains, at SH, **12.** 164
HW locks up, at SH assembly, **33.** 61n
HW's correspondence with, **42.** 396
HW thanks, for verses probably by her
brother, **42.** 396
HW visits, **12.** 167
Hertford, Cts of, entertains, **33.** 283
Hobart, Mrs, entertains, at play at Ham
Common, **33.** 370
slighted after father's fall, **33.** 338
Somerton, Lady, visited by, **12.** 164
North, Hon. Brownlow (1741–1820), Bp of
Lichfield 1771–4, of Worcester 1774–81, of
Winchester 1781–1820:
brother gives Worcester bishopric to, **24.** 63
elected fellow of All Souls, **1.** 351
(?) Gray seen by, at Grafton's installation at
Cambridge, **10.** 284
Montagu pleased by appointment of, as Dean
of Canterbury, **10.** 321
prospects of, **10.** 321
wife of, takes three hours to undress, **28.** 391
Worcester bishopric given to, **39.** 220
North, Mrs Brownlow. *See* Bannister, Henrietta
Maria
North, Hon. (after 1790, Lady) Catherine Anne
(1760–1817), m. (1789) Sylvester Douglas,
cr. (1800) Bn Glenbervie:
father cared for by, during his blindness,
33. 580–1
HW entertains, at SH, **12.** 164
Hertford, Cts of, entertains, **33.** 283
Hobart, Mrs, entertains, at play at Ham
Common, **33.** 370
husband of, **12.** 116
marriage of, **11.** 114n
slighted after father's fall, **33.** 338
SH visited by, **12.** 235
North, Hon. (after 1790, Lady) Charlotte
(1770–1849), m. (1800) Hon. Lt-Col. John
Lindsay:
HW dines with, at Bushey House, **11.** *114*
HW entertains, at SH, **12.** 164
HW exchanges visits with, **11.** 317, **12.** 167
Hobart, Mrs, entertains at play at Ham Com-
mon, **33.** 370
slighted after father's fall, **33.** 338
Somerton, Lady, visited by, **12.** 164
North, Hon. Dorothy (ca 1605–98), m. 1 (1625)
Richard Lennard, 13th Lord Dacre; m. 2
(1650) Chaloner Chute:
Germain, Lady Elizabeth, mentions, to Chute,
19. 372
portraits of, **35.** 73, 639
North, Dudley (ca 1602–77), 4th Bn North:
(?) portrait of, **35.** 73

North, Edward (ca 1496–1564), cr. (1554) Bn North, M.P.:
Erasmus's portrait owned by, **10**. 285

North, Francis (1637–85), cr. (1683) Bn of Guilford; lord keeper:
portrait of, **35**. 73

North, Francis (1704–90), 7th Bn North, cr. (1752) E. of Guilford:
Anecdotes of Painting liked by, **10**. 20
Archer, Lady Elizabeth, to be visited by, at Hale, **10**. 280
Argyll, Ds of, entertained by, **9**. 358
ass's milk drunk by, **10**. 164
Bath visited by, **10**. 169, 173, 178, 264, 266, 268, 308
Canterbury races attended by, **10**. 164
chamberlain's post sought by, **10**. 29
daughter of, **10**. 286n
death of, would deprive Montagu of secretary-ship, **10**. 252
earldom for, **20**. 203
Erasmus's portrait brought by, from Kirtling Hall, **10**. 284
genealogy of, **10**. 352
George II notified by, of son's death, **20**. 233
George III's governor, **20**. 203, 246
gives wedding dinner, **10**. 210n
HW dreamed, was sent to American Congress, **32**. 304
HW entertained by, **9**. 358
HW may visit, **9**. 36, 156
HW regrets unfortunate circumstances of SH visit of, **10**. 320
HW sends thanks to, **9**. 155–6, **10**. 320, 322
HW's ill health regretted by, **10**. 319, 321
HW's legs as big as those of, **9**. 291
HW's opinion of, **10**. 312
HW's party for French visitors praised by, **10**. 76
HW's relations with, over information about Customs place, **10**. 317–22
HW's state of health reported by, to Montagu, **10**. 217
HW's verses to French visitors praised by, **10**. 76
HW to receive regrets of, for inability to attend SH dinner, **10**. 308–9
Halifax's length of stay in Ireland predicted by, **9**. 355
Harris compared with, **32**. 183
health of: **10**. 252, 257, 264, 266, 268, 270, 284, 302, 306, 308–9; erysipelas, **9**. 293; fever, **9**. 293; gout, **9**. 293, **10**. 164, (?) 321; stone, **39**. 92n
Hinchingbroke entertained by, **10**. 209–10
house of, 'regular,' **10**. 210
Jekyll, Lady Anne, to visit, **10**. 169
letters brought by, from Kirtling Hall, **10**. 284
library at Wroxton added by, **35**. 72
London Chronicle report of HW's illness worries, **10**. 164
London visited by, **10**. 190, 197, 302, 319

made Treasurer to Q. Charlotte, **32**. 176
may be 'Queen Dowager,' **33**. 394
marriage of: expected, **9**. 85; reported, **9**. 116
Montagu allowed by, to do honours at Wroxton, **35**. 72
—— asked to accompany, to Lady Anne Jekyll's funeral, **10**. 220
—— called on by, at Adderbury, **10**. 308–9
—— entertained by, **10**. 209–10
—— finds print of Sidney picture in library of, **10**. 128
—— hopes to see, in London, **10**. 190
—— may accompany, to London, **10**. 281
——'s appointment pleases, **9**. 358
——'s correspondence with, **9**. 352, **10**. 30, 76, 164, 217, 220, 257, 266, 268, **43**. 137
—— sees, in London, **10**. 319
——'s relations with, **10**. 284
—— tells, about Customs place, **10**. 318
—— thanked by, for news of HW. **10**. 164
—— to accompany: to Bath, **10**. 264; to Wroxton, **10**. 264
—— to be visited by, at Greatworth, **9**. 291
—— told by, of Lady Anne Jekyll's death, **10**. 220
—— to meet, at Lady Elizabeth Archer's, **10**. 280
—— to thank, for message to HW. **10**. 322
—— visits: at Waldershare, **10**. 319, 320, 321; at Wroxton, **9**. 352–3, **10**. 30, 128, 169, 185, 217, 284, 287, 312
Montagu, John, visits, at Wroxton, **10**. 312
Montagu, Hon. William Augustus, entertained by, **10**. 209–10
North avoids political separation from, **39**. 92
—— not mentioned by, **10**. 217
—— son of, **7**. 237n, **10**. 234, 321n, **22**. 552n
—— to be told by, of HW's information about Customs place, **10**. 319
Osborn, Sir George, tells, of Montagu's appointment, **9**. 352
pension of, may revert to son, **22**. 552, 561
political sympathies of, akin to Montagu's, **10**. 217
Sandwich entertained by, **10**. 209–10
Wroxton occupied by, **10**. 263–4, 308

North, Francis (1761–1817), 4th E. of Guilford, 1802:
(?) attends Mrs Hobart's play, **33**. 370
avoids HW's visit at Bushey House, **12**. 167
brother succeeds, **11**. 302n
(?) dancing of, **33**. 284
Kentish Barons, The, by, **11**. 302, **43**. 149
Lausanne visited by, **11**. 302
(?) slighted after father's fall, **33**. 338
wife of, **11**. 195n
witty verses of, **11**. 302

North, Frederick (1732–92), styled Bn North; 2d E. of Guilford, 1790; prime minister:
Adam attacks, in speeches, **24**. 537, **28**. 481
—— vents discontent against, **28**. 481n
Additional Militia Bill of, **33**. 108n
administration dissolved by, **33**. 333, 388

[North, Frederick (1732–92), *continued*]

administration of: **28.** 124n; Americans ill-disposed towards, **24.** 143; Americans provoked, not intimidated, by, **24.** 137; American treaty not arranged by, **25.** 259; America's loss by, will not help it confront France, Spain, and Irish rebels, **39.** 326; Bourbons hated by, for making England lose America, **39.** 333; brings bad consequences, **33.** 16, 26–7; Camden may be dismissed by, **23.** 168; cared for nothing but their own power, **25.** 276; Chatham attacks, over America, **32.** 228–9, **39.** 246; Conway not to anathematize, like Burke, **39.** 239; Conway should continue opposing, **39.** 288; Cornwallis's defeat has not further weakened, in House of Commons, **25.** 212; defeat of, would have helped King and country, **39.** 325–6; disgraced, extremely angry, **25.** 264; dissolution of, announced by North, **25.** 258; East India Co. injured by, **41.** 300–1; fall of, unexpected, **25.** 263; foreigners wonder why military defeats have not overthrown, **25.** 255, 268; four wars provoked by, all unsuccessful, **24.** 490, **25.** 267–8; Fox, C. J., opposes, **34.** 253–4; 'full good enough for the people,' **33.** 222; Gibbon attacks, shortly before voting for it and accepting a place, **35.** 615; Gloucester, D. of, not apt to be given aid by, **36.** 101; Gordon Riots said to have saved, **39.** 369n; Grafton and Lyttelton see difficulties of, **41.** 314; grows less sage and makes people less sober, **35.** 363; HW does not expect immediate change in, **25.** 251–2; HW sees no prospect of victories to improve situation of, **25.** 244, 255; HW tells Richmond to give no respite to, **41.** 310; Hardinge praises, **35.** 559; has majority in Ireland, **23.** 530; intelligence received by, is dubious, **39.** 340; Ireland mismanaged by, **25.** 267; Keppel refuses to serve under, **24.** 449; Lexington battle leaves, 'thunderstruck,' **41.** 303; Lord Mayor's committal offered by, **25.** 290–1; Minorca's danger blamed upon, **24.** 468; Murray's letters to, sent by Mann to England, **25.** 233; must fall, **25.** 19; no longer gives up America as lost, **24.** 348; Opposition honester but not abler than, **24.** 448; Opposition will blame St Eustatius's loss on, **25.** 236; pacification with France may be feared by, because of Opposition, **39.** 301–2, 303–4; Parliamentary majority the only aim of, **39.** 325; Parliament grants requests of, **24.** 142; peace not sought by, though they bungled war, **25.** 276; rails against American independence, **35.** 528; raises rebellions not revenues, **33.** 82; reported victory strengthens position of, **25.** 253; Richmond, D. of, defeats, over India House, **23.** 546; Rigby, Thurlow and Weymouth might wreck, to satisfy Oppo-

sition, **24.** 447; Roman Catholics in Ireland said to be aroused by, **41.** 312–13; Roman Catholic toleration advocated by, **39.** 326; secret committee on India carried by, **39.** 369–70; Shelburne blames, **24.** 424n; Spanish negotiations of, questioned, **39.** 324; Spanish war not blamed upon, **24.** 492; split by faction, **25.** 259; total reversal of, needed, **41.** 304; totters, **35.** 617–18, 619; unashamed though all at variance, **25.** 218; unpopular, **36.** 194; Walpole, Sir Robert, never took risks like, **39.** 330; waste and negligence of, **25.** 267; Westminster and Middlesex candidates may be lacking to, **24.** 45n

American papers sent to Parliament by, **6.** 139

American papers submitted by, to House of Commons, asking for Address, **24.** 75n

American peace proposed by, **24.** 348, 354, 358–9, **32.** 404

at Guilford's, **10.** 210n

appointment of, as joint paymaster, **30.** 233

attacked in Parliament: **7.** 216; by Adam, **28.** 481; by Fox, **28.** 249, 359; by Macdonald, **28.** 486

Banbury constituents to be placed by, **9.** 262

—'s representative, **24.** 187

— to be visited by, **10.** 287

Bankes opposes, in Parliamentary debate, over East India Co., **39.** 380–1

Barré attacks, in speech, **23.** 186

— gets witticism from, on their blindness, **33.** 585

— the dread of, **38.** 508

Bedford faction throws out militia bill of, in House of Lords, **24.** 497n

Bedford's death leaves, in full security, **31.** 151

bellows to revive his comrades, **38.** 321

blindness of, **33.** 580–1, 585, 587

brother given Worcester bishopric by, **24.** 63

Burke defended by, **25.** 408n

—'s speech amuses, **28.** 354

Bushey Park the home of, **32.** 193

— too solitary for, **33.** 347

Cabinet Council empowers, against Gordon Riots, **33.** 175

—'s authorization to order magistrates to keep peace forgotten by, **25.** 53

—'s instructions disregarded by, **29.** 53

Carlisle offered position by, in Board of Trade, **7.** 185n

Chancellor cannot be made by, **23.** 268

chancellor of the Exchequer, **10.** 249, 256

Chatham said to have asked, to be chancellor of Exchequer, **22.** 494n

(?) —'s conduct interpreted by, **39.** 356

children of, not to be brought to Banbury, **10.** 287

Cider Bill vote of, costs him Pynsent's bequest, **38.** 493–4

Cinque Ports' government given to, **7.** 49

conciliatory bill not carried by, till Wedderburn explained it, **41.** 316

continues in ministry, **3.** 400n

Conway's prospects from, good, **39.** 164

——'s resignation from Ordnance to be conveyed to, **39.** 163

Cooke to be joint paymaster with, **22.** 440n

Courtenay 'deputy buffoon' to, **29.** 116

Court partly will rally to, **35.** 617

Customs post at disposal of, subject of information sent by HW through Montagu and Guilford, **10.** 316–21

Dampier a friend of, **32.** 168

daughters of, not at HW's ball, **28.** 447

declaims against Opposition, **28.** 155

defeated on Navy half-pay bill, **32.** 98

defeat of, may strengthen him, **29.** 191

dilatory, **29.** 177n

downfall of, **2.** 310n

Drake, Lady, visited by, **10.** 197

Du Deffand, Mme, interested in, **6.** 200

——'s opinion of, **7.** 221, 222, 226, 236, 237

Dundas's letter to, **29.** 177

Dutch war to be averted by, **33.** 156n

East India Co. defeats, at India House, in bargain, **25.** 18

—— inquiry moved by, in Parliament, **23.** 442n

—— threatened by, with loss of charter, **29.** 133

East Indian affairs debated by, **28.** 86n

Eden deserts, for Pitt, **33.** 513n

Exchequer accepted by, **39.** 97

—— declined by, **39.** 92

—— predicted for, **39.** 88

expected benefactor of Miss Legge and Col. Keene, **32.** 48

eyes 'goggled' by, **10.** 215

father not to be separated from, politically, **39.** 92

finances of, **10.** 215

flippancies of, severely handled by successors, **25.** 285

Fox, C. J., and, cause fall of Shelburne, **25.** 369–70, 372, 377, 379, **33.** 388

Fox, C. J., attacks, in House of Commons, **6.** 24, 145, **24.** 139, **39.** 369

—— begins coalition with, **25.** 369

—— charges, with promising Woodfall indemnity for betraying Horne, **23.** 557n

—— dismissed for disrespect to, **23.** 557

——'s coalition with: **25.** 369–70, 372, 377, 379, **29.** 287, 289, 328n, **33.** 395; falls, **29.** 320, 330n; ridiculed, **36.** 209

French army expected by, to invade, **28.** 453, **33.** 118

French Court believed by, **24.** 262n

French disarming misrepresented by, in House of Commons, **41.** 299

Furnese, Lady Anne, gives ball for, **35.** 80

Garter of, surprises Castries, **28.** 222

Garter to be conferred upon, **23.** 391, 415

genealogy of, **10.** 352

George III acts revengefully towards, **25.** 488

—— and D. of Portland differ from, about cabinet post, **25.** 379

George III asks for seals of, as secretary of state, **25.** 460

—— consults, about future ministry, **33.** 391n

—— deserted by, **29.** 206

(?) —— does not easily stomach, as minister, **25.** 418n

—— might be offended by dismissal of, **39.** 343

—— not treated by, with great gratitude, **25.** 381

—— orders: to form new administration headed by D. of Portland, **25.** 379–80, 387; to have Calais-Dover mails stopped, **24.** 496n

—— praises, for opposing increased naval pay, **32.** 99n

——'s letter from, **33.** 331

——'s message of American-French treaty, given by, to House of Commons, **24.** 364n

——'s request for war funds granted by House of Commons to, **39.** 324–5

——'s request to Parliament presented by, **7.** 40n

—— tells D. of Portland through, that his arrangement is accepted, **25.** 390–1

—— told by, of Dutch peace overtures, **25.** 188n

—— tries to detach, from alliance with C. J. Fox, **25.** 378

—— wants Conway to form ministry replacing, **39.** 348n

(?) George IV's establishment urged by, **25.** 418n

Germain differs with, over Carleton, **25.** 241n

——'s dismissal notified by, **33.** 327

Gloucester, D. of, appeals to, for provision for his family, **36.** 306

—— gets George III's leave from, for absence, **36.** 308

—— makes overtures to George III through, **24.** 314n

Gordon, Lord George, examined before, **25.** 71n

Gordon rioters told by, that religious laws would be considered, **25.** 54

Gower rumoured as successor to, **7.** 49

——'s defeat of Militia Bill resented by, **24.** 497

Grafton succeeded by, **4.** 349n, **28.** 431n

Grantham to be succeeded by, as secretary of state, **25.** 372n

Grenville dependent on, **38.** 508

——'s and Bedford's deaths leave, in full security, **31.** 151

Grenville's election bill opposed by, **32.** 189n

guards procured by, to clear way in Gordon riots, **33.** 177

Guilford does not mention political affairs of, **10.** 217

HW advises C. J. Fox to attack, **33.** 326n

[North, Frederick (1732–92), continued]

HW and brother will accept any Customs arrangement by, **41.** 328

HW asked by, for price list of articles procured in Exchequer ushership, **41.** 358

HW asks Montagu to solicit pension from, for Bentley, **9.** 261, 262

HW calls: 'egregious,' **29.** 102; 'our dictator,' **33.** 327; 'Punch,' **33.** 328

HW considers, a dexterous politician but fatal minister and selfish man, **25.** 381

HW credits, with good answer to London's remonstrance, **23.** 197

HW dines with, at Bushey House, **11.** 114

HW does not read of reception of, at Oxford, **23.** 497

HW entertains, at breakfast at SH, **32.** 156

HW expects to visit, at Bushey, **29.** 210

HW forwards Montagu's letter to, **24.** 268

HW has more to do with others' business than, **32.** 229

HW has no desire to supplant, **32.** 206

HW hopes, will not retire, **23.** 490

HW mentions, **29.** 187, 197, 314, 317

HW notified by, for E. of Orford, of transfer of park rangership, **41.** 378–80

HW offers dancing partner to, **33.** 284

HW pleased at Montagu's secretaryship to, **10.** 250, 251

HW praises, **23.** 186, 197, 199, 217, **25.** 275

HW rejects offer from, of Customs place for his lifetime, **29.** 327n, **39.** 289

HW's correspondence with, **41.** 378–80, **42.** 469

HW's cribbage partner, **33.** 232

HW's fête not attended by, **7.** 78, 81

HW's ill health regretted by, **10.** 319

HW's letter from, about E. of Orford's authorization for Lord William Gordon, **36.** 157–8

HW's little respect for, **33.** 304

HW's notes on, **4.** 311

HW's relations with, over Customs place, **10.** 316–21

HW submits question of Mann's place in Customs to, **24.** 177–8

HW tells story of, **32.** 242

HW thanked by, **42.** 469

HW to be pleased by Montagu's favours from, **10.** 317

HW visits, at Bushey House, **33.** 214, 235, 580–1

Halifax rumoured to be succeeded by, in Board of Trade, **9.** 340

Harcourt promised by, that absentee tax will be passed, **35.** 348n

Hardinge calls, 'ministerial highwayman,' **35.** 604

——— prefers HW's friendship to that of, **35.** 558

health of: fever, **25.** 97

Hertford, Cts of, entertains, **33.** 284

highwayman wounds postilion of, **24.** 47

Hobart, Mrs, entertains, at play at Ham Common, **33.** 370

holidays of, **33.** 49

House of Commons notified by, of Spanish rescript, **24.** 483n, 491n

——— tears Shelburne and, from power in one year, **25.** 402n

——— told by, about governmental loan, **24.** 448

idleness of, **33.** 393

indifference of: 'Roman,' **33.** 327–8; to Thirty-Nine Articles, **28.** 72n

inferior to Charles Townshend in talents, **39.** 88

ingratitude of, **25.** 218

Irish Parliament said to be feared by, more than English, **33.** 127

Irish popularity of, **33.** 153

Irish revenue board disapproved by, **23.** 380n

joint paymaster-general's place obtained by, **30.** 233, **38.** 370n

Keene, Mrs, entertains, **33.** 232

Keppel, Mrs, entertains, at Isleworth, **33.** 481

lacking in temper, feeling, activity, and good breeding, **25.** 275

levee of, **33.** 83

loan attempt brings attacks on, for partiality and corruption, **36.** 194n

loan negotiated by, **29.** 123

loan proposed by, **24.** 361n, **29.** 188n

London house of: assaulted by mob, **23.** 305; may be attacked by Gordon rioters, **33.** 184n; 'put off,' **10.** 197; windows of, broken by mob, **24.** 442

London visited by, **10.** 319

Luttrell accuses, of buying a borough, **25.** 29

Mackreth now ranks with, **41.** 400–1

Mann grateful to, for letting Suckling be deputy in his place, **24.** 184

———'s correspondence with, over Tortola lands, **24.** 264, 281

Mason deplores, **28.** 287, 289, 326, 328n, 330n

——— mentions, **28.** 437, **29.** 67, 121

———'s aversion to, **29.** 353n

mentioned, **29.** 86n

merchants urge, to send Keppel against French, **28.** 409

mines boasted of by, **39.** 325

(?) ministry may include, **9.** 201, 203

mob attacks, and tears his chariot to pieces, **23.** 291

Montagu hints at place for, **9.** 201n

——— leaves reversion to family of, **2.** 211n

——— may be required by, to come to London, **10.** 281

——— offered post by, as private secretary, **3.** 352n, **10.** 249, 252

———'s correspondence with, **10.** 249

——— sees, in London, **10.** 319

———'s freedom as secretary to, **10.** 266

———'s relations with, **10.** 316

——— thinks secretaryship to, temporary, **10.** 251–2, 267

—— to be entertained by, **10.** 256
—— visits, at Wroxton, **9.** 352–3
most popular man in England, **25.** 381
Nivernais's *Jardins modernes* given to, **12.** 259
Norton accuses, in Parliament, of breach of promise, **25.** 27
—— attacks, prompted by C. J. Fox, **25.** 28n
Opposition defeats, in Parliament, **23.** 461–2
Orford, E. of, gets letter from, about Parks rangership, **36.** 158
Osborn, Sir George, jokes about, **10.** 234
Oxford and Staffordshire visited by, **33.** 347
Oxford installs, as chancellor, **32.** 137n
Palliser defended by, in House of Commons, **33.** 248n
Parliamentary amendment by, to Fox's motion on Palliser, **25.** 119n
Parliamentary majority of, **25.** 466
Parliamentary motion on Chatham's burial approved by, **33.** 20n
Parliamentary motions by: **28.** 179n; for bill to stop trade with America, **24.** 158n; on *North Briton*, **38.** 225
Parliamentary reform opposed by, **29.** 280, 328n, 351
Parliamentary speeches by: cool after escape from mob, **23.** 290; praised by HW, **23.** 186; prudent, **23.** 248
Parliamentary support of, unsure, **25.** 379
Parliamentary victories of: over disenfranchisement of revenue officers, **25.** 37–8; over St Vincent, **23.** 462
Parliament to hear 'plan' of, **32.** 236
Parr praises, **34.** 45n
Peace of Paris vote of, costs him Pynsent's bequest, **38.** 494n
pension reversion not given to, **22.** 552, 561
'pitiful chicane' of, **35.** 616
Pitt, Thomas, denounces, for England's decline, **25.** 35
Pitt, William II, demolishes, in debate over accounts, **39.** 380
place of, **39.** 388
political connections of, **10.** 215–16
popularity of, **9.** 166
Portland, D. of, and C. J. Fox confer with, **25.** 387n
Portland, D. of, proposed by, as first lord of Treasury, **25.** 377, 379
—— resigns Treasury post immediately on dismissal of, **25.** 46on
prime minister, **23.** 182
prime minister's office offered to, **36.** 208–9
promises of Treasury places not kept by, **32.** 354
Pynsent expected to leave money to, **22.** 277n, **38.** 493, 494n
Quieting Bill brought by, into Parliament, **24.** 542n
rebellion rumoured if, turned out, **33.** 107
refuses to become prime minister again, **25.** 372

regulating bill for East India Co. promoted by, **23.** 490
removal of: planned, **24.** 439n; Rigby plots, **24.** 533n
resignation of: **29.** 201–2, 203, 351–2; expected, **25.** 256; suggested, **24.** 447n
reversion of father's pension accepted by, **22.** 552
Richmond contrasts Necker with, **7.** 95
Rigby plots removal of, **24.** 533n
—— summoned by, to inquiry, **24.** 474n
robbed by highwayman, **32.** 213
Robinson told by, to send to HW the customs commissioners' report to Treasury, **41.** 325–9
Rockingham's correspondence with, **10.** 215
——'s replacement of, **39.** 388
Royal Marriage Bill disliked but supported by, **23.** 390
rumbles about his mustard-bowl, **38.** 309
rumoured attempt to terrify, from keeping office, **24.** 533–4
sacrifice of, will not suffice when 'real authors' of measures are not removed, **41.** 304
Savile moves for inquiry into behaviour of, **29.** 123n
second reading of Burke's bill of reformation deferred by, **25.** 20
secretary of state, **22.** 552, **25.** 391, 460
sensible and moderate, offending nobody, **23.** 217
soldiers and sailors offended by, through sheer laziness, **25.** 208
Somersetshire house let by, **33.** 232
sons of: to receive Customs post, **10.** 317; tutored by Dampier, **32.** 168n
Spanish disarmament agreement signed by, **23.** 297n
Storer shows best side to, **11.** 114n
SH pleases, **10.** 319
SH visited by, **9.** 174, **10.** 319, 320, **12.** 225
taxes to be laid by, before House of Commons, **25.** 254
tax on pensions voted in committee against wishes of, **28.** 373
temper and prudence of, prevail over rash counsel, **23.** 199, 203
thunders in Parliamentary debate, **38.** 309, 321
Thurlow's dismissal demanded by, **25.** 381
—— vainly asks, for deanery for Bp Thurlow, **39.** 388
Thurlow, Bp, opposed by, for deanery of St Paul's, **33.** 339n
Tories may regret following, against Shelburne, **25.** 379
Torrington, Lord, opposed to, **33.** 225
Townshend, Charles, attacks, in Parliament, **38.** 309
—— may be succeeded by, in Exchequer, **39.** 88, 90, 94, 97
—— ridicules, over Dr Brocklesby, **38.** 273
Treasury post rumoured for, **22.** 37n

[North, Frederick (1732–92), *continued*]
unanimity recommended by, **28**. 373
vice-treasurership of Ireland reluctantly refused by, **10**. 215–16
Wedderburn made chief justice by, despite promise to Norton, **25**. 27n
Westcote's letter to, about going over to Pitt, **33**. 587
Weymouth's correspondence with, on resignation, **24**. 533n
wife of, **9**. 203n, **11**. 82n
Wilkes demands impeachment of, **23**. 246n
——'s prosecution undertaken by, **10**. 215–16, **38**. 225
Williams, G. J., commends, **9**. 203
Willoughby de Broke may be favoured by, to lead Yeomen of the Guard, **25**. 241n
wit and good humour of, **25**. 275
witticism by: **31**. 327; on cuckolds, **25**. 246; to Barré on blindness, **33**. 585
See also Bushey Park
North, Hon. Frederick (1766–1827), 5th E. of Guilford, 1817; M.P.:
Bushey Park revisited by, **42**. 385
dancing of, **33**. 284
England reached by, **11**. 302
HW misses seeing, **42**. 385
HW's social relations with, **31**. 297
(?) Hobart, Mrs, entertains, at play at Ham Common, **33**. 370
More, Hannah, praises, **31**. 297
Pindaric ode by, on Catherine II, **42**. 396n
(?) slighted after father's fall, **33**. 338
travels of, stopped by plague at Constantinople, **11**. 302
verses probably by, **42**. 396
North, George (1710–72):
Cole's life of, **2**. 226n
North, Hon. George Augustus (1757–1802), styled Lord North 1790–2; 3d E. of Guilford, 1792:
brother succeeds, **11**. 302n
dances in boots, **33**. 284
Egerton, Miss, rumoured to marry, **32**. 330–1
Hertford, Cts of, entertains, **33**. 284
(?) Hobart, Mrs, entertains, at play at Ham Common, **33**. 370
Hotham, Miss, entertains, **12**. 154
house of, in Old Burlington St, **25**. 369n
Molesworth, Frances, said to be marrying, **33**. 506n
portrait of Prince Henry owned by, at Wroxton, **34**. 189
second marriage of, announced, **12**. 147–8
(?) slighted after father's fall, **33**. 338
SH visited by, **12**. 232
See also Bushey House
North, Mrs George Augustus. *See* Hobart, Maria Frances Mary
North, John (1645–83), scholar:
Life of, **1**. 372, 373
North, John:

Müller told by, about HW's *Historic Doubts*, **41**. 353n
North, Louisa (1737–98), m. (1761) John Verney, Lord Willoughby de Broke:
marriage of, **10**. 286n
North, Lady Maria Frances Mary. *See* Hobart, Maria Frances Mary
North, Roger (1653–1734), lawyer; historian:
Life of . . . Sir Dudley North . . . and of Dr John North, The, by, **1**. 372, 373, **43**. 63
North, William (1678–1734), 6th Bn North; 2d Bn Grey:
birth date of, corrected, **43**. 115
Copt Hall sold by, **9**. 92–3
widow of, **16**. 293
North. *See also* North family
Northampton, Cts of. *See* Hougham, Anne (d. 1781); Lawton, Jane (d. 1767); Payne, Frances (1719–1800); Shirley, Elizabeth (1694–1741); Somerset, Lady Anne (1741–63); Spencer, Elizabeth (d. 1632)
Northampton, E. of. *See* Compton, Charles (1737–63); Compton, Hon. George (1692–1758); Compton, James (1687–1754); Compton, Spencer (1601–43); Compton, Spencer (1738–96); Compton, William (ca 1560–1630); Howard, Henry (1540–1614)
Northampton, M. of. *See* Parr, William (1513–71)
Northampton:
ale of, 'nasty,' **10**. 256
Althorp near, **9**. 299
bad roads near, **9**. 201
Compton stands as M.P. for, **9**. 141
distances from, **9**. 292
election at: **43**. 135; expensive, **10**. 287
extravagance of, **10**. 256
Glass visits, to get venison, **10**. 296
Halifax's death falsely rumoured in, **10**. 296
Horton near, **9**. 134n
London climate milder than that of, **10**. 199
Montagu hopes that HW will visit, **10**. 80
—— stands as M.P. for, **9**. 141
—— to procure in, for HW, a print of Backwell, **10**. 301
Montagu, Frederick, not to be re-elected from, **10**. 194
Northampton, Cts of, from, **10**. 337
Osborn, Sir George, benefits from election at, **10**. 288
sandy country near, **9**. 201
Northampton Mercury:
arsonist's letter printed in, **34**. 5n
Sydney and Ossory advertise in, for detection of Ampthill arsonist, **34**. 4n
Northampton races:
visitors to: Drury, Mary Anne, **9**. 300; Halifax, **9**. 300, **10**. 178–9; Northampton, E. of, **9**. 247; Osborn, Sir George, **10**. 179
Northamptonshire:
Bedfordshire clashes with, over Turnpike Bill, **20**. 112

Bridges's *History and Antiquities* of, 1. 7, 2.
  277
Cardigan's seat in, 12. 164
Cole and HW tour, 1. 67n, 212
draining of fens, 1. 132
Giberne's prebendal estates in, 20. 82n
Graftons to return to, 38. 67
Graham, M. of, to visit, 31. 199
Gray to visit Montagu in, 2. 212
Grey, Archdeacon, lives in, 10. 345
HW concludes Lady Ossory is still in, 34. 80
HW not pleased by, 35. 70
HW visits Lady Betty Germain's seat in, 30.
  171
lack of dust in, 10. 83–4
map of, sent by HW to Montagu, 9. 155
Militia Bill causes riots in, 21. 137n
Montagu delays return to, 10. 213
—— moves to, 9. 146
Montagu, D. of, lord lieutenant and custos
  rotulorum of, 20. 79n
Montagu, Henrietta, may suffer from climate
  of, 9. 170–1
Morton's *Natural History of*, 2. 277
mud of, 10. 88, 211, 256
Ossorys in, for hunting, 33. 495
Parliamentary reform measures rejected by,
  29. 26
Pipwell in, 35. 537
poverty and distress in, 10. 257
Powys, M.P. for, 25. 175n
roads in, bad, 9. 201, 10. 214–15, 256
Robinson, Sir George, lives in, 10. 188
Spencer disappointed by moderate petition
  from, 25. 10
verdure in, 10. 83–4
North and Grey, Bn. *See* North, William
North and Grey, Bns. *See* Jong, Maria Mar-
  garitta de
'North and Grey, Miss.' *See* Scotland
North Audley St, London:
  Berrys in, 11. 112n, 145, 149, 160, 162, 231,
    304, 347, 360, 372n, 374n, 12. 58, 85, 159,
    161, 30. 363, 373
  Dickenson, Mrs, addressed in, 31. 367
  Leveson Gower, Catherine, has house in, 32.
    173n
  Ligonier in, 9. 117n
North Berwick, Scotland:
  Bury lands at, 19. 247
North Briton. See under Wilkes, John
North Carolina. *See under* Carolina
Northcote, James (1746–1813), painter:
  Farrer a friend of, 15. 162n
  HW praises Shakespearian paintings of, 15.
    206
  SH visited by, 12. 229
North Court, Shorwell, Isle of Wight:
  Bull rents, and later buys it, 42. 127n
North Duffield, Yorks:
  Salvin of, 2. 38n
North Eagle, Russian war ship:

made at Portsmouth into hospital ship, 23.
  187n
North End House, Hampstead Heath:
  Chatham ill at, 22. 541n
  —— retires to, 36. 45n
  Dingley's house, 31. 122n
Northern Ocean (? Arctic Sea):
  Siberia will not lure people across, 30. 63
Northesk, E. of. *See* Carnegie, George (1716–
  92)
Northey, William (? 1723–70), M.P.:
  George III appoints, to Bedchamber, 21. 460
  Parliamentary Address debated by, 37. 414
  Parliamentary debate by, on Scotch Bill,
    26. 32
  Philipps opposed by, at Horn Tavern con-
    clave, 35. 137n
  Shelburne buys Calne from, 29. 24n
  Tory, 21. 460
North family:
  Guilford thanks HW for kindness to, 10.
    318–19
  Keppel, Mrs, entertains, at fête, 33. 481
  monument of, in Mildenhall church, 41. 104
  Montagu leaves reversion to, 29. 37n
North Foreland, Kent:
  Berrys in, 12. 113
'North Indies':
  England may become, 21. 306
Northington, E. of. *See* Henley, Robert (ca
  1708–72); Henley, Robert (1747–86)
Northmore, Thomas, of Upper Seymour St,
  Portman Sq.:
  (?) SH visited by, 12. 238
North Pole:
  England's wings reach from, to 'farthest East,'
    11. 227
  HW thinks Berrys at, 12. 110
  Stormont's Polish marriage will lead him to,
    38. 36
North Sea:
  Whaley and Dodd see, from Isle of Thanet,
    40. 4
North Stoke, Oxon:
  Heald vicar of, 2. 347n
Northumberland, Cts of. *See* Howard, Lady
  Elizabeth (ca 1623–1705); Seymour, Lady
  Elizabeth (1716–76); Wriothesley, Elizabeth
  (d. 1690)
Northumberland, Ds of. *See* Burrell, Frances
  Julia (1752–1822); Seymour, Lady Elizabeth
  (1716–76)
Northumberland, D. of. *See* Brithnoth (d. 991);
  Dudley, John (1502–53); Dudley, Sir Robert
  (1573–1649); Percy, Hugh (1742–1817);
  Smithson, Sir Hugh (1715–86)
Northumberland, E. of. *See* Neville, John (ca
  1431–71); Percy, Algernon (1602–68); Percy,
  Henry de (1341–1408); Percy, Henry (ca
  1502–37); Percy, Joceline (1644–70); Puiset,
  Hugh de (? 1125–95); Smithson, Sir Hugh
  (1715–86); Walcher (d. 1080)

Northumberland (county):
  Blackett a Jacobite in, **15.** 293
  Carshalton resembles rural village in, **33.** 111
  colliers in, fight militia at Hexham, **21.** 491
  Grafton, Ds of, visits father in, **22.** 80
  Hutchinson's *A View of*, **2.** 204
  king of, **16.** 108
  riots in: **9.** 341; over militia balloting, **30.** 163
Northumberland, earldom of:
  descent of, **20.** 81
  Somerset, D. of, wants Sir Charles Wyndham to have, **20.** 12
Northumberland family:
  vault of, **2.** 103
Northumberland Herald. *See under* Herald
Northumberland House, London:
  assemblies at, **32.** 27, **38.** 400, 401
  Blamire, stationer in Strand near, **29.** 278
  dinner at, lasts till 11 P.M. due to waiting for House of Lords to end, **38.** 529–30
  festino at, with illuminations, **10.** 34–5
  fire at, **41.** 412
  gallery at: **20.** 328n; HW sees, by candlelight, **21.** 88; Northumberland, D. of, gets painting copied for, **20.** 507n; Northumberland, D. of, sends drawing of, to Mann, **21.** 209
  garden at, lighted, **35.** 301, **38.** 401
  gateway to, **41.** 106
  HW among crowd entertained at, **35.** 107
  HW meets Ps Dashkov at, **33.** 172
  HW passes, on way to Adelphi, **11.** 249
  HW sends letter to Percy to, **41.** 397
  HW to go to, **37.** 522
  Hertford writes from, **39.** 132
  Northumberlands build at, **20.** 341
  —— entertain at, **9.** 334, **10.** 34–5
  one of few remaining palaces in London, **12.** 254
  paintings in, taken to Syon House, **20.** 329n
  Somerset, D. of, leaves furniture of, to E. of Hertford, **20.** 10n
  visitors to Cock Lane séance change clothes at, **10.** 6
  visitors to Magdalen House meet at, **9.** 273
Northumberland Household-Book:
  Percy gives, to HW in D. of Northumberland's name, **41.** 182
'Northumberland rout':
  Mann's assembly compared to, by Vcts Spencer, **22.** 180
North Wales:
  Cole proposes to visit, **1.** 34, 87
  Halifax shown beauties of, by Salusbury, **9.** 340n
Norton, ——, surgeon in Golden Sq., Piccadilly:
  Maredant's drops invented by, **1.** 298n, **43.** 58
Norton, Sir Fletcher (1716–89), Kt; cr. (1782) Bn Grantley; Speaker of the House of Commons 1770–80; attorney-general 1763–5; M.P.:
  attorney-general, **22.** 209, 227, **38.** 285
  brutality of, **38.** 241–2

Churchill satirizes, in *The Duellist*, **38.** 290
Clarke to be succeeded by, as Master of the Rolls, **22.** 263, **38.** 468, 471
complains that he was dismissed without notice, **25.** 95
defeated as Speaker, **29.** 86n, 87n
dismissed, as attorney-general, **22.** 323, **30.** 196
Dunning annoys, by *Inquiry*, **38.** 474
Éon object of information filed by, **38.** 377–8
George III orders, to prosecute d'Éon, **22.** 227
Grafton's meeting attended by, **7.** 367
—— with North's assent promised chief justice's post to, yet North gave it elsewhere, **25.** 27n
Guerchy's application for *Nolle prosequi* denied by, **38.** 523n
HW describes, **23.** 176
HW identifies, **16.** 346
Horne Tooke accused of attacking, **23.** 555
House of Commons opened by, **29.** 58n
—— passes vote of thanks to, **25.** 100
illness of, adjourns House of Commons, **25.** 18, 38, 40–1
imprudence of, weakens Opposition, **25.** 28
impudence of, forsakes him, **38.** 316
Inquiry into the Doctrine attacks, **22.** 274n
Keppel answers oration by, in House of Commons, **24.** 445
land enclosures in Norfolk blamed on, **23.** 555n
lord chancellor's post not desired by, **23.** 179–80
Lowther's candidate at Appleby, **20.** 435n
Master of the Rolls, **38.** 468
mercenaries will support, in Parliament, **25.** 27
ministry's champion, **22.** 209
mob breaks windows of, **23.** 305
mother would have been moved by, to better house if landlord would leave pictures in it, **38.** 454
newspaper attacks, **28.** 135n
North accused by, in Parliament, of breach of promise, **25.** 27
—— attacked by, **29.** 14
Onslow would have felled, with mace, for contempt, **38.** 325
Opposition to propose, as Speaker, **36.** 183
Parliamentary adjournment proposed by, **38.** 325
Parliamentary speeches by: 'beastly and brutal,' **22.** 209n; mentioned by HW. **28.** 309
peerage obtained by, **22.** 263n, **25.** 264
pension of, **38.** 468
Pitt answered by, in debate over *North Briton*, **38.** 226
—— 's return desired by, **7.** 273
predecessor of, succeeds him as attorney-general, **38.** 468
'Repeal, The,' caricatures, **22.** 400

resignation said to be contemplated by, **25.** 38
retires as Speaker, **29.** 28
Rushout clashes with, in Parliamentary debate having been prosecuted by him, **38.** 242
salary and pension of, **38.** 468
solicitor-general, **9.** 413, **22.** 189
Speaker of the House of Commons, **22.** 263n, **23.** 176, 179, 305
stays attorney-general, not Master of the Rolls, **38.** 471
tooth of, pulled, **25.** 40
to return to House of Commons, **25.** 41
treachery of, **22.** 283
Vestris jokingly predicted as being thanked by, **33.** 258
Wedderburn threatened by, with impeachment, **28.** 401
Wilkes's authorship of *North Briton* not proved by, **22.** 189, **38.** 259
—— writes refusal to, **23.** 281
Woodfall quarrels with, **32.** 188–9
Yorke's promotion opposed by, **23.** 176
—— to succeed, **14.** 137n
—— would not return to Court during attorney-generalship of, **38.** 285
See also under *Epistle to Dr Shebbeare*
Norton, Grace (ca 1676–97), m. (1697) Sir Richard Gethin, 2d Bt:
Bibliothèque du Roi has Faithorne's print of, **7.** 358
Norton, Richard (d. 1732):
estate of, left by Whithed to Thistlethwayte, **20.** 238
Whithed's great-grandfather, **14.** 49n
will of, set aside for insanity, **20.** 237n
Norton, Thomas (1532–84), dramatist:
Gorboduc by Sackville and, **35.** 134n
Norton, Mrs Thomas. See Serjeantson, Elizabeth
Norton, William (1742–1822), 2d Bn Grantley, 1789; minister to the Swiss cantons 1765–82, 'un Anglais':
Du Deffand, Mme, gives account of, **4.** 65
—— sends parcels by, **4.** 62, 64, 66, 69
social relations of, in Paris, **4.** 64, 66
Norton, Glos:
Keyt burns his house at, in suicide, **30.** 23
Norton Hall, Derbyshire:
Shore of, **29.** 140n
Norway:
Caroline Matilda may be sent to, **23.** 387
Gray's odes from, **10.** 255
Karl Wilhelm Ferdinand and wife may be driven to, **38.** 311
Macpherson ignorant of manners and customs of, **16.** 377
tar from, **18.** 452n
Norwegians:
Scottish Highlands and Isles controlled by, **16.** 379, 380
Norwich, Bp of:
HW holds leasehold estates of, **30.** 344–5, 347
See also Bagot, Lewis (1740–1802); Gooch,

Sir Thomas (1674–1754); Hall, Joseph (1574–1656); Hayter, Thomas (1702–62); Montagu, Richard (1577–1641); Trimnell, Charles (1663–1723); Yonge, Philip (ca 1709–83)
Norwich, E. of. See Goring, Charles (ca 1615–71); Goring, Sir George (1585–1663)
Norwich, Norfolk:
assizes at, Horatio Walpole (1678–1757) might find peace congress in Holland more exciting than, **30.** 72
Beevor, Dr, physician from, attends E. of Orford, **24.** 293, 294, **32.** 349, **36.** 120, 335
bookseller of, **2.** 282
Crostwight near, **12.** 21n
damask of, **21.** 458n
Deeker's balloon ascents at, **25.** 596n
election expense at, **21.** 56
French may be rumoured to occupy, **21.** 326
Gardiner recruits men at, **42.** 334n
geese and turkeys to race from, to London, **21.** 7
Grey Friars of, **40.** 247
HW visits, **40.** 21
Hardinge's law case at, **35.** 633–4
Hobart, candidate for, **19.** 421n
Hoveton Hall near, **42.** 441
Kerrison of, **42.** 338n
militia's quartering at, opposed by Wodehouse, **39.** 297–8
musically gifted child at, **43.** 351
Nasmith at, **1.** 290
Nesling ordained priest at, **1.** 51n
Orford, E. of, marches militia to, **34.** 47
—— wants to burn suburbs of, **34.** 48
revolutionary spirit at, **15.** 243
Walpole, Horatio (1678–1757) abandons scheme to set up Thomas Walpole against Edward Bacon for, **21.** 56n
weavers from, prevented from joining London mob, **38.** 560, 563
Windham, M. P. for, **24.** 524n, **25.** 579
Norwich Cathedral:
Anstey, priest at, **13.** 5n
Norwood, Middlesex:
Hinton curate of, **12.** 168
'Nos dames doivent leurs attraits':
Du Deffand, Mme, quotes, **6.** 379
Nose; noses:
blowing of, considered disrespectful to D. of Cumberland, **19.** 464
Christian VII picks, **23.** 43n
Curzon's, drips, **20.** 12
Gondi, Mme, loses, **18.** 87
Nosebleed; nosebleeds:
occurrences of, **24.** 145, **33.** 325
Nosegay; nosegays:
Athenry, Bns, has, **37.** 442
Englishmen carry large, with ribbons, at Massereene's ball, **30.** 211
from Covent Garden, **37.** 197
Macaronies', **23.** 467
Nuneham's garden of, **28.** 105

[Nosegay; nosegays, *continued*]
  of holly and ivy, for Christmas, **25.** 639
  subterranean apartment at Pantheon crammed with, **39.** 330
  vases of flowers for, **35.** 301
  worn by young members of Parliament, **28.** 87
Nos filles de Ste-Marie, church of. *See* Filles de Ste-Marie
'Nos filles de Ste-Marie,' Paris convent:
  Mme de Sévigné's letter written from, **34.** 82
No Song, No Supper. See under Hoare, Prince
Nostell Priory, Yorks:
  HW's MSS at, **36.** 315
  materials relating to *Anecdotes of Painting* at, **16.** 51n
  More family painting at, **16.** 48
Nostradamus (Michel de Notredame *or* Nostredame) (1503–66), astrologer:
  HW compares himself with, **33.** 156
  Northampton resembles, **9.** 137
Nostra Signora della Misericordia, tartan:
  burnt to prevent plague, **18.** 252n
Nostra Signora del Rosario, Tuscan ship:
  Glasgow captures, while bound from Marseille to Leghorn, **21.** 288n
  Pachio, Giovanni Battista, master of, **21.** 288n
Nostredames. *See* Notredame
Notables, Assembly of (French):
  Necker poses questions to, **34.** 32
Notary; notaries:
  at Paris, toasts dying man after making his will, **32.** 260
  at Rome, **26.** 5
  Florentine: declaration by, **25.** 120; Mann, Horace II, derided by, for drawing up deed for servants' benefit, **25.** 670
  Kingston, Ds of, must execute order attested by, to have furniture and jewels released from Rome, **24.** 83–4
  mousquetaire confiscates parliamentary registers from, **39.** 65–6
  parliament of Paris to try, for breach of trust, **39.** 66
Notebook, HW's:
  HW to consult about portrait, **41.** 442
Notes:
  HW's reflections on, **15.** 106
Notes on the Statute Law of Scotland. See under Dalrymple, Sir David
Notes to the Portraits at Woburn Abbey by HW:
  HW pleased by D. of Bedford's acceptance of, **42.** 340
  HW's work on, **34.** 115, 121, 125, 127–9, 130–1
Nothing:
  HW discusses E. of Rochester's poem on, **12.** 173–4
  King Lear, line from, on, **12.** 174
Notitia monastica. See under Tanner, Thomas
Notizie del Mondo:
  formerly *Gazzetta di Firenze,* **23.** 532n
Notredame, Jean de (d. 1590):

Vie des . . . poètes provençaux, Les, by, **40.** 115, 298, **43.** 274
Notredame, Michel de. *See* Nostradamus
Notre Dame de la Garde:
  Scudéry, governor of, **5.** 188
Notre-Dame de Paris:
  catafalque at: **6.** 90; for Dauphin's funeral oration, **7.** 304
  Dauphiness may visit, **4.** 458
  HW recommends treasure at, **39.** 202–3
  HW visits, **7.** 274, 304
  Marie-Josèphe's funeral oration at, **31.** 134
  solemn Te Deum at, for French successes, **21.** 502n
  sweeper of, left annuity, **7.** 451
  Te Deum sung at, **7.** 428
Notre-Dame-des-Champs, Rue, in Paris:
  Chartreux near, **13.** 169n
'Notte, La.' *See under* Allegri, Antonio (Correggio)
Nottingham, E. of. *See* Finch, Daniel (1689–1769); Finch, George (1752–1826); Howard, Charles (ca 1536–1634)
Nottingham, Capt.:
  Sandwich commanded by, **25.** 167n
Nottingham, Notts:
  distance from, to Northampton, **9.** 292
  Dodd and Whaley to visit, **40.** 17
  HW does not stir about, **35.** 278
  Harcourt visits house near, **29.** 81
  Howe, Vcts, addresses voters of, **39.** 571
  Lenton Abbey near, **41.** 93
  Markham visits, **28.** 316n
  Mason passes through, **28.** 429n
  stocking-weaver at, **25.** 104n
Nottingham, English ship:
  believed safe, despite storm, **30.** 112
  French ships pursued by, **19.** 411
Nottingham ale. *See under* Ale
Nottingham Castle:
  HW does not see, **35.** 278
Nottinghamshire:
  barons in, war with one another over game, **35.** 266
  Belle-Isle may be sent to, like Tallard, **18.** 563, **19.** 18
  club of gentlemen of, dine at Star and Garter, **38.** 503
  county club of, **22.** 284n
  HW contrasts, with Yorkshire, **35.** 266–72
  HW's tour in, **1.** 152n, **35.** 266–72
  HW would visit Lincoln in, **30.** 178
  Sussex, Cts of, from, **10.** 339
Notting Hill, Middlesex:
  Beaufort, Ds of, advised to remove to, **33.** 185
  Lady Mary Coke's house at: alterations at, approved by HW, **31.** 138, 141; Coke, Lady Mary, away from, **33.** 185; Coke, Lady Mary, lives at, **31.** 155n; dinner at, **31.** 139; HW designs frames for library at, **31.** 141; HW dines at, **33.** 343, **35.** 341; HW visits, **31.** 138–9, 141, 154; loo at, **31.** 155; men-

tioned, **31**. 163; views at, please HW, **31.** 138; visited for dinner by Ladies Powis and Holdernesse, Pelhams, and Lord Frederick Cavendish, **35.** 341

Noue. *See* La Noue

Nouet, ——:

attends session of parliament of Paris, **8.** 173

Nougaret, Pierre-Jean-Baptiste (1742–1823):

Mille et une folies by, owned by Mme du Deffand, **8.** 33

Nourmanzor, Sultan:

Persian tale about, **23.** 152

Nourse, (?) Charles (d. 1741):

suicide of, after Windsor refuses to duel with him for slandering Shuttleworth, **17.** 248

Nourse, John:

book shop of, in Catherine St, **10.** 349, 350

Candide published by, in English and French, **10.** 349–50

'Nousvoullone':

Florentine name for nobles raised by Francis I, **22.** 351, 360n

HW's philosophy of indifference would be good for, **22.** 360

Maria Louisa insulted by small attendance at her reception for, **22.** 357, 467

——'s birthday to be celebrated by, **22.** 371

Nouveau de Chennevières, Barthélemy-Antoine:

(?) attends session of parliament of Paris, **8.** 173

Nouveau dictionnaire. See under Chauffepié, Jacques-Georges

Nouveau théâtre français, Le:

Hénault's *François II* in, *see under* Hénault, Charles-Jean-François

(?) story in, **43.** 149

Nouvel abrégé de l'histoire de France. See Hénault, Charles-Jean-François: *Abrégé chronologique*

Nouvelle bibliothèque de littérature. See under Grivel, Guillaume

Nouvelle Héloïse, La. See Rousseau, Jean-Jacques: *Julie ou la nouvelle Héloïse*

Nouvelles lettres du Chevalier d'Éon. See under Beaumont, Charles-Geneviève-Louis-Auguste-André-Timothée de, Chevalier d'Éon

Nouvelles lettres intéressantes du Pape Clément XIV:

HW calls, spurious, **31.** 278

Nouvelles récréations, Les. See under Des Périers, Bonaventure

Nova progenies. See Williams, Sir Charles Hanbury: *New Ode*

Nova Scotia ('Acadia'):

Brest fleet probably goes to, **20.** 538

Cornwallis, lt-gov. of, **9.** 145n, **19.** 177n, **43.** 259

England now is, **32.** 404

Ezekiel's prophecy about, **35.** 219

fate of, dubious, **41.** 314

Halifax to colonize, under Cornwallis, **20.** 40–1

Hay, Lord Charles, arrested for criticizing Loudoun in, **21.** 367n

Knights of, **32.** 279

lands in, granted to disbanded soldiers, discharged sailors, poor artificers, and labourers, **20.** 40n

Perrier de Salvert thought to be bound for, **20.** 538n

Novati, Marchese (d. 1748), army officer:

capture or death of, rumoured, **18.** 489

Florence visited by, **18.** *514*

Pernklö aided by, **19.** 271

Po crossed by, at Quingentoli, **19.** 206n

Var to be crossed by, **19.** 330n

Novel; novels:

by 'ladies of quality,' common and bad, **31.** 273

Conway wishes HW would write, **37.** 263

female writers of: attempt unsuccessfully to imitate *Evelina* and *Cecilia*, **31.** 271; nauseate HW, **31.** 271

HW buried in, **37.** 189

modern, not read by HW, **39.** 509

More, Hannah, does not read, without recommendation, **31.** 274

Novellara, Ricciarda di. *See* Gonzaga, Ricciarda

Novellara (Italy):

Francis III may give duchy of, to daughter, **19.** 335

Massa, Ds of, regent of, **17.** 47n

Novelle letterarie. See under Lami, Giovanni

November:

HW's opinion of, **1.** 243

people should move to town on first day of, **35.** 390

Novena; novenas:

opera promoters dread, in Florence, **18.** 295

Noverre, Chevalier, dancer:

Amants réunis, Les, ballet by, **35.** 363n

troupe of, at Stuttgart, Paris, and London, **25.** 575n

Noverre, M. Augustine:

Twickenham resident, **42.** 485

Noverre family, dancers:

riots against, **35.** 261

Novgorod, Abp. of. *See* Sechenov, Daniil Andreievich

Novi, governor of. *See* Lomellini, Bartolommeo

Novi (Italy):

Botta approaches, **19.** 297

French retire near, **19.** 231

Gages tries to pass by, **19.** 58

HW and Gray at, **13.** 192n

joint Spanish armies to cross Genoese state at, **19.** 36

La Bocchetta between Genoa and, **13.** 230n

Lomellini denies entrance to, to Austrians, **19.** 67

Maillebois near, **19.** 237

Schulenburg occupies, before the Genoese do, **19.** 58

Novillars, —— de, Chevalier:

[Novillars, —— de, Chevalier, *continued*]
body of, pulled up by hair, **10.** 12
death of, at Carrickfergus, **10.** 11–12
Montagu gets pocket-book of, **10.** 11–12
—— has, buried, **10.** 12
pictures of mistresses of, **10.** 12
'Novogorod, primate of.' *See* Stone, George, Abp
of Armagh
Novogorod. *See also* Novgorod
Novum Aratrum, Dutch ship:
Blenheim captures, **21.** 287n
Novum Organum. See under Bacon, Francis
Nowell, Thomas (1730–1801), D.D.:
HW ridicules sermon by, **28.** 40
Noyon, Bp of. *See* Broglie, Charles de
Noyon. *See also* Noyoun
Noyoun, Lady. *See* FitzOsbert, Alice
Noyoun, Sir John (d. ? 1341):
marriage of, **1.** 387
Noyseau. *See* Le Fèvre d'Ormesson de Noyseau
Nubecourt, Château de, near Clermont:
Churchills at, **22.** 244n, **38.** 495
Nubia:
Norden's voyage to, **9.** 414
sport in, **33.** 134
Nuestra Señora del Cabadonga, Spanish ship:
Anson takes, to Portsmouth, **18.** 463
HW needs to capture, to defray expenses, **21.**
561
Montero, Don Geronimo, commander of, **18.**
463n
Nugæ antiquæ. See under Harington, Sir John
Nugent, Cts. *See* Drax, Elizabeth
Nugent, ——, English naval Capt.:
Havana news brought by, **22.** 82n
Nugent, Miss (d. 1775):
death of, **7.** 398
Nugent, Charles Edmund (ca 1759–1844), Adm.:
Howe's capture of French ships reported by,
12. 81–2
wife of, **11.** 264n
Nugent, Mrs Charles Edmund. *See* Dee, Deborah Charlotte
Nugent, Edmund (1731–71), army officer; M.P.:
birth date of, corrected, **43.** 326
father distinguished from, **37.** 447
groom of the Bedchamber, **21.** 460n
Trevanion promises to secure election of, **30.**
332n
Nugent, Jane, m. (1757) Edmund Burke:
pension during life of, **34.** 214n
Nugent, Lady Louisa (ca 1757–1841), m. (1784)
Eliab Harvey, K.C.B., 1815:
father disowns, **24.** 418, 422n
Florence visited by, **24.** 417–18
Nugent calls, 'Chance,' **24.** 417
Nugent, Margaret (ca 1724–94):
Nugents visited by, **9.** 65
Nugent, Lady Mary Elizabeth (d. 1812), m.
(1775) George Grenville (later Nugent Temple Grenville), 2d[3d] E. Temple, 1779; cr.
(1784) M. of Buckingham; she was cr.
(1800) Bns Nugent, s.j.:

HW hopes to see picture by, of *Mysterious
Mother*, **42.** 256
SH visited by, **12.** 240
Temple marries, **24.** 422n
Temple, Cts, gives diamonds to, **39.** 238
Nugent, Robert (1709–88), cr. (1767) Vct
Clare, (1776) E. Nugent; M.P.:
amours of, **9.** 65
Barrington may be succeeded by, as secretary
at war, **39.** 93
'bashful,' **17.** 254
Berkeley, Cts of, jokes about, with Lucan,
24. 418
biographical information about, corrected,
43. 68, 114, 182, 238
bishops accused by, in Parliament, **17.** 431
Bristol dislikes voting by, for Jew Bill, **35.**
179
child attributed to, **9.** 104
Cobham's wager with, about spitting in Hervey's hat, **20.** 123–4, **26.** 29–30
Cole treated with incivility by, **2.** 119n
converted Irish Catholic, **17.** 255, 431
daughters of, by Cts of Berkeley, **24.** 422n
Eliot, Mrs Edward, visits, **9.** 65
'ethic epistles' by, **34.** 35n
faction of P. of Wales led by, **20.** 32
first lord of trade, **22.** 473
Frederick, P. of Wales's follower, **20.** 3n
——'s friend, **30.** 332
Gloucester, D. of, snubs, at Bath, **33.** 136–7
Goldsmith befriended by, **17.** 165n
Grafton recommends, as war secretary, **39.** 93
HW coins 'nugentize' from fortune-hunting
marriages of, **18.** 481
HW identifies, **16.** 346
HW mentions, **18.** 374
HW quotes, on 'jurisdictions,' **19.** 396
HW visits, **9.** 63–5
(?) Hertford not informed by, of war, **35.** 220
'indifferent speaker' in Parliament, **17.** 431
Irish bills introduced by, **28.** 395n
Irish Jacobite, **18.** 219n
(?) Irvine's quarrel with, at opera, **37.** 443,
446–7
lady's affair with, **37.** 447
Leveson Gower insults, at masquerade, **20.**
124
loud voice of, **37.** 415, **39.** 224
Mann compares, with town bull, **17.** 322
Marriage Bill opposed by, **9.** 147, **20.** 383,
37. 362
marriage of, **9.** 127n
Mountjoy, Lady, pays, **17.** 271
—— said to be wife of, **17.** 271n
Newcastle, D. of, flattered by, **20.** 454n
—— has, appointed commissioner of Treasury, **20.** 425n
Nugent, Lady Louisa, called 'Chance' by, **24.**
417
Nugent, Margaret, visits, **9.** 65
Ode on Mr Pultney, An, by: HW likes, **9.**

65; HW quotes, **31.** 269; HW thinks, not written by Nugent, **14.** 36

old woman offered proof by, that he is Irish not Jewish, **35.** 179

Parliamentary Address debated by, **37.** 415

Parliamentary bill against clandestine marriages opposed by, **9.** 147, **20.** 383, **37.** 362

Parliamentary speeches by: on privately-raised regiments, **26.** 13, 17; opposing Clandestine Marriage Act, **37.** 362; repeated to wife on road, **17.** 271

Parliamentary vote by, on privately-raised regiments, **26.** 19

peerage granted to, **10.** 237

Pelham's 'humble servant,' **20.** 32

Pelham, Lady Catherine, talks to, at masquerade, **20.** 124

Pitt and Fox opposed by, **20.** 454

Pitt-Bedford negotiation at Bath arranged by, **30.** 236

Pitt's speech makes, fear for his vice-treasurership, **38.** 320

poet, Patriot, author, and lord of the Treasury, **17.** 254n

poetry composed by, **9.** 65

Protestant conversion of, **9.** 65

Rigby introduced to Frederick, P. of Wales, by, **30.** 331n

Roman Catholic Church rejoined by, **17.** 431n

Sandwich attacked by, in Parliament, **20.** 124

sick in the night, **17.** 271

son of, **12.** 82n

(?) speech for George III written by, **9.** 89

Stanhope imitates late remarriage of, **35.** 298

Temples visit, at Gosfield Hall, **35.** 467

Townshend, Vcts, jokes about gray muff and ugly wife of, **17.** 165

Treasury post given to, **17.** 254n, **21.** 24

Trevanion obtains office through, in return for election of his son, **30.** 332n

Tweeddales visit, **9.** 65

verse about Anson attributed to, **9.** 90

Walpole, Sir Robert, refuses to hear charge of bigamy against, **17.** 271n

wife of: **2.** 343n; 'old she-goat,' **17.** 271

wife parts with, **24.** 451n

wife tells Chesterfield to urge, to speak in Parliament, **17.** 254–5

(?) Williams's ode to Hussey ascribed to, **30.** 312n

wit attributed to, **17.** 271

Nugent, Mrs Robert. *See* Craggs, Anna

Nugent, Thomas:
Cellini's autobiography translated by, **23.** 383n, **35.** 342n

Nugent, Thomas (fl. 1785–98), engraver: engraving by, **9.** 98n

Nugent Temple Grenville. *See* Grenville (from 1779 Nugent Temple Grenville)

Nuis. *See* Neuss

Nuit et le moment, La. See under Crébillon, Claude-Prosper Jolyot de

Nuits, Les. See Young, Edward: *Night Thoughts*

Nuits-sur-Armançon, Baron de. *See* Clugny, Jean-Étienne-Bernard de

'Nullum tempus . . .':
HW paraphrases, from common-law maxim, **39.** 159

Numero Due, Russian war ship: dismasted, **23.** 202

Numidia, K. of. *See* Juba II

Numismata. See under Evelyn, John

Numismata antiqua. See under Herbert, Thomas

Nun; nuns:
at St-Cyr, **10.** 292–4

choral, Scarlatti, Giovanna, becomes, **17.** 53n

confirmation of, at Florence, attended by Mann, **18.** 45

disguised to visit bagnios, **20.** 464

elopement of, from Venice, **17.** 86

Englefield, Martha, in convent for, at Bruges, **37.** 118

Ferdinando, P., gets picture from, **17.** 199

Finch, Lady Isabella, wears costume of, **17.** 495

HW in Paris to be treated as if about to become, **38.** 469

Louis XV influenced by, **23.** 414

Mann does not think Joseph II should turn, out of nunneries, **25.** 239

—— thinks, should be allowed to die off, and not become a burden to society, **25.** 239

negro: Louis XIV's alleged daughter, **7.** 305; picture of, **7.** 305

return of, to families, would cause derangement because of dispersal of fortunes, **25.** 239

Saliciennes' convent to be staffed by, **20.** 333–4

Spain, Q. of, portrayed as, **40.** 283

Ursuline, pray for D. of Gloucester's recovery, **36.** 144

Nun Appleton Hall, Yorks:
Milner's seat, **11.** 141n

Nunc Dimittis:
HW parodies, **33.** 319

Nunciata. *See* Annunciata

Nunciature:
Venetians shut up, **20.** 173

Nuncio; nuncios:
at Brussels, *see* Crivelli, Ignazio Michele (1698–1768); Molinari, Giovanni Carlo (ca 1717–63); Tempi, Luca Melchior (1688–1762)

at Cologne, *see* Crivelli, Ignazio Michele (1698–1768); Serbelloni, Fabrizio (1695–1775); Tempi, Luca Melchior (1688–1762)

at Florence, *see* Archinto, Alberigo (1698–1758); Biglia, Antonio (ca 1708–55); Borromeo, Vitaliano (1720–93); Crivelli, Carlo (1736–1818); Manciforte Sperelli, Giovanni Ottavio (1730–81); Onorati, Bernardino (fl. 1759–67)

at Frankfurt, *see* Doria, Giorgio (1708–59); Stoppani, Giovanni Francesco (1695–1775)

[Nuncio; nuncios, *continued*]

at Henry VII's marriage, *see* Pasarella, Jacopo (d. 1495)

at Lisbon, *see* Acciaioli, Filippo (1700–66); Tempi, Luca Melchior (1688–1762)

at Paris, *see* Bentivoglio, Cornelio (1668–1732); Crescenzi, Marcello (1694–1768); Doria Pamfili, Giuseppe (1751–1816); Durini, Carlo Francesco (1693–1769); Giraud, Bernardino (1721–82)

at Venice, *see* Caracciolo, Martino Innico (d. 1754)

at Vienna, *see* Crivelli, Ignazio Michele (1698–1768); Garampi, Giuseppe; Paolucci, Camillo (1692–1763)

at Warsaw: Brühl's son excluded as, 22. 192; disappears after Russian ambassador ill-treats him, 22. 577n; *see also* Durini, Angelo Maria (1725–96)

Clement XIII notifies, of quarrel with Genoa, 21. 405, 411

in Switzerland, *see* Acciaioli, Filippo (1700–66)

Pallavicini formerly was, at Spain and Naples, 23. 118

shifting of, 18. 288

to Saxony-Poland, and to the Empire, *see* Serbelloni, Fabrizio (1695–1775)

Nuneham, Vct. *See* Harcourt, George Simon (1736–1809)

Nuneham, Vcts. *See* Venables Vernon, Elizabeth (1746–1826)

'Nuneham, Catalogue of.' See *Nuneham-Courtenay*

Nuneham Courtenay, Oxon, seat of Vct Nuneham, later E. Harcourt:

alterations at, 28. 340, 29. 73, 161, 262–3, 269–70, 274, 360

apartment built at, for maps, 16. 195n

bower at, 35. 484

Brown's improvements at, 33. 417

'capabilities' of, 28. 105

church at: Mason's altar-piece painted for, 29. 312, 35. 527; worthy of Abelard and Heloise and of Jerningham's hero and heroine, 35. 460

English poets' heads collected at, 35. 516

Farington to depict, 35. 542

Fitzpatrick's *Dorinda* may pass time at, 35. 470

flower garden at, 29. 310, 35. 460, 461, 473

'Frencheries' at, 29. 274

French might burn, before it is rebuilt, 35. 488

Gothic tower to be built at, 29. 263, 268, 270, 310

HW admires, 11. 75

HW asked to accompany Lady Elizabeth Laura Waldegrave to, 35. 492–3

HW at first disappointed in, 28. 105, 106

HW avoids, for fear of gout, 35. 524

HW cannot visit, because house is not ready, 35. 368

HW describes, 32. 136

HW hopes to meet Mason at, 28. 330, 404, 433, 29. 71, 73, 77, 83

HW impatient to hear of Mason's renovations at, 35. 520–1

HW may visit, 31. 199

HW misses Mason at, 29. 85

HW plans to visit, 28. 100, 444, 29. 49, 154, 156, 273, 357

HW's fondness for, 34. 94

HW's nieces at, 28. 470

HW suspects he is not in favour at, 28. 400

HW thinks of, with pleasure, 28. 338, 464

HW to visit, 25. 428, 35. 456–7, 469–70, 489, 506, 508, 524, 531, 534–5, 539, 39. 249, 385, 392

HW unable to visit, 35. 495–6, 536

Harcourt, 1st E., dies at, 24. 328, 28. 327

——'s seat in Oxfordshire, 25. 428n

Harcourt, 2d E., seeks treillage paper for 'bower' at, 35. 383–4

——'s etchings should do justice to landscape at, 35. 459

—— should develop beauties of, 35. 482

Harcourts to 'pull,' 35. 488

improvements at, please HW, 35. 375

landscape at, left unimproved by 1st E. Harcourt, 35. 459

Mason busy at, 35. 368

—— hopes to see HW at, 28. 334, 408, 418, 429, 29. 75

——'s visit to, postponed, 28. 407

—— to visit, 28. 399, 29. 80, 93, 190, 259–60, 304, 35. 519

—— visits, 28. 45

Noailles, Marquis and Marquise de, to visit, 35. 475

'paradise on earth,' 29. 88

park at, is ploughed up, 12. 153n

royal family to visit, 36. 246n

tapestry maps, given by HW, in special room at, 12. 100, 35. 539–40

visitors to: Berry, Mary, 12. 100; Butler, Bp, 35. 535; Conways, 12. 38; (?) Damer, Mrs, 12. 38; Fauquier, Miss, 33. 54; Gloucester, D. and Ds of, 35. 456–7; HW, 2. 118n, 5. 385, 391, 29. 360–1, 32. 136, 242, 247, 33. 51, 53–5, 211, 231, 234, 417, 35. 374, 375, 458–9, 469–70, 490–2, 494; Jerningham, 11. 145; Jersey, Lady, 32. 247; Johnstons, 11. 123, 12. 169; Lee, Sir William and Lady, 32. 136; Mason, 28. 45, 33. 54, 234, 35. 368, 375; Miller, Charles, 33. 164; Orange, P. and Ps of, 12. 203; Ossory, Lady, 34. 94; Reynolds, Sir Joshua and nieces, 33. 54; 'Rosette,' 35. 460, 464; Villiers, Lady Charlotte, 32. 247; Waldegrave, Lady Anna Horatia, 28. 470, 33. 164; Waldegrave, Lady Charlotte Maria, 28. 470, 35. 529; Waldegrave, Lady Elizabeth Laura, 28. 470, 35. 492–4; Whitehead, 32. 247; 35. 531

Whitehead's verses on, 29. 180, 183, 189

Nuneham-Courtenay (catalogue):
HW's gifts mentioned in, **35**. 535
HW thanks Harcourt for, **35**. 535
Nuneham Paddox. *See* Newnham Paddox
Nunez, Isaac Fernandez (ca 1732–62):
biographical information about, **43**. 77
sale of, **2**. 368
suicide of, **2**. 368, **38**. 167
Twickenham resident, **42**. 480, 487
Nunnery. *See* Convent
Nunziata. *See* Annunziata
Nuremberg (Germany):
Aulic Council issues decree against, for Prussian recruiting, **21**. 29
avocatoria disappear from, before von Mayr's arrival, **21**. 102n
Conway and Scott visit, **39**. 538
Frederick II's troops approach, **21**. 102
Henry, P., captures, **21**. 294n
Hentzner's *Itinerarium* published at, **13**. 28n
Holdernesse intercepted near, by hussars, **18**. 517
Mathews waits at, for passports, **18**. 517
medal showing rhinoceros made at, **20**. 128n
Nurse [? Nourse], Capt.:
Admiralty gets news from, of landing at St-Lunaire Bay, **21**. 243n
Nurse; nurses:
godparent might give money to, at child's christening, **24**. 199
Louis XV's, **18**. 544
Pope's, *see* Beach, Mary
present in bedroom of P. and Ps of Orange, **37**. 287
saying by, of heaven taking those too good for earth, **37**. 43
volunteer, offensive, **40**. 52
See also under Servant
Nursery (room):
two-coloured brocatelle suitable for furniture of, **21**. 468
Nursery; nurseries (for trees and plants):
Boutin's garden resembles, **35**. 126
on Thames, near Asgill's, **32**. 318n
royal, at Kew, **32**. 317n
See also under Gray, Christopher; Strawberry Hill: nursery at
Nursery-garden:
Germany is, for military laurels, **38**. 173
Nurseryman; nurserymen:
HW talks learnedly with, **37**. 292
Nut; nuts:
apples as inedible as, for the toothless, **33**. 533
enchanted, HW tells story of, **13**. 200
See also Almond; Filbert; Pignut; Walnut
Nuthall, Benjamin, mayor of King's Lynn:
HW to write to, if unable to attend election, **36**. 33
Nuthall, Thomas (d. 1775), solicitor:
Chatham's power of attorney reported by, **39**. 89

connection of, with Nicoll affair, **14**. 196, 197, 200, 212, 217, 230, 231
death date of, corrected, **43**. 189, 269
embezzlements by, **41**. 311n
letters of, to Horatio Walpole (1678–1757), **14**. 224–5, 226–8
treachery of, **20**. 273
Nuthall, Mrs Thomas (formerly wife of Hambleton Costance):
HW tells Richmond to inquire about scandalous pension to, **41**. 311
Nuthall Temple, Notts:
Sedley's seat, **29**. 81n
Nutini, ——, Florentine silk merchant:
bankruptcy of, **17**. 62
Nutmeg:
brought by the ancients from India, **11**. 295
Holland to bewail loss of Ceylon monopoly of, **25**. 283
Nutshell; nutshells:
silk enclosed in, **35**. 49
Nutting, Joseph (ca 1660–1722), engraver:
prints by: of Ds of Beaufort, **1**. 181; of Scheuchzer, **16**. 67
Nut-tree:
Desmond, Cts of, falls from, **40**. 113n
Nuvulloni. *See* Nousvoullone
'Nykin.' *See* Bosville, Godfrey
Nymph; nymphs:
Lyttelton retires with, to Epsom, **24**. 537
Salamander and Water, in Darwin's *Botanic Garden*, **42**. 269–71
unmasked, at Vauxhall party, **10**. 279
Nymphenburg, Treaty of:
conditions of, **17**. 151n
rumoured, **17**. 182–3

O

Oak; oaks:
aspen leaf and, **33**. 311
at: Hardwick, **9**. 298, **35**. 304; Newstead Abbey, **9**. 299; Sandleford Priory, **31**. 321; Wentworth Castle, **9**. 295
balustrade of, at Horton, **10**. 336
bank of, at Hardwick, **35**. 304
chair of, from Glastonbury, **35**. 106n
destroyed at Mt Edgcumbe, **33**. 212
donation of, for making images, **42**. 68n
'good fire of British,' **32**. 359
Greendale, killed by cutting a passage through it, **35**. 271
HW's constitution unlike, **35**. 218
HW would rather sleep in, than in a French inn, **33**. 459
Harcourt fails to engrave, **35**. 459
heart of: box of, **33**. 95n; Exeter sends box of, to Pitt and Legge, **21**. 87n; Keppel given freedom of London in box of, **24**. 444n
in Berkeley Sq., **31**. 235
in Windsor Forest, **35**. 161
lopping of, in France, **35**. 336

[Oak; oaks, *continued*]

Northington's, cut down, **23.** 368

Norway, Montagu does not like painting of, **10.** 309

Oxford fells, at Welbeck, **35.** 271–2

posterity will move, as easily as tulips, **37.** 292

tables and cabinets of, at Hardwick, **9.** 297

Wanstead apartment constructed of, **35.** 238

Oakhampton. *See* Okehampton

Oaks, The, Epsom, Stanley's seat:

Stanley, Bn, to entertain fiancée at, **24.** 14

Oakum:

sailor mends wooden leg with, **24.** 283–4

Oat; oats:

Cole raises, **1.** 276

farmers discuss price of, **10.** 259

HW tired of talk about, at Houghton, **23.** 122

high price of, may make them fashionable, **35.** 391

poison thought to be as plentiful as, in racing stables, **41.** 6

ship brings, to Fiumicino and Nettuno, **18.** 453

Oates:

Locke lived at, **16.** 137n

Oath; oaths:

Ciudadela magistrates give, on surrender, **20.** 552

Gray takes, at Cambridge, **13.** 59

of matriculation at Cambridge, sent by Gray to HW, **13.** 75

Russian troops take, upon their sabres, **21.** 255

violation of, in France, **31.** 361

Oatlands Park, Weybridge, Surrey, seat of Lord Lincoln (later D. of Newcastle), and of Frederick, D. of York:

Anderson, Mrs, at, **12.** 13

bonfires at, **12.** 98

Budé, Gen., at, **12.** 13

Conway should have mastered, **38.** 75

George III and Q. Charlotte visit, **38.** 418

grotto at, visited by HW, **34.** 7, 8

HW too lame to visit, **39.** 390

HW visits, **12.** 11, 13, **34.** 7, 8

Henry, D. of Gloucester, born at, **34.** 7

Hertford visits, **39.** 286

Lincoln's seat, **1.** 44

Newcastle, D. of, cannot sell, without son's consent, **39.** 390

—— entertains Fitzroy, George, P. of Wales, Hertfords, Holdernesses and George Onslows at, **32.** 250

SH compared with, **9.** 169, **35.** 237

York, Ds of, at, **12.** 98

—— entertains at, **39.** 493

York, D. of, at, **12.** 188n, **42.** 472n

—— buys, **34.** 7, **36.** 252

O'Beirne, Rev. Thomas Lewis (ca 1748–1823), writer:

Generous Impostor, The, by: **43.** 353; indifferent, **33.** 244; protected by Mrs Crewe, **33.** 243

Obelisk; obelisks:

at Chanteloup, *see* Chanteloup: pagoda ('obélisque') at

at the Vyne, **35.** 640

at Wentworth Castle and Wentworth Woodhouse, **35.** 267

at Wroxton, to Frederick, P. of Wales, **35.** 74

Dudley's, at Teddington, **35.** 389

Egyptian, **33.** 258

in Lord Radnor's garden, **35.** 174

in tableau for Q. Charlotte's birthday, **38.** 204

on tomb, **35.** 151

Oberea *or* Oberiea. *See* Tevahine

Oberg, Christian Ludwig von (1689–1778), Hanoverian Maj.-Gen.:

defeat of, at Lutterbourg, **40.** 144

Isenburg joins, at Velmar, **21.** 251n

Soubise defeats, **21.** 251

Oberiea. *See* Tevahine

Obernam, Capt., Austrian officer:

Lobkowitz sends, to Mann, **18.** 484

'Oberon':

character in 'Sequel to Gulliver's Travels,' **32.** 71–2

'Oberon':

Choiseul, Duc de, called, **10.** 198

Pygmalion a better name than, **39.** 461

verses mention, **10.** 114–17

'O Bessy Bell and Mary Gray,' ballad:

HW quotes, **12.** 147, 153

O'Birne, ——, Irish gamester:

Harvey gambles with, at the Cocoa Tree, **25.** 12

Irish gamester, **25.** 12

Obligations:

HW's reflections on, **10.** 318

Oblivion:

HW to anticipate, **25.** 542

Oboe. *See* Hautbois

Obreskov, Alexei Mikhailovich (1719–87); Russian minister to Turkey 1751–68:

Bucharest congress left by, **23.** 469n

release of, **23.** 308

O'Brian, Dennis, surgeon. *See* O'Bryen, Dennis

Obrien, Mr ——:

HW jokes about, **9.** 110

Manchester, Ds of, pursued by, **9.** 110

O'Brien, Charles (1699–1761), Vct Clare; Comte de Thomond; Maréchal de France:

Choiseul, Comtesse de, daughter of, **7.** 346

O'Brien, Daniel (1683–1759), cr. (1726) Bn Castle Lyons, (1746) E. of Lismore (Jacobite peerage):

France honours, **20.** 27

Maurepas hates, **20.** 28n

Old Pretender dismisses, at son's request, **20.** 45

wife of, banished, **20.** 27–8, 45

O'Brien, Henry (1688–1741), 7th E. of Thomond:

wife's nephew inherits estate of, **20.** 24n

O'Brien, Lucius (d. 1771), Capt. of the *Sheerness*:
booty shared by, 37. 236

O'Brien, Margaret Josepha (living 1763), m. (1735) Daniel O'Brien, cr. (1726) Bn Castle Lyons, (1746) E. of Lismore:
banished from Paris, 20. 27–8, 45
innocence of, established, permitting return to Paris after Maurepas's disgrace, 20. 28n
Maurepas hates, 20. 28n
Tencin's secrets disclosed by, to Spain, 20. 28

O'Brien, Lady Mary (1692–1780), m. (1709) Robert Fitzgerald, E. of Kildare:
letters of, about illness of Lady Williams, 18. 104n
son tells, that Firmian is model man of the world, 21. 271n

O'Brien, Murrough (1726–1808), 5th E. of Inchiquin, 1777; cr. (1800) M. of Thomond:
Bland loses to, at hazard, 35. 209
debts and captaincy the only assets of, 35. 209

O'Brien, Nelly (d. 1768), courtesan:
Bolingbroke's affair with, 10. 53
—— tells Reynolds to copy eyes of, for Vcts Bolingbroke's portrait, 10. 53

O'Brien, Percy Wyndham. *See* Wyndham O'Brien, Percy

O'Brien, Lady Susan. *See* Fox Strangways, Lady Susan (1743–1827)

O'Brien, William (ca 1700–77), 4th E. of Inchiquin, 1719; M.P.:
birth date of, 43. 255
Frederick, P. of Wales, appoints, 18. 551
Hertford leases Taplow House from, 38. 26

O'Brien, William (d. 1815), actor and playwright:
Conway dismisses, from Ordnance post in America which he refuses to return to, 39. 138
Drury Lane Theatre riotous during play acted by, 22. 120n
Duel, The, by: failure of, undeserved, 28. 58–9; HW sheds tears over, 28. 59
Fox Strangways, Lady Susan, elopes with, 38. 366–8
Garrick surpassed by, in acting men of fashion, 38. 524
HW refuses to give G. Bedford's position to, 41. 209
High Life Below Stairs acted by, 31. 14n
marriage of, 22. 219
'Ohio' lands for, 38. 421–2
Roman Catholicism of, bars him from employment, 38. 379
villa of, at Dunstable, 38. 367
wife of, 9. 335n

O'Brien. *See also* Wyndham O'Brien

O'Brien de Clare, Laure (ca 1696–1781), m. (1720) Claude-Charles le Tonnelier, Comte de Breteuil:
son of, 22. 385

O'Brien de Thomond, Charlotte-Antoinette-Marie-Septimanie (1759–1808), m. (1775) Antoine-César de Choiseul, Comte de Praslin, Comte de Choiseul, later Duc de Praslin:
social relations of, in Paris, 7. 346, 349, 426, 430, 451
son born to, 7. 457
Thomond's daughter, 7. 346

O'Bryen, Dennis (1755–1832), surgeon, dramatist and political writer:
death date of, corrected, 43. 352
Defence of the Right Honourable the Earl of Shelburne by, 29. 280n
Mason attributes pamphlets by, to Burke, 29. 280–1
(?) Sandwich's letter from, 33. 101

Observant Friars. *See* Grey Friars

Observations and Reflections Made in the Course of a Journey through France, Italy, and Germany. See under Salusbury, Hester Lynch, Mrs Piozzi

Observations intéressantes sur la cure de la goutte, et du rhumatisme. See under Bruhier d'Ablaincourt, J. J.

Observations on a Late Publication Entitled 'Memoirs of Great Britain, by Sir John Dalrymple':
published, 28. 85n

Observations on Ancient Castles. See under King, Edward

Observations on a Pamphlet entitled Thoughts on the Cause of the Present Discontents. See under Sawbridge, Catherine, Mrs Macaulay

'Observations on Celts.' *See under* Lort, Michael

Observations on Civil Liberty. See under Price, Richard

Observations on Dr Price's Theory and Principles of Civil Liberty. See under Goodricke, Henry

Observations on Modern Gardening. See under Whately, Thomas

Observations on Mount Vesuvius. See under Hamilton, Sir William

Observations on Several Parts of England. See under Gilpin, William

Observations on the Account . . . of . . . Royal and Noble Authors. See under Hill, John

'Observations on the Barberini Vase.' *See under* King, John Glen

Observations on the Conversion and Apostleship of St Paul. See under Lyttelton, George

Observations on the Diseases of the Army. See under Pringle, Sir John

Observations on the Faerie Queen of Spenser. See under Warton, Thomas

Observations on the Introductory Discourse. See under Stebbing, Henry

Observations on the Poems Attributed to Rowley. See under Fell, John; Hickford, Rayner

Observations on the River Wye. See under Gilpin, William

Observations sur le Cid. See under Scudéry, Georges de

Observations sur le Mémoire justificatif de la cour de Londres. See under Beaumarchais, Pierre-Augustin Caron de

Observations upon the Poems of Thomas Rowley. See under Bryant, Jacob

Observatory; observatories:
at Blenheim, 33. 531n
Beauclerk's, 32. 122n
Parisian ladies assemble at, to see eclipse, 38. 372

Obsidian:
Dee's 'black stone' is, 43. 389n

Obstetrics:
Lyttelton discusses, 32. 387
Vespa teaches, at Pisa, 22. 460n

'O'Bull':
HW expert in MSS of, 33. 414

Occasional Discourse . . . on the Subject of the African Slave Trade, An. See under Mason, Rev. William

Occasional Meditations upon Several Subjects. See under Boyle, Lady Mary

Occasional Reflections upon Several Subjects. See under Boyle, Hon. Robert

Occhiali, Gabriele degli. *See* Wittel, Gaspar Adriaensz van

Occhines. *See* Ochino

Occleve. *See* Hoccleve

Ocean; oceans:
HW calls, England's 'capital,' 25. 277
HW compares Mrs Clive to sun rising out of, 39. 133
HW jokes about Lady Mary Coke taming, 38. 83
See also Sea

Ochino, Bernardino (1487–1564), Italian Protestant theologian:
Elizabeth, Q., translates Italian sermon by, 40. 296n

Ochre:
parchment rubbed with, 16. 342, 350

O'Connor, Roderic (ca 1116–98), K. of Ireland, 1166:
Harcourt should imitate, by shifting fealty to England, 35. 457
Henry II acknowledged by, 28. 467n

O'Connor Sligo, Sir Donogh (d. 1609):
marriage of, 40. 109

Octavia (ca 69–11 B.C.), m. 1 Caius Claudius Marcellus; m. 2 Marcus Antonius:
daughter of, 15. 12n
fame of, 31. 21
HW's medal of, 6. 54, 15. 14, 37. 111

'Octavia and Cleopatra':
meeting of, 20. 201

Octavian. *See* Augustus

Octavius (1779–83), P., of England:
birth of, 24. 454, 33. 95
death of: 25. 403; has not checked inoculation in England, 25. 413, 420, 422; not imputed to inoculation since he recovered from smallpox, 25. 413
HW imagines offer of, to Lady Gertrude Fitzpatrick, 33. 277
Leyden gazette attributes death of, to inoculation, 25. 405–6, 412n
parents devoted to, 25. 403

Octavius Cæsar. *See* Augustus

October:
HW's 'only comfortable' month at SH, 33. 502
only month to be trusted, 34. 50

Oculist; oculists:
George II's, 18. 240n
See also Ilmer (b. ca 1720); Taylor, John (1703–72)

Odcombe, Somerset:
Coryate, rector of, 1. 55n

Oddi, Giovanni (1697–1770), cardinal, 1743:
Benedict XIV makes, cardinal, 18. 302n

'Oddities, 1757':
print entitled, 43. 259

'Odd man!':
prime ministers may call, to get partners, 33. 394

Ode; odes:
English poets pour forth, 25. 612
Grecian graces of, not understood by Dr Johnson, 33. 287
HW has no talent for writing, like Dryden or Gray, 16. 257
HW promises to write, for Ps Amelia's birthday, 39. 441
HW's, for Lady Lucan, 33. 260–1
in *Arno Miscellany*, 25. 507
Legge writes, 37. 81
Newmarket race-horses should compete for, 16. 298
on Dettingen victory, 35. 39
Ossory, Lady, writes to HW, 32. 220
St Cecilian, Pope not successful in, 16. 257
West's, on Q. Caroline, 17. 468n
Whitehead's, to George III, 32. 247–8
Williams's: mentions Finches, 21. 345n; to Pulteney, 18. 73–5, 90–1, 319–21, 334

Ode Addressed to the Savoir Vivre Club, An:
(?) HW has not read, 35. 462

Ode for Music. See under Gray, Thomas

Ode for St Cecilia's Day, An. See under Handel, George Frideric

Ode for the Fourteenth of July. See under Merry, Robert

'Ode from Earl Powlett to Francis Fane, Esq.' *See under* Bubb Dodington, George

'Ode Humbly Inscribed to the Earl of Bath, An.' *See under* Williams, Sir Charles Hanbury

'Ode Inscribed to the Memory of the Honourable Col. George Villiers, An.' *See under* Prior, Matthew

Ode on a Distant Prospect of Eton College; Ode on the Death of a Favourite Cat. See under Gray, Thomas

'Ode on the Death of Matzel, a Favourite Bull-

finch, An'; 'Ode on the Marriage of the Duchess of Manchester.' *See under* Williams, Sir Charles Hanbury

Ode on the Powers of Poetry. See under Cook, Thomas (1703–56)

Oder river:
Frederick II said to be driven across, **21.** 241
Russians may cross, **21.** 308

Odes. See under Gray, Thomas; Horace

Odescalchi, Livio (1725–1805), Duca di Bracciano:
Gloucester, D. of, entertained by, at Rome, **23.** 388–9
Rosenberg keeps, waiting, **23.** 104n

Odes, Songs, Choruses, etc. for the Concert in Commemoration of Chatterton. See under Jenkins, Richard

'Ode to Henry Earl of Lincoln'; 'Ode to Lord Chesterfield.' *See under* Williams, Sir Charles Hanbury

''Ode to Mary Magdalene,' by West:
sent in letter to HW, **13.** 110

'Ode to Mr Poyntz.' *See under* Williams, Sir Charles Hanbury

Ode to Mr Pulteney, An. See under Nugent, Robert

'Ode to Sir Charles Hanbury Williams, An.' *See under* Jenyns, Soame

'Ode . . . to the Earl of Bath, An.' *See under* Williams, Sir Charles Hanbury

Ode to the Honourable William Pitt; Ode to the Naval Officers of Great Britain. See under Mason, Rev. William

Odiarne, Wentworth (d. 1762), serjeant-at-arms to House of Commons:
Lever committed to, **17.** *251*, 272–3
Murray in custody of, **20.** 249
Paxton committed to, **17.** 397

Odieuvre, Michel:
Hénault's *Abrégé* illustrated by, **7.** 211n

Odiham, Hants:
Pinkerton marries at, **12.** 10n

Odin:
HW mentions hall of, **10.** 255

Odo (d. 1097), Bp of Bayeux; E. of Kent:
titles of, **2.** 182

Odo *or* Eudes. *See* Urban II

Odoardo of England. *See* Edward III

O'Donell, Charles, Lt; O'Donell, Joseph, Ensign:
captured at Velletri, **18.** 492

O'Donell (*or* O'Donnell, *or* O'Donel), Karl Claudius (1715–71), Austrian Gen.:
Daun succeeded by, **21.** 470n

O'Donell. *See also* O'Donnell; Oionell

Odongir, ——, volunteer:
captured at Velletri, **18.** 493

O'Donnell, Mrs ——:
Frenchwoman, married to Irish officer, **25.** 536
Stuart, Charlotte, accompanied by, to Florence, **25.** *522*, 536

O'Donnell, Colombe-Hyacinthe (ca 1725–89),

Chevalier; Comte; Irish officer in French service:
(?) wife of, **25.** 536

O'Donnell. *See also* O'Donell; Oionell

O'Dunn; O'Dunne, Comte. *See* Dunn, James

O'Dunne, Comtesse. *See* Parsons, Sarah

Odysseus. *See* Ulysses

Odyssey. See under Homer

Œdipe. See under Voltaire

Œdipe chez Admète. See under Ducis, Jean-François

Œdipus. See under Dryden, John; Lee, Nathaniel

Œdipus; Œdipuses:
Conway the master-general of, **39.** 445
could not guess the truth of political news, **34.** 34
not an, at Stapleton's Club, **32.** 362

Oeillarde. *See* Hilliard

Oeiras, Conde de. *See* Carvalho e Melo, Sebastião José de (1699–1782)

Oels. *See* Württemberg-Oels

Oenade. See *Æneid*

Œuvres du philosophe de Sans-Souci:
Frederick II disowns, **21.** 413
Muzell promises to get copy of, for Mann, **21.** 413
See also under Frederick II

Œuvres posthumes. See under Frederick II

Œyras. *See* Oeiras

Ofaly. *See* Offaly

O'Farrell, ——, Lt-Col.:
regiment of, **17.** 300n

'Of Education.' *See under* Milton, John

Offa (d. 796), K. of Mercia:
reign of, **16.** 108

Offaly, E. of. *See* Fitzgerald, George (1748–65)

Office of Public Decency, Florence:
officers of, make arrests, **18.** 112n

'Office of the Madonna.' *See under* Pergolesi, Giovanni Battista

Officer; officers:
ball given by, in honour of Francis I's election, **19.** 115
belts of, **18.** 261
Dutch: **38.** 4; may lead German-Swiss regiment in America, **20.** 531; sketched by Anne Seymour Conway, **38.** 156
English army: Ailesbury, Cts of, sends, to HW with medal, **38.** 153–4; Braddock's, sacrificed by his troops, **35.** 245; Brown, Lady, honours, **30.** 84; courts martial upon, at Inverness, **37.** 248–9; Dettingen casualties of, **18.** 258–61; dismissals of, for Parliamentary conduct, **22.** 274, **30.** 188, **38.** 497–9, 502, 509, 533; Edgcumbe brings, to Florence, **20.** 536; every packet carries, to Germany, **38.** 156–7; fifty, killed at Ticonderoga, **30.** 148; from Minorca, report its fall, **25.** 269; fruit shop guarded by, **38.** 109; George III promises Pitt to reinstate, after dismissals, **30.** 188; Goodwood frightens HW with crowds of, **39.** 295; HW

[Officer; officers: English army, *continued*]
visited by, at Paris, and they quarrel, **39.** 23; in Flanders, Olimphant's alleged letter to, **19.** 170; Lincoln's insult from, **17.** 411–12, **30.** 32; militia, **24.** 372, **39.** 179, 183; non-commissioned, find Conway's orders too long to understand, **38.** 148; of privately-raised regiments, **19.** 158, **26.** 14–19; on Irish establishment ordered there, **35.** 220; on way to Flanders, **17.** 410, **18.** 179; Parliament examines list of, at Port Mahon, **17.** 300; Peachey beats, **30.** 84; Pitt's and Grenville's speeches on dismission of, **38.** 320; pretend zeal for active service, **17.** 410; sketched by Anne Seymour Conway, **38.** 156; Vernon hated by, **18.** 251

English half-pay: attentive to HW, **17.** 270–1; Maclaine quarrels with, **20.** 169

English naval: bribed to let artillery pass, **19.** 147; conduct of, greatly criticized, **21.** 69; court martial for, **19.** 33; recalled from Mediterranean for examination, **19.** 12; Vernon revered by, **18.** 151

Ferdinand's, told to give thanks, **35.** 305

Florentine: buy horses at low prices, **21.** 179; Franchini driven into retirement by, **18.** 111

Florentine gendarme: offers to fight San Vitali, **18.** 368; sbirri at odds with, **17.** 225

Forrester's, **18.** 107

Francis I's, said to debauch Spanish deserters, **17.** 349

French: believe story about Granby's avoidance of wigs, **38.** 481; captured by Conway, **37.** 273n; captured by Murray, **25.** 207; French losses at Assietta admitted by, **19.** 427; Genoese orchestra composed of, **19.** 505; HW may send watch to Mann through, **21.** 306; in Corsica, **33.** 37, 124; in Holland, **38.** 3–4; may have to rejoin regiments, **24.** 357; prevent publication of paper on Louis XV, **23.** 231; punishment of, for undivulged crime, **21.** 382; said to arouse Irish unrest, **22.** 24; seen by HW arriving at Calais, **10.** 283; sent to America, **24.** 309; sent to Poland, **23.** 338, **39.** 146; shoot holes in hats to show off at balls, **20.** 159; sketched by Anne Seymour Conway, **38.** 156; wounded or killed at Dettingen, **18.** 258, 261

German: sketched by Anne Seymour Conway, **38.** 156; supposed author of letter in *Oxford Journal*, **9.** 196, 198; will not serve with Vane unless he fights duel, **17.** 486

Hanoverian regiment's, all killed at Roucour, **30.** 107

Hessian, challenges Hampshire justice to duel, **20.** 563

Irish: Craon, Princesse de, accompanied by, **22.** 536; in French service, **23.** 402; in French service, brings news of French mobilization, **24.** 357

Lorraine, *see under* Lorraine

of Swiss Guards, **17.** 236

Östergötland's, delivers HW's letter to Ds of Gloucester, **24.** 247

Piedmontese, in Reggio, **17.** 46

Portuguese, prosecuted for not paying taxes, **23.** 166

Prussian: Berlin approached by, with message, **21.** 242; Berrue talks with, **17.** 206

Russian: Chernyshev recommends, to Mann, **25.** 84; Orlov promotes, **24.** 84; Orlov receives dispatches through, **23.** 444; Orlov's, sail from Kronstadt, **23.** 222; reaches Florence from Leghorn, **23.** 235; tells Mann about arrival of Houghton collection, **25.** 2; Spiridorf's, notifies Orlov, **23.** 162

Scotch, entertained by Mrs Bentley, **10.** 196

Spanish: at Bologna, **18.** 154; brings horses to Orbetello, **17.** 214; deposit effects in banks and convents, **17.** 427; letters from, to Prato and Pistoia, **17.** 238; Montemar's mismanagement enrages, **17.** 262; Philip V notifies, of Montemar's dismissal, **18.** 59

Swiss, in Holland, **38.** 4, 10

Officer's Answer, The:
ascribed to Conway, **37.** 523n

Officina Arbuteana. *See* Strawberry Hill Press

Offley, Charles (living, 1817), wine-merchant:
Farington paints landscape for, **12.** 187n, **15.** 322

Offley, John (? 1717–84), M.P.:
(?) alternative identification, **13.** 166n
birth date of, corrected, **43.** 267
Conway's costume might be aped by, **38.** 2, 11
flitch of bacon might be given by, to Conway and wife, **38.** 70–1
gambles at Twelfth Night, **35.** 204
George II honours, **35.** 204
groom of the Bedchamber, **35.** 281
HW entertains, at SH, **10.** 70–1
HW's distress compared with that of, for Münchhausen, **30.** 266
HW visits, at Wichnor, **9.** 294
(?) mob knocks down, **20.** 156

Offley, Laurence (ca 1719–49), of Clare Hall, Cambridge:
(?) Paris visited by, **13.** 166

'Of His Majesty's Receiving the News of the Duke of Buckingham's Death.' *See under* Waller, Edmund

O filii:
verses to air of, **5.** 354

'O'Flaharty, Dr':
character in 'The Peach in Brandy,' **32.** 61

O'Flaherty, Roderic (1629–1718):
Ogygia by, not seen by HW, **16.** 282

Of London. See under Pennant, Thomas

Of the Art of Sinking in Poetry. See under Pope, Alexander

Of the Origin and Progress of Language. See under Burnett, James, Lord Monboddo

Of the Patagonians. See under Pennant, Thomas

Of the Use and Abuse of Parliaments. See under Ralph, James

Ogborne, John (1755–1837), engraver:
print by, of Turenne, **16**. 323
Ogden, James (d. 1781):
Clinton's messenger, captured by Americans, **25**. 135
Ogden, Samuel (1716–78), D.D.:
Ashton's letter to, **15**. 303
name of, corrected, **43**. 212
Ogg, Roderick, King's messenger:
Keith sends, with dispatches, **23**. 385n
Oghinski. *See* Ogiński
Ogier, Jean-François (1704–75), president of parliament of Paris:
Breton parliament to be attended by, **3**. 370
Le Prestre secures office expected by, **4**. 442
Ogilby, John (1600–76):
Dryden's Virgil uses Hollar's illustrations to Virgil translation by, **37**. 299n
Fuller's portrait of, **42**. 380n
Ogilvie, Bns. *See* Johnstone, Margaret
Ogilvie, Cecilia Margaret (1775–1824), m. (1795) Charles Lock:
Aubigny visited by, **6**. 333
biographical information about, corrected, **43**. 100, 150
engagement of, to Lord Chichester, broken, **11**. 326
gossip about, **11**. 329
Ogilvie, David (1725–1803), styled Bn Ogilvie 1731–33; titular E. of Airlie, 1761:
capture of, rumoured, **19**. 254
death of, rumoured, **19**. 248
wife of, captured, **37**. 245
Ogilvie, Emily Charlotte (1778–1832), m. (1799) Charles George Beauclerk:
at Goodwood, **11**. 118
birth of, **7**. 16
dates of, corrected, **43**. 103
Ogilvie, William (1740–1832):
Conolly, Lady Louisa, corresponds with, **43**. 103
daughter of, **11**. 326n
Du Deffand, Mme, has no news of, **6**. 436
—— hears from, of Ds of Leinster's miscarriage, **6**. 331
—— mistakes, for O'Kelly, **6**. 421
(?) ——'s correspondence with, **7**. 155
——'s opinion of, **6**. 319, 328, 338, 342, **7**. 128, 156
—— to receive partridges from, **7**. 108
gored by elk at Goodwood, **11**. 118
HW asks for news of Mme du Deffand from, **7**. 231–2
HW jokes about fondness of, for wife, **30**. 270
Leinster, Ds of, marries, **7**. 173n, **11**. 211n, **32**. 204n
Paris to be visited by, **7**. 19
recovering from accident, **31**. 355
social relations of, in Paris, **6**. 319, 329, 330, 421
wife of, **9**. 376n
Ogilvie. *See also* Ogilvy

Ogilvy, Alexander (1718–46), 6th Bn Banff, 1738; Capt.:
Spanish register ship captured by, **17**. 377
Ogilvy, James (ca 1714–70), styled Lord Deskford 1730–64; 6th E. of Findlater, 1764:
Albani called on by HW and, at Conclave door, **17**. 9
anecdote told by, **15**. 151n
Castle of Otranto carried to Edinburgh by, **15**. 105
Conway saw, at Geneva, **37**. 58
England visited by, **15**. 151
HW and Coke claimed by, as friends, **17**. 371
HW congratulated by, **17**. 320
HW gives Mann's packet to, **17**. 24
HW praises, from Rome, **37**. 58
HW receives letter for, **17**. 26
HW's acquaintance with, **15**. 151, **23**. 312, **35**. 124
letter from, containing equivocal observations, **17**. 371
Mann's acquaintance with, **23**. 312
Northumberland House dinner attended by, with (?) Mackye, **38**. 530
Santo Buono talks with, about Porto Bello, **17**. 7
son of, **23**. 312
Ogilvy, James (1750–1811), styled Lord Deskford 1764–70; 7th E. of Findlater, 1770:
(?) affair of, with 'Irish Baroness,' **32**. 283
Bute's daughter to marry, **23**. 312
HW at same hotel with, in Paris, **35**. 124
marriage of, rumoured, **32**. 55
Northumberland House dinner attended by, **38**. 529–30
Paris visited by, **32**. 55
quietness of, **32**. 55
Ogiński, Michal Kasimierz (1731–1800), Prince; hetman of Lithuania:
Cosway, Mrs, entertains, **33**. 511
Poland's king for 24 hours, **33**. 511
pretender to Polish throne: **33**. 511; stripped of estate, **35**. 386
Prussian king's ring worn by, **35**. 386
SH visited by, **12**. 226, **35**. 386
Oglander, Lady. *See* Fitzroy, Maria Anne
Ogle, Cts of. *See* Percy, Lady Elizabeth (ca 1667–1722)
Ogle, Miss [? Catherine (d. 1790)]:
Damer, Mrs, teaches, **25**. 577
models, **25**. 577
Ogle, Sir Chaloner (ca 1680–1750), Kt, 1723; naval officer; M.P.:
American news comes from, **17**. 35
French ships mistaken for Spanish by, **17**. 46n
Frye prosecutes, **19**. 328
Knowles subordinate to, in West Indies, **18**. 279n
Santiago attack advised by, **17**. 175
Vernon joined by, in attack on enemy ships, **17**. 35n
Ogle, Capt. (?) Robert (d. 1762), lunatic murderer:

[Ogle, Capt. (?) Robert, *continued*]
death of, in fire at Newgate Prison, 38. 167,
168n
'Ogleby, Lord.' *See under* Garrick, David:
Clandestine Marriage
Ogle family:
portraits of, at Welbeck, 35. 270
Oglethorpe, Eleanor (1684–1775), m. (1707)
Eugène-Marie de Béthisy, Marquis de
Mézières:
Albemarle, Cts of, ridiculed by, 37. 353
arrival of, from Paris, 37. 353
biographical information about, corrected,
43. 99, 137
daughter of, 39. 44
death of, 6. 213
HW discusses, with her daughter, 10. 290–1
Selwyn mentions relatives of, and calls her
laundress to Ds of Portsmouth, 37. 353
Oglethorpe, James Edward (1696–1785), Gen.;
founder of Georgia:
age and preservation of, 25. 570, 31. 214,
33. 477
Birch thinks, ignorant of his profession, 19.
321n
death of, 33. 476
Dutch regiment to be commanded by, 30.
97n
fox-hunters converted by, into hussars, 19.
127
HW sees, for first time in 20 years, 33. 389–90
hussars to be commanded by, 18. 409
Indians brought to England by, 30. 94
Lort sees house of, 16. 196–7
Mathews's friend, 19. 33n
Methodists follow, to Georgia, 20. 41
neighbour challenged by, for trespassing,
25. 570
niece of, 4. 230n, 10. 290
Paoli lauded by, 23. 31n
rebels pursued by, 19. 185–6
regiment of, in Georgia, 19. 69n
Royal Regiment of Hunters under, at Durham, 19. 127n
Senauki, Q., and Tomo Chachi brought by,
from Georgia, 42. 236
sister of, 37. 353
social relations of, with Mrs Vesey, 31. 214
teeth of, gone, 25. 570
trial of, for cowardice, 19. 320–1
vigour of, at '95', 25. 570
Oglethorpe, Sir Theophilus (1650–1702):
Westbrook bought by, 16. 196n
Oglethorpe, Mrs Theophilus. *See* Wall, Eleanor
Oguelvit. *See* Ogilvie
Ogygia. See under O'Flaherty, Roderic
O'Hara, ——, English sea-capt.:
Andromache commanded by, 25. 645n
O'Hara, Charles (ca 1705 *or* 15–76), Irish M.P.:
deals at faro, at Dublin, 39. 40
HW's correspondence with, 40. 107–12
O'Hara, Charles (ca 1740–1802), army officer;
gov. of Gibraltar 1795–1802:

appearance of, 11. 246–7
Berry, Mary, engaged to, 12. 171–3, 210, 211,
43. 156
Berrys see, at Cheltenham, 12. 158, 161
Craven, Lady, attended by, at Drury Lane,
29. 43
Damer, Mrs, visited by, in Lisbon, 11. 203
England reached by, 11. 201
father of, 18. 104n
fondness of, for Berrys, 11. 246–7
Fowke and Byng send minutes of Gibraltar
council of war by, to Admiralty, 20. 560n
French horrors seen by, 12. 170
Gibraltar's governor, 39. 383n
—— the destination of, 12. 173, 42. 364
HW has not seen, even at Conway's, 11. 236
(?) HW's correspondence with, 42. 364
HW sympathizes with, for lack of promotion,
11. *119*, 203
imprisonment of, after siege of Toulon, 12.
158n, 18. 104n
London visited by, 11. 203
London Gazette mentions wounds of, 39. 383
Paris embassy secretaryship might go to, 33.
420n, 42. 73n
(?) presentation of, 42. 364
'sober advice' by, 12. 167
Toulon reached by, 12. 57, 67
—— troops to be commanded by, 12. 7, 18
O'Hara, Eugene, Ensign:
captured at Velletri, 18. 492
O'Hara, James (1690–1773), 2d Bn Tyrawley,
1724; diplomatist; army officer:
army command not to go to, 37. 583n
(?) at Chesterfield's assembly, 37. 327
comment by, on fog, whist, and House of
Commons, 18. 148
comments by, on Grantham and Pulteney,
18. 104
English troops in Portugal to be commanded
by, 22. 43
Fowke replaced by, at Gibraltar, 20. 561n
HW might ask, about Correggio painting,
18. 373
Jefferies not told by, of succour intended for
St Philip's, 21. 3
Lippe-Bückeburg's appointment sends, home
in disgust, 22. 48
Lisbon post left by, 17. 135n
—— post to go to, 22. 7
mission of, to Gibraltar, to punish Fowke
and Stuart, 20. 562
natural son of, 11. 119n
officers to accompany, to Portugal, 14. 120
Paris wigs and, 21. 191, 37. 526
Pope mentions seraglio of, 18. 104n
Portugal the station of, for 15 years, 18. 148
Portuguese forces said to be commanded by,
22. 34
returns from Portugal, with scorn for 'war'
there, 22. 70
Sackville, Lord George, abused by, 30. 158
Spanish post might go to, 21. 166

witticism by, to HW. on Col. Caesar, and Margaret Woffington, **21**. 157

wives and children brought to England by, from Portugal, **18**. 104

O'Hara, James (d. 1769), Capt.:
father of, **18**. 104n

O'Hara, Kane (ca 1714–82), dramatist:
Two Misers by, seen by George III, **32**. 235

Ohio River:
England can compensate Frederick II with lands on, **21**. 326
France builds forts on, on land owned by London and Virginia gentlemen, **20**. 440n
—— knows more than England about, **35**. 196
—— wants all forts destroyed, south of, **35**. 212n
George II hires Russians and Hessians to recover, **37**. 407
HW would prefer SH to lands on, **21**. 306
Hillsborough opposes plan for settlements on, **23**. 424
—— resigns because of land grant on, **23**. 423n
Jumonville may have been killed near, **41**. 157, 159
O'Briens said to have lands on, **38**. 421–2
Parliamentary campaign eclipses events on, **20**. 455
Popple's map omits, **20**. 497
Virginia militia fight Shawnees over valley of, **41**. 312n

Oil:
Del Montes steal, **20**. 428
England could have grown olives for, in hot summer, **24**. 407
Florentine: cost of, in London, **17**. 240; Mazzei to sell, in England, **21**. 495
for painting, HW to send, to Bentley, **35**. 352
Genoese have, **19**. 352
Lucca gives, to D. of York, **22**. 221
olive, tax on, in Spain, **39**. 63
pigments of, **40**. 215, 219
scorpion's, **30**. 197
used in making artificial stone, **41**. 229

Oil and vinegar:
Bentley sometimes dipped brush in, **28**. 195

Oilcloth; oilcloths:
Dutch wagon covered with, **38**. 4
painted: HW jokes about advertising Lady Mary Coke's travels on, **31**. 149; Hogarth's 'Bartholomew Fair' shows advertising posters of, **31**. 149n
picture on, advertises sights, **20**. 40
Roman pavements copied in, **34**. 222–3, 225

Oil painting:
Bentley's first attempt at, **35**. 207
—— to work away at, **35**. 208
invention of, in Italy, **42**. 65–6
Mason's experiments with, **29**. 311, 316
Stubbs invents method of enamelling, **29**. 137

varnished tempera mistaken for, **42**. 66
See also under Painting, *and under* Raspe, Rudolf Erich

Oil-paper:
emblems painted on, by servants, **38**. 204

Oilskin:
bootikins made of, **23**. 464, **24**. 494
coats of, **37**. 420
HW's letters wrapped in, **20**. 23

Ointment; ointments:
for wounds, **17**. 97
Henry VIII's receipts for, **2**. 332, 334
maids leave, in Mann's house, **17**. 395
Masses deemed better than, **35**. 388
of sulphur and hellebore, **23**. 460, **36**. 332
sore foot treated with, **9**. 83

Oionell, Jean, Ensign:
captured at Velletri, **18**. 492

Oise, river:
bridge on, **13**. 178n

Oiseau, L', French ship:
English ships pursue, **21**. 303
Glasgow's engagement with, **21**. 292
in Mediterranean, **21**. 249
St-Pierre the refuge of, **21**. 292n
Sardinian port sought by, **21**. 292

'Oiseaux de Steinkerque, Les.' *See* Alsace-Hénin-Liétard, Gabrielle-Françoise-Charlotte d' (Vicomtesse de Cambis); Beauvau, Marie-Françoise-Catherine de (Marquise de Boufflers); Boufflers, Louise-Julie de (Comtesse de Boisgelin)

Oisi, Comtesse d'. *See* Massuau, Bénigne de

O'Keeffe, John (1747–1833), dramatist:
Agreeable Surprise, The, by, **12**. 151, **16**. 256, **33**. 341, 348, 467
Beggar on Horseback by, **33**. 466–7
one of HW's favourite authors, **33**. 466

Okehampton, Devon, borough:
Lyttelton not elected at, **20**. 39
—— steals, from Thomas Pitt, **20**. 39

O'Kelly, (?) William (d. 1767), Freiherr; Irish officer in Austrian service:
(?) gone into the country, **17**. 67
governor of Pistoia, **19**. 454n
horses bought by, in England, **19**. 454n
Mill's substitute for English trip from Vienna, **19**. 454
Niccolini probably accused by, **20**. 2
Porto Ferraio reached by, from Leghorn, **20**. 98n
secret projects of, in England, **20**. 2

O'Kelly, (?) Mrs William:
(?) gone into the country, **17**. 67

O'Kelly-Farrell, Jean-Jacques (1749–1800), cr. (1776) Comte O'Kelly:
Caraman's social relations with, **7**. 346
Du Deffand, Mme, mistakes Ogilvie for, **6**. 421
Roissy visited by, **6**. *210*

Okeover, Leake (1710–63):
Fleet Prison confinement of, **20**. 257

[Okeover, Leake, *continued*]
Nicoll, Margaret, harshly treated by, 14. 194, 195
—— maintained by, 20. 256-7
runs away for debt, 14. 198-9
Okeover, Mrs Leake. *See* Nicoll, Mary
Okeover, Staffs:
Okeover of, 14. 194n
Olan. *See* Aulan
Olbach. *See* Holbach
Olbreuse, Éléonore d' (fl. 1665-90), Ds of Zell:
resents George I's treatment of her daughter, 2. 125
Old age. *See* Age, old; Youth and old age
Old Bachelor. See under Congreve, William
Old Bailey, the, in London:
Bentley, Mrs, not directed to, 9. 187
criminals' aliases at, 34. 177
Derwentwater to be tried at, 19. 180-1
felons at, deny their crimes, 23. 195
Grey's trial at, 19. 450n
HW compares *Old English Baron* to murder trial at, 28. 381-2
Hackman's trial at, 24. 459n, 460n
Keys, Riley, and Smith condemned at, 20. 199n
Lempster tried at, 20. 303n
Maclaine's trial at, 20. 188n
Mason, confectioner, to be tried at, 16. 204n
Page acquitted at, 21. 184n
prisoners at, 11. 298n
Rudd, Mrs, tried at, 24. 153
Salisbury, Sally, tried at, 19. 389n
streetwalkers at, known under aliases, 23. 520
Theodore of Corsica visits, 21. 45
trial at, for counterfeiting, 19. 242
Old Batchelour, The. See under Congreve, William
Old Bond St, London:
Buckingham's house in, 32. 371
Grafton, D. of, lives in, 33. 556
Gretton's book shop in, 10. 349
Hotham, Lady Dorothy, lives in, 34. 2n
Lort has been at, for fortnight, 16. 189
——'s lodgings in, 1. 313n, 2. 16
Strawbridge, Mrs, has house in, 33. 556
'Oldboy.' *See under* Bickerstaffe, Isaac: *Lionel and Clarissa*
Old Broad St, London:
Cranch writes from, 42. 257
Darell, of Union Court in, 22. 279n
Old Burlington St, London:
Hoper of, 12. 176n
Ilchester's house in, robbed, 32. 77
North, George, has house in, 25. 369n
Oldcastle, Sir John (ca 1370-1417), Lord Oldcastle, styled Lord Cobham; Lollard leader:
allegiance professed by, to Richard II, 16. 4
HW cannot say more about works of, 16. 4
in *Royal and Noble Authors*, 12. 257
Old 'Change, London:
Protestant Association marches past, 25. 53n

Old Coachman, The. See under Williams, Sir Charles Hanbury
Oldcotes, Derbyshire:
Bess of Hardwick builds, 9. 298, 40. 182
Old Durham House, London:
Adelphi on site of, 28. 102n
Oldenburg, Maj.-Gen. Jürgen Friedrich von:
(?) Erfurt attacked by, 21. 102n
Old England (periodical):
HW's contributions to, 13. 13, 14, 18
Mann receives issues of, 18. 411
Mann, Galfridus, sends numbers of, to HW, 35. 50
readers of, condemn Londoners' lack of modesty, 18. 316
Old English Baron, The. See under Reeve, Clara
Oldershaw, Mrs John. *See* Cotton, Anne
Oldfield, ——, physician:
Williams, Lady, treated by, 18. 104n
Oldfield, Anne (1683-1730), actress:
'become a nun,' 13. 66
chair conveys, from theatre, 17. *435*
Churchill, Charles, son of, 11. 42n, 97n, 13. 183, 28. 389n
Cibber's expression on, in preface to *Provoked Husband*, 23. 132n, 31. 157
Farren, Miss, compared to, 33. 563-4
granddaughter of, 18. 481
Hedges reputed lover of, 13. 183
house left by, to son, 11. 95n
older generation can talk of, 23. 351
played genteel comedy well, 33. 563
Swift criticizes acting of, 10. 219
Old Hall Green, near Ware, Herts:
Standon school transferred to, 40. 198n
Oldham, Rev. John (ca 1629-1716), nonconformist minister:
son's supposed 'Character' of, 13. 189
Oldham, John (1653-83), poet:
'Character' by, 13. 189
'Old Hat, The,' (?) inn:
near Acton, Montagu portraits to be left at, 10. 104
Oldisworth, William (1680-1734):
'character' of Smith by, 29. 111n
'Old King Cole':
song of, paraphrased, 32. 186
Old Maids. See under Hayley, William
'Old Man of the Mountain.' *See* Hasan ibn-al-Sabbah
'Old Palace [Palazzo Vecchio], gentleman of.'
See Nay, Emmanuel de, Comte de Richecourt
'Old Palace.' *See* Palazzo Vecchio
Old Park, Durham:
Gray visits, 1. 169n
Wharton of, 14. 58n
Old people:
follies of, 31. 345
HW calls, censors of modes, 25. 641
HW's reflections on, 25. 298, 308, 332
men, agreeable when lively but ridiculous when pretentious, 35. 376

women, next generation of, will be artistic, not mere devout scandal-mongering card-players, **35**. 390

Old Pretender, The. *See* James Francis Edward (Stuart)

Old Sarum, Wilts:
air traffic will revive, **39**. 425

'Old Sir Simon the King':
tune of, **17**. 292

'Old Tarleton's Song':
HW paraphrases, **9**. 50

Old Windsor. *See* Windsor, Old

'Old Woman Cloathed in Grey, An':
Gossips-toast sung to tune of, **37**. 84

Old Woman's Oratory. See under Smart, Christopher

Old Woman's Will of Ratcliffe Highway:
Montagu, D. of, binds, with mother-in-law's will, **18**. 566

Oldys, William (1696–1761):
Biographia Britannica includes articles by, **14**. 62n

Oleron. *See* Île d'Oleron

Olier, Mrs:
SH visited by, **12**. 231

Olimphant, Col. [? Laurence Oliphant (ca 1692–1767) of Gask; cr. (1760) Lord Oliphant in Jacobite peerage]:
alleged letter from, to officer in Flanders, **19**. 170

Olimpiade, L', opera. *See under* Metastasio, Pietro; Pergolesi, Giovanni Battista; Traetta, Tommaso

Olimpie. See under Voltaire

Olio:
HW might write, on Jews and Pagans, **35**. 384

Oliphant, Laurence (ca 1692–1767) of Gask, cr. (1760) Lord Oliphant in Jacobite peerage:
Jacobite governor of Perth, **19**. 170n
See also Olimphant

Oliva, Giovanni Paolo (1600–81), Gen. of the Jesuits:
correspondence by, in Jesuit archives, **23**. 517n, 518n

Oliva, treaty of:
Poland renews, **22**. 574n

Olivares, 'Duc' d'. *See* Guzman, Gaspar de

Olive; olives:
cypress with, **34**. 147

Olive Branch, merchant ship:
sinks off Falmouth, **35**. 196

Olive oil. *See under* Oil

Oliver, 'Mother' (fl. 1730), fruit-woman at Eton:
Cole when buying apples from, alleged to pinch her for being Presbyterian, **2**. 86

Oliver, Isaac (d. 1617), miniature painter:
dates of, corrected, **43**. 292
Herbert, Lord, of Chirbury, depicted in miniature by, **1**. 71n, **10**. 133n, **43**. 132

Hilliard's pupil, **16**. 148
Lucan, Bns, copies, **41**. 418n
Mary, Q. of Scots' portrait by, dubious, **42**. 320–1
miniatures by, **1**. 170, 173, **15**. 112n, 191n, 192n
Oliver, Isaac (d. 1687), may be identical with, **42**. 43
works by, burnt, **16**. 322n

Oliver *or* Olivier, Isaac (d. 1687), fellow of King's College, Cambridge:
verses by, on death of Edward King and on Charles I's child, **42**. 43–4

Oliver, Peter (ca ?1589–1647), miniature painter:
dates of, corrected, **43**. 292
miniatures by, of Digby family, **2**. 43n, **28**. 180, **32**. 165; of Jonson, **1**. 170; of Venus and Adonis, at Burghley House, **10**. 345

Oliver, Mrs Peter. *See* Harding, Anne

Oliver, Richard (1735–84), alderman; M.P.:
at liberty when Parliament is prorogued, **23**. 303
biographical information about, corrected, **43**. 283
candidate for lord mayor, **23**. 520n
elected sheriff, **23**. 419n
House of Commons sentences, to the Tower, **23**. 288
—— to examine, **23**. 283
Mansfield attacked by, in House of Commons, **23**. 256n
printer released by, **23**. 280
refuses to run for sheriff, **23**. 314n
Townsend carries, in London election, **39**. 196
——'s election as lord mayor blamed on, **23**. 441n
voting for, **23**. 315n
Wilkes summoned by, as Middlesex M.P., **23**. 475n
—— triumphs over, **32**. 53

Oliver, Silver, Irish M.P.:
absentee tax moved by, **23**. 530n

Oliver, Thomas (1734–1815), Lt-Gov. of Massachusetts:
Whately's letters from, **32**. 167n

Oliver, William (1695–1764), M.D.: physician:
Anson treated by, at Bath, **22**. 33n
death date of, corrected, **43**. 184
(?) Granville, Cts, attended by, **19**. 133
Practical Essay on the Use and Abuse of Warm Bathing in Gouty Cases by, **14**. 87n

Oliver Cromwell. See under Crébillon, Prosper Jolyot de

Olivet, Abbé d'. *See* Thoulier, Pierre-Joseph

Olive tree; olive trees:
branches of, **37**. 400, **38**. 163
HW lacks, for Bentley, **35**. 161
lacking, in England, **37**. 551
Lante, Cardinal, remonstrates at destruction of, **18**. 344n
Spaniards cut down, **18**. 344

[Olive tree; olive trees, *continued*]
Tuscan, warriors hang their arms on, 23. 159

Olivier, Mme:
Favart's verses for, 3. 129

Olivier, Francis, courier:
Englishman, formerly in Mann's service, 25. 197n
letters between London and Florence carried by, 25. 196, 197, 198
returns to Florence, 25. 208

Olivier, Jean-Antoine, Comte de Sénozan:
heiress of, 7. 92

Olivier de Sénozan de Viriville, Madeleine-Henriette-Sabine (ca 1763–94), m. (1778) Archambaud-Joseph de Talleyrand, Vicomte de Périgord, Duc de Talleyrand-Périgord:
marriage of, 7. 92

Ollerhead, Richard, mayor of Chester:
Hertford received by, 39. 18

Ollerton, Notts:
Markham of, 1. 6n

Ollières. *See* Félix d'Ollières

Olliffe, Mrs William. *See* Antrobus, Jane

Ollioules (near Toulon, France):
battle at, 12. 8n

Ollivier, B.:
elegy by, on Stafford's death, 42. 44

Ollivier, Michel-Barthélemy:
paintings by, of Paris concerts, 43. 107

Olmius, John (1711–62), cr. (1762) Bn Waltham; M.P.:
New Hall, home of, 9. 92
Weymouth election influenced for, 17. 421n

Olmütz (Moravia):
Conway and Scott visit, 39. 538
Frederick II besieges, 21. 204
—— blamed for leaving his country defenceless while attacking, 21. 227n
—— forced to raise siege of, 21. 224, 37. 549
—— leaves, 21. 237
—— leaves Prague for headquarters at, 17. 315n
——'s outposts approached, 22. 63
—— wastes time at, 21. 225
Prussians retreat towards, by Austerlitz, 17. 401n

Olonne, Comtesse d'. *See* Angennes, Catherine-Henriette d'

Olonne, Duc d'. *See* Montmorency-Luxembourg, Charles-Anne-Sigismond de

Olton. *See* Oulton

Olympiade. See Olimpiade

Olympic games:
Gray alludes to, 14. 12
West, Gilbert, describes, 9. 84

Olympus, Mt:
imitated in French garden, 32. 57
mentioned, 33. 116

Omaggio, L'. See under Bianchi, Giovanni Battista; Giordani; Rauzzini

Omaggio poetico. See under Belforte, D. of

O'Mahony. *See* Mahony

Omai:

Conway breakfasts with, 24. 175
England visited by, 16. 303n
ice called 'stone water' by, 24. 175
learns to skate, 24. 175
native of Otaheite, 24. 175

Omar (ca 581–644), caliph:
Ferdinand of Naples compared with, 31. 279
library at Alexandria burnt by, 31. 279

Ombersley, Worcs, Sandys's seat:
Dodd and Whaley visit, 40. 13–14

Ombre (game):
Craon, Princesse de, addicted to, 18. 101
foreign ministers play, at Tuscan Court, with Maria Louisa and Archduchess of Milan, 25. 51
HW and Pope use term from, 32. 123
Mann hopes to play with Maria Louisa, 25. 301
played: 17. 416; at Turin, 13. 191

Omelet; omelets:
Cori eats, on Fridays, 17. 254

Omens:
HW discusses, 33. 25, 426
See also Superstitions

Omer, d'. *See* Domer

Omiah. *See* Omai

Omnia quæ extant . . . quibus accedunt epistolæ . . . See under Busbecq, Augier-Ghislain

Omoa, Honduras:
capture of, 24. 543, 33. 150n

O'More, Rory (d. 1578):
Fitzpatrick killed, 1. 215n

'Omphale':
HW's name for Cts of Orford, 20. 439

Omrah:
Clive's right to be, at Mogul Court, 38. 348

'Oncle, l'.' *See* Hénault, Charles-Jean-François

'Oncle, le petit.' *See* Crozat, Louis-Antoine

'On Dr Johnson's Biographers,' verses by HW:
quoted, 12. 258

'One':
pronunciation of, 7. 373

Oneal, Mr:
social relations of, in Paris, 7. 271, 274

O'Neal, Mrs. *See* Cameron, Jeanie

O'Neal, Rev. Mr, Roman Catholic priest:
witticism by, 12. 265

O'Neal. *See also* O'Neil; O'Neill; Onel

Onebye, Mary (d. 1669), m. (1656) Thomas Staveley:
HW asks for print of, from *Bibliotheca topographica Britannica*, 42. 289

Oneglia (Italy):
Piedmontese said to defeat Spanish at, 37. 159–60
Spaniards occupy, 18. 454, 559
—— retire from, 18. 461

'O'Neil, King':
title of, to Irish throne, 21. 371
See also O'Neill, Hugh

O'Neil *or* O'Neille, Felix, Irish Capt. in French service:

Young Pretender accompanied by, in Scottish wanderings, **37**. 251–3

O'Neil. *See also* Oneal; O'Neal; O'Neill; Onel

O'Neill, Hugh (d. 1230), 'King of Ulster': HW inquires about, **14**. 104

O'Neill, John (ca 1740–98), cr. (1793) Bn, (1795) Vct O'Neill; M.P.:
(?) Hertford's daughter rumoured to be engaged to, **10**. 194
(?) wealth of, **10**. 194

O'Neill. *See also* Oneal; O'Neal; O'Neil; Onel

Oneille. *See* Oneglia

Onel [? O'Neill], Capt. Felix: captured at Velletri, **18**. 492

Onesti. *See* Braschi Onesti

One Thousand Seven Hundred and Forty-Four, a Poem. See *Discord*

Ongar, Essex: Bull of, **1**. 288n, **15**. 161n

Ongley, Bn. *See* Henley Ongley, Robert

Oniglia. *See* Oneglia

Onion; onions:
French flavour gravy with, **35**. 485n
Orford, E. of, distributes, to militia, **25**. 11
—— fond of, **25**. 11
ropes of, **33**. 261
skin of, Bentley might draw with, **35**. 243

'On Legacy Hunters.' *See* Williams, Sir Charles Hanbury: 'Peter and My Lord Quidam'

On Modern Gardening by HW. *See Essay on Modern Gardening*

Onofrio, ——, musician:
plays at Esher party, **10**. 73

Onorati, Bernardino, titular Abp of Sida; nuncio at Florence 1759–66, at Venice, 1767;
Botta takes precedence of, **22**. *44*
Leopold's relations with, **22**. 319
Mann debates with, over Young Pretender, **22**. 384
—— preceded only by, **22**. 349
—— to thank, for attentions to D. of York, **22**. 179
told to give D. of York invitation to Rome, **22**. 171
York, D. of, greeted by, at Florence, **22**. 213, 215

Onslow, Bns and Cts of. *See* Shelley, Henrietta

Onslow, Mrs ——:
George III civil to, **36**. 323

Onslow, Anne (d. 1751):
parents of, **30**. 289n

Onslow, Arthur (1691–1768), speaker of the House of Commons 1728–61; M.P.:
anecdotes by, **7**. 362
army voted by, in Committee, **30**. 301n
Barnard humiliated by, over trade bills, **20**. 135
——'s character sketch by, **17**. 252n
biographical information about, corrected, **43**. 240, 295
'body-coach' of, **37**. 378
brother of, **9**. 275n

Byng's expulsion from Hosue of Commons demanded by, **21**. 63

Caroline, Q., replies to boasting of, **30**. 292n

chair of, **18**. 191

Clutterbuck might succeed, **17**. 391n
—— persuaded, to resign treasurership of Navy, **30**. 293n

Coke's retort to, about Taaffe and Wortley Montagu belonging to Parliament and not to White's, **20**. 289

Commons' privileges maintained by, **30**. 301n

Conway and HW dread, **37**. 180, 183

Conway should deflect, from impartiality, **37**. 453

death of, painful, **22**. 585

declamations by, on grandeur of ancient English kings, **30**. 291n

dominant characteristics of, impartiality and bullying, **30**. 301n

election of, as Speaker, **35**. 17

Etonians proposed by, for King's fellowship, **40**. 39

family of, **30**. 288, 289n

Frenchman's note-taking in House of Commons would be disliked by, **35**. 162

German treaties opposed by, **20**. 501

Grenville, George, said to succeed, as Speaker, **21**. 491

HW addresses, **26**. 25

HW and Tonson meet at house of, **20**. 165

HW answers comments of, on *Anecdotes of Painting*, **40**. 309–11

HW asked by, about *Letter from the late E[arl] of H[arrington]*, **40**. 99

HW calls on, **35**. 97

HW expects his endurance to be tried by, **30**. 81

HW hears from, story of 'illegitimate' son of Cts of Rutland, **43**. 269

HW inquires about health of, **41**. 122

HW mentions, **14**. 120, **18**. 519

HW referred by, to journals of the House of Commons, **20**. 139

HW's correspondence with, **40**. 98, 309–11

HW sends *Historic Doubts* at request of, **41**. 122

HW's 'Patapan' satirizes, **13**. 14n, **30**. 287–306

HW's quarrel with, **13**. 20

HW thanked by, for Gray's *Odes*, **40**. 98

HW to be visited by, at SH, **40**. 98

HW told by, of Conway's intimacy with son, **38**. 35

Hampden's and Pym's portraits in library of, **30**. 304n

Hardwicke's dispute with, **9**. 149

heir of, **38**. 33, 35

Hessian and Russian treaties opposed by, **35**. 88

High Bailiff of Westminster assured by, of support of House of Commons, **20**. 123n

Hoadly's tracts presented to, **16**. 283n

Hyde's letter to, **37**. 340

[Onslow, Arthur, *continued*]
'immortal in the chair,' 38. 232
impartiality of: boasted of by him, 30. 292n; Gybbon and Rushout praise, 30. 292n; his foible, 30. 293n
impostor pretends to be son of, 19. 505–7, 510n
language used by, to control disorders in House of Commons, 30. 299n
Liddell and Talbot named by, to Secret Committee list, 17. 386, 391
Murray's insubordination provokes storm from, 20. 225
Navy post resigned by, 17. 391
Newcastle, D. of, forwards battle reports to, 30. 156n
Norton would have been felled with a mace by, 38. 325
officer's quarrel with, 9. 143
Parliamentary bill against clandestine marriages opposed by, 20. 383
Parliamentary speeches by: against House of Lords, 30. 301n; on Regency Bill, 20. 257; on retirement, promises complete retreat, 30. 164; pompous, 19. 412; prorogation, filled with pompous rhetoric, 30. 301n; reprimanding Westminster J.P., Williams's witticism on, 30. 301n
Parliamentary triumph over ministers hailed by, 18. 540
Pelham, Henry, proposes, as Speaker, 17. 219n
pension for, urged in address to George III, 30. 164
Philipps moves address of thanks to, 30. 164
Pitt attacked by, on stay of execution granted to Byng, 21. 64n
Popery Unmasked distributed by: cheap abridgement of Middleton's *Letter from Rome*, 30. 56–7; publication of, 30. 56; to discourage Roman Catholicism, 30. 57n
retirement of, as Speaker, 9. 346, 30. 164
rioters at Ember Court exact promise from, against militia, 35. 285–6
Ryder opposed by, on Clandestine Marriages Act, 37. 365
sits up late in Parliament though retired from being Speaker, 38. 321
son and nephew of, 23. 279
Speaker of House of Commons, 17. 219, 19. 446
Strange wants to exempt, from place tax, 21. 199
Walpole party might have been supported by vote of, 17. 251
Onslow, Mrs Arthur. *See* Bridges, Anne
Onslow, Denzil (ca 1698–1765), M.P.:
Selwyn succeeds, as paymaster of the Board of Works, 20. 518
Sutton, Thomas, replaced by, as salt commissioner, 20. 518n
Onslow, George (1731–92), M.P.:
(?) Dalrymple's answer to, concerning Sidney, 28. 85–6, 92, 95

Heroic Postscript attacked by, 28. 137
mob mistakes Sulivan for, 23. 288
Onslow, Thomas, 'jockeyed' by, at Guildford, 36. 174
Parliamentary membership of, corrected, 43. 295
printers of House of Commons debates arrested at request of, because speeches abuse him, 23. 279–80
Onslow, George (1731–1814), cr. (1776) Bn Cranley; 4th Bn Onslow, 1776; cr. (1801) E. of Onslow; M.P.:
Belgioioso's escape confirmed by, 39. 455
Boufflers, Mme de, visited by, 11. 248
Carlisle succeeded by, as treasurer of the Household, 33. 104n
Conway sees, at Chatham, 38. 33, 35
cousin ousted by, as M.P. for Guildford, 36. 174
(?) Dalrymple's answer to, concerning Sidney, 28. 85–6, 92, 95
declines running for Surrey, 36. 178n
Douglas, Lady, visited by, 12. 117
Ellis's motion against Oliver seconded by, 23. 288n
George III's encounter with Mme du Barry described by, 34. 127
———'s levee attended by, 39. 455
Grenville denounced by, 38. 499
HW annoyed with, for sending 17 French visitors to SH, 12. 27
HW cannot persuade, to abstain from voting on Regency Bill, 38. 548
HW dines at house of, with clergy, 32. 156
HW entertains: at breakfast, 32. 156; at dinner, 12. 5
HW hears news from, 32. 148
HW hears of American accommodation from, 39. 252
HW in carriage accident with, coming from Mrs Crewe's in Richmond, 39. 454
HW informed by, 23. 175n
HW mentions, 12. 70
HW resents implication by, that HW votes from interest, 38. 551
HW's correspondence with, 41. 122
HW tells story told him by father of, 43. 269
Horne Tooke sued by, 35. 553n
ingratitude of, to Chatham's memory, 28. 395
Jeffreys, Mr, visited by, 12. 25
Lords' expulsion from House of Commons moved by, 23. 256n
Malden, Vct, visited by, in Herefordshire, 31. 288
militia's reduction proposed by, 22. 413n
(?) Morton known to, 31. 427
Newcastle, D. of, entertains, at Oatlands, 32. 250
——— may take, to SH, 40. 361
———'s nephew, 40. 361
——— told by, of Ds of Leeds's death, 38. 419
news of battle of Charleston from, 32. 318
news of, rarely true, 39. 252

'panic-master-general,' **12.** 25, 27, 39
parents of, **30.** 289n
Parliamentary activity of, on Regency Bill, **38.** 548–9, 551-2
peerage of, corrected, **43.** 144, 340
printers of House of Commons debates arrested at request of, because speeches abuse him, **23.** 279–80
rangership and surveyorship lost by, **22.** 109n
Richmond residence of, **11.** 148, **31.** 288
son of, **36.** 174
Speaker's heir, **38.** 33
SH visited by, **12.** 228
SH visitors sent by, **12.** 27, 240, 245
wife entertains Major in absence of, **34.** 18
Onslow, Mrs George. *See* Shelley, Henrietta
'Onslow, Richard.' *See* Veers, Daniel
Onslow, Richard (1528–71), Speaker of the House of Commons 1566–71:
Onslow, Arthur, emulates, **30.** 288
Onslow, Sir Richard (1654–1717), 2d Bt; cr. (1716) Bn Onslow; Speaker of House of Commons 1708–10:
Onslow, Arthur, emulates, **30.** 288
Onslow, Richard (ca 1697–1760), M.P.; army officer:
death of, dissolves Lord Charles Hay's court martial, **21.** 385
illness of, delays Sackville's court martial, **21.** 377n
regiment of, **17.** 451n
Sackville's court martial avoided by, **21.** 366n
——'s court martial to be supervised by, **9.** 275
Onslow, Richard (1713–76), 3d Bn Onslow, 1740; M.P.:
red ribbon conferred on, **20.** 311
Onslow, Thomas (1754–1827), 2d E. Onslow, 1814; M.P.:
cousin ousts, from Guildford election, and Keppel displaces him for Surrey, **36.** 174, 178
SH visited by, **12.** 245
'On Sonnets,' verses by HW:
quoted, **12.** 271
Ontaouanouc Indians:
HW reads about 'purest dialect' of, **35.** 186–8
Ontario, Lake:
Amherst proceeds down, **9.** 308n
On the Character and Privileges of Sir Robert Walpole. See under Pownall, Thomas
On the Death of Richard West, Esq. See under Ashton, Thomas
'On the Destruction of the French Navy,' by HW:
HW sends, to Beauchamp, eliciting criticism from (?) tutors, **38.** 50-1, 52–3
Hertford receives, from son and forwards it to HW, **38.** 54–5
'On the Fireworks for the Peace,' by HW:
not printed, **13.** 22
'On the Foregoing Divine Poems.' *See under* Waller, Edmund

On the Sonatas of Bendall Martyn. See Bentley, Richard (1708–82): ode by
On the Virtues of Sage in Lengthening Human Life. See under Hill, John
Onyx:
cornelian resembles, **16.** 69
in mourning ring, **31.** 131n
seal of, on HW's watch, **40.** 64n
Opalinska, Katharina (1680–1747), m. (1698) Stanislas I (Leszczyński), K. of Poland; D. of Lorraine:
apartment of, **20.** 116
Opera; operas (general topic; *see also* Opera, English; Opera, French; Opera, Tuscan, etc.):
Alexander costumed in plumes in, **24.** 222
Bayreuth, Margravine of, composes, **20.** 478
Colisée resembles, **39.** 145
Conway thinks, vulgar diversions, **37.** 232
copied by hand in Italy, **17.** 181n
costume and hair-dressing at, **35.** 363
German princes waste money on, **24.** 186
HW would rather see than hear, **35.** 514
Italian castrati singers in: **9.** 236–7; ridiculed by HW's 'Persian Letter,' **30.** 36
making of, a 'civil' act, **35.** 335–6
Methodists do not attend, on Sunday, **20.** 86
omitted in jubilee year in papal states, **20.** 83
Palais Royal's pictures painted and varnished like scenes in, **39.** 202
.perpetual, life in Paris is, **35.** 115
politics less dignified than, **21.** 542
rivalry between singers a method of promoting, **16.** 280
Rolli, composer of, **18.** 468n
Rousseau's remarks on, **35.** 514
Russel's puppet-show burlesques Italian, **19.** 28
St-Germain composes songs for, **26.** 20
Spanish expedition in Italy has, **18.** 228
Walpole, Bns, prefers tragedies to, **18.** 128
Opera, at Bologna:
HW and Gray to hear Viscontina sing at, **17.** 31n
Opera, at Fontainebleau:
once a week, **38.** 448, 451
Richelieu orders operas for, **31.** 56, 64
Opera, at Reggio:
HW attends, **17.** 39–40, 47
masking optional at, **13.** 242
Opera, at Rome:
Conway dresses after, **37.** 324
Friedrich II of Hesse visited by D. of Gloucester in box at, **24.** 275
reportedly fine, **30.** 5
Opera, English (in London):
admission price to, **25.** 646
Ailesbury, Cts of, misses, **38.** 87
—— wants box at, **37.** 476–7, 480
Amelia, Ps, will displease guests if her parties conflict with, **38.** 81
Amorevoli not to sing in, **17.** 185, 190, **18.** 342
—— perhaps to sing in, **30.** 5
—— retained by, **17.** 170, 211, 358, 478, **18.** 32

[Opera, English, *continued*]

——'s part in, to be read, 37. 116

at Haymarket: **35.** 80; costumes of performers and spectators described in newspapers, **35.** 363; eclipsed by those at play-houses, **20.** 410; *see also under* Haymarket: King's Theatre in

at little theatre in Haymarket, **21.** 506, **37.** 50; *see also* Haymarket: little theatre in

attendants at, hired from Bear Garden, **17.** 166

attended by: Ailesbury, Cts of, **22.** 304, **38.** 470; Albany, Cts of, **11.** 272; Allen, **38.** 247; Arenberg, **18.** 137; Banks, Margaret, **19.** 234; Bedford, D. and Ds of, **22.** 498; Bernstorff, **10.** 265; Buckingham, Ds of, **17.** 254; Caroline, Q., **13.** 142; Charlotte, Q., **38.** 123, 126; Chewton, Lady, and sisters, **33.** 335; Christian VII, **10.** 265, **23.** 42–3, **35.** 328; Churchill, Lady Mary, **17.** 359, **18.** 180–1, 196, **21.** 278; Chute, **19.** 372; Coke, Lady Mary, **10.** 6; Conway, **30.** 239, **37.** 50, **38.** 470; Cornwallis, **38.** 247; Cumberland, D. of, **38.** 512; Dashwood, Lady, **19.** 224; Douglas, Lady Mary, **32.** 28; Éon, **38.** 378; Foote, Mrs (Mary Mann), **17.** 359, **22.** 304; Francis III, **20.** 57; Frederick, P. of Wales, **9.** 27; Grafton, Ds of, **32.** 28; HW, **1.** 52, **9.** 264, 358, **10.** 6, 79, 139, **17.** 412, **18.** 137, 180–1, **19.** 224, **20.** 57, **22.** 264, 304, **23.** 403, **25.** 242–3, 648, **28.** 391, **30.** 239, **32.** 29, 106, **33.** 586–7, **37.** 157n, **38.** 354, 466, 494; Hamilton, **9.** 358; Heathcote, Lady Margaret, **32.** 28; Hertford, **10.** 6; Hervey, Bn, **19.** 372; Hesse, Landgrave of, **9.** 27, 30; Holck, **10.** 265; Karl Wilhelm Ferdinand, **38.** 289–90; Lincoln, E. of, **17.** 411–12; Northumberland, Cts of, **10.** 6; Orford, Cts of, **18.** 234; Pecquigny, **38.** 307; Pitt, **30.** 239; royal family, **38.** 289–90; Salisbury, Lady, **11.** 248; Stanley, **38.** 466; Tavistock, Marchioness of, **22.** 498; Virette, **38.** 307; Whithed, **19.** 372; York, Edward, D. of, **9.** 264, **10.** 6

Auretti popular in, **18.** 131

ballad, HW's opinion of, **10.** 298

bankers usually recruit singers for, **17.** 191

Barbarina to be retained by, **17.** 358, **18.** 31, 131

bass in, Montagu's witticism on, **18.** 342

begins: after George II's birthday, **17.** 165, 170; despite prejudice against Roman Catholics and Italians, **19.** 177n; with pasticcio, **18.** 96

benefit performance, **25.** 134

Bettina dances in, **17.** 256, 421

Carrara sings in, **32.** 106

Charlotte, Q., may substitute concerts for, **38.** 101

Chiaretta may not appear in, **18.** 31–2

Christian VII sees *Buona figliuola* at, **23.** 42–3

comic, Paganini popular in, **21.** 491

comic operas the best at, **23.** 82

commended but deserted, **31.** 144

'consumptive,' **19.** 464

Conway a director of, **17.** 190, **37.** 112–13

Conway and wife to hear Manzuoli in, **38.** 470

Conway hopes HW will attend, often, **37.** 112

—— prefers, to that at Paris, **37.** 50

——'s directorship of, worries HW, **37.** 116–17

—— sorry to hear, are over, forever, **37.** 158

Cori, prompter at, **17.** 254n

Cornelys, Theresa, has Guadagni open in, **23.** 271

Cornwallis and Allen attend, drunk, **38.** 247

crowded: on Saturdays but not on Tuesdays, **17.** 256; on Tuesdays, **9.** 337; when George III and Q. Charlotte attend, **38.** 123

Cythère assiégée at, **32.** 259

dancers in: at Pantheon fête, **39.** 331; cannot dance, **38.** 250; capital, **25.** 243; Sodi pleases as much as Faussan in, **18.** 104

dances in: charming, **19.** 302; church music used for, **19.** 369; mended, **19.** 454; on French system, **17.** 166, **19.** 369; unpopular, **17.** 190, 197

Dauberval needed by, **38.** 467

—— to rejoin, **38.** 460

Davies, Cecilia, returns to, in spite of Mrs Yates, **39.** 238

—— succeeds in, **23.** 547, 570–1

deplorable, **39.** 211

deteriorated, **18.** 342

Dilettanti collect subscriptions for, **18.** 211

directors of: **17.** 190–1; advised by HW, **16.** 280; are Whigs, **17.** 191n; arrested for alleged plot, **35.** 229, 230; enrage HW, **18.** 293–4; fear that Amorevoli may not return, **17.** 478; HW to tell, about Gizziello's return, **17.** 424; hire Fumagalli and Visconti, **17.** 421; replace Visconti by Fumagalli, **17.** 398, 423; retain Muscovita to please Middlesex, **17.** 358; ruin it by importing abbés and mistresses, **18.** 210–11; spend money, **17.** 166

discussed at 'guzzling affair,' **13.** 64

Dorset asks George II not to subscribe to, **18.** 226

Drury Lane theatre deserted by men of quality on night of, **35.** 261

elephant breaks stage in, **17.** 358

Elisi has not appeared in, **21.** 459

—— sings in, **20.** 86n

empty, **31.** 4

English fondness for, on eve of war, **20.** 469

'English' when given at play-houses, **20.** 410

expense of, **17.** 166, 191, 216, 240, **18.** 226, 293

Farinelli in, **17.** 190, 478

fashionable ladies at, **34.** 262

Faussans in, **17.** 358

five a week, **20.** 410

flourish even before Christmas, **38.** 142

Frederick, P. of Wales, and George II to attend, on different nights, **17.** 186

Frederick, P. of Wales, sponsors, 19. 342
French invasion forgotten because of, 37. 459
French system imitated in, 17. 166
'full' when HW attends, 35. 323
Galuppi's *Scipione* in, 17. 358
Garrick, Mrs, danced in, 20. 74n
George II's quarrel with son suggested by, 18. 104
Gluck's operas flourish at, 19. 234
HW and Stanley hear Manzuoli in, 38. 466
HW as a child saw almost the first, 25. 558
HW ashamed to see so few contemporaries at, 38. 470
HW a subscriber to, 17. 358, 18. 293–4
HW attends, only once in 1786, 25. 648
HW attends Conway and Pitt alternately at, 30. 239
HW avoids, in cold weather, 9. 268
HW calls, 'woeful,' 10. 238
HW criticizes, 31. 144
HW doubts reopening of, 19. 442
HW has heard Rubinelli at, 25. 648
HW hears, are woeful, 31. 93
HW hears Allegranti in, 25. 242–3
HW's box at: 10. 139; D. of York visits, 22. 264; silver ticket to, 10. 139n, 43. 391; *see also under* Haymarket: King's Theatre at
HW sees Conway at, 38. 354
HW's opinion of, 9. 157
HW talks with Williams at, of Fox's wedding, 37. 157n
HW tired of defraying expenses of, 18. 293–4
HW to attend, 38. 313
HW to give up, 32. 117
HW to see Hertford at, 38. 81
HW unable to attend, 33. 322
HW will no longer attend, 31. 141
HW wishes George III and Q. Charlotte would not go to, 38. 128
Handel sets up oratorios to oppose, 18. 180
Harmonic Meetings given in, 23. 271
Hertford submits, for HW's inspection, 39. 169
hissing popular in, 18. 131
horses in, slow, 19. 369–70
houses' rivalry in, 11. 191, 202, 232
Hume Campbell prides himself on not attending, 20. 5
Il Cidde, admired, 32. 89
imported from France, 11. 208
in decline, 21. 363
Italian: 42. 506; arias from, 36. 53n; Chatterton might credit Hengist with invention of, 16. 221; Giardini unpopular as manager of, 38. 250; less popular than English operas, 10. 138; *Midsummer Night's Dream* more nonsensical than, 35. 209–10; parodies of, 25. 174n; subscribers of, to have ball and supper, 10. 138; unpopular on Tuesdays, 10. 138
Karl Wilhelm Ferdinand and Ps Augusta to attend, 22. 197
ladies attend Parliament after, 38. 318

lapse of, 37. 158
lasts almost to midnight, 32. 39
license for, at Pantheon, 11. 95
Lincoln's scuffle with drunken officer at, 17. 411–12, 30. 32
London takes to, when given at play-house, 20. 410
Lyttelton, Bns, and Lady Mary Churchill take no boxes at, 37. 477
Mancini's performance at, 18. 342
Mattei's absence retards, 35. 286–7
Middlesex and Holdernesse the managers of, 18. 110
Middlesex chief undertaker of, 30. 5
—— does not pay performers in, 19. 370
——'s mismanagement of, 19. 226, 293
—— sponsors, 19. 342
——'s wife's fortune may be spent on, 18. 501
—— the contribution of, to politics, 18. 365
Millico sings in, 23. 403
Mingotti hissed in, 35. 256–7
—— to sing in, 38. 233
miserable, 18. 104
mob may silence, 17. 166
Monticelli retained by, 17. 185, 190, 211, 358, 401, 30. 5
Muscovita retained in, by Middlesex, 17. 358
music unpopular in, 17. 190
none, in London, 13. 197
Nugent-Irvine quarrel at, 37. 446–7
officials give, for Friedrich Wilhelm, 19. 265
Olimpiade given at, 17. 401
omitted because of actors' illnesses, 17. 190
Ossory will tell wife about, 32. 164
Pacchierotti admired in, 25. 243
Parsons, Nancy, former dancer in, 23. 344n
parties forming against, may prevent full season, 30. 30–1
performers in, have not yet sung even in private, 30. 31
Pescetti's, shows Venetians with gondolas and masks, 17. 302
politics moves to, 38. 2, 11
popular, 17. 211, 331, 38. 2
popular when prices are equal to those of plays, 20. 410
prevalent in London, 35. 192, 39. 322
races eclipse, 23. 570–1
Reginello acts in, 19. 370
Rich, Lady, patroness of, 30. 295n
Ricimero at, 33. 250
Royal Academy of Music begins, 25. 558n
Rubinelli's voice better at Handel jubilee than at, 25. 648
Saturdays at, 'prodigious,' 38. 503
season for, almost over, 17. 421, 434
seating arrangements at, 38. 289
serenata at, 20. 49
serious operas seldom given in, 22. 484
shepherdesses change to gods and goddesses in, 12. 164
Sheridan's interest in, 33. 301
side-box at, flirtation in, 35. 558

[Opera, English, *continued*]
subject of dinner conversation, **38.** 530
subscription for, **17.** 358
succeeds well, **35.** 160
to be fine, **30.** 5
to begin: **38.** 244; at end of October, **30.** 30
Tuesday's and Monday's, exchanged, to suit George III and Q. Charlotte, **38.** 142–3
undertakers of, always cheat, **38.** 208–9
unfrequented, **18.** 119, **19.** 342, **23.** 547
unpopular, **31.** 141
unsuccessful, **38.** 250
Vaneschi and Mingotti set up rival companies for, **37.** 459
Vaneschi, manager of, through Lord Middlesex, **17.** 191, 216, **35.** 229
—— 's, **18.** 198
—— to be discarded by, **17.** 358
Vauxhall eclipses, **13.** 102, **17.** 421
'very bad,' **32.** 117
Vestris benefit eclipses opera for hurricane sufferers, **25.** 134
—— 's fête ends in, **39.** 382
—— 's success in, **33.** 254–5
Viaggiatori felici, I, at, **33.** 322
Virette seeks Pecquigny after attendance at, **38.** 307
Viscontina in, **17.** 190, **30.** 5
visitors to, adjourn to tavern, **37.** 54
Wales, Caroline, Ps of, receives acclamations at, **12.** 185–6, 187
would be thought magnificent at Florence, **17.** 208
Yates, Mrs, and La Bastardella disagree about, **39.** 223–4
Zanaida at, forsaken by HW to go to SH, **38.** 201
Opera, French, at Paris:
attended by: Cornbury, **20.** 213–14; Du Deffand, Mme, **7.** 339, **30.** 263; Fontenelle, **20.** 213–14; HW, **7.** 328, 334, 339, **18.** 495, **30.** 263; Maurepas, **6.** 194, **24.** 61; Pont-de-Veyle, **5.** 418, 424; Richmonds, **7.** 328; Sanadon, Mlle, **5.** 155, 325, **7.** 339
ball at, **4.** 154, **5.** 179
Barrymore, Lady, to have box at, **32.** 55
begins, **38.** 298
Conway prefers London opera to, **37.** 50
Cornbury and Fontenelle discourse at, **20.** 213–14
Dauberval cannot be spared from, **38.** 477, 483
directors of, *see* Auvergne, Antoine d'; Berton, Pierre-Montan; Joliveau, Nicolas-René; Rebel, François
English opera imitates, **17.** 165–6, **19.** 369
'figurantes' in, wear festoons of flowers, **30.** 265
Frederick II might compose opera for, **35.** 221
frequent, **38.** 574
Garrick thinks to rival, **39.** 133

HW comments on, **32.** 22
HW disgusted by, **31.** 45–6
HW disparages, **4.** 128
HW first sees, in Paris, **18.** 495
HW recognizes Englishwoman at, by her costume, **30.** 264
HW will miss, **38.** 505
HW will send Mason latest improvements at, **28.** 219
HW would like Elizabeth of Russia's amours made into, **18.** 495
heroines of, quaver, **18.** 495
Hertford has good box at, shared with Marigny, **38.** 298
—— introduces English visitors to, **38.** 222
lowered musical taste makes dancing more important in, **38.** 483
Maurepas applauded at, **24.** 61
music of, inharmonious, **13.** 162
Réduction de Paris at, **32.** 268
singers in, distressed when not squalling in usual French taste, **7.** 338
Spitalfields weavers can outdo dancers in, **38.** 461
support needed by, **38.** 477, 483
Opera, Genoese:
at Teatro del Falcone, **22.** 201n
French exclude Genoese from, and act all parts, **19.** 505
Opera, Irish:
Arne's, at Dublin, **37.** 412n
Opera, Italian. *See* Opera, at Bologna; Opera, at Reggio; Opera, at Rome; Opera, English, at London: Italian; Opera, Genoese; Opera, Lucchese; Opera, Neapolitan; Opera, Paduan; Opera, Tuscan; Opera, Venetian; Opéra-Comique
Opera, Lucchese:
Vaneschi cheats Middlesex and Raymond at, **17.** 216
Opera, Neapolitan:
glorious, **19.** 442
Gray's MSS of, **43.** 61
plans for cantata at, **19.** 437–8
Opera, Paduan:
Murray takes English visitors to, from Venice, **21.** 512–13
Opera, Tuscan:
accademici deny use of theatre for St John's Day, **18.** 439
advantages (social) of, **19.** 311
Amorevoli in, **17.** 80, 81
Andreoni acts in, **19.** 455
Astrua in, **19.** 438
at Leghorn: Babbi hired for, for carnival, **18.** 525–6; Braitwitz takes Mann to Francis I's box in, **17.** 259; Goldsworthy, Mrs, receives Mann at, **17.** 260; opera to be given at, for carnival, **22.** 354; restored, **19.** 1; Sani sings in, **18.** 160
Babbi in, **19.** 438
bad: at beginning of carnival, **17.** 284, **18.**

128, 555, **19.** 454, **20.** 115, 210–11; at great theatre, **18.** 555, **20.** 357; for St John's Day, **17.** 79–80

Bagnano not to give, in Via del Cocomero, **17.** 56

Barlocci sings in, **18.** 302

Barrett Lennard, Mrs, will not attend, on Sunday, **20.** 86

Barrett Lennards miss, **20.** 92

Bernacchi chief actor in, **17.** 239

Botta wants, in autumn at Florentine great theatre, **22.** 166

boxes at, *see under* Teatro della Pergola; Theatre: Florentine

Caffarelli sings in, **19.** 437, 439

Chimenti not worth hearing in, **18.** 361

Chute and Whithed at, **18.** 322

Chute attends, in chair, **18.** 386

clergyman, English, does not attend, on Sunday, **18.** 162–3

Craon attends, **19.** 440

Craon, Princesse de, attends, **17.** 40, 83, **18.** 302, **19.** 357, 439–40

—— offended by incidents at, **19.** 439–40

dance in, represents siege of Vienna, **25.** 360

dances in, **17.** 48, **18.** 322, **19.** 355–6, 454–5

dances in, unsuccessful, **18.** 361, **20.** 357

Du Châtelet attends, **19.** 439

Egizziello (Giziello) singer in, **17.** 56, 449, 454, **18.** 1, 12, **19.** 438

Electress's courtiers attend, **18.** 160

—— 's death cuts, short, **18.** 163

Elisi shines in, **20.** 86

Elmi and Turcotti women impresarie for, **17.** 80

Estevenon attends, **17.** 217

Feroni, Mme, attends, **17.** 81

first woman in, has no voice, **30.** 14

Forbes and Laurence attend, **19.** 192

for Joseph II, **22.** 564

for Joseph II's birth, **37.** 96

for Maria Elizabeth's birth, **18.** 294, 302

for Maria Theresa's coronation celebrations, **17.** 100, 101

for Maria Theresa's name day, **18.** 322, **22.** 558–9

for St John's Day, **17.** 449, 463, **18.** 435, 445

for the Carnival, **19.** 355–6

fourth, recently begun, **19.** 439–40

Francis I's box at, **17.** 60, 83

frequented, **19.** 207

Gabburri, Mme, attends, in Mann's box, **17.** 136

Galli, Mme, has box in, **19.** 505

gay, at Carnival, **19.** 364

Gloucester, D. of, hears Tenducci in, **23.** 353

gossip lacking at, **19.** 439

Gray, Sir James, lured from Venice by, **19.** 433

Grifoni, Mme, attends, **17.** 48, 51, 78, **18.** 54

HW admires accounts of, **19.** 442

HW goes to, at 9 P.M., **37.** 78

histrioni take place of, **18.** 462

illumination after, unfrequented, **18.** 303

illumination at, **18.** 322

impresario of, dies, but wife goes on singing, **20.** 298

Incontri, Abp, dislikes mingling of sexes at, **18.** 41

in morning, at end of Carnival, **19.** 465

intermezzi bad in, **20.** 210–11

in Via del Cocomero, *see* Teatro del Cocomero

in Via della Pergola, *see* Teatro della Pergola

last night of, **17.** 304

last of season, **18.** 60

Leopold regulates, **22.** 559

Lorraine faction impresarii for, **18.** 555

Lucchi, Angiola, appears in, **18.** 368

Mann and Chute avoid, **17.** 269

Mann attends, **17.** 69, 74, 81, 104, 106, 136, **18.** 12, 29, 54, 60, 307, **19.** 354–6, 357, 505

—— cannot attend: because of cold, **18.** 322; because of gout, **25.** 360

—— has rehearsal for, in his terreno hall, **18.** 294

—— indifferent to, **20.** 404

—— meets Gustav III at, **33.** 449

—— prefers HW's letters to, **20.** 15

—— 's boxes at, *see* Teatro della Pergola: Mann's box at; Theatre: Florentine, Mann's boxes at

—— 's spirits not raised by, **18.** 307

—— to attend, with special chairs, **17.** 69

—— to take Bns Lucan to, **20.** 418

masks alone keep audience from slumbering at, **19.** 439

masks permitted at, while Caffarelli remains, **19.** 439

Medici, Filippo de', impresario for, **18.** 439

Modenese princess attends, **17.** 60, 69, 99, 101

Modenese princess gives money to, **17.** 65

Narni and Valenti dance in, **19.** 455

Neri courts Mme Gondi at, **18.** 86

Orford, Cts of, supports, **18.** 555

Philipps attends, in Mann's box, **17.** 81

Pinacci roars in, **18.** 361

planned for Maria Josefa, **22.** 525

poor, **30.** 14

prices of tickets for, **23.** 458

promoters of, dread Novena, **18.** 295

resumed in Florence, **18.** 1

Riccardi disputes with Mann at, **19.** 505

Richecourt's orders about, **19.** 8

Ridolfi produces, with Bernacchi and Bagnolese, **17.** 239–40

—— will lose by, **17.** 284, **18.** 128

Rosenberg regulates, **22.** 559

Sade attends, **17.** 283

Salimbeni in, **17.** 79, 81

Santarelli's performance in, **18.** 353, 361

Santi Barbieri sings in, **18.** 302

Sauveterre choreographer at, **17.** 45n

—— dances in, **18.** 361, **19.** 355–6

—— directs, **18.** 303

[Opera, Tuscan, *continued*]

—— hissed by pit at, from respect to Denis, 19. 439

second one: at great theatre, 22. 477; to begin, 19. 437

Serristori, Andreo, attends, 17. 136

singers' box at, 17. 60

Suares, Francesco, attends, 17. 81, 149

Suares, Mme, attends, 17. 81, 18. 29, 19. 311

supper after, avoided, 18. 303

Tesi insulted at, 18. 368

—— may be in, 18. 438

——'s: promoted by Mme Suares, 18. 280–1; rehearsal at Mann's house, 18. 294; successful, 18. 302; unsuccessful, 18. 361

——'s costume for, 18. 353, 361

——'s fee for singing in, 18. 281

——'s ostentation ruins, 18. 361

Trionfo della gloria, Il, given at, during Carnival, 19. 354n

two, at Teatro della Pergola, 35. 16, 28

unfrequented, 17. 284, 18. 128, 20. 115, 357

unlikely to be given, 30. 5

Visconti sings in, 19. 437

visitors prefer, to seeing Mann, 17. 97

weddings interfere with, 18. 59–60

worst ever, 18. 128, 19. 207

Opera, Venetian:

Andreoni sings in, 17. 248n

Elmi sings in, 17. 80n

Paganini, Rosa, sings in, 17. 45

Sauveterre, choreographer in, 17. 45n

Opera books:

Italian, call plot of opera the *argomento,* 23. 281

Opéra-Comique (Comédie Italienne):

attended by: Bussy, Marquise de, 5. 361; Christian VII, 4. 154; Conway, 6. 109; Craufurd, 3. 345; Crewe, Mrs, 5. 361, 376; Du Deffand, Mme, 3. 345, 4. 274–6; Du Deffand, Mme, women servants of, 7. 453; Dunmore, 4. 276; Greville, Mrs, 5. 361, 376; HW, 7. 260, 262, 272, 305, 316, 319, 331, 351, 22. 342, 32. 266–7; Hertford, 38. 217–18; Louis XVI, 5. 376, 377; Luxembourg, Mme de, 3. 345; Marie-Antoinette, 5. 376, 378; Mirepoix, Mme de, 3. 345, 32. 266–7; Richmond, D. and Ds of, 4. 274–6; Roncée, Comtesse de, 5. 361; Selwyn, 3. 345

better than Comédie-Française, 14. 145

Caillot of, 28. 285

characters of, 11. 365, 18. 103

Comédie-Italienne united with, in Paris, 10. 175

Du Deffand, Mme, invited to, 4. 281

—— mentions, 3. 239

Farmain de Rozoi's *Henri IV* at, 6. 116, 39. 217–18

Fermor, Lady Sophia, resembles Columbine in, and Lincoln resembles Valere, 18. 103

HW admires, 10. 175–6, 31. 46

HW and Mme de Mirepoix see *Réduction de Paris* at, 32. 266–7

(?) HW to have box at, 6. 217

management of, 6. 28

Pont-de-Veyle frequents, 5. 117, 6. 75

Sedoine's *Deserteur* to be given at, 5. 376

Opera girl; opera girls:

auction of effects of, 7. 369

Beauvillier's marriage to, dissolved by his family after having her confined, 30. 59

elocution of, 4. 72

Vernon spends money on, 17. 126

Opera glass; opera glasses:

French might see England through, from Calais, 35. 370

Opera House, English. *See* Haymarket: King's Theatre in

Opera House, Florentine. *See* Teatro degl'Intrepidi; Teatro del Cocomero; Teatro della Pergola

Opera singer; opera singers:

fee of, 18. 281

French, seem comic to HW, 18. 495–6

hussars frighten, into a fever at Bologna, 18. 302

See also Singer

Opera ticket; opera tickets:

Wrey gives, to Margaret Banks, 19. 234

Operation; operations:

on breast, 30. 171

on D. of Bedford's eyes, 41. 110, 137

Ophaly. *See* Offaly

'Ophelia' in Shakespeare's *Hamlet:*

Mrs Jordan to play, at Richmond, 12. 142

Ophir:

mines of, 11. 72

Opiates:

HW takes, 31. 191

Waldegrave takes, in last illness, 10. 58

Walpole, Sir Robert, takes, 19. 16

See also Opium

Opie, John (1761–1807), painter:

HW describes style of, 29. 184–5

HW to assess the genius of, 34. 10n

'Jephthah's Vow' by, 15. 206

portraits by: of Hannah More, 31. 258, 279; of Mrs Delany, 29. 185

Opiner:

French parliamentary councillor too modest to, 6. 72, 12. 193

Opium:

bark as soporific as, 29. 311, 35. 376

Godschall's dullness suggests addiction to, 17. 295

HW calls, 'false friend,' 39. 149

soothing effects of, 31. 241

taken by: Beauchamp, Vcts, 39. 149; Beauclerk, Topham, 33. 107; Bolingbroke, Vct, 33. 107; Stafford, Cts of, 9. 119; Voltaire, 7. 44, 46, 28. 408, 410

Turkish, Hume's histories full of, 42. 78

Voltaire dies of overdose of, 28. 408, 410

—— takes, 7. 44, 46

young people are, to the elderly, 10. 305

Oporto, Portugal:

chaplain at, **1**. 163n

Opossum:
Piozzi, Mrs, comments on, **9**. 142n

Oppidans. *See under* Eton

Oppido (Italy):
earthquake account mentions, **25**. 376

Opposition, The. See under Hamilton, William Gerard

Opposition, the:
Bute may yet receive support of, **30**. 185
contradicts the whole nation, **31**. 94
Fox's low opinion of, **30**. 189
HW not to change opinions or language on quitting, **30**. 196
necessity of, for free nations, **15**. 63, 131
old, Barnard and Egmont the last survivors of, **35**. 195–6
support of George III against Grenville ministry declared by, **30**. 185
Tory destruction fundamental point of, **30**. 190
See also Parliament: Opposition in

Opposition Mornings. See under Tickell, Richard

Opposition Not Faction:
Faction Detected answered by, **18**. 319n

Oppression on the breast:
occurrences of, **16**. 243, **18**. 139, 172, **22**. 42, **25**. 280, **38**. 338, 523

Opy. *See* Opie

'O'Quarrel':
HW's name for Malone, **33**. 308

Oracle, The (periodical):
Fagnani, Maria, called Queensberry's daughter by, **33**. 64n

Oracles des sibylles:
Du Deffand, Mme, owns, **8**. 26

Oraison funèbre de . . . Louis, dauphin. See under Loménie de Brienne, Étienne-Charles de

Oraison funèbre de Stanislas I. . . . See under Copel, Jean-François

Orange, P. of. *See* Frederik Hendrik (1584–1647); William I (1533–84); William III (1650–1702); William IV (1711–51); William V (1748–1806)

Orange, Princes of:
print collection of, **43**. 382

Orange, Ps of. *See* Anne (1709–59); Frederika Sophia Wilhelmina (1751–1820); Marie Luise (1688–1765); Mary (1631–60); Wilhelmina Carolina (1743–87)

Orange (France):
national guard reaches Avignon from, **11**. 85n

Orange; oranges:
Brown, Sir Robert, saves money by not having, on his sideboard, **25**. 609
China: measles caused by, **17**. 352; served at Versailles ball, **32**. 256
climate of India suitable for ripening, to shaddocks, **25**. 153
Du Barry, Mme, tosses, **23**. 85

Frederick William discusses sellers of, with George III, **9**. 237
lady carries, in pocket, **37**. 22
Magdalen House chapel decorated with, **9**. 273
roses wither when SH has, **9**. 190

Orange, House of:
Conway describes bedchamber of, **37**. 287, 289
Cowper's claim to Nassau title opposed by, **25**. 78n
Frederick II tells Dutch to uphold, **33**. 384
minorities prevalent in, **20**. 279
See also under Holland; Nassau family

Orange flower; orange flowers:
Cole wants, for potpourri, **1**. 67, 69–70, 72
Dublin nymphs make, **37**. 412
Guimar, Mlle, to have, outside dining-room windows, **23**. 323
HW's at SH: **10**. 127, **11**. 290, 296; drowned, **32**. 302; HW gathers, **32**. 241; profusion of, **1**. 69; ruined by rain, **39**. 176
Hertford, Cts of, wants HW to bring, **39**. 160
Johnstons thank HW for, **12**. 196
June's, not yet in bloom, **33**. 334
Mann sends, dried, to Horatio Walpole (1678–1757), **20**. 255
price of, in Florence, **18**. 230

Orange flower water:
curative properties of, **19**. 330n
distilled, Mann uses, against Cocchi's advice, **22**. 469
English seek, from Florence, **19**. 330
HW seeks, for Bns Hervey, **31**. 60
HW will be able to send, if warm weather continues, **20**. 131
Mann gets, from Malta, **19**. 330
—— sends, to Horatio Walpole (1678–1757), **19**. 330, **20**. 255

Orange groves:
Mann's, at Florence, **35**. 41

Orange jelly:
cost of ingredients of, **4**. 45
Du Deffand, Mme, asks for recipe for, **4**. 45
—— makes, according to HW's recipe, **4**. 63

Orange juice:
HW drinks, **29**. 133

Orange peach. *See under* Peach

Orangerie:
at Sceaux, **7**. 322

Orange-tawney:
Macaronies and Cts of Hertford's footmen wear, **32**. 191n

Orange tree; orange trees:
at Chantilly, **7**. 260
at Ranelagh, **20**. 47
at Stowe, **10**. 315
Conway's commission about, to HW, **38**. 13
Duane's, at Twickenham, **33**. 355
emblem for Princes William Henry, Henry Frederick, and Frederick William, **38**. 204
HW's, at SH: blooming, **10**. 224; HW breaks, looking for nests, **40**. 252; HW to protect,

[Orange tree; orange trees, *continued*]
21. 361, 369; in winter quarters, 33. 529;
HW sends, to Bentley, 35. 161
in Mann's garden, 17. 104, 499
Lorenzi praises colour scheme of, 21. 501
Mann's, in bloom, 18. 230
Martin's, sold at auction, 21. 121
not yet in bloom in June, 33. 334
pomegranates used with, in Paris, 33. 293
Stanley buys, around London, for fête champêtre, 24. 14

Orange tubs:
at Lady Diana Beauclerk's, 33. 225

Orange-wood:
bergamotes lined with, 31. 100n

Oratio de novo physiologiæ explicandæ munere.
See under Middleton, Conyers

Oratoire, L'. *See* Pères de l'Oratoire

Oratorio; oratorios:
at Hinchingbrooke, 33. 99
Granville, Cts, attends, 18. 537
HW attends, 18. 537
Handel's: *Alexander's Feast*, 32. 106; HW
asks if Mann has received, 22. 73; Mann
wants, for Mme Branchi, 22. 35, 36, 41–2;
Mann, James, to have selected, 22. 49;
Samson, not attended by HW, 32. 109; set
up by Handel to oppose operas, 18. 180
poor singers of, 18. 180, 186
popularity of, 18. 180, 186
too ephemeral to be printed in Italy, 17.
181n

Oratory:
Greeks' grace in, 16. 270

Oratory; oratories (devotional structures):
Henley preaches at, 18. 465n
popularity of, 35. 200
private, Giovanni Gastone has, in Palazzo
Pitti, 20. 489

Orazio, burletta:
composed by Latilla, Resta, and Ciampi, and
sung at Haymarket, 20. 4n

Orbetello (Italy):
air of, bad, 18. 16
Modena, Ds of, not to visit, 18. 222, 223
Montemar may leave garrison at, 18. 27
—— may visit, 17. 182n, 198, 204, 206, 214,
18. 7, 16, 27
——'s agreement with Ferretti signed at, 17.
214n
—— sends courier from, 17. 226
Neapolitan governor repels Spanish xebecs
from, 18. 287
Neapolitan troops at, 19. 378
Philip, Don, may land at, 17. 389
Sienese approach-route covered by, 17. 289
Spaniards prefer Foligno to, as headquarters,
18. 27
Spanish army leaves garrison at, 17. 289
Spanish army to leave, for Foligno, 17. 265
Spanish baggage approaches, 18. 243, 253
Spanish invalids may embark at, 19. 55

Spanish officers buy horses at, for baggage,
17. 214
Spanish troops at, 17. 154, 178, 179, 192, 197,
204, 206, 262, 289, 350

Orcades. *See* Orkney Islands

Orchard, Rev. Arthur (? 1640–1706):
godfather to Cole's uncle, 2. 351

Orchard, Paul (1739–1812), M.P.:
M.P. for Callington, 42. 350n

Orchard; orchards:
has not been in Queen Square since reign of
Canute, 39. 418

Orchard St, Portman Sq.:
Timms of, 33. 369n

Orchard Wyndham, Somerset:
Wyndham of, 15. 151n

Orchestra; orchestras:
at Genoa, entirely composed of French officers, 19. 505
double, at Birthday serenata, 38. 87
Florentines expect Mann to have, to celebrate George III's coronation, 21. 533
for fête champêtre in Boboli amphitheatre,
25. 586
See also Music: band of

'Orco,' Cardinal di:
Romans' name for Cardinal York, 19. 428

Ord, Anne Dillingham:
Burney, Fanny, travels with, 42. 330n

Ord, Craven (1756–1832), antiquary:
believes in Ireland's MSS, 15. 321
Nivernais's *Jardins modernes* given to, 12. 260

Ord, Robert (1700–78), M.P.:
biographical information about, corrected,
43. 251
Sandys's secretary, 18. 320n
Williams, Sir Charles Hanbury, satirizes,
18. 320

Ord, Mrs William. *See* Dillingham, Anne

Ord. *See also* Orde

Orde (from 1795, Orde-Powlett), Thomas
(1746–1807), cr. (1797) Bn Bolton; M.P.:
France visited by, 1. 213, 216
Irish bill withdrawn by, 33. 491
print by, of Malden, 1. 188
prints by, 1. 207, 210, 212, 213, 216

Orde. *See also* Ord

Orde family:
SH visited by, 12. 244

Order; orders:
wearing of, 9. 56, 10. 235

Order of La Croix étoilée. *See* Croix étoilée,
Order of the

Order of Malta. *See* St John of Jerusalem,
Knights of

Order of Maria Theresa. *See* Maria Theresa,
Order of

Order of St Andrew. *See* St Andrew, Order of

Order of St Catherine. *See* St Catherine, Order
of

Order of St January. *See* St January, Order of

Order of St-Louis. *See* St-Louis, Ordre de

Order of St Patrick. *See* St Patrick, Order of
Order of St Stephen. *See* St Stephen, Order of
Order of the Bath. *See* Bath, Order of the
Order of the Elephant. *See* Elephant, Order of
  the
Order of the Garter. *See* Garter, Order of the
Order of the Thistle. *See* Thistle, Order of the
Ordinary of Newgate's Account, The. See under
  Moore, Joseph
Ordine di Cristo, in Portugal:
  Acciaioli, knight of, **17**. 444n
Ordnance:
  Amherst succeeds Conway in, **36**. 83n
  Argyll restored to post in, **17**. 345
  Conway content with salary in, **22**. 560
  —— may be deprived of post in, by George
    III, **39**. 160n
  —— ponders over salary as master-general of,
    39. 123-4
  —— resigns from, **39**. 164
  ——'s post in, incompatible with one in Ex-
    chequer, **39**. 93-4
  —— succeeds George Townshend in, **22**. 549
  —— succeeds Granby in, without accepting
    salary, **23**. 179
  —— to be lt-gen. of, **39**. 83-4
  —— to resign from, **39**. 163
  debt from, **33**. 433n
  Frederick's post in, fits him to put on fire-
    works, **37**. 297
  Gashry treasurer and paymaster of, **18**. 81n
  Granby gets post in, **21**. 328n, **35**. 295
  —— resigns as master of, **22**. 170, 175, **39**. 122
  Marlborough, D. of, becomes master of, **20**.
    517
  Montagu, D. of, master-general of, **25**. 264n
  O'Brien's post in, **39**. 138
  Pelham procures, for D. of Cumberland, **20**.
    120
  Richmond, D. of, becomes master-general of,
    25. 262, 264n
  —— resigns from, **25**. 392
  ——'s willingness to retain trifling post of,
    shows his disinterestedness, **25**. 296
  Townshend, George, may become head of,
    39. 160, 163, 164n
  —— obtains mastership of, **25**. 53
  vacated by D. of Montagu's death, **20**. 120n
  Vilett seeks post in, **36**. 79-80
Ordre de St-Louis. *See* St-Louis, Ordre de
Odre du St-Esprit. *See* St-Esprit, Ordre du
Odre du Saint-Esprit, l'. See Poullain de St-Foix,
  Germain-François: *Histoire de l'ordre du
  Saint-Esprit*
Ore; ores:
  in Ds of Portland's collection, **36**. 237
  Kennon, Mrs, had, **37**. 439n
O'Reilly, Alexander (1725-94), Conde de
  O'Reilly; Spanish army officer:
  honour lost by, in previous attack on Algiers,
    25. 416

Spanish expedition led by, against Algiers,
  24. 111n, 119n, *121-2*
Spanish expedition to be led by, against Al-
  giers, **25**. 416
O'Reilly, Robert Bray, proprietor of the King's
  Theatre, Haymarket:
  manager of opera house, **11**. 191n
  Salisbury issues license to, for operas at Pan-
    theon, **11**. 95
  ——'s agreement with, about free opera tick-
    ets, **11**. 227-8
Oreste. See under Voltaire
Orestes:
  HW and Mann compared to Pylades and, **22**.
    274, **23**. 309, **24**. 283, **25**. 5, 9, 312, 615
  HW refers to Wilkes as, **38**. 234
  Vicomte du Barry called, **33**. 72
Orfeo ed Euridice. See under Gluck, Christoph
  Willibald
Orford, Cts of. *See* Cavendish, Lady Rachel
  (1727-1805); Rolle, Margaret (1709-81)
Orford, E. of. *See* Russell, Edward (1653-1727);
  Walpole, George (1730-91); Walpole, Horatio
  [HW] (1717-97); Walpole, Horatio (1723-
  1809); Walpole, Horatio (1752-1822); Wal-
  pole, Horatio (1783-1858); Walpole, Sir
  Robert (1676-1745); Walpole, Robert (1701-
  51)
Orford, Suffolk:
  Clarck's connection with, **37**. 402-3
  Conway, M.P., for, **12**. 40n
  Hertford lives in retirement at, **39**. 401
  Hertford, Richards, and Hon. Henry Sey-
    mour-Conway choose Joseph Probart as
    mayor of, **39**. 265
  Hertford's interest in borough of, **37**. 402n
Orford, English ship:
  Fitzroy, Lord Augustus, capt. of, **17**. 116n
Orford, earldom of:
  creation of, **17**. 318, **43**. 170
  HW's reflections on accession to, **34**. 133-7,
    145
  Sandys enraged at Sir Robert Walpole for
    taking, **17**. 333
'Orford, House of':
  Chute attached to, **35**. 26
Orford Castle, Suffolk:
  HW visits, **35**. 247
Orford estate:
  entail of, **9**. 186-7, **23**. 367, **36**. 24-32, 163-
    5, 295-304
  See also Houghton
Orford House. *See under* Chelsea
Organ; organs:
  apothecary makes, of glyster pipes, **36**. 8
  at Magdalen House chapel, **9**. 273
  at York Minster: Charles I removes, **16**. 47;
    Finch replaces, **16**. 48
  Beckford's, at Fonthill, **35**. 211n
  Bute invents, **23**. 96n
  French ladies hear Lord Fitzwilliam's, **11**.
    285

[Organ; organs, *continued*]
imitation of, at Mass, **4**. 211
Young buys, **20**. 331
See also Hand-organ
Organist; organists:
at Aschaffenburg, **18**. 342
bellows-blower and, **35**. 565
Schauensee, at St Leodegar, **19**. 354n
Oribasius (A.D. ca 325–ca 403), physician:
Cocchi publishes Greek and Latin versions of, from collection of Nicetas, **20**. 34n
Oriel College, Oxford:
Hodges the provost of, **15**. 304
Orient, the:
'cradle of science,' **34**. 132
Ginori's felucca brings materials from, **18**. 184n
See also East, the
Oriental gardening. *See under* Chambers, Sir William
Oriental tales. *See* Literature, eastern; *see also* *Arabian Nights*; Arabian tales; Persian tales; Pétis de la Croix, François: *Mille et un jours*
Oriflamme, French ship:
runs aground, **21**. 188n
Oriflamme:
États' discussion of, ridiculed by HW, **11**. 100
Origany:
used in tincture for the eyes, **18**. 365n
Original and Growth of Printing, The. See under Atkyns, Richard
Originality:
perseverance nearer allied to madness than to, **33**. 490
Original Letters of the Late King James. See under Fuller, William
Original Letters to an Honest Sailor:
letters to Vernon, published by him, **19**. 459n
Original Letters, Written during the Reigns of Henry VI, Edward IV, and Richard III, ed. Sir John Fenn:
HW praises, **33**. 558–9
publication date of, corrected, **43**. 358
Original Papers, Containing the Secret History of Great Britain. See under Macpherson, James
Original Speech of Sir W——m St——pe, The, by HW:
makes 'great noise,' **13**. 21
Origine des mœurs. See Toussaint, François-Vincent: *Mœurs, Les*
Origin of nations:
HW's reflections on lack of interest in, **16**. 282
Orignal (moose):
Orford's, sought by Dr Hunter, **41**. 264
Orinoco River:
current of, might be mistaken for circulation of the blood, **33**. 366
England's empire from Japan to, **33**. 208
Mason's lines will be repeated on banks of, **28**. 406

Ralegh's voyage to, **14**. 107n
Oriuna:
uncertainty about, **7**. 358
Orkney, Cts of. *See* Villiers, Elizabeth
Orkney Islands:
Christian I pledges, **37**. 298n
HW jokes about Bute being sent to, **10**. 39
highlanders from, as gardeners in England, **32**. 359
Sheerness captures American ship in Jacobite service near, **37**. 237
ships near Deer Sound in, **37**. 246
used as symbol for distance, **28**. 260, **32**. 250
Orlandi, Casimirro, Florentine postmaster:
(?) Vorontsov consorts with, **21**. 249
Orlandi, Pellegrino Antonio (1660–1727):
Abcedario pittorico by: Dobson article in, amuses HW, **18**. 312; English version of, **42**. 69; quotation from, **16**. 96n; Sassoferrato not included in, **18**. 93–4
Orlandini, Mme, —— (? *née* Butler):
Albany, Cts of, breakfasts with, **25**. 101
Orlandini, Ipolito Gaspero del Beccuto (ca 1696–1771), Austrian Maj.-Gen.:
(?) widow of, **25**. 101n
Orlandini, Mme Teresa:
Mann's legacy to, **25**. 667n
Orlandini del Beccuto, Giulio Ranieri (1699–1782), Priore:
ball to be given by, for Tempi's wedding, **18**. 435, 438
'Orlando Furioso':
Stair compared with, **18**. 48
Orlando Furioso. See under Ariosto, Lodovico
Orlaw. *See* Orlov
Orléans, Bp of. *See* Gérente de la Bruyère, Louis-Sextius (d. 1788)
Orléans, Duc d'. *See* Bourbon, Louis de (1703–52); Bourbon, Louis-Philippe de (1725–85); Bourbon, Louis-Philippe-Joseph de (1747–93); Bourbon, Philippe de (1640–1701); Bourbon, Philippe de (1674–1723); Gaston-Jean-Baptiste (1608–60); Louis-Philippe (1773–1850); Orléans, Charles d' (1391–1465); Orléans, Charles d' (d. 1545)
Orléans, Duchesse de. *See* Bourbon, Françoise-Marie de (1677–1749); Bourbon, Louise-Marie-Adélaïde de (1753–1821); Bourbon-Conti, Louise de (1726–59); Élisabeth-Charlotte (1652–1722); Henrietta Anne (1644–70), of England; Isabella (1387–1410) of Valois
Orléans, Mlle d'. *See* Bourbon d'Orléans, —— de (1777–82)
Orléans, Mayor of:
HW cites, **36**. 208
Orléans, Princesses de. *See* Bourbon d'Orléans, —— de (1777–82); Bourbon d'Orléans, Louise-Marie-Adélaïde-Eugénie de (1777–1848)
Orléans, Régent d'. *See* Bourbon, Philippe de (1674–1723)
Orléans, —— de (d. 1688), Chevalier de Longueville:

legitimated, **7.** 276
Orléans, Charles (1391–1465), Duc d':
English verses by, **31.** 270–1, 273, **34.** 6–7
HW's account of, **31.** 270–1, 273
Margaret of Anjou's proxy wedding attended by, **14.** 71–2
Orléans, Charles (d. 1545), Duc d':
Raynal describes inflammatory genius of, **34.** 65
Orléans, Charles-Paris d' (1640–72), Duc de Longueville:
La Ferté, Duchesse de, mistress of, **7.** 276
Orléans (France):
Barthélemy praises bridge at, **8.** 201
Choiseul imprisoned at, **11.** 301n
Choiseuls spend night at, **41.** 197
cotignac from, **3.** 361
crammed with state prisoners, **34.** 144
HW visits, **13.** 11
Joseph II not to visit, **8.** 202
municipal officers ordered to, for trials, **11.** 233n
prisoners dragged to Paris from, **12.** 28n, **15.** 237, **35.** 446
suggested as place of exile for Mrs O'Brien, **20.** 28
turned into a jail, **34.** 152, 158
visitors to: Arras, Bp of, **5.** 239–40; Du Châtelet, Comtesse, **5.** 239; Du Deffand, Mme, **5.** 239–40, 251; Gramont, Duchesse de, **5.** 239–41; Ligne, Princesse de, **5.** 239–40
Orléans, Hôtel de, at Paris:
Cole lodges at, **1.** 99
Craufurd, James, lodges at, **4.** 283
Orléans, Siège d'. See *Siège d'Orléans*
Orléans chapel:
at Célestins' church, **7.** 308
Orléans de Longueville, Marie d' (1625–1707), m. (1657) Henri de Savoie, Duc de Nemours:
Mémoires of, owned by Mme du Deffand, **8.** 34
Orléans family:
Barbantane, Mme de, dismissed by, **23.** 480
Orleans House, Twickenham:
Pitt, Mrs, lives in, **9.** 263n
Orley, Bernart van (ca 1492–1542):
tapestries designed by, attributed to Raphael, **16.** 157
Orlingbury, Northants:
Whitehouse rector of, **12.** 11n
Orlov ('Orloff'; 'Orlow'), Alexeï Grigor'evich (1737–1808), Gen.:
agent in St Petersburg revolution, **23.** 185
Catherine II's accomplice in murder, **23.** 207
——'s favourite, **23.** 149
—— warned by, **22.** 64
Constantinople's capture by, would be known in Paris before Florence, **23.** 311
courier brings peace treaty to, at Florence, **24.** 40
courier from Venice tells, that Russian fleet reaches coast of Morea, **23.** 204
determined to sail, **23.** 309

Dick receives black boy from, **23.** 228
—— receives letters from, about Russo-Turkish battle, **23.** 232
—— receives Order of St Anne from, **24.** 84, 96
Dick, Lady, receives Turkish girls from, **23.** 228
disgrace of, **32.** 174
Dolgorukov accompanied by, to Florence, **23.** 191
English intervention against France must please, in Greek islands, **23.** 478
English visit of, thought by French to be intrigue, **25.** 61
Eubœa bombarded by, **23.** 331n
fleet of, repaired at Leghorn, goes to Ægean Sea, **23.** 307
Florence visited by, **23.** 149, 185, 191, **24.** 113
HW does not believe denial by, of Peter III's murder, **23.** 195, 207
Leopold receives Egyptian horse from, **23.** 228
Mann often sees, in Florence but cannot easily talk with him, **23.** 185
—— receives black boy from, **23.** 228
—— repulses hints by, of giving him Russian honours, **24.** 84
—— rides with, in coach, **24.** 84
Maria Louisa receives Turkish girls from, **23.** 228
messenger from St Petersburg tells, of Russian victories, **23.** 160
name of, corrected, **43.** 278
officers of guards regiment of, sail from Cronstadt, **23.** 222
officers promoted by, **24.** 84
peace terms unknown to, **24.** 33
returns to St Petersburg after closing accounts with Dick and Rutherfurd, **24.** 114
Rumiantsev's operations reported to, at Florence, **24.** 29
Russia consults, about Ægean campaign, **23.** 146n
Russian fleet commanded by, as Lord Admiral, **23.** 234
Russian fleet found by, in gulf of Napoli di Romania, **23.** 226
Russian officer and courier sent by, from Leghorn with dispatches for Russian Court, **23.** 235
Russian officer carries dispatches to, through Florence to Greek Islands, **23.** 444
Russian ships at Leghorn to fetch, **23.** 191
Russians not permitted by, to land on Chios, **23.** 233
Rutherfurd made agent for Russian fleet by, **23.** 161, **24.** 114
St Petersburg courier awaited by, at Florence, **24.** 33
scourge of the Turks at sea, **24.** 114
Spiridov's fleet to be joined by, from Paros, **23.** 326n
Orlov, Count Fedor Grigor'evich (1741–96):

[Orlov, Count Fedor, *continued*]
  Catherine II's favourite, **23**. 149
  disgrace of, **32**. 174
  escapes burning ship, **23**. 227, 233
  Florence visited by, **23**. 149
  Russia consults, about Ægean campaign, **23**. 146n
Orlov, Grigorii Grigor'evich (1734–83), Count;
  Catherine II's favourite:
  Catherine II may discard, as favourite, while he is at Congress of Fokshani, **23**. 441
  —— put on her throne by, **24**. 114
  ——'s favourite lover, **23**. 75n, **24**. 143n
  dances and loves of, gigantic, **24**. 143
  diamonds carried by, **24**. 114, 143
  disgrace of, **32**. 174
  displaced as favourite but not as courtier, **23**. 444
  enemies of, foment Moscow riots, **22**. 205n
  England visited by, **24**. 113, 143
  English itinerary of, **24**. 143n
  Florence visited by, **24**. 95, 113
  Fokshani congress's breakdown blamed on, **23**. 438n
  Joseph II does not see, **24**. 113n
  nonsense talked by, **24**. 144
  Samoyed's reply to, **28**. 477
  Spa to be visited by, for health, **24**. 113
  two men to fill place of, with Catherine II, **24**. 143
  youthful prowess of, proved by loads of diamonds, **24**. 114
Orme, Capt. Robert (d. 1790), Braddock's aide-de-camp:
  reward offered by, for Braddock's rescue, **20**. 495
  Townshend family do not consent to marriage of, to Lady Audrey Townshend, **20**. 495n
  wife of, **9**. 188n
Orme, Hon. Mrs Robert. *See* Townshend, Hon. Audrey
Ormea, Marchese d'. *See* Ferrero di Roasio, Carlo Vincenzo (1680–1745)
Ormer shells:
  Bentley sends, to HW who may give them to Bns Lyttelton's grotto, **35**. 175
  HW offers, to Lyttelton for Hagley grotto, **40**. 81
  HW thanks Bentley for, **35**. 258
Ormesson, Marquis d'. *See* Le Fèvre, Marie-François de Paule
Ormesson. *See also* Le Fèvre d'Ormesson
Ormolu:
  armoires decorated with, **31**. 80
  commodes decorated with, **31**. 98
  funnel adorned with, **39**. 15
  HW thinks, contraband in England, **31**. 98
  in Colebrooke's sale, **23**. 569n
  inventor of, *see* Boulton, Matthew
  not contraband in England, **31**. 110
  popularity of, in England, **23**. 211–12
  sconces of, **32**. 261
  teakettle of, sold at auction, **23**. 212

Ormond, D. of:
  patient in madhouse fancies himself to be, **24**. 187; *see also* Butler, Charles (1671–1758); Butler, James (1610–88); Butler, James (1665–1745)
Ormond, E. of. *See* Butler, Sir James (1420–61); Butler, Thomas (ca 1424–1515)
Ormond, M. of:
  Irishman and, **30**. 247
Ormond, earldom of:
  Calcraft aspires to, **32**. 38
Ormond, house of:
  'heiress of ninety-nine' the sole survivor of, **21**. 261
Ormond Mews, back of St James's Sq., London:
  Pitt's horses to be sold at, **38**. 136n
Ormoulu. *See* Ormolu
Ormus. *See* Ormuz
Ormuz (Iran):
  wealth of, **13**. 138
Ormuzd:
  Ahriman gets the better of, by turns, **23**. 192
Ornament; ornaments:
  French, excel English, **25**. 635
Ornaments of Churches Considered. See under Hole, Rev. William H.
Ornano, Bianca Colonna. *See* Colonna, Bianca
Orne (France):
  Priestly elected member for, in National Convention, **15**. 236n
Orny, —— d':
  Young Pretender's project known to, **18**. 379n
'Orondates,' character in La Calprenède's *Cassandre*:
  Conway has person and courage of, **37**. 195
  HW's name for George II, **20**. 213, 218
  suffering of, compared to HW's, **11**. 312
  See also under Costes de la Calprenède, Gautier: *Cassandre*
Oronooko; Oronooque; Oroonoko. *See* Orinoco
'Oronooko.' *See* Chetwynd, William Richard
'Oroondates.' *See* 'Orondates'
Oroonoko. See under Amis, Aphra, Mrs Behn; Southerne, Thomas
'Orosmades' ('Orozmades'). *See* Gray, Thomas
Orozmades. *See* Ormuzd
Orphan, The. See under Otway, Thomas
Orphée, French ship:
  capture of, **21**. 188n
Orphée et Eurydice. See under Gluck, Christoph Willibald
Orpheline angloise, L'. See under Fielding, Sarah; La Place, Pierre-Antoine de
Orpheline léguée, L'. See under Saurin, Bernard-Joseph
Orpheus:
  bear would be tolerated by, if it danced to his music, **20**. 427
  Boufflers, Comtesse Amélie de, compared with, **11**. 148
  HW not to be, **37**. 93
  letters of, miscarry, **10**. 282
  Lincoln compared with, **30**. 296
  lost art of, **35**. 336

Orpheus and Eurydice:
pun on, in London theatre, 17. 172
serpent in, made by watchmaker, 11. 214–15
See also under Rich, John; Theobald, Lewis
Orpheus Caledonicus:
ballad printed in, 12. 147n
Orrery, Cts of. *See* Hamilton, Margaret (1710–58)
Orrery, E. of. *See* Boyle, Charles (1674–1731); Boyle, Hon. Hamilton (1730–64); Boyle, John (1707–62); Boyle, Roger (1621–79)
'Orrery, Lord':
print of, 40. 236
Orrery; orreries:
Lady Anne Fitzpatrick's, 33. 477
Orris root; orris roots:
delayed at customs, 5. 160–1
Du Deffand, Mme, receives, 5. 182
Orsan, Marquis d'. *See* Cambis, Henri-Marc-Amable de
Orsan, Marquise d'. *See* Grave, Augustine de
Orsi, Donato, Florentine banker:
(?) Cholmondeley's credit with, 25. 314
(?) Cowper notifies, of consignment of plate, 25. 661
Mann's legacy to, 25. 667n
Orford, Cts of, shows account to, 25. 113
Orsi, Giusto, Florentine banker:
(?) Cholmondeley's credit with, 25. 314
(?) Cowper notifies, of consignment of plate, 25. 661
Mann leaves legacy and ring to, as executor, 25. 667n
——'s executor, 25. 669n
——'s funeral monument to be planned by, 25. 665n
Orsi, Messrs, Florentine bankers:
bills on Sneyd drawn in favour of, 25. 303n
Orsi (pro-Spanish Florentine faction):
Ascanio's death depresses, 17. 87
Austrian defeat encourages, 17. 433
Cartagena victory confuses, 17. 68
Castellar talks with member of, about Spanish plans, 17. 349
English-Spanish peace wished by, 17. 263
Francis I disliked by, 18. 2
——'s retreat from Prague proclaimed by, 17. 488–9
Galli a member of, 18. 46
Mann asked by, about fleets, 17. 39
——'s reports not believed by, 19. 198
Modena's resistance predicted by, 17. 443
Montemar's conquest of Lombardy hoped by, 17. 481
Philip, Don, wanted by, as Grand Duke of Tuscany, 17. 68n
report circulated by, that Maria Theresa's allies may make her conclude peace, 18. 241
Spanish and Neapolitan defeat expected by, 17. 427
Te Deum avoided by, 18. 241
Tencin's supplanting of Fleury wished by, 17. 481

Volterra exile predicted for, because of their indiscreet talk, 18. 46
Orsini, Domenico Amadeo (1719–89), cardinal, 1743; Neapolitan minister at Rome:
announcement by, at Conclave door, 23. 90
audience with Clement XIII demanded by, to protest against treatment of Parma, 23. 15–16
Benedict XIV makes, cardinal, 18. 302n
Clement XIII sought by, 23. 10
—— told by, to discard Torreggiani, 23. 35
confers with French and Spanish ministers, 23. 10
Cumberland, D. of, entertained by, 23. 566n
Ferdinand of Naples orders, to rebuke Neapolitan cardinals, 23. 26
Jesuits' suppression again demanded by, 23. 214
Neapolitan Court disavows homage of, to Young Pretender, 22. 399
Young Pretender given royal honours by, 22. 392
Orsini, Eleonora (d. 1634), m. (1592) Alessandro Attendolo Sforza, Duca di Segni:
letters of, about Francavilla statues, sent by Mann to HW, 21. 480, 497, 22. 583, 587, 25. 657
Orsolene, convent of, at Rome:
Albany, Cts of, retires to, 25. 106
Sobieski, Ps, fled to, from husband's tyranny, 25. 106
Orthodoxy:
HW on, 2. 283
Orto, Via dell', parish of San Frediano, Florence:
Orford, Cts of, in, in 1773, 43. 284
Ortolan; ortolans:
HW's letter as fat as, 35. 27
Ortolani, Dominico, of Montereggi:
Lady Orford's Declaration signed by, 43. 288
Orton, Westmorland:
Burn, vicar of, 29. 115n
Orton Longueville, Hunts:
Cope of, 9. 146n
Orvilliers, Comte d'. *See* Guillouet, Louis
Orwell, Bn and Vct. *See* Vernon, Francis
Osbaldeston, Mrs George. *See* Head, Jane
Osbaldeston, Richard (1690–1764), Bp of Carlisle, 1747, of London, 1762:
appoints chaplain, 14. 131n
George IV said to be baptized by, 38. 174, 180–1
Osbern de Crepon (d. ca 1040), seneschal:
family of, 1. 387
Osbern. *See also* FitzOsbern; Osborn; Osborne
Osborn, Lady. *See* Finch, Lady Heneage
Osborn, ——, bookseller:
HW buys volume of pamphlets at shop of, 35. 163n
Osborn, Sir Danvers (1715–53), 3d Bt; M.P.:
Bentley seeks employment from, through Montagu, 9. 149
genealogy of, 10. 352

[Osborn, Sir Danvers, *continued*]
governor of New York, 9. *149*
inscription by, on columbarium at Chicksands, 10. 170
inscription to, by tutor, 10. 170
son of, 9. 248n
Osborn, George, Jacobite:
(?) author of pamphlet attacking HW, 13. 31-2, 14. 258-9
Mitre and Crown by, Manby sends, to Middleton, 43. 190
Osborn, Sir George (1742-1818), 4th Bt, 1753; M.P.; Muster-Master-Gen.:
avenue and columbarium of, 10. 170
Bedford, D. of, politically attacked by, 10. 235
claret drunk by, at Adderbury, 10. 297
cricket played by, 10. 235
gambles at Adderbury, 10. 297
genealogy of, 10. 352
Guilford told by, of Montagu's appointment, 9. 352
HW regrets reading by, of *Mysterious Mother*, 10. 298
HW to frank letter for, 10. 86, 97
Halifax gracious to, at Northampton races, 10. 179
Hessian troops on rolls of, 24. 285n
Hinchingbrooke visits, 10. 235
Horton visited by, 9. 248
joke by, about Lord North, 10. 234
major of Bedford militia, 9. 248
Montagu considers, too young, 10. 85
—— may be visited by, at Greatworth, 10. 225
—— not to visit, 10. 85
——'s youth restored by, 10. 296-7
—— visited by, at Adderbury, 10. 288, 295-6
—— visited by, at Greatworth, 9. 248, 10. 225, 234
—— visits, at Chicksands, 10. 169, 263
Montagu, Hon. William Augustus, visits, 10. 235
Mysterious Mother acted by, at Adderbury, 10. 297, 300
Northampton election benefits, 10. 288
Northampton races attended by, 10. 179
quinze played by, at Adderbury, 10. 297
Sandwich visits, 10. 235
SH visited by, 12. 243
(?) Talbot, William, lives on farm of, during vacation, 10. 170
Trinity College attended by, 9. 248
Osborn, John (1743-1814), minister to Saxony 1771-5:
drinks claret and gambles at quinze at Adderbury, 10. 297
genealogy of, 10. 352
HW regrets reading by, of *Mysterious Mother*, 10. 298
Montagu's youth restored by, 10. 296-7
—— visited by, at Adderbury, 10. *288*, 295-6
Mysterious Mother acted by, at Adderbury, 10. 297, 300
Osborn, Mrs John. *See* Byng, Hon. Sarah

Osborn, Lady Mary. *See* Montagu, Lady Mary
Osborn, Peter (d. 1754), naval Capt.:
Ambrose succeeds, 19. 12n
Craon comments on, 18. 477
entertained at Florence, 18. 98, 99
Goldsworthy's correspondence with, 18. 28
HW's cases said to have been conveyed by, 18. 477, 514
Leghorn to be defended by, with four ships, 18. 38n
Lestock conveyed by, to England, 18. 477, 514
Mann may be visited by, 18. 67
Marciana and Porto Longone devastated by, 18. *28*, 59
Osborn. *See also* Osbern; Osborne
Osborne, Lord:
print of, with sisters, 40. 236
Osborne, Lady Anne (d. 1722), m. 1 Robert Coke; m. 2 Col. Horace Walpole:
grandson of, 34. 38n
Leneve, Isabella, and Dorothy Walpole brought up by, 21. 353n
Osborne, Lady Bridget:
Pomfrets entertain, 17. 169n
'Osborne, Francis.' *See* Pitt, James
Osborne, Francis (1593-1659), writer:
Advice to a Son by, quoted, 1. 154
Works of, 43. 53
Osborne, Francis Godolphin (1751-99), styled M. of Carmarthen 1761-89; 5th D. of Leeds, 1789; foreign secretary of state 1783-91:
ancestry of, 2. 26
ball given by, at Beverley, 28. 471
Batheaston's verse contributions from, 32. 225n
Buckingham's writings criticized by, 42. 368n
Coke, Lady Mary, angry at engagement of, to Catherine Anguish, 31. 288
Cosway, Mrs, entertains, 33. 511
Cowper notified by, of George III's permission to accept Order of St Hubert, 25. 470
death of, 11. 161n
dinner of, attended by C. J. Fox, Conway, E. of Buckinghamshire, Macartney, M. of Buckingham, 33. 554
disbelieves in Ireland's MSS, 15. 321
dispatches received by, 11. 130n
Dorset's letter to, 11. 40n
engagement of, rumoured, 7. 128
estate of, settled on children by first wife, 25. 75n
foreigners talk of ignorance of, 25. 486
Fortescue's social relations with, in Paris, 7. 326
Germain attacked by, in House of Lords, 29. 184, 33. 326n
Glover's youngest son the friend of, 28. 288
Godolphin's bequest to, 25. 583
Grenville succeeds, as foreign secretary, 34. 109n
HW accompanies, to theatre, 7. 331
HW detains, with old stories, 33. 584-5
HW to inquire about packets of, 11. 157

health of, bad, 11. 256

Holdernesse, Cts of, has law suit with, 29. 303, 305

Holdernesses accompanied by wife and, 28. 321

—' daughter to marry, 28. 112, 117

K.G., 11. 161, 163

Mann, Horace II, asked by, to be chargé d'affaires after uncle's death, 25. 666–7

— rejects salary offer from, 25. 672–3

— told by, of successor's appointment, 25. 675–6

manor of Aston passes to, 28. 43n

marriage of, 28. 91n, 32. 166, 35. 467

mother-in-law stinted by, 25. 486n

Newcastle, Ds of, makes, her chief heir, 32. 308n

office of: 11. 134n, 166, 167; Baisly sent from, for copies of stolen dispatches, 25. 619n

Paris post assigned to, 25. 363

protests against Germain's elevation, 29. 178n

resignation of: as chamberlain to Q. Charlotte, 33. 162; as foreign secretary of state, 11. 251, 256, 257, 25. 583, 34. 108

Rockingham's house guarded by, 33. 187n

secretary of state (foreign), 25. 460n, 583

unable to dine at Ps Amelia's, 32. 308

verses by, 39. 241

Waldegrave, Lady Elizabeth Laura, fails to marry, 25. 75

Wales, Caroline, Ps of, advised by, at the opera, 12. 185–6

wife writes to, acknowledging adultery, 31. 194

Osborne, Lord Francis Godolphin (1777–1850), cr. (1832) Bn Godolphin:

Godolphin's bequest to, 25. 583

Osborne, Henry (ca 1698–1771), naval Capt., Adm., 1757:

brother of, married to Byng's sister, 21. 191n

Byng's friend, 21. 191

courier of, does not feel earthquake, 21. 133

Dick visited by, at Leghorn, 21. 123

Du Quesne fights, off Cartagena, 21. 187n

fleet of: French fleet fights with, 21. 188, 191; harasses French Mediterranean coast, 21. 135; Mann obtains provisions for, at Leghorn, 21. 114

health of: apoplexy, 21. 197; eye lost, 21. 197

Hervey advises, not to return to Gibraltar, 21. 135n

— with, at Gibraltar, 21. 197

Leghorn saluted by, 21. 122n

Mann induces, to send courier to England, 21. 122

—'s correspondence with, 21. 197

Saunders sails to Gibraltar with, 21. 97n

squadron of, cruises off Malta and Sardinia, 21. 135n

Vado visited by, on the Essex, 19. 10n

Osborne, J., publisher:

Frederick II's address to English people published by, 30. 68n

—'s Rescrit published by, 18. 500n

Osborne, John:

Byng's sister married, 21. 191n

Osborne, John, Vcts Townshend's coachman:

testifies on mistress's arrest, 38. 502n

Osborne, Peregrine (1659–1729), 2d D. of Leeds:

Gates's mother housekeeper to, 10. 22n, 25. 92n

HW's anecdotes about, to great-grandson, 33. 585

Osborne, Peter. See Osborn, Peter

Osborne, Sophia (d. 1746), m. 1 Donough O'Brien, styled Lord O'Brien; m. 2 William Fermor, cr. (1692) Bn Leominster:

Pomfrets entertain, 17. 169n

Osborne, Sir Thomas (1632–1712), 1st E. of Danby; cr. (1694) D. of Leeds; lord high treasurer:

Burnet's treatment of, 16. 20–1

descendants of, 2. 26

Osborne, Thomas (1713–89), 4th D. of Leeds:

ancestry of, 2. 26

Aston not redeemed by, 28. 172

becomes Cabinet councillor, 21. 489

cofferer of the Household, 9. 181, 35. 263

Court attended by, 9. 89

George II makes, K.G., 9. 89, 10. 29, 20. 71, 72

Grenville succeeds, as Cofferer, 9. 341, 343, 21. 489

Halifax's former salary turned over to 21. 489

Holdernesse lends money to, 33. 13n

Kiveton a seat of, 28. 471n, 35. 270

Knight of the Garter, 9. 89, 10. 29

Lyttelton succeeded by, as Cofferer, 20. 517

mastership of the Horse may go to, 20. 182–3

may become George III's governor, 20. 345

may become Groom of the Stole, 30. 163n

Newcastle, D. of, considers, for Cofferer, 20. 518n

offices exchanged by, 30. 162

resignation of, expected, 21. 98

Sandys succeeded by, as chief justice in eyre, 21. 489

— succeeds, as chief justice in eyre, 20. 518

son of, 7. 128n, 25. 75n, 363n, 486n, 583n

to return as chief justice in eyre, 9. 341

wife of, 16. 157n

Osborne, Thomas (d. 1767), bookseller in Gray's Inn:

Cornwallis's Essayes sold by, 14. 176

death of, 7. 397

HW asked by, for publication material, 9. 86

HW presented by, with print, 9. 86

print of Bns Cutts sought by, 9. 187

Osborne. See also Osbern; Osborn

Oslenghi, ——, Roman courier:

Young Pretender to be notified by, of father's death, 22. 383

Osman III (1696–1757), Sultan of Turkey:

Cumberland, D. of, compared with, 35. 206

Osman, Lettres d'. See under St-Foix, Philippe-Auguste de

Osman Effendi:
Crimean independence denied by, at Fokshani congress, **23.** 438n

Osmaston, Derbyshire:
Montagu of, **10.** 158n

Osmond, René-Eustache (1751–1838), Marquis d':
(?) social relations of, with Mme de Luxembourg, **7.** 352

Osmond. *See also* Médaby d'Osmond

Osnabrück ('Osnaburg'), Bp of. *See* Frederick (1763–1827); Klemens August (1700–61)

Osnabrück (Germany):
Conway, wife, and daughter in winter quarters at, **21.** 554, **38.** 155n
French find bad hay only, in allied stores at, **21.** 545n
Legge takes negotiations over bishopric of, out of hands of George II's agent in Berlin, **20.** 39n
nearer to Vienna than Brabant, **34.** 90
Paganzikar, Mme, of, **38.** 156

Osnabrug, Osnaburgh. *See* Osnabrück

Osney Abbey:
Huddesford's account of, (?) given to HW, **41.** 202

Osorio-Alarcon, Cavaliere Giuseppe (ca 1697–1763), Sardinian ambassador to England 1730–43:
Charles Emmanuel III's communications to, **19.** 306n, 431n
—— shocked by news from, **19.** 258
—— to tell, to write to George II or D. of Newcastle about disloyal English officer, **19.** 147, 150
fashionable in England, **17.** 186
first minister of Sardinia after being minister to England, **18.** 342n
Gorsegno's correspondence with, **19.** 87, 95, 150
HW discusses Hanoverians with, **18.** 342–3
HW knows, **17.** 186
Macartney, (?) Alice *or* Frances, pursued by, **17.** *186*, **30.** 45
Mann told by, of D. of Newcastle's appointment, **20.** 421–2
name of, corrected, **43.** 251, 252
Worms treaty attended by, **18.** 311n

Ossa:
parliament of Paris relieved of, **24.** 265

Ossegovich, Basile *or* Basilio (d. 1784), Slavonian sailor:
Great Duchess of Tuscany seized by, **25.** 479–81

Osservazioni letterarie. See under Maffei, Marchese Scipione

Osservazioni per ben regolare il coro. See under Adami, Andrea

'Ossian':
controversy over, **42.** 14
favourable reception of, **16.** 379
HW compares, to 'Rowley,' **16.** 124, 350

Holbach and guests dispute about, **7.** 267

Ossianic poems. *See under* Macpherson, James

Ossorio. *See* Osorio-Alarcon

Ossory, Bp of. *See* Newcome, William (1729–1800); Pococke, Richard (1704–65)

Ossory, Bn of Upper. *See* Fitzpatrick, Sir Barnaby (? 1535–81)

Ossory, Cts of Upper. *See* Liddell, Hon. Anne (ca 1738–1804); Leveson Gower, Hon. Evelyn (1725–63)

Ossory, E. of Upper. *See* Fitzpatrick, John (1745–1818)

Ossuarium; ossuaria:
HW buys, at Mead's sale, **20.** 470n
HW jokes about preparing, for cat, **10.** 155

Ossulston, Vct. *See* Bennet, Charles

Ossun, Mme d':
acts at Chanteloup, **5.** 382n

Ossun, Pierre-Paul (1713–88), Marquis d'; French ambassador to Naples and Spain:
Chanteloup visited by, **8.** 202
Charles III reassured by, **21.** 275
Grimaldi's instructions to, **23.** 306n
may get French cabinet post, **23.** 264
Potter gets passport from, **21.** 557n
social relations of, with Duc and Duchesse de Fitzjames, **7.** 300
talk of recall of, **4.** 380
Voltaire's verses to Aranda sent to, **41.** 203–4

Ostade, Adrien (1610–85), *or* Isaac (1621–57), painters:
Praslin has paintings by, **7.** 353

Ostein, Johann Friedrich Karl von (d. 1763), Abp and Elector of Mainz 1743–63:
Frankfurt fine to be levied by, **21.** 28–9
subsidies for, **19.** 229

Osten, Greve Adolph Siegfried von der (1726–97), Danish ambassador to Naples 1768–70:
Danish revolution involves, **23.** 380
Ogiński supported by, **33.** 511n

Ostend, governor of. *See* Chanclos de Rets Brisuila, Charles-Urbain, Comte de

Ostend:
Anson receives letter from, minimizing Prussian defeat at Kunersdorf, **30.** 156–7
boisterous weather at, may have detained Mann's courier, **25.** 334
Coke, Lady Mary, misses packet-boat at, **33.** 293
convenient for invasion of England, **19.** 88
East India Co. buys tea at, **25.** 577–8
Elliot embarks for, **12.** 19n
English embarkation lands at, **37.** 156
English sends troops to, **18.** 457, **19.** 78
fortifications of, weak, **19.** 69
France may offer, to Holland, **19.** 88
—— may use, as Dunkirk's substitute, **21.** 527
French besiege, **37.** 204
French embark Fitzjames's regiment at, **19.** 208
French progress in Flanders reported from, **19.** 67

French repulsed at, **12.** 49, 51, 53
French threaten, **18.** 456–7, **19.** 69, 92, 96
Gloucester, D. and Ds of, embark at Margate for, **33.** 336n
ineffectual reinforcement of, when troops needed at home, **30.** 96
Joseph II should keep, open, so that Mann and HW can correspond, **25.** 105
letter addressed to Munich by way of, **36.** 227
letters pass through, **5.** 1n, **7.** 157, 159, 161–3, 165, 169, 170, 172, 227, 232, 422, 423, 426
letter to Paris by way of, **36.** 170, 176, 178, 181, 185, 188
Leyden gazetteer gets news from more accessible port than, **23.** 110
lieutenant de Roi at, *see* St-Aldegonde
Løvendal conducts siege of, **19.** 90n
Macbride sends account of Dumouriez from, **12.** 3
mails between Dover and, **12.** 3n
Mann hopes English will give, to the Dutch, **18.** 290
Mann, Horace II, rumoured lost on packet-boat from, **25.** 210
Maria Theresa gives, to the French, **21.** 117
messengers from, **12.** 76n
Morice sends valuables back to, on sighting a privateer, **25.** 89
Newport Gat near, **21.** 338n
passage to, from England, makes post to Italy irregular, **23.** 541, **24.** 141, **25.** 383
Piennes, Duc de, goes to, **11.** 256n
post by way of, **4.** 355n
Riccardi's jewels may be sent through, to Brussels, **19.** 94
Robinson, Mrs, sends cassolettes by way of, **8.** 204
Spencers embark at, **7.** 177n
Stair negotiates for English base at, **17.** 400n
Thurot said to have put in at, **21.** 349
Tylney driven ashore at, **37.** 325
visitors to: Conway, **21.** 261n, **37.** 151, 152, **38.** 3; Dieskau, **38.** 4, 43. 374; Mann, Horace II, **24.** 517; Mount Stuart, **33.** 134n
Wade demands artillery for, **19.** 69
Young Pretender said to have landed at, **19.** 311
'Ostensible'; 'ostensibly':
Bromfield's hints about, **40.** 316
Ostentation:
French love of, HW comments on meanness of, **7.** 357, **13.** 164
HW averse to, **22.** 480
Östergötland, D. of. *See* Fredrik Adolf (1750–1803)
Osterley Park, Heston, Middlesex, Child family's seat:
Child, Robert, of, **11.** 176n, **12.** 63n, **32.** 361
HW shocked by tragedy at, **10.** 104
HW visits and describes, **10.** 103, **28.** 413–14, **32.** 125–6, **33.** 26, **34.** 237–9

Houghton's towers inspired by, **32.** 128n
Montagu visits, **10.** 103
to be kept up as in Child's lifetime, **12.** 72
wedding preparations at, **10.** 103
See also Menagerie
Osterly. *See* Osterley
Ostermann, Heinrich Johann Friedrich (1679–1747), Graf von:
Catalogue of French Books, A, mentions, **18.** 53
Osterode Castle:
Belle-Isle and suite prisoners in, **18.** 563n
Ost Frize. *See* East Friesland
Ostia (Italy):
York, Cardinal, cardinal-archbishop of, **17.** 10n
Ostler; ostlers. *See under* Servant
Ostrich; ostriches:
Bentley designs plumes of, for Great North Bedchamber at SH, **20.** 375n
discretion compared with, **32.** 187
Ducarel described as, **36.** 39
feathers of, Howe and Mrs Fitzherbert should be 'nodding under,' **34.** 201
Ostrog, Disposition of the:
Williams, Sir C. H., quarrels with Brühl after espousing Poniatowski family's interest in, **30.** 322
Ostrogothia. *See* Östergötland
O'Sullivan, John William (b. ca 1700):
Young Pretender accompanied by, **37.** 251–2
Oswald, George (d. 1742), Sir Robert Walpole's steward:
HW's art shipments from Italy sent to, **17.** 68n, **26.** 6
HW's correspondence with, **17.** *6*
Mann's correspondence with, **17.** 108, 113
—— sends bill of lading for HW's cases to, **17.** 31
——'s parcels mistakenly addressed by, to Goldsworthy, **17.** 302
Mann, Galfridus, to be paid by, at Sir Robert Walpole's order, **17.** 228
—— to tell, of HW's illness, **17.** 51
melon seeds desired by, for Sir Robert Walpole, **17.** 34
Oswald, James (1715–69), M.P.; commissioner of Trade and Plantations; lord of the Treasury:
brother of, **10.** 9
Chatham said to have asked, to be chancellor of Exchequer, **22.** 494n
commissioner of Trade and Plantations, **17.** 299n
Irish vice-treasurership to be exchanged by, for pension, **22.** 569n
Leicester House believed by, to come to terms with D. of Newcastle, **21.** 75n
Newcastle, D. of, betrayed by, **22.** 37n
Parliamentary debate by, on Scottish heritable jurisdictions, **37.** 268

[Oswald, James, *continued*]
Parliamentary memberships of corrected, **43.** 242
Parliamentary speech by, **18.** 440n
Treasury post rumoured for, **22.** 37n
Walpole party voted against by, **17.** 299

Oswald, Dr John (d. 1780), Bp of Clonfert, 1762, of Dromore, 1763, of Raphoe, 1763:
appointment of, as Bp of Clonfert, **10.** 9

Oswald, Richard (1705–84):
peace negotiations by, **25.** 342n
peace preliminaries signed by, **25.** 347n

Oswego, N.Y.:
Amherst prepares invasion force for Canada at, **21.** 421n
capture of, **21.** 14
force embarks at, **9.** 308n
French and Indian force under Montcalm captures, **21.** 12n
more important than Minorca, **21.** 14
prisoners from, forwarded from Quebec to Plymouth, **21.** 18

Osyth, St. *See* St Osyth

Otaheite, Q. of. *See* Tevahine (ca 1722–?–ca 1775–6)

Otaheite (Tahiti):
Banks and Solander guilty of exposing, to Europe's 'abominable passions,' **2.** 225
forgotten, **24.** 21
HW unacquainted with, **16.** 303
inhabitants of, fortunate to have no gold mines, **33.** 359
living with the young is like living in, **25.** 538
macaw from, **32.** 111
not exploited because it has no wealth, **25.** 545
Omai native of, **24.** 175
rites of love in, **32.** 128

Otes, Essex:
Masham of, **16.** 371n
Palmer of, **33.** 521n

Othello. See under Shakespeare, William

'Othello,' E. of Orford's horse:
races won by, **32.** 131n

Otho, Marcus Salvius (A.D. 32–69), Roman Emperor, A.D. 69:
Du Deffand, Mme, admires suicide of, **6.** 1

O'Toole, Arthur (1538–?1622), soldier of fortune:
print of, by Delaram, **1.** 62, 63

'O'Torture, Phelim':
character in HW's 'Peach in Brandy,' **32.** 61

Otranto (Italy):
Aikin, A. L., asks to see, **32.** 197
Alhambra equally suitable with, for scene of novel, **2.** 152
Bute would have written from, to HW, **23.** 103, 107n
castle of: Craven, Lady, sends drawing of, to HW. **42.** 177; HW imagines, as like (?) Trinity College, Cambridge, **6.** 145; HW

receives drawing of, **35.** 435, 438; nobles and inferior classes imprisoned in, **35.** 438
in Naples, not Sicily, **23.** 107
See also Castle of Otranto, by HW

'Otranto':
HW's name for SH, **23.** 350

Ottajano ('Ottajaro'), Principe d'. *See* Medici, Giuseppe de'

Otter, English sloop:
Gordon, capt. of, **17.** 298n
shipwrecked, **17.** 298

Otterbourne, Thomas (fl. 1393–1420), chronicler:
Chronica regum Angliæ by, quoted by Gray, **14.** 78

Ottingen, Bavaria:
(?) Chute confuses Dettingen with, **35.** 41

Ottley (Otley), William Young (1771–1836), writer on art:
(?) SH visited by, **12.** 235

Otto, Mr:
SH visited by, **12.** 225

Otto, Henry (fl. 1759–74), King's messenger:
Austrians capture, **21.** 507n
Pitt sends, to Lyttelton, **21.** 507

Otto, Rudolph (d. 1811), Ritter von; Gen.:
Mansel sent to support, **12.** 97n

Ottoboni, Pietro (1610–91). *See* Alexander VIII

Ottoboni, Pietro (1667–1740), cardinal:
Alexander VIII's nephew, **15.** 247
collection of, sold, **13.** 214, **19.** 420n
dies in Conclave, **13.** 214
HW buys bust at sale of, **13.** 232–3, **15.** 12
ostentation of, shown by gift of cameos to E. of Carlisle, **13.** 214
See also under Vatican

Ottoman Emperor. *See* Mustafa III

Ottoman Empire:
Catherine II and Joseph II might destroy tyranny of, **42.** 183–4
present rulers of, have as valid a title as European nations, **35.** 392
See also Turkey

Ottomans:
dignity of, **33.** 212
ravages of, **34.** 161
See also Turkey; Turks

Otway, Gen. Charles (d. 1764):
Fletcher succeeds, **38.** 432n

Otway, Thomas (1652–85), dramatist:
HW compares, with Shakespeare, **9.** 356n
HW prefers Southerne's tragic scenes to those in *Venice Preserved* and *The Orphan* by, **41.** 290
miscarries in *Don Carlos*, **41.** 290
next to Shakespeare in boldness, but next but one in strokes of nature, **41.** 290
Orphan, The, by: acted at Queensberry House, **19.** 468n; at Drury Lane, **37.** 16; 'Castalio' and 'Polidore' characters in, **9.** 124–5; inspired by ballad, **40.** 374; said to

be based on story of E. of Bedford's sons, **34.** 126

Shakespeare's *King John* surpasses, **29.** 370

Ouches. *See* Owches

Oudenarde:
battle of: George II hero of, **9.** 311; HW's dancing is of era of, **33.** 283; tapestry of, at Windsor, **9.** 18n
Conway and Scott visit, **39.** 536
English army near, **37.** 152

Oudenbosch:
Mitchell's report on, **19.** 465n

Oudh, Nawab-Vazir of. *See* Asaf-ud-daulah (ca 1750–97)

Oudh (India):
army, revenue, and population of, **25.** 13
Begums of: Hastings might treat Ds of Bedford like, **33.** 525; mistreated by Hastings, **33.** 525n, **35.** 392
England acquires, **25.** 13

Oudry, Jean-Baptiste (1686–1755), painter:
HW buys pictures by, **7.** 403

Ouel, *or* Ouells; *or* Ouels. *See* Württemberg-Oels

Ouessant (France):
Conflans may attack ships at, **21.** 358n
naval battle near, **7.** 63n

Oughton, Sir James Adolphus Dickenson (1720–80), K.B., 1773; army officer:
Harcourt, Cts of, dies at house of, **38.** 495

Oulmont, ——:
picture of Mme du Deffand left in legacy by, **8.** 216

Oulton, Yorks:
Bentley of, **13.** 173n

Oulton family:
notes on, **1.** 251

Oulton Low, Cheshire:
Starkeys from, **1.** 251

Oundle, Northants:
Barnwell church near, **2.** 275, 277, **16.** 192n
Cole and HW visit, **10.** 343
Farming Woods near, **34.** 190, 204, 225
Rockingham Forest keeper lives near, **10.** 238, 241

Ourches, Marguerite-Jeanne d', m. (1751) Louis, Marquis de Choisy:
social relations of, in Paris, **7.** 298, 329

Oursin, ——:
attends session of parliament of Paris, **8.** 173

Ouseley, (?) Sir William (1767–1842), Kt, 1800; orientalist:
Essex poem to be shown by, to HW, **42.** 254
Walker delivers parcel and letter to HW by means of, **42.** 253

Ousterwick:
Ligonier and Conway at, **37.** 280

Outfangthief:
of Saxon ancestors, **12.** 178

Outremont, ——:
attends session of parliament of Paris, **8.** 173

Outwell, Norfolk:

Bell of, **1.** 10n
stained glass at, **40.** 225

Ouwerkerk, Heer van. *See* Nassau, Jan Nicolas Floris (1709–82), Rijksgraaf van; Nassau, Willem Maurits, Graaf van

Ouwerkerk, Mevrouw van. *See* Testas, Maria Anna

Ovada:
Maillebois near, **19.** 258

Oven; ovens:
MSS used for, **35.** 104
Pont-de-Veyle's letters burnt in, **32.** 263
volcanos compared with, **35.** 414
See also Coke-oven

Over, Cheshire:
seat of Starkey family, **1.** 251

Overbury, Sir Thomas (1581–1613), Kt; poet; courtier:
imprisonment of, **16.** 161
Northampton thought to have abetted murder of, **16.** 162
Somerset's letters from, **16.** 161
Somersets convicted of murder of, **15.** 192n
Stent said to have engraved portrait of, **16.** 64
supposedly poisoned, **9.** 124n
Weston executed for murder of, **16.** 163

'Overkirk, P. and Ps':
Cowpers to become, **24.** 353

Overkirk; Overquerque. *See* Auverquerque; Ouwerkerk

Overstone, Northants:
Drury of, **9.** 278n

Overton, Arlingham, Glos:
Butt of, **12.** 75n

Overture; overtures:
audience bawls for, at theatre, **24.** 348
Handel's, *see under* Handel

Ovid (Publius Ovidius Naso) (43 B.C.–A.D. ca 18), Roman poet:
Amores, quoted by Whaley, **40.** 9
Ars amatoria by, quoted, **17.** 466, **18.** 74
De tristibus by, Ovid complains of barbarous dialects in, **30.** 73
elegiac, **33.** 43
Epistulæ ex ponto by, quoted, **30.** 73
Fasti by, Chute quotes, **35.** 63
flow of expression in, lacked by HW, **34.** 169
Guibert's comparisons resemble those of, **5.** 341
HW might have compared *Georgics* to, **13.** 198
HW takes Mason for, **28.** 160
Heroides by, **9.** 26, **12.** 204, **14.** 235, **33.** 209, 397, **34.** 86, **37.** 102, **40.** 5
Hungary's equivalent to, **39.** 182
lamentations of, in banishment, **16.** 272
Metamorphoses by: Cambridge cooks to surpass transformations in, **20.** 71; crop of soldiers in, **9.** 83; Fox family's political shift reminiscent of, **25.** 11; Gray quotes, **13.** 145; HW mentions nymph in, **9.** 79; (?) HW misquotes, **35.** 175; HW quotes,

[Ovid, *continued*]

11. 140, 28. 31, 38. 172; HW reads, 10. 38; Nivernais quotes, 41. 20; transformations in, 33. 92; West alludes to, 13. 100; West quotes, 13. 124; Whaley quotes, 40. 4

More, Hannah, jokes about exile of, 31. 289

Rowley's knowledge of, 2. 289

scenes from *Metamorphoses* of: on cabinet, 1. 94; on plates, 2. 152–3

Tristia by: Conway quotes, 37. 30, 122; HW quotes, 33. 469; (?) More, Hannah, paraphrases, 31. 289–90

West refers to, 13. 134

Owches:

HW reads about, in Sidney papers, 9. 25

Owen, ——, Capt.:

Halifax left by, in *Baltimore*, 21. 130n

Owen, Mrs:

SH visited by, 12. 234

Owen, Humphrey (1702–68), librarian of the Bodleian 1747–68; principal of Jesus College, Oxon, 1763–8:

Bowle persuaded by, to give Q. Elizabeth's MS to the Bodleian, 40. 305

Owen, John (? 1560–1622):

Epigrammata by, 38. 567n

Owen, Sir John (1600–66), Kt; royalist:

picture of, 2. 43, 77

Owen, Col. John (?1698–1776):

Whiteboys pursued by regiment of, from Cork, 22. 24n

Owen, Thomas, attorney:

Cambridge, R. O., spends vacations with, 13. 112n

Owen, William (d. 1793), bookseller, at Homer's Head, London; printer of *The Gazetteer*:

Camden defends, over publication of *Case of the Hon. Alexander Murray*, 35. 551n

Gazetteer, The, published by, 40. 256n

(?) HW's correspondence with, 40. 256–7

(?) HW's pamphlet seized at shop of, 13. 22n, 23

Magazine of Magazines published by, 14. 44

printer, 43. 171

Sackville's trial published by, 21. 407n

Owens, Mrs, butter-woman:

Tracy marries daughter of, 9. 75–6

Owens, Susannah, m. (1748) Robert Tracy:

Tracy pursues and marries, 9. 75–6

—— takes, to France, 9. 76

Owl; owls:

Fitzpatrick, Lady Anne, wants stories about, 32. 188, 193

HW as drunk as, from noise in Parliament, 38. 327

HW's story about, 10. 197

HW to be, to hoot in evening, 33. 200

mice's feet bitten off by, to keep them quiet to fatten, 39. 9

Temple, Cts, mentions, in verses, 10. 115

Owyhees (Hawaians):

unexploited because they have no wealth, 25. 545

Ox; oxen:

artillery conveyed by, 18. 530

bones of, used to make false teeth, 18. 289n

Clinton captures, 24. 419

curricles drawn by, in Sussex, 35. 139

Doria wounded by, 21. 386

HW jokes about, of patriarchs, 37. 290

live, Bruce breakfasts on, with Abyssinian maids, 24. 21

Mann obtains, for English fleet, 21. 114

market of, at Tunbridge, 35. 135

Murray orders, to be salted at Leghorn, 24. 381n

negroes compared to, 31. 328

picture of, at Burghley House, 10. 345

Powis, E. of, has, roasted in every town, 32. 302n

prayers of, lead to discovery of Madonna dell' Impruneta, 30. 4

Rowley hoped to find, for English fleet, 18. 503n

Sunday to be kept holy by, 31. 365, 435

Tuscan Regency begrudges, for Austrian artillery, 18. 541

Oxburgh, Norfolk:

Parkin writes from, 40. 222

Oxcheek:

centaur's rump resembles, 35. 46

Oxenden, Lady. *See* Dunch, Elizabeth

Oxenden, Sir George (1694–1775), 5th Bt, 1720; M.P.:

biographical information about, corrected, 43. 256, 353

Deane House the seat of, 40. 4

HW's account of, 33. 222, 34. 257

Mrs Dunch's pictures reserved by, 9. 412

Orford, Cts of, had affair with, 15. 324, 19. 5, 33. 222

Orford, E. of, rumoured to be son of, 15. 324

portraits of, 33. 223

sister-in-law made pregnant and perhaps killed by, 34. 257

son of, 19. 5

Oxenden, Sir Henry (1721–1803), 6th Bt, 1775:

brother to join, in Italy, 43. 256

Bulgarini, Mme, cicisbea to, 43. 279

Florence to be visited by, with introductory letter from HW to Mann, 19. 5

Fortini's affair with, 19. 374

groom of the Bedchamber to Frederick, P. of Wales, 43. 256

lame, 19. 232

Mann entertains, and accompanies him to Mme Grifoni's, 19. 232

—— not to worry about HW's recommendation of, 19. 250

—— receives HW's letter through, 19. 232

——'s coach to be used by, in Siena, 19. 232

——'s correspondence with, 43. 256

(?) print of, 40. 236

Siena may be visited by, to learn Italian, 19. 232

Wittenham Hill on estate of, 32. 298n

Oxenden family:

Deane a seat of, 33. 222

Oxford, Bp of. *See* Butler, John (1717–1802); Compton, Hon. Henry (1632–1713); Crew, Nathaniel (1633–1721); Hough, John (1651–1743); Hume, John (ca 1706–82); Lowth, Robert (1710–87); Parker, Samuel (d. 1688); Potter, John (? 1674–1747); Secker, Thomas (1693–1768)

Oxford, Cts of. *See* Cecil, Lady Diana (d. 1654); Holles, Henrietta Cavendish (1694–1755); Nevill, Margaret (d. after 1488); Philippa de Couci (1367–1411 *or* 12); Scott, Jane Elizabeth (ca 1773–1824); Sergaux, Alice (d. 1452)

Oxford, E. of. *See* Harley, Edward (1689–1741); Harley, Edward (ca 1699–1755); Harley, Edward (1726–90); Harley, Robert (1661–1724); Vere, Aubrey de (d. 1194); Vere, Aubrey de (1626–1703); Vere, John de (1408–62); Vere, John de (d. 1540); Vere, Richard de (ca 1385–1417); Vere, Robert de (1362–92)

Oxford, Earls of:

tombs of, at Colne Priory, 42. 59n

Oxford, Mayor of. *See* Ward, Philip

Oxford, Oxon.:

Batt, Charles William dies at, 11. 322

Beauchamp calls, 'a retired town,' not drunken, 38. 45, 46

—— invites HW to visit, 38. 45–6

Bentley's friend at, forwards Johnson's life of Gray, 35. 272

Berry, Mary, delighted with, 12. 100

Bullock's Lane at, 10. 86

Busbecq's epistles printed at, 16. 151

Cerretesi taken to, by Venetians, 18. 166

Charles I joined at, by lords, 40. 131

Christian VII gives masquerade tickets to, 23. 58

—— visits, 23. 57n

Clarendon Printing-House at, 33. 98, 34. 36n; *see also under* Oxford University

Clarendon's *Life* expected from, 16. 23

clergy of, admire Burke's *Reflections*, 34. 99n

college servant dies at, 19. 387

Conway meets HW at, 9. 288

Corporation of, punished by House of Commons, 22. 584

Dammartin, Catherine, exhumed and reburied at, 29. 107n

dirges at, on P. of Wales's death, 20. 261

Dodd and Whaley visit, 40. 10, 12

Élie de Beaumont visits, 38. 461

Fitzpatrick's balloon ascent at, 25. 591, 33. 469

Fürstenberg, Landgrave of, and family visit, 11. 133

Gibson publishes James V's ballad at, 16. 141

HW does not read of North's reception at, 23. 497

HW fears to visit, alone, 35. 71

HW goes through, without stopping, 9. 120

HW learns at, of fall of Louisbourg, 30. 149

HW's landlord at, 37. 560

HW's passion, 33. 54, 417

HW to visit Beauchamp at, 9. 282, 285–7

HW visits, 9. 4, 228–9, 30. 149, 33. 54–5, 57, 417–18, 35. 147, 155–6, 37. 560, 38. 59, 61, 62, 40. 19–20

Harcourt's vale bounded by, 35. 459

Hardinge on circuit at, 35. 585, 591, 593, 608

High St at, 13. 100n

'Holbeins' at, probably by Scorel, 43. 123

letter from royalist lords at, to the Scots Privy Council, 40. 131

lines composed at, on Gunpowder Plot, 32. 76

Lives of Leland, Hearne, and Wood printed at, 28. 40

'Louse Hall' near, 40. 322n

map of, 2. 356

Martyr's bones said to be dug up at, and burnt, 29. 107

Methodists at, 22. 17n

—— replaced at, by Hutchinsonians, 35. 156

Montagu, Charles, visits, 10. 41–2

Montagu, George, to consult physician at, 10. 61, 67, 68

—— to meet HW at, 9. 285, 286, 288

—— visits, 10. 41–2

muses unknown even to bedmakers of, 35. 368

music meeting at, 12. 258

North, Lord, visits, 33. 347

Orange, P. and Ps of, visit, 12. 203

Paoli visits, 23. 150

Parker and Sir Edward Turner present petition about election at, 20. 435n

Parliament to chastise, 20. 50

patent dated at, 40. 223

Pomfret, Cts of, wants to be buried at, 21. 562

Prince, bookseller at, 16. 194

Radcliffe Camera opened at, 20. 50

riots at, 20. 6, 50

St Mary's Church at, Pomfret, Cts of, buried in, 21. 562n

Secker becomes bishop of, 17. 451n

singers from, to sing *Miserere*, 18. 211

Sot's Hole near, 10. 86

surgeons from, attend Temple at Stowe, 24. 516n

tavern at, Rigby and Selwyn in riot at, 30. 88n

waterman near, 10. 210

Wood, Anthony à, should describe antiquities of, 40. 12

See also Oxford University

Oxford, English ship:

at Mahon, 17. 285

Martin commands, 18. 15n

[*Oxford*, English ship, *continued*]
Mathews sends, to seize xebecs, **18.** 300
misconduct of, **18.** 325n
Oxford, English transport ship:
Americans capture, **24.** 229
Oxford, earldom of:
Crew's resolution about, **22.** 303n
Oxford Arms, The, London:
Baldwin, Ann, bookseller at, **9.** 138n
Oxford Blues. *See* Blues
Oxford Chapel, London:
Moss, Mrs, lives near, **38.** 24
Oxford coach:
Mason asks HW to send 'delineator' by, **28.** 338
Oxford Guide. See New Oxford Guide
Oxford Journal:
German officer's letter in, **9.** 196, 198
Oxford Road, London:
Bonus's shop in, **16.** 184
Craufurd robbed in, **33.** 413
Mortimer St near, **35.** 644
Pantheon erected in, **23.** 210, 298
See also Oxford Street
Oxfordshire:
election in, **9.** 320, **11.** 82, **20.** 435, 469, **35.** 192, 208
HW jokes about Montagu being stuck in clay of, **10.** 306
High Church tendencies of, **9.** 320
Jacobite tendencies in, **9.** 320, **21.** 531
jailor in, suggests hanging a prisoner ahead of time, **19.** 418
map of, sent by HW to Montagu, **9.** 155
Nuneham in, **25.** 428n, **29.** 259–60
Parliamentary candidates for, **37.** 371n
roads in, good, **10.** 258
Oxford St, London:
Herbert helps build, **33.** 376n
Wells St near, **31.** 368
See also Oxford Road
Oxford University:
'act' at, explained, **20.** 71n
Beauchamp and Hon. Henry Seymour-Conway go to, **38.** 99
Beauchamp describes life at, **38.** 45–6
—— unpopular at, **38.** 44n
'bellmen' of, usurp poetic throne, **29.** 135
Bodleian Library in: catalogue of, **1.** 249; 'Charles Christ and Jesus Christ' portraits in, **9.** 114, **34.** 179; picture gallery in, **35.** 155
Bonus employed by, to repair Guise's pictures, **21.** 429
books in, first kept in St Mary's Church, **28.** 147–8
Botanic Garden at, **13.** 123
Burgh is refused M.A. at, **28.** 199, 204
chancellor of: installed, **9.** 241–2; presents address, **9.** 321; table of, **9.** 219
chancellors of, never distinguish royalty from pretenders, **32.** 3

chancellor's post at, will be bone of contention, **22.** 72
chapels of, seen by Montagu brothers, **10.** 40–1
Christian VII fortunate in not having tutor from, **23.** 40
Church and Dodwell honoured at, for attacking Middleton, **15.** 298
Clarendon Press at: Johnson's bookselling arrangements with, **34.** 36n; prints petition against dissenters, **33.** 98; to print edition of Strabo, **28.** 198, 209
Clarendon's *Life* given to, **38.** 47
clergy of, oppose Lord Charles Spencer, **9.** 320
college of, puts blue glass in east window, **9.** 290
college plate of, should be seized by John Paul Jones, **35.** 497
counsel for, argues that vice-chancellor should not be compelled to testify against himself, **20.** 6n
Croxall attends, **20.** 208n
deserted during Long Vacation, **38.** 62
(?) Divinity School at, **16.** 14
drunkenness and prerogative taught at, **33.** 483
encænia at, **23.** 497n, **32.** 137
Esther performed at public act of, **20.** 71n
Fellow of, accused of scandalous conduct, **30.** 89
Fox, Henry, attends, **13.** 33
Genlis, Mme de, visits, 'to take her Doctor's degree,' **33.** 482–3
gossip and coffee-house disputes at, **38.** 45
'Gothic scene' with monkish Fellows 'stealing to their pleasures,' **35.** 147
Guise's collection at, **33.** 55
HW and Conway to visit Beauchamp at, **38.** 54, 59–60, 61, 62
HW asks West for account of Etonians at, **13.** 94
HW asserts liberties of, in pamphlet, **13.** 22–3
HW not again to exhaust Beauchamp at, **38.** 68
HW quotes language of, **25.** 454
HW's enthusiasm for, **9.** 288
HW to visit, **38.** 44, 62
HW visits, *see* Oxford, Oxon: HW visits
HW will not give his collection to, **20.** 471
HW would like to live at, **10.** 92
Harcourt unlikely to regale voters from, at election time, **35.** 507
Hardwicke made LL.D. at, **10.** 309
heads of houses at, expulsion of two, for scandalous conduct, **30.** 89
Humphrey's benefactions to, **16.** 14
Jacobites always elected as vice-chancellors of, **20.** 18n
Jacobitism of, **9.** 288, **30.** 88, 98, 149, 330
Johnson honoured by, **28.** 199
——'s criticism of Gray: pleases, from rivalry

with Cambridge, **35.** 272; will make, happy, **29.** 117, 119

Jones, Sir William, Parliamentary candidate for, **29.** 35

king may nominate chancellor of, **20.** 18

King's Bench, Court of, refuses to let attorney-general and solicitor-general see statutes of, **20.** 18n

Laud's portrait subject of offer by, **2.** 160

'loungers' at, **38.** 45–6

loyal address from: duplicate of, probably sent to Young Pretender at Edinburgh, **30.** 98; sent to Abp of Canterbury, **30.** 98

Mason is benumbed by being near, **29.** 270

——'s *Gray* not admired at, **28.** 198, 199

Meeke a Fellow of college at, **10.** 105

Methodism and, **1.** 135

Orford, 2d E. of, 'attached' to, **30.** 87

—— to receive and ignore request of, against Rigby, **30.** 88

orthodoxy of, **29.** 198

Pelham ministry proposes that Crown nominate chancellor of, **13.** 22–3

Phelps, fellow at, **19.** 196

Phipps studies at, **18.** 185

Pitture antiche d'Ercolano received by, **22.** 25n

Pomfret, Cts of, presents husband's collection of statues to, **9.** 122n, 193n, **20.** 390n, 470, 579, **21.** 562n

pro-proctor of, Rigby's altercation with, **30.** 330

public act at: **20.** 71; Pomfret, Cts of, lauded by, **20.** 579, 584

public orator of, *see* Mather, Roger

Radcliffe Camera at, Mason sees, from Nuneham, **28.** 337

Radcliffe Observatory at, **33.** 54–5

Radcliffe's and Hyde's benefactions to, **38.** 30

Rawlinson's antiquities bequeathed to, **42.** 239

Rigby and Sir C. H. Williams visit Selwyn at, **30.** 330n

Rigby's Castle Rising candidacy opposed by, **30.** 87, **36.** 16n

——'s insult to, **30.** 87

St John's College: garden at, **33.** 57; Percy's nephew a fellow of, **42.** 367; Rawlinson's bequests to, **42.** 239n

scholars of, condemned for treason, **20.** 6

Selwyn criticized by, for recommending La Rochefoucauld's maxims, **30.** 88

——'s expulsion from, **30.** 85, 88, 93

Seymour-Conway, Hon. Henry, at, **35.** 179–80

Sheldonian Theatre at: **13.** 100; presentation ceremonies at, **9.** 193–4; vice-chancellor at, **9.** 193

Smyth acquainted with Spence at, **17.** 10n

Spence a professor at, **17.** 51n

topics of conversation at, **38.** 45

Tories of, disgusted with Bute's packing House of Lords, **38.** 159

variety of students at, **38.** 45–6

verses written at, mere juvenile exercises, **16.** 15

vice-chancellor of: HW jokes about Selwyn and, **30.** 149; said to mistake Lady Sarah Bunbury for Q. Charlotte, **21.** 531n; *see also* Huddesford, George (ca 1699–1776); Isham, Euseby (1676–1753); Purnell, John (ca 1708–64)

Walpole, Sir Robert, opposed by, **30.** 97

West attends, **13.** 233

—— to return to, **13.** 157

Westmorland chancellor of, **21.** 531, **22.** 72

Wilbraham, deputy steward of, **19.** 287n

Williams, Sir C. H., to receive deputation from, **30.** 88

windows, painted, of, **1.** 21

Wolsey founds lectures at, **1.** 266, 269

Wood's history of colleges of, **35.** 387

Young Pretender's health no longer drunk by, **23.** 329

See also Balliol College; Christ Church; Jesus College; Magdalen College; Merton College; New College; Oriel College; Pembroke College; Queen's College; Trinity College

See also under Oxford, Oxon

Oxford University Press:

Strabo edition to be printed by, **28.** 198, 209

Oxted, Surrey:

Fetherstonhaugh of, **42.** 210n

Oxwich Castle, Glamorgan:

Mansel of, **41.** 117n

Oxydracæ:

Alexander the Great at, **33.** 354

Oyly. *See* D'Oyly

Oynhausen, Georg Ludwig (d. 1759), Graf von; Maj.-Gen.:

brother sends, on embassy, **19.** 64

Florence reached by, **19.** 64n

Kendal, Ds of, aunt of, **19.** 64

Oyo. *See* Ohio

Oyras. *See* Oeiras

Oyster; oysters:

Fitzwalter consumes 14 barrels of, weekly, **20.** 518–19

forks for, **4.** 262

hors d'oeuvre of, **19.** 356n

'large stewing' of, **37.** 430

Vorontsov's soul little more animated than, **21.** 247

Oyster-shells, scraped:

lantern of, **37.** 439

Oysterwoman; oysterwomen:

États généraux insulted by, **34.** 72

Parliament's members more abusive than, **35.** 379

Townshend imitates street-cry of, **37.** 430

Voltaire mentions, **35.** 413

Ozernicheff, ——, Russian Gen.:

Soltykov's vanguard led by, **21.** 419n

Oziosi society:

Arno Miscellany written by, **25.** 506n, 507n, **26.** 46

P

'P——, Lady.' *See* Herbert, Barbara, Cts of Powis

'P——, Miss.' *See* Pelham, Frances

'P——, Mother.' *See* Jeffreys, Hon. Henrietta, Cts of Pomfret

'P.P.':
HW's letter to Lincoln signed, **30.** 46

Paar, Thérèse, m. Johann, Graf Bucquoy von Longueval:
Spa to be visited by, **20.** 460

Paar, Wenzel Johann Joseph (1719–92), Count (later Prince):
(?) manner of speaking of, **3.** 269
(?) mistake of, in speaking of Socrates, **3.** *214*
(?) social relations of, in Paris, **3.** 214, **7.** 313, 325, 332

Pacchiarotti, Gasparo (1740–1821), male soprano:
biographical information about, corrected, **43.** 149
Duncan, Lady Mary, connected with, **11.** 153n, 307
Mann has not heard, **25.** 426
many prefer, to Marchesi, **25.** 426
much admired in London, **25.** 243, **29.** 174
Sheridan does not pay, **31.** 343
sings at Pantheon, **11.** 202n

Pace, Clemente de, Mozzi's lawyer:
Lady Orford's will presented for probate by, **43.** 288–9
Lady Orford's will probably opened in presence of, **43.** 288
Mozzi consults, **25.** 456, **43.** 291

Pace, the:
Spaniards to pass, **17.** 342

Pachio, Giovanni Battista:
Nostra Signora del Rosario, ship of, **21.** 288n

Pacific Ocean:
islands of, used to be safe before Banks exposed them, **39.** 459

Packer, John Hayman (1730–1806), actor:
insignificant in *Braganza*, **28.** 177, **41.** 295n

Packet; packets:
Mann's expense allowance for, **18.** 516
price for delivery of, **17.** 262n

Packet-boat; packet-boats:
at Minorca, **37.** 313
at Ostend: delays English post, **23.** 541; missed by Lady Mary Coke, **33.** 293
captain of: has affair with Lady Ligonier, **30.** 255; to take HW's letter to Montagu, **10.** 283
capture of, rumoured, **12.** 121
Carteret detains, at Harwich, **19.** 213
cross-Channel, stoppage of, interrupts HW's correspondence with Mme du Deffand, **30.** 266–8, 271
delays of, frequent in winter, **19.** 453
detained at Flushing, for fear of the French, **21.** 465, 474

English: delayed or captured by French, **19.** 430, **21.** 75, 84, 168, 541, **24.** 302, 504; privateer carries, to Dunkirk, **24.** 302; stopped, **18.** 401
English capture, from Lisbon, **20.** 320
Flushing the worst port for, **21.** 141, 464
French must have captured or delayed, **19.** 430
from Dublin, about to sail, **38.** 115, **39.** 59
Gloucester family travel in, **36.** 155
HW dislikes vessels smaller than, **11.** 116
HW prefers balloon to, **33.** 459
HW's anecdotes of characters in, **30.** 19–20
HW's letter lost on, **21.** 186
mail thrown from, into sea, **21.** 168, 541, **24.** 504
Mann, Horace II, rumoured lost on, **25.** 210
officers carried to Germany in every sailing of, **38.** 156–7
pass between England and France, despite undeclared war, **24.** 399
Port Mahon, Tuscan government almost destroys, **24.** 416
post delayed by: to Dublin, **37.** 418, 441; to England, **17.** 476, **21.** 75, 84, 465, 474; to Italy, **19.** 196, 430, 453, **21.** 141, 464, **23.** 541, **24.** 504
weather storm, **11.** 162, 166, 167, 170
winds prevent, from reaching Holland, **19.** 196

Pack horse; pack horses:
wagons supersede, **10.** 348

Packing:
Du Deffand, Mme, gives directions for, to HW, **3.** 297
expense of, **5.** 233
waterproof cover to be used in, **5.** 125
See also Transportation

Packing case; packing cases:
expense of, **17.** 130, **26.** 4

Packington. *See also* Pakington

Packington Hall, Warwickshire, seat of Lord Aylesford:
Gloucester, Ds of, praises hospitality of, **34.** 75, **43.** 369
—— visits, **36.** 268, **43.** 387
visitors to: Waldegrave, Cts, **43.** 386–7; Waldegrave, Lady Elizabeth, **43.** 387; Waldegrave, Hon. William, **43.** 386–7
Waldegrave, Cts, writes from, **36.** 257, 258, 259, 262, 269
Waldegrave, 4th E. and Cts at, **36.** 257–61, **43.** 386–7
Waldegrave, 4th E., ill at, **34.** 68
Waldegrave, Hon. William, addressed at, **43.** 386
—— writes from, **36.** 264

'Pacte de famille,' Bourbon. *See* Bourbon family: family compact of

Pactolus:
dry in Bengal and at Almack's, **32.** 184
Hippocrene should not be taken for, **31.** 222

Pad; pads (horses):
fish to set forth on arrival of, **37.** 378
Mann's great-great-grandmother famous for breaking, **20.** 13
Paddington, London:
Bedford, D. of, disputes with D. of Grafton over proposed road through, **37.** 452–3, 457–8
Cole crosses, to Hyde Park and Twickenham, **2.** 370
hanging prevalent in, **20.** 65
route of, from Islington to Edgeware Road, **20.** 549n
Townshend, Vcts, takes villa in, near Tyburn, **22.** 165
Paddle; paddles:
Coke, Lady Mary, carries, in garden, **31.** 138
Paddock; paddocks:
at Sion House, made for ball, **35.** 331
at Wentworth House, **35.** 280
Paderborn:
Conway and Scott visit, **39.** 537
Ferdinand, P., as well in, as in the other world, **38.** 82
—— retires to, **9.** 353, **21.** 498
Paderni, Camillo (fl. 1738–69), Neapolitan artist:
(?) plates by, **15.** 20n
Padlock, The, comic opera:
at Drury Lane, **23.** 82n
Padlock; padlocks:
Bird puts, in park gate, **20.** 323
Padnag; padnags:
Montagu's, **10.** 111
Padona. *See* Padua
Padri di famiglie:
Florentine, ask Leopold to curb extravagance in ladies' dress, **25.** 175
Padroni:
of barks, **22.** 546
Padstow, Cornwall:
Orford, E. of, presents Paxton to living at, **40.** 39n
Padua, John of. *See* John of Padua
Padua (Italy):
Abano near, **24.** 9
Abercorn, 3d E. of, dies at, **42.** 89n
Berry, Mary, writes from, **11.** 367, 368
cattle distemper appears around, **19.** 174n
Cordus studies at, **14.** 126n
couriers from Lombardy and Germany do not pass through, **24.** 136
Courtenay dies at, **9.** 123
Eleonora's death announced from, **17.** 362
—— visits, **17.** 74
lady of, **17.** 74
letters from, reach Florence on Wednesdays only, **24.** 136
Mann's letters from, about D. of Gloucester's health, **24.** 144
Marlborough takes house at, **21.** 512
Niccolini may live at, **20.** 24

opera at, will detain English, **21.** 512
visitors to: Abercorn, 3d E. of, **42.** 89n; Cowper, 3d E., **43.** 277; Gloucester, Ds of, **24.** 144; Gloucester, D. of, **24.** 135, 144, 314; Lincoln, **17.** 72n; Marlborough, D. of, **21.** 512–13; Murray, **21.** 512–13; Naylor, **17.** 72n; Niccoli, **17.** 224; Niccolini, **20.** 145n; Orford, Cts of (Bns Walpole), **17.** 72n, 217, 224, 235; Pitt, Anne, **24.** 22; Richecourt, **17.** 217, 224, 235, 419n, **18.** 216; Steavens, Thomas, **20.** 175n
Paduan; Paduans:
Ennery has medals of, in silver, **7.** 325
Paduasoy:
red, gown of, **42.** 236
Pætus, Cecina (d. A.D. 42):
Arria's remark to, **32.** 230, **35.** 466
suicide of, **5.** 424
Paéz, Pedro (1564–1622), Spanish Jesuit:
palaces and convents said to be built by, in Abyssinia, **39.** 476–7
Pagan; pagans:
HW might write olio on, **35.** 384
sexual intercourse encouraged by religion of, **31.** 434
Pagani, Anton Giuseppe, printer:
Pignotti's *Shakespear* printed by, **24.** 536n
Paganini, Carlo:
Paganini, Rosa, may belong to family of, **17.** 45n
Paganini, Giuditta. *See* Giuditta
Paganini, Maria Angela (fl. 1743–?60), opera singer:
Paganini, Rosa, may belong to family of, **17.** 45n
popular in comic opera in London, **21.** 459
Paganini, Rosa, m. (?) Francesco Sauveterre:
HW mentions, **17.** 42
Rangoni pursued by, **17.** 45
Paganism:
pageantry of, HW regrets loss of, **11.** 22
Paganzikar, Mme, of Osnabrück:
sketch of, by Anne Seymour Conway, **38.** 156
Page, Mr, of Harrow, Middlesex:
SH visited by, **12.** 245
Page, Sir Gregory (ca 1695–1775), 2d Bt, 1720, of Greenwich, Kent:
Blackheath house of, **33.** 125n
pictures formerly belonging to, **33.** 137
Howe's bequest from, **39.** 252
Wricklemarsh, house of, demolished, **36.** 246
Page, Mary (d. 1817), m. Charles Bedford:
family of, **42.** 492
unprovided for, **42.** 58
Page, Mrs Thomas. *See* Howe, Hon. Judith *or* Juliana
Page, William (d. 1758), highwayman:
Ferrers appears against, at Hertford assizes, **21.** 184
Page; pages:
Court, title of nobility necessary for, **4.** 413n, 425, 491–2

[Page; pages, *continued*]
Frederick II's, escapes lashing by giving letter to a Jew, 43. 145–6
to Comtesse de Provence, costs and prerequisites for being, 4. 484–5, 491–2
See also under Servant

Pageantry:
HW and Mary Berry like, 11. 22
HW's news will be all of, 21. 515

Page-surgeon; page-surgeons:
D. of Gloucester's, *see* Bryant, Robert (d. 1788); Charlton, John

Paget, Bn. *See* Bayly, Henry (1744–1812)

Paget, Caroline (d. 1766), m. (1737) Sir Nicholas Bayly, 2d Bt:
death of, 7. 397

Paget, Dorothy (d. 1734), m. (ca 1706) Edward Irby, cr. (1704) Bt:
house of, near Lowther's in Pall Mall, 34. 256
invasion to be escaped by, by going to China, 37. 206

Paget (formerly Bayly) Henry (1744–1812), Bn Paget, 1769; cr. (1784) E. of Uxbridge, n.c.:
peerage creation for, 39. 410n

Paget, Henry William (1768–1854), styled Lord Paget, 1784; 2d E. of Uxbridge, 1812; cr. (1815) M. of Anglesey:
peerage of, corrected, 43. 146
Rutland, Ds of, rumoured to be marrying, 11. 187, 244, 12. 120
wife of, 11. 108n

Pagett, Thomas (d. 1741), army officer:
Canterbury assembly attended by, 40. 4

Pagholo, Fra Bartolommeo di. *See* Bartolommeo della Porta, Fra

Paglio. *See* Palio

Paglioni. *See* Pallione

'Pagod':
HW calls Hénault, 39. 12

Pagoda; pagodas:
at Kew, 35. 308
Bateman's, converted from Chinese to Gothic, 35. 359
cathedral tiles would be desecrated in, 36. 39
See also Chanteloup: pagoda (obélisque) at; Kew

'Pagode, la grande.' *See* Temple, Le

'Pagode, le dieu de la.' *See* Bourbon, Louis-François de, Prince de Conti

Pail; pails:
HW buys, 7. 399
HW fishes with, 9. 155
HW uses, full of cold water, to dip his head in, 21. 168

Pailly, Mme. *See* Malevieux, Marie

Pain; pains:
absence of, the pleasure of old age, 24. 327
HW's reflections on advantages of, 23. 462–3
HW's reflections on reactions to, in youth and age, 33. 436
HW's variety of, 33. 163
in back, 17. 67

in bowels, 19. 192, 32. 219
in breast: 32. 192, 199; gout supposed to cure, 20. 335; occurrences of, 19. 8, 207, 20. 225, 335, 22. 110, 24. 210, 38. 463–4; remedy for, hot sponge, 19. 8
in hands, 25. 100
in head, 20. 225, 38. 65; *see also* Headache
in stomach: 33. 251; Bath waters do not remove, from HW, 22. 461; occurrences of, 22. 110, 450, 454–5, 461, 468, 24. 68, 38. 65, 276, 39. 79
in the face, 33. 285

Paine, James (ca 1716–89), architect:
birth date of, corrected, 43. 135
HW should have had Haddon Hall drawn by, 40. 183
Kedleston designed by Adam and, 10. 230n
Stone's notebooks acquired by, 43. 38

Paine, Thomas (1737–1809), writer:
banditti army may be raised by, 34. 143
Burke's *Appeal* attacks, 34. 116
——'s remark on vote of, for Louis XVI, 34. 180
disciples of, arrested, 11. 320
England indifferent to proposals of, 11. 322
France's happiness not proved by, 11. 336
HW calls, 'demon,' and 'philosophizing serpent,' 31. 373
HW compares Knight to, 29. 339
message worthy of, 11. 330
Revolution Society's meeting attended by, 11. 319
Rights of Man by: denounced by HW, 31. 373; distribution of, 11. 260, 314, 318, 319; HW's opinion of, 11. 239; quoted, 11. 239–40; 'seditious,' 11. 260
Rights of Man, Part the Second by, wide distribution of, 15. 224–5
Sièyes, Abbé, has controversy with, 11. 319

Paine. *See also* Payne

Painshill, Surrey, Hon. Charles Hamilton's seat:
a show place, 1. 44, 9. 71n
HW visits, 9. 71

Paint; paints:
Bentley to receive supply of, 35. 182, 243, 252, 264
for china, *see* Cobalt; Zinc
Francis III uses, on face, 20. 75
gout as affected by, 1. 371, 373
green, for house-painting, Lady Diana Beauclerk asks about, 35. 530
HW 'sick of smell of,' in book reviews, 35. 515
Mann to send, to Sir Edward and (?) Mary Walpole, 19. 368–9
SH 'commodity,' 9. 170
Sturgis promises, to academician, 17. 462
sun not to be imitated in white, 10. 239
Wharncliffe Lodge lacks, 35. 268
white, as cosmetic, 37. 78–9, 81
See also Whitewash

Paint-brush. *See* Brush

Painted glass. *See* Stained glass

Painter; painters:

at SH, **10.** 61, 63, **38.** 207

'crooked,' HW sees, **10.** 394

Dutch: flower-paintings by, over-finished, **29.** 285; HW on, **2.** 189; HW's distaste for, **29.** 298; Hogarth less indelicate than, **41.** 449

English: do animals and landscapes well, **24.** 93; London overrun with, **29.** 299; Montagu's remarks on, **16.** 146–7; obscure, in HW's *Anecdotes*, **28.** 2–3; obstinacy of, **28.** 301, **29.** 137; scarce because never immortalized, **38.** 151; very indifferent, **16.** 27; *see also Anecdotes of Painting* by HW

engravers' prices exceed those formerly charged by, **25.** 532

Flemish: 'delineator' should enable Reynolds and West to excel, **28.** 329; HW on, **2.** 189; Hogarth less indelicate than, **41.** 449

foreign, HW to ignore, unless they settled in England, **16.** 37

HW hears from, at Rome, about Old Pretender's movements, **17.** 15

HW's reflections on impertinence of, **9.** 259

modern, heads by, crowd Uffizi, **25.** 170

Piozzi, Mrs, comments on, **9.** 259n

Reeve copies portraits of, **40.** 231

reported to number 2,000 in London, **15.** 47

Scottish, **40.** 251, 260–9, 284–5, **42.** 72

Venetian, process of, discovered, **15.** 335

Painting; paintings:

Agincourt's project on monuments of, **42.** 63–9, 101–4

Anson's, of sea victory, **20.** 38

Arundel's taste for, **42.** 422

at Cornbury, **40.** 12

at Deane House, **40.** 4

at Gloucester House and Lady Dysart's, to be seen by Humphry, **42.** 463–4

at Hatfield House, **40.** 199, 248

at Hinchingbrooke, **10.** 79, **40.** 283–4

at Houghton, in finest preservation, **39.** 172; *see also under* Houghton

at New College, Oxford, **38.** 43–4

at Palais-Royal, **38.** 308, **39.** 202

at Standon, **40.** 198–9

at Waldershare, **40.** 5

Boyle, Charlotte, mistress of, **31.** 251n

Butler's, **40.** 273

Cardigans', **38.** 357

classical, seldom expresses passion, **35.** 444

Conway sees, at Rome, **37.** 324

—— wants to know about, **37.** 73

copies of, pretend to be originals, **15.** 66–7, 95

Devonshire, D. of, invites HW to see, from Hardwick Hall, **38.** 120

Dutch: flowers and fruits of all seasons combined in, **10.** 304; seen by Conway and wife in Holland, **37.** 286

early, in oil and tempera, on wood and canvas, **42.** 64–9

encaustic: HW's account of, discontinued, **13.** 34; English painters too obstinate to adopt, **29.** 137; Müntz writes on, **16.** 170, **28.** 301; use of, by Protogenes and Caylus, **28.** 300

English: Chatterton's fictitious accounts of, **16.** 101–5, 107–12, 219–20; had no intrinsic merit before Holbein, **16.** 234

etiquette in, for painters in royal service, **40.** 150

exhibitions of: at Louvre, over, **39.** 202; at Paris inferior to those shown in London, **31.** 134; HW and Lady Mary Coke attend, at Louvre, **31.** 134, 183; in London, **23.** 210–11

export of, forbidden, **20.** 465–6

Ferdinand of Naples develops taste for, **35.** 433

Flemish school of: Mann thinks painters of, inferior to Italian school, **20.** 398; masters of, in Joseph II's collection, **33.** 487; Reynolds ascribes HW's Henry VII to, **33.** 466; Schaub has examples of, **21.** 200; Zoffany exceeds, **23.** 435; Zoffany imitates, but avoids its degrading features, **24.** 527

Florentine school of, HW wants a few drawings by, **18.** 284

flower, to be left by HW for Lady Ailesbury, **37.** 475

French neglect, or over-clean, **35.** 344–5

French spoil, with varnish, **35.** 425, 429

Fuller's, on wood, of Charles II's escape, **42.** 380–1

George III likes, **21.** 449, 451–2

Gothic: in Sicily, **35.** 409; on shields, **35.** 419

Greeks perhaps set standards for, **33.** 479

—— probably graceful at, **16.** 270

HW and Hogarth discuss, **9.** 366

HW brings 'cartloads' of, from abroad, **37.** 107

HW buys, **31.** 339

HW considered good judge of, by Cole, **10.** 332

HW criticizes grotesque horrors in, **31.** 221–2

HW discusses, with Stanley, **30.** 71

HW eschews tawdry use of, at SH, **20.** 382

HW has no room to spare for, at SH, **30.** 149

HW's, Mann packs in case to be sent to England, **18.** 152

HW said to take, into retirement, **37.** 257, 258

HW's changing taste in, **9.** 348

HW sees, in Paris, **7.** 261–353

HW sends, with list, to Conway, **37.** 487

HW's knowledge of, **21.** 368

HW to receive, from Fox through Selwyn, **30.** 171

HW wishes to have, cleaned before sending them to Houghton, **15.** 322, 325

high price of, in England, **23.** 210–12, 466

historical, West imitates Poussin, in, **23.** 210–11

Indian, **35.** 301

[Painting; paintings, *continued*]
in reign of Henry VI, **2.** 221
Italian, **2.** 221
Jamesone's: catalogue of, **40.** 263–9; resemble Van Dyck's, **40.** 263–4
list of, in HW's Berkeley Sq. house, **30.** 370–1
Louis XVI's, piled in house at Versailles, **39.** 201
Louvre exhibit of, over, **39.** 202
Lund's remarks on upholstering and, **30.** 62
Leopold buys, of Gaddi family, **25.** 170
MS on, sent by Hinchliffe to HW, **16.** 196
Mason's new technique in, **35.** 375
Mirepoix, Mme de, has, in closet, **31.** 99
Morton refuses to buy, for mother's 'hut,' **38.** 454
of P. of Monaco, ill-used, **39.** 202
oil: Mason experiments with, **29.** 311, 316; Pars does, **24.** 135, 144, **35.** 424; Raspe's book on discovery of, **15.** 145; Stubbs invents method of enamelling, **29.** 137; Van Eyck said to have discovered, **16.** 106
on Cornwall monument, **42.** 387
on wood, **42.** 67, 380n
prices of, high, **35.** 428
Proctor's prize in, **25.** 577
'reservoirs' of, at Marigny's, **39.** 15
Reynolds's, sold, **42.** 414
Scottish, **15.** 141, 155, 164, 190–2, 208–9, **16.** 51; *see also under* Jamesone, George
Shelburne buys, cheap, **37.** 460
Spanish grandees deem, 'a mere mechanical art,' **16.** 170
Strafford thanks HW for information about, **37.** 559
transfer of, to new canvases, **35.** 429
Walker's plan for promoting, in Ireland, **42.** 305
Walpole, Sir Edward, makes witticism about modern miracles in, **25.** 577
washed drawings by Pars, **24.** 135, 144
Wright's, of judges, **40.** 267
See also Hunting scenes; Landscape; Miniature; Picture; Portrait; Seascape, *and under names of collectors and painters*
Painting of the Ancients. See under Junius, Franciscus
Pairet, Juan Pablo, French quack:
Floridablanca stabbed by, **11.** 76–7
Pair of colours (ensign's commission):
Baldwyn gets, **39.** 431, 441
Sturgis offers to procure, in England, **43.** 245
Paisiello, Giovanni (1741–1815), composer:
Gli schiavi per amore by, **33.** 586n, 587n
Il re Teodoro in Venetia by, heard by HW, **33.** 586–7
Paisley, Bn. *See* Hamilton, James (1712–89)
Paisley, ——:
(?) HW's letter to Craufurd carried by, **41.** 277n
Paisley, Scotland:
Morvo directs mason-work at, **42.** 69n

Pajet, Mme de:
dances at ball in honour of Dauphin's marriage, **4.** 410
Pakington, Lady. *See* Coventry, Dorothy
Pakington, Sir Herbert Perrot (ca 1701–48), M.P.:
amatory renown of, **40.** 14
Perrot portrait said to be owned by, **40.** 271
Westwood, seat of, **40.** 14, 271n
Pakington, Sir John (ca 1722–62), 6th Bt:
father succeeded by, at Westwood, **40.** 271n
Palace; palaces:
little princes specialize in, in Italy, **25.** 587, 589
plan of, bought by HW, **26.** 4
Soubise can build, free of cost, **21.** 178
'Palace, old,' at Florence. *See* Palazzo Vecchio
Palace, the, High St, Newmarket:
Cumberland, D. of, sometimes lives at, **20.** 373n
Granby, Marchioness of, inherits Crown's lease of, **20.** 373n
'Palace, the,' at Florence. *See* Pitti, Palazzo
Palace of the Sun:
Osterley borrows from, **32.** 127
See also Palmyra: Temple of the Sun at
Palace Yard, Westminster:
Bedford's house in, **3.** 380n
Coronation display in, **38.** 126
crowded for Coronation ceremonies, **9.** 386
HW sleeps in, on night before George III's Coronation, **21.** 534
HW thanks Bedfords for hospitality at, **40.** 206
King's Arms Tavern in, **20.** 359n
Williams in pillory in, **38.** 512
See also New Palace Yard
Palæologi, the:
HW unwilling to serve the modern successors to, **28.** 371
Palafox y Mendoza, Juan de (1600–59), Bp of Puebla:
Benedict XIII begins canonization of, **43.** 282
Clement XIV to resume attempt to canonize, **23.** 123–4
Jesuits delay canonization of, **23.** 124
'Palagio o Ponte a Mensola':
Bracci's villa called, **20.** 221n
Palairet, John (1697–1774):
French grammar by, **13.** 6n
Palais, the, at Paris (Palais de Justice):
fire at, **6.** 256–7
HW visits, **7.** 276
Hertford goes to hearing at, **38.** 360
Rigaut bookseller near, **30.** 263n
Palais-Égalité, at Paris. *See* Palais Royal
Palais Marchand, Paris:
damaged by fire, **6.** 256
HW probably not tempted to buy at, **39.** 47
HW visits, **7.** 291, **31.** 93, **32.** 26
Richmond, Ds of, visits, **32.** 26

Palais Royal, at Paris:
Bingham, Lady, given studio at, **6.** 333, **32.** 298
Conway enjoys pictures at, **37.** 308
'dame du,' *see* Vaulserre des Adretz, Marie-Olympe de
Du Deffand, Mme, dreams she is shopping at, **5.** 272
Genlis, Mme de, lives at, **6.** 293
Knight worthy to be erected in, **29.** 340
La Frenaye's shop at, **5.** 307n, **17.** 98–9
Orléans's little house next to, **8.** 127
paintings at: badly restored, **39.** 202; over-varnished, **35.** 425, 429; transferred to new canvases, **35.** 429
Polignac, Mme de, of, **3.** 123
Raphael painting at, **7.** 287
Santini's watch would discredit performances at, **21.** 322
Selwyn loses money at, **3.** 208
visitors to: Boufflers, Comtesse de, **3.** 396; Choiseul, Duchesse de, **6.** 293; Forcalquier, Mme de, **4.** 224; HW, **7.** 272, 336; Pembroke, Cts of, **4.** 159
'Palamon' in Dryden's 'Palamon and Arcite': Lady Diana Beauclerk's drawing of, **11.** 247
Palaprat, Jean (1650–1721), dramatist:
Grondeur, Le, by, cited, **3.** 194, 309, **7.** 55
Palatinate, the:
Conway and Scott visit, **39.** 537
England may recover, **37.** 563
ministers from and to, *see under* Minister
troops of, object to crossing Rhine into Germany, **21.** 94n
Valtravers, councillor of legation of, in London, **20.** 393n
'Palatine, la.' *See* Rodet, Marie-Thérèse, Mme Geoffrin
Palatine, Elector. *See* Elector Palatine
Palatine, Electress. *See* Electress Palatine
Palatine, Mount. *See under* Rome
Palatine, Princesse. *See* Élisabeth-Charlotte
Palatine Hill. *See under* Rome
Palavicini, Lady. *See* Hoostman, Anne
Palavicini, Sir Horatio (d. 1600), architect:
Cole's account of, **1.** 2–5, 12
estate of, at Babraham, **1.** 2–3, 3n, 5, 170, **2.** 181n
family of, **1.** 3
MS epitaph on, **1.** 4
Palavicini, Tobias (Toby) (b. 1593):
family of, **1.** 3
house of, at Little Shelford, **1.** 3n
puts up chimney-piece, **1.** 170
Palavicini. *See also* Pallavicini
Palazzi, Contessa:
son brings Lady Mary Wortley Montagu to house of, near Brescia, **20.** 235n
Palazzi, Conte Ugolino (b. ca 1715):
biographical information on, corrected, **43.** 106
Montagu, Lady Mary Wortley, at Brescia with, **20.** 235, 272, 279, 281

—— escorted by, from Avignon to Brescia, **20.** 235n
—— keeps, as lover, **7.** 281
Palazzo Cesaroni. *See* Manetti, Casa
Palazzo del Governo; Palazzo del Senato. *See* Palazzo Madama
Palazzo di Spagna, Rome:
misquelets on duty at, **19.** 113n
Palazzo Franceschi. *See* Franceschi family: palazzo of
Palazzo Lanfredini, Florence:
Mann's house opposite, **11.** 154n
Palazzo Madama, at Rome:
Francis I sells, to the French, **20.** 264
Rome's governor housed in, **20.** 264n
Palazzo Monti, at Bologna:
Guido painting at Wimbledon may be copied from one at, **21.** 173n
Palazzo Pitti. *See* Pitti, Palazzo
'Palazzo Pitti.' *See under* Twickenham
Palazzo Pubblico, at Florence:
Accademia degli Intronati in, **20.** 391n
Palazzo Rosso, Brignole palace at Genoa:
Conway sees, **37.** 319
Palazzo Vecchio:
balcony in for viewing presentation ceremony, **22.** 245n
corridor from, to Pitti Palace, **18.** 391
English sculptor at Florence makes chimney-pieces for, **25.** 93
fireworks at, **17.** 100
'gentleman of,' *see* Nay, Emmanuel de, Comte de Richecourt
gold from furnishings at, made into plate for Leopold, **25.** 231
Leopold's accession ceremony in Grand Salon of, **22.** 412n
Niccoli visits, daily, **20.** 335
Orford, Cts of, visits, **17.** 283
poor girls given a dinner and ball at, after marriage, **22.** 491
Richecourt may keep Mrs Richmond in, **19.** 97, 101
——'s apartment in, **17.** 224, 283, **18.** 391, **19.** 385
sales from, **25.** 230–1
Siries, Louis, at, **15.** 279, **17.** 93n, 213, **20.** 475n, **24.** 500
Pale; pales:
road strewn with, after storm, **33.** 81
Paleotti, Adelaide (d. 1726), m. 1 Alessandro Roffeni; m. 2 (1705) Charles Talbot, 12th E. of Shrewsbury, cr. (1694) D. of Shrewsbury:
Bubb Dodington's ballad mentions, **33.** 557, **34.** 262
first husband of, **43.** 268
Montagu, Lady Mary Wortley, mentions, **33.** 557
portrait of, at Easton Maudit, **10.** 88, 338
silver tube used by, to ventilate bed, **20.** 203
Strawbridge, Mrs, surpasses, **34.** 262

Palermo, Sicily:
  bishopric of Malta belongs to archdiocese of, **20.** 405n
  Corsini lives at, **18.** 262n
  Mann, Horace II and Lady Lucy, to sail to, **24.** 222, 225
  Messina plague described in letters from, **18.** 269
  rebellion at, **32.** 159
Palestina (Italy):
  earthquake damages, **25.** 376
Palestine:
  crusaders to, imagined by HW as in Cyprus, **35.** 222
  Russia unlikely to take, from Turkey, **23.** 194–5
  visitors to: La Condamine, **22.** 147n; Wortley Montagu, Edward, **22.** 113n
  See also Holy Land
Palestrina, Principe di. *See* Colonna Barberini, Carlo
Palestrina (Italy):
  HW and Gray visit, **17.** 26
Palette; palettes:
  Müntz prefers foreign gazette to, **35.** 265
Pálffy, Maria Anna (1716–73), Cts, m. (1739) Gerolamo Luigi Malabaila di Canale, Conte di Canale; Maria Theresa's maid of honour; Wachtendonck's 'cousin':
  Richecourt's recall procured by, **17.** 490
Pálffy, Maria Leopoldine (b. 1729), m. Franz Joseph, Fürst Kinsky:
  (?) Louis XV rejects, **5.** 285
  (?) Maria Theresa cheats, of daughter's property, **7.** 292
  Paris adopted as residence by, **7.** 292
  social relations of, in Paris, **7.** 292, 297, 298, 346
Palfrey; palfreys:
  Clement XIII unlikely to be assisted to, by Joseph II, **22.** 555
  Gramont's characters ride, on pillions, **35.** 136
Palgowan, Kirkcudbright Stewartry:
  Mackye of, **41.** 277n
Palgrave, Rev. William (ca 1735–99), Fellow of Pembroke College, Cambridge:
  anecdote of uncle of, **28.** 465
  drawings by Lady Diana Beauclerk seen by, **28.** 259
  Gray sends HW information from, **14.** 184
  ——'s friend, **22.** 272
  HW can write nothing to entertain, **29.** 100, 101, 106, 107
  HW invites, to SH, **29.** 117
  (?) HW mentions, **6.** 202
  HW sends compliments to, **28.** 167, **29.** 99
  HW's tale entertains, **29.** 113
  HW to be visited by, **28.** 28
  ill with influenza, **29.** 254
  Mann asked by, to ask HW for life of Lord Herbert of Chirbury, **22.** 273

Mason tries to persuade, to change arms on chaise, **29.** 365
  —— visits, **28.** 129
  —— visits Scarborough with, **28.** 165
  Mémoires of Gramont to be given to, **28.** 119, 120
  mentioned, **28.** 124, 278, 284, 429, **29.** 38, 94
  Nivernais's *Jardins modernes* to be given to, **12.** 260
  original humour and good heart of, **29.** 112
  reports universal admiration for Mason's Gray, **28.** 198
Palgrave, Suffolk:
  Martin of, **2.** 30n
  Palgrave at, **28.** 124
Palhava brothers. *See* Antonio (1714–1800); José (1720–after 1777)
Palifox. *See* Palafox y Mendoza
Palio:
  at Siena, **22.** 515n
  Francis I's horse wins, **17.** 79, 456
  Mann and guests attend, **18.** 251
  on St John's Day at Florence, **22.** 532n
Palio dei cocchi. *See* Corso dei cocchi
Palisser. *See* Palliser
Palissot de Montenoy, Charles (1730–1814):
  article on Voltaire in Sabatier de Castres's *Trois siècles* may be by, **5.** 314
  Éloge de M. de Voltaire by, **7.** 82, 94, 96–7, 180
Palk, Lady Mary. *See* Bligh, Lady Mary
Palk, Robert (1717–98), cr. (1782) Bt; M.P.:
  Ashburton to be borough of, **36.** 47
  Callington borough of, **39.** 192n
Pall; palls:
  made at Monaco for D. of York, **22.** 354
Palladio, Andrea (1508–80), architect:
  bridge in style of, at Stowe, **10.** 315
  Chambers influenced by, **16.** 187n
  HW contrasts bridges of, with that at Park Place, **10.** 105
  Mereworth in 'taste' of, **35.** 143
  Villa Rotondo by, **35.** 143
Palladis Tamia. See under Meres, Francis
Palladius and Irene:
  imitates Gray and Shakespeare, **28.** 118
Pallas, Peter Simon (1741–1811), explorer:
  Pennant's collaborator, **2.** 191–2n
Pallas:
  Cleveland, Ds of, painted by Lely as, **30.** 326
  Fitzroy, Lady Caroline, compared to, **30.** 326
Pallas, English frigate:
  Thurot pursued by, **21.** 376
Pallas, French ship:
  English seize, **8.** 209, **28.** 405n, 408n
Pallavacini, Annetta:
  art treasures restored to, **19.** 352n
Pallavacini, Gian Luca (1697–1773), Austrian army officer; gov. of Lombardy:
  artillery carriages sent by, from Milan, **19.** 406
  Batthyáni and Schulenburg refuse to serve under, **19.** 50

Lobkowitz succeeded by, as governor of Lombardy, **19**. 30n

Maria Theresa said to authorize, to treat with Genoese mob, **19**. 359

Maricone advised by, to report Spanish fleet's arrival, **17**. 309

Milan exposed by retreat of, **19**. 120

palace of, plundered, **19**. 352n

regiment of: (?) **17**. 154n; embarks at Fiumicino for Loano, to aid Charles Emmanuel III, **18**. 502n; reinforces Lobkowitz, **19**. *30*

Spaniards escape from, **19**. 244

Pallavacini, Lazzaro Opizio (1719–85), cardinal, 1766:

Clement XIV's secretary of state, **23**. 118

Cumberland, D. of, entertained by, **23**. 566n

former nuncio to Spain and Naples, **23**. 118

York, Cardinal, asked by, about Young Pretender, **23**. 324

Pallavicini, Marchese (?) Nicolò Maria:

Maratti's painting includes, **21**. 208, 231, 478–9

Pallavicini, Hotel. *See under* Parma

Pallavicini, Palazzo, at Genoa:

Genoese mob plunders, **19**. 352n

Pallavicini. *See also* Palavicini

Pallavicini Collection:

Maratti's paintings from, bought by Sir Robert Walpole, **17**. 56n

Pallazi *or* Pallazio, (?) Roman art dealer:

attestation fee of, **26**. 4

medals, pictures and urn bought from, by HW, **26**. 7

Pallio. *See* Palio

Pallione:

Guido's painting of, *see under* Guido Reni

Palliser, Alice, m. John Clough:

(?) Du Deffand, Mme, pities, **7**. 116

(?) mob makes insane, by demolishing her house, **33**. 96

Palliser, Sir Hugh (1723–96), cr. (1773) Bt; Adm.; M.P.:

Admiralty and Parliamentary posts vacated by, **24**. 444

Admiralty reached by, after escape from Portsmouth, **24**. 442

at Court, **29**. 27

coat of, pulled by mob, **24**. 442

conduct of, at Ushant, **29**. 48

court martial of: **33**. 75n; begins, **24**. 459; demanded by the Admiralty, **24**. 444; ends in acquittal, **24**. 474–5; expected to end in acquittal, **24**. 464; Mann interested in, **24**. 478; oblivion preferable to, **24**. 453

Craufurd, but not HW, sorry for, **33**. 85

disgrace of, **33**. 96, 98

Fox's motion for censuring preferment of, defeated, **29**. 100–1

furniture of, removed, **24**. 442

Greenwich Hospital appointment of: **33**. 207–9; not censured by Parliament, **25**. 118

house of, in Pall Mall: **24**. 442n, **33**. 141n; stoned, **28**. 450n

House of Commons may ask George III to remove, as Gen. of the Marines and gov. of Scarborough, **24**. 446

Keppel exonerated from charges of, **7**. 106, 112, 116

—— risks reputation to save that of, **24**. 474

——'s court martial caused by, **24**. 427, **28**. 453n

——'s court martial will probably be regretted by, **24**. 435

——'s debate with, in House of Commons, **33**. 248n

——'s duel with, falsely reported, **28**. 434

——'s quarrel with: **24**. 424n; rumoured, **24**. *406*; to be investigated again, **25**. 103

——'s signals disobeyed by, because of rotten mast, **24**. 474

La Rochemaure to be pursued by, in *Shrewsbury*, **21**. 431n

Mann not solicitous for fate of, **24**. 434

mob breaks into house of, despite soldiers and constables, **24**. 442

North defends, in House of Commons, **33**. 248n

'Palisser'd' used to mean plundered, **33**. 141

Sandwich toasts, **29**. 47

sister of, has house demolished, **33**. 96

squadron of, sailing of, **24**. 384n, 408n

unpopularity of, **31**. 193

wounded in leg, **7**. 112

Palliser, Rebecca (d. before 1789), m. William Walters:

(?) Du Deffand, Mme, sorry for, **7**. 116

(?) mob makes insane, by demolishing her house, **33**. 96

Palliser, Ursula (ca 1722–96), m. John Fletcher:

(?) Du Deffand, Mme, sorry for, **7**. 116

(?) mob makes insane, by demolishing her house, **33**. 96

Pall Mall, London:

Almack's Club in, **28**. 104n, **38**. 511

Anson's 'Aquapulca' triumph passes through, **30**. 54

Augusta, Ps of Brunswick lives in, **32**. 68n

Backwell's bank at 'Grasshopper' in, **22**. 279n

Bedford, Ds of, has house in, **11**. 121, 199

—— takes Cowper's house in, **33**. 522n

Bland's guests pelt mob in, with bottles and glasses, **30**. 84

Calthorpe walks down, **9**. 56

Carlton House in, **33**. 498

——'s screen and front on, **42**. 274n

Chenevix, Mrs, has shop near, **13**. 103n

Chidley Court in, **42**. 47n

Christie's rooms in, **12**. 270, **23**. 210n, **25**. 543n

Clement, Jane, returns to Sir Edward Walpole's house in, **36**. 321–2

Cocoa Tree in, **25**. 12n

Conway's house in, **3**. 275n

—— wants cheap, snug house near, **37**. 184

[Pall Mall, London, *continued*]

Cosway addressed in, **42.** 187

——'s house in, **11.** 15n

Croft and Backwell in, **33.** 116n

Croft, banker in, **42.** 198

Cumberland, D. of, lives in, **23.** 7n

—— moves furniture from house in, **23.** 358n

Dalton's print warehouse in, acquired by Christie, **32.** 289n

Deards, William, has shop in, **21.** 296n

Dodsley, bookseller in, **33.** 579n, **40.** 148

Douglas, Sir John, lives in, **22.** 155n

Edwards, bookseller in, **15.** 212n, **35.** 436n

fight in, next to Dr Graham's, **33.** 335

Friedrich III of Saxe-Gotha takes house in, **17.** 331n

George III and Q. Charlotte stoned in, **34.** 212n

Germain's house in, **24.** 255n

Gloucester, D. of, gives up house in, to D. of Cumberland, **7.** 366

Graham takes Schomberg House in, **33.** 335n

Gunning, Mrs, returns to, **11.** 201n

Gunnings move from, **11.** 205n

HW sees woman through window in, **38.** 199

HW tries to call on De Saussure in, **41.** 165

Hamilton's studio in, **32.** 140n

Harrises' house in, visited and criticized by HW, **38.** 42

house in, Cts of Orford's claim to money from sale of, **25.** 162–3

Jervais's window after Reynolds's 'Nativity' exhibited in, **33.** 417

Keppel, Mrs, has house in, **33.** 191, **34.** 189n

looking-glasses sought in shops of, **20.** 141

mail from France robbed in, **25.** 619

Marlborough's house in, **21.** 512n

Nicol addressed in, **42.** 375

'nymphs and shepherds tend their flocks in,' **11.** 290

Palliser's house in, **24.** 442n, **33.** 141n

paving of, Holbach thinks, composed of lava or deluge stones, **30.** 208

Rinuccini arrives at his lodgings in, **19.** 307n

robbery committed in, **29.** 59, **35.** 505

Royal Academy exhibits at Christie's in, **32.** 289n

—— in, **23.** 210n

Royal Hotel in, **33.** 351n, 399n

Russell, Lord John, in, **11.** 205n

Russell, Lord William, has house in, **12.** 150

St Alban's Tavern near, **20.** 50

Sandwich's house in, **9.** 314

Schomberg House in, **9.** 316, **33.** 335n

Seyffert, printer in, **21.** 403n

Shakespeare Gallery in, **42.** 283n

Shrewsburys live in, **17.** 140n

Smyrna Coffee-House in, **29.** 159n

Star and Garter tavern in, **34.** 23n, **38.** 501, 503

taverns in, **37.** 444

Temple's house in, **23.** 132n

'tirewomen' of, **35.** 249

Vemberght, Mme, milliner in, **32.** 120n

Waldegrave, Cts, gives loo party in, **38.** 371

Walpole, Sir Edward, lives in, **9.** 235, **30.** 136

—— turns house in, over to Mrs Keppel, **24.** 349n

—— writes from, **36.** 14, 62, 105, 106

Walpole, Sir Robert, gives freehold in, to son Edward, **36.** 14n

Yates, Mrs, has house in, **33.** 301n

York House in, **22.** 270n

Pallon grosso:

English travellers to introduce, at home, **17.** 132

Ferdinand of Naples enjoys, **25.** 600

public game performed outside Florentine walls, **25.** 600

Palluau, Comtesse de. *See* Bouthillier de Chavigny, Louise-Françoise

Pallucci, Natalis Joseph (1719–97), Florentine physician and surgeon:

Young Pretender treated by, **25.** *394*

(?) ——'s approaching apoplexy predicted by, **25.** 245

Palma, Jacopo (1544–1628):

paintings by, at the Escurial, **16.** 180n

Palma città (Italy):

earthquake account mentions, **25.** 376

Palmer, ——:

Bedford sends on, to Honiton, **23.** 139n

Palmer, ——, glazier:

HW calls on, to pay bill and complain about it, **20.** 391, 396, 401

HW mentions, **20.** 326

silk waistcoat and wife's and son's portraits owned by, **20.** 396

Palmer, Miss:

Burney calls on, **42.** 330n

Palmer, Mr:

Berry, Mary, as cold as, **11.** 16

HW to be visited by, in Berkeley Sq., **12.** 139

Palmer, Mrs:

HW to be visited by, in Berkeley Sq., **12.** 139

Palmer, Anne (1662–1722) otherwise Fitzroy, m. (1674) Thomas Lennard, cr. (1674) E. of Sussex:

marriage of, **35.** 138

Palmer, (?) Charles (d. 1769):

HW objected to 'pretensions' of, **41.** 206

HW tells G. Bedford not to connive at failure of, to give accounts, **41.** 172

Palmer, John (ca 1742–98), actor:

School for Scandal well acted by, **41.** 363

Palmer, John (1742–1818):

mail coaches of, **33.** 480n

Palmer, John Fysche (1741–1814), M.D.:

Carter to send proposals to, **16.** 193

head comes to HW from, **2.** 275n, **16.** 192–3

Palmer, Mary (d. 1757), m. (1738) Daniel Finch, 7th E. of Winchilsea:

Haszlang ogled by, **9.** 185

Selwyn expects, to ogle Moroccan ambassador, **9.** 185

Palmer, Mary, m. Hon. Dr Coote Molesworth: escapes fire at sister-in-law's house, **22.** 139, **38.** 201

Palmer, Mary (ca 1750–1820), m. (1792) Murrough O'Brien, 4th E. of Inchiquin, cr. (1800) M. of Thomond: Nuneham visited by, **33.** 54

social relations of, with Mrs Ord, **31.** 213

Palmer, Robert (d. 1787), solicitor; agent of D. of Bedford: Bedford, D. of, orders, to have houses ready, **33.** 521

Palmer, Theophila (ca 1756–1848), m. (1781) Robert Lovell Gwatkin: Nuneham visited by, **33.** 54

Palmer, Thomas Fysche (1747–1802): brother of, **16.** 193n

Palmer, W., artist: Louisa drawn by, **33.** 490n

Palmerston, Vct. See Temple, Henry (ca 1673–1757); Temple, Henry (1739–1802); Temple, Henry John (1784–1865)

Palmerston, Vcts. See Mee, Mary

Palmieri, Villa (Villa de Tre Visi), near Fiesole, Italy: Cowper acquires, **20.** 191n

—— gives concert at, **23.** 64

farces performed at, **23.** 325–6

HW has picture of, **20.** 191

Mann rides from, on horseback, **20.** 191

Palmira. See Palmyra

Palm tree; palm trees: at Petraia, astonishes Morice by its size, **22.** 29

in Cook's *Voyage*, **33.** 436

Johnson says that Palmyra is an Irish bog planted with, **25.** 638

state coach adorned with, **22.** 104

Wilkes and daughter depicted under, **33.** 138

Palmyra: effects of, imitated in modern landscape, **21.** 418

Johnson says, is a bog in Ireland, **25.** 638

London may resemble, **23.** 569

ruins of: St Paul's will resemble, **24.** 62; *see also* Wood, Robert: *Ruins of Palmyra*

small trading city, not capital of empire, **35.** 160

Temple of the Sun at, London Pantheon more beautiful than, **31.** 167

Wood's tombstone must stress his achievements at, **41.** 247

Paloma, La, ship: in Spanish fleet, **17.** 286

Palombo, Domenico, Mann's secretary at Florence: accused of being cheat and liar, **17.** 38n

Chute gives Penny's letter to, **35.** 17

'does not love trouble,' **17.** 38

French not familiar to, **20.** 329

George II's speech copied by, **17.** 38

greenhouse collapse in Mann's garden first discovered by, **20.** 94

HW may remember, **20.** 465, **22.** 466

Hollands receive messages through, from Mann, **22.** 466

Lami's request to, **22.** 13, 24

Lucchese secretary tells, of lack of news, **20.** 465

Mann informed by, of would-be duellist, **13.** 202

—— quotes, **17.** 240, 432

——'s correspondence with abbé at Rome kept from, **17.** 114

—— sends message by, **17.** 342

——'s letters copied by, **17.** 97, **20.** 275

—— supposes, to be faithful, **20.** 275

—— told by, of edict against export of antiquities, **20.** 465

—— wishes to replace, **17.** 157–8, 172, 189

office letters copied by, in Mann's letter-books, **20.** 275

paper carried by, in hat, **20.** 465

'sedate,' **22.** 466

solemn and stupid as ever, **22.** 13

spelling of, bad, **18.** 240

Voltaire's epistle copied by, **20.** 329

wages and duties of, **17.** 157–8

Palpitation; palpitations: HW has, **34.** 199

Palsa, Johann (1752–92), player of French horn: HW hears, **33.** 471

Palsy: Bath, Cts of, attributes paralytic stroke to, **21.** 232, 234

gout may turn into, **2.** 298, **24.** 67, **25.** 402

Keck, Lady Susan, harangues Shaw about, **30.** 54

Kingston, Ds of, said to have, **28.** 235

Milles's, **2.** 242

Montagu jokes about, **10.** 275

newspapers attribute, to HW, **22.** 461

occurrences of, **9.** 300, **10.** 269, 275, **18.** 225, **36.** 210, **37.** 341

Shirley, Lady Frances, dies of, **28.** 412

strokes of: **29.** 296, **33.** 130, 373, **35.** 350–1, **37.** 580, **39.** 197; rumoured, **31.** 9, 127; *see also* Stroke, paralytic

symptoms of, described, **39.** 280

treatment for, bleeding and blisters, **21.** 15

See also Apoplexy

Paltzig. See Palzig

Palude Pontine. See Pontine marshes

Palzig (Germany): battle of: **21.** 316, **38.** 23–4; falsely reported as Prussian victory, **21.** 315n, **30.** 156, **35.** 293

Pam (knave of clubs in loo game): card of, HW fixes up, with verses for Ds of Grafton, **38.** 89

'coterie of', Viry, Contessa di, sends regards to, **41.** 203

HW jokes about levees of, **35.** 334

HW looks like father of, **35.** 304

HW might raise regiment dressed as, **38.** 40

HW will raise altar to, **22.** 17

[Pam, *continued*]
trump, in loo, **43**. 123
See also under Loo
Pamela —— (ca 1773–1831), m. 1 (1792) Lord Edward Fitzgerald; m. 2 (1800) Joseph Pitcairn:
Bath and London visited by, **34**. 138n
marriage of, **34**. 177
Orléans's death unfortunate for, **12**. 61–2
relation of Mme de Genlis, **33**. 482, 490
SH visited by, **33**. 482–3
'Pamela' (of Richardson's *Pamela*):
Du Deffand, Mme, does 'portrait' of, **4**. 32–3
Pamela. See under Goldoni, Carlo; Richardson, Samuel
Pamfili, Benedetto (1675–1760), Duca di San Martino; Principe di Valmontone, Mendola, and San Martino, 1747:
belly of, large, **19**. 445
clothes of, **19**. 445
Doria has former palace of, **23**. 109
Florence visited by, **19**. 444
parsimony of, **19**. 445
Pisa the home of, **19**. 445
Pamfili, Camillo (ca 1673–1747), Principe di Meldola:
brother is heir to fortune of, **19**. 444–5
Doria has former palace of, **23**. 109
Pamfili. *See also* Doria Pamfili
Pamfili palace, Rome:
sarcophagus in, **42**. 268n
Pamphili. *See* Pamfili
Pamphlet; pamphlets:
about India, **38**. 344–5
against Franklin, **39**. 326
anti-Jesuit, **21**. 383
Bolingbroke's, **37**. 112
Egmont's, **20**. 43
HW abused in, **38**. 439
HW buys old volumes of, **35**. 163
HW does not read, political, **39**. 509
HW enjoys, **9**. 195
HW has no taste for, **25**. 503
HW sends: to Chute, **35**. 48; to Hertford, **38**. 422, 424; to Mann, **18**. 31, 89, 353–4, **21**. 90, 554
HW suspected of writing, **9**. 416
impertinent, **3**. 202
Italian, given to HW by Walker, **42**. 365
Kildare abused in, **37**. 410
Lort returns, to HW. **16**. 202
Mann, Horace II, seeks list of, from HW for Mann, **24**. 451
Marchmont's, **37**. 450
Meredith, Sir William, writes, **39**. 318
newspaper letters supersede, **42**. 501
on Byng, **37**. 473
on colonies and Stamp Act, HW jokes about, **31**. 97
on East India Co.'s affairs, **30**. 237
on Ireland, **25**. 11
on Maclaine, **20**. 188
on Pitt, sometimes attributed to HW. **38**. 144

on Sackville, **38**. 32–3, 35
political: are scurrilous, **38**. 187; HW dislikes, **31**. 60, 74; new, read only by Common Council, **31**. 153
scarcer, now that anonymous letters can be printed in newspapers, **22**. 169n, **24**. 451
slavery defended in, **31**. 280
Wren's, sold, **40**. 348
Pamphleteers:
now writers of letters to newspapers, **24**. 451
Pamphlet shop; pamphlet shops:
Frederick II's death little noticed in, **36**. 241
Pan; pans:
earthen, Clement XIV's bowels break, by fermentation, **24**. 43
HW buys, old broken, at Mrs Kennon's sale, **37**. 439
water-souchy kept in, **35**. 182
Panama, president of. *See* Martínez de la Vega, Dionisio
Panama:
Anson captures ships off coast of, **18**. 478
Pan and Syrinx:
HW buys cups and saucer decorated with, **7**. 414
Panaro (river in Italy):
almost dry, **17**. 464
Austrian army nearer, **17**. 432–3, 464
Berrys' crossing of, described, **11**. 149n
campaign to reopen on, **18**. 45
Charles Emmanuel III may cross, **17**. 472
——'s troops await his permission to cross, **18**. 197
—— tries to bridge, **17**. 449
Gages crosses, **19**. 35
—— to reopen campaign on, **18**. 55
German cavalry crosses, **18**. 197
Lobkowitz crosses, **19**. 30
—— retires to, **19**. 22
Montemar approaches, **17**. 427
—— said to have crossed, **17**. 455
Sardinian troops near, **17**. 424, 432–3
skirmishes near, **17**. 432
Spaniards blow up bridges over, after retreat, **18**. 154, 161
Spaniards cross: **18**. 151, **19**. 30; at Bondeno, **17**. 464, 472
—— may return to, **18**. 76
—— watched by Austrians and Sardinians near, **17**. 489
Spanish army retreats from, **18**. 196
Spanish retreat from, **18**. 163
Traun does not dare to leave, **18**. 76
—— does not expect to cross, **18**. 66
—— on other side of, **18**. 154
'Pancake, John.' *See* Panciatichi, Giovanni Gualberto
Pancalier, Marquis de:
Benedict XIV's act of acknowledgment sent to Vienna by, **19**. 158n
Panchaud, Isaac (1726–89), Paris banker:
bankruptcy of, over East India stock, **23**. 133

Broglie, Marquise de, to send to, for pimpernel seeds left by Fox, 30. 251

Conway addressed in care of, Rue St-Sauveur, 39. 245

—— to direct HW's letter to, 39. 252

(?) Du Deffand, Mme, hopes, can dispose of Bp of Mirepoix's purchase, 6. 252, 255, 257

(?) —— paid by, 6. 349

(?) Echlin's debt guaranteed by, 7. 122

false American reports sent by, to manipulate stocks, 32. 396

HW meets, on road to Calais, 31. 117

HW to be repaid by, for ruffles and shoes for Cts of Hertford, 39. 264

HW to pay: for Gibbon's snuff-box, 6. 303; in behalf of Mme de Mirepoix, 6. 136, 149

Hertford, Cts of, to pay, for watches, 39. 118

(?) Leroy knows, 6. 255

letter to Craufurd to be directed to, 32. 271

(?) social relations of, in Paris, 7. 272, (?) 284, 285, 294, 353

Panchaud, Isabella, m. (1767) William Knight, brother of 'E. of Catherlough':

(?) social relations of, in Paris, 7. 294, 307, 309

Panchot. See Panchaud

Panciatichi, Signora. See Corsi, Giulia (d. 1744)

Panciatichi, Bandino (1719–61):

health of, smallpox, 17. 148, 150, 416

house of, not good for ball, 17. 122

Rinuccini discusses Albizzi's fistula with, in Mann's presence, 17. 481

son born to, 18. 121

wedding feast of, 17. 416

wedding night of, 17. 150, 169

wife's present from, on birth of heir, 18. 121

Panciatichi, Giovanni Gualberto (1721–50), 'young Panciatichi'; 'Giovannino':

Cambridge visited by, 14. 31

darkened but enlivened, 19. 371

England to be visited by, 19. 308

English visit improves the mind but ruins the constitution of, 20. 117

fashionable at The Hague, 19. 371

Franchi, Cocchi, and French and German surgeons attend, 20. 36

Grifoni, Mme, attended by, 17. 37

HW's civilities to, in England, deeply appreciated by, 20. 36

health of: fever, 20. 36; humour in the knee, 20. 36; knee-pan broken, 17. 202; measles, 17. 381, 416

London visited by, 19. 371

Lovat's execution attended by, 19. 387

Malta knight, 17. 381, 18. 121

Mann calls on, 20. 36

Parigi receives settlement from, 17. 111

Paris visited by, 20. 36

sister-in-law's present from, on birth of heir, 18. 121

Suares, Teresa, may be married by, 18. 197

to leave England, 19. 435

Vitelli, Mme, abandoned by, 18. 197, 333

—— deserted by, for the Parigi, 17. 111

—— pursued by, 18. 520

Panciatichi, Niccolò (1742–1811):

birth of, 18. 121

Electress godmother to, 18. 121

Mann attends baptism of, 18. 121

Panciatichi, Palazzo, at Florence:

HW mentions, 11. 154

Panciatichi family:

HW hopes that 'Onslow' affair discredited English knowledge of, 19. 510

Panciatichi-Ximenes, Palazzo, at Florence:

in Via de' Pinti, 17. 122n

Pancoucke, André-Joseph (1700–53), bookseller:

Dictionnaire des proverbes françois by, (?) owned by Mme du Deffand, 8. 25

Pancras Lane, London:

Hillier, merchant in, 40. 290n

'Pancrazio, Signor':

Pertici acts, 20. 357

'Pandæmonium.' See under Milton, John: Paradise Lost

'Pandæmonium, The.' See under Williams, Sir Charles Hanbury

'Pandæmonium':

National Convention called, 12. 23, 71, 86, 120

Pandolfini, Mme. See Bardi, Maria Costanza

Pandolfini, Elisabetta (d. 1750), m. (1737) Giuseppe Maria Gabburri:

(?) Libri or Nerli to be cicisbeo to, 17. 150

(?) opera attended by, in Mann's box, 17. 136

(?) returns to Spain and husband, 18. 46

(?) Ricasolis entertain, 17. 136

(?) Serristori, Andrea, dismissed by, 17. 136, 150

Pandolfini, Conte Ferdinando (1716–80); Col. of militia; Gen.:

Albizzi, Marchesa degli, attended by, 17. 33

—— brings, to Mann's concert, 18. 12

—— cicisbea of, 18. 12, 29

—— deprived of company of, 17. 156

—— quarrels with, 18. 369

—— would enjoy telling Buckingham's story to, 18. 307

brother of, breaks with the Ginori, 17. 52

Feroni, Mme, entertains, 17. 33

HW mentions, 17. 42

HW sends muff and tippet to, 17. 45, 47, 52

(?) hæmorrhoid operation avoided by, 17. 59

Mann called on by, 17. 52

—— discusses HW with, 17. 33

—— engages Leghorn lawyer to draw up reply to, 21. 21n

—— to entertain, at dinner, 19. 501

militia regiment of: arrives at Prato and Pistoia, 18. 100n; at Leghorn, 17. 156, 266, 288

sings, at Mann's entertainment, 18. 12, 29

Pandolfini, Conte Roberto (1705–83):

(?) acting Grand Chambellan, 25. 249n

[Pandolfini, Conte Roberto, *continued*]
becomes Count and secretary of Regency, 19. 501
Cambridge visited by, 14. 31
Capponi, Abbé, lives with, 18. 149–50
English visit of: 14. 31, 19. 72, 308, 329, 331, 348, 353–4, 435, 501; ruins his mind and constitution, 20. 117
Eszterházys entertained by, at dinner, 20. 50
Francis I's death notified by, 22. 329n
Ginori, Signora, has affair with, 17. 52, 111
HW entertains, on fast day, 19. 331
HW knew, in England, 19. 501
HW's friend, 19. 72
Harrach accompanies, from England, 19. 435
health of: (?) hæmorrhoids, 17. 59; ill, 19. 353–4, 20. 2
Mannelli's correspondence with, 19. 369
(?) Mann informed by, about audience with Leopold, 25. 249n
——'s correspondence with, about captured Tuscan ships, 21. 288n
—— to entertain, at dinner, 19. 501
—— writes to, about Rubens's heads copied by Maria Hadfield, 25. 646n
mother's dowry must be equalled by wife of, 17. 137–8
Niccolini receives letter of banishment from, 20. 2, 24
permit to export vases to Sir Robert Walpole requested of, 17. 24n
promoter of music, 18. 150
put to bed, 19. 348
ships' seizures protested by, 21. 269n
Suares, Teresa, might marry, 17. 137–8, 171, 202
Pandolfini, Palazzo, in Florence:
Raphael the designer of, 11. 154
Pandolfini family:
HW hopes that 'Onslow' affair discredited English knowledge of, 19. 510
'Pandolfo.' See under *Commèdia in commèdia, La*
Pandora:
box of, 9. 1
Pandour; pandours ('panduri'):
Conway sees, at review, 37. 141–2
Frederick II renders, powerless, 9. 206
HW expects Austrians to have, 33. 530
left at Prague to annoy the French, 18. 58
Rhine crossed by, at Walluf, 37. 159
Sauromatæ sometimes stands for, 30. 73
to be placed outside Vienna, 17. 144
Panel; panels:
Boyle, Charlotte, paints, for Boyle Farm library, 31. 251, 35. 390
Panettien, François:
Boncifort's letter from, 24. 437n
Pange, Marquise de. See Espinoy, Jacquette-Philippe-Renée d'
Pangbourne, Berks:
auction at, missed by HW, 40. 197

Panin, Count:
Bender captured by, 23. 245n
Panin, Nikita Ivanovich (1718–83), 'governor' of Paul I:
Catherine II advised by, to befriend both France and England, 24. 520n
—— persuaded by, not to attend Peter III's funeral, 22. 71n
——'s rejection of English alliance drafted by, 25. 26n
Goertz to alert, to Austrian designs on Poland, 25. 45n
(?) in power, 22. 59
Paul I's education by, aided by French and Russian masters, 32. 59n
Panmure, E. of. See Maule, William
Pannier; panniers:
Robinson, Sir Thomas, has no space for, in ballroom, 37. 55
Pannilini, Porzia (b. 1729), m. (1746) Giovanni Sansedoni:
York, D. of, entertained by, 22. 224
Pannini, Giovanni Paolo (1691 or 2–1765), painter:
HW buys architectural drawings by, 35. 428n
pictures by, bought by HW, 26. 7
Pannocchieschi d'Elci, Marchese Lodovico (1706–88):
HW civil to, in England, 18. 459
HW met, at Mme Grifoni's, 18. 459
Mann to attend ball given by, 18. 60
Niccolini's relative married by, 18. 60, 85
Pannocchieschi d'Elci, Ranieri (1670–1761), cardinal:
'dying' candidate of Corsini faction in Conclave, 37. 57–8
Pannoni's coffee-house at Florence ('Pannonia'):
abbés spread false reports in, 18. 557
Cerretesi's English notes to entertain, 17. 503
Florentine coffee-house, 17. 97n, 503n, 19. 460n
Florentine nobility meet at, 17. 503n, 20. 496
gazettes print 'news' worthy of gossipers at, 17. 417
gossip at: about Mann and Niccolini, 20. 7; more enduring than that of London, 19. 460
gossiping material lacking at, 19. 459
HW says that England could be routed by a detachment from, 20. 496
Richecourt's departure discussed at, 17. 97
scandal banished from, 19. 476
Sturgis avoids, 17. 462
See also under Manzuoli, Giovanni
'Panone'. See Manzuoli, Giovanni
Panshaw. See Panchaud
Pansy; pansies:
Flora throws, 30. 328
Pantagruel. See under Rabelais, François
Pantaléon, Jacques. *See* Urban IV

Pantalon, character in pantomime and Italian comedy:
HW takes Friday's father for, 33. 362
looks like real Venetian, 11. 365
Panthémont, Abbess of. *See* Béthisy de Mézières, Marie-Catherine de
Panthémont, Abbey of, at Paris:
Browne, Miss, goes to, 9. 152n
Cholmondeley, Henrietta Maria, denied return to, 4. 400
—— to be pupil at, 4. 230, 233
Cholmondeley, Hester Frances, remains at, 4. 404
—— to be pupil at, 4. 230, 233
Du Deffand, Mme, to send to, for news of Maria Fagnani, 7. 148
Fagnani, Maria, at, 7. 145
—— to be pupil at, 7. 80, 141
HW sends kisses to Cholmondeley girls at, 36. 55
visitors to: Choiseul, Duchesse de, 4. 273; Cholmondeley, Mrs, 7. 332; Du Deffand, Mme, 4. 300; (?) Gergy, Comtesse de, 7. 332; HW, 7. 332
Pantheon (classical):
Kedleston has statues of gods of, 10. 230
Pantheon, Oxford St, London:
Aguiari, Lucrezia, sings at, 39. 224
Albany, Cts of, sits in King's box at, 11. 272
almost finished, 23. 298
burnt, 34. 137
Damer, Mrs, meets Mrs Cholmondeley at, 11. 235n
dome of, painted with gods and goddesses, 28. 31
erected in Oxford Road, 23. 210
George III supports, 11. 203
HW calls, most beautiful edifice in England, 28. 102
HW describes, 11. 202
HW describes as 'new winter Ranelagh,' 23. 210, 298
HW praises, 31. 167
HW takes Guines and Lévis to, 23. 298
Haymarket vanquished by, 11. 206
Lunardi's exhibitions at, 25. 543
masked ball at, 23. 476n
masquerade at, 1. 311n, 5. 230, 24. 103, 28. 31
Pacchierotti sings at, 11. 307
reopens, 5. 230n
Salisbury gives O'Reilly licence for operas at, 11. 95
Savoir Vivre Club's masquerade at, 24. 103n
subscription ball to be held at, 24. 481
subscription fête at, 39. 330–1
Panthéon, at Paris:
French 'gods' in, 12. 192
Rousseau's body removed to, 29. 282n, 31. 383n
Pantheon, at Rome:
Alexander VII first proposes modernization of, 21. 37n

Benedict XIV authorizes repairs to, 21. 37n
cupola to be added to, 21. 37
frieze of, Greek buildings at Paris said to be copied from, 23. 158
HW dislikes, 21. 31
London Pantheon's dome resembles that of, 23. 298
Posio, Paolo, plans modernization of, 21. 37n
said to have fallen down, 21. 31, 37
St Hedwig's portal in Berlin imitates, 20. 329n
Pantheon, The:
people of fashion satirized in, 32. 147–8
'Pantheon chapel':
HW's name for SH cabinet, 22. 523
Panther, English ship:
at Port Mahon, 17. 285
Martin commands, 18. 15n
Panther; panthers:
exhibited at York, 28. 91
Panthou, Mme de. *See* La Martillière de Chançay, Anne-Louise-Thérèse
Panthous:
Euphorbus, son of, 12. 33
Pantiles. *See under* Tunbridge Wells
Pantin; pantins:
HW compares himself with, 31. 100
no longer fashionable in Paris, 31. 99, 40. 385
See also Puppet shows
Pantolomina:
Sauveterre and 'Spaccatavola' compared with, 19. 356
Pantomime; pantomimes:
at Richmond, for Edwin's benefit, attended by HW, 35. 399
Boyle, Miss, writes, and dances in it, 42. 204
Fleetwood supports, 18. 538
Hawkins, Sir John, on, 32. 334
London tries to expel, from theatres, 18. 538
of Bastille horrors, 34. 71
of Garrick's *Cymon*, 34. 135n
transformations in, 33. 361n
Wales, P. of (George IV), too young to understand, 33. 135
See also Choice of Harlequin; *Lun's Ghost*; Sheridan, Richard B.: *Robinson Crusoe*
Panton, Mary (d. 1793), m. (1750) Peregrine Bertie, 3d D. of Ancaster, 1742:
Buckingham House ball attended by, 38. 290
Charlotte, Q., followed by, in Coronation procession, 38. 127
—— has, as first lady of Bedchamber, and Mistress of the Robes, 21. 518, 38. 96
—— to include, in Household, 9. 377
children of, 11. 255
Claverings elope from house of, 34. 18n
consents to daughter's marriage to 4th E. of Cholmondeley, 11. 241
(?) Court ball attended by, 9. 403
dances little, at private Court ball, 38. 143

[Panton, Mary, *continued*]
Dauberval's patroness, **38**. 483
daughter married at Berkeley Sq. house of, **33**. 96n
death of, **12**. 43–4
Florence visited by, **25**. 618n
French prefer, to other English duchesses, **22**. 155
HW ridicules, **21**. 156
HW summoned by, to sign E. of Cholmondeley's marriage articles, **11**. 250–1
health of, bad, **11**. 255
house of, in Berkeley Sq., **11**. 255n, **33**. 96n, **34**. 108n
marriage date of, corrected, **43**. 72
misfortunes of, **33**. 202–3
never sober, **24**. 499
Paris visited by, **22**. 155
print of, at Park Place, **39**. 550
son's attentions to, **33**. 110
son's bequest to, **24**. 494
son's engagement acknowledged by, **33**. 114
Spa visited by, **11**. 255
to winter in France, **2**. 235
Waldegrave, Lady Anna Horatia, taken by, to Lady Elizabeth Burrell's, **33**. 164
—— told by, that son would have married her, **24**. 494
weeps at daughter's wedding, **11**. 255
Panton, Paul (1727–97), antiquary; barrister:
HW's correspondence with, **41**. 160
HW tells Ann Bransom to admit, to SH, **43**. 164
Panton, Thomas (ca 1697–1782), Master of the King's Running Horses:
daughter of, **2**. 235n, **11**. 241n, **21**. 156n, **24**. 499
'disreputable horse jock of Newmarket,' **24**. 499
horse of, entered in race, **13**. 89n
son of, **1**. 200
Panton, Thomas (1731–1808), sportsman:
suggested for Cambridgeshire seat, **1**. 200
Pantoufles:
HW's 'high historical,' **20**. 503
sentiments in, **9**. 83
Paoletti, Gaspare (1727–1813), architect:
Villa Medici remodelled by, **24**. 190n
Paoli, Fra. *See* Sarpi, Paolo
Paoli, Clemente (1715–93), Corsican general:
Corsican rebellion financed by, **24**. 26n
Leghorn visited by, **23**. *130*
prays at Vallombrosa, **23**. 159
prays for enemies before shooting them with perfect aim, **23**. 130, 159
retreat sought by, at Vallombrosa or La Verna, **23**. 130
Paoli, Pasquale (1725–1807), Corsican patriot:
alleged French negotiations with, fabricated to discredit him, **23**. 37–8
Barbaggio representative of, **21**. 412n
Bath and Oxford visited by, **23**. 150
birth date of, corrected, **43**. 87, 152

birthday of, celebrated by Boswell, **23**. 31n
Boswell's account of: **14**. 170, 174; *see also* Boswell, James: *Account of Corsica, An*
—— the friend of, **28**. 209
Boufflers, Chevalier de, intended to see, **8**. 137
Caprara may be taken from, **23**. 46
Chauvelin sends Louis XV's edict to, **23**. 53n
Choiseul's perfidy can be exposed by his own letters to, **23**. 154
Cocchi with, **23**. 68
Corsica fled by, to Leghorn, **23**. 96n
Corsican independence still awaited by, **23**. 130
Cosway child's godfather, **42**. 233n
defeat of, is England's disgrace, **23**. 125
dressed in scarlet and gold, **23**. 150
Du Barry, Mme, might save, **23**. 75, 81, 87, 90–1, 124
Du Deffand, Mme, enthusiastic over, **4**. 109
England approves of, **23**. 145
—— expects, to hold out in Corsican fastnesses, **23**. 121
—— may some day espouse the cause of, **23**. 159
—— pensions, **25**. 242n
—— visited by, **23**. 139, 142, 150
—— will be glad of diverting news of, **23**. 121
English supporters of, demand help for Corsica, **23**. 31
followers of, near Leghorn and Florence, **23**. 159
France said to resent English visit of, **23**. 139–40
Franco-Genoese treaty over Corsica dooms, **23**. 27
French decry, as a coward, **23**. 142
French defeated by, **23**. 75
French invasion threats alarm, **23**. 96
French offers rejected by, **23**. 36
French say, acquired a fortune on the continent, **23**. 142
French slander, **23**. 154
French try to take Corsica from, **23**. 45–7
Genoese under Matta defeated by, **22**. 156n
George III and Q. Charlotte notice, **23**. 150
goddaughter of, **11**. 285n
HW despises conduct of, in fleeing from Corsica, **15**. 332
HW sees, at Court, **23**. 150, 159
HW suggests, as fit company for Benedict Arnold, **25**. 242
HW wishes Lord Hood had not recognized, **12**. 63
Johnson, Dr Samuel, speaks to, **29**. 104n
Joseph II confers with, at Mantua, **23**. 137, 140
——'s letter about, quoted by Beauvau to HW, **23**. 142, 154
—— writes about, to Leopold, **23**. 137, 154
Leghorn visited by, **23**. 130, **43**. 282

Leopold talks with, at Florence, **23**. 130, 136–7

letter of, enclosed by Mann to HW, **23**. 68

life of, in danger, **23**. 81

London visited by, **7**. 368

Louenberg confers with, **22**. 157n

Louis XV's expulsion of Mme du Barry would undo, **23**. 90–1

Macaulay, Mrs, does not blight English visit of, **23**. 150

—— quarrels with, **36**. 55–6

Mann should persuade Joseph II to rescue, **23**. 107

——'s letters from, probably intercepted, **23**. 150

—— told by, that Corsicans will submit to France unless aided by England, **23**. 51–2

—— to write to, **23**. 159

Marbeuf's ultimatum to, **23**. 46

Martin's portrait of, **23**. 211n

Pembroke might escort to London, **23**. 138

—— to accompany, through Germany, **23**. 137n

plot against, discovered, **23**. 68

SH visited by, **12**. 222

troops of, to occupy ports evacuated by the French, **22**. 536

Versailles said to be visited by, for peerage and pension, **23**. 31

Viennese mob tries to honour, **23**. 140

Paolo; paoli (coins). See Paul

Paolucci, Camillo (1692–1763), cardinal, 1743; nuncio to Vienna 1738–46:

Benedict XIV gets information from, **17**. 465

—— makes, cardinal, **18**. 302n

Maria Theresa may dismiss, from Vienna, if Valenti is still supported by Benedict XIV, **18**. 56

Paolucci, Marchese Giuseppe (1726–85), Modenese envoy to England 1754–7, 1763–4, to France 1760–3; Modenese minister of commerce:

dishonest, **38**. 306

Pecquigny warns, against Virrette, **38**. 306

Papacy, the:

Calvin's opposition to, **34**. 111

Fénelon submits to, **6**. 435

Jansenists opposed by, **21**. 48n

National Assembly's treatment of, **34**. 120

now a mere gouty chair, **22**. 254

power of, restrained by parliament of Paris, **5**. 213–14

Quietists opposed by, **21**. 48n

See also Roman Catholic Church

Papal states, the, in Italy:

Alfieri banished from, **25**. 397

ambassadors to and from Holy See at, see under Ambassador

armies in, **18**. 473

bandits in, **17**. 29n

Del Monte family invades, **20**. 423, 428–9, 442, 445, 446

food shortage in, acute, **22**. 453

French ships in, should be burnt, **18**. 453

grain not to be exported by, to other parts of Italy till French and Spanish wants are filled, **23**. 430

incident similar to plot of *Mysterious Mother* occurred in, **24**. 517

Jesuits' colleges in, seized, **23**. 504

—— excluded from, **22**. 517

——'s wealth in, **23**. 517

—— to be distributed in, **23**. 473

map of, Newcastle asks Mann to procure, **20**. 459

Montemar may pass through, **17**. 226, 229, 261, 342

Neapolitan convoys in ports of, should be burnt by English, **18**. 453

Neapolitans may invade, **18**. 295–6, 443–4, **19**. 364

neutrality of, violated at Civita Vecchia, **17**. 8n

opera omitted in, in jubilee year, **20**. 83

ports of, neutral, **18**. 301

recalcitrant Jesuits to be banished from, **23**. 507

Sardinians ask leave to pass through, **17**. 472, 482

seamen of, fear enslavement by Turkish pirates, **17**. 16

secretary of state for, see Secretary of State, Papal

ship of: carried to Spezia, **17**. 16; from Pesaro, **17**. 8

ships of, destroyed by Colvill, **19**. 246

Spaniards may invade, **18**. 444

Spanish troops pass through, **17**. 323

Traun to march through, to Bologna, **17**. 350

Ubaldini, Cts, banished from, **19**. 497

Young Pretender to be offered residence in, **20**. 12

Paparini. See Paperini

Papa Silvia (Italy):

Spaniards at, **18**. 531

'Papefigues'; 'Papafiguière'. See Rabelais, François: *Pantagruel*

Paper:

Bowen's paper, **37**. 475

broken window in E. of Bath's house stopped up with, for four years, **30**. 89

brown and white, for Harcourt's etchings, **35**. 451

burnt, 'parson and clerk' is played with, **30**. 60

carta cerulea, **25**. 88, 93

Chute's, large, **35**. 3

coarse, in Onslow's *Popery Unmasked*, **30**. 57

common in 15th century, **16**. 241, 243

Dacre procures, for HW, **42**. 72

Florentine, **25**. 507

foolscap, HW jokes about, **18**. 204, **31**. 154

for printing, HW gets, from Tonson, **40**. 117

[Paper, *continued*]

furniture [?wall-paper]: Florence should manufacture, **20**. 362; HW and Conway buy, for Mann, **20**. 362

gilt: chimney-sweepers wear crowns of, on May 1, **25**. 275; HW wants, **40**. 308

HW writes on, to Mann, **18**. 204

green, used by Mme Roland in La Malle plan, **10**. 196

green-edged, used in 18th-century French letters and 17th-century English ones, **9**. 224

HW changes size of, for letters, **17**. 426, 502

HW furnishes, in Exchequer office, **9**. 117n

HW's: for letters, **17**. 426n; for writing, **3**. 105, 106, 121, 131; French, abominable, **31**. 63; sucks up ink, **11**. 165

HW uses Miss Hotham's, **40**. 363

HW wants Jenkins to send, **36**. 2

imperial, HW jokes about, **31**. 154

India: at Cornbury, **20**. 182; HW seems to be made of, **24**. 66; HW's 'Persian Letter' to Lincoln written on red, **30**. 35

Italian, thin but good, **11**. 300

large, HW writes on, **33**. 21

mosaics of, by Mrs Delany, **42**. 179n

nautilus of, HW is, **34**. 105

note, HW uses small size of, **10**. 197

oil, *see* Oil paper

printers' cancelled sheets consigned to trunk-makers, **42**. 368

scarce, at Ghent, **37**. 119

scraps of, with holy words, made into soup, **20**. 430

Sévigné, Mme de, has cabinet for, **33**. 150

small, HW writes on, **34**. 99

SH Press's, 'magnificent,' **31**. 316

thread, documents made into, **16**. 356

Townshend, Vcts, carries, to Brompton lodgings, **30**. 70

treillage, HW seeks, for Harcourt, **35**. 383–4

Uguccioni's poems will provide pastry shops with, **18**. 554

wall, *see* Wallpaper

wet brown: HW compares Mann to, **18**. 467, **19**. 61n, 127, **24**. 66, 521, **25**. 656; HW has iron stamina in case of, like Mann's, **24**. 521; the 18th-century adhesive tape, **43**. 257

windows of, at Florence, **24**. 232

Paper; papers (documents):

HW asks Sir C. H. Williams to bring all his books and, to Houghton, **30**. 64

HW finds missing, desired by H. Fox, **30**. 253

HW sorts and burns, **32**. 216

scurrilous, written by Lord Townshend and G. Townshend against each other, **30**. 142

Paper-Buildings. *See under* Temple, The

Paper-hanger; paper-hangers:

HW's, at SH, *see* Bromwich, Thomas

HW scolds, at SH, **20**. 371

Paperini, ——, Florentine publisher:

Lunario per la Toscana by: earthquake to be indicated in, **20**. *143*; HW to consult, **17**. 155; Roman hurricane described by, **20**. 69

Paperini, Giuseppe, Florentine postmaster:

(?) Vorontsov consorts with, **21**. 249

Paper money. *See* Money, paper

Paper Office. *See* State Paper Office

'Papers on the New Indulgence to Catholics':

Lort sends, to Cole and HW, **16**. 172

Paphos (Cyprus):

'church' of, **33**. 98

HW should not hobble to, on crutches, **31**. 69

Paris will be HW's, **32**. 25

roses of, **32**. 219

verses allude to, **37**. 76

Paphos, 'la nymphe de.' *See* Bécu, Jeanne, Mme du Barry

Papillotes:

Frederick makes squibs from, **37**. 297

See also Curling-papers

Papio, Jean, Capt.:

captured at Velletri, **18**. 494

'Papist':

Johnson, Dr Samuel, called, **32**. 225

Papist, Papists. *See* Roman Catholic; Roman Catholics

Pappenheim, Graf von:

Cowper's proxy at St Hubert installation, **25**. 568n

Papplewick, Notts:

Mason visits, **29**. 84n

Montagu, Charles, of, **9**. 238n, 361n, **10**. 352, **28**. 312n, 429n

Papyrus, Egyptian:

Latin MS on, in Pinelli sale, **42**. 240

Paraclete (France):

HW names SH hall after, **20**. 372

Haistwell's etching of, **42**. 53n

Héloïse buried at, **5**. 234n

Parade, The, St James's Park, London:

Amherst, Lady, has 'assemblies' in, **33**. 215

Paradis, Rue de, in Paris:

Soubise, Hôtel de, near, **7**. 283n

Paradis de Moncrif, François-Augustin (1687–1770), member of Académie française:

death of, **4**. 489n

Essai sur la nécessité et sur les moyens de plaire by, **5**. 43

Marquise de Monconseil's social relations with, **7**. 296, 297

Paradise:

poetic descriptions of, **35**. 397

St Augustine's, Conway likes HW's idea of, **37**. 127

Paradise Lost; *Paradise Regained*. *See under* Milton, John

Paradis terrestre (? by HW):

Mann's opinion of, **17**. 108

Paradox:

on Richard III, **42**. 302

Paraguay:
Jesuits said to endanger Portuguese sovereignty of, 21. 217n
Portugal and Spain to exchange territories in, 21. 341
Parakeet; parakeets ('perroquet'):
at Bois Prévu, 7. 293, 35. 116
cicisbeos compared to, 37. 77
duchess's, Lady Mary Coke weeps over moulting of, 31. 70n
HW cannot abandon, 9. 306
HW glad to see, 9. 350
HW's: dies, 38. 129; on his shoulder, 35. 308
one of, has clipped wings, 37. 551
Strafford, Cts of, has, 35. 275n
Parallèle de la conduite. See under La Ville, Abbé Jean-Ignace de
Parallel in the Manner of Plutarch . . . See under Spence, Joseph
Paralysis:
Acquaviva's eyesight threatened by, 19. 136
in bowels, 35. 460
Montagu has symptoms of, 10. 164
occurrences of, 20. 463, 22. 211, 23. 175, 25. 562n, 604n, 32. 309, 39. 278, 279, 280–1
See also Palsy; Stroke, paralytic
Paralytic disorder:
HW said by gazetteer to have, 22. 459, 468, 43. 48
Paralytic stroke. *See* Paralysis; Stroke: paralytic
Par and impar (game):
Roman matrons played, 30. 221
Paraphrasis poetica Genesios. See Junius, Franciscus: *Cædmonis monachi paraphrasis*
Parc-aux-Cerfs:
Louis XV's mistresses in, 22. 239n
Parchment; parchments:
deed on, 20. 547
deeds and rolls of, 16. 242
éloges of deceased written on, in Italy, to be put into tombs, 21. 170
gospel accounts on, 40. 285
HW furnishes, 9. 117n
not used except for legal documents, etc., 16. 241
ochre rubbed on, to make it appear old, 16. 342, 350
petitions inscribed upon, 25. 34
See also under Manuscript
Parc-Royal, Hôtel du, at Paris:
Beaufort's ball at, 22. 365
enlarged, 6. 81
guests at: Beaufort, 31. 71n; Buccleuch, 31. 100; Crewe, Mrs, 5. 358, 361; (?) Findlater, 32. 55, 35. 124; Fortescues, 7. 325n; Greville, Mrs, 5. 358, 361; HW, 1. 99, 4. 258, 268, 6. 81, 7. 266, 267, 10. 201n, 22. 365, 31. 109, 32. 54–5, 35. 124, 41. 61n; Hume, 41. 61n; Scott, Hon. Campbell, 31. 109; Selwyn, 7. 127n; Smith, Adam, 31. 109
HW addressed at, 41. 8

HW confined by gout in bedchamber at, 22. 348
HW's apartment at, 3. 340, 4. 258, 270–1, 384, 5. 85, 6. 209, 210, 214
St-Germain-des-Prés near, 39. 204
Simonetti, Mme, landlady of, 3. 342
Parc-Royal, Rue du, in Paris:
Canillac, Hôtel de, in, 4. 23n
Pardaillan de Gondrin, Antoine-François de (1709–41), Marquis d'Antin:
death of, reported, 17. 46
fleet of, disappears, 17. 36
half-brother of, 3. 112n, 4. 68n, 77n, 393n
marriage of, 3. 5n, 92n, 99n
squadron commanded by, 13. 228n
wife of, 3. 4n, 14. 144n
Pardaillan de Gondrin, Madeleine-Julie-Victoire de (b. 1731), m. (1753) François-Emmanuel de Crussol, Duc d'Uzès:
social relations of, in Paris, 6. 431
Pardo (Spain):
Elizabeth Farnese wins 'battle' of, 18. 195
Pardo, Convention of:
Parliamentary address on, 37. 90n
Williams, Sir C. H., opens debate on, 30. 311
Parent; parents:
HW never counsels sons to go against inclinations of, 25. 259
trials of, HW's reflections on, 25. 414
Parentalia. See under Wren, Christopher (1675–1747)
Parere (medical opinion):
Cocchi's, 19. 329
Parfaict, Claude (ca 1701–77) *and* François (1698–1753):
Histoire du Théâtre-françois, L' by: Du Deffand, Mme, owns, 8. 33n; (?) HW tells story from, 11. 292
Parfilage:
Du Deffand, Mme, gives Mme de Luxembourg a box of, 5. 298
(?) —— makes suit for HW with, 5. 270, 439
—— orders, 7. 438
verses on, 5. 439
vogue of, 3. 45n, 5. 284, 295, 383, 431, 7. 197
Parham, Sussex:
Bisshopp family of, 9. 140n, 11. 242n
Parigi, (?) Maddalena (d. ?1774), opera singer:
Panciatichi, Giovanni, makes settlement on, 17. 111
Pecori deserts the Pepi for, 17. 111, 136
Pepi, the, to shoot, for giving disease to Pecori, 17. 136–7, 144, 19. 136
Tesi's creature, 18. 302
Vitelli, Mme, jealous of Giovanni Panciatichi's attentions to, 17. 136
Parini, Abbate:
'Della Cruscan,' 25. 612n
Paris, ——, French butcher:
Mme du Deffand's receipt from, 8. 42
Paris, Matthew (ca 1200–59), historian:
Colchester, Walter de, praised by, 42. 42

[Paris, Matthew, *continued*]
Cole's correction concerning, 1. 81
Historia by, 43. 74
lives by, of Abbots of St Albans, 2. 278–9
Paris, classical hero:
HW compared with, 32. 108, 220
infant, bust of, 35. 437
Petersham, Lord, compared with, 30. 326
statue of, destroyed in Uffizi fire, 22. 68n
young, Mrs Damer's bust of, 12. 272, 273
Paris, Abp of. *See* Beaumont de Péréfixe, Hardouin de (1605–71); Beaumont du Repaire, Christophe de (1703–81)
Paris (*streets and buildings are listed under their own names*):
See Vols 3–8 *passim*
air of, 'can do wonders,' 38. 514, 516
'À la mains' from, 2. 123, 37. 103
Albany, Cts of, may be at, 24. 102
Albemarle dies at, 20. 459–60, 35. 201
—— retires from, with Mlle Gaucher, 20. 156
——'s entertainments at, 20. 156
——'s goods at, bought by Hertford and offered to Bedford, 38. 170
—— when ambassador, did not let his wife come to, 37. 353
Alexander, Alexandre, banker at, 17. 23n
Alincourt on road from, 41. 309
architecture of, 32. 260–1, 35. 429; *see also under* Architecture
aristocrats not safe in, 11. 85–6
army deserters threaten, 11. 27, 67, 39. 471
Artois to return to, *colle trombe in sacco*, 25. 334
assemblies at, better than Dublin's, 39. 39
Astley's amphitheatre brought to, 35. 375
Athens excelled by, in tragedy and comedy, 41. 155
Aubeterre would be disavowed by, if he acknowledged Young Pretender, 25. 526
Austrian and Prussian kings should be at gates of, 34. 144
Austrian and Russian peace delegates to reside at, 21. 498
Baccelli dances in opera at, wearing ribbon of Garter, 31. 268
Balagni fights Pinocin in streets of, 40. 357
balloon made in, 39. 419
bankers in, lend to Veers, 19. 507, 510n
Barbantane supposed to have sent Mann snuffbox from, 25. 206
barbarity of, 22. 421
Barrymore, Lady, admired at, 30. 264
Barthélemy's *Anarcharsis* popular at, 34. 70
Bastille at: fall of, 31. 321, 323; Malesherbes releases prisoners from, 28. 226
Bastille Day at: fête to draw money at, 39. 477; quiet, 11. 95
Beaufort gives ball at, 22. 365
Beauvau hopes to see HW in, 40. 31
Beauvillier sent to, by family, 30. 59
Bedford, Ds of, to go to, when peace is assured, 38. 176, 177

Bedford, D. of, hissed on way to, 38. 176
—— may negotiate at The Hague on way to, 38. 170
—— popular at, 38. 184
——'s mission to, 38. 166
Benedictines at, ask parliament's leave to doff habits and rules, 22. 325
Bibliothèque du Roi at, permits no fires, 15. 108
bickerings at, may be fruitful, 34. 205–6
Bishop becomes actor and dancer at, 36. 106
bloody Monday at, 34. 163
Boisgelin recalled to, 22. 330
bon mots non-existent in, 30. 208
bon ton in, to be grave and learned, 31. 50
Boufflers, Comtesse de, will not return to, till HW is gone, 22. 554
bourgeois militia protects, 11. 67
'breeding' influenced by, 32. 16
Bretons march to, 11. 99
bridge at, *see* Pont Neuf
Broglie, Comte de, banished from, 23. 521
Broglie, Maréchal de, has partisans at, to enjoy defeat of Estrées and Soubise, 22. 50–1
Brunswick, D. of, may not reach, to rescue Louis XVI and Queen, 34. 141–2
buildings at, *see* Abbaye, L'; Académie royale de chirurgie; Arsenal; Asturies, Hôtel des; Augustins' church (*see also* Grands Augustins); Aumont, Hôtel de; Bastille; Beaupréau, Hôtel de; Bellechasse convent; Bibliothèque du Roi; Bouillon, Hôtel de; Bourbon, Palais de; Bourgogne, Hôtel de; Brancas, Hôtel de; Bretagne, Hôtel de; Brienne, Hôtel de; Broglie, Hôtel de; Brunswick, Hôtel de; Caraman, Hôtel de; Carnavalet, Hôtel de; Castries, Hôtel de; Célestins, church of; Chartreuse; Château du Taureau; Châtelet, Le; Choiseul, Hôtel de; Colisée; Collège de Louis le Grand; Collège des Quatres Nations; Collège du Plessis; Conciergerie; Condé, Hôtel de; Cour des Aides; Cours de la Reine; Danemark, Hôtel de; Deux, Ponts, Hôtel de; Duc de York, Hôtel du; Du Châtelet, Hôtel; Dunquerque, Au petit (shop); École de chirurgie; École royale militaire; École veterinaire; Empereur, Hôtel de l'; English Benedictines, church of; Entragues, Petit Hôtel d'; Evreux, Hôtel d'; Filles de l'Assomption; Filles de l'Ave Maria; Filles de Ste-Marie; Filles du Calvaire; Filles du St-Sacrément; Grande Écurie; Grands-Augustins, church and convent of; Great Jesuits' Church; Grimbergh, Hôtel de, Rue St-Dominique; Halles, Les; Hanovre, Pavillon d'; Holy Innocents Church; Holy Sepulchre convent, Rue St-Dominique; Hôpital des enfants trouvés, l'; Hospice des quinze vingts; Hôtel de ville; Invalides, church and hospital; Italiens, Théâtre des; Lachine, Hôtel; Lambert, Hôtel de; La Mothe,

Hôtel de; Langlée, Hôtel de; La Roche-foucauld, Hôtel de; Lesrocs; Louvre, the; Luxembourg, Hôtel de; Luxembourg, Hôtel de, Rue des Petits-Augustins; Luxembourg Palace; Luynes, Hôtel de; Magasin, Le; Mars, Hôtel de; Maurepas, Hôtel de; Mazarin, Hôtel de; Mirepoix, Hôtel de; Miséricorde convent; Modène, Hôtel de; Monaco, Hôtel de; Mouchy, Hôtel de; Moulin-Joli, le; Nicolet, théâtre de; Notre-Dame; Opéra; Opéra-comique; Orléans, Hôtel d'; Palais, le; Palais Marchand; Palais Royal; Panthéon; Parc-Royal, Hôtel du; Pères de l'Oratoire; Petites-Maisons; Praslin, Hôtel de; Provence, Hôtel de; Rambouillet, Hôtel de; Richelieu, Hôtel de; St-André-des-Arts, church of; St-Antoine, château de; St-Antoine, convent of; Ste-Geneviève, Abbey of; St-Esprit, Hôtel du; St-Eustache, church of; St-Germain-des-Prés, church of; St-Germain l'Auxerrois, church of; St-Gervais, church of; St-Jacques, convent of; St-Jean-en-Grève, church of; St-Joseph, church of; St-Joseph, convent of; St-Landri, church of; St-Louis-du-Louvre, church of; St-Louis-la-Couture, church of; St-Magloire, seminary of; St-Merry, church of; St-Nicolas-du-Chardonnet, church of; St-Paul, church of; St-Roch, church of; St-Sulpice, church of; St-Sulpice, seminary of; Scots College; Soubise, Hôtel de; Soyecourt, Hôtel de; Sully, Hôtel de; Temple, the; Toulouse, Hôtel de; Trocadéro; Tuileries; Turenne, Hôtel de; Uzés, Hôtel d'; Val-de-Grâce; Vauxhall; 'Veau qui tette'
Busoni, banker at, 25. 113
Campoflorido, Ps, avoids, because it lacks macaroni, 18. 315
Carmarthen appointed to embassy at, 25. 363
Carnival festivities at, 38. 336–7, 485
cases for scissors best made at, 31. 85
Caylus discovers encaustic method at, 21. 239
Chabot, Comtesse de, sets out for, 38. 430
change in English ministry called *malheureux pour la France* in, 25. 287
Chantilly 5 hours from, 3. 1
china at, *see under* China
Choiseul suddenly returns to, 32. 268
Choiseul-Beaupré brought to, 11. 301
civil war may arise in, 21. 435
clergy sitting in assembly at, 39. 2
coffee-houses in, have English newspapers, 28. 356–7
coffee taken as snuff a new fashion in, 38. 215
coiffures from, 35. 477
colder than Lapland, 35. 115
cold weather in: 31. 78; deters HW from sight-seeing, 31. 91, 95; equal to Russia's, 31. 93; resembles Siberia, 31. 90
Conclave sends courier to, to complain of Bourbon cardinals, 24. 79
confusion at, increases, 34. 96
Constantinople news would reach, before it reached Florence, 23. 311
conventual treasures of, 42. 286–7
conversation at: 38. 238; petty and disgusting, 14. 143–4
Conway thought to be in, on political errand, 39. 204
—— to be fetched from, by wife and daughter, 35. 422
—— to visit, 37. 327
—— writes from, 37. 45
Cordon, Abbé Comte, attacked by mob in, 11. 87
Cornélie vestale damned at, 10. 260
cost of Cole's visit to, 1. 97
counter-revolution in, expected, 11. 325, 12. 91
courier escorts Stuart to, 25. 513
courier, couriers from: about peace, 22. 65, 105; outruns one from Rome, 22. 407; reaches Florence after departure of courier from Rome, 22. 405; with news of Lestock's raid, 19. 330
courier sent to, for copy of dispatch stolen from French mail, 25. 619
Court residence at Fontainebleau leaves, a desert, 31. 62
court to be held at, 5. 30n
Cowper's valet-de-chambre goes through, without stopping for HW's letter, 22. 380
Craon and Richecourt hear news from, of Young Pretender, 19. 86–7
Craon gets condolences from, by post, 17. 463
Craven, Lady, may be kept busy by, 42. 181–2
Dacre to try new physician at, 10. 290
Damas d'Antigny brought to, 11. 301
Dauphin's death: closes theatres, 31. 92, 93; stifles diversions, 31. 88
——'s death will bring people to, 31. 88
—— to be mourned by, 32. 24
Dauphin (Louis XVI)'s marriage celebrated at, 4. 402, 418–20, 424
deaths, marriages, and promotions the only events in, 31. 92, 136
deserted, 4. 242, 265, 411, 440, 10. 181, 31. 49, 62, 71, 75, 32. 54, 38. 573
dinners for literati in, 32. 3
dirt of, 31. 45–6, 49, 64, 73, 35. 342
distracted, 39. 493
Dorset inefficient as ambassador at, 25. 486
dress at, simple, 10. 176
Du Barry, Comtesse, rumoured at, to have died, 24. 18
—— the only topic in, 23. 133
Duclos dies at, 5. 209n
Du Deffand, Mme, dies at, 25. 90
—— ill at, 33. 228, 229–30
—— only person Montagu wants to see at, 10. 296
—— plans trips with HW to suburbs of, 4. 266
——'s annuities from, 8. 38, 39, 45–6
—— wants to drive about, at 1 A.M., 30. 263

[Paris, *continued*]

Dumouriez sets out for, 12. 2

—— vengeance on, demanded by, 12. 1

earthquake felt at, 20. 531n

easy, empty, and quiet, 38. 573

emigration caused by uproar at, 34. 110

émigrés tremble for friends at, 34. 114

England compared with, 32. 23, 27, 29–30

—'s ultimatum to, for peace, 25. 342

—'s war with France rumoured in, 32. 328

English allowed to go to, despite undeclared war, 24. 399

English ambassador to be sent to, 35. 207

English army expected to capture, 19. 91, 21. 228, 352

English assemblies more vulgar than anything at, 39. 37

English at: 15. 7; as troublesome as at Florence, 38. 458; entertained by Hertford, 38. 398, 516; fewer than usual, 31. 109; HW avoids, 30. 207, 31. 48; HW diverted by, 30. 211; HW does not cultivate, 30. 265; HW does not wish to know, 30. 207; Lennox, Lady George, adored by, 31. 124; not received at all in the 1740s, 38. 458; numerous, 30. 207, 215, 265, 31. 79, 100, 38. 404, 39. 8; on way to Rome, 20. 82; received everywhere, 31. 49; return, 22. 175; see inferior company, 32. 182; spend large sums there since the peace, 22. 152; swarm, 22. 365; treated like Russians, 31. 107; use fashions discarded at, 10. 176

English books may be bought at, 10. 170, 172, 174

English desert, when Parliament summons, 38. 485

English embassy at: chapel services at, free to all, 38. 279; Hume replaces Bunbury as secretary to, 38. 578; Hume's secretaryship at, not officially announced, 39. 1–2; secretaryship to, in doubt, 33. 420; secretary to, leaves, 20. 490n; will probably cease at Albemarle's death, 20. 460; *see also under names listed under* Ambassador: from England to France

English formerly not well received at, 38. 458

English gamble at, 38. 506

English gardening gains at, 35. 125

Englishman asks what town it is, when changing horses in, 39. 185

English should not go to, 42. 374

Éon's accent not of, 33. 510

ephemeral plays successful at, 41. 156

equipages at: bring everything near, 37. 41; simple, 10. 176

exchange at, 1. 98

expense of living in: 10. 296; Cole's costs from, 1. 97

experiments with diamonds in, 7. 372, 31. 158

Exposé succinct of Hume-Rousseau trial printed in, 41. 48

factions in, 12. 89

faïence factories in Faubourg St-Antoine in, 7. 337n

fashion, fashions in: for feathers in headdresses, 30. 264; of brief duration, 31. 100; to speak broken French, 33. 399

ferment of, causes French to come to England, 34. 95

Fête de la Féderation at, 31. 340

fire at fête in, 8. 166

fireworks at: on the peace, 22. 163; produce accidents, 20. 48, 23. 217–18; to celebrate 'victories' over English and Hessians, 21. 246

firing of cannon in, 11. 36

Fleury incurs debt for carriages in, 12. 79

fogs and damps in: 1. 99, 103; rival London's, 31. 73; worse than in England, 30. 204

Foljambe seeks recommendatory letters to people in, 28. 49

Fontainebleau does not depopulate, 31. 78

Fontenelle's opera revived at, 20. 213

Forbes challenges Wilkes in, 22. 162

foreigner at, wears orders of different countries, 24. 360–1, 25. 572

'fountain of age,' 31. 96

Francis I sends courier to, 17. 216

Franklin should have English come to, 32. 404

French ignorance of everything outside of, 12. 28

French noblemen exiled to, 23. 298

French often in country instead of staying in, 38. 404

from Peru to, French are defeated, 21. 352

Fronsac brings news of St Philip's surrender to, 20. 572

Fullarton lately Stormont's secretary at, 25. 31

funeral orations at, 20. 403–4, 31. 111

Gage and Lady Mary Herbert reunited in, 30. 215

Galluzzi's history being translated at, 25. 238

gates of, customs' search at, 37. 40

gates of, *see* Porte St-Antoine

Gatti lived long at, 24. 67n

gazette extract from, 21. 344

Gem attended Charlotte Stuart at, 25. 516, 26. 47

—— English physician at, 25. 516

Genlis, Mme de, has hôtel at, 33. 483

Genoa's courier to, 20. 588

George II's death reported from, 20. 388

Gloucester, Ds of, hopes to see Mme du Deffand at, 36. 142

Gloucester family not to visit, 36. 132

governor of, *see* Albert de Luynes, Marie-Charles-Louis d'

gowns from, *see under* Gown

Gramont, Comtesse de, banished from, 4. 436–7

Grands Augustins convent at, *see under* Grands Augustins

Grecian buildings in, 23. 158

greenery absent in, **30.** 218

Grimaldi receives *cordon bleu* at, **21.** 560

HW advised by Cts of Suffolk to delay visit to, **38.** 431

HW already forgotten at, **39.** 462

HW amused but not comfortable in, **31.** 51

HW and Voltaire on men of taste at, **4.** 129

HW anxious for Ds of Richmond to follow him to, **30.** 202

HW arrives at, **3.** 342, **4.** 272n, **5.** 42n, 87n, **7.** 260, 316, 324–5, 334, 343

HW avoids trip to, for fear of gout, **39.** 184, 186, 198–9, 208–9, 223

HW cannot spend winter in, though he wants to, **24.** 117

HW can occupy Beauchamp's apartment in, **38.** 477, 481, 485

HW could find silver plate at, for Montagu, **10.** 288

HW defers visit to, **35.** 414

HW denies explicitly asking Hertford to resign embassy at, **38.** 390–2

HW describes pleasures of, **13.** 162

HW describes society at, **32.** 18, 22, 27, 29–30, **35.** 112, 115–16

HW does not hear news at, **10.** 197

HW drops correspondence with Bns Craven at, **25.** 615

HW expects Selwyn to revisit, **30.** 218

HW expects to hear from, of Mme du Deffand's death, **35.** 507–8

HW expects to shop at, **38.** 276

HW finds, monotonous, **10.** 184

HW had no correspondents left in, **16.** 281

HW has seen few of the beauties in, **31.** 72

HW hopes that Arlington St and SH will not be carried to, **35.** 235

HW hopes to meet Craufurd at, **32.** 246

HW hurts himself in, by ridiculing whist and Richardson, **30.** 208

HW imagines trip to, by balloon, **33.** 459

HW indifferent about visit to, **10.** 175

HW jokes about Cts of Hertford becoming a rake and Wilkes a pious man at, **38.** 343

HW jokes about decrepitude being the fashion in, **30.** 204, 220

HW jokes about remaining permanently in, **31.** 93

HW kindly treated in, **30.** 211

HW knew Gatti in, **22.** 342, **23.** 468

HW leaves, **3.** 1, 344, **4.** 272, **5.** 90, **7.** 314, 324, 333, 342, 353

HW likes: as little as London, **22.** 451; better than he expected, **31.** 44, 48

HW likes suppers at, **10.** 175

HW lodges at Hôtel du Parc-Royal in, **1.** 99

HW may find visit to, too expensive, **38.** 415, 431

HW may not like, now that Hertford has left, **22.** 492

HW may visit, **1.** 66, 69, 89, 94, **39.** 4

HW might amuse himself in, with papal bull Unigenitus, **20.** 337

HW might prefer Bath, Tunbridge Wells, or Italy to, **22.** 492

HW more pleased with, than ever, **39.** 259

HW not made ill by life at, **41.** 45–6

HW not pleased by, **39.** 25

HW not to go beyond, **22.** 332

HW observed nothing in, in 1739 and 1741, **39.** 10

HW offers to execute commissions for Henry Fox in, **30.** 202

HW orders clothes at, **17.** 176

HW pleased with, **30.** 204, 211

HW proposes to visit, **1.** 34, 82, 215n, 217, 218, **17.** 127, **22.** 135, 152, 175, 247, 270–1, 285, 289, 484, 544; **23.** 128–9, 133–4, 304, 311, **24.** 120, **28.** 211, 213, 214, 219, **30.** 176, 177, 194–5, 196, 246, **31.** 142, 154, **32.** 17, 239, 241, 246, **35.** 316–17, 333, 341–3, 470–1, 506, 539, **37.** 300, 301, **38.** 203, 249, 351, 363, 379, 387, 399, 408–10, 415, 422, 426–7, 430, 431, 439, 463–4, 469–71, 477, 481, 485, 497–8, 504–5, 509, 513, 514, 516, 525, 531, 535, 569–70, 573–4, **39.** 85–6, 138, 531, **40.** 378, 380, **41.** 94

HW reached in, 7 days from Calais on first trip, **38.** 380

HW receives copy of illumination from, **2.** 195

HW receives letter from, **23.** 568

HW returns from, **1.** 111–12, **30.** 250

HW's acquaintance in: **11.** 285, **31.** 78–9; narrow, **31.** 70; well-established, **31.** 137

HW satirizes life in, **35.** 334–7

HW saw *Lettere pittoriche* in, **23.** 266

HW's conversation on declining monasticism during his last visit to, **34.** 193

HW's curiosity in, **30.** 204

HW's 'dear old friend' at, *see* Vichy-Champrond, Marie de, Marquise du Deffand

HW's dream about King's Library at, **32.** 74

HW seldom writes to, by the post, **40.** 364

HW sends letter by way of, **22.** 294, 301, 398, **24.** 137

HW sets date for departure from, **10.** 283

HW sets out for, **10.** 247n, **32.** 17

HW's expense from Boulogne to, **39.** 8

HW's favour in, **31.** 103

HW's first visit to opera in, **18.** 495

HW's hotel at, *see* Parc-Royal, Hôtel du

HW should bring suit and ruffles from, **37.** 105

HW's hours at, **41.** 1

HW's letter from: about D. of York's death, may have miscarried, **22.** 560; not to be specifically answered by Mann, **24.** 127; received by Mann, **24.** 130

HW's life in, 'perfectly French,' **31.** 93

HW's news may be welcome at, **36.** 56

HW's opinion of, **10.** 175–7, 208

HW's Paphos, **32.** 25

[Paris, *continued*]

HW's popularity in, **10.** 175, 206

HW's purchase of Francis I's armour from, **1.** 243

HW's purchases in, **7.** 399–414, **30.** 217, **31.** 73

HW's reasons for visiting, **3.** 104

HW's services at, to Lady Mary Coke, **24.** 179

HW's set at, not the most agreeable, **39.** 45, 48

HW suffers from cold at, **10.** 242

HW surprised Bn Holland does not visit, **31.** 97

HW's visit to: fills his mind with new ideas, **31.** 103; may be prevented by Parliamentary session, **22.** 247; postponed, **1.** 84–5

HW's writings known in, because he lived there, **39.** 462

HW tells Mann not to write to him at, **22.** 411, 548, **23.** 134, 139, 311, **24.** 128

HW thinks Hertford should resign embassy at, **38.** 388–9, 397–8, 411–12, 425–7

HW too indolent to visit, **28.** 167

HW took a week to get to, from Calais, **38.** 380

HW took 6 days from Calais to, **32.** 253

HW to revisit: as 'the way of all flesh,' **22.** 152; in Feb. 1767, **41.** 43; to see Mme du Deffand, **22.** 484, **23.** 311, **24.** 120; when Parliament rises, **22.** 285

HW to vent vagaries in, **31.** 93

HW tried to see a little of, on first visit, **22.** 175

HW visits garden near, **32.** 55–6

HW walks along boulevards at, **10.** 285

HW warns Conway and wife against theft at, **39.** 190

HW will execute commissions for Ossorys in, **32.** 50, 52, 53–4

HW will have news of, **32.** 20, 49

HW will regret, **39.** 42

HW would like to be at, when Pitt returned to power, **22.** 441

HW writes from, **17.** 124–7, **22.** 340–4, 347–8, 358–60, 363–6, 371–3, 380–3, 394–7, 400–5, 409–11, 550–5, **24.** 123–7, 132–4, **35.** 111–18, 120–2, 125–8, **39.** 87–9, **40.** 381, 384, 387, **41.** 99, 210, 215

Hamilton, Lady Archibald, to be buried at, perhaps at Val-de-Grâce, **35.** 68

Harcourt to get embassy at, **23.** 65–6

Hardinge expects, to 'be the seat of empire,' **35.** 584

—— gets letters to HW's friends at, **35.** 581, 583

—— to visit, **35.** 579, 580, 581

—— wants HW to recommend cicerone for, **35.** 579

—— wonders when HW next goes to, **35.** 574

Harrington expected in, **30.** 264

headdress from, for Mme Grifoni, **17.** 239

Hertford, Cts of, jokingly said to live riotously at, **38.** 494

—— leaves, **40.** 385

—— to leave, **30.** 202

Hertford, E. of, ambassador at, **1.** 34, **20.** 467–8, **22.** 130, 135, 175, 315–16, 341, **30.** 194–5, **38.** 211–578, **39.** 1–5

—— finds, expensive, **38.** 220

—— hopes HW will soon return from, to SH, **39.** 25

—— invites HW to, **38.** 192

—— regrets leaving, **38.** 408, **39.** 19, 45

——'s resignation disrupts HW's plans to visit, **22.** 316

——'s stay at, makes provincial England seem odd, **39.** 18–19

—— to visit, **31.** 30. **39.** 77, 78

Hertfords' inclination to embassy at, **38.** 166, 168–9

—— on way to, **38.** 212

Hervey, Bns, introduces fashion from, **9.** 166

Hervey, Bp, ejected from, **25.** 454

Holland, Bn, rumoured to have died at, **10.** 83

Holland said to have sent Wassenaer to, with peace terms, **19.** 216

Honoré III probably notifies, of D. of York's illness, **22.** 556

houses at, all alike, **23.** 312, **32.** 218

Hume admires *ton* of, **35.** 112

—— causes sensation by letter to a private gentleman at, **41.** 60

——'s popularity in, **30.** 209

Hume-Rousseau quarrel famous in, **22.** 465, **41.** 24–6, 43–5, 46–57, 59–64

indignant about Calonne's treachery, **11.** 44

iron wig brought from, by Wortley Montagu, **20.** 226

Italian playhouse in, unpopular, **13.** 162

Italy used to get *ton* from, **25.** 495

Jacobite emissary at, **18.** 426

James II said to have deposited funds at Hôtel de Ville in, **22.** 385

Jersey, Cts of, to visit, **25.** 411

Jersey attack announced by post from, **24.** 471

Jesuits banished from, **38.** 339

Julienne's sale at, **22.** 323

Karl Wilhelm Ferdinand to visit, **30.** 220

Kingston, Ds of, summoned to, to meet agents of Ecclesiastical Court, **24.** 83

—— to rent palace at, **24.** 242

ladies of: better attended than ministers are, **38.** 262; HW kissed by, **31.** 182; Hertford describes, **38.** 267–8; life of, **10.** 70

'Lapland,' **1.** 110

laughing, pantins, and bilboquets out of fashion in, **40.** 385

length of journey from, to London, **10.** 213

Lennox, Lady Sarah, admired in, **30.** 240

Lent at, **38.** 485, 504

letters from: about French invasion of Jersey, **24.** 471; about Mme du Barry, **23.** 151; about peace negotiations, **22.** 86; about storm-tossed English fleet, **24.** 436–7; bewail French situation, **24.** 466; encourage Lo-

renzi, **22.** 370; lament Laeffeld battle, **19.** 426; report English damage to Lorient, **30.** 109; says France will defend Holland against Austria, **25.** 545; speak of breakup of French camps, **24.** 413; to Florence, take 9 or 10 days, **22.** 352; to Rome about new schemes of Young Pretender, **19.** 451; written in terror, **34.** 185

letters from Ds of Gloucester sent from, **32.** 376

linen washed in river at, **10.** 232

Liotard's prices higher in England than in, **20.** 362

London compared to, **23.** 121

Lorenzi says that his clothes come from, **21.** 501

Lorenzi, Comtesse de, follows styles of, **21.** 501

Louis XVI and Marie-Antoinette return to, **11.** 298, 300, 303

Louis XVI invites D. and Ds of Gloucester to, **24.** 125

Louisbourg news at, **21.** 230, 234–5

Macartney not allowed to go to, **30.** 274

magnificent living in, **38.** 220

Maillebois posts Louis XV's reprimand to, **23.** 284

Manchester, D. of, takes embassy at, **25.** 398

Mann encloses letter to Stanley at, **22.** 340

—— sends iris roots for, **23.** 333

——'s letter probably detained at, by Thompson, **18.** 412

—— tries to get gossip from, about visit of Cts of Coventry and Lady Caroline Petersham, **20.** 333

—— would learn news of peace from, before HW could send it, **25.** 347

Marie Leszczyńska's triumphal entry into, **18.** 524

married women expect men's attentions in, **39.** 201

massacres at, **15.** 218–19, 237, **42.** 373

Mauduit's *Considerations* appear at, **21.** 469

Maurepas ablest and most agreeable man HW knew at, **39.** 198

Medina Sidonia, D. of, dies on way to, **24.** 440

men at: inferior to women, **35.** 111–12; take up gravity, **14.** 149–50

men of taste at, exceed those of Athens, **41.** 155

mendicants at, **18.** 72

mentioned, **11.** 87–8, 140n, 142n, 143, 144, 147, 155, 157, 170, 348, **12.** 12, 14, 40, 66, 67, 77, 87, 98, 118

merchants at, report Choiseul's fall, **39.** 112

Mercy-Argenteau and Starhemberg make statements at, about Austrian-Dutch quarrel, **25.** 561

Mesmer practises animal magnetism in, **31.** 280

Minden victory may open, to English army, **35.** 292

Mirabeau's book burnt at, **34.** 44

Mirepoix family seldom at, **20.** 87

mob of: slaughters pheasants, **34.** 64, 69; tramples old woman for cheering Louis XV, **21.** 56; turns against Esprémesnil, **34.** 155

models of good breeding at, surpassed by HW, **35.** 586

Modena, Ds of, to stay at, **18.** 222

modern: manners of, prevail in French tragedies, **41.** 296; tirewomen of, **35.** 249

Montagu asks HW to shop for him, at, **10.** 170, 174, 285–6, 295

—— hopes HW enjoys, **10.** 188

—— mentions, **10.** 284

National Assembly's fête at, **39.** 477

National Convention fears losing control in, **12.** 132–3

——'s report to, **12.** 8

news from, mentioned, **11.** 32, 37, 43, 45, 104

newspapers are correct about uprisings in, **39.** 467

Niccoli is Tuscan agent at, **24.** 362

nothing new in literature, theatre, fashions, or shops in, **39.** 144–6

nuncio at, *see under* Nuncio

O'Brien, Mrs, banished from, **20.** 27–8, 45

old age fashionable in, **32.** 27, 29–30

opera at, *see* Opera, French, at Paris

Ossory, Lady, requests gossip about, **32.** 312

Panchaud a banker in, **23.** 133

Papal election to be influenced from, **17.** 21

Parliamentary opposition goes to, **24.** 262

parliament of, *see* Parliament of Paris

parliament of Paris's retirement causes loss of money by, **23.** 322

parliament will not reform pleasure-loving people of, **38.** 339

'Patapan' barks at Frenchmen in, **18.** 221

Payba flees to, after fraudulent bankruptcy, **20.** 288n

peace might be made under walls of, **38.** 105

peace of, *see* Paris, Peace Treaty of

peaches in, **2.** 111

people of: HW calls, assassins and devils, **34.** 161–2; HW calls, frantic fiends, **34.** 191; HW calls, monsters, **34.** 182; HW calls, wild beasts, **34.** 181; HW dissatisfied with, **14.** 143–4

Pius VI burnt in effigy in, **11.** 270

plays published at, authorized by censor, **29.** 323

poissardes in, **11.** 208

Polish king's proxy wedding at, **38.** 83n

pomegranate and orange trees mixed at, **33.** 298

post from and to, *see under* Post

président's family from, argue over dinner courses, **22.** 163

Presle's collection at, **26.** 46

prisoners dragged to, from Orléans, **35.** 446

provinces gayer than, **24.** 498

public opinion and religion in, governed by fashion, **22.** 412

quays of, Mme du Deffand takes HW on tour of, **32.** 260

[Paris, *continued*]

rainwater from, **17.** 414

ramparts of, Stanley lives on, **37.** 308

Rennes said to be closer to London than to, **39.** 33

reports of Wilkes's trial sent to, **23.** 12

revolutionary outrages in, **11.** 39–40, 42–3, 260, **12.** 31, 47, 101, **15.** 218–19, 237, **31.** 372, **34.** 56, 109, 143–4, 151–5, 161–3, 181, 182, **42.** 373–4; *see also* French Revolution

Richardson's popularity in, **30.** 208–9

Richmond, Ds of, dislikes, **31.** 93

—— goes to Aubigny from, **40.** 28

Richmond, D. of, becomes ambassador at, **22.** 323, 341, 369, **30.** 200, **32.** 16

—— sends his dogs to, **41.** 11n

riots at: **6.** 184, 187; over children being sent to the colonies, **20.** 170; over corn prices, **24.** 101–2

robberies at, **39.** 190

Rochford, E. of, and Villettes to meet at, **20.** 76

Rochford, E. of, may be ambassador at, **20.** 420, 426, 467, **22.** 420

—— sets out for embassy at, **39.** 90

Rohan, Cardinal, to be imprisoned in, **25.** 603

Roland, Mme, may be dazzled by, **10.** 207–8

—— to visit, **10.** 188

rouge fashionable in, **18.** 220

Rousseau's possible opinion of, **24.** 62

routes from England to, **31.** 118, **37.** 38–42

royal academy of, Sloane's museum offered to, **20.** 358

St-Florentin has amusements of, under his jurisdiction, **38.** 477

St Paul, Horace, flees to, **9.** 113n

St-Simon's *Mémoires* in, **34.** 29

Sandwich, Cts of, dies at, **35.** 99

Saxe's house at, offered to Ligonier, **37.** 280

Schaub, English minister at, **9.** 88n

Scots College at, *see under* Scots College

Selwin, banker at, **17.** 93, 115n, **26.** 29

Selwyn likes anything fashionable in, **30.** 210

—— returns from, **30.** 240

sensational news from, **4.** 407

Sévigné, Mme de, leaves daughter at, **35.** 198

'Sévigné, Mme de,' urges HW to visit, **3.** 51

Seymour's visit to, might be inspired by Young Pretender's wife, **24.** 102

shops in, sell parrots, macaws, cockatoos, **33.** 515

snow in, **22.** 396

Sorba, Genoese minister to, **21.** 509, **23.** 363

——'s birth and death at, **23.** 363

Stafford, E. and Cts of, to live half-time at, **18.** 277

Stainville envoy at, **20.** 29

Stanhope, Lady Harriet, expected in, **30.** 264

Stanley's missions to, **21.** 504, 514, **22.** 300

Stormont ordered to quit, **24.** 373

——'s courier leaves, **24.** 1

streets in, narrow, **31.** 45

streets of. *See* Anjou, Rue d'; Armandiers,

Rue des; Augustins, Quai des; Bac, Rue du; Beaune, Rue de; Beaurepaire, Rue; Bergère, Rue; Bernardins, Rue des; Boulevard; Boulogne, Bois de; Bourbon, Rue de; Capucines, Rue des; Carrousel, Place du; Champ de Mars; Champs-Élysées, les; Châtelet, Place du; Chaume, Rue de; Colombier, Rue du; Condé, Rue de; Coq-Héron, Rue; Cordeliers, Rue des; Croix des Petits-Champs, Rue; Culture-St-Catherine, Rue de la; Dauphine, Place; Dauphine, Rue; Desmarais, Rue; Deux Écus, Rue des; Enfer, Rue de l'; Faubourg St-Antoine, Rue du; Faubourg St-Honoré, Rue de; Faubourg St-Jacques, Rue du; Férraille, Quai de la; Fossés-St-Germain-des-Prés, Rue des; Fossés-St-Victor, Rue des; Four, Rue du; Grands-Augustins, Quai des; Grands-Augustins, Rue des; Grange-Batelière, Rue de la; Grenelle, Plaine de; Grenelle, Rue de; Grève, Place de; Guillotine, Place de la; Huchette, Rue de la; Jacob, Rue; Jardin Royal; Jouy, Rue de; Judas, Rue; Lafitte, Rue; Lille, Rue de; Louis-le-Grand, Place de; Louis XV, Place de; Luxembourg, Jardins du; Marais, Rue des; Mauconseil, Rue; Minimes, Rue des; Montmartre, Rue; Mouton, Rue du; Notre-Dame-des-Champs, Rue; Paradis, Rue de; Parc-Royal, Rue du; Petit-Musc, Rue de; Petits-Augustins, Rue des; Petits-Champs, Rue des; Place Royale; Quatre-Fils, Rue, du; Richelieu, Rue de; Roquette, Rue de la; St-André-des-Arts, Rue; St-Augustin, Rue Neuve; St-Benoît, Rue; St-Bernard, Quai; St-Croix-de-la-Bretonnerie, Rue; St-Denis, Rue; St-Dominique, Rue; Ste-Anne, Rue; Ste-Anne-Butte-St-Roch, Rue; Ste-Apolline, Rue; Ste-Marguerite, Rue; St-Germain, Boulevard; St-Germain l'Auxerrois, Rue; St-Louis-en-l'Isle, Rue; St-Marc, Rue; St-Martin, Rue; St-Nicaise, Rue; St-Paul, Rue; St-Roch, Rue; Sts-Pères, Rue des; St-Thomas-du-Louvre, Rue; Seine, Rue de; Sépulcre, Rue du; Temple, Rue du; Thérèse, Rue; Tire-Boudin, Rue; Tisséranderie, Rue de la; Tournon, Rue de; Université, Rue de l'; Varenne, Rue de; Vaugirard, Rue de; Vendôme, Place; Victoires, Place des; Vieilles-Audriettes, Rue des; Vieux Colombier, Rue du; Vivienne, Rue; Vrillière, Rue de la; Vuide Gousses, Rue de

Stuart, Charlotte, brings new modes from, **25.** 535

—— educated in convent at, **25.** 512, **26.** 47

—— registered in, as Ds of Albany, **25.** 513, 516n, 521–2

summer the fine season at, **10.** 167

surgeons of, fail to cure Panciatichi's knee, **20.** 36

surgeon would never leave, for private service, **17.** 81

Sussex, hostage at, **10.** 339

Sutton rumoured to be at, **24.** 2
talk at, of invading England, **33.** 129
Tancred not successful in, **16.** 44
'that kennel of a place,' **1.** 113
theatre in, *see* Theatre: Paris; *see also under* Opera, French, at Paris
topics of conversation in: horse-races, **31.** 106–8; parliaments, **31.** 79, 106–8; politics, **31.** 79; trivial, **31.** 92
toys from, at Leghorn fair, **22.** 423
tracasseries of, **41.** 7
trade dull in, **32.** 54
travelling time from, to Florence, **22.** 352
Trinity in, consists of Hume, Richardson, and whist, **30.** 208–9
Tuileries outrages at, **31.** 372, **34.** 143–4
Turgot rumoured to be in charge of, **6.** 300
Turner expects to visit, annually, **13.** 137
turns out for Lauraguais-Forbes race, **1.** 110
Tuscan embassy in, run by chargé d'affaires, **20.** 192n
Tyrawley's wigs from, **21.** 191
ugly and beastly, **14.** 143
university of, *see* Sorbonne; University of Paris
Vaugirard, barrière of, **4.** 211, 212, **6.** 189n
Versailles preferred to, by French ministers, **33.** 273
view of, from terrace of Comtesse de Boufflers, **28.** 223
Viry, Sardinian ambassador to, **9.** 406n
Viry, Mme de, dazzles, **41.** 343
visiting of churches unfashionable in, **31.** 73
visitor brings news from, **33.** 309
visitors to: A. A., Mr, **30.** 215; Abington, Mrs, **41.** 215–16; Adams, John, **28.** 382; Ailesbury, Cts of, **6.** 99, 115–55, **32.** 200, **35.** 351, **39.** 188, 189, 194, 195n, 200–5, 206–9, 216–19, 229, 234, 237, 539; Albany, Cts of, **23.** 398; Alford, **7.** 310; Almódovar, **7.** 428–31; Althorp, Vct, **6.** 219, 483–4, 488, 490; Ancaster, Ds of, **22.** 155; Andrews, Francis, **38.** 427; Anglesea, **38.** 514–15; Anhalt, P. of, **7.** 318, 322; Anhalt-Zerbst, Ps of, **22.** 65; Artois, Comtesse d', **11.** 96; Astley, **25.** 451; Aston, Lady, **7.** 271; Aubrey, **7.** 268; Bache, B. F., **6.** 383; Baillie, Griselda, **25.** 2; Baretti, **4.** 230–7; Bariatinsky, Ps, **7.** 345, 346, 349; Barré, **7.** 272, 377, **22.** 365, **38.** 413; Barret, **7.** 325; Barrymore, Cts of, **6.** 229–82, **7.** 345–51, **30.** 264, **32.** 55; Bath, E. of, **20.** 155, **22.** 343n; Beauchamp, **5.** 219, 384–8, **7.** 265, 404, **22.** 344; Beauclerk, Topham, **7.** 270–85; Beaufort, Ds of, **7.** 334; Beaufort, D. of, **7.** 271, **31.** 71–2, **32.** 24; Beauvau, **19.** 426n; Bedford, Ds of, **22.** 78, 105, **31.** 30; Bedford, D. of, **22.** 69–70, 90, 92–3, **31.** 30; Bentinck, **7.** 293–301; Bentinck, Lord Edward, **7.** 282–312; Berkeley, Cts of, **7.** 269–306, **31.** 79, 93, **32.** 24, **35.** 317, **39.** 37; Berkeley, E. of, **7.** 277, 294, **31.** 79; Bernstorff, **4.** 128–64; Berrys, **11.** 122, 124,

372, 34. 24; Bertie family, **2.** 235; Berwick, Ds of, **7.** 261–311, **38.** 298–9, 337; Berwick, D. of, **7.** 272–92, **38.** 298–9, 337; Bingham, Miss, **6.** 357–66; Bingham, Hon. Richard, **36.** 192; Biron, K. E., **4.** 7; Bishop, **6.** 28–55, 160, **7.** 344; Bland, **20.** 338; Blaquiere, Col., **5.** 91–153, **6.** 496, **7.** 16, 40, 341–2, 41. 215; Blaquiere, Mrs, **6.** 496, **7.** 16, 26; Blome, Bn von, **7.** 429–30; Blome, Mme de, **7.** 431; Boswell, **41.** 138; Bragança, **7.** 9, 26; Bridgwater, Ds of, **22.** 155; (?) Brodrick, Hon. Henry, **7.** 349–50, 353; Brodrick, Hon. Thomas, **7.** 349, (?) 350, 353, **30.** 262; Brown, (?) Lancelot and (?) Lancelot, jr, **7.** 325, 327; Browne, Lady, **31.** 49; Bruce, Thomas (?) **7.** 380; Brusby, **7.** 285, 300; Buccleuch, D. of, **3.** 92, 157, 160, **7.** 305–9, **31.** 109, **38.** 337; Buckner, **7.** 281, 303–14; Buller, Mrs, **7.** 351; Bunbury, Lady Sarah, **3.** 199–234, **35.** 318, **38.** 553n, 537, 556; Bunbury, Sir T. C., **3.** 205–31, **4.** 105–24, **35.** 318; Burdett, **20.** 20; Burford, E. of, **37.** 309; Burgoyne, **5.** 269–76; Burke, Edmund, **5.** 329–39, **32.** 103; Burke, Richard, **6.** 41, 56; Burrell, Sir William, **7.** 267, 377, 404; Bute, **4.** 127; Butler, Mme, **7.** 272; Byng, **4.** 363, 365; Byres, **42.** 101; Caher, Bn, **7.** 311; Campbell, **7.** 380; Caracciolo, (?) Carlo Maria, **6.** 30; Carignan, **7.** 352; Carlisle, Cts of, **7.** 50–84, **35.** 317; Carlisle, E. of, **3.** 152–170, **4.** 190–205, **5.** 205–17, **7.** 321, 323, **22.** 554, **30.** 251; Carmarthen, **7.** 326, 331; Carmichael, **6.** 427; Carteret, Lady Sophia, **20.** 97; Caswall, **7.** 317–21, 385; Cathcart, Hon. Charlotte, Hon. Mary, and Hon. William, **6.** 401; Chamier, **4.** 228, **5.** 8; Chesterfield, **17.** 232; (?) Chevalier, **7.** 205, 209; Chewton, Vct, **7.** 288, 289, 319; Cholmondeley, 3d E. of, **4.** 210–35; Cholmondeley, 4th E. of, **4.** 210–35, **5.** 430, 435, **39.** 204, **42.** 352; Cholmondeley, Henrietta Maria, **4.** 217–445; Cholmondeley, Hester Frances, **4** 217–369; Cholmondeley, Mrs Robert, **4.** 208–480, **7.** 325–33, **10.** 291–4; Cholmondeley, Robert Francis, **7.** 343; Christian VII, **4.** 153–69; Churchill, Charles, **5.** 2–89, **7.** 318–36, **20.** 324–5, 329, **22.** 262, **35.** 123, **38.** 409–10, **39.** 144, 146, 148; Churchill, Charles (poet), **20.** 261, 272; Churchill, Lady Maria, **5.** 2–86, **6.** 207, **7.** 334–6, **20.** 324–5, 339, **22.** 262, **35.** 123, **38.** 409–10, **39.** 144, 146, 148; Churchill, Mary, **5.** 2–89, **7.** 334–6; Clanbrassill, **3.** 347, 369, **4.** 16; Clarke, **7.** 260, 293–4; Clarke, Mrs, **7.** 294; Clermont, Bn, **4.** (?) 271, **6.** 172, 175, 395, **7.** 261, 325–8; Clermont, Bns, **4.** (?) 271, **6.** 282, 383, **7.** 260, 262, 329, 352–3; Clermont, E. and Cts of, **25.** 357n; Clinton, **18.** 429; Coke, Lady Mary, **4.** 404, 432, 439, **5.** 69, **6.** 56–60, 216, **7.** 317–50, **22.** 94, **23.** 568, **24.** 179, **30.** 264, **31.** 61, 133–5, 182–5, **35.** 317, **38.** 373, 411; Cole, Rev. William, **1.** 94–8, 99, 104–5,

[Paris, *continued*]

111n, **7.** 268, 273, 377, 404; Coleraine, **30.** 264; Colloredo, **6.** 440, 443; Colomb, Philip, **7.** 405–13; Colonna, **7.** 80–141; Conolly, Lady Louisa, **6.** 28, **7.** 32–9, **38.** 537, 556; Conway, Hon. Henry Seymour, **6.** 61n, 90–156, **10.** 154, **35.** 351, **37.** 45–7, 48, 51, 81, 307–9, 324, **39.** 188–91, 194, 195n, 200–15, 218, 220, 223–4, 228–30, 233–4, 236–7, 242–5, 247–9, 536, 539; Conyers, **3.** 184; Cornbury, **19.** 188n, **20.** 213–14; Cosway, Mrs, **42.** 200; Coventry, Cts of, **20.** 324, 333, 337–8, 376, **37.** 341; Coventry, E. of, **20.** 324, 337–9, 376, **38.** 430, 440; Crammond, **7.** 309, 316; Craufurd, James, **4.** 283–93, **5.** 228–33, **6.** 481–3; Craufurd, John, **4.** 161–477, **5.** 265–89, **6.** 228, 481–9, **7.** 260–323, **30.** 207, 264, **31.** 91, **32.** 24, 38; Craven, Bns, **7.** 271, 294; Craven, Hon. Keppel Richard, **25.** 611n; Crébillons, **20.** 325; Crewe, Mrs, **5.** 358–80; Cumberland, D. and Ds of, **23.** 344, 349, 519–20, 525–6; Czernieski, **7.** 300; Czernieski, Mme, **7.** 277–313; Dacre, Bn and Bns, **7.** 326–30, **10.** 290, **35.** 121; Dalrymple, Vct, **5.** 153, 164, 320; Damer, Hon. John, **5.** 384, 386, **7.** 285, 288, 293; Damer, Hon. Mrs John, **5.** 259–63, **6.** 99–156, **7.** 88–91, **11.** 265, **33.** 520, **34.** 29, **35.** 351, **39.** 188n, 195n, 539; Dampier, Mr, **6.** 207; Dampier, Mrs, **5.** 2, **6.** 207; Deane, Lady, and son, **4.** 271; Denbigh, Cts of, **37.** 51; Devonshire, Ds of, **5.** 280–403, **11.** 27, **39.** 467; Devonshire, 5th D. of, **4.** 327–52, **11.** 27; Dickinson, **3.** 156, 311, **7.** 268, 270, 320; Diede, **4.** 156; Diede, Baroness von, **6.** 347; Dorset, D. of, **4.** 296, 306, **6.** 395, **7.** (?) 380, (?) 404; Douglas, Ds of, **7.** 259, **22.** 155, **39.** 9; Douglas, Sylvester, **4.** 461; Downe, **20.** 324; Duncannon, **7.** 344–50, 396, **30.** 264–5; Duncannon, Cts of, **4.** 283, 371, 374, **6.** 284; Dunmore, E. of, **4.** 276–7, 283; Echlin, **7.** 110–46, 300–10; Echlin, Lady, **38.** 514–15; Edmondson, **7.** 345, 389–96; Eglintoun, **6.** 357; Elcho, **9.** 272; Elliot, Lady, **6.** 416–18; Elliot, Sir Gilbert, 3d Bt, **7.** 261–8, **31.** 49, **38.** 413, 427, 440, 444; Elliot, Sir Gilbert, 4th Bt, **4.** 427–42, **6.** 364–426, **7.** 288–304, 380; Elliot, Hugh, **4.** 427–43, **7.** 213–304, 380, (?) 446; Elliot, Isabella, **6.** 407–18; English sympathizers with French Revolution, **42.** 374; Erne, Bns, **7.** 14–15; Estaing, **24.** 545; Eszterházy, Comte, **6.** 23, 30; Eszterházy, Valentin-Ladislas, **6.** 23, 30; Evelyn, **16.** 63; Exeter, E. of, **10.** 344–5; Fagels, **7.** 329; Fagnani, Maria, **7.** 137–48; Fanshawes, **4.** 241–2, 247; Farnham, **4.** 74, **38.** 440, 448; Fawkener, **32.** 299; Felicità d'Este, **18.** 378; Fermor, Lady Juliana, **20.** 97; Fermor, Lady Sophia, **37.** 81; Ferrers, Cts of, **20.** 298; Fife, Cts of, **7.** 271, 277, 292, 294, **31.** 72; Fife, E. of, **7.** 270–302, **31.** 72; Findlater, **32.** 55; Fitzgerald, Lord Charles, **6.** 330;

Fitzgerald, Lady Charlotte, **6.** 330; Fitzherbert, **4.** 327–45, **7.** 271, **25.** 311; Fitzpatrick, Hon. Richard, **5.** 2–11, **6.** 385–409, **32.** 343; Fitzroy, Charles, **3.** 152–67, **6.** 86–96, **31.** 125; Fitzroy, Mrs Charles, **3.** 149–57, **6.** 86, 89, **31.** 125; Fitzwilliam, 2d E., **4.** 184, 186, **7.** 261, 310; Foley, Lady, **7.** 293, 300, 309; Foote, **40.** 386; Forbes, Bn, **7.** 271, 294, 304, **22.** 162, **31.** 107; Foster, Lady Elizabeth, **25.** 459n; Fox, Lady Caroline (Bns Holland), **3.** 369, 375, **4.** 283–327, **22.** 163, **30.** 230, 250, **38.** 222, 314, 337, 533, 537, 556; Fox, Charles James, **4.** 301–28, **5.** 2–11, **6.** 375–92, **7.** 342, **32.** 343; Fox, Henry (Bn Holland), **3.** 375, **4.** 319, 327, **7.** 324, **10.** 60, 83, **22.** 129, 163, 554, **30.** 230, 250, **32.** 38, **38.** 222, 296, 314, 373, 414; Fox, Lady Mary (Bns Holland), **5.** 98–101; Fox, Stephen, (2d Bn Holland), **38.** 222, 337, 485, 517; Franchini, Abbé, **18.** 131; Franklin, Benjamin, **6.** 380–98, **7.** 33, 86, 320, **32.** 337; Franklin, William Temple, **6.** 383; Frederick, Charles, **37.** 47; Freeman, **38.** 498, 508; Friesendorff, **7.** 300, 303, 314; Fuentes, **38.** 340; Fuser, **7.** 306; Garrick, **38.** 478–9, 484, 517–18; Gatti, Dr, **3.** 241, 337, **4.** 234–431, **5.** 7, **6.** 340, **7.** 266–331; Gibbon, **6.** 441–89, **8.** 90; Glenorchy, Bns, **7.** 270; Gloucester, D. of, **31.** 126; Gordon, Col., **7.** 288–90, 379; Gordon, Lord William, **7.** 267–77, 378, **32.** 24; Graham, Mr and Mrs Thomas, **6.** 401; Grantham, 2d Bn, **5.** 87; Gray, Sir James, **7.** 316–21; Gray, Thomas, **13.** 8, 162n; (?) Gray, William, **33.** 496–7; Gregory, Dorothea, **6.** 357; Grenville, Henry, **6.** 225–82, **7.** 347–52, **30.** 264, **39.** 259; Grenville, Mrs Henry, **6.** 225–54, **7.** 347–52, **30.** 264, **39.** 259; Grenville, Louisa, **6.** 225–82, **7.** 347–8; Grenville, Thomas, **25.** 279; Greville, Hon. Charles Francis, **6.** 379; Greville, Mrs Fulke, **3.** 124–55, **5.** 361–73; Grimm, **8.** 64; Guasco, **3.** 335, **7.** 311, **22.** 529; Gurowski, **7.** 302, 312–13; Gustav III, **5.** 26–40, **39.** 419; HW, **1.** 34n, 95–9, 103, 109–10, 120n, 124, 157, 189, 190n, 228, 229, 235, 358, 381, 384, **7.** 257–417, **10.** 129, 131, 139–41, 146, 148, 149, 154, 157, 158, 160, 167–9, 171, 174–214, 244–51, 260, 282–98, **11.** 44, 341, **12.** 269, **13.** 8, 11, 41, 42, 46, 49–50, 162n, **14.** 140, 142, **15.** 6–7, 107, 126, 16. 128, 199, **17.** 24–7, 131, 164, 176, **18.** 495, **22.** 332–3, 340–4, 347–8, 358–60, 363–6, 371–3, 380–3, 394–7, 400–5, 409–11, 434, 441, 524, 548, 550–5, **23.** 133, 139, 141–5, 157, 158, 266, 311, 319, 320–3, 330–1, 398, 524, **24.** 116–17, 123–7, 132–4, 179–1, **25.** 516, 558, **28.** 18, 19, 51, 58, 219–23, 225–7, **30.** 18–19, 203–21, 262–5, **31.** 44–114, 65, 133–7, 157–9, 182–5, **32.** 17–18, 21–8, 46, 53–7, 69, 252–69, 298, **33.** 35, 235, **35.** 111–18, 120–8, 335–8, 343–5, 411, 425, **37.** 105, 106, 108, **39.** 87–98, 117–18, 141–9, 201, 222, 233, 255–72, **40.** 381–8, **41.** 1–8,

12–13, 99, 210, 213–16, 309, 343; Hamilton, Ds of, **22.** 155; Hamilton, Lady, **6.** 345, 350; Hamilton, Lady Archibald, **19.** 361n; Hamilton, Sir William, **6.** 345, 350, 364; Harrington, 2d E. of, **6.** 118, 220, 240, **39.** 186, 215, 269; Hart, Mrs, **4.** 275, **7.** 326–32, 349, **10.** 291–4; Hartley, **7.** 328–9; Hay, Sir George, **7.** 261; Hays, Mrs, **7.** 265, 272, 311; Herbert, Bn, **4.** 86, **7.** 230–1, 453; Hertford, Cts of, **7.** 261–3, 376, 404, **10.** 129, 163, 175, **31.** 44, **38.** 213–578, **39.** 1–5; Hertford, E. of, **1.** 34, **10.** 129, 163, **15.** 99, 106, **38.** 213–578, **39.** 1–5; Hervey, Hon. Felton, **4.** 333, 357; Hervey Aston, Henry, **7.** 301; Hessenstein, Edvard von, **7.** 328; Hessenstein, Fredrik Wilhelm von, **4.** 280, 317, 333, **5.** 39–40, **7.** 319, 330, 333, 336; Hillsborough, E. and Cts of, **7.** 263–4; Hobart, Hon. George, **6.** 348, 358, **7.** 108–9; Holdernesse, Cts of, (?) **10.** 288, **22.** 173n, **38.** 373; Holdernesse, E. of, **3.** 69–117, **6.** 187–91, **22.** 173n, **38.** 373; Honywood, Gen. and Mrs, **7.** 318; Howard, Mrs, **7.** 288–9, 297; Hume, **7.** 262–92, **10.** 176, **15.** 108, **41.** 24–6; Hunt, **19.** 477; Hyde, Bn, **37.** 307–8; Ikerrin, Vct, **7.** 389; Irwin, Gen. John, **4.** 93–311, 370, **7.** 329–34; Izard, Mrs, **6.** 62–8, 186; Izard, Ralph, **6.** 62–8, 186, **24.** 102; Janes, Rev. Mr, **7.** 352–3; Janssen, Sir Henry, **7.** 282, 312; Jenkinson, **3.** 104–10, 152–63; Jennings, **7.** 300–1, 344–51, 380; Jerningham, Charles, **3.** 301, **5.** 186, **6.** 43–5, **7.** 297, **11.** 67; Johnston, James and Lady Cecilia, **7.** 268; Joseph II, **6.** 394–455, **24.** 281, 298, 367, **32.** 343; Karl XIII, **5.** 26–40; Karl Alexander, **20.** 376; Karl Wilhelm Ferdinand, **3.** 13–49, **22.** 414; Keene, **3.** 47–132, **7.** 261–2; Keith, **38.** 354; Ker, Mr and Mrs, **7.** 301, 304, 309; Kildare, M. of, **7.** 326; Kilmorey, Vcts, **20.** 298; Kingston, Ds of, **6.** 311, **24.** 84, 242; Kinský, Fürstin, **7.** 292, 297–8, 346; Knight, Mrs, **7.** 294, 307, 309; Koch, **6.** 316, 362, **7.** 344–6; Krasicki, Bp, **7.** 329; Lambert, Lady, **7.** 271, 322; La Mina, Marquesa de, **9.** 9; Lee, (?) Arthur, **6.** 69; Leinster, Ds of, **6.** 319–38, **7.** 16–160, 449; Lennox, Lady Cecilia Margaret, **4.** 274–5; Lennox, Lord and Lady George, **35.** 317; (?) Lethieulliers, **37.** 47; (?) Lewenhaupt, **7.** 433; Ligonier, Vct, **7.** 270–4, 377; Lincoln, E. and Cts of, **24.** 420; Lincoln, E. of, **7.** 177, **17.** 165, **30.** 18, 19, 29; Livingston, **7.** 169–72, 427–33; Lloyd, Rachel, **3.** 149–57, 396, 404, 406, **4.** 7–86, 116, 159–64; Long, Mrs, **7.** 330; Lorenzi, Chevalier de, **20.** 542; Lorraine, Duchesse de, **18.** 298n; Lorraine, Primate of, **35.** 28; Lort, **2.** 16, **16.** 190; (?) Loss, Graf and Gräfin von, **7.** 349; Louis, **10.** 202; Lucan, Bn, **6.** 330–75, **7.** 157, 159, 423, **32.** 293, **36.** 192, **39.** 414; Lucan, Bns, **6.** 328–66, **7.** 157, 423, **32.** 293, 312, **39.** 414; Lumley, Vct, **6.** 362; Lyell, Mrs, **5.** 414,

416; Lyte, **4.** 329, **7.** 268; Lyttelton, 2d Bn, **6.** 395, **7.** 309; Macartney, **7.** 177–89, 433; Macaulay, Mrs, **6.** 486–97; Macclesfield, Cts of, **7.** 309–10; Macdonald, Sir James, **7.** 261–6, **22.** 343; Magnan, **18.** 564; Mahon, Vct, **6.** 29; Mallet, **3.** 385, 394, **4.** 11; Manchester, D. and Ds of, **5.** 283–328, **7.** 111; Mann, Sir Horatio, **25.** 2; Mar, Lady, **34.** 255; March, E. of (D. of Queensberry), **3.** 349–69, **7.** 321–3, **30.** 177, 251, **31.** 136, **38.** 413, 440, 448, 481, 485, 506, 511, 514, 516; Marlay, Rev. Richard, **7.** 351–3; Martin, **5.** 95, **7.** 337–41, **22.** 198, **38.** 270, 280; Masserano, **6.** 438; Massereene, E. of, **7.** 271, 294; Mathew, Mrs, **7.** 291, 294, **41.** 331; Maximilian, Archduke, **6.** 148–63; Meade, **7.** 297; Meynell, Hugo, jr, **6.** 455; Meynell, Mrs Hugo, sr, **6.** 455, 460; Miller, (?) Charles, **5.** 74; Miller, Mr and Mrs John, **5.** 189, 197, 205, **6.** 402, **24.** 197; Mitchell, **7.** 272; Modenese Duchess, **18.** 385–6; Monnerat, David, **5.** 91, 93, **6.** 214n, **7.** 410, 412–13; Montagu, Mrs Edward, **6.** 357, 362; Montagu, George, **9.** 9–11; Montagu, Lady Mary Wortley, **7.** 281; Montfort, Bn, **1.** 381n, **20.** 155–6; (?) Moore, Misses, **7.** 271; Morant, Mr and Mrs, **7.** 350, 352; Morehead, Mrs, **19.** 477; Morgan, **7.** 396; Morice, **5.** 265–6, **7.** 234, (?) 425, **23.** 140, 146, **25.** 74; Morton, E. of, **7.** 154–72, 425–57; Mountmorres, Vct, **5.** 320, **7.** 353; Mount Stuart, Lord, **33.** 134; Mozzi, **23.** 141–2; Murray, Hon. Alexander, **20.** 286; Nassau-Siegen, P. of, **5.** 175, **6.** 23, **7.** 32, **31.** 112; Nesbitt, **7.** 380; Nicholson, **7.** 308–9; Nicol, **7.** 317; Nolcken, **6.** 276, 281–3; Northumberland, Ds of, **3.** 191; Norton, William, **4.** 62–9; Ogilvie, **6.** 319–30, 421; Oneal, **7.** 271, 274; Orford, Cts of, **20.** 335, 439, **23.** 2, 120, 141–2, 230; Ossory, E. of Upper, **7.** 261–84, **30.** 207, **31.** 62, **38.** 517, **40.** 386; Oswald, **25.** 279; Paar, **3.** 214, 269, **7.** 313, 325, 332; Paine, **11.** 319; Palmerston, Vct, **5.** 401, 410; Panciatichi, **20.** 36; Pars, **6.** 236, 238, 240–1, **24.** 144, **26.** 48; Parsons family, **17.** 185, **37.** 114; Pater, Mme, **3.** 13, **7.** 296, 317, 320; Pembroke, Cts of, **3.** 396, 406, **4.** 7–201; Pembroke, 10th E. of, **3.** 396, **4.** 7–37, 82, 116, 139; Penn, Mrs, **20.** 20; Percy, Lord Algernon, **31.** 137; Petersham, Lady Caroline, **20.** 324, 333, 337–9; Pierson, **7.** 271; Pitt, Anne, **5.** 292–318; Pitt, Mr and Mrs Thomas, **5.** 130; Pomfret, Cts of, **20.** 97; Poyntz, Mrs, **22.** 163–4; Price, **5.** 317; Priestley, **42.** 374; Pringle, **7.** 319–20; Prior, Matthew, **20.** 62n; Pulteney, Vct, **20.** 155n; Pye, Mrs, **6.** 117; Radziwill, Ps, **4.** 93; Ramsay, Allan, **7.** 266–8, 376, 404, **31.** 59; Ramsay, Mrs Allan, **7.** 266, 268, 344, **31.** 59; Razumovskiĭ, **7.** 277; Rena, Contessa, **7.** 312, **30.** 220; Reynolds, Sir Joshua, **7.** 338; Richards, **7.** 261–3, **38.** 507; Richmond, Ds of, **4.** 114,

[Paris, *continued*]

7. 270, 327, 10. 163, 172, 181, 22. 155, 31. 125, 32. 16, 35. 317, 337, 38. 222, 384, 39. 47; Richmond, D. of, 4. 114, 6. 346, 438, 7. 270, 327, 10. 163, 172, 181, 289, 22. 163, 364, 31. 125, 32. 16, 35. 317, 337, 38. 222, 39. 47, 42. 104n; Rigby, 38. 190, 427, 434; Riggs, Mrs, 5. 189, 197, 205, 24. 197; Robinson, Hon. Frederick, 5. 87; (?) Rzewuski, 7. 327, 329; St George, Bns, 7. 270-1; St John, Hon. Henry, 4. 73, 77, 82; Salm, P. of, 7. 274, 290, 352; Salm, Ps of, 6. 279, 7. 280, 290, 295, 23. 398; Sandwich, Cts of, 5. 309, 7. 283, 286; Saxe, P. of, 4. 288; Sayer, Frances Julia, 35. 393; Schomberg, 7. 328; Schutz, 4. 77; (?) Scott, Hon. Campbell, 7. 309, 31. 109; Scott, David, 39. 536, 539; Selwyn, George, 3. 83-170, 184, 204, 210, 317, 345-69, 7. 76-7, 131-47, 321-4, 22. 105, 163, 30. 171, 250, 31. 136, 33. 64, 38. 409, 413, 440, 448, 452, 481-2, 485, 492, 503, 506, 511, 514, 516; Sempill, 18. 426; Seymour-Conway, Hon. Henry, 5. 384-95, 39. 117; Seymour-Conway, Hon. Hugh, 42. 104n; Shadwell family, 37. 46; Shelburne, E. of, 5. 144-63, 6. 100, 352-5, 39. 212n; Shirley, Mrs, 7. 277, 291, 293, 298, 379, 404; Shuvalov, Comte and Comtesse André, 6. 496, 7. 26, 54, 73, 429, 431, 8. 205; Shuvalov, Ivan, 3. 41-6, 111-12, 365, 381, 6. 72, 86, 442, 7. 263-353, 415; Sloane, 7. 266; Smith, Adam, 7. 302-12, 360, 31. 109; (?) Smyth, Edward S., 4. 258; Smyth, Elizabeth, 40. 331; (?) Smyth, James, 4. 258; Snelling, Miss, 4. 241; Somerset, D. of, 20. 139; Spencer, Cts, 5. 280, 351-403, 6. 219, 482-8; Spencer, 1st E., 5. 403-4, 6. 219, 221, 482-8; Spencer, Lady Henrietta Frances, 6. 482-8; Spencer, Lord Robert, 3. 396, 4. 16, 31, 37, 5. 8-11, 120, 135-6, 139-44; Stafford, Cts of, 18. 429-30, 42. 90; Stafford, E. of, 18. 429-30; Staley, 7. 378; Stanhope, 2d E., 6. 29, 39; Stanhope, Lady Harriet, 6. 99-110, 134-56, 229-40, 39. 186, 195n, 215, 219, 269, 539; Stanley, 21. 504, 514, 22. 300, 327, 340, 31. 49, 35. 230, 37. 307-8, 38. 427, 452; Staunton, 7. 206, 210-11, 213; Stavordale, Bn, 4. 328; Stephenson, 7. 288; Sterne, 40. 386; Stevenson, 7. 283; Stolberg-Gedern, Ps of, 5. 218; Storer, 7. 342; Stormont, 5. 258, 31. *passim*, 37. 309, 324; Strange, (?) 3. 389, 7. 262, 314; (?) Strathmore, 22. 23; Strogonov, 6. 228-9, 7. 346-9; Strogonov, Cts, 6. 228-9, 7. 346, 349; Stuart, Alexander, 7. 279, 284, 378; Sutherland, Lady, and son, 34. 156-7; (?) Sutton, Robert, 6. 75; Taaffe, John, 3. 12n; Taaffe, Theobald, 3. 12n, 19. 450n, 20. 287-8, 21. 473n; Tate, 7. 396; Tavistock, 38. 358, 359; Thanet, E. of, 35. 230; Taylor, 7. 377, 380; Thompson, 7. 344, 348-50; Tissot, 7. 235, 241, 437, 453, 458; Townsend, James, 6. 352-5; Tracys, 9. 76; Tra-

paud, Mrs, 7. 304; Tufton, Lady Charlotte, 7. 330; Tylney, 37. 309; Van Hoey, 19. 264; Veers, 19. 507; Vernon, Gen. Charles, 7. 294, 298-9, 310, 30. 215, 39. 42; Vernon, Lady Henrietta, 6. 364, 24. 242; Vespasiano, Abbé, 7. 264; Vestris, 43. 265; Voltaire, 7. 17, 24. 356, 28. 357, 365, 31. 270; Wachmeister, Baron, 7. 319; Walker, 42. 365, 384; Walpole, Lt-Col. Edward, 3. 253, 272-301; Walpole, Hon. Robert, 4. 133-480, 5. 29, 82-3, 86, 89, 23. 141, 39. 88; Walpole, Hon. Thomas, 4. 133-8, 446, 461, 464, 470, 5. 91-100, 7. 180-90, 205, 209, 240-51, 272-4, 279, 289-90, 336-41, 431-5, 446, 458, 461, 36. 168, 169-205, 211-24, 248-50; Walpole, Thomas, jr, 7. 189, 209, 243-9, 432, 435, 36. 206; Walpole of Wolterton, Bns, 38. 482; Ward, 4. 42, 5. 329; Webb, Lady, 7. 270-1; Welderen, 7. 350, 352, 396; Wenman, 7. 294; Werthein, 7. 341; Werthern, 7. 306; West, Richard, 43. 180; Wilkes, 3. 322n, 7. 266-306, 10. 180, 22. 162, 194, 198, 261, 272, 282, 365, 23. 28, 38. 279-80, 289-90, 297-8, 352-3, 361-2, 484, 39. 16-17, 40. 386; Williams, Jonathan, 6. 383; Williams, Miss, 25. 459n; Wilton, Joseph, 20. 391n; Wood, Robert, 7. 319-20, 39. 89; Wortley Montagu, 19. 450n, 20. 226, 287-8, 294, 21. 473n; Wrottesley, 22. 554; Wroughton, 4. 241; (?) Württemberg-Oels, Ds of, 7. 449, 460; Wynn, 37. 309; Yertzin, Mme de, 38. 401; York, Edward, D. of, 7. 364-6, 22. 245, 550, 558, 31. 134, 38. 430; Young, Mr, 7. 284-5, 289, 293, 296, 299-301, 309-10, 316; Young, Mrs, 20. 327; Young Pretender, 7. 274-5, 8. 58, 18. 378, 385, 389, 393, 394, 402, 404, 415, 433-4, 19. 86-7, 140, 319-20, 368, 376, 378, 509, 20. 8, 9, 15, 22-3, 35, 44, 21. 59n, 22. 106, 385, 389, 393, 23. 351, 398

vivacity uncommon in, except among rash young men, 24. 498

Voltaire arrives at, 28. 357, 365
—— banished from, 4. 293, 307
—— praises dramatic appreciation of, 8. 142
—— to see performance of *Irène* at, 31. 270

wager over ride from, to Fontainebleau, 35. 190

Waldegrave, Cts, may accompany HW to, 38. 343

Waldegrave, E., ambassador at, 2. 125n, 19. 564

Walkinshaws in convent at, 26. 47, 33. 442

Walpole, Horatio (1678-1757), ambassador at, 9. 116n

Walpole, Robert, secretary of embassy at, 4. 133n

Walpole, Hon. Thomas, banker in, 4. 132n
—— marries at, 33. 587

Washington's founding of Cincinnati society stirs, 33. 431

watches from, for Riccardi and Niccolini girls, 21. 343

weather in: **1.** 99, 103, 109, 110n; severe, **30.** 211; *see also* cold weather in

Whately's book printed in French at, **16.** 191

whist popular in, **30.** 208–9

wigs from, **37.** 526

will of Ds of Kingston lodged in, **31.** 288–9

Williams, G. J., tells HW that half of, is mad after his *Account of the Giants,* **30.** 238

witticism at, about Estaing, **24.** 450

women of, often well-informed and witty, **14.** 150

Wortley Montagu told to leave, because father is there, **20.** 226n

York, D. of, takes hôtel in, **38.** 440

Yorke may replace Stormont at, **24.** 179

Young Pretender collects volunteers at, **19.** 87

—— may enter French army at, **18.** 378

—— probably visits Princesse de Talmond at, **20.** 44

—— reported to be hiding near, **20.** 35n

——'s arrest at, **20.** 8, 15

——'s disappearance reported from, **19.** 367

—— sends Stuart to, to fetch daughter, **25.** 513

——'s income rumoured at, **23.** 402

——'s non-recognition from Clement XIII variously interpreted at, **22.** 394

Paris, Parlement de. *See* Parliament of Paris

Paris, Peace Treaty of, (1763):

carpenters might resent, for reducing demand for wooden legs, **38.** 509

concluding, **22.** 116

conclusion of, **15.** 54n

couriers announce, **22.** 105

deferred, **22.** 99–100

definitive treaty for, awaited, **22.** 118

England's conquests 'refunded' by, **33.** 215

English negotiators for, **21.** 504, 514, **22.** 69–70, 86, 90, 92–3, 300

English victories sacrificed by delegates to, **22.** 401

Éon's part in bringing, to England, **38.** 243–4

France has not forgotten, **29.** 65

HW does not wish, inscribed on his tomb, **32.** 318

Hertford ordered to press France for fulfilment of, **38.** 217n

in progress, **22.** 52, 60, 65

Melo e Castro, Portuguese minister at, **21.** 45n

North's vote for, costs him Pynsent's fortune, **38.** 494n

opposed, **22.** 89, 91, 95

Pitt carried into Parliament to oppose, **32.** 44n

Pompadour, Mme de, buys English stocks to profit by rise at news of, **25.** 357

Pynsent, Sir William, angered by, **38.** 493

—— lived to see, **22.** 277, 284

said to be broken off, **22.** 81

signing and terms of, **22.** 95–6

stocks fluctuate according to expectations of, **22.** 38, 81

Townshend, Charles, applauds, though he had opposed it, **38.** 496

Paris, Treaty of (1783):

declared, **33.** 381, 383

England's ultimatum about, **25.** 342

English negotiators for, **25.** 279, 311

Gibraltar's defence may influence, **25.** 352

HW expected England to be more ruined than it was by, **35.** 369

HW hopes, will confirm England's blessings, **35.** 372

HW relieved by signing of, **35.** 375

Hunter, Dr, might negotiate, **33.** 318

ignominious but hardly mentioned after Parliament's approval, **25.** 373–4

in progress, **25.** 279, 311

not yet concluded, **25.** 354, 355

preliminaries for, **25.** 356–7, 362

scandalous, **34.** 230

signed, **25.** 426–7

to be adhered to, despite English political shift, **25.** 372

unpopular in England, **25.** 362, 366–7

Paris à la main. See under À la main

Paris de Montmartel, Mlle:

(?) engagement of, rumoured, **5.** 147

Paris de Montmartel, Armand-Louis-Joseph (1748–81), Marquis de Brunoy:

Aranda takes house of, **5.** 406

Brunoy sold by, **6.** 365n

Paris de Montmartel, Jean (1690–1766), Marquis de Brunoy; banker:

Brunoy owned by, **6.** 365n

(?) daughter of, **5.** 147n

wealthy, **3.** 101

Paris de Treffonds, Louis (d. before 1779), receiver-gen. of finances for Rouen:

Du Deffand, Mme, inquires of, about parcel, **4.** 22–4

Durand sends parcel to, **4.** 23–4

Paris associations:

for defence in Gordon Riots, **35.** 505n

Pariset, D. P.:

Ibbot's print by, **42.** 22n

'Parish Register of Twickenham, The':

HW mentions Chesterfield's amour with Lady Fanny Shirley in, **10.** 2n

HW quotes from, **43.** 118

remarkable persons listed in, **13.** 33

text of, **42.** 488–90

Paris plate. *See under* Plate

Paris sauvé. See Sedaine, Michel-Jean: *Maillard ou Paris sauvé*

Park, Thomas, high constable of Furness 1642–7:

book contains extracts from MSS of, **2.** 289n

diary of, says troubled times are hard on constables, **39.** 237

Park, Thomas (1759–1834), engraver and antiquary:

Percy considers, for editing Surrey, **42.** 367n

SH visited by, **12.** 229

Park, Mrs Thomas. *See* Hughes, Maria Hester

Park; parks:
Cascines reminiscent of, 23. 6
HW's aversion for, around a house, 34. 196
rangership of, *see under* Hyde Park; Richmond: New Park; St James's Park
royal, arrests forbidden in, 9. 153
Parker, Capt.:
Bath installation attended by, as proxy, 23. 410n
Parker, Dr, rector of St James's, Piccadilly:
Osbaldeston appoints, 14. 131n
Parker, Vcts. *See* Drake, Mary Frances
Parker, Catharine, m. (ca 1630) John Savage, 2d E. Rivers:
HW asks about portrait of, at Kimbolton, 10. 78
Parker, Dorothea (d. 1768), m. Robert Gates:
intimate with Lady Walpole's woman, 25. 92n
son of, 25. 92n
Parker, G.:
print of, 40. 236
Parker, George (ca 1697–1764), 2d E. of Macclesfield, 1732; M.P.; president of Royal Society 1752–64:
chairman of trustees of Sloane's museum, 20. 359
Cherokees and Mrs Clive entertained by, 10. 36
crowd sees, lying in state, 38. 358
death of: 22. 211; releases tellership of Exchequer, 38. 346
Grenville succeeds, as teller of the Exchequer, 22. 211
HW to send papers to, 20. 557
house of, in St James's Sq., 22. 211n
in cavalcade at Henley, 37. 371n
longitude investigated by, 20. 359
mistress marries, 22. 211
Morton succeeds, in presidency of Royal Society, 38. 463
president of Royal Society and Sloane trustee, 20. 557n
wife's bequest from, 38. 348
Parker, Hon. Mrs George Lane. *See* Cæsar, Jane
Parker, Sir Hyde (1714–82), 5th Bt, 1782; naval officer:
fleet of, inspected by George III, 29. 150
French transports defeated by, 25. 21
George III thanks, for doubtful victory over Dutch, 25. 176–7
Rodney joins, at St Lucia, 25. 24n
—— 'pallisered' by, 29. 48
St Eustatius convoy should have been protected by, 25. 159–60
ships of, off Nantucket, 33. 52n
Parker, John (ca 1730–ca 1765), painter; art agent:
antiquarian at Rome, 43. 267
(?) Pulteney warned against, 20. 174
Parker, John (?1735–88), cr. (1784) Bn Boringdon; M.P.:
Devonshire electors tell, to oppose Cider Tax, 38. 459n

Parker, Capt. John (fl. 1781–2), sea-capt. in Tuscany:
Mann commissions, 25. 249
Minorcan news brought by, 25. *196*
Murray commissions, to get supplies for Minorca, 25. 198n, 249n
Udny to question, about Murray's correspondence with Crillon, 25. 208n
Parker, Mark (ca 1698–1775), papal naval capt.; art dealer at Rome:
Compagni and Libri to pay money to, 17. *81–2*
Cybo's collection known to, 18. 236
expenses of, over statue, 18. 178
HW's correspondence with, 17. 291, 26. *3–5*
HW's views of Rome billed by, 17. 81–2
HW's views of Rome sent by, to Howe, 17. 395
Lanfranco painting may be owned by, 18. 275
list of pictures owned by, forwarded to HW, 18. 243
Mann pays, 18. 214
—— regrets not having bought collection of, for Sir Robert Walpole, 18. 273
——'s correspondence with, about 'views' and statue for HW, 17. 81–2, 268, 291, 317, 18. 56, 133, 152, 161, 177–8, 190, 197, 236, 239–40
prices of, excessive, 18. 296
(?) Pulteney warned against, 20. 174
Raphael painting bought by, from Cybo collection, 18. 239–40
statue procured for HW through, 17. 82, 212, 268, 291, 317, 18. 56, 133, 152, 161, 177–8, 190, 197, 26. 5
Valle does not trust, 18. 152
—— paid by, for statue, 17. 212n
—— to be threatened by, 17. 317
Parker, Matthew (1504–75), Abp of Canterbury, 1559:
Anne Boleyn's chaplain, 40. 159
Cole's life of, 2. 226n
De antiquitate Britannicæ ecclesiæ by: William of Wykeham's architectural prowess mentioned in, 16. 35; Zouch cites, 16. 46, 47
editions by: of *Ælfredi regis gestæ*, 1. 172; of 'monkish' historians, 1. 172
Edward VI's letter inscribed by, 40. 159
Elizabeth, Q., sends stag to, 1. 224, 227
MSS given by, to Corpus Christi College, 1. 185, 194, 222, 223–4
Tyson's print of, 1. 193n
Parker, Sir Peter (?1721–1811), Kt, 1772; cr. (1783) Bt; naval officer; M.P.:
Admiralty post to go to, 34. 9n
baronetcy of, corrected, 43. 350
Byron's ships commanded by, off New York, 33. 52n
Charleston expedition of, fails, 6. 354, 24. 236
fleet of Byron and, sails to America, 33. 31n
Grasse dines with, 33. 351n
Jamaica shipping reported by, 39. 353n

renown of, will not equal Marlborough's, **28.** 280–1

Rowley to reinforce fleet of, at Jamaica, **33.** 245n

said to be wounded in 6 places, **24.** 236, **32.** 318

Parker, Richard (1572–1629), historian:

History and Antiquities of the University of Cambridge by, cited, **1.** 148

Parker, Samuel (1640–88), Bp of Oxford 1686–8:

Bishop Parker's History of His Own Times, 'Impartial Account' in, based on Wood, **20.** 188n

conversion of, from Presbyterianism, **20.** 188

James II's master of Magdalen College, **20.** 188

Parker, Thomas (1723–95), 3d E. of Macclesfield:

candidacy of, for Oxfordshire, **37.** 371n

Clarke's fortune goes to, as his alleged halfbrother, **38.** 468

petition about Oxford election presented by, **20.** 435n

Parker, William (1575–1622), 5th Bn Monteagle and 13th Bn Morley, 1618:

warned of Gunpowder Plot, **32.** 76

Parker, William (1714–1802), D.D.:

Expediency of the Miraculous Powers of the Christian Fathers, The, by, **15.** 298

Parker-Jervis, W. R.:

Mme du Deffand's and HW's MSS owned by, **3.** xxxvii-xl, xlvi-xlviii, **36.** 312

Parkers, manor at Brumstead, Norfolk:

HW's will mentions, **30.** 368

Parkes, Ann, Lady Strathmore's housemaid:

Strathmore, Lady, elopes with, **33.** 460

Park Hall, Warwickshire:

Ardens' seat, **1.** 147

Parkhouse, Hannah (1743–1809), m. (ca 1768) —— Cowley; dramatist and poet:

Merry's interchange with, in *The World,* **31.** 271n

plays of, considered indelicate, **33.** 594

School for Greybeards by: HW to attend, **33.** 544; HW's opinion of, **33.** 546

Parkin, Rev. Charles (1689–1765), antiquary:

account of Houghton by, **1.** 75n

HW receives information from, for *Anecdotes of Painting,* **40.** 222–7

HW's correspondence with, **40.** 222–7

Partridge lends *Anecdotes of Painting* to, **40.** 222

Parkinson, Sydney (ca 1745–71), draughtsman:

Journal of a Voyage to the South Seas by: HW criticizes, **32.** 127; publication of, delayed, **28.** 86n

Park-keepers:

landholders might massacre, **35.** 266

Park Lane, London:

St John, Lady Mary, dies at, **11.** 190n

Park Place, Berks, Conway's seat:

acting at, not known to HW, **33.** 580

Ailesbury, Cts of, invites HW to, **37.** 504–5

—— takes Bryant's *Observations* to, **33.** 316

alterations to, **34.** 204, **39.** 500

animals at, all diminutive, **37.** 347

beauties of, **34.** 15

bedchamber and new passage added to, **37.** 350

bow-window room of, **37.** 475

bridge at: **10.** 104–5, **34.** 15; finished, **38.** 470, **39.** 461

Ceunot employed at, **37.** 329

Chinese pheasants swarm at, **38.** 179

Coke, Lady Mary, to visit, **31.** 200

Conway, Anne Seymour, to be taken to, by Mathews, **37.** 330

Conway, Henry Seymour, and Cts of Ailesbury buy, **20.** 316–17

Conway, Henry Seymour, and Cts of Ailesbury confer about placing HW's drawing at, **37.** 475

Conway, Henry Seymour, and Cts of Ailesbury invite HW to, **37.** 466, 468, 470, 483, 484–5, 487, 489

Conway, Henry Seymour, and Cts of Ailesbury owners of, **10.** 99

Conway, Henry Seymour, and Cts of Ailesbury stay at, **11.** 145

Conway, Henry Seymour, at, **9.** 288, **11.** 317, **22.** 413, **29.** 96n, **33.** 70, 270

—— calls, 'House of Riddles,' **37.** 411

—— goes to: **30.** 233, **33.** 70, 270; in winter, **22.** 413; when his bridge cracks, **35.** 428; 'with his usual phlegm,' **38.** 554

—— hopes, will be green for HW, **37.** 377

—— ill in bed at, **25.** 115

—— in state department should not pine for sugar-plums of, **39.** 31

—— invites HW to, **37.** 360

—— longs for plough and cabbages of, **37.** 450

—— on way to, **35.** 361

—— plants small trees at, for small deer, **37.** 347

—— returns to, from Ireland, **37.** 366

—— 's comedy should be acted at, **35.** 395

—— seldom at: **35.** 365; even when not on military duty, **38.** 59

—— 's return to, predicted by Duncannon, **37.** 460

—— 's seat, **25.** 428n, 576n

—— unlikely to return to plough at, **37.** 437

Cooper, Gislingham, at, **9.** 142

cottage at: **39.** 549–50; HW likes, **10.** 104; Powys's verses written in, **39.** 533–5

Damer, Mrs, at, **11.** 48, 307, 310, 357, 360, **12.** 145n, 302n, **35.** 386

—— does modelling at, **12.** 271, 272

—— sends plants from, **12.** 36

description of: in *The Times,* **39.** 549–52; in *The World,* **39.** 549–52

dressing-room at: Conway hangs prints in, **37.** 350; fitted up by Cts of Ailesbury, **37.** 475

drought at: dries up ponds and kills trees and grass, **37.** 367; rain relieves, **37.** 368

[Park Place, *continued*]

'Druidic Temple' at: **34**. 14–15, 21, **35**. 395, 396; called 'little Stonehenge,' **39**. 460

French noblemen's 'invasion' of, averted, **39**. 292

gardens at, **43**. 379

goldfish at, *see under* Goldfish

grass seed planted at, **37**. 368

HW and Anne Seymour Conway run down the 'precipices' of, **38**. 155n

HW and Churchills to attend party at, **37**. 522–3, 537, 538

HW and Jerningham to visit, **39**. 436, 437, **42**. 147

HW calls: 'coldest house in the world,' **12**. 37; 'Sabine Farm,' **22**. 413, **39**. 179

HW dines at, **35**. 147

HW has not been further than, for 4 years, **11**. 97

HW hears news at, **33**. 299

HW jokes about fetching Lady Ailesbury from, **31**. 25

HW may visit, **6**. 181, 337n, **14**. 83, **20**. 443n, **42**. 474

HW postpones visit to, because of weather, **33**. 455

HW praises beauties of, **11**. 75, **12**. 177

HW prefers to visit: going or coming from Nuneham, **39**. 385, 392; in November rather than July, **39**. 296

HW reads Rousseau's *Émile* at, **38**. 181

HW returns from, **16**. 290

HW's 'Mi Li' describes, **39**. 461

HW's reason for not going to, **32**. 283–4, 309

HW to be attended at, by Philip Colomb, **42**. 299

HW to bring Anne Seymour Conway back to, **37**. 336

HW to send Anne Seymour Conway to, **37**. 343

HW to spend night at, en route to Matson, **30**. 260

HW to visit: **29**. 72, 99, 156, 161, **32**. 242, 309, 327, 408, **33**. 211, 231, **35**. 289, **36**. 243, **37**. 366, 369, 383, **39**. 107, 138, 157–9, 249–50, 384–5, 392, 403, 406, 419, 444–5, 470–2, 485, **41**. 404, **42**. 384; to see great arch, 'Druidic temple,' Lady Ailesbury's needlework and Mrs Damer's sculpture, **35**. 395

HW unable to visit, **35**. 496

HW would like to see the Fitzroys or Richmonds at, but not the Cavendishes, **39**. 101

Hague, The, contrasted with, **38**. 100

Henley near, **25**. 428n, 576n

Holdernesses in raptures over, **38**. 60

improvements at, **37**. 350

India-room chimney at, **37**. 331

landscape effects at: Conway's plantings, **37**. 350; HW's advice needed on, **37**. 487; Lombardy poplar, **11**. 146n, **33**. 480, **39**. 133n; plantations thriving, **38**. 179

lawn at, dry, **37**. 492

lawns and shrubs at, green, **37**. 486

Malmesbury, Lord, buys, **15**. 334, **43**. 379

—— considers purchase of, **12**. 176, 177

Mount Edgcumbe probably puts Conway out of humour with, **39**. 294

near Henley, not Chatham, **42**. 131

neighbours all overlooked by, from hall, **37**. 350

nightingales at, **12**. 97

note on, **11**. 74–5n

occupants of, to visit HW, **10**. 99

Parliament may keep Conway away from, **6**. 177

pond prepared at, for goldfish, **37**. 370

previous owners of, **20**. 316–17

progress of work at, **10**. 104–5

repairs at, **12**. 37

Rochford brings poplar to, from Turin, **39**. 133n

rosary field at, cows to do quarantine in, **37**. 345

sideboard and chair frames needed for, **37**. 465

stucco at, raised by nightingale, **39**. 505

terraces at, HW unable to compass, after gout, **39**. 3

too high to be flooded, **38**. 277

trees do not intercept view from, **37**. 350

'unroofed and unceiled,' **12**. 37–8

visitors to: Amelia, Ps, **10**. 310, 311, **31**. 146; Banks, Miss, **37**. 380; Berrys, **11**. 48, 74, **12**. 100, 103, 167, 169, 170, 173, **39**. 474; Brandenburg-Ansbach, Margrave and Margravine of, **39**. 500; Cambis, Mme de, **11**. 357, 360; Campbell, Lady Frederick, **35**. 386, (?) **39**. 419n; Campbell, Lord Frederick, **35**. 386, **37**. 350, 527, (?) **39**. 419n; Campbell, John (1723–1806), **37**. (?) 350, 527; Campbell, Lady William and children, **33**. 50–1; Campbell, Lord and Lady William, **38**. 436; Churchills, **39**. 419n; Coke, Lady Mary, **31**. 139, 146, 156; Conway, Hon. Anne Seymour (Mrs Harris), **37**. 349, 368, 369, 385; Conway, Hon. Henrietta Seymour, **38**. 13; Damer, Mrs, **35**. 386; Devonshire, D. of, **37**. 483, 486; Fox, Henry and Lady Caroline, **37**. 483, 486; Guerchy, **38**. 461, 478; HW, **1**. 119n, 177, 256, **2**. 18, 118n, **4**. 445n, **6**. 83n, 207n, **9**. 141–2, 163n, 192, 288, **10**. 44, 103–5, 124, 126, 157, 159n, 227n, 310, 311, **11**. 48, 71, 72, 129, 134, 135, 357, 360, 362, **12**. 103, 167, 169, 170, **14**. 158n, **15**. 251, 269–70, **16**. 290, **22**. 263, **23**. 339, **25**. 119, 428, 659, **29**. 156n, **30**. 268, **31**. 12, 139, 146, 156, 187, **32**. 136, **33**. 47, 50, 52, 231, 272, 415, 417, 438, 484, 504, 524, **34**. 14–16, 65, 203–4, **35**. 71, 297, 333, 338, 374, 375, 386, 396, 414, 489, **37**. 343, 558, **38**. 34, 37, 39, 59, 175, 179, 181, 430, 436, 439, 461, 470, **39**. 179, 419, **40**. 133, 442; Hamilton, Lady, **23**. 339, **37**. 527; Hamilton, Sir William, **23**. 339, **33**. 415, **35**. 375, **37**. 527; Harrowbys, **39**. 419n; Hertford, E. of, **31**. 146;

Hervey, Mrs, **42**. 303; Hervey, Elizabeth, **11**. 135, **39**. 419n; Hervey, Mrs William Thomas, **11**. 135, **39**. 500; Howard, Lady Anne, **31**. 146; Jerningham, Edward, **11**. 145, **33**. 484; Johnston, Lady Cecilia, **11**. 57, 123, **12**. 169, **38**. 165, **39**. 453; Johnston, Gen. James, **11**. 57, 123, **12**. 169, **39**. 453; Ker, Lady Louisa, **37**. 543, 548; Kildare, Cts of, **37**. 483, 486; Lennox, Ladies Louisa and Sarah, **37**. 486; Lockhart, Mrs, **12**. 103; Lyttelton, Bn, **37**. 349, **40**. 133; Lyttelton, Bns, **37**. 349, **38**. 35, 165, **39**. 300; Middleton, Catherine, **31**. 146; O'Hara, **12**. 158n; Pitt, **37**. 380; Rich, Mary, **37**. 505; Richmond, Ds of, **35**. 289, **37**. 483, 528, 534, 537n, **39**. 283, 419n, 526; Richmond, D. of, **39**. 419n; Seymour-Conway, Hon. Henry, **39**. 281; Strafford, E. and Cts of, **37**. 483; Temple, E. and Cts, **37**. 380; Townshend, Mary, **37**. (?) 350

Park Place, St James's, London:
  Shorter, Erasmus, lived in, **37**. 372n

Park St, Grosvenor Sq., London:
  Huntingdon, Cts of, lives in, **20**. 52n
  St John dies in, **12**. 29n
  Wallingford, Vcts, dies at her house in, **42**. 387n

Park St Chapel, Grosvenor Sq.:
  Hackman ordained at, **33**. 100n

Parlement; parlements (French). *See* Parliament

Parley, Mrs:
  HW mentions, **6**. 297

Parliament; parliaments:
  kings' attempts to break, **39**. 222

Parliament (English):
  See sub-sections: House of Commons *and* House of Lords *for entries not in main sequence below*
  accuracy of reports of speeches in, **17**. 230n, **25**. 58
  action of, at beginning of George II's reign, **9**. 316
  actors' fatigue nothing compared to that endured in, **38**. 317
  acts and bills of: act for abolishing sinecures, **25**. 273; Act for Better Preventing . . . Murder, **9**. 279, **20**. 317, **21**. 388; act for preventing theft of dogs, **4**. 405; Act for Relief of Insolvent Debtors, **9**. 85–6, **40**. 192; Act of Dependency, **25**. 682n, **43**. 292; Act of Insolvency, **21**. 45, 140, 148; Act of Settlement, **19**. 142; Act of Succession, **9**. 143; Acts of Attainder, **41**. 92, 322–3; Additional Militia Bill, **33**. 108; Adultery Bill, **24**. 455n; against arming without authority, **19**. 102n; American acts, **24**. 77; American Commissioners Bill and American Declaratory Bill, **24**. 359n, 429n; American Congress demands repeal of, **39**. 227, 231–2; American trade restriction bill, **24**. 158, **28**. 179, 217; Annuity and Lottery bill, **18**. 141n, **25**. 402n; army supply bills, **19**. 4–5; bill against importing foreign clothes, **35**. 36; bill against importing gold and silver fabrics, **35**. 36n; bill for disqualifying customs officers as voters, **25**. 66n, 257n; bill for increasing judges' salaries, **9**. 235; bill for reform of public offices, **25**. 20, 26–8, 29. 109, 116, **33**. 407n, **42**. 58n (*see also* regulation of the King's civil establishments); bill for regulating election trials, **25**. 573n; bill for Sulgrave enclosure, **9**. 336–7; Bill of Conciliation, **41**. 316; Bill of Pains and Penalties, **17**. 330; bill of perpetual insolvency, **35**. 644; Bill of Protection, **22**. 473n; Bill of Rights, **23**. 114, 209; bills for reform of, **25**. 20, 26–7, 272, 273; bill to regulate trial of controverted elections, **24**. 45, 273, **32**. 189; Boston Port Act, **23**. 561n, **24**. 158n, **41**. 304; Bribery Bill, **22**. 584–5; Buckinghamshire Assizes Bill, **13**. 19–20, **19**. 468n; burnt in explosion, **13**. 104; Cambric Bill, **18**. 192; Catholic relief bill, **25**. 54n, **28**. 395, **29**. 66, **33**. 98n, 177n, 187n, **39**. 350; Charter Act, **25**. 159n; Chatham Annuity Bill, **24**. 382n; chimney-sweepers' regulation act, **39**. 428n; Cider Bill, **10**. 57–8, **22**. 129, 132–3, **38**. 292–3, 307, 326n, 459n, 493, **41**. 10; Clandestine Marriages Act, **9**. 147, 149, 154, 231, **20**. 383, **22**. 294, **23**. 399n, 400n, **30**. 125, **31**. 292n, **37**. 361–4, 365, 366–7, 407, **38**. 318, **39**. 375–6; Contractors' Bill, **25**. 28, 38–9, 47, 257n, **29**. 28, 230–1; Correspondence with the Pretender Bill, **18**. 440; Crown lands can only be disposed by, **15**. 90; Declaratory Act, **32**. 234, **33**. 328n, **41**. 9n; Defence by Counsel Bill, **19**. 396; Detention of Suspected Persons Bill, **18**. 408; Devonshire Canal bill, **34**. 184n; Disabling Act, **23**. 194n, **25**. 38n, 66n; Dissenters' Bill, **33**. 98n; duty on imported china to favour Bristol manufacturers, **32**. 270; East India Co., altered by, **41**. 301; East India Co. Dividend Bill, **22**. 513, 534; East India Judicature Bill, **23**. 399; Election Laws Bill, **17**. 484; Exchequer reform bill, **33**. 406n; Excise Bill, **34**. 229, **39**. 318–19; Excise Bill on Cider, *see under* Cider Bill; Exclusion Bill, **20**. 222; Ferrers separation bill, **21**. 184, 367, 396, **37**. 529; Five Mile Act, **28**. 46; forbidding correspondence with the Pretender's sons, **30**. 91; for building tow-path in Surrey, **29**. 70; Game Act, **36**. 221; Gaming Act, **37**. 201; Gin Act, **20**. 48, **30**. 315, **33**. 190; Gold Coin Act, **23**. 498; Grafton's divorce bill, **23**. 99; Grenville Act, **24**. 45, 273, **32**. 189n; HW imitates language of, **25**. 358; Habeas Corpus Extension, **21**. 182, 199, 205, **37**. 526, 528–9, **41**. 182n; Habeas Corpus Suspension, **18**. 408, **28**. 283, **32**. 402n; Hanover troops, *see under* Hanover; Indemnity Bill, **17**. 425, 428–9, 436–7, 448, 454, 520n, **35**. 29; India Bills, **25**. 448–9, 451–2, 457, 458n, 459,

[Parliament (English), *continued*]
484–5, 488, 490–1, **29.** 320, 329n, 331–2, 333, 347–8, **31.** 285, **35.** 381, **36.** 214, 218n, 219n, 221, 231n (*see also* Regulating Bill); Irish commercial intercourse bill, **26.** 564n, 573n, 578n; Irish commercial regulations, **33.** 491n; Irish Mutiny Bill, **33.** 173n; Jacobites deny validity of, **30.** 97; Jacobites restored by, to forfeited Scottish estates, **25.** 520; Jew Bill, **9.** 157, 333, **35.** 70n, 179; Judicature Act, **25.** 159n; Kyrwood, Mrs, wants, to prevent distilleries from exploding, **39.** 153; Licensing Act, **37.** 25–6; make war but cannot repeal it, **24.** 355; Marriage Act, *see* Clandestine Marriages *and* Royal Marriage Act; Massachusetts Bay Act, **23.** 568; Massachusetts Trade Act, **24.** 158n; Militia Bills, **21.** 12n, 137, 552, **24.** 497, **30.** 126, 142, **32.** 278–9, **35.** 285n, 286, 291n, **37.** 441, 444, 452, 456, 458, 461, 575, **38.** 145n, 315 (*see also* Additional Militia Bill); Money Bills, **9.** 402, **37.** 389n; Murder Preventing Act, *see* Act for Better Preventing . . . Murder; Mutiny Bill, **9.** 143, 276, **20.** 30n, 33, 38, 51, 54, 112, 229, 265n, **30.** 319, **35.** 162; naturalization of Karl Wilhelm Ferdinand, **38.** 289; Navigation Act, **28.** 211, **32.** 231n; Navy Bills, **20.** 33, 38, 54, **21.** 182, **38.** 307; Northumberland, D. of, procures, for erection of powder mills, **23.** 365; Paddington Road Bill, **37.** 452–3, 456, 457–8, 459, 461, 464; Pension Bill, **17.** 392; Place Bill, **17.** 295–6, 391–2, 431, **18.** 19, **37.** 87, 227; Players of Interludes Act, **23.** 471; Poor Bill, **10.** 150, **38.** 528–9, 535, 536; Popish Relief Act, *see* Catholic Relief Bill; postal regulation acts, **31.** 234n; Posthorse Act, **33.** 108n; Poynning's Act, **23.** 156n; private bills, **20.** 50 *and passim*; Prize Bill, **37.** 420; Quaker Bill, **19.** 503n; Qualification Bill, **38.** 48; Quartering Act, **24.** 14n, **33.** 179n; Quebec Government Bill, **11.** 263, **24.** 13, 161n, **39.** 175, 227, **41.** 300, 304, 312n; Quieting Bill, **24.** 542, **33.** 152–3; Regency Bill, **9.** 113, **10.** 153, 154, **20.** 239–40, 247, 249, 257, 263, 434, **22.** 294–9, **31.** 1, **34.** 43n, **35.** 176, **38.** 533, 541–5, 547–53, 556, 557, 568, **42.** 495; Regulating Bill (East India Bill), **23.** 490n, **29.** 320, 329n, 331–2, 333, 347–8, **31.** 285, **32.** 119, 129; regulation of the King's civil establishments, **25.** 20, 26–7, 28 (*see also* bill for reform of public offices); relating to monuments in Westminster Abbey, **28.** 166; relief acts, *see* Catholic relief bill *and* Dissenters' Bill; Renunciation Bill, **33.** 382n; Restraining Bill, **41.** 304; Richmond's, for annual Parliaments, **29.** 54, 67; Riot Act, **17.** 252, **33.** 196, **38.** 562; Roman Catholic Relief Bill, *see* Catholic relief bill; Royal Marriage Act, **5.** 207, **23.** 390, 396, 398, **25.** 629, **33.** 455, **36.** 66, 67n, 84, 144, 307, **39.** 160n; Scottish bills, **19.** 388, 396, **20.** 310, **26.** 31–3; Seditious Meetings Bill,

34. 209n; Self-Denying Ordinance, **22.** 585n; Septennial Act, **17.** 386, **32.** 29n; Shop Tax Bill, **25.** 578n, 583n; sneered at in France, **28.** 221–2; Somerset, D. of, disinherits son by, **18.** 523; Stamp Act, **10.** 192n, **22.** 401–2, 408, 409–10, 494, **24.** 208, **25.** 213, 252, 279, **29.** 168, **30.** 221, **31.** 97, 285, **33.** 232, 303, **38.** 508–9, **39.** 40, 61, **41.** 9, **42.** 506; Strutt's, for increasing Parliamentary qualifications, **29.** 50; SH sold by, to HW, **13.** 17; Test Act, **11.** 317, **33.** 127; Trade Bills, **20.** 135; Treasonable Practices Bill, **34.** 209n; Triennial Act, **17.** 392; turnpike bills, **20.** 112, 120–1, **23.** 455 (*see also* Paddington Road Bill); Winchester Bill, **33.** 179n; Wrought Silks and Velvets Bill, **22.** 301, **30.** 181n, **38.** 558n
Adam brothers aided by, **28.** 108
addresses in, disgust Montagu, **9.** 328
addresses may be procured by, on national disgraces, **24.** 132
addresses to George II from, **18.** 418
adjourned, **9.** 205, **10.** 236, **32.** 119, 336, **33.** 190–1, 214
adjournments of: delay conclusion of Wilkes controversies, **22.** 200; during Gordon riots, **25.** 67, 76; expected, **20.** 554, **25.** 167, **31.** 32; for re-elections, **22.** 31; for three weeks, **22.** 194, 200, 455; Grenville ministry to oppose, **30.** 181; in summer of 1778, to be short, **24.** 384; over Christmas holidays, **18.** 366, 552, **19.** 194, 455, **20.** 409, **21.** 35, 558, **22.** 194, 200, 478, **24.** 341, **25.** 103, 116, 222, **37.** 425–6, **38.** 272; over Easter holidays, **19.** 234, **20.** 240, **21.** 75, **24.** 458, **25.** 30–1, 264, **38.** 527; to see *Othello*, **20.** 231; to settle things, **17.** 319; when members seek Newmarket, **39.** 145
administration change depends on next meeting of, **25.** 462
Admiralty attacked in, **7.** 112, 114
African Co.'s slave trade discussed in, **20.** 126
agenda of, **23.** 66, **25.** 562, 563, 566
aimless, **9.** 205
Aix treaty debated in, **20.** 3
allusions to, often obscure to HW, **25.** 612
Almack's Club resembled by, **24.** 81
America and India absorb attention of, **24.** 46
America may receive virtual declaration of war from, **24.** 75
American affairs before, **6.** 138–40, 145–6
American affairs' effect upon, **32.** 326
American affairs to be discussed by, **38.** 490
American agitation in, must be intense, **24.** 87
American disputes should be laid before, **22.** 390, 407, 408
American negotiations proposed in, **24.** 141–2, 354, 355, 358–9
Americans laugh at, **31.** 94
American subjection upheld in, by Pitt's followers alone, **24.** 371
American war eagerly promoted by, **24.** 81, 85

American war favoured by votes in, **28.** 178

animosity in, **24.** 434

annuity settled by, on earldom of Chatham, **24.** 382

anti-American acts of, arouse movement for repeal, **32.** 227–8, 234–5

'archiepiscopal seat of folly and knavery,' **24.** 284

Arcot, Nawab of, influences members of, **25.** 117, **33.** 244

Arenberg-Wade feud may divide, **37.** 183

'army and navy days' in, **39.** 232

army officers who are members of: have not left, **18.** 203; may get leave to come home on 'private affairs' to 'drop in' at House of Commons, **18.** 97; nearly all return to England, **18.** 102

army's disgust may be felt in, **21.** 252

assembly of, will produce news, **31.** 144

associations seek to reform, **25.** 29

associations to petition, **7.** 202, 210, **25.** 6

attainder acts can be undone by, **41.** 113

Austria promised support by, **17.** 133

Aylett committed to Newgate by, **23.** 74

balls and masquerades not disturbed by, **20.** 469

Barré taunts Sandwich in, **38.** 513

battles no longer fought in, **21.** 344

Beauforts legitimated by, **41.** 114

Belloni avenges himself on, **19.** 77

——'s letter burnt by common hangman by order of, **43.** 258

Benfield said to have bribed members of, for Nawab of Arcot, **25.** 117

Berne Gazette's lies about, **35.** 12

bills in, the proving ground for ministerial leaders, **26.** 27

Birmingham petitions, to enforce American acts, **24.** 77

bishops accused in, by Nugent, **17.** 431

'blockish stupidity' of, **32.** 404

Bostonians will not drink tea with, **23.** 550

Buckingham grand jury thanks, for lowering land tax, **22.** 494–5

Burgoyne's surrender arouses no consternation in, **24.** 341

business of: deferred till after the holidays, **20.** 240; left off, **25.** 146; over for the session, **38.** 360

Bute does not secure support of, **9.** 315

Byng cannot be tried until meeting of, **21.** 3

calendar changed by, **12.** 152–3

campaign in: **10.** 45; almost over, **20.** 538–9; heat of, **24.** 349; opens warmly, **20.** 455

cannot do worse than it did last year, **24.** 133

Caribs unrepresented in, **23.** 462

Carter, Elizabeth, asks HW to get act of, for putting down faro, **34.** 172

chamber of, Mansfield wants Ds of Kingston to have private hearing in, **24.** 150

change in, since Cromwell's day, **20.** 339

Charles I and, **40.** 130–2

—— denied pay for army by, until priest is hanged, **42.** 235

Chatham may appear in, **6.** 38, 138–9

Chavigny's observation about, **22.** 294

chimney-sweepers' betterment obtained from, **16.** 217

Cholmondeley to travel before opening of, **23.** 316

Christmas not to disperse, from London, **24.** 542–3

church more fashionable than, **20.** 357–8

Chute's hopes about minority in, **35.** 20

clergy's adherence to Thirty-Nine Articles to be debated by, **23.** 366

common business alone transacted by, **24.** 67

condemned by Abp of Florence to pay large sum to Northumberland, **25.** 225

confusion in, **25.** 66

Constitutional Queries subject of motions in, **20.** 222

controlled by ministers, **12.** 256

convention with Frederick II to be considered by, **21.** 190

Conway elected to, **6.** 177

—— hopes for meeting of, to release him from army, **37.** 257, 296

—— looks forward to meeting of, **37.** 130

—— may open, with éclat if Canada bills are settled with France, **39.** 30

—— not returning to, **37.** 321

—— regrets time lost due to, **37.** 188

——'s conduct in: does not affect Hertford's self-interest, **38.** 330; not approved by Hertford, **38.** 244, 384

——'s friends reflect on him in, **41.** 82

—— should come for opening of, **39.** 242

——'s success in: pleases half-sister, **38.** 384; pleases Hertford, **38.** 314

——'s voting in, displeases George III, **38.** 384–5, 386–7

—— to be candidate for, **37.** 71, 74

—— to leave Flanders for opening of, **37.** 180, 182–3, 184, 185

—— votes in, against army, **37.** 188n

Cornwallis's surrender makes no impression on, **25.** 218

Count of Narbonne to appear before meeting of, **41.** 454

county associations send petitions to, **7.** 202, 210, **25.** 6

Courier de l'Europe translates speeches of, **7.** 19, 114

Court majority in, **11.** 161, 162, 248

Court must resist dissolution of, **23.** 151

Court of Requests links Houses of, **20.** 123n

—— within, is prerogative court for civil causes, **20.** 123n

Court party in: prevails, **25.** 482, 502; will rally to Lord North, **35.** 617

Court wins victory in, over new-raised regiments, **25.** 34

Craufurd attends debate in, **32.** 99

—— will not return for meeting of, **32.** 38

[Parliament (English), *continued*]

Crébillon may dedicate *Oliver Cromwell* to, **20.** 339

crowd at opening of, greater than at Coronation, **22.** 104

Crown's prerogative excited against, **15.** 128

Cumberland, D. of, influences votes in, **9.** 72

debates in: accuracy of reporting of, **17.** 230n, **25.** 58; on Mutiny Bill, **30.** 319; on Spanish peace and new taxes, **11.** 173; on West Indian regiment, **20.** 531; over burning of queries, **20.** 222; over foreign situation, **24.** 341; written up by Gordon for *London Magazine*, **20.** 167n

deep game must be played by, **24.** 61

dissolution must be: **1.** 347, **2.** 217, **19.** 412, 418, 421, **22.** 587, **23.** 5, **24.** 44, **25.** 481-2, **29.** 64, 72, 75, 77, 78, 323; advised by Hardwicke and Newcastle, but opposed by Pelham, **19.** 412n; blamed by Cts of Orford for mismanagement of her boroughs, **24.** 57, 66-7; by Pitt or Rockingham would leave Wilkes to control the next one, **23.** 181; Court must resist, **23.** 151; disrupts Hardinge's politics, **35.** 612; Dunning seeks to delay, **25.** 41; expected, **9.** 159-60, **15.** 131, **20.** 187, 337, **25.** 465, 467, 474, **33.** 204, 211, 212, 220, 221-2, **37.** 270, **41.** 279; feared, **36.** 219; George II's speech on, **19.** 418; irregular, **24.** 44; Mann hopes for, **18.** 4; not expected, **36.** 217; not surprising, **25.** 85-6; reported falsely, **33.** 216, 220; rumoured, **25.** 461; rumoured, provokes Newcastle's express to D. of Bedford, **30.** 246; thought imminent, **15.** 131; threatened, **23.** 176, 182, 186, 188, **35.** 617, 619; unlikely, **35.** 619; will empty London and send HW to SH, **25.** 461

'division bell' of, **19.** 4n

divisions of, **10.** 236

does nothing, **5.** 321

does nothing for want of an Opposition, **23.** 454

Droit le Roi ordered by, to be burnt, **38.** 333

Du Deffand, Mme, comments on singularity and beauties of, **3.** 306

—— mentions, **4.** 332

——'s interest in doings of, **4.** 336, 342, 346, **7.** 189

Dunning seeks to prevent prorogation or dissolution of, until petitions are satisfied, **25.** 41

duration of, **3.** 267, 288, 290, 311, 315, 317, **4.** 232, **5.** 355, **6.** 83, 352, 354

East India Co. settles affairs with, **22.** 478-9

—— to be regulated by, **23.** 442

East Indian squadron to be voted funds by, **20.** 410

Edgcumbe to attend opening of, **40.** 54

elections to, after dissolution, **12.** 190, **36.** 172, 173-4, 177, 178, 179-80, 184

ending of: **18.** 440; pleases Mann, **17.** 14; pleases Sir Robert Walpole, **17.** 502; Speaker

addresses King upon, **30.** 301n; to precipitate politics, **22.** 219

English counties and towns send petitions to, **25.** 6, 10

English diversions undisturbed by, **20.** 469

English extravagance cannot be curbed by, **24.** 231

English-German negotiations may not please, **20.** 493

English mistakes authorized by, **24.** 474

Exchequer building incorporated in, **17.** 300n

exiled members of Paris Parliament should be elected to, **37.** 364

factions will not arise till next session of, **21.** 504

Fairfax receives watch from, after Naseby battle, **38.** 340n

fate of leaders of, compared to that of generals, **25.** 255

first session of, apt to be dull, **20.** 456

forage contracts giving share to Robert investigated by, **21.** 185n

Fox, C. J., the first figure in, **25.** 154

Fox, Henry, disapproves of dissolution of, **21.** 98n

freedom of press is expected to be subject of message to, **28.** 112, 116

French aid to America discussed in, **24.** 254

French insult to be communicated to, by ministry, **22.** 364

French invasion set after assembling of, **17.** 160

French parliaments less lively than, **38.** 271

French parliaments resembled by, **20.** 286-7

French people ask Hertford about procedure of, **38.** 304

galleries for members of, at fireworks, **20.** 48

Garrick's family not to be provided for by, **24.** 435

George II adjourns, **17.** 319

—— congratulated by, on Porto Bello, **37.** 53

—— expects neutrality convention to be applauded by, **37.** 112

—— notifies, of French invasion threat, **37.** 452

—— receives loyal address from, **18.** 430

—— said to be urged by, to give Hanover to D. of Cumberland, **17.** 328

—— should not call for election lest Tories dominate, **18.** 356n

——'s messages to: incites resolution to aid Lisbon sufferers, **25.** 520; on French crisis, answered by loyal addresses, **35.** 216

——'s speech to: **35.** 17; Franco-Hanoverian convention of neutrality said to contradict, **30.** 23

—— tells: of Drummond's proposal to exchange prisoners, **19.** 187; of invasion threats, **18.** 399

—— to address, **17.** 220, **18.** 429

—— to adjourn, **35.** 95

—— to be addressed by, about court martial for naval officers, **19.** 33

George III appears at, to recommend Regency Bill, **38.** 533, 541
—— buys the virtues of both Houses of, **41.** 108, 110
—— disapproves of provision by, for D. of Gloucester's children, **36.** 108n
—— drafts abdication message to, **25.** 381n
—— may denounce son to, if he weds Mrs Fitzherbert, **25.** 629
—— passes bills in, by commission when ill, **38.** 523
——'s disability to result in measures by, **42.** 232
——'s martial message adopted by, **11.** 231
——'s messages to: about French notification, **24.** 374; about Wilkes's arrest, read by Grenville, **38.** 223–4, 225
——'s speeches to: **22.** 274, **33.** 106; at closing, **39.** 175; at opening, **25.** 352, **38** 486–7; at opening, about colonies' rebellion, **39.** 225; disordered by Cornwallis's defeat, **25.** 209; unpromising, **24.** 423
——'s sudden visit to, **23.** 303
—— to address, on Gordon Riots, **33.** 196–7
—— to recommend Regency Bill to, **38.** 533
—— visits, **9.** 325, 412
—— wants, adjourned not prorogued, **38.** 557
Gloucester, D. of, advised by HW not to apply to, for financial support, **36.** 100–3, 107–12
—— does not expect his debts to be paid by, **36.** 306–7
—— intends to ask, for financial provision, **37.** 100n, 104n
(?) ——'s marriage to be announced to, **5.** 265
good sense of, **36.** 222
Gordon rioters assault members of, **25.** 53–4
Gower and Weymouth resign on eve of, **24.** 533–4
Grenville's friends avoid, **23.** 248, 251
—— tired of, **22.** 520
—— wants peace preliminaries referred to, before signing, **22.** 91n
Guines astonished by uproar in, **23.** 256–7
gunpowder discovered beneath, **35.** 199
Gunpowder Plot unlikely to produce methodical debates in, **35.** 413–14
HW alludes to his service in, **33.** 407
HW as angry old man out of, would be ridiculous, **39.** 290
HW asks West for news of, **13.** 238
HW attends, **1.** 120
HW avoids, **32.** 210
HW calls: prostitute, **39.** 327; 'Temple of Concord,' **28.** 155, **38.** 187; 'Temple of Janus,' **11.** 230
HW considers, infamous, **36.** 109
HW describes typical course of events in, **38.** 272–3
HW discusses his career in, **10.** 318
HW 'dismembers' himself from, **35.** 334
HW does not head debates in, about war and generals' conduct, **24.** 485

HW glad to leave, **1.** 124
HW has quitted, **32.** 195
HW hates, **31.** 111
HW ignorant of proceedings at, **35.** 527
HW in, **3.** 266
HW jokes about members of, **10.** 289
HW jokes about returning to, when he wants money, **31.** 47
HW knows little of, **32.** 278
HW may delay letter for session of, **25.** 427
HW mentions, **11.** 203, 222, **12.** 40
HW peaceful at SH during turmoil in, **37.** 270
HW pleased not to have to attend, with gout, **10.** 266
HW proposes dissolution of, to dissipate Newcastle's influence, **21.** 98n
HW quits, **4.** 39, 80, 178, **13.** 42, 44, **15.** 155
HW quitted and abjured, near 30 years ago, **34.** 172
HW ready to quit, on issue of Ps of Wales and Regency Bill, **22.** 298n
HW's abandonment of, leaves him without influence, **41.** 163
HW's conduct in, displeasing to Hertford, **37.** 244
HW's dispatches will be overpowering after meeting of, **35.** 259
HW sends news of, to Conway, **6.** 151
HW's friends concerned with affairs of, **10.** 268
HW's membership in, occupied his time, **15.** 74
HW's quitting of, called taking up his 'freedom,' **24.** 46
HWs sojourn at SH may be delayed for breakup of, **10.** 24, 26
HW's speeches in, make Sir Edward Walpole jealous, **36.** 19
HW wants act by, about master-builders' fire liability, **20.** 185
HW will regret ending of, **18.** 186
[*for other references to HW and Parliament see under* Parliament: House of Commons]
Hamilton's Etruscan vases bought by, **26.** 46
Hanover's safety insured by, **17.** 46
harmony of, about war, pleases Mann, **21.** 263
Henry VI and, in engraving, **40.** 217
Hertford disapproves of revenge for voting in, **38.** 260
Hervey, Augustus, to apply for divorce in, **31.** 139
Hessian and Hanoverian troops discussed in, **37.** 452
Hessian and Russian treaties face defeat in, **35.** 88, 91
Holland may ask, to make war on America, **24.** 77
House of Commons: address against Hanover troops proposed in, **18.** 355; address against rank for officers of privately-raised regiments carried in, **18.** 154, 158; address attacked in, by new Opposition, **35.** 260;

[Parliament (English), *continued*]

addresses in, venal, **35.** 363; address from gets amendment proposal, **25.** 368n; address from, omits mention of treaties, **37.** 413–14; address in, scarcely opposed, **20.** 286, **25.** 437; address moved in, **17.** 375–6, **18.** 351, 399; address of, almost thanks Hanover troops, **21.** 30–1; address of, on accommodation with America, passed unanimously, **25.** 352; address passed and privilege to be discussed in, **38.** 231; adjourned, **17.** 484, **22.** 508, **23.** 292; adjourned for Speaker's illness, **25.** 18, 38, 40–1, **38.** 232; adjourned to choose a Speaker, **23.** 176; adjournment of, moved by Grenville, **22.** 382n; adjourns during Gordon riots, **33.** 190–1; adjourns for subscription masquerade, **23.** 193; adjourns from day to day, to avoid opposition from Grenville ministry, **30.** 181; adjourns on Rigby's motion, **38.** 308; adjourns to see *Othello*, **20.** 231; admirals' and generals' conduct examined by, **24.** 481; Adultery Bill dropped in, **24.** 455n; ailments of, compared to HW's gout, **25.** 402; amendment to Address debated in, **19.** 188, **26.** 22–4; American Congress's petition to, **39.** 227; American taxes considered in, **38.** 508–9; America to be discussed by, day and night, **22.** 513; Appleby election and militia discussed in, **37.** 429; Apsley does not doff hat when getting bill from, **36.** 84–5; approach to, through Wesminster Hall, **17.** 300; Argyll, D. of, brings Sir Henry Erskine into, **20.** 229n; army and navy corruption should be resisted in, **26.** 15; army estimates debated in, **38.** 498–501; army increases voted by, **17.** 410; army in Flanders discussed in, **18.** 123, 382–3; army reduction proposed in, **42.** 55n; army remittances examined in, **18.** 191; army's augmentation argued in, **37.** 420; army voted on by, **17.** 343; as acquisitive as if composed of Catherine II, Frederick II, and Maria Theresa, **24.** 562; Ashburton seats in, compromised, **36.** 47; Ashton preaches before, **14.** 236; Astley proposes in, to make Grenville's election bill permanent, **32.** 189n; attacked by false patriots, **15.** 128; attendance at, severe, **15.** 94; Augusta's dowry voted by, **38.** 249; authority of, must not be weakened by the Crown or the mob, **23.** 181; balloting in, **38.** 192; Baltimore, Bn, to present motion in, **9.** 31; bar of, prisoners to kneel at, **20.** 224; bar of, Wilkes has March, Sandwich, and Temple summoned to, **23.** 73–4, 77; bar of, Wilkes to be heard at, **23.** 73, 78; barons abused by, **9.** 149; Barré and Saville leave, in rage, **23.** 289, 291; Barré's motion in, for American dispatches, **24.** 205n; Barré's motion in, for Chatham's burial, **33.** 20n; Barré speaks in, on dismission of officers, **38.** 321;

Barré's pension debated in, **33.** 348n; barricaded in Gordon riots, **33.** 174; Barrington, Lord, expelled from, **2.** 121–2, **15.** 147–8, **33.** 470; Barrington informs, of George II's order to arrest Mordaunt, **21.** 163n; Barrington informs, of Sackville's arrest, **21.** 374n; Barrington's estimate to, of army, **24.** 347n; Baskerville's plight might be brought before, **40.** 275–6; Bavarian treaty to be ratified in, **20.** 212; Beckford attacks Knowles in, **37.** 432; Beckford conducts Chatham's business in, **22.** 506–7; becomes a mere war office, **21.** 344; Bedfords do not want Conway to lead, **22.** 542, 570; Bedford's followers desert, **22.** 464; Berry, Mary, compares National Assembly with, **11.** 127n; bill passed in, absolving Keppel and Norris from oath of secrecy about Byng trial, **21.** 63–4; bill to encourage iron importation from America debated in, **20.** 135n; bill to increase judges' salaries debated in, **9.** 235; Blackett's and Clavering's motion in, against denial of Parliament's validity, **39.** 126; Blaquiere's speech in, **32.** 161n; Boone's two speeches in, give him high reputation, **30.** 31; bribery and corruption investigated by, **23.** 584; Buckinghamshire assizes cause of controversy in, **19.** 470–1, **26.** 25–8; Buckinghamshire petition committee not chosen by, **25.** 572; Bunbury fails to make motion in, against German war, **22.** 7–8, **43.** 185; Bunbury said to be needed in, **38.** 222; Burgoyne appears in, **33.** 12; Burgoyne discussed in, **24.** 383, **32.** 400n; Burgoyne's resolutions in, on East India Co.'s corruption, **23.** 483n; Burgoyne's speeches in, laboured, **28.** 337; Burke and C. J. Fox debate in, **11.** 263–4; Burke and Saville accuse North in, of concealing Spanish belligerency, **24.** 491n; Burke attacks, **23.** 170, 184; Burke defends himself in, for restoring dismissed men to Pay Office, **25.** 407–8; Burke denounces sinecures in, **31.** 241n; Burke in, deplores military suppression of Gordon riots, **25.** 77n; Burke predicts Spanish war to, during prorogation debate, **24.** 483n; Burke's motion in, for inquiry into Rodney and Vaughan, **25.** 218n; Burke's motion in, for papers on India, **25.** 630n; Burke's motion in, on American conciliation, **32.** 274n; Burke's motion in, on St Eustatius, **36.** 199; Burke's reform bill in, **25.** 20, 26–7, 28, 32n; Burke's speech in, on American taxation, **32.** 222n; Burke's speech in, on civil establishments' reform, **33.** 169; Burke's speech in, on French Revolution, **34.** 104n; Burke's speech in debate in, on address to Q. Charlotte and George IV, **34.** 41n; Bury election voided by, **35.** 196n; Bute jeopardizes, by creating so many peers, **38.** 159; Bute may be protected from, by ministerial office, **9.** 341; Byng may have

to face, **20.** 578, **21.** 55; Byng's court martial discussed in, **21.** 63–5; call of, **17.** 440, **21.** 35; Camden's expulsion weakens Court party in, **23.** 182; Carrington examined by, **38.** 317; Carteret might be sent to Tower by, **19.** 213; Carteret's ministry has majority in, **18.** 96; Cavendish, Lord George, succeeds nephew in, **36.** 205; Cavendish, Lord John, introduces resolutions in, against treaty, **25.** 367n; Cavendish, Lord John, makes motion in, against preliminary peace articles, **25.** 371n, **33.** 388n; Cavendish, Lord John, moves in, for amendment to Address, **24.** 533n; Cavendish, Lord John, moves in, for George IV's allowance, **25.** 418n; Cavendish, Lord John, proposes resolutions in, against American war, **25.** 253n; chairman of, **20.** 35; chairman of the Committee on Privileges and Elections chosen by, **17.** 220, 242, 250; changes in, rumoured at Florence, **17.** 325; chaos in, **19.** 202; Chatham's children fathered by, **28.** 394, **29.** 248; chief clerk to, *see* Hatsell, John (1743–1820); Chippenham election decided in, **17.** 318–19; Churchill supports government party in, **40.** 177; Chute, Francis, may be kept from, by gout, **35.** 21; Chute, John, hopes for majority in, **35.** 22; Cider Bill debated in, **38.** 307, **41.** 10; Clandestine Marriages Act 'nursed' through, by lawyers, **37.** 362–4, 365; Clandestine Marriages Act's repeal discussed by, **39.** 375–6; Clavering's motion to ask George III to lay London's petition before, **23.** 198; clerk of, *see* Dyson, Jeremiah (1722–66), Hatsell, John (1743–1820), Ley, John (ca 1732–1814); clerks forced by, to sit in empty walls, **25.** 572–3; Clive exonerated by, **23.** 484–5, 562; Clive names 10 members to, **24.** 61; Clive's and Johnstone's speeches in, on India, **23.** 399n; coffee-girl attends, in Speaker's chambers, **22.** 284; coffee-house resembled by, **21.** 52; Coke, Edward, sits 22 hours in, **17.** 383; Coke, Thomas William, and Grosvenor move in, against Pitt administration, **25.** 471n; Coke, Thomas William, moves in, for partial disavowal of peace commissioners' manifesto, **24.** 426n, 429n; committee compared to Roman senate, **9.** 3; committee in, on elections, **43.** 242; committee of, examines Independents, **19.** 387–8; committee of, to study reform, **29.** 214, 220, 226; Committee of Privileges and Elections in, includes HW, **35.** 208n; Committee of Ways and Means in, **30.** 244n; committees formed in, on riots, **23.** 291, 297, 303; complaint in, of Dunn's arrest for threatening Wilkes, **38.** 264–5; composition of, uncertain, **18.** 327; constitution involves, **11.** 264; contested election in, **13.** 26; contested elections reviewed by, **24.** 67; Conway and C. J. Fox attack

Court party in, **24.** 139; Conway and Sackville attack Grenville administration in, **38.** 308–9; Conway answers Egmont in, **35.** 162; Conway debates with Grenville in, **22.** 274; Conway does not hear debate in, on Sir Robert Walpole, **37.** 90–1; Conway does not seek power through, **35.** 510n; Conway does not seek prime ministry through, **35.** 510; Conway hopes HW will be called home by, **37.** 46; Conway inspires, in Gordon riots, **33.** 176–7; Conway leaves, **39.** 407–8; Conway may act jointly with Charles Townshend in, **39.** 84; Conway may be summoned to, from army, **38.** 141; Conway might come back for opening of, **39.** 222; Conway miscounts, but Sandwich counted correctly, **39.** 79; Conway moves address to George III in, **25.** 244, 251–2, 259; Conway must leave Jersey to attend, **39.** 339–40; Conway opposed as leader of, by D. of Bedford, **22.** 542, 570; Conway's anti-Court votes in, may bring reprisals, **38.** 239–40, **40.** 328–42; Conway's colleagues should protect HW from long sessions in, **22.** 317; Conway's distinction in, **20.** 265; Conway's membership in, impediment to his going to Scotland, **19.** 204; Conway's motion in, leads to Opposition's victory, **33.** 330; Conway's motions in, for making peace with America, **33.** 328n, 329, 330n, 332n, **35.** 616n, **39.** 353–4; Conway's speech in, on why he stayed in office, **25.** 294n; Conway's treatment in, by Lord John Cavendish, **41.** 65–6; Conway's unlucky day in, following Pitt in opposition, **37.** 321; Conway's victory in, **35.** 615–16; Conway's voting for popular bills in, worries Pelham, **37.** 226–7; Conway takes seat in, **38.** 76; Conway the sole target of attacks in, **39.** 92; Conway to remain as leader of, **22.** 571; Conway to stand for, **37.** 71, 74; Conway unable to attend, **31.** 117; Conway wants to share leadership of, with Charles Townshend, **39.** 84; Cooper's motion in, on British Museum, **24.** 304n; Cornewall's monument in, **37.** 271; Cornish and Scottish vote in, overturns Sir Robert Walpole, **17.** 346n; Cornish election (Bossiney) settled by, **17.** 233, 247, 263; Cornwall becomes Speaker of, **25.** 95; Cornwallis's surrender has not further weakened administration supporters in, **25.** 212; Corsica noticed by, **23.** 66, 69; country gentlemen desert, **22.** 520; country gentlemen in, oppose land tax, **22.** 487; country gentlemen in, probably bribe their constituencies to present anti-American addresses, **24.** 132; Courtenay attacks Flood in, **35.** 381; Court of King's Bench proposed by Glynn and Oliver for investigation by, **23.** 256n; Court party rallies in, **35.** 619; Court party wins in, **18.** 96, **22.** 109, **23.** 168, 194; Court puts Luttrell into,

[Parliament (English), *continued*]

in Wilkes's place, **23**. 344, 346; Crewe's bill in, rejected, **25**. 38n, 66n; Crosby summoned before, **14**. 189n; Crowle calls, *brutum fulmen*, **20**. 224; Cumberland, D. of, exposed by, **20**. 33; Cumberland, D. of, said in, to be made captain-general, **30**. 181; Cumberland election engages, **10**. 273; Cust as Speaker of, negligent in restraining speeches, **23**. 175n; Cust resigns as Speaker of, **23**. 175; *Daily Advertiser* advertisement said to be condemned by, **19**. 353, 362; Deal representatives ask Horace Mann II to inquire in, about Dutch ships, **25**. 222–3; debate in, delays guests at fête, **33**. 481; debate in, on privilege, postponed, **38**. 240–1; debate in, on procedure, fatiguing and dull, **38**. 223; debate in, over abolition of Thirty-Nine Articles, **23**. 376; debates in, **28**. 141, **29**. 264–5, **32**. 401–2, **33**. 248; debates in, of little consequence because of unshaken majority, **25**. 153, debates in, on Treaty of Dresden, sent by HW to D. of Bedford, **40**. 71–2; De Grey cannot be spared from, **23**. 175; Denbighshire election settled by, **17**. 343–4, **31**. 394, 401; (?) dinner at, **30**. 252; Diogenes's witticism would not raise smile in, **34**. 39; division in, advocated by Jacobites and opposed by Patriots, **17**. 231; division in, over congratulating George II on Treaty of Madrid, **20**. 221n; Dowdeswell and George Grenville amuse, with squabble, **22**. 566; Dresden treaty's supporters and opponents speak in, **20**. 299n; Dresden treaty to be laid before, **20**. 299n; Drury Lane riots surpassed by combats in, **37**. 419; duels prevalent in, **38**. 270; Dundas brings bills in, against Rumbold, **25**. 274n; Dundas should be given more places by, **41**. 321; Dunning denounces Crown's influence in, **25**. 34–5, 45n, 66n, **29**. 17, 22, 187, 350; Dunning deserts minority in, **23**. 168; Dunning moves *by authority* for adjournment of, **25**. 262; Dunning's motion in, against prorogation of Parliament, **25**. 66n; Easter adjournment impossible for, **25**. 572; East India Co. discussed in, **39**. 82; East India Co. enrages, by voting irregular dividend, **22**. 513; East India Co. examined by, **22**. 493, 495–7, 504, **23**. 392, 399, 401, 451–2, 490; East India Co. investigated by conflicting committees in, **23**. 455n; East India Co.'s profits debated in, **39**. 380–1; East Indian affairs debated in, **28**. 86, 87; Eden's motion in, for repeal of Irish regulations, **25**. 267n; Egmont and Opposition walk out of, on Mutiny Bill, **20**. 112; Egmont attacked in, by Charles Townshend, **35**. 195n; Egmont's speech in, on Mutiny Bill, **35**. 162; elections embroil, **20**. 469; elections for, **20**. 388, 456, **21**. 484; elections heard by, **35**. 192, 208; election vot-

ing in, requires 100 members, **24**. 273; Elliot moves in, for Impey's impeachment, **34**. 3n; Ellis's motion in, for anti-Papist bill, **25**. 66n, 67n; English-Spanish negotiations to be discussed in, **21**. 553; *Essay on Woman* discussed in, **22**. 181–5, 186–8; estimated strengths of factions in, **22**. 489n; Exchequer, chancellor of, must be member of, **20**. 422n; Exchequer house has door to, **17**. 299–300; Exchequer reform debated in, **33**. 406n; excise discussed in, **17**. 458; Feilding to have moved Address in, **35**. 363n; Firebrace in, to have repeated Poulett's motion, **35**. 224; Fitzpatrick in supply committee in, proposes new army, **33**. 433n; Fitzpatrick speaks in, **32**. 275, 276; Flood's maiden speech in, **35**. 381; foreign estimates debated in, **21**. 553n; Fordwich, Vct, loses seat in, by staying in Florence, **21**. 543; Fortrose a member of, **19**. 233; Fox, C. J., and William Pitt II will clash in, **35**. 519; Fox, C. J., attacks North in, **39**. 369; Fox, C. J., attacks Sandwich in, **24**. 460, 464n, **25**. 244; Fox, C. J., compliments Conway on triumphs in, **25**. 251–2; Fox, C. J., criticizes war conduct in, **39**. 396n; Fox, C. J., does not explain resignation to, **35**. 519n; Fox, C. J., has majority in, **25**. 449, 466; Fox, C. J., influential in, **34**. 253; Fox, C. J., makes motion in, against Sandwich, **35**. 616n; Fox, C. J., makes motion in, amended by North, for censuring Palliser's Greenwich appointment, **25**. 118n; Fox, C. J., makes motion in, for inquiry into Sandwich's naval mismanagement, **33**. 328n; Fox, C. J., makes motion in, for resuming committee on state of nation, **33**. 432n; Fox, C. J., makes motion in, on naval abuses, **33**. 326n; Fox, C. J., makes motions in, for data on Burgoyne and for not sending old army corps overseas, **24**. 351n; Fox, C. J., may be carried to, in procession, **25**. 563; Fox, C. J., might by violence provoke Tories of, against North and Fox, **25**. 379; Fox, C. J., moves in, about state of navy, **24**. 449n, 452n; Fox, C. J., moves in, for inquiry about Burgoyne, **24**. 341n; Fox, C. J., persuades, to reverse itself, **28**. 309; Fox, C. J., prevents Pitt's ministers from speaking in, **25**. 467n; Fox, C. J., proposes India bill in, **25**. 448–9; Fox, C. J., questions Mulgrave in, about Palliser, **24**. 444n; Fox, C. J., shines in, **23**. 188, **25**. 154, 437; Fox, Henry, and Pitt [Chatham] have daily altercations in, **21**. 65; Fox, Henry, and Pitt preempt debates in, **37**. 436; Fox, Henry, at first assured of management of, **35**. 168; Fox, Henry, becomes manager of, for Bute, **22**. 92; Fox, Henry, defers motion in, on continuing term of privately-raised regiments, **19**. 209; Fox, Henry, expects HW's more regular attendance in,

30. 167–8; Fox, Henry, expects HW to show himself a friend at any opportunity in, 30. 130–1; Fox, Henry, originally unpopular and ungraceful speaker in, 30. 334; Fox, Henry, persuaded by Carteret to be leader of, 20. 502; Fox, Henry, presents Hessian and Russian treaties to, 35. 88n; Fox, Henry, promised to resign leadership of, 38. 195; Fox, Henry, refuses secretaryship of state because he cannot have control of, 20. 417; Fox, Henry, reported to 'give up,' 30. 129; Fox, Henry, resented because he has responsibility for, without support, 21. 6n; Fox, Henry's, absence from, to be governed by events, 30. 130; Fox, Henry's, cabinet post not to interfere with secretary of state's priority in, 20. 461n; Fox, Henry, should manage, more easily, 22. 112; Fox, Henry's, position in, likely to be awkward, 30. 130; Fox, Henry, to lead, 10. 45, 35. 253, 38. 184, 185–6, 195; Fox, Henry, to manage, 35. 88; Fox, Henry, to preside at Cockpit on eve of session of, 20. 503; Fox, Henry, vacates seat for, 22. 201; franking abuses discussed in, 38. 368; Frederick, P. of Wales, said to be buying, 37. 270; French prisoners' compensation settled by, 38. 495–6; French war opposed in, by Wycombe, Tarleton, and Courtenay, 39. 508n; Fullarton's regiment discussed in, 25. 34; full attendance by, 25. 368n; Fuller condemned by, 16. 366; full of curiosity-seekers, 35. 183; Gage expected to get Patriots to, and keep them from, 30. 291n; Gage preserved from arrest by membership in, 17. 255n; Gage's son to enter, 17. 255n; galleries at, closed to visiting Amazons, 38. 327; generals at bar of, say that America cannot be conquered, 24. 474; general warrants considered by, 22. 374–5, 283, 38. 318–21, 325–7, 490, 505; George II and Sir Robert Walpole said to dread change in, 17. 203; George II asks, through Fox, to send relief to Lisbon after earthquake, 20. 512n; George II does not go to, 21. 345; George II notifies, of sending Hessians to Scotland, 19. 188; George II tells Pulteney to quit, 17. 494; George II voted money by, for Maria Theresa, 17. 390; George II wants, to tell him not to give rank to officers of privately-raised regiments, 19. 154; George II wants to prorogue, 20. 469; George II yielded to, 33. 331; George III astonished at slender majority in, 25. 19n; George III hissed by mob on way to, 23. 291; George III never applauded at, 38. 276; George III notifies, of militia's mobilization, 24. 367n; George III recommends increased pensions for his brothers, and dowry for his sister, to, 22. 425; George III's message to, 11. 230; George III's message to, delayed reading

of, 38. 223, 225; George III's request for war funds granted by, to North, 39. 324–5; George III's speech to, 21. 344–5; George III visits, 9. 325, 412; George III visits, and announces its dissolution, 25. 481; George III visits, for bill for D. of Grafton's divorce, 23. 99; Germain lays peace commissioners' manifesto before, 24. 426n; Germain's motion in, for using peers' sons to carry bills to Lords, 23. 256n; German war unpopular with, 21. 553; Gibbon supports North ministry in, 35. 615; Gibson and Murray sentenced by, 20. 224–5; Glover to enter, 9. 398; Glynn's motion in, for Wilkes to explain his complaint against Frewen, 23. 475n; Gordon, Lord George, a candidate for, 25. 183, 187; Gordon, Lord George, divides, 33. 169; Gordon, Lord George, has followers marching to, 33. 173; Gordon, Lord George, presents anti-Catholic petitions to, and makes motions, 24. 475n; Gordon, Sir William, attends, wearing blister and flannel, 17. 298; Granby deserts to minority in, 23. 168; Granby to move question in, 38. 324, 327; Granville ministry not permitted by, 19. 212; Great Seal's cast used for death-warrant of, 25. 481; Grenville administration mortified in, 38. 498–501; Grenville administration's overthrow depends on leadership in, 30. 190; Grenville defeated in, 22. 381–2; Grenville opens budget discussion in, 38. 341; Grenville proposes election bill in, 24. 45, 273; Grenville rarely attends, 30. 240; Grenville said to succeed Onslow as Speaker of, 21. 491; Grenville's bill in, for regulating election trials, 25. 573n; Grenville's faction in, in Whately's charge, 39. 100n; Grenville to be manager but not Speaker of, 21. 541, 38. 132, 136; Grenville was manager of, for Bute, 22. 91; Grenville-Bedford faction worn out in, 41. 10; Grenville-Pitt debate in, 22. 401n, 405n; HW absent from, during re-election, 21. 63; HW and Sir Edward Walpole decline to stand again for, 39. 95; HW approves of recent behaviour of, 31. 93; HW attends, 10. (?)55; HW attends constantly, but never stays long, 17. 344; HW attends prayers at, to reserve a place, 38. 323; HW avoids, 21. 344; HW calls, 'Sanhedrin,' 23. 555; HW calls, 'Temple of Janus,' 11. 230; HW calls, 'Temple of Concord,' 24. 341, 28. 155, 35. 260; HW calls, 'Temple of Virtue,' 24. 341; HW calls, 'that scold,' 22. 316; HW compares, with Arthur's Club, 9. 263; HW declines to run again for, 41. 77–9; HW defends, against Mason, 29. 208, 210; HW describes, in stock-exchange terms, 38. 1; HW deserts, to attend book sale, 38. 341; HW detests, 30. 196; HW did not attend, 30. 236; HW dines after leaving, 18. 351; HW does not attend discussions

[Parliament (English), *continued*]

in, of private business, **16.** 28–9; HW dreads entering, **17.** 109, 176; HW drinks wine after fatigue in, **35.** 264; HW fatigued by attendance at, **17.** 294, **18.** 381, **21.** 28, **22.** 506; HW fears his gout may be brought on by, **40.** 388; HW finds, monotonous, **10.** 184; HW for once wishes himself in, **33.** 146; HW forsakes, **35.** 334; HW glad to be out of, **22.** 316, 570, **23.** 66, 128–9, 351, **24.** 46, 101, 284, **25.** 476, **28.** 93; HW goes to, to hear C. J. Fox, **23.** 399–400; HW has avoided, for a month, **38.** 355; HW has seen no member of, **25.** 578; HW hates, **31.** 93; HW helped by heat of, **38.** 236; HW kept busy by, **18.** 381, 392, **20.** 30, 522; HW leaves, before vote, in order not to vote against Henry Fox, **21.** 86; HW loath to leave, though despising it, **38.** 504; HW looks back on career in, **25.** 558; HW may forsake, for Paris, **38.** 463, 485, 497–8, 504–5, 509, 516; HW must go to, though knowing all that will happen there, **38.** 187; HW not sorry to miss Stamp Act debate in, **30.** 221; HW paraphrases Bible verse to apply to, **25.** 262; HW resolves never to set foot in, **23.** 399–400; HW's absorption in, **9.** 178; HW's aversion to, **22.** 348, **24.** 101; HW's career in, praised by King's Lynn electors, **41.** 89–91; HW's conduct in, reviewed, **40.** 336, **41.** 77–9; HW's election to, **17.** 73, 84; HW's Exchequer ushership attacked in, **42.** 57; HW's first speech in, falsely reported in magazines, **13.** 12; HW's health impaired by attendance in, **22.** 285, **24.** 146, **38.** 511; HW sick of, **30.** 203; HW sick of, but attends merely from devotion to Whigs, **38.** 243; HW sits in, from 2 P.M. till 5 A.M., **35.** 260; HW sits in dark corner under window in, **39.** 222; HW's motion in, for the Address, **20.** 227; HW's notes on debate in, lost by Conway, **37.** 389; HW's notes on debate in, of 22 Jan. 1752 OS, **42.** 493–7; HW's notes on debate in, of 13 Nov. 1761, **30.** xxviii, **43.** 312; HW's refusal to return to, alienates his friends, **22.** 359; HW's rule for behaviour in, is obedience to Henry Fox's commands, **30.** 129; HW's seat in, requires his return, **37.** 93; HW's 'severe attendance' in, **16.** 53; HW stays late at debates and committees in, **35.** 212–13; HW 'stewing' in, **22.** 514; HW's voting in, **19.** 154, **20.** 126, **26.** 19; HW takes Gisors to, but stops his notetaking, **35.** 162; HW tells story related in, **28.** 360; HW to bring bill of perpetual insolvency into, **35.** 644; HW to forsake, **22.** 522; HW waits for general warrants, officers' dismissals, and Manila ransom to be considered by, **38.** 497; HW wearied by long hours in, **38.** 315; HW will attend, when C. Townshend is re-elected, **30.** 237;

HW would feel gout if he returned to, **23.** 66; HW would like to forsake, **10.** 147; habeas corpus suspension voted down in, **18.** 408n; Hamilton, John James, speaks in, **35.** 381–2; Hamilton, Sir William, might stand for, **35.** 417; Hanover and Madrid treaties presented to, for ratification, **20.** 212n; Hanover troops debated in, **18.** 123, 180, 382, **19.** 241; Hardinge could not endure Scots orators in, **35.** 620; Hardinge defends Rumbold in, **35.** 623; Hardinge seeks to enter, **35.** 618; Hartington and Wyndham move for address of loyalty to George II from, **18.** 399; Hartington sits 22 hours in, **17.** 383; (?) Hartley opens unsuccessfully in, **39.** 232–3; Hartley's motion in, for making peace with America, **39.** 374–5; Hastings's impeachment committee in, **33.** 560n; Hastings's trial at, **25.** 630, 639, 642, 651, 653; Hay not permitted by George III to become member of, **21.** 73; Heberden and Hawkins sent by, to Wilkes, **38.** 274; Hedon election in, **17.** 355, **35.** 20n; Hertford may have 6 sons in, **25.** 488; Hervey not to attend, till majority is certain, **17.** 275; Hessian and Prussian treaties debated in, **38.** 7–8; Hickey and Reynolds punished by, **22.** 584; Hillsborough moves Address in, **37.** 413, 416; *History* of, by Cæsar Ward, **29.** 295; Holroyd's motion in, defending North, **25.** 29n; Hood to have replaced Rodney in, **25.** 284–5; Horne Tooke's petition to, **11.** 194; Horne Tooke summoned before, for attacking Norton, **23.** 555; House of Lords agrees to resolutions of, **22.** 187; House of Lords asked by, for peers to appear at their bar, **23.** 73–4, 77; House of Lords' quarrel with, vainly provoked, **23.** 256; Howe moves in, to summon Cornwallis, **24.** 474n; Howe's motion in, for American papers to be laid before the House, **24.** 439n, 474n; Hume Campbell again frequents, **20.** 111; imperialistic, **23.** 562; India's affairs examined by, *see under* East India Co.; 'ingenious buffoonery' in, **39.** 82; inquiry by, into paymastership of Marines, **30.** 312; inquiry in, about American war, **39.** 321, 325; Ireland considered by, **25.** 583; Ireland's independence signed by, **25.** 279–80; Irish commercial propositions debated in, **33.** 491n; Irish-establishment troops permitted by, to go to America, **32.** 296n; Jacobites expect, to thwart George II and Sir Robert Walpole, **17.** 203; Jacobites in, instructed to oppose Sir Robert Walpole, **17.** 232n; Jacobites in, oppose suspension of habeas corpus, **19.** 138–9; Jacobites incite instructions to members of, **21.** 12, 19; Jacobites want division in, **17.** 231; Jacobites will try to buy seats in, **20.** 131; Jenkinson's motion in, for orders of the day, **25.** 253n, 256n; Johnstone abuses Germain in, **23.** 255–6;

Johnstone attacks HW and Keppel in, 24. 465n; Johnstone talks in, of Deane's mission to Paris, 24. 254n; Jones, Inigo, charged before, 40. 207; journals of, consulted by HW, 20. 139; Kentish counter-petition to, 25. 45n; Keppel has not been to, 33. 94; Keppel informs, that Byng court martial members want release from oath, 35. 97; key-hole of, stopped, 17. 300; king and lords a balance against, 35. 379; king and lords alternate with, in preponderance of power, 34. 102; king and lords balanced by, in constitution, 11. 264, 42. 402; King's Bench remands prisoner committed by, 20. 249–50; ladies attend, 38. 317–18; ladies excluded from, 38. 327; land tax reduction voted by, 30. 243n; late hours at, 35. 262–3; late servility of, to the Crown, 25. 273; Lee opposes Pitt in, 19. 241; Legge refuses to aid Hessian subsidy in, 21. 486n, 30. 164n; Legge speaks in, on supplies and taxes, 37. 444–5; Leheup investigated by, 35. 158; literary property debated in, 28. 135, 149, 154–5; loan and lottery authorized by, 9. 263; London and Westminster members of, vote for Address, 18. 125; London Bridge repairs debated in, 38. 347; London city's quarrel with, over Wilkes, 3. 56n, 23. 196–7, 198, 199–200, 279–81, 288–9; London's members in, instructed, 38. 139; London's remonstrance debated in, 39. 125–6; long day in, causes HW's cold, 10. 147; long session in, 17. 294, 383; Lord Mayor summoned by, 23. 281, 288; Lords' amendments to Militia Bill opposed by, 21. 137n; Lords' expulsion from, moved by Onslow, 23. 256n; Lords told by, to 'withdraw,' 17. 431; Luttrell's motion in, for Palliser's court martial, 24. 427n, 33. 75n; Luttrell's motion in, for treating with America, 24. 141n, 158n; Luttrell's opening speech in, 39. 233; Luttrell to be instated by, 10. 277; Luttrell to do penance in, 32. 77; Lyttelton attacked by Pitt on budget in, 37. 432; Lyttelton's reports to, confused, 15. 331; Macartney to enter, 22. 586; Macklin's letter on debates in, on King's speech, printed in newspaper, 37. 426; Mackreth a member of, 24. 53n, 60; Madrid treaty to be ratified by, 20. 212; Malpas's vote in, sought by ministry, 38. 345n; malt tax debated in, 39. 482; Manchester council heard by, against taxes, 25. 573; Manchester petition to, 25. 578n; Mann asks how often Wilkes can be chosen for, and rejected, 23. 96, 110; Mann fears that HW's health may suffer from late hours of, 18. 114, 395; Mann hopes that Wilkes will never sit in, 23. 96; Mann pleased by HW's release from, 20. 42; Mann pleased by Opposition's defeat in, 22. 111–12; Mann pleased by Wilkes's expulsion from, 23. 88; Mann surprised that Middlesex does not obey decision of, 23. 119; Mann

wishes that HW's moderation and prudence could be felt in, 23. 184; Mann, Horace II, advised by Mann to quit, 25. 474; Mann, Horace II, an 'unconnected' member of, 25. 223; Mann, Horace II, as member of, is better informed than HW, 25. 209, 236; Mann, Horace II, attends, 24. 425, 477; Mann, Horace II, entered, under illusions, 24. 518, 25. 560; Mann, Horace II, enters, 24. 54; Mann, Horace II, hurries back to, 24. 363, 396, 530, 25. 200; Mann, Horace II, is asked to institute inquiry at, 25. 222–3, 234; Mann, Horace II, may cause resentment in constituents by his absence from, 24. 146; Mann, Horace II, not at, 24. 146, 25. 367; Mann, Horace II, offers to resign from, 24. 275, 281; Mann, Horace II, re-elected to, 25. 86; Mann, Horace II, retires from, 25. 461, 465, 476, 488, 505, 523; Mann, Horace II, sends regular accounts of, to Mann, 25. 475; Mann, Horace II, should quit, if he votes against Mann's wishes, 24. 452; Mann, Horace II, to report news of, to Mann, 24. 532, 542; Mann, Horace II, votes for Court party in, 24. 455; Mann, Horace II, would never benefit by seat in, 25. 465; Mansfield will not express opinion to, about Ps of Wales as possible regency member, 22. 297; March may be examined in, 10. 272; Marchmont's peerage stops his career in, 19. 5; Maria Theresa voted aid by, 17. 133n; Marriage Bill debated in, 9. 147; Martin attacks Burke in, 25. 408n; Martin clashes with, over Wilkes, 38. 226–7; Mason's name supposedly mentioned in, 28. 149, 155; Mediterranean naval investigation by, 19. 12, 25, 32–3, 47; members of, can be sent to Tower, if House so votes, 30. 299n; members of, consider themselves superior to titular lords, 22. 482; members of, divide with every new minister, 19. 4; members of, go to political dinners at taverns, 17. 243; members of, instructed by constituents through newspapers, 17. 392; members of, meet at Cockpit to hear George II's speech, 18. 103; members of, mentioned, 15. 326; members of, oppose peace, 36. 209; members of, return from Ghent and Antwerp, 18. 97n; members of, speculate in East India Co.'s stock, 22. 498; members of, superior to Tuscan nobles, 22. 483; mercenaries will support Norton in, 25. 27; merchants' petition discussed in, 17. 353–4; merchants petition, for reconciliation with America, 39. 247, 248; merchants' petitions considered by, 32. 231; Meredith and C. J. Fox drive Clive out of, 23. 490–1; Meredith complains to, about abusive publications, 39. 125n; Meredith moves in, for depositions on Wilkes, 38. 307–8; Meredith puts off discussion of warrants in, 38. 490; Meredith's motion in, on illegality of warrants, 38. 318–9; Middlesex

[Parliament (English), *continued*]

election discussed by, **23.** 181–2; Middlesex sheriffs summon Wilkes as member of, **23.** 475; Middlesex will be enraged by performance of, in rejecting Wilkes and electing Luttrell, **23.** 105; Militia Bill and Murray's affair cause long sessions at, **38.** 315; Militia Bill debated in, **32.** 279n; militia's reduction proposed in, **22.** 413n; millions voted by, **21.** 256; ministries not overturned by, **21.** 261; ministry defeated in, over land tax, **22.** 487–8; ministry without influence in, **21.** 57; Minorca's loss investigated by, **21.** 56, 76–7, 85–6, 95; minutes of, see *Votes* of; Mitchell election debated in, **35.** 215–16; money to be blindly voted by, since Prerogative Proclamation, **41.** 314; money to be raised by, **20.** 212; Morton's motion in, on Regency Bill, **22.** 299n; motion in, for account of proceeds of place tax, **40.** 153–4; motion in, on officers' dismissals, **38.** 502, 509; motion in, on Sir Robert Walpole, *see under* Walpole, Sir Robert; Mulgrave's motion in, on Westminster election, **25.** 502n; Müntz needs no protection from, **40.** 169; Murray, Alexander, denied pen, ink, paper, and visitors by, **20.** 225n; Murray, Alexander, sentenced by, **16.** 293, **20.** 286; Murray, William, cannot be spared from, **20.** 557; Murray, William, refuses to stay in, to aid Newcastle, **20.** 557n; Murray, William, successful in, **18.** 383–4; Mutiny Bill debated in, **35.** 162; nabobs called to account by, **25.** 277; naval augmentation defeated in, **19.** 168; naval captains' petition to, for increased half-pay, **23.** 462; naval estimates considered by, **38.** 496; naval investigation proposed in, **18.** 399–400, 427; naval salary increase advocated by resolution in, **32.** 99n; navy bills debated in, **38.** 307; navy-estimates debate in, with Palliser-Keppel clash, **29.** 180; navy's censure defeated in, **29.** 180; Newcastle, D. of, has devotion from, **21.** 11; Newfoundland merchants complain to, on French encroachments, **38.** 527–8; Newhaven urges, to ease Irish trade restrictions, **24.** 473n; 'New Interest' candidates for, **37.** 371; newly-raised regiments and county and town petitions considered in, **25.** 34; new peerages may remove property-holders from, **38.** 159; North and C. J. Fox have majority in, **25.** 466; North and Shelburne torn from power by, in a year, **25.** 402n; North announces resignation in, **25.** 258–9; North defeated in, **32.** 99; North defeated in, on revenue question, **23.** 461–2; North delivers George III's message of American-French treaty to, **24.** 364n; North misrepresents French disarming to, **41.** 299; North moves in, for inquiry into East India Co., **23.** 442n; North notifies, of Spanish rescript, **24.** 483n, 491n;

North proposes loan in, **24.** 361n; North's fever will probably postpone first debate in, **25.** 97; North's government overturned by, **29.** 201, 204–5, 208; North's motion in, for bill to stop American trade, **24.** 158n; North's motion in, for prosecuting *North Briton*, **38.** 225n; North submits American papers to, and asks for address, **24.** 75n; North's victory in, over St-Vincent, **23.** 462; North tells about government loan, **24.** 448; North to lay taxes before, **25.** 254–5; North wins victory in, over disenfranchisement of revenue officers, **25.** 37–8; *North Briton* and Wilkes, subjects of debate in, **38.** 225–6; Norton attacks North in, **25.** 27, 28n; Norton becomes Speaker of, **22.** 263n, **23.** 176, 179–80; Norton thanked by vote of, **25.** 100; Norton to return to, **25.** 41; nothing but jobs in, **25.** 140; not in a mood to be dallied with, **25.** 261–2; not well attended, **19.** 138, 272, **24.** 148, 273, **25.** 572–3, 583; Nugent attacks Sandwich in, **20.** 123, 124; Nugent, Mrs, wants her husband to speak in, **17.** 254–5; officers' dismissal for conduct in, opposed by Granby, **22.** 274; Old Pretender hopes, will lack spirit, **17.** 202; Oliver sentenced by, to Tower, **23.** 288; Onslow commissioned by, to reprimand Westminster J.P.'s, **30.** 301n; Onslow demands Byng's expulsion from, **21.** 63; Onslow elected Speaker of, **17.** 219–20, **19.** 446, **35.** 17; Onslow's language in controlling disorders in, **30.** 299; Onslow's speech on superiority of, to House of Lords, **30.** 301n; opening debate in, avoided by Bedford party, **30.** 236; opening debate in, languid, **30.** 236; opening session of, discusses George III's complaint against Wilkes for *North Briton*, **22.** 181–2; opens with debate over reading a bill or hearing a privilege complaint, **38.** 223–4; Opposition has best speakers in, **22.** 208; Opposition has majority of, **25.** 471n; Opposition in, alarms Mann, **17.** 133; Opposition in, HW advises withdrawal of, from House, **22.** 298n; Opposition in, humbled, **25.** 449, 451; Opposition in, strengthened by faction in ministry, **25.** 259; Opposition in, to oppose George II's speech, **18.** 102; Opposition in, to propose Norton as Speaker, **36.** 183; Opposition in, wants Parliament to continue sitting, **39.** 329; Opposition in, will decry North's taxes, **25.** 255; Opposition in, will have no effect, **20.** 513; ordnance debt discussed in, **33.** 433n; Orford, Cts of, corresponds with HW about her members of, **24.** 534; Ossory moves address of thanks to George III's speech in, **33.** 429n; Ossory released from, with HW's congratulations, **34.** 202; Ossory's speech in, **32.** 274–5; outside pressure may force, to bow to Pitt, **21.** 13; Oxenden a speaker in, **33.** 222; Oxford corporation punished by, **22.** 584;

Oxford petition to, against dissenters' relief, 33. 98n; Palliser resigns seat in, 24. 444; Palliser's removal may be asked by, in petition to George III, 24. 446; parties in, almost equally balanced, 25. 256; party violence in, leads to duels, 38. 270; path to, from Change Alley, 22. 498; peace articles may be resented by, 25. 362; peace with Spain declared in, 23. 268; peers' regiments voted by, 19. 128n; Pelham absent from, 17. 484; Pelham has majorities in, 19. 202; Pelham ministry triumphant in, 19. 458; Pelham ministry unpopular in, 19. 4; Pelham mortified by speeches in, 20. 257; Pelham visits, just before death, 20. 413; Pennsylvania regiment debated in, 37. 444; petitions to, about roads and poor rates, 31. 5n; petition to, for reform of expenditure of public money, 35. 501; petition to, for relief at Barbados, 25. 109n; Philipps proposes Commission of accounts in, 38. 192; Philipps's committal wanted by, 20. 250; Pigot's bill in, to authorize naval court martials, 33. 76n; Pitt absent from, 38. 369; Pitt and Henry Fox debate in, on Pennsylvania regiments, 37. 436; Pitt and Powys attack Adam and Dundas in, 35. 620–1; Pitt answers Conway in, 25. 467n; Pitt asks Newcastle not to meddle in, 21. 91; Pitt attacks Carteret in, 18. 383; Pitt attacks Newcastle in, on Minorca, 20. 554n; Pitt attacks Rockingham ministry in, 31. 117; Pitt attends, only twice in winter, 21. 182; Pitt carried into, to oppose Treaty of Paris, 32. 44n; Pitt charms, with speeches, 10. 203; Pitt debates with Hume Campbell in, 35. 262; Pitt defies, 29. 333, 349; Pitt does not quit, but has less power, 38. 131–2; Pitt holds, in commendam, 21. 56; Pitt may lose control of, 22. 501; Pitt might become leader of, 20. 493n; Pitt might leave, to Grenville by accepting peerage, 30. 188; Pitt must manage, 22. 490; Pitt probably controls, better in absentia, 21. 58; Pitt's absence from, encourages Charles Townshend, 22. 492–3; Pitt's administration defeated in, over Fox's motion, 33. 432–3; Pitt's burial to be attended by, 24. 379; Pitt's demand for increased navy defeated in, 19. 168–9; Pitt's departure from, disliked, 22. 443; Pitt's expression in, about Clive, 22. 176, 243n, 23. 381n, 387; Pitt should sing ariette in, 38. 11; Pitt silent in, against Fox's attacks, 36. 222; Pitt's motion in, on dockyards, 25. 629n; Pitt's resolution and Dolben's bills in, on slave trade, 31. 269n; Pitt's resolutions for Irish trade-equality laid before, 25. 565n; Pitt's speeches in, attacking Newcastle, 35. 194; Pitt still unable to attend, 21. 33, 35; Pitt tells Beckford to lay plans before, for East India Co., 22. 493; Pitt the meteor of, though some Tories

oppose him, 19. 202; Pitt to address, 11. 226; Pitt voted a funeral and monument by, at public expense, 24. 379; Pitt walks out of, in debate with Grenville, 22. 401n; Pitt, Thomas, moves in, to amend Address, 25. 368n; Pitt, William II, behaves well in, 25. 437; Pitt, William II, debates in, for bill for reform of public offices, 42. 58n; Pitt, William II, defeated in, over fortification plan, 25. 629–30, Pitt, William II, demolishes North in, in debate over accounts, 39. 380; Pitt, William II's Irish propositions in, see under Parliament: Irish propositions; Pitt, William II's loan to Francis II approved by, 12. 124; Pitt, William II's ministry weak in, 36. 215; Pitt, William II's motion for reform of, defeated, 25. 401–2, 404–5; Pitt, William II, supported by George III against majority in, 25. 471n; Pitt, William II, to address, 11. 226; Pitt, William II, wounds, in way which may be fatal to Constitution, 25. 484–5; placemen in, 17. 296, 43. 242; place tax debated in, 21. 199; plate tax debated in, 37. 451; Poor Bill passed by, 38. 528; Popish laws to be considered by, 33. 178; Powys may be successful in, 25. 474; 'Pride's Purge' of, 15. 129; printers of debates of, arrested, 23. 280; printing of Secret Committee's report not decided by, 17. 475–6; privately-raised regiments discussed in, 19. 154–5, 26. 13–19; privilege debated by, in Wilkes's absence, 38. 226, 231, 240–3; privileges of, maintained by Onslow against House of Lords, 30. 301n; proceedings in, when a member is 'named,' 30. 299n; Pulteney called by name by, 37. 91; Pulteney kept from, by daughter's illness, 17. 363; Pulteney leads Patriots in, 17. 231; Pulteney leaves, 18. 23; Pulteney quells disputes in, 17. 355; Pulteney's motion for examination of foreign negotiations defeated in, 17. 250–1; Rawlinson informs, of Hood's success at St Kitts, 25. 253; reform in, see Parliament: reform of representation in; Regency Bill debated in, 38. 545, 547–53; rejects abolition of slave trade, 11. 252; renewing of new regiments debated in, 40. 50; resolution to deny validity of proceedings of, 39. 125–6; Rigby's motion in, over Stamp Act, 22. 382n; right of sovereignty decided by, 28. 87; riots over North Briton investigated by, 38. 258; Rockingham ministry to include members of, 22. 311; Rockingham ministry triumphant in, 22. 381; Rolle's motion in, against Pigot's superseding Rodney, 25. 278n; Ross under age when elected to, 17. 244n; Rous's motion in, against North administration, 25. 256n, 258n; Royal African Co. petitions, for support of its forts and settlements, 20. 126n; royal household members of, have not yet kissed hands, 20.

[Parliament (English), *continued*]
247; Rumbold to be squeezed by, **25**. 277; Rushout leads Carteret's party in, **19**. 212; Rushout oldest member of, **39**. 78; Sackville (Germain) does not attend, **21**. 345; Sackville tells, that America must give unlimited submission, **24**. 282n; Sackville wants Tyrawley to be censured by, **30**. 158n; St Stephen's chapel in, **17**. 245n; St Vincent's island debated in, **32**. 99, 100; Sandwich may be examined in, **10**. 272; Sandwich's prosecution in, **25**. 243; Sandwich 'whitewashed' by, **33**. 326, 328; Sandys, 1st Bn, considers, unfair tribunal, **19**. 25–6; Sandys, 2d Bn, vacates seat in, **23**. 206; Saturday sessions may be introduced at, **17**. 247; Savile and Burke attack, **15**. 130; Savile attacks, **23**. 169–70, 184; Savile introduces Roman Catholic Relief Bill in, **33**. 177n; Savile's motion in, for inquiry into North's loan, **36**. 194n; Savile's motion in, for petition from county delegates favouring reform, **36**. 198n; Savile's violent conduct in, **39**. 121; Sawbridge's motion in, for shortening parliaments, **25**. 290n; Sawbridge's motion in, for Westminster election return, **25**. 562n; Sayre said to have planned seizure of George III on way to, **24**. 138; 'scene of folly and billingsgate,' **28**. 401; Scottish bill debated in, **26**. 31–3; Scottish election decided in, **17**. 294; Scottish heritable jurisdictions debated in, **37**. 268; Scottish members of, **17**. 496; Seaforth election debated in, **19**. 449; seamen to be voted by, for American war, **24**. 127; seat in, unprofitable, **20**. 11, **25**. 465; seat in, vacated for Robinson, **20**. 17; seats in, high-priced, **35**. 176; Secret Committee again proposed in, and defeated, **18**. 117–18; Secret Committee of, on East India Co., **39**. 168; Secret Committee on India carried in, **39**. 369–70; Secret Committee proposed in, against Sir Robert Walpole, **17**. 297, 355, 364, 375, 379, 383–6, 388, 425, 475–6, 484, **30**. 292n, 304n; Selwyn, Downe, and Stone remain in, despite appointment to Household by George II, **20**. 247n; Selwyn's absence from, noticed, **38**. 492; sensible members of, probably disgusted by Opposition orators, **25**. 57; serjeant-at-arms to, *see* Bonfoy, Nicholas (d. 1775); Odiarne, Wentworth (d. 1762); Spence, Thomas (d. 1737); seventeen-hour session the longest ever in, **38**. 315; Shelburne defeated in, **25**. 368, **33**. 388; Shelburne's friends in, vote against Court on privilege issue, **38**. 248; Sheridan opposes Burke in, on French Revolution, **31**. 343n; sits eternally, though half empty, **24**. 148; sits for 22 hours, **17**. 383; Sloane's Harleian and Cottonian collections bought by act of, **20**. 358n; small majority in, equivalent to defeat, **38**. 320, 326; Smithson vacates

seat in, **20**. 125; Solomon's Porch behind Speaker's chair in, **17**. 245n; Somerset, Lord Noel, leads Jacobites in, **17**. 231; Speaker and clerk wearied by long hours in, **38**. 317; Speaker of, *see* Addington, Henry; Chute, Chaloner; Cornwall, Charles Wolfran; Norton, Sir Fletcher; Onslow, Arthur; Speaker's chair in, Mansfield frightened out of, **23**. 247; Speaker's chamber in, **17**. 300n; Speaker's chamber in, used by HW for writing letter, **17**. 246; Speaker's chambers at, crowded for voting Secret Committee lists, **17**. 383; Speaker's chamber visitors locked out by under-doorkeeper, **17**. 244–5; speakership in, **9**. 398; Speaker's mace, **23**. 175–6, **24**. 356; Speaker's retiring-room in, **17**. 245n; Speaker's speeches in, hint at Sir Robert Walpole's impeachment, **17**. 354–5; speeches in, incorrectly reported, **25**. 58n; Spencer's motion in, for removal of ministers, **33**. 432n; spiritless, **33**. 325; spirit of, shows that Constitution is not quite gone, **25**. 262; Stamp Act repeal passed by, **41**. 9; Stanhope, Sir William, too deaf to hear debates in, **22**. 183; Stanley's first speech in, **39**. 248; strangers excluded from gallery of, **23**. 168n; Stratton et al. tried by order of, **25**. 12n; subsidy treaties attacked in, **37**. 405 (*see also* Hessian, Prussian, etc.); supply bill for militia debated in, **31**. 117n; Surrey ridicules Eden in, for changing party, **25**. 623n; Surrey to make motion in, against North administration, **25**. 258n; Taaffe and Wortley Montagu belong to, **19**. 450n, **20**. 289; tapestry in room near, **40**. 213; taxes considered by, **25**. 583; taxes debated in, **19**. 458, **37**. 445; taxes should be heaped by, on those who present flattering addresses, **24**. 193–4; Temple to be examined in, **10**. 272; Tindal's and Toland's writings condemned by, **20**. 454n; toast drunk in, **17**. 354; too small to vote on election, **24**. 273; Tories avoid voting in, **18**. 383, **25**. 19; Tories in, opposed subsidiary treaties, **20**. 300; Tory side of, popular, **19**. 4; Townshend absent from, on day of his own business, **30**. 244; Townshend attacks North and Forrester in, **38**. 309; Townshend blames arbitrary conduct of, on Ps of Wales, **23**. 289; Townshend returns to, and supports ministry, **30**. 244; Townshend's death leaves Conway more exposed in, **39**. 92; Townshend's motion in, for Renunciation Bill, **33**. 382n; Townshend's successor will not speak so well in, **39**. 90; Townshend suggests facetious Address by, to George II, **37**. 474; Townshend's witticism in, on recruiting, **37**. 446; Townshend, George, moves in, for inquiry on Anstruther, **20**. 229n; Townshend, Thomas, attacks East India Co.'s purchase of seats in, **33**. 244n; Townshend, Thomas

jr, divides, **38**. 224; treaty with Saxony opposed in, by Cobham and Horatio Walpole (1678–1757), **20**. 299–300; Turner ridicules Gordon in, **33**. 177n; turnpikes and poor rates occupy, **31**. 5; two prime ministers overturned by, in one year, **25**. 402; Tyrawley comments on, **18**. 148; vacillations of, over prerogative and petitions, **25**. 66–7; Van's rumoured motion for Wilkes's expulsion from, **39**. 225; Verney brings petition into, against Buckinghamshire election, **25**. 572n; vote in, mistaken by Conway, **39**. 79; *Votes* of, sales of, decline, **22**. 406n; *Votes* of, seen by Mann, **20**. 304, **21**. 58, 163, **22**. 406; voting in, about naval questions, **24**. 449; wainscot of, **25**. 35; Waller abandons, because of deafness, **30**. 291n; Walpole, Horatio (1678–1757) cannot be spared by, **19**. 469; Walpole, Horatio (1678–1757), shocks Mann by opposition in, **20**. 304; Walpole, Horatio (1678–1757), told by, to withdraw, **17**. 431; Walpole, Richard, to succeed Sir Edward Walpole in, **39**. 95n; Walpole, Sir Robert, expelled from, **2**. 121–2; Walpole, Sir Robert, hurries HW to, **18**. 394; Walpole, Sir Robert, manages, against Dr Sacheverel, **22**. 26; Walpole, Sir Robert, member of, from 1700 on, **22**. 26; Walpole, Sir Robert, the only K.G. in, since Q. Elizabeth's day, **23**. 391; Walpole, Sir Robert, to have been removed from George II's councils by motion made in, **17**. 83, 142, 232n, **30**. 304n, **37**. 89–92; Walpole, Sir Robert, wins majority in, **37**. 89–91; Walsh offers to resign seat in, **38**. 249; Wareham election discussed in, **19**. 458; war inquiry started and halted by, **24**. 474; warm campaign in, might cause Conway to be sent for, **38**. 141; warmth in, rekindles, **25**. 212; warrants, general, debated by, **22**. 374–5, 283, **38**. 318–21, 325–7, 490, 505; Wenman and Dashwood take seats in, **20**. 435n; Weobley election contested in, **20**. 31; Westminster election causes longest day in, **38**. 315; Westminster election examined by, **17**. 220, 233, 246, 247, 250–2, 272–3, 298, 322, **20**. 107–8, 113, 122–3, 156, 223–4, **25**. 502, 565; Whig union saves Pelham's mastery of, **18**. 118; Whithed enters, **19**. 446–7; Wilberforce talks against slavery in, **31**. 296n; Wilkes and warrants debated in, **38**. 324–7; Wilkes dull in, **22**. 136; Wilkes expelled from, **4**. 193n, **10**. 277, **22**. 181–5, 186–8, 199, 207, **23**. 86, 316–17; Wilkes fails to appear before, **22**. 198; Wilkes prints manifestos against, but hopes to re-enter it, **23**. 205–6; Wilkes proposes Mackreth as Speaker of, **39**. 221; Wilkes rejected by, **10**. 277, **23**. 97; Wilkes's appearance before, prevented by members' fears, **23**. 303; Wilkes's attempted assassination complained of in, **38**. 264–5;

Wilkes's complaint on privilege to be heard by, despite Grenville's opposition, **38**. 292; Wilkes's examination by, **23**. 73–4, 82, 84; Wilkes's expulsion from, protested in London petition, **39**. 114, 115; Wilkes's friends in, petition against Luttrell, **23**. 114–15; Wilkes's hearings in, **10**. 272; Wilkes's medical attention debated in, **38**. 273–4; Wilkes's papers illegally seized, according to Opposition in, **22**. 207–8; Wilkes's re-election to, **10**. 277; Wilkes's speech in, on British Museum's acquiring printed books and Houghton paintings, **43**. 286; Wilkes summoned by, but refuses unless he can occupy his seat, **23**. 281; Wilkes to carry 12 members in, **39**. 196; Wilkes wants more equal representation in, **24**. 187; Wilkes will be harmless in, **23**. 8; Wilkes will control, **23**. 181; Williams, Sir C. H., moves Address in, **30**. 311n; Winchester Bill passes, **33**. 179; Wood, Webb, and messengers examined by, about Wilkes, **38**. 316; Worms treaty to be discussed in, **18**. 383; Wortley Montagu enters, **19**. 450; Wraxall explicit in, **33**. 276; Wyndham speaks in, **15**. 152; Wynn, Sir W. Williams, enters, **18**. 344; Yorke brothers stay away from, **24**. 178; Young Pretender's Scottish scheme depends on, **17**. 202; *see also under* Parliament: acts and bills of; speeches in, etc.

House of Lords in: Abingdon's buffoon speech in, delivering 'Coalition' caricature, **35**. 381; address against Hanoverian troops proposed in, **18**. 158; address against Massachusetts act considered by, **22**. 507; address debated in, **37**. 416; address in, almost ruined by clause of thanks for Hanoverian troops, **21**. 30; address moved and debated in, **38**. 229; address of, on accommodation with America, passed unanimously, **25**. 352; address to George II debated in, **18**. 230–1; address to George II not made by, **18**. 409; address to George III voted in, against London's remonstrances, **23**. 200; adjourns, **10**. 272; adjourns in Gordon riots, **33**. 176, 214; adjourns out of respect for Lord Chatham, **24**. 371; Albany, Cts of, visits, **11**. 296; antiquated and idle, **25**. 153; Argyll does not attend, **37**. 338, **18**. 159; aristocratic tendencies of, at end of George II's reign, **23**. 164; Armada tapestries in, **1**. 10–11, 13, **9**. 18, **18**. 126–7, **23**. 242, **34**. 84–5; army should not include too many from, **26**. 13; Arran carried to, **37**. 458; assizes bill amended by, **13**. 20; authors numerous among members of, **16**. 294; bar of, scene of conversation, **40**. 334; Barrington, Bp, brings Adultery Bill into, **24**. 455n; Bedford asks, to investigate toasts to Old Pretender, **20**. 365–6, 375; Bedford attends, **17**. 338; Bedford's moderation in open-

[Parliament (English), *continued*]
ing debate in, **30.** 236; Bedford's motion in, to stop war in Germany and make peace, **22.** 7, 15, **38.** 154; Bedford speaks in, for Address, **37.** 416; Bedford's petition in, against (and Ossory's for) Seditious Meetings and Treasonable Practices bills, **34.** 209n; Bedford faction defeats militia bill in, **24.** 497n; Bell may be huzzahed by mob on way to, **17.** 503; Berkeley claims Botetourt barony in, **38.** 368; Berkshire attends, **17.** 338; bills defeated in, **17.** 391–2, **21.** 182, **25.** 38, 47, 459; bishops and Scottish peers in, considered household 'troops,' **25.** 368, **29.** 215; Bristol moves in, for Sandwich's removal, **24.** 464n; Brooke's son cannot enter, **9.** 36; Buckingham assizes dispute may go to, **19.** 470; Bute attends, **38.** 354; Bute attends Berkeley's peerage case at, **22.** 219n, **36.** 40n; Bute said to be filling, with 'old-fashioned country boobs,' **38.** 159; Byng court martial called to bar of, **21.** 65; Byron may be tried in, **38.** 503; Byron's trial by, **38.** 511, 527, 534–5; Camden absent from, because outvoted by Court and Scotch peers, **35.** 588; Camden attacks Mansfield in, **23.** 256n; Camden's motion in, on Quebec Bill, **41.** 299–300; censures tract, **10.** 154n; Chamberlayne informs, of message from Fielding, **33.** 176n; Chandos moves in, for adjournment, **25.** 459n; Chatham and Grafton prepare motions in, **24.** 341n; Chatham appears in, **23.** 167, **24.** 14, 208; Chatham does not draw magic circle around, **39.** 245; Chatham forsakes, **23.** 194, 197–200, 256; Chatham has fit in, **28.** 379; Chatham has little influence in, **21.** 205–6, **23.** 186; Chatham in, praises Choiseul, **41.** 201; Chatham is expected in, **28.** 349; Chatham preparing news for, **32.** 232; Chatham proposes, should probe Middlesex election, **23.** 167; Chatham's bill in, for pacifying America, debated, **32.** 234–5; Chatham's death in, **34.** 210; Chatham's last speech in, **24.** 370–1, **34.** 210; Chatham's long motions in, **32.** 66; Chatham's motion in, to ask George III to withdraw troops from Boston, **32.** 226n, 228, **39.** 245–6; Chatham's motion in, to withdraw troops to conciliate America, **32.** 401n; Chatham's motions in, **23.** 180, **24.** 75; Chatham's speech in, for recall of troops from Boston, **32.** 228; Chatham visits, for last time, **24.** 370–1; Chatham wants Temple to stay in, **21.** 485; Chesterfield attends, **17.** 338; Chute pleased by defeat in, of Indemnity Bill, **35.** 29; Committee appointed in, on public schools and education, **16.** 151; Commons abused by, **9.** 149; Commons' resolutions condemning *North Briton* approved by, **38.** 247; Commons' resolutions on Wilkes agreed to by,

22. 187; constitution involves, **11.** 264; Contractors Bill debated in, **29.** 28, 244; controversy to be expected in, **25.** 398; Conway's witticism on, **38.** 548; Cooke and Fall testify to, about riot, **38.** 257; Cornwallis, Abp, and Bp Moss testify in, about Roman Catholic decrease, **25.** 66n; counter-resolutions expected from, **36.** 224; Cromwell's, composed of dregs, **33.** 53, 144; Cromwell, Richard, replies in, to Bathurst, **34.** 443; crowds from Charing Cross to, **21.** 389; Cumberland, Henry, D. of, votes in, **22.** 521; Cumberland, William, D. of, enters, **17.** 398; Cumberland, William, D. of, leads minority in, **22.** 187; Cumberland, William, D. of, not present in, on day of Mutiny Bill, **20.** 38n; Cumberland, William, D. of, votes in, **20.** 38; Dashwood to enter, **22.** 130; debate in, on state of nation, **28.** 356; debates in, **32.** 403; debates in, on American conciliatory bills, **24.** 359n; Denbigh and Pomfret attack Bedford in, **38.** 529; Denbigh's brutality in, **9.** 334; divorce case in, **25.** 228; divorce should not be granted by, after proof of collusion, **24.** 227; divorce trial possibly to be in, **13.** 219; Douglas case considered by, **32.** 90n, **38.** 368; Douglas case decided by, **22.** 155n; Douglas case to be tried before, **23.** 83; dragoons guard, after Gordon riots, **29.** 65; *Essay on Woman* examined by, **22.** 195, 199, **38.** 229–31, 293; Ferrers's paper attacks, **21.** 398–9; Ferrers's separation trial at, **21.** 183n, 184, 396; Ferrers, Cts, testifies to, that her husband is sane, **21.** 399; Fielding and magistrates examined by, on weavers' riots, **38.** 559; Fitzwilliam active in, **35.** 377; Foley bill rejected in, **34.** 10; Fox's East India bill defeated in, **29.** 320, 329n, 331–3, 348, 350; Fox to enter, **10.** 60, **30.** 249; Frederick, P. of Wales, attends, **20.** 232; Frederick, P. of Wales's party suffers rift in, **20.** 38; Fullarton censured in, **29.** 13; George II at, **20.** 231n; George II's bills passed in, **20.** 232; George II's speech debated in, **17.** 230; George III goes to prorogue, **23.** 115; George III humbles, **22.** 97; George III stoned on way to, **34.** 212n; George III wants India Bill defeated in, **25.** 458n; Gerbier's academy and Museum Minervæ may have resulted from committee in, **16.** 152; Germain blackened by, **33.** 326; Gloucester, D. of, to entreat, to mediate with George III, **36.** 110–11; Gloucester, D. of, votes in, **22.** 521; Gordon riots endanger members of, **33.** 175–6; Grafton and Lyttelton attack Court party in, **24.** 139, **41.** 314n; Grafton disputes with Pomfret in, **33.** 238; Grenville-Bedford faction pert in, **41.** 10; Grenville's death keeps Chatham and Temple from, **23.** 248; HW calls, 'Temple of Honour,' **24.** 341; HW declines 'duty' to speak

in, **34**. 210; HW listens to speeches in, **18**. 356; HW mentions, **10**. 153; HW not to take seat in, **15**. 216, **42**. 349; HW permitted by, to dispose of property, **33**. 11, 14; HW rejects Lady Ossory's sending him to take his seat in, **33**. 171–2, 210; HW's bill for purchase of SH passed by, **9**. 82; HW talks to D. of Richmond in, **22**. 297n; HW urged to take his seat in, or name a proxy, **31**. 363; HW visits, **1**. 52; habeas corpus extension debated in, **37**. 526–7, 528–9; habeas corpus extension to be defeated in, **21**. 199, 205–6; habeas corpus revision rejected by, **21**. 182n; Halifax attends, **17**. 338; Halifax proposes adjournment of, before Bute's or Ps of Wales's friends come, **22**. 297n; Halifax proposes motion in, on Regency Bill, **22**. 297; Halifax speaks in, **9**. 229; Halifax-Temple and Gower-Temple exchanges in, **38**. 233; Hanoverian troops not debated in, by Tories, **18**. 141; Hanoverian troops to be discussed in, **37**. 452; Harcourt endangered by rioters at, **35**. 503; Harcourt should vote in, for American independence, **35**. 528; Hardinge hopes HW will meet Chatham at, **35**. 565; Hardinge outlines appellant jurisdiction of, **35**. 622; Hardwicke attacks Henry Fox in, **20**. 383; Harrington dragged to, from coffin, **37**. 458; Hastings trial subject of special reports in, **11**. 269; Herbert offends, by speech, **16**. 5; Herbert of Chepstow not a member of, **40**. 130; Hertford grateful for reparation from, **38**. 353; Hertford's vote in, inconsequential to Opposition **38**. 416; holiday-time interrupts business in, **39**. 70; 'household troops' in, **25**. 368, **29**. 215; House of Commons asks, for peers to appear at their bar, **23**. 73–4, 77; House of Commons opposes amendment of, to Militia Bill, **21**. 137n; House of Commons provoked to quarrel with, **23**. 256; House of Commons tells members of, to 'withdraw,' **17**. 431; Ilchester to inform H. Fox of debate in, **30**. 236; inactive, **20**. 111; Ireland's independence signed by, **25**. 279–80; Irish bankruptcy tried by, **21**. 65; Irish relief moved in, by Rockingham and Shelburne, **39**. 324n; Italians ignorant of founding of, **18**. 126; Karl Wilhelm Ferdinand naturalized by, **38**. 289; Kidgell called to, as witness, **43**. 186; king and commons a balance against, **35**. 379; king and commons alternate with, in preponderance of power, **34**. 102; Kingston, Ds of, petitions, for her trial, **24**. 143, 149–50; Kingston, Ds of, says, acknowledges her to be Countess, **24**. 220; Kingston, Ds of, tried by, **2**. 10n, **24**. 191–3, 195–6, 198–9, **28**. 234–5, 260–6, **33**. 299–300; Kingston, Ds of, wants to defer trial by, **39**. 272; last, under Sir Robert Walpole, **15**. 153; Limerick's scheme in, for allowing secular Roman

Catholic priests, **37**. 426–7, 428; Lincoln proposes motion at, **9**. 38; Lincoln rarely attends, **30**. 179; literary property debated in, **28**. 135, 149; *London Gazette* defended by Suffolk in, **24**. 205n; London sheriffs warn, of new riot, **38**. 562; Lyttelton attacks Court party in, **24**. 139, 534; Lyttelton complains to, about *Droit le Roi*, **38**. 333; Lyttelton (2d Bn)'s comment in, on Gower, **24**. 534n; Manchester and Rockingham oppose misrepresentation in, of Canadian affairs, **32**. 284n; Manchester's motion in, for American dispatches, **24**. 205n; Mann shocked by mob's treatment of member of, **22**. 112; Marchmont and Somerset complain to, of newspaper attack on Hertford, **38**. 347, 353; Marchmont to succeed Crawford in, **20**. 110–11; Marlborough moves for address of loyalty to George II from, **18**. 399; Massachusetts assembly's act examined by, **22**. 507, 520; Militia Bill to be stopped in, **37**. 458; ministry's majority in, dwindles, **22**. 525; Morton ridicules bishops in, **35**. 587; motion in, against use of Hanover troops, **18**. 356; motion in, for address for removing Sir Robert Walpole, **37**. 87; naval investigation proposed in, **18**. 400; Newcastle and Hardwicke formerly treated subserviently in, **22**. 109–10; Newcastle avoids voting in, **22**. 508; Newcastle expects Chatham to attack him in, **22**. 494n; new members convert, into house of invalids, **40**. 89–90; new peerages not allowed for, **38**. 377; new peers to add to silence in, **37**. 270; no division in, **18**. 351, **22**. 109; Northington and Camden clash in, with Mansfield, **22**. 520; North's government would have been retained by, **29**. 208, 210; nothing passes in, **25**. 140; Onslow maintains privileges of House of Commons against, **30**. 301n; Onslow's speech on inferiority of, to House of Commons, **30**. 301n; Opposition a majority in, **38**. 529; Opposition in, led by Bedford, **17**. 497n; Opposition in, mere 'dignified ciphers,' **25**. 295; Opposition lords in, a minority, **30**. 210; Opposition wastes time of, **12**. 257; Opposition withdraws from, **23**. 256; origin of hereditary peerages in, **18**. 126n; Orrery, E. of, Jacobite leader in, **20**. 499n; Oxford, E. of, augments, **35**. 15; peers' eldest sons proposed as carriers of bills to, **23**. 256n; Pepys and, **11**. 46; Pitt, William II, influential in, **11**. 269–70; plays to be acted by, in HW's newspaper parody, **9**. 129; Pomfret committed by, to Tower, **36**. 187n; Poor Bill debated in, **38**. 528–9, 535, 536; Port Mahon officers' lists examined by, **17**. 300; Poulett's motion in, **35**. 223–4; Poulett's motion in, Pratt does not testify to, on Habeas Corpus Bill, **21**. 205n; prime minister not usually a member of, **35**. 183; princes' pensions de-

[Parliament (English), *continued*]

layed in, by Conway, **22**. 425; printer taken up by, for printing Weymouth's letter, **23**. 77; profligacy of members of, **32**. 191; prophesying in, **32**. 44; Pulteney, E. of Bath, dashes peerage patent on floor of, **34**. 148; Pulteney, E. of Bath, enters, **17**. 485n, **18**. 23; Radnor's Regency proposal in, **25**. 684n; Ravensworth makes motion in, for Hanover troops, **20**. 526; rebel lords tried by, **19**. 280–7; Regency Bill in, **38**. 541–5, 547–8, 552–3; registration rules for membership in, **42**. 349n; report upon cessation of trials, **11**. 269; Richmond, 2d D. of, defends Sir Robert Walpole in, **17**. 330; Richmond, 3d D. of, answers Portland in, **25**. 458n; Richmond, 3d D. of, debates in, on naval and military affairs, **41**. 314n; Richmond, 3d D. of, in, questions military suppression of Gordon riots, **25**. 77n; Richmond, 3d D. of, makes motion in, for address to George III, **24**. 370n; Richmond, 3d D. of, makes motion in, for American conciliation after Penn's examination, **24**. 142n; Richmond, 3d D. of, makes motions in, for inquiry into state of nation, **24**. 341n; Richmond, 3d D. of, makes resolutions in, for civil regulation of Quebec, **41**. 84n; Rochford misrepresents French disarming to, **41**. 299; Rockingham and Grafton agree and disagree in, **28**. 304; Rockingham attacks Sandwich in, **25**. 221; Rockingham introduces Roman Catholic Relief Bill in, **33**. 187n; Rockingham makes motion in, **23**. 180; Rockingham's motion in, for amendment to Address, **24**. 533n; Rockingham speaks in, only by necessity, **25**. 288; Rockingham ministry triumphant in, **22**. 381; Rockingham unable to cope with opponents in, **41**. 88; Sandwich denounces *Essay on Woman* in, **22**. 184; Sandwich runs gauntlet in, **28**. 402; Sandys's entrance into, satirized by HW, **18**. 257–8; Sandys succeeds Hardwicke as Speaker of, **21**. 25; Secret Committee may be hampered by, **17**. 400; secretaries of state in, hint that Bute fomented mob, **30**. 182; Shelburne can expect little opposition in, **35**. 528; Shelburne defeated in, **25**. 368; Shelburne in, mentions American-French trade, **24**. 254n; Shelburne opposes loan in, **25**. 402; Shelburne ridiculous in, **25**. 407; Shelburne's motion in, for walking at Chatham's burial, **24**. 379n; sheriffs of London inform, of intended weavers' riot, **30**. 181; sheriffs testify to, about riot for burning *North Briton*, **38**. 257; slavery defended in, **31**. 280; Southampton moves Address in, **35**. 363n; spiritless, **33**. 325; Stamp Act repeal may be passed by, **41**. 9; Stanhope, 2d E., moves Address in, **18**. 158, 178; Stormont questions Radnor's Regency amendment in, **25**. 684n; Stormont's speech in, on Spain, **24**. 463n; Suffolk's motion in, for amendment to Address, **22**. 381n; Suffolk urges, to ask George III to reward Harley, **23**. 21; Talbot's statement in, about Ferrers, **9**. 272–3; taxes called heavy in, **18**. 158; Temple assembles, without giving reason, **22**. 507; Temple does not attend, **23**. 251; Temple proposes first minister in, **21**. 546; Temple's remarks in, on Spain, objected to, **38**. 233; Temple to stay in, **21**. 485; Temple unable to attend, **38**. 489; Thurlow in, **11**. 151; Thurlow resists Parliamentary reform in, **25**. 273; Thurlow ridiculous in, **25**. 407; Townshend in, advocates enlisting Irish Papists, **41**. 313n; treaty with Saxony debated in, **20**. 300; twelve peerages conferred to alter, **25**. 605; uproar in, brings Chatham's secession, **23**. 256; Wales, Augusta, Ps of, stigmatized by, **38**. 549; Walpole, Sir Robert, sends proxy to, **18**. 159; Walpole, Sir Robert, to be removed by motion to be made by, **37**. 87; Walpole, Sir Robert, to enter, **17**. 319, 325, 333, 335, 338; Walpole, Sir Robert, wins majority in, **37**. 89–91; Warburton, Bp, tells Bp Lyttelton in, about rejecting Helvétius, **38**. 365; Warburton, Gen., hears in, that Conway is turned out, **38**. 375; weavers' relief bill thrown out of, by D. of Bedford, **22**. 301; weavers surround, **22**. 301; weavers threaten to come to, for redress, **38**. 560; Weymouth lays regimental returns before, **24**. 351n; Weymouth notifies Spanish war to, **24**. 483n; Wilkes not to be heard by, **23**. 77; Wilkes's demand perplexes, **10**. 272; Wilkes's writs of error to be argued before, **23**. 81; Winchester Bill thrown out by, **33**. 179; Winchilsea's complaint in, on Vcts Townshend's arrest, **38**. 502n; York, Edward, D. of, speaks but does not vote in, **22**. 521

Howe, Mrs, asks votes for son's election to, **37**. 571

'important' issues in, soon forgotten, **25**. 365

inactivity of, **28**. 347

India discussed in, **23**. 490, **24**. 46, **25**. 159; *see also under* House of Commons; House of Lords

India's plunder winked at by, **24**. 231

infirm, **25**. 565

inquiry in: about Dutch ships at Deal, proposed by Horace Mann II but dropped on Mann's advice, **25**. 222–3, 234; about war conduct, **24**. 348, 351

invalids brought to, **17**. 298

inviolability of members of, Rigby assumes, **30**. 330

Ireland defies, **25**. 681

—— may be offended by rising of, without redressing their wrongs, **39**. 330

—— receives concessions from, **24**. 542

Irish bills opposed in, **33**. 10

Irish deliberations deferred by adjournment of, **20.** 409

Irish propositions considered by, **25.** 564–5, 578, 589, 596

Irish would throw off, and also amend it, **39.** 405

Jacobites avowed enemies of, **30.** 97

—— prefer invasion to disputes in, **18.** 417

—— to make attempt after meeting of, **17.** 160

James II would have adjourned without, **34.** 119

Jews give money to, **21.** 341

——'s naturalization revoked by, **35.** 70n, 179n

jokes while provoking a civil war, **24.** 133

journals of, may contradict Hume's facts, **35.** 214

Keppel-Palliser affair again to be examined by, **25.** 103

lack of opposition in, results in lack of interest, **24.** 278

ladies attend, **38.** 317–18

La Rochefoucauld, Duc de, interested in, **4.** 180

last, under Sir Robert Walpole, **15.** 153

Lestock vindicated by, **19.** 33

list of, newspapers could avoid errors by consulting, **22.** 325

London deserted till meeting of, **25.** 105, **38.** 214

—— does not throng to see, **19.** 118

—— not to be vacated by, at Christmas, **24.** 542–3

——'s American-trading merchants to petition, **39.** 231n

——'s remonstrances to, **23.** 196–8, **25.** 218

—— will be empty till meeting of, **25.** 105

'Long' Parliament, **40.** 130

long sessions in, **35.** 262–3

Louis XV might dissolve, if George III changed places with him, **35.** 344

Lucas tends E. of Orford's boroughs in case of dissolution of, **25.** 462

madwoman presents her speech at opening of, as Q. Elizabeth, **24.** 361

Mann awaits new system for, **21.** 492–3

—— calls, 'great scene of discord,' **24.** 39

—— expects to hear echoes from, of victory at Gibraltar, **25.** 340

—— fails to understand debates in, **20.** 54

—— fears for HW's health at, **22.** 469, 532

—— glad that HW is not in, during riots, **23.** 300

—— hopes that Wilkes and Lord Mayor will be humbled by, **23.** 296

—— impatient to see opening addresses of, **23.** 253

—— indignant at anti-administration agitation in, **23.** 203

Mann, Horace II, discusses, with Grand Duke, **25.** 58

Mansfield to be baited by, **23.** 268

Mason expects next, to be worse than last, **29.** 80

—— is apprehensive about meeting of, **28.** 224

masquerades undisturbed by, **20.** 469

Massachusetts assembly said to have usurped powers of, **22.** 507

meeting of, expected, **9.** 250, **36.** 135, 183

meets in 'Temple of Concord,' **28.** 155

members of: avoid arrest for debt, **19.** 418; bribed by sinecures and pensions, **29.** 127, 138, 208; frank letters, **31.** 226; more abusive than oyster-women, **35.** 379; mostly frozen in the country, **24.** 175; paid for secret services, **25.** 605; rapacious, **22.** 395; should not be protected when libellous, **38.** 245; though unable to raise money for war, prey upon government, **24.** 465; tired or absent, **22.** 519–20; to return for trials of rebel lords, **19.** 273; turn to army instead of horse-racing, **24.** 384; *see also* Parliament: House of Commons: members of

messages to be delivered to, on war with France, **28.** 273

Middlesex election writ delayed beyond opening of, **35.** 324

ministers during fight in, forget foreign enemies, **39.** 121

ministry might not be arranged before rising of, **41.** 87

ministry's requests granted by, **24.** 142

ministry wins in, **7.** 220

mob tries to take Wilkes from prison and put him in, **23.** 20

moderate, **11.** 162

Montagu glad HW is no longer concerned with, **10.** 261, 266

—— unacquainted with activities of, **10.** 199

more confined to personalities than to divisions, **25.** 98

Morgan more powerful in, than D. of Beaufort, **23.** 174

motions in, over Falkland Islands, **23.** 251

navy strengthened soon after meeting of, **24.** 252

new: but little changed, **25.** 95; ends Sir Robert Walpole's administration, **13.** 11; is no better than previous one, **29.** 86; Ossory to give news of, **33.** 236

Newcastle ministry will have to explain loss of Minorca to, **20.** 578

Newcastle's influence would be dissipated by dissolution of, **37.** 487n

—— will be deserted by, **21.** 93

new parties in, **20.** 509–10

news during recesses of, like fruit out of season, **33.** 382

newspaper and pamphlet ordered by, to be burnt, **28.** 179–80

newspapers are adequate journals of, **25.** 464, **32.** 231, 235–6

no longer of consequence, **28.** 351

North administration cares only for majority in, **39.** 325

[Parliament (English), *continued*]

North and C. J. Fox not sure of following of,
25. 379

North said to fear Irish Parliament more
than, **33.** 127

Norton leaves estate to, for use of the poor,
20. 237n

nothing likely to be decided by, **24.** 254

nothing settled about, **21.** 244

not to meet until after Christmas, **32.** 148

not yet prorogued by languishing, **22.** 23

Onslow hails triumph of, over ministers, **18.**
540

opening of: **1.** 120, **33.** 6, **38.** 184, **39.** 262;
Conway and wife to break up Park Place
before, **37.** 348; Conway may bring great
éclat to, **37.** 30; HW hopes Selwyn comes
to London before, **30.** 272; HW waits for,
before writing to H. Fox, **30.** 235; *see also*
session of: begins

opposition but no division at meeting of, on
the Address, **20.** 100

Opposition in: abandons it for Paris and
country, **24.** 262; Address attacked by, **35.**
260; address on George II's speech to be
opposed by, **18.** 102; admits total defeat,
25. 488; Aix treaty to be attacked by, **20.**
30; alarms Mann, **19.** 372, **21.** 552; American sovereignty acknowledged by all but
Pitt's followers in, **24.** 371; American war
may be halted by, **36.** 222–3; American
war should have been opposed by, more
strongly, **24.** 491; as weak as the ministry,
38. 258; Augusta, Ps, connected with, **38.**
291; awaits move by opponents, **17.** 168;
awaits its opening, **22.** 559; Baltimore
leads, **19.** 360; Barré dismissed for joining, **22.** 189; Bathurst prominent in, **20.**
32; Bedford faction only one that does not
support, **22.** 382; bedridden and tongue-
tied, **38.** 258; Bentley's comedy libels, **29.**
219; Boston Port Bill opposed by, **23.** 561n;
Bubb Dodington ineffective as leader of,
20. 51, 96; Burke and C. J. Fox only effi-
cient members of, **25.** 295; Bute negotiates
with, **38.** 342; Bute opposed by, **22.** 52–3,
508; Bute regarded by George II as closely
connected with, **20.** 570n; Chatham stared
and shrugged at by, **39.** 245–6; checked a
little, **25.** 28, 30; Chesterfield included in,
17. 232n, **18.** 102; cider counties and Yorke
family join, **38.** 459; Conway has no cause
to be grateful to, **39.** 408; county associations eclipse, in power, **25.** 29; Cumberland, Henry, D. of, joins, **24.** 74, **25.** 140;
Cumberland, Henry, D. of, slighted by,
because of marriage, **23.** 434; Cumberland,
William, D. of, in relation to, **20.** 300,
21. 145, **22.** 310; Dashwood supports, **17.**
247; dear to the Americans, **41.** 305; defeat of, will enhance Bedford's reputation,
22. 172; defeats Shelburne, **25.** 368, 369,
371–2, 402; demolishes Westminster scru-

tiny, **25.** 562; did not start county committees, **25.** 30; disjointed, **25.** 437, **38.**
281; disunited, **36.** 48; divisions in, **29.** 26,
32, 42, 63, 197–8, 314, 317; does not lurk
at Knightsbridge, **23.** 461–2; Earle opposed
by, as chairman of committee, **17.** 220, 242;
East India Co. debates divide, **39.** 82n;
East India Co. examination disappoints,
22. 506; Eden deserts, **25.** 623–4; Egmont
and Barnard last of the old, **35.** 195–6;
finds its warnings unheeded, **24.** 491–2;
Fountain meeting-place of, **17.** 429n; Fox,
C. J., shines in, **25.** 212; Frederick, P. of
Wales, forms, **19.** 360, 372, **20.** 30, **21.** 145;
Frederick, P. of Wales, recruits members
for, **19.** 449; George II and D. of Newcastle may join in suppressing, **20.** 513;
George II's speech to be opposed by, **18.**
102; George III's own servants lead, **22.** 7;
George III would dislike ministry exclu-
sively of, **39.** 343; Gower joins, **18.** 159;
Grafton, Lyttelton, and Bp of Peterborough
vote with, **28.** 229; Grafton will probably
head, **22.** 109; Grenville laughed at by, **38.**
500; Grenville ministry diminishes, by encouragement, **38.** 553; Grenville ministry
may ward off, till after recess, **38.** 328;
Grenville odious in, **22.** 483; HW and Conway vote with, over Parliamentary privilege, **38.** 224–5; HW compares, to wet
dishclout, **28.** 337; HW hopes, will remain
in minority, **38.** 323; HW speculates on
Chatham's possibly being asked to lead,
28. 377; HW's reflections on, **29.** 269; HW
wonders where North finds, to declaim
against, **28.** 155; Halifax joins, **18.** 159;
Hardwicke approaches, slowly, **22.** 109;
Hardwicke may forsake, **38.** 195; has majority in House of Commons, **25.** 471n;
Hastings opposed by, **25.** 630; Hertford
might need Conway's favour with, **38.** 283;
Hertford's chief allies are in, **38.** 416;
Hertford's reasons for not joining, **38.** 424–
6; Hertford wants to keep Conway from
joining, **38.** 283, 330–1; Hertford wonders
about future of, **38.** 336; 'heterogeneous
assemblage,' **29.** 27; honester but not abler
than administration, **24.** 448; Hunter attacks, in lecture, **29.** 86; hurries to Court,
28. 142; inactive, except on India's affairs,
25. 623; ineffectual in both Houses, **17.**
241; invigorated by hope, **25.** 19; Karl Wilhelm Ferdinand sees leaders of, **38.** 287;
Keppel a member of, **24.** 263; lacking, **24.**
278, **25.** 386; lacks leadership, **29.** 42; Lee,
George, wanted by, as chairman of Committee on Elections, **17.** 220, 242–3; liberty
of the press opposed and then abused by,
22. 315; Lord Mayor gives dinner for, **23.**
200; Lyttelton included in, **18.** 102; majority of, diminishes, **29.** 23; Mann used
to be terrified by, **20.** 43; Mason prefers
ministers to Rockingham faction of, **28.**

398; meeting of, at St Alban's Tavern, **20.** 50, **21.** 552; Michell's ties with, provoke his recall, **38.** 393; might profit by resentment against Keppel's persecution, **24.** 447; moneyed interests oppose, **36.** 219; moves for Wilkes's complaint of breach of privilege, **38.** 292; Mutiny Bill opposed by, **20.** 112; Newcastle encouraged by votes for, **38.** 261; Newcastle expects to be blamed by, for loss of Minorca, **20.** 578n; Newcastle joins, **22.** 98; Newcastle may chastise, **20.** 513; Newcastle not to join, **22.** 464; Newgate not ransacked by, for writers, **38.** 422; North agrees with, about Americans, **28.** 357; North's conciliatory bills accepted by, **28.** 359; North's government displaced by, **29.** 201; North's peace terms virtually acknowledge arguments of, **24.** 354; Norton's impudence weakens, **25.** 28; not unanimous, **25.** 47; not very able, **24.** 447; now includes powerful men, **20.** 516; officers' dismissal question deferred ostensibly to await Pitt, **38.** 508–9; opposes Address, **37.** 414–16; Ossory and brother join, **32.** 216n; pacification with France may be opposed by, **39.** 301–2, 303–4; perpetual militia demanded by, **21.** 552; petitions encourage, **25.** 29; Pitt (Chatham) encourages, to form ministry, **22.** 310; Pitt (Chatham) leads, **18.** 102, **20.** 516, **21.** 552, **24.** 341; Pitt (Chatham) not to join, **22.** 78; Pitt (Chatham)'s rapprochement with Bute weakens, **38.** 355; Pitt, William II, 'purchases' members of, **25.** 623n; Pitt, William II, shines in, **25.** 212, 407; Potter aids, **19.** 449, **20.** 32; Powys tries to reconcile William Pitt II with, **25.** 475n; prepares address, **24.** 254; proposes amendment to address, **24.** 534; prorogation opposed by, **39.** 329; Pulteney persuades Frederick, P. of Wales, to form, **19.** 229; punctilious, **25.** 275; Quarendon supports, **17.** 247; quelled, **25.** 556; quiet, **24.** 546; recovers spirit, **25.** 218; refuses to be led by Bubb Dodington, **20.** 96; resists attempts of Court to divide it, **29.** 205, 207; resorts to private bargains, **35.** 418; Rigby might wreck administration to satisfy, **24.** 447; roars at Grenville, **38.** 500; Rockingham declares against, though opposing, **22.** 549; Rockingham does not come to London to lead, **24.** 546; Rockingham not to join, **22.** 464; Sackville carries 5 into, **38.** 311; Sandwich attacked by, **25.** 221; Shelburne dismissed for joining, **22.** 189; should not prevail until more strongly popular, **35.** 617; shows strength on Savile's motion, **36.** 197–8; Smelt blames, for tearing 'sacred veil' from George III, **28.** 492; sold for pensions, **22.** 274; stays away, **24.** 273; successful not because of abilities but because of reverses in war, **25.** 244; tactics of ministers against, **29.** 299; Tavistock inclines

towards, **38.** 433; temperate and tame, **11.** 161; Temple, 1st E., does not attract followers into, **22.** 382; Temple, 1st E., to be nominal head of, **22.** 549; Temple, 2d E., supports D. of Richmond at meeting of, **25.** 295; Thurlow might have wrecked administration to satisfy, **24.** 447; time wasted by, **12.** 257; to lie low, and not discuss officers' dismissals, **38.** 533; too dull to produce ballads or epigrams, **22.** 110; Tories dislike, **19.** 370; Townshend may join, **38.** 285–6; Townshend to have betrayed administration to, **22.** 552; troublesome, **35.** 61; two at same time, **22.** 483; two factions of, headed by Chatham and Rockingham, **28.** 383; unlikely to aid D. of Gloucester, **36.** 108–9; unpopular, **36.** 194; upholds clause in Burke's bill, **25.** 26; victory of, on petitions for Parliamentary reform, **29.** 17; waits for Pitt (Chatham's) recovery, **38.** 508–9; Wales, Augusta, Ps of, ill-treated by, **38.** 568–9; Wasner said to work with, **17.** 325–6; weak in numbers, **25.** 295; Weymouth might wreck administration to satisfy, **24.** 447; Wildman's Club set up by, **38.** 294; Wilkes's support from, shows how united it is, **38.** 284–5; Wilkes supported by, in complaint on privilege, **38.** 292; will be strengthened, **19.** 449; William Henry, P., inclines towards, **38.** 435; will impute shame of St Eustatius's loss to ministry, **25.** 236; wins victory, **25.** 251–2; Yorke and Charles Townshend desert, **38.** 496–7; Yorke ridiculed by, **38.** 472; Yorke's and Mansfield's speeches reduce, **38.** 248; Yorkes blame father for forcing them into, **38.** 472; Yorkes fixed in, **38.** 341; Yorkes join, to oppose D. of Bedford on Marriage Bill, **38.** 318; Yorkes leave, **38.** 468; Yorkes may join, **38.** 285, 459; Yorkes may join after Wilkes affair, **38.** 285

orators in, should speak by inch of candle, or by hour glass, **25.** 58

oratory improves in, **35.** 263

Orford's boroughs in, **35.** 416–18

Ossory knows news of, **33.** 271, **34.** 138

ousted ministers do not propose divisions in, **25.** 407

Oxford to be chastised by, **20.** 50

Palliser's appointment not censured by, **25.** 118

party struggles in, before Sir R. Walpole's fall, Gen. Churchill's witticism on, **30.** 29–30

pattern of usual events at, **38.** 273

Peace of Aix not brought before, **19.** 464, **20.** 30

—— probably will be approved by, **20.** 27

Peace of Paris (1763) probably will not be made until meeting of, **22.** 78

Peace of Paris (1783) hardly mentioned after its approval by, **25.** 374

[Parliament (English), *continued*]

——'s preliminaries awaited by, **25.** 352, 356, 357

peace proposals to be passed by, **24.** 359

Pelham congratulates HW on happy conclusion of session of, **40.** 40

Penn family compensated by, **34.** 14n

petitions attack, **23.** 133

petitions to, **17.** 232–3, 295, 344, **25.** 29, *see also under* Parliament: House of Commons

Pitt (Chatham) attacks, for taxing America, **22.** 395–6

—— may lead George III's forces in, **24.** 350

—— might sing ariette in, **38.** 11

——'s adulation from, a farce, **24.** 415

——'s burial poorly attended by members of, **24.** 393, 415

——'s death during session of, lucky for his family, **24.** 389

——'s debts to be paid by allotment by, **24.** 382

—— the meteor of, **19.** 202

—— will be buried by, in Westminster Abbey or St Paul's, **24.** 382

polemic geniuses in, **37.** 183

politics move from, to opera, **38.** 2, 11

Portland ministry should show strength in, **33.** 429

prerogative subject of vacillation by, **25.** 66

Price's toast to, **11.** 135

Prince's chamber in, George II's funeral from, **9.** 321

prorogation of: **9.** 314, **11.** 282, 293, 296, **17.** 484, 503, **18.** 211, 227, **20.** 135, 212, 410–11, 435, **21.** 290, 294, 409, 491, **22.** 227, 285, 424, 533, 537, **23.** 115, 214, 308, 416, **24.** 34, 497, **25.** 295, 418, 519, **38.** 195, **39.** 329, 370, **40.** 367; enormous crowd at, **30.** 164; expected, **19.** 29, 35, **22.** 519–20, **24.** 483, **39.** 370; HW attends, to hear Onslow's last speech, **30.** 164; HW denounces, **30.** 97; may lengthen HW's holidays, **38.** 187; may offend Ireland, **39.** 330; may quell tumults, **23.** 301; produces few changes, **24.** 386; sudden, **23.** 303; Walpole, Sir Robert, may be saved by, **18.** 4, 9; wanted by George II, **20.** 469; will be brief, **24.** 14; will make HW's letters less frequent, **24.** 385

proxies for, sent to Scotland, **37.** 458

quack medicine rewarded by, **40.** 275–6

quartering of government places might be attacked in, **24.** 276

quiet: **21.** 267; during Easter and Newmarket season, **25.** 398

recess of, *see* Parliament: adjournment of

reform of representation in: **2.** 209, 210; begun, **25.** 373; Burke wrangles with Fitzwilliam about, **29.** 281; county delegates present petition for, **36.** 198n; deferred, **25.** 573; different views of, **29.** 63; feared by Mann to be unconstitutional, **25.** 49; HW opposes, **25.** 399, 541–2, **29.** 21–2, 226, 230; North opposes, **29.** 280; not genuinely

admired in England, **25.** 273–4; opposed by Rockingham and Cavendishes, and backed by Shelburne and C. J. Fox, **25.** 29–30; Pitt, William II, makes motion for, **25.** 399, 401, 405; Pitt, William II, supports, but later opposes it, **29.** 333, 349; Quintuple Alliance seeks, **25.** 401–2; repulsed, **25.** 406; to be discussed, **25.** 566; Wilkes wants, **24.** 187; would have been opposed by Horace Mann II, **25.** 399, 404; *see also under* Mason, William: HW's relations with

Regency Act not passed by, before George III's recovery, **25.** 682–4

Regency may be established by, **20.** 239

Richmond, Ds of, has fever from attendance at, **38.** 327

Richmond, D. of, alone debates in, **32.** 184

Rigby's election to, opposed by Oxford University, **30.** 87

rioters insult, by attacking Speaker, **35.** 285–6

rising of, *see* prorogation of

Rochefort affair may be probed in, **21.** 165, **37.** 521

Rockingham faction does not require dissolution of, **39.** 123

Rockingham ministry victorious in, **10.** 192

rôle of, in English constitution, **42.** 402–3

rolls and records of, **30.** 288

rolls of: HW differs with More about, **35.** 609; searched for HW, **41.** 92

Rome gets news of, through Goddard, **17.** 368–9

Rowley to allay fears of, **18.** 526

Russian war unpopular with, **11.** 231

Sackville (Germain)'s resignation to be announced to, **25.** 236

—— will probably attempt revenge after meeting of, **21.** 328

sailors' petition to, **23.** 21

St Stephen's Chapel in: HW calls, 'hot house,' **10.** 263; play to be acted in, **9.** 129

Sandwich, E. of, attacked in, **20.** 123, 124, **24.** 445, 460, 464, **25.** 221, 244

—— receives vote of approbation in, **25.** 243

satires on neutrality to be commented upon in, **17.** 189

Saxon treaty debated in, **20.** 299–300

Sayers satirizes members of, **33.** 401

seat in, does not lead to government posts, **35.** 418

serene, **19.** 341–2

session of: **11.** 119, 136, 147, 182, 190, **28.** 124, **29.** 299; awaited with suspense, **15.** 11, **24.** 71; begins, **11.** 119, 136, 147, 182, 190, **12.** 169, **17.** 160, 170, 171, 211, 335, **18.** 327, 349, 429, 526, 529, 537, 556, 561, 564, **19.** 134, 138, 446, 511, **20.** 3, 221, 280, 286, 434, 506, **21.** 7, 30, 39, 158, 263, 344, 452, 562, **22.** 101, 104, 463, 478, 573, **23.** 61, 66, 150, 167, 172, 219, 245, 247, 248, 316, 326, 368, 442, **24.** 61, 133, 252, 423, 529, 532–3, **25.** 209, 236, 319, 351; country ladies lay in supplies after, **18.** 498; ends, **18.**

341, **19**. 107, **21**. 12, 153, **25**. 321, 341, **38**. 377, **39**. 325, 370; HW expects, to be inactive, **30**. 235; HW hopes, will be less sensational, **35**. 379; has lasted a week, **22**. 565; imprudent to postpone, **23**. 150; may be violent, **18**. 511; may end unexpectedly, from weariness, **25**. 47; may prevent HW's Paris visit, **22**. 247; not to begin till after Christmas, **22**. 169, 256, **23**. 150, 520, **25**. 103, 519–20, 608; quiet, **9**. 229; should have novelty because of new administration, **25**. 95; Speaker addresses King on throne at end of, **30**. 301n; to begin and then adjourn for re-elections, **21**. 22; to begin in October, **25**. 296; to end before ministry changes, **20**. 212; to last 5 days, **35**. 176; to open, **35**. 183, **38**. 184, 186–7, 191, 415, 443, 465, **39**. 508; will revive set of poets, **25**. 612

Shelburne administration should give novelty to, **25**. 95

—— defeated in, **25**. 368, 369, 371–2, 402

sheriffs examined by, for failure to burn *North Briton*, **22**. 188

sits only on necessary business, **25**. 506

Sloane's museum offered to, **20**. 358

sold and despised, **23**. 499

Spanish rescript and George III's reply read to, **33**. 103n

Speaker's Chamber in, Gordon, Lord George, harangues mob from, **33**. 177

Speaker's rooms in, ladies dine in, and maybe play loo, **38**. 327

speeches in, by: Adam, William, **24**. 537; Alston, **37**. 415; Baltimore, 5th Bn, **26**. 14, 18; Bankes, **39**. 380; Barnard, Sir John, **20**. 257, **26**. 10; Barré, Isaac, **23**. 186, 248, **33**. 348n, **38**. 321, 496, 508, **39**. 325; Barrington, Lord, **26**. 13, 14, 15, 16, 17, 18, **37**. 415, **39**. 125n; Bathurst, **26**. 17; Beauchamp, **39**. 126n; Beckford, **37**. 415, **38**. 487, 499; Bedford, D. of, **20**. 310, **22**. 463–4, **37**. 416, **38**. 257–8; Bennet, **26**. 17; Bladen, **26**. 14; Blaquiere, **32**. 161n; Boone, **26**. 15; Bubb Dodington, **17**. 354, **26**. 14, 23, **37**. 415; Burgoyne, **24**. 387n; Burke, Edmund, **23**. 170, 184, 248, **25**. 31, 408, **31**. 241n, **32**. 222n, 400n, 34. 41n, 98n, 104n, **39**. 126n, 232, 325; Bute, **32**. 22n; Byng, George, **36**. 194n; Calvert, **26**. 23; Camden, Earl, **22**. 520; Campbell, Gen., **26**. 28, 31; Campbell, Lord Frederick, **38**. 319; Carew, **26**. 23; Carteret, John (Lord Granville), **18**. 158; Cholmondeley, 3d E. of, **18**. 230, **38**. 257; Cholmondeley, Richard, **17**. 296; Chute, Francis, **17**. 234, 297; Clive, **23**. 399n; Coke, Edward, Vct. **17**. 298, **26**. 23, 32; Conway, Hon. Henry Seymour, **22**. 208, 274, **24**. 139, **25**. 294n, 467n, **26**. 15, **33**. 432n, **38**. 48–9, 308–9, 325–6, 487–8, 500–1, 547–8, **39**. 126n, 353–4; Cornbury, Lord, **26**. 22, 24; Cotes, **26**. 18; Cotton, Sir John, **17**. 355, **26**. 15; Danvers, **26**. 15; Dash-

wood, **17**. 298, **26**. 15, 18; Doneraile, Lord, **17**. 354, **26**. 14; Dowdeswell, **22**. 556, **38**. 496; Dunning, **25**. 35–6, **39**. 126n; Egmont, E. of, **20**. 51, 222, **37**. 415; Elliot, **38**. 325; Erskine, **20**. 229–30; Fazakerley, **26**. 16; Fitzpatrick, Hon. Richard, **32**. 275n, 42. 55n; Fox, C. J., **24**. 139, 444n, 447n, **25**. 369n, **31**. 396n, **32**. 275n, **33**. 432n, **39**. 369, 375n; Fox, Henry (Lord Holland), **17**. 297, 355, **26**. 15, 16, 17, 24, **37**. 363, 365, 415; Gordon, Lord George, **39**. 325; Gower, **38**. 233; Grafton, D. of, **24**. 139, **38**. 248; Granby, **38**. 488; Grenville, George, **17**. 297, **22**. 274, 382, 444–5, 464, 496, 566, **26**. 19, 23, **37**. 415, **38**. 231, 320, 341, 487–8, 549n; Grenville, James, **38**. 242–3; HW, **17**. 376–7, 494, **18**. 406, **30**. 331n; Halifax, George, E. of, **17**. 230, **18**. 356, **38**. 233; Hamilton, William Gerard, **37**. 416, 443, 444; Harrington, 3d E. of, **39**. 325; Hay, George, **37**. 415; Henley, Robert, Lord Northington, **22**. 520; Hervey, Hon. Augustus John, **38**. 488; Hervey, John, Bn, **18**. 159; Hillsborough, **26**. 14, 22, 32, 33; Howe, Richard, Bn, **24**. 450n; Hume Campbell, **26**. 24; Hussey, **38**. 241; Johnstone, **23**. 399n, **39**. 325; Keppel, Augustus, **24**. 445, 450n; Lee, Sir George, **19**. 470, **26**. 16, 17, 18, **37**. 415; Legge, **26**. 18, 23, 32, **37**. 415, 444–5; **38**. 226; Lyttelton, George, Bn, **24**. 139, **26**. 18, **37**. 415, **38**. 248; Lyttelton, Sir Richard, **20**. 33, **37**. 415; Mann, Horace II, **24**. 451–2, 457, 458; Mansfield, E. of, **17**. 123, **22**. 520, **23**. 167, **37**. 415, 529, **38**. 248, 257–8; Martin, **37**. 415, **38**. 549; Mellish, **26**. 18, 23; Meredith, **39**. 232; Minchin, **33**. 433n; Mordaunt, **26**. 14, 18, 31, 32, 33; Morton, **38**. 549n; Murray, William (*see* Mansfield, *above*); Newcastle, D. of, **26**. 10; Newdigate, **26**. 10; North, Bn, **23**. 186, 248, 290, **38**. 309; Northey, **26**. 32; Norton, Sir Fletcher (Bn Grantley), **24**. 445, **38**. 241–2, 325; Nugent, **26**. 13, 17, **37**. 362; Ossory, **32**. 274n; Pelham, Henry, **19**. 470–1, **20**. 300, **26**. 10, 14, 16, 17, 18, 22, 24, **37**. (?) 223; Philipps, Sir J., **26**. 13, 14, 16; Pitt, Thomas, **25**. 35; Pitt, William, E. of Chatham, **17**. 297, **18**. 383, 19. 4–5, 168, 370, **20**. 453, **21**. 256–7, 344–5, 547, **22**. 208, **23**. 167, 180, **24**. 371, **26**. 10, 14, 15, 17, 18, 24, **31**. 117n, **32**. 228n, 400–1, **35**. 194n, **37**. (?) 223, 416, **38**. 231, 241, 319, 320, 326, **39**. 380; Pitt, William II, **25**. 467n, **33**. 432n, **42**. 56n; Pomfret, E. of, **20**. 470; Portland, D. of, **38**. 248; Potter, **19**. 470, **37**. 415; Powlett, Lord Harry, **38**. 500; Prowse, **26**. 23; Raymond, **18**. 230; Rigby, **33**. 432n, **38**. 242–3, 499, 501; Robinson, **26**. 32, 33, **37**. 415; Rockingham, M. of, **23**. 180, **25**. 221; Rushout, **26**. 17, 18, **38**. 242; Ryder, **17**. 297, **26**. 18, 23, 31, 33; Sackville (Germain), **22**. 208, **37**. 452, **38**. 308n, 309; Sandwich, E. of, **18**. 158, 230–1,

[Parliament (English), *continued*]
356, **20**. 300, **23**. 167, **38**. 229–30; Savile, **23**. 169–70, 184; Shelburne, **38**. 248; Sheridan, **31**. 343n, **33**. 432n, 560n; Stanhope, Earl, **18**. 158; Stanhope, Philip, **37**. 415; Strange, Lord, **26**. 10, 14, 16, 17, 18, 23, 24; Suffolk, E. of, **24**. 359n; Sydenham, **26**. 23, 31; Temple, George, 2d E., **25**. 437; Temple, Richard, 1st E., **20**. 257, **22**. 464, **24**. 362, **38**. 233; Thornton, **26**. 32; Townshend, Hon. Charles, **22**. 208, 493–4, 512, **37**. 363, **38**. 285, 308n, 309, 325, 496, 508, 552, **39**. 46n; Townshend, George, Vct, **37**. 415, 419, **38**. 489; Townshend, Thomas, **38**. 488, 499; Townshend, Thomas jr, **33**. 244n; Tracy, **26**. 31; Vernon, Adm., **18**. 206, **37**. 415; Vyner, **26**. 15, 31, 32; Waller, Edmund, **17**. 354–5; Walpole, Horatio (1st Bn Walpole of Wolterton), **18**. 467, **19**. 168–9, **26**. 16; Walpole, Sir Robert, E. of Orford, **18**. 409, **34**. 229n; Warburton, **38**. 230; White, **26**. 18; Wilberforce, **31**. 296n; Wilkes, **24**. 304, **32**. 400n; Willes, John, **19**. 471; Williams Wynn, **26**. 17; Winnington, **17**. 484, **26**. 16, 17, 18, 22, 23; Wraxall, **25**. 137–8; Yonge, **17**. 297, **26**. 13, 14, 15, 16, 17, 18; York, Edward, D. of, **22**. 521; Yorke, Charles, **22**. 208, **38**. 241, 248, 325; Yorke, Philip, E. of Hardwicke, **20**. 383
Stair said to have obeyed, in defiance of George II, **18**. 289
Stamp Act repealed by, **22**. 400–1, 404–5, 408, 409–10
strain of life in, **3**. 161, 166, 168, 258, 265, 286, **4**. 480
success in America needed before meeting of, **32**. 380
supporters of Bill of Rights decrease in, **23**. 209
'Test Act' of, **4**. 424
to meet, **33**. 258, 270, **34**. 3
too corrupt to be a court of correction, **25**. 400
Tories avoid voting in, **25**. 19
transactions of, known to HW mainly from newspapers, **28**. 155
treasurer and pensions indispensable to, **25**. 97
triennial, Blachford inquires about, **21**. 12n
turnpike bill would upset, more than India or West Indies do, **23**. 455
unable to raise money for American war, **24**. 465
unable to say no, **33**. 254
unanimity of: **20**. 286; makes it unsensational, **24**. 85
unshaken, **24**. 426
'venal and false,' **22**. 382
vote of, will not clear Cornwallis in his conduct towards loyalist Americans, **25**. 211
Wales, Ps of, stigmatized by act of, **22**. 396
Walpole, Sir Robert, accused of bribing, **25**. 605

—— attends opening of, from St James's, **24**. 361
—— loses favour in, **28**. 70
—— rechosen by King's Lynn as M.P., after expulsion, **41**. 78
——'s last, **15**. 153
—— vindicated in both Houses of, **37**. 90–2, 96
war plan for America rumoured for, **39**. 247
'wars' in, indecisive, **38**. 324
weavers' mob besets, **38**. 558–61
Westminster electors desire dissolution of, **7**. 367
——'s remonstrance to, **25**. 218
Wilkes recommends purchase by, of Houghton collection, **24**. 304
——'s seat in, **4**. 89, 91, 198, 204, 205, **5**. 131
will be thronged, **35**. 258
William III's way of influencing, **28**. 387
will probably meet again under gloomy circumstances, **24**. 432
winter equivalent to, in HW's opinion, **25**. 358
Witenagemot becomes 'wit and a gamut' in, **39**. 207
wit suggests that voting in, should precede debates, **24**. 533
wives of members of, revive in London, **22**. 451
young members of, should not endanger England just to show off their talents, **21**. 565
Young Pretender threatens those who might attend, **19**. 138
Parliament; parliaments, French:
See also under Aix-en-Provence, parliament of; Avignon, parliament of; Bordeaux, parliament of; Dijon, parliament of; Douai, parliament of; Grenoble, parliament of; Parliament of Paris; Pau, parliament of; Rennes, parliament of; Rouen, parliament of; Toulouse, parliament of
Aiguillon detested by, **23**. 259
amusement furnished by, **38**. 280
aroused over Louis XV's action in d'Aiguillon affair, **4**. 449
brochures of, less illuminating than HW's letters, **23**. 331
broken daily, **31**. 157, **35**. 344
Chauvelin denounces Jesuits to, **22**. 514
Choiseul ministry opposed by, **38**. 271, 280
—— said to give clandestine support to, **23**. 259
constitution may be changed by Whig tendencies of, **38**. 245
controversies between clergy and, **31**. 69
Crown resisted by, **34**. 2–3
Dauphin would crush, **21**. 44
discussed in Paris, **31**. 79
Du Deffand, Mme, mentions, **5**. 35
edict of 7 Dec. 1770 affecting, **4**. 493, **5**. 14
English Parliament more lively than, **38**. 271
English Parliament resembles, **20**. 287
HW bored by affairs of, **10**. 177

HW jokes about probable occupation of, **30.** 218

HW not to read remonstrances of, **30.** 203

HW prefers English cause to that of, **38.** 245

HW ridicules activities of, **10.** 201

increasing popularity of, **38.** 262

Irish parliament treated like, **20.** 440

king's formula when turning over, to his chancellor, **22.** 244

London Chronicle has paper on, **7.** 300

Louis XV determined to discipline, **30.** 218

—— forbids, to dispute his acts, **22.** 415n

—— getting the better of, **7.** 285

—— permits remonstrances by, about Fitzjames, **38.** 303n

——'s dispute with, **20.** 293, **22.** 412, **23.** 317

——'s temporizing to govern, **20.** 440

—— survives rage of, **23.** 329

Louis XVI hears philippics from, **33.** 582

—— restores, **34.** 176

Machault leads faction of, **21.** 56

mutinous, **23.** 270

Orléans, Duc d', and Duc de Chartres refuse to recognize, **32.** 201

Parliament of Paris forbidden to unite with, **39.** 55

—— may be imitated by, **23.** 259

——'s pretensions resented by, **38.** 539–40

présidents of, **35.** 337

proceed heavily, **20.** 432

reform of, **23.** 320

remonstrances of, hushed by bribery, **23.** 320

struggles of, merely bring on despotism, **23.** 376

troublesome, **38.** 280

Voltaire, idol of members of, **31.** 69

war with England repugnant to, **23.** 253

Parliament, Irish:

See also under sub-sections: House of Commons *and* House of Lords

absentee tax and, **32.** 161–2

absentee tax on land defeated but tax on salaries carried by, **23.** 530n

acts and bills of: bill for better accommodation of the army, **33.** 179–80; money bills, **20.** 402n, 409n, **23.** 155–6, 163, 166, 359, **38.** 138, 148, **43.** 125–6; Mutiny Bill, **39.** 350n, 354n; Septennial Bill, **38.** 149, **39.** 67–8, 70–1; Test Act, **24.** 430n

address from: improper, **39.** 67; to George II, apologetic, **37.** 404–5; too loyal to suit HW, **37.** 406

adjourned and to be prorogued, **20.** 409–10

adjournment of: **39.** 59, 70; releases Conway, **37.** 455

adjourns quietly after voting augmentation of troops, **37.** 456

anecdote of Speaker of, and Mr Smith, **30.** 299n

Anglo-French trade treaty passed by, **39.** 439n

Belturbet represented in, **37.** 336

bills from, ready to go to England, **37.** 435

bills returned to, from England, **39.** 67, 70, 72

Boyle, the Speaker, heads faction in, against D. of Dorset, **20.** 316, 401–2

Bristol, E. of, to attend sessions of, **22.** 450

Buckingham suppresses votes of, for regency, **34.** 44

budget discussed in, **32.** 161–2

Clanricarde said to be first earl of, **41.** 331

Conolly advocates Irish independence in, **33.** 332

Conway exhausted by, **37.** 450

——'s attendance in, **37.** 426–7

dignity of, talked of, **37.** 410

dull, with no divisions, **37.** 443

Egmont spoke in, **20.** 31

elections for, explained, **37.** 74n

Fitzgibbon reminds Grattan of procedure in, for legislation, **25.** 682n

free trade demanded by, **24.** 525n

George II prorogues, **20.** 432n

George III may get protest from, against new board, **23.** 380

—— might prorogue, **23.** 359

grand juries seek re-sitting of, **35.** 162

HW does not love loyal expressions from, **37.** 406

Halifax's speech at opening of, **9.** 399

Hamilton's speech causes fears in, **10.** 8, 10

Harcourt might flee from, **35.** 460

Hertford pays court to members of, and their wives, **39.** 40

—— reaches Dublin in time for, **39.** 25–6

——'s speech to, answered by addresses, **39.** 26

—— when permitted by, will give Fitzgerald a commission, **39.** 28

Hertfords kept by, in Dublin, **39.** 72

Hervey, Bp, urges admittance of Roman Catholics to, **25.** 438n

House of Commons of: all considerable people in, support the government, **37.** 462; Boyle, Hon. Henry, Speaker of, **20.** 316n; broken into by mob, in protest against failure to pass Protecting Duties, **25.** 491; Burgh is member of, **28.** 200; Butler proposes in, augmentation for Halifax, **10.** 18, 19; coerced by 'independent army,' **33.** 140–1; commercial regulations with England passed by, **33.** 491n; Forster's resolutions in, on Quieting Bill, **33.** 153n; George III addressed by, for augmentation for Halifax, **10.** 18, 19; Gore family in, support Devonshire administration, **37.** 463; government has powerful majority in, **39.** 45; Halifax attended by, in Presence Chamber, **10.** 19; Halifax attends, **10.** 20; Halifax's refusal of augmentation astonishes, **10.** 19; Hamilton's speech converts, **10.** 10; Hamilton's speech to, **9.** 399; Irish government opposed by, **9.** 130, 157; Lucas declared by, to be an enemy of his country, **20.** 156n; Nevill, Arthur Jones, expelled for contempt of,

[Parliament, Irish, *continued*]

20. 402n; resolution by, on Irish pensions, 38. 148; Speaker of, *see* Boyle, Hon. Henry (1682–1764), E. of Shannon; Ponsonby, John (1713–89); speeches in, on address to George II, 37. 410; Stone, Abp, disclaims interfering in, 21. 154n; Yelverton's bill in, for regulating legislation, 25. 682n

House of Lords of: adjournments of, long and frequent, 9. 399; business of, to be finished, 10. 8; De Courcy takes seat in, 10. 8; Dublin rioters have oath administered in, 9. 266; Montagu visits, when he pleases, 9. 399, 10. 3; (?) private bills introduced in, 10. 11; Shannon, E. of, enters, 37. 462; sittings of, rare, 10. 3

incendiary delegates repulsed by, with resolutions of loyalty, 25. 452–3

independence from Parliament wanted by, 39. 405n

independent army besieges, in support of free trade, 24. 535n

Irish pensions and Dublin election-contest preoccupy, 31. 165n

journey to, a relief for Conway, 37. 442

juries, insolvent debtors, and turnpikes debated by, 37. 426, 428

Lord Lieutenant prorogues, 23. 166, 170

lords justices' friends in, 38. 147

lords justices' rôle in, 38. 147–50

may cause Harcourt to resign, 35. 460–1

meets every other year, 9. 355

Montagu ill after opening of, 9. 400

North, Lord, fears, more than British Parliament, 33. 127

Northumberland reports to Halifax about, 43. 131

Opposition in: disgracefully beaten, 39. 68; Hamilton placates heads of, 38. 147; Hamilton said to vote with, 38. 251; Hertford abused by, 39. 71n, 72; Hertford well received by, 39. 27; Ponsonby temporarily joins, 39. 68; unchanged, 37. 462

Orde withdraws bill in, 33. 491

peace terms not accepted by, as 'adequate,' 10. 108

Pitt, William II's, resolutions for trade-equality laid before, 25. 565n

political turmoil in, 20. 315

Ponsonby becomes Speaker of, 37. 462

—— carries question in, against Hertford, 39. 70

Privy Council's money bills the pretence for new sessions of, 23. 156n

proceeds heavily, 20. 432

prorogation of: 31. 5; deferred till passing of money bills, 23. 155–6, 163, 166

prorogations and adjournments for, 37. 409

Quieting Bill well received by, 33. 152–3

recess of, 10. 18

reform resisted by, 35. 382

Roman Catholics should not vote for members of, 25. 529

rumoured abolition of, resented by rioters, 21. 382n

shortening of, attempted, 35. 377

Stewart to enter, 23. 4

still sitting, because of public bills, 39. 67

Stone brings Cunningham into, 20. 316

to meet, 39. 49

treated like a French parliament, 20. 432, 440

troop augmentation in Ireland rejected by, 39. 100

troop bill passed and money bill rejected by, 20. 155–6

Yelverton's resolution and Conolly's motion in, against reform, 25. 453n

Parliament, Scottish:

Young Pretender calls, 19. 118

Parliamentary Debates:

Saye and Sele, Vct, quoted in, 35. 614

Parliamentary or Constitutional History of England:

Herbert of Chepstow in, 40. 130–1

Lords' Journals the basis of, 40. 131

Parliamentary privilege:

Hertford's reflections on, 39. 244–5

Parliamentary Spy, The:

Augusta, Ps of Wales, denounced in, 23. 196

Conway not to prosecute, for attacking Ps of Wales and Bute, 39. 124

Parliament House, Dublin:

Conway's visits to, a relief, 37. 442

Parliament House, London:

Conway's lodgings a great distance from, 37. 184

Parliament of Aix. See Aix, parliament of

Parliament of Avignon. *See under* Avignon

Parliament of Bordeaux. *See* Bordeaux, parliament of

Parliament of Bretagne; Parliament of Brittany. *See* Rennes, parliament of

Parliament of Dijon. *See* Dijon, parliament of

Parliament of Douai. *See* Douai, parliament of

Parliament of Grenoble. *See* Grenoble, parliament of

Parliament of Paris:

affairs of: French are occupied with, 31. 109; prominent, 4. 491, 5. 30

Aiguillon asks investigation by, 4. 197–9

—— 's suit in: 4. 427, 429–30, 459, 470; judgment in, 4. 430, 8. 168–9; Louis XV reverses decision and suppresses documents in, 4. 427–30, 449n, 459, 8. 169–70, 173–5

arrêt of: Clement XIII rebuked by, 23. 4, 10; condemns books, 5. 203

Aubigny peerage registered by, 6. 455

banished, 20. 440, 23. 270, 322

Barbantane dislikes behaviour of, 23. 278

Beauvau opposed fate of, 23. 322

Benedictines and Cordeliers ask permission of, to doff habits and rules, 22. 325

Bertin resigns because unpopular with, 38. 261–2

bishops ordered by, to stay at their sees, 38. 339

cabals of, may injure the cause of inoculation, **22**. 153

carriages and liveries of, splendid, **24**. 61n

Chauvelin attacks Jesuits before, **22**. 514n

Choiseul desires support of, **4**. 202

—— does not wish to quarrel with, **28**. 153

——'s ministry asks, for financial advice and care of sinking fund, **38**. 301

——'s ministry dreads union of, with provincial parliaments, **38**. 301

clergy's squabbles with, **35**. 173

Conti's notion that the sole house of peers is, **38**. 539–40

convents to be regulated by, **4**. 48

declaration by, of 8 March 1772, **5**. 213

Del'Averdi approved by, **38**. 262

Du Deffand, Mme, and HW indifferent to, **6**. 82

Du Deffand, Mme, characterizes, **3**. 261

—— mentions, **4**. 29, 326, **5**. 33

edicts presented to, 9 Feb. 1776, **6**. 265, 274

expected back after Louis XV's death, **39**. 184

financial remonstrances of, **4**. 377

Fitzjames's arrest voided by, **38**. 271n

Goëzmann case decided by, **6**. 23

Guines judged by, **6**. 421

HW glad not to be standing for, **35**. 118

HW's friends in, have retired to provinces, **28**. 51

HW visits, **39**. 222

Jesuits exiled by, unless they take oath, **38**. 339n, 349

—— expelled by, **3**. 291, 293–4, **8**. 133–4, **43**. 47

La Chalotais's trial by commission objected to by, **30**. 206

Lamottes and Rétaux de Villette sentenced by, **25**. 653n

Le Breton may be tried by, for breach of trust, **39**. 65–6

letters to ask recall of, **5**. 40, 47

lettres de cachet expected for, **5**. 15

Louis XV addresses Grande Chambre, of, **31**. 111

Louis XV and Louis XVI show despotism by reversing, **39**. 222

Louis XV annihilates, **39**. 143

—— at odds with, over: Aiguillon, **4**. 427–30, 449n, 458, 459, **8**. 168–70, 173–5; Brittany, **4**. 429–30, 458, 459, **7**. 279–80, 303, **8**. 168–75, **31**. 106–7, 111; edict of 7 Dec. 1770, **4**. 493, **5**. 14; Séguier affair, **4**. 450n, 470, 491

—— cows, **41**. 3

—— divides, into 6 courts, **5**. 30n, 52, 58

—— establishes new, **5**. 17, 58–9, 61–3, 66n

—— exiles, **5**. 17, **8**. 181–2, **20**. 432n, 440, **23**. 270, 322, **37**. 364

—— gets condolences from, on Stanislas I's death, **39**. 56

—— intervenes when *Instruction pastorale* by Abp of Paris is denounced by, **38**. 303

—— orders registers of, sent to Versailles, **31**. 109

—— rebukes and threatens, **39**. 55–6

——'s dispute with, **37**. 446

——'s lit de justice occasioned by remonstrances of, **10**. 202

—— stops proceedings of, about Fitzjames, **38**. 302–3

——'s tyranny opposed by, **22**. 153

—— suppresses remonstrances of, concerning Hôpital Général, **20**. 293n

—— visits, **7**. 306, **31**. 109

—— waited on by deputation from, at Versailles, **20**. 293n

Louis XVI expected to make, submit, **6**. 278

—— receives deputation from, **6**. 60, 277

——'s response to, **6**. 61

Malesherbes and Turgot opposed by, **41**. 346–7

Marie-Antoinette's response to, **6**. 61

Maupeou suppresses, **32**. 49, 54

Maurepas restores, **28**. 221, 227

Mirabeau's book ordered burnt by, **34**. 44n

Monaco, P. and Ps of, separated by act of, **5**. 14

Morangiès to appeal to, **5**. 364

most flexible French parliament, **38**. 271

new: appointed, **23**. 270; HW expects no results from, **39**. 231; Louis XVI angry with, **24**. 102; Maupeou's declaration against arrêt of 1762 attacked by, **23**. 398; members of, urged by wives to resign, **23**. 303; Orléans and Chartres refuse to salute, **6**. 77, **24**. 26; (?) speeches at opening of, sent by Conway to HW, **39**. 230

old: exiled, **5**. 17, **8**. 181–2, **20**. 432n, 440, **23**. 270, 322, **37**. 364; HW prefers, to new, **39**. 214; lit de justice restores, **39**. 216; restoration of, **6**. 108, 110–12, **20**. 440, **24**. 55, 61, **39**. 207; restoration of, expected, **24**. 19, 25, 35; restoration of, makes no difference, **39**. 222–3

Orléans and Condé disgraced for espousing the cause of, after Maupeou banished it, **39**. 143n

Orléans's exile evokes remonstrance from, **34**. 2n

Papal power restrained by declaration of, **5**. 213

Paris, Abp of, at odds with, **7**. 284

—— denounced by, for pastoral letter favouring Jesuits, **38**. 303

Paris loses money by retirement of, **23**. 322

Parliament of Toulouse's arrest of Fitzjames annulled by, **38**. 302

parliaments may imitate suspension of, **23**. 259

Parma defended by, against Rome, **23**. 4

pleasure-loving Parisians will not easily be reformed by, **38**. 339

policy of diminishing influence of, **4**. 197

(?) Pompadour, Mme de, opposed by, **38**. 338

[Parliament of Paris, *continued*]
présidents à mortier of, summoned by Louis XV in middle of night, **31.** 107
Princes and nobles ask recall of, **5.** 40, 47
quits its functions, **23.** 259
recess of, **4.** 430
registers of, seized by mousquetaire, **39.** 65–6
religious requirement for registry of title in, **4.** 297, 418, 423, 424, 428
remonstrances of: **31.** 109; about parliament of Rennes, **10.** 202
resolutions of: against Jesuits, **22.** 519; on Breton parliament's dissolution, **39.** 33
Richelieu-St-Vincent trial attended by, **6.** 292–3
Rousseau proscribed by, **3.** 310
royal family's devotion to be changed by, **38.** 338
Séguier at odds with, **4.** 450n, 470, 491
suppressed, **5.** 61, 66n
suspends sessions, **5.** 14
temporary tribunal replaces banished members of, **5.** 17–18
threatens to resign, **4.** 493
Versailles to compromise with, **23.** 265
verses on division of, **5.** 52
verses on expulsion of new members of, **6.** 118
Wilkes must fight, to retrieve honour, **22.** 198
writings libelling Unigenitus suppressed by, **20.** 337n
Young Pretender wants daughter registered by, as Ds of Albany, **25.** 513, 516n
Parliament of Pau. *See* Pau, parliament of
Parliament of Rennes. *See* Rennes, parliament of
Parliament of Rouen. *See* Rouen, parliament of
Parliament of Saragossa. *See* Saragossa, parliament of
Parliament of Toulouse. *See* Toulouse, parliament of
Parliaments of Love:
Coke, Lady Mary, should study, in Provence, **31.** 144
HW jokes about acts of, **31.** 164
Parliament St, Westminster, London:
coffee-house near, **22.** 189n
Green and Gold Lamp in, **20.** 389n
Parma, Ds of. *See* Élisabeth (1727–59) of France; Maria Amalia (1746–1804) of Austria
Parma, D. of. *See* Ferdinand-Marie-Philippe-Louis (1751–1802); Philip, Don (1720–65)
Parma, Ps of. *See* Elizabeth (Farnese) (1692–1766)
Parma (Italy):
Acquaviva asks Benedict XIV for, for Don Philip, **17.** 201
Aix treaty's provisions for, **19.** 479n
arrêt of 1762 caused by excommunication of, **23.** 398–9
Aubeterre and Orsini protest to Clement XIII against treatment of, **23.** 15–16
Austria guaranteed her possessions in Italy by, **20.** 294n

— may have designs upon, **22.** 379
battle expected near, **19.** 236
besieged, **19.** 231, 236
Bodoni at, prints Castle of Otranto, **11.** 149, 150, 170, **35.** 436
Boisgelin recalled to Paris because of court squabble at, **23.** 330
Braitwitz's letter from, **18.** 161, 163–4
bridge at, **11.** 149n
Brown blockades, **19.** 236
Castellar evacuates, **19.** 244
— occupies, **19.** 236
castle of, captured, **19.** 245
Castro and Ronciglione to be seized by, **23.** 24
Charles III sends message about, to Joseph II and Maria Theresa, and recalls his minister, **23.** 446
Charles Emmanuel III and Mann might appear before, **21.** 266
Clement XIII's brief against, **22.** 582, **23.** 26, 38
—'s death puts a stop to his opposition to, **23.** 88
—'s quarrel with, **23.** 10
Clement XIV resigns pretensions to, **23.** 518
Coke, Lady Mary, afraid to visit, **31.** 177
— wants to avoid, **23.** 543
convent at, Correggio painting in church of San Antonio Abbate at, **17.** 167, 196, 199, 268, **18.** 323, 337, 351, 355, 370, 373, **35.** 5, 12
Correggio's angel at, **11.** 149, 150n
duke of, may be preceded by Richecourt, **20.** 295
Du Tillot and Llano dismissed from, **23.** 445
Elizabeth Farnese might have bought, **18.** 345
Ferdinand of Naples to visit, **25.** 586–7
Fiorenzuola near, **19.** 47
France and Austria give up, to Don Philip, **21.** 280n
France sends couriers to, about Louis XV's escape from assassin, **21.** 48
Francis I guarantees possessions of, **20.** 294n
Francis III of Modena might have had, **13.** 242
—'s new road leads to, **37.** 320
French subsidy to, **42.** 495
HW contrasts Newmarket with, **18.** 315
HW prefers Canterbury to, **17.** 142
Hampden's poems printed at, **42.** 397
Hôtel Pallavicini at, **22.** 241n
hussars at, **18.** 338
Illustri fatti Farnesiani may be found at, **25.** 403, 411–12
Joseph II wants, as fief of the Empire, **22.** 395
Leopold's letter rejected by, **22.** 378–9
— told by mother to go to, to lecture his sister, **23.** 411–12
Liechtenstein awaits cannon from, **19.** 258
Llano goes to, **23.** 325, 445, 518–19
Lobkowitz's army near, **19.** 36–7, 40, 50

Maria Theresa gives, to Charles Emmanuel III, **17**. 379

—— not to demand reversion of, to Austria under Aix treaty, **21**. 280n

ministers from and to, *see under* Minister

Monteil predicted as French minister to, **5**. 209

Parliament of Paris defends, against Rome, **23**. 4

Philip, Don, disliked by people of, **20**. 45

—— may be transferred from, to Naples, **21**. 264

——'s pretensions to, not mentioned in complaints to Benedict XIV, **17**. 201n

—— to bring Duchess to, **20**. 45

—— to receive, by Aix treaty, **19**. 481

Pignatelli, Gian Domenico, Spanish ambassador at, **31**. 91

preliminary Aranjuez treaty guarantees territorial integrity of, **20**. 294n

Revilla formerly Spanish minister at, **22**. 330

—— returns to, **23**. 518–19

revolution at, **23**. 444–6

Richelieu's arrival expected by, to conclude treaty with France, **20**. 576n

San Vitale, Contessa, detains Strathmore at, **22**. 88

Sardinian troops enter, **17**. 342n, 392n

Servi church at, 'Madonna of the Long Neck' in, released to Medici, **17**. 199n

Spain ends dissension in, by removing Du Tillot, **23**. 324–5

Spaniards and Neapolitans may march to, **19**. 65

Spaniards escape from, **19**. 244

—— evacuate, **19**. 231n

—— may take, **17**. 198, 204, 214, **18**. 454, **19**. 22

Spanish weekly couriers to avoid, **23**. 446

visitors to: Berrys, **11**. 149n; Coke, Lady Mary, **23**. 535, 539; Edwards, James, **35**. 436; Flavigny, **5**. 209n; Gray, **13**. 9, 192n; Gustav III, **25**. 499; HW, **13**. 9, 192n; Liechtenstein, **22**. 153n; Strathmore, **21**. 524, **22**. 23, 88; York, D. of, **22**. 232, 241

Parmeggiano. *See* Parmigiano

Parmigiano *or* Parmigianino, Il (Girolamo Francesco Maria Mazzola 1503–40), painter:

Furnese has pictures by, **21**. 172n

(?) Larue has drawings by, **7**. 356

'Madonna degli Angeli' (? Madonna of the Long Neck) by, acquired by Medici, **17**. 199n

Mariette has drawings by, **7**. 273

Monaco, P. of, has painting of Venus and Cupid by, **7**. 335

pictures by, at Mariette's sale, **32**. 266

Parnassus, Mt:

coffee-houses on, **33**. 527

empire of, **31**. 157

foolish, in Batheaston miscellany, **32**. 225

HW compares Castle Howard with, **30**. 258

HW might sue for divorce in forum of, **11**. 21

HW with gout cannot hobble up slopes of, **31**. 69

headdress resembles description of, **9**. 64

Ida, Mt, seems to counterbalance, in Boutin's garden, **32**. 57

Luxborough, Lady, retired to, **32**. 283

Miller, Mrs, has, at Bath, **32**. 196

More, Hannah, has testimonials for, **31**. 318

—— jokes about, **31**. 273

of pasteboard, Lady Ossory's house is not, **32**. 223

parish of: charged with Muses' bantlings, **31**. 244; SH lowest in, **11**. 1

Pope's house carved out of, **21**. 417

portrait-painters grow old soon in, **34**. 226

'puppet-show' at Batheaston, **32**. 221

'turnpike' of, **42**. 364

Parnassus fair:

Millers hold, on Thursdays, **39**. 241

Parne, Rev. Thomas (ca 1694–1751), D.D.:

Cole officiates for, **15**. 315

Parnell, Sir John (1744–1801), 2d Bt:

chancellor of Exchequer in Ireland, **12**. 117n

Parochial Antiquities. See under Kennett, White

Parodies du Théâtre italien:

Du Deffand, Mme, owns, **8**. 33

Parolet. *See* Paroli

Paroli; parolis:

at faro, **24**. 370, **34**. 46, **39**. 377, 391

coat of arms depicts, **9**. 186

HW compares politics to, **10**. 139

Paroquet; paroquets. *See* Parakeet

Paros (Greece):

Orlov writes from, **23**. 226

Russian fleet sails to, **23**. 226

Russian fleet winters at, **23**. 307

Russian frigates from, reach Leghorn, **23**. 326

Parotides:

swelling of, **17**. 52

Parr, Mr, of Isleworth:

SH visited by, **12**. 249

Parr, Catherine (1512–48), m. 1 Sir Edward Burgh; m. 2 (1533) John Nevill, 3d Bn Latimer; m. 3 (1543) Henry VIII of England; m. 4 (1547) Thomas Seymour, 1st Bn Seymour:

birth date of, corrected, **43**. 155

(?) *Birth of Mankind* dedicated to, **40**. 306n

corpse of, exhumed at Sudeley Castle, **42**. 112–17, **43**. 385

Edward VI's letter to, **14**. 104n, **40**. 158–60

Elizabeth, Q., writes to, **42**. 115–16

Fermor sends HW account of discovery of coffin of, **31**. 217

grave of, at Sudeley Castle, **10**. 285, **12**. 165

HW descended from second husband of, **12**. 165

HW's reason for attributing prayers to, **16**. 207

Horton associations of, **10**. 82

jealous of her last husband, **16**. 207

portraits of, **34**. 208

[Parr, Catherine, *continued*]
Prayers or Medytacions attributed to: Ashby questions authorship of, **16.** 203–4, 207n; Lort argues against Catherine of Aragon's authorship of, **16.** 209
pregnancy of, **42.** 114–16
print of seal of, **2.** 163n
Ross's print of corpse of, sent by Nash to HW, **43.** 385
sister-in-law of, **9.** 98n
Parr, Rev. Samuel (1747–1825), LL.D. (Cambridge, 1781); scholar:
believes in Ireland's MSS, **15.** 321
Bellendus of, 'old carriage on new wheels,' **34.** 45
Beloe's translation of Aulus Gellius approved by, **15.** 255
dedication of Aulus Gellius written by, **15.** 256n
Middleton's *Life of Cicero* attacked by, **15.** 8n
school of, at Stanmore, **15.** 215n
Tracts by Warburton and a Warburtonian by, attacks Bp Hurd, **34.** 45
Parr, Thomas (d. 1635), 'old Parr':
age of, **33.** 567
Ellis compared with, **33.** 326
HW would be despised by, **42.** 408
none in Jamaica, **34.** 218
prints of, **28.** 28
Parr, William (d. 1546), cr. (1543) Bn Parr of Horton:
lived at Horton, **10.** 82n
Parr, William (1513–71), cr. (1539) Bn Parr, cr. (1543) E. of Essex, (1547) M. of Northampton:
tomb of, at Horton, **10.** 333
Parratt, ——, writer:
World contributions by, **20.** 400n
Parre. *See* Paar
Parrot; parrots:
Bute gives, to Ps of Wales, **38.** 462
Cayenne, Duchesse de la Vallière lacks, **5.** 128
Craon, Princesse de, has, **18.** 78
death of Duchesse de la Vallière's, **5.** 342
'Fitz-Arbuthnot' painting of, **32.** 51–2
Hôtel de Bouillon has, **7.** 317
Lespinasse, Mlle de, said to have bequeathed, to Vichy, **6.** 328
Paris shops sell, **33.** 515
rival suitors seek, for French lady, **33.** 515–16
ships' language might be repeated by, in polite circles, **23.** 66
waddles obliquely, **39.** 183
Parry, Lady: SH visited by, **43.** 160
Parry, Mr:
Mason's counsel, **28.** 322n
Parry, Rev. (?) Gregory (ca 1717–85):
cause of, for Eton fellowship deserted by E. of Sandwich, **20.** 121
Churchill gets HW to use influence for, **40.** 65
Pars, William (1742–82), painter; draughtsman:
accounts of, **6.** 236, **26.** 48

death of, at Rome, **24.** 173, **26.** 48
drawings by, for 'Description of SH,' **1.** 379n, **33.** 576n, **43.** 72
HW gives, letter of recommendation to Sir William Hamilton, **24.** 135, **35.** 424–5
HW provides, with letters of recommendation, **6.** 236
HW recommends, to Mann, **24.** *134–5*, 144, 173
HW wants view of Fiesole done by, **24.** 135
HW writes to, through Mme du Deffand, **6.** (?) 235, 238
Italy to be visited by, to improve his oil painting, **35.** 424–5
loses trunk and letters, **6.** 236, 238, 240–1
Mann to recommend, to Cardinal Albani, and at Rome, **24.** 135
Naples visited by, **35.** 424n
not yet appeared at Florence, **24.** 173, 189, 232
oil paintings and portraits now done by, **24.** 135, 144
Palmerston employs, to draw Swiss views, **35.** 424–5
—— has volume of washed drawings done by, **24.** 135, **26.** 48
—— the patron of, **24.** 135, 144
portmanteau lost by, between Calais and Paris, **24.** 144, **26.** 48
Rome to be visited by, for study, **24.** 144
washed drawings of SH done by, **2.** 249n, **24.** 135, 144, **25.** 532n, **35.** 424, **43.** 72
'Parsley-bed':
HW's name for his nursery, **9.** 176
Parsnip; parsnips:
sowing of, Rider's almanac discusses time of, **30.** 34
Parson, Samuel Pearce, LL.D., 1792, surrogate of the Master of the Prerogative Court of Canterbury:
HW's will probated before, **30.** 377
Parson; parsons:
country, unaccustomed to eat turtle, **35.** 70
Fielding's, are gross, **16.** 270
HW's irate letter to, for oppressing tenants, **39.** 494
popular, Charles II's witticism about, **22.** 57, **24.** 52
See also Clergy; Clergyman
Parsonage; parsonages:
children sleep at foot of the bed in, **35.** 186
'pasnidge-house,' **24.** 293
'Parson and clerk,' game:
HW alludes to, **30.** 60, **31.** 283, **33.** 121
Parsons, Mrs:
SH visited by, **12.** 249
Parsons, Anne (d. 1769), m. (1754) Sir John Hinde Cotton, 4th Bt:
marriage of, **2.** 281
Paris visited by, **37.** 114
Robinson's ball attended by, though not of 'first fashion,' **17.** 185, **37.** 114

Parsons, Anne (ca 1735– ca 1814) m. (1776) Charles Maynard, 2d Vct Maynard; 'Nancy'; 'Mrs Haughton, *or* Houghton'; 'Mrs Horton':
Bedford, D. of, connected with, 33. 522, 525
Berkeley, Cts of, and Cts of Orford the only people who do not call on, 24. 451
bishops might sup with, at Vauxhall, to get her influence for promotion, 39. 105
Cumberland, Ds of, mistaken for, 5. 132, 23. 344
Dorset as badly off as if he had married, 24. 435
——'s mistress, 23. 344, 24. 435n
'Duchess Nancy,' 33. 525
Grafton accompanied by, at Ascot races and at Whittlebury Forest, 38. 435
—— keeps, 38. 435, 39. 101, 105
——'s mistress, 9. 364n, 23. 344, 24. 435n, 32. 12n, 34. 240–2
James's Powder dispensed by, at Court of Naples, 24. 451
Maynard has not yet married, 32. 293
Neapolitan Court presentation of, prevented by Ferdinand, 24. 451n
Reynolds's portrait of, 43. 375
Rigby's relations with, 34. 241–2
Santo Marco, Mme, friendly with, 24. 451n
Stuart, Lady Louisa, gives account of, 43. 375
Parsons, Hon. Catherine (d. 1766), m. (1705) James Hussey:
Ailesbury, Cts of, meets, 37. 435
septleva of, enviable, 37. 439
Parsons, Elizabeth (1749–1807):
Cock Lane Ghost an imposture by, 10. 6, 282n, 22. 8
HW fears, will not survive treatment at Cock Lane séances, 10. 6
Parsons, Humphrey (?1676–1741), lord mayor of London, 1730, 1740:
brewer, 17. 185n, 22. 7
daughter of: 2. 281n, 20. 9, 22. 7; elopes, 4. 117n
France often visited by, 17. 185n
George II notices, 17. 185n
injury by brewery of, to Cotton estate, 2. 281
Jacobite, 17. 185n, 270n, 22. 7n
lord mayor, 22. 7n
West mentions, 13. 236
widow of: 1. 379; gives Conway a dog, 13. 189n
Parsons, Mrs Humphrey. *See* Crowley, Sarah
Parsons, James (1705–70), physician:
Remains of Japhet by, 1. 211
Parsons, John:
dances at Robinson's ball, though not of the 'first fashion,' 17. 185, 37. 114, 115
Paris visited by, 37. 114
Parsons, John (1761–1819), Master of Balliol College, Oxford; Bp of Peterborough 1813–19:
HW reads review by, 34. 83
Parsons, 'Nancy.' *See* Parsons, Anne

Parsons, Richard (ca 1656–1703), cr. (1681) Vct Rosse:
wife of, 42. 89, 90n
Parsons, Richard, parish clerk:
Cock Lane ghost instigated by, 10. 6
Parsons, Robert (1546–1610), Jesuit:
on William Thomas, 1. 273
Parsons, Sarah, m. James Dunn, called Jacques, Comte O'Dunne:
(?) dances at Robinson's ball, 37. 115
husband of, 20. 9, 22. 7
Paris visited by, 37. 114
Robinson's ball attended by, though not 'of the first fashion,' 17. 185, 37. 114
Parsons, W.:
print of, 40. 236
Parsons, William (1736–95), actor and painter:
bad performance of, in Lady Craven's comedy, 29. 44
Congreve's *Love for Love* acted by, 11. 9n
School for Scandal well acted by, 41. 363
Parsons, William (ca 1764–1828), poet:
Berry, Mary, calls, 'high priest of ennui,' 12. 113
'Della Cruscan,' 25. 612n
Florence Miscellany has poems by, 25. 633
Florence visited by, 11. 177, 25. 612n
Germany visited by, 11. 177
HW's correspondence with, 42. 215–16, 263
HW sends *Mysterious Mother* to, 42. 275–6
Kent visited by, 12. 113
Meget's Inn visited by, at Florence, 25. 612n
(?) Nivernais's *Jardins modernes* given to, 12. 260, 42. 263
SH visited by, 12. 229
Parsons family:
brewery of, 2. 281, 43. 74
Paris visited by, 17. 185
Robinson entertains, 17. 185
Parson's Green, London:
Thomas, Lady Sophia, lives at, 9. 82
Parthenissa. See under Boyle, Roger
Partie de chasse de Henri IV, La. See under Collé, Charles
Partridge, Mrs (1) and Mrs (2):
SH visited by, 12. 249
Partridge, Henry (1711–93), Recorder of Lynn, 1745:
Parkin lent *Anecdotes of Painting* by, 40. 222
Partridge, John (1644–1715), almanac-maker:
Newton, Sir Isaac, probably envied by, 28. 277
Partridge, John (ca 1719–1809), clerk of Stationers' Company:
(?) HW mentions, 14. 120,
Partridge; partridges:
at Sandywell, 37. 107
availability of, determines French Court's stay at Compiègne, 38. 404
brace of, HW has not killed, 30. 100
campaign opened for, with waste of gunpowder, 25. 188
Conway's, devoured by vermin, 37. 476
covey of, Russian army compared to, 21. 237

[Partridge; partridges, *continued*]
English politicians kill, in summer vacation, **25.** 596
English should kill, in autumn for winter food, **35.** 474
Ferdinand of Naples rises at 2 A.M. to catch, when leaving roosts, **25.** 600
HW receives, from Lady Browne, **31.** 170
HW thanks Bentley for, **35.** 260
HW thanks Mrs Bentley for, **35.** 241
HW thinks grouse-poults a new sort of, **31.** 344
Hertford sends brace of, to HW, **39.** 164
hors d'œuvre of, **19.** 356n
large entremets of, **19.** 357n
Leinster, Ds of, sends, to Mme du Deffand, **6.** 395
Ogilvie sends, to Mme du Deffand, **7.** 108
Ossory, Lord, shoots, **33.** 49, **34.** 205
Parisians might use guns on others besides, **34.** 69
pie of, **33.** 387n
shooting of: **1.** 256, 263, **33.** 292; should be shooting robbers, **33.** 355
shunned, when wings tremble, **30.** 295
soldier shoots at, **18.** 286
wooden, on wainscot, **31.** 80
See also under Game
Partridge-net; partridge-nets:
Prussian troops caught as if by, **21.** 354
Parts (talents), men of:
HW's reflections on, **12.** 258, **31.** 92
Party; parties, political:
HW discusses, with Stanley, **30.** 71
HW obtains ambition of pleasing himself without being tied to, **30.** 196
HW to withdraw even from discussion of, **30.** 196
Temple probably wants to break, to govern them all, **30.** 186
'Party, make a':
HW's expression, **35.** 95, 167n, 254, 260
Pasarella, Jacopo (d. 1495), Bp of Imola 1479–88; Bp of Rimini 1488–95:
dispensation granted by, for Henry VII's marriage, **14.** 79
figure of, in Gossaert's painting, **20.** 390n
Henry VII's marriage benediction pronounced by, **16.** 47, 52
Innocent VIII's nuncio at Henry VII's marriage, **20.** 390n
Pascal, Blaise (1623–62):
hallucination of, **7.** 117
Pasetti, Capt. ——:
Albani sends, to Mann, **19.** 2, 7
Mann receives from, an 'exact list' of Spanish and Neapolitan troops, **19.** 2n
Pasquale, (?) Gaetano (ca 1700–45), Livornese physician:
English not known by, **18.** 11
satire 'translated' by, **18.** 11
Sturgis's death not expected by, **18.** 198–9

Pasquali, Mme. *See* Capponi, Elisabetta (1729–1800)
Pasquali, Cosimo (1716–82), senator; 'eldest Pasquale':
marriage of, planned, **19.** 438
Pasquali, Giovanni Battista (fl. 1738–73), Venetian bookseller and printer:
seeks music books wanted by HW, **21.** 477, 482
Pasqualini, Nicodemo:
Corsican rebellion by, **24.** 26n
Pasquier, Denis-Louis:
(?) attends session of parliament of Paris, **8.** 171, 173
Pasquier, Étienne (1529–1615):
Recherches de la France by: English credit mentioned by, **20.** 48–9; execution of Mary, Q. of Scots, described in, **9.** 83; Mary, Q. of Scots, described by, **15.** 113; HW mentions, **19.** 486
Pasquier, 'Nicolas' (? Étienne):
portrait of, **30.** 370
'Pasquin':
Benedict XIV attacked by, **20.** 189
HW wants epigrams by, about Clement XIII, **21.** 491
York, Cardinal, satirized by, **21.** 259
Pasquinade; pasquinades:
HW likes, **20.** 199
in Ireland, on Sackville family and Stone, **20.** 316
in style of Forum, **17.** 351, 372
Pass, Crispin van de (1564–1637) the elder; engraver:
print by, of Thomas Percy (1560–1605), **1.** 182
Pass, Simon (1595?–1647), engraver:
(?) print by, of Gondomar, **2.** 44
print by, of Sir Thomas Overbury, **16.** 64n
silver plates by, **41.** 219
Pass, William (ca 1598–ca 1637), engraver:
HW's article on, **1.** 173n
Haywood's portrait engraved by, **16.** 67
print by, offered by Bull to HW, **42.** 458
prints by, **1.** 173, **2.** 44
Passau, Bp of. *See* Thun, Josef Maria von (d. 1763)
Passau (Germany):
Bavarian elector said to have entered, **17.** 108
Passavant; passavants:
baggage exempted from search by, **37.** 39–40
Passeck, Peter Bogdanovich (1736–1804), Capt.-Lt:
arrest of, **22.** 64
'Pass eldest.' *See under* Loo
Passerini, Cavaliere:
Del Monte, Giambattista, threatens and injures, **20.** 422n
Passerini, Signora:
Fairies, The, sung by, **35.** 209
Passion; passions:
ambition the most detestable of, **35.** 355–6

Du Deffand, Mme, asks HW's opinion of, **6**. 446
—— on, **3**. 296, **4**. 247
HW says: 'embrace their opposites,' when carried too far, **20**. 449; form 'airy balloons,' **25**. 532
Passion des Jésuites, La:
Du Deffand, Mme, sends, to HW, **5**. 314–15
Passionei, Domenico (1682–1761), cardinal, 1738:
Almada directed by, **21**. 383
anti-Jesuit champion, **21**. 475
Benedict XIV consults, about Young Pretender, **20**. 22
——'s brief against Jesuits drafted by, **21**. 217n
cardinal-priests headed by, **21**. 207n
Dutch minister's rejoinder from, on proposed toasts, **12**. 266
Niccolini invited by, to Rome, **21**. 127
—— reproved by, for not giving him HW's inscription on Benedict XIV, **21**. 127
permission of, necessary for copying Vatican MSS, **21**. 170
Stosch's MSS bought by, for Ottoboni collection, **21**. 284n
Passion flower; passion flowers:
HW to receive, from Montagu, **9**. 144
Passionist monastery, Monte Cavo, Italy:
cabbage garden of, walled with temple fragments, **42**. 406
Passionist monks ('Discalced clerics'):
York, Cardinal, builds monastery for, **42**. 406n
Passion play:
Leopold stops theatre manager from presenting, in Lent, **23**. 459
Passions, Des. See under Darlus, Marie-Geneviève-Charlotte
Passion week:
Clive, Mrs, retires to country during, **9**. 344
Stabat mater sung during, **9**. 219
Passport; passports:
Acquaviva obtains, for Young Pretender, **18**. 378, 388
—— withholds, from English visitors, **19**. 15
Agdollo carries, **17**. 149
Bedford, D. of, and Nivernais exchange, **22**. 70n
Belle-Isle imprisoned for travelling without, **18**. 563n
Belloni procures, from Acquaviva for Shuttleworth, **19**. 77
Berrys show, at Bourgoin, **11**. 138n
Boothby to get, at Venice, **21**. 482
Cholmondeley, George James, needs, **7**. 87
Conway gets, to take wife to England, **37**. 291
eliminated by general amnesty in France, **11**. 355
English, Austrian, and Dutch, sent by Sandwich to Puisieux for plenipotentiaries, **19**. 446n

English, for French bark, *Union*, **19**. 383n
France abolishes, **31**. 360
Francis III applies for, under assumed name, **19**. 314n
French: Lorenzi may obtain, from France for Thomas Pitt, **21**. 524; Pitt, Thomas, fails to get, for French journey, **21**. 543, 545, 550; Strathmore obtains, **22**. 22–3; Young Pretender travels with, **22**. 389
George II's, to be treated with respect, **19**. 384
HW jokes about, for London, **10**. 277
HW seeks, for Müntz, **40**. 93
La Ensenada seeks, for furniture, **18**. 253
Maillebois receives, **19**. 231
Mann makes out, **18**. 46
—— obtains, from Rome for Stuart Mackenzie, **24**. 337n
—— procures, for Cholmondeley's journey through France, **25**. 348
Maria Theresa's ministers monopolize, **21**. 482
Mathews awaits, at Nuremberg, **18**. 517
Modena, Ds of, wants, for Tuscany, **18**. 223
Montemar and Castellara want, **18**. 44
Mountrath fails to get, for Naples, **19**. 15
Polignacs have Swiss merchant's, **34**. 67n
Potter's, to travel through France, **21**. 557n
Selwyn needs, **7**. 36–8, 40, 65, 66, 67, 123, 152
Simolin gets, for French royal family, **34**. 229n
Stanley to demand, for return to England after peace mission, **21**. 536n
Tuscan, declared invalid, **21**. 482
Passy (France), seat of Duc de Penthièvre:
château near, **3**. 122n
Franklin at, **6**. 386n
Valentinois, Comtesse de, entertains at, **5**. 147
visible from Comtesse de Boufflers's terrace, **28**. 223
Paste:
British, should be undisguised, **35**. 36
coloured, table of, resembles marble, **10**. 336
See also Scagliola
Pasteboard:
Colisée made of, **39**. 145
Pastel; pastels:
Chute's and Whithed's portraits in, **18**. 243, **24**. 222
Lucan, Bns, paints in, **41**. 418n
Mann to send, to HW's cousin, **19**. 368–9
See also Crayon
Pastilles:
burned: at Holdernesse's *repas*, **18**. 130n; in churches, **21**. 554
Cole orders, **1**. 102
Florentine, in cakes or drops, **21**. 565
HW brings, for Cole, **1**. 111, 115, 116, 117, 119, 120
HW mentions, **6**. 297
HW obtains, from Mann, **21**. 554, 565
HW orders, **1**. 103n
HW to bring, **1**. 103, 108
Nancy, sent by Mme du Deffand to Lady Mary Churchill, **6**. 325

[Pastilles, *continued*]
Stormont to take, to HW, **6.** 292, 294, 296, 305
Paston, Lady. *See* Hewitt, Margaret
Paston, Sir John: (1442–79), Kt, 1463:
Warwick, E. of, borrows from, **42.** 192
Paston, John (1421–66):
letter addressed to, **16.** 241n
Paston, Rebecca, m. (1708) Sir Stafford Fairborne, Kt:
HW's relationship to, **7.** 258
Paston, Mrs Thomas. *See* Darcy, Dorothy
Paston, William (ca 1654–1732), 2d E. of Yarmouth, 1683:
Raphael painting belonged to, **2.** 169n
Paston letters:
Fenn buys, **16.** 231n
——'s edition of, praised by HW, **33.** 558–9
—— to edit, **42.** 105
HW does not expect to find any mention of Rowley in, **16.** 237
HW praises, **42.** 100
HW returns, to Fenn, advising publication, **42.** 95
HW's preface or advertisement to, **42.** 142
HW supplies footnote to, about E. of Warwick, **42.** 192–3
Henry VI's picture to be frontispiece to, **42.** 98
Pastor; pastors:
at The Hague, **38.** 87
See also Clergyman; Parson
Pastora:
Selwyn said to be in love with, **30.** 271
Yearsley, Mrs, a Lactilla, not a, **31.** 221
Pastoral; pastorals:
in *Arno Miscellany*, **25.** 507
Pastor Fido, Il: See under Guarini, Giovanni Battista
Pastor se torna Aprile, Il:
Mann sends, to HW, **17.** 181, 212
Rich, Elizabeth, wants, **17.** 166
Past, present, and future:
HW's reflections on, **38.** 110
Pastry-cook; pastry-cooks:
French, English show frivolity in trading with, **37.** 56, 59
laurel from, **37.** 197
Twelfth-cakes displayed by, at Christmas, **34.** 231
Pastry-shop; pastry-shops:
Uguccioni's poems will provide paper for, **18.** 554
Pastry-ware:
recipes for, **35.** 48
Pasty:
venison, HW tries, for gout cure, **22.** 322
Pastyme of People, The. See under Rastell, John
Patagonia (South America):
Byron discovers giants in, **22.** 421
ladies' promenade suggests, **25.** 174
Patagonians:
HW not to write another account of, **33.** 365

HW's account of, *see Account of the Giants Lately Discovered, An*
Hall, Bp, mentions, **1.** 130
height of, exaggerated, **42.** 182
See also under Coyer, Gabriel-François
'Patapan' (d. 1745), HW's dog:
barks at Frenchmen in Paris, **18.** 221
beauty of, **17.** 352, 452
'Brunette' salutes, **37.** 158
Chute alludes to Wootton's painting of, **35.** 38, 44–6
—— calls: 'Knight of the Silver Fleece,' and promises him the succession to 'Geoffrey,' **35.** 12, **37.** 98; 'Pope,' **35.** 56
—— dreams of, **35.** 55
—— inquires about, **35.** 22
—— offers to kiss, **35.** 6
—— receives letter from HW and, **35.** 50–1
——'s dream inspires poem about, **18.** 314n, **35.** 44–6, 48–9
Conway sends compliments to, **37.** 87, 93, 95
death of, **19.** 39, 59, **37.** 192
'Geoffrey' makes, his heir, **35.** 9, 12
Grifoni, Signora, becomes, in HW's 'Patapan,' **30.** 296
—— gave, to HW, **30.** 296n
HW accompanied by: at Downing St, **17.** 495; at Houghton, **18.** 36, 299, 498; to New Park, **18.** 136; while writing letter, **18.** 36
HW expects captive French officers to kiss the foot of, **30.** 38
HW jokes about 'Horace' (Stair's dog) and, **30.** 54
HW's 'common expressions' about, **30.** 296
HW's joke about, **17.** 76
HW's 'light horse' led by, **37.** 181
HW's poem on, **30.** 287–306, **35.** 48
hates gazettes but loves Sir C. H. Williams's odes, **30.** 55
Houghton visitors curious about, **18.** 299
Italy not regretted by, **17.** 143
'knight of the silver fleece,' **35.** 12, **37.** 98
Mann and Chute to visualize, in HW's room at Houghton, **18.** 17, 36, 60
Mann asks about, **17.** 41, 53, 56, **18.** 243, 264
—— jokes about, **18.** 174
Martial thrown by, into fire, **18.** 339
'Patapan, Miss,' corresponds with, **18.** 530
'Patapanino' resembles, **35.** 4
pointer shakes and bruises, **18.** 71
rainbow ribbon tied around neck of, **18.** 317
Roman, **18.** 220
'Rosette' the successor of, **23.** 200
sleeps in HW's lap, **30.** 18
to celebrate Dettingen victory, **35.** 39
Walpole, Sir Robert, amused by, **18.** 71, 299
Whithed's puppy had, as godfather, **18.** 333
'wife' of, **37.** 98
'wife' of, would be made less humble by HW's flattery, **40.** 45
Wootton's picture of, **35.** 38, 41, 44–6, **43.** 170
—— to paint, **18.** 221, 243
wormed, **18.** 317

'Patapan, Miss,' friend of HW's dog:
'Patapan' corresponds with, 18. 530
'Patapanino' or 'Pettapanino' ('Patapan's' puppy):
Chute delivers, at Florence from Venice, 35. 4
Eleonora called godmother to, 17. 149
HW sends, to Florence, 17. 112
HW's joke about, 17. 76
sire resembled by, 35. 4
'Patapan or The Little White Dog':
HW to write, 35. 48
never printed, 13. 14
text of, 30. 287–306
'Patavinity':
Livy's, 9. 22
Patch, James (d. 1791), surgeon:
brother's engravings distributed by, 23. 276
brother to send case to, 23. 447
HW receives, kindly, 23. 301
HW receives Thomas Patch's engravings and Donatello bas-relief from, 23. 459
HW to talk to, about subscription for brother's engravings, 23. 288
surgeon in Norfolk St, 23. 276
Patch, Thomas (1725–82), painter:
Beauchamp has picture by, 26. 45
brother to receive case from, 23. 447
career of, 23. 275–6, 26. 45
caricatures and conversation pieces of, 23. 275
caricatures by, 23. 5, 267, 422, 427, 429, 26. 45
conversation piece by, showing Lord Tylney, 43. 281–2
dies of apoplexy, 25. 272, 280
English in Florence caricatured by, 23. 5, 26. 45
English painter in Florence, 23. 287n, 26. 45
Florentine baptistery doors engraved by, 23. 429–30, 435
Florentine landscapes by: 30. 370; sent to HW, 23. 287–8, 301, 333, 360, 362
Giotto's paintings engraved by, 23. 459, 465
HW's account of, 26. 45
HW's criticism of his engravings approved by, 23. 371, 468–9
HW's dedication from, in book of engravings, 23. 371–2, 382, 465
HW wants drawing by, of Mann, 23. 267
HW will aid subscription of, 23. 288, 435
Hawkwood's portrait engraved by, 23. 428
Italian painter told by, that Madonna is not member of Trinity, 23. 459
Mann sends tabernacle through, 23. 447
——'s house visited by, daily, 23. 275
Masaccio's frescoes engraved by, 23. 267–8, 276, 287, 315, 362, 371, 422, 465, 469, 25. 280, 26. 45
Mead, Dalton, and Vernet aid, 23. 275
Michelangelo pictures engraved by, 23. 276
paintings by Andrea del Sarto engraved by, 23. 276
paintings of Fra Bartolommeo engraved by, 23. 268, 276, 362, 371, 459, 465, 468–9

Piccolomini aids, when expelled from Rome for religion, 23. 275
Poussin pictures sought by, for Lowther, 21. 209
Rome visited by, 23. 390
'Sterne and Death' by, 23. 5, 27, 33, 37
Strada Felice, Roman home of, 20. 392n
Patch; patches:
black, Cathcart hides battle scar with, 36. 12n
HW would not put, on St Ethelburgh's statue, 21. 471
Harley wears, over scratched forehead, 38. 256
ladies use, on Whig and Tory side of face, 16. 258
Patch box. See under Box
Patchwork:
frieze of, 39. 139
room full of, at Cannons, 30. 61
Pâté; pâtés:
Périgueux, 4. 152, 155
petit, in white sauce, hors d'œuvre of, 19. 356n
pineapple recipe for, sent by HW to Mme du Deffand, 6. 269
Patent; patents:
for Customs place, 24. 178, 26. 52–4
for fish supply, 23. 448
Hotham, Henrietta, brings, to Cts Temple, 10. 116
pension deduction for, 20. 204
Patent place:
Sackville's, in Ireland, 21. 328
Pater, Mme Gerhard. See Nieukirchen de Nyvenheim, Sophie-Gertrude-Adélaïde-Dorothée-Catherine-Albertine-Frédérique-Élisabeth de
Patera; pateræ (antique dishes):
HW's, Etruscan, 15. 13, 22
Middleton's, bronze, 15. 16, 22
on eagle's pedestal, 19. 122
on monument in Trinity Hospital, Greenwich, 16. 88
Pater noster:
mock, by Barthélemy, in imitation of Credo, 4. 343
Paternoster Row, London:
Beecroft's house in, 2. 81
Cooper, T., bookseller at Globe in, 17. 334n
Fielding and Walker of, 16. 177n
Johnson and Payne, booksellers in, 41. 170n
Paul's Alley in, 41. 280n
Richardson, bookseller in, 16. 45
Robinsons, booksellers in, 33. 476
Scott's book shop at 'Black Swan' in, 10. 349
Stephens of, 13. 63n
Walker, J., in, 43. 290
Woodfall's address, 41. 226
Woodgate in, 14. 105n
Paterson, Capt.:
Sardinian galleys under, 19. 82n
Paterson, James:
witness at trial of rebel lords, 19. 283n

Paterson, Col. James (d. ca 1789):
arrives from New York, 28. 434n
Paterson, John:
Blackfriars Bridge built by, 32. 153n
Paterson, John (?1705–89), M.P.:
Committee of Ways and Means headed by,
22. 488n
HW meets, at Lady Shelburne's, 32. 153
London election candidate, 23. 5
Paterson, Mrs John. See Hope, ——
Paterson, S., auctioneer:
Beauclerk's library sold by, 33. 136n
Paterson. See also Patterson; Pattinson
'Patience,' Catherine of Aragon's maid in wait-
ing:
Catherine attended by, in Henry VIII, 18.
537
Patience:
'desperate substitute to hope,' 24. 178
HW cultivates, 24. 178, 342
HW defines, 11. 249
Patience (card game):
HW hopes to play again, at Mme du Def-
fand's, 41. 42
HW likes, 3. 21, 337
'Patient Grisel,' tune:
Craon's sonnet on Lady Sophia Fermor to be
sung in part to, 30. 13
Patin, Guy (1602–72), physician and writer:
Nouvelles lettres by, quoted by HW, 39. 157
Patino, Don Lucas Fernando (ca 1701–51),
Marqués de Castelar, 1733; Spanish army
officer:
command of, in Italy, restored, 17. 349n
Gages may permit capture of, 19. 237
Montemar wants passport for, through Tus-
cany, 18. 44
Orso talks with, about Spanish plans, 17. 349
Parma occupied by, 19. 236, 245
Philip, Don, arranges troop passage with,
19. 51
returned to Spain, 17. 349n
Spanish agent at Florence told by, to threaten
Regency with blockade unless deserters
were returned, 17. 349
Patinson. See Pattinson
Patmos (Greece):
HW jokes about, 17. 495
HW wishes Wilkes were in, 35. 322
St John in, 11. 347
Patoon, ——:
Mann escorted by, 23. 60n
Patouillet, Louis (1699–1700), Jesuit:
Voltaire's enemy, 8. 156
Patriarchate:
of Venice, to be transferred, 20. 206
Patriarch of Lisbon. See Saldanha, Francisco de
Patrick, St:
Burke compared with, 32. 103
'fire' of, 35. 158
order of, should have members' portraits
done, starting with its institution, 42. 155–7

'Patrick Brian Macgill':
seated in Ireland, 33. 474
Patrick, Penelope, m. (1730) Edward Weston:
(?) Conway to be visited by, 37. 302
Patrick, Simon (1626–1707), Bp of Chichester
1689–91, of Ely 1691–1707:
blunders of, 1. 16
Patrick Fleming. See Peter Fleming
'Patrimoine de St-Pierre,' near Rome:
Spaniards and Neapolitans at, 18. 546
Patrimonio, Corsica:
capture of, 23. 46
Patrington, Yorks:
Nichols rector of, 2. 371n
Patriot, The:
HW and Hardinge discuss theme of, 35. 561,
562
Patriot, The. See under Anstey, Christopher
Patriot; Patriots (political faction):
Admiral Hosier's Ghost cried up by, 37. 64, 69
and courtier, the same, 32. 214
Bedford formerly associated with, 20. 72
Bolingbroke's letters on spirit of, 20. 59–62
Bubb Dodington headed, young, 30. 292n
Butler disapproves of toleration of, 28. 458
called discontented Whigs, 17. 231n
'cheat at eloquence,' 30. 221
Chesterfield and Pitt to receive legacies as,
18. 540
coffee-house politicians are, 37. 108
Conway is, by turns, 37. 92
Country Girl, The, satirizes, 18. 23
Coventry of the 'breed' of, 20. 302
Cox belongs to, 20. 156
dismissal of, from St James's, used to turn
them towards Albano, 22. 257
dismissal of Hanover troops discredits, 19. 17
Earle satirizes, 17. 243
English losses attributed to, 19. 255
first ministers used to be attacked, not pro-
posed by, 21. 546–7
Frederick, P. of Wales, builds up Opposition
after desertion of, 20. 30
Gage became whip for, 20. 291n
George II expected by Carteret to reward,
18. 81
—— wins over, by giving them places, 19. 229
Glover's Leonidas praised by, 18. 124n
HW disparages, 9. 87
HW pleased by dissension among, 20. 61,
65–6
HW's altar-piece would be attacked by, as
popish, 2. 186n
HW's description of, in 'Spectator,' 32. 81–2
HW's 'friends,' 2. 156n
HW would dread title of, 30. 104
Hardinge answers HW's remarks on, 35. 561
——'s feelings as, 35. 556
has become an opprobrious term, 28. 315
Houghton lantern excites wit of, 20. 163
House of Commons's keyhole stopped by,
17. 300

in Florence, pretends to know all English politics, **20.** 227

Jacobites and Tories join, in Parliament, **17.** 231n

Jacobites join, in opposing Sir Robert Walpole, **22.** 93

Labour in Vain satirizes, **18.** 18

Lyttelton a member of, **30.** 303n

Methodists no more virtuous than, **35.** 324

'ministerial' synonymous with, though formerly its opposite, **21.** 277

ministers outbid by, to demonstrate patriotism, **37.** 271

mutual accusations by, **20.** 65–6

Newmarket the resort of, to imbibe principles of honour, **41.** 344

no less harmful than the Stuarts to England, **19.** 456

Parliamentary division opposed by, **17.** 231

Pelham must bring in, **18.** 537

perseverance seldom typical of, **38.** 342

portraits of, at Gosfield, **9.** 64

privately-owned regiments opposed by, **19.** 154

Pulteney (E. of Bath) abused by, **20.** 31

—— leads, in Parliament, **17.** 231

——'s period with, **20.** 257

——'s treatment of, satirized, **18.** 91

ruinous activity of, **18.** 425

Sandwich an adherent of, **20.** 198

Walpole, Sir Robert, blames, **17.** 232

—— cannot conciliate, **17.** 330–1

wives of, attend Court in Queen Anne dresses, **18.** 95

See also Whig-Patriots

Patriot; patriots (general term):

Frederick II misunderstands English connotation of, **30.** 69

HW reflects on, **28.** 228

Patriot; Patriots, Dutch:

defeated, **39.** 459n

oppose William V, **39.** 450

Patriot; Patriots, Irish:

downfall of, **37.** 456

groan at playhouse, **37.** 449

'Patriot Exalted,' print:

(?) HW returns, to Lady Ossory, **34.** 140

Patriotism. See under Bentley, Richard (1708–82)

Patriotism:

emanation of self-love, **7.** 360, **33.** 202

faction distinguished from, **33.** 25

flourishes in beds of dung and filth, **42.** 502

HW advocates, though it makes one a bad citizen of the world, **33.** 158

HW explains his, **33.** 103

HW's, would be stronger were it not for his compatriots, **33.** 35

HW's reflections on, **18.** 423, **28.** 228

HW's reflections on uselessness of, **10.** 263

love of country because one is born in it, **33.** 580

'love of one's country makes one a wicked animal,' **33.** 429

massacres sole test of, in France, **31.** 392

modern, political moderation incompatible with, **25.** 50

power and prostitution inevitably succeed, **21.** 546

Patriots Are Come, The. See under Hervey, John (1696–1743)

Patrique, Russian frigate:

Denison commands, **25.** 60n

Patrizi, Agostino (d. 1496), Bp of Pienza:

story by, of founding of Siena, **13.** 204n

Patrizi, Giovanni Battista (1658–1727), cardinal:

Villa Patrizi built for, **17.** 25n

Patrizi, Marchese Giovanni Chigi Montoro:

ball given by, **17.** 25n

Patrizi, Villa, at Rome:

(?) ball at, **37.** 63

Charles of Naples at, **18.** 532

entertainment at, **17.** 25

Patrizii:

first rank of Tuscan nobility, **20.** 192

old Florentine noble families called, **22.** 350–1

Patrol:

House-Guard, **35.** 189

in Hyde Park, **35.** 189

Patten, Mary (1674–1705), m. (1698) Thomas Wilson, Bp of Sodor and Man:

Waynflete's descendant, **41.** 139

Pattens:

Bedford, Ds of, said to wear, **33.** 525

Bracegirdle, Anne, wears, **17.** 435

lowest Englishwomen tramp in, **24.** 126

Pattern; patterns:

scalloped, HW takes Selwyn's, to Betts, **30.** 242

Pattern doll. *See under* Doll

Pattern papers:

tailor's, **35.** 125

Patterson, Mrs, Lady Molesworth's maid:

dies in fire, **22.** 138

Patterson. *See also* Paterson; Pattinson

Pattinson, Thomas, deputy mayor of Carlisle:

boastful letter of, about repulsing rebels, nullified by his surrender, **19.** 165–6

Patton. *See* Patten, Pattyn

'Patty.' *See* Blount, Martha; Turk, Martha

'Patty was a Pretty Maid':

HW quotes, **33.** 465

Patyn *or* Patten, Richard, of Wainfleet, Lincs:

son of, **41.** 139

Pau, Parliament of:

reduced by Louis XV, **7.** 285

submits, **39.** 35

Paucefort, Mrs:

Isleworth house of, **33.** 524n

Paul, St (d. ?A.D. 67):

Bolingbroke writes *Craftsman* against, **20.** 454

disagreed with St Peter, **2.** 283

Du Deffand, Mme, cites, **4.** 83

[Paul, St, *continued*]
—— mentions, **3.** 146
feast of Conversion of, **37.** 3
Festus tells, that much learning had made him mad, **33.** 396
HW's model for letter-writing, **32.** 385
history of, in tapestry, **16.** 147
Mason quotes, **28.** 418
painting of conversion of, **2.** 4, 7, 7–8
peace announced by, to the Corinthians, **33.** 379
preaching of, **32.** 227
Raphael cartoon of, **35.** 37
sword of, **37.** 15
verses by Cts Harcourt would make, mad, **35.** 462
Voltaire mentions, **35.** 413
See also Rose Tavern: painting at
Paul III (Alexander Farnese) (1468–1549), pope 1534–49:
medal of, **21.** 189n, 201
Paul IV (Giovanni Pietro Caraffa) (1476–1559), pope 1555–9:
Galluzzi disparages, **25.** 224n
Paul V (Camillo Borghese) (1552–1621), pope 1605–21:
Henri IV induces, to compromise on excommunication of Venice, **20.** 198n
'Pastoralis' of, **22.** 582n
supposed opulence of England did not weigh with, to induce him to grant dispensation to James I, **25.** 224, 226
Venetians quarrel with, **25.** 198
Paul I (1754–1801), grand duke; Czar of Russia 1796–1801:
birth of, **20.** 457, **35.** 199
children of, **33.** 562
education of, **32.** 59
father doubts legitimacy of, **22.** 57, 75, **23.** 215, **35.** 314–15
Florence to be visited by, **25.** 250–1
HW hopes, will be childless so that his family's history may be published, **25.** 87
impostor claims to be father of, **23.** 547
Louis XVIII's gracious message from, **34.** 229
mother confers Order of St Anne in the name of, **24.** 84
mother has, inoculated, **23.** 76
mother may poison, **22.** 253, **23.** 236
mother might give Turkey to, **23.** 236
mother sends, on travels, **33.** 312
murdered, **12.** 54n
Naples left by, sooner than expected, **25.** 250
oath taken to, as heir, **35.** 315n
party of, foments Moscow riots, **22.** 205n
Pitt, Anne, jokes about, **10.** 39
Pugachev demands crown for, **32.** 184
Rome visited by, **25.** 250
Russian plot in favour of, **23.** 440n
Shuvalov praises, **8.** 206
—— received by, **6.** 492
still alive, **33.** 562

Paul (d. 1093), Abbot of St Albans 1077–93:
Paris's life of, **2.** 278–9
Paul (d. 1779), Armenian interpreter:
Arabs waylay, **24.** 510n
Paul, Father. *See* Sarpi, Pietro
Paul, George (d. 1755), LL.D.; King's Advocate:
Duke of Newcastle's Letter attributed to, **21.** 281
Paul, Horace. *See* St Paul, Horace
Paul, St (surname). *See* St Paul
Paul; pauls (Italian coins):
worth of, **17.** 227
'Paul before Felix':
Hogarth ridicules Dutch and Flemish painters in, **41.** 449
Paulet, Sir Charles (1661–1722), 2d D. of Bolton:
forces his son's marriage, **2.** 329
Paulet, Charles (1685–1754), 3d D. of Bolton:
first marriage of, **2.** 328–9
horse of, **13.** 89
Paulet, Elizabeth (d. 1656), m. 1 Robert Devereux, E. of Essex; m. 2 (1647 *or* 1648) Thomas Higgons, Kt, 1663:
funeral oration for, **2.** 271–2
Paulet *or* Powlett, William (ca 1483–1572), cr. (1551) M. of Winchester:
biographical information on, corrected, **43.** 56
print of, **1.** 213
Paulet. *See also* Pawlet; Poulett; Powlett
Paulin, Comte de. *See* La Tour du Pin-Gouvernet, Jean-Frédéric de
Paulin, Miss, m. (1768) James Mawhood:
husband parts from, **39.** 250–1
Paulis, Giacinto de:
Theodore of Corsica calls, traitor, **18.** 156
Paulmier, François:
Traité méthodique . . . de la goutte, **43.** 90
Paulmy, Marquis de. *See* Voyer, Marc-Antoine-René de
Paulmy, Marquise de. *See* Fyot, Suzanne-Marguerite
Paulo, Don. *See* Borghese, Paolo
Paulone. *See* Paulin
Paul's Alley, Paternoster Row, London:
Chapter Coffee-House in, **41.** 280n
Paul's Cross. *See* St Paul's Cross
Paulton Park, Hants:
Stanley of, **11.** 41n
Paultons, Hants:
Mendip, Lady, and Mrs D'Oyly own, **12.** 148n
Paume, ——:
Paris visited by, **7.** 458
Pausanias (fl. A.D. 174) of Magnesia:
Chandler's *Travels in Greece* follows, **28.** 257
Description of Greece by, quotes Homeric poem, **16.** 179
Pauw, Cornelius de (1739–99), writer:
name of, corrected, **43.** 358
Recherches philosophiques sur les Grecs by, read by HW, **34.** 40, 42

Pavée de Villevieille, Philippe-Charles (d. 1825), Marquis de Villevieille:
Voltaire's confession of faith signed by, **7.** 25–6
Pavement; pavements:
French remove, from St-Malo streets for defence, **37.** 502
marble, Mann orders made, for Bubb Dodington, **20.** 54, 253
new, **42.** 506
Roman, near Dorchester, **37.** 491
Pavey, Charles (fl. 1769–70), churchwarden of Twickenham:
(?) sells land to HW, **32.** 122
Pavia (Italy):
battle of (1525), **1.** 383
Botta's nephew from, **22.** 14
—— to retire to, **22.** 448, 454
Charles Emmanuel III and Lobkowitz to join at, **19.** 55
Philip, Don, retires to, **19.** 231
Spaniards may invade, **19.** 41
Pavie, M. de:
SH visited by, **12.** 231
Pavilion:
Mann uses, to mean 'flag,' **21.** 270, 277–8
Richelieu's, see Pavillon d'Hanovre
Pavilions, the D. of Gloucester's house. See under Hampton Court
Pavillon d'Aurore:
at Sceaux, **7.** 322
'Pavillon d'Hanovre':
HW visits and describes, **23.** 329
Richelieu's garden pavilion called, **21.** 172n, **23.** 329
Paving:
of Piccadilly, **42.** 499
Paving-stones:
in London, painful to horseback riders, **35.** 549
new road to avoid, **37.** 452
Pavizzoni, Abbé:
Cicognani college to be directed by, **23.** 513n
Pavonarius, Frederick (d. 1783), page:
(?) Wales, Frederick, P. of, attended by, **20.** 232
Pavon e Moncastello (Italy):
Charles Emmanuel III and Austrians near, **19.** 84
Pawlet (?Powlett), Mrs:
at the Vyne, **14.** 93, 95
Pawlet. See also Paulet; Poulett; Powlett
Pawnbroker; pawnbrokers:
Cates is, **40.** 65n
Jewish, Mme Suares rents her own jewels from, **17.** 137
Maclaine takes waistcoat to, **20.** 168
tax on, **25.** 578n
Pawning:
at Monte di Pietà in Tuscany, **17.** 304n
of jewels, **17.** 137, 484, **19.** 181
of Newcastle's gold plate, **19.** 485n
of Whithed's clothes, **18.** 4

Paxton, Mr:
Norsa, Hannah, travels with, **9.** 109n
Paxton, Mrs:
SH visited by, **12.** 226
Paxton, Nicholas (d. 1744), solicitor to the Treasury:
Fitzwilliam kisses, at Chelsea in HW's presence after release from Newgate, **17.** 502
Florentines call, Sir Robert Walpole's secretary, **17.** 417
Newgate may be the prison of, **17.** 397, 400n
Secret Committee causes loss of place by, **17.** 502
—— examines, about money given at Limerick election, **17.** 397
——'s report exposes, **17.** 425
Paxton, Rev. William (1723–95), fellow of King's College, Cambridge 1745–51:
King's College fellowship sought by, **40.** 39–40
Orford, E. of, presents, to livings at Padstow and Buckland, **40.** 39n
Payba, Abraham, (?d. 1776) alias James Roberts:
death date of, **43.** 270
Jews to commemorate losses of, in HW's newspaper parody, **9.** 129
Paris the refuge of, after fraudulent bankruptcy in London, **20.** 288n
Taaffe and Wortley Montagu arrested in Paris for cheating, **19.** 450n, **20.** 288, **21.** 473n
Taaffe, Wortley Montagu, and Southwell said to have extorted notes from, on his banker Waters, **20.** 288n
Payen, Pierre (d. ca 1664), Sieur Deslandes:
Nanteuil's print of, **15.** 100
Payerback; Payersberg. See Poymont
Paymaster (of the Land Forces):
Burke becomes, **25.** 264n, 392
Chandos's profits as, **30.** 60n
changes in post of, **9.** 32, 39, 180, 210, 233, **10.** 153
Cooke and North to be, **22.** 440n
Fox, Henry, is, **21.** 74, 92, 99, 103, **22.** 92, 134
—— must be, **21.** 91n
——'s dismissal from, **30.** 183–4, 190, 230, 248, 249
—— to remain as, **38.** 184
—— willing to be, under Pitt, **21.** 98n
—— will not make room for new people as, **38.** 370, 377
George II appoints Pitt as, **20.** 138
—— insists on Fox's retention as, **21.** 99
—— retracts offer of, to Fox, **21.** 77n
—— tells Holdernesse to send for Fox as, without notice to Dupplin, **21.** 74n
George III promised not to take, from Fox without giving him an earldom, **30.** 230–1
joint: Darlington and Dupplin become, **20.** 517, **35.** 263; North is, **30.** 233; Potter succeeds Darlington as, **21.** 25
Leicester's witticism on Pitt's appointment as, **19.** 286

[Paymaster (of the Land Forces), *continued*]
Newcastle to give position of, to Fox, **21**. 86n
Pelham retires as, **18**. 313
Pitt (Chatham) is, **19**. 256, 286, **20**. 138, 512, 517
salary of, **22**. 440
Townshend, Charles, not to be, **22**. 440
—— succeeds H. Fox as, **22**. 302, 304
—— to be, **38**. 496
Townshend, Thomas (1733–1800), resigns on Rigby's succeeding Cooke and himself as, **39**. 98–9
Vane becomes, **37**. 424
Walpole, Sir Robert, is, **22**. 26
—— profits by place of, **42**. 81
Winnington is, **17**. 172n, **18**. 350, 356, **19**. 211, **30**. 291n
Paymaster of Chelsea Hospital:
Pelham's resignation as, **18**. 313
Paymaster of the Board of Works:
Gilmour succeeds Brown as, **17**. 493, **37**. 132n
Selwyn succeeds Onslow as, **20**. 518
Paymaster of the Marines:
Pitt, John, to become, **21**. 26
See also Williams, Sir Charles Hanbury
Paymaster of the Pensions:
Gage succeeds Compton as, **20**. 517
Jeffries said to succeed Stewart as, **17**. 495
value of the office of, **17**. 384n
See also Hooper, Edward; Keene, Benjamin
Payne, Lady. *See* Keeling, Maria (d. 1802); Kolbel, Frances Lambertina Christiana Charlotte Harriet Theresa (d. 1830)
Payne, Rev. ——, rector of Moulsho:
sister of, **10**. 337
Payne, Benjamin (d. 1768), footpad:
execution of, **1**. 135n
Payne, Catherine (d. 1801), m. (1749) Lord Francis Seymour:
sister of, **10**. 337
Payne, Frances (1719–1800), m. 1 (1748) Hon. George Compton, 6th E. of Northampton, 1754; m. 2 (1761) Claudius Amyand:
fortune of, **9**. 401
husband's jointure returned to Compton family by, **10**. 337
marriage of, expected, **9**. 401
marriages of, **10**. 337
Payne, Sir Gillies (1720–1801), Bt, of Tempsford Hall:
member of committee, **2**. 208n
wife of, **12**. 252n
Payne, John (d. ca 1647), engraver:
Bolton's portrait engraved by, **16**. 65
Payne, John (1719–99), publisher:
Evelyn's *Sculptura* published by, **43**. 54
memoir by, **16**. 62n
Payne, Sir Ralph (1739–1807), K.B., 1771; cr. (1795) Bn Lavington; M.P.:
Burgoyne to be answered by, **33**. 136
'centricality' of house of, in Grafton Street, **32**. 343

HW's correspondence with, about Poles visiting SH, **33**. 501–2
HW visited by, **32**. 343
made K.B., **23**. 272
North, Lady, entertains, at dance, **33**. 284
oratory of, **32**. 180
SH visited by, **12**. 224
West Indian, **23**. 272
Payne, Roger (1739–97):
finds books for Cole, **1**. 35
Payne, Rev. Thomas:
daughter of, **10**. 337
Payne, Thomas (1719–99), bookseller:
Burgess's *Lives* printed by, **40**. 238
'Guirlande de Julie' bought by, **42**. 93n
publisher of *British Topography*, **1**. 255, 263
SH visited by, **12**. 247
Wood's *Essay* published by Elmsly and, **41**. 306n
Payne. *See also* Paine
Pay Office:
Burke restores Bembridge and Powell to, **25**. 407–8
—— succeeds Barré in, **25**. 407
Grafton removes Townshend from, **23**. 186n
HW's verses on splitting, **14**. 88
Powell dismissed from, for deficiency in accounts, **25**. 407
—— placed in, by Holland, **25**. 407
Rigby's hold on, **39**. 99
Townshend, Vcts, gossips about, **9**. 32
Townshend, Thomas, long notified of destination of, **39**. 99
See also Paymaster
'Paysan du Danube.' *See* Hume, David
Paysan gentilhomme, Le. See Contant d'Orville, André-Guillaume: *Paysan parvenu, Le*
Paysan parvenu, Le. See under Contant d'Orville, André-Guillaume; Marivaux, Pierre Carlet de Chamblain de
Pays de Vaud, Switzerland:
Budé born in, **12**. 9n
Payta:
Anson captures *Nuestra Señora del Carmen* near, **18**. 478n
Pazzi, Antonio (1706–66), engraver:
Gherardini's portrait of Bianca Cappello engraved by, **21**. 561n
Pazzi, St Maria Maddalena de' (1566–1607), nun:
painting by, **18**. 171, 207
Pea; peas:
Cole raises, **1**. 276
cost 4 livres in Paris, **7**. 452
Du Deffand, Mme, cannot resist, **4**. 244, 247, 252, **5**. 371
frost said to have killed, in England, **23**. 200
Goldsworthy makes profit by sale of, to English ships, **18**. 107
HW and Richelieu resemble old withered grey, **31**. 58
HW's parched, **39**. 499

Ireland to send, to Lisbon earthquake sufferers, 37. 423n
Peace:
Anglo-French, HW anxious for success of rumoured Dutch plan for, 30. 48–9
and war, alternate, 32. 7
bad way of, 37. 296–7
Cole on, 2. 247
Conway dreads, 37. 533
—— hears, is signed, 37. 295
——'s reflections on, 37. 284
—— thinks, *summum bonum*, 37. 193
—— wishes for, 37. 195
does not advance, 37. 101
Du Deffand, Mme, wishes, to conclude English-French war, 7. 103, 112, 114, 126–7, 129, 132, 138, 149, 157, 163, 164, 168–70, 172, 174, 194, 212, 221, 222, 226, 233, 239 (*see also* War: English-French: Du Deffand, Mme, fears)
Empresses may interpose to make, 30. 274
England cannot expect, good, 37. 285
France must try for, 38. 37–8
Frederick, Charles, prepares spectacle to celebrate proclamation of, 37. 295
HW, above all, desires, 33. 160
HW anxious for, 30. 274
HW calls: 'jack-o-lantern,' 38. 185; 'old hen,' 35. 341
HW favours, 9. 31, 353
HW hopes for, 38. 95
HW ignorant of rumours about, 10. 44
HW prefers: 35. 341, 366; to doctrines, 25. 39–40
HW's reflections on, 2. 246, 24. 393
HW thinks bad, better than a worse, 30. 49
Letter to Two Great Men proposes, 9. 270
Montagu hopes for, 9. 253
not so catching as war, 25. 188
Pope's line about Fleury's love of, applied to Necker and Sir Robert Walpole, 34. 19
returns to heaven with Virtue, 38. 130
rumours of, 9. 31, 10. 36, 45
victory less desirable than, 22. 85
Peace, justice of. *See* Justice of the peace
'Peace as long as the moon endureth':
Churchill's father's text, 7. 374
Peace in Europe, serenata:
performed at London opera, 20. 49
Wall's witticism at, 20. 51–2
Peace of Aix-la-Chapelle. *See* Aix-la-Chapelle: treaty of
Peace of Paris. *See* Paris, Treaty of (1763); Paris, Treaty of (1783)
Peace treaties:
HW's reflections on, 33. 379, 579–80
Peach, Edward. *See* Petch, Edward
Peach, Mrs Joseph. *See* Witts, Apphia
Peach, Mary (d. 1791), m. Samuel Lysons:
SH visited by, 12. 233

Peach; peaches:
apricots and, sugared and chilled, 3. 405–6, 4. 3n
baskets of, served at Versailles ball, 32. 256
Cole's, 2. 113
England has to import, 32. 359, 33. 561
expense of growing, in England, 10. 290
HW receives, from Mme de Marchais, 39. 258
HW's, 2. 111
Holdernesse's guests eat, from Dutch stoves, 38. 60
in Paris, 2. 111
orange-, complexion compared to, 9. 388
Paris has better, sold on street corners than grown in England, 10. 290
skins of, 35. 473
stewed, eaten by Mann at dinner, 17. 104
Peacham, Edmond (d. 1616), Puritan divine:
HW asks about, 15. 77–8
Peacham, Henry (ca 1576–ca 1643):
Compleat Gentleman, The, by, mentions Raphael's tapestry designs, 16. 147, 43. 219
Peach colour:
fades rapidly, 21. 471
Peachey, Mrs:
SH visited by, 12. 229
Peachey ('Peachy'), James (1723–1808), 4th Bt, 1765; cr. (1794) Bn Selsey; groom of the Bedchamber to George III 1751–91; Master of the Robes 1792–1808; M.P.:
biographical information about, corrected, 43. 269, 314
George III's groom of the Bedchamber, 20. 247, 21. 460n
HW calls, 'solemn,' 30. 84
Lyttelton, Bns, might be persuaded that Sir James Morgan is, 39. 222
officer beaten by, 30. 84
snobbishness of, 30. 101
Sussex election lost by, 39. 207
'Peach in Brandy, The,' by HW:
fœtus in, 19. 447n
HW uses title of, as euphemism for 'miscarriage,' 32. 359
(?) Hardinge alludes to, 35. 572
text of, 32. 59–63
Peach tree; peach trees:
dead of 'influenza,' 33. 335
Plat's directions for growing pomegranates on, 28. 275
Peacock, G.:
Ward, Ann, succeeded by, 29. 190n
Peacock, Irish wherry:
Americans capture, and call it *Surprize*, 24. 302n
Peacock; peacocks:
eggs of, 35. 282
in Noah's ark, 33. 148
Juno and, 32. 178
pied, Tylney to provide, 35. 275
York, D. of, receives, at Rome, 22. 228

Peafowl; peafowls:
Stafford, Lady, will find that embargo will make more food for her, **35.** 320
Pea-green:
and silver, worn by Lady Mary Coke, **39.** 7
'Peak, Sir James of the.' *See* James of the Peak
Peak, the, Derbyshire:
Devonshire, D. of, called 'king' of, **33.** 405
Dodd and Whaley visit, **40.** 15–17
giant of, **9.** 296
HW's Whiggism not confined to, **33.** 342
Pear; pears:
between cheese and, **35.** 230n
bury: HW cannot stir because of, **39.** 258;
HW receives, from Mme de Marchais, **39.** 258
HW eats, for supper, **22.** 110
HW should not eat, cold, **22.** 114
Marchais, Mme de, sends, to Mme du Deffand, **6.** 232, 251, 259
Pearce, William (b. ca 1741), Gen. Gunning's groom; 'Carloman':
Gunning affair involves, **11.** *197–201*, 204, 225, 252, 279
Pearce, Zachary (1690–1774), Bp of Bangor, 1748; of Rochester, 1756; Dean of Westminster, 1756:
Archbishop and bishops oppose resignation of, from Rochester see, **38.** 364
Aymer de Valence's tomb said to be permitted by, to be replaced by Wolfe's, **38.** 110
crucifix removed by order of, from window in St Margaret's, Westminster, **10.** 339–40
Faction Detected attributed to, **18.** 319
Ferrers declines services of, **21.** 398
George II's funeral service read by, **9.** 322
George III hears, preach at Chapel Royal, **38.** 526n
HW's correspondence with, about Aymer de Valence's tomb, **38.** 110–11, **40.** 200–2
Longinus edited by, **15.** 295
objects to erecting painted windows, **2.** 186n
pagan mythology permitted by, in Westminster Abbey monuments, **10.** 339–40
Pulteney, E. of Bath, makes, dean, **18.** 319
—— recommends, to Newcastle, for Peterborough bishopric on resigning Westminster deanery, **43.** 251
—— supplies, with material, **18.** 319
Reply to the Defence of the Letter to Dr Waterland, A, by, **15.** 295
Reply to the Letter to Dr Waterland, A, by, **15.** 295
Westminster Abbey monument's removal justified by, **40.** 201–2
Pearce. *See also* Pearse; Peirce; Peirse; Pierce
Pearl; pearls:
chain of, **42.** 12
Charlotte's mantle fastened with, **21.** 529
Choiseul, Mme de, preferable to necklace of, **41.** 108, 110
Clive may not again return with, **22.** 243

Coke, Lady Mary, robbed of, by French maid, **23.** 535n
decorate Ds of Queensberry's gown, **32.** 112
from India, imported by Romans, **11.** 295
in Tudor portraits, perhaps taken from convents, **33.** 487
Joseph II's, to be sold by auction at Brussels, **33.** 487
necklace of, **18.** 291, **22.** 540n, **41.** 108, 110
objects made or ornamented with, in Q. Elizabeth's collection, **32.** 323–5
'Patapan' said to shed, instead of fleas, **30.** 297
Waldegrave, Cts, wears, **23.** 193
wedding gown trimmed with, **23.** 93
Pear-monger; pear-mongers:
Bussy compared to, **37.** 127
pert, **37.** 127
Pear pie. *See under* Pie
Pearse, Thomas (d. 1743), M.P.:
Weymouth election influenced for, **17.** 421n
Pearse. *See also* Pearce; Peirce; Peirse; Pierce
Pearson, Capt.:
news from, of Burgoyne's surrender, **24.** 340n
Pearson, James (d. 1805), glass-painter:
paints glass for SH, **1.** 201n
slow with Ely window, **1.** 201, 206, 214
Pearson, Sir Richard:
Kempenfelt sends, with news to Admiralty, **25.** 221n
Pearson. *See also* Peirson; Pierson
Peart, Mary, m. (1768) Lord George Manners Sutton (formerly Manners):
regimental uniform worn by, **33.** 20n
Pear tree. *See* Iron-pear-tree-water
Peasant; peasants:
Beauclerk, Lady Diana, paints, **42.** 490
Frederik of Denmark liberates, **31.** 274
French: ball for, at Roissy, **7.** 334; dirty, disliked by HW, **10.** 298
Peasinghall, Suffolk:
Derehaugh family's lands in, **1.** 376–7
Peaux d'âne. *See* Fairy tales
Pebmarsh, Essex:
Luckyn, rector of, **9.** 92n
Pecari; Peccori. *See* Pecori
Pecci, Cavaliere:
Richecourt has the Tuscan finances examined by, **20.** 327n
Pecci. *See also* Pucci
Peche, Elizabeth de (fl. *temp.* Edward II); m. John Walpole:
pedigree of, **2.** 115
Peche, Gilbert de (fl. *temp.* Edward II):
daughter of, **2.** 115
Peche, Sir Hamon de (fl. *temp.* Henry I):
family of, **2.** 115
Peche, Isolda de (fl. *temp.* Edward II):
daughter of, **2.** 115
Peche family:
pedigree of, **2.** 115

Pêché-mortel (furniture):
HW wants to loll in, **18**. 315
Mann not familiar with, **18**. 332

Peck, Francis (1692–1743), antiquary:
Academia tertia Anglicana by, **43**. 54
Antiquarian Annals of Stamford by, **1**. 176
Desiderata curiosa by: **1**. 5, **43**. 38; Cole mentions description in, of Burghley House, **10**. 344, 346; HW imitates, **13**. 48n, **28**. 37; HW mistakes, for *Memoirs of Cromwell*, **40**. 157; social customs in, **40**. 210

Peck, Rev. Wharton (d. 1777):
death of, **2**. 51

Peckitt, William (1731–95), glass-painter:
Exeter Cathedral's west window by, **41**. 102
HW employs, **1**. 145n
HW's commissions for, at SH, **1**. 145, **28**. *213*, 216, 227, 253–4
HW to present Harcourt with glass for window to be assembled by, **35**. 520n
Mason forwards parcel to, **6**. 202n
painting by, at SH, **40**. 312n
to work at Ely, **1**. 146
to work at Exeter, **1**. 146–7
windows by: **9**. 267n; at Hinchingbrooke, **40**. 284

Pecori, Contessa. *See* Berzichelli, Maria Leopolda (1704–82); Suares de la Concha, Maria Theresa (1728–1809)

Pecori, Antonfrancesco (1682–1743), Conte:
death of, **18**. 150
house of, on corner of Via di Santo Spirito and Via Maffia, **18**. 150n
marries to spite nephew, **18**. 150

Pecori, Bernardo (1720–63), Conte:
Chesupiades shared by, **18**. 345
Mann describes, **19**. 145
Parigi, the, is rival of the Pepi with, **17**. *111*, 136, 444, **19**. 136
Pepi, the, cicisbea to, **18**. 150
——'s engagement with, broken, **17**. 111, 136
—— to shoot the Parigi for giving disease to, **17**. 444, **19**. 136
—— tries to kill, **17**. 136
Suares, Teresa, to marry, **19**. 136, 145
uncle marries to displease, **18**. 150
wife said to arouse jealousy of, **19**. 311

Pecquigny, Duc de. *See* Albert d'Ailly, Marie-Joseph-Louis d'

Pedant; pedants:
'a just volume' required by, **11**. 77

Pedantry:
French Revolution aided by, **34**. 73, 159

Pedestal; pedestals:
Damer, Mrs, falls from, **42**. 291
for Boccapadugli eagle, *see under* Eagle, Boccapadugli
for bust of Vespasian, *see under* Vespasian
Montfort will need, to lead Cambridgeshire militia, **21**. 312
of buried column used as rubbish for foundation of arch, **21**. 343

Pedigree; pedigrees:
Chesterfield's, of Stanhope family, **20**. 181, 195
HW's, for registration in House of Lords, **42**. 349n
illuminated, of Earls of Warwick, **35**. 606
in MS for Gough, **2**. 232
Italians hang, in conspicuous places, **20**. 205
Manchester's, depicts Richard III, **41**. 134, 144
Mann's, *see* Mann family: pedigree of
(?) of Greville family, **37**. 305–6
on brass, in Mereworth Church, **35**. 144
Pomfret, Cts of, devises scheme for, **20**. 180–1, 194
Walpole, returned by HW to Heard, with corrections, **42**. 349
See also Genealogy

'Pedigree of Reginald de Walpole,' by HW:
Blomefield cited in, **20**. 381n

Pediment; pediments:
Pitt, Thomas, recommends portico without, for green-house, **38**. 198

Pedlar; pedlars:
HW's news no better than that of, **37**. 497
Jewish, Mme de Marchais resembles, **30**. 265

Pedro III (1717–86), K. consort of Portugal 1777–86:
niece's marriage to, **21**. 422
wife of, **11**. 361n

Pedro IV (1319–87), K. of Aragon 1336–87:
Calveley said to have married widow of, **41**. 445
wife said to have given love-potions to, **41**. 445

Peekskill, N.Y.:
Bird's expedition to, **24**. 306n

Peel Castle, Isle of Man:
Gloucester, Ds of, dies in, **14**. 75n

Peep into the Principal Seats and Gardens in and about Twickenham, A. See under Mendez, Jael

Peer; peers, English:
Coronation preparations of, **35**. 310–11, 313
costume of, unbecoming, **38**. 126
creation of: expected, **29**. 215, 228, 289, **37**. 270; not to take place, **38**. 377
Cromwell made, of cobblers, **31**. 267
George II creates, **12**. 271
Irish peers contrasted with, **28**. 17
lay themselves in the kennel, **35**. 399
old English, arms of, in stained glass, **35**. 77
to kiss hands on promotions, **30**. 163
trials of: decorated in crimson, **19**. 280n; more interesting than a Coronation, **21**. 535
See also Nobility; Peerage; Peeress

Peer; peers, French:
business enjoyed by, but army will not permit it, **38**. 304
Fitzjames's arrest causes meeting of, not attended by Louis XV, **38**. 302

[Peer; peers, French, *continued*]
  not at parliament where d'Aiguillon was discussed, 4. 429–30
  parliamentary business of, 4. 429
  protest honour to house of Lorraine, 4. 408–9, 412
  protest illegal parliament, 5. 61, 63
  summoned to lit de justice, 4. 427, 429, 5. 61
Peer; peers, Irish:
  English peers contrasted with, 28. 17
  George III permits, to walk at Coronation if they were at his marriage, 35. 313
  newly created: 33. 260, 268, 420; HW saw only a third of, 25. 433; HW ridicules, 21. 24, 24. 227, 30. 165; numerous, 32. 304, 33. 268, 301, 405, 420, 520
Peerage. See under Collins, Arthur
Peerage; peerages, English and Irish:
  Anson to receive, for victory, 37. 273
  authors and authoresses among members of, 16. 294
  Bampfylde and Tynte said to be bribed with, 38. 326
  Bouverie gets, by bribery, 19. 419
  cheesemongers elevated to, 41. 361
  Clinton barony's descent in, 25. 165
  conferred upon: Anson, 19. 414; Archer, 19. 419; Bagot, 25. 86; Bateman, 24. 227; Beauclerk, Lord Vere, 20. 135; Bessborough, 20. 66; Blakeney, 21. 24, 52; Boyle, 37. 448n; Brooke, 17. 391n; Brudenell, 25. 86; Bubb Dodington, 21. 490; Bute, Cts of, 21. 490; Carpenter, 21. 490; Conway, Francis, 20. 135; Courtenay, 22. 31; Curzon, 21. 484, 490; Damer, 22. 31; De Grey, 25. 86; De la Warr, 21. 490; Duncombe, 19. 419; Dunning, 25. 264; Edgcumbe, 17. 399n; Edward Augustus, P., 21. 389; Egmont, 22. 32; Fauconberg, 20. 563; Fitzroy, 25. 86; Fitzwilliam, 17. 399, 19. 296; Fox, Lady Georgiana, 22. 31; Fox, Henry, 20. 502n, 22. 129; Fox Lane, 22. 31; Gage, 25. 86; Garth Turnour, 21. 490; Grosvenor, 21. 490; Harrington, 17. 333; Henley, 21. 389; Herbert, 25. 86; Hillsborough, 17. 436n, 20. 26; Hobart, 19. 296, 307; Hunsdon, 25. 166; Ilchester, 20. 563; Irby, 21. 490; Keppel, 25. 264; Kildare, 19. 371, 21. 485; Liddell, 19. 419; Ligonier, 22. 449–50; Lyttelton, 21. 18, 24, 26; Norton, 25. 264; Phipps, 22. 548; Pitt, 20. 442–3; Pitt, Lady Hester, 21. 541, 38. 131–2, 134, 135–7; Pulteney, 17. 485n; Rawdon, 20. 135–6; Robinson, 21. 490; Rolle, 19. 419; Sandys, 17. 249n, 18. 142, 357–8, 365; Shelburne, 25. 542; Spencer, 21. 490; Talbot, 21. 489, 490, 25. 86, 37. 70; Temple, 25. 542; Vernon, 22. 31; Vesey, 20. 136; Walpole, Horatio (1678–1757), 17. 469n, 20. 556, 563; Walpole, Sir Robert, 17. 318, 319, 20. 27; Wentworth, 22. 31; Wyndham O'Brien, 21. 24, 26; Yorke, Philip (1690–1764), 37. 70

creation of: 37. 270; rumoured, 36. 172, 173, 174, 209; to convert House of Lords, 25. 605
Dutchwoman lowers, 38. 266
elevations in, hard to obtain from George III, 30. 247
excessive number of, 33. 520, 523
for sale but no buyers, 33. 430
Fox, Henry, wants, for wife, 21. 75
George II prefers to advance peers in, by stages, 37. 449n
HW's comments on new members of, 24. 227
Hamilton, James, fails to get, 42. 88
Heathcote had promise of, 20. 81
hereditary origins of, 18. 126n
House of Lords's orders for registration of, 42. 349n
Irish, may be bought by Duc d'Orléans, 11. 85
Jack Pudding may be concealed by ermine and velvet of, 35. 400
ladies extend, to husbands, 10. 240
Lowther to receive, 23. 58
Malone declines, 37. 449n
Mann expects, to be given to Sir James Gray, 22. 469
new creations for: 24. 205, 32. 7, 37. 270, 39. 410; rumoured, 36. 172, 173, 174, 209, 38. 159
Northumberland and Somerset titles perpetuated in, 20. 81
Northumberland's list for, not granted, 38. 377
offers of, rejected, 33. 430
old, kept ceremonious state, 42. 380
Paoli said to get, from France, 23. 31
patent of, 17. 485n
Pitt's, disliked by London, 22. 442–3
Ryder almost gets, 20. 557
Sackville to receive, 25. 237, 241
Saye and Sele descent, 25. 165
Scotch dukes said to join, 36. 222, 223
Townshend's wife's, perhaps given too soon, 39. 85
Peerage of England, The. See under Collins, Arthur
Peerage of Ireland, The. See under Lodge, John (d. 1774)
Peerage of Scotland. See under Douglas, Sir Robert (1694–1770)
Peeress; peeresses, English:
  commoners' marriages with, exclude them from Coronation parade, 35. 310
  dancing avoided by, at Ps of Wales's ball, 10. 186
  heralds advertise for names and addresses of, 21. 535
  sleep, dressed, in arm-chairs on night before Coronation, 38. 122
  travel as much as their eldest sons, 25. 649
Peeress; peeresses, Irish:
  creation of, ridiculed by HW, 12. 164

Peers, Col. Newsham (d. 1743):
killed at Dettingen, 18. 258
Pégase, French ship:
Jervis captures, 29. 251n
Pegasus, English ship:
Rodney detaches, 25. 24n
Pegasus:
HW will bespeak side-saddle for, 32. 88
HW will turn his, to grass, 32. 131
Pegge, Samuel (1704–96), antiquary:
Carter, Charles, paints, 43. 295
Forme of Cury, The, edited by, 2. 223
'Observations on the History of St George'
by, 2. 162, 163–4, 43. 69
Whittington subject of discussion by, 1. 265n,
14. 47n
Peggi, Pier Francesco (1688–1780), canon, 1710:
Benedict XIV's letter to, 21. 126, 196
Peggy, English ship:
Keppel joined by, 39. 306
Windham and Sadler rescued by, 25. 579n
Peirce ('Pearce'), Mr; surgeon:
Essex, Cts of, attended by, 30. 321
Williams, Sir C. H., writes ode to, 30. 321
Peirce. *See also* Pearce; Pearse; Peirse; Pierce
Peirenc de Moras, François-Marie de (1718–
71), controller-general:
satire on, 7. 331
Peirse, Henry (?1754–1824), M.P.:
(?) Gabrielli, Caterina, kept by, 24. 148–9
Peirson, Francis (1756–81), army officer:
Conway's epitaph for, 39. 411
Peirson, Maj. James:
Jersey forces commanded by, 25. 110n, 111n
Peisley, Mrs. *See* Caulfeild, Lettice
Pekin; Peking (China):
Coke, Lady Mary, might be at Paris or, 31.
185
HW's friend at, *see Letter from Xo Ho*
HW speculates about Rousseau's opinion of,
24. 62
Iris searches from London to, 31. 120
'pure,' used to describe Vcts Townshend's
house, 40. 52
Pelasgians:
HW has no regard for, 33. 479
Peldon ('Pelden'), Essex:
advowson of church of: 30. 350, 36. 53; Daye
family's interest in, 30. 359
Pelée de Varennes, Marie-Louise-Antoinette-
Anne, m. Barthélemy de Vougny:
social relations of, with Mme de Lambert,
7. 302
Pelet, Jean-François (1725–1804), Comte de
Narbonne-Pelet-Fritzlar:
(?) Corsican rebellion crushed by, 24. 26n
Peletier. *See* Le Peletier; Le Pelletier
Peleus et Thétis. See under Le Bovier de Fon-
tenelle
Pelew Islands:
English ship sent to, 34. 29
See also under Keate, George

Pelham, Bn. *See* Pelham, Sir John (1650–1712);
Pelham Holles, Thomas (1693–1768)
Pelham, Bns. *See* Frankland, Anne (ca 1734–
1813); Holles, Lady Grace (ca 1668–1700)
Pelham, ——, Hon. Henrietta Seymour Con-
way's maid:
HW remembers, 38. 52
HW thanked by, for remembering her, 38.
160
Pelham, ——:
Hardinge hears from, Montagu's story about
Nicholas Hardinge, 35. 605
Pelham, Mrs:
portrait of, 10. 338
Pelham, Lady Catherine. *See* Manners, Lady
Catherine (ca 1701–80)
Pelham, Catherine (1727–60), m. (1744) Henry
Fiennes Clinton (later Pelham Clinton), 9th
E. of Lincoln; 2d D. of Newcastle-under-
Line, 1768:
approaching marriage of, 30. 64, 74
assembly given by, at Exchequer House, 37.
453–4
(?) at Chesterfield's assembly, 37. 325
Capello, Signora, does not invite, 19. 18
dances at Robinson's ball, 37. 114
death of, 21. 428
Falmouth, Vcts, singled out by, because Ds
of Bedford had snubbed her, 37. 454
HW anxious to be well-thought-of by, 30. 76
Lincoln promises to be good husband to,
30. 47
marriage of, 18. 245, 277, 483, 21. 18n
pregnant, 9. 16
Richmond's fireworks attended by, 9. 81
Sandwich's ball not attended by, 20. 121
Scott, Lady Jane, only person to be visited by,
37. 454
sings, 9. 81
ugly, 37. 114
younger sister of, 43. 113
youthfulness of, 30. 74
Pelham, Dorothy (fl. 1740):
death of, 21. 362, 30. 22
Pelham, Elizabeth (d. 1723), m. (1678) Edward Montagu:
genealogy of, 10. 352
Montagu's grandmother, 9. 103n, 196n, 304n
Pelham, Frances (d. 1756), m. (1715 *or* 1717)
Christopher Wandesford, 2d Vct Castlecomer:
Ferrers, Cts of, and, the 'generals' of Twickenham, 37. 292
HW calls, 'old rock,' 11. 56
'inconvenient for my Lord Castlecomer' is
comment of, on tutor's broken leg, 10.
311n, 11. 55–6
(?) Montagu may buy chariot of, 9. 196, 197
Pelham, Frances (1728–1804), daughter of
Henry Pelham:
admirers of, 32. 7
(?) at Chesterfield's assembly, 37. 325
Bedford, Ds of, entertains, 33. 544

[Pelham, Frances (1728–1804), *continued*]
biographical information about, corrected, **43.** 151
Bower's theory about earthquake known to, **20.** 157
club at Almack's founded by, **10.** 305
Coke, Lady Mary, quarrels with, **28.** 402–3
cousin has hardly seen, **20.** 180
cousin of, **10.** 72n
cousin should go to England to wed, **20.** 115, 129, 172–3
cousin's marriage to, will make him the chief Pelham heir, **20.** 173
Dillon and Bessborough scolded by, at quinze game, **32.** 345
earrings lost by, in hackney chair, **20.** *114*, 129
elder sister of, **43.** 113
Fitzroy, Mrs, quarrels with, **32.** 103, 106–7, 112
(?) frantic, **38.** 203
gains of, at loo, **9.** 412
gambling of, **9.** 412, **32.** 7, 121, 160, 169–70
Grafton, Ds of, not amused by oddness of, **38.** 89
guests of, at Esher: Coke, Lady Mary; Graftons; Holdernesses; Nivernais; Pelham, Mr and Mrs Thomas, and Mary; Pembrokes; Pitt, Mrs George and Anne; Rockingham, Marchioness of; (?) Shelley, John; Sondes, Bns; Usson, Comtesse d'; Villiers; Vorontsov; **10.** 72–3
HW and Mary Rich seen by, on fall from stile, **35.** 276
HW dines with, **12.** 5
HW unable to attract, **32.** 92
HW walks with, **31.** 36
HW writes song to, **10.** 54–5, **43.** 128–9
loo liked by, **32.** 7
Magdalen-House visited by, **9.** 273–4
marriage of, predicted, **9.** 53, **32.** 6
neglected at Anne Pitt's ball, **38.** 475–6
Nivernais's verses on, **10.** 73
orgies of, **32.** 121
popularity of, changes with father's status, **38.** 476
'quite mad,' **32.** 160
Richmond, D. of, entertains, **10.** 54
Selwyn presents to the Rena a rose given by, to March, **32.** 6n
sings at Esher party, **10.** 73
temper of, **32.** 92
'Thomyris,' **32.** 106
Vauxhall visited by, with Lady Mary Coke, **37.** 557
volatility of, **32.** 28, 92
weeps at Magdalen-House sermon, **9.** 274
Pelham, Frances (1760–83), m. (1778) George Brodrick, 4th Vct Midleton, 1765:
death of, **33.** 405
Pelham, Grace (ca 1731–77), m. (1752) Hon. Lewis Watson, cr. (1760) Bn Sondes:
(?) at Chesterfield's assembly, **37.** 325

birth date of, corrected, **43.** 129
HW's naiads produce less water than the tears of, **35.** 325
health of, cold, **38.** 342
House of Commons never left by, in long session, **38.** 317
marriage of, **37.** 339, 341
Pelham, Frances, entertains, at Esher, **10.** 72–3
Queensberry, Ds of, rejects tardy answer by, to ball invitation, **38.** 342
tears not to be shed by, till her accouchement, **35.** 170
Pelham, Henrietta (1730–68), m. 1 (1748) Hon. Richard Temple; m. 2 (1753) George Nevill, Bn Abergavenny:
brother to seek, at Hanover, **20.** 172, 180
husband's separation from, **38.** 510–11
second marriage of, **20.** 180n
suggested as Bedchamber lady to Q. Charlotte, **38.** 96
Sussex visited by, **20.** 180
Pelham, Hon. Henry (1695–1754), prime minister; M.P.:
absent from Parliament, **17.** 484
address of thanks proposed by, **19.** 188
administration of: Arenberg supported by, against Wade, **37.** 183; collapse of, expected, **30.** 49; Conway may be prevented by, from going to Scotland, **19.** 204; discord in, ridiculed by poem, **30.** 49; falls, and is restored, **37.** 220–1; follies involve, **20.** 74n; Frederick II distresses, by manifesto, **30.** 68; George II forced by, to assign Beefeaters to Falmouth, **19.** 397; HW blames rebels' progress on, **30.** 96–7; HW's low opinion of, **30.** 49; HW unconnected with, **30.** 68; has seen its best days, **19.** 17; ignorance of, **30.** 97; Jacobites bribed by, **37.** 271; Mann glad that Granville's association with, did not wreck it, **19.** 225; Maria Theresa's towns will not be fortified by, **19.** 69; Scottish taxes of, **20.** 310–11; triumphant in Parliament, **19.** 458; Walpole, Sir Robert, fails to compose discord in, **30.** 49; Williams, Sir C. H., disliked by, **19.** 16
Admiralty and Navy Bill opposed by, **20.** 38
Amelia, Ps, tells, of North's appointment, **20.** 203n
Anstruther inquiry disliked by, **20.** 230n
appointment of, as first lord of Treasury, **30.** 39
Ashton encouraged by, to seek Newcastle's aid, **43.** 189
Augusta, Ps of Wales, made regent by, **20.** 249
Barnard defends discipleship of, to Granville, **26.** 10
—— influences, **20.** 111
Bath, E. of, displeased with, **20.** 3n
Beauclerk's peerage requested by, **20.** 135
Bedford, D. of, aided by, **19.** 154, **20.** 120

—— to punish, **20**. 38

Bentley's satirical petition to, **35**. 643

biographical information about, corrected, **43**. 178

birth date of, **20**. 413n, **43**. 178, 313

bishops flock to house of, **18**. 231

Bower consulted by, about earthquake, **20**. 157

brother and himself the sole concerns of, **33**. 440n

brother of, **12**. 5n

Burdett promises to present Castle-Durrow and Rodney to, **20**. 20

Cabinet Council to resist removal by, **18**. 537

Capello's letters to, **43**. 253

Carteret (Granville) and Newcastle might be warned by, not to trust Richecourt's insinuations against Mann, **18**. 363

Carteret (Granville) arouses jealousy of, **18**. 535

—— betrays, into losing sugar tax, **22**. 489

—— makes Admiralty appointments unbeknownst to, **18**. 349

—— opposes, about privately-raised regiments, **19**. 158

—— reconciled with, **18**. 349

——'s conflicts with, **30**. 49

——'s failure to form new ministry strengthens, **19**. 213

——'s vengeance might be feared by, **19**. 17

Chancellor of the Exchequer, **20**. 114n, 180n, 233n

'character' of, as 'Plumbosus' in *Discord*, **30**. 49, **37**. 162

Chelsea Hospital paymastership resigned by, **18**. 313n

Chesterfield discontented with, **31**. 173

Chesterfield, Pitt, Patriots, and Tories to be brought in by, **18**. 537

Chesterfield's witticism on, **20**. 214

children of, die of fever and sore throats, **13**. 196–7, **17**. 399, **21**. 362, **30**. 22

Clutterbuck infuses scruples into, **17**. 391n

Cockpit meeting to be presided over by, **18**. 103

Conway regrets time lost due to, **37**. 188

——'s voting worries, **37**. 226–7

counterpart of, lacking at Laughton Place, **35**. 140

Cumberland, D. of, gets ordnance from, **20**. 120

——'s quarrel with Newcastle calmed by, **20**. 120

Custom House place secured by, for E. of Lincoln and his son, **20**. 18

daughter; daughters of: **10**. 72n, **12**. 5n, **20**. 121n, 180n, **21**. 18n, 428n, **28**. 402n; prevented by him from marrying E. of March, **32**. 6n; said to be engaged, **9**. 53

death of: **9**. 159, 210, **14**. 80–1, **20**. 411–14, 419, **25**. 288, **35**. 84, 164–7; proves he was not essential to England's political calm, **35**. 167, 173

debt interest reduced by, **42**. 497

Discord satirizes, as 'Plumbosus,' **30**. 49, **37**. 162

distribution of patronage difficult for, **18**. 550

Dupplin settles 61 Parliamentary boroughs with, at Richmond, **20**. 411n

Egmont formerly preferred Fox to, **20**. 224

—— helped by, in Weobley election contest, **20**. 31

——'s pamphlet attacks, **20**. 32

——'s party heaps incense on, **20**. 224

England's shift to New World might be proposed by, **37**. 249

Esher the seat of, **14**. 60n

eulogies on, not forthcoming, **35**. 170

Euston visited by, **18**. 254

Exchequer auditorship controlled by, **20**. 233n

Exchequer resigned to, by Sandys, **18**. 350, 356

faction of, unpopular in House of Commons, **19**. 4

Fanshawe a parasite of, **10**. 68n

far from rich, **20**. 413

Fawkener's letter forwarded to, by Poyntz, **40**. 59

first lord of the Treasury, **18**. 299, **20**. 233n, **25**. 20n, **30**. 39

Fox, Henry, and his friends courted by, **18**. 451

Fox, Henry, may succeed as prime minister, **20**. 411, 419

—— opposes, on Clandestine Marriages Act, **37**. 365

——'s marriage disapproved by, **37**. 157n

—— visits Pitt and Hartington after death of, **20**. 412n

Fraigneau tells, about George I's intentions for Bolingbroke, **20**. 452

Frederick, P. of Wales's adherents bribed by, **20**. 30

——'s opposition shows strength of, **19**. 158–9

—— speaks to, at Carlton House, **17**. 337

—— toasts Fox for opposing, **19**. 161

Garter may be expected by, **20**. 84

genealogy of, **10**. 352

George II approached by, about Berlin post for Sir James Gray, **19**. 444

—— asks Winnington to recall, to ministry, **19**. 212

—— displeased by plan of, to make D. of Bedford Master of the Horse, **20**. 235n

—— on distant terms with, **18**. 552

—— permitted by, to choose Admiralty candidate, **20**. 17

—— sick of timidity and compromises of, **19**. 212

—— to remove, to make room for Carteret, **21**. 100n

—— will hardly speak to, **19**. 159

Gisors appraises, **31**. 3n

Gower in the hands of, **20**. 258

Grafton to head dependents of, **20**. 120

Granville, Cts, distresses, by assembly, **18**. 562

[Pelham, Hon. Henry, *continued*]
Gray, Sir James, promised Berlin post by, 19. 444, 453
great ministerial power of, 29. 79
Grodno's diet breakup would disturb, 18. 562
Gunnings eclipse, 20. 260
HW asks: about troops going abroad, 37. 226; for preferment for Ashton, 17. 430n
HW attacks, 13. 18n
HW calls, 'Saturnus,' 35. 263
HW calls on, 9. 11
HW on 'ill terms' with, 35. 164n
HW preferred company of George Selwyn to that of, 32. 191
HW's applications to, regarding his Customs place, 43. 314
HW satirizes, in his imitation of Corneille's *Cinna*, 13. 14, 18. 465n
HW's contempt for, vindicated by Melcombe's diary, 25. 503, 33. 440
HW's correspondence with, 13. 249n, 30. 119, 40. 36–7, 39–40, 73–5
HW solicits reversion from, 29. 327n
HW's praise of Lincoln pleases, 30. 26
HW told by, that George II mentioned D. of Cumberland's recommendation of Conway, 37. 226
HW to speak to, about Mann, 18. 382
HW to visit, 30. 26
Harcourt a creature of, 20. 246
Hardwicke bows to, at trial of rebel lords, 19. 280
—— discusses retirement with, 20. 202
—— forces, to support Clandestine Marriages Act, 37. 363–4
Harrington sacrificed by, 21. 100n
—— visits, to ask, how he offended George II, 20. 207n
Hartington a favourite of, 20. 74n
—— proposed by, to George II for Master of the Horse, to secure Devonshire interest, 20. 258n
health of, 20. 413, 35. 158
Henley's tribute to, in sermon, 35. 170
Hervey hated by, 17. 430
house of, at Esher, *see* Esher
house of, at Spring Garden, 30. 22
house of, in Arlington St: 13. 12, 33. 340; built by him on site of Sir Robert Walpole's, 35. 199n; Gower leaves, 10. 271; Grafton occupies, 10. 271; on former site of Sir Robert Walpole's, 10. 271; opposite HW's, 18. 231, 21. 167n
House of Commons mortifies, 20. 257
—— visited by, just before death, 20. 413
Hume Campbell paid by, for political silence, 20. 5n
illness of, attributed to Irish troubles, 35. 158
interest reduction planned by, 20. 111
Jackson may apply to, for Leghorn post, 17. 409, 430
Lee and Potter speak against, 19. 470
Legge courts, 19. 458

—— defended by, 20. 39n
Leigh resembles, 9. 103
lenient measures preferred by, 23. 86
levee of, 18. 231, 19. 20
Leveson family subject of invectives by, 20. 201
Leveson Gower, Hon. William, to preach before, in HW's newspaper parody, 9. 129–30
Lincoln's love for Lady Sophia Fermor might be mentioned by, 30. 24
——'s uncle, 30. 22, 29
—— to inherit property of, 18. 245
Lovat calls to, at trial, 19. 347
Lyttelton a supporter of, 13. 19
Mann fears that Robert Mann may be injured by retirement of, from paymastership, 18. 313
—— surprised at news of, 18. 557
Mathews's friend, 19. 33n
Murray a protégé of, 18. 384
—— examined before, 19. 391n
—— may succeed, as prime minister, 18. 411, 419
naval reduction proposed by, but opposed by Pitt faction, 20. 223
Newcastle, D. of, converses with, 9. 12
—— jealous of, 17. 430
—— links, in 'passion' against Harrington, 26. 10
—— shares leadership with, 10. 192n
—— succeeds, 9. 12n
Nugent attached to, 20. 32
old politicians hate Egmont because of, 20. 32
Onslow's election as Speaker moved by, 17. 219
Orford's Bedchamber appointment promised by, 20. 470n
——'s death would vacate place in the gift of, 20. 233
overshoots himself, 20. 259
Parliamentary debates by: on amendment to the Address, 26. 22, 24; on privately-raised regiments, 26. 16, 17, 18; on Scotch bill, 26. 33; on the Pretender, 18. 440n; on unanimity in the Army, 26. 10
Parliamentary majorities commanded by, 19. 202
Parliamentary motion's alteration proposed by, 17. 354
Parliamentary oratory improves since time of, 35. 263
(?) Parliamentary speech by, 37. 223
Parliamentary speeches by: on Dresden treaty, 42. 493; on renewing regiments, 40. 50
Parliament's dissolution opposed by, 19. 412n
Patriots' dismissal of Hanover troops discredits, after his attack on Whigs for similar acts, 19. 17
peace may be restored by, in absence of George II and Newcastle, 20. 143
peace professed by, 42. 497
peace will secure position of, 19. 5

peace with France urged by, **30**. 109n

Pitt and (Henry) Fox injure, in their strife, **20**. 230

Pitt and Halifax favoured by, for secretaries of state, **20**. 202n

Pitt (Chatham) attacks, **19**. 169

—— bullies and flatters, **19**. 155

—— cannot be got by, into place, **19**. 159

—— courted by, **18**. 327

—— faction flatters, despite disagreement, **20**. 224

—— may succeed, as prime minister, **20**. 411, 419

—— might get concessions from, **20**. 223

—— praises, **26**. 10

political situation of, resembles that of 1765, **22**. 303

Prowse favours, **20**. 32

pusillanimity of, **20**. 483

regent, **18**. 209

resignation proposed by, **19**. 105

resigns, as first lord of the Treasury, **19**. 211

Richmonds friendly with, **18**. 451

Rutland wanted by, as Master of the Horse, **20**. 183

sacrifice of political embroils, **20**. 39

sacrifices all, to jealousy and ambition, **18**. 535, 537

Sandwich's connection with Pretender told to, by Horatio Walpole (1678–1757), **17**. 231n

—— 's dismissal by, **9**. 115n

Scarborough visited by, to cure scurvy, **20**. 413

Selwyn's witticism at sale of plate of, **35**. 220–1

sides with HW, **13**. 23n

successor of: not likely to dismiss Robert Mann, **18**. 326; proposed, **35**. 165–6; unfit for post, **20**. 431

supporters of, may overturn him, **19**. 6

Townshend, Vcts, hates followers of, **18**. 497

Treasury to be headed by, **18**. 147, 265, 277, 299, 313

treaty with Saxony defended by, in Parliament, **20**. 300

Trevor given Durham bishopric by, over George II's objections, **20**. 323n

—— related to, **17**. 366

Walpole, Horace (1678–1757), intimate with, and admired by him, **20**. 420n

Walpole, Sir Robert, apt to yield to, against his better judgment, **39**. 318–19

—— asks, to secure pension, **17**. 229n, **18**. 465–6

—— follows suggestion of, to stay in the country, **18**. 536n

—— had, as friend and pupil, **17**. 229n

—— ill-used by, **13**. 19

—— not to be replaced by, **17**. 319

—— said to be ungratefully treated by, **19**. 471

—— sends letter to Loudoun through, **36**. 7

—— visited by, at Houghton, **18**. 245, 248, 254

—— wants George II warned by, against Carteret's Hanoverian policy, **18**. 356n

—— would write to, if Bedford's place were endangered, **40**. 41

war opposed by, **19**. 448

West secretary to, as chancellor of Exchequer, **20**. 371n

Whitehall no longer the residence of, **30**. 22

wife of, **9**. 128n, **13**. 328n, **20**. 114n, **25**. 20n

wife said to keep, from revealing Greenwich Park affair, **26**. 10

Williams, Sir C. H., clashes with, over Hereford appointment, **30**. 312n

—— compliments, in ode to Lincoln, **30**. 318

—— frequently slighted by, **30**. 312

—— receives K.B. from, **30**. 311

—— satirizes, and compares unfavourably with Sir Robert Walpole and Winnington, **30**. 318

—— 's candidacy for K.B. opposed by, **18**. 451

Pelham, Henry (ca 1736–9):
death of, **17**. 399, **21**. 362, 369, **30**. 22

Pelham, Henry (?1729–1803), of Lee, Kent; M.P.:
dismissal of, from Customs post, feared, **22**. 109n

Pelham, Henry (1759–97), son of Sir Thomas Pelham, Bt:
SH visited by, **12**. 224

wife of, **12**. 201n

Pelham, Mrs Henry. See Cobbe, Catherine (ca 1762–1839)

Pelham, Henry Cresset:
Hardinge, Jane, wife of, **30**. 178n

Pelham, Col. James (ca 1683–1761), M.P.:
bequests by, to dishonest servants, **9**. 417

biographical information about, corrected, **43**. 126, 267

death of, **9**. 417

Pelham, Thomas, corresponds with, **20**. 172, 195

secretaryship of, to lord chamberlain, coveted by HW for Charles Churchill, **40**. 177–8

Pelham, Sir John (ca 1623–1703), 3d Bt; M.P.:
genealogy of, **10**. 352

guests asked by, about length of stay, **9**. 371

Montagu's great-grandfather, **9**. 196n, 371

wife of, **10**. 125n

Pelham, Louisa or Lucy (ca 1728–40):
death of, **21**. 362

Pelham, Lucy (ca 1728–40):
death of, **30**. 22

Pelham, Lady Lucy. See Sidney, Lady Lucy

Pelham, Lucy (d. 1736), m. (1717) Henry Clinton, 7th E. of Lincoln:
husband's death a blow never surmounted by, **21**. 93

portrait of, **10**. 338

'Treaty, The,' said to cast aspersions on, **21**. 93

Pelham, Margaret (ca 1700–58), m. (1727) Sir John Shelley, 4th Bt, 1703:
husband long outlives, **34**. 258

Pelham, Mary (1739–94), youngest dau. of Henry Pelham:
(?) at Chesterfield's assembly, 37. 325
Bedford, Ds of, entertains, 33. 544
House of Commons never left by, in long session, 38. 317
neglected at Anne Pitt's ball, 38. 475–6
Pelham, Frances, entertains, at Esher, 10. 72–3
Shelley rejected by, 43. 122
Pelham, Sir Nicholas (ca 1519–59), Kt, 1549:
gamekeeper of, killed by Dacre, 35. 139–40
Pelham, Sir Thomas (ca 1650–1712), 4th Bt, cr. (1706) Bn Pelham; M.P.:
genealogy of, 10. 352
Pelham, Thomas (ca 1705–37) of Stanmer; M.P.:
Stanmer house of, to be dined at by Dodd and Whaley, 40. 6
Pelham, Thomas (1728–1805), 2d Bn Pelham of Stanmer, 1768; cr. (1801) E. of Chichester:
Acciaioli, Mme, has affair with, 20. 115–16, 129, 158, 172, 180, 284, 37. 323
—— visited by, in the country, 20. 115–16
Acciaioli family likes, 20. 115–16, 172
Admiralty post lost by, 22. 109n
—— post obtained by, 21. 490
Amelia, Ps, entertains, 33. 104, 39. 441
—— leaves legacy to, as her executor, 33. 535
appearance of, not very good, 20. 195n
cannot dance, 38. 250
chief justice in eyre, 23. 562
Coke, Lady Mary, entertains, at Notting Hill, 35. 341
Customs reversion to go to, 21. 26
entail of Newcastle's peerage granted to, 10. 27
family of, use subterfuges to lure him home, 20. 180
George II commends dancing of, 20. 200
HW called on by, 20. 207
HW calls on, 20. 200
HW's opinion of, 20. 225
Halland inherited and abandoned by, 10. 287n
heir should be produced by, to D. of Newcastle, 20. 116
Holdernesse, Cts of, to entertain, 35. 341
last keeper of the Great Wardrobe, 20. 115n
leaves Florence, 20. 171
lively and well-bred, 20. 195n
Mann accompanied by, in riding parties, 20. 172
—— assured by, of receiving baronetcy, 20. 459n, 462
—— entertains, regularly at supper, 20. 115
(?) —— escorted by, 23. 60n
—— might be aided by, in case of recall from Florence, 21. 129
—— might be helped by, to become K.B., 22. 381
——'s arrears solicited by, at Hanover, 20. 173, 195
——'s friend, 21. 490, 22. 32, 23. 562

—— should seek intercession of, for himself, not Milbanke, 20. 180
——'s 'little waxen friend,' 21. 26
——'s opinion of, 20. 171
—— thanks HW for civilities to, 20. 211
—— thinks of joining, at Hanover, 20. 150
Mann, Galfridus, to press, about Mann's affairs, 20. 211
marriage of, to Frances Pelham would make him chief Pelham heir, 20. 172–3
Milbanke, John, met, at The Hague, 20. 55n
neutrality promised by, in Sussex election, 39. 207n
Newcastle, D. of, retirement of, announced by, 22. 579n
—— to be approached by, about Mann's arrears, 20. 173
—— visited by, at Hanover, 20. 195n
Newcastle House the abode of, 20. 207
Newcastles accompanied by, from Hanover, 20. 195n
not in town for reading of Ps Amelia's will, 33. 535
Pelham, Frances, entertains, at Esher, 10. 72–3
—— should marry, 20. 115, 129, 180
Pelham, Col. James, told by, to intercede with D. of Newcastle for Mann's salary arrears, 20. 195
Pisa baths visited by, 20. 158
reversion of Newcastle's new peerage to go to, 22. 32
sister will not be found by, in Hanover, 20. 180
son of, 12. 201n
Spence, Elizabeth, leaves reversion to, 38. 459
(?) Stone advises, about Mann's salary arrears, 20. 195
surveyor-general of the customs of London, 21. 26n
to be master of the Great Wardrobe, 24. 142
Pelham, Thomas (1729–39):
death of, 17. 399, 21. 362, 369, 30. 22
Pelham, Hon. Thomas (1756–1826) of Stanmer, styled Bn Pelham 1801–5; 2d E. of Chichester, 1805; M.P.:
English peerage declined by, 33. 430n
to be secretary to lord lieutenant of Ireland, 12. 117n
wife of, 28. 470n
Pelham, Mrs Thomas. See Frankland, Anne (ca 1734–1813)
Pelham Clinton, Lady Catherine Fiennes (1776–1804), m. (1800) William Pleydell Bouverie, styled Vct Folkestone, 1779; 3d E. of Radnor, 1828:
Clinton barony to revert to, HW thinks, 25. 165
Pelham Clinton, Henry (1720–94). See Fiennes Clinton, Henry
Pelham Clinton, Henry (1777–9), styled E. of Lincoln:
death of, 7. 177, 33. 123

HW sends servant to inquire after, **30.** 272

probable death of, distresses Hertfords, **30.** 272

still living, **30.** 273

Pelham Clinton, Henry Fiennes (1750–78), styled Bn Clinton 1752–68, E. of Lincoln 1768–78; M.P.:

Chamberlayne accompanies, **23.** 224

cheated and poxed, **23.** 378

death of, **24.** 420

English at Florence have not gambled heavily since affair of, **23.** 536

Florence visited by, on way from Rome to England, **24.** 252

France visited by, for health, **24.** 420

HW recommends, to Mann, **23.** 223, 228

house of, in Arlington St, **24.** 420n

marriage of, **24.** 71, 420, **28.** 303n

Newcastle, Ds of, aggrieved at, **24.** 52n

story about, repeated from Tuscany, and printed in newspapers, **23.** 368

wife of, **6.** 132n

Pelham Clinton, Lord John (1755–81), M.P.:

HW's Customs place might provide for, **40.** 146

Mann to present, at Tuscan Court, **24.** 251

Pelham Clinton, Lord Thomas (1752–95), styled E. of Lincoln 1779–94; 3d D. of Newcastle-under-Line, 1794; M.P.:

America to be station of, as Clinton's aide-de-camp, **24.** 263n

—— visited by, **33.** 123

biographical information about, corrected, **43.** 286, 368

contingent heir of D. of Kingston, **32.** 150

defeat of, by C. J. Fox, **33.** 227

elected for Westminster by Ds of Northumberland's efforts, **24.** 52

father cannot sell Oatlands without consent of, **39.** 390

HW intended to recommend, to Mann, **24.** 263

HW's Customs place might provide for, **40.** 146n

Newcastle, Ds dowager of, opposes election of, **24.** 52n

Westminster election won by, **39.** 196

—— scrutiny asked by, after defeat by C. J. Fox, **36.** 177

wife of, **26.** 403n

Pelham Clinton. *See also* Fiennes Clinton

Pelham coterie:

Bedfords entertain, **9.** 232

Pelham faction:

Capello, Signora, excludes, **19.** 18

resignations expected from, **21.** 98

Pelham family:

armour of, at Halland, **10.** 287

HW never loved, **22.** 109

HW on good terms with, **31.** 173

HW predicts that rule of, will end in October, **21.** 93

Legge ingratiates himself with, **19.** 458

Milbanke should be aided by, **20.** 171

Monitor, The, attacks, **21.** 39n

Montagu asks HW to buy ancestral portraits of, **9.** 196, 197, **10.** 281

—— related to, **10.** 281, 352

no less harmful than the Stuarts to England, **19.** 456

Parliamentary act would give regency powers to, if George III ascended as a minor, **9.** 113

Pelham, Thomas, will be chief heir to, if he marries Frances Pelham, **20.** 172–3

Pelham Holles, Thomas (1693–1768), 2d Bn Pelham; cr. (1715) D. of Newcastle-upon-Tyne, (1756) D. of Newcastle-under-Line; prime minister:

absurdity of, **22.** 102–3

Addison to be supported by, in Pembroke College election, **14.** 90

administration of: **2.** 310n; addled, **37.** 485; alterations in, **30.** 162; beginning of, **35.** 169, 281; Byng quarrels with, **21.** 3; Byng said to have compassion of, **21.** 63; cannot endure at same time with two others, **21.** 465; dismissal of, inexpedient, **37.** 417; Fox, Henry, and Mansfield and Waldegrave consider, hopeless, **21.** 99; has seen its best days, **19.** 17; Hertford under no obligations to, **38.** 98, 108; Mirepoix complains to, of attack on French ships, **20.** 489; Oxford Loungers discuss, over custards and syllabubs, **38.** 46; Parliament will expect explanation of Minorca's loss from, **20.** 578; Pitt disclaims responsibility for Halifax's omission from, **30.** 135; Townshend, George, disapproves of, **30.** 135

affronted but omnipotent, **35.** 194

alarmed by disapproval of Hessian and Russian treaties, **35.** 87–8

alleged disinterestedness of, **21.** 26

ambition of, to be prime minister, **18.** 535

Amelia, Ps, and D. of Cumberland said to ill-use, **20.** 120n

Amelia, Ps, might be defending, to HW, **10.** 50

appointment of friends urged by, **30.** 194, 196

Arenberg entertained by, **18.** 97n

Ashburnham, Lady Catherine Pelham, and Lincoln approve of, **43.** 274

Ashburnham the favourite of, **35.** 246

Ashton asks, to have Aldingham living transferred to Ashton's brother, **43.** 189

auction of effects of, **10.** 281, 287

Augusta, Ps of Brunswick, has visit connected with, **32.** 17

Augusta, Ps of Wales, made regent by, **20.** 249

Austrian leanings of, **20.** 38n

authority of, established, **20.** 425

barber rewarded by, in HW's newspaper parody, **9.** 128

Barrington not wanted by, to replace Legge, **21.** 486n

[Pelham Holles, Thomas, *continued*]
——'s transfer probably owing to, **30**. 196
Bath, E. of, Carteret, Furnese, and Limerick entertained by, **17**. 503, **18**. 20–1
Bath, E. of, displeased with, **20**. 3n
—— frightens, at Lovat's trial, **19**. 347
——'s letter to Pitt and, **9**. 270n
Bath (Somerset) visited by, **22**. 566–7, 579n
Beauclerk's peerage requested by, **20**. 135
Bedford, D. of, about to clash with, over Turnpike Bill, **20**. 112
—— cannot be ousted by, because of D. of Cumberland, and Ps Amelia, **20**. 201n
—— embraced and then avoided by, **20**. 201
—— given aid by, **20**. 120
—— receives express at Woburn from, about rumoured Parliament dissolution, **30**. 246
——'s breach with, **20**. 38
——'s misconduct may provoke shift by, from secretary of state to president of the Council, **20**. 201n
——'s removal pressed by, **20**. 235n
——'s union with, proposed, **40**. 344n
Bedford, D. and Ds of, entertain, **9**. 232–3, 363
——'s guests ignore, at ball, **9**. 232–3
Bedford faction and Rockingham to be reconciled by, **22**. 549
Bedford House visited by, to unite Bedford and Rockingham factions, **22**. 566
bed of, at Chelsea, **9**. 40–1
behaves as usual in ministerial crisis, **30**. 185
Belle-Île expedition stopped by orders of, **21**. 466n
Belle-Isle interviewed by, at Windsor Castle, **19**. 3n
Bentley's *Patriotism* mentions, **14**. 134n, **31**. 69n, **43**. 131
—— writes as seldom as if in a country under sole control of, **35**. 187–8
'betrayals' by, **30**. 96
bishops appointed by: **31**. 69; avoid him after his fall, **10**. 32, **22**. 36–7, 323–4; flee Opposition, **38**. 248
bishop tells, he should have led Blues at Minden, **39**. 105
Bolingbroke may be aped by, **22**. 442
Botta believes, must return to government, **22**. 44
Breda delegates chosen by, **21**. 355n
breeches-strings burst by, **37**. 267
Bristol, E. of, promised ambassadorship to Spain by, **21**. 166n
brother-in-law of, **9**. 19n
brother might be succeeded by, **35**. 165
Bruce's appointment not announced to, **9**. 328–9
Brudenell a follower of, **9**. 184n
—— perhaps assured of interest with, **37**. 387
Brunswick-Wolfenbüttel's pension arranged by, **2**. 124, 125
Brussels dinner party with Botta involves, in question of precedence, **22**. 44

—— visited by, on way from Calais to The Hague and Hanover, **22**. 44n
Bunbury's motion attacks, **22**. 8n
Burdett promises to present Castle-Durrow and Rodney to, **20**. 20
Burghley, Godolphin, and Q. Elizabeth might be equalled by, **35**. 240
Burnaby instructed by, to prevent Young Pretender from living at Fribourg, **19**. 509n
Bute advised by, to be secretary of state, **21**. 488
—— and Hardwicke join, against Pitt, **21**. 539n
Bute and Temple meet, at Bute's Garter installation, **22**. 79
Bute conciliated by, **9**. 341
—— informs, that George III will permit choosing a new Parliament, **21**. 444n
—— opposed by, **38**. 186
——'s dismissal of, implies certainty of peace, **22**. 38
—— settles changes with, **21**. 487n
—— to be won over by, **21**. 86n
Byng blamed by, for loss of Minorca, **20**. 578n
——'s courage compared to timidity of, **21**. 67
——'s sacrifice said to be determined by, **21**. 55n
Cabinet and Parliament will oppose, **21**. 93
Cabinet Council place may be kept by, **22**. 79
Calvert attends, at installation, as Cambridge chancellor, **9**. 242
Cambridge Address presented by, to George III, **9**. 321, **22**. 78n, **30**. 98n
Cambridge chancellorship sought by, **9**. 71
Cambridge clergy appointments regulated by, **22**. 324n
Cambridge clergy ungrateful to, **22**. 38
Cambridge college head might be recommended by, for K.B., **22**. 332
Cambridge steward's election to be influenced by, **14**. 131
Cambridge to celebrate installation of, as chancellor, **20**. 71, 83
Cambridge turned half-Jacobite by ordinances of, **20**. 346–7
Canterbury, Abp of, avoids last levee of, **10**. 35
caricatures of: in 'Pillars of State,' **35**. 280n; in 'The Duke of N——tle and His Cook,' **17**. 485n; in 'The Treaty,' **21**. 93
Carteret (Granville) and, **35**. 21
—— approved of by, for using victories to procure peace, **18**. 230n
—— arouses jealousy of, **18**. 535
—— calls, to witness that Sir Robert Walpole aided Hanover troops measure, **18**. 382
—— makes Admiralty appointments unbeknownst to, **18**. 349
—— mediates between Henry Fox and, **20**. 502
—— never writes to, **18**. 382
—— reconciled with, **18**. 349
—— said to leave, in place, but without power, **18**. 82

——'s conflicts with, **30.** 49

——'s discomfiture at rebels' progress enjoyed by, **19.** 109

——'s letter with Dettingen news copied by, **18.** 258

——'s measures thought by, to be aimed at flattering George II, **18.** 327n

——'s negotiations with, to strengthen Newcastle against D. of Cumberland, Bedford, and Sandwich, **20.** 72n

——'s union with, **17.** 301

——'s vengeance might be feared by, **19.** 17

—— told by, about venison, **17.** 506

Charles Emmanuel III denied troops by, **18.** 462n

Charlotte, Q., finds, in her retiring-room at Westminster Abbey during Coronation, **21.** 535, **38.** 122

Chatham, E. of, and, *see below under* Pitt, William (Chatham)

Chesterfield and H. Fox discuss downfall of, **20.** 502

Chesterfield discontented with, **31.** 173

—— may arouse jealousy of, **19.** 413

—— not obligated to defend, **35.** 224

——'s witticism on, **20.** 214

Chloé, French cook of, **17.** 485n

Churchill, Lady Mary, holds place of which reversion was granted by, **40.** 177

churchyard epitaph appropriate to, **37.** 368

Clandestine Marriages Act not voted for by, **37.** 362, 364n

Claremont the seat of, **1.** 44

—— to be retreat of, for a few days, **21.** 92

clergy patronized by, **22.** 323–4

clerks and tide-waiters restored by, to office, **22.** 323

Clinton's new title solicited for him by, **9.** 36

Cofferer candidates considered by, **20.** 518n

contradictory characteristics of, **30.** 185

Conway advised by, about policy towards Boyle and Stone, **37.** 399n

—— consults: **22.** 432n; about Bedchamber vacancy, **37.** 386, 387

—— led by, **38.** 569

—— reimprisoned due to delay by, **9.** 52

——'s friends led by, towards Bedford faction, **22.** 533

——'s speech on Qualification Bill hostile to, **38.** 49

—— tells, that HW cannot come to Claremont, **41.** 36

—— to be entertained by, at dinner at Claremont, **22.** 332

—— urges, to drop Stone from Irish Regency, **20.** 503n

Cornwallises thank, for bishopric, **43.** 278

Cornwallis the only bishop to attend last levee of, **10.** 32

country's fate the only threat not feared by, **38.** 187

Couraud, protégé of, **18.** 125n

——, secretary to, **17.** 24n

Court frequented by, **30.** 236

—— visited by, with ease, **30.** 236

credit of, decays, **20.** 505

crocodile tears of, in HW's newspaper parody, **9.** 130

Crown livings at disposal of, **40.** 37

Cumberland, D. of, at odds with, **20.** 120

—— observed by, to have altered, **38.** 445

——'s train stepped on by, at George II's funeral, **9.** 323

—— summons, **22.** 310n

—— supports Bedford and Sandwich against, **20.** 113n

—— told by, of intrigues by Horatio Walpole (1678–1757), **19.** 474n

—— to meet with, **19.** 485n

Darlington made paymaster by, **35.** 263

death of: **23.** 70; expected, **10.** 269

Delaval's letter to, about Andover election, **43.** 276

Denbigh's appointment not opposed by, **9.** 334

dessert designed by, **20.** 126

dessert prepared by, for P. of Brunswick, **40.** 386

Dettingen battle reported to, by Harcourt and Richmond, **18.** 259n

Devonshire, D. of, leaves Bath after fall of, **22.** 96

—— replaces, as prime minister, **21.** 24

—— rumoured to be succeeded by, as first lord of Treasury, **21.** 91n

——'s fit and sister-in-law's death announced to, **38.** 419

dinner given by, **3.** 84

Dixon's miniatures acquired by, **41.** 96n

doctor's gown worn by, **9.** 321

Dowdeswell chosen by, to move land tax reduction, **22.** 487n

dukedom of, entailed on E. of Lincoln, **21.** 18, 26

Dunmore's letter from, recommending Hon. George Townshend, **36.** 7n

dupes must be re-employed by, **20.** 518

Dupplin a follower of, **21.** 74

Durand informs, of Louis XV's order to arrest Young Pretender, **20.** 35n

Egmont and Northington opposed by, at Cabinet meeting, **22.** 425n

Egmont continues to support, in Parliament, **20.** 31

—— praises Hanoverian loyalty of, **20.** 222n

——'s pamphlet attacks, **20.** 32

England's defeat hoped by, in order to blame Pitt, **38.** 75

——'s relations with France not approved by, **20.** 38n

English success attributed by HW to loss by, of absolute power, **21.** 499

English victories not ascribed to, by people, **9.** 251

(?) engrossers of power support, **35.** 216

[Pelham Holles, Thomas, *continued*]

epigram recommends Cambridge school of politics to, **38.** 30

exchange of provinces by, as secretary of state, **19.** 463

extravagance by, at elections, satirized in ballad, **18.** 82

eyeglass used by, **9.** 323

faction of: **9.** 212n, **19.** 4, **21.** 27; concerned in Regency Bill, **38.** 550; Conway calls, 'old branch,' **37.** 491; HW avoids, **37.** 581

Fane offended by letter from, **23.** 550

fear of, of doing right or doing wrong, **37.** 267

Finch informs, about Bedchamber, at Cts of Yarmouth's, **21.** 460n

followers of: not to resign, **30.** 234; oppose hostilities to Pitt, **30.** 236; weary of following, **22.** 444; will desert to George III and D. of Cumberland, **21.** 93; would find no room if Winchilsea and Fox remained, **21.** 99

folly of, complicates debate over Regency Bill, **22.** 299

footman sleeps in room with, **9.** 41

forces people to dine at Claremont, **30.** 194

Fox, Henry, advised by HW against joining, **30.** 122–3

—— allowed no scope by, **21.** 6

—— and D. of Bedford oppose, **13.** 26n

Fox, Henry, and his friends courted by, **18.** 451

Fox, Henry, contends with, for favours to protégés, **9.** 180

—— denied power by, **35.** 169

—— discourages overtures of, **22.** 91n

—— disliked by, **20.** 412, **21.** 23n

—— makes advances to, after Pelham's death, **20.** 412n

—— may receive trifle from, **21.** 91

—— might be replaced by, **38.** 134

—— offends, **21.** 17

—— persuaded by, to lead House of Commons, **20.** 502

—— proposes no cordiality to, **20.** 502

—— ridicules jealousy of, of Granville's assemblies, **18.** 562

——'s accommodation reported by, **37.** 411

——'s alliance with: **35.** 260; marred by squabbles, **20.** 516

——'s marriage disapproved by, **37.** 157

——'s negotiations with, broken off, **21.** 73

——'s promises from, regarding secretaryship of state, broken, **30.** 123

——'s rivalry with, **37.** 458

——'s rupture with, **20.** 417

——'s unpopularity terrifies, **21.** 76

—— temporarily gets the better of, **35.** 256

—— to be given paymastership by, **21.** 86n

—— to be imprisoned by, in HW's joking prophecy, **9.** 159

—— to benefit from wrong-thinking by friends of, **21.** 91n

—— unlikely to agree with, **37.** 413

—— unlikely to be conciliated by, **21.** 93

—— wishes to have the privilege of abusing, **21.** 98n

Francis I's candidacy for emperor supported by, **19.** 7n

Francis III entertained by, at Lincoln's Inn Fields, **20.** 56n

Frederick II and Elector of Cologne pressed by, to stop blocking election of K. of the Romans, **20.** 394n

Frederick II blamed by, for leaving Prussia defenceless while attacking Olmütz, **21.** 227n

Frederick, P. of Wales's adherents bribed by, **20.** 30

—— speaks to, at Carlton House, **17.** 337

French invasion feared by, **37.** 436–7, 450

French peace offers believed by, **21.** 504n

friends of, dismissed from government, **22.** 109

'frisking while his grave is digging,' **22.** 102

gazette money summoned by, **20.** 270

genealogy of, **10.** 352

geographical ignorance of, **19.** 485, **30.** 146

George II abuses Pitt and the Grenvilles to, **20.** 223

—— acquainted by, with Harcourt's and Lincoln's requests for the Garter, **20.** 73n

—— alarmed by, over fate of German treaties, **20.** 501

—— and Pitt reconciled by, **20.** 138

George II approached by, on Conway's behalf, **37.** 386

—— called on by, at Kensington, **21.** 93, 97

—— calls, 'puppy,' **18.** 535

—— charges Pitt to form ministry with, **37.** 487

—— discards Sir Robert Walpole in favour of, **40.** 88

—— discusses ambition of, with Barrington, **21.** 74n

—— discusses H. Fox with, **21.** 205n

—— dismisses, **10.** 153n

—— feels, has broken faith with him, **21.** 97, 99

—— forces Chesterfield to demand election of, as chancellor of Cambridge, **20.** 10n

—— given consent of, to be sole minister with Fox as paymaster, **21.** 92

—— gives Mansfield full powers to negotiate with, **21.** 99n

—— induced by, to discard 6 secretaries of state, **40.** 88

—— may join in suppressing opposition, **20.** 513

—— mourned by, **9.** 316

—— on distant terms with, **18.** 552

—— said to be sent to sea by, **9.** 55

——'s Cambridge orders must be justified by, **9.** 72

—— sees, while excluding Holdernesse, **20.** 346

——'s funeral attended by, **9.** 322–3

——'s interview with, at start of ministry, **35.** 169–70

——'s relations with, **21.** 76

——'s speech partly drafted by, **21.** 344n

—— tells Mansfield of displeasure with, **21.** 76n

—— tired by, **19.** 212

—— to be accompanied by, to Hanover, **20.** 39, 143

—— to be entertained by, at Claremont, **20.** 72

—— to consult, before confirming sentence on Byng, **21.** 51n

—— told by, of Mann's hint of Dashwood's treachery, **17.** 412

—— to remove, to make room for Carteret, **21.** 100n

—— transmits commands of, **9.** 71

—— wants, to resume Seals, **21.** 76

George III ascertains attitude of, to peace, **22.** 78n

—— consults, as 'oldest knight of the Garter,' **22.** 80n

—— grants less power to, than his predecessors did, **22.** 36

—— orders Conway to send dismissal to, **22.** 439n

——'s levee attended by, **9.** 321

—— to be appeased by, **21.** 76

German measures must be taken by, to regain George II's favour, **21.** 93

German war's end feared by, lest it unloose the French, **21.** 552n

Germany and Holland to be visited by, **19.** 484–5

Gisors appraises, **31.** 3n

'gives everything,' **21.** 257

godfather to Thomas Charles Townshend, **37.** 550

gold plate carried by, to Hanover, **19.** 485n

Goldsworthy probably sent Roman letter to, **19.** 226

—— recommended to protection of, **18.** 346n; **43.** 252

——'s correspondence with, **43.** 252

government members proposed by, **21.** 86n

Gower in the hands of, **20.** 258

Grafton on sickbed intruded upon by, **21.** 78–9

—— to head dependents of, **20.** 120

grandson of, might pay fortune for posterity's inventions, **37.** 293

Grantham and Hardwicke said to be recommended by, as secretaries of state, **30.** 185

Granville, Cts, distresses, by her assemblies, **18.** 562

Gray, Sir James, promised Berlin post by, **19.** 444, 453

Gray, Thomas, hopes, will check Sandwich at Cambridge, **14.** 131

Grenvilles might have Treasury headed by, **41.** 86

Grodno diet's breakup would disturb, **18.** 562

Gunnings eclipse, **20.** 260

HW always ridiculed, **39.** 530

HW and Conway invited by, to Claremont, **41.** 35–7

HW asked by, to recommend Blanshard to Hertford, **40.** 364

HW at levee of, **13.** 38, **28.** 184n

HW calls: 'Duke Trinculo,' **20.** 502; 'Lepidus,' **21.** 79; 'Lindamira,' **20.** 214n; 'Mamamouchi,' **20.** 72; 'Mazarine,' **9.** 228; 'old busy sinner,' **22.** 508; 'old simpleton,' **38.** 548; 'weathercock Duke,' **30.** 164

HW calls on, and advises Opposition's withdrawing from House, **22.** 298n

HW charges, with betraying 4 prime ministers, **19.** 463n

HW compares, with old monkey, **31.** 68–9

HW compares Duchesse de Nivernais with, **31.** 76

HW contemptuous of, **29.** 327n

HW denounces, **30.** 96

HW describes, **38.** 420

HW did not admire, **23.** 265

HW dines with, at Claremont, **38.** 418–20, 427

HW does not connect with, **10.** 111

HW does not find, at home, **30.** 26

HW drafts letter to, for Cts of Suffolk, **31.** 24, 427

HW embraced by, at D. of Cumberland's levee, and invited to eat Sussex mutton, **38.** 256

HW entertains, at breakfast at SH. **38.** 445

HW has laughed at, for 20 years, **38.** 256

HW inquires for, **30.** 175

HW invited by, to dinner, **40.** 343–4

HW jokes about bishopric for, **35.** 281

HW jokes about future grandson of, **37.** 293

HW lacks ambition of, **22.** 38

HW lacks persistence of, **22.** 570

HW listed by, among 'sure friends' in Parliament, **22.** 209n

HW may be expected to write *palinodia* on, **38.** 255–6

HW mentions, **9.** 211, **37.** 186

HW needs newer people than, to write about, **38.** 144

HW not to make plans for next reign like, **32.** 303, 306, **33.** 360

HW preferred company of George Selwyn to wisdom of, **32.** 191

HW proposes dissolution of Parliament to dissipate influence of, **21.** 98n

HW proposes plan to, about Customs House place, **40.** 145–7

HW puns on, as 'Castelnuovo,' **35.** 253

HW receives inquiries from, when ill, **35.** 331

HW recommended Ashton to, for Lancashire living, **40.** 39

HW's appearance at Court may astonish, **9.** 305

[Pelham Holles, Thomas, *continued*]

HW's contempt for, justified by Melcombe's diary, **25.** 503, **33.** 440

HW's correspondence with, **13.** 38, **40.** 145–7, 343–4, 361–4, **41.** 35–7

HW's letter to Rockingham forwarded to, **22.** 395n

HW's reception by, pleases Hertford, **38.** 427

HW's verses attack, **21.** 7n

HW's witticism about God not taking the word of, **37.** 550

HW taken around garden by, in one-horse chair, **38.** 419

HW to be called on by, at SH, **40.** 361–4

HW to call on, at Claremont, **40.** 343–4, 362–4

HW wishes, would order him to send for Lincoln for King's Birthday, **30.** 28

HW witnesses reception by, of news of sister-in-law's death, **30.** 175

Habeas Corpus extension racks, **37.** 527

—— revision opposed by, **21.** 182n

Halifax may succeed, as secretary of state, **9.** 159

—— negotiates with, to defeat Bubb Dodington's plans, **39.** 412n

—— rejects Chesterfield's proposal of meeting with, **21.** 111n

—— resents broken promise by, of secretary-ship of state, **30.** 135n

Halland owned by, **10.** 287n

—— scene of auction of effects of, **10.** 287

Hanoverian and noblemen's regiments rejected by, **37.** 452

Hanoverian troop proposal to be considered by, **37.** 452

'Hanoverizes,' **22.** 39

Hanover left by, for England, **20.** 201n

—— to be visited by, **19.** 484–5, 490, **20.** 39, 143

—— visited by, **9.** 71, **30.** 320

Harcourt a creature of, **20.** 246

—— told by, that Bp Hayter must be dismissed, **20.** 343

Hardinge, Mrs, makes witticism about George III's choice of, **21.** 460

Hardwicke advises, to urge Regency provision on George II, **20.** 239n

—— asks, to put Anson into Privy Council, **20.** 135n

—— prevents, from joining Fox, **21.** 87

——'s alliance with, may cause trouble, **22.** 107

—— suggested by, as lord privy seal, **21.** 541n

—— to succeed, as High Steward of Cambridge, **20.** 19

—— upheld by, at rebels' trial, **19.** 286

Harrington and Holdernesse abandon George II's favour, in order to please, **21.** 100

Harrington and Pelham attacked by, **26.** 10

Harrington corresponds with, about French invasion, **19.** 78n

—— disagrees with, about orders to be sent to Sandwich, **19.** 326n

—— may quarrel with, **19.** 326

Hartington notifies decision to, **37.** 398n

—— reveals broken promises of, **30.** 123n

——'s policy deemed by, a concession to Boyle, **37.** 398n

health of: out of danger, **22.** 579; stroke of the palsy, **10.** 269, **23.** 70; teeth gone, **9.** 363

Hertford asks for news of, **38.** 184

—— not treated with political friendship by, **38.** 424

——'s indifference to, **38.** 329–30

Hervey hated by, **17.** 430

Hervey, Bns, detests, **31.** 83

Hesse, P. of, dines with, **19.** 265n

Holdernesse deserts, for Pitt, **9.** 341

——'s dismissal pleases, **30.** 162

——'s fall outwardly lamented by, **9.** 341

Holland not soon to be visited by, **19.** 484–5

hopes to be minister for 30 or 40 years more, **38.** 75, 173

house of, in Lincoln's Inn Fields, **10.** 281

House of Commons devoted to, **21.** 11

House of Lords formerly subservient to, **22.** 209–10

Hume, Bp, in household of, **30.** 2n

Hume Campbell retained by, to abuse Pitt and perhaps Fox, **35.** 262

Hussey Montagu accompanies, at Bedfords' ball, **9.** 232

impropriety of return of, to St James's, **30.** 196

incompetence of, **30.** 96, 141

indecision of, **9.** 178

Indemnity Bill opposition led by, **17.** 436n

in political minority, **10.** 111

intrigues of, **22.** 566–7

invasion threats frighten, **35.** 255

Jackson hopes to get Leghorn post through, **17.** 218, 409, 430

—— proposes letter of thanks to, from Leghorn merchants, **17.** 260

Jones secretary to, **21.** 26

(?) journal of trip to Hanover by, **28.** 165

Karl Wilhelm Ferdinand presented to wife of, at Newcastle House, **38.** 290–1

—— writes to, **38.** 287

Keene receives information from, **19.** 306n

—— the tool of, at Cambridge, **20.** 346

kisses hands as prime minister, **35.** 169

knight of the Garter, **10.** 29

Law arrives on *Spence* with letters for, **17.** 71n

Lee, Sir George, courted by, **20.** 245

—— wanted by, for Exchequer, **21.** 92n

Legge avenges coldness from, **35.** 253

—— complains about, **20.** 453n

—— courts, **19.** 458

—— frowned upon by, though formerly his protégé, **20.** 493

—— replaced by, in Treasury, **21.** 103

Leicester's witticism to, at rebels' trial, **19.** 286

Letter from the Cocoa Tree abuses, **22.** 102n
letters against, **42.** 505
letter to, **9.** 367n
Letter to Two Great Men refers to, **9.** 270n
levee of, **10.** 32, 35, **13.** 38, **20.** 20, **22.** 37
Lincoln, E. of, advised by, to return home, **17.** 41n, **30.** 13n
—— calls, 'factious old fool,' **30.** 178
—— favourite nephew and heir of, **30.** 178
—— forced to resign and go into Opposition by, **30.** 178
—— informs, of love for Lady Sophia Fermor, **30.** 6n
—— liked by, **17.** 210
—— pleases, **30.** 31
—— resentful at not receiving places from, **30.** 179
—— 's ingratitude to, **30.** 178
—— 's love for Lady Sophia Fermor might be mentioned by, **30.** 24
—— 's marriage to niece of, disconcerting, **43.** 250
—— takes message to P. of Wales from, promising to support him when king, **30.** 178
—— to inherit property of, **18.** 245
London approves of, **20.** 493
lord privy seal's post of, aided by Secker for clerical patronage, **22.** 324n
Lyttelton preferred by, after Legge and Treasury lords fail, **40.** 88
—— 's overture to Bedford disclaimed by, **35.** 194–5
Mann advises Townshend to write to, **19.** 375
—— asked by, for information about Young Pretender, **17.** 159, 160, 203
—— delays writing to, **17.** 265, **18.** 374
—— directed to send dispatches to, **17.** 113n
—— doubtful about his favour with, **18.** 115–16, **19.** 383–4
—— encloses letter to, **19.** 99
—— fails to understand how Treasury can be headed by, **20.** 422
—— informs, of Young Pretender's departure, **18.** 375, 376, 380
—— in letter to, contradicts *London Gazette*'s report, **18.** 205–6
—— kept waiting for credentials by servants of, **17.** 24
—— may benefit from Lincoln's influence with, **17.** 373n
—— may send HW's coffee-pot to, **18.** 115–16, 137
—— ordered by, to send duplicate dispatches to Hanover, **18.** 229
—— prepares, to expect few letters, **17.** 97
—— 's baronetcy delayed by, **20.** 458, 467
—— scolded by, for not asking for salary until too late, **21.** 483
—— 's correspondence with, **17.** 97, 203, 311, 315, 341, 369, **18.** 93n, 174n, 190, 272n, 328n, 374, 375, 376, 379, 380, 392, 411, 412, 420, 488, 516–17, 557, **19.** 56, 99, 158, 474, **20.** 195, 467, **21.** 483
—— 's dispatch to, predicts Young Pretender's departure from Rome, **17.** 315n
—— seeks salary arrears from, **18.** 516–17, **19.** 56, 338, 474, **20.** 195–6, 467, **21.** 483
—— sends Benedict XIV's speech to, **19.** 422
—— sends Charles of Naples's manifesto to, **18.** 420
—— sends duplicates of dispatches for, to HW, **18.** 488
—— sends duplicates of his letters to, **17.** 311
—— sends list of Electress's jewels to, **17.** 266n, **43.** 241
—— sends medals to, **17.** 19n, 218
—— 's information sent to, about Young Pretender's being impersonated in Scotland: **19.** 141, 198; discussed with Horatio Walpole (1678–1757), **19.** 172
—— 's inquiries about Theodore of Corsica unanswered by, **18.** 205
—— surprised at news about, **17.** 361, **18.** 557, **21.** 106
—— thinks of seeing, in Hanover, **20.** 151
—— told by, to assure Francis I of continued English support, **18.** 557
—— told by HW and Galfridus Mann not to give presents to, **18.** 137, 151–2
—— to send Roman account of rebels' successes to, **19.** 158
—— wants Sir Robert Walpole to write to, **18.** 517
—— wonders how his conduct impresses, **17.** 119
—— would like hint conveyed to, about measures in case of his recall from Tuscany, **21.** 115
Mann, Edward Louisa, writes to, about Mann baronetcy, **20.** 459n
Manners family intimidates, into substituting Rutland for Gower, **20.** 418
Maria Theresa's difficulties told to Hardwicke by, **17.** 144n
Marius compared with, **10.** 192
marriage contract of Ps Mary read by, **37.** 61n
Mason's attitude towards, **29.** 67
Mathews displeased by, **18.** 346, 361
may be lord treasurer, **20.** 412
may end at head of mob, **38.** 183
may hope to return to power under George IV, **22.** 442
Michell delivers pamphlet to, **20.** 348n
—— receives refutation of Prussian claims from, **20.** 348n
minister for 20 years, **30.** 96
ministry excludes, **9.** 202
ministry may be quitted by, **37.** 478
Mirepoix complains of being overreached by, **35.** 240
Mitchell election shows allegiance of Tories to, **35.** 216

[Pelham Holles, Thomas, *continued*]

Montagu calls, 'King of Clare Market,' 9. 333

—— cousin of, 9. 199, 333, 10. 352

—— thinks Beaufort abler than, 9. 333

—— wants effects from auction of, 10. 281

Montfort asks, for lucrative posts, 35. 201

Morley agent for, in behalf of Lord Middlesex, 17. 400n

most promotions owing to, 30. 196

Murray (E. of Mansfield) cannot be spared by, from House of Commons, 20. 557

—— examined before, 19. 288n, 391n

—— refuses to stay in House of Commons to aid, 20. 558n

—— upheld by, against Pratt, 21. 205

mushroom beds at Claremont ordered destroyed by, 31. 10–11

nation's infatuation for, disillusioned, 35. 253

Navy Bill support sought by, 21. 182n

nephew of, 35. 199n

Newcastle House left by, from fear of contagious sore throats, 21. 312–13

New England governor's report to, of galleon's capture, 37. 246n

new ministers entertained by, at Claremont, 17. 503, 18. 20

niece and brother of, 12. 5n

niece's marriage to Lincoln to please, 18. 277

Nivernais entertained by, 10. 72

Nivernais, Duchesse de, resembles, 30. 214, 39. 215

northern province of state department coveted by, 19. 326

Northington abuses, 22. 109

Nottingham Castle of, resembles him in promising much but containing little, 35. 278

Nugent flatters, 20. 454n

——'s appointment as commissioner of the Treasury arranged by, 20. 425n

office refused by, 30. 185

office-seekers and clergy patronized by, 22. 323–4

office under George III coveted by, 30. 178

old age of, degrading, 9. 348

Old Coachman, The, mentions, 18. 20

Old Pretender's resignation of pretensions reported to, by Mann, 17. 19n

Onslow gets battle reports from, 30. 156n

—— may be taken by, to SH, 40. 361

—— notifies, of death of Ds of Leeds, 38. 419

Opposition expected by, to blame him for loss of Minorca, 20. 578n

—— joined by, 22. 98

—— may be chastised by, 20. 513

—— not to be joined by, 22. 464

—— of, has majority, 38. 529

——'s voting interpreted by, as presaging his political return, 38. 261

Orange, P. of, urged by, to carry on the war against France, 19. 403n

Orford, 3d E. of, told by, of intended resignation, 30. 128

Osorio to write to, about disloyal English officer, 19. 147

Oswald and Bute believe Leicester House will come to terms with, 21. 75n

overshoots himself, 20. 259

Oxford's appointment not announced to, 9. 328–9

Parliamentary activity of, on Regency Bill, 38. 542, 543, 548, 550, 553

Parliamentary report opposed by, 35. 216

Parliamentary speech by: 9. 31; on Habeas Corpus, 37. 529

Parliamentary voting avoided by, 22. 508

Parliamentary voting by, on Poor Bill, 38. 529

Parliament's dissolution opposed by, 19. 412n

——'s dissolution would dissipate influence of, 37. 487

—— will desert, 21. 93

party of, lies quiet, 21. 34

peerage granted to, 10. 27, 22. 32

Pelham arouses jealousy of, 17. 430

—— attacked by, 26. 10

—— converses with, 9. 12

—— might warn, not to trust Richecourt's insinuations against Mann, 18. 363

—— pensioner of, 9. 417n

—— succeeded by, 14. 8on

Pelham, Thomas, leaves Hanover for England with, 20. 195n

—— should produce heir to, 20. 116

—— to approach, about Mann's arrears, 20. 151, 173, 195

—— visits, at Hanover, 20. 195n

'Pillars of State' satirizes, 35. 28on

Piozzi, Mrs, comments upon, 9. 316n, 323n

Pitt (Chatham) and friends to avoid provoking, 21. 77

Pitt (Chatham) and H. Fox contend over, 21. 79

Pitt (Chatham) and H. Fox fail to terrify, 20. 454

Pitt (Chatham) and Legge oppose, 20. 509

Pitt (Chatham) and Leicester House supposedly engaged with, 21. 98n

Pitt (Chatham) asks, not to meddle in House of Commons or state department, but stick to Treasury, 21. 91

—— attacks: 22. 395, 37. 416; in House of Commons on Minorca, 20. 554n; in Parliamentary speeches, 35. 194

—— blames, for Treasury's mismanagement, 21. 290n

—— breaks with, 20. 453

—— charged by, with fiscal irresponsibility, 21. 290n

—— complimented by, 22. 207n, 208n

—— confers with: 21. 97, 22. 160; at Royston's house, 21. 92n

—— connection denied by, 21. 74

—— content to manage war under, 21. 448

—— demands exclusion of, **21**. 11

—— dismissed for opposition to, **14**. 88n

—— expected by, to attack him over land tax, **22**. 494n

—— given overtures from, **21**. 23

—— may be betrayed by, **9**. 232

—— might join, to oust Bute, **22**. 102n

—— needs support of, **9**. 202

—— negotiates with, to regain Halifax for Board of Trade, **21**. 111n

—— not chosen by, for colleague, **20**. 248

—— object of protest by, **22**. 471n

—— praises, **20**. 222

—— preferred by, to H. Fox, **21**. 6n

—— proposes government posts for, **22**. 161

—— refuses to join, **22**. 78

——'s administration not to include, **10**. 222

—— said to reject overtures of, **22**. 93

——'s appointments opposed by, **22**. 442

——'s coalition with, **9**. 205n, **21**. 103–4

——'s demands rejected by, and conferences broken off, **21**. 91, 92

—— seeks support of, for Habeas Corpus Bill, **21**. 205n

——'s friends want union with, **21**. 87

——'s ministry proposed to include, **22**. 302n

——'s rapprochement with, **37**. 485n

——'s refusal to serve with, would cause his resignation, **21**. 6n

——'s relations with, discussed by George II and Holdernesse, **21**. 74n

——'s rumoured rupture with, **9**. 210

——'s sneering remark about his union with, **30**. 136

——'s Spanish War proposal opposed by, **38**. 131n

—— supports, against Sandwich and the Bedfords, **20**. 222

—— unlikely to get along with, **21**. 99–100

—— upsets power of, **20**. 230

Pitt faction mutinous against, **20**. 248

Pitt faction not to provoke, **21**. 77

Pitt-Fox coalition might sacrifice, **20**. 557n

plate of, in pawn, **19**. 485n

plate tax's loss feared by, **37**. 451

policy of, becomes very military, **19**. 464

political secrets kept from, **30**. 246

political situation in 1765 like that of era of, **22**. 303

politics said to be renounced by, **22**. 579, **23**. 70

Portland urged by, not to resign, **22**. 442n

Port Mahon officers' list discussed by, in House of Lords, **17**. 300

Portsmouth approached by, to favour Delaval in Andover election, **21**. 484n

——'s correspondence with, **43**. 276

Portuguese subsidy advocated by, **22**. 31n

Pratt (Camden)'s rift with, **21**. 205

predicted as sole minister, **9**. 210

pretends to be willing to retire, **21**. 448

Prevereau in office of, **17**. 98

previous dukes of Newcastle as foolish-looking as, **35**. 271

prime minister, **9**. 159, **14**. 87–8, **35**. 183

prime minister's post may go to, **35**. 165, 168

private resentment should be stifled by, **21**. 28

privy seal, but not lord presidency, would be accepted by, **30**. 185n

promises frequently broken by, **30**. 207

proposes himself as first lord of the Treasury, **21**. 86n

Pulteney (E. of Bath) parodies speech of, to Regency, in ballad, **19**. 106

—— recommends Pearce to, for Peterborough bishopric, **43**. 251

——'s and Gower's letters to, **18**. 89n

—— will break with Carteret sooner than with, **18**. 328n

pusillanimity abandoned by, **20**. 483

Regency Bill of 1751 the work of, **38**. 542

regent, **18**. 209n

'regicide-descent' of, mentioned in verses, **30**. 126

regulations instituted by, **28**. 73n

resignation of, as prime minister, **21**. 11, 17, **22**. 36, **43**. 119

resignation of, expected, **38**. 156

resignation proposed by, **9**. 199, 316, 328, **10**. 32

resigns as secretary of state, **19**. 211

Richecourt's attempts to oust Mann would not please, **18**. 363

——'s brother negotiates with, at Hanover, over Joseph II's election, **20**. 178n

Richmond, D. of, may influence, against Mann, **17**. 334

—— rumoured to be succeeded by, as Master of the Horse, **17**. 330n

Richmonds friendly with, **18**. 451

Rinking's letter to, about Sir C. H. Williams, **43**. 274

rivalry between P. of Wales and, **13**. 18n

Robinson, Sir Thomas, favoured by, for secretary of state, **20**. 202n

Rochefort expedition planned by, **21**. 117n

Rockingham made political heir of, **22**. 579n

Rockingham ministry displeases, **30**. 196

Rockingham ministry's resignation delayed by, **22**. 432

Rutland substituted for Gower by, **20**. 418

—— wanted by, as Master of the Horse, **20**. 183

Sackville's sentence not notified to, until after delay, **21**. 384n

sacrifices all, to jealousy and ambition, **18**. 535, 537

St-Germain's retort to, **26**. 20, 21

Sainthill and Cholwick recommended by, to Mann, **17**. 483

Sandwich asks, for Paris embassy, **20**. 29n

—— not admitted by, to full reconciliation, **20**. 120n

[Pelham Holles, Thomas, *continued*]
—— opposed by: **20.** 120, 222; over Wilkes, in House of Lords, **38.** 293
—— receives instructions from, about negotiations, **19.** 289n, 448n
——'s conduct at Aix-la-Chapelle makes irreconcilable breach with, **20.** 120n
——'s dismissal by, **9.** 115
Seaforth election disturbed by, **19.** 449
Secker plies, with smelling-bottle, **9.** 323
Selwyn, Brand, and HW deride, in stage whispers, **9.** 233
Selwyn jokes about faction of, **9.** 202
—— jokes about unpopularity of, **10.** 35
Shaw physician to, **31.** 10n
——'s dosing Bute would make, jealous, **38.** 83
Shebbeare's letter to, **21.** 87
Shelley nephew of, **20.** 26
——'s preferment regarded by, as insult, **22.** 471n
sheriffs' controversy with, about Lovat's head, **37.** 267
ship brings news from West Indies, to, **37.** 246
sister of, **9.** 196n, **11.** 55n, **34.** 258
Smithson carries letter of, on Hertford's behalf to George II, **20.** 12n
smugglers and, **35.** 141
Somerset succeeded by, as chancellor of Cambridge, **20.** 9–10
Stanley dines with, at Claremont, **31.** 11
Stone, Andrew, consulted by, **19.** 347
—— secretary to, **17.** 6, 24n, **18.** 137n, **19.** 347n, **23.** 538n
Stone, George, brother of favourite of, **20.** 505
Stosch might have written to, about Mann's illness, **17.** 51
—— reports to, on D. of Modena, **18.** 238n
stronger than ever, **20.** 510
Suffolk, Cts of, wants, to make Morton master of Charterhouse, **31.** 427
supporters of, may overturn him, **19.** 6
Sussex men kissed by, at army review, **19.** 495
Sussex post might be begged by, **21.** 499
Taaffe attends, at Lewes races, **20.** 289
Tabuerniga employed by, to report on Leicester House, **17.** 277n
—— reports to, on P. of Wales's intention to form party against Pelhams, **19.** 360n
Talbot advises, on Pitt's resignation, **21.** 540
——'s witticism about, **22.** 79
Theodore of Corsica claims that aid was promised him by, **18.** 188
——'s speculations told to, **18.** 234
Thompson forwards Mann's packet to, **18.** 397
Tories abused by court of, **9.** 329
—— given positions by, **9.** 129
Townshend, Charles, makes witticism about, **35.** 93
Townshend, George, and Tories do not push Port Mahon investigation for fear of reuniting, with H. Fox, **21.** 56

Townshend, George, caricatures, **37.** 444
—— slighted by, **30.** 193n
transport hired by, to hold his travelling furniture, **19.** 484
'treachery' of, **30.** 164
Treasury post taken by, **20.** 417, 422
—— to be headed by, **35.** 168
Trevor, Bp, given Durham bishopric by, over George II's objections, **20.** 323n
Trevor, John, related to, **17.** 366
Turner the London steward of, **40.** 343n
Twickenham Park to be occupied by widow after death of, **31.** 123
'Uncle Thomson's' epitaph would suit, **37.** 568
unintelligible, **37.** 529
Vane paid by, to cut off entail of Newcastle estate, **17.** 209–10
venison procured by, from New Park, **17.** 506
Vernon appeals to, for Wentworth's recall, **18.** 143n
—— publishes letters from, **19.** 459n
——'s letter to, **17.** 76n
verses attack, **30.** 126
Villettes in good standing with, **19.** 431n
Villiers's name replaced by Keith's by, for Vienna post, **20.** 16n
Violette's performances concern the politics of, **20.** 74n
vote lost through ill-treatment by, **17.** 243
Waldegrave said to be favourite of, **20.** 505
Walpole, Horatio (1678–1757), accuses, of obstructing Mann's appointment, **43.** 233
—— approaches, about Mann's salary arrears, **19.** 474
—— asks, to stifle rumour of sham Young Pretender, **19.** 174, 199
—— attacks, **19.** 474n
—— informed by, of George II's intention of making him a peer, **21.** 56n
Walpole, Sir Robert, arouses jealousy of, **18.** 535
—— dissatisfies, **17.** 301n
—— gets support from, for friends, **17.** 336n
—— hears complaints of, about HW's attending Granvilles' assembly, **18.** 562
—— kept ignorant of foreign affairs by, **18.** 30
—— makes witticisms about dinner guests of, **17.** 506
—— receives Dettingen news from, **18.** 258
—— said to have been betrayed by, **18.** 82
——'s successor as prime minister not known to, **40.** 48
—— supposedly friend of, **9.** 348
war's continuation supported by, **30.** 109n
war's end reminds, of end of Q. Anne's reign, **38.** 173
Westmorland arouses jealousy of, **9.** 321
West to be given post as sop to, **30.** 196n
'whets his busy blunted sting,' **22.** 505

White, M. P. for East Redford in time of, **29.** 354

wife frightened by, with account of D. of Grafton, **21.** 79

wife of, **9.** 40n

wife's illness delays, at Dover, **20.** 201n

wife's illness forces, to cancel party for Fuentes family, **21.** 417n

Williams, Sir C. H., listed by, for appointment to Turin, **19.** 456n

——'s candidacy for K.B. opposed by, **18.** 451

—— writes much-admired letter to, on Poland, **30.** 320

Winchester bishopric jokingly suggested for, **9.** 209

wishes to succeed Somerset as chancellor of Cambridge, **14.** 21n

witticism on George III's being the only surviving member of government brought in by, **22.** 110

yacht of, **19.** 484

Yarmouth, Cts of, tells, of Leicester House's confidence in Sackville, **21.** 387n

Yonge consults, about cider counties' opposition, **38.** 459n

York, D. of, buys Oatlands from, **12.** 11n

Yorke, Charles, dislikes preference of, for Pitt, in privilege dispute, **38.** 285

Yorke, Sir Joseph, offends, by not writing him since retirement, **38.** 420

Young Pretender's declaration burnt by order of, at Royal Exchange, **19.** 161

—— would probably be entertained by, **30.** 91

Pelham Manor, N. Y.:
British land at, **24.** 268n

Pelican; pelicans (bird):
Montagu's term for himself, **10.** 197

Pelican; pelicans (artillery shot):
Guise, at Cartagena, says, would make a pelican pie, **17.** 485, **20.** 450

Pelion:
Parliament of Paris relieved of, **23.** 265

Pelisse; pelisses:
of blue fox, sent to Mme du Deffand by Shuvalov, **7.** 72, 80–1

Pella:
coffee-houses of, **32.** 388

Pellam, J.:
Joan, Q., committed to custody of, **42.** 218n

Pellatt, William (living 1797), attorney:
Beddington occupied by, **28.** 456

Pellegrini, Antonio (1674–1741) of Padua; painter:
Cowdray staircase painted by, **41.** 105n
paintings of story of Phaeton by, in hall at Castle Howard, **30.** 258

Pellegrini, Ignazio (b. ca 1716, d. after 1777), army officer:
Pitti palace altered by, **22.** 258–9, 291

Pellegrino, Bolognese inn:
Borsini keeps, **22.** 232n

Pellepore. See La Fite de Pellepore

Pelletier. See Le Peletier; Le Pelletier

Pellew, Sir Edward (1757–1833), Kt, 1793; cr. (1796) Bt, (1814) Bn, and (1816) Vct Exmouth; M.P.:
biographical information about, corrected, **43.** 153
ships taken by, **12.** 81n

Pellew. See also Bellew

Pell Office Exchequer:
Roberts of, copies D. of Gloucester's letter, **36.** 306n

Pells:
Vilett may get clerkship of, **36.** 90
See also Clerk of the Pells

Pélopides, Les. See under Voltaire

Peloponnesus. See Morea

Pemberton, Henry (d. 1741), Fellow of St Catherine's, Cambridge:
verses by, **13.** 145–6

Pemberton, Jeremiah or Christopher, Cole's friend:
Cole calls on, **1.** 287, 288

Pemberton family:
Knight buys Milton manor from, **1.** 267n

Pemble, Mrs:
SH visited by, **12.** 229

Pembroke, Cts of. See Beauclerk, Elizabeth (ca 1767–93); Clifford, Anne (1590–1676); Devereux, Anne (fl. 1455–86); Fitzwilliam, Hon. Mary (1707–69); Howe, Hon. Mary (d. 1749); Penancoët de Keroualle, Henriette-Mauricette de (ca 1649–1728); Sidney, Mary (1561–1621); Slingsby, Barbara (ca 1669–1721); Spencer, Lady Elizabeth (1737–1831); Talbot, Mary (d. 1650); Vere, Susan de (1587–1629)

Pembroke, E. of. See Hastings, Laurence de (1320–48); Herbert, George Augustus (1759–1827); Herbert, Henry (ca 1538–1601); Herbert, Henry (ca 1689–1750); Herbert, Henry (1734–94); Herbert, Philip (1584–1650); Herbert, Thomas (ca 1656–1733); Herbert, William (ca 1506–70); Herbert, William (1580–1630); Marshal, William (ca 1146–1219); Tudor, Jasper (ca 1430–95); Valence, Aymer de (ca 1270–1324)

'Pembroke, le petit.' See Herbert, George Augustus

Pembroke, Mr:
SH visited by, **12.** 249

Pembroke, English ship:
arrival of, in England, **18.** 267
at Leghorn, **17.** 455
at Port Mahon, **17.** 285
HW's pictures listed in quarantine orders of, **18.** 282n
HW's shipment goes by, **18.** 196n, 214–15, 234, 250
Lee captain of, **18.** 234
quarantine might be performed by, **18.** 275, 282

Pembroke and Montgomery, E. and Cts of. *See* Pembroke

Pembroke College, Cambridge:
Brown will leave Gray's portrait to, 1. 238, 2. 171n
chapel at: HW prefers Westminster Abbey to, for Gray's monument, 28. 276; Long's and Gray's funerals in, 1. 231–2
electioneering at, 14. 89–92
Gray's removal to, 28. 159
HW to give book to, 28. 27
Mason at, 28. 73
Meeke a fellow of, 10. 105
portrait of Bp Felton at, 1. 19
Tories at, 13. 58

Pembroke Hall. *See* Pembroke College

Pembrokeshire:
Picton Castle in, 19. 310n

'Pen, Lady.' *See* Barry, Lady Penelope

Pen (surname). *See* Penn

Pen; pens:
enshrinement desirable for Hannah More's, 31. 398
HW borrows, from governor of Radicofani, 37. 67, 73
HW furnishes, 9. 117n
HW's: 'old scribbling' and 'subject to babble,' 42. 287; shared with Gray, 43. 392
HW's French, abominable, 31. 63
HW to continue to write as wind sets in, 39. 12
HW to send, to Mme Galli, 17. 193
HW uses Miss Hotham's, 40. 363
hard-nibbed, 2. 70
Lyttelton, Bns, has, which always needs mending, 42. 466
Mann can hardly hold, because of bitter cold, 22. 385
quills for, 40. 48
scarce, at Ghent, 37. 119
Sévigné, Mme de, has cabinet for, 33. 150
—— has old man mend, 33. 150

Penance:
one station's luxury is another's, 37. 172

Penancoët de Kéroualle, Henriette-Mauricette de (ca 1649–1728), m. 1 (1675) Philip Herbert, 7th E. of Pembroke; m. 2 (1685) Jean-Timoléon Gouffier, Marquis de Thois:
name of, corrected, 43. 90, 111
second marriage of, 4. 299

Penancoët de Kéroualle, Louise-Renée de (1649–1734), cr. (1673) Ds of Portsmouth; Charles II's mistress:
Aubigny, duchy of, 4. 417–18, 423, 424, 43. 363
biographical information about, corrected, 43. 90, 111
Charles II's mistress, 15. 158n
Dixon's portrait of, 41. 97
granddaughter of, 9. 307n
Hamilton, Lady Archibald, contrasted with, 9. 16
—— to accompany, in death, 35. 68

'laundress' of, 37. 353
Louis XIV gives Aubigny to, 4. 287n, 40. 28n
marriage of sister of, 4. 299
medal of, 16. 301, (?)317
meeting of, with other royal mistresses at Windsor, 33. 528–9, 34. 260
Rochester accuses, of having bad breath, 7. 355
Villette, Marquise de, tells anecdote of, 7. 354–5
Wren's designs for St Paul's rejected by influence of, 40. 353
Yarmouth, Cts of, a successor to, 20. 90

Penancoët de Kéroualle ('Querouaille') family:
alliances of, 4. 299

Penaro. *See* Panaro

Penates:
HW's, in Berkeley Sq., 42. 202

Penautier. *See* Reich de Pennautier

Penbedw, Flintshire:
Digby miniatures found at, 41. 253n

Pen-box ('*pennino*'):
set with brilliants, 17. 64–5

Pencester, Sir Stephen de (d. 1299), warden of the Cinque Ports:
tomb of, at Penshurst, 35. 142

Penchester. *See* Pencester

Pencil; pencils:
card written with, 42. 83
Choiseul, Duchesse de, wants, from HW, 7. 144, 146, 152, 154
HW inserts words in, in blank place, 24. 209
HW sends, to Mme du Deffand, 3. 404, 4. 5, 10, 19, 5. 145, 172
price of, 31. 400
seldom apparent in Jamesone's paintings, 40. 264
silver, 17. 194

Pendarves, Mrs Alexander. *See* Granville, Mary

Pendennis Castle, Cornwall:
Barrell governor of, 19. 248n

Pender, Francis, Commander:
Dutch colonies captured by, 25. 145n

Penderel, Humphrey:
(?) HW mentions house of, 10. 105

Penderel, Richard (d. 1672), royalist:
(?) house of, 10. 105
print of, 1. 197

Pendergass. *See* Prendergast

Pendrell. *See* Penderel

Penelope. *See under* Galuppi, Baldassare; Rolli, Paolo Antonio

Penelope:
HW to imitate patience of, 23. 365
Lyttelton describes his first wife under name of, 21. 409
web of HW's health unravelled like, 24. 148

Penet, Peter (d. ca 1827), of Nantes:
Franklin accompanied by, 6. 383

Penicuik House, Midlothian:
ceiling paintings at, 15. 189n

Penkethman. *See* Pinkethman

Penknife; penknives:
  Crowe's suicide with, **20.** 1n
  HW furnishes, **9.** 117n
  HW wants, **40.** 308
  names carved by, on window, **34.** 7
Penmaenmaur, mountain:
  imitations of, recommended by Girardin for gardens. **29.** 283
Penn, Granville (1761–1844), writer:
  SH visited by, **12.** 246
Penn, John (1760–1834), writer:
  Florence visited by, **11.** 159, 243
  letters from England received by, **11.** 159, 162
  Penn, Lady Juliana, receives letter from, **11.** 243
  Penn family estates valued by, **34.** 14n
Penn, Lady Juliana. *See* Fermor, Lady Juliana
Penn, Richard (?1734–1811), colonist; M.P.:
  birth date of, corrected, **43.** 377
  Congress's petition said to be brought by, **39.** 253n
  Mann wants to know about mediation attempts of, in America, **24.** 128
  SH visited by, **12.** 242
Penn, Mrs Richard. *See* Masters, Mary
Penn, Sophia Margaret (1764–1847), m. (1796) Hon. William Stuart, Bp of St Davids 1793–1800; Abp of Armagh 1800–22:
  Boyle Walsingham, Mrs, entertains, at dinner, **11.** 41
  Florentine news reported by, **11.** 159
  HW sees letter to, from Paris, **11.** 36–7
  Richmond visited by, **11.** 148
  Stuart Mackenzie, Lady Elizabeth, visited by, **11.** 124
Penn, Thomas (1702–75):
  Fermor, Lady Juliana, marries, **19.** 565n, **20.** 97, 248
  Pennsylvania's 'sovereign,' **20.** 248
  pistol wounds, in post-chaise accident, **20.** 248
  wife of, **3.** 184n, **11.** 7n, **30.** 328n
Penn, William (1703–47), Quaker:
  converted to Quakerism, **20.** 20n
  wife of, **20.** 20
Penn, Mrs William. *See* Vaux, Ann
Pennacchi da Trevigi, Girolamo (1497–1544), painter and sculptor:
  Gray sends name of, to HW, **14.** 117
Pennant, Mrs:
  HW mentions, **12.** 190
Pennant, Arabella (d. 1828), m. Edward Hanmer:
  struck out of aunt's will, **2.** 266
Pennant, Catharine (1729–97):
  generous to her brother, **2.** 266, 267
Pennant, Richard (d. 1808), cr. (1783) Bn Penrhyn; M.P.:
  peerage of, **25.** 433
Pennant, Thomas (1726–98), traveller, naturalist, and writer:
  Backwell's portrait seen by, **10.** 301n
  British Zoology by, **1.** 330n
  Bull's correspondence with, **43.** 60

Cole corresponds with, **2.** 20–1, 42–3, 247, 322
—— receives prints and drawing from, **2.** 42–3, 77
—— receives prints from, **2.** 167, 191
——'s help acknowledged by, **2.** 270, 271
comes into wealth, **2.** 265–6, 267
daughter of, **2.** 266
does not lose by his works, **2.** 265–6
Genera of Birds by, **1.** 330n
Granger's correspondence with, **43.** 60
HW congratulates, on forthcoming volume, **41.** 444
HW does not know first name of, **41.** 250
HW expected to receive Nash's prints from, **43.** 384
HW receives print from, **2.** 170
HW's correspondence with, **41.** 250–4, 394–5, 442–6, **42.** 16–17, 19–21, 37–9, 198–9, 214–17, 234–6, 238–41, 278–9, **43.** 384
HW sends coin to, and will send print, **42.** 278–9
HW's opinion of, **1.** 328–30, **2.** 20, 245, 259, 328, **43.** 60
HW talks with, **34.** 121
health of, influenza, **42.** 17
high sheriff of Flintshire, **2.** 330
History of Quadrupeds by, **2.** 191
Johnson ridicules, for credulity, **32.** 225
Journey from Chester to London, The, by: **2.** 191, 323, 325–6, **41.** 251n, 395; anticipates HW's account of pictures at Woburn Abbey, **34.** 121–3; HW thanks Pennant for, **42.** 16; mistakes in, **34.** 122
Journey to Snowdon, The, by, **2.** 265n, 270, 271
Literary Life of the Late Thomas Pennant by, **41.** 394n, **43.** 384n
miniature of himself shown by, to HW, **41.** 394
Myddelton may have told, of his gift to HW of a painting, **42.** 215
oddities of, **15.** 332
Of London by: **43.** 143; errors in, **11.** 93–4; HW's contributions to, **11.** 93, **42.** 199n; story of 'White Widow' in, **28.** 388n
Of the Patagonians by: based on Father Falkener's relation, **42.** 214; HW thanks Pennant for, **42.** 214
portrait of, **2.** 191, 203
print by, of Rembrandt's mother, **42.** 12–13
print of Cts of Desmond said to be owned by, **1.** 329, 332, 339
print of himself sent by, to HW, **41.** 394
punctiliousness of, **2.** 170
reported to be deranged, **2.** 256, 259, 265, 267
rumour of knighthood for, **2.** 330
sister of, **2.** 266
SH visitor sent by, **12.** 243
Tollemache's portrait seen by, in Scotland, **16.** 285
Tour from Downing to Alston-Moor by, **41.** 250n
Tour in North Wales by, **28.** 381

[Pennant, Thomas, *continued*]
  Tour in Scotland, 1769, by, **1**. 329, 336
  Tour in Scotland and Voyage to the Hebrides,
  A, by, **1**. 328–9, 332, 334, 336, **2**. 20
  Tour in Wales, A, 1773, by: **41**. 395n, **43**. 69;
    Cole has not seen, **2**. 77; continuation of, **2**.
    265; engravings for, **2**. 42–3, 77; HW reads,
    2. 75; remainder of, at press, **42**. 38
  travels of, **2**. 250
  Welsh, **42**. 19, 21
Pennautier. *See* Reich de Pennautier
Penné. *See* Penny
Penneck, Rev. Richard (ca 1728–1803); chap-
  lain to George, 3d E. of Orford; keeper of
  reading-room of British Museum:
  Colman assaulted by, **32**. 97–8
  nurse of, **2**. 164
  Orford, 3d E. of, said by, to have parted with
    his housekeeper on doctors' orders, **15**. 333
  SH visited by, **12**. 238
Pennée. *See* Penny
Pennicott, Rev. William (1726–1811), rector of
  Long Ditton, Surrey:
  Gloucester, Ds of, summons, to Pavilions, **36**.
    263
  —— tells HW to keep, from going to Pa-
    vilions, **36**. 261
  —— to receive gratitude of, **36**. 90
  —— visited by, **36**. 254
  (?) HW mentions, **14**. 120
  HW receives painting from, **29**. 45n
  HW sees picture shown by, **2**. 200
  Nivernais's *Jardins modernes* given to, **12**. 259
  SH visited by, **12**. 224, 232, 238, 239, 251
Pennington, Sir Isaac (1745–1817) Kt, 1795;
  physician:
  Cole asks information of, **2**. 69, 72, 230
  HW's life of Baker mentioned to, **2**. 230
  Hodson's contest with, for chemistry chair at
    Cambridge, **32**. 165n
  lends volume with Baker's notes, **2**. 344
Pennington, John (1737–1813), cr. (1783) Bn
  Muncaster; M.P.:
  peerage of, **25**. 433
Pennington, Lowther (1745–1818), 2d Bn Mun-
  caster, 1813; army officer:
  Charleville, Cts of, leaves Isleworth house to,
    33. 524n
  Tollemache, Capt., killed by, in duel, **32**. 398
Pennino, Del. *See* Del Pennino
Pennino (pen-box). *See* Pen-box
Pennsylvania:
  Germans and Swiss in, may form regiment,
    20. 531
  Jesuits tolerated in, **22**. 233n
  Penn, John, of, **11**. 159n
  Penn, Lady Juliana, 'late Queen of,' **34**. 14
  Penn, Thomas, 'sovereign' of, **20**. 248
  Penns of, **11**. 7n, 37n
  regiments of, debated in House of Commons,
    37. 436, 444

Pennsylvania Packet:
  Parliament's resolutions on Lafayette printed
    in, **24**. 456n
Penny ('Pennée'), Edward (1714–91), painter:
  Chute informed by, from Bologna, about
    Domenichino painting, **17**. 267–8, **35**. 17
  Creti communicates to, his doubts about
    Domenichino painting, **35**. 17, 18–19
  ——'s pupil talks with, **18**. 334
  Mann employs, to buy alleged Domenichino
    painting at Bologna, for HW, **17**. 226,
    227–8, 241, 257, 267, **18**. 334, **35**. 17, 18
  —— receives 'Magdalen' by Torri from, **17**.
    268
  ——'s correspondence with, **17**. 227, 257, 268
  (?) —— to seek Correggio painting through,
    17. 199
  Venice visited by, **35**. 19
Penny or Penné, Peter (d. ca 1779):
  death of, **16**. 181–2
Penny, Mrs Peter. *See* Hughes, Anne
Penny, Richard, printer's devil:
  House of Commons summons, **23**. 555n
Penny; pennies, silver:
  Buckinger wrote Lord's Prayer in compass
    of, **10**. 113–14
  Channel Islands small enough to fill, **39**. 299
  HW could dance minuet on, **9**. 293
  HW offers, at Harcourt's shrine, **35**. 535
  new, Henrietta Hotham brings, to Cts Tem-
    ple, **10**. 116
  tiny, **25**. 15, **38**. 335
Penny post:
  rebus sent to Lovel by, **30**. 42
  See also under Post
Penobscot Bay, Maine:
  American fleet destroyed in battle at, **28**.
    467, **33**. 123, 124
Pen Park, Glos:
  Lambert of, **16**. 123n
Penrhyn, Bn. *See* Pennant, Richard
Penrith, Cumberland:
  rebels said to have reached, **19**. 165
Penrose, Mr:
  SH visited by, **12**. 234
Pensacola, Florida:
  taken by Spaniards, **25**. 172
Pensées de Pope. See under Pope, Alexander
Pensées philosophiques. See under Diderot,
  Denis
Penseroso, Il. See under Milton, John
Penshurst Place, Kent:
  celebrated by Jonson and Waller, **2**. 240
  Chute and HW make Perry vacate his dress-
    ing-room at, **20**. 389
  Chute and HW visit, **35**. 135, 141–2
  Edward VI gives manor of, to Sidney, **35**. 141
  HW compares Marble Hill to, **32**. 31
  HW compares Nuneham to, **28**. 464
  HW recommends, to Conway, **39**. 310
  half of glory of, ends at Yonge auction, **10**.
    124

Leicester, E. of, visits, and wants to purchase it, **34.** 28

Sherard, Lady, owns half-interest in, **10.** 122n

Van Dyck's double portrait at, of Countesses of Carlisle and Leicester, **41.** 443

Pension; pensions:

Acton's, from Tuscan grand dukes, **22.** 548

Affry's, **5.** 168

Albany, Cts of, gets: from Cardinal York, **25.** 150; from French Court, **25.** 150, 536; from popes, **25.** 107

Alembert's, **5.** 209, 222, **41.** 62

Amherst refuses, **23.** 44

Arundel gets, on Ireland, **20.** 517

Barré's, **33.** 345n, 348n

Barthélemy's, **5.** 168, 173

Beauvau's, **5.** 220, 225

Bentley desires, **9.** 261–2

Boyle receives, **37.** 448n

Bradshaw and family get, **35.** 350n

Broglie's, **3.** 57

Burke's, **34.** 214

Burney, Fanny, gets, **42.** 330n, 331

Camden's, 'flying,' **23.** 174n

Cameron, Jeanie, seeks, from Young Pretender, **22.** 453

Chamfort's, **6.** 374

Charles III grants, to expelled Jesuits, **22.** 516

Charles Emmanuel III said to continue, to Modenese princesses, **18.** 223

Chauvelin family's, **5.** 431, 435

Chesterfield asks, for Lady Frances Shirley, **19.** 463n

Choiseul's, **5.** 155, 159, 162, 166–7, **23.** 363

Chudleigh, Elizabeth, jokingly suggested as seeking, **10.** 76

Cocchi's, **20.** 204

——'s widow's, **21.** 194

Cowper gives, to aunt's old friend, **23.** 416

Craon's, **20.** 25–6

Cybo's, **17.** 47

Dartmouth and Rochford offered, on resigning, **24.** 142n

deduction from, for patent, **20.** 204

Dorset, D. of, rejects, **21.** 104, 109

Du Barry, Mme, receives, **24.** 10n

Du Deffand, Mme, interested in, **4.** 48

—— may lose, **39.** 136, 189

——'s: **3.** 378, 397, **4.** 79, 91, 315, 317–18, 379; amount of, **3.** 5n, **4.** 354, 375; because of services of her aunt, **3.** 5n, **4.** 354, 386; Choiseul secures payment of, **4.** 406; continued after Marie Leszczyńska's death, **4.** 97, 103, 107; delay in payment of, **4.** 183, 189, 235, 289, **5.** 29; Du Barry, Mme, threatens to stop, if Mme du Deffand visits the Choiseuls, **5.** 43–4; Du Deffand, Mme, seeks addition to, **4.** 354–5, 359, 364; HW's offer to supplement, **4.** 358–9, 364–6, 375; Louis XVI may cancel, **6.** 306; Louis XVI not to cancel, **6.** 307; Necker to facilitate payment of, **6.** 370, 372; paid after Choi-

seul's fall, **5.** 29, 175, **6.** 100; reduced, **4.** 353–5, 364; taxed, **4.** 386; Terray might not continue, **4.** 334, 341–2, 352; Terray restores, to full amount, **4.** 375–6; through Marie Leszczyńska, **4.** 354

Du Muy, Maréchale, granted, **6.** 218

Electress's, to servants, Serristori, and Mme Uguccioni, taxed, **19.** 23–4

English Opposition sold for, **22.** 274

Éon's, **6.** 474

Essex's, **22.** 570n

Ferdinand's, **21.** 491

Finch, Hon. William, said to receive, **22.** 311

for Dukes of Gloucester and Cumberland, **43.** 281

for Dukes of York, Gloucester, and Cumberland, **22.** 424–5, 428

for Henrietta Maria's attendants, **41.** 160–1

Francis I and Leopold pay, to East India Co. employees, **22.** 548

friends of Gascoigne and Damer give, to wife of man injured by them, **22.** 286

French: may not be paid, **5.** 214, 344; reduced, **4.** 353, 6, 218; rulings about, **6.** 394; taxed, **4.** 353, 386; to be paid, **5.** 169

George II gives: to Carteret, **18.** 556; to Cts of Albemarle, **20.** 460, 467

George III's, Savile demands list of, **25.** 18

granted to persuade office-holders to accept salaries, **23.** 247

Grantham's, to go to Fitzwalter, **35.** 195

(?) Grey, Hon. Mrs John, receives, **9.** 344

Guilford's, North to have reversion of, **22.** 552

HW does not expect, in Ireland for being Gates's godfather, **10.** 23

HW expects, for damage from explosion, **39.** 153

HW jokes about, **30.** 165

HW's gardener declines, **35.** 479–80

HW tells Richmond to ask for lists of, to complain, **41.** 311

HW will never seek, **35.** 502

hackney writer seeks, **42.** 504

Hamilton, Lady Archibald, receives, **19.** 62, 361

—— refuses, **19.** 361

heralds get, for registering the nobility, **21.** 535

Hertford not to procure, for friends, **39.** 19

Hertford, Cts of, resigns, as lady of the Bedchamber, **17.** 346

Holdernesse's, **9.** 395n

Hume's, **4.** 87, 92, **29.** 111

Hume Campbell accepts, **20.** 5

Irish: **35.** 290; for Bedford's followers, **21.** 485n; Gizziello should get, **37.** 427; Irish Parliament's resolution on, **38.** 148; Waldegrave, Cts, receives, **23.** 415n

Irish unrest over, **21.** 154

Jenison's, **18.** 551

Jephson loses, **39.** 49

[Pension; pensions, *continued*]

Jersey's, **9.** 33

Jesuits', **23.** 191, 508

Johnson's, **29.** 111

Kilmarnock's, **19.** 283–4

La Chalotais's, restored by Aiguillon, **39.** 144

Lami's, **22.** 13

Le Courayer's, **9.** 116n

Ligonier's, **22.** 450

Lorenzi's, disappoints him, **22.** 346, 351, 356, 370–1

Louis XVI gives, to Cts of Albany, **25.** 150

Louis XVIII's, **34.** 213n

Lowther's, from Tuscany, **22.** 548

Macpherson's, **28.** 431

Magnan's, **19.** 564

Mann should expect, on retirement, **24.** 160

Massa duchess and princesses have, **17.** 47

Mill receives, from Tuscany, **22.** 548

Molesworth family's, from George II and George III, **37.** 356n

Monclar's, **4.** 285

Monro's, **19.** 400

Montagu, D. of, pays, **20.** 79

Montazet's, **5.** 435–6

Murray seeks, for his children, **25.** 364

new, announced, **36.** 209

North accuses Opposition of seeking, **28.** 155

—— does not get, **22.** 561

Northington's, **22.** 443, 571, **30.** 233

Norton's, **38.** 468

O'Brien, Mrs, loses, **20.** 28

Old Pretender's: from France and Spain, **22.** 387; son secures reversion of, **21.** 391, **22.** 368

Onslow's, **30.** 164

Oswald to get, **22.** 569n

Paoli's, **23.** 31, **25.** 242n

Parliament cannot do without, **25.** 97

paymastership of: Hooper receives, from Bath, **30.** 305n; value of, **30.** 305n; *see also* Paymaster of the Pensions

Pitt, Anne, gets: **38.** 468, 475; from Bute, not from her brother, **31.** 40n

—— has, increased, **31.** 3n

Pitt, Lady Hester, receives, **9.** 395

Pitt, William (E. of Chatham) accepts, **38.** 131, 134, 135–7

—— gets dispensation for, from Common Council, **21.** 546

—— must regret acceptance of, **22.** 277

——'s: **10.** 45, **21.** 548, **24.** 389; said to be first to be printed in *London Gazette*, **21.** 541n

—— should spurn, **38.** 188

Porter's, **24.** 160

proposal to tax, defeated, **28.** 369, 373

Quarles's, **41.** 191

Rantzau dismissed with, **23.** 426

Razumovskiĭ gets, from Catherine II, **22.** 456

Robinson's, on Ireland, **20.** 502

Rochford gets, on Ireland, **3.** 392, **21.** 460

Roman proconsuls', **25.** 118

Rousseau's: from Frederick II, **3.** 94; from George III, **3.** 24, 57, 91, 94–5, 98, 250, 257, 259–60, 267, 281, 320, 322, **4.** 434, **10.** 242, 243

St-Germain's, **6.** 226

satirized in *Labour in Vain*, **18.** 20

Scottish and Cornish outcry against, **17.** 347

secret service, **35.** 281n

Smelt resigns his, **28.** 491

Sorba family's, **5.** 170

Stanhope's, **18.** 178

Stanislas I's, **22.** 403

Stosch's, **17.** 212n, **20.** 53

Suffolk's, **31.** 420

Sundon, Lady, receives, **17.** 276n

Sussex's, **10.** 339

Tabuerniga brothers', **17.** 278

Tencin's, discontinued, **17.** 19n

Thurlow's, **33.** 405n

Thurn, Comtesse, receives, **23.** 253

Tickell's, **33.** 145n

Tighe's, **32.** 230n

Torreggiani's, from Jesuits, **21.** 425

Torrington may receive, **19.** 155

Tourville's, **4.** 353–4

Townshend sends list of, from Ireland to London, **23.** 362n

unpaid, in France, **35.** 126, **39.** 143

Walkinshaw, Mrs, gets, **26.** 47

Walpole, Sir Robert, secures, after first refusing it, **17.** 329n, **18.** 465

Wilkinson, Mrs, to be given, on presentation of memorial, **10.** 186

York, Cardinal, gives: to Cts of Albany, **25.** 150; to Jesuits, **23.** 191

—— receives, **21.** 391, 392

Young Pretender assured of, by Clement XIII, **22.** 368

——'s, Pius VI to give half of, to Cts of Albany, **25.** 107

—— to receive, from Spain, **19.** 392

See also Annuity; Ireland: pensions on

Pension Bill. *See under* Parliament: acts of

Pensioners, band of. *See* Yeomen of the Guard

Pensions, Paymaster of the. *See* Paymaster of the Pensions

Pentachord:

invented by Sir Edward Walpole, **28.** 196, 200, **36.** 53n

Penthièvre, Duc de. *See* Bourbon, Louis-Jean-Marie de

Penthièvre, Duchesse de. *See* Maria Theresa Felicità

Penticross. *See* Pentycross

Pentland, Alexander (ca 1750–1816), surgeon: (?) SH visited by, **12.** 231

Pentolino (pot):

Walpole, Bns, takes ptisan in, to Richecourt, **18.** 67

Penton, Henry (?1705–62), M.P.:

death of, **38.** 167

Pentons, manor in Norfolk:
HW's will mentions, **30**. 368

Pentonville, London:
Law dies in, **16**. 239n

Pentraeth, Dolly (1685–1777 *or* 8), m. ——
Jeffers *or* Jeffery; Cornish fisherwoman:
death date of, corrected, **43**. 69
HW diverted by, **2**. 164
said to be last speaker of Cornish language,
2. 164n

Pentycross, Rev. Thomas (1749–1808):
'Blue-coat boy' from Kingston, **12**. 207
Cole does not know, **2**. 15–16
HW's account of, **2**. 18–19, **12**. 207–8, **15**. 287
requests print of HW, **12**. 207
SH visited by, **12**. 207
verses written by, **12**. 207, 208, **43**. 64
Wittenham-Hill by, **32**. 298

Penzance, Cornwall:
Admiralty gets news of Lord Howe from,
12. 81

People, the:
Du Deffand, Mme, detests, **3**. 107, **7**. 232

Pepi, Signora. *See* Macinghi, Ottavia (1717–77)

Pepi, Francesco Gaspero (1708–64):
Florence, Abp of, does not permit, to let
Don Pilogio be acted, **18**. *41*, 63
Uguccioni informs HW of changed plans of,
40. 32
wife goes home to, **17**. 137
wife's child attributed by, to Suares, **18**. 345

Pepi, Maria Giulia Gaspera (b. 1743):
birth of, **18**. 345

'Pepin, Le roi.' *See* 'Le roi Pepin'

Pepper:
caravan of, from India, **24**. 510n
England will get, from Ceylon conquest, **25**.
277
French will be unable to get, for ragoûts,
21. 523
Holland to bewail loss of Ceylon's monopoly
of, **25**. 283

Peppercorn; peppercorns:
as quit-rent payment, **32**. 302
HW's letters as worthless as, **25**. 530, 576
'of affection,' HW's letter is, **35**. 316

Peppermint water:
HW sends, to England from Paris, **7**. 379
HW uses, for summer sickness, **33**. 412

Pepperrell, Sir William (1696–1759), cr. (1746)
Bt:
regiment of, arrives at Plymouth, **21**. 18n

Pepper warehouse:
Oswald appointed keeper of, **17**. 6n

Pepusch, John Christopher (1667–1752):
wife of, **13**. 64n

Pepys, Lady. *See* Dowdeswell, Elizabeth

Pepys, Charles Christopher (1781–1851), cr.
(1836) Bn and (1850) E. of Cottenham, lord
high chancellor:
father of, **11**. 30n

Pepys, Henry (1783–1860), Bp of Sodor and
Man 1840–1, of Worcester 1841–60:
broken arm of, prevents Pepyses from din-
ing at SH, **11**. 55

Pepys, Sir Lucas (1742–1830), cr. (1784) Bt;
M.D.:
George III's illness declared by, to have
ceased, **25**. 682n
Piozzi, Mrs, writes to, attacking Boswell, **43**.
292
small, **11**. 31n
social relations of, with Mrs Ord, **31**. 213
wife of, **11**. 71n

Pepys, Samuel (1633–1703), secretary to the Admiralty; diarist:
*Account of the Preservation of King Charles
II after the Battle of Worcester* by, edited
by Dalrymple, **15**. 103–4n
ballads collected by, **1**. 89, **15**. 63
prints in library of, **1**. 173, **2**. 253

Pepys, William Weller (1741–1825), cr. (1801)
Bt; lawyer:
believes in Ireland's MSS, **15**. 321
Berry, Mary, identifies, **11**. 30n
—— receives news from, **11**. 236
—— writes to, **11**. 37
Berrys' neighbour at Teddington, **11**. 56
Bishop Bonner's Ghost sent to, **31**. 310, 313
Bognor Rocks visited by, **12**. 200
Damer, Mrs, invites, **11**. 286
Dudley, Lady, house of, rented by, **11**. *30–1*
French Revolution approved by, **11**. 264
HW consults, about lease, **11**. 73
HW invites, to dinner, **11**. 54–5
HW learns Hannah More's address from, **31**.
327
HW's meetings with, infrequent, **11**. 211
HW's 'small dealings' with, **11**. 46
HW visits, **11**. 243
Hamilton, Mary, talks with, **31**. 206
Hesketh, Lady, visited by, **11**. 236
household effects of, lost, **11**. 31, 37
long nose of, **11**. 30–1
More, Hannah, chooses company for party
given by, **31**. 242–3
—— has letter from, **31**. 370n
shrewdness of, **11**. 31
sister-in-law of, **11**. 71n
social relations of, with: Burney, Charles and
Fanny, **31**. 243; Cambridge, Richard Owen,
31. 243; Garrick, Mrs, **31**. 206, 213, 228;
HW, **31**. 228, 243, 260; Hamilton, Mary,
31. 228; Montagu, Mrs, **31**. 243; More,
Hannah, **31**. 213, 228, 260; Ord, Mrs, **31**.
213
SH visited by, **31**. 206, 327
Wimpole St residence of, **31**. 228

Pepys, Sir William Weller (1778–1845), 2d Bt,
1825:
HW shows eagle to, **31**. 327n

Pepys, Mrs William Weller. *See* Dowdeswell,
Elizabeth

Perambulation of Kent. See under Lambarde, William

Perceval, Lady Catharine (1713–48), m. (1733) Thomas Hanmer:
Bland carries, to Scarborough, **30.** 84n

Perceval, Charles George (1756–1840), 2d Bn Arden, 1784:
SH visited by, **12.** 251

Perceval, John (1683–1748), 1st E. of Egmont; M.P.:
death of, **20.** 31
notes taken by, of curious pictures and paintings, **40.** 247–8
Walpole, Lady, disparaged by, **17.** 403n

Perceval, John (1711–70), styled Vct Perceval 1733–48; 2d E. of Egmont, 1748; M.P.:
Address debated by, at, **37.** 414, 415
address of thanks to George II opposed by, **20.** 222n
address opposed by, **20.** 510n
Admiralty headed by, **22.** 167
Augusta, Ps of Wales's appointment of, as treasurer, rejected on Townshend's attack, **35.** 195n
Cabinet overrules, **22.** 425n
collection of, **40.** 247
continues as first commissioner of the Admiralty, **3.** 104–5
Craftsman prints work of, **20.** 31
death of, expected, **23.** 247
despairs, **35.** 255
election of, at Westminster, **17.** 220n, 253, 272, **20.** 31
English peerage as Bn Lovel and Holland given to, **10.** 26, **22.** 32
Examination of the Principles of Conduct of the Two Brothers published by, **20.** 32, 43
Faction Detected by: **35.** 49; antagonizes Pitts and Lytteltons, **20.** 31; Mann wants to see, **18.** 334; Mann, Galfridus, mentions, **18.** 334; meeting described in, **17.** 335n; Williams's verses mention, **18.** 320
Fitzwalter may be succeeded by, as treasurer of the Household, **35.** 195
Fox, Henry, formerly preferred by, to Pelham, **20.** 224
—— handles, severely, **20.** 224
—— obtains amended return in favour of, for Weobley elections, **20.** 31n
——'s inclusion in ministry required by, **20.** 502n
Frederick, P. of Wales, favours, **20.** 31
—— makes, lord of the Bedchamber, **20.** 32
——'s faction summoned by, for post mortem conference, **20.** 239–40
——'s follower, **20.** 3n
—— warned by, against cold, **20.** 232
Genealogical History of the House of Yvery by, **17.** 272n, **20.** 31
Guerchy barred from Portsmouth by, **38.** 401–2
HW calls Vandeput a puppet of, **20.** 224n
HW may be subject of whisperings of, **9.** 306

HW mentions, **20.** 292
HW's opinion of, **20.** 31–2
health of, gout, **42.** 497
Hessian and Russian treaties opposed by, **35.** 88
House of Commons left by, on Mutiny Bill, **20.** 112
Jacobites to be united by, with P. of Wales's party, **20.** 50
last survivor of old Opposition, save Barnard, **35.** 196
lord privy seal, **23.** 173n
Mann shocked by behaviour of, **20.** 244
—— wishes to see pamphlets by, **18.** 334, **20.** 43
may become secretary of state, **22.** 159
Mutiny Bill opposed by, **20.** 51, **35.** 162
Newcastle praised and Granville blamed by, for Hanoverian loyalty, **20.** 222n
newspapers advertise pamphlet by, **20.** 43
nomination of, **17.** 272n
old politicians hate, on account of Pelham and Sir Robert Walpole, **20.** 32
Opposition assembly addressed by, at St Alban's Tavern, **20.** 50
Parliamentary motion by, in House of Lords, to uncover plot by summoning Union Coffee-House mistress, **38.** 257
Parliamentary motion to resume sentence against Murray opposed by, **20.** 286n
Parliamentary speeches by, against Mutiny Bill, **35.** 162; on burning *Constitutional Queries*, **20.** 222
Parliament threatened by, with long sitting, **20.** 50
party of, heaps incense on Pelham and Pitt, **20.** 224
Pelham helps, in Weobley election contest, **20.** 31
Pelhams aided by, in Parliament, **20.** 31
Pitt ministry proposed to include, **22.** 302n
Pitt's oratory compared to that of, **20.** 32
Poor Bill opposed by, **38.** 528
porter at house of, disparages political guests, **17.** 301
Saunders succeeds, in Admiralty, **22.** 449
Secret Committee called by, 'of Accusation,' **17.** 297
speech by, in Irish Parliament, **20.** 31
Strange clashes with, **20.** 32
title of, may indicate descent from Cts of Holland, **22.** 32
Vandeput's petition presented by, **20.** 224
Williams's epigram on, **20.** 51, **30.** 319

Perceval, Thomas (1740–1804), M.D.; F.R.S.; writer:
Speculations on the Perceptive Power of Vegetables by, sent by him to Hannah More, **31.** 295

Percevale, Walter (fl. 1440–3):
received into fraternity of Bury Abbey, **2.** 38

Perch:
HW's goldfish as big as, **9.** 134
Irish rarely have, **10.** 18
Perci, Agnes de, m. (ca 1150) Jocelyn de Louvaine:
marriage of, **9.** 97n
Percy, Cts. See Burrell, Frances Julia (1752–1820); Stuart, Lady Anne (1746–ca 1819)
'Percy, Lady':
in Shakespeare's *Henry IV*, Pt II, **41.** 294–5
Percy, Algernon (1602–68), 4th E. of Northumberland, 1632:
Percy, Thomas, asks HW about tract by, **12.** 32
wife of, **12.** 32n, **16.** 172n, **42.** 382
Percy, Lord Algernon (1750–1830), 2d Bn Lovaine, 1786; cr. (1790) E. of Beverley:
boarded at Edinburgh with Blair, not Ferguson, **29.** 239
created Earl, **11.** 127
HW does not know, and only saw him once, **25.** 422
health of: flimsy, **21.** 514–15; Mediterranean cruise restores, **24.** 203
Illustri fatti Farnesiani sent from Leghorn in case belonging to, **25.** 420, 448, 459
Mann entertains, at Florence, **25.** 420
—— to be accompanied by, at investiture, **23.** 60
marriage of, **24.** 499
Paris visited by, **31.** 137
Percy, Thomas, tutor to, **43.** 309
Percy, Lady Algernon. See Burrell, Isabella Susanna (1750–1812)
Percy, Lady Dorothy (1598–1659), m. (ca 1615) Robert Sidney, 2d E. of Leicester:
Van Dyck's portrait of: **21.** 420n; at Penshurst, **41.** 443; bought by HW at Yonge auction, **10.** 123
Percy, Eleanor (d. 1530), m. (1490) Edward Stafford, 3d D. of Buckingham, 1483:
Brandon's codpiece supposedly admired by, **35.** 360
Percy, Lady Elizabeth (1667–1722), m. 1 (1679) Henry Cavendish, styled E. of Ogle; m. 2 (1681) Thomas Thynne; m. 3 (1682) Charles Seymour, 6th D. of Somerset:
dates of, corrected, **43.** 265
father and husband of, **40.** 318
never sits before grandmother without leave, **42.** 380
Northumberland title descends through, **23.** 365n
print of, **40.** 236
settlement by, of her estate, **20.** 11n
Percy, Lady Elizabeth Anne Frances (1744–61):
death of, **21.** 515
funeral of, in St Nicholas Chapel, Westminster Abbey, **38.** 111
Percy, Henry de (1341–1408), cr. (1377) E. of Northumberland:
HW identifies, **42.** 138

Percy, Henry (ca 1502–37), 5th E. of Northumberland, 1527:
Boleyn, Anne, loved by, **35.** 248
portrait of, **35.** 248
Percy, Hugh (1715–86). See Smithson, Hugh (1715–86)
Percy (till 1750, Smithson) Hugh (1742–1817), styled Bn Warkworth 1750–66, E. Percy 1766; 2d D. of Northumberland, 1786; M.P.:
accommodation with America may be brought by, **24.** 313, 315
address moved by, in Parliament, **38.** 489
Ansbach, Margrave and Margravine of, will eclipse, **34.** 133
enclosure of Hounslow Heath opposed by, **12.** 153
English troops reinforced by, at battle of Lexington, **24.** 110
Gage sends out party under, **28.** 206n
health of: Mediterranean cruise restores, **24.** 203; miserable constitution, **21.** 514–15
Howe disgusts, **24.** 309
marriage of, **22.** 302n
Muzell might be travelling companion of, **21.** 512
Naples the destination of, **21.** 512n
Percy, Rev. Thomas and Lord Algernon, visit seat of, **43.** 309
Pisa visited by, **21.** 512n
predictions ascribed to, **24.** 315
returns to England, **24.** 309
separation of wife from, rumoured, **14.** 141
steward of, avaricious, **11.** 16–17, 56, **12.** 169
Westminster election won by, **24.** 52, **39.** 196
Westminster seat vacated by, on getting mother's barony, **32.** 336n
Percy, Joceline (1644–70), 5th E. of Northumberland, 1668:
descendant of, **9.** 265n
heiress of, **40.** 318
Percy, Lady Lucy, m. Sir Edward Stanley, mother of Venetia, Lady Digby:
HW praises miniature of, **1.** 358n
mother of Lady Digby, **28.** 180n
Percy, Lady Lucy (ca 1600–60), m. (1617) James Hay, 1st E. of Carlisle:
portrait of, at Ham, engraved by Lombart, **41.** 443
portrait of, by Van Dyck: **21.** 420n; HW buys, at Yonge auction, **10.** 123
portraits of, **41.** 442–3
Percy, Robert, of Knaresborough:
attainted, **41.** 92n
Percy, Thomas (1560–1605), conspirator:
print of, **1.** 182
Percy, Rev. Thomas (1729–1811), D.D.; Bp of Dromore, 1782:
ballads of, to be sung by Montagu as deputy ranger, **10.** 191
bishopric of, corrected, **43.** 213
Blair's letters shown by, **29.** 239–40
Boswell abuses, in *Life of Johnson*, **11.** 275

[Percy, Rev. Thomas, *continued*]
Buckingham's works to have been edited by, **41**. 321n, **42**. 366–8
Chambers's letter vindicates, **16**. 228
Chatterton does not deceive, **2**. 81
—— to be published by, **2**. 114n
Chattertonian materials collected by, **16**. 131
Cole and Lort spend evening with, **1**. 313n
Dallington visited by, **10**. 185
disbelieves in Ireland's MSS, **15**. 321
Farmer, Richard, aids, in compiling *Reliques*, **40**. 372n
Gough's *Sepulchral Monuments* quotes, **34**. 227
——'s correspondence with, **42**. 366n
HW asks advice of, about Chatterton affair, **41**. 395–7
HW calls on, after fire at Northumberland House, **41**. 412
HW grateful for glimpses of editions by, of Buckingham, Wyatt, and Surrey, **42**. 369
HW identifies, **16**. 350
HW offers to, his version of Rochford's alleged poem, **42**. 381–3
HW receives letter from, **12**. 32
HW receives *Northumberland Household-Book* from, and gives him a book, **41**. 181–2
HW receives unpublished proof-sheets from, **42**. 366
HW ridicules interest of, in Percy family, **12**. 32
HW's correspondence with, **40**. 372–4, **41**. 181–2, 320, 395–7, 411–13, **42**. 207–8, 366–70, 378–83, 423
HW's kindness appreciated by, **10**. 185
HW sorry to miss calls by, **41**. 320
HW tells, to call on him in London, **40**. 372
HW thanks, for new edition of *Reliques*, **42**. 423
HW to call on, **41**. 320
HW to furnish, with drawings and Wyatt's speeches, **41**. 320
HW to get copy from, of Cts of Northumberland's prayers, **42**. 379–80
HW to give 1st vol. of *Miscellaneous Antiquities* to, **42**. 379
HW wrongly attributes publication of Rowley poem to, **28**. 36
Hau Kiou Chouan edited by, **15**. 75n
Henry's letter to, **43**. 200
identifies subject of painting, **2**. 7
incumbent at Easton Maudit, **15**. 114
itinerary of, with Lord Algernon Percy, **43**. 309
MS of HW's *Letter to the Editor* given by him to, **43**. 218, 304
Montagu meets, **10**. 185
Nash's correspondence with, **43**. 390n
Northumberland, Cts of, suggested by, for inclusion in *Royal and Noble Authors*, **12**. 32
Northumberland, D. of, employs, as domestic chaplain and as tutor to younger son, **43**. 309–10

Northumberland, D. and Ds of, may be approached by, as intercessor, **1**. 164, 169, 177
Northumberland, E. of, tract of, inquired about by, **12**. 32
Northumberland House the address of, **41**. 397
parchment said by, to have been rubbed with ochre, **16**. 342, 350
Percy family history contributed by, to Collins's *Peerage*, **34**. 227n
Percy family history known by, **34**. 224–5
Pinkerton calls on Lort by wish of, **16**. 280n
Reliques of Ancient English Poetry by: **1**. 89–90; authorship of *Hardyknute* revealed in, **15**. 65n; 'Chevy Chace' in, **23**. 264; Dalrymple contributes to, **15**. 106; HW's editions of, **43**. 47; presented by Percy to HW, **40**. 372–4; 'Sir Cauline' and 'Ditty of Glasgerion' in, **40**. 374; Warton doubtless enjoyed, **40**. 377
Ritson's attack on, **2**. 335
SH visited by, with family, **12**. 241
Surrey and Buckingham editions by, started by Tonson, to be finished by Percy's nephew, **42**. 367–8
takes his degree, **1**. 193, 193n
Tonson asks, to edit Wyatt and Surrey, **41**. 320n
Percy, Rev. Thomas II (1768–1808):
fellow of St John's, Oxford, **42**. 367
uncle's edition of Surrey and Buckingham to be continued by, **42**. 367
Percy, Mrs Thomas. *See* Gutteridge, Anne
Percy. See under More, Hannah
Percy, barony of:
Somerset, Ds of, inherited, **20**. 11n
Percy family:
beheadings frequent in, **12**. 32
Brébeuf family wish genealogical connection with, **38**. 555
estate of, settled, **19**. 11–12
HW honours, **41**. 411
heralds of, **40**. 178–9
Hotham family's alleged connection with, **34**. 224–5
kicks not received by, **9**. 264
Osterley Park must be envied by, **32**. 125
Petworth expresses spirit of, **9**. 97
title of, goes to coachman's grandson, **20**. 124–5
tombs of, in Beverley Minster, **34**. 224–5, 227
Westminster Abbey vault of, in St Nicholas chapel, **41**. 411n
Wyndham family deny access to library of, at Petworth, **40**. 317
Percy Herald. *See under* Herald
Percy Lodge, Iver, Bucks:
Somerset, D. of, dies at, **20**. 124n
Père de famille, Le. See under Diderot, Denis
Péréfixe. *See* Beaumont de Péréfixe
Peregrinaggio di tre giovani figliuoli. See under Christoforo ('Armeno')

Pereira, Ephraim Lopez (1739–1802) Baron d'Aquilar (of Portugal), 1759; HW's neighbour:
biographical information about, corrected, 43. 306
coach of, shot at, 29. 59
shot at, in Twickenham, 35. 355
Perelli, Tommaso (1704–83), Professor of Astronomy at University of Pisa 1739–80:
English understood by, 21. 390
financial backers of, angry at him for expense, 21. 430
letter of, to Sisson: HW delivers to Sisson, 21. 354, 359–60; Mann sends, to HW, 21. 348
machine for raising water sent to, by Sisson, 21. 406
Pisa visited by, 21. 390
professor of astronomy, 21. *348*
Sisson says, has description of drawing, 21. 407
——'s letter to, 21. 414
——'s plan praised by, 21. 430, 432–3
——'s plan to be sent to, 21. 390
witticism by, about Host being carried everywhere during epidemic, 22. 511–12
Pères de l'Oratoire, church of, at Paris:
HW visits, 7. 280
Jerningham, George and William, packed up to go to, 39. 437
Peretti, Felice. See Sixtus V
Perey, David (1711–98):
music by, for *Didone Abandonata*, 9. 342n
Pérez de Alderete, Juan Manuel (1705–86), Spanish naval officer:
(?) tender of, captured, 17. 381
'Perfidion':
drunken lady invokes, 35. 306
Perfume; perfumes:
Gontaut's anecdote about, 5. 106
Mann sends, to HW, 18. 201
monks of St Mark make, 18. 177n
silver trunk for, 23. 407, 26. 56
See also Essences; Sweet bags
Perfume bottles:
Montagu sends, to Mme Roland, in casket, 10. 246, 248
Perfumer; perfumers:
Colomb leaves effects with, requiring trip to Windsor, 42. 297–8
French, wrote on harmony of essences, 33. 262
See also Hugenien, Moses
Pergama, Bp of. See Attems, Charles-Michel d'
Pergola, Via della, Florence:
theatre in, see Teatro della Pergola
Pergolesi, Giovanni Battista (1710–36), composer:
first hearing in England of compositions of, 17. 401n
Gray collects compositions of, 13. 233n
intermezzo by, performed between acts of his *Il prigionero superbo*, 17. 166n
Olimpiade by: 39. 119; at the Haymarket, 17. 411n; Chute promises to get, at Naples, 19.

149; HW mentions, 19. 70; Mann seeks, for Lady Maria Walpole, 19. 95; Monticelli sings in, 17. 401
Rousseau advises study of, at Naples, 35. 514n
Serva padrona, La, by: Mann has Chute send, to Leghorn to be sent to HW, 17. 262, 263; Rich, Elizabeth, wants, 17. *166*
Virgin of the Seven Sorrows, office of, composed by, 17. 39n, 166, 408
Periam, John (b. ca 1702), M.P.:
(?) Gray searches for, 13. 142–3
Periam, Zachary (ca 1703–38):
of Inner Temple, 13. 142n
Pericles (ca 495–429 B.C.), Athenian statesman:
fame of, 31. 21
'Pericles':
Lyttelton uses name of, for Pitt, 21. 409
Pericles and Aristides. See under Brown, John (1715–66)
Perier de Salvert, Antoine-Alexis (d. 1757), naval officer:
Acadia or Gulf of St Lawrence thought to be destination of, 20. 538n
(?) Brest left by, for West Indies, 20. 538n
Périers. *See* Des Périers
Périgord, Comte de. *See* Talleyrand, Gabriel-Marie de
Périgord, Vicomte de. *See* Talleyrand, Archambaud-Joseph de
Périgord, Vicomtesse de. *See* Olivier de Sénozan de Viriville, Madeleine-Henriette-Sabine
'Périgord, Monsieur':
should be restricted to one suit of clothes, 35. 36
Périgueux pâtés:
Wilkes fears his, are poisoned, 4. 152, 155
Periodical; periodicals. *See Annual Register*; *Archæologia*; *Bee*; *British Critic*; *Chronique de Paris*; *Common Sense*; *Courier de l'Europe*; *Craftsman*; *Crisis, The*; *Critical Review*; *Daily Advertiser*; *Éclair, L'*; *Esprit de journaux, L'*; *European Magazine*; *Fog's Journal*; *Gazette de Leyde*; *Gazette d'Utrecht*; *Gazetteer, The*; *Gazette littéraire de l'Europe*; *General Advertiser*; *Gentleman's Magazine*; *Historical Register*; *Independent London Journalist*; *Lady's Magazine*; *Lloyd's Evening Post*; *London Chronicle*; *London Courant*; *London Evening Post*; *London Gazette*; *London Magazine*; *London Packet*; *London Review*; *Monthly Review*; *Morning Chronicle*; *Morning Herald*; *Morning Post*; *New Review*; *New York Gazette*; *Northampton Mercury*; *Oracle, The*; *Oxford Journal*; *Public Advertiser*; *Reading Mercury and Oxford Gazette*; *Saint James's Chronicle*; *Saint James's Evening Post*; *Saint James's Magazine*; *Scots Magazine*; *Spectator*; *Tatler*; *Test*; *Times*; *Town and Country Magazine*; *True Briton*; *Whitehall Evening Post*; *Woodfall's Register*; *World, The*
See also Magazine; Newspaper

Periphrases:
modern age eliminates, **39.** 316
Peritchone, Padre:
Shirley engages, to support James, **15.** 80
Periwig; periwigs:
Balmerinoch doffs, at execution, **19.** 302
black, of generals, lose their horror, **37.** 278
campaign, **37.** 143
Carteret rubs off, **37.** 92
Charlotte, Q., would wear, if George III
asked, **21.** 529, **38.** 116
Granville's, **9.** 89
See also Wig
Periwig-maker; periwig-makers:
George III gets complaint from, about men
wearing their own hair, **38.** 509
HW's, in Paris, **31.** 44
London shops of, staffed by French, **9.** 246
Menard, Mme, suspects, of theft, **7.** 268
Perjury:
men commit, to women and to the nation,
35. 213
most harmless of French sins, **35.** 447
Perkins, Dr, of Hampton:
SH visited by, **12.** 233
Perkins, Mr:
print of, **40.** 237
Perkins, Mr:
rudeness of, **12.** 222n
SH visited by, **12.** 222
Perkins, Mrs Francis. *See* Fermor, Arabella
Perkins, Mary (d. 1784), m. (1751) William
Dodd:
Sandwich's former mistress, **32.** 185
Perlas. *See* Vilana Perlas
Perlin, Estienne (fl. 1550), ecclesiastic and
traveller:
*Description des royaulmes d'Angleterre et
d'Escosse*, HW ignorant of, **33.** 280
'Permaloso':
Huntingdon's favourite word, **21.** 545
Permasens (Germany):
Frederick William II goes to, **12.** 29n
Pernety, Jacques (1696–1777), abbé:
letter to, sent by Mme du Deffand to HW,
20. 98
social relations of, with Duchesse de la Val-
lière, **5.** 234
Pernklö (called Bernklau *or* Bärnklau), Johann
Leopold (1700–46), Freiherr von Schönreuth;
Gen.:
Charles Emmanuel III joined by, at the
Trebbia, **19.** 269
Elector Palatine's troops may be given by,
to Maria Theresa, **19.** 41
name of, corrected, **43.** 257
Ripalta castle taken by, **19.** 262n
successes of infantry under, at Piacenza, **19.**
271
Peronne, Maria (ca 1739–83), Contessa di Bor-
ringe (Genève-Borringe), m. (1755) Vittorio

Amadeo Sallier de la Tour, Marchese di
Cordon:
Carmarthen, Lady, confesses adultery to,
31. 194
Péronne (France):
Joseph the deaf-mute found near, **7.** 134
visitors to: Craufurd, **5.** 294; HW, **7.** 315, 342,
343
Peroz, Admiral. *See* Pérez
Perpetuity; perpetuities:
Scottish law more favourable than English to,
42. 13n
Perpignan, mayor of. *See* Aguilar, ——
Perpignan (France):
Du Barry, Jean-Baptiste, to be imprisoned in,
6. 52
Mann, Horace II and Lady Lucy, visit, **24.**
246
Spanish victory near, **12.** 40n
Perrault, Charles (1628–1703), writer:
Boileau not to link HW with, **37.** 293
*Contes du Tems Passé de ma Mère L'Oye . . .
Tales of Passed Times by Mother Goose* by,
4. 220
Hommes illustres by, **7.** 356
Perreau, Daniel (d. 1776), and Robert (d.
1776), forgers:
Rudd, Mrs, involved with, **11.** 208n, **24.**
152n, **28.** 192
Perrenot de Granvelle, Antoine (1517–86),
cardinal:
Watson's *History of . . . Philip II* treats,
32. 339–40
Perrier *or* Perrière. *See* La Perrière; Perier
Perrin, Denis-Marius de (ca 1684–1754) cheva-
lier:
Belle-Isle accompanied by, **9.** 22
Sévigné letters published by, **9.** 22
Perrin. *See also* Perryn
Perrin de Cypièrre de Chevilly, Adrien-Phili-
bert:
(?) attends session of parliament of Paris,
8. 173
Perron. *See* Perrin; Perrone
Perrone, Carlo Francesco, Sardinian envoy to
England:
Fox, Henry, suggests to, exchanging Gibraltar
for Port Mahon with Spain, **20.** 574n
HW gives goldfish to, to take to Turin in
post-chaise, **35.** 225–6
treaties by, on commerce, lent by him to HW,
35. 81
Perroni, Cts. *See* Zambecarri, ——
Perroni, Lodovico (d. 1757), Conte; (?) Hungarian consul at Ancona:
(?) Spaniards accuse, of circulating seditious
papers at Naples, **18.** 253–4
(?) —— capture, **18.** 253
(?) —— confine, in Rimini prison, **18.** 253,
257
Perroquet. *See* Parakeet

Perrot, Anne (d. ca 1610), m. Sir John Philipps:
husband of, **1**. 375n

Perrot, Humphrey, sexton of St Mary Redcliff,
Bristol 1748–56:
parchments lightly given away by, **16**. 354

Perrot, Sir John (ca 1527–92), Kt:
Chambars's chalk copy of portrait of, **40**.
272n, **43**. 384n
daughter of, **1**. 375n
HW seeks portrait of, **40**. 271
Henry VIII's alleged son, **40**. 271, 272
print of, **1**. 182, **43**. 54, 384

Perrot, Thomas (16th cent.):
Berkley, Mary, marries, **1**. 375n
wife of, **1**. 182n

Perrot d'Ablancourt, Nicolas (1606–64):
Apophtegmes des anciens, Les, by, owned by
Mme du Deffand, **8**. 33

Perruque; perruques:
hair differs from, **41**. 390

Perry, Mr and Mrs:
SH visited by, **12**. 229

Perry, Anne (d. 1741), m. Richard Rigby:
son of, **30**. 330n

Perry, Francis (d. 1765), engraver; antiquary:
Ducarel's letter delivered to HW by, **40**. 222
HW lends medals to, **40**, 218
HW to be shown plates by, **40**. 222
Henry III's coin seen by, **40**. 221
plates engraved by, for Ducarel's *Series of
. . . Coins,* and *Series of English Medals,*
40. 222n
Series of English Medals, A, by: in progress,
16. 157; medals of the Wadhams in, **16**. 210

Perry, George (d. 1757), army officer:
regiment received by, **30**. 136n
suicide of, **30**. 137, **37**. 502

Perry, Micajah (d. 1753), M.P.; alderman; lord
mayor:
Barnard's bust at Stowe confused with, **35**.
76
Scrope almost fights duel with, **17**. 458

Perry, Richard Vining, surgeon and apothecary:
elopes with Clementina Clerke, **11**. 253

Perry, Mrs Richard Vining. *See* Clerke, Clementina

Perry, William (d. 1757), of Penshurst:
Florence visited by, **20**. 379
HW and Chute drive, from dressing-room at
Penshurst, **20**. 389
Mann likes, because he claims to know HW,
20. 379
marriage of, **20**. 398n
obesity of, diminishes after leaving England,
20. 379
wife of, **10**. 122n

Perry, Mrs William. *See* Sidney, Elizabeth

Perry. *See also* Pery

Perryn, Lady. *See* Browne, Mary

Perryn, —— (b. ca 1755–6):
(?) absconds for debt, **33**. 30

Perryn, James (ca 1760–96), army officer:
(?) absconds for debt, **33**. 30
SH visited by, **12**. 224

Perryn, John (ca 1758–1805), army officer:
(?) absconds for debt, **33**. 30

Perryn, Sir Richard (1723–1803), Kt; jurist:
daughters brought by, to HW's ball, **28**. 447–8
robbed, **33**. 30
son of, absconds for debt, **33**. 30

Perryn, Rev. Richard (ca 1754–1825):
(?) absconds for debt, **33**. 30

Persecution:
politics as well as religion thrive on, **23**. 87

Persée. See under Quinault, Philippe

Perseo. See under Sacchini, Antonio

'Perseus,' statue of. *See under* Cellini, Benve-
nuto

Perseverance:
HW's reflections on, **30**. 269
nearer allied to madness than to originality,
33. 490

Persia:
character in *Alonzo* goes to, **32**. 107
England might send Shirley to, to hire troops,
37. 498, 500
Erekle II pretender to throne of, **20**. 401n
etiquette in, **23**. 550
maidens of, **30**. 36
princes of, love duels, **32**. 107
shield from, at SH, **31**. 26
silk of, HW's 'Persian Letter' to Lincoln
wrapped in, **30**. 35
sultana of, Ds of Richmond dressed as, **22**.
148

Persian; Persians:
Raynal discusses, **39**. 168

Persian and the Turkish Tales, The:
HW's copy of, **43**. 93
Pope sends, to Atterbury, **11**. 20
See also Pétis de la Croix, François: *Mille
et un jours*

'Persian friend.' *See* Patapan

'Persian letter':
HW's, **18**. 167n

'Persians':
in England, **5**. 199

Persian Tale; Persian Tales:
HW alludes to, **31**. 56
HW tells, about Sultan Nourmanzor, **23**.
152–3, 162
See also Arabian Nights; Arabian tales;
Pétis de la Croix, François: *Mille et un
jours*

Persius Flaccus, Aulus (A.D. 34–62), satirist:
Satires by, quoted by HW. **10**. 233

Persons. *See* Parsons

Perspective:
classical art lacks, **35**. 445

Perspiration:
bootikins induce, **24**. 280
checking of, for medicinal purposes, **19**. 250

[Perspiration, *continued*]
Franklin walks naked about room at night to bring on, 24. 430
HW tells Mann not to check, for gout, 25. 595
Mann attributes Princesse de Craon's ailments to checking of, by heavy clothing, 18. 110

Persse, Mr:
SH visited by, 12. 237

Perth, Ds of. *See* Gordon, Lady Jean

Perth, D. of. *See* Drummond, James (1648–1716); Drummond, James (ca 1673–1720); Drummond, James (1713–46); Drummond, Lord John (1714–47)

Perth, Scotland:
Conway stationed at, 37. 216–22
English brigade goes to, 37. 249
Gowrie conspiracy at, 29. 262n
Murray lord lieutenant and M.P. for, 29. 53n
Stormont, Vcts, aids rebels in, 19. 283
Young Pretender at, 19. 102n, 105, 107, 167, 208, 283

Pertici, Signora. *See* Isola, Anna

Pertici, Caterina:
acts in burlettas in London, 43. 265

Pertici, Pietro, 'buffo man'; singer; comedian:
becomes actor on losing singing voice, 18. 198n
burletta of, to rival Tesi's opera, 18. 294
English theatre engagement wanted by, 18. *198*
Garrick admires acting of, in burlettas, 20. 4, 357
HW praises, 18. 198, 20. 41
'Pandolfo' in *La Commèdia in commèdia* successfully played by, 20. 4n
Smith tries to hire, for English performances, 18. 198

Pertinax (d. A.D. 193), Roman emperor:
death of, 6. 465

Pertusati, Conte, Austrian gen.:
wounded at Campo Santo, 18. 164

Peru:
Anson to have conquered, 9. 55
Atahualpa the last Inca of, 29. 102n
bark of, 43. 76–7
conquered by Spain, 28. 175, 217
England might aid revolution in, 25. 292n
English fleet mighty enough to capture, 11. 124
Englishman's life worth more than conquest of, 21. 558
European usurpations in, 34. 202
from Paris to, French are defeated, 21. 352
gold and silver thread cheap in, 33. 262
gold of, 30. 297
HW wishes to correspond no more in language of, 33. 266
inhumanities in, 36. 221
Inquisition in, 12. 120
'king' of, crowned at Quito, 22. 426

language of, 33. 261–2, 266–7
Londoners would soon forget conqueror of, 38. 182
Marmontel's drama on conquest of, 28. 299–301
masters of, supposedly generous, 24. 413
milk-maid of, 39. 292
riches of, for English crown, 32. 325
Robertson gives no account of conquest of, 15. 125n
Spain finds, a burden, 32. 328
Spaniards in: atrocities by, 29. 102; outdone by English in India, 23. 387, 396–7; savages and barbarians, 34. 177
Spanish domination of, 32. 272
treasures of, diverted to the Thames, 38. 188
verses in language of, 33. 258, 262–3
viceroy of, *see* Amat y Junient Planella Aimeric y Saint Pau, Manuel de
wealth of, 13. 138

Perugia (Italy):
Lobkowitz at, 18. 529
Richecourt grand prior of, 19. 394
Spanish army active at, 18. 42, 76, 542, 19. 7, 10
Stosch's correspondence with learned man at, interrupted by Inquisitor on suspicion of freemasonry, 34. 11–12

Peruke-maker. *See* Rogers, ——

Pérusse, Marquise de. *See* Artaguette d'Iron, Jeanne-Victoire-Marie d'

Pérusse. *See also* Pérusse des Cars

Pérusseau *or* Perussault, Sylvain (ca 1678–1753), Louis XV's confessor:
(?) Louis XV's lessons from, 22. 415
Pompadour, Marquise de, retires in order to appease, 20. 236

Pérusse des Cars, Françoise-Émilie (1747–1823), m. (1767) Armand-Louis-Joseph Paris de Montmartel, Marquis de Brunoy:
social relations of, with Duchesse de la Vallière, 7. 345

Pérusse des Cars, Louis-François-Marie (1737–1813), Comte des Cars:
social relations of, in Paris, 7. 446, 447

Peruvians:
destruction of, 34. 161
ghosts of, must insult European usurpers, 25. 109
Jephson might do a tragedy about, 41. 292
religion of, 41. 292

Peruzzi, Palazzo:
(?) Cowper takes, 23. 449n

Peruzzi, Leopolda. *See* Berzichelli, Maria Leopolda

Perversion, sexual:
frequency of, with Greek and Roman poets, 37. 8
instances of, 18. 369, 20. 41, 53
offensiveness of, to modern taste, 37. 8
rumour of, 37. 244
scandal about, among Irish rulers, 20. 316
verses on, 18. 369, 20. 316

Winstanley's joke on, **20.** 317–18

Pery, Edmond Sexten (1719–1806), cr. (1785) Vct Pery; Speaker of the Irish House of Commons 1771–85:

chief of the Patriots, **10.** 8

Halifax permits, to support popular Septennial Bill, **38.** 149

Hamilton's eloquence convinces, **10.** 8

name of, corrected, **43.** 374

teller for minority in Irish Parliament, **37.** 463

Pesaro, Francesco (1739–1819), Venetian diplomatist:

(?) Mann told by, of Greek refugees in Venice, **23.** 226

Pesaro (Italy):

Lobkowitz may shut Spaniards up in, **18.** 405

—— retreats to, **18.** 542

Montemar visits, **17.** 323, 342, 350

pope's ship from, **17.** 8

Spaniards at, **17.** 323, 342, 350, 379, **18.** 76, 335, 339, 412, 419

—— may retire to, **18.** 174

Spanish barks may escape to, **18.** 288

Velluti to visit, **17.** 323

Pescara, Marchese di. *See* Avalos, Ferdinando Francesco d'

Pescara (Italy):

Austrians hope to capture, **18.** 460

Landini governor of, **19.** 55n

Neapolitan troops assembled in, **19.** 345

Pescetti, Giovanni Battista (1704–66):

Alexander in Persia by, **17.** 184n

Arsaces by, **13.** 142n

dates of, corrected, **43.** 242

Manzuoli sings arias by, **22.** 264n

Polidoro by, **17.** 302, **43.** 242

Pesciolini. *See* Venerosi Pesciolini

Pest (Hungary):

Conway and Scott visit, **39.** 538

Pestalozzi, Giuseppe (ca 1683–1751), Barone; Gen.:

capture of, **18.** 460, 478

Pesters, John de:

Prestage auctions effects of, **37.** 465

Pesters, Nikolaus de, Cts of Denbigh's nephew:

Fontenoy accounts of, agree with HW's, **19.** 56

in Dutch service in Flanders, **19.** 56

(?) Lobkowitz's retreat described by, **18.** 529

Mann's old friend, **18.** 514, **19.** 56

Pestilence. *See* Plague

Pestre. *See* Pesters

Pet (surname). *See* Pett

Petch *or* Peach, William, page to D. of York:

(?) illness of, **22.** 225n

Petempaucum (India):

English defeat at, **25.** 149n

Pet en l'air (dressing-gown):

eccentric Englishwoman wears, to assembly in Florence, **24.** 260

HW mentions, in verses, **10.** 115

Montagu, Lady Mary Wortley, wears riding coat as, **22.** 3

verses about, **18.** 369

Peter, St:

cock-crowing and, **37.** 67

HW imagines Cts of Bath's squabble with, **18.** 8

HW jokes about countesses received by, **9.** 226

jail delivery of, **35.** 355

Joseph II might dethrone, **23.** 117

keys of: **37.** 15, 77; Kingston, Ds of, secures her treasures under, **24.** 234

Matilda gives patrimony to, **22.** 562

paintings of: **2.** 152, 155; by Lanfranco, **10.** 346; by Steenwyk, **16.** 155; by Titian, **15.** 335

patrimony of, **20.** 459, **22.** 562

Paul, St, disagreed with, **2.** 283

popes the successors of, **17.** 204, **21.** 291

saints probably more familiar to, than Mme de Sévigné is, **35.** 393

Westminster Abbey dedicated to, **24.** 382n

Peter I (1672–1725) (the Great), Czar of Russia 1682–1725:

Catherine II has celebration at tomb of, **23.** 249

civilized everything but himself, **12.** 257

Magnan privy councillor of, **18.** 548n

Maintenon, Mme de, visited by, at St-Cyr, **10.** 292

niece of, **13.** 217n

portrait of, offered to HW, **6.** 305

Reynolds might paint Deptford episode of, **31.** 243

Russians taught by, to read, **22.** 71

Stanislas I profited by wars of, **22.** 404

tyranny of, **11.** 207

Peter II (1715–30), Czar of Russia 1727–30:

Anne succeeds, **13.** 217n

Peter III (1728–62), Czar of Russia Jan.–July 1762:

abdication of, **22.** 58, 74

Austrian and Prussian adherents contend for favour of, **22.** 14

Austrians rejoice at any misfortunes of, **22.** 52

Bestuchev allegedly placates, by favouring Prussians, **21.** 144n

—— expects, to succeed Elizabeth, **21.** 159n

Bologna Gazette's report about, **22.** 19

Botta says, will never join Frederick II against Maria Theresa, **22.** 40–1

Catherine II buried beside, **34.** 229

—— deprives Frederick II of friendship of, **23.** 145

—— dethrones, **10.** 38–9, **22.** 54, 56–60, 61–2, 81, **23.** 329, **35.** 314–15, **38.** 162

——'s execution never intended by, **23.** 207

——'s manifesto on death of, **22.** 64, 74–6, 570n, **33.** 36–7

——'s supposed part in murder of, **29.** 60n, **31.** 162, **32.** 390, **34.** 153

——'s treatment of, **3.** 298, 299

[Peter III, *continued*]
—— weeps for, and wants to go to his funeral, **22.** 71
—— would have been divorced by, **22.** 57
—— would have been imprisoned by, **22.** 68, **23.** 215
children's legitimacy doubted by, **35.** 314
China, Emperor of, reminds Catherine II of murder of, **23.** 116, **24.** 333
Colberg's conquest may induce, to keep foothold in Pomerania, **22.** 10–11
——'s inhabitants generously treated by, **22.** 22
'cooped,' **10.** 38–9
Danish crown to have descended to, **10.** 39
death of: asserted by Russians to have been non-violent, **23.** 215; attributed by Orlov to despair and drink, **23.** 185; preferable to exile in Siberia, **22.** 68
Elisaveta Vorontsova's letter from, given to HW by Buckinghamshire, **22.** 55n
embarkation attempt of, at Cronstadt, **22.** 58
English revolutions pale beside murder of, **22.** 91
Frederick II friend of, **10.** 39
—— object of enthusiasm of, **22.** 16, 54, 61, **23.** 145
—— said to be likely to get aid from, **22.** 19
——'s peace treaty with, **38.** 154n
—— the only beneficiary of, so far, **22.** 23
German campaign will reveal allegiance of, **22.** 40
ghost of, should hail Russian fleet from dome at Constantinople, **23.** 195
Gudovich aide-de-camp or adjutant to, **22.** 11n, 58n
HW curious about fate of, **22.** 59–60
HW hails accession of, **38.** 154
HW hopes, is not assassinated, **10.** 39
HW tells Hertford more about, than he could hear in London, **38.** 166
impostor claims to be, **23.** 547, **32.** 184
Ivan VI to have been made heir to, **22.** 57
leniency of, augurs well, **22.** 22
Maria Theresa's assurances from, **22.** 10
mistress of, is Vorontsov's niece, **22.** 55
mistress said to have received Order of St Catherine from, **22.** 58
mistress to have been married by, **23.** 215
murder of: makes past crimes seem more credible, **22.** 65; Orlov said to have committed, **28.** 477n; rumoured, **38.** 164
Muscovy owned by, **10.** 39
nobles to erect statue to, in gratitude for freedom, **22.** 22
Orlov's denial of murder of, not believed by HW, **23.** 195
Pitt, Anne, jokes about dethronement of, **10.** 39
proclaimed czar at army in Pomerania, **22.** 1
Prussia liked by, **22.** 7
Pugachev impersonates, **23.** 547
Razumovskiï forced into conspiracy against, **22.** 456

Reynolds should paint Catherine II strangling, **36.** 237
said to be impotent, **22.** 57
Schleswig claimed by, from Denmark, **22.** 54n
son born to, **20.** 457
son said to have been repudiated by, **22.** 57, 75, **23.** 215
Swedish crown to have descended to, **10.** 39
Voltaire will probably claim that Catherine II did not murder, **22.** 253
Vorontsov may be banished by, **22.** 11
—— scolds, for zeal for Frederick II, **22.** 62n
Vorontsova, Mme, attracts, **22.** 173
Vorontsova, Elisaveta, informs sister of intention of, to imprison Catherine II, **22.** 68
——'s letter from, given to HW by E. of Buckinghamshire, **22.** 55n
Peter (1745–98), P. of Brunswick:
Catherine II releases, in care of Juliane of Denmark, **34.** 3n
Peter, ——, HW's (?) coachman:
fish begged by, for HW, **35.** 205
Montagu wants chariot to be inspected by, **9.** 196
signs himself as 'Ham' in HW's letter, **35.** 228
'Peter':
robbing, to pay '*Peter*,' **33.** 572
'Peter,' Conway's greyhound:
HW, when gouty, glad to be away from, **38.** 66
'Peter and My Lord Quidam.' *See under* Williams, Sir Charles Hanbury
Peterborough, Bp of. *See* Hinchliffe, John (1731–94); Kennett, White (1660–1728); Lamb, Robert (ca 1703–69); Parsons, John (1761–1819); Terrick, Richard (1710–77); Thomas, John (1696–1781)
Peterborough, Cts of. *See* Browne, Robiniana (d. 1794); Robinson, Anastasia (d. 1755)
Peterborough, Dean of. *See* Lockyer, Francis (ca 1666–1740)
Peterborough, E. of. *See* Mordaunt, Charles (ca 1658–1735); Mordaunt, Henry (1621–97)
Peterborough, Northants:
bishops of: palace of, **10.** 347; portraits of, **10.** 347
cathedral at: façade of, noble, **33.** 420; HW has seen, twice, **33.** 420; HW likes only the façade of, **10.** 92; whitewashed, **10.** 346
Cole and HW propose to visit, **16.** 194
Cole describes, **10.** 346–7
deanery at, **10.** 347
Gunton's *History* of, **1.** 16, 175, 351
—— vicar of, **1.** 16n
HW dines at, **28.** 36n
HW mentions, **10.** 86
HW to visit, **40.** 288
Jacob, bookseller at, **16.** 194
Lort receives MS on painting from, **16.** 196
Palmer of, **16.** 192n, 193
Pulteney recommends Pearce for bishopric of, **43.** 251
St John's Church at, described by Cole, **10.** 347

Terrick obtains see of, from D. of Devonshire, 30. 209n
visitors to: Chute, 10. 82; Cole, 10. 91, 92, 346–7; HW, 10. 82, 91, 92, 346–7; Montagu, 10. 82; Terrick, 10. 347
Peterborough, Earls of:
Dee's black stone owned by, 33. 324, 43. 389
Peterborough collection:
Germain, Lady Elizabeth, disperses natural philosophy part of, 23. 286
Peterborough Court, Fleet St, London:
Rickaby, printer in, 43. 390n
Peter Fleming, ballad:
Selwyn mentions, 10. 32–3
'Peter Gore':
freemason's name for Pythagoras, 39. 158
Peterhoff (Russia):
Catherine II at, when told that Peter III may kill her, 22. 57
Peterhouse, Cambridge:
Gray of, 15. 314, 43. 191
——'s hyperbolic description of quadrangle of, 13. 137
——'s removal from, 28. 152
——'s residence at, 13. 78
Keene, Edmund, master of, 20. 346n
master of, *see* Keene, Edmund; Whalley, John
resembles Presbyterian meeting-houses, 13. 80
Tories at, 13. 58
Peter Leopold, Grand D. of Tuscany. *See* Leopold II
Peter Martyr. *See* Vermigli, Pietro Martire
Peter Peloquin, ship:
Sally captured by, 21. 16n
Peter Regalatus (1392–1456), St:
canonization of, 19. 171n
Peters, ——, 'Russia merchant':
Cony gets introduction to Musin-Pushkin from, 26. 55
Peters, Eugenia (d. 1783), m. (before 1757), Philip Stanhope:
advertisement by, to Chesterfield's *Letters*, 28. 157
Chesterfield's letters published by, 28. 144n, 42. 122
——'s portraits of his contemporaries copied by, 28. *145*
HW might dissatisfy, as editor of Chesterfield's letters, 31. 173–4
Peters, Hugh (1598–1660), Independent divine:
HW does not love, 15. 131
Petersberg: Petersbourgh: Petersburg. *See* Petersburg
Petersfield, Hants:
Beckford's candidate for election at, 35. 171n, 43. 361
Bertie, Lord Robert, meets George III at, 32. 129
Petersham, Vct. *See* Stanhope, Charles (1753–1829); Stanhope, William (1719–79)
Petersham, Vcts; Petersham, Lady Caroline. *See* Fitzroy, Lady Caroline (1722–84)
Petersham, Surrey:
Bellenden's villa in, 9. 359n

Brooke at, 9. 135
Campbell, Lord Frederick, inherits Bellenden's house at, 43. 347
Douglas House at: D. of Queensberry's house, left to Lady Jane Scott, 33. 67; left by Lady Jane Scott to Lady Frances Scott, 33. 146
drought at, 10. 38
Egremont offers house at, to Cts Waldegrave, 40. 280–2
HW calls on Lady Cecilia Johnston at, 35. 474
HW to visit D. of Clarence (William IV) at, 11. 332
HW visits Lady Elizabeth Stuart Mackenzie at, 12. 12
Ham House at, 10. 306n
Hertford, Cts of, says she is as demanding as the lady at, 39. 268
highwaymen endanger route to, 35. 525
Johnston, Lady Cecilia, afraid to leave, because of highwaymen, 33. 353
—— at, 33. 347, 35. 474
Jordan, Mrs, frequents D. of Clarence's villa at, 11. 368
Mordaunt, Lady Mary, visits Lady Cecilia Johnston, at, 35. 521
Penn, Lady Juliana, lives at, 11. 7n, 34. 14
Rutland, Ds of, at, 9. 135
Stuart Mackenzie's villa at, 11. 35n, 31. 287–8
Walpole, Elizabeth, dies at, 11. 28n
Petersham Lane, near Richmond:
island off bottom of, 11. 341n
Petersham Lodge, Richmond, Harrington's seat:
Foxes, HW, and Waldegraves to breakfast at, 31. 13–14
Ligonier and Harrington to play whist at, 19. 166
Peterson, Christabella (ca 1733–91), m. (1751) Solomon Dayrolles:
SH visited by, 12. 234
Peter the Great. See Voltaire: *Histoire de l'Empire de Russie sous Pierre le Grand*
Peter the Hermit (Peter of Amiens) (1050–1113):
British situation could not be worse if directed by, 33. 9
Crusades started by, might be imitated by Lady Craven, 42. 184
Peter the Wild Boy (ca 1712–85):
Ossory, Lady, has woodland life of, 33. 526
Pether, Abraham (1756–1812), landscape painter:
SH visited by, 12. 251
Petherton, Somerset:
Venner practised at, 1. 180n
Pétion de Villeneuve, Jérôme (1756–94) mayor of Paris:
rises from Mirabeau's ashes, 34. 154
Pétis de la Croix, François (1653–1713) orientalist:
Mille et un jours, Les, by, 4. 261, 11. 20n

[Pétis de la Croix, François, *continued*]
Persian and Turkish Tales by, **9.** 230–1, **20.** 347, **35.** 313, **37.** 466

Thousand and One Days, The, by, **9.** 230–1

Petit, ——, priest:
song about, **4.** 164

'Petit Chien, Le.' *See under* La Fontaine, Jean de

Petit de Bachaumont, Louis (1690–1771), author:
Mémoires secrets . . . by Pidansat de Mairobert and: **6.** 478, 483, **28.** 328n, **43.** 102; anecdote in, about Voltaire, **33.** 377–8; HW describes contents and style of, **28.** 324–5; HW quotes anecdote from, **28.** 326; HW sends to Mason, **28.** 324, 331, 333, 338; printing of, **28.** 324n, **43.** 301

Petites-Maisons (Paris insane asylum):
Du Deffand, Mme, mentions, **3.** 326, 329
Selwyn fit for, **5.** 189

Petit Hôtel d'Entragues, at Paris:
recommended, **37.** 41

Petition; petitions:
about Appleby and Oxfordshire elections, **20.** 435n
about roads and poor rates, **31.** 5n
African trade the subject of, **20.** 126n
against Fonnereau, **30.** 331n
against North's administration, unsuccessful, **33.** 166–7
against Rigby's election for Sudbury, **30.** 331n
American, to George III, **24.** 128n
American Congress's, to George III, House of Commons, and English people, **39.** 227, 231
answer to, should have been more prudent, **23.** 197
Barbados seeks relief by, **25.** 109n
Bedford's opposing (and Ossory's favouring) Seditious Meetings and Treasonable Practices Bills, **34.** 209n
Birmingham's, for enforcement of American acts, **24.** 77
bluster about, ends, **23.** 168
Buckinghamshire's, **25.** 572
Bury election may produce, **35.** 612
carpenters might present, lamenting lack of demand for wooden legs, **38.** 509
Conway said to be threatened with, **39.** 222
Cornish, **17.** 233
counties and towns send, to Parliament, **25.** 6, 10, 12, 18, 29, 34, 41
Dunning seeks to prevent Parliament's dissolution or prorogation until demands of, are satisfied, **25.** 41
elections will produce, **23.** 66
fashionable in Dec. 1779, **25.** 66
for and against new Paddington Road, **37.** 452n, 453n
Fox, Henry, said to be made ill by, **23.** 152
Frederick's and Hume's, **17.** 318
French remonstrances compared with, **35.** 337
from Berwick, **20.** 453n
from Manchester, **25.** 578n

from Surrey and London, **35.** 334
Gordon, Lord George, sends, to National Assembly, **34.** 62n
HW's, in verse, to Pitt, **38.** 41
HW will not sign, for reform of expenditure of public money, **35.** 501
half-pay naval captains', **23.** 462
Heathcote proposes, at meeting, **19.** 107
Irish, from Belfast and Dublin, **23.** 529n
Kirkwall and Westminster present, against C. J. Fox, **25.** 488n
livery of London's, **23.** 132
London merchants', drafted by Glover, **37.** 200
London's: against Quebec Bill, **39.** 175; hasten Bute's downfall, **22.** 129; to Crown, against Wilkes's expulsion from Commons, **39.** 114, 115
London's American-trading merchants to send, to Parliament, **39.** 231n
Mann distrusts, **25.** 23
merchants': **17.** 295, 353; for reconciliation with America, **39.** 247, 248
Middlesex freeholders', **23.** 114, 120, 130
Mountrath's and Berkeley's, over Hedon election, **35.** 20n
Northamptonshire's, **25.** 10
on Hedon election, **17.** 234n, **35.** 20n
Opposition encouraged by, **25.** 29
Oxford's, against dissenters' relief, **33.** 98n
Parliamentary vacillation over, **23.** 223
Parliament's postponement encourages, **23.** 150
—— to receive, **17.** 232–3, 295, 343–4
periwig-makers', to George III, **38.** 509
presented in House of Commons, **25.** 34
Protestant Association's, carried to Parliament, **25.** 52–3
Pulteney presents, **43.** 240
reform associations', through county delegates, **36.** 198n
sailors', to Parliament, **23.** 21
Scottish, **23.** 151; anti-Catholic, **24.** 475n
supporters of Bill of Rights present, **23.** 114
undertakers for, in English counties, **23.** 163
West Indies should issue, **41.** 315
Westminster: **17.** 232–3, 298, **20.** 223–4, 235; election, **20.** 223n
Whigs apt to resort to, **33.** 167
Wiltshire, Worcester, and Yorkshire to present, **23.** 132

Petitioning:
in Cambridge, **2.** 207–8

Petition to the R.H. Mr Pelham in Favour of Mr Maclean, A. See under Bentley, Richard (1708–82)

Petit-maître; petit-maîtres:
HW's fine costume considered characteristic of, **18.** 181
in cantata, **35.** 106

Petit Musc, Rue du, in Paris:
Célestins church in, **13.** 163n
Dumont de Valdagou in, **4.** 353n

Petitot, Jean (1607–91), painter in enamel:
Anecdotes of Painting mentions, **40.** 238

enamels by: **5.** 417n, **15.** 190, 191n; HW buys, at Caylus's auction, **39.** 32n

Ennery collects paintings by, **6.** 136, **7.** 325

HW covets painting by, of Mme d' Olonne, **14.** 146

HW mentions Ds of Portland's bequest of miniature by, to Mrs Delany, **42.** 179n, 254

Harenc de Presle collects paintings by, **6.** 136

Mayerne introduces, to Charles I, **40.** 238

painted only in enamel, **1.** 25

paintings by, of: Godfrey, Mrs, **22.** 485n; Gramont, Comtesse de, **10.** 4; James II, **9.** 412; Maintenon, Mme de, **10.** 293; Middleton, Mrs, **16.** 324n; Olonne, Mme d', **6.** 96–8, 102, 111, 116, 119, 125, 128, 129, 140–2, 150, 153, 168, 181, 215, 217, 239, 245, 251, 254, 255, 258, 260, 262, 263, 266, 267, 269, 271, 274–5, 280, 282–3, 288, 368, **14.** 146, **32.** 282, **39.** 198, 208, 215; Petitot (self-portrait), **12.** 255n, **42.** 179n, 254; (?) Richmond, Ds of, **1.** 24; Sévigné, Mme de, **3.** 73, **7.** 313

Walker tells HW of portraits of, **42.** 302

Petit prophète de Boemischbroda, Le. See under Grimm, Friedrich Melchior

Petits-Augustins, Rue des, Faubourg St-Germain, Paris:

Cole lodges in, **1.** 99

Craufurd, James, lodges in, **4.** 283

Hôtel de Luxembourg in, **13.** 11n, 162n, **37.** 41n

Petits-Champs, Rue des, Paris:

Aranda and Brunoy live in, **5.** 406

Hôtel du Controle in, **6.** 455n

Petit Trianon, Versailles:

HW visits, **7.** 334

Louis XVI gives, to Marie-Antoinette, **6.** 57

Marie-Antoinette entertains at, **6.** 60

Petra, Vincenzo (1662–1747), cardinal, 1724:

Louis XV wants French candidate elected by, **17.** 20–1

Sinzendorf reproved by, in Conclave, **13.** 212

Petraia, near Florence; Grand Ducal villa:

Barbantane on way to, **22.** 537

cannon at Modena may be audible at, **17.** 443

Craon at, **17.** 95, 100, 109, 122, 443, 463, **18.** 1, 17, **19.** 498

—— rented, **20.** 116

——'s summer residence, **17.** 390n

Craon, Princesse de, at, **17.** 109, 443, 463, 481, **18.** 1, **19.** 407, 500, **20.** 14, **22.** 29, 536, **23.** 296

—— passes summers at, **22.** 224–5

Craons invite Mann, Chute, and Whithed to visit, **17.** 443

—— sorrowful at, **35.** 28

—— write from, **40.** 38

destitute of necessary furniture, **22.** 536

Francis I gave life use of, to Princesse de Craon, **23.** 296

—— owns, **17.** 390n

furniture supplied to, by Craons, **20.** 116

George II's condition discussed at, **17.** 390

Grafton, Ds of, to visit, on horseback, **22.** 29

HW's favourite, **22.** 224

HW's 'sweet,' **22.** 29

HW to visit Craons at, **37.** 69

Mann might pick up news at, **17.** 116

—— takes D. of York to, **22.** 224–5

Morice astonished at size of palm tree at, **22.** 29

Rosenberg drives Princesse de Craon from, **23.** 296

terrace of, has large palm tree, **22.** 29

Tuscan Court prefers Lappeggi to, **22.** 412

visitors to: Beauvau, **19.** 500; (?) Chute, **17.** 443, **18.** 1; HW, **22.** 29, 224; Mann, **17.** 443, 463, 481, **18.** 1, **19.** 498, 500, **22.** 537; Morice, **22.** 29; Richecourt, **20.** 15; Whithed, **17.** 443, **18.** 1

water at, bad, **17.** 481

Wilczek occupies, **23.** 296

Petrarch (Francesco Petrarca) (1304–74), poet:

Du Deffand, Mme, gives opinion of, **4.** 46

HW's appraisal of, **40.** 377–8

harmony and grace of, **16.** 272

life of, *see under* Sade, Jacques-François-Paul-Aldonce de

Mason would like to be, **28.** 341

notes by, on Vatican MS, **21.** 169

Sade's life of, **4.** 22n, 24, 28, 33, 37n, 46, 56, **31.** 143

sonnet form used by, **29.** 342

sonnets by: HW comments on, **15.** 260–1; Italians give titles to best of, **16.** 270

West would 'rifle,' **13.** 135

Petre, Dorothy (1534–1618), m. (1555) Nicholas Wadham:

medal of, **16.** 210

Petre, Edward (1631–99) confessor of James II:

a fool, **28.** 72

in Stratford's tragedy, **29.** 223

Petre, Robert Edward (1742–1801), 9th Bn Petre, 1742:

Charlotte, Q., to visit, **33.** 66

estate repurchased from, by D. of Norfolk, **32.** 384

George III and Q. Charlotte accept invitation of, **28.** 446n, **43.** 304

George III to be entertained at house of, **28.** 446

Southcote, Mrs, leaves Woburn Farm to, **31.** 210n

Petre, Robert James (1713–42), 8th Bn Petre, 1713:

buildings of, cracked and without prospects, **9.** 164

evergreens planted by, at Worksop, **35.** 270

Thorndon Hall of, visited by Barrett Lennard and HW, **35.** 184

Petrie, Mr:

SH visited by, **12.** 221

Petrie, Robert (ca 1727–1803), M.D.; physician to Tower of London:

SH visited by, **12.** 222

Petrignani, Giacomo, officer of Corsican recruits for Minorca:

sails to Minorca, **25.** 199

Petrillo, ——:
Tesi's dependent, **17**. 130
Walsegg insults at burletta, **17**. 130
Petrockstow, Devon:
Heanton Satchville at, **14**. 50n
Petroni, Conte Alessandro (ca 1704–71), Papal official:
Albani's substitute, **37**. 57
assembly of: attended by Giuseppe, Riviera, and Whithed, **19**. 85; Dunbar harangues, **19**. 218
HW ushered about by, in Rome, at Albani's request, **17**. 9
Petronius Arbiter, Gaius (d. ca 66), Roman writer:
Conway quotes, **37**. 16
explanatory notes needed for, **32**. 320
HW's copies of, **37**. 16n
Montagu imitates, **9**. 6
Satyricon by: HW quotes, **35**. 196; West quotes, **13**. 101
'Petruchio,' character in Shakespeare's *Taming of the Shrew*:
Kemble the 'representative' of, **11**. 236
Petry, Nicolas-Antoine (ca 1734–1812), Mme du Deffand's reader; 'mon Invalide':
Du Deffand, Mme, dictates letter to, **7**. 75–7, 89, 96, 104–6, 119–20, 142–3, 156–7, 159, 160, 204, 430
—— dictates morning letters to, **7**. 81, 223
—— dictates part of letter to, **5**. 376, **7**. 62–4, 81–4, 131–4, 146–7
—— read to by, **6**. 324n
—— settles annuity on, **7**. 39, 192
——'s services from, as reader, begin: 6–7 A.M., **4**. 471, **6**. 428; 7–8 A.M., **7**. 204, 217
—— to dictate letter to, **7**. 83
—— wears out, **6**. 445
reads well, **4**. 471
Richelieu, Cardinal de, hated by, **4**. 471
Pett, Robert (d. 1776), naval Capt.:
Mann meets, at Leghorn, **18**. 509
Walpole family favours, **18**. 509
Pettalazzi. *See* Pestalozzi
'Pettapanino.' *See* 'Patapanino'
'Pettegola.' *See* Vanbrugh, Philippia, Mrs Goldsworthy
Petticoat; petticoats:
Blount, Martha, pins up, in rain, **33**. 511
canvas, **37**. 78, 81
Caroline's, for Coronation, **38**. 109–10
dimity: **22**. 3; worn by Lady Mary Wortley Montagu, **10**. 5
figure clad in, in Raphael painting, **35**. 37
HW to hide under Mme de Sévigné's, **35**. 604
Queen Anne's, at Blenheim, **9**. 289
red flannel, **38**. 510
Rich, Mary, displays, when falling, **35**. 276
Senauki's, **42**. 236
swanskin, **38**. 196
trapes in short, **33**. 313
under, *see* Underpetticoat
woman puts jordan under, **18**. 307
women think little of, **28**. 131

Pettiward, Mrs Roger Mortlock. *See* Sandwell, Douglas
Pettman, William, of Sandwich:
Letter to Robert Heron, A, by, **16**. 278n
Petty, Henry (1675–1751), 1st E. of Shelburne; M.P.:
Fox, Lady Caroline, receives legacy from, **20**. 248
Petty (after 1818 Petty-Fitzmaurice), Henry (1790–1863), 3d M. of Lansdowne, 1809:
birth of, **33**. 204
Petty, James (ca 1708–50), styled Vct Dunkeron:
Mirepoix lives at house of, at Turnham Green, **9**. 154
Petty, John (1706–61), cr. (1753) E. of Shelburne, n.c.:
art purchases by, at (?) Batt's sale, **37**. 460
riches compensate, for lack of parts, **37**. 459–60
wife of, **5**. 88n, **10**. 216n
Petty, Mrs John. *See* Fitzmaurice, Mary
Petty, John Henry (1726–1809), styled Vct Fitzmaurice 1765–84, and E. Wycombe 1784–1805, 2d M. of Lansdowne, 1805; M.P.:
French war opposed by, in Parliament, **39**. 508n
(?) Pitt administration need not fear, **39**. 509
Petty, Sir William (1623–89):
phrase invented by, **29**. 86n
Petty (formerly Fitzmaurice), William (1737–1805), 2d E. of Shelburne, cr. (1784) M. of Lansdowne:
(?) acts unlike anybody else, **39**. 212
administration of: begins, **25**. 293–4, 299; Carlisle's resignation blows up, **33**. 385n; defeated, **33**. 388–9; formation of, **29**. 173n; HW hopes, will be pacific, **25**. 337; will give Parliament novelty, **22**. 336
American conciliatory bills opposed by, **24**. 359n
American prisoners rather than Berkeley Sq. house benefited by, **33**. 6n
anti-papist, **29**. 63
army disgusted by appointment of, **9**. 329
arrival of coach at house of, allays HW's fears in Gordon riots, **33**. 174
Barbados thanks, for recalling Cuninghame, **33**. 357n
Barré friend of, **23**. 65
—— gets pension through, **33**. 345n, 348n
—— intended by, for Bengal, **38**. 378
Barrington preferred by, for Salisbury diocese, **33**. 338n
Bedford, D. of, defeated by, **7**. 367
Bedford faction objects to, **22**. 571
Berkeley Sq. called 'demesnes' of, **31**. 235
—— the home of, **29**. 193, **33**. 394, 396
biographical information about, corrected, **43**. 143, 369
Board of Trade to be headed by, **22**. 130
Bordeaux to be visited by, **6**. 352, 354, 355
Bunbury's intimacy with, connects him with H. Fox, **22**. 7n
Burke attacks, **29**. 280–1

Bute flattered by, **38**. 248n, 255n

—— may be negotiating with Pitt through, **38**. 334

(?) Calcraft and, keep up the Court's spirits, **38**. 201

Caracciolo friend of, **5**. 145

Carmarthen's dinner not attended by, **33**. 554n

Cavendish, Lord John, declines to serve under, **25**. 293

—— makes motion against, **33**. 388n

Cavendish faction deserts, **29**. 264

Charlotte's house visited by, for conference on new ministry, **25**. 260–1

Chatham answered by, in Middlesex election debate, **23**. 209n

—— complains of removal of, **23**. 61

—— shields, **22**. 571n

—— proscribes, **22**. 161

—— 's American bill violently opposed by, **32**. 235

—— 's faction headed by, **28**. 383

—— supported by, in debate over Wilkes, **23**. 209n

—— upheld by, **39**. 246

—— would give essential post to, **28**. 377

Cholmondeley not preferred by, **25**. 319

Clavering's and Blackett's motion opposed by, **39**. 126

continues in ministry, **3**. 400n

Conway's connection with, **6**. 235

declines to form ministry, **29**. 205, 207

Dick to carry letters from, to Italy, **23**. 55

dismissal of, for anti-Court voting, **22**. 189, **38**. 254–5

Du Deffand, Mme, has not met, **5**. 153, 157, 163

—— 's social relations with, **6**. 100, 352, 354, 355

Dunning friend of, **25**. 262

Edgcumbe's dismissal announced to him by, **22**. 470n

engagement of, rumoured, **5**. 456, 460

English-French trade mentioned by, in House of Lords, **24**. 254n

faction of, urges recall of British troops from Germany, **21**. 552n

Fitzpatrick brother-in-law of, follows C. J. Fox instead of, **33**. 341n

Florence visited by, **25**. 271

Fox, C. J., bluntly announces his resignation to, **25**. 393

—— quarrels with, **25**. 320

Fox, Henry, quarrels with, **30**. 191n, 230n

—— 's opinion of, **30**. 230

—— 's resignation plans reported by, to George III and Bute, **22**. 134n

Franklin's acquaintance with, **25**. 454n

Fullarton attacked by, **29**. 13n

—— 's duel with, **7**. 218n, **25**. 31, 37, **29**. 13–14

Garter given to, **25**. 273

George III confers with, **25**. 260

—— makes, aide-de-camp, **9**. 329

—— persuaded by, to ask Victor Amadeus III to pardon Virys, **24**. 328n, **35**. 522n

—— sees, in Closet, **39**. 83

—— 's messages to Rockingham carried by, **29**. 215n

—— 's negotiations with, without Rockingham's consent, **25**. 372n

—— 's wish to patch up administration seconded by, **25**. 379

Glapion's appeal to, for Jesuits, **22**. 233n

goes abroad, **23**. 263

Gray inquires about resignation of, **14**. 128

Guines's ball attended by, **32**. 96n

HW alludes to political troubles of, **33**. 216

HW always civilly treated by, **25**. 310, **33**. 129–30

HW and Bedford ready to inform, about Exchequer place, **42**. 33

HW calls: 'ridiculous,' **25**. 407, 437; 'the minister paramount,' **25**. 296

HW condemns faults of, **25**. 372, 380–1, 402, 407

HW criticizes 'finesses' of, **36**. 215

HW expects, to oppose constitutional bills, **29**. 214

HW has omen that prime ministry will go to, **33**. 340

HW imagines, as Master of Ceremonies at Bath, **33**. 468

HW informed by, of omission in *Anecdotes of Painting*, **33**. 246

HW mentions, **29**. 352

HW not friend of, **5**. 157

HW quotes, **23**. 175n

HW's correspondence with, **42**. 57–9, 327–9

HW's opinion of, **33**. 105–6

HW suspects motives of, in supporting Parliamentary reform, **29**. 24, 26, 329n

HW tells, to reform Exchequer ushership but provide for its employees, **42**. 57–8

HW thanked by, for accepting diminished Exchequer income, **42**. 327–8

HW will not attend levee of, **29**. 193n

Hertford not sorry for, **38**. 260–1

Hervey, Bp, rejects offer of, to go to Versailles as peace delegate, **25**. 454

Hillsborough may succeed, as secretary of state, **22**. 569

Horne Tooke's relations with, **11**. 78

house of, in Berkeley Sq., **29**. 193, **31**. 235, **33**. 394, 396

House of Commons tears North and, from power in one year, **25**. 402n

in the country, **25**. 437

Kennett papers bought by, **15**. 98n

'lives on hips and haws,' **33**. 526–7

loan opposed by, in House of Lords, **25**. 402

London to be visited by, **6**. 352, 354, 355

Louis XV talks with, **5**. 163

Mann praised by, **25**. 271

—— sends courier to, **23**. 51, 60, 71

—— 's letters from: convey George III's approbation, **22**. 500–1; do not mention MS ac-

[Petty, William, *continued*]
count of Tuscany, **23**. 27–8; on assuming secretary of state's office, **22**. 447; show continuance as secretary of state, **22**. 581
——'s MS account of Tuscany sent to, through Capt. Steward for George III, **23**. 27–8
——'s 'master and friend,' **25**. 271
(?) —— thinks new ministry might be headed by, **25**. 553–4
Mann, Horace II, acquainted with, **25**. 271
Markham answered by, **2**. 99n
—— provoked by, **28**. 313n
marquessate conferred on, **25**. 542
marriage of, **30**. 271, **33**. 104–6, 107, 109, 115
marriage of, to Miss Molesworth, rumoured, **33**. 6
marriage plans of, announced, **22**. 275
may consider himself Chatham's political heir, **24**. 379
may resign America in secretary of state's office, **22**. 569
ministers may be opposed by, over peace treaties, **25**. 428
ministry formed by, would fail, **25**. 260
ministry might include, **24**. 447n
Molesworth, Frances, rejects, **6**. 13, **24**. 417
North accused by, of rum contract, **33**. 269n
—— administration blamed by, for Keppel's case, conciliatory bills, etc., **24**. 424n
North and C. J. Fox unite to defeat, in Parliament, **25**. 368, 372
opinion of, on combined fleets, **33**. 131
opposition by, in House of Lords, **41**. 9
opposition expected by, from those averse to American independence, **35**. 528
Opposition split by, **29**. 314, 317, 322, 325–6
Ossory aloof to, forfeiting aid in getting peerage, **33**. 346n
Ossory, Lady, sister-in-law of, **33**. 339
—— has letter from, **33**. (?) 246, 251–2
packet sent by courier to, **43**. 282
Paolists drink to health of, **23**. 31n
Paris to be visited by, **6**. 352, 354, 355
—— visited by, **5**. 144–5, **39**. 212n
Parliamentary activity of, on Regency Bill, **38**. 541, 542
Parliamentary motion by, for Irish relief, **39**. 324
Parliamentary motion introduced by, **28**. 485n
Parliamentary motions of: defeated, **29**. 394n; for members to walk at Chatham's burial, **24**. 379n
Parliamentary reforms backed by, **25**. 30
Parliamentary speeches by: against Court, **38**. 248; in House of Lords, **28**. 203n, **29**. 22n
Pitt, William II, may want, in administration, **25**. 553n
popularity falsely vaunted by, **25**. 402
Portland succeeds, as prime minister, **36**. 208
Powys refuses to be secretary at war under, **25**. 474n
Pratt's and James Grenville's continuance will place, in awkward position, **23**. 65
predecessors severely handled by, for their flippancies, **25**. 285

Priestley librarian to, **31**. 329n
prime ministry alone would satisfy, **24**. 493
protest by, **22**. 7
recent Irish earl and more recent English baron, **25**. 273
'reciprocity' a favourite term of, much used and ridiculed at time of peace with America, **25**. 519n
reading by, idle, **33**. 247–8
Regulating Bill supported by, **32**. 129
reports naval preparations on French coast, **6**. 360n
resignation of: **33**. 527; arranged at parley at Calcraft's, **22**. 168n; as first lord of trade, **22**. 167; as prime minister, **25**. 377; as secretary of state, **23**. 62
Richmond, D. of, offended by appointment of, as secretary of state, **30**. 228, 230
—— presents memorial against, **9**. 329
—— replaced by, **3**. 103n
ridiculed, **36**. 209
Rigby supports, against Henry Fox, **41**. 68n
rioters respect, **33**. 175n
Rockingham at odds with, **29**. 63
——'s appointment as prime minister negotiated by, **25**. 260–1
——'s friends averse to, if he takes office, **35**. 516
—— succeeded by, as prime minister, **29**. 258, 263
——'s Whigs' breach with those of, unhealed, **25**. 294
—— will always contend with, **35**. 513
Roscoe's *Poesie del magnifico Lorenzo de' Medici* in library of, **43**. 210
Rose directed by, to explain to HW the Exchequer inquiry, **42**. 31
rumoured as Rockingham's successor, **25**. 389
rumoured as secretary of state for the colonies, **24**. 350n
secretary of state, **3**. 103n, 104, **22**. 439, 443, 571, **25**. 262, 319, **29**. 208, **30**. 228, 230
secretary of state's position coveted by, **22**. 159
(?) speaks well, but lacks judgment and sincerity, **39**. 212
Stanhope's doctrines considered sensible by, **34**. 98
suspected of revolutionary leanings, **11**. 78
Sydney may be succeeded by, as Home Secretary, **25**. 487
system of, for numbering letters, **22**. 563
Temple, dupe of, **36**. 215
Thurlow candidate of, for Bp of Salisbury, **33**. 339
to go abroad after wife's death, **31**. 153
Tories may regret following North against, **25**. 379
Townshend a follower of, **10**. 309n
—— to be succeeded by, **10**. 60
Treasury post named for, **35**. 517
unpopularity of, mounts, **29**. 266
(?) vanity and confidence of, needed to keep up spirits of Court, **38**. 201
Viry, Contessa di, friend of, **24**. 328n, **35**. 522n
Walpole, Sir Robert, praised by, **42**. 327

West, Mrs, sells MSS to, **40**. 253
Weymouth succeeds, as secretary of state, **23**. 62
wife of, **7**. 190n, **9**. 193n
wife of, dies, **23**. 263
wife's separation from, falsely rumoured, **14**. 141
Wiltshire the county of, **29**. 24, 26
witticism by, about D. of Dorset's ignorance, **25**. 487
Woburn to be visited by, with new wife, **30**. 271
would disapprove of HW's lack of interest in Rockingham, **33**. 337
Petty France:
HW makes pun about, **9**. 254
'Petulant.' *See under* Congreve, William: *Way of the World*
Petworth, Sussex:
Bromfield stays with relatives at, **40**. 317
—— writes from, **40**. 313–20, 324–8
Petworth House, Sussex:
Bromfield unable to complete list of paintings at, **40**. 324, 327
Egremont goes to, **21**. 76n
HW compares, with Hampton Court and Tuileries, **9**. 97
HW recommends, to Mary Berry, **12**. 206
in Sussex, not Surrey, **42**. 131
paintings at, unidentified because lists are lost, **40**. 318
portrait at, **10**. 78n
Somerset, D. of, dies at, **20**. 9n
—— leaves furniture of, to E. of Hertford, **20**. 10n
visitors to: Chute, **9**. 97–8; Conway, **39**. 309; HW, **9**. 97–8
Welderen sees Egremont's new liveries at, **32**. 154
Wyndham, Sir Charles, succeeds to, **20**. 11n
Pevensey, Vct. *See* Holroyd, George Augustus Frederick Charles
Peverel, Alicia (fl. *temp*. Henry I), m. Sir Hamon de Peche:
family of, **2**. 115
Peverel, Ingelrica (fl. 1070), m. Ranulph de Peverel:
stone effigies of, in Hatfield Priory, **2**. 175
Peverel, Pagan (fl. *temp*. Henry I):
founder of Barnwell Abbey, **2**. 115
Peverel family:
pedigree of, **2**. 115
Pevol, Choiseul's servant:
escapes injury, **5**. 122
Pew; pews:
at Gloucester Cathedral, hung with damask and furnished with birdcage, **35**. 154
Mann family's, at Linton, **21**. 250
Pewit; pewits:
HW receives eggs of, from Lord Orford, **34**. 130
HW tripped like a, **32**. 252, **34**. 118, **43**. 314
Pewter:
alms-boxes of, **21**. 238

English bury, on approach of rebel army, **19**. 173
shillings counterfeited from, **19**. 242
Pewterer. *See* Cleeve, Bourchier
Pewter mines:
cobalt and zinc by-products of, **18**. 323
Peyre, Comtesse de. *See* Gassion, Jeanne de
Peyre, Mme de:
daughter of, banished, **30**. 213
Jansenist lady, **41**. 258
Les Rochers home of, **30**. 213, **41**. 258
Peyrère, La. *See* La Peyrère
Peyrousse. *See* Maury de la Peyrousse
Peyton, Sir Henry (1736–89), 1st Bt; M.P.:
Manners, Lord Robert, nominated by, **2**. 219
Orford, E. of, appoints, his executor, **42**. 344
Peyto Verney. *See* Verney
Pezay, Marquis de. *See* Masson, Alexandre-Frédéric-Jacques de
Pezay, Marquise de. *See* Murat, Charlotte
Pezay (France):
Pezay dies at, **6**. 499n
Pézennes, Marquis de. *See* Girard, Pierre-Maurice-Emmanuel de
Pezzana, Abbé Giuseppe (d. 1802):
Guines recommends, to HW, **36**. 193, **41**. 423–4, 425
Metastasio edited by, **41**. 423–4
Pezzo; pezzi:
value of, **18**. 448n
Pfütschner, Charles de (d. ca 1766), Bn; 'Fishner':
Craon's correspondence with, **17**. 287, 472
Dumesnil accuses, of heresy for frequenting Mass, **19**. 491
Francis I's decision on Leghorn conversions conveyed by, **22**. 250n
Khevenhüller's progress into Bavaria reported by, **17**. 288
Leopold of Lorraine's sons taught German by, **17**. 287n
negotiates between Maria Theresa and Frederick II, **17**. 315n
Phædra and Hippolitus. See under Smith, Edmund
Phaeton (mythological):
Apollo's curricle must have been seized by, **39**. 472
HW's verses compare Carlisle with, **30**. 258
Necker refers to, **5**. 407
Pellegrini's paintings of story of, in Castle Howard Hall, **30**. 258
stairs for, in old stage properties, **11**. 292
Phaeton. See under Quinault, Philippe
Phaeton, English ship:
Waldegrave transferred to, **33**. 323n
Phaeton; phaetons (vehicles):
Craon, Princesse de, uses, **17**. 83
Fitzherbert, Mrs, drives in, at Margate, **12**. 113
high, Ds of York arrives in, **12**. 11
horses of, in English opera, **19**. 370
ladies visit Cascines in, **25**. 558n
low, North drives with wife in, **33**. 581n

[Phaeton; phaetons, *continued*]
Markham dislikes, 29. 159
open, belonging to Lady Montfort, 1. 335
tides of, in London, 11. 249
Whalley drives wife in, 31. 307
York, Ds of, arrives at SH in, 12. 11
Phalli:
bronze, in Middleton's *Monumenta*, 15. 16
HW approves of Middleton's describing, in Latin, 15. 22
Phaon:
HW charmed to be Lady Ossory's, 32. 89
HW signs himself 'Phaon the Second,' 32. 91
Pharamond. See Faramond
Pharaoh; pharaohs (Egyptian):
lice uncontrollable by, 30. 275
priests of, 34. 102
soothsayers sent for by, 32. 206
Pharaoh (game). *See* Faro
Pharisee; pharisees:
England's internal dissensions like those of, with Jews, 33. 24, 167
HW confesses that he is, 23. 528
prudes compared with, 31. 437
squabbles of, 33. 133
story of, and Magdalen, most beautiful in New Testament, 33. 38–9
Pharmacopœia. See under Salmon, William
Pharos:
at Boulogne, 16. 211, 37. 41
at Dover, 16. 211
Pharsalia:
Penobscot as well known as, 33. 123
Pharsalia. See under Lucan
Pharsalia and Philippi. See under Holdsworth, Edward
Pheasant; pheasants:
Ailesbury, Cts of, and Bns Lyttelton feed, 39. 158
a penny each, at Paris, 34. 64, 69
campaign opened for, with waste of gunpowder, 25. 188
Chinese: at Park Place, 38. 179; Mann sends, to Leopold, 22. 368; prices of, at auction of stuffed birds, 23. 210
Du Deffand, Mme, receives, 7. 440
eggs of, 35. 282
English should kill, in autumn for winter food, 35. 474
Ferdinand of Naples rises at 2 A.M. to catch, when leaving roosts, 25. 600
from Houghton, for HW, 12. 56, 164
Gibbons's carving includes, 35. 138
gold: heroes scarcer than, 35. 277; sold at Covent Garden market, 21. 294
HW tries to get, from Tylney, for Lady Strafford, 35. 275, 277
highwaymen compared to, 33. 353
hunting of, 33. 292
Irish rarely have, 10. 18
roast, as 'remove' for soups, 19. 357n
Strafford's, stolen, 35. 367
Strafford, Lady, has, 35. 324
'Pheasantry':
Ailesbury, Cts of, must oversee, 39. 138

Phèdre, rôle in Racine's *Phèdre*:
Clairon, Mlle, acts, 7. 316
Phèdre. See under Racine, Jean
Phélipot, Louise-Gabrielle, m. (1712) Louis-Ignace Tournemine, Baron de Camsillon:
(?) social relations of, with Mme Geoffrin, 7. 273
Phelippe, ——:
attends session of parliament of Paris, 8. 173
Phelipps *or* Phillipps, Ann, m. John Horner:
(?) HW mentions, 17. 475
Phelp, Mr:
SH visited by, 12. 241
Phelps, Mr:
SH visited by, 12. 248
Phelps, Richard (ca 1720–71), diplomatist:
Beaufort, D. of, and Dawkins accompanied by, 19. 191n
Bouverie accompanied by, at Rome, 19. *191*, 196
—— pays travelling expenses of, 19. 196
Conway's friend, 21. 113
fellow at Oxford, 19. 196
Florence hurriedly visited by, on way to England, 21. 113
Grevilles accompanied by, to Italy, 21. 124
Italy often visited by, as tutor or governor, 21. 124
Mann cites information from, about peace parleys, 22. 89n
—— has known, for years, 21. 113
—— sends HW's letters back to England by, 21. 113, 118, 124, 26. 36
Old Pretender entertains, after being congratulated by him, 19. 191, 196
Peter III's declaration announced by, 22. 19n
Sicily secretly visited by, 21. 124
to be secretary of embassy in Spain, 22. 112
York, D. of, discusses Young Pretender and Cardinal York with, 22. 106n
Phélypeaux, Jean-Frédéric (1701–81), Comte de Maurepas:
ablest and most agreeable man HW knew in Paris, 39. 198
agreeable and sensible, 39. 34
Aiguillon, Duc d', advised by, to resign, 24. 10n, 14n
—— nephew of, 6. 257, 314, 315
——'s return asked by, 6. 314, 315, 323
——'s return to be announced to, 6. 333
Aiguillon, Duchesse d', shares opera box with, 7. 318
Amelot wanted by, to succeed Malesherbes but Turgot objects, 24. 207n
Artois, Comte d', and, 32. 226
Bernin, Mlle, to give brother's books to, 5. 287
—— writes to, 5. 287
brother of, married, 6. 5
Châteauroux, Duchesse de, said to have been poisoned by, 7. 278
Choisy visited by, 6. 53
Clugny to work under supervision of, 6. 315
council attended by, 6. 55
Deane applies to, 24. 254n

death of: Choiseul thought to profit by, **25.** 291n; reported in papers, **25.** 212

disgraced for attacks on Mme de Pompadour, **13.** 152–3

disgrace of: caused by Mme de Pompadour, **7.** 278, **30.** 205; will benefit England, **20.** 51, **30.** 205

does not gain ground, **24.** 13

Dorat's *Adélaïde* hails return of, **6.** 85

Du Barry, Mlle, former occupant of apartment given to, **6.** 57

Du Deffand, Mme, approves of conduct of, **6.** 85

—— may fear, **39.** 189

—— mentions, **3.** 318

English-French naval disarmament pact signed by, **24.** 299n

Fontainebleau visited by, **6.** 236

Forcalquier, Mme de, reproved by, for quarrel with Mme du Deffand, **4.** 390

Forth sent by England to, with war threats, **24.** 324n

French navy promoted by, **20.** 51

HW accompanies, to opera, **7.** 318

HW converses with, on Seven Years War, **7.** 285–6

HW glad, is not a minister, **39.** 34

HW mentions, **6.** 64n

HW might give Conway a letter to, **39.** 198

HW pressed by, to visit him in country, **39.** 198

HW's acquaintance with, **30.** 205

HW's opinion of, **30.** 205

HW sups with, **39.** 34

HW to converse with, **41.** 7

Hardwicke resembles, **30.** 205, 214, **39.** 215

health of: **6.** 134, 232, 233, 235, 236, (?) 238, 240, 370, 372, 418, **7.** 58, 81, (?) 84, 195, 448; bled for gout, **6.** 232, 233

indecisions of, **6.** 365

invasion not abetted by, **18.** 413

jokes made about Pezay and, **6.** 38

jokes made about successor to, **7.** 129

Joseph II's absence said to please, **6.** 39

——'s Paris visit perhaps prevented by, **29.** 278n

La Fayette interviews, **7.** 113

Lauraguais's conversation with, **3.** 370

Liancourt visited by, **5.** 95

Linguet's *Journal* suppressed by, **6.** 416n

Louis XV sends messages by, **18.** 544n

——'s secretary of state and minister of marine, **43.** 86

Louis XVI asked by, for La Chalotais's release, **24.** 10n

—— found by, to be disposed towards war, **24.** 316n

—— hesitates to promote, **6.** 59

——'s letter soliciting advice from, **6.** 52–3

——'s meetings with ministers to be attended by, **6.** 315, 372

——'s reception of Senegal news attended by, **7.** 123

made head of finance council, **6.** 315, 317

Maillebois protected by, **6.** 322

Malesherbes incited by, to ask Marie-Antoinette to dismiss Guines, **24.** 207

—— undertakes awkward mission for, **6.** 299

Marie-Antoinette receives, **6.** 53

——'s relations with, **6.** 314, 323, 333

Marly visited by, **6.** 67

Maurepas, Comtesse de, illness of, distresses, **5.** 137, 141

Mémoires of, HW's opinion of, **12.** 29

Mesdames de France receive, **6.** 53

mob applauds, at opera, for restoring parliament, **24.** 61

mocks at everything, **6.** 278

'Monfort, M. de,' **7.** 84

naval funds for, diverted to Prussia, **20.** 51

Necker needs support of, **6.** 459

——'s appointment due to, **24.** 255n

—— to intercede with, for Macartney, **7.** 210

Nivernais, brother-in-law of, is expected to succeed him as minister of finance, **25.** 212

O'Briens hated by, **20.** 28n

parliament of Paris restored by, **28.** 221

Pezay thwarted by, **6.** 499n

Pompadour, Mme de, accuses, of trying to poison her, **20.** 51n

—— caused disgrace of, **7.** 278, **13.** 152–3, **30.** 205

—— ridiculed by, in chansons, **7.** 283, **20.** 51n

Pontchartrain, Marquis de, has accident riding with, **4.** 248

Pontchartrain, seat of, **3.** 65n

possible colleagues of, **6.** 397

Racine quoted by, on Cornwallis's surrender, **25.** 211

Rueil visited by, **5.** 40

St-Germain confers with, **6.** 228

—— defers to, **6.** 251, 300

secrecy maintained by, **7.** 67–8

secretary of state for marine department, **20.** 51n

social relations of, in Paris, *see index entries ante* 8. 469

Stormont protests to, **24.** 316n

success of, **6.** 85, 154, 323, 326, **7.** 58

Talmond, Princesse de, leaves porcelain and a watch to, **5.** 438

—— saved by, from banishment, because she is Queen's cousin, **20.** 44n

Terray ordered by, to resign, **24.** 34

Toulouse, Abp of, would profit by death of, **6.** 28

Turgot a friend of, **6.** 77, **32.** 200

—— makes, jealous, **24.** 207

verses on, at time of Versailles revolt, **6.** 194

Voltaire promised by, to be free from molestation, **28.** 365

weak, **6.** 277

Wilkes inquired about by, **7.** 337

younger minister than, would declare war on England at once, **24.** 300

Young Pretender flouts, as emissary of Louis XV, **20.** 8n

——'s departure known to, **18.** 379n

Phélypeaux, Louis (1705–77), Comte de St-Florentin; Duc de la Vrillière, 1770; statesman; 'le lord-trésorier':
advises on choice of controller, 4. 326
Bauffremont close friend of, 4. 354
Choiseul receives Louis XV's dismissal order from, 41. 196–7
Colisée subsidized by, 39. 145n
Conflans's alleged letter to, called spurious, 21. 356n
copy of Louis XV's answer certified by, 4. 412
'courtier-wretch,' 11. 43
Dauphin stays with, before marriage, 4. 406
dismissal of, expected, 6. 59
divides office of ministre d'état, 14. 153n
Du Deffand, Mme, asks, to seek new pension for her, 4. 354, 359
——'s pension continued by appeal to, 4. 97, 103
dukedom given to, 4. 425
envoys at house of, 5. 7
envoys work with, 5. 30
HW addresses to, case of SH books for library at Paris, 41. 58
hand of, cut off by bursting gun, 22. 342
health of, 6. 55, 308
Hertford to speak to, about Dauberval, 38. 477, 483
likely to fall, 24. 12
Louis XV's letter of banishment delivered to Comte de Broglie by, 5. 402
——'s letter to, dismissing Monteynard, 6. 12
——'s letter to exiled members of parliament of Paris signed by, 8. 182
——'s orders signed by, 8. 170
Louis XVI's letter to Maurepas delivered by, 6. 52
Malesherbes replaces, 6. 207, 213
Maupeou ordered by, to give up seals, 24. 34n
Monclar's pension and, 4. 285
Monteynard's dismissal brought by, 6. 10, 12
not at fault in matter of HW's books, 3. 262–3, 263
Paris and its amusements under care of, 38. 477
permission to visit Choiseuls may be held up by, 5. 43, 45
resigns as minister of King's household, 6. 207, 43. 99
Sabatin, Mme, mistress of, sells lettres de cachet, 11. 43, 23. 339, 28. 226–7
secretary of state, 22. 342
social relations of, in Paris, 4. 288, 7. 291, 298, 309, 312
Sutton banished by, 24. 2n
treachery of, to La Chalotais, 11. 43–4
Phélypeaux, Paul-Jérôme (1703–75), Marquis de Pontchartrain:
accident to, 4. 248, 251, 254, 261
health of, 6. 178
marriage of, 6. 5
Maurepas brother of, 6. 5
social relations of, in Paris, 7. 303, 339

Phélypeaux de la Vrillière, Marie-Jeanne (1704–93), m. (1718) Jean-Frédéric Phélypeaux, Comte de Maurepas:
Bernin, Mlle, not to give brother's ring to, 5. 287
Céreste's relations with, 5. 287
Du Deffand, Mme, mentions, 3. 318
——'s opinion of, 6. 370
ill, 5. 129, 134, 137, 141, 169, 6. 180
Liancourt visited by, 5. 95
Necker entertains friends of, 6. 493
Paris visited by, 5. 141
Pontchartrain visited by, 6. 53
social relations of, in Paris, see index entries ante 8. 470
Phélypeaux de Pontchartrain, Hélène-Angélique-Françoise (1715–82), m. (1730) Louis-Jules-Barbon Mancini-Mazarini, Duc de Nivernais:
Borghese, Ps, acts as hostess for, 20. 285–6
Hertford, Cts of, directed by, 38. 216–17
—— favoured by, 38. 221
—— has Court dress ordered by, 38. 237
Hervey, Bns, would be amused by, 31. 76
—— would detest, 31. 83
Newcastle, D. of, out-chattered by, 14. 154
—— resembles, 30. 214, 31. 76, 39. 215
social relations of, in Paris, see index entries ante 8. 470
Phélypeaux d'Herbault, Georges-Louis (1729–87), Bp of Bourges 1757–87:
may be grand aumônier, 6. 404
Phenicians. See Phœnicians
Pheon, heraldic term:
in arms of Sir Philip Sidney, 32. 47
Phidias (ca 500– ca 432 B.C.), sculptor:
Jupiter by, imitated in stained glass, 40. 225
Mason alludes to George III's statue as 'Phidian,' 28. 472
Philadelphia, Pennsylvania:
battle for, won by English, 32. 393, 394
Bedford, Grosvenor, collector of customs for, 42. 491
Boston commended by assembly of, for dumping tea, 23. 550n
Carlisle, E. of, writes from, 7. 63
Clinton abandons, 28. 409, 411
commissioners for peace with America arrive in, 33. 28
Congress sitting at, 28. 210n, 217
Cornwallis fails to advance to, 28. 282n
(?) customs collectorship at, 40. 41
England and Europe may have to take laws from, 24. 229
English army under Howe captures and occupies, 24. 281, 282, 336, 338–9, 342, 348, 352, 361–2, 393
English evacuation of, 28. 422n, 434n
English troops to go to, 32. 380
evacuation of, predicted by Lady Ossory, 35. 25
exports to, 32. 242
Franklin boasts, will be starved into surrender, 24. 361–2

—— might abandon, to save New York, **24.** 342

—— of, **7.** 320

Howe, Gen., at, **28.** 342n

—— marching to, **32.** 388

Howes miscarry in attempt on, **28.** 329

Mason expects his and HW's books to be reprinted at, **28.** 232

news about, via Halifax, **32.** 397

Quakers of, **28.** 284

Washington encamped near, **28.** 350n

—— said to have foiled Howe's attempt to capture, **24.** 327

'Philalethes':

Some Reflexions upon the 7, 8, and 9th Verses of the 2d Chapter of Genesis, **15.** 304, **43.** 212

'Philander':

'dirty,' HW objects to Conway's appearing as, at masquerade, **38.** 206

Tankerville's and Rochfort's nom-de-plume, **18.** 220

Philanthrope, Le. See under Legrand, Marc-Antoine

Philaster. See under Beaumont, Francis, and Fletcher, John

Philibeg; philibegs:

Young Pretender wears, **19.** 320n

Philibert, Philipp (d. 1753), Freiherr von; Austrian Gen.:

Leghorn may be commanded by, **17.** 406–7

Toussaint's father-in-law, **17.** 406

Philibert, French ship of India Co.:

captured off Cape Finisterre, **19.** 410

Philidor or Philidore. See Danican, François-André

Philip, Roman Emperor. See Marcus Julius Philippus

Philip (1478–1506) of Burgundy, K. of Castile:

Wolfeton House lodges, **37.** 491

Philip, K. of France. See Philippe

Philip II (382–336 B.C.), K. of Macedonia 359–356 B.C.:

Demosthenes and, **33.** 288, **37.** 200

Philip II (1527–98), K. of Spain 1556–98:

ambassador's remark to, **33.** 489

and Mary, 'an insipid pair,' **34.** 122

believed himself warranted to slaughter, **34.** 161

Carlos, Don, victim of 'dark and cruel vengeance of,' **41.** 290–1

—— writes Travels of, **12.** 24

European monarchs mostly descended from, but would not defend his character, **42.** 122

HW detests, **3.** 318

Henry VIII's family group includes, **42.** 247

Holland could not be conquered by, **24.** 127

insurrection to prevent Q. Mary's marriage to, **1.** 255n

marriage of, **1.** 187

medal of, with Mary, **16.** 157n

Mercado physician to, **14.** 126

Popes bullied, **18.** 344

portraits of, **9.** 124

Titian calls, K. of England, **7.** 355

Vie de, see under Leti, Gregorio

Voltaire's Universal History treats, **34.** 79

Watson's life of, **15.** 156, **32.** 339–40

Philip III (1578–1621), K. of Spain 1598–1621:

Charles of England woos daughter of, **15.** 341

daughter of, **1.** 58n, **11.** 109n, **15.** 341

James I's 'opposite,' **15.** 80–1

Mercado physician to, **14.** 126

Philip IV (1605–65), K. of Spain 1621–65:

James I's letter probably written to be shown to, **15.** 342n

Olivares congratulates, on rebellion, **34.** 48

Philip V (1683–1746), K. of Spain 1700–46:

army of, Electress's jewels endangered by, **3.** 241–2

army officers notified by, of Montemar's dismissal, **18.** 59

Catalogue of French Books, A, satirizes, **18.** 54

Catalonia oppressed by, despite English protests, **23.** 212n

Court of, **12.** 183n

death of: **19.** 277–8; England disappointed by results of, **22.** 1; falsely rumoured, **19.** 19, 25; Tabuerniga returns to Spain after, **17.** 277n

English invasion plans approved by, **18.** 379n

Haddock intercepts packet for, **17.** 53

Louis XIV's correspondence with, **6.** 433

——'s grandson, **28.** 296

Louis XV said to influence, about papal election, **17.** 20–1

marriage of, **4.** 44

match of, with Ps of Modena, broken off by her father, **13.** 242–3

memoirs concerning reign of, **15.** 137

Neapolitan alliance with, **18.** 43

Old Pretender gets 'grandeeship' from, for Craon, **17.** 10n

prime minister to, **6.** 434n

sea victory attributed to, **18.** 413

Silva consul of, **19.** 57

son dislikes policies of, **19.** 278

son of, **13.** 243n

Vendôme aids, **6.** 429

Viviani wants to be minister of, to Francis I, **18.** 129

wife of, **13.** 213n

Philip, D. of Burgundy. See Philippe

Philip, 'Don' (1720–65) of Spain, D. of Parma 1749–65:

Acquaviva may lend Caprarola palace to, **17.** 389

Aix to be visited by, **17.** 361–2

Aix treaty had destined a Neapolitan crown for, **21.** 330

Albenga reached by, **19.** 58

Antibes to be visited by, **17.** 362, 380, 388–9, **18.** 395, **19.** 313–14

army of: advances to join other Spanish army, **19.** 36, 47; has not started from Nice, **19.** 36; moves towards Provence to join Conti, **18.** 371n

[Philip, 'Don' (1720–65), *continued*]

Austria persuades Louis XV to leave, at Parma, despite Aix treaty, **21.** 323n

baggage of, at Barcelona, **17.** 182

Barcelona left by, for Roussillon, **17.** 362n

Bavarian elector may give Milan to, **17.** 290

Beauvau to join, **19.** 54

Castel Ceriolo e St Giuliano captured by, **19.** 84

Castellar arranges troop passage for, **19.** 51

Catalogue of French Books, A, satirizes, **18.** 53

Chambéry may be station of, **18.** 513

Charles III to be met by, at Lerici, **21.** 264n, 280

—— will not relinquish Naples to, **21.** 264, 270

Charles Emmanuel III may be persuaded by, to permit Spanish invasion, **17.** 323

—— threatened by, with retaliations in Piedmont for English bombardment of Genoese coast, **19.** 121

—— to expel, from Savoy, **18.** 65

—— to resist, at Nice, **18.** 395

—— wants to transfer, to Naples, **21.** 264

Chute, Mann, and Whithed unlikely to be injured by, **35.** 11

Coni and Demonte may be approached by, through Mondovi, **19.** 58

Cuneo's resistance may force back, to Savoy, **18.** 513

daughter's letters from, **22.** 313

death of, **22.** 313, 364

embarked at S. Pier d'Arena, **19.** 304n

England may acknowledge, **17.** 196

English fleet impedes, **17.** 405, 408, **19.** 51

Ferdinand VI cannot set up, **19.** 432

—— orders, to propose suspension of arms to Charles Emmanuel III, **19.** 279n

flees from Nice and Antibes to Aix, **19.** 314n

flees to Sestri, **19.** 304

France and Austria give up Parma to, **21.** 280n

France will lose face by abandoning interests of, **21.** 323

Francis III given equal rank with, in army, **18.** 235

—— prevented by Charles Emmanuel III from joining, **18.** 322

—— sells Guastella allodials to, **22.** 144

—— vies with, **20.** 45

—— with, at Nice, **19.** 432n

French and other galleys to escort, **17.** 362

French galleys to bring, to Orbetello, **18.** 397n

French may join, in Savoy, **18.** 295

funeral orations on, **31.** 111

Gages may join army to that of, **18.** 556, **19.** 2, 36

(?) Galli 'ministro degli alloggi' to, **17.** 56n

—— thinks of asking, to be godfather, **18.** 46

Genoese house prepared for, **17.** 389, **18.** 454, 554

George II's instructions about, **19.** 278n

Glimes and, retreat to Ft Barraux, **18.** 95n

HW did not know, **22.** 325

Henry Benedict (Stuart) may join, **19.** 99

'horridly French,' **20.** 45

Italy to be invaded by, **17.** 195, 215, 350, 380, 388–9

Keene and Villettes receive instructions concerning provisions for, **19.** 278n

La Ensenada secretary of state to, **18.** 253

letters for, from Naples, **21.** 280

Liechtenstein visits, at Parma, **22.** 153n

Lombardy to be domain of, **17.** 427

Maillebois ordered by, to join Spanish army at Piacenza, **19.** 263n

Mann praises generosity and civility of, **22.** 314, 325

Mari head tutor to, **17.** 226n

—— to attend, **17.** 226

—— to prepare house for, **17.** 389

may have to fight his way through Nice, **17.** 408

Montemar's actions to be guided by acts of army of, **18.** 27

——'s preference for Charles of Naples to, said to irritate their mother, **18.** 5

—— to obtain Tuscan conquests for, **18.** 16

mother might have bought Parma Placentia for, **18.** 345

mother seeks title for, **18.** 389

Naples may be visited by, **17.** 323

—— may be winter home of, **19.** 144

—— should be kingdom of, **35.** 14

news of: awaited, **19.** 267; from Rome, **17.** 389

Nice and Villefranche to be attacked by, **18.** 371n

Nice may be entered by, **17.** 408, **18.** 271

—— the headquarters of, **19.** 36, 432

Orbetello may be visited by, **17.** 389

Parma and Placentia asked for, by Acquaviva, of Benedict XIV, **17.** 201

Parma and Placentia assigned to, by Aix treaty, **19.** 481

Parmesans dislike, **20.** 45

Pavia the refuge of, **19.** 231

Piedmont entered by, through the Barcelonetta valley, **17.** 389n

poor, **20.** 45

reigned virtuously with absolute power, **22.** 404

retreat of, to Venice, alleged, **19.** 269

Savoy invasion of, angers Charles Emmanuel III, **18.** 58–9

Savoy rule of, ended, **18.** 95

servants quartered by, on chief families, **20.** 45

soldiers desert, **20.** 45

Spain makes demands for Italian state for, **19.** 393n

Spanish and Neapolitan troops in Italy commanded by, **17.** 182n

Spanish army to be commanded by, at Nice, **18.** 547

Spanish convoy to include, **17**. 215, 323

Spanish invasion of Tuscany and Neapolitan advance depend on success of, **18**. 312

Spanish party at Florence want, **17**. 68n, **19**. 498

Spanish plan to instate, in Maria Theresa's dominions, **18**. 43

title of D. of Savoy taken by, **18**. 65

Turin approached by, **19**. 164n

Tuscan title may be given to, **17**. 380, 389

Tuscany to be seized by, **17**. 196

wife of: **20**. 147–8; allegedly leaked secrets to Louis XV, **20**. 28n

York, D. of, to be entertained by, **22**. 232

Young Pretender expected by Amelot to assist, **18**. 415

Philip, HW's servant, *see* Colomb, Philip

'Philip':

character in Pinkerton's play, **16**. 253

Philip. *See also* Philippe

Philip, Lady. *See* Chaucer, Alice

Philip, Sir John (d. 1418), K.B.:

marriage of, **9**. 68

Philip Anton (1747–77), D. of Calabria:

birth of, **19**. 423

cantata for, **19**. 437–8

death of, **24**. 330

father sets aside, for imbecility, **21**. 322–3, 329, 333, 337, 347, **22**. 570

medical commission examines, **21**. 322–3, 324–5, 329

miracle might restore, **21**. 329, 333

Philip Augustus, K. of France. *See* Philippe II

Philipe, Mr:

SH visited by, **12**. 250

Philipon la Madelaine, Louis:

Modèles de lettres by, owned by Mme du Deffand, **8**. 35

Philippa (?1314–69) of Hainault, m. (1328) Edward III of England:

effigy of, in Westminster Abbey, **12**. 105

estate given by, to York Minster, **1**. 275, **28**. 42, 44

portrait of, **1**. 148

Philippa de Couci (1367–1411 *or* 12), m. (1378) Robert de Vere, 9th E. of Oxford, cr. (1386) D. of Ireland:

effigy represents, **9**. 68n

husband divorces, **9**. 67

Philippe, Roman Emperor. *See* Marcus Julius Philippus

Philippe II (1165–1223), (Philippe-Auguste), K. of France 1180–1223:

fictional memoirs of, **28**. 291

Gaillard's account of, **5**. 68

Vie de, (?) owned by Mme du Deffand, **8**. 34

Philippe IV (1268–1314), K. of France, 1285:

Cocchi's *Lettera critica sopra un manoscritto in cera* on household expenses of, **20**. 107n

Quinze-Vingts ordered by, to wear fleurs-de-lys, **20**. 107n

Philippe VI (1293–1350) (de Valois), K. of France, 1328–50:

Gaillard's account of, **5**. 69

Philippe II, III, and IV of Spain. *See* Philip

Philippe III (1396–1467), D. of Burgundy 1419–67; 'Philip the Good':

Doumenil has portrait of, **7**. 313

entry of, into Ghent, **14**. 78

La Marche's account of, **42**. 192

Philippe (1478–1506) of Burgundy. *See* Philip, K. of Castile

Philippe, HW's servant. *See* Colomb, Philip

Philippe-Auguste, K. of France. *See* Philippe II

Philippi:

Brentford serves as, to Wilkes and Luttrell, **10**. 274

See also under Virgil: *Georgics*

Philippoleos, Abp:

print of, **43**. 64

Philipps, Lady. *See* Darcy, Catharine (1641–?1713); Shepherd, Elizabeth (ca 1700–88)

Philipps, Catharine (ca 1736–1801), HW's cousin:

HW visits, **11**. 70, **34**. 29, 63

SH visited by, **12**. 232n

Philipps, 'Dolly':

HW asks about, **36**. 1, 2, 4

Philipps, Elizabeth (d. 1728), m. John Shorter:

family of, **1**. 52n, **43**. 45

HW's grandmother, **1**. 52n, **9**. 69n, **13**. 81n

Hertford sends humble duty to, **39**. 517

Philipps, Sir Erasmus (ca 1623–97), 3d Bt:

daughter of, **28**. 24n

descendants of, **1**. 52n

HW's descent from, **1**. 375n, **7**. 258n, **9**. 69n, **13**. 81n

Philipps, Sir Erasmus (1699–1743), 5th Bt, 1737, M.P.:

arrives at Florence, **17**. 67

biographical information on, corrected, **43**. 236

Craon avoided by, **17**. 81

death of, **18**. 343–4

family of, **43**. 45

HW exchanges compliments with, **17**. 81

health of: pain in back, **17**. 67; recovers, **17**. 81

lean, **17**. 121

leaves Florence for Turin, **17**. 138

Mann avoided by, **17**. 80–1

—— entertains, **17**. 70

—— exchanges calls with, **17**. 67

—— meets, at Franceschi's sale, **17**. 121

Martin accompanies, **13**. 202n, **17**. 81

monument of, at Bath, **10**. 232

name of, corrected, **43**. 242

servant of, **17**. 67

Walpole, Lady, cousin of, **17**. 67n

Wright friend of, **17**. 423

Philipps, Sir John (d. 1629), 1st Bt, of Picton Castle:

HW's ancestor, **1**. 375n

Philipps, Sir John (?1701–64), 6th Bt, 1743; M.P.:
afterwards lord of trade and baronet, 17. *384*n
Board of Trade office of, corrected, 43. 244
Chatham's satirical panegyric on, 35. 560
Commissioner of Trade, 18. 551
commission of accounts proposed by, in Parliament, 38. 192
Frederick, P. of Wales, adds, to his party, 20. 3n
HW mentions, 17. 418
HW's cousin, 9. 27, 20. 249
House of Commons would like to commit, 20. 250
Jacobite, 19. 168, 310n
Jacobite tendency of, approved by George III, 33. 455
King's Bench moved by, to produce Murray, 20. 249
militia's styling as 'perpetual' opposed by, 21. 552n
named in Secret Committee lists, 17. 384
not elected as commissioner to examine accounts, 17. 438
Parliamentary address of thanks to Onslow moved by, but bungled, 30. 164
Parliamentary debate by, on privately-raised regiments, 26. 13, 14, 16
Parliamentary speech by, compared to still-life painting, 37. 470
pedigree drawn by, 9. 69, 33. 454–5
pedigree presented by, to Sir Robert Walpole, 13. 81n
peerage rumoured for, 38. 159n
resigns, 19. 27–8
Tories desert, when he moves for a void election, 35. 216
Vernon complains to, about provisions, 19. 168
Walpole, Lady, cousin of, 17. 384n
Philipps, Joyce (ca 1737–1820), HW's cousin:
HW visits, 11. *70*, 34. 29, 63
SH visited by, 12. 232n
Philipps, Mary (ca 1734–1820), HW's cousin:
HW visits, 11. *70*, 34. 29, 63
SH visited by, 12. 232n
Philipps, Sir Richard (d. 1648), 2d Bt, 1629, of Picton Castle; HW's great-great-grandfather:
'Republicans' capture, when besieging Picton Castle, 34. 93
wife of, 1. 375n
Philipps, Sir Richard (1744–1823), 7th Bt, 1764; cr. (1776) Bn Milford:
father of, 33. 454
sisters of, 34. 29
Philipps family:
HW's Welsh ancestors, 42. 19
Magnus Maximus, ancestor of, 43. 114
pedigree of, 1. 375, 9. 69
Picton Castle the seat of, 9. 112, 19. 310n

Philips, (?) Mr:
SH visitor sent by, 12. 234
Philips, Ambrose (ca 1675–1749), poet:
Collection of Old Ballads, A, by, 1. 89–90
Distressed Mother by, disliked by HW, 13. 75
Jeffreys's epigram attributed to, 2. 202n
translation by, of Sappho, quoted, 32. 91
Philips, Mrs Catherine. *See* Fowler, Katherine
Philips, Con. *See* Phillips, Teresia Constantia
Philips, John (1676–1709), Oxford poet:
poems of Edmund Smith and, published together, 14. 27
Philips, Thomas:
song attributed to, 24. 401n, 28. 412n
Philips. *See also* Phelipps; Philip; Philipps; Phillips
Philipson. *See* Phillipson
Philistis, Queen:
medal of, 21. 358
Phillips, Mrs. *See* Amis, Judith; Burney, Susanna
Phillips, Col. ——:
40th Ft, regiment of, 19. 69n
Phillips, John:
Tavernier's *Six Voyages* translated by, 24. 433n
Phillips, John (fl. 1739–76):
Hertford's builder, in Brook St, 38. 18
Phillips, Judith. *See* Amis, Judith
Phillips, Molesworth (ca 1755–1832), Capt. (later Maj.) of Marines:
SH visited by, 12. 243
Phillips, Teresia Constantia (1709–65), courtesan; m. (1723) Henry Muilman:
HW would not distinguish between Catherine II and, 24. 35
Phillips, Thomas (fl. 1765):
Cole writes to, 1. 93
Phillips. *See also* Phelipps; Philip; Philipps; Philips
Phillipson, John (1698–1756), M.P.:
Admiralty post lost by, 18. 550
birth date of, 43. 252
Carteret appoints, to Admiralty, 18. 349
not of Carteret or Pulteney faction, 18. 551
Surveyor of the Roads, 19. 34
Phillipson, Richard Burton (d. 1792):
(?) HW sends letters by, 21. 389
'Phillis':
HW refers to Lady Browne as, 41. 278
HW's name for fish, 35. 205
Phillis:
referred to as beloved by poets, 33. 334
Phillis, servant maid:
fights Downing St fire, 17. 496
Phillis. *See also* Phyllis
Phillis Court, Freeman's seat, near Henley:
Conway and wife to visit Coopers at, 37. 345
Cooper formerly of, 41. 218–19
Freeman buys, from Cooper and his mother, 41. 219n
Howe, Mrs, and Miss Harvey visit, 39. 266

Park Place overlooks landscaping at, **37**. 345

'Philo Christus.' *See* Moseley, Richard

Philoctète. See under La Harpe, Jean-François de, Sophocles' *Philoctète*; Sophocles

Philodamus. See under Bentley, Richard (1708–82)

'Philo-Gray of Salisbury':

  Mason scolded by, in newspaper, **28**. 209

Philological Inquiries. See under Harris, James

Philosophe, Le. See under Voltaire

Philosophe anglais, Le. See under Prévost d'Exiles, Antoine-François

Philosophe ignorant, Le. See under Voltaire

Philosophe marié, Le, ou le mari honteux de l'être. See under Néricault, Philippe

Philosophe moderne, Le. See under Berkeley, Lady Elizabeth, Bns Craven

Philosopher; philosophers:

  always affect to act in character, **22**. 151

  ambassador should be, **21**. 335

  Anacreon the only sensible, **33**. 286

  Ashton said to be a Christian, **37**. 258

  characteristics of, **31**. 439–40

  Conway far from being, **37**. 259

  —— is, **37**. 176–7, **38**. 446

  death as viewed by, **41**. 162

  deathbed affectations of, **22**. 557

  Du Deffand, Mme, sings her song on, for Gustav III, **5**. 40

  French: affectations of, **22**. 271; at Holbach's, **30**. 208; Burke disputes with, **32**. 103; Catherine II and Frederick II receive incense from, **25**. 39; Catherine II charms, **22**. 570; 'compounded of d'Urfé and Diogenes,' **39**. 292; Dauphin expected by, to restore Jesuits, **39**. 22; Du Deffand, Mme, dislikes, **39**. 190; dullness of, **28**. 311; Frenchmen become, while Englishmen dance, **24**. 112; HW avoids, in Paris, **35**. 116; HW condemns, **41**. 1; HW discusses, **39**. 22–3; HW's reflections on, **28**. 30, **41**. 48, 56–7; HW's unflattering opinion of, **14**. 144, **30**. 204, 208; HW unlike, **39**. 292; irreligion of, **30**. 204; merely bring on despotism, **23**. 376; monastic professions discouraged by, **34**. 193; morality expunged by, **34**. 192; regard volcanos as orderly, **35**. 414; responsible for outrages, **34**. 166, 172; Rousseau imagines persecution from, **29**. 48; Sévigné, Mme de, unlike, **39**. 292; 'solemn, arrogant, and dictatorial,' **24**. 498

  French disgrace and debase name of, **31**. 384

  French Revolution caused by, **31**. 385

  God to be replaced by, with matter, **41**. 55

  Gray's opinion of, **14**. 12

  greatest of actors, **21**. 335

  Grecian, often impertinent, **32**. 148

  HW does not want to be taken for, **22**. 271

  HW greatest in world unintentionally, **39**. 180

  HW honours natural, **33**. 128

  HW jokes about, **11**. 209

  HW on, **1**. 104, 105, **31**. 322–3, **41**. 46, 48, 54–5

  HW prefers being, to being a rich man, **39**. 276

  HW said to be, **39**. 186, 292

  HW thinks that systems of, are as foolish as simpleton's collections, **25**. 604

  HW to converse with, **41**. 7

  hair-splitting by, **37**. 576

  Hamilton should not imitate, by too closely studying volcanos, **35**. 437

  Hume defends, against HW. **41**. 62–3

  in great countries, are usually those who have no philosophy, **25**. 105

  in religious times, write against immorality, **33**. 335

  modern: Du Deffand, Mme, disparages, **3**. 207; mot on, attributed to Mme du Deffand, **4**. 53

  motives of, for travel, **24**. 186

  name of, disgraced and debased by the French, **31**. 384

  Necker, Mme, calls HW, **39**. 292

  phenomena ascribed by, to deluge and conflagrations, **38**. 385

  predictions of, invalidated by unforeseen events, **25**. 369

  priests hated by, while erecting altars of their own, **35**. 117

  'sported on the verge of the tomb,' **35**. 362

  statesmen and, contrasted by Mme du Deffand, **3**. 101

  suicide an affectation of, **39**. 79

  system of antediluvian deluges invented by, to prove eternity of matter, **30**. 208

  unfit for political reformation, **34**. 172

  wisdom of, trifling, **39**. 446

  world said by, to be enlightened, **32**. 266

Philosopher's stone:

  Bentley's scheme for discovering, **35**. 190–1

  Chute disparages, **35**. 7

  discoveries made when in search of, **20**. 415

  HW has not found, **28**. 168

  HW's regimen turns him golden, as if by, **31**. 128

  indifference of, **4**. 314

  laughter is, **35**. 32

  virtues resemble chemists' vessels used in pursuit of, **33**. 435

Philosophes. *See* Philosopher; philosophers: French

Philosophe sans le savoir, Le. See under Sedaine, Michel-Jean (1719–97)

Philosophical and Mathematical Commentaries of Proclus. See under Taylor, Thomas

Philosophical, Historical and Moral Essay on Old Maids, A. See under Hayley, William

Philosophical Reflections . . . Concerning . . . Tar Water. See Berkeley, George (1685–1753): *Siris*

Philosophical Transactions of the Royal Society:

[*Philosophical Transactions*, continued]
    fish discussed and illustrated in, **1.** 282
    Grand Lama's letter printed in, **25.** 15
    HW does not want to be recorded in, **34.** 188
    HW will search, for Brounker, **16.** 12
    Wren's method of etching said to be mentioned in, **16.** 35
Philosophy:
    and enthusiasm have met, **34.** 161
    civilization undermined by, **34.** 169
    Conway and HW discuss, **37.** 257–9
    Conway's 'little natural stock of,' **37.** 187
    ——'s slow progress in, **37.** 575–6
    crimes encouraged more quickly by, than by religious mania, **34.** 139
    eighteenth century's close reveals bad effects of, **34.** 178
    excusable when exertion is in vain, **24.** 370
    fashionable in France, **39.** 270
    French affect, **10.** 176
    Gray's reflections on, **13.** 74
    HW and Mme du Deffand discuss, **4.** 213
    HW defines, as presence of mind, **21.** 335
    HW despises affectation of, **22.** 451
    HW discusses contemporary, **32.** 79–83
    HW hears Trevigar's lectures on, **13.** 6
    HW moves, from Windsor to SH, **37.** 270
    HW scorns, **11.** 249
    HW's: **39.** 180; is to paint his thoughts *couleur de rose*, **33.** 550; of indifference, **11.** 112, 251; *see also under* HW
    HW's opinion of, **9.** 349, **10.** 176, 184, 231
    HW's reflections on, **4.** 357, **13.** 108
    Helvétius's, new in France but exhausted in England, **16.** 23
    Mann's, will keep loss of Bath knighthood from making him unhappy, **22.** 407
    —— unable to accept HW's, **22.** 376, 381
    materialist, condemned by HW, **22.** 410
    natural, Edwards prays for deliverance from, **9.** 270
    only a command of the muscles, **33.** 338
    the truest, to think only of the present, **32.** 328
Philosophy of Earthquakes. See under Stukeley, William
'Philothée.' *See* Duchâtel, Louise
'Philotheos':
    Deist Doctor, The, by, **15.** 299
    Dissertation on 2d of Peter 1.19, A, **15.** 304
Philpot:
    Queenborough constables listed by, **35.** 142n
Phipps, Miss:
    'West Indian fortune' promised by Mrs Grieve to Charles Fox, **32.** 162
Phipps, Hon. Charles (1753–86):
    Scarborough elects, M.P., **24.** 444n
Phipps, Constantine (1722–75), cr. (1767) Bn Mulgrave:
    Bristol's brother-in-law, **22.** 548
    death of, **7.** 398
    made Irish baron, **22.** 548
    marriage of, **17.** 274n, **18.** 185, **30.** 325n

Oxford attended by, **18.** 185
Townshend, Vcts, jokes about Hervey family's 'quarrel' with, **30.** 51
    wedding of, in HW's 'Fairy Tale,' **30.** 325n
    wife of, **9.** 150n, **17.** 274n, **31.** 416
Phipps, Mrs Constantine. *See* Hervey, Hon. Lepell
Phipps, Constantine John (1744–92), 2d Bn Mulgrave, 1775; M.P.:
    Fox, C. J., questions, about Palliser in House of Commons, **24.** 444n
    Keppel answers, in House of Commons, **24.** 449n
    Parliamentary motion by, on Westminster election, **25.** 502n
    returns from unsuccessful design against Flushing, **25.** 167
    safety of, uncertain, **32.** 367
    sister's dowry increased by, **32.** 312n
Phipps, Hon. Edmund (1760–1837); army officer:
    declines invitation to ball at Windsor, **11.** 329
Phipps, Hannah, m. Charles Long:
    Tylney's legacy to, **25.** 534n
Phipps, Henrietta Maria (1757–82), m. (1776) Charles Dillon (after 1776, Dillon Lee), 12th Vct Dillon, 1787:
    marriage of, **32.** 312
Phipps, Hon. Henry (1755–1831), 3d Bn Mulgrave, 1792; cr. (1812) E. of Mulgrave:
    declines invitation to ball at Windsor, **11.** 329
    (?) HW mentions, **7.** 142
    wins victory, **12.** 56n
Phipps, 'Lady Lepell.' *See* Hervey, Hon. Lepell
'Phiz, King.' *See under* Villiers, George (1628–87): *Rehearsal*
Phlipon, Marie-Jeanne (1754–93), m. (1780) Jean-Marie Roland de la Platière:
    execution of, **15.** 248n
'Phocias.' *See* Hughes, John: *Siege of Damascus*
'Phoebe is Gone' (?song):
    HW reminded of, **28.** 30
Phœbus:
    Berry, Mary, is offered HW's services as, **11.** 1
    HW charmed to be Lady Ossory's, **32.** 89
    HW's verses mention, **10.** 316
    'le dieu Phœbus,' **32.** 372
    See also Apollo
Phœnician; Phœnicians:
    Anecdotes of Painting mentions, **40.** 228
    applied to an antiquary. **32.** 94
    HW has no regard for, **33.** 479
    Irish connections of, **33.** 474
    lore of, **34.** 244
    Venetians said to be confused with, **39.** 158
    Warburton not offended by HW's passage on, **13.** 39
    West alludes to, mistakenly, **32.** 196
Phœnix:
    HW mentions, **25.** 599
    Wilkes compared to, **24.** 45
Phœnix, English ship:
    Brodrick commands, **18.** 392n

French fired on by, **19.** 336n

Goldsworthy, Augustus, put on books of, as midshipman, by Hervey his godfather, **20.** 93n

involved in war, **19.** 313

Phoenix Court, Newgate St, London:

fire damages stocking-trimmer's house in, **38.** 168n

Phoenix Insurance:

Houghton's fire damage estimated by, **34.** 88n

Phoenix Park, near Dublin:

Rigby falsely reported to get Sackville's deputy rangership of, **21.** 328n

Westmorland, Lady, dies at, **12.** 64n

'Phraates':

HW's name for Bute, **38.** 316

Phyllis, (?) Mrs Boyle Walsingham's maid:

HW offers to take a pot with, at alehouse, **42.** 222

Phyllis. *See also* Phillis

Phyn, Mrs:

SH visited by, **12.** 228

'Phys, King.' *See under* Villiers, George (1628–87): *Rehearsal, The*

Physic:

degree in, HW scoffs at, **25.** 316

doctor of, to attend HW's second assembly, **10.** 107

Electress's, **35.** 35

HW does not believe in, **22.** 257

HW does not understand, **20.** 440

HW knows no more of, than a physician does, **21.** 368

life to be swallowed like a dose of, **37.** 176

professor of, refuses to aid Gray, **23.** 329

world should be taken like dose of, **37.** 176

Wren should have used his talents in, **40.** 349

See also Medicine; Physician

Physic garden:

at Chelsea, **18.** 250, **20.** 358n

Physician; physicians:

absurdity of, **31.** 97

Akenside is, to Q. Charlotte, **35.** 566n

and surgeons, limitations of, **2.** 338

at Florence, for the insane, **25.** 270

at Marseille, **35.** 25

at Pisa: Orford, Cts of, not hopefully regarded by, **25.** 112; supplies drugs for D. of Gloucester, **23.** 369

at Valdagno, promises complete recovery to Lady Lucy Mann, **24.** 122

Beelzebub 'President of,' **33.** 230

—— the devil's name as, **24.** 71

bootikins at first praised but later condemned by, **24.** 70–1

bootikins decried by, **23.** 76

Campbell, Lady William, accompanied by, at Florence, **25.** 271

Carteret's, order him to Spa, **19.** 26

Charles Emmanuel III sends, to Hercules III, **17.** 489

Chute needs braziers more than, at the Vyne, **35.** 109

——'s, **35.** 96

——'s aversion to, **24.** 210

Clement XIV's, forbids his *villeggiatura*, **24.** 39

——'s, *see also* Adinolfi, Pasquale

Clive's, prescribes laudanum, **24.** 60, 68

College of, HW's poor opinion of, **11.** 60

commit more deaths than soldiers do, **25.** 342

Conway does not bring wife to, again, **39.** 423

—— gets advice of, on goldfish's tympany, **37.** 476

Cromarty's remarks on, **15.** 30

Dacre's faith in, **10.** 290

Dalkeith's, **20.** 138

Devonshire's, suggest visit to Spa, **38.** 422

Du Deffand, Mme, has poor opinion of, **3.** 135, 139, **4.** 150, 177–8, 464, **5.** 133, 183, **6.** 234, 255, **7.** 241

—— suggests that HW consult, **4** 464, **5.** 322

English weather benefits, **25.** 582

epidemic fever deplored by, **36.** 288

fever and sore throat baffling to, **21.** 362

'flying gout' a term showing ignorance of, **22.** 114

from Rome, attends Cts of Orford, **24.** 312

from York, joins rebels, **19.** 180

frowsy tied wig typical of, **37.** 12–13

George III's, cannot be consulted by HW, **25.** 413

German: fears Leopold's exposure to smallpox, **22.** 559; Maria Louisa overdosed by, **22.** 459–60

Gloucester's: fear effects of autumn campaign, **24.** 401; give contradictory statements, **24.** 76; prevent him from going to Rome, **23.** 357; tell him he must go abroad, **39.** 247–8

gout does not require, **23.** 451, **31.** 97

Grafton's, optimistic, **37.** 482

grave face and tied wigs of, **24.** 71

HW abhors, **32.** 37, **33.** 229, 230, 460

HW agrees with, about warm weather helping Mann, **24.** 311

HW confers with, about nephew, **16.** 314, **32.** 121

HW disparages knowledge of, **21.** 368, **22.** 110, **24.** 76, **25.** 441

HW does not haggle with, over names, **35.** 319

HW has little faith in, **28.** 101

HW modifies his aversion to, **33.** 460

HW's life invaded by, **23.** 497

HW's pen compared to that of, **11.** 337

HW's poor opinion of, **4.** 464, **5.** 322n, **6.** 144, **9.** 359, **10.** 277, 290, **38.** 276, **39.** 31

Italian: at Reggio, **42.** 204; HW has less faith in, than in English ones, **24.** 206, 281; HW has no opinion of, **24.** 432; Mann tells Rainsford to consult, **23.** 393; take gloomy view of D. of Gloucester's illness, **23.** 337, 341

[Physician; physicians, *continued*]

James, Dr, summoned by, only in hopeless cases, **41**. 305

James's powders not prescribed by, for Waldegrave till too late, **22**. 127

James's powders opposed by, **36**. 40

Jesuits' fate should be shared by, **23**. 76

lawyers surpassed by, as poets, **42**. 364

Mann quite ready to distrust, **24**. 83

——'s: believes his rheumatism to be gout in the head, **24**. 479; feeds him ice creams and uses bleedings and senapisms, **25**. 560; gives him false encouragement, **25**. 567; Mann tells, that he must get well to entertain Hollands, **22**. 467; orders him to stay in bed, **25**. 555, 556; reassures Horace Mann II, **25**. 607; tells him that chalkstones are painful, **25**. 626; *see also* Muri, ——

—— suggests, for Lady William Campbell, **25**. 270

Maria Louisa may choose, **22**. 460

Marlborough, Ds of, repulses, **17**. 235

materia medica cannot be despised by, **35**. 569

More, Hannah, jokes about sources of fondness for, **31**. 318

—— prefers James's powders to, **31**. 272

Mozzi invites, to houses of pleasure, **23**. 158

murrain explained by, **19**. 174

Northampton, Cts of, attended by, **22**. 142

old Greek, Cocchi to edit works of, **20**. 34

Orford, Cts of, and Mozzi accompanied by, **23**. 158

Orford, 2d E. of, rejects, **20**. 233

Orford, 3d E. of, advised by, to part with housekeeper, **15**. 333

—— has no opinion of, **24**. 294

——'s, **41**. 260–1, 266

——'s to be discharged, **28**. 126, 130

—— wished by, to be secluded, **23**. 482

Pelham sons neglected by, **21**. 369

Pitt (Chatham)'s, order him to be kept quiet, **30**. 224

—— told by, not to go to Parliament, **24**. 370

Pius VI's, consider his illness serious, **24**. 461

Pompadour, Mme de, pronounced by, to be out of danger, **38**. 350

quack, fee of, **23**. 251

quacks preferred to, by HW, **21**. 378

Rome should not be prescribed by, **23**. 451

Royal College of, **29**. 95

Selwyn, John, and, **37**. 88, 93

smell of, **40**. 51

stuffed birds bought by, **23**. 210

tuberculosis attributed by, to verdigris, **40**. 257

vocation pretended by, **34**. 51

Voisin's, **41**. 174

Wilkes may have additional, **38**. 273

wine recommended by, for gout, **10**. 277

Young Pretender's, consider him to be in great danger, **25**. 394, 467; *see also* Pallucci, Natalis Joseph

See also under Medicine; Quack

Physiognomische Fragmente. See under Lavater, Johann Caspar

Physiognomy. See under Clubbe, John

'Physionomie, la':

French hair-dressing fashion, **39**. 271

Piacenza ('Placentia'; 'Plaisance'), Italy:

Aix treaty's provisions for, **19**. 479n

Bartolommei at, with Charles Emmanuel III and P. of Piedmont, **17**. 392n

battle at, **9**. 33–4, 48, **19**. 274n, **40**. 56–7

capture of, prematurely reported, **19**. 291

Charles Emmanuel III at, **17**. 392

—— insists on evacuation of, **19**. 279

—— joins Traun at, **17**. 312n

—— reluctantly exchanges, for Savoy and Nice, **19**. 508n

Choiseul proposes to Solaro that France pay Sardinia equivalent of revenue of, **21**. 275n

French and Spaniards said to have escaped from, **19**. 275

Gages at, **19**. 253

garrison of, escapes battle, **19**. 279

HW and Gray visit, **13**. 9

list of casualties and captures at, **19**. 266–7, 270–1

Maillebois joins Spaniards at, **19**. 266

Maria Theresa gives, to Charles Emmanuel III, **17**. 379

—— not to meddle in Sardinia's claims to, under Aix treaty, **21**. 280n

Modena, D. of, might have had, **13**. 242

Neapolitan-Sardinian war might start over reversion of, **21**. 275n

Ormea visits, **17**. 392n

Parma, Ds of, visits, **20**. 45n

—— seeks, **17**. 201

—— to receive, **19**. 481

Philip, Don, orders Maillebois to join Spanish army at, **19**. 263n

reversionary rights to, **21**. 283n

second battle of, **19**. 302–3

Spaniards and French cannot hold, **19**. 268

Spaniards bombarded by Austrians at, **19**. 276

—— may take, **17**. 198, 204–5, 214

—— prevent couriers from crossing, **19**. 156

—— retire to defences of, **19**. 266

Spanish army at, **19**. 258, 262

Villettes visits, **17**. 392n

Piaga aperta:

Tencin has, **17**. 481

Pianoforte; pianofortes:

Du Deffand, Mme, enthusiastic over, **4**. 451

—— to have Balbastre play, **6**. 115, 118

Lucans bring, to Mme du Deffand, **6**. 356–7

note on, **4**. 451–2

Pianoro (Italy):

Cocchi, Dr, travels from, to Florence, **17**. 54n

Piantanida:
  Lenten concerts arranged by, 19. 374
Piatti, Signora:
  in burletta company, 22. 474n
Piazza, Girolamo Bartolommeo (d. ca 1745),
  teacher at Cambridge:
  HW learns Italian from, 13. 6
Piazza del Carmine:
  Tylney's house in, 23. 468n
Piazza del Gran Duca, Florence:
  Craon, Princesse de, not well received in,
    17. 178–9
  impostor would not have succeeded at, 20. 29
Piazza della Signoria, Florence:
  'festa degli omaggi' in, 18. 251
Piazza di San Stefano:
  Pannoni's coffee-house overlooks, 17. 97n
Piazza di Santa Maria Novella, Florence:
  chariot races in, 17. 79n
Piazza di Santo Spirito, Florence:
  cocchiata begins at, 18. 485
  Santo Spirito convent on, 17. 65n
Piazza di Spagna at Rome. See under Spagna
Piazza Madama, Rome:
  Palazzo Madama on, 20. 264n
Piazza San Luigi, Rome:
  Palazzo Madama on, 20. 264n
Picard, Rev. Thomas (d. 1801), vicar of St
  Martin's, York:
  SH visited by, 12. 245
Picardy:
  Abbeville in, 11. 229n
  Belle-Isle plans invasion of British isles from,
    20. 535n
  English visitors' chaises enrich, 39. 8
  flax cultivated in, 7. 259
  HW expects to see regiment of, in London
    street scrawls, 33. 193
  intendant of, see Agay, Marie-François-
    Bruno d'
  Maillebois to command in, 6. 322
Picardy Canal. See St-Quentin Canal
Picart, Charles (ca 1780– ca 1837), engraver:
  engraving of Roscoe by, 15. 281n
Piccadilly, London:
  Arlington St extends from, 13. 3n
  Bath's house in, see under Pulteney, William,
    E. of Bath
  Burlington House in, 20. 66n
  butcher in, rents lodging to Giustinianis, 23.
    287
  Cholmondeley, E. of, lives in, 23. 217n, 316n,
    36. 60n
  Clarges St off of, 31. 234, 42. 99, 186n
  Clarke, Anna Maria, addressed in, 42. 186
  Devonshire's house in, 4. 352n, 32. 392n
  Egremont's house in, 22. 96n
  —— writes from, 40. 281
  Fitzwilliam's house in, 25. 294n
  Fores's 'Caricature Warehouse' in, 25. 641n
  Fox's house in, 30. 247
  HW astonished at stone houses instead of
    livery stables in, 9. 255–6
  HW is contented with, 28. 58
  HW mistakes crowds in, for mob, 11. 249,
    287
  highwayman attacks post-chaise in, 20. 188
  illuminated during Gordon riots, 33. 188
  mob takes possession of, 23. 6
  noisy, 10. 271
  paving of, subject of newspaper letters, 42.
    499
  parade in, 32. 331
  Selwyn and Maria Fagnani in, during Gordon
    riots, 33. 184
  statuary's yard in, 32. 342
  Stockdale bookseller in, 29. 157
  White, bookseller in, 31. 396n
  White Horse Cellar in: Bristol coach leaves
    from, 31. 313; place of stage-coaches' de-
    parture, 21. 313
  Williams, White Horse innkeeper in, de-
    nounces Independents, 19. 387n
Piccenza. See Piacenza
Piccinni, Niccolò (1728–1800), composer:
  Barone di Torre Forte, Il, by, at Haymarket,
    25. 134n
  Caracciolo defends, 7. 19
  Cecchina ossia la buona figliuola by: at the
    Haymarket, 23. 82n; Christian VII sees,
    played by Lovatini and Guadagni, 23. 42,
    35. 328; George III and Q. Charlotte praise,
    22. 474; HW praises, 22. 473–4; second
    part of, not so popular as first, 22. 484
  Gluck's rivalry with, 6. 478n, 7. 9, 19, 28.
    374n
  Marmontel revises Quinault's opera for music
    of, 6. 413
  name of, corrected, 43. 363
  Roland by, 6. 445, 7. 9
Piccolomini, Eneo Silvio (1708–68), cardinal,
  1766; gov. of Rome, 1761:
  (?) Chute and Whithed would like to send
    Young Pretender's limb to, 19. 318
  edict of, declares narrative to be false, 22.
    328
  Gascoigne and Hon. George Damer pro-
    tected by, from consequences of drunken
    brawl, 22. 286
  Patch aided by, when gov. of Rome, 23. 275
Piccolomini, Ottavio Eneo Giuseppe (1698–
  1757), Gen.:
  advantageous situation of, will keep Fred-
    erick II in winter quarters, 21. 15
  Austrian troops in Moravia commanded by,
    21. 5n
  Botta surrenders command to, temporarily,
    19. 363n
  Gavi surrenders to, 19. 301n
  —— to surrender to, 19. 315
  (?) Königgrätz headquarters of, 21. 15n
  (?) regiment of, 18. 331n
  too strongly entrenched to be attacked, 21. 5
Piccolomini, Senatore Cavaliere Priore Tommaso (d. 1784), Tuscan minister for foreign
  affairs 1771–84:

[Piccolomini, Tommaso, *continued*]
Billerey delivers French threat to, **24.** 508n
George III's letter promoting Mann presented to, **25.** 249n
government post given to, **23.** 294
HW hopes that letters are not opened by, **23.** 38
Mann notifies, of English manifesto, **25.** 112
——'s complaint answered by, **24.** 416n
Pichault de la Martinière, Germain (1696–1783), surgeon:
French rumour concerning, **32.** 386–7
Louis XV treated by, **6.** 48
Pichegru, Jean-Charles (1761–1804), Gen.:
armistice signed by, **34.** 213n
campaign of, in Holland, **12.** 121
Pickard. *See* Picard; Picart
Pick-ax:
England sends to Portugal, **20.** 512n
HW wields, in fancy, **15.** 19
Pickering, Elizabeth (ca 1679–97), m. (1697) John Cutts, 1st Bn Cutts:
Montagu wonders if Cowslade has portrait of, **9.** 252
sermon by Atterbury at funeral of, **9.** 261
Pickering, William (d. 1770) and John; tea merchants:
(?) Du Deffand, Mme, sends address of, to Craufurd, **5.** 331
Hyson tea bought at, **7.** 125n
Pickering, York:
Cayley's seat near, **11.** 13n
near Middleton, **11.** 18n
Picket; pickets:
for army camp, **37.** 121
French, in Scotland, surrender, **37.** 240
Tuscan, **18.** 100
Picket guard:
English, in Germany, **37.** 136
Pickle; pickles:
Corsican questions to be preserved in, **23.** 128
Howe's troops eat, at Boston, **28.** 294
Pickpocket; pickpockets:
statesmen become, **37.** 176
Picnics:
HW dislikes, **10.** 314
Pico, Lodovico (1668–1743), cardinal, 1712:
death of, **18.** 288
Picquet (game). *See* Piquet
Picquet de la Motte, Toussaint-Guillaume (1720–91), Comte de la Motte Picquet; French naval officer:
Digby's fleet pursues, **39.** 378n
—— to intercept fleet of, **24.** 361n
English convoy captured by, **25.** 152, 159–60
fleet of, sails from Brest, **24.** 473n
St Eustatius ships captured by, **36.** 198–9
St Vincent captured by, aided by Caribs, **24.** 503n
wounded, **7.** 451
Picquigny, Duc de. *See* Pecquigny
Picquigny (France):
HW visits, **7.** 259
Pict; Picts:

Pinkerton describes origin of, **16.** 303
Pictet, Marc (1693–1768), treasurer of Geneva:
(?) Veers forges signature of, **19.** 507
Picton, Maj.:
Hervey Aston's duel with, **25.** 566n
Picton Castle, Pembrokeshire:
HW hopes Sir John Philip lived at, **9.** 68
HW regrets not seeing ancestral seat of, **34.** 93
HW's ancestral home, **9.** 112
HW wishes to visit, **9.** 112
Philipps's home, **1.** 52n, 375n, **11.** 70n, **13.** 81n, 19. 310n
Pictorum aliquot celebrium præcipue Germaniæ inferioris effigies. See under Hondius, Hendrik
Picture; pictures. *See* Drawing; Enamel; Engraving; Etching; Hunting scene; Landscape; Miniature; Painting; Portrait; Print; Seascape; Silhouette; Water-colour
Picture, Moving. *See* Moving Picture
Picture-cleaner; picture-cleaners:
Montagu's opinion of, **10.** 285
Van der Gucht is, **33.** 538n
working in Gallery at SH, **10.** 84
See also Beckwith; Bonus; Collevaux; Donjeu
Picture frame; picture frames:
at Navestock, **9.** 244
coronet on, **9.** 282
HW injures, by too-quick gilding, **40.** 288
Montagu orders, **9.** 276, 282
Picture shop; picture shops:
at Dublin, **9.** 404
Pidansat de Mairobert, Mathieu-François de (1707–79):
Anecdotes sur la vie de Mme du Barry by, **6.** 273, 283, **43.** 99
(?) *Correspondance secrète et familière de M. de Maupeou avec M. de Sor . . .* , by, **5.** 104, **7.** 335
Mémoires secrets by Bachaumont and, **6.** 478, **33.** 377–8
(?) *Suite de la correspondance entre M. le Chancelier* by, **5.** 203
Piddlecombe. *See* Piddletown
Piddletown, Dorset:
HW visited, in 1745, **42.** 389
not an old Rolle estate, **25.** 148
Orford, E. of, bequeaths estate of, to Mrs Turk, **15.** 324
—— may sell, **25.** 148
——'s seat at, **25.** 227
Walpole, Horatio (1752–1822), owns estate in, with portrait, **42.** 389
Pidford, Isle of Wight:
Worsley of, **22.** 477n
Pidgeon, Tom, Granger's parish clerk:
Granger's mistake in psalms corrected by, **41.** 186–7
Pie, La. See under La Motte, Antoine Houdart de: *Fables*
Pie; pies:
Austro-Britons should eat plain, not French, **35.** 36

chicken, Mann's English guest prefers, to beef, **18.** 162
gooseberry, **13.** 174
macaroni, refused admittance to Florentine theatre, **20.** 219
mince: **13.** 76, **18.** 367; costs a penny **35.** 175n
of black cock, **36.** 324
of fat or meat, forbidden in theatre, **20.** 219
partridge, cold, **33.** 387n
pear, second course of, **19.** 357n
'pelican,' **17.** 485, **20.** 450
pigeon, 'remove' for soups, **19.** 357n
'rebel,' Townshend, Vcts, fears to encounter, **19.** 302, **24.** 21, **35.** 485
umble, may be part of deputy ranger's salary, **10.** 188
Pièce:
for Genoese opera, read by Mann, **19.** 505
Piece of eight; pieces of eight:
England sends Portugal £20,000 in, **20.** 512n
Nuestra Señora del Cabadonga has cargo of, **18.** 463n
San Antonio carries, **18.** 344n
Pièces de théâtre. See under Hénault, Charles-Jean-François
Pièces fugitives. See Fugitive Pieces in Prose and Verse, by HW
Pièces intéressantes et peu connues pour servir à l'histoire. See under La Place, Pierre-Antoine de
Pièces relatives aux lettres . . . du Chevalier d'Éon. See under Beaumont, Charles-Geneviève-Auguste-André-Timothée de, Chevalier d'Éon
Piedmont, P. of. *See* Charles Emmanuel IV (1751–1819)
Piedmont, Ps of. *See* Marie-Adélaïde-Clotilde-Xavière (1759–1802)
Piedmont:
Alfieri from, **25.** 538n
army of, Wentworth said to favour, **19.** 451
Austrian troops in, destitute of supplies, **19.** 431n
Beauvau said to be in, **19.** 70
Broglie, Comte de, was to have fetched Comtesse d'Artois from, **23.** 521
Broglie family from, **23.** 521
émigrés in, **11.** 140n
French attempts upon, **18.** 504–5, **19.** 417, 426–7, 436
French break power of, **12.** 191
Genoa campaign to follow campaign in, **19.** 437
Guasco from, **22.** 529
invasion threatens, **19.** 429n
Lobkowitz to send regiment to, **18.** 512
militia of, defeats Spaniards, **37.** 159
officers of, in Reggio, **17.** 46
Philip, Don, advances into, through Barcelonetta Valley, **17.** 389n
—— threatens to burn places in, **19.** 121
Richecourt, Cts, from, **20.** 90n

Spaniards' defeat secures, **37.** 159
troops of: cross the Var, **19.** 335–6; officers of, executed at Metz, **21.** 382–3; retreat towards Ventimiglia, **19.** 409
Piedmonte, Marchese Ippolito:
'Della Cruscan,' **25.** 612n
Piennes, Duc de. *See* Aumont de Rochebaron, Louis-Marie-Céleste de
Pierce, Mrs:
SH ticket not used by, **12.** 250
Pierce (*or* Pearce), Edward (d. 1658), sculptor:
Fuller's portrait of, **42.** 380n
Pierce. *See also* Pearce
Piercy family:
arms of, **1.** 28
Piercy. *See also* Percy
Pier glasses:
St John offers, to Mann, **17.** 283, 292
Pieri, Pietro Maria (1676–1743), cardinal, 1734:
death of, **18.** 150
Pierot. *See* Pierrot
Pierpoint. *See* Pierrepont
Pierpont Morgan Library, New York:
HW's MSS at, **36.** 314
Pierrecourt, Marquise de. *See* Rothe, Antoinette-Catherine-Josèphe de
Pierre d'Arena (Italy):
Spaniards reach, **19.** 47
Pierre de Bernis, François-Joachim de (1715–94), Cardinal de Bernis:
Aiguillon orders, to support Azpuru's efforts at Rome, **23.** 373n
anecdotes illustrating 'genteel address' of, **12.** 270
appointed ambassador to Holy See, **4.** 243–4
Ayen's witticism on recall of, from exile, **38.** 298
circular letter of, sent by Mann to HW, **21.** 218
Chesterfield disparages, **6.** 37
Clement XIV's election secured by, **23.** 134n
——'s negotiations with, over Jesuits, **23.** 414
Conclave attendance in hot months feared by, **24.** 461–2
—— expects, **23.** 95n
cost of administration of foreign affairs under, **4.** 371
Cumberland, D. of, entertained by, **23.** 566n
death of, falsely reported, **12.** 119
disgrace of, perhaps caused by disapproval of his Franco-Austrian treaty, **21.** 262n
dismissal of, **21.** 262–3, 265
embonpoint of, extraordinary, **24.** 462
French ambassador at Rome, **42.** 104
French relatives of, recommended by him to Mann, **24.** 375
Gloucester, D. of, entertained at dinner by, **23.** 389
goods of, confiscated when he rejects oath, **39.** 483
Gustav III discouraged by, at Rome, from aiding Young Pretender, **25.** 475
HW to write to Agincourt in care of, **42.** 104

[Pierre de Bernis, François-Joachim de, *cont.*]
Jesuits no longer opposed by, 23. 431n
——'s suppression again demanded by, 23. 214
——'s suppression demanded from, without mention of Avignon or Benevento, 23. 527n
lavish expenditure of, 23. 389
Louis XVI is said to have recalled, 25. 222
——'s aunts lodge with, 12. 222n
Mann, Horace II, to dine with, at Rome, 25. 675
Maurepas may be replaced by, 6. 323
——'s possible colleague, 6. 397
Maximilian's social relations with, 6. 156–7
may be fetched back to France to become prime minister, 24. 10
may get French cabinet post, 23. 264
party of, at Conclave of 1774, 24. 59n
Pius VI asked by, to receive Duchesse de Chartres like Archduchess Maria Christine, 24. 222n
——'s visit to Joseph II opposed by, 25. 239n
Pompadour, Mme de, advances, to be a cardinal, 21. 242
—— disputes with, over Soubise, 21. 263n
—— may have caused banishment of, 21. 262n
—— overturns, because of insults, 23. 144
print of, given to HW by Berrys, 11. 4
publishes erroneous news of French victory, 25. 127
recent ambassador to Vienna, 6. 156n
Santacroce, Principessa di, maintained by, 25. 675
satire on, 21. 265
Soissons place of exile of, 21. 262n
Starhemberg told by, that France cannot send troops to Moravia, 20. 589n
wit of, belied by heavy features, 11. 4
Young Pretender's journey discussed by, 23. 324

Pierre le Grand. See under Dorat, Claude-Joseph

Pierrepont, Lady Anne (b. 1631), m. (1658) John Manners, later 1st D. of Rutland:
husband of, resembles her 'illegitimate' son, 43. 269

Pierrepont, Lady Caroline (d. 1753), m. (1749) Thomas Brand:
death of, 9. 150, 20. 434–5
family of, 34. 257
marriage of, 20. 434–5
tavern visited by, after opera, 37. 54

Pierrepont, Charles. *See* Medows, Charles Pierrepont

Pierrepont, Evelyn (ca 1665–1726), 1st D. of Kingston-upon-Hull:
Bentinck, Lady Isabella, courted by, 14. 243
daughters of, 9. 150n, 14. 38n, 20. 281n, 434n
Montagu, Lady Mary Wortley, ordered by, to choose husband, 14. 244
wives and children of, 34. 255, 257

Pierrepont, Lady Evelyn (1691–1727), m. (1712) John Leveson Gower, 2d Bn Gower, cr. (1746) E. Gower:
relatives of, 20. 281n, 34. 256

Pierrepont, Evelyn (1711–73), 2d D. of Kingston-upon-Hull, 1726:
army camp at Newport visited by, 37. 503
(?) at Chesterfield's assembly, 37. 327
beauty of, fades, 9. 107
breaks trips to London at Grantham, 28. 224n
chamberlain's post sought by, 10. 29
Chudleigh, Elizabeth, kept by, 9. 412, 10. 29
—— preserves virtue from, 10. 274
——'s ball attended by, 35. 301
—— to marry, 23. 93
death of, leaving all to 'wife,' 23. 520, 32. 145–6, 149–50, 151–2
'dreadfully altered,' 37. 116
dying, 35. 347–8
family of, 34. 257
frock worn by, at Chudleigh ball, 38. 205
Hervey said to have connived at marriage of, for money, 24. 192n
K.G., 10. 29
La Touche, Mme de, comes to England with, 6. 130n
Light Horse of: 37. 230; at Culloden, 37. 240; dislodge rebels from the Spey, 37. 238n
losses of, by fires at Lincoln's Inn and Thoresby, 20. 321
marriage of: 20. 213n; House of Lords invalidates, 32. 299–300; not certain, 39. 105–6
Medows family mourns for Ds of Kingston out or respect for, 31. 289
milliner taken by, to Thoresby, 38. 473
mistress and Le Blanc accompany, to England, 20. 228n
mob pelts, by mistake for D. of Bedford, 23. 99
Mordaunt, Lt-Col. to, 26. 14
nephews hope to intercept estate of, 24. 56
nephews may deserve wealth of, 24. 30
nephews of, 24. 227n
nephews sue E. of Bristol for estate of, 24. 227
Petersham, Lady Caroline, entertains, at Vauxhall, 9. 107–10
—— pursues, 9. 107
relatives of, might be aided by Bp of Derry in proving his marriage invalid, 24. 55–6
sister of, 6. 185
soldier of, claims to have wounded Stewart, 37. 230
Thoresby the seat of, 28. 224n
Townshend, Vcts, challenged by, 35. 81
unmarried, 10. 29
wedding coach, favours, and liveries of, covered with mud, 23. 99
wife may swoon at name of, 24. 187
wife of: 2. 10n, 5. 406n; 9. 148n, 11. 219n, 28. 261n, 32. 169; tried for bigamy, 5. 406

wife reminded of, in Florentine Cascines, **24**. 6

wife said to terrify, with pistol, **24**. 198

wife should have divorced former husband before marrying, **24**. 88–9

wife should have permitted, to leave most of his estates to his family, **24**. 31

wife swoons at name of, **28**. 263

will of: **23**. 520, **32**. 145–6, 149–50, 151–2; lawyers may try to break, despite aliases, **24**. 30; nephews dispute, **24**. 20–1; widow wins Chancery case in regard to, **24**. 118

Pierrepont, Lady Frances (d. 1761), m. (1714) John Erskine, 6th E. of Mar:

Bedford, D. of, lends house to, **20**. 281

daughter tends, **20**. 281

HW's notes to her sister's letters to, **34**. 255–61

insane, **20**. 281

sister ill-treats, **14**. 243–5, **20**. 281

sister's letters to, **20**. 281

Pierrepont, Lady Frances (1713–95), m. (1734) Philip Medows:

bill brought by, **6**. 185n

family of, **34**. 257–8

Kingston trial not to benefit, **24**. 150n

sons of, **24**. 227n

Pierrepont, Gertrude (ca 1663–1732), m. (1680) Charles Cheyne, styled Bn Cheyne; 2d Vct Newhaven, 1698:

Bedford, Ds of, 'bred up' by, **34**. 257

Pierrepont, Lady Grace (d. 1703):

(?) Garth's *Dispensary* mentions, **34**. 256

Pierrepont, Lady Mary (1689–1762), m. (1712) Edward Wortley Montagu:

'acquired deformities of,' **30**. 15

Algarotti and, **43**. 190

appearance, avarice, and costume of, **10**. 5, **22**. 3, **37**. 78, 81

arrival of, in England: **10**. 5; denied, **9**. 395; rumoured, **9**. 392, **21**. 540, **31**. 24

avarice of, **10**. 5, **21**. 472–3, **22**. 3, **37**. 78, 81

Barnett takes on shipboard at Genoa, **21**. 473

Bedford House entertainment attended by, **22**. 17

bed in Roman lodging spoiled by, **30**. 8

Birtles disliked by, **17**. 98, 103–4

Brescia official entertains, at dinner, **20**. 279

Buondelmonti incited by, to satirize English at Florence, **17**. 92

château of, a mere hovel, **23**. 315

'cheats horse and foot' in faro at Princesse de Craon's, **13**. 234

clothes of, coarse and unclean, **18**. 306, **22**. 3

costume of, **10**. 5, **22**. 3, 17, **37**. 78, 81

Craven, Lady, discredits travel accounts by, **42**. 183

Crébillon fils sought as paramour by, **7**. 281

daughter inoculated by, **34**. 255

daughter of, **13**. 36n, **28**. 164n

death and will of, **22**. 72

death date of, corrected, **43**. 128

death of: **38**. 167; expected, **10**. 36, **22**. 76, **35**. 315

decayed though still graceful when HW first saw her, **42**. 507

description of, drawn in *Sortes Virgilianæ*, **10**. 5

dirt and economy of, shown in quarrel over sheets, **34**. 255

dirt of, should make her stay in quarantine, **21**. 540

doge to be reconciled by, with George II, **17**. 98

eclogues of: **43**. 182; Chute praises, **19**. 450; Gray deplores dislike of, in London and Cambridge, **14**. 38–9; inspired by Pope and Gay, **14**. 242; printed, **19**. 449, 450; Shrewsbury, Ds of, mentioned in, **33**. 557

England to be visited by, **21**. 472, 545

English consul at Venice insulted by, **17**. 98

English foreign ministers disparaged by, **17**. 98n

English reputation at Florence lowered by, **18**. 309

Epistle from Arthur Gray by: **19**. 450; Murray, Lady, mentioned in, **21**. 301n

false emeralds would still be fobbed off by, despite husband's death, **21**. 483

Firmian may be asked by, for book, **21**. 447

Florence to be visited by, **10**. 5

—— visited by, **17**. 91–2, **30**. 10, **37**. 78–9, 81

Florentines hear boasts of, **23**. 315

Genoa visited by, **17**. 91–2, 138, **21**. 473

Genoese abbé reported to be cicisbeo of, **30**. 11

Genoese supported by, in their dispute with English captain, **17**. 92, 104

Goldsworthy said by, to have discarded his wife, **18**. 13n

HW abhors, **35**. 489

HW calls: 'better specific against lust than all the bawdy prohibitions of the Fathers,' **30**. 10; 'most extraordinary in all her concerns,' **30**. 8; 'old, foul, tawdry, painted, plastered,' **13**. 234

HW calls on, **22**. 3

HW characterizes, **30**. 310n

HW expects, to form 'triple alliance' with Ladies Pomfret and Walpole, **13**. 227–8

HW goes in coach alone with, **30**. 10

HW jokes about morals of, **9**. 392

HW reads works of, in manuscript, **13**. 234

HW's account of, diverts Mann, **22**. 13

HW's anecdotes of, **14**. 242–7

HW sees MS of eclogues of, in Florence, **19**. 449n

HW's lines on post-chaise of, **14**. 246–7

HW's notes to letters of, **34**. 255–61

HW's opinion of, **10**. 5

HW to call on, **17**. 92

HW to send *Royal and Noble Authors* to, **21**. 458, 472

HW unattracted by, **30**. 10

half-sister of, **20**. 434

[Pierrepont, Lady Mary, *continued*]
Hamilton, Ds of, calls on, **22**. 4
health of: cancer of the breast, **22**. 56; dropsy, **10**. 36; ill at Brescia, **20**. 235n; pox, **37**. 78, 81
Hervey's effeminacy remarked upon by, **17**. 274n
husband of, **9**. 338n
inoculation introduced by, **13**. 3n, **34**. 255
itinerary of, **17**. 91n
languages spoken by, **10**. 5
letters of: **6**. 282, **28**. 243n; copied at Venice, **22**. 141; from Constantinople, **22**. 85n; HW's notes to, **34**. 255-6; HW interested in, **17**. 1n; HW quarrels with Macartney over, **33**. 317-18; published, **2**. 152n, **38**. 202; to her sister, seen by HW, **20**. 281, **34**. 255-61
Lincoln, E. of, claimed by, as blood relative, **30**. 10
——'s relations with, **30**. 10
—— to call on, **17**. 91
Mann asked by, for *Royal and Noble Authors*, **21**. 447
—— to get news of, through Niccolini, **20**. 285
manuscripts of: given to clergyman in Holland, **22**. 84; HW would like to see, **22**. 84; volumes of prose and verse bequeathed to daughter, **22**. 84
Marlborough, Ds of, discusses Bns Sundon with, **17**. 276-7
masquerade attended by, **7**. 281
memoirs of, compared to Mme del Pozzo's, **22**. 84
Micheli, Mme, told by, that Palazzi stops their correspondence, **20**. 279
Mohammedanism preferred by, **2**. 152
Muzell brings HW a scolding from, **21**. 458
Naples visited by, **17**. 91-2
nieces of, **20**. 281
not yet arrived, **21**. 560
Palazzi, Conte, attentive to, **7**. 281
—— escorts, from Avignon to Brescia, **20**. 235n
—— said to have imprisoned, in Brescia, **20**. 235, 272, 279, 281
——'s house near Gottolengo bought and occupied by, **20**. 235n
Pinkerton prefers, to Mme de Sévigné, **16**. 265-6
Pitt, George, admired by, in Italy, **17**. 468n
—— known by, **20**. 58
Pomfret, Cts of, forced to air the bedchamber of, **19**. 72
Pomfret, E. of, host to, while she tries to play a joke on him, **17**. 92
Pomfrets accompanied by, to Casa Giraldi, **43**. 179
Pope, Alexander, alleged lover of, **34**. 255
—— frequently mentions, **30**. 310
—— might have visited, at Wharncliffe before satirizing her, **35**. 268
—— satirizes, **20**. 282, **21**. 472n

portrait of, as authoress, at Welbeck by (?) Rusca, **35**. 271
'poxed, foul, malicious, black blood of,' **30**. 10
Raper brings diamond crochette to, **17**. 138
Rawdon accused by, of buying title and pictures for the same reason, **20**. 135n
—— meets, in Venice, **17**. 400n
Rémond de St-Mard almost cheated by, **20**. 281-2
—— lover of, **20**. 281-2
republics preferred by, **17**. 98
Richelieu converses with, **7**. 281
ring given by, to Barnard, **21**. 473
Rome visited by, **17**. 91-2, **30**. 8, 10
secretary of, *see* Moro, Dr Bartolommeo
Simonetti, Contessa, compared with, **20**. 148
sister ill-treated by, **20**. 281
Six Town Eclogues by, *see under* eclogues by
Skerrett, Maria, friend and relative of, **13**. 8n, **17**. 320n, **34**. 256
son awaits, at Montélimar and accompanies her to Orange, **18**. 567n
son left one guinea by, **20**. 81
son not supplied by, **20**. 235
son of, **20**. 226
son's conversation with, at Geneva, **18**. 567
son's relations with, **30**. 10
Stafford, Cts of, friend of, **9**. 119
Stair, E. of, lover of, **34**. 257
statue at Luton Hoo to honour, **32**. 91
tedious in her narrations, **22**. 17
Town Eclogues by, *see under* eclogues by
Townshend, Charles, exaggerates quantity of MSS of, **22**. 85-6
Townshend, Vcts, imitates ogling of, **17**. 468
Turin visited and abused by, **17**. 91
Tweeddale, Lady, called ugly by, **17**. 278n
Twickenham house of, **9**. 119, **34**. 255, **42**. 486, 488, 490
Venetian doge and senate assured by, that she will reconcile them with George II, **17**. 98
Venice visited by, **17**. 91-2, 98
verses by, on shipboard, **21**. 473
Villettes praised by, **17**. 98n
Walpole, Bns, competes with, for Oxonian's favour, **13**. 233-4
—— ridiculed, and Cts of Pomfret scolded by, **37**. 78
Walpole, Sir Robert, sent letter by, **17**. 98
wishes her enemies to suffer from gout or stone, instead of dying, **35**. 489
wit of, attracts lovers, **37**. 81
witticism by, about Adam, **20**. 282
Wrottesley, Lady Mary, confused with, **21**. 540
Pierrepont, William (1692-1713), styled E. of Kingston 1706-13:
family of, **34**. 257-8
'Pierrot':
'Harlequin's' dialogues with, **18**. 501
Piers, Lt Riccarde:
captured at Velletri, **18**. 492
Piers. *See also* Peers; Peirse

Pierson, Maj. (d. 1781):
killed in Jersey attack, 39. 360n
Pierson, Mr:
Beaufort's social relations with, in Paris, 7.
271
Pierson, James Bradshaw (1741–ca 1818), col-
lector:
Christie's fails to sell alleged Van Dyck
Madonna auctioned by, 35. 428
Duncombe buys a Guido from paintings
brought by, mostly from Venice, 23. 569–70
marriage of, 23. 569–70
Pierson, Mrs James Bradshaw. See Giacomazzi,
Teresa
Pierson, Gen. Richard (d. 1781):
death of, 29. 88n
Pietas Academiæ Cantabrigiensis:
compilation of: 13. 145–6
'Pietra'; 'Pietraccia.' *See* Stone, Andrew
Pietraja. *See* Petraia
Pietra Mala (Italy):
Botta to meet Leopold at, 22. 334
Modena, Ps of, entertained at, by Botta's
delegates, 22. 202
Pietra River (Italy):
earthquake destroys, 33. 397
Pietra Santa (Italy):
Spaniards to cross, 19. 35
Spanish army crosses Tuscany at, 19. 40
Pieyre, Pierre-Alexandre (1752–1830), play-
wright:
Amis à l'épreuve and *École des pères* by, 42.
214
Pig; pigs:
Chinese, offered by HW to Conway, 37. 344,
345–6, 349
country fellow thrusts, in D. of Somerset's
face, 20. 10n
gout cured by, freshly slaughtered, 17. 11n
HW may be sticking, in Chinese fashion,
40. 17
HW might have promoted interest of Ds of
Newcastle's, 20. 83
HW's coachman admires, 37. 347–8
Middleton's bronze figure of, 15. 16
Newcastle, Ds of, brings, from Hanover, 20.
72
Ossory, Lady, puzzles HW by allusion to,
33. 266
St Anthony's, 13. 145, 43. 176
St-Antoine, Abbess of, should be escorted by,
34. 77
Pigage, Nicolas de (1723–96):
Galerie électorale de Dusseldorff by, 33. 148
Pigalle, Jean-Baptiste (1714–85), sculptor:
verses on statue by, of Voltaire, 5. 354
Voltaire's verses to, 5. 327–8, 7. 20–1, 23
Pigeon; pigeons:
as hors d'œuvres, 19. 356n
fat, coveted by Italian wives, 32. 148
HW receives news as if by, 35. 228
Irishman's saying about, 24. 64
Lunardi takes, in balloon, 25. 528n

See also Wood pigeon
Pigeon pie. *See under* Pie
Pigeon wood:
Hervey, Bns, to have shoes of, 9. 18
Pigmalion. See under Rousseau, Jean-Jacques
Pigmy; pigmies:
Conway's temple to be *chorea* of, 39. 460
existence of, not believed, 42. 182–3
Pignataro, Carmine (fl. 1760–70 at Naples),
engraver:
Hamilton employs, 35. 429n
Pignatelli, Gian Domenico (*or* Juan Domingo)
(d. 1765); Spanish ambassador to Parma:
death of, 31. 91
Egmont, Comtesse d', raised, 31. 91
intended bride of, 31. 91
Pignatelli, Luís (1749–1801), Conde de Fuentes;
Duque de Solferino:
Fuentes's house shared by, 5. 405–6
Pignatelli de Aragón, Juan Joaquín Atanasio
(1724–76), Conde de Fuentes; Spanish am-
bassador to England and to France:
Aiguillon supported by, against the Church,
5. 213–14
Aranda in house of, 5. 405
arrival of, in England, 21. *417*
Bubb Dodington entertains, at Hammersmith,
35. 301–2
Castromonte planned to call on, 4. 367
Charles III's declaration delivered by, to
foreign ministers in England, 21. 559
Chudleigh ball attended by, 35. 300–1
Cumberland, D. of, points to, 9. 318n
Du Barry, Mme, avoided by, 5. 108, 110
—— refused homage by, 23. 321, 338
Egremont's negotiations with, 22. 5n
family of, 9. 338
Forcalquier, Mme de, has social relations
with, 7. 317, 318
French declaration opposed by, 23. 322
(?) Huntingdon resembles, 35. 300
Joseph II's and Maria Theresa's declaration
to, about Jesuits, 23. 477n
leaves for Spain, 21. 558
Maupeou ignored by, 23. 321
negotiations of, may be resumed, 22. 30n
Newcastle, D. of, cancels party for, 21. 417n
Northumberland, Ds of, entertains, 35. 301
out-of-town invitations declined by, ungra-
ciously, 21. 417
Paris house, taken by, offered to Hertford,
his friend, 38. 340
public places avoided by, according to vow,
21. 428
son of, 5. 158n
Spanish memorials delivered by, 21. 553n,
558n
Toison d'Or conferred on, 21. 560
Tylney's ball not attended by, 21. 417
Pignatelli d'Egmont, Alphonsine-Louise-Julie-
Félicie (1751–86), m. (1768) Luís Pignatelli,
Conde de Fuentes, Duque de Solferino:
Egmont, Comtesse d', grandmother of, 31. 91

[Pignatelli d'Egmont, Alphonsine, *continued*]
immense heiress, **31.** 91
intended husband of, **31.** 91
social relations of, in Paris, **7.** 286, 301
Pignatelli d'Egmont, Casimir (1727–1801),
Comte d'Egmont:
command rumoured to be given to, **7.** 151
Compiègne instead of Madrid visited by, **20.**
572n
Du Deffand, Mme, mentions, **3.** 318
father-in-law sends, to Madrid, **20.** 572
marriage of, **3.** 42n
social relations of, *see index entries ante* **8.** 471
wife of, **3.** 42n, **14.** 156n
Pignatelli y Gonzaga, José (1744–74), Marqués
de Mora:
Bubb Dodington entertains, at Hammersmith,
35. 301–2
Chudleigh ball attended by, **35.** 300–1
father of, **9.** 338n
Du Deffand, Mme, has social relations with,
5. 158
Fuentes' house shared by, **5.** 406
high-born ugliness of, **35.** 300
Norfolks entertain, **9.** *338*
Northumberland, Ds of, entertains, **35.** 301
Pignotti, Abbate Lorenzo (1739–1812), M.D.;
poet and scientist:
'Della Cruscan,' **25.** 612n
Lady Orford's death certificate signed by, **43.**
288
Roberto Manners by, **25.** 636
Shakespear by, **24.** 536
Pignuts:
Lansdowne said to live on, **33.** 527
Pigot, George (1719–77), cr. (1764) Bt and
(1766) Bn Pigot; gov. of Madras:
arrest of, in India, **28.** 293, 304, **35.** 486
Benfield helps to depose, **29.** 103
death of, reported, **33.** 5
diamond of, **31.** 159
dies under suspicious circumstances, **28.** 344,
348–9, **29.** 123
East India Co. in London votes to restore,
after his illegal imprisonment, **24.** 288
gambling loss of, at Ps Amelia's, **39.** 238
Stuart arrests, **35.** 486
Tanjore's conquest condemned by, **23.** 562n
trials of those who deposed, **25.** 13n
Pigot, Hugh (1722–92), Adm., M.P.:
Bedford, Ds of, entertains, **33.** 544
fleet of, near Sandy Hook, **25.** 351n
George III's remonstrance from, for Keppel's
trial, **24.** 432n
news of schooner taken by, should not have
been put in gazette, **25.** 318
Parliamentary bill by, authorizing naval
courts martial, **33.** 76n
West Indian fleet to be commanded by, **25.**
311n, 318n
wife of, **4.** 9n, **9.** 69n
Pigot, Mrs Hugh. *See* Le Neve, Elizabeth (1720–
before 1759); Wrottesley, Frances (d. 1811)

Pigott, Arthur Leary (1749–1819), Kt, 1806;
solicitor-gen. to P. of Wales 1783–92:
Revolution Society's jubilee attended by, **11.**
314
Pigott, Granado:
Cole's legal representative, **2.** 379
Pigott, Mrs John. *See* Brownlow, Mary (1719–
85); Tyrrell, Christobella (1695–1789)
Pigott, Margaret (ca 1714–88), m. Edward
Riggs:
chatters metaphysics, **5.** 205
Du Deffand, Mme, dislikes, **5.** 205
——'s social relations with, **5.** 189, 197
HW entertained by, **10.** 233
Miller, Mrs, daughter of, has 'Parnassus' at
Batheaston, **39.** 240–1
Millers leave children with, in France, **24.** 197
—— live with, at Batheaston, **24.** 197
Montagu, Lady Barbara, friend and neigh-
bour of, **10.** 234
rough English humourist, **24.** 197
Pigou, Frederick (d. 1804), banker:
(?) Little Marble Hill to be vacated by,
12. 36
——, Twickenham, occupied by, **42.** 484
SH visited by, **12.** 241, 249
Pigou, Frederick John (son of Frederick Pigou):
(?) Little Marble Hill to be vacated by,
12. 36
Pig's blood:
prescribed for gout, **13.** 213
Pigtail. *See* Queue
Pigtail tobacco. *See under* Tobacco
'Pigwiggen':
fairy, in Drayton's *Nimphidia*, **18.** 70n
'Pigwiggin.' *See* Walpole, Horatio (1723–1809)
'Pigwigginhood':
Astley draws pictures of, **20.** 341
Pike, Lt (?) Edward (d. 1776):
killed in expedition against Charleston, **24.**
237, **32.** 318
Pike (fish):
ragoût of, **7.** 446
Pike; pikes (weapons):
Jacobins have, **15.** 221
Piked horns. *See under* Head-dress
Pilar, María Ignacía del (ca 1745–64), m. (1756
and 1760) José Pignatelli y Gonzaga, Marqués
de Mora:
biographical information on, corrected, **43.**
124, 362
Bubb Dodington entertains, at Hammersmith, **35.** 301–2
dances first, at Norfolk House ball, **9.** 338
Norfolks entertain, **9.** 338
(?) Northumberland, Ds of, entertains, **35.**
301
sick and lacks teeth, **35.** 300
Pilaster; pilasters:
glass, at Boyle Farm, **35.** 390
Pilate, Pontius:
on truth, **32.** 348, **34.** 43

'Pilate':
Florentine children's name for Richecourt, 21. 85
Pilâtre de Rosier, Jean-François (1754–85), aeronaut:
balloon ascent of, 25. 450
balloon voyage of, 25. 527n
biographical information on, corrected, 43. 291, 292, 357
death of: 33. 467, 468; chills but does not stop rage for balloons, 25. 596; in balloon accident, 25. 590; lamented by Mann, 25. 593
Orford, E. of, said to entertain, 25. 596n
Pilchards:
Hervey, Bns, sends, to HW, 31. 34
Piles, Roger de (1635–1709), artist; writer:
Art of Painting by, has omitted painters, 40. 238
English painters lack, 38. 151
Piles. See Hæmorrhoids
Pilgrim; pilgrims:
masqueraders costumed as, 17. 339, 343, 368
raggedness of, 30. 219
to Rome, in jubilee year, estimated at three million, 20. 43n
'Pilgrim's Progress':
HW should write, 35. 33
Pilgrim's Progress. See under Bunyan, John
Pilkington, Mrs Matthew. See Lewen, Lætitia van
'Pillars of State, The' (print). See under Townshend, George (1724–1807)
Pill; pills:
quack, 41. 15
Pill box:
Mann sends cameo in, to HW, 25. 560
Pillion; pillions:
palfreys ridden with, 35. 136
Pillnitz (Germany):
declaration of, 11. 262n, 352n
Pillori, Antonio (d. ?1782), translator:
Caractacus being translated by, 28. 172
Elfrida translated by, 28. 171
Pillory; pillories:
Billard in, 5. 190
Du Deffand, Mme, mentions, 6. 21
Fuller sentenced to, 16. 366
hackney writer may write himself into, 42. 504
in Palace Yard, Williams stands in, 38. 512–13
Shebbeare may be punished by, 21. 39
—— will end in, 21. 87
Wilkes threatened with, 22. 183
—— unlikely to be put in, 23. 30
Pillow; pillows:
Craon, Princesse de, has all sizes of, 17. 481
in Anne of Denmark's collection, 32. 325
Walpole, Sir Robert, snores upon, 17. 171
Pill to Purge State-Melancholy, A:
Estcourt's ballads in, 33. 215n
song in, quoted, 33. 215
Pilon, Frederick:
Invasion by, 33. 135n

Pilot; pilots:
English seek, at Leghorn for Adriatic, 17. 455–6
of barge, Ferdinand of Naples reprimands, 25. 581
Pilpay. See Bīdpaī
Pilsen (Bohemia):
Austrians advance on, 18. 58
—— capture, 17. 466n
Pimpernel:
HW mentions, 3. 341
seeds of, sent to Marquise de Broglie, 30. 251
Pin; pins:
Amelia, Ps, uses, for her napkin, 33. 164
black, for curling hair, 30. 275n
Galli, Mme, to have, 17. 239
HW sends, to Mme Galli, 17. 416, 422
Wharton borrows, from guardian, 34. 94
Pinacci, Angela (fl. 1757–92), m. (1757) Casimiro Branchi; singer:
'divine singer,' 22. 35
Grafton, Ds of, charmed by, 22. 35
Mann wants Handel's oratorios for, 22. 35–6
—— wants music for, on Ds of Grafton's account, 22. 50
sings at musical accademia, 23. 405n
Pinacci, Giovanni Battista (b. 1696), singer:
roars, 18. 361
Pinasters:
HW to send, to Montagu, 9. 177
Pinchbeck, Christopher (ca 1670–1732), watch and toy-maker in Fleet St:
metal alloy of, 30. 54n
Pinchbeck, Christopher (ca 1710–83), inventor and shopkeeper:
great room of, at Tunbridge Wells, 33. 129
Jervais exhibits works at shop of, in Cockspur St, 2. 222n
Queen's zebra bought by, 28. 90
Pinchbeck, Lincs:
Walpole of, 1. 130n
'Pinchbeck,' alloy of copper and zinc:
buckles of, 30. 54
Pinchy. See Pinchbeck
Pincot, Daniel (d. 1797):
(?) attendance charge of, at Mrs Coade's stone factory, 41. 229
Essay on . . . Artificial Stone, 23. 311n, 41. 229n
Pincushion:
HW asks Lady Anne Fitzpatrick to make, 33. 260
Pindar (?518– ca 448 B.C.), poet:
abrupt transitions of, 11. 175, 39. 206
bust of, 29. 296
Cumberland might imitate, 29. 146
HW compares Gray to, 28. 20, 174
HW compares Mason to, 28. 204
HW compares Ossianic specimens to, 15. 61
HW uses adjective derived from, 32. 112, 228, 33. 12, 434, 34. 14
HW wishes that odes like those of, were made for Newmarket races, 16. 298

[Pindar, poet, *continued*]
Jerningham's passage superior to poetry of, **41**. 382
Mason compares Gray to, **28**. 276, 279
ode by, **43**. 227
odes of, unsuitable for a mass meeting, **16**. 297
seal may depict, **19**. 483
Stanley translates, **29**. 8
West's translation of, **9**. 84, **43**. 115
'Pindar, Peter.' *See* Wolcot, John
'Pindar, stroller':
Temple as vain as if descended from, **9**. 259
Pindemonte, Ippolito (1753–1828), Veronese writer:
SH visited by, **12**. 235
Pindus:
Batheaston becomes, **39**. 241
Hannah More's heart worth all of, **33**. 533
Pine, John (1690–1756), engraver; printer:
engraving by, of Henry VI and Parliament, **40**. 217
Hogarth represents, **15**. 142n, **41**. 449
print of Magna Carta by, **2**. 47n
Tapestry Hangings of the House of Lords by, **9**. 18n, **18**. 126–7
Pine; pines:
Florentine commissary has, cut down in Lucca, **20**. 514
hurricane uproots, at Villa Negrone, **20**. 69
Lombardy, in French garden, **28**. 220
See also Pinaster; Stone pines; White pines
Pineapple; pineapples:
at Claremont Park, **9**. 71
Botta's room hot enough to produce, **21**. 370
Churchill, Lady Mary, sends, to Mme du Deffand, **6**. 325
confection of, given by HW to Beauvau, **41**. 330
culture of, in England, **1**. 177, **2**. 200, 239
Damer, Mrs, sends, to Mme du Deffand, **5**. 386
England imports, from the south, **32**. 359
HW and Montagu bring, from Wroxton, **35**. 72
Hanover, destination of, **9**. 71
Italians first see, in England, **19**. 331
Pomfret pedigree depicts, **20**. 180–1
preserves of, **6**. 378, **7**. 417
recipe for pâté of, sent by HW to Mme du Deffand, **6**. 269
sold at Covent Garden market, **21**. 294
Taaffe brings, to Marquise de Pompadour, **20**. 289
Young Pretender first tastes, at Blair Atholl, **19**. 106
'Pineapples, The,' in Lincoln's Inn Fields:
Fanshawe, Lady, rents, **34**. 148n
Pineda, Juan de (d. ca 1593), of Medina del Campo:
Monarquía eclesiastica, La, by, cited by HW from Bayle, **37**. 293

Pineda, Juan de (1557 *or* 8–1637), Spanish Jesuit:
HW confuses, with namesake, **37**. 293
Pinelli, Maffeo (1736–85), of Venice; collector:
library of: Edwards visits, **11**. 150n; sale of, **42**. 240n
Pinfold, Joseph, banker at Leghorn:
Crowe clerk in bank of, **20**. 1n
Pini, (?) Alessandro:
Museum Florentinum directed by, **18**. 390–1
Pink; pinks:
at SH, **10**. 127
Edward VI carries, in portrait, **16**. 232
'language' of, **33**. 262
More, Hannah, mentions, **31**. 295
—— raises, **31**. 250
propagation of, by piping, **31**. 264
transitory, **35**. 461
Pinkerton, Lady:
endorsement by, **43**. 226
Pinkerton, John (1758–1826), antiquary; historian; HW's correspondent:
Ancient Scotish Poems by: **43**. 226; HW praises, **16**. 288; (?) Pinkerton gives, to HW, **16**. 287; published, **16**. 326n
Anderson's letter to, **16**. 373–6
Batsford's letter to, **16**. 382
Beauclerk, Lady Diana, writes to Abp Moore about, **16**. 286
Berry, Mary, receives gift from, **16**. 316, 381
—— writes to, **16**. 381
Berry family hopes to see, when he visits HW at SH, **16**. 381
British Museum post sought by: **16**. 294–5, 311–12, 325–6; by HW through Banks, **42**. 212–13
Buchan sends HW a message for, **15**. 192
catalogue of Charles I's collection discovered by, **16**. 289–90
Grace's letter from, **16**. 382
Craigmillar Castle by, **16**. 251n
Dissertation on the Origin and Progress of the Scythians or Goths, A, by, **16**. 280n
Elibank's publications to be listed by, for HW, **42**. 197
Essay on Medals, An, by: (?) Berry, Mary, thanks Pinkerton for, **16**. 381; dedicated to HW, **16**. 325; HW admires, **16**. 254; HW declines dedication of, **42**. 262n; HW meets Pinkerton through, **29**. 359; HW sends plate from, to Bull, **42**. 262; new edn of, **42**. 262; revision of, **16**. 299n; second edn of, dedicated to HW, **15**. 256n, 262n; Southgate aids second edn of, **42**. 212n
Gentleman's Magazine prints inquiry by, **16**. 382
HW asked by: to consult Bp Douglas, **12**. 9; to get Abp Moore's permission to see Lambeth books, **16**. 280
HW asks, not to address him 'humbly,' **16**. 277
HW congratulated by, on becoming E. of Orford, **16**. 313

HW declines to buy picture suggested by, **16**. 320

HW does not want, to 'throw a few daisies' on his grave, **16**. 309

HW encloses order to, for visitors' admission to SH, **42**. 197

HW gives SH edns to, **16**. 274

HW glad to show medals to, at SH, **42**. 111

HW hopes that Mary Berry will know, better, **16**. 316–17

HW informed by, of pictures to be bought, **16**. 284–5

HW invites to SH, **16**. 252, 267, 273, 290–1, 293, 299, 316, **42**. 197, 225

HW reads preface of, **16**. 262

HW receives medal from, **16**. 317

HW receives 'old MS' from, **16**. 251

HW recommends, to (?) Astle, **42**. 279–80

HW's correspondence with: **12**. 9, **16**. 251–328, **42**. 111–12, 197, 225, 288; MSS of, **36**. 314

HW sends servant to Nichols, bookseller of, **42**. 277

HW's friendship with: Boswell's account of, **29**. 358; Harcourt's account of, **29**. 359

HW's social relations with, **16**. 274, 277, 287, 288, 290

HW to give *Royal and Noble Authors* to, **16**. 274

HW to send books to, **16**. 259

HW to show to, Vertue's MS on coins, **12**. 256n

HW unable to comply with request of, **16**. 318–19

HW unable to set date for receiving, at SH, **42**. 111–12

HW warns, about project of writing history of George II's reign, **16**. 261

History of Scotland, The, by: HW consents to read MS of, **16**. 314–15; HW has read and corrected, **16**. 319; published, **12**. 10n

'Hymn to Liberty' by: Anderson's suggestions for, **16**. 375–6; Pinkerton asks HW's advice on, **16**. 297; printing of, **16**. 373; text of, **16**. 373–4

Iconographia Scotica: portraits sought for, **16**. 321–4; prints in, inferior to biographies, **16**. 324; published, **15**. 138n

Inquiry into the History of Scotland, An, by: (?) Berry, Mary, thanks Pinkerton for, **16**. 381; HW's opinion of, **16**. 302–7; published, **16**. 280n

James IV's portrait sought by, **16**. 382

Kentish town the address of, **42**. 288

Knight borrows HW's *Mysterious Mother* from, **16**. 372

——'s letter to, **16**. 372

Knightsbridge the address of, **42**. 111

Lambeth Palace books sought by, through HW's aid, **16**. 281–2

learned, **11**. 177

Letters of Literature by: **43**. 224; attributed to HW, **29**. 358, **33**. 491–2; Colman praised in, **16**. 265; HW advises Pinkerton not to answer criticism of, **16**. 278–80; HW did not see, until it was in print, **33**. 492; HW has read, three times, **33**. 490; HW sends, to Colman, **16**. 265, 267; HW's opinion of, **33**. 471, 491–2; HW thanks Pinkerton for, **16**. 263, 268; Harcourt finds 'coarse Johnsonian arrogance' in, **29**. 358; Ossory, Lady, to send for, **33**. 477; 'Pilkington' said to be author of, **16**. 274; Pinkerton does not puff, **16**. 283; plan in, for improvement of English language, **16**. 264; published under pseudonym of 'Robert Heron,' **29**. 357–8; publishers of, **33**. 476; purchasers of, will not all be admirers, **16**. 283; Ravensworth, Lady, reads, on HW's recommendation, **33**. 490; second edn of, should list reviewers' misquotations, **16**. 283–4

Lives of the Scottish Saints by, (?) HW is urged to print, **16**. 276

Lorimer's controversy with, in *Gentleman's Magazine*, **16**. 311

marriage of, **12**. 10

Medallic History of England, The, by: **16**. 381n; Snelling's *Thirty-Three Plates* the basis of, **16**. 299

Nicol approaches HW through, **42**. 371

Nivernais's *Jardins modernes* given to, **12**. 259

obnoxious to the clergy, **16**. 327

play by: criticized by HW, **16**. 253–4; HW gives, to Colman, **16**. 254, 259, 265

Rimes by, (?) HW thanks Pinkerton for, **16**. 251

'Robert Heron' the pseudonym of, **29**. 357–8, **33**. 471

Scotish Gallery, The, by, **15**. 138n, **16**. 321n

Scotish Poems by, **16**. 326n

Scotish Tragic Ballads and *Select Scotish Ballads* edited by, **16**. 251n

Scotland's ancient history is being written by, **16**. 286

Scottish charters and documents sought by, **42**. 280

SH visitors sent by, **12**. 226, 227, 228, 234, 236, 240, 241 *bis*

Tales in Verse by, (?) HW thanks Pinkerton for, **16**. 251

Two Dithyrambic Odes by, HW thanks Pinkerton for, **16**. 251

Vitæ antiquæ sanctorum edited by: **16**. 326n; sent by HW to E. of Carlisle, **42**. 278

works published by, from MSS, **16**. 326

Pinkethman, William (fl. 1692–1724), actor:
acts in *Dioclesian*, **18**. 565

HW did not admire, **23**. 265

petition of, in *Spectator*, **18**. 565

Pinkie House, Midlothian:
Holbein painting said to be at, **16**. 51

Pink Room. *See* SH: Star Chamber

Pinnacle; pinnacles:
of SH Library bookcases, **35**. 157, 200

on SH Library chimneypiece, **35**. 158

Pinner, Middlesex:
Hamilton, Miss, lives at, **33.** 364
Pinners' Hall, London:
Foster, James, pastor of Independent church at, **19.** 299n
Pinocin (d. 1612):
Balagny kills, but is mortally wounded, **40.** 357
Pinot Duclos, Charles (1704–72), writer:
Académie française member and secretary, **5.** 209, 222, 234
Alembert and, **43.** 93
Alembert bequeathed diamond by, **5.** 211
—— replaces, as secretary, **5.** 222
Considération sur les mœurs de ce siècle by, **5.** 209n, **8.** 35n
costume of, **10.** 70–1
death of, **5.** 209
five vacancies left by, **5.** 209
HW entertains, at SH, **10.** 70–1
Histoire de Louis XI by, **10.** 70, **14.** 41, **43.** 129
Hume prefers, **41.** 25n
La Chalotais receives offers through, **23.** 207
Montesquieu's letters infuriate, **22.** 531
——'s *Lettres familières* to be taken by, to France, **22.** 531
Pisa visited by, **22.** 531
Quinault, Olympe, gets bequest from, **5.** 211
secretary of Académie des Sciences, **22.** 531
social relations of, in Paris, **7.** 267, 271, 280, 307
Suard elected to replace, **5.** 234
Pinsent. *See* Pynsent
Pinterel de Neufchâtel, Oger (d. 1781), Chevalier:
(?) attends session of parliament of Paris, **8.** 173
Pinti, Via de', at Florence:
Palazzo Pantiatichi-Ximenes in, **17.** 122n
Pinto, Chevalier de; Portuguese envoy extraordinary to England:
Maria I tells, about Bns Craven, **34.** 133n
Pinto, Mme de, wife of Portuguese minister:
HW complimented by, on verses, **32.** 372
Pinto, Don Tommaso:
Neapolitan physician, **21.** 325
Pinto de Fonseca, Emmanuel (1681–1773), Grand Master of the Order of the Knights of St John of Jerusalem:
consuls at Malta to be named by, **22.** 201n
Dodsworth imprisoned by, **22.** 201n
does not declare war on England for affair of *La Rose*, **21.** 335
Rohan, Prince Camille de, sent by, with galleys, to Leopold II, **22.** 556
Pioche de la Vergne, Marie-Madeleine de (1634–93), m. (1655) François, Comte de la Fayette; novelist:
Du Deffand, Mme, writes letters like those of, **6.** 286
HW's verses mention, **31.** 12
letters of, printed, **6.** 275

letters of, to Mme de Sévigné: Du Deffand, Mme, enjoys, **4.** 139, 144; HW finds, dry, **4.** 141, 144
medallion of, at Livry, **10.** 212
memoirs of, quoted by HW. **19.** 5
Princesse de Clèves, La, by, **4.** 24, 32, 71, **6.** 284, 476, **37.** 203
Sévigné, Mme de, friend of, **19.** 5n
Zaïde and the *Princesse de Clèves* by, wean HW from romances, **37.** 203
Piombanti, Teresa (ca 1711– after 1774), m. (ca 1734) Antonio Cocchi:
pension of, **21.** 194
Piombino, P. of. *See* Boncompagni, Gaetano (1707–77)
Piombino, Ps of. *See* Boncompagni, Maria (1686–1745)
Piombino, gulf of:
Medley orders Hodsol and Proby to cruise in, **19.** 235n
Piombino, straits of:
Charles Emmanuel III's galleys cruise in, **19.** 236n
English ships cruise in, **19.** 235–6
Ferdinand and Maria Carolina detained in, **25.** 581
Mann hopes to capture prizes in, **19.** 236
Neapolitans intercept grain ships in, **22.** 206
Piovene, Conte Agostino:
Tamerlano by: **18.** 280–2, 294; *Giramondo* may surpass, **18.** 294
Piozzi, Gabriel (1739–1809), musician:
favourite pupil of, **12.** 64n
Florence visited by, with wife, **25.** 611n
Italian fiddler, **25.** 633n
Mann cannot invite, with Italian nobility, **25.** 633n
Meget's Inn visited by, at Florence, **25.** 612n
wife of, **11.** 21n, 106n
Piozzi, Mrs Gabriel. *See* Salusbury, Hester Lynch
Pipe; pipes (musical instruments):
at Haymarket entertainment, **39.** 382n
militiaman plays, badly, at Stowe, **10.** 314
people dance to, around maypole, **20.** 47
played at Bedford House, **9.** 369
Pipe; pipes (for tobacco):
country fellows walk down lanes holding, in mouth, **21.** 417
Stanislas I smokes, **20.** 26
Turkish, bought by HW at Mrs Kennon's sale, **37.** 439
Van Tromp's, **35.** 430n
Westmorland, Lady, died smoking, **32.** 200
Pipe; pipes (for water):
in London street, broken to get water for fire-fighting, **35.** 210
Piper; pipers:
Northumberland, Ds of, has, **20.** 341
Piperno ('Privernum'), Italy:
Austrian hussars capture convoy near, **18.** 460
Camilla of, **29.** 89

Pipkin; pipkins:
  HW buys old broken, from Mrs Kennon's sale, **37**. 439
Pipon, Thomas:
  Conway's letter from, from Jersey, **39**. 359n
Pippi, Giulio (ca 1492–1546), called Giulio Romano; painter:
  Clovio, pupil of, **42**. 165n
  Faenza ware said to be designed by, **25**. 591n
  Houghton picture assigned to, **35**. 421n
  Palazzo de Te at Mantua decorated by, **35**. 4n
  Sala di Troia at Mantua painted by, **35**. 5
Pippin; pippins:
  Conway withers and moulds like, **37**. 124
  golden, true breed of, lost, **35**. 191
Pipwell Abbey, Northants
  paving tiles from, **35**. 537
Piquer. *See* Ponz y Piquer
Piquet (game):
  Ayen's witticism based on discards in, **38**. 298
  Chesterfield plays, at Bath, with Moravian baron, **35**. 258
  Farren, Miss, plays, with E. of Derby, **12**. 17–18
  Ferrers plays, with warder, **21**. 397
  Florentine society's chief diversion, **20**. 115
  HW's fondness for, **13**. 154
  Hénault plays, daily, **4**. 444
  Jeffreys and Fawkener play, **9**. 145
  played, **4**. 201, 393, **5**. 140, **6**. 378, **7**. 135, **17**. 61–2
Piquet. *See also* Picquet de la Motte
Piracy:
  instance of, **42**. 102
  more practicable than victory, **25**. 108
  See also Pirate
Piranesi, Giovanni Battista (1720–78), engraver and architect:
  Cumberland, D. of, receives works of, at Rome, **23**. 576
  might do justice to Duncan's Castle in *Macbeth*, **33**. 547
  York, D. of, receives prints by, **22**. 233n
Pirate; pirates:
  Mann calls Algerians, **25**. 270
  —— grants commissions to foreign officers to protect them from being treated as, **25**. 199, 249
  Mediterranean islands inhabited by, **25**. 493
  Pepys's goods stolen by, **11**. 31
  Slavonian soldiers become, after seizing *Great Duchess of Tuscany*, **25**. 479–81
  Turkish, Pope's seamen fear enslavement by, **17**. 15–16
Pirated editions:
  to be forestalled, **4**. 29
Pirgo, Essex:
  Cheke of, **10**. 123n
Pirmasens (Germany):
  Brunswick, D. of, attacked near, **12**. 7n
Pirner, William (living 1824), apothecary:
  Robinson's daughter marries, **28**. 297

Pirner, Mrs William. *See* Robinson, Anne
Piron, Alexis (1689–1773), dramatist; poet:
  Gustave, praised by West, **13**. 175
  verses by, on ship *Voltaire*, **4**. 122
  witticism by, **28**. 326
Pironi. *See* Perroni
Pirski, Mr, of Isleworth:
  SH visited by, **12**. 233
Pisa, Abp of. *See* Franceschi, Angelo (d. 1806); Guidi, Paolo Francesco Salvatico (1694–1778)
Pisa:
  abbey of, suppressed by Leopold without consulting Rome, **23**. 504
  Austrian troops encamped at, **19**. 254
  balls at: **23**. 262, **25**. 581; end at Leopold's retirement, **23**. 171
  baths of: Barrett Lennards do not ask Mann to go to, **20**. 194; Cocchi advises Mann to visit, **19**. 477; Cocchi's book on, *see* Cocchi, Antonio: *Dei bagni di Pisa*; Craon asks Cocchi about, **17**. 342; cutaneous disorders thought to be cured by, **24**. 83; HW hopes that Mann will enjoy his visit to, **20**. 91; Leopold and Maria Louisa to visit, **23**. 108; Mann and Barrett Lennards visit, **20**. 84, 85; Mann prefers, to all places in Tuscany, **20**. 158; Mann to see Pelham and Milbanks at, **20**. 158; Orford, Cts of, may go to, **24**. 83; Pitt, Anne, not benefited by, **23**. 567; Richecourt to visit, **20**. 252; Richecourt visits, **20**. 480; York, D. of, may visit, **22**. 236; Young Pretender to visit, **23**. 226
  Battle of the Bridge at: **24**. 189n, **25**. 582; Leopold may defer, till Ferdinand of Naples's visit, **25**. 569; Leopold often forbids, **25**. 568n; Mann not to attend triennial celebration of, **20**. 473; popular with Pisans, **25**. 569; preferable to Scheldt invasion, **25**. 583; Regency may forbid, **20**. 473; scaffolds for, **24**. 188; too violent to please Leopold, **22**. 515
  Berrys' correspondence with HW from, **11**. 208, 215, 246, 247
  —— to visit, **11**. 165n, **31**. 343
  Bona, St, takes veil at, **13**. 88n
  bridges at, **20**. 473n
  burletta to be held at, **22**. 424
  capitolo of San Stefano order held at: **19**. 238, 245; Ginori presides over, **20**. 473
  Capponi to visit, with troops, **18**. 85
  cavaliere of, sent to Volterra for indiscreet talk about Spaniards, **18**. 46
  certificate of Cts of Orford's death to be procured from, **25**. 114
  Chute might land at Leghorn to make acquaintances at, **20**. 114
  climate and weather of, **23**. 71–2, 80, 94, 149–50
  courier from, tells Mann of Cts of Orford's illness, **25**. 113
  Court's stay at, will be expensive for Mann, **23**. 55, 64, 80

[Pisa, *continued*]

Dante's comment on, applied to France, 12. 122

death of Cts of Orford reported from, 25. 129

Diharce, sea-consul at, 20. 421n

dragoons from, 11. 78n

Empoli on way to, 18. 54

English absurd at, 20. 352

Englishmen at, send home story about Lincoln, 23. 368

Ferdinand of Naples and Maria Carolina welcomed at, 25. 581–2

floods at: averted, 23. 378; feared, 13. 237

Florentine nobility despise, as provincial, 23. 80

foreign ministers (except Spanish) no longer need to attend Court at, 25. 548

galley slaves escape from, 20. 206

Gloucester, D. of, may visit, 23. 336, 342, 347

—— to say at Mann's house at, 23. 347

Gustav III coolly received at, 25. 458

HW advises Berrys to go to, 11. 143

HW doubts safety of, 11 78, 84

HW mentions, 11. 204, 207, 209, 238, 248

HW never saw, 13. 230, 23. 79

illumination at, 17. 66

Joseph II may visit, 25. 350, 352, 367, 457, 468

Karl Wilhelm Ferdinand to visit, 22. 458

learned men at, 11. 177

Leghorn residents flee to, 17. 303

Leghorn visitors at, inconvenience Mann, 19. 487, 20. 85, 91

Leopold has more liberty at, 23. 278

—— loves place but not the inhabitants of, 23. 254

—— may conduct Joseph II to, 25. 367, 468

—— passes winter of 1782–3 at, 25. 421

—— 's statue may be erected in, 23. 95

—— to return from, 25. 393

—— to return to, in Sept. 1783 for 10 months, 25. 421

—— to spend winter of 1783–4 at, but without his or foreign ministers, 25. 425

—— to stay at Leghorn and, till February, 23. 71–2

—— to visit, 22. 453, 23. 336–7, 342, 348

lodgings at, awaited by Mann and Barrett Lennards, 20. 84

London compared to, 11. 218, 250

Mann and Barrett Lennards postpone departure for, 20. 86

Mann benefited by baths of, 19. 486–7, 20. 84, 85

—— 's coolness from D. of Gloucester at, 24. 247, 296–7

—— secures house at, 23. 254

—— sees Battle of the Bridge at, for first time, 11. 499

—— sends furniture to, for D. of Gloucester, 23. 342

—— 's expenses at, will be ruinous, 23. 150, 254, 278, 293

—— 's finances will be ruined by sojourns at, 23. 129, 254, 278, 293

—— 's house at: arrangements at, for D. of Gloucester's occupancy, 23. 394, 397; Beaufort, Ds of, borrows, 23. 372

—— 's occupations at, 20. 91–2

—— 's sojourn at, better than being at a military camp, 23. 88

—— 's visit to, makes him want a villa, 20. 25

—— to avoid visit to, 24. 188

—— to entertain lady from, 18. 353

—— to go to, from Leghorn, 23. 337

—— to prepare to go to, 23. 64

—— to return to Florence to prepare to go to, 23. 337

—— to visit, 19. 477, 22. 511, 23. 149

—— writes from, 23. 153, 159, 171, 184, 260, 273, 277, 347, 351, 355, 356, 369

Maria Louisa does not enjoy, 23. 72, 342

—— to have child at, 25. 425

ministers found removal to, expensive, 25. 548

Modenese princess distributes presents at, 17. 70

noble English couple at, 20. 352

nobles of, to be enrolled in two classes, 20. 192n

O'Kelly commissary at, 17. 67n

Orford, Cts of, defers visit to, 25. 107

—— dies at, 25. 112, 113–14, 195, 29. 106n

palace at, Rosenberg to examine, 23. 253

Pamfili loves lady of, 19. 445

people of, unworthy of Leopold's favour, 23. 95

physicians at; not hopeful about Cts of Orford, 25. 112; supplies drugs for D. of Gloucester, 23. 369

Pitt, Anne, surprises HW by visit to, 24. 194

—— to visit, 23. 557

prices at: higher than at Florence, 23. 278; of apartment, 23. 55

pumps at baths of, 25. 442

report from, that Austrian-Dutch quarrel is not healed, 25. 561

Richecourt patronizes baths of, 19. 487

riot at, 20. 473

Roccettini convent at, suppressed, 23. 504

Russians at, rejoice over peace with Turkey, 24. 84

—— spend lavishly at, 24. 95

St Ranieri celebration at, 18. 455

scaffold at, for Battle of the Bridge, drives Anne Pitt away, 24. 188

shows at, for Tuscan Court, uninteresting, 22. 515

snow in, in late March, 23. 294

Suares, Mme, conducts lady from, 18. 353

surgeon at, 11. 235

Teatro dei Ravvivati at, new, 23. 353

theatre at: impresario of, has burletta performed by bad company, 23. 171; Mann to attend, 23. 72; new, 23. 353

troops may be sent to, **18**. 77

Tuscan Court at, **25**. 436, 548

—— gives weekly ball and supper at, **23**. 171, 191, 262

—— goes to, **22**. 511, **23**. 149, 352, **25**. 334

—— returns to, from Leghorn, **23**. 80

—— to visit, **22**. 417, **23**. 325, **24**. 188

—— university of, *see* Pisa, University of

visitors to: Acciaioli, Mme, **20**. 158; Barbantane and family, **23**. 480; Barrett Lennards, **20**. 91–2; Beaufort, Ds of, **23**. 372, 397; Benedict XIV's niece, **19**. 487; Berrys, **11**. 175, 177, 179, 189, 208, 215, 216, 235, 236, 246, 247, 319; Bouverie, **17**. 67; Chute, **18**. 455; Clephane, **17**. 67; Compton, Lady Elizabeth, **23**. 372, 397; Cork, E. and Cts of, **20**. 451; Corsini, P. and Ps, **22**. 424; Davison, **19**. 407; Dick, Sir John and Lady, **23**. 262, 395; Duclos, **22**. 531; Du Muy, **22**. 153n; Eszterházys, **20**. 351; Fuller, **17**. 67; Gloucester, D. of, **23**. 352–3, 355–6, 356–8, 392–6, 404–7, 502, **24**. 247; Grifoni, Mme, **17**. 33; Gustav III, **25**. 442, 458; Hervey, **22**. 430; Heywood, **23**. 394; Joseph II and Leopold, **23**. 108–9, **24**. 129; Leopold, **22**. 422, 515, **23**. 185, **25**. 383; Liechtenstein, P. of, **22**. 153n, 154; Lyttelton, Sir Richard, **21**. 509n; Mann, **19**. 486–7, 494, 500, **20**. 25, 91, 158, **21**. 499, 503, **22**. 422–3, 427, 514, 515, 531; **23**. 67–8, 71–2, 79–80, 88–92, 94–7, 117–20, 153–5, 260–2, 269–73, 277–9, 347–9, 351–8, 369–72, 392–7, 404–7; Mann, Horace II, **25**. 581; Maria Louisa, **22**. 423; Milbanke, **20**. 158; Mill, **19**. 407; Minifie, **25**. 559; Minto, **15**. 107n; Mozzi, **25**. 421; Orford, Cts of, **24**. 105, **25**. 112, 113; Pelham, **20**. 158; Perelli, **21**. 390; Pitt, Anne, **23**. 564, 567, **24**. 188; (?) Pratt, Caroline, **20**. 91; Rena, Mme, **23**. 119; Richecourt, **20**. 162; Rinuccini, **19**. 245; Smollett, **23**. 189; Somerset, Lady Mary Isabella, **23**. 372, 397; Stampa, **20**. 24; Suares family, **19**. 238; Sudleys, **23**. 203; Trapp, **17**. 67; Vorontsov family, **22**. 202–3, 204–5; Warkworth, Bn, **21**. 512n; Whithed, **18**. 455; York, Cardinal, **22**. 164, 250, (?)256; York, D. of, **22**. 220, 223

Vorontsov family returns to Florence from, **22**. 204

West meets Berrys at, **11**. 319

York, D. of, entertained at park near, **22**. 221

Young Pretender quits, for Siena, **23**. 318

Pisa, University of:

Branchi, professor at, **18**. 177n

Cerati *provveditore generale* of, **21**. 147n

Gualtieri a professor of, **18**. 88

Pasquali a professor at, **18**. 11n

Perelli, Tommaso, professor of astronomy at, **21**. 348n

Rucellai professor of civil law at, **17**. 30n

Sapienza court of, prepared for ball, **25**. 581

Vespa teaches obstetrics at, **22**. 460n

Pisa Forest:

does from, eaten by Leghorn galley-slaves, **20**. 83

Pisan, Christine de (1364–ca 1430), writer, m. (ca 1379) Étienne de Castel:

amour of, with E. of Salisbury, **2**. 195

biographical information about, corrected, **43**. 70, 358

Cité des dames by: HW lends, to Hannah More, **31**. 245; More, Hannah, deserves lodging in, **31**. 244

HW compares Hannah More with, **31**. 244

HW's account of, **31**. 245; *see also Postscript to the Royal and Noble Authors*

HW secures copy of miniature of, **7**. 197, 199, 200, 203–5, 226

Mémoires . . . du sage roi Charles V by: *Collection universelle des mémoires* contains, **31**. 245; HW lends, to Hannah More, **31**. 245

portrait of, from *La Cité des dames*, **2**. 195

Pisani, Luigi (1663–1741), Doge of Venice 1735–41:

burial of, **17**. 75

Montagu, Lady Mary Wortley, promises to reconcile, with George II, **17**. 98

Pisarro. *See* Pizarro

Pisgah:

Dover compared with, **40**. 5

Pishiobury, Herts:

seat of Edward Gardiner and of Sir W. Mildmay, **2**. 227

Pismire; pismires:

China as seen by, **33**. 569–70

Conway should not injure, for HW's visit, **39**. 419

earwigs and mites in comparison with, **33**. 570

Wolverhampton's people as black as, **40**. 42–3

Piso:

Horace's *Ars Poetica* criticizes tragedy by son of, **42**. 51

Pison, Charles, French physician:

rheumatism defined by, **22**. 451n

Pisselieu, Anne de (1508–ca 76), m. (1536) Jean de Brosse, Duc d'Étampes; François I's mistress:

Doumenil has portrait of, **7**. 313

Pistoia (Italy):

Braitwitz to make, his headquarters, **18**. 98

German troops reach Bagni della Porretta near, **18**. 98

Grifoni, Mme, visits, **17**. 100

gun barrels from, **18**. 242, 329

HW has not seen, **13**. 230

iron worker at, leaves for Seravezza, **18**. 242

Leopold and Maria Louisa to meet Ferdinand of Naples and Maria Carolina at, **25**. 294

letters to, from Spanish officers, **17**. 238

new road from Modena to, **25**. 594

nobles of, to be enrolled in two classes, **20**. 192n

O'Kelly governor of, **17**. 67n, **19**. 454n

post-house outside walls of, **22**. 222

[Pistoia (Italy), *continued*]
Te Deum sung at, **21.** 112
Tuscan troops to go to, **18.** 98, 100
visitors to: Modenese princess, **17.** 100; Serristori, **20.** 442; Suares, 'Cecco,' **17.** 103; York, D. of, **22.** 222
York, D. of, and Mann greeted by governor of, but do not enter town, **22.** 222
Pistol; pistols:
Acquaviva's guard armed with, **19.** 113
Adam and Fullarton use the same, for their duels, **25.** 37
Anckarström loads, with crooked nails, **15.** 237
Chudleigh, Mrs, threatened with, by footpads, **24.** 198
Conway busy with, **37.** 336
Damer's suicide with, **24.** 234–5
discharged when being cleaned, **33.** 370
double-barrelled, owned by C. J. Fox, **33.** 267n
duel fought with, **20.** 364, **25.** 37, **38.** 228
extra, carried by Maclaine, **20.** 184
Ferrers carries, to bed, **21** 396
—— pulls, against robber, **22.** 184
firing of, at Hampton Court, **35.** 526
Flobert guards mistress's house with, **21.** 386
Florentine silver coin depicts, **42.** 439
footpads at SH armed with, **33.** 476
Fortescue said to have killed himself with, **22.** 333
Gascoigne discharges, without bullets, at Roman populace, **22.** 287
HW cannot fire, **25.** 570
HW does not shoot, **11.** 25
Hackman shoots Martha Ray with, **33.** 100
horse—, **33.** 445n
Keyt expels family with, before suicide, **30.** 23
Kingston, Ds of, said to terrify husband with, **24.** 198
loaded with crooked nails, **15.** 237, **34.** 175
Maclaine says he fired, accidentally, **40.** 63–4
Montfort uses, for suicide, **35.** 202
Nourse proposes duel with, **17.** 248
pandours carry, **37.** 142
Penn's, goes off accidentally, **20.** 248
Pepi takes, in pockets, **17.** 136
Pitt has, in Gorgon's head, **35.** 262
pocket, of Q. Elizabeth, **35.** 373
servants armed with, against highwayman, **33.** 296
Spanish agent at Florence buys, for Montemar, **17.** 207
suicide with, **23.** 420n
Townshend offers to arm a courtier with, **33.** 83
Walpole, George, wants, **37.** 73
Wilkes and Martin duel with, **38.** 228
with nails, small shot, and round and square balls, **34.** 175n
Wright's confiscated, **17.** 449
Young Pretender always carries, **25.** 101n
See also Gun; Weapon

Pistole; pistoles (coin):
Spanish, captured by English feluccas, **18.** 116
value of, **19.** 372n
Pistro (Italy):
Mann surprised at accounts of, **18.** 381
Pitaval. *See* Gayot de Pitaval
Pitcairn, David (1749–1809), M.D.:
SH visited by, **12.** 248
Pitcairn, Mrs Joseph. *See* Pamela —— (ca 1773–1831)
Pitch:
Southwark magazines of, **25.** 577
Pitcher; pitchers:
German, bought by HW, **39.** 32n
on monument in Trinity Hospital, Greenwich, **16.** 89
Pitfield, Mrs Charles. *See* Ashley, Dorothy
Pitfirrane, Fifeshire:
Halkett of, **14.** 106n
Pithou, François (1543–1621):
Lettres d'un François by, (?) owned by Mme du Deffand, **8.** 35
Pitigliano, gov. of. *See* Borghesi, Domenico Antonio
Pitman, Jeffrey, of Woodbridge, Suffolk:
HW's ancestor, **1.** 374
Pitman, Mary (fl. 1635), m. Edmund (*or* Edward) Burwell:
mother of Sir Jeffrey Burwell, **1.** 374
Pitman family:
arms of, **1.** 374
Pitonessa:
imprisoned, together with her confessor, for publishing their dreams, **24.** 30
Pitreavie, Fifeshire:
Wardlaw of, **14.** 106n
Pitroddie, Perthshire:
Lindsay of, **15.** 80n
Pitrot, Antonio *or* Giovanni, dancer:
(?) smiles on himself, **35.** 468–9
Pits *or* Pitseus, Rev. John (1560–1616), historian:
Relationum historicarum de rebus Anglicis by: Humphrey said by, to be author, **16.** 15; Rowley not mentioned by, **2.** 105, 106; Starkey described by, **1.** 250–1
'Pitsburg.' *See under* Pitt, Anne: house of, at Knightsbridge
Pitsligo, Lord. *See* Forbes, Alexander
Pitt, Lady. *See* Howe, Hon. Mary
Pitt, Miss:
note to, **11.** 110n
Pitt, Mrs (fl. 1774) of Maddox St:
gives letter of Nell Gwyn's to Apthorpe, **1.** 348–9
Pitt, Amelia, m. (1761) Dr William Spry:
brother gives portion to, **21.** 365
Pitt, Anne (1712–81), HW's correspondent:
Abano baths to be visited by, **24.** 9, 22, 105, 108, 220
Abano visited by, **24.** 220, 233
Abano waters benefit, **24.** 22, 233

a great politician, **33**. 10

appearance of, unherculean, **31**. 67

artistic talents of, **23**. 457

Augusta, Ps of Wales's keeper of Privy Purse, **23**. 451n, 558n, **31**. 1

ball given by, **24**. 16, **31**. 33, **32**. 48n, **38**. 335, 475–6

ball planned by, for Lord Villiers, **32**. 48

Bolingbroke, Cts of, returns with, to England, **30**. 51

Berkeley Sq. address of, **31**. 98

brother mourned by, on her return to England, **24**. 415

brother's fluctuating health explained by, **39**. 95

brother's talents and ambition shared by, **24**. 379

Bute gets pension for, when Chatham refuses, **31**. 40n

Bute, Cts of, corresponds with, **31**. 41, 187

—— thanks HW through, for Erskine's appointment, **31**. 40–1

Bute's calamity will distress, **24**. 378

Caraman entertained by, **38**. 527

Cardigan, Cts of, informs, of HW's inquiries, **31**. 4

—— may not have visit from, **31**. 2

cats hated by, **31**. 54

Chelsea Old Church to be visited by, **31**. 139

Chesterfield's conversation with, **10**. 219

——'s witticism to, on Pitt's intention to speak in a horizontal posture, **23**. 177

—— to be invited by, to SH, **31**. 111

Coke, Lady Mary, corresponds with, **31**. 139

—— thinks, dislikes her, **31**. 139

corbeilles to be introduced by, at Knightsbridge, **31**. 54–5

Craon, Princesse de, resembles, **24**. 6

Cumberland, Ds of, may be subject of liberties taken by, **23**. 558n

curiosities eagerly pursued by, in Rome, **24**. 105

death of Ds of Montagu afflicts, **24**. 105

dies in madhouse, **25**. 127

dismissal of, as Ps of Wales's keeper of Privy Purse, **23**. 558

Du Deffand, Mme, gives opinion of, **5**. 309, 406

——'s social relations with, **5**. 295, 309, 311, 317, 318

early fame of, as wit, **30**. 51

England expects, daily, **24**. 401

—— reached by, **24**. 411

English people would be found by, to be as mad as herself, **24**. 349

finances of: pension increased, **31**. 3n; pension obtained, **31**. 40n; third pension for, **38**. 468, 475

Florence left by: **24**. 9; for Bologna, **24**. 381

—— visited by, **33**. 10

France visited by, **31**. 3–4

French female servant nursed by, at Rome, **24**. 344, 353

French horns brought by, to SH. **35**. 225

French hospitality to, will be returned by HW, **31**. 3

French sojourn of, adds to her *ton*, **24**. 6

Geneva visited by, **24**. 118, 131

HW asks about, **24**. 227

HW attends 'fairy entertainment' of, **24**. 8

HW calls house of, 'Pittsburgh' and 'Temple of Vesta,' **24**. 15, **31**. 55–6

HW compares: with doctor in *Don Quixote*, **31**. 67; with fairy, **31**. 33

HW congratulates, **31**. 1

HW consulted by, on plan for room, **31**. 87–8, 90

HW, Ds of Bedford, and Mme de Guerchy attend ball of, **38**. 335

HW entertains, at SH, **10**. 127, **35**. 225, **39**. 104

HW esteemed by, **23**. 567

HW expects, to become reigning fashion, **30**. 51

HW glad that Mann's verdigris was mentioned by, **24**. 15

HW informed by, of Kensington Palace change, **38**. 457

HW invited by, to ball, **32**. 48, 52

HW invites: to Arlington St, **31**. 140; to SH, **31**. 41

HW mentions, **5**. 439

HW not sorry that Mann has been forsaken by, **24**. 17

HW often mentioned by, **23**. 456

HW receives invitation from, **31**. 404

HW recommended by, to Comtesse de Rochefort, **31**. 53–4

HW recommends, to Mann, **23**. 557–8

HW's compliments to be conveyed to, by Mann, **24**. 233

HW's correspondence with: **7**. 376–80, **31**. 1–5, 31–3, 40–2, 53–8, 66–9, 87–90, 98–101, 103, 106–8, 110–12, 139–40, 404; MSS of, **36**. 310

HW sends message to Chesterfield through, **10**. 219

HW sends plan to, **7**. 380

(?) HW's ill health alarms, **4**. 160

HW's witticism about brother's resemblance to, **38**. 527

HW tells Mann to beware of, **24**. 3

HW thanked by, for Mann's civilities to her, **24**. 3

HW told by: about nephew, **40**. 271; of Chesterfield's remark, **10**. 219

haymaking given by, **38**. 400, 401

health of: **5**. 314, 318; Abano waters benefit, **24**. 233; better, **24**. 374; gout suspected, **31**. 89; HW concerned for, **31**. 4; insanity, **23**. 558n, **24**. 421, **31**. 189; Pisa baths might benefit, **24**. 188; relapse in, makes her return to Abano despite hot weather, **24**. 22;

[Pitt, Anne, *continued*]

weak and emaciated, **24.** 9; weak nerves, **24.** 6

Holdernesse, Cts of, has social relations with, **31.** 139

Holland, Bns, reported by, to be wounded by sons' ingratitude, **24.** 30

house of: at Knightsbridge, design for ceiling in, **31.** 99, 106, 110; design for room in, **31.** 87–8, 90; French inquire about, **31.** 55; HW calls, 'Pitsburg,' **24.** 15, **31.** 55, 56; HW consulted about bow window for, **31.** 35; HW jokes about, **31.** 55; trees at, **31.** 55, 68

Italy may be winter home of, for fear of English journey, **24.** 381

Kingston, Ds of, believed by, to enjoy her trial, **24.** 199

—— blamed by, for mentioning Ps of Wales, **24.** 203

—— does not see, but exchanges messages with her, **24.** 7

Knightsbridge address of, **24.** 15, **31.** 139

Lorraine visited by, **24.** 131, 188

(?) Lyttelton's 'Delia,' **21.** 531n

Mann charmed with, **24.** 6

—— exchanges affectionate letters with, **24.** 233

—— exchanges kind messages with, **24.** 188

—— may tell, about her brother's alliance with Temple, **24.** 14

—— receives notes from, **24.** 6

——'s correspondence with, **23.** 564, **24.** 6, 22, 131, 233, 405

—— sends newspapers to, **24.** 233

——'s house occupied by, **23.** 567

——'s regard for, **23.** 567

—— to ask, if Mme Grifoni is still beautiful, **24.** 17

—— told by, of C. J. Fox's ingratitude to mother, **24.** 22

—— to tell: about neighbour's elopement, **24.** 15; that English ladies weep no more, **24.** 112

Maria Louisa tells news to, **33.** 10–11

—— tells, of her father's remarks on Spanish policy, **24.** 375

milk and chocolate taken by, for breakfast, **23.** 567

Mirepoix, Mme de, gives opinion of, **5.** 292

—— may recover E. W. Montagu's note through, **5.** 434

Nancy to be visited by, **24.** 131

Naples to be visited by, **24.** 344

neighbours of, at Knightsbridge, **24.** 15

nephew gives sad account of, **24.** 431, 462

Nevers visited by, **31.** 4n

Nivernais sends compliments to, **41.** 19

nose of, large, **32.** 48

once sprightly, **24.** 462

Padua visited by, **24.** 22

Paris should be visited by, **31.** 90

—— visited by, **5.** 292

Pelham, Frances, describes HW's accident to, **35.** 276

—— entertains, at Esher, **10.** 72–3

perches contrived by, for guests at overcrowded party, **24.** 8

Pisa visited by, **23.** 557, 564, 567, **24.** 188, 194

Pitt, Hon. William, shocks, by illness and travel plans, **31.** 189n

Pius VI might make, 'Ps Fossani,' **24.** 360

Provence visited by, **24.** 194

Rochefort, Mme de, a friend of, **31.** 54–5, 111, **32.** 23, **40.** 387

—— consulted by HW about room for, **7.** 287

—— neglected by, **41.** 22

Rome visited by, **24.** 105, 344, 357–8, 374, **31.** 187

(?) St-Priest, Vicomtesse de, inquires for, **31.** 58

(?) Selwyn, Charles, corresponds with, **31.** 31–2

—— recommended by, to HW, **31.** 31–2

Spa to be visited by, **20.** 116n

SH visited by, **31.** 139

Surgères, Marquise de, acquainted with, **31.** 88

Tessés recommended by, to Mann, **24.** 253

troop movements detain, at Trent, **24.** 389

unlimited power of, to invite to SH, **31.** 111

Vauxhall visited by, **10.** 127

wild, and may be confined, **24.** 421

witticisms by: about Bp Hervey's title, **24.** 430–1, 462; about Catherine II's coup d'état, **10.** 39; about Ds of Kingston, **24.** 6

Pitt, Hon. Anne (1772–1864), m. (1792) William Wyndham Grenville, cr. (1790) Bn Grenville:

father to take, to Italy, **24.** 411

mother of, should be well-informed, **39.** 506

Pitt, Christian (d. 1761), m. (1760) Thomas Saunders:

brother gives portion to, **21.** 365

death of, **22.** 2

Pitt, Christopher (1699–1748), poet:

Spence's letter to, **2.** 214

Pitt, Elizabeth 'Villiers' (1712–70), m. (1761) John Hanham (*or* Hannam):

Augusta, Ps of Wales, has, as maid of honour, **20.** 507n

brother attacked by, **20.** 507n

brother's affair with, **20.** 411

brother's kindness to, ill-requited, **21.** 46

calls herself by her middle name, **20.** *406*

conversion of, to Roman Catholicism, **20.** 416, 507n

Cork, Cts of, to shun, despite former intimacy, **20.** 452

England revisited by, **21.** 46

Florence visited by, **20.** 406, 410–11, 416

Germany to be the wedding-place and Holland the winter residence of, **20.** 499

HW considers, a dangerous 'inmate,' **20.** 507

HW warns Mann against, **20.** 410–11

Mann has no connection with, **20**. 452
—— has bad accounts of, **20**. 416
marriage of, **20**. 507n
Popish chapel the resort of, **21**. 46
Preston accompanies, perhaps to marry her,
   20. 499
Prujean writes letter to, **20**. 499
Prujean, Mrs, quarrels with, about religion,
   20. 499
pseudonym of, **20**. 507n
returns from Italy, **20**. 507n
Talbot's mistress, **20**. 507n
Test given brother's letters by, to prove that
   he cheated her, **21**. 46
Warren a friend of, **20**. 499
writings of, **20**. 507n
Pitt, Lady Frances. *See* Ridgeway, Lady Frances
Pitt, George (1721–1803), cr. (1776) Bn Rivers;
   M.P.:
appointment of, as minister to Savoy, **9**. 406
'attitudes' of, **32**. 13
Bristol to be visited by, with Stuart Macken-
   zie, **30**. 59
brutal and half-mad, **23**. 451
Charlotte, Q., might appoint, grand harper,
   38. 101
Chatham's distant relative, **22**. 572n
Churchill entertained by, at ball, **20**. 367
Coventrys entertained by, at ball, **20**. 367
daughter of, **11**. 268n, **25**. 538n, **26**. 48
English at Turin recommended by, to Mann,
   22. 41n
Fermor, Lady Charlotte, loved by, **17**. 468
—— renounced by, **18**. 103
George III appoints, to Bedchamber, **21**. 460
Graftons' house at Turin to be taken by, **22**. 2
(?) 'grave, rich, and shallow,' **13**. 233
Greville, Fulke, made secretary of legation at
   Turin by, **21**. 124n
HW entertained by, at Ball, **20**. 367
HW sends compliments to, **30**. 7
Halifax's orders to, about D. of York, **22**.
   173n
handsome, **17**. 468n
Holdernesse entertained by, at ball, **20**. 367
Holdsworth tutor to, **19**. 139n
Italy to be visited by, **20**. 58
Jermyn St residence of, **20**. 367n
Lincoln to entertain, **17**. 468
Mann may remember, **21**. 460
—— remembers, **20**. 58
minister to Turin, **22**. 2n
Montagu, Lady Mary Wortley, admires, in
   Italy, **17**. 468n
(?) —— and Bns Walpole compete for favour
   of, **13**. 233–4
—— knows, **20**. 58
receipts by, for buttered muffins, as 'Corydon,'
   39. 241
Rome visited by, **30**. 7
St James's Palace guard fires on, after assault,
   30. 330n

Spanish post may be offered to, **22**. 500
Stratfieldsaye residence of, **17**. 468
Sudeley Castle owned by, **42**. 113
Tory, **21**. 460
Townshend, Vcts, ogles, **17**. 468n
Turin post to go to, **21**. 548, **22**. 2n
uncle of, **19**. 458
wife ill-treated by, **23**. 451
wife loves, **20**. 58
wife of, **9**. 81n, **11**. 96n, **30**. 328n
York, D. of, embarrasses, at Turin by incog-
   nito, **22**. 230n
Pitt, George (1751–1828), 2d Bn Rivers, 1803:
mother cannot communicate with, **23**. 451
mother's letter to, about atrocity at Lyon, **34**.
   121
Pitt, Mrs George. *See* Atkins, Penelope
Pitt, George Morton (d. 1756), gov. of Fort St
   George (Madras); M.P.:
biographical information about, corrected,
   43. 122
HW sceptical about death of, **9**. 263, 264
Twickenham resident, **42**. 483
woman at house of, detects burglar, **9**. 132–3
Pitt, Mrs George Morton. *See* Bugden, Sophia
Pitt, Harriet (1745–63), m. (1762) Brownlow
   Bertie, 5th D. of Ancaster:
biographical information about, corrected, **43**.
   121–2
Buckinghamshire, E. of, rejected by, **38**. 57
Halifax might take, **38**. 58
marriage of, expected, **9**. 263
Malmesbury mentions, **10**. 70n
Pitt, Lady Harriot (1758–86), m. (1785) Hon.
   Edward James Eliot:
death of, **33**. 527
(?) Grenville family resembled by, **39**. 76
mother puts, under uncles' protection, **23**. 74
Pitt, Lady Hester (1720–1803). *See* Grenville,
   Lady Hester
Pitt, Lady Hester (1755–80), m. (1774) Charles
   Stanhope, styled Vct Mahon, later 3d E. Stan-
   hope:
(?) Grenville family resembled by, **39**. 76
husband of, **28**. 207n
marriage of, **24**. 67
mother puts, under uncles' protection, **23**. 74
Pitt, James ('Francis Osborne') (ca 1680–1763),
   journalist:
called 'old woman,' **17**. 346n
Gazetteer and, **14**. 28
hack writer, **10**. 207n
Pitt, Hon. James Charles (1761–1800):
father attended by, **24**. 371
(?) Grenville family resembled by, **39**. 76
mother puts, under uncles' protection, **23**. 74
Pitt, John:
Hagley temple designed by, **35**. 148n
Pitt, John (ca 1706–87), M.P., of Encombe,
   Dorset:
Admiralty post temporarily given to, **21**. 25–6

[Pitt, John (ca 1706–87), *continued*]
biographical information about, corrected, 43.
119, 255
Commissioner of Trade, 18. 551, 19. 458n
dismissed from Board of Trade, 9. 181, 20. 517
Drax contests Wareham election with, 19.
458–9
election of, 19. 459n
George II coldly receives, as Admiralty lord,
37. 481
HW sarcastically calls, 'Whig,' 9. 329
Jacobite, 19. 458
to be paymaster of Marines, 21. 56
wife of, 11. 241n
Pitt, John (1756–1835), 2d E. of Chatham, 1778:
Admiralty headed by, 39. 462n
Admiralty post to go to, 34. 9n
father attended by, 24. 371
godfather to Chatham Horace Churchill, 11.
264
(?) Grenville family resembled by, 39. 76
K.G., 11. 161, 163
Mann hears, is to be envoy to Berlin, 25. 314
mother puts, under uncles' protection, 23. 74
pension reversion to, 21. 541n, 24. 389
Seymour-Conway, Hon. Hugh, kindly treated
by, 11. 262
Pitt, Mrs John. *See* Morgan, Marcia
Pitt, Louisa (ca 1756–91), m. (1773) Peter
Beckford:
HW not acquainted with, 11. 268
mother cannot communicate with, 23. 451
Pitt, Marcia (1759–1808), m. (1790) George
James Cholmondeley, HW's grand-nephew:
Cholmondeley, Lord, displeases, by his mar-
riage, 11. 241
HW visited by, 11. 317
marriage settlements of, 11. *83*
stillborn child of, 11. 256, 275
Pitt, Marcia Lucy (1756–1822), m. James Lane
Fox:
mother cannot communicate with, 23. 451
Pitt, Hon. Penelope (1749–1827), m. 1 (1766)
Edward Ligonier, 2d Vct Ligonier; m. 2
(1784) Capt. Smith:
adulteries of, 5. 77, 30. 255–6
Alfieri gives up, after her affair with tugboat
captain, 30. 256
——'s affair with, 5. 77n, 23. 451n, 25. 538n,
26. 48, 35. 453
Cumberland, D. of, entertains, at Calais ball,
23. 351n
death date of, 43. 284
HW calls: 'fiancée du Roi de Garbe,' 30. 255;
'Mme Messaline,' 5. 77
HW wishes, would replace Comtesse du Barry,
30. 256
Harding's affair with, 30. 256, 35. 453
husband divorces, 5. 77n, 23. 451n, 25. 538n,
26. 48
Pitt, Thomas (1653–1726), gov. of Madras:
diamond of, 9. 2, 12. 4, 86, 191, 29. 4, 31.
158–9, 43. 110

Pitt, Thomas (ca 1705–61), M.P.:
birth date of, corrected, 43. 243
Cornish boroughs managed by, 17. 346n
death of: probably mentioned in letters forwarded by Mann, 21. 524; soon after second
marriage, 21. 517
jointure given by, to second wife, 21. 517
Lyttelton steals Okehampton borough from,
20. 39
Opposition assembly addressed by, at St
Alban's Tavern, 20. 50
sister's affair with, 20. 411
son cuts off entail to pay debts of, 21. 365
son of, 21. 364n
Waldegrave replaces, as Warden of the Stan-
naries, 20. 246–7
Pitt, Thomas (1737–93), cr. (1784) Bn Camelford; M.P.:
Bedfordshire visited by, 10. 57
Carlisle, Bp of, visits, 10. 57
Chatham's return to ministry said to be arranged by, 24. 366n
Dagge praises, 21. 365
death of, expected, 10. 57
Ditton Park visited by, 10. 100
draws Gothic ornaments for HW's cabinet and
gallery ornaments 22. 25
Du Deffand, Mme, to meet, 5. 130
entail cut off by, to pay father's debts and
sisters' portions, 21. 365
father of, dies, 21. 517
foreign tours of, show him England's waning
prestige, 25. 35
fraudulent vote of, 14. 133n
French passport for, 21. 524
French passport not received by, 21. 543, 545,
550
Granada and Italy to be visited by, with
Strathmore, 21. 364
Grenville's alleged statement at house of, 40.
328–42
——'s correspondence with, 40. 328–9
Greville, Mrs, praises, 5. 130
HW and, should bring Gothic trowels to
episcopal palaces, 40. 288
HW consults, about architectural books for
planning Conway's greenhouse, 38. 198
HW delivers Mann's letter to, 22. 2
HW discusses attribution of French pamph-
let to, 11. 53
HW exchanges calls with, 21. 558
HW gives letter of introduction for, to Mann,
21. 365
HW has not seen, 40. 271, 287
HW needs, for SH designs, 40. 273
HW praises, 10. 101
HW's and Grenville's correspondence with,
about Grenville's alleged remark on Con-
way at meeting, 38. 395–6
HW's apartment in Mann's house may be
occupied by, 21. 543, 545
HW's conference with, about Conway, 38.
253

HW's correspondence with, **40.** 328–42
HW sends messages to, **21.** 505
HW's 'present architect,' **38.** 198
HW's relations with, cool since George Grenville's era, **24.** 411
HW's reply to Elliot criticized by, **10.** 94
HW undeceived by feigned mourning of, for deceased uncle, **24.** 415
Harcourt's tomb should be designed by, **35.** 487
health of: crippled knees, **24.** 411, **43.** 286; fever, **10.** 57
hears of son's safety, **11.** 92
Hobart, Mrs, entertains, at play at Ham Common, **33.** 370
house of, called Palazzo Pitti, **22.** 33
house taken by, at Twickenham, **22.** 18, 25
Italy to be visited by, with family, **24.** 411
itinerary of, from Rome, **21.** 543, 545
Kinnoull accompanied by, to Lisbon, **21.** 364
letters from, enclosed by Mann, **21.** 543
Lyttelton, Charles, to be visited by, **40.** 271
—— visits, **10.** 57
(?) Lyttelton (Thomas)'s ill temper not to be mentioned to, **22.** 251
Mann forwards letters probably about death of father of, **21.** 524
—— greets, on arrival in Florence from Leghorn, **21.** 500
—— (?) hears sad account from, of aunt, **24.** 431, 462
—— impatient for arrival of, **21.** 380
—— may arrange for return of, to England, **21.** 524
—— sends remembrances to, **22.** 46, 49
—— sends word to, that Strathmore returns to England, **22.** 22–3
—— takes, to Uffizi, **21.** 500
—— to take, to burletta, **21.** 501
—— visited by, **21.** 550
Mann, Horace II, quotes letter of, about salary, **25.** 672–3
marriage of, approaching, **32.** 52
Montagu praises, **10.** 100
Naples to be visited by, **21.** 545
—— visited by, **24.** 486
Parliamentary address moved by, **38.** 489
Parliamentary motion by, for amendment to Address, **25.** 368n
Parliamentary speech of, denounces North for England's declining prestige, **25.** 35
Piozzi, Mrs, comments on, **10.** 101n
Pitt, William II, and Gower in memorandum by, **25.** 378n
probably on way back from Rome, **21.** 543
(?) Richardson sends compliments to, **40.** 234
San Casciano baths visited by, with Sir Richard Lyttelton, **21.** 524
sets out for Germany, **21.** 550
Strathmore awaits, **21.** 524
—— calls on, at Twickenham, **22.** 152
—— friend of, **21.** 543
——'s conduct will surprise, **22.** 45

—— separates from, in Spain, **21.** 501
SH Gallery arranged by, **10.** 94
Sunning Hill visited by, to drink waters for health, **22.** 73
swears by uncle's ghost, despite previous dislike, **24.** 412
Twickenham resident, **42.** 480
Venice to be visited by, to attend Ascension celebrations, **21.** 500
—— visited by, **21.** 512
villa of, **11.** 332n
wife sends courier to, **24.** 486
Windsor boarded by, for Portugal, **21.** 364n
Pitt, Thomas (1775–1804), 2d Bn Camelford, 1793:
father to take, to Italy, **24.** 411
saved in shipwreck, **11.** 92
Pitt, Mrs Thomas. *See* Murray, Maria; Wilkinson, Anne (1738–1803)
Pitt, William (1708–78), cr. (1766) E. of Chatham; M.P.; prime minister:
absent from Parliament, **42.** 497
abuse answered by, with victories, **39.** 327
achievements of, in opposition, surpass his former efforts, **20.** 516
Addington attends, **22.** 505
—— forbids, to transact any business, **22.** 505
administration declined by, **22.** 541, **30.** 180, 188
administration might be assumed by, to oust Bute, **22.** 102n
administration of: cannot endure at same time with two others, **21.** 455; may be dissolved, **9.** 203–4; to be short-lived without Newcastle or Henry Fox, **9.** 202; to produce few changes, **10.** 223
administration of, with Grafton: **3.** 254–5; Cavendishes oppose, **30.** 238–9; formation of, accompanied by confusion and absurdity, **30.** 228; formation of, surrounded by rumours and guesses, **30.** 221–2; George III's and Bute's friends support, **30.** 243; HW violent in support of, **30.** 288; HW will dislike if Richmond not a part of, **30.** 234; strength of, **30.** 234
administration of, with Newcastle: alterations in, **30.** 162; cannot endure with two others at same time, **21.** 465; Pitt disclaims responsibility for Halifax's exclusion from, **30.** 135; Townshend, G., disapproves of, **30.** 135
administration to be accepted by, **32.** 10
Admiralty and Navy Bill opposed by, **20.** 38
Admiralty board selected by, **21.** 104
Admiralty demanded by, for Temple, **21.** 12n
Africa's conqueror, **21.** 541
Allen the friend of, **9.** 394n
alone politically, **23.** 264
Alt congratulated by, on Russian defeat, **21.** 316
Amelia, Ps, questions HW about oratorical ability of, **10.** 50
amendment proposed by, to Address, **23.** 167

[Pitt, William (1708–78), *continued*]

amendments on Wilkes's warrant not opposed by, **38**. 325

American Congress praised by, **39**. 228

American independence opposed by, **24**. 350n, **28**. 379

American offer to George III may be transmitted by, **6**. 139

American pacification bill of, debated, **32**. 232, 234–5

American sovereignty upheld in Parliament by followers of, **24**. 371

Americans the chief supporters of, **22**. 396

America said by, to be conquered in Germany, **22**. 1n, **23**. 551, **24**. 187, **31**. 67n

Anson quarrels with, **9**. 236

—— referred to as, 'great and respectable name,' **38**. 545

Anstruther inquiry urged by, **20**. 230n

anti-Hanoverian 'trumpet' scoured by, **35**. 89

appears in House of Lords, **24**. 13

appointment not given to, **18**. 551

appointments by, opposed by D. of Newcastle, **22**. 442

ariette should be sung by, in Parliament, **38**. 11

army appropriation bill to be supported by, **19**. 4

army post jokingly suggested for, **9**. 209

army to be forced to submission by, by breaking officers of court martial, **21**. 165n

assertion by, that English troops would never be sent to Germany, **23**. 258

at end of his reckoning, **23**. 270

attorney-general to be a follower of, **21**. 110

Baltic squadron might be sent by, to reinstate Peter III, **10**. 39

Barnard compared with, **22**. 84

Barré apologizes for attack upon, **35**. 32

—— a substitute for, **38**. 508

—— should write an oration, and Wilkes a satire on, **38**. 255

Bath, E. of, makes witticism on exclusion of, from ministry with Fox remaining, **35**. 199

——'s letter to Newcastle and, **9**. 270n

Bath, Exeter, London, Worcester, and Yarmouth give freedom of city to, **21**. 87

Bath to be visited by, **31**. 125, **35**. 263, **41**. 35

—— visited by, **10**. 229, **21**. 540, **22**. 413n, 425, 449, 461, 462, 472, 479, 483, 488, 492, 567, **30**. 236, 240, **31**. 130, **35**. 120, 199, 319, **41**. 41

Bath, common council of, presents gold box to, **41**. 77n

Beckford confers with, **22**. 160

—— desired by, to lay reorganization plan for East India Co. before House of Commons, **22**. 493

—— friend of, **22**. 39n, **24**. 132

—— made lord mayor by, **38**. 183

—— quarrels with, **9**. 325

——'s, Granby's, and Grenville's deaths deprive, of support, **23**. 246

Beckford transacts business of, in Parliament, **22**. 506–7

becomes lord privy seal and E. of Chatham, **22**. 442

Bedchamber post to Frederick, P. of Wales, resigned by, in friendship to Lyttelton, **19**. 27

Bedford, Ds of, should be conciliated by, **41**. 71

——strong for, **30**. 236

Bedford, D. of, close to, at Bath, **41**. 41

—— may make overtures to, **38**. 434

—— may succeed, as secretary of state, **9**. 341

—— no longer wants return of, **22**. 167

—— notifies, of Lyttelton's overture, **35**. 195

——'s adherents opposed by, **22**. 308

——'s Bath negotiation with, **30**. 236

——'s connection with, wished by Bedford's family, **41**. 72

——'s demands on: few but considerable, **30**. 236; rejected by him, **22**. 472

——'s faction bargains with, **10**. 236

——'s Irish post instigated by Henry Fox to spite, **21**. 31

——'s overture refused by, **7**. 279

—— speaks like, **20**. 310

——'s union with, likely if places can be found, **30**. 236

—— to punish, **20**. 38

Bedfords forsaken by, **20**. 138

Belle-Île expedition proposed by, **21**. 438n

belligerency makes, 'errant knight,' **37**. 419

Bentley's *Patriotism* satirizes, **10**. 128n, **14**. 134n

—— uses, as character in *Philodamus*, **9**. 414

bequests to, **30**. 104, 217

big words used by, **23**. 163

Blackfriars Bridge has inscription in honour of, **21**. 449

blazing meteor, successful in war but not in peace, **25**. 275

Bolingbroke's *Letters* formerly read by, **20**. 59

—— wanes in esteem of, **20**. 59

Botta sends Pucci's credentials to, **21**. 179n

—— to write to, **21**. 180

Bourbon family compact said to be procured by, in copy, for £4,000, **21**. 539n

Breda delegates chosen by, **21**. 355n

Brest and Rochefort suggested by, as points for attacks, **21**. 213n

Bristol, E. of, declines lord chamberlain's post from regard for, **32**. 8n

—— friend of, **23**. 65

—— ordered by, to leave Madrid, **38**. 128

—— recalled by, from Spain, **38**. 120

——'s recall wished by, **21**. 536–7

brother of, **21**. 517n

Brunswick, Ps of, visit of, connected with, **32**. 16–17

Buckingham House visited by, in chair, **22**. 159

budget opened by, in private, **22**. 439

burial of: 2. 80, 82, 84; Barré's motion about, 33. 20n; poorly attended by Parliament members despite their affected concern, 24. 393

Bussy complains to, of English haughtiness, 38. 112

bust of, at Stowe, 10. 155n, 35. 75, 41. 6n

Bute could have been deposed earlier by, 22. 129

—— does not relinquish keys to, 22. 130

—— may be approached closer by, 22. 490

—— may dispute leadership with, in state department, 9. 340

—— may negotiate with, through Shelburne, 38. 334

——, Newcastle, and Parliamentary oppression of America all attacked by, 22. 395–6

Bute not trusted by, 10. 222

—— said to be treating with, 38. 405, 533

——'s alliance may cause unpopularity of, 22. 433

——'s alliance with: 22. 473; suggested, 22. 78n

——'s chief rival at George II's death, 23. 152

—— sends for, 22. 159–60

——'s friendship with, would please George III but alienate the people, 22. 440

—— should enlist under, 38. 553

——'s interview with, after Egremont's death, 22. 159n, 160n

——'s junction with, rejected, 22. 93n

——'s negotiations with, worry Bedford faction, 38. 405

——'s relations with, 10. 45

——'s 'treaty' with, 33. 64

—— suggests, to George III to head ministry, 22. 431n

—— to be ousted by, 7. 273

—— treats with, 38. 355

Cabinet Council at odds with, 38. 131n, 140

Camden at Bath may confer with, 39. 95

—— joins, in attacking George III's Parliamentary address, 41. 183n

—— reportedly sent for by, 30. 227

——, Shelburne, and Temple do not desert, 39. 246

Camden's peerage a compliment to, 30. 194n

Canada and Cabinet Council to be conquered by, 21. 290

Canada's conqueror, 21. 541

Canadian government or chancellorship of Duchy said to be offered to, 21. 540n

Canning, Elizabeth, may have met, at Englefield Wash, 38. 131

cannon and colours lost at St-Cast should be retrieved by, 37. 570–1

cannon sent by, against St-Malo but not against Rochefort, 21. 213

career of, ended, 24. 376

caricature of, in 'The Turnstile,' 21. 93

(?) Caroline, Q., connected with, 17. 146

Carteret abused by, in Parliament, 18. 383

Carteret (Granville) unimpressed by diction and views of, 30. 229

Cavendish thinks style of, too high, 22. 444n

Cavendishes think Rockingham and Lord John Cavendish equal to, 39. 101

characteristics of, 37. 416

Charles III, Louis XV, and Great Mogul threatened by, 22. 276

Charles III might be pressed by, to have a pro-British ministry, 22. 441n

——'s declaration against, 21. 559

Chesterfield discusses, 6. 38

——'s witticism on intention of, to speak in a horizontal posture, 23. 177

children of: fathered by House of Commons, 28. 394, 29. 248; resemble Grenvilles, 39. 76

Choiseul does not forgive, 39. 236

—— probably dreads, 23. 134

——'s peace negotiations with, 21. 515n, 526n

Churchill could now attack, 22. 304

—— longed to satirize, 22. 261

Cicero and Demosthenes surpassed by, 35. 260, 262

clamour to be stopped by, 37. 479

Clarke, Col., describes Rochefort fortifications to, 7. 357

Clement XIII fears, 30. 216

Clerk's rejection by, brings rift with Bute, 37. 574n

Clive called 'heaven-born' by, 23. 381n, 387

—— called 'heaven-born hero' by, 22. 176, 243

—— presents, with Shah Goest, 21. 378n

——'s father makes offer to, 21. 404

coach-horses advertised by, for sale, 38. 135–6

Cockpit meeting attended by, 37. 413

coinage of a word attributed to, 11. 348

Coke, Lady Mary, compared with, 37. 572

—— early admirer of, 31. 21

—— might inspire orations of, 31. 22

Cole indifferent about, 9. 86

complains of Shelburne's removal, 23. 61–2

concessions might be obtained by, from Pelham, 20. 223

content to manage war under D. of Newcastle, 21. 448

Continental entanglements disliked by, 19. 168

Conway and Mordaunt braved by, 9. 217n

Conway calls on, seeking army command, 37. 582n

(?) —— coldly treated by, 37. 556

—— displeases, over East India Co. affair, 22. 509

—— must despise mustard-bowl of, 39. 239

—— on bad terms with, 3. 200n

—— praised by, 38. 434

—— rejected by, for army command, 37. 567

——'s friends take liberties with, 41. 82

—— should be advised by, to abandon Lord John Cavendish's faction, 41. 66

—— should not feel obligated to, for army command, 37. 579–83

[Pitt, William (1708–78), *continued*]
—— should thank, for not letting him serve, **37**. 544
——'s speech may bring, to town from Hayes, **38**. 500–1
——'s speech praised by, **26**. 15
——'s unsealed letter may be taken to, **37**. 568–9
——'s victories useless when not ascribed to, **38**. 141
—— urged by, to stay in office, **22**. 472
(?) —— visited by, at Park Place, **37**. 380
—— will be vindicated by rashness of, **37**. 581
Copley's painting of death of, **29**. 185, **34**. 210
Cornbury joined by, in opposing George II's use of Hessian troops, **19**. 188
Cotes abuses, for refusing Gower, **30**. 230
Court often attended by, after resignation, **38**. 134
Court supports, **22**. 497
Court would not get much quarter from, **22**. 102
crutch of, will not solve American crisis, **39**. 227–8
crutch used by, **32**. 18
Cumberland, D. of, confers with, **22**. 102
—— hears conditions made by, **30**. 188n
—— sees, at Hayes, but his offer is refused, **38**. 558, 562
—— sent to, **22**. 302
—— to make overtures to, **22**. 300n
—— wanted by, as army leader, **22**. 161
daughter of, marries, **24**. 67
death of: **24**. 379, **28**. 394, 398, 410; Copley's painting of, **29**. 185, **34**. 210; during Parliamentary session, lucky for family, **24**. 388–9; HW does not wish to imitate, **34**. 210; makes him seem indispensable, **24**. 382
defeat in America arouses call for, **32**. 399
defeat of, in absence, over question of land tax reduction, **22**. 488
Demosthenes surpassed and pensions spurned by, **38**. 188
departure of, from House of Commons disliked, **22**. 440
descendants of, will think him flawless, **37**. 271
designs of, on secretary of state, **20**. 223
Despenser the only friend to ask about health of, on his return to Parliament, **24**. 393
despotism of, based on his popularity, **23**. 100
Devonshire, D. of, disgusts Fox by favour to, **21**. 31
—— told by, he will await George II's orders before resigning, **21**. 74n
—— urges, to become minister, **21**. 11
—— urges George II to give place to, to placate Leicester House, **21**. 86n
difficult times preferred by, to halcyon days, **39**. 95
Dingley's house at Hampstead occupied by, **30**. 221, **31**. 122

dismissal of: as Paymaster, **9**. 179, **20**. 512, 517; as secretary of state, **21**. 74
does not appear, **23**. 115
doughty rather than courteous, in Parliamentary debate, **37**. 419
Du Barry, Mme, may anticipate, in saving Paoli, **23**. 75
Du Deffand, Mme, fears return of, **4**. 264
—— inquires after, **3**. 16, 227
—— mentions, **3**. 119, 120
—— receives word of, **3**. 249
——'s hatred for, **3**. 22
——'s knowledge of, **3**. 107–8
——'s opinion of, **3**. 64, 104
Duke St reported to be residence of, **31**. 86
Dupplin and Darlington succeed, as Paymaster, **14**. 87n
earldom may be won by, **38**. 135 (*see also under* Peerage of)
eastern monarchs and Borealian electors attend, in his Sabine farm, **21**. 518
East India affairs distract attention from, **38**. 368
East India Co. 'begot' by, **23**. 400
East India Co. crisis will be weathered by, **22**. 496
East India Co.'s general courts displease, **23**. 132n
——'s investigation demanded by, **30**. 240n, 244n
——'s restrictions from, opposed by Conway at C. Townshend's instigation, **22**. 493
Edgcumbe dismissed by, **22**. 470–1, **30**. 237n
Edinburgh may give freedom of city to, **21**. 87
Egmont's oratory compared to that of, **20**. 32
——'s party heaps incense on, **20**. 244
Élie de Beaumont visits, **38**. 461
Elliot said to mimic, **39**. 13
eloquence of, inspired British arms, **31**. 21
embassy to, expected, **32**. 238
England brought to glory under, **23**. 82
—— can still conquer even without, **22**. 82
—— must be saved by, **38**. 445
—— needs, **36**. 47
—— now lacks, **24**. 485
—— owes its security to, **21**. 261
——'s debt to, **9**. 395
——'s dependence upon sole abilities of, alarms Mann, **21**. 84
——'s empire extended by, **33**. 208
——'s glory bought by, but dearly, **33**. 389
——'s greatness buried with, **33**. 89
——'s pension from, is more war, **38**. 132
—— will clamour for return of, at first calamity, **21**. 558
—— would prefer, to Bute, in victory or defeat, **22**. 47–8
English disgraces must be removed by, **21**. 31
English expedition a sacrifice to vain-glorious whims of, **21**. 244
English ignoramuses mistake Frederick II for, **21**. 237–8

English troops said by, never to be used in Germany, **23.** 258
English victories ascribed to, by people, **9.** 251
Éon's alleged letter to, **22.** 248n, **38.** 507n
epigram on Bath's and London's gifts to, **21.** 87
events 'watered and pruned' by, **37.** 533
Exchequer demanded by, for Legge, **21.** 12n
—— said to be offered by, to North and Oswald, **22.** 494n
Exeter sends, box of heart of oak, **21.** 87n
expected in London, **30.** 240
faction of: **9.** 212n, **21.** 27; Conway distrusts, **37.** 491; does not resign, **19.** 27; Fox would like HW's criticism of, in *Xo Ho* strengthened, **30.** 133–4; HW avoids, **37.** 581; HW calls, 'third and least' in *Letter from Xo Ho*, **30.** 133n; Lyttelton abandons, **20.** 512; may be led by him, **10.** 274; only Whigs that do not vote with the Court, **18.** 118; Pelham flattered by, **20.** 224; Regency Bill opposed by, **20.** 248; to avoid provoking D. of Newcastle in order to lay Minorcan blame on Fox, **21.** 77
faith defined by, **35.** 614
falls from virtue by accepting place, **37.** 453
fame of, will be eclipsed by Dundas's, **29.** 135
family attend, at messenger's house, **24.** 371
family reconciliations of, **7.** 272, 367
fatigue of long Parliamentary session will be borne by, **38.** 321
favours strong measures against France, **9.** 389n
fear defined by, **9.** 238
festival for, cancelled, **3.** 108n
Finch misquotes, **9.** 308
fitter for raising storm than laying one, **39.** 228
Fitzroy's interview with, **30.** 189
followers of: alone, in Parliament, acknowledge American sovereignty, **24.** 371; headed by Shelburne, **28.** 383; would find no places if Winchilsea and Henry Fox remained, **21.** 99
foreigners' curiosity about, **38.** 527, 571
foreigners should be made to think that all English soldiers and sailors inherit cloak of, **25.** 15
foreigners watch, making speech at 5 A.M., **22.** 209
fortune still constant to, even though he sees no one, **22.** 508–9
Fox, C. J., and Lord North would not be timidly opposed by, **29.** 314n
Fox, C. J., usurps oratorical throne of, **28.** 349
Fox, Henry, and D. of Richmond may join with, **5.** 193
Fox, Henry, and Onslow attack, on stay of execution granted to Byng, **21.** 64n
Fox, Henry, answers, on Minorca, **20.** 554n
—— confers with, at Saville House, **21.** 11n
—— debates with, on Pennsylvania regiments, **37.** 436

—— is expected to unite with, and then attack, **20.** 453
—— may be succeeded by, as secretary of state, **21.** 6–7, 11
—— not to be joined by, in ministry, **21.** 11
—— opposes, **9.** 178, 179
—— proscribed by, **22.** 161
——'s breach with, widens, **21.** 34
——'s daily altercations with, in House of Commons, **21.** 65
——'s dispute with, resembled by actors' disputes in Paris, **38.** 539
—— seconds, **35.** 194
——'s inclusion in ministry required by, **20.** 502n
——'s relations with, **10.** 45
——'s rivalry with, **20.** 230
——'s 'war' with, **35.** 258
——'s witticism to, on tombstone epitaph, **37.** 426, 429, 441–2
—— visits, after Pelham's death, **20.** 412n
—— willing to be paymaster under, **21.** 98n
—— wishes to serve with, and under, **20.** 417n, **30.** 128n
France and Spain will be humbled by England during rule of, **22.** 441
France dreaded crutch of, to the last, **24.** 379
—— must be tied up by next treaty of, **21.** 338
—— no longer opposed by crutch of, **24.** 381
—— not to come begging to, **39.** 8
Franklin said to commission, to offer £350,000 a year from America, **32.** 227–8
Frederick II and P. Ferdinand the heroes of, **22.** 440–1
Frederick II's idea of expedition to Rochefort abandoned by, **21.** 117n
Frederick, P. of Wales, approached by faction of, **20.** 223n
—— calls Elizabeth Chudleigh better candidate than, for secretary at war, **19.** 175
—— hates, since Carteret's fall, **19.** 175
—— may dismiss, **18.** 118
——'s follower, **18.** 102
—— warns, **18.** 102
French Court obliged to, **37.** 201
French declaration sent by, to Mann, to be communicated to Regency, **21.** 502–3
French deem war synonymous with, **38.** 571
French destitution exaggerated by, **39.** 8
French expeditions of, unsuccessful, **23.** 186
French fear of: **10.** 201, 202, **30.** 216, **31.** 61; discovered by HW at Paris, **22.** 441
French fear wild beast of Gévaudan as much as, **22.** 289
French invasion discredited by, **18.** 399n
French invasion expected by, **21.** 299
French onslaught not yet expected by, **38.** 15
French peace offers distrusted by, **21.** 504n
French puzzled by refusal of, to lead administration, **22.** 342
friends of: advocate firmness, **22.** 513; want union with D. of Newcastle, **21.** 86–7

[Pitt, William (1708–78), *continued*]

funeral of: 7. 44, 28. 401, 406, 417, 29. 283, 33. 19–20; had not as many noble coaches as Garrick's, 33. 89 (*see also* burial of)

further legacies may be sought by, 18. 541

future descendants of, will think him spotless, 37. 271

Garrick equivalent to, in HW's opinion, 23. 41

—— less attentive than, to worldly riches, 24. 435

——'s verses from, 35. 564

general warrants, opposed by, bring him a bequest, 22. 277n

genius of, still constant, 22. 463

George II abuses, to D. of Newcastle, 20. 223

—— cannot place, in power, 19. 159

—— charges, to form ministry with Newcastle, 37. 487

—— confers with, once, 21. 43

—— dislikes, 20. 412, 21. 91n, 473

—— enjoys defeat of, 20. 223

—— expresses dissatisfaction with, 21. 205n

—— fears unwillingness of, to do his German business, 21. 6n

—— gives Mansfield full powers to negotiate with, 21. 99n

—— invites, into administration because of anger with Fox, 21. 6n

—— laughed at by, for liking military shows, 21. 238

—— loves Fox for opposing, 21. 91n

—— makes, Paymaster, 20. 138

—— might be carried by, to Tower on French cannon, 37. 571

—— orders Holdernesse and Devonshire to visit, in country on business, 21. 22n

—— pleased by, in Closet, 21. 31

—— receives Shah Goest from, 21. 378

—— reconciled with, by D. of Newcastle, 20. 138

—— regards Bute as closely connected with, 20. 570n

—— rejects, as secretary at war, at Pulteney's instigation, 19. 168n, 194n, 209, 211

—— revolted by demand of, to dismiss Holdernesse, 21. 17n

—— said to be approached by, on Sackville's behalf, 21. 320n

—— sends Holdernesse for seals of, 21. 74n

—— should charge, to form ministry under Dorset, 37. 487

——'s speech partly drafted by, 21. 344n

—— to see, 9. 203

George III and, cannot agree, 10. 99

George III and Bute prefer war measures of, 21. 527n

George III and royal family eclipsed by, at Lord Mayor's dinner, 21. 547

George III arranges ministry with, 22. 439

—— asked by, to dismiss peace supporters, 22. 160–1

—— confers with, 14. 128, 23. 132, 39. 116

—— dissatisfied with, 21. 205n

—— does not consult, on Bute's appointment as secretary of state, 21. 487–8

—— favours, 21. 93n

—— gives Fox an account of negotiations with, 30. 230

—— has to summon, to ministry, 22. 302

—— may send for, 39. 221, 227–8

—— notified by, of willingness to continue, 21. 448

—— orders, to offer Irish post to Bristol, 22. 450n

—— receives, 38. 209, 210

——'s conference with: 14. 128; variously reported, 22. 168

—— sees, 22. 497n

—— sends for, 10. 221–2, 22. 432, 31. 121–2

—— sends Grafton to ask, for interview, 22. 307

——'s forces may be led by, in Parliament, 24. 350

——'s interview with, delayed, 30. 226

——'s levee attended by, 22. 161, 39. 115, 116

——'s marriage declaration in circular letters signed by, 21. 520n

——'s offers to, 30. 188

——'s opinion of, 9. 340–1

——'s overtures rejected by, in audience, 32. 11n

——'s rebuke to, about proposing his friends, 22. 161

——'s separation from Bute said to be demanded by, 38. 210–11

—— summons: 31. 121–2; to plan new administration, 30. 221n

—— summons Temple at desire of, 22. 435

—— told by, that Bedford must be excluded, 22. 167n

—— treats firmly, 22. 495

—— tries to appease, by Grenville's appointment and restoration of West Indies department, 21. 488

—— will support, after loss of land tax, 22. 489

—— would not send for, a third time, 22. 419

German subsidy advocated by, 21. 65

German treaties opposed by, 20. 501

German victory pleases, 9. 379

German war supported by, in debates on foreign estimates, 21. 553n

German war supported by reputation of, 21. 549

Germany must be conquered by, since Frederick II is unlikely to do so, 21. 354

Gévaudan beast exhibited like, 39. 14

gold procured by, for city friends, 38. 120

gout and smell of war will bring back, to the stage, 23. 70

gout keeps, from House of Lords, 28. 350

gout of, may be political, 38. 69

gouty chair of, 22. 159n

government leadership offered to, 22. 159

government may be led by, 23. 182

government offers waived by, **21**. 540

Gower notified by, of new ministry, **41**. 7on

—— opposes, **32**. 403

—— refused office by, despite Temple's request, **30**. 228, 230

—— sent by, with overtures to D. of Bedford, **22**. 472

Grafton, D. of, calls on, **38**. 210

—— hears complaints of, **23**. 61

—— not seen by, though summoned, **36**. 434

—— seen by, at George III's request, **41**. 87n

—— to see, **30**. 226

—— unable to see, **22**. 436, **30**. 224, **31**. 124

Granby made commander-in-chief by, **23**. 168n

——'s resignation urged by, **23**. 175n

grandfather of, **29**. 4n

Grattan's 'character' of, **32**. 177–8

'Great Commoner' a common term for, **22**. 425n

Grenville, G., and Temple reconciled with, **7**. 367, **23**. 74

Grenville, G., and Temple said to be reconciled with, **38**. 571

Grenville, G. and Temple unite with, **7**. 367n

Grenville, G., attempts to prevent Bedford's union with, **30**. 236

—— may have underhand dealings with, **22**. 91

—— provokes, to speech on dismission of officials, **38**. 320

—— reconciled with, **10**. 272

—— refused office by, despite Temple's request, **30**. 222, 223

—— relies on waywardness of, **38**. 286

——'s death keeps, from House of Lords, **23**. 248

——'s debate with, **22**. 401n, 405n

——'s hatred from, exceeds deference to Temple, **23**. 115n

——'s match of silence with, **38**. 326

——'s visit from, boasted of by late ministers, **30**. 197

—— would have Exchequer post according to demands of, **21**. 92

Grenville, James, attacked by, **35**. 75–6

—— made cofferer to appease, **9**. 341

——'s promotion assuages, **30**. 162

Grenville ministry's failure shows need for, as minister, **38**. 323

Grenvilles condescendingly treated by, **22**. 419

—— driven by, **19**. 194

—— reconciled with, **36**. 56

—— the only allies of, **19**. 169

Greville, Mrs, compares, with Thomas Pitt, **5**. 130

'grey-headed experience' boast of by, **19**. 169

grows impatient for power, **3**. 22n

Grub St papers about, printed in Vienna court gazette, **22**. 178

HW advises Conway and Richmond to recommend, to George III, **22**. 432n

HW ascribes English victories to, **21**. 347

HW asks Edgcumbe about, **35**. 195

HW attacks, **13**. 18n

HW attends Conway and, alternately at opera, **30**. 239

HW attributes capture of Martinique to eloquence of, **10**. 22

HW blames Belle-île expedition on, **9**. 366

HW calls: 'Almanzor,' **37**. 543, **39**. 115; 'arrant cheat and gipsy,' **38**. 131; 'Colbert,' **9**. 228; 'Conqueror of America,' **38**. 558; 'Demosthenes,' **21**. 365, **23**. 163; 'Don William Quixote,' **37**. 550; 'giant,' **38**. 131; 'Gorgon,' **20**. 454; 'Hannibal,' **22**. 211; 'Irishman,' **32**. 400; 'Leonidas,' **38**. 334; 'minister who carried our glory to its highest pitch,' **29**. 351; 'mountebank of history' and 'impostor,' **10**. 184; 'Mr Secretary Cortez,' **38**. 120; 'old Myra,' **23**. 168; 'popular young orator,' **30**. 303n; 'Solomon,' **9**. 164

HW calls on, **35**. 97, **40**. 170, 171

HW compares, to: Bath, E. of, **38**. 131; Cæsar, **23**. 82, **38**. 140; Capet, Hugh, **38**. 140; Cromwell, **38**. 140; Dr Rock, **21**. 547; Fabius, **21**. 337; Garrick, **28**. 206, 207; Kings of Bantam, **10**. 153

HW considers, as mad, **38**. 136, **39**. 88–9, 95

HW converses with, at Bath, **22**. 461n

HW discusses possible administration of, **10**. 222

HW disillusioned by acceptance by, of peerage and gifts, **21**. 541

HW doubted, would join proposed administration, **30**. 180

HW dreams of Mme de Bentheim and, **39**. 4

HW expects 'resurrection' of, **30**. 176

HW gives Lucan's *Pharsalia* to, **40**. 191

HW hints to Choiseul's friends that Wilkes might bring, back to power, **23**. 143

HW honours, for victories, **35**. 297

HW hopes for administration of Grafton and, **41**. 73

HW imagines, 'more eloquent than Demosthenes,' **38**. 188

HW implies that illnesses of, are feigned, **30**. 217

HW jokes on: **30**. 146, 205; about Bute's possible deposition by, **10**. 39–40; about Lady Mary Coke and, **31**. 14, 21–2; about regiment for, **35**. 281

HW listed among 'friends' of, **43**. 277

HW may call on, at Bath, **39**. 76, 78

HW mentions, **3**. 90, **10**. 224, 242

HW more interested in, than in his son, **25**. 487

HW pleased by George III's summons to, **31**. 122

HW praises, **40**. 171–2

HW predicts new administration by, **22**. 308

HW predicts political downfall of, **10**. 222

HW proposes George II should send carte blanche to, to form ministry under Dorset, **21**. 98n

[Pitt, William (1708–78), *continued*]

HW quotes, **22.** 1

HW ridicules disinterestedness of, **9.** 394

HW's admiration for, **33.** 360

HW's appraisal of, **24.** 415

HW saw whole career of, **25.** 559

HW's correspondence with, **40.** 92, 170–3, 191, 355–6, 359

HW sees coach of, at Bath, full of children, **39.** 76

HW sends Lord Herbert of Chirbury's *Life* to, **40.** 355–6

HW's 'epitaph' on, **38.** 136–7

HW's friends might enlist under, **38.** 557

HW's letter about Lady Mary Coke might be intercepted by, **37.** 568–9

HW's letters to, disinterested, **13.** 38

HW's 'morsels of criticism' mention, **31.** 281

HW's opinion of, **21.** 541, 547, **32.** 177–8

HW's 'petition' in verse to, **38.** 41

HW's speech praised by, **17.** 377

HW subject of proposal by, to Conway, **39.** 78

HW substitutes print of, for Fox's picture, **30.** 125

HW's verses mention, **14.** 88

HW's verses to, **31.** 15

HW's witticism about sister's resemblance to, **38.** 527

HW's witticism to, on not kissing hands, **35.** 263

HW talks with, **35.** 120

HW thanks, for accepting Lord Herbert's *Life*, **40.** 359

HW thinks, mad, **38.** 136, **39.** 88–9, 95

HW thinks of sending for, **32.** 218

HW threatens the French with new administration by, **41.** 7

HW undeceived by mourning feigned for, by nephew, **24.** 415

HW wishes to have Conway vindicated by rashness of, **37.** 581

HW writes to Mme du Deffand about, **7.** 382

habeas corpus voting shunned by, **18.** 408–9

Halifax, E. of, proscribed by, **20.** 161

——'s demand for West Indies secretaryship of state, refused by, **9.** 212

——'s disappointment not fault of, **30.** 135

Hampden covets office of, **20.** 224

——'s quarrel with, **20.** 224, 235

Hanoverian troop bill supported by, **19.** 241

Hanover said by, to be preferred to America by Administration, **21.** 553n

harangues in House of Commons, **21.** 547

Hardinge a worshipper of, **35.** 582

—— hopes HW will meet, in House of Lords, **35.** 565

Hardinge, Mrs, makes witticism on George III's choice of, **21.** 459–60

Hardwicke alarmed at popularity of, **21.** 87

—— and D. of Newcastle join Bute against, **21.** 539n

Hardwicke supports, to keep down Henry Fox and D. of Cumberland, **20.** 412n

—— takes terms of, to George III, **21.** 109n

—— tells, of his and Newcastle's dislike of Fox, **21.** 23n

Hartington opposes, **20.** 222

'has kicked and cuffed,' **22.** 416

haughtiness pushed too far by, **22.** 419

Hay loses seat in service of, **21.** 73

health and spirits of, good, **22.** 462

health but not popularity enjoyed by, **22.** 552

health of: **3.** 290, 365, **7.** 42, **8.** 162; apoplectic fit, **24.** 371, **28.** 324, 379–80; as bad as his situation, **21.** 67; better, **22.** 559; better, but unlikely to recover, **24.** 378; cannot yet walk, **21.** 39; eyesight affected by gout, **21.** 484; fat and well, **23.** 132; fever, **22.** 436, **30.** 221, 226, **31.** 122; fever and gout, **38.** 240; fever, symptomatic, **22.** 505; fever, worse, **30.** 224; gout, **9.** 203, 205, **21.** 22, 31, 33, 35, 39, 43, 52, 171, 177–8, 198, 261, 286, 374, 381n, 484, 518, **22.** 101, 169n, 208, 211, 277, 284, 298, 307n, 449, 479, 501, 521, 578, **23.** 70, 74, 194, 199, **24.** 126, **28.** 350, **30.** 216, **31.** 62, 125, 131, **37.** 268, 451, **38.** 258, 332, 379, 493; gout, preventing attendance on Regency Bill, **38.** 547; gouty fever, **30.** 188; ill, **22.** 488; looks and walks well, **35.** 120; mental derangement rumoured, **22.** 505; mental disorder still suspected, **22.** 513; poor, **20.** 412; recovered, **39.** 115; recovery rumoured, **39.** 95; sister explains fluctuations of, **39.** 95; sleepless for 14 nights, **21.** 484; Temple's return may bring recovery of, **36.** 45; worse, **31.** 124

Hertford considers, as prime minister, **38.** 211

——'s respect for, **38.** 330

—— told by, that he will not obstruct Conway's military appointment, **37.** 577

—— vainly expects, to be secretary of state, **39.** 1

(?) Hervey, Bns, hopes, will not form new administration, **31.** 86

Hessian and Russian treaties opposed by, **35.** 89

Hillsborough has no connection with, **22.** 439

Holdernesse deserts D. of Newcastle for, **9.** 341

——'s dismissal angers, **30.** 162

—— to be attacked by, over release of Hanoverian soldier at Maidstone, **21.** 34

Hopson's and Moore's dispatches to, **21.** 277n

house of, in St James's Sq., to be let, **38.** 136n

House of Commons defeats demand of, for increased navy, **19.** 168–9

—— held by, *in commendam*, **21.** 56

—— left by, in debate with Grenville, **22.** 401n

—— may be snatched from leadership of, **22.** 501

—— member, but now powerless, **38.** 132

—— might be led by, **20.** 493n

—— must be managed by, **22.** 490

—— not attended by, **37.** 268

—— not visited by, **38.** 369

—— prevented by, from adjourning, **38.** 316

—— to attend burial of, **24.** 379

—— votes funeral and monument to, at public expense, **24.** 379

House of Lords attended by, **32.** 402

—— gets motions from, **32.** 66, 403

—— little influenced by, **21.** 205–6

—— may be attended by, with a proposal, **6.** 138–9

—— not attended by, **23.** 194, 199–200

—— visited by, against physicians's orders, probably for last time, **24.** 371

—— will be as little impressed by, as France was by his coastal attacks, **23.** 186

Hume Campbell demolished by, in Parliamentary debate on subsidy treaties, **35.** 262

hunts, **23.** 387

ignorance of, of the world, **39.** 78

illumination in honour of, countermanded, **3.** 108

imagination of, gigantic but unable to entertain England's present delusion, **39.** 356

importance of, **2.** 84

incompetence of, **30.** 141

Indians have eloquence of, **35.** 187

India's 'conqueror,' **21.** 541

'iota' an expression of, **38.** 7

Irish vice-treasurership accepted by, **19.** 221n, **37.** 453

Irvine, Vcts, toasts, **9.** 207

Jacobite county and city corporations won by eloquence of, **35.** 291

Karl Wilhelm Ferdinand writes to, and calls on him at Hayes, **38.** 287

Keene allowed by, to retire, **21.** 150n, 159n

Keppel thinks, neglected him, **30.** 234

La Chalotais said to correspond with, **30.** 216, **39.** 33

lamentable in House of Commons, **37.** 445

land officers in Rochefort affair blamed by, **37.** 521n

Lee opposes, in Parliament, **19.** 241

—— resigns post from resentment towards, **21.** 104

Legge avoids dispute with, **20.** 453

—— ignored by, **22.** 161

—— would have peerage and Admiralty according to demands of, **21.** 92

Leicester House said to countenance, **21.** 13

Leicester's witticism on appointment of, as Paymaster, **19.** 286

letter of, speaks of no longer guiding Cabinet Council, **38.** 140

letters against, **42.** 505

Letter to Two Great Men refers to, **9.** 270n

likes to bid on others' haughtiness, **21.** 536

Lincoln vacillates between Bute and, **30.** 179

London Common Council gives freedom of city to, **21.** 77

—— receives letter from, explaining his acceptance of pension, **21.** 546

—— thanks, **9.** 397, **38.** 139–40

London crisis avoided by, **38.** 561

London dislikes acceptance by, of peerage and pension, **22.** 442–3, **38.** 132, 135

—— lured by, with hope of Spanish plunder, **21.** 549

—— ready to tear, to pieces, **38.** 135

——'s policy towards, **21.** 90

—— tavern might satirize Bath and, **38.** 137

—— to be visited by, **9.** 203

Lord Mayor's dinner attended by, in chariot and pair, **21.** 547

lord privy seal, **3.** 104, **35.** 319

Louis XV almost tossed in blanket by, **22.** 276

lying-in-state of, **33.** 19

Lyttelton calls, 'Pericles,' **21.** 408–9

—— debates against, **35.** 260

—— does not aid, antagonizing Grenvilles, **35.** 194–5

—— reconciled with, **38.** 364

—— refused office by, despite Temple's request, **30.** 225, 227

—— related to, **22.** 251

——'s budget attacked by, on sinking fund, **37.** 432

——'s friendship with, **19.** 27

—— to receive messenger from, with offer of Turin post, **21.** 507–8

Lytteltons and Grenvilles driven by, **19.** 194

Lytteltons and Grenvilles the only allies of, **19.** 169

makes exorbitant demands, **14.** 128n

makes high demands of France, **9.** 353n

Mann congratulated by, **21.** 522n

—— expects, as new superior, **21.** 16

—— favourably mentioned by, to Wood, **22.** 469

—— informs, of Old Pretender's ill health, **21.** 390

—— must be haughty, now that he represents, **22.** 441

—— not likely to be opposed by, **22.** 433

—— ordered by: to direct his letters by way of Holland, **21.** 134n; to send letters through Flushing in Zeeland, **21.** 141n

—— receives letter by order of, **21.** 381

—— receives letter from, on death of George II, **21.** 453, 455

——'s correspondence with, **21.** 36

——'s credentials from, **21.** 463–4

——'s obligation to, stressed by Chute, **21.** 338

——'s political remarks should first be authorized by, **21.** 465–6

——'s truculence to Tuscan Court would be backed by, **22.** 483

—— to inform, of Botta's reception of George III's letter, **21.** 464

—— will think HW has succeeded, **21.** 539

—— would be surprised to find, secretary of state, **20.** 235

Mann, Galfridus, favoured by, **21.** 166

Mansfield attacked by, **39.** 246

——'s language compared with that of, **35.** 515

[Pitt, William (1708–78), *continued*]
——'s prosecution dropped by, **23.** 282
——'s speech cowed by right of, **22.** 464
Marlborough visited by, **22.** 488
Marlborough, Ds of, leaves legacy to, as 'patriot,' **1.** 112n, **9.** 34n, **18.** 540, **22.** 277
marriage of, **9.** 166, **35.** 194
Masserano frightened by return of, **22.** 441
Maurepas to be frowned on by, in the other world, **25.** 212
may become secretary at war, **19.** 155
may be sent for, after debate on Regency Bill, **22.** 300
may emerge with Wilkes, **23.** 82
medallion of, **41.** 348
memorial arouses retort from, **38.** 31
'meteor' of House of Commons, **19.** 202
Mexico might be attacked by, **38.** 120, 128
Middlesex election discussed by, till nobody will answer him, **23.** 208–9
Middlesex election heated and reheated by, **23.** 215
Middlesex election referred by, to House of Lords, **23.** 167
military men may be preferred by, **22.** 439
military success due to, **21.** 277
militia bills sponsored by, **35.** 291n
militia plan of, **37.** 441
ministers, Opposition, Wilkes, and London abused by, **23.** 251
ministry might engage Paoli against, **23.** 145
ministry of, *see* administration of
ministry predicted for, **38.** 486
ministry refused by, **30.** 180, 188
miscarriages and derision suffered by, **23.** 216
mob angry at, over food prices, **35.** 320
mob cheers, **22.** 405
mob has not put, into St James's Palace, **21.** 541
mob ill-treats, **22.** 449
mob might be ordered by, to oppose the ministry, **43.** 275
Mogul frightened by, **22.** 276
Molineux admires, **39.** 96n
Monckton and Townshend send news to, of Quebec's capture, **21.** 337n
money and people both impossible to be raised by, **23.** 218
Montagu admires, **9.** 394, **10.** 203
Mordaunt and Hawke get letter from, on Rochefort expedition, **37.** 503n
Mount Edgcumbe visited by, **23.** 387n
Murray answered by, in House of Commons, **18.** 123
—— attacked by, on army estimates, **20.** 454n
mysteriousness of, **30.** 186
nation may call for, **23.** 100
naval investigation supported by, in Parliament, **18.** 399
naval reduction opposed by, **20.** 223
nephew of, **21.** 364–5
nephew swears by ghost of, despite previous dislike, **23.** 412

Neville said to be abused by, **38.** 360, 368–9
Newcastle, D. of, abandoned by, **20.** 453
—— and Fox opposed by, **20.** 509–10
Newcastle, D. of, asked by, not to meddle in House of Commons or state department, **21.** 91
—— attacked by: in House of Commons, over Minorca, **20.** 554n; in Parliamentary speeches, **35.** 194
—— charges, with fiscal irresponsibility, **21.** 290n
—— compliments, **22.** 207n, 208n
—— confers with: **22.** 160; at Royston's house, **21.** 92n
—— denies engagements with, **21.** 74, 98n
—— does not choose, as colleague, **20.** 248
—— expects attack from, over land tax, **22.** 494n
—— fears coalition between Fox and, might sacrifice him, **20.** 557n
—— first minister under, **10.** 192n
—— may betray, **9.** 232
—— negotiates with, to regain Halifax for Board of Trade, **21.** 111n
—— not to be joined by, **22.** 78
—— prefers, to Fox, **21.** 6n
—— proposes, as secretary of state, **21.** 86n
—— rejects demands of, and breaks off conferences, **21.** 92
—— resumes conference with, **21.** 97
—— retains Hume Campbell to abuse, **35.** 262
—— said by George II to be negotiating with, **21.** 74n
—— said to have rejected extravagant terms of, **21.** 91
——'s and Holdernesse's support sought by, for Habeas Corpus Bill, **21.** 205n
Newcastle's coalition with: **9.** 205n, **21.** 103–5; sneered at by him, **30.** 136
——'s exclusion demanded by, **21.** 11
——'s friends oppose having hostilities to, **30.** 236
——'s overtures rejected by, **21.** 23, **22.** 93
——'s rapprochement with, **37.** 485n
——'s rumoured rupture with, **9.** 210
—— supported by, against Sandwich and the Bedfords, **20.** 222
—— unlikely to get along with, **21.** 99–100
—— upset by, **20.** 230
—— wants England defeated to put the blame on, **38.** 75
—— would resign if, refused to serve with him, **21.** 6n
new Opposition led by, **21.** 552, **35.** 260
nominee for secretaryship, **20.** 202
Norton desires return of, to power, **7.** 273
Northington responsible for recall of, according to Bute's friends, **30.** 222
nose of, large, **32.** 48
not to stay in power, **41.** 88
not turned out, **35.** 194
not yet in place, **19.** 202
Nugent opposes, **20.** 454

offers refused by, if known to be unhelpful to his popularity, **30.** 188

officers' appointments by, criticized, **37.** 580

Opposition encouraged by, to form ministry, **22.** 310

—— led by, in Parliament, **9.** 180, **24.** 341

—— not to be joined by, **22.** 78

—— ostensibly suspends officers' dismission question during gout of, **38.** 508–9

—— ready to join, **38.** 557

—— requested by, to lie still, **38.** 53

—— shrugs and stares at, but courtiers laugh, **39.** 246

orations of, nobler than Greek or Roman, **31.** 22

oratory of, **10.** 22, 203, 254

'outlived himself and the duration of the empire,' **28.** 234

pamphlets on, sometimes attributed to HW, **38.** 144

(?) Park Place visited by, **37.** 380

Parliamentary Address debated by, **37.** 414, 416

Parliamentary Address displeases, **37.** 414

Parliamentary appearance again made by, **24.** 308

Parliamentary appearance of, borne by servants, to oppose Treaty of Paris, **32.** 44n

Parliamentary attendance still impossible for, **21.** 33, 55

Parliamentary debate by, on privilege and the *North Briton*, **38.** 225–6

Parliamentary membership of, corrected, **43.** 242

Parliamentary motions by: about American affairs, **24.** 341n; in House of Lords, **23.** 180, **24.** 75, **32.** 403; long, in House of Lords, **32.** 66; to recall troops and deny independence to America, **32.** 400–1; to recall troops from Boston, **24.** 75n, **32.** 226n, 228, 401n, **39.** 245–6

Parliamentary Opposition to be led by, **18.** 102

Parliamentary question on dismission of officers warmly supported by, **38.** 509

Parliamentary resolution of, about administration, **32.** 11

Parliamentary speeches by: **10.** 203, **17.** 297, **21.** 345n, **31.** 67, (?) **37.** 223, **43.** 256; alarms House of Commons, **20.** 453; HW quotes, **35.** 194; long, **30.** 197; implies world conquest, **21.** 344–5; mimicked by Charles Townshend, **38.** 28; Newcastle praised and stand on Spanish war reversed in, **20.** 222; not up to his old standard, **23.** 167; on Address, **38.** 231; on amendment to the Address, **26.** 24; on conquering America in Germany, **31.** 67n; on finance, poor, **37.** 445; on liberty, **38.** 320; on Old Pretender and sons, **18.** 440n; on privately-raised regiments, **19.** 154, **26.** 14, 15, 17, 18; on recall of troops from Boston, **32.** 228; on Secret Committee, **19.** 370; on seizure of Wilkes's

papers, **22.** 208; on supply bill for militia, **31.** 117n; on unanimity on the Army, **26.** 10; on Wilkes, shows exhaustion, **38.** 326; Parliament charmed by, **10.** 203; Parliament swayed by, **21.** 256–7; 'sketched' by HW, **37.** 470; unheeded, **37.** 444

Parliamentary vote by, on privately-raised regiments, **26.** 19

Parliament attacked by, for taxing America, **22.** 395–6

—— attended by: in flannel on crutches, **38.** 240–1; only twice in winter, **21.** 182

—— avoided by: in debate on Manila ransom, **38.** 488; in Regency dispute, **38.** 547; since war of privilege, **38.** 369

—— begins without, **22.** 101

—— charmed by speeches of, **10.** 203

—— may be forced by outside pressure to bow to, **21.** 13

——'s adulation of, a farce, **24.** 415

—— said to be object of London visit of, **6.** 38

——'s dissolution by, would leave Wilkes in control, **23.** 181

—— told by, that Choiseul is greatest French premier since Richelieu, **41.** 201

—— to pay debts of, **24.** 382

—— will bury, in either Westminster Abbey or St Paul's, **24.** 382

Paymaster, **9.** 32, **19.** 256, **20.** 138, 406

paymastership given to, to appease his followers' demands, **9.** 39

peaceable, and has reason to be pleased, **23.** 65

peace called 'inadequate' by, **10.** 108n

peace conditions not auspicious for, **10.** 222

peace made by, will be a good one, **21.** 355

peace negotiations by, **21.** 527n, 536n

Peace of Paris (1763) condemned by, **22.** 95–6

peace prevented and war avoided by, **38.** 132

peerage for: **3.** 105, **30.** 188, **43.** 321–2; Commons Council angered by, **30.** 234; Monument illumination cancelled because of, **30.** 234

peerage for wife of, **9.** 395, **38.** 131–2, 134, 135–7

Pelham attacked by, **19.** 169

—— bullied and flattered by, **19.** 155

—— courts, **18.** 327

—— favours, for secretary of state, **20.** 202n

—— may be succeeded by, as prime minister, **20.** 411, 419

—— must bring in, **18.** 537

pension acceptance must be regretted by, **22.** 277

pension and peerage for wife accepted by, **9.** 395, **38.** 131–2, 134, 135–7

pension of, **21.** 546, **24.** 389

pension will not stop, from political victories, **10.** 45

perpetual militia bill may be necessary to, **21.** 552

personally very expensive, **24.** 389

[Pitt, William (1708–78), *continued*]
Philipps satirized in 'panegyric' by, **35.** 560
Piozzi, Mrs, comments on, **10.** 254n
Pitt, George, a distant relative of, **22.** 572n
Pitt, Mrs George, visited by, at Wandsworth Hill, **22.** 572
Pitt, Thomas, nephew of, **5.** 130
political disappearance of, **10.** 153
political enemies injured but not defeated by, **38.** 324
political faction may be led by, **10.** 274
political prospects of, on becoming secretary of state, **21.** 17
political success of, **10.** 236
popularity of: **9.** 223; even in illness would have made new ministry difficult, **24.** 381
possible return of, to power, **28.** 206, 349, 370, 376–7
Potter, Thomas, may rival, **17.** 449
praises his own administration, and denounces dismission of officers, **38.** 320
Pratt devises Habeas Corpus Bill with, **21.** 205n
—— named by, for lord chancellor, **22.** 161 (*see also under* Camden)
—— preferred by, to Charles Yorke for chancellor, **38.** 285
——'s peerage virtually ignored by, **30.** 197
prerogative called 'master wing of the eagle' by, **39.** 122
prime minister, **10.** 223
print of, inscribed by HW with lines from Dryden, **35.** 262
Privy Seal to be taken by, **22.** 442
proposes adding M.P.s, **15.** 130
proud prejudices of, **37.** 580
prudence may be added by, to courage, **37.** 569
Pynsent estate mostly sold by, **39.** 95
——'s bequest to: **22.** 276–7, 284, **30.** 217, **32.** 18, **38.** 493; equalled only in England, **22.** 280–1
Queensberry friend of, **19.** 175
Queensberry, Ds of, governs, **19.** 195
—— 'orders,' to have the gout, **37.** 268
Reading visited by, **22.** 490, 572
recovery of, would quash opposition, **22.** 506
refusal of, to form government, results in recall of former ministers, **10.** 152n, **38.** 558, 562
Regency Bill opposed by, **22.** 298, **38.** 545
regiments allowed by, to be raised by anybody, **38.** 40
reported to have kissed hands, **30.** 135
Ré's capture urged by, **30.** 142n
resignation of: **9.** 392, **21.** 537, **23.** 61, **31.** 24, 140; threatened, **21.** 30–1; will make Spain bolder, **21.** 538, 539
resigns, when Cabinet Council rejects Spanish war, **38.** 131, 134
restoration of: in sight, **21.** 557–8; rumoured, **24.** 366

resumption of 'throne' by Temple and, may resemble revolution in *The Rehearsal*, **30.** 222
retirement of, probably permanent, **10.** 272
returns to Hayes, **38.** 210
reversion of, **10.** 234n
(?) Richardson sends compliments to, **40.** 234
Richmond, D. of, vainly tries to plan new ministry with, **41.** 304n
rioting could be stopped by, **38.** 561
Robinson attacked by, **20.** 453
Rochefort expedition advocated by, **21.** 117n, **37.** 501n
Rochefort instructions of, for Hawke and Mordaunt approved, **21.** 119n
Rochford opposed to, **3.** 254
Rockingham called on by, though he was formerly ejected from the house, **23.** 181
Rockingham faction's opposition may force, into alliance with Bedford faction, **30.** 232
Rockingham faction to be divided by, **41.** 67n
Rockingham ministry attacked by, in House of Commons, **31.** 117
Rockingham ministry charged by, with perfidy, **22.** 425
Rockingham ministry favoured by, **22.** 382
Rockingham ministry to be approved by, **39.** 40
Rockingham ministry turned against by, **22.** 413
Rockingham must aid, **23.** 246
——'s coolness with, **24.** 350
——'s faction deserts, **23.** 199
——'s faction's opposition may force, into alliance with Bedford faction, **30.** 232
Rousseau's fame compared to that of, **41.** 60
royal wedding and Coronation the only topics allowed to, **38.** 118
rumour of acceptance by, of administration, **22.** 410
Russian alliance desired by, **30.** 233n
Russia's desertion of Prussia to concern, **10.** 39
'Sabine farm' of, **21.** 518
Sackville thought by, to deserve a hearing, **38.** 22n
St Alban's Tavern meeting opposes, **21.** 552n
St-Malo's capture never intended by, **21.** 213
Sandwich arouses jealousy of, **20.** 138
—— hated by, **20.** 38
—— opposed by, **20.** 222
—— proscribed by, **22.** 161
Scott's praise or abuse of, depends on Sandwich's status, **22.** 410n
Scrope almost fights with, **17.** 458
Seals to be taken by, **21.** 22
seat of, *see* Hayes
secession from Parliamentary majority threatened but retracted by, **21.** 86
secession of, in House of Lords, **23.** 256
secluded at Hayes, **38.** 368–9

second son of: **25.** 487n; in opposition, proves that eloquence has not degenerated, **25.** 212

secretary at war application of, rejected, **18.** 552

secretary at war's post coveted by, **19.** 168

secretary at war's post rumoured for, **37.** 219

secretary at war's reversion sought by, **37.** 200–1

secretaryship of state expected for, **20.** 461, **21.** 12

secretaryship of state for West Indies not permitted by, **21.** 104

secretaryship of state goes to, **9.** 202, **21.** 103

self-sacrifice of, jokingly expected, **10.** 112

Selwyn might be brained by, with crutch, **30.** 217

——'s description of, amuses HW, **30.** 216

Shelburne may consider himself political heir to, **24.** 379

—— proscribed by, **22.** 161

—— shielded by, **22.** 571n

Shelley apes, **22.** 470n

sides with HW, **13.** 23n

sings, **39.** 89

sister attacks, **20.** 507n

sister mourns for, **24.** 415

sister of, **5.** 292n, **20.** 406, **23.** 451n, **24.** 194n

sister of, resembles him, **23.** 557, **24.** 379

sister refused a pension by, **31.** 40n

sister sends letters of, to the *Test* to show that he cheated her, **21.** 46

situation of, unchanged, **22.** 543

Somersetshire man at Bath calls, 'your Majesty,' **22.** 425–6

son almost equals oratory of, **39.** 380

son compared with, **25.** 407, 449, 452, 487, 512, **29.** 116

son's popularity based on, **39.** 431

son will enable France to avenge her defeats by, **36.** 223

Spain's fear of, **29.** 138

Spanish negotiations wanted by, to be discussed in House, **21.** 553

Spanish war should be avoided by, **21.** 544

Spencer, Hon. John, leaves reversion of estate to, **9.** 34, **22.** 277

Stanley recalled by, **21.** 536

——'s post in Russia suggested by, **22.** 444n

Sterne's *Tristram Shandy* dedicated to, **21.** 407n

Stowe monuments to, **10.** 314

Strange as harshly treated as Hume Campbell by, **38.** 8

strong administration expected by, **30.** 227

Stuart Mackenzie asks Mann about chances of help from, **22.** 469

subsidy treaty might be digested by, from compliment to George II, **35.** 253

success of, probably unexpected by him, **24.** 388

Sulivan directed by, **22.** 497n

summons to power expected by, **39.** 221

sun of, broke forth after Seven Years War, **24.** 356

Talbot's advice to D. of Newcastle on resignation of, **21.** 540

Tanucci's letter from, about Gray's Bath investiture, **21.** 507n

tasks of, in George III's reign, **9.** 314

taste defined by, **35.** 569n

tavern sign to show Bath and, embracing, **38.** 137

Temple again unites with, **24.** 14

Temple and Grenville unite with, **7.** 267, **23.** 74

Temple asks, about intentions towards Stuart Mackenzie and Northumberland, **30.** 226

—— demands equal power with, **22.** 538

—— denied prime ministry by, to exclude George Grenville, **36.** 45n

—— deplores violence of, **23.** 167

—— enjoys reflected glory of, **24.** 517

—— entertains, at dinner, **23.** 132n

—— made by, to refuse Irish post, and stay in House of Lords, **21.** 485

—— may be proposed by, for Treasury post, **22.** 433

—— offended at promise of, to aid Bute's friends, **22.** 436

—— probably abused by, **30.** 225, 226

—— quarrels with, **3.** 101n, **23.** 263, **28.** 286, **31.** 151

—— reconciled with, **10.** 272

—— refuses aid to, **7.** 273

——'s brother-in-law, **9.** 261n

——'s consent needed by, to join administration, **22.** 307–8

——'s demand for George Grenville refused by, **22.** 436, **41.** 23n

——'s demands increase with popularity of, **9.** 261

——'s recommendation of Grenville and Lyttelton rejected by, **41.** 23n

——'s reconciliation with Grenville implies sincerity in negotiation of, with D. of Cumberland, **30.** 184

——'s reconciliation with Grenville probably not desired by, although willing to profit by it, **30.** 186

——'s threatened opposition scoffed at by, **30.** 227

——'s treachery disappoints, **22.** 309–10

——'s unsuccessful ministerial recommendations to, **30.** 222, 225, 227, 228, 230

—— supports, in using Byng's trial as political weapon, **21.** 55n

——'s visit agitates, **30.** 24

—— to visit, at Hayes, and take him to town, **23.** 115n

—— urges, to retain his place, **21.** 346

—— visits, at Hampstead, **30.** 222, **31.** 122, 124

—— would have Irish post and blue ribbon according to demands of, **21.** 92

[Pitt, William (1708–78), *continued*]
Test, The, attacks, 21. 38
third expedition planned by, 21. 243
threatened with expulsion, 35. 194
'thunder' of, 28. 303
titles of anti-American acts entered by Franklin in speech of, 32. 235n
Tories abandon, 21. 553
—— hate, 20. 510
—— promised by, that he would shun House of Commons, 22. 101n
—— safe under Grenville ministry supported by, 30. 190
—— support, in attempt to oust Hessian troops, 21. 33–4
(?) Tothill's suit against, 8. 162
town house of, in Bond St not Duke St, 31. 86n
Townshend, Vcts, gossips about, 9. 32
—— nicknames, 9. 166
Townshend, Charles, assists, 38. 142
—— encouraged by absence of, from House of Commons, 22. 492–3
—— fears, 38. 502
—— half-ally of, 21. 553
—— meets, at Newcastle House, 30. 136
—— now applauds Paris peace treaty after retirement of, 38. 496
—— opposes, 30. 243–4
—— rejected by, as chancellor of the Exchequer, 22. 442
—— resents being made chancellor of the Exchequer by, 22. 493
—— supports Parliamentary speech of, 38. 319
—— told by, to become chancellor of Exchequer, not Paymaster, 22. 439–40
—— visits, at Hampstead, 30. 227
Townshend, George, might urge, to storm Rochefort with militia, 37. 572–3
—— refuses office from, 30. 133
Townshend, Thomas, brings overtures to, 22. 413n
Townshend brothers' interview with, 30. 134–5
Treasury mismanagement blamed on Newcastle and Legge by, 21. 290n
treaty with, over Bedford coalition, 41. 70–1
Turin candidate to be proposed by, to George III, 21. 507–8
Turkey would oblige, by impertinence, 21. 537
turns against Rockingham administration, 22. 413
undependable in Opposition, 38. 286
vanity of, 30. 217
venal, 21. 541
verses by, to Garrick, disclaim ambition, 23. 387
vice-treasury of Ireland granted to, 19. 241
victory does not resign with, 22. 15
'vicinage' a word coined by, 11. 348

vote of credit to be limited by, 21. 91n
voted for, as commissioner, 17. 437–8
Wales, Augusta, Ps of, denounced by, as 'secret influence,' 23. 195
Wales, Frederick, P. of, persuaded by, to seek chancellorship of Cambridge, 20. 10n
Walpole, Sir Edward, calls on, 19. 371
Walpole, Horatio (1678–1757) connected with, 35. 88n
—— debates with, 19. 168–9
—— rebukes, for forwardness, 2. 205–6
—— thanks, 19. 371
Walpole, Sir Robert, acquitted by, in speech, 19. 370
—— criticized by, for keeping peace, 37. 200
—— opposed by, 9. 64n
Walpole, Hon. Thomas, asked by, to return Hayes to him, 36. 46
—— converses with, 7. 273
—— corresponds with, 7. 272, 22. 93n
—— lends to HW a letter by, 36. 45
war declaration against Spain demanded by, 21. 537n
war declaration expected from, 38. 121
war hints will certainly cure, 23. 32
war's continuation urged by, 38. 75
war's ending should have been followed by retirement of, 42. 229
war talk revives, 23. 156
war would restore faculties of, 23. 78
West, Gilbert, inscribes book to, 9. 84
Westminster Abbey chapel has monument to, with Mrs Wright's wax head, 32. 98n
Westminster scrutiny investigation demanded by, 20. 123
Weymouth said to be in league with, 23. 259
Whigs may detain Hessian troops to thwart, 21. 33–4
Widdrington resembled by, 23. 264
wife gets power of attorney from, before he leaves for Burton Pynsent, 39. 88–9, 95
wife might lean on brothers if despairing of recovery of, 41. 88
wife of: receives peerage and pension, 9. 395; said to think him imbecile, 23. 74
Wilkes is deserted by, 38. 255
—— quarrels with, in print, 23. 163
Williams's witticism on resignation of, 19. 27
Wilton does bust of, 20. 397n
Winchilsea will not act with, 21. 99
Winnington answers charges of, against Carteret, 18. 351
——'s witticisms: on resignation of, 19. 27; on turncoat politics of, 18. 540
witticisms by: on Boscawen's burning the French fleet, 35. 294; to Bussy, on French prisoners, 38. 112; to malapropism about Indigo Jones, 12. 256
Wolfe and Saunders write to, 21. 336n
Wood reprimanded by, 38. 318
—— to mention to, Mann's request for promotion, 21. 483

Wright, Mrs, does wax figure of, **32**. 98

Yarmouth, Cts of, notices coolness between Bute and, **21**. 13n

—— urged by, to persuade George II to favour Habeas Corpus bill in return for support of Hessian subsidy, **21**. 205n

Yorke, Charles, angry with Newcastle's compliance to, **38**. 285

——'s approval of amendments keeps, from attacking them, **38**. 325

Pitt, Hon. William (1759–1806), prime minister, M.P.:

Abercorn's influence with, **11**. 104n

ability of, recognized by himself, **12**. 258

abolition of slave trade favoured by, **11**. 252

administration of: bets on George III's recovery, **34**. 46; defeated in Commons over Fox's motion, **33**. 432–3; despicable save for a few, **36**. 222; Fox, C. J., prevents, from speaking, **25**. 467n; George III's allegiance from, may get Parliament dissolved, **36**. 219; Russian war may overthrow, **34**. 109n; (?) Wycombe not to be feared by, **39**. 509

aunt shocked at illness and travel plans of, **31**. 189n

Austrian victories confirmed by, **12**. 177

Batt's friendship with, **11**. 17n

behaviour of, in House of Commons, praised, **25**. 437

Boswell sketches, **33**. 462n

brother of, **11**. 161n

Burke's motion for papers on India opposed by, **25**. 630n

burnt in effigy, **25**. 604

(?) Carmarthen's dinner attended by, **33**. 554n

chancellor of the Exchequer, **29**. 329n

Charlotte, Q., indifferent between Fox and, **11**. 227n

—— protects, **25**. 680, 683

Conway answered by, **25**. 467n

defects of, not seen by him, **12**. 258

Dundas attacked by, in Parliament, **35**. 620–1

Eden deserts Fox and North for, **33**. 513n

eloquence of, resembles his father's, **29**. 116

English-French commercial treaty initiated by, **36**. 248n

English indifference will permit, to do anything he chooses, **39**. 432

Exchequer or secretaryship of state may be taken by, **35**. 518

father attended by, **24**. 371

father compared with, **25**. 407, 449, 452, 487

——'s oratory almost equalled by, **29**. 116, **39**. 380

Fitzwilliam's misunderstanding with, **12**. 120n

foreign ministers declare C. J. Fox as superior to, **25**. 486

fortification plan of, adopted to please D. of Richmond, but defeated, **25**. 629–30

Fox, C. J., compared with, **25**. 407, 452, 487

—— debates with, over making P. of Wales regent, **42**. 232n

—— disliked by, **11**. 324

—— loved and courted, **25**. 452

—— reported to be succeeded by, as secretary of state at age of 22, **25**. 295

——'s attacks no longer answered by, in House of Commons, **36**. 222

——'s opposition makes success of, remarkable, **25**. 407

—— surpasses, **35**. 621

—— will clash with, in House of Commons, **35**. 519

—— wrests majority from, in House of Commons, **36**. 223–4

France will be enabled by, to avenge defeats from his father, **36**. 223

Frederick William II said to be bribed by, **12**. 86n

George III abuses, while raving, **25**. 685

—— alienated by, from sons, **25**. 680

—— and Parliament dominated by, **39**. 431–2

George III appoints, first lord of Treasury, **29**. 320n

—— averse to, before insanity, **25**. 680–1

—— sees, **25**. 679n

——'s message on state of Europe to be delivered by, **11**. 226

——'s offer of prime ministry said to be rejected by, **25**. 377, 379

——'s support to William V of Orange endangers French negotiations with, **39**. 450n

—— supports, against majority in House of Commons, **25**. 471n

——'s views served by ambitions of, **36**. 223

George IV and D. of York averse to, **25**. 683

George IV omits, from ball, **25**. 476n

Gordon, Ds of, receives retort from, **34**. 216

Gordon, Lady Charlotte, fails to marry, despite mother's intention, **34**. 216

government to be assumed by, **25**. 683

Grattan opposes Irish plan of, **25**. 589

(?) Grenville family resembled by, **39**. 76

HW as 'immaculate' as, **36**. 223

HW calls: 'our young Cicero,' **25**. 278; 'tool of the Crown,' **29**. 351

HW cites, to show that eloquence has not degenerated, **25**. 212

HW criticizes ministry of, **36**. 214–15

HW more interested in father of, than in the son, **25**. 487

HW's 'morsels of criticism' mention, **31**. 281

HW's poor opinion of, **25**. 566

HW's satiric verses on, **12**. 259

half ripe before others blossom, **39**. 407

Hardinge disappointed by, **35**. 621

Hastings condemned by, **33**. 560n, 561

—— opposed by, **25**. 653

Hawkesbury said to be at odds with, **25**. 683

House of Commons defied by, **29**. 333, 349

—— wounded by, in way which may be fatal to the Constitution, **25**. 484

[Pitt, Hon. William (1759–1806), *continued*]
India Bill not opposed by, despite boast, **25.** 451
indiscreet, **25.** 683
influence of, on House of Lords, **11.** 269–70
Ireland promised equal trade by, **25.** 564–5
Irish courtiers fly in the face of, **25.** 681
Irish propositions of: Grattan opposes, **25.** 589; loss of, affects him, **12.** 259; will be passed by House of Commons, **25.** 578
Jenkinson joined by, **29.** 322
loan to Francis II sponsored by, **12.** 214
London mob besets, in Downing St, **39.** 431n
malt tax dispute embarrasses, **39.** 482
Mann's opinion of, **25.** 405
Mann, Horace II, gets no answer from letters to, **25.** 678
—— pleased by rejection of Parliamentary reform motion of, **25.** 405
Mason hints, should resign, **29.** 267
——'s ode to, **29.** 247–8, 329n
may become first lord of the Treasury, **25.** 460
member of committee to restore freedom of Parliament, **2.** 208n
modesty of, **39.** 381
More, Hannah, makes pun on, **31.** 213
mother puts, under uncles' protection, **23.** 74
new, to expel Potemkin from Bulgaria, **11.** 230
new party may be formed by, **25.** 380
North demolished by, in Parliamentary debate on accounts, **39.** 380
Opposition members 'purchased' by, **25.** 623n
oratory of, extempore, **33.** 543
Ossory, Lady, admires, **34.** 47
Parliamentary bills by: for reform of public offices, **33.** 407n; for regulating commerce with Ireland, **33.** 491n
Parliamentary motion by, for resolution for consideration of slave trade, **31.** 269n
Parliamentary reform motion of: defeated, **25.** 401–2, 405; to be moved, **25.** 399
Parliamentary reform supported but later opposed by, **29.** 328–9n, 333, 349
Parliament controlled by, **12.** 256n
popularity of: French trade negotiations may reduce, **39.** 439–40; lost, **39.** 431
position of, conspicuous, **25.** 314
Powys alienated by rejection by, of reconciliation attempt, **25.** 475n
—— tries to reconcile Portland and, **25.** 476n
'premature boy,' **36.** 222
prime minister, **29.** 330n, 357
prime minister's office offered to, **36.** 208
prime ministry rumoured for, **33.** 390
resignation of, talked of, **34.** 433
Rolliad aimed at, **15.** 202n
rumour of place for, **29.** 262
Russian war to be avoided by, **11.** 242
Rutland advises, to confer marquisate on Shelburne, **25.** 554n

——'s letter from, about Irish trade equality, **25.** 564n
satiric print of adherents of, includes Mason, **29.** 330n
second son of a second son, **25.** 487n
secretaryship of state rumoured for, **29.** 262
Selwyn's witticism on, **33.** 393, **36.** 209
Shelburne may be wanted by, in administration, **25.** 553n
shines in Parliament though ill supported, **25.** 407
Strafford imitated by, **36.** 221
Temple, E., is expected to be secretary of state with, **25.** 295
thanked for his proposals, **29.** 313n
Versailles cabinet upholds, **25.** 485
Westcote to go over to side of, **33.** 587
Westminster candidacy declined by, **25.** 284n
Westminster nominates, for Parliament, **25.** 278
Wilberforce supported by, against slavery, **31.** 296n
would not be timid opponent of C. J. Fox and North, **29.** 314n
Wraxall's *Short Review* favours, **35.** 558n
youths attached to, **25.** 380
Pitt, Lt-Col. Sir William Augustus (ca 1728–1809), K.B.; M.P.; army officer:
at camp at Cox Heath, **25.** 320
(?) Montagu, Charles, friend of, **9.** 314
taken prisoner, **9.** 314
wife of, **9.** 264n, **21.** 245, **25.** 320
Pitt, Mrs William Augustus. *See* Howe, Mary
Pitt, India ship:
news of East Indies brought by, **21.** 378n
Pitt Diamond. *See under* Pitt, Thomas (1653–1726)
Pitt family:
army increase opposed by, in Parliament, **17.** 410
Egmont's *Faction Detected* never forgotten by, **20.** 31
Pitt's death during Parliament's session lucky for, **24.** 388
Secret Committee not attended by, **17.** 366
Walpole, Sir Robert, derided by, for preserving peace, **37.** 200
Pitti, Cavaliere:
Del Vernaccia, Mme, attended by, **18.** 112
Rinaldi's duel with, prevented, **17.** 111–12
sale of effects of, **17.** 53
Pitti, Nerozzo, Capt. in Tuscan army:
Franchini tells lies about, **21.** 510–11
Pitti, Palazzo, at Florence:
apartment and guardhouse added to, **22.** 258, 290–1
approaches to, levelled, **22.** 124
architect alters additions to, **22.** 291
Boboli amphitheatre faces back of, **25.** 586
Boboli Gardens at, **11.** 168n
Botta changes pictures and furniture in, **22.** 206

—— furnishes apartment in, for Leopold, **22**. 157

—— lowers place before, after first raising it, **22**. 290

—— plans guardhouses for, **22**. 124

—— prepares, for Leopold, **22**. 123

—— rearranges pictures in, according to gilding of frames, **22**. 246, 291

——'s discourse about his alterations at, **22**. 178–9

Calvin's and Luther's portraits expelled from, **22**. 179, 246, 291

casino at, **22**. 258, 290–1

Charles III shoots at tapestry in, **23**. 237–8

church to be added to, **22**. 258

Cocchi and Mann visit, to see *cenacolo*, **20**. 489

corridor from, to Palazzo Vecchio, **18**. 391

Cosimo III's travels said to be preserved in, **25**. 97

dinner served in great hall in, **22**. 367

English houses cost more than, **24**. 93

Fox, Henry, permitted to visit most sacred parts of, in sedan chair, **22**. 528

Francis I has not as yet stripped, **19**. 82–3

Francis III covets furniture of, **18**. 323

Giovanni Gastone's oratory in, **20**. 489

gold damask hangings in, **22**. 178n

gold taken from furnishings in, made into plate for Leopold, **25**. 231

Grande Maîtresse's apartment in, drawing-rooms held at, **22**. 368

guards at, doubled, **17**. 238

(?) HW has seen Craon receive homage at, for Francis I, **22**. 427

hailstorm damages, **22**. 77

heating arrangements at, **22**. 291

kitchenware from, sold, **17**. 53

Leopold's aversion to, **23**. 253

—— transfers paintings from, to the Uffizi, **25**. 531n

Mann escorts Karl Alexander to, **22**. 376

—— must not apologize for writing so much about alterations in, **22**. 303

—— performs New Year's ceremonies at, **24**. 346

Maria Amelia prefers stables to, **25**. 301

Modena, Ds of, shows, to daughter, **17**. 237–38

new chapel in, Maria's Louisa's churching in, **22**. 487n

pictures in, rearranged by Botta, **22**. 178–9, 246, 291

Pietro da Cortona's ceiling at, cleaned, **21**. 556

Pitt, Thomas, names his house after, **22**. 33

posterity will be indifferent to revolutions at, **22**. 303

refurnished for Leopold, **21**. 556–7

Richecourt fears that the Spaniards may rob, **19**. 295

Rubens's heads at, **25**. 646n

stoves installed in, **22**. 576

Strange copies paintings in, **21**. 448n

Te Deum in chapel of, **22**. 532n

Titian painting banished from state apartment in, **22**. 179

treasures of, not removed, **17**. 380

Walpole, Bns, takes Franceschi's house near, **18**. 391

Walpole, Sir Robert, would enjoy, **18**. 212

Zoffany had right to take down any painting in, **24**. 540

Pitti Gaddi. *See also* Gaddi, Gaspero

Pitti Gaddi family:

collection of: Mann sends catalogues of, to England, **24**. 80; to be sold, **24**. 80

Leopold buys bust and pictures of, **25**. 170

Pitti Palace. *See* Pitti, Palazzo

Pitts, Miss, m. (1770) Sir Robert Goodere, Kt, 1762:

HW's civility to, **11**. 124

SH visited by, **12**. 227

Twickenham resident, **42**. 480

Pitts, Thomas:

Caroline's page of the back stairs, **17**. 146n

Pitts. *See also* Pits

'Pitts, the':

'Mis-sow' visits, at (?) Richmond, **31**. 287

Pitt's Buildings, Kensington (mad-house):

Brown and Sir Charles Hanbury Williams inmates of, **9**. 219

Clark, Mrs, keeps, **9**. 219, **21**. 183n

Pittsburgh, Pennsylvania:

Washington surrenders fort on present site of, to French, **20**. 449n

'Pittsburgh':

HW's name for Anne Pitt's house, **24**. 15

Pitture antiche di Ercolano:

Albani might procure, for HW, **21**. 262

await shipment at Leghorn, **21**. 318–19

Charles III does not distribute, generously, **21**. 142

—— hedges publication of, with precaution, **22**. 457

—— restricts new volume of, that recipients may not sell their copies, **22**. 35

edition of, at a stand, **35**. 419

expected at Leghorn from Naples, **22**. 533

HW has only first volume and catalogue of, **22**. 452

HW receives, **21**. 363, **22**. 568

HW sees copy of, **21**. 291

HW thanks Mann for procuring, **21**. 278, 327

HW wants, **21**. 131, 262, 363, **22**. 25, 422, 452

HW would exchange SH imprints for, **21**. 131, 262

Hamilton might be jealous of Mann over, **22**. 547

Mann hopes, is on way to England, **22**. 533

—— obtains, for HW, **22**. 457

——'s efforts to find, for HW, **21**. 142, 272, **22**. 35, 547

—— sends bills of lading for, **21**. 324, **22**. 547, 557, 559, 561, 562, **23**. 109, *559*

[*Pitture antiche di Ercolano*, continued]
—— should have bought, from Viviani instead of waiting for Sir James Gray, 21. 299
prints in, flatter the originals, 21. 379
published by Reale Accademia Ercolanese di Archeologia, 14. 123n
remaining volumes of, said to have gone to Leghorn, 22. 477
unlikely to be completed after Charles III's departure for Spain, 21. 363

Pius V (Antonio, *later* Michele Ghislieri) (1504–72); pope 1566–72; saint:
Cosimo I said to have been forced by, to wed Camilla Martelli, 24. 16
Elizabeth, Q., excommunicated by, 22. 177n

Pius VI (Giovanni Angelo Braschi) (1717–99), pope 1775–99:
Albany, Cts of, invited by, to convent at Rome, 25. 106
Alfieri imposes upon, 25. 397
antidotes said to be taken by, against poison, 24. 467
Avignon men hanged for refusing to disavow, 11. 84
Belgioioso's expulsion from Flanders probably aided by, 39. 456
blessings distributed by, 25. 283
Bologna's dispute with, 25. 85
bulls of, have blunted horns, 25. 85
burnt in effigy at Paris, 11. 270
Butta su used by, for *couvre salope*, 24. 107
Canadian adherents of, joined American colonists, 24. 161
cardinals' hats sold by, 25. 568
cardinals' promotion postponed by, to save money for his family, 25. 568
cardinals to be created by, in bedchamber, 24. 470
cardinals to be made by, 24. 479
Catherine II asks, to reestablish Jesuits in Russia, 25. 389
—— persuades, to let Jesuits have novices, 16. 191
——'s correspondence with, about Jesuits, 25. 390n
ceremony for, of taking possession, 24. 131, 136, 145
Cesena, Bp of, ordered by, to reward girls, 24. 107
Charles III may be persuaded by, to admit Jesuits, 24. 106
clergy regulated by edicts of, 24. 107
consistory appointed by, to consider Joseph II's reply to request to visit him, 25. 239
Cowper might get cardinal's hat from, 25. 572
—— should ask, for bishopric for one of his sons, 25. 606
crowned as pope, 43. 285
despised at Rome, 25. 383
education of, not so polite as his predecessor's, 24. 275
election of, 32. 209
emissary of, in London, 12. 77

England may get another Augustine from, 33. 209
Falconieri, Ps, appointed by, to wait on Ds of Gloucester, 24. 164
family of, might be provided for by wealth from suppressed convents, 25. 594
Florentine carnival's non-suppression does not compliment, 25. 243
French not spoken by, 24. 275
French seize property of, 34. 120, 157
(?) Friedrich II of Hesse visits, by back stairs, 24. 275
Gloucester, D. and Ds of, courteously treated by, 24. 174, 190
Gloucester, D. of, pleases, by giving surgical instruments to hospital at Rome, 24. 129
Gordon, Lord George, would be sent to devil by, 25. 131
Gordon rioters plunder more Protestants than followers of, 25. 61
grandmother of, consumed by internal fire, 24. 467
HW calls: 'Madam of Babylon,' 24. 162; 'Pontifex Maximus,' 25. 589; 'your holy neighbour,' 25. 544
HW expects Mann to tell him of lamentations of, 25. 243
HW inquires about return of, to Italy after visiting Joseph II, 25. 275
HW mentions, 25. 272
HW prefers, to Joseph II, 25. 596
HW wonders whether, will be most afraid of France, Spain, or poison, 24. 86
health of: better, 24. 470; illness concealed at Rome, 24. 467; illness considered serious, 24. 461; much better, 24. 479; rheumatism, 24. 467; very ill, 24. 467
Hervey, Bp, urges, to put Irish bishops on footing with Gallican church, 24. 430
indifference of, to earthquake, 25. 383, 391
Jesuits at Castel St Angelo might have been released by, had not Charles III intervened, 24. 115
—— released by, 24. 99
Joseph II consents to receive, but visit will be futile, 25. 245
—— humbles, 25. 400
—— said to wall up doors at time of visit of, 25. 275
——'s attack on Holland instead of attacking church property probably pleases, 25. 544
——'s letter to, 33. 390
——'s suppression of convents provokes, to cancel Carnival, 2. 306
jubilee extended by, 6. 284n
Kingston, Ds of, can get her treasure from, only when her authorization is proved not to be a forced one, 24. 234
—— cannot be cleansed by, with all the holy water in the Tiber, 24. 126
—— entrusted, with her treasure, 24. 123
—— friend of, 24. 175

—— gets promise from, never to give up her treasure without well-authenticated order, **24**. 167

—— may find her valuables appropriated by, **24**. 162

—— may fly to, for dispensation, **24**. 123

—— may prove an embarrassment to, by leaving treasure in his custody, **24**. 167

—— may revisit Rome under protection of, **24**. 123

—— said to have bequeathed jewels to, **35**. 397

—— told by, that her jewels and furniture will be kept for her at Rome, **24**. 83–4

—— will shock, by her trial, **24**. 149

leave asked by, of Joseph II, to pay him visit in Vienna, **25**. 238–9

legate sent by, to appease tumult in Rome, **12**. 77

Leopold does not compliment, with suppression of carnival, **25**. 243

Lepri gives wealth to, **25**. 384–5

——'s donation to, declared invalid, **25**. 587, 589

Macartney visits, **12**. 191

Mann gets weekly bulletin of illness of, **24**. 461, 467

—— informs, of Rodney's victory, **25**. 24

—— might have to demand Ds of Kingston's treasures from, **24**. 191

Marie-Antoinette's daughter's birth disappoints, **24**. 470

meat will be less permitted by, if Necker roots out the monks, **25**. 21

Messina earthquake attributed by, to suppression of Inquisition in Sicily, **25**. 383

nephew of, in France, might receive rich benefice on Dauphin's birth, **24**. 470

Orford, Cts of, carried in litter of, **24**. 317

Pitt, Anne, might be made 'Ps Fossani' by, **24**. 360

pompous, simple, and at heart a Jesuit, **24**. 106

Pontine marsh drainage project of, **24**. 343, 379, **25**. 383

priests' costume regulated by, forbidding powdered hair, **24**. 107

protector for, **33**. 245

Rohan's censure by, imprudent, **25**. 658

Roman Catholics permitted by, to eat meat in Lent because of fish shortage, **25**. 17, 24

Roman governor's proposal to close theatres and stop carnival rejected by, **25**. 383

Rome crowded with strangers to see ceremony of *possesso* of, **24**. 145

Russian minister asks, to reestablish Jesuits in Russia, **25**. 389–90

St Peter's might be sent to London by, for safe-keeping from French atheists, **12**. 56

—— to be provided with new sacristy built by, **24**. 343, **25**. 383–4

Scottish Presbyterians forswear, tooth and nail, **24**. 475

Sforza Cesarini will dispute Lepri inheritance with, **25**. 385

simple man, **24**. 115

Stuart, Charlotte, receives congratulatory answer from, **25**. 550

suppression of Galluzzi's history might have been demanded by, as price for making Maximilian, Bp of Münster, **25**. 80

uncle ordered by, to reward pretty and virtuous girls, **24**. 107

unpopularity of, **25**. 587–8

Venetians threatened by, with interdiction, **24**. 189

Vienna to be visited by, **25**. 250

Vienna visit of: a farce to balance tragic wars, **25**. 283; disapproved by cardinals, **25**. 250; does not interrupt Joseph II's suppression of convents, **25**. 283; expensive, humiliating, and useless, **25**. 384

York, Cardinal, persuades, to banish Alfieri, **25**. 397

—— will not be permitted by, to assume crown, **25**. 526

Young Pretender given allowance by, but not recognized as king, **24**. 244

—— never permitted by, to assume crown, **25**. 526

——'s pension from, partly granted to Cts of Albany, **25**. 107

—— though denied royal rank, is allowed by, to make his daughter a duchess, **25**. 552–3

Zelanti member, **24**. 86n

Pizarro, Francisco (1475–1541), explorer:

HW compares Sandwich with, **10**. 202

Pizzaná. *See* Pezzana

Pizzighettone (Italy):

Lobkowitz to garrison, **18**. 513

Maria Theresa gives, to Charles Emmanuel III, **17**. 379

Pizzo (Italy):

earthquake account mentions, **25**. 376

Pizzoni, ——, Venetian Resident in London:

Almodóvar quarrels with, **24**. 413n

Place, Barbara, m. Rev. William Middleton:

Conyers Middleton's mother, **15**. 308n

Place, Rev. Conyers (ca 1665–1738):

'High Church parson', **15**. 292

Remarks on a Treatise (by Hoadly), by, **15**. 292

Place, Mary (ca 1707–45), m. (ca 1734) Rev. Conyers Middleton:

Cole's unflattering account of, **15**. 308

death of, **15**. 293, 308, 309

HW sends compliments to, **15**. 7, 9, 11, 21, 24

Middleton marries, **15**. 292

Place. *See also* La Place

Place Bill. *See under* Parliament: acts of

Place de la Concorde. *See* Louis XV, Place de

Place de la Guillotine, Paris:

French may amass looted art in, **34**. 217

Place de Louis le Grand, Paris:

HW sees burial in, **13**. 163

Place de Louis XV, Paris. *See* Louis XV, Place de

Place d'Espagne, Naples:
Pontano lives in, **18.** 56

Place des Victoires. *See* Victoires, Place des

Place House, Titchfield, Hants, Ds of Portland's seat:
Southampton family portraits brought from, to Bulstrode Park, **10.** 102

Placentia, Italy. *See* Piacenza

Placentius, Johannes Leo (ca 1500–ca 1550), versifier:
Pugna Porcorum per P. Porcium Poetam, quoted by Gray, **14.** 27

Place Royale, Paris:
Carnavalet, Hôtel de, in, **39.** 201

Place Tax. *See under* Tax

Place Vendôme. *See* Vendôme, Place

Plague; plagues:
at Constantinople, **11.** 302
at Cyprus, Toulon, and Marseille, **18.** 271n
at Danzig, **25.** 422
at Messina, **18.** 252, 256, 261–2, 269–70, 274
at Reggio, **18.** 282, 288, 301–2
at Smyrna, **26.** 48
Boccaccio's *Decameron* written during, **33.** 410
Egyptian, **25.** 582
England threatened with, **33.** 409, 412–13
English naval captains seize vessels, regardless of fear of, **18.** 256
Florentines guard against, **18.** 252, 288
French ship brings, to Leghorn, **17.** 105, **23.** 24
HW hears, is spreading, **18.** 294
HW wants to hear about, **18.** 284
in Asia and Russia, **18.** 271n
in Bengal, **23.** 282
in Calabria, **18.** 270, 282–3, 288
in Hungary, **18.** 122
in Sicily, **18.** 283
Italian, HW does not like, **21.** 369
Laura dies of, **40.** 377
Leghorn alarmed by arrival of, in ship from Algiers, **17.** 105
—— repels ship because of, **18.** 262
London merchants object to precautions about, **18.** 282
Mathews may bring, **18.** 279
Messa has return of, **18.** 282n
Neapolitan Court may flee from to Aquila, **18.** 302
Neapolitans hoard provisions against, **18.** 288
—— mass troops on borders, under pretence of guarding against, **18.** 295–6
Orlov fears, on Chios, **23.** 233
quarantine 40 days for, **18.** 275
Rome quarantines against, **18.** 263n
Rosso and Moncada request aid for victims of, **18.** 262n
rumour of, in London: **21.** 427; attracts sight-seers, **13.** 203
1711 not a year for, **11.** 106

Tiber closed to ships to prevent, **18.** 252n
Tuscan precautions against, **18.** 270, 285
Tuscan quarantines against, futile, **18.** 295
Tuscany mobilizes under pretence of guarding against, **18.** 285
vinegar used, to prevent, **18.** 270

Plaid:
offensive to England, **19.** 471
Queensberry, D. of, dressed in, **19.** 471
Scotch, nightcap of, **19.** 302
suppression of, in Scotland, **26.** 32
waistcoat of, worn by Frederick, P. of Wales, **20.** 131
Young Pretender's, **19.** 320n

Plaideurs, Les. See under Racine, Jean

Plain Dealer, The. See under Wycherley, William

Plaine de Sablon, Paris:
horse races in, **1.** 110, **39.** 270

Plainsong:
(?) charade on, **39.** 545

Plaisance. *See* Piacenza

Plaisanteri, the (Italy):
Alberoni's lands in, seized by Traun, **18.** 199

Plaistow, Kent:
Thellusson of, **12.** 176n

'Planetæ sunt habitabiles.' *See under* Bryant, Jacob

Planning for the future:
HW's reflections on folly of, **10.** 290

Plan of a Supplement to Dr Middleton's Free Inquiry:
pamphlet in the 'miracles' controversy, **15.** 298

Plan of the French Constitution:
HW may have seen, **31.** 385n

Plans, Elevations, and Sections . . . of Houghton. See under Ware, Isaac

Plant; plants:
HW to send, to Montagu, **9.** 177–9
Mann sends, to Bubb Dodington, **20.** 253
Montagu receives from HW, **9.** 180
Moone's collection of, rare, **32.** 135n
sensibility of, discussed by 'amiable but romantic' philosophers, **31.** 295
See also under Flower; Shrub; Tree; Vegetable; Vine, *and under names of individual plants*

Planta, Joseph (1744–1827), keeper of MSS and medals at the British Museum:
Pinkerton wants to succeed the successor of, **42.** 212
Thorkelin would succeed, at British Museum, **16.** 295
Thurlow refuses permission to, to go abroad, **16.** 294–5

Planta, (?) Margaret:
HW asks, to give 'Des. of SH' to Ps Elizabeth for him, **42.** 445–6
HW's correspondence with, **42.** 445–6, **43.** 390

Plantagenet, Edward (1475–99), 2d E. of Warwick, n.c.:
in Tower of London, **2.** 364

(?) Rous's roll done for, **35**. 607

Other members of the royal dynasty of Plantagenet are to be found under their first names

Plantagenet family:
Geoffrey a name in, **35**. 9
Hardinge interested in, from wife's ancestry, **35**. 611
Huntingdon and Ds of Beaufort represent, in Florence, **23**. 406
Moira, Lord, descended from, **12**. 156
scene of, reenacted, **22**. 303
Warbeck may really belong to, **41**. 126

Plantations:
Board of Trade to control, **20**. 259

Planting:
growth of, coincides with planters' decay, **37**. 303

Plas Gwyn, Anglesey, North Wales:
Panton writes from, **41**. 160

Plas Teg, Flintshire:
Trevor family of, **9**. 191n, **10**. 352

Plaster (of Paris):
and gold, ancestral statue covered with, **35**. 267
busts of, **34**. 184, 258
for artificial stone, **41**. 228, 229
HW prefers Morpheus statue in, **18**. 561
statues of, at Kedleston, **10**. 230
Zoffany depicts statues in Tribune as if they were casts in, **24**. 527

Plaster, cosmetic:
Benedetta, Ps, wears, **33**. 531

Plaster; plasters (medicinal):
applications of, **21**. 78
broken heads may create demand for, **33**. 108
for gout, **32**. 267
quack, supposedly a cancer cure, **20**. 291
use of, **37**. 78, 81

Plasterer; plasterers:
Conway's, does nothing but tombstone face, **37**. 345
HW hurries, at SH, **20**. 371

Plat (*or* Platt), Sir Hugh (1552–1608), Kt; inventor and writer:
Garden of Eden, The, by, recommended by HW to Mason, **28**. 275
HW's bibliography of, **43**. 300

Plata, La. *See* La Plata

Plate (metal services for ecclesiastical and dinner-table use):
Botta prepares, for Leopold, **22**. 123
carried abroad by Cts of Orford, **25**. 158
cases of, (?) Cowper to send, to banker at Florence, **25**. 661
chest of, brought to Young Pretender from Rome, by his staff, **18**. 433–4
church, in Florence: may be sacrificed to import food, **22**. 447, 448; sent to mint without Clement XIII's permission, **22**. 475–6
college and church, considered sacred by churchmen, **35**. 497

Cowper to have, fetched from England to Florence, **23**. 449
Craon may pawn, **18**. 134
Craon, Princesse de, sends, by sea to Leghorn, **22**. 536
diplomatists', **17**. 135n
diplomatists' allowance for, **18**. 472n
Elizabeth, Q., has, inventoried, **32**. 323–4
embossed, for Vyne chapel, **35**. 640
Fairfax, Brian, has list of, **42**. 354
Fane's, **17**. 135, **18**. 472
Fermor lacks, **19**. 148
Florentine, may have to be carried to mint, **17**. 239
Franceschi's, sold, **17**. 122
Frederick II gives, to Hyndford, **18**. 89, 107
George III gives: to godchildren, **24**. 206; to Mrs Delany, **33**. 497
gilt, sent by Spain to Del Campo for ball for Q. Charlotte, **39**. 465n
gold: for Leopold's household, made from furnishings at Palazzo Vecchio, **25**. 231; Newcastle carries his, to Hanover, **19**. 485n
Gothic, architectural, of Mercers' Co., **16**. 84
HW's, at Arlington St, untouched by housebreakers, **23**. 285
Jesuits', seized, **23**. 506
Lepri gives, to Pius VI, **25**. 384
Mann buys, **22**. 357
—— lacks, for 16, **20**. 387
—— pawns, for Theodore of Corsica, **20**. 378–9
——'s, to be sold by nephew to settle estate, **25**. 678
—— to buy, **18**. 472
Molesworths' servant steals, **22**. 140n
Montagu wishes, from Paris, **10**. 98
Old Pretender's, **22**. 385
Orford, Cts of, had: list of, sent to England by Mozzi, **25**. 163; Orford's claims for, on mother, **25**. 158, 169; Orford, Cts of, exchanged, in England for small set taken to Italy, **25**. 144
Pelham's, sold, **35**. 220–1
pewter, sugar-dish of, used to serve water at Wellingborough inn, **10**. 89
Rinuccini leaves piece of, to daughter-in-law, **19**. 461
Rosenberg's, not sold for debts, **23**. 294
set of, Du Quesne has, on shipboard, **21**. 255
Seymour, Lady Frances, buys, **20**. 183
sideboard of, belonging to Pesters, **37**. 465n
silver: Montagu wishes, from Paris, **10**. 286, 295, 300; Secker receives, from Hardwicke, **30**. 304n; *see also under* Silver
silver-gilt: of Charles V and François I meeting, given to HW by Hamilton, **35**. 423n; (?) travelling, Tencin gives, to Young Pretender, **17**. 114
Stuart Mackenzie gets, for Spanish embassy, **21**. 508
tax on, **21**. 199n, **37**. 445, 451

[Plate, *continued*]
Tylney's, at Naples, to be sold for servants' benefit, **25.** 534
Wade stores, at Antwerp, **37.** 154
Williams, Sir Charles Hanbury, has, **18.** 472n
wrought, tax on, proposed, **21.** 199n
Young Pretender receives, **25.** 525
Plate; plates, china:
attributed to Rubens, **2.** 152–3, 155–8
of Chelsea china, **22.** 121–2
striped, at Northumberland House dinner, **38.** 530
Plate; plates, engravers':
copper, for Hancarville's book, **23.** 448–9
cost of, **1.** 160
Plate; plates, glass:
Athenry, Lady, has, of Bohemian glass, **37.** 442
HW has, for dessert, of Venetian glass, **17.** 73n
Plate-covers. *See* Dish-covers
Platel ('Platell'), Rev. Peter (d. ?1769):
(?) comical, **10.** 330, 331
(?) Scotts often visited by, **10.** 330, 331
Platen, ——, Prussian Lt-Gen.:
Austrians check, **24.** 411n
Platen, Mme de (living 1690), mistress of Elector Ernst August:
Königsmarck loved and betrayed by, **7.** 278
Platen und Hallermand, Sophia Charlotte, Gräfin von (ca 1673–1725), m. Johann Adolph, Bn von Kielmensegge; she was cr. (1772) Cts of Darlington:
daughter of, marries Vct Howe, **10.** 10n
Plato (?427–?347 B.C.), philosopher:
Aristophanes' censure by, would be ridiculous, **41.** 55
cannot end conjectures for Cato, **33.** 129
Cole does not 'dissert' on divinity of, **2.** 104
Conway does not read, **37.** 576
Fordyce cites, **39.** 157
HW cannot find parallel to C. J. Fox in, **39.** 157
HW does not call, 'a Quixote,' **30.** 176
Herbert of Chirbury's philosophy as austere as that of, **30.** 176
majesty of, missed by Shaftesbury, **41.** 374
Taylor's translation of Proclus on, **34.** 83
'unintelligible,' **34.** 83
West alludes to, **13.** 172
'Plato' (unidentified Etonian):
health of, improves, **13.** 68, 94
West has supper with, **13.** 173
—— inquires about, **13.** 92
'Plato, Bishop.' *See* Markham, William
'Platon, Father.' *See* Levshin, Petr Georgievich
Platonic Wife, The. See under Griffith, Elizabeth
Platt, Sir John:
Westbrook built by, **16.** 196n
Platter; platters:
HW sends, to Mme du Deffand, **5.** 172

Platz, ——, Gen.:
Artimiso attacked by, **18.** 488
Leutrum joined by, **19.** 227
Plautus, Titus Maccius (ca 250–184 B.C.), dramatist:
Amphitryon, (?) paraphrased by Mann, **17.** 120
Colman translates, **41.** 401n
Comédies, owned by Mme du Deffand, **8.** 33
Plaw, Priscilla:
lines on, **32.** 247, 251
Play; plays:
Conway borrows, from HW, **37.** 189
ephemeral, successful at Paris, **41.** 156
fashionable in London, **19.** 342
fashionable people act, in England, **24.** 86
more dignified than politics, **21.** 542
no new, at Paris, **39.** 144
numerous in London, **19.** 464, **39.** 322
officers give, for Friedrich Wilhelm, **19.** 265
opera prices made equal to those of, in London, **20.** 410
politics less dignified than, **21.** 542
Portici, Signora, considers, inferior to burlettas, **20.** 357
strolling companies act, in barns, **24.** 371
Suares family give, for Modenese princess, **17.** 65, 99, 100, 104
unfashionable in London, **18.** 119
Walpole, Sir Edward, might take granddaughters to, **36.** 325
Seee also under Comedy; Theatre; Tragedy
Player; players. *See* Actor
Playfair, John (1748–1819), mathematician and geologist:
SH visited by, **12.** 244
Playford, J.:
print of, **40.** 236
Playhouse; playhouses. *See* Theatre
Pleasure:
English make a business of, **25.** 110
Londoners in pursuit of, ignore want of money and weight of taxes, **25.** 243
Pleasures of the Imagination, The. See under Akenside, Mark
Pléiade, the, French ship:
English ships pursue, **21.** 303
escape of, **21.** 188
Plélo, Comte de. *See* Bréhant, Louis-Robert-Hippolyte de
Pleneuf, Mme Jean-Étienne Berthelot de. *See* Rioult de Douilly, Agnès
Plenipotentiary (diplomatic rank):
Hamilton becomes, **23.** 293
Mann wants to become, **23.** 293
Stuart Mackenzie becomes, **21.** 471–2
Plessis, Du. *See* Du Plessis
Plessis-Châtillon, Du. *See* Du Plessis-Châtillon
Pleurisy:
claret and port do not induce, in Montagu, **10.** 101
Italians get, in cold spell, **20.** 143

occurrences of, 3. 330, 20. 232, 244, 22. 560, 38. 473

Pleuritic fever; pleuritic inflammatory fever. *See under* Fever

Pleydell, ——, nephew of Maria Skerrett:
Walpole, Sir Robert, leaves legacy to, 19. 32n

Pleydell, Mr and Mrs:
Montagu asks HW for SH ticket for, 10. 215

Pleydell, Mrs, of Twickenham:
SH visited by, 12. 227

Pleydell, John Cleeve (ca 1736–1816), army officer; equerry to D. of Gloucester:
Dick's bequest to, 23. 404
Gloucester, D. of, accompanied by, 24. 311
Udny gets letter from, 24. 311

Pleydell Bouverie, Jacob (1750–1828), 2d E. of Radnor, n.c., 1776:
Barrington questioned by, 24. 196n
Regency proposal by, in House of Lords, 25. 684n

'Pliant Sir Paul.' *See under* Congreve, William: *Double-Dealer*

Plimouth. *See* Plymouth

Pliny the Elder (Caius Plinius Secundus) (A.D. 23 *or* 24–79):
HW reads, on ancient music, 35. 419
Historia naturalis (Natural History) by: 43. 97; cestrum in, 9. 251–2; encaustic painting discussed in, 28. 300; French translation of, stimulates HW's imagination, 28. 159–61; HW amused by, 6. 47, 69; Juba mentioned in, 16. 35
probes nature of earthquakes, 33. 108
Spence's *Polymetis* quotes, 14. 20
Voltaire quotes, forgetting he was killed by a volcano, 35. 414
Xeuxis's painting described by, 30. 324

Pliny the Younger (Caius Plinius Cæcilius Secundus) (?62–ca 113), orator and statesman:
Cork's letters would not have pleased, 28. 89
Damer, Mrs, writes Latin like, 25. 184
English architecture as classic as villas of, 23. 313
Epistles of: HW's epigraph from, 43. 233; translated by Cork, 20. 454n
HW cannot compose letters like, 33. 504
HW's letter to be placed with those of, 40. 173
Hervey's epigram mentions, 15. 3
Letters of: 43. 97; Conway paraphrases, 37. 243; Conway quotes, 37. 59; Cork translates, 20. 454n; Du Deffand, Mme, likes, and compares to HW's, 3. 303, 6. 68, 73; HW dislikes, 6. 69–70, 73
Sharp quotes, 40. 158
Trajan's praise from, mentioned by Hervey, 40. 22
West fears influence of, on SH, 40. 311

Plokof, Jean. *See* Voltaire: *Traduction du poème de Jean Plokof*

Plombières (France):
Richecourt to take baths at, 21. 62
visitors to: Aulan, 7. 53, 219, 235, 454; Aulan, Marquise d', 7. 235, 454; Beauvau, 6. 461, 7. 427; Boufflers, Comtesse Amélie de, 7. 53; Boufflers, Comtesse de, 7. 48, 53; Gramont, Duchesse de, 6. 124, 295, 319, 347, 348

Plomer, ——:
Wilkes's friend, now alderman, 23. 441n

Plomer, Sheriff:
George III asked by, to receive address when on throne, 24. 116n

Plot, Robert (1640–96), natural scientist:
Natural History of Oxfordshire by, Bird's colouring of marble mentioned in, 16. 36
Natural History of Staffordshire by, HW sends picture from, to Fox, 40. 76–7

Plotho, Erich Christoph Edler (1707–88), Herr von; Prussian ambassador to the Empire:
(?) Frederick II's *Pro-Memoria* delivered by, to Diet at Ratisbon, 21. 102n

Plough; ploughs:
army will not leave Conway at, 37. 437
Conway wants to forsake Ireland for, 37. 450
for sugar cultivation, 31. 328
HW wishes Conway had returned to, 39. 178–9
HW wishes he understood, 31. 331
Sabbath abstention from, 31. 365

Ploughman; ploughmen:
Gray's references to, 35. 399–400
HW praises simplicity of, 10. 184

Plough Monday:
Cole dates Jan. 11 as, 2. 137
procession of, described by Gray, 13. 73–4

Ploughshares:
Montagu does not convert, into falchions, 10. 274

Plovers' eggs:
(?) Ailesbury, Cts of, thanks HW and E. of Orford for, 37. 484, 485, 489
HW receives, from E. of Orford, 25. 143
to be set, 37. 489

Plowden, Francis:
James II's comptroller of the Household, 41. 470n
——'s Court at St-Germain includes, 41. 470n

Plowden, Mrs Francis:
Mary of Modena's lady in waiting, 41. 470n

Plowden, Mary (ca 1703–85), m. (1733) Sir George Jerningham, 5th Bt:
(?) Du Deffand, Mme, angry with, 7. 58
HW asked by, for works of Mme Roland, 10. 197
HW to return her son to, 42. 109–10
Hamilton remembered by, at St-Germain, 41. 470
health of: palsy, 36. 210; revived, 42. 147
sees woman in white in tree at SH, 35. 534

Plowman, Capt.:
Tartar commanded by, 25. 480n

'Plucknet, Col., of Cold-Blow Lane':
  Conway's Irish friend, 37. 434
Plum; plums:
  bought at chandler's shop, 35. 521
  cake of, 17. 263
  green, HW to send, to Princesse de Beauvau,
    7. 417
  See also Plum porridge; Plum pudding; Plum
    tree
Plumard de Dangeul, René-Joseph (b. 1722),
    maître des comptes:
  HW accompanied by, to Bois Prévu, 35. 115
  (?) HW sends seal to, 6. 260
  HW takes, in coach to Cts of Hertford, 23. 6
  lives in Rue St-André-des-Arts, 7. 417
  social relations of, in Paris, 7. 291, 293, 298,
    336, 344, 352
Plumbe, ——, alderman of London:
  voting for, 23. 315n
Plumber (surname). See Plomer; Plumer
'Plumbosus.' See Pelham, Henry
Plume; plumes:
  Abington, Mrs, wears, 32. 216
  Alexander wears, in opera, 24. 222
  American, Mann should flaunt, before Riche-
    court, 21. 347
  Chartres, Duchesse de, wears, 24. 222
  Coke, Lady Mary, wears, for Niagara's cap-
    ture, 38. 27
  elderly soldiers wear, 9. 269
  fashionable in head-dresses, 35. 428
  HW mentions, 20. 375
  ladies covered with, in England, 24. 86
  Mann should not be paid with, 22. 226
  of knights of the Bath, 38. 122
  Richelieu's might be imitated by HW, 32. 246
  song about, 6. 379
  vogue of, in England, 6. 139, 148
  See also Ostrich feathers
Plumer (Plummer), Mrs:
  SH visited by, 12. 229, 230
Plumer, Anne (1690–1776), m. (1711) James
    Hamilton, 7th E. of Abercorn:
  auction attended by, 17. 477–8
  Devonshire, Ds of, talks to, of 'ugly women,'
    17. 478
  ugly, 17. 478
Plumer, Richard (ca 1689–1750), M.P.:
  Robinson replaces, as lord of trade, 20. 17n
  Weymouth election influenced for, 17. 421n
Plumer, (?) Walter (?1682–1746), M.P.:
  birth date of, corrected, 43. 252
  witticism by, on Pulteney's Treasury appoint-
    ments, 18. 350
Plumley (alias Williams), Christopher:
  respited, 25. 67n
Plummer. See Plomer; Plumer
Plum porridge:
  out of fashion among people of rank, 25. 124
Plumptre, Dorothea (d. before 1815), m. John
    Ward:
  Cole dines with, 2. 139, 266

Plumptre, John (1679–1751), M.P.:
  named in Secret Committee lists, 17. 384
Plumptre, John (1711–91), M.P.:
  birth date of, corrected, 43. 68
  visited by nephew, 2. 154
Plumptre, Rev. Joseph (1759–1810):
  conveys MS to London for Cole, 2. 154
  dines with Cole, 2. 265
Plumptre, Robert (1723–88), Master of Queen's
    College, Cambridge:
  Hardwicke usually gives his publications to,
    2. 262n, 265
  son of, 2. 154, 265
Plumptre, Dr Russell (1709–93), Regius Pro-
    fessor of Physic at Cambridge:
  daughter of, 2. 139n
  Gray attended by, 1. 298
  ——'s refusal from, when asked for assistance
    at night, 1. 231, 236, 23. 329
  Middleton attended by, 15. 313
  Orford, 3d E. of, attended by, 1. 298, 23.
    46on, 28. 126n, 36. 331
Plumptre, Rev. Septimus (1717–82):
  death of, 2. 304n
Plum pudding:
  ditchers have, once a week, 37. 172
Plum tree; plum trees:
  HW sees, on Amiens-Clermont road, 7. 259
Plunder, John; smuggler:
  outlawed, 9. 105
Plunket, William, journeyman apothecary:
  HW robbed by, 13. 23
  Maclaine's accomplice, 20. 168
'Plunkett, Mr':
  HW calls himself, 30. 76, 77
Plunkett, Mrs James. See Gunning, Elizabeth
    (1769–1823)
Plutarch (A.D. ca 46–ca 120), Greek biographer:
  Conway alludes to Aristides' life by, 37. 95
  —— quotes, 37. 74
  HW paraphrases conversation from life of
    Pyrrhus by, 31. 160–1
  HW quotes from life of Cæsar by, 19. 288n
  Œuvres of, owned by Mme du Deffand, 8. 32
  Pitt will look well in future edition of, 21. 558
Pluto:
  Elysian fields of, 10. 282
  Ethiopian mistaken for, 30. 300
  HW calls: 'Lord Pluto,' 10. 282; 'old Nich-
    olas Pluto,' 11. 22
  HW's name for D. of Cumberland, 32. 130
  HW's verses mention, 31. 120–1
  'iron,' Burke's term for Thurlow, 25. 684
  'iron tears' of, 34. 41
Pluto, English fireship:
  Portsmouth reached by, 30. 112n
Pluto, French ship:
  Hood captures, 29. 250n
Plutus:
  Clive compared to, 23. 381
  more persuasive than Parliamentary orators,
    38. 309

Plymouth, E. of. *See* Windsor, Other Hickman (1751–99); Windsor, Other Lewis (1731–71)

Plymouth, Devon:
Boscawen's fleet sails from, **20.** 480n, 487n
Conway on frigate driven to, by storm, **25.** 115, **29.** 96, **33.** 143, 270, **39.** 361, 366n
Dunmore succeeds Churchill as governor of, **19.** 62
embarkations from, to America, **39.** 197n
English men of war chased into, **24.** 506
English naval strength at, **23.** 40
English prisoners from Oswego and Quebec arrive at, **21.** 18
Feilding brings captured Dutch convoy to, **25.** 3, **29.** 2
fires set at, by John the Painter, **28.** 287
fortifications at, strengthened, **25.** 183
France may seek to destroy, **39.** 332
French and Spanish fleet approaches, **16.** 189n, **24.** 506, **25.** 183
French and Spanish fleet disappears from, **24.** 511, **28.** 464n
French fleet at, **29.** 33, **33.** 190
French merchant at, has concealed weapons, **18.** 402
French prisoners from Jersey arrive at, **25.** 115
George III and Q. Charlotte visit, **11.** 32n
Goldsworthy, Mrs, to visit her father at, **18.** 158
HW promises to fire cannon at, for Conway's victory, **37.** 202
Hawke returns to, **21.** 336n
—'s fleet driven back to, **38.** 37
Howe's fleet said to have been sent off, **12.** 82
Keppel is said to have been insulted at, **28.** 435
—— returns to, **24.** 400, **33.** 31
—'s fleet at, **39.** 306–7
Maker Tower near, **12.** 82–3n
men of war from, to join Norris, **18.** 393
Montagu, Charles, visits, **9.** 194
Mount Edgcumbe near, **30.** 67
Mudge retires to, **1.** 282n
regiments at, **9.** 196n
rumours at, **28.** 434n
Russian squadron near, **33.** 214
Shrewsbury sails from, **39.** 307
two hoys lost off, **11.** 117

Plymouth, English ship:
at Port Mahon, **17.** 285

Plymouth in an Uproar. See under Neville, Edward

Pneumonia:
occurrences of, **3.** 112, 330

Po, Italian river:
Charles Emmanuel III crosses, **19.** 292n
—— on other side of, **19.** 156
English ships to guard mouth of, **17.** 455
forces retreat across, **9.** 48n
Gages recrosses, **19.** 291
German troops oppose Spaniards at, **19.** 267
Lobkowitz builds bridges across, **19.** 41

Novati crosses, **19.** 206n
overflows, **19.** 163, **21.** 510
Patapan not to drown in, **17.** 56
Spaniards control, **19.** 276

Poblet (monastery), Spain:
Wharton, D. of, dies at, **16.** 6n

Pocket; pockets:
breeches', **37.** 74
coach passenger's, compared to cornucopia, **37.** 22
coat, canonici and abbés forbidden to wear, **21.** 224
HW could import plate in, **10.** 289
in abbé's costume, **17.** 136
Louis XV carries bread in, **20.** 340
Montagu's muff to fit into, **10.** 146
Sandwich carries dice in, **20.** 113

Pocket-book; pocket-books:
Cerretesi enters inscriptions in, **17.** 503
Cole's, HW makes notes in, **10.** 346
Craon wants, **17.** 194
Craon, Princesse de, shows, to Electress, **17.** 424
Craufurd wants to exchange, with highwayman, **33.** 413, 415
Ferrers sends, by Vaillant, to Mrs Clifford, **21.** 402
Fitzroy loses, with dispatches, **38.** 109
HW's, filled with notes, **10.** 346
Novillars's, obtained by Montagu, **10.** 11–12
Nugent's payments from Lady Mountjoy revealed in, **17.** 271
red leather, stolen from Harrington, **38.** 259n
Rudd, Mrs, pulls out, **24.** 153
sardonyx, received by Craon from HW, **17.** 222, 324n, 414
SH's, will record Cts of Ailesbury's neglect, **39.** 138

Pocket-glass:
Coventry, Cts of, looks at, in last illness, **21.** 451
old women should carry, to remind them of their own death's heads, **25.** 584

Pocock, Lady. *See* Drake, Sophia

Pocock, Beatrice, m. Rev. Dr David Campbell:
sister tended by, **31.** 287

Pocock, Sir George (1706–92), K.B., 1756; naval officer:
Aché does not battle with, off Gondelour and Ft St David, **21.** 283n
at Twickenham, **31.** 287
battle off Ft St David lost by, from lack of support, **21.** 296n
houses of, in Charles St, Berkeley Sq. and Orléans House, Twickenham, **33.** 347n
London Gazette tells activities of, in India, **21.** 337n
SH visited by, **31.** 202
SH visitors sent by, **12.** 229
Twickenham resident, **42.** 483
Walpole, Thomas jr, thanked by, for civilities to son, **36.** 252
West Indies expedition led by, **22.** 7n

Pocock, Sir George (1765–1840), cr. (1820) Bt:
Gosling, Mrs, at house of, in Twickenham, 12. 249
SH visited by, 12. 248
Walpole, Thomas jr, gracious to, 36. 252
Pocock, Joyce:
'disordered,' 31. 287
Pocock, Nicholas (ca 1741–1821), painter:
SH visited by, 12. 239
Pocock, Sarah, m. Capt. Philip Vincent:
at Twickenham, 31. 287
returns to London, 31. 199
Pocock, Sophia (d. 1811), m. (1782) John Poulett, styled Vct Hinton 1764–88, 4th E. Poulett 1788:
marriage of, 33. 347
Pocock family:
HW to visit, 31. 203
Pocock. See also Pococke
Pococke, Edward (1604–91), orientalist:
HW's notes on Arabic words from life of, 31. 248n
Pococke, Richard (1704–65), D.C.L.; Bp of Ossory 1756–65, of Meath 1765:
Bruce abuses, 28. 249
death of, 7. 391
Description of the East and Some Other Countries, HW's copy of, 28. 249n
early visitor to Chamouni, 30. 2n
(?) HW disparages learned hypotheses of, 35. 78
Pococke. See also Pocock
Podagre:
definition of, 22. 451n
Poder, Spanish ship:
capture of, 18. 403n, 414
in Spanish fleet, 17. 286
sunk, 18. 417
Urrutia, captain of, 18. 415n
Podestà, Palazzo del, Florence:
Bargello's prison, 17. 137n
prison in Via del Proconsolo, 17. 137n
Podewils, Otto Christoph (1719–81), Graf von:
Frederick II's secretary of state, 17. 456n
minister at the Hague, 18. 61n
treaties signed by, 17. 456n
Poelenburg, Cornelius van (1586–1667), painter:
'Adoration of Magi' by, at Julienne's, 7. 287
Blœmaert's and Elsheimer's pupil, 7. 355
painting after, 30. 371
paintings by: at Ham House, 10. 306; of Christ and apostles, at Julienne's, 7. 287
Poellnitz, Baroness von. See Stuart, Lady Anne (1746–ca 1819)
Poellnitz, Friedrich Karl Hans Bruno, Baron von:
Percy, Bns, weds, 14. 141n
Poellnitz. See also Pöllnitz
Poem; poems:
Conway finds, in Scottish Highlands, 37. 260
metaphysical, in blank verse, fashionable, 37. 261
See also Verse

Poemata. See under Hardinge, Nicholas
Poème sur la loi naturelle. See under Voltaire
Poems by Anna Chamber Countess Temple. See under Chambers, Anne
Poems by Mr Gray. See under Gray, Thomas
Poems Consisting Chiefly of Translations from the Asiatic Languages. See under Jones, Sir William
Poems in Latin and English on the Late Royal Nuptials:
Montagu gives, to HW, 43. 127
Poems of Mr Gray to which are Prefixed Memoirs of his Life and Writings by W. Mason. See under Gray, Thomas
Poems on Several Occasions; Poems on Various Subjects. See under Cromartie, Ann
Poems Supposed to Have Been written at Bristol. See under Chatterton, Thomas
Poesie del magnifico Lorenzo de' Medici. See under Medici, Lorenzo de'
Poet; poets:
artisans and labourers became, after Stephen Duck, 31. 220
black costume worn by, 9. 305
English: collection of heads of, at Nuneham, 35. 516; epigrams poured forth by, 25. 612
faults of bad, 31. 218
Florentine, derided by HW, 25. 612
great, have right to command, 30. 53
HW and Hannah More discuss, 31. 211
HW's reflections on impertinence of, 9. 259
HW's verses on a dull, 12. 267
HW thinks C. H. Williams only true, since Pope's death, 30. 53
HW would dread title of, more than that of patriot, 30. 104
insipid, HW's reflections on, 19. 27–8
season sympathizes with, 33. 334
truth told only by, 31. 22
Poetaster; poetasters:
modern, decried by HW, 11. 34
Poetess; poetesses:
English, extravagances of, 16. 257
Poetical Amusements at a Villa near Bath:
Palmerston contributes to, 28. 385n
Poetical Remains of James I King of Scotland. See under Tytler, William
Poetical Tales by Sir Gregory Gander. See under Ellis, George
Poet laureate; poets laureate:
Cibber recommends Jones as, 20. 214
HW jokes about, 10. 115
Hardwicke predicted to be, 9. 345
post of, a sinecure, 33. 314
Poetry:
Albany, Cts of, reads, 25. 106
Arabian, HW's opinion of, 12. 205
Bentley's verse epistle on decay of, 35. 645
cannot be translated, 29. 156
English: history of, see under Warton, Thomas; loses in French translation, 42. 353; Surrey improves, 42. 422; Voltaire introduces, to France, 41. 152

epic: explanation of critics for scant mention of heroes in, 30. 105; Hayley's *Essay* on, discussed by HW, 29. 255–7, 262; Macpherson kills, 28. 41, 282, 29. 256

Erse: Dalrymple sends, to HW, Macpherson's account of, for Gray, 15. 67; Ossianic specimens called, by Gray, 15. 64

French, said to owe its quality to overcoming difficulties, 35. 465–6

gone to bed, or into prose, 23. 212

good sense in, needed by the middle-aged, 41. 28

Greeks' grace in, 16. 270

—— set standards for, 33. 479

HW desires new touchstones for, 11. 121

HW prefers, natural, easy, full of sense and humour, 34. 91

HW requires new images in, 11. 34

HW requires novelty, plan, and suite in, 11. 211

HW's knowledge of, 21. 368

HW's reflections on, 16. 257

HW thinks, excusable only to amuse friends, 30. 104

how to be patroness of, 32. 31–2

Icelandic, HW comments on absurd figure in, 29. 30–1

Irish, Montagu offers to send, to HW, 9. 355

Johnson, Dr Samuel, and, discussed by HW, 33. 287–8

—— criticizes use of mythology in, 31. 241

Lucan, Bns, has turn for, 24. 475

lyric, thought obscure by Hannah More, 31. 211

modern: Conway's opinion of, 37. 18–19; hours of love are quintessence of, 37. 345

new imagery for, from astronomy, 28. 160–1

of passion, soon forgotten, 41. 28

power of: discussed by HW, 32. 223–4; in conveying fame, 31. 21–2

Scandinavian, Jerningham's poem on, 29. 331

sense required in, 34. 92

suffers from virtue of ladies, 32. 32

Twickenham's, 32. 31

writing of: most men try, 13. 121; West's reflections on, 13. 123–5

See also Poet; Prosody; verse

Poggelini, Cavaliere:

Berrys aided by, at Bologna, 11. 364–5n

—— see, at Florence, 11. 364n

complaisance of, 11. 364–5

Poggio a Caiano, Grand Ducal villa in Tuscany:

Cappello, Bianca, and Francesco I die at, 23. 296

Cowper to be entertained at, 23. 296

HW has print of, 22. 222

Leopold and Maria Louisa to take Ferdinand and Maria Carolina of Naples to, for hunting, 25. 594

Leopold and Maria Louisa to spend autumn at, 24. 123n

Tuscan Court moves to, 23. 296

—— to visit, to hear Cowper's farces, 23. 325–6

York, D. of, eats dinner at, prepared by Mann's servants, 22. 222

Poggio Imperiale, Grand Ducal villa in Tuscany:

Botta's French horns at, announce Peter III's overthrow, 22. 63

Craon not allowed to sleep at, 24. 23

Craon, Princesse de, obtains apartment at, for herself only, 24. 23

—— pays court at, to Leopold, 22. 536

Craons play cards at, 24. 23

Electress hoped to live at, 20. 414–15

enlarged and redecorated since HW saw it, but façade towards avenue is still ugly, 25. 598

enlarged but not yet completed, 23. 296

Ferdinand of Naples and Maria Carolina live quietly at, with Leopold and Maria Louisa, 25. 598

furniture at, 20. 116

Gloucester, D. and Ds of, see all Leopold's family at, 24. 297

guards dismissed from, by Joseph II's request, 23. 112

HW's favourite palace, 22. 41

hangings in, display Bianca Cappello's portrait, 20. 414–15

Joseph II expected at, 24. 108

Joseph II, Leopold, and Maria Louisa at, 23. 111–12

Leopold and family move to, from Castello, 25. 421

Leopold and Maria Louisa retire to, with two servants only, 23. 449

Leopold and Maria Louisa stay shut up at, during mourning, 22. 526

Leopold and Maria Louisa to take Ferdinand of Naples and Maria Carolina to, 25. 594

Leopold and Maria Louisa visit, 22. 424, 427

Leopold lives at, like a country gentleman, 25. 498–9

—— met by people in lanes and roads near, 23. 122

—— must have, as summer residence, 23. 296

—— transfers statues from, to Uffizi, 25. 531n

Mann's and P. of Mecklenburg's entertainment at Court at, more flattering than in Florence, 22. 438

Mann sends news of Clinton's success to, 25. 71

—— visits Botta at, 22. 40–1

Maria Amelia is lodged at, 25. 301

Paul I and wife to be lodged at, 25. 250–1

Tuscan Court in retreat at, while princes are inoculated, 24. 7

water-colours of Medici grand duchesses and of Marie de Médicis and Louis XIII copied from, 20. 414n

Pohen water:

Holland, Bn, to take, at Spa, 22. 129n

'Poinçon, Roi.' *See* Christian VII

Poinsinet, Antoine-Alexandre-Henri (1735–69), dramatist:
Alix et Alexis by, given at Choisy, 4. 257–9
Tom Jones by: 7. 305, 319, 38. 519; HW has not seen, 30. 215; performed in Paris and commended, 30. 215
Poinsinet de Sivry, Louis (1733–1804):
Pliny's Historia naturalis translated by, 28. 159–61, 35. 419n
Pointer; pointers:
HW does not turn, to grass, 23. 497
HW gives away, 32. 142
Latin might be read by, 35. 48
Mirepoix has, 9. 154
Orford's: wanted by Hertford, 39. 171; wanted by Townshend for Ireland, 41. 261
Patapan shaken and bruised by, 18. 71
Point Levi, Quebec:
Saunders writes to Pitt from, 21. 336n
Pointz. See Poyntz
Poiré, M.:
acts at Chanteloup, 5. 382n
Poirier, Mme (?wife of Simon-Philippe Poirier), china merchant in Paris:
armour of François I to be packed by, 5. 121, 124
Craufurd's purchases from, 5. 362n
—— to receive porcelain from, 5. 307, 323
Du Deffand, Mme, buys bowl from, 5. 223
—— pays, for Craufurd, 5. 331, 342
—— seeks information from, 6. 97
—— to pay: for Craufurd, 5. 323; for HW, 4. 356, 361, 365
HW's cups from, 4. 335, 338, 348–9, 352, 356, 361, 366, 377, 385
HW sends cup to Mme du Deffand from, 4. 331, 333, 338, 352
Henri IV, medallion of, sold by, 5. 267
Poirier, Simon-Philippe, china merchant in Paris:
Cole buys china at shop of, 1. 108
HW buys from, 7. 262
HW calls at shop of, 7. 269–71, 296, 310, 326, 328, 334
HW orders designs of commodes from, 31. 110
HW's bill from, 7. 401, 408, 412, 413
HW's purchases from, sent to England, 7. 405
nothing new in shop of, 39. 145–6
shop of, 43. 90
Poirot, Domenico Matteo de (d. 1775), Barone di Saint-Odile, 1752; Tuscan minister to Rome 1752–74:
Benedict XIV's purchase of Medici estates at Urbino arranged by, 20. 306n
Clement XIII does not summon, because he does not wait in Torreggiani's ante-chamber, 22. 573
Florence to be visited by, on way to settle Tuscan disputes with Benedict XIV at Rome, 20. 305

Migazzi replaced by, as Tuscan minister to Rome, 20. 305n
minister to Rome, to aggrandize priests and Inquisition, 20. 308
Regency council to be joined by, in Florence, 20. 305–6
Richecourt bars visitors from, 20. 308
——'s antagonist, in Vienna, 20. 305, 308
Valenti asked by, about Benedict XIV's claim to Monte Santa Maria, 20. 428
Poison:
Clement XIV and his confectioner said to have died of, 24. 42–4, 49–50
in 'vipers' of the Church, 25. 245
Pius VI may fear France or Spain more than, 24. 86
race-horse dies of, 41. 6
rat, eaten by Marsan's guests, 5. 192
Poissardes (fishwomen); poissonières:
absent from meeting at Crown and Anchor, 11. 320
Adélaïde and Victoire, Mmes, detained by, 11. 207
Artois, Comtesse d', invited by, to return to Paris, 11. 96
Burke refers to Mrs Macaulay and Mrs Barbauld as, 11. 169–70
Catherine II should be confronted by, 34. 146
États afraid of, 11. 100
French give liberty to, to hang people, 34. 99
HW mentions, 11. 97, 208, 234–5, 240
Louis XVI and Marie-Antoinette cheered by, 11. 79
Louis XVI and Marie-Antoinette insulted by, 34. 72
patricians disguise as, 15. 236
Poisson, Abel-François (1727–81), Seigneur de Vandières; Marquis de Marigny:
Argenson asked by, for cordon bleu, 20. 228
brother of Mme de Pompadour, 20. 227
Frenchman seeks, in church of San Lorenzo, 20. 228
HW permitted by, to copy Gramont's portrait, 5. 222, 7. 283
HW sees collection of, 7. 266
HW sees 'refuse' of pictures of, 39. 15
HW to send SH Lucan to, 7. 415
(?) Hertford shares Paris opera box with, 38. 298
house of, at Versailles, has unhung royal pictures, 39. 15, 201
Le Blanc accompanies, to Florence, 20. 228
Leghorn visited by, 20. 236
nickname of, 20. 228
Rena, the, captivates, 21. 162
sister's bequest to, 38. 374
social relations of, with Mme Geoffrin, 7. 283, 291, 304, 345
statues ordered by, 7. 23
wife of, 4. 370n
Poisson, Jeanne-Antoinette (1721–64), m. (1741) Charles-Guillaume Le Normand d'Étoilles;

cr. Marquise de Pompadour s.j.; Louis XV's mistress:

Anson might carry off, **37.** 535

apartment at Capuchins in Paris taken by, for religious retreat, **20.** 530n

Bellevue, château of, **3.** 27n

Bernis and Choiseul advanced by, **21.** 242

Bernis disputes with, over Soubise, **21.** 263n

—— fell because of insults to, **23.** 144

—— may have disobliged, **21.** 262n

Berryer, protégé of, **21.** 263n

brother of, **5.** 222n, **20.** 227, **21.** 162, **38.** 298

cameos made popular by, **7.** 201

Capuchins' chapel decorated in honour of, **7.** 281, **20.** 236n

Choiseul owed his favour to, **4.** 301n, **21.** 242

—— persuades, not to publish minutes condemning Broglie, **21.** 519n

death of: **4.** 214n, **38.** 373, 374; expected, **22.** 212

devotional turn of, **20.** 530, **37.** 446

Du Barry, Comtesse, more powerful than, **5.** 48

Durini refuses to visit, **21.** 216

dying, **38.** 372

endangered if France does not invade British isles, **38.** 38

English fleet thought by, too weak to fight, **21.** 358n

English should thank, for Maurepas's mistake, **30.** 205

English stocks bought by, to profit by Peace of Paris, **25.** 357

engraving done by, **7.** 201

epigram against, **9.** 249, **12.** 29n, **28.** 221n

eye said to be lost by, **22.** 30

finances and debts of, **38** 374

fireworks given by, **20.** 338

former apartment of, **3.** 286

France undone by, **38.** 35

German studied by, **21.** 514

Guerchy, Comtesse de, may be successor to, **22.** 239

HW calls, 'Bathsheba,' **22.** 4

HW hopes to see, **38.** 357

HW translates French epigram on, **9.** 249

health of: fever and oppression on breast, **38.** 338, 344; recovering, **38.** 350, 357

Hertford attends opera with brother of, **38.** 298

——'s conversation with, **38.** 218

Hôtel d'Evreux bequeathed by, to Louis XV, **38.** 374

jubilee said to be observed by, at Capuchins', **20.** 236

letters attributed to, *see Lettres de Mme la Marquise de Pompadour*

Louis XV asks Soubise to dismiss, after Damiens's attempt, **21.** 56n

—— attached to, merely from habit, **38.** 350–1

—— exiles Machault for dismissing, **21.** 56n

—— influenced by love of, for peace, **20.** 530

—— makes, *dame du palais* to his wife, **20.** 530

—— mismanaged by, **22.** 30

—— provided by, with Irish mistress after her own physical inadequacy, **20.** 542

—— said to be abandoned by, **20.** 236

—— said to be separated from, **20.** 530, 542

——'s expenses not all caused by, **20.** 500

——'s extravagant diversions contrived by, to keep him from clergy, **37.** 340

——'s mistress, **22.** 212

——'s stabbing frightens, **14.** 152

—— tends, constantly but gaily, in her illness, **38.** 350

Maria Theresa reportedly asked by, to abolish Inquisition so she might have pleasant stay in Vienna, **21.** 258n

——'s correspondence with, **21.** 258

Mariette offered 50 louis by, for print, **14.** 146

Matignon, Mme de, said to have been introduced by, to Louis XV, **22.** 4

Maurepas's disgrace caused by, **7.** 278

——'s disgrace plotted by, for lampooning and trying to poison her, **20.** 51n

——'s epigram on, **12.** 29n

—— writes scurrilous verses on, **7.** 283, **14.** 152–3

Mirepoix, Duchesse de, rides with, after courting Queen, **14.** 152

Morphy, Mlle, unlikely to quarrel with, **35.** 173

name of first husband of, corrected, **43.** 268

(?) Paris parliament opposes, **38.** 338

(?) Petitot miniature sought by, **5.** 417n, **7.** 269

political changes after death of, **22.** 227n

Pont-de-Veyle's verses on, **8.** 194–5, **14.** 152–3, **43.** 109

Presle has china formerly owned by, **7.** 346

rouge may be abandoned by, **20.** 530

Sacy, Père, confessor to, **20.** 530n

'sick of the war,' **22.** 30n

Souvré's witticism when at home of, **21.** 514

Starhemberg delivers letters from Maria Theresa to, **21.** 258n

successors to, not at once in evidence, **38.** 389–90

Taaffe brings turtles and pineapples to, in post-chaise, **20.** 289

Thétis played by, in *Thétis et Pelée*, **20.** 213n

title of, corrected, **43.** 375

will and effects of, **38.** 372, 374

Yarmouth, Cts of, the counterpart of, **20.** 91

Poisson, Raymond (1633–90):

Baron de La Crasse, Le, by, **6.** 381

Poisson de Malvoisin, Jeanne-Charlotte (d. 1814), m. (1779) Alexandre-Paul-Augustin-Félix-Élisabeth Barrin, Comte de la Galissonnière:

(?) social relations of, with Mme du Deffand, **7.** 426

Poissonnier, Pierre (1720–98), physician; chemist:
Chanteloup visited by, 8. 207, 208
Du Deffand, Mme, asks HW's good offices for, 3. 338
—— continues with Bouvart instead of, 6. 241
—— introduces, to HW, 5. 359
——'s account of, 3. 334
——'s consulting physician, 5. 359, 401, 6. 106
——'s correspondence with, 5. 369
—— sees, 5. 377, 7. 299
—— sends book to HW by, 3. 334
—— sends messages to, 5. 369
——'s social relations with, 5. 384, 6. 182
HW described to Mme du Deffand by, 5. 381
HW receives parcel by, 5. 377
HW sends Mme du Deffand news of return of, 5. 372
(?) HW to dine with, 32. 122
leaves Paris, 6. 106, 222
London to be visited by, 5. 359
returns to Paris, 6. 234
Poissy (France):
Artois obtains capitainerie of, 6. 397
Louis XVI's edict concerning, 6. 265n
Poitevin de Villiers, Jacques (d. 1780):
(?) attends session of parliament of Paris, 8. 171
Poitier, Miss, m. (1755) Joseph Vernon:
(?) Fairies, The, sung by, 35. 209
Poitiers, Diane de (1499–1566), m. (1512) Louis de Brézé, Comte de Maulevrier; cr. Duchesse de Valentinois; Henri II's mistress:
Doumenil has portrait of, 7. 313
HW mistakes cipher for that of, 7. 260
in HW's World, 9. 154n
Melbourne, Vcts, the counterpart of, 35. 532
portraits of, 7. 313, 32. 282
supposed portrait of, 1. 142n
Poitiers (France):
court to be held at, 5. 30n
HW fancies himself at, 21. 212
Joseph II visits, 6. 453, 8. 202
Ruffec near, 5. 402
Poitiers, battle of:
English deterioration since, 9. 17
Poitiers-de-Rye, Élisabeth-Philippine de (1715–73), m. (1728) Guy-Michel de Durfort, Duc de Lorges:
social relations of, in Paris, 7. 272, 339
Poix, Prince de. See Noailles, Antonin-Claude-Dominique-Juste de (1777–1846); Noailles, Philippe-Louis-Marc-Antoine de (1752–1819)
Poix, Princesse de. See Beauvau, Anne-Louise-Marie de (1750–1833)
Poker; pokers:
at Ham House, 10. 306
red-hot, 35. 95
Polacca. See Polacre
Polacre, French:
plague abroad, 17. 105n

Poland, K. of. See Frederick Augustus I (1670–1733); Frederick Augustus II (1696–1763); John II (Kasimir) (1609–72); John (Sobieski) (1629–96); Stanislas I (Leszczyński) (1677–1766); Stanislas II (Poniatowski) (1732–98); Wladislaw IV (1595–1648)
Poland, Primate of. See Poniatowski, Michael George
Poland, Q. of. See Gonzaga, Luisa Maria (1611–67); La Grange, Marie-Casimire-Louise de (1639–1716); Maria Josefa (1699–1757); Opalinska, Katharina (1680–1747)
Poland:
acquisitiveness and cupidity of, 17. 168
ambassadors from and to, see under Ambassador
Annual Register's article on, 28. 101
Austria and Russia may dismantle Turkey in fashion of, 25. 399
Austrian claims on Dalmatia as clear as those upon, 24. 11–12
Austrians march into, 23. 145
Broglie ambassador to, 4. 214n
Brühl's son excluded as nuncio to, 22. 192
Catherine II and Joseph II to meet in, 25. 61
Catherine II asked by, to restore Biron to Courland, 22. 118–19
—— defeats, 31. 369–70, 373, 391
—— to visit her acquisitions in, 25. 44
Choiseul might espouse quarrel of, 24. 11
Clairon, Mlle, to visit, 3. 268
Condorcet worse than partitioners of, 39. 496
confederates of: Jablonowsky, Ps, sent by, to England as ambassadress, 23. 319; Louis XV and French ministers vainly encourage, 23. 331; Talmond, Princesse de, emissary of, 23. 319; Turks unable to aid, 23. 319; Young Pretender may be invited by, 23. 318; see also under Bar, Confederacy of
constitution of, stifled by Catherine II, 34. 144, 153–4
Conti seeks throne of, 4. 214
Conway not to usurp, 39. 178
Craven, Lady, writes from, to HW, 42. 176
Czartoryska, Ps, to return to, 42. 308
Diet of: 22. 181n; better than the new one, 34. 159; Dissidents favoured by, 22. 574n; Malachowski marshal of, 34. 153; National Assembly contrasted with, 34. 157; Parliament as tedious as, 38. 223
dissidents in: Clement XIII cannot persuade Catholic princes to crusade against, 22. 574; Clement XIII orders mass and procession for destruction of, 22. 577; emerging from 'servitude of symmetry,' 42. 164; have not a cheeseparing left, 23. 328; Louis XVI might want to destroy, 24. 11
dissension in, 8. 165
Dresden treaty between England, Holland, and, 20. 299n
Durand de Distroff ambassador to, 3. 184n
English fleet should come to aid of, 23. 475

France and Spain may be inspired by partition of, to divide Milan with Sardinia, **23.** 469

France cannot confer crown of, **42.** 496

—— got Lorraine when trying to make a king for, **42.** 496

—— may interfere in, **5.** 338n

—— sends officers to, **23.** 338, **39.** 146

—— turns, against Catherine II, **23.** 338

Frederick II a plunderer of, **35.** 386

—— defeats Russians in, **21.** 237

—— drives Russians into, **21.** 246–7

—— quarters, **23.** 437

—— said to receive assurances from, **18.** 512

—— 'swears through,' **12.** 45

—— the pickpocket of, **24.** 55

—— to meet Catherine II and Joseph II in, **25.** 44

—— to review troops in area newly-acquired from, **24.** 18

French elegance in, **38.** 33

Gage fails to win crown of, **35.** 349

Gaven tries to sell alleged Raphael in, **35.** 37n

Geoffrin, Mme, to visit, **31.** 101–2

HW would not aid quixotic plan to save, from Russians, **34.** 156

Henri III flees from, to avoid Diet, **35.** 460

Holland might be divided like, **25.** 539

Joseph II said to have reported disturbances in, to Leopold, **25.** 44

—— to visit his acquisitions in, **25.** 44

king chosen for, **22.** 248

king's death may cause war in, **22.** 177

letter from, reveals Russian news, **17.** 20

Mann suspects authorship of English letters about, **23.** 502–3

Maria Theresa's reasons for reluctantly consenting to partition of, **23.** 439

ministers from and to, *see under* Minister

More, Hannah, horrified by events in, **31.** 370–1

Müntz brings views of, to England, **12.** 263

—— in, **16.** 168n

new constitution of, should be imitated in France, **39.** 487

news must be sought in, **23.** 505

nobility caused ruin of, **23.** 436

nuncio to, expelled, **22.** 192

Ogiński aspired to throne of, **35.** 386

Old Pretender's revenue from wife's lands in, **22.** 387

partitioners of, scourged by one another, **33.** 32

partition of: **5.** 346, **11.** 78, **12.** 170, **25.** 613n, **33.** 36, 280, 502, **41.** 347; accomplished in short time, **25.** 201; dialogue satirizes, **23.** 556; France dared not interfere in, **33.** 14; HW approves of, after Ps Lubomirska's rudeness, **39.** 447; HW displeased by, **39.** 178; HW ridicules, **24.** 55; impudent force the cause of, **24.** 365; Joseph II's invasion of Venice made credible by, **24.** 37–8; Mann

enjoys dialogue about, **23.** 564; Maria I might accede to, **24.** 310; said to be planned, **23.** 419; three monarchs 'jump at,' **32.** 266; violates law of nations, **39.** 302, 303

pomp and hospitality of, two centuries behind times, **38.** 33

Pope mentions, in *Moral Essays,* **35.** 349n

——'s lines on Gage's offer from, **33.** 280

prime minister of, *see* Brühl, Heinrich

'Queen-Mother' of, *see* Rodet, Marie-Thérèse, Mme Geoffrin

revolution in: **11.** 286, 296, **33.** 511; 'noble, wise and moderate,' **34.** 159; shows possibility of improving government, **34.** 120

revolution shown by, to be possible without assassination, **34.** 163

Roman Catholics of, invited by Turkish Grand Signor to turn Mohammedan, **23.** 81

ruby supposedly pawned by, to Prince James Sobieski, **25.** 525

Russia draws, upon her shoulders, **34.** 32

Russian army retires to, **37.** 556

Russians invade, **21.** 419

—— may destroy 'noble new constitution' of, **36.** 281

Sidney said to be considered for kingship of, **9.** 26, **40.** 136

Stanislas I not re-elected by, **22.** 402

Stanislas II and Sulkowsky competed for throne of, **33.** 279–80

Stanislas II king of, **22.** 253

Stormont visits, **38.** 33

SH visitors from, **12.** 224, 233, **33.** 501–2

subscription for defence of, fraudulent and futile, **15.** 224–5

subsidies from England may prevent war in, **42.** 496

Talmond, Princesse de, from, **20.** 44, **38.** 465

Turkish sultan withdraws protection from, **24.** 40

Usson expected to be French ambassador to, **39.** 24

Voltaire lauds ravagers of, **23.** 515

wars in, out of England's reach, **23.** 432

Williams, Sir C. H. writes to D. of Newcastle a much-admired letter about, **30.** 320

Wroughton minister to, **4.** 241n

Young Pretender may have gone to be king of, **23.** 324

—— may marry in, **20.** 44

—— said to have joined Catholics and Dissidents in, **23.** 337

——'s alleged journey to, reported to Stanislas II, **23.** 352

Poland St, London:
Lunardi's London address, **25.** 543n

Polar Star, Knights of the. *See* Knights of the Polar Star

Polastron, Vicomtesse de. *See* Bouchard d'Esparbez de Lussan, Marie-Louise-Françoise

Polastron, Denis-Gabriel-Adhémar (1762–1812), Vicomte (later Comte) de:
marriage of, 7. 453

Polastron, Gabrielle-Yolande-Claude-Martine de (ca 1749–93), m. (1767) Armand-Jules-François, Comte (Duc, 1780) de Polignac:
Basle reached by, from Paris, 34. 67n
biographical information about, corrected, 43. 91
Clermont's letter from, 25. 356–7
dances at ball in honour of Dauphin's marriage, 4. 410
Devonshire, Ds of, advised by, to leave Paris, 39. 467n
—— exchanges presents with, 25. 427
dirty as if she walked from Bath, 39. 449
England left by, 39. 449–50
HW cares for Princesse de Lamballe as little as for, 39. 456
HW pities, less than he does Mme de Boufflers, 34. 68
HW would rather see haycock than, 39. 448
Hertford's ball not attended by, 39. 449
husband of, 25. 409
Marie-Antoinette's friendship for, 7. 153, 25. 357n, 409, 33. 309, 34. 68
mockery of, 34. 68
Necker's 'magnificence' to, 34. 67–8
print satirizes, 11. 54n
social relations of, in Paris, 7. 453
son born to, 7. 452
(?) Voltaire aided by, 28. 365n
would have been murdered in Paris, 34. 73–4

Polastron, Marie-Henriette de (d. 1792 or 1793), m. (1736) François-Léonor, Comte d'Andlau:
(?) HW to visit, 33. 461
reinstated at Court, 33. 310

Polcevera, valley of (Italy):
Genoese mob joined by people of, 19. 343

Pole, Anne (d. 1833), m. (1772) Charles Cocks, cr. (1784) Bn Somers:
SH visited by, 12. 250

Pole, Catherine (d. 1576), m. (1532) Francis Hastings, 2d E. of Huntingdon:
Moira descended from, 12. 156n

Pole, Edmund de la (ca 1471–1513), E. of Suffolk:
executed, 42. 208n

Pole, Edward:
Bedford, D. of, orders regiment of, assembled, 21. 373n

Pole, Henry (ca 1492–1539), Lord Montagu:
executed, 42. 208n

Pole, John de la (1442–91), 2d D. of Suffolk:
position of, at Henry VII's Court, 2. 365
survived his son, 2. 364

Pole, John de la (ca 1462–87), E. of Lincoln:
attainder act against, 41. 92
banishment of, 2. 364
death of, 2. 364
Simnel supported by, 15. 172

Pole, Lady Margaret. See Margaret (Plantagenet) (1473–1541)

Pole, Millicent (d. 1825) m. (1774) Arthur Acheson, 2d Vct Gosford, 1790; cr. (1806) E. of Gosford; 'Miss Poole':
(?) quadrille danced by, 32. 116

Pole, Mrs Ralph. See Cole, Anne

Pole, Reginald (1500–58), cardinal:
portrait of: Du Deffand, Mme, wishes to send, to HW, 5. 178; HW fortunate to have escaped getting, 5. 184; Thiers has, 5. 148n, 7. 372

Pole, Sir Richard (d. 1504), K.G.:
marriage of, 2. 364
wife of, 9. 98n, 14. 177n

Pole, Lady Sarah. See Moore, Lady Sarah

Pole, William de la (1396–1450), 4th E. of Suffolk; cr. (1444) M. and (1448) D. of Suffolk:
Bute compared with, 22. 53
execution of, Fenn sends account of, to HW, 16. 231
marriage of, 9. 68

Pole; Poles:
drinking loved by, 38. 61
HW thinks, ought to be admired and imitated, 39. 487
SH visited by, 12. 224 bis, 233, 33. 501–2

Pole; poles:
green, Mann's garden lamps suspended from, 18. 479

Polemburgh. See Poelenburg

Polemo-Middinia. See under Gibson, Edmund

Polenburgh. See Poelenburg

Polhill, Charles (1725–1805), of Chipstead, Kent:
SH visited by, 12. 239 bis

Polhill, David (d. 1754):
genealogy of, 10. 352

Polhill, Mrs David. See Trevor, Elizabeth (1683–1706)

Polhill, Nathaniel:
Wilkesite candidate in Southwark election, 39. 197n

Poli, Duca:
Rosenberg keeps, waiting, 23. 104n

Poli, Anna Teresa (Sister Maria Teresa) of Valentano:
Clement XIV's death foretold by, 24. 30, 41–2
prosecution of, 24. 30, 41–2

Polibin, ——, Russian Rear-Adm.:
squadron under, goes to Mediterranean, 25. 60n

Police:
English riots a disgrace to, 23. 13
London lacks, 39. 99
Parisian, reformed, 6. 184
Townsend a factotum of, 12. 115

Policy:
'honour of nations,' 39. 302

'Polidore':
in Otway's Orphan, 40. 374

Polidore. See Polidoro Caldara

Polidoro. See under Pescetti, Giovanni Battista

Polidoro Caldara (ca 1495–1500 – ca 1543), styled Polidoro da Caravaggio:
(?) shields painted by, **35.** 419, 420–1
Polignac, Comtesse de. *See* Le Vicomte de Rumain de Coëtanfao, Constance-Gabrielle-Bonne (ca 1747–83); Polastron, Gabrielle-Yolande-Claude-Martine de (ca 1749–93)
Polignac, Duchesse de. *See* Polastron, Gabrielle-Yolande-Claude-Martine de (ca 1749–93)
Polignac, Marquise de. *See* La Garde, Marie-Louise de (d. 1779); Rioult de Douilly, Marie (1712–84)
Polignac, Armand-Jules-François (1745–1817), Comte, and (1780) Duc de:
Artois's premier écuyer, **5.** 220
balloon ascent attested by, **25.** 450n
Basle reached by, from Paris, **34.** 67n
birth date of, corrected, **43.** 94
England left by, without taking leave, **39.** 449–50
—— visited by, **25.** 408–9, **29.** 306n
George III receives, on Windsor terrace, **39.** 449
Hertford's ball put off by, **39.** 449
print satirizes, **4.** 410n
social relations of, in Paris, **7.** 294, 320, 332
wife of, **4.** 410n
Polignac, Auguste-Jules-Armand-Marie (1780–1847), Prince de:
birth of, **7.** 452
Polignac, Diane-Françoise-Zéphyrine de (b. 1740 or 1746):
(?) anecdote about, at French Court, **33.** 309
(?) Basle reached by, from Paris, **34.** 67n
friend of Ds of Devonshire, **11.** 27n
(?) illegitimate child of, **33.** 309
(?) SH visited by, **12.** 227
Polignac, Diane-Louise-Augustine de (b. 1742 or 1748):
(?) anecdote about, at French Court, **33.** 309
(?) Basle reached by, from Paris, **34.** 67n
(?) illegitimate child of, **33.** 309
(?) SH visited by, **12.** 227
Polignac, Henriette-Zéphyrine de (b. 1753), m. (1776) Amédée-Claude-Rosalie Testu, Marquis de Balincourt:
(?) Du Deffand, Mme, plans supper party for, before ball, **4.** 415
(?) Hénault's social relations with, **7.** 332
Polignac, Louise-Gabrielle-Aglaé de (ca 1768–1803), m. (1780) Antoine-Louis-Marie de Gramont, Duc de Guiche; Duc de Gramont:
England left by, **39.** 449–50
George III receives, on Windsor terrace, **39.** 449
marriage of, **7.** 153, 456
Polignac, Melchior de (1661–1742), cardinal:
Anti-Lucretius by, sent by Saxe to Chesterfield through D. of Cumberland, **9.** 52
conclave not attended by, **17.** 21n
Du Deffand, Mme, makes witticism to, on St Denis, **3.** 305, **8.** 60
Tencin disgraced by information of, **17.** 19n

Polimetis. See *Polymetis*
Poliorcetes (Demetrius I):
Conway is not, **37.** 543
Polishing:
English tempers need friction with others for, **39.** 277
Polish language:
musical when sung, **42.** 230
St-Germain understands, **26.** 20
Polish Partition, The. See under Lind, John
'Polite':
vulgarity of, **12.** 254
Political and Military Rhapsody. See under Lloyd, Henry
'Political Eclogue, A.' *See under* Williams, Sir Charles Hanbury
Political illness:
HW has excuse for, **35.** 259
Political parties:
English, changeable, **12.** 253
Roman, HW comments on 'blues' and 'greens,' **12.** 253
Political Register:
HW mentioned in, **35.** 539
HW sends, to England, **7.** 407
Political Survey of Britain, A. See under Campbell, John
Politician; politicians:
arts of, less effective than chance, **25.** 248
coffee-house, **39.** 108
HW after Paris trip can inform, **39.** 150
HW meets, at Lady Elizabeth Stuart Mackenzie's, **12.** 28
HW speculative, not practical as, **34.** 101
HW timid as, **34.** 119
HW would have made a miserable, **33.** 338
Ossory, Lady, is, **32.** 277
red hot, in petticoats, **33.** 560
See also under Politics
Politics:
a profession of calculation, **33.** 348
assemblies, balls, operas, and plays more dignified than, **21.** 542
balls and masquerades replace, in England, **23.** 476
Cole on, **1.** 86, **2.** 86, 208, 210–11, 227, 310
——'s 'flaming,' **2.** 296, 298
conversation spoiled by, **31.** 213
Conway hates, **37.** 176
—— thinks HW has learned, from ladies at Ranelagh, **37.** 165–6
—— wishes world were of one mind in, **37.** 193
depth of, is seeming to know contrary of truth, **33.** 276
Du Deffand, Mme, abhors, **30.** 272
Dutch, Stair does not interfere with, **37.** 149
English: asleep in London, but active in country, **30.** 250; calm in, **30.** 240; Conway indifferent to, **37.** 86, 92, 484; Conway knows nothing of, **37.** 102; Conway pleased by HW's 'scraps' of, **37.** 421; Du Deffand, Mme, interested in, **3.** 33, 64, 69, 90, 100–

[Politics, *continued*]

1, 104–5, 107–8, 110, 119–21, 137, 160, 163, 178, 188, 227, 252, 254–5, 258, 261, 273, 316, 326, 355, 365, 399–400, 407, **4.** 144, 204, 336, 342, 344, 349, 374, **5.** 56, **6.** 235, 241, 259, 261; Du Deffand, Mme interested in, only as relating to HW, **4.** 255; English taste corrupted by, **39.** 120; French do not understand English way of, **38.** 571; go as HW wishes, **30.** 176; HW abandons, **31.** 109; HW abhors, **31.** 105–6, 111, 372; HW anxious to escape from, **30.** 182; HW busy with, **39.** 312; HW engaged in, on account of others, **10.** 157; HW engrossed in, **30.** 239; HW forgets ancient quarrels in, **31.** 173; HW forsakes, **10.** 197, 198, 219, 258, 311, **35.** 317, 372; HW glad to leave, **1.** 124, **22.** 572, **23.** 128–9; HW goes to Paris to escape from, **38.** 470; HW not to meddle with, **31.** 109; HW quits, **39.** 31; HW persists in avoiding, **23.** 145, 570, 579; HW's aversion to, **10.** 49, 109, 113, 118, 154, 155, 157, 158, 162, 163, 167, 168, 170, 177, 184, 263, 267, 273, 301, **32.** 10, 40, **33.** 106, 180, 357, 398, **38.** 463, 470, **39.** 31, 244–5, 300, 415; HW's interest in, **4.** 480; HW's part in, **3.** 29, 35, 53, 69, 101, 103–4, 161, 164, 167, 181, 184, 185, 222, 265, 266, 271, 301–2, 306, 311, 326–7, 331, 343, 391, 404, **4.** 2, 175, 178, 344; HW to quit, forever, **30.** 194; HW uninterested in, **30.** 211, 215, 218; HW weary of, **30.** 196; Hertford no longer has ambitions in, **38.** 569; Hertford's aversion to, **38.** 329, 387, 389, 411; incessant revolutions in, **30.** 224; Milton outlived, **39.** 120; Newcastle, D. of, should found school for, at Cambridge, **38.** 30; Oxford Loungers peruse, over coffee, **38.** 46; Parliament relinquishes, to opera, **38.** 2, 11; Petersham, Lady Caroline, does not let town relapse into, **37.** 433; Rochford explains, to Mme du Deffand, **3.** 261; war and, tire London, **37.** 53

English absorption in, **23.** 157–8
English credulity about, **18.** 305
English indifference to, **20.** 260
English ladies addicted to, **25.** 476, 483, 495
ephemeral character of, **25.** 604
four ways of viewing, **33.** 521
Fox inquires about Orford's opinions concerning, **30.** 167
French: Du Deffand, Mme, characterizes, **4.** 480; Du Deffand, Mme, hates, **39.** 189; HW indifferent to, **4.** 144; HW tired of, **11.** 286; must lead to civil war, despotism, or assassination, **35.** 342
German, Stormont scarce enters, **37.** 472–3
great rather than small alterations more effective in, **16.** 264
HW a coward on points of, **34.** 160
HW adopts from no side, and preaches to nobody, **24.** 351
HW and Lady Ossory avoid, **33.** 521, **34.** 34

HW calls, 'poison of all English connections,' **35.** 332
HW changes scene of, by going to Paris, **35.** 342
HW compares: to paroli, **10.** 139; to stage, **23.** 41
HW considers, a farce except when war is concerned, **25.** 365
HW cool to, **35.** 334
HW does not discuss, at Stowe, **10.** 313
HW engaged with, on account of others, **10.** 157
HW hates, **22.** 550, **41.** 7
HW indifferent to, **1.** 206
HW is done with, **25.** 309
HW preferred Newmarket to, as topic at White's, **25.** 483
HW proposes fine for discussing, **31.** 213
HW refuses to write about, to Montagu, **10.** 113, 197
HW retreats from, **22.** 300, 304, 308–9, 316, 348, 359–60, 365, 436
HW's: **33.** 25; attachment to Fox out of power HW's 'passionate principle' in, **30.** 131; differ from Lord Derby's, **12.** 90; disinterested, **30.** 170; influenced by Lady Mary Churchill's Windsor appointment, **30.** 176; to be governed by Fox's commands, **30.** 129
HW's aversion to, *see under* Walpole, Horatio (1717–97): aversions of
HW's disinterestedness in, **31.** 60
HW's gout connected with, **31.** 39, 41
HW sick of, **24.** 117
HW's melancholy reflections on, **32.** 272
HW's mind worn out by, **22.** 316
HW's proposals for success in, **32.** 316–17
HW's pun about, **10.** 219
HW's reflections on, **2.** 73, 83–5, 89, 193–4, 209, 217, **15.** 89–90, **32.** 272
HW's reflections on inability to decide merits of, in heat of events, **25.** 142
HW tells Mann not to mention, except to ministers, **25.** 459
HW tired of witnessing, **22.** 110
HW to be neutral in, **10.** 277
HW to forsake, **10.** 147, 167, 197, **30.** 194
influence in: Caroline's, powerful, **31.** 420; HW does not cultivate, **30.** 199; HW's, for obtaining appointments, slight, **31.** 41; HW's, slight with Rockingham ministry, **30.** 199; Suffolk, Cts of, had little, **31.** 420
Irish: Conway confounded by, **37.** 395; Conway describes, **37.** 448–50; quieter, **37.** 376; ladies understand, better than HW does, **33.** 558
Mann's letters avoid subjects of, **23.** 71
moderation in, incompatible with modern patriotism, **25.** 50
Montagu compares, to horses, **10.** 238
—— compares administrations of, to annual flowers, **10.** 222–3

—— regrets eclipse of, by amusements, **10.** 141

——'s opinion of, **10.** 119, 170

morality in, **35.** 613–14

never end, **25.** 370

news of, unreliable, **33.** 34–5

newspapers abandon, **30.** 237

objects of entertainment to HW, **34.** 34

Orford, 3d E. of, rarely thinks about, **30.** 167n

Ossory's, **33.** 25

people forced by, into alliance with their enemies, **23.** 145

piddling, HW's aversion to, **23.** 420

Pineda believed Adam understood all sciences but, **37.** 293

public's absorption in, diminishes Cadell's sales, **31.** 387

Selwyn can strike wit out of, **32.** 38

——'s indifference to, **30.** 271

too inauspicious for HW's letter, **12.** 137

vanity of, HW's reflections on, **19.** 4

Poll, Jan van de (? 1721–?1801), Dutch deputy to England, 1759:

English mission of, **21.** 290–1

Poll, Margarethe Cornelia van de (1726–93), m. 1 (1743) Cornelis Munter; m. 2 (1754) Pierre-Chrysostome d'Usson de Bonac, Comte d'Usson:

Beauvau, Princesse de, takes, to theatre, **7.** 344

biographical information about, corrected, **43.** 84, 129

Calvinist, **10.** 71

(?) Coke, Lady Mary, mentions, **4.** 16n

Dutch, **10.** 70, 71

England disliked by, **38.** 214

English not spoken by, **10.** 71

HW did not like, in England, **38.** 480

HW entertains, at SH, **10.** 70–1

HW mentions, **3.** 341

HW's verses to, at SH party, **10.** 69, 71, 73, 74

HW to be received by, in Paris, **38.** 504

HW to sup with, in Paris, **39.** 16

Hertford and Comtesse de Boufflers entertained by, **38.** 350–1

Hertford has not seen, **38.** 337

—— sups with, at Fontainebleau, **38.** 218

husband of, **10.** 71–2

La Tuilerie visited by, **7.** 345

London visited by, **22.** 135

Pelham, Frances, entertains, at Esher, **10.** 72–3

(?) Polish embassy may be given to husband of, **31.** 102

polite but not well thought of, and loves abuse, **38.** 221

Selwyn's friend disparaged by, **7.** 93

social relations of, in Paris, *see index entries ante* 8. 533–4 *where she is wrongly identified*

Spa visited by, **7.** 239

Polliaiolo, Simone del (1457–1508), called Cronaca:

cornice by, for Strozzi palace, **13.** 201n

Pollard, Arthur (d. 1754), English consul at Aleppo 1745–53:

Rena persuades, to spend fortune, **21.** 162

'Pollard, the.' *See* Ashe, Elizabeth

Pollington, Vct. *See* Savile, Sir John (1719–78)

Pollio, Gaius Asinius (76 B.C.–A.D. 5), Virgil's patron:

anecdote on, in Wyndham's letter, **42.** 122

Bubb Dodington's name for Bute, **28.** 242

HW compares Holdernesse to, **28.** 207

Mason would like to make Effingham his, **28.** 208

Pollio. See under Virgil: *Eclogues*

Pöllnitz, Bns. *See* Stuart, Lady Anne

Pöllnitz, Karl Ludwig (1692–1775), Freiherr von; memoir-writer:

HW does not imitate, **22.** 343

Lettres et mémoires by, **31.** 154

writings of, **22.** 343n

Pöllnitz. *See also* Poellnitz

Pollock, ——, of Downing St:

Macartney wants book sent in care of, **32.** 386n

Pollock, William, King's Messenger:

(?) Hertford sends letter to HW through, **38.** 570

—— to send letter and dispatch through, **38.** 351–2

Polly Honeycombe. See under Colman, George

'Polly Peachum.' *See under* Gay, John: *Beggar's Opera*

Polmood, Peebleshire:

Murray seized at brother-in-law's house at, **19.** 274n

Polnitz. *See* Poellnitz; Pöllnitz

'Pologne, Mme de.' *See* Czernieski, Mme

Polonaise; polonaises (women's apparel):

Florentine ladies dress in, **25.** 175

Mann ignorant about, **17.** 152

old ladies ridiculous in, **33.** 420

Polish women's dress suggests, **17.** 152n

'Polonaise, sa majesté.' *See* Bourbon, Louis-François de, Prince de Conti

'Polonius':

HW is, to Ps Amelia, **39.** 127

See also under Shakespeare, William: *Hamlet*

Polotsk:

Jesuit novitiate at, **16.** 192n

Polruan, Cornwall:

Adam of, **14.** 75n

'Poltis, King.' *See under* Prior, Matthew: *Alma*

Polviglio:

Uguccioni gives, to Granvilles, **18.** 553–4

Polwarth, Vcts. *See* Yorke, Amabel

Polybius (d. ? 122 B.C.), Greek historian:

English generals not tried by rules of, **38.** 128

Histories by, describe Demetrius, **18.** 422

Zouch prefers Clarendon to, **16.** 18

Polycarpe, Joseph:

(?) José Manoel attacked by, **21.** 250, **43.** 275

Polycraticus. See under John of Salisbury
Polyeucte. See under Corneille, Pierre
Polygraphy or Shorthand Made Easy. See under Macaulay, Aulay
Polymetis. See under Spence, Joseph
Poly-Olbion. See under Drayton, Michael
Polypus:
    occurrence of, 24. 211
Pomatum; pomatums:
    Boufflers, Comtesse de, sends, to Bns Hervey, 31. 103
    Mann sends, to HW, 23. 407
Pombal, Marqués de. *See* Carvalho e Melo, Sebastião José
Pomegranate; pomegranates:
    and rose, on font owned by Catherine of Aragon, 32. 323–4
    HW could as soon find, as cherries, in Twickenham, 39. 407
    in 15th-century embroidery, 14. 78
    on clothes, in painting, 40. 216, 219
    'standard': HW grows, in pot, 33. 293; Parisians mix, with orange trees, 33. 293
Pomenars, Marquis de:
    crimes of, 31. 74
Pomerania:
    Calmucks wanted to set fire to villages of, 22. 14
    Frederick II drives Russians into, 21. 246–7
    Peter III may be induced to keep a foothold in, 22. 10–11
    —— proclaimed in, as czar, 22. 1
    Ungern-Sternberg assembles force in, 21. 119n
Pomeroy, Lt-Col.:
    battalions to be raised by, in Ireland, 38. 148n
Pomeroy, Miss, Twickenham schoolmistress:
    SH visited by, 12. 247
Pomeroy, Arthur (1723–98), cr. (1783) Bn and (1791) Vct Harberton:
    peerage of, 25. 433
Pomfret, Cts of. *See* Draycott, Anna Maria (ca 1736–87); Jeffreys, Hon. Henrietta Louisa (ca 1700–61)
Pomfret, E. of. *See* Fermor, George (1722–85); Fermor, Thomas (1698–1752)
Pomfret, Yorks:
    executions at, ordered by Richard III, 14. 179
Pomfret Castle. *See* Pontefract Castle
Pomfret family. *See* Fermor family
Pomme, Pierre (1735–1812), physician:
    Arles to be visited by, 6. 349, 355
    Boufflers, Comtesse Amélie de, attended by, 6. 349, 355
    Craufurd attended by, 3. 363
    — suited by, 3. 360
    Dacre consults, in Paris, 10. 290, 35. 121, 43. 137
    Du Deffand, Mme, alludes to, 3. 367
    (?) —— attended by, 6. 100
    —— considers consulting, 4. 168, 170, 177, 224

—— talks with, 3. 363
Noyon, Bp of, attended by, 4. 108, 119
Provence visited by, 5. 183
system of, 3. 367–8, 4. 127, 5. 183
wine proscribed by, 35. 121
Pommyer, ——:
    attends session of parliament of Paris, 8. 171
'Pomona.' *See* Venables Vernon, Lady Elizabeth, Cts Harcourt
Pomona:
    HW's name for Mrs Garrick, 31. 374
    hothouses of, 35. 473
    Marchais, Mme de, is, 39. 258
    Pitt, Mrs George, compared with, 30. 328
    Shelburne, Lady, compared with, 33. 139
    Vertumnus and, 35. 459
'Pomone'; 'Flore-Pomone.' *See* La Borde, Élisabeth-Josèphe de, Mme de Marchais
Pompadour, Marquise de. *See* Poisson, Jeanne-Antoinette
Pompadour, Françoise de (d. 1777), m. (1708) Philippe-Égon, Marquis de Courcillon:
    anecdote of Cardinal d'Estrées and, 4. 56
Pompeati, dancer:
    Cornelys, Theresa, married to, 23. 271n
'Pompeiata':
    Cornelys, Theresa, sang under name of, 23. 271
Pompeii:
    Almack's as devastating as earthquake at, 35. 423
    art objects from, brought by Hamilton, 32. 70
    Hamilton should list utensils from, 35. 419
    —— to seek silver flutes at, 35. 419
    —— to sift, 35. 415
    Pars will draw, well, 35. 424
Pomperant, Sieur de (fl. 1525):
    at surrender of François I, 1. 383
Pompey (Cneius Pompeius Magnus) (106–48 B.C.); Roman general:
    Dashkov a 'tolerable,' 33. 172
    HW jokes about hearing, scold in Temple of Concord, 38. 187
    Roman Capitol scene of triumph of, 8. 156
'Pompey':
    Boscawen's negro servant called, by HW, 9. 141
'Pompey,' (?) Mann's dog:
    Patapan's 'correspondence' said to excite, 18. 530
Pompey. See Corneille, Pierre; *Pompée*
'Pompey, old':
    HW visits, in London, 12. 153
Pompey the Little. See under Coventry, Francis
Pomphett. *See* Pomfret
Pompignan, Marquis de. *See* Le Franc, Jean-Jacques
'Pompom.' *See* Wiart, Auguste-Nicolas-Marie
Pompon; pompons:
    Hale's, 38. 41
    Luna to wear diamond in, 35. 86
    mahonnoises replace, in France, 21. 52

Pomponne, Marquis de. *See* Arnauld, Simon
Ponce, Signora:
in burletta company, **22.** 474n
Ponce de Guerrero, Don Manuel, 4th Conde de Selva Florida:
Peruvians hail as king, **22.** 426
Ponce de Léon y Spinola, Antonio (1726–80), Duque de Arcos:
mob forces, to carry demands to Charles III, **39.** 63
Ponce de Léon y Spinola, Don Joaquín (d. 1743), Duque de Arcos y Maqueda:
wounded, **18.** 154
Pond, Arthur (ca 1705–58), painter; F.R.S.:
HW's article on, **1.** 175n
member of Society of Antiquaries, **2.** 189n
might have supplied frontispiece for Golding, **14.** 27
print collection of, sold, **41.** 145
Pond; ponds:
Conway's, for goldfish, **37.** 367, 370
of goldfish, at SH, **20.** 188
See also Po-Yang
Pondevelle. *See* Pont-de-Veyle
Pondichéry; Pondicherry, French town in India:
Boscawen, Adm., fails to capture, **20.** 113n
——'s fleet sent to, **20.** 113
capture of, **21.** 515, **24.** 454, **38.** 105
courier carries news of capture of, through Turkey to Italy, **21.** 523
earlier peace would have spared France the loss of, **21.** 534
English victory at, **9.** 369
HW jokes about, **9.** 378
Lally's administration of, **3.** 30n
——'s alleged treason at, **9.** 52–3
——'s property to be confiscated and used for poor of, **3.** 30n
Mann will read about, in gazette, **21.** 516
reduction of, known in Florence, **24.** 461
war extends from, to Canada, **21.** 290
Pondisi, ——:
social relations of, with Marquise de Monconseil, **7.** 297
Poniatowski, Prince Andrea (1734–73):
death of, **5.** 346n
Poniatowski, Prince Michael George (1736–94), brother of Stanislas II; Abp of Gnesen; Primate of Poland and Lithuania:
arrested for debt, **11.** 243
English books sent by, to Stanislas II, **11.** 243
London visited by, **11.** 242
Merlin's scientific toys bought by, **11.** 242
Poniatowski, Prince Stanislas (1754–1833):
England visited by, **31.** 164–5
English ladies admire, **31.** 164
Lind said to be tutor to, at Cambridge, **23.** 556n, 564–5
Poniatowski, Stanislas Augustus. *See* Stanislas II
Poniatowski family:
Williams, Sir C. H., quarrels with Brühl over affairs of, **30.** 322

Pons, Marquise de. *See* Cossé-Brissac, Emmanuelle-Marie-Anne de
Pons, Vicomtesse de. *See* Le Tonnelier de Breteuil, Louise-Gabrielle-Rosalie
Pons, Antoinette-Rosalie de (1751–1824), m. (1766) Paul-François de Quélen de Stuer de Caussade, Marquis (later Duc) de St-Maigrin, later Duc de la Vauguyon:
HW never saw, **39.** 214
invited to Choisy, **4.** 259
Mirepoix ball attended by, **3.** 219, 221
social relations of, with Louis XVI and Marie-Antoinette, **6.** 105
Pons, Charles-Armand-Augustin (1744–94), Comte de:
Louis XVI gives grandes entrées to, **6.** 52
Pons, Louis-Marie (1744–ca 86), Marquis de:
French minister to Prussia, **5.** 146–7
social relations of, in Paris, **7.** 301, 337
Ponsonby, Bns. *See* Molesworth, Hon. Louisa (1749–1824)
Ponsonby, Capt.:
death of, rumoured, **37.** 33n
Ponsonby, Brabazon (1679–1758), 2d Vct Duncannon; cr. (1739) E. of Bessborough:
Devonshire obtains peerage for, **20.** 66
family of, lose Irish election, **37.** 422
Irish dissensions reported by, **20.** 455n
nominated lord justice in Ireland, **20.** 426
Ponsonby, Hon. Caroline (d. 1756):
death of, **21.** 362
Ponsonby, Catharine (1746–1827), m. (1763) Richard Boyle, styled Vct Boyle; 2d E. of Shannon, 1764:
birth date of, corrected, **43.** 131
marriage of: **38.** 235; expected, **10.** 110
Stone asks to perform marriage ceremony of, **10.** 110
—— opposes marriage of, **10.** 110
Ponsonby, Lady Catherine (1742–89), m. (1763) Hon. Aubrey Beauclerk, 2d Bn Vere, 1781; 5th D. of St Albans, 1787:
Addington church visited by, **10.** 343
appearance of, **10.** 343
death of, **11.** 110n
Devonshires entertain, at Chatsworth, **9.** 295
dying of cancer, **11.** 59–60
HW and Cole entertained by, at Drayton, **10.** 90, 342
HW thinks Mann has seen, with husband, **25.** 191
HW visits, at Hanworth, **33.** 294
health of: cancer, **11.** 59–60; fever and sore throat, **21.** 362; sore throat, **9.** 272
lives abroad, from debt, **33.** 294n
marriage of, **10.** 342
name of, corrected, **43.** 140
Penn, Lady Juliana, not congenial with, **11.** 23
returned to England, **33.** 293
'the new Veres,' **33.** 293

Ponsonby, Lady Charlotte (1747–1822), m. (1770) William Fitzwilliam, 4th E. Fitzwilliam:
Berry, Mary, identifies, 11. 59n
Devonshires entertain, at Chatsworth, 9. 295
engagement of, 10. 304
Fitzwilliam to wed, 23. 213
HW always liked, 35. 377
sister of, ill, 11. 59–60
SH visited by, 12. 247
Wales, P. of, and D. of York to be entertained by, 11. 59
Ponsonby, Lady Elizabeth. See Cavendish, Lady Elizabeth
Ponsonby, Frederick (1758–1844)), styled Vct Duncannon, 3d E. of Bessborough, 1793:
Amelia, Ps, entertains, 33. 416n, 35. 533n
Barrymore, Lady, visits Colisée with, 7. 350n
Cholmondeley House, Richmond, may be occupied by, 35. 357
emissary to George III about Ps Amelia's will, 33. 535
fiancée may not be gentle enough for, 35. 357
HW asks, to let Ps Amelia's portrait of her grandmother be copied, 42. 180–1
HW's correspondence with, 42. 180–1
HW sends letter by, 7. 396, 30. 265
HW's social relations with, in Paris, 7. 344, 348–9
Hobart, Mrs, entertains at play, at Ham Common, 33. 370
Mariette's sale attended by, 7. 350
member of Committee, 2. 208n
Paris not left by, as expected, 30. 265
—— visited by, 32. 265
reads petition at Cambridge, 2. 207
SH visited by, 12. 232
wife of, 6. 482n, 11. 213n, 29. 185n
Ponsonby, Hon. Henry (d. 1745), Maj.-Gen.:
killed at Fontenoy, 19. 42–3, 36. 11, 37. 192
regiment of, 17. 450n, 451n
Ponsonby, Hon. Henry (d. ? ca 1756):
death of, 31. 362
Ponsonby, John (1713–89), Irish Speaker 1756–71:
administration opposed by, on Septennial Bill, 39. 67–8, 70–1
daughter of, 10. 110, 38. 235
Gore supports, 37. 449n
Halifax attended by, in Presence Chamber, 10. 18
—— leaves, as lord justice in Ireland, to retrieve reputation in England, 38. 147
Hertford accepts nomination from, of aide-de-camp, 30. 200
—— does not expect to be deceived by, 39. 27
—— well treated by, 39. 27
lord justice in Ireland, 38. 28n, 147
Montagu wants to present Catalogue of the Collections of Pictures of the Duke of Devonshire . . . to, 9. 396, 398

Selwyn's witticism about gambling of, at Newmarket, 21. 7
Speaker's chair quietly entered by, 37. 462
speakership of, arranged, 37. 448n
Stone, Abp, denounces, 37. 463
—— to be opposed by, 38. 28
SH visited by members of family of, 12. 246
Wexford and Navan elections lost by, 37. 422–3
wife of, 28. 323n
Ponsonby, Hon. John (d. ca 1756):
death of, 21. 362
Ponsonby, Lady Sarah (d. 1765):
Devonshires entertain, at Chatsworth, 9. 295
Ponsonby, Sarah (ca 1755–1831), recluse of Llangollen:
HW does not know, 34. 94–5
Ponsonby, Stephen:
Irish faction led by, 21. 154n
Ponsonby, William (ca 1704–93), styled Vct Duncannon; 2d E. of Bessborough, 1758; M.P.:
absentee tax opposed by, 23. 524n
Admiralty post given to, 9. 33, 19. 256, 20. 157
Admiralty post taken from, 21. 25
Amelia, Ps, leaves legacy to, as executor, 33. 535
(?) at Chesterfield's assembly, 37. 325
biographical information about, corrected, 43. 91, 112, 194, 240, 322, 366, 373
bronzes owned by, 15. 12
Chatham, E. of, object of protest by, 22. 471n
daughter of, 10. 342, 11. 23n, 59n, 23. 213, 25. 191n
daughter's engagement pleases, 10. 304
daughter visited by, at Hanworth, 33. 294n
Devonshire, D. of, visited by, at Chatsworth, 38. 19
Devonshires entertain, at Chatsworth, 9. 295
family of, suffers from epidemic, 9. 271
Gray, Sir James, hoped to supplant, as secretary in Ireland, 19. 472
HW calls on, 43. 381
HW hears from, of Conway's approach, 37. 460
HW resists climbing Stowe column with, 39. 127
HW's correspondence with, 43. 379–82
HW's opinion of, 10. 313
HW to approach, about house for Lady Malpas, 36. 42
HW to receive answer from, to Riccardi's offer, 19. 387
HW visits, 32. 11
health of: fever and sore throat, 21. 362; illness, 33. 535; sore throat, 9. 272
Malpas, Vcts, wants house of, 36. 42
Mann buys marble fragment for, from Stosch's collection, 21. 192
—— expects Riccardi's offer to be rejected by, 19. 392

—— sends gladiator intaglio to, **20.** 159

Mann, Galfridus, procures seeds for, **20.** 25

marriage of, **20.** 66

North's letter from, on absentee tax, **32.** 164n

Pelham, Miss, and Dillon play quinze with, **32.** 345

postmaster, **22.** 311

resignation of: **41.** 67n; as joint postmaster-general, **22.** 97, 471; successfully discouraged, **30.** 234

Riccardi's jewelry may be bought by, **19.** 361, 372–3, 382, 398

Richmond's invitation to, **19.** 308n

son acts for, as Ps Amelia's executor, **42.** 180n

Stosch corresponds with, about Meleager, **20.** 159

—— gives or sells intaglio of Gladiator to, for procuring arrears of his pension, **17.** 212, **20.** 157, 159, **21.** 151

——'s affairs executed by, **20.** 70

Temples entertain, at Stowe, **4.** 432, **10.** 313–16

Treasury post goes to, **21.** 24

verses by, on Lady Sarah Lennox, **38.** 88

voting shunned by, **22.** 508n

Wexford and Navan elections lost by, **37.** 422–3

Ponsonby, Hon. William (d. ? ca 1756):
death of, **21.** 362

Ponsonby, William:
Paris secretaryship of embassy may go to, **33.** 420n, **42.** 73n

Pont, Miss, of Twickenham:
SH visited by, **12.** 244

Pontano, Don Cicio, Neapolitan abbé:
Acquaviva orders seizure of papers and arrest of, on suspicion of treasonable correspondence, despite Maria Theresa's patent of protection, **18.** 55–6

Place d'Espagne, residence of, **18.** 56

Thun claims, **18.** 56

Pont-aux-Dames, convent of:
Du Barry, Mme, exiled to, **6.** 52

Pont Beauvoisin. See Pont-de-Beauvoisin

Pontchartrain, Comtesse de. See L'Aubespine, Hélène-Rosalie-Angélique de

Pontchartrain, Marquis de. See Phélypeaux, Paul-Jérôme

Pontchartrain, Marquise de. See Galard de Béarn, Angélique-Marie-Gabrielle de

Pontchartrain (France), Maurepas's seat:
Aiguillon, Duchesse d', not at, **5.** 138

Maurepas, Comtesse de, returns from, **6.** 53

Pontchartrain's accident at, **4.** 248

visitors to: Agen, Bp of, **5.** 98; Aiguillon, Duchesse d', **3.** 65, 370, **5.** 127, 129, 134, 137; Estaing, **7.** 439; Pont-de-Veyle, **4.** 471, **5.** 410, 413

Pont-de-Beauvoisin (France):
Artois, Comtesse d', to be received at, **5.** 402

Berrys pass, **11.** 139n

HW and Gray at, **13.** 181n

letter to Louis XV from, about Comtesse d'Artois, **5.** 420

village near, **11.** 87n

Young Pretender said to be banished to, with Sheridan and Stafford, **20.** 9

Pont de Neuilly:
medal of, **6.** 27n

Pont d'Espierre:
English march to, **37.** 179

Pont-de-Veyle, Comte de. See Ferriol, Antoine

Pont du Gard, Nîmes (France):
example of Roman power and skill, **15.** 202

Ponte, Jacopo da (1510–92), called Bassan; painter:
Furnese has pictures by, **21.** 172n

Hôtel de Lambert has painting by, **7.** 337

Monaco, P. of, has paintings by, **7.** 335

New Oxford Guide mentions, **35.** 462

paintings by, in Colebrooke's sale, **23.** 569n

Ponte alle Grazie, Florence:
HW's lodging near, **37.** 68

Ponte a Santa Trinità, Florence:
Azzi attacked on, by coachmen, **17.** 448

Bosville, Mrs, misbehaves upon, **18.** 286, **35.** 41

cocchiata moves to, **18.** 485

Florentines gather on, in the evening, **17.** 77n

frequented, **17.** 473

HW prowls about, after supper, **17.** 473

HW recalls 'delicious nights' on, **11.** 287

Henley bridge excelled only by, **25.** 613, **33.** 485

ladies to walk in Mann's garden instead of, **17.** 498

Mann frequents, **17.** 77

——'s house near, **11.** 154

masquerades on, at night, **17.** 97

people prefer, to seeing Mann, **17.** 97

promenade on, **13.** 228, 229

Via Maggio leads from, to church of San Felice, **17.** 488n

Vincent calls, unsuitable for duel, **18.** 111

whimsical dresses worn by Florentine ladies on, **25.** 174

Ponte d'Albaret, Joseph de (d. 1792):
(?) Du Deffand, Mme, learns song from, **4.** 77

(?) St-Ouen visited by, **6.** 229, **7.** 348

(?) social relations of, in Paris, **3.** 24, 100, **7.** 321, 348

Ponte della Madelena, at Naples:
San Gennaro's kinsman harangues mob at, **24.** 541

Ponte del Reno (Italy):
Charles Emmanuel III and Traun at, **17.** 500

Pontedera (Italy):
Pucci and Riccardi have houses at, **22.** 220n

Ponte di Trinità. See Ponte a Santa Trinità

'Pontefract':
HW uses, for 'Pomfret,' **17.** 339

Pontefract (or Pomfret) Castle:
HW sees ruins of, where Edward V's attendants were killed, **35.** 269

Ponte Molle (Italy):
  hussars demolish part of, **18**. 444
  Lobkowitz's army at, **18**. 531
Ponte Vecchio, at Florence:
  cracks during flood, **13**. 237
  HW's lodgings near, **37**. 68
  Riccardi must have bought his jewels on, **19**. 73
  Siries at, **15**. 279
  Strozzi, Principessa, seeks stolen jewels on, **19**. 350
  York, D. of, looks forward to walking on, **22**. 236
Pontiac (ca 1720–69), Indian chief:
  conspiracy of, **22**. 177n
Pontifex Maximus:
  HW's name for Conway, **39**. 150
  HW's term for Pius VI, **25**. 589
  Wilkes more conspicuous than, **24**. 48
Pontine Marshes:
  drainage project not needed for, in drought, **24**. 479
  Pius VI's drainage project for: expensive failure, **25**. 383, 588; may fail from lack of declivity, **24**. 479; Romans failed to do it, **24**. 343–4
Pontius Pilate (fl. A.D. 26):
  Benedict XIV makes pun on name of, **21**. 37
Pont Neuf, in Paris:
  Dal Pozzo, Mme, could build, with penises, **17**. 8on
  Du Deffand, Mme, mentions, **6**. 102
  Louis XV kneels before sacrament at, **39**. 55–6
  Mazuel, bookseller on, **30**. 263n
  statue of Henri IV on, **31**. 99, **34**. 176
  Thomas stationed at, **3**. 250, **5**. 202
  threatening verses posted at, **20**. 287
'Ponto,' HW's pet:
  Montagu to kiss, for HW, **10**. 205
  (?) ossuarium not to be made for, till dead, **10**. 155
Pontoise (France):
  French parliament exiled to, **20**. 293, 432n, **37**. 365
  HW may go to, **10**. 190
  St Martin's near, **10**. 12n
Ponton, Daniel, chairman of quarter session, Lambeth:
  Weymouth's letter to, **23**. 77n
Pontoon bridges. *See under* Bridge
Pontorson (France):
  battle near, **12**. 84n
Pontremoli (Italy):
  Fivizano near, **19**. 35
  Lobkowitz sends Gorani to, **19**. 36
  Spanish army threatens approach from, to Tuscany, **17**. 289
  Spanish troops approach, **19**. 245
  Traun's troops must enter Tuscany through, **18**. 76
Pont Ste-Maxence (France):
  HW visits, **7**. 316

Pony:
  Montagu's, eats trees at Waldershare, **10**. 321
Ponzio, Pietro, Benedict XIV's surgeon:
  Benedict XIV's witticism to, on use of syringe, **21**. 37
Ponz y Piquer, Antonio (1725–92), abbé; art critic; writer:
  HW's account of Raphael's cartoons questioned by, **16**. 169
  Viage de España and *Viage fuera de España* by, **16**. 169n
Pool, Mrs:
  SH visited by, **12**. 251
Pool. *See also* Poole
Poole, Dr:
  print of, **40**. 237
'Poole, Miss.' *See* Pole, Millicent
Poole, Sir Ferdinando (d. 1804), 4th Bt, 1767:
  post lost by, **22**. 109n
Poole, Sir Henry (d. 1767), 3d Bt, 1763:
  Excise post lost by, **22**. 109n
Poole, Dorset:
  anti-American address from, **24**. 132n, **39**. 270n, **41**. 311n
  custom house at, robbed, **9**. 106n
  George III and Q. Charlotte meet Mt Edgcumbes at, **11**. 32
Poona. *See* Puna
Poor, Enoch (1736–80), American Gen.:
  (?) British escape from, at Monmouth, **24**. 405n
Poor, the:
  aged, sufferings of, **31**. 402
  Cambridge, R. O., to provide potatoes for, **12**. 177
  charity for, **31**. 397
  Gloucester, Ds of, aids, **31**. 396
  Grenvilles propose Treasury relief for, **30**. 235
  HW contributes towards relief of, **42**. 455
Poor Bill. *See under* Parliament: acts of
Poor rate; poor rates:
  House of Commons busy about, **31**. 5
  petitions about, **31**. 5n
  Scotland does not have, **15**. 91
Poor Robin:
  in book of ballads, **32**. 200n
Poor Robin's Almanac:
  HW parodies, **31**. 13
  prognostications in, **13**. 123
Pope, Mr, brother of Jane Pope:
  SH visited by, **12**. 228
Pope, Mrs:
  Louis XV's mistress, **9**. 189
Pope, Alexander (ca 1641–1717), 'hatter,' father of the poet:
  Cooper brother-in-law of, **29**. 279
  son of, satirized in *New Lesson for Pope*, **18**. 34
Pope, Alexander (1688–1744), poet:
  Addison and, professionally jealous of each other, **2**. 252

Addison called 'perfect monster' by, **35.** 563

Answer to Mrs Howe by, mentions Bns Hervey, **31.** 417

Are These Things So, misattributed to, **17.** 387, 410, **35.** 25

Art of Sinking in Poetry by, perhaps mentioned by Hannah More, **31.** 264

Ashe, nurseryman to, **35.** 157n

Ashton's translation of epitaph by, **14.** 235

——'s verses show influence of, **13.** 138–40

Atterbury a correspondent of, **11.** 20n

—— receives remark from, **11.** 20n

——'s witticism on, **20.** 66

'Baker, Sir James,' pseudonym of, **18.** 317n

Bathurst's correspondence with, said to have been burnt, **28.** 239

'begotten in a grotto by the headache upon the gripes,' **35.** 25

Bevois Mount associated with, **33.** 42–3

Blenheim's description should be prescribed by, **40.** 12

Blount, Martha, and, **32.** 32n, **33.** 520

Bolingbroke admired by, **28.** 440, **29.** 169

Bolingbroke and Swift admired by, **25.** 6

Bolingbroke 'celebrated' by, **35.** 466

—— often visits, at Twickenham, **42.** 488, 490

—— persuaded by friends of, to pay for printing of book, **20.** 66

——'s *Idea of a Patriot King* privately printed by, **20.** 59n

——'s *Letters* printed and altered by, **20.** 61

——'s letter to, introducing *Essays*, **37.** 354

——, Swift, and, flatter one another, **35.** 568

Bubb Dodington's verses echo, **28.** 242

Burlington, Cts of, said to have been furnished by, with inscription for her daughter's picture, **18.** 482

—— talks with, at Chiswick, **18.** 449

'Charms of the Athenians,' paraphrased by HW, **35.** 478

Charteris mentioned by, **13.** 138n, **19.** 148n

Chatterton's pillage from, **2.** 305–6

Chaucer not improved by, according to Warburton, **17.** 144

Chiswick visited by, **43.** 253

Churchill's *The Times* mentions admiration of, for Bns Hervey, **31.** 417

Cibber attacks, **18.** 8

——'s *Letter to Mr Pope* ridicules, **30.** 310, **37.** 125

——'s quarrel with, satirized in *New Lesson for Pope*, **18.** 34–6

Cobham deified, at Stowe, despite quarrel, **35.** 76

correspondence of: **30.** 24; shows good heart and great mind, **14.** 3

Court Poems published under name of, **19.** 449n

death of: **19.** 229; leaves Sir C. H. Williams the only true poet in England, **30.** 53

Dennis abused by, **13.** 65n

Discord attributed to, **37.** 162, 165

Du Deffand, Mme, asks for print of, **4.** 241, 266

—— cites letters of, **6.** 146–7

Dunciad, The, by: **1.** 227; adapted or quoted, **32.** 86, 132, **33.** 362, 529; Conway quotes, **37.** 89, **43.** 372; Gray alludes to, **13.** 147, (?) **14.** 14; Gray drops poem because it resembles, **15.** 53, **43.** 191; HW alludes to, **11.** 170, **13.** 122, **38.** 309, **43.** 377; HW compares *Heroic Epistle* to, **28.** 77, 81, **32.** 101; HW paraphrases, **9.** 180; HW quotes, **12.** 261, **17.** 451, **29.** 118, 322, **35.** 136, 173, 251, **36.** 241, **38.** 543, **39.** 150; HW's criticism of, **16.** 272; HW transcribes, for Mann, **17.** 403; Hayley discusses, in *Essay on Epic Poetry*, **29.** 256; Mallet subject of sonnet affixed to, **20.** 62; *Rolliad* compared with, **25.** 612; Selwyn quotes, to Wilkes, **38.** 223; West alludes to, **13.** 118, 127, 131

Elegy to the Memory of an Unfortunate Lady by: HW quotes, **39.** 209; Johnson's comment on, **29.** 130; said to be written about Miss Scudamore, **42.** 123n

Eloisa to Abelard by: **35.** 529; admired by Dr Johnson, **29.** 130; HW quotes, **30.** 78, **33.** 335, 526; translated by Duchesse d'Aiguillon, **3.** 190–1; West paraphrases, **13.** 93; Yearsley, Mrs, knows no work by Pope except, **31.** 218

English still prefer Shakespeare and Milton to, **40.** 379

engraving from Brown's drawing of, **15.** 189

epigram 'To Sir R[obert] W[alpole]' attributed to, by HW, **30.** 4–5

Epilogue to the Satires by: **32.** 305; HW quotes, **2.** 314, **9.** 311; *Epistle* by Bubb Dodington mentioned in, **30.** 316

Epistles by, quoted, **33.** 511, **43.** 357

Epistles of Horace by, quoted by HW, **35.** 250

Epistle to Cobham by, quoted by HW, **24.** 301

Epistle to Dr Arbuthnot by: **43.** 176; 'Bufo' in, **15.** 26n; Gray alludes to, **14.** 46; Gray is charmed by, **13.** 75; HW alludes to, **13.** 121, **14.** 169; HW parodies, **35.** 500; HW quotes, **2.** 233, **9.** 373, **11.** 175, 364, **12.** 10, **31.** 300, **32.** 372, **33.** 523, **34.** 44, **35.** 524, **39.** 460; Hardinge quotes, **35.** 577; Mason alludes to, **28.** 436, **29.** 278; More, Hannah, quotes, **31.** 389; West paraphrases, **13.** 93; West quotes, **13.** 133

Epistle to Jervas by, 'Wortley' changed to 'Worsley' in, **29.** 285

Epistle to Lord Burlington by: **2.** 275n; discusses gardens at Cannons, **30.** 60–1

'Epitaph for Himself' and 'On the Grotto' by, sent by HW to Spence, **40.** 35

epitaph 'On Charles Earl of Dorset' alluded to, **32.** 145, 178

[Pope, Alexander, poet, *continued*]

Essay on Criticism by: HW parodies, **35.** 101; HW paraphrases, **32.** 298; HW quotes, **10.** 192, **18.** 129; Pillori translates, **28.** 171n; West paraphrases, **13.** 93

Essay on Man by: **4.** 84, **43.** 364; adapted or quoted, **32.** 50, 130, **33.** 25, 396, 511, 520, **34.** 5, 206; critics called later parts of, inferior to first, **28.** 127; HW alludes to lines on Newton in, **28.** 408; HW paraphrases, **13.** 94; HW quotes, **18.** 36, **28.** 397, **31.** 191; influenced by Shaftesbury, **13.** 133; Nivernais translates, **42.** 393; style of, would harm *Paradise Lost*, **41.** 297; Warburton's notes to, **22.** 184; Wilkes's parody of, **22.** 184–5

faults of, **20.** 65–6

First Ode of the Fourth Book of Horace by, Conway encloses, to HW, **37.** 7–8, 11

First Satire of Second Book of Horace by: HW paraphrases, **16.** 18; HW quotes, **39.** 342

Frederick, P. of Wales, talks with, **17.** 143

friends of, publish pamphlets against Bolingbroke, **20.** 65

garden of: art and deception used in design of, to make it appear larger, **25.** 177; 'improved' by Stanhope, **25.** 177–8

ghost of, flits under SH window, **37.** 270

Glover is preferred to, by newspaper, **13.** 133

Gray alludes to, **14.** 35

——'s interview with, **14.** 3

grotto of, at Twickenham: **10.** 38, 279; Pope's lines on, travestied by West, **14.** 235; visited by Boswell, Courtenay, Malone, and Malone's sisters and sister-in-law, **42.** 143n

HW and Mrs Spence discuss, **20.** 189

HW cannot 'compose' letters like, **33.** 504

HW compares Mason to, **28.** 279, 325, 400, 440, **29.** 103, 312

HW disclaims authorship of verses on, **18.** 505

HW prefers Dryden to, **31.** 213

HW quotes, **2.** 177, 233, 314, **18.** 129, **24.** 301 (*see also under titles of individual works*)

HW quotes lines from English newspaper on death of, **18.** 467–8

HW reads letters of, to Digby, **28.** 280

HW's letters better than 'studied style' of, **31.** 365n

HW's notes to poems of, **43.** 106

HW's opinion of, **1.** 310

Halifax's contribution towards Dryden's monument satirized by, **21.** 140

Harte a disciple of, **15.** 53

Hayley imitates, **31.** 266n

health of: dropsy, **18.** 449

Herbert, Lady Mary, and Gage satirized by, **7.** 288

Heroic Epistle could have been written by, **28.** 86

Hervey satirized by, **31.** 416

Hervey, Bns, mentioned in letters of, **31.** 416–17

Horace imitated by, **33.** 501, **37.** 7–8, 25

house of, at Twickenham: **9.** 72n, **10.** 83n, 15. 319, **29.** 130, 178, **37.** 270, **42.** 481; Ellis lives in, **11.** 41n; occupied by Lord Mendip, **12.** 158, 160, 164, 198; Shirley's field next to, **39.** 310–11; visited by Archduke and Archduchess of Austria, **33.** 532

Iliad, The, completion of translation of, delayed, **29.** 130

Imitations of Horace by: **33.** 501, **37.** 7–8, 25; dedication in, to Murray, **17.** 250n; HW quotes, **32.** 33, 305, **34.** 19, **41.** 191, **42.** 285; Kinnoull and Tyrawley satirized in, **18.** 104; Wortley Montagu and wife satirized in, **21.** 472n; *see also under titles of the books of Horace*

Jervas taught painting to, **15.** 144n

Johnson's life of, HW comments on, **18.** 130–1

lack of poetry at Twickenham since death of, **32.** 31, **33.** 465

Lansdown the patron of, **28.** 208n

letter of, on death of Fenton, **2.** 259

letters of: affected, **9.** 29; stiff, **35.** 568

Letters of the Late Alexander Pope, Esq., stiff and laboured, **28.** 17, 292

Letter to a Noble Lord by: Mason alludes to, **28.** 225; suppressed at wish of Horatio Walpole (1678–1757), **9.** 116

Lyttelton a friend of, **20.** 61

——'s advice to give up satire disregarded by, **29.** 255

Mallet's relations with, **20.** 62

Mann dislikes, **17.** 403

map of, corrected by Wood, **41.** 177

Marchmont a 'hero' of, **20.** 5

Mason mentions, in verses, **28.** 440

Memoirs of Martinus Scriblerus (with Arbuthnot): 'Crambe, Conradus' in, **43.** 247; HW alludes to, **28.** 61

Memoirs of P. P., by, **29.** 150, **34.** 64

Messiah by: **43.** 176; quoted by HW, **12.** 170, **35.** 268

model of purity and taste, **16.** 257

Monro mentions, in epigram on doctors, **17.** 168, **30.** 30

Montagu, Lady Mary Wortley, allegedly loved by, but quarrelled over sheets, **34.** 255

—— frequently mentioned by, **30.** 309–10

—— quarrels with, over his song on Mrs Howard, **14.** 243

—— satirized by, **14.** 242–3, **20.** 282, **21.** 472n

——'s eclogue attributed to, **14.** 38n

Montagu, Mrs, prefers Dryden to, **31.** 213

monument of, in Twickenham church, **2.** 368

Moral Essays by: Gage and Lady Mary Herbert mentioned in, **30.** 215; HW paraphrases, **31.** 341; HW quotes, **2.** 177, **28.** 104, **29.** 150, 173, **32.** 317, 364, **33.** 280, **35.** 526, **37.** 269; Hardinge quotes, **35.** 556; Mason quotes, **29.** 259; Poland and the Asturian mines mentioned in, **35.** 349n

More, Hannah, prefers, to Dryden, **31.** 213

Morning Herald prints parody of, **34.** 55, 60

mother of, **29.** 278, 279
Murray's friendship with, **17.** 250n, 344n
New Lesson for Pope satirizes, **18.** 34–6
new poets unlikely to equal, **16.** 265
Nivernais translates, well, **33.** 496
not a prolific author, **33.** 501
nurse of, *see* Beach, Mary
Of the Art of Sinking in Poetry by, quoted, **36.** 283
out of his senses, **18.** 449
Oxford, E. of, a friend of, **2.** 144n, **20.** 61
Pensées of, owned by Mme du Deffand, **8.** 33n
Persian and Turkish Tales recommended by, **11.** 20
Peterborough celebrated by, **24.** 112
Pinkerton dislikes, **16.** 265
pleases but does not surprise, **41.** 297
poetry elevated by, **15.** 202
prefaces by, to Shakespeare, **24.** 267n
Prologue to the Satires by, quoted by HW, **20.** 189, **25.** 321
Queensberry, Ds of, a friend of, **9.** 61n
—— mentioned in letters of, **19.** 195n
Rape of the Lock, The, by: 'Belinda' in, **12.** 206; Bonducci's translation of, **17.** 64; Buondelmonti's translation of, **13.** 231n; Gray alludes to, **13.** 65; HW quotes, **28.** 30, 32. 123, **33.** 404, **35.** 304; Johnson's comment on, **29.** 130; standard of grace and elegance, **16.** 272; West alludes to, **13.** 131
Rolli's epitaph on, quoted by HW, **18.** 468, 485
Satires and Epistles of Horace, paraphrased by West, **13.** 93
satires of: Chute quotes, **35.** 40; HW paraphrases, and applies to Selwyn, **30.** 271; HW quotes, **15.** 202; struck too low, **28.** 78
Satires of Dr John Donne Versified by: HW quotes, **28.** 46, 32. 302, **33.** 172, **39.** 230; Janssen's cheating of Bedford hinted at in, **18.** 124n; Mason quotes, **28.** 338
Second Epistle of the Second Book of Horace by: Conway quotes, **37.** 484; HW quotes, **30.** 43, 77; published, **37.** 25
Second Satire of the First Book of Horace by: quoted by HW, **29.** 178; Wortley Montagu satirized in, **35.** 268–9
Shakespeare edited by Warburton and, **40.** 228
'Sharawaggi' used by, **20.** 127n
Sixth Epistle of the First Book of Horace by, mentioned by Mason, **28.** 436
Sixth Satire of the Second Book of Horace by, paraphrased by Mason, **29.** 204
Southcote, friend of, **9.** 116
Spence defends, in pamphlet, **20.** 62n
——'s blindness to mortality of, **35.** 262
Stanhope alters house and garden of, **21.** 417
—— lives in house of, **2.** 368
Stowe visit brings memories of, to HW, **10.** 314
Suffolk, Cts of, often mentioned by, **22.** 544
Swift's lines on, **9.** 305n

—— urged by, to burn history of Anne's reign, **21.** 184
taste for poetry kept alive by, **13.** 248
Thompson treats, **9.** 66n
Three Hours After Marriage by, fails on the stage, **18.** 34
translations of Homer by, profitable, **18.** 35n
Twickenham resident, **42.** 481, 488, 490
unsuccessful in St Cecilian ode, **16.** 257
vanities and weaknesses of, **14.** 3
'Verses Upon the Late D——ss of M——,' Gray comments on, **14.** 2–3
villa of, *see* house of, at Twickenham
Voltaire introduced, to France, **41.** 152
—— told by, that Milton did not rhyme because he could not, **41.** 156
Walpole, Bns, commends satire supposedly by, **17.** 491
Walpole, Horatio (1678–1757), wishes poem of, suppressed, **9.** 116
Walpole, Sir Robert, never reviled by, **25.** 6–7
Warburton 'explains,' by metaphysical notes, **16.** 38
——'s edition of, **9.** 116–17, **13.** 38, 39
—— to defend, **20.** 62
Warton's *Essay* on, **29.** 178
West would make angry by publishing HW's letters, **13.** 198
——'s verses imitated from letter of, **14.** 15
Whitehead attracts attention of, **13.** 146n
'Windsor Forest' by: (?) HW echoes, **31.** 246n; paraphrased by West, **13.** 118
Works of, said to be printed by Baskerville, **40.** 228
Works of, in Prose, Vol. II: correspondence among Bolingbroke, Arbuthnot, Swift and Pope published in, **30.** 24–5; HW has not seen, **30.** 25; much commended, **30.** 25; Warburton's notes to, mention *Castle of Otranto,* **41.** 409–10
Zouch quotes, **16.** 34
Pope, Alexander (1763–1835), actor; painter: marriage of, **29.** 166n
Siege of Berwick acted by, **12.** 83
SH visited by, **12.** 237
wife of, **12.** 70n
Pope, Mrs Alexander (actress). *See* Younge, Elizabeth (ca 1744–97)
Pope, Mrs Alexander (mother of the poet). *See* Turner, Edith (1642–1733)
Pope, Dramley, Leghorn merchant: dishonesty of, **17.** 68
failure of, results in tea shortage, **17.** 59
Rome the refuge of, **17.** 68
Pope, Jane (1742–1818), actress: acts in *The Critic,* **28.** 487n
Clive, Mrs, friend of, **11.** 124n
—— visited by, **33.** 407, **35.** 533–4
Goodere has not paid HW the rent due to, **42.** 306
Great Queen St the address of, **42.** 306
HW's correspondence with, **42.** 306–7
HW's pun on name of, **33.** 407

[Pope, Jane, *continued*]
School for Scandal well acted by, 41. 363
SH visited by, 12. 224
SH visitors sent by, 12. 230, 243, 245
tears shed by, over Lady Diana Beauclerk's drawings, 28. 318
Pope, Sir Thomas (1508–59), founder of Trinity College, Oxford:
portrait of, 35. 73
Warton's life of, 28. 30
Pope, Sir William (1573–1631), K.B., 1603; cr. (1628) E. of Downe:
portrait of, 35. 72
tomb of, 35. 74
Wroxton built by, 35. 72
'Pope':
Walpole, Sir Robert, and Bns Sundon joke about, 17. 278
Pope; popes:
alchemist receives purse from, 32. 157
Bathurst called, 33. 176
burnt in effigy in London, 34. 113
Calvin worse than, 34. 111
dispensation from, 15. 341
dominions of, HW's lines on, praised by Gray, 14. 36
ease of governing astonishes, after accession, 21. 10
effigy of, paraded at bonfires, 10. 254
election of, *see* Conclave
England, having taken over authority of, has their excuse for tyranny and rapine, 25. 642
Galluzzi consulted Leopold II concerning publication of infamy of, 25. 238
—— exposes iniquity of, 25. 80, 202, 224, 238
Gibbon's account of, 42. 221
HW calls, succession of rascals, 25. 224
HW imagines poisoning of, 35. 222
HW jokes about himself as, 30. 8
HW on, 2. 78, 100
HW wishes, were extinct like Medici so that their true history could be published, 25. 224
illegitimate children no longer begotten by, 22. 254
imperial fiefs usurped by, may be coveted by Joseph II, 25. 224
Joseph II may dethrone, 23. 117
later history of, as dull as that of later Byzantine emperors, 24. 48
lies to be expected from, 11. 288
Maximilian I lacks bribe-money to become, 25. 468
medals of: at Burghley House, 10. 345; Stosch's, 21. 231
Monte Cavallo the summer home of, 24. 344
names chosen by, 36. 233
nolo episcopare of, means 'I lie,' 11. 288
office of, compared by Mann to doge's, 17. 87
old saying about thinking no more of, 23. 128
Ossory, Lady, might choose, 32. 209
Passionei's toast to, at conference, 12. 266

Philip II bullied by, 18. 344
quotation from, about ease of governing, 20. 425
ring of, 21. 52
rose-water baptism case to be decided by, 17. 62–3
saying attributed to, 10. 142
ship of, captured by English, 17. 8, 15–16
state of, *see* Papal States
testoons of, 17. 4
whole world claimed by, as heirs of Christ, 25. 642
York, D. of, makes witticism on kissing toe of. 7. 365
Young Pretender denied royal title by, 11. 270–1
See also Alexander VI (1431–1503); Alexander VII (1599–1667); Alexander VIII (1610–91); Benedict XIV (1675–1758); Boniface III (1235–1303); Clement VII (d. 1534); Clement VIII (1536–1605); Clement XI (1649–1721); Clement XII (1652–1740); Clement XIII (1693–1769); Clement XIV (1705–74); Gregory XIII (1502–85); Honorius III (d. 1227); Innocent III (ca 1161–1216); Innocent IV (d. 1254); Innocent VIII (1432–92); Innocent X (1572–1655); Innocent XII (1615–1700); Innocent XIII (1655–1724); Julius II (1445–1513); Julius III (1487–1555); Leo X (1475–1521); Paul III (1468–1549); Paul IV (1476–1559); Paul V (1552–1621); Pius V (1504–72); Pius VI (1717–99); Sixtus V (1521–90); Urban II (ca 1042–99); Urban IV (d. 1264); Urban V (1310–70); Urban VIII (1568–1644)
'Pope Joan':
Bathurst addressed as, by Gordon Rioters, 33. 176
brought to bed, 22. 450
Elizabeth, Q., may have fancied herself as, 32. 323
Walpole, Sir Robert, calls Bns Sundon, 17. 278
'Popery':
totters, though bolstered up by England, 25. 237
See also Roman Catholic Church
Popery Act. *See* Parliament: acts of: Popish Relief Act
Popery Unmasked. See under Onslow, Arthur
Popes:
West's poems written at, 14. 16n
'Pope's Head,' Edinburgh:
Donaldson at, 10. 350
Pope's Head Alley, London:
Kentish's shop in, 16. 70
Pop-gun; pop-guns:
Abercrombie might be terrified by child with, 21. 56
citadels not captured with, 22. 116
HW may mount, in castle battlements, 21. 311
Popham, Edward (d. ?1772):
Hawkins dedicates book to, 15. 70n

Popham, Elizabeth (d. 1761), m. 1 (1707) Edward Richard Montagu, Vct Hinchingbrooke; m. 2 (1728) Francis Seymour:
death of: 9. 346; expected, 9. 345
Montagu, D. of, leaves reversion of estate to, 9. 94
portrait of, 40. 284
Sandwich's mother, 20. 216n
Popkin, Rebecca Eleonora (d. 1799), m. (before 1773) Sir Watkin Lewes:
unable to come to SH, 15. 198
Poplar; poplars:
HW quivers like a, 33. 157
leaves of, turn according to wind, 33. 35
Lombardy: Conway sends, to HW, 39. 133, 134; grown by HW, Conway, and Lord Ossory, 33. 480; in fashion, 11. 146; Rochford brings, to Conway from Turin, 39. 133n; would be encouraged by wet season, 39. 133
Poplar pine. See under Poplar: Lombardy; see also Lombardy pine
Popple, Henry (d. 1743), F.R.S.:
map of, omits Ohio River, 20. 497
Poppy; poppies:
harvest pure from, 35. 372
Lichfield Cathedral's beds of, make clergy sleepy, 40. 43
symbolic of Ceres, 30. 326
Temple, Cts, mentions, in verses, 10. 114
Poppyhead; poppyheads:
infusion of, taken by Chute for gout, 14. 93, 94
Popularity:
HW's reflections on mortality of, 37. 266
Population:
of English cities, increasing, 11. 287–8
Poquelin, Jean-Baptiste (1622–73). See Molière
Porbus, Franz (1540–80) or Franz (1570–1622), Flemish painters:
portrait attributed to, at Knole, 35. 133
Porcelain:
Chinese, collected by Colquhoun, 42. 322n
Choiseul gives, to Mme du Deffand, 41. 197
Dresden, snuff-box of, 42. 464
Du Deffand, Mme, offers to leave, to HW, 36. 181, 182
English, HW sends, to Mme du Deffand, 6. 429
first HW has read of, in Q. Mary's reign, 32. 323
Francis I gives special privilege to Ginori to make, 18. 184n
Frankenthal, see under China
French, in lottery, 34. 142
HW compares varieties of, 25. 635
HW's collection of, 25. 591
HW's folly in collecting, 25. 604
Louis XVI gives, to Joseph II, 6. 449
porringer of, 32. 323
Sèvres, exchanged by HW and Mrs Gostling, 41. 437–8

Tuscan: HW wants Horace Mann II to bring him specimen of, 25. 590–1; see also under China factory: Tuscan
See also China
Porchester, Bn. See Herbert, Henry (1741–1811)
Porchester, Bns. See Wyndham, Lady Elizabeth Alicia Maria
Porchester, Hants:
Margaret of Anjou lands at, 14. 72
Porchet. See Porquet
Porci, Ciccio. See Cicciaporci, F.
Porcia (first name). See Marcia; Portia
Porcia, Leandro (1673–1740), cardinal, 1728:
Conclave abandoned by, after quarrel with Benedictines, 17. 22
death of, 17. 22n
rage of, at Conclave, causes him to spit blood, 13. 215–16
Porcupine; porcupines:
exhibited at York, 28. 91
HW's serenity not as ruffleable as, 33. 316
See also Hedgehog
Pordenone, Giovanni de' Sacchis (1484–1539), called:
painting attributed to, 22. 291
Pore; pores:
Mann attributes Princesse de Craon's ailments to checking of perspiration in, by heavy clothing, 18. 109–10
Pork:
Ireland to send, to Lisbon earthquake sufferers, 37. 423n
Montagu sends, to HW, 9. 183
season too far advanced for salting of, 24. 381n
Pornography:
earthquake said to be a judgment against, 20. 133–4
See also under Chorier, Nicolas; Cleland, John; Gervais de la Touche, Jean-Charles; Godart de Beauchamps, Pierre-François
Porphyria:
(?) occurrences of, 43. 285
See also George III: health of: 'insanity'
Porphyrogeniti:
HW imagines sharing Mary Berry with, 12. 131
HW not to 'twinkle under the auspices of,' 28. 371
Mann too discreet to send anecdotes of, 33. 450
Porphyry:
chimney-pieces inlaid with, 25. 93n
in mosaic, 35. 409
tables of, 26. 7
urns of, 31. 80
Porpora, Nicola Antonio (1686–1768), composer:
biographical information about, corrected, 43. 249
Temistocle by, 18. 180

Porquet, Pierre-Charles-François (1728–96), abbé; tutor to Chevalier de Boufflers:
Cholmondeley, Mrs, gives book to, **4.** 454
social relations of, in Paris, **7.** 338, 339
verses by: **5.** 284n; for bust of Stanislas I, **4.** 325; HW mentions, **5.** 439; on Holbach's *Système de la Nature*, **4.** 454; on Mme du Deffand, with rhymes in 'ec' and "eugle,' **4.** 454; on Mme du Deffand's tonneau, **4.** 454
(?) verses from, **4.** 295–6
(?) wit of, **4.** 296
Porriante, Cesare:
Mann's annuity to, **25.** 667n
Porridge, plum. *See* Plum porridge
Porringer:
porcelain, owned by Q. Elizabeth, **32.** 323
Porson, Richard (1759–1808), Greek scholar:
disbelieves in Ireland's MSS, **15.** 321
Port, George Rowe (ca 1775–94), Mrs Delany's great-nephew:
great-aunt to be visited by, at Windsor, **33.** 498
Port, Georgina Mary Ann (1771–1805), Mrs Delany's great-niece; m. (1789) Benjamin Waddington:
biographical information about, corrected, **43.** 213
great-aunt accompanied by, at Windsor, **33.** 498
not favoured by George III and Q. Charlotte, **15.** 334
Port (wine):
Chute to get, from Hackwood Park, **35.** 86
clergyman drinks, **10.** 297
Fitzwalter consumes 24 bottles of, weekly, **20.** 518–19
HW nauseated but cured by, **12.** 38
Mason does honours to Nicholls in, **28.** 418
—— drinks Haidar 'Ali's health in, **29.** 133
—— unable to drink more than a pint of, **28.** 208
Montagu addicted to, **9.** 293, 390, 393, **10.** 101, 258
Oxford Loungers peruse divinity over, **38.** 46
Pembroke, E. of, makes his own, **25.** 497
Wilkes's ghost laid in a sea of, **23.** 5
Port; ports:
English, guarded against smuggling, **10.** 288–9
See also Seaport
Porta alla Croce, Florence:
race ends near, **17.** 79n
Porta al Prato ('Cascine Gate') at Florence:
Corsini's house near, **17.** 101
Craon's lodge on piazza near, **17.** 79n
races start near, **17.** 79n
Porta del Popolo, at Rome:
Neapolitan troops reach, **19.** 144
Porta di Bacco, Florence:
church to be erected near, **22.** 258
Porta di San Gallo, Florence. *See* Porta San Gallo
Portail, Jean-Louis (1705–ca 81), président:
social relations of, in Paris, **7.** 291

Port-à-l'Anglois, le, house near Choisy (France):
Du Deffand, Mme, cancels visit to, **5.** 73, 79, 402
location of, **5.** 79
Mirepoix, Mme de, occupies, **5.** 66, 69, 73, 97, 264, 370, 396, 402, **6.** 53, 55, 92
——'s country house at, **7.** 7n
—— takes, **4.** 472
visitors to: Beauvau, **6.** 53, 54; Cambis, Vicomtesse de, **5.** 396; Du Deffand, Mme, **5.** 69, 78, 396, **6.** 55, 92, 93; Luxembourg, Mme de, **6.** 56
Porta Pia, Rome:
Villa Patrizi near, **17.** 25n
Portarlington, Cts of. *See* Stuart, Lady Caroline
Porta San Gallo, Florence:
appointment at, for duel, **13.** 202
arch at, Viviani displays, to San Severino, **20.** 369
deserters attack, **20.** 424
Florentines flock to, **18.** 445
Francis I's 'lying arch' at, **37.** 97
Grafton, Ds of, declines to visit, **22.** 29
house near, designed by Raphael, **11.** 154
Karl Alexander received by ladies at, **20.** 376
Porta San Lorenzo, Rome:
Negroni, Villa, near, **20.** 69n
Porta Santa Maria, Via, Florence:
Pannoni's coffee house in, **17.** 97n
Portchester. *See* Porchester
Porte, La. *See* La Porte
Porte-dieu:
Guasco serves as, in French church, **22.** 529–30
Port Eliot, Cornwall:
Eliot, of, **9.** 65
Porten, Mary, m. (1724) Robert Darell:
son of, **12.** 103n
Porten, Sir Stanier (d. 1789), Kt, 1772; secretary of embassy at Paris 1766–8:
HW mentions, **3.** 341
in London, **3.** *313*
Mann's letter docketed in handwriting of, **25.** 349n
social relations of, with Cts of Rochford, **7.** 318
Porteous, John (d. 1736):
affair of, **20.** 230
death of, **43.** 268
Edinburgh mob hangs, after acquittal for firing on execution crowd, **20.** 230n
Porteous. *See also* Porteus
Porter, David (ca 1747–1819), master chimney-sweeper:
(?) benevolent efforts proposed by, in letter sent by HW to Horace Mann II, **25.** 353
chimney-sweepers' betterment sought by, **16.** 217, **39.** 428
HW has not heard of Lort's interview with, **16.** 222
HW praises, **16.** 219
HW seeks Lort's aid for son of, **16.** 217–18
HW will ask, to call on Lort, **16.** 219

Hanway, Tyrwhitt, and Sir Edward Walpole friendly with, **16**. 217

Lort advises, to defer son's going to Cambridge, **16**. 224

—— wishes to see, **16**. 218

son may be handicapped by occupation of, **16**. 217–18

Porter, Endymion (1587–1649), groom of the Bedchamber:

Faithorne's print of, **42**. 126

portrait of, at Knole, **35**. 133

Porter, Sir James (1710–86), ambassador at Constantinople 1746–62; minister plenipotentiary at Brussels 1763–5; Kt, 1763:

former minister at Constantinople, **19**. 100n, **24**. 160

Frederick II will be the only possible protector of, **21**. 248

Gordon secretary to, **32**. 263n

pension of, **24**. 160

Vorontsov displeased by conduct of, at Constantinople, **21**. 247–8

Porter, Mary (d. 1765), actress:

appears as Clytemnestra, **13**. 151

benefit for, **17**. 336

Dumesnil resembles, **35**. 122

Garrick surpassed by, in passionate tragedy, **38**. 524

Gray is not to see, in *Albion Queens*, **13**. *96*

HW prefers, to Mrs Siddons, **33**. 360

HW reverences, **33**. 87

HW's correspondence with, **40**. 27

(?) HW's essay on performance by, of Clytemnestra in Thomson's *Agamemnon*, **13**. 151, **40**. 27

health of, 'indisposed,' **40**. 27

Hyde's comedy published by, **13**. 29

Porter, Rev. Moses (d. 1791), curate at Clapham, Surrey:

(?) SH visited by, **12**. 232n

Porter, Solomon (d. 1771) (*alias* Solomon Moses):

hanged at Tyburn for Slew's murder, **32**. 68n

Porter, Stephen (b. 1772), translator:

father's occupation may be handicap to, **16**. *217–18*

HW asks Lort for recommendation for, to enter Trinity College, Cambridge, **16**. 217–18

Lort advises father to defer college entrance by, **16**. 224

—— to write to Postlethwaite in behalf of, **16**. 218

—— wishes to see, **16**. 218

passages from Horace and Greek Testament translated by, **16**. 224

probably not a Greek student, **16**. 219

Porter (beverage):

Ferrers obtains, from brother, **21**. 397

Granby orders, for army in Germany, **38**. 75

verdigris contaminates, **40**. 257

Porter; porters:

expense of, **17**. 130

HW's fee to, **7**. 399

Mann entrusts letter to, **21**. 461

Richecourt's litter carried by, **21**. 80

See also under Servant

Porter's lodge:

Houghton lantern compared to, **20**. 163n

Portes, Mme de. See Mignot, Marie *or* Claudine-Françoise

Portes, Pierre de:

marriage of, **20**. 132

Porte Ste-Antoine, Paris:

HW visits faïence factories near, **7**. 337

Porteus, Beilby (1731–1809), Bp of Chester 1776–87, of London 1787–1809:

approves tolerance of Roman Catholics, **29**. 125

Beattie praises, excessively, **29**. 309

charity sermon preached by, at Twickenham, **11**. 311, **31**. 359

common friend of Mason and HW, **29**. 342

corrected date for Downman's pastel of, **43**. 326, 343

Darwin's *Botanic Garden* read by, and returned to HW, **31**. 303

dinner party of, **11**. 291

Garrick, Mrs, visited by, **11**. 33

goodness of, combined with agreeableness, **31**. 351

HW and Frederick Campbells entertained by, at Fulham, **39**. 497

HW and Hannah More would like to see, Abp of Canterbury, **31**. 342–3

HW called on by, at SH, **16**. 222

HW calls, Hannah More's 'confessor,' **31**. 383

HW concerned for, on Mrs Porteus's accident, **31**. 359

HW dines with, **11**. 42, 45, 288, 291

HW does not know address of, **31**. 359

HW flattered by, in letter to Hannah More, **31**. 313

HW gives copies of *Bishop Bonner's Ghost* to, **11**. 41, **31**. 304, 306, 313, **34**. 54

HW hears sermon by, at Twickenham church, **11**. 311, **31**. 359, **34**. 115n

HW mentions, **11**. 46

HW returns Hannah More's letter from, **31**. 314

HW sends to D. Lysons a message from, **15**. 270

HW's wit praised by, **31**. 313

HW's witticism on 'sugar-candied' attitude of, to slave trade, **31**. 260n

HW urges, to enjoin clergy to denounce French atheism, **31**. 383

HW visits, **11**. 240, 253, **12**. 169

Lort visits, **16**. 282

Marcus Flaminius read by, **34**. 168n

More, Hannah, attempts to acquaint HW with, **31**. 311–12

—— corresponds with, **31**. 303, 311, 314, 358, 387

[Porteus, Beilby, *continued*]
—— forced by, to acknowledge *Remarks on the Speech of M. Dupont*, **31**. 382, 383
—— informed by, of HW's health, **31**. 358
—— inquires for, **31**. 351
—— pleased by HW's acquaintance with, **31**. 316
—— sends letter from, to HW, **31**. 311
—— shows HW's letter to, **31**. 311
—— to visit, at Fulham, **31**. 295
—— urged by, to print London edition of *Bishop Bonner's Ghost*, **31**. 319
—— writes poem on visit to, **11**. 33, **42**. 250
opens walk to Bonner's bench at Fulham, **11**. 33
social relations of, with: Beattie, Dr, **11**. 291; Boscawen, Mrs, **11**. 45, 291, **31**. 319; Garrick, Mrs, **11**. 291; HW, **11**. 42, 45, 288, 291, **31**. 312, 313, 319, 351; More, Hannah, **11**. 288, 291, **31**. 258, 303, 351, 388, 399
SH visited by, **12**. 232n, 233
Sturges describes visit to, at Fulham, **43**. 342
winding walk made by, at Fulham, **34**. 54n
See also Fulham Palace
Porteus, Mrs Beilby. *See* Hodgson, Margaret
Porteus. *See also* Porteous
Portfolio, Mme du Deffand's:
Conway to lock, when in Paris, **39**. 190
Du Deffand, Mme, requests return of, **4**. 228
HW returns, **4**. 233, 237
lent to Craufurd, **3**. 356
lent to HW, **3**. 356, 367, 383, 384
Porthole; portholes:
left open, on French ship, **21**. 357
'Portia.' *See under* Shakespeare, William: *Merchant of Venice*
Portia. *See also* Porcia
Portici (Italy):
built above Herculaneum, **13**. 222
Ferdinand of Naples tosses Florentines in blanket at, **23**. 254
garden at, **35**. 433
Mann, Lady Lucy, not benefited by air of, **24**. 203
museum at, for antiquities from Herculaneum, **21**. 364n
Portico; porticos:
at Mereworth, **35**. 143
at the Vyne, **35**. 641
for green-house, **38**. 198
'pert,' at Gloucester, **35**. 153
Roman, HW suggests, at Mistley, **30**. 87
round, at Mereworth Church and St-Mary-le-Strand, **35**. 144
Portier des Chartreux, Le. See under Gervaise de la Touche, Jean-Charles
Portland, Cts of. *See* Temple, Jane Martha (1672–1751)
Portland, Ds of. *See* Cavendish, Lady Dorothy (1750–94); Harley, Lady Margaret Cavendish (1715–85); Noel, Elizabeth (1688–1737); Scott, Henrietta (1774–1844)

Portland, D. of. *See* Bentinck, William (1709–62); Bentinck, William Henry Cavendish (1738–1809); Cavendish-Scott-Bentinck, William Henry Cavendish (1768–1854)
Portland, E. of. *See* Bentinck, Hans Willem (1649–1709); Weston, Richard (1577–1635)
Portland, English war ship:
Dutch contraband seized by, **25**. 3n
endangered, **21**. 350
Portland, Dorset:
English fleet near, **21**. 232, **30**. 148
Portland Castle, governor of. *See* Clapcott, William
Portland Place, London:
Chartres's house in: **29**. 302n; occupied by Mme de Genlis, **33**. 483
Foley's garden in, **39**. 425n
Portland St, London:
Goulburn dies in, **12**. 79n
Portland vase. *See under* Vase
Portlethen, Kincardineshire:
Thomson of, **40**. 266, 269
Port l'Orient, France:
English damage to, reported, **30**. 109
English discover bay near, in French war, **9**. 198, **37**. 536
Sinclair bungles, **19**. 456
Port Louis (France):
English capture of, would ruin French East Indian trade, **30**. 109
English reportedly besieging, **30**. 109
French carry valuables to, from Lorient, **30**. 109
Port Mahon, Minorca:
Ailesbury, Cts of, may be at, **20**. 285
air of, considered bad, **20**. 293
Beauvau behaves well at, **20**. 579
Belle-Isle plans to attack, from Toulon, **20**. 528n
Blakeney ennobled for loss of, **21**. 52
Byng encounters French fleet near, **9**. 191n, **28**. 219n
—— said to be at, **35**. 95
—— said to have captured, **21**. 15
Cabinet meeting on loss of, **20**. 578n
Colvill takes HW's eagle to, **19**. 268
Conway does not wish to take wife to, **20**. 293
—— may have lost weight at, **20**. 313
—— stationed at, **37**. 310–15
Dartmouth at, **17**. 285
Edgcumbe escapes from harbour of, **20**. 559
endangered, **20**. 538, **24**. 490
England must be anxious over, **20**. 558
English fleet at, **19**. 9
Englishman and wife come to Florence from, **19**. 304
English ships at, listed, **17**. 285–6
English ships take French prizes to, **18**. 438
English ship takes Venetian prize to, **19**. 81
English troops from, **18**. 312
French announce intention of attacking, **20**. 541
—— capture, **21**. 135

—— may intend to attack, **20.** 537

—— said to be attacking, **9.** 183

garrison of, weak, **24.** 375, 380

Gibraltar's exchange for, suggested by H. Fox, **20.** 574n

Gloucester, D. of, to visit, **23.** 294

governor of, prepares for French attack, **20.** 528–9

HW's shipments delayed at, **18.** 445

Haddock advised at, of Spanish fleet's arrival, **17.** 306

—— anchors fleet at, **17.** 314

—— at, **17.** 17n, 23n, 84n, 267, 290, 291n

House of Lords examines list of officers at, **17.** 300

Kingston at, **17.** 285n

Leghorn might be exchanged by, for England, **17.** 267

——'s supplies to replace missing ones from Ireland for, **24.** 375

Lestock joins Haddock at, **17.** 291n

—— to visit, **17.** 290

letters from, **37.** 470n, 471

loss of, expected, **35.** 92

Mann ignorant of Conway's departure from, **20.** 290

—— may send Domenichino painting to Anstruther at, **18.** 144

—— should plan secret expedition against, **21.** 239

——'s ship from Leghorn to visit, **19.** 206

—— to write to, about pedestal for eagle, **19.** 427

Mann, Horace II and Lady Lucy, to visit, **24.** 233

man-of-war may leave HW's shipment at, **19.** 216

Mathews at, **18.** 420

Medley sends ships from, to Leghorn, **19.** 192

—— still at, **19.** 216

news from, that Elphinston's division is at Gibraltar, **23.** 162

old tar's letter about captures of, **21.** 51–2

packet-boat of, *see Earl of Besborough*

Parliamentary investigation of fall of, languidly pursued, **21.** 55–6

Postillion obliged to refit at, **19.** 235

races at, on St John's Day, **37.** 311

Richelieu captures town of, **20.** 552

Rowley at, **19.** 146

—— may leave, **18.** 555

Rupert at, **17.** 285n

Russian ships at, **23.** 162, 172, 189, 192

sea captain formerly of, talks to Mann after Algiers visit, **25.** 416

Severn to stop at, **20.** 27

ship from: reaches Leghorn, **17.** 314; visits Leghorn in search of Rowley, **19.** 132

Spanish artillery diverted from, to Genoa, **18.** 257

Spanish expedition against, from Cadiz, would have little chance of success, **25.** 59

Spiridorf at, **23.** 162, 185

Stanhope captures, **21.** 52

Te Deums sung at, for Spanish landing on Minorca, **25.** 189

Toulon squadron might have been bound for, **24.** 375

Townshend leaves Corsica for, **20.** 385

—— pretends to be driven to, **20.** 274

—— puts in at, for repairs, **19.** 207

—— to be court-martialled at, **19.** 324

—— writes from, to Mann, **19.** 216

Villettes arrives at, **19.** 81

visitors to: Arbuthnot, **20.** 284; Conway, **20.** 284–5

Windham hopes for loss of, to embarrass the government, **25.** 50

York, D. of, to visit, **22.** 179

Young to leave, to sail in *Colchester* to Byng's trial, **20.** 590n

Portman, Mr:

SH visited by, **12.** 226

Portman Sq., London:

Chartres to have house in, **25.** 363n

French ambassador lives in, **11.** 91n

La Luzerne's house in, **11.** 38n, **39.** 465n

Montagu, Mrs, lives in, **31.** 258, **35.** 495n, **42.** 468n

—— writes from, **42.** 468

Montagu House in, **11.** 290n, **29.** 184n

Waldegrave, Cts, in, **4.** 9n

Portman St, London:

Castelcicalas live in, **11.** 341n

Portmanteau; portmanteaux:

chaise's capacity for, **37.** 40

embroidered, HW jokes about laurels kept in, **18.** 61

French mail carried in, **25.** 619

HW loses, at Chantilly, **39.** 17

HW uses, for blankets, **18.** 315

Ligonier has no time to pack, **35.** 292

Mann, Horace II, has not yet unpacked, **25.** 417

Pars loses, **24.** 144

Portmore, E. of. See Colyear, Charles (1700–85)

Porto Bello, governor of. See Martínez de la Vega y Retes, Don Francisco Xavier

Porto Bello (Puerto Bello), Panama:

American war may produce successor to, **20.** 449

capture of: **9.** 52n, 235, **13.** 211, 218, 219, **17.** 5n, **37.** 53, 56; depicted on medals, **13.** 226; hailed in song, **37.** 83; not believed at Rome, **17.** 29; Pulteney's letter to Vernon on, **19.** 459

Hosier, Adm., lets crew sicken by delaying at, **37.** 65

news of, reaches HW at Rome, **17.** 5, **43.** 179

(?) Old Pretender's movements may be influenced by capture of, **17.** 23–4

Santo Buono pronounces, impregnable, **17.** 7

Portocarrero, Joaquín Fernando (1681–1760), Marqués de Almanara:

Benedict XIV creates, cardinal, **18.** 302n

Porto Ferrajo (Porto Ferraio), Italy:
capable of receiving large fleet, **21.** 36
Francis I tells Braitwitz to defend, **17.** 229
frigate sails from, to pursue pirates, **25.** 480
grenadiers relegated to, **24.** 8–9
Mann, Lady Lucy, not improved by water of, **24.** 322
—— takes waters of, in hopes of getting a son, **24.** 318
Mill's associates travel to, through Leghorn, **20.** 98n
next best port to Leghorn, **21.** 59
Townshend driven from, by storm, **19.** 206–7
tunny fish caught near fortress of, **23.** 131
Tuscan Court at, **23.** 131
Tuscan ships outfitted at, **20.** 472n
Wright's prizes take refuge in, **21.** 69
Porto Ferraro, Italy:
garrison at, **19.** 11
procaccia banished to, **20.** 447
Porto Longone, Italy:
boats at, ready to follow Capt. Wright, **21.** 69
Charles of Naples owns, **18.** 28
iron mines near, **23.** 131
Leopold not to visit, **23.** 131
Mann hopes that troops may be prevented from reaching, **19.** 410
Marciana near, **18.** 28
Osborne devastates, **18.** 28
soldiers at, **17.** 154
Spanish possession, **23.** 131
Porto Praya, Santiago:
naval battle off, **29.** 146n
Porto Rico (Puerto Rico), West Indies:
capture of, not believed at Rome, **17.** 29
Dutch ship captured on way from, **17.** 53
possible compensation for Havana, at peace, **22.** 92n
Porto San Stefano, Italy:
Jesuits remain before, **22.** 532
Spaniards arrive at, **17.** 197
Porto Spezia ('Spezie' or 'Spezza'). See Spezia
Portpool:
Secker allowed to hold prebend of, **20.** 187n
Portpool Lane, Leather Lane, Holborn, London:
Hirons's address, **41.** 389
Portrait; portraits:
Albany, Cts of, gives, to Coke, **39.** 180
at Althorp, **35.** 305
at Belhus, **35.** 184
at Boughton, **10.** 340–1
at Burford Priory, **35.** 155
at Burghley, **10.** 345–6
at Castle-Ashby, **10.** 336–7
at Castle Howard, **30.** 258
at Deane, **33.** 222–4
at Drayton, **10.** 342
at Easton Maudit, **10.** 338
at Gothurst, **10.** 333
at Hagley, **35.** 147–8
at Horton, **10.** 334–5
at Kiveton, **35.** 270

at Knole, **33.** 222–4, **35.** 132
at Leeds Castle, **35.** 145
at Letheringham, **35.** 247–8
at Matson, **35.** 152
at Oxford, **35.** 155
at Penshurst, **35.** 141
at Petworth, **40.** 317–19, 320, 324, 327
at Piddletown, **42.** 389, 390
at Raynham, housekeeper does not know, **30.** 81
at SH, shown to Storer, **33.** 273
at the Vyne, **35.** 69
at Wanstead, **35.** 238
at Welbeck Abbey, **35.** 270–1
at Wroxton, **35.** 72
bad, at Wentworth Castle, **35.** 267
Bess of Hardwick's, at Hardwick Hall, **42.** 314
book of, of reigns of François I and Henri II, **32.** 282
Doumenil's, old French, **39.** 204
Drouais's, of Mme du Barry, **35.** 121
English: HW collects, **23.** 423, **25.** 448; in Bibliothèque du Roi, **39.** 236
English care about no paintings but, **35.** 424
Geoffrin, Mme, consents to Selwyn's having copy of her, **30.** 213
HW buys, of Gramont's personages, **35.** 227–8
HW has no more room for, at SH, **10.** 54
HW wishes to have, cleaned before sending them to Houghton, **15.** 322, 325
Hampden's and Pym's, **30.** 304n
in SH Blue Bedchamber, **35.** 174
in Tribune, at Florence, **33.** 286
large enamelled, in ante-chapel of Ste-Chapelle, **39.** 203
list of, in HW's Berkeley Sq. house, **30.** 270–1
new peers should have Worlidge paint, **40.** 90
of Abercorn, probably copied from Cooper's miniature, **42.** 89
of Carew, **33.** 111
of Knights of St Patrick, suggested, **42.** 155–6
of Raleighs, **33.** 272
of St-Esprit knights, **5.** 222, **7.** 276, 284, **42.** 155–6, 157
of Wilkes and daughter, **33.** 137–8
oil, at Little Strawberry Hill, **42.** 307
painters of, may be aided by the Delineator, **29.** 371
Rosalba's, in pastel, **18.** 243n
Scottish, **15.** 141, 155, 164, 190–2, 208–9
Sheffield and (?) Gibbon want HW's opinion about, **42.** 206
show character, not passion, **35.** 445
See also under Miniature; Painting, and under names of painters and sitters
Portrait de Mme Geoffrin. See under Morellet, André
Port-Royal, (France), Abbess of. See Dio-Palatin de Montpeyroux, Marie-Antoinette-Éléonore
Port Royal (Jamaica):
William IV at, **25.** 684n

Port St Mary (Spain):
Goldsworthy succeeds Hay as consul at, **20.** 433n

Portsdown Hundred, Hants:
Whithed inherits estates in, from Richard Norton, **20.** 238n

Portsmouth, Cts of. *See* Griffin, Hon. Elizabeth

Portsmouth, Ds of. *See* Penancoët de Kéroualle, Louise-Renée de

Portsmouth, E. of. *See* Wallop, John

Portsmouth, Hants:
Abercromby sails from, **12.** 213n
accident at, shocks Mann, **23.** 228
alleged attempt to set fire to, **24.** 273
Anson takes Acapulco ship to, **18.** 463
Burgoyne lands at, **28.** 395n
Byng's trial aboard *St George* in harbour of, **21.** 39n
chaplain to docks at, **33.** 424n
Cherbourg cannon brought from, **21.** 238
Clarence, D. of (William IV) at, **11.** 152n
Conway, Henry Seymour, embarks at, for Jersey, **25.** 111, 115
—— lands at, in *Champion,* **33.** 142–3
—— ordered to stay at, **30.** 141–2
——'s expedition disembarks at, **21.** 143
——'s groom refuses to go to, to see horses embarked, **21.** 155
—— writes from, **37.** 503, 512
cutter sails from, to Guernsey, **39.** 361–2
Darby's fleet returns to, **39.** 378n
Dodd and Whaley to visit, **40.** 6, 8
earthquake at, **20.** 133n
Edgeworth, Father, arrives at, **12.** 46n
embarkations from, to America, **39.** 197n
English expedition sails from, **21.** 210
English expedition to sail from, **12.** 158n
English fleet at, **5.** 228n, **28.** 462, **33.** 120
English naval strength at, **23.** 40
fires set at, **21.** 419–20, **28.** 287, **39.** 151
Foot Guards to march to, **9.** 196n
force assembled at, **9.** 303n
France may seek to destroy, **39.** 332
French may attack, **24.** 500
French men of war reported to be towed into, **33.** 315
French princes do not visit the equivalent of, **40.** 387
George III to visit, to see the fleet, **23.** 491, 497, **32.** 119
—— visits, **32.** 128–9, 132
Gray and Chute visit, **14.** 83
HW and Rigby to visit, **30.** 92
HW directs letter to Conway to, **37.** 516
HW has avoided, **28.** 92
HW's shyness in dockyard at, witnessed by Rigby, **30.** 103
Hardy at, **24.** 511, 516
—— dies at, **25.** 48
Harvey, governor of, **9.** 314n, **11.** 61n
Hertford to visit, **39.** 171
Hillsea barracks at, **21.** 300n

Jersey may be relieved by force from, **25.** 111
Keppel revisits, **24.** 420
——'s court martial at, **24.** 433, 435, 438, **28.** 435n
marines embark from, **24.** 74n
Moira sets off for, **12.** 71n
Norris at, **18.** 393
Orford, E. of, takes Norfolk militia to, **21.** 300
Palliser escapes from, **24.** 442
—— returns to, despite rotten mast, **24.** 474
picture of attack in 1545 on, **2.** 8
postmark of, on HW's strayed letter, **10.** 40
review at, **28.** 110, 112, 113
Richmond tries to take Guerchy to, but Egmont forbids it, **38.** 401–2
rumours at, **28.** 434n
sailors from, stopped from joining London mob, **38.** 560
Sandwich, E. of, said to have detained fleet at, to entertain George III and Q. Charlotte, **24.** 377
Saunders's fleet prepared at, **23.** 475n
Scottish regiment mutinies at, **25.** 362, **33.** 384
secret expedition beats about near, **21.** 461
ship-carpenters at, **35.** 178
ships arrive at, **28.** 425n
ships in port at, **25.** 221
ships to leave, for America, **24.** 46n
Spencer, Seymour, and Dundas to go to, **12.** 179n
storm at, **12.** 175n, **25.** 115
visitors to: Barrington, **37.** 580; Boscawen, **20.** 468n; HW, **19.** 92n, **30.** 92, 103; Kinnoull, **21.** 364n; Pitt, Thomas, **21.** 364n; Richmond, D. of, **39.** 318; Rigby, **19.** 92n, **30.** 92, 103; Wallace, **29.** 96n
Walter, clergyman at, **33.** 424

Portsmouth (Virginia):
Leslie builds fortifications at, **29.** 90n

Portsoken ward, London:
Parsons, alderman of, **1.** 379n

'Portugaise, la religieuse.' *See* Alcoforado, Marianna

Portugal, Anton von (d. 1769), Graf von Puebla, Imperial envoy to Prussia 1748–56:
Dresden connections of, intimate, **20.** 187n
Serbelloni and Daun order, to join P. Charles near Prague, **21.** 96n
Williams, Sir C. H., negotiates with, **20.** 186–7, **30.** 320

Portugal, K. of. *See* Henry I (1512–80); João V (1689–1750); José Manoel (1714–77); Pedro III (1717–86); Sebastian (1554–78)

Portugal, Princes (bastard) of. *See* Antonio (1714–1800); José (1720–after 1777)

Portugal, Q. of. *See* Maria I (1734–1816); Maria Anna Josephine Antoinette (1683–1754); Maria Anna Vittoria (1718–81)

Portugal:
Acciaioli expelled by, **21.** 422, 475
ambassadors from and to, *see under* Ambassador

[Portugal, *continued*]

American independence rumoured to be recognized by, **28**. 376

animosity of, towards Spain, may make up for military deficiencies, **22**. 41

arms of, removed from Almada's door in Rome, **21**. 426

arrests in, after attack on José Manoel, **38**. 5

banker from, *see* Rosa, Lopez

Boscawen to ask pardon of, for defeating La Clue in Portuguese waters, **21**. 35

Braganza, D. of, of illegitimate branch of royal family of, **22**. 174

Brisbane sent to Court of, **15**. 103n

Catherine II's manifesto illiterate enough to be from, **22**. 71

chess games formal in, **9**. 2

Clement XIII authorizes Mensa di conscienza e ordini to proceed against clergy conspiring against crown of, **21**. 340n

—'s death may keep, in the Church, **22**. 331

—'s quarrel with, **21**. 422–6, 428, 436–7

Clement XIV detaches, from Franco-Spanish cabal, **23**. 221

coast of, Boscawen burns French fleet off of, **35**. 294

conspiracy in: **21**. 264–5, 267, 275–6; said to be fabricated to discredit the Jesuits, **21**. 342; to be subject of book printed at Rome, **21**. 275

Correggio painting might be sold to, **18**. 373

Corsini the Protector of, **21**. 423

Cours de l'Europe satirizes, **17**. 177

Dee, Miss, lives in, **11**. 264n

England recommends Jews to, **21**. 341

— should send aid to, to humble Spain, **22**. 100

—'s subsidy to, attacked by Grenville, **22**. 31n

— to send troops to aid, **22**. 23

East Indies lost by, **39**. 354

English destroy French ships on coast of, **21**. 334

English fleet returns safely from, **24**. 412

English leaders divided over question of aiding, **22**. 30–1

English plans to aid, may be disconcerted, **22**. 41

English-Spanish war fought in, **22**. 34–5, 43

envoys from and to, *see under* Envoy

Fane said to be appointed ambassador to, **17**. 135

Ferdinand VI kind to, **20**. 512

— orders unlimited export from Spain to, after Lisbon earthquake, **20**. 512n

France not to join Spain in war with, **24**. 262n

— tempts Charles III into designs on, **22**. 99

— to make peace with, **12**. 148n

general of, cowardly, **22**. 94

Gregory XIII's bull to, allegedly does not cover punishment of Jesuits, **21**. 308n

Guy Fawkes Day might be imitated by, **21**. 477

havocked world for gold, **25**. 142

hostilities in, almost the only sign of war in Europe, **22**. 40

Ireland sends food to, **37**. 423

island of, seized by Spain, **24**. 309–10

Jesuits' attempt in, **21**. 267

— from, reach Genoa, **21**. 348

— mortified by, **21**. 217

—' part in conspiracy in, unconcealed, **21**. 275–6

— precipitate Clement XIII's rupture with, **21**. 425–6

— probably did not promote assassination plot in, **23**. 173

—' suppression determined by, **23**. 136, **26**. 49

Judaistic tendencies of, **21**. 430

Kinnoull to beg pardon of, for English violation of neutrality, **21**. 352

Lippe to command troops of, **22**. 43

London embassy of, in Audley St, scene of Garrick's marriage, **20**. 74n

Melo e Castro recalled to, **4**. 329n

ministers from and to, *see under* Minister

Nightingale goes to Minorca and Italy from, **37**. 313–14

officer of, prosecuted for not paying taxes, **23**. 166

papers sent to, during Reformation, **15**. 187

patriarch of, might appease his king by curtailing Rome's power, **21**. 348–9

Peace of Paris saves, **22**. 95

Pombal accuses Jesuits of assaults on South American sovereignty of, **21**. 275

Pulteney on way home from, **22**. 121

queen of, in Jephson's *Braganza*, **32**. 233

relation from, of negro mutiny in Brazil, **23**. 452

religion used by, as excuse for plunder, **25**. 400

revolution in, treated in Jephson's *Braganza*, **6**. 151

Riccardi's jewels to be sold in, **19**. 349

Rome's quarrel with, over Jesuits, **21**. 475–7

royal family of: may have to live at Somerset House, **22**. 38, 95; might be sheltered by Charles III, **21**. 560

Saldanha made visitor and reformer to Jesuits in, **21**. 217n

secretary of war in, *see* Secretary at war, Portuguese

ship from, delivers message to Keppel, **33**. 48

Souza imports birds from, **5**. 129

Spain about to conquer, **38**. 186

— at odds with, **6**. 339

— continues conquest of, **22**. 78

— disappointed by not getting, **22**. 95

— has not enslaved, **22**. 1

— may attack, **24**. 253

— may be unable to conquer or keep, **22**. 51

—— may push conquest of, to exchange it for Havana, **22**. 99–100

—— may take, from the Portuguese but not from the English, **38**. 178–9

—— more interested in the conquest of, than in Havana's loss, **22**. 48, 51, 92

——'s campaign in, fails to live up to boastful manifestos, **22**. 66

——'s invasion of, violates law of nations, **39**. 202

——'s preoccupation with, pleases HW, **22**. 31

——'s success in, **22**. 48, 51, 94

—— threatens to invade, if it does not declare war on England, **21**. 559

—— to exchange territories with, in Paraguay, **21**. 341

—— to renounce claims to, **22**. 76n

Spanish attack upon, reported, **22**. 34

Spanish conquest of, would make France more insolent, **22**. 76

Spanish settlement at Rio Grande attacked by, **24**. 223–4

(?) *Triton* goes to Minorca from, **20**. 280n

Twiss describes, as dull, depopulated, and despotic, **28**. 190–1

Tyrawley returns from, with wives and children, **18**. 104

—— said to command forces of, **22**. 34

—— says that war in, is scheme to get English money, **22**. 70

—— sent to relieve, **14**. 120n

—— spends 15 years in, **18**. 148

—— to command English troops in, **22**. 43

—— to leave post in, **17**. 135n

visitors to: English officers and wives, **10**. 29; Gizziello, **37**. 427; Walpole, Col. Edward, **10**. 63; *see also under* Lisbon: visitors to

'votre cousin de.' *See* Walpole, Hon. Robert

Walpole, Col. Edward, has low opinion of people of, **10**. 63

Walpole, Hon. Robert, arrives from, **33**. 400

—— minister to, **4**. 133n

—— to go to, **5**. 163

war in, seems more interesting than that in Germany, **22**. 41

Portugal St, Hyde Park, London:

Edgcumbe child born in, **11**. 323n

HW to see Bns Lyttelton in, **42**. 118

Lyttelton, Bns in, **39**. 430

Portuguese, the:

in East and West Indies, **39**. 168

Raynal's *Histoire* tells of, **39**. 168

rebellious negroes of, called 'disaffected,' **23**. 452, 462

Portuguese banker at Rome. *See* Rosa, Lopez

Portuguese Hospital at Rome:

Almada posts notice at, **21**. 423

Portuguese language:

(?) St-Germain's native tongue, **26**. 20

Porus (d. 321 B.C.), king in India:

Alexander the Great did not despoil, after victory, **25**. 545

——'s plea for seizing wealth of, **25**. 642

Posi, Paolo (1708–76), architect:

church of Santi Apostoli prepared by, for Old Pretender's body, **21**. 392n

Pantheon's modernization projected by, **21**. 37n

Posidippus (fl. 289 B.C.), poet:

West's translation of epigram by, **14**. 16

Posse comitatis:

Montagu to come to London with, **10**. 121

Possesso, Papal:

Pius VI to celebrate, **23**. 131, 136

Post, the:

abuse of franking in, **38**. 368

'actually setting out,' from Florence, **21**. 342

administrators of, in France, suppressed, **6**. 470, 483

afternoon too late for, at Twickenham, **42**. 288

ambassadors', not opened, **5**. 70, 74

arrival of: expected in Florence with impatience, **25**. 302; in Florence, from Leghorn, Reggio, and Bologna, **17**. 47; with alarming news of French and Spanish fleets, **25**. 173

at Paris, from and to England, **39**. 257

binding removed, to enable book to be sent by, **17**. 64

book of, **3**. 5, 10n

cancellation mark of, **4**. 428

carried in coaches, **31**. 264–5

censored, **10**. 183, 197

Chanteloup, arrival and departure of, **5**. 243, 244, 246, 255

Choiseul, Duchesse de, ceases to write by, **5**. 18

common, HW risks a letter in, **35**. 168

cost of, *see* price of

countersigning of letter, **3**. 53

countersigning of parcel, **3**. 132, **4**. 99, 101

courier forgets English mail, **25**. 366

courier, private, swifter than, **4**. 91

daily, at Ragley, **38**. 81

days for, **37**. 21

delay of, between England and Florence: **18**. 233, 343, 352, **19**. 360, 362, 365, 405, 430, **21**. 270, **23**. 378; by bad weather, **19**. 333, 360, **20**. 467, **24**. 433, **30**. 8; by floods, **19**. 135; by Maria Amalia's visit, **25**. 299; by winds in Mediterranean, **17**. 393; facilitates false rumours by England's enemies in Italy, **19**. 362–3; from England, **23**. 110; from Florence, **23**. 537; from France, by snow, **17**. 207; in reaching Florence, **23**. 203; makes 3 or 4 arrive together, **24**. 513; probably caused by bad weather, **21**. 369

delays of: always at most critical junctures, **21**. 543, **25**. 492; could be endured by long-lived patriarchs, **23**. 240; in winter, **23**. 273–4; to Ireland, **37**. 441

Dutch, **17**. 84

Dutch route longer than French, **18**. 92

[Post, the, *continued*]

Dutch route more hazardous than French, **18**. 102

Dutch route not yet followed by, **18**. 437

English, to Italy: goes by way of Flushing, **21**. 215; Ostend packet-boat often delays, **23**. 541

English merchants at Leghorn receive, regularly, **18**. 442–3

English visitors at Florence assemble on arrival of, **21**. 445

expected at Houghton, **18**. 247, 259

expense of, HW and Montagu careful not to let each other incur, **10**. 263

expense of sending watch by, from England, would be heavy, **21**. 322

extension of daily deliveries by, **37**. 411n

Flemish mails arrive, **11**. 167

floods prevent, **35**. 265

foreign: cost of, **10**. 183; from London, **23**. 500n, **24**. 527n; HW puts Mme Roland's letter into, **10**. 145, 261; Montagu ignores regulations of, **10**. 143

for Germany, awaits letter from Leghorn, **23**. 232

four mails from England reach Florence together, **21**. 410, **25**. 399, 553

France establishes, for men supposed to be fighting in England, **21**. 326

franking of, **16**. 71n, **38**. 368, **42**. 384n

French capture fishing-boats carrying, to England, **19**. 143, 146

French local ('la petite poste'): **3**. 344, **4**. 290, 295, **6**. 98, 241; Necker receives charge of, **7**. 453

French mail robbed in Pall Mall, **25**. 619

from Adderbury, **10**. 261, 300

from Bath to London, **3**. 138

from Bologna to Florence, **17**. 32, 47

from Brompton (Yorks) to Twickenham, **12**. 21

from Calais to Paris, arrives Tuesday and Saturday, **3**. 5

from Cambridge, schedule of, **2**. 97, 106, 267

from Dover to Calais, stopped, **7**. 157, 161

from England, opened in France, **31**. 144

from England through Mediterranean, 'out of repair,' **25**. 191

from England to Florence: delayed by bad weather, **30**. 8; not expected till next day, **24**. 495; reaches Florence twice a week, except sometimes in winter, **24**. 368; retarded, **24**. 461; three posts missing from, **21**. 406

from England to France: price of, **4**. 355n; regular route of, no longer available, **30**. 267

from England to Italy, becomes irregular, **24**. 140–1

from Florence to London, **11**. 245

from France, said to be stopped, **34**. 165

from France to England: HW suspects that letters sent by, do not always arrive, **30**. 214; slowness of, **10**. 177

from Genoa, delayed by bad weather, **19**. 360

from Holland, **17**. 84, **36**. 11

from Ireland to England, slow, **10**. 177

from Leghorn, **17**. 47, **19**. 22, **25**. 313

from London: does not leave on Sunday nights, **12**. 57; none on Sunday to Ampthill, **33**. 581, **34**. 134

from London to Paris: arrives Friday (via Ostend), **7**. 187–8; arrives irregularly, **4**. 48, 76, **6**. 306; *and passim*; arrives ordinarily on Sunday, **3**. 353, **7**. 117, *and passim*; arrives ordinarily on Wednesday, **3**. 213, **7**. 117, *and passim*; departs Friday, **7**. 155

from London to Park Place, **11**. 130

from Norfolk, brings business letters to HW, **34**. 135

from Paris: **17**. 463; announces Jersey attack, **24**. 471; to England, **35**. 124; to Florence, **22**. 352, 353

from Paris to Calais, departs Sunday only, **3**. 5

from Paris to London: departs Monday, **3**. 167, 184, 213, 243, 378, **4**. 167, 176, 177, 281, 337, 352, 364, 467, 494, **5**. 9, 32, 150, **6**. 244, 257 425, **7**. 22; departs Sunday, **3**. 16; departs Thursday, **3**. 378, **4**. 116–17, 312, 316, 384, **5**. 22, **6**. 28, 88, **7**. 4, 22; hour of departure of, **4**. 38, 94

from Pisa to London, **11**. 208, 236

from Pougues to Lyon, **11**. 126

from Rome, **24**. 250

from Venice to Florence, **17**. 88, **19**. 439

from Yorkshire: to London, **11**. 38–9, **12**. 16, 43; to Twickenham, **11**. 13

George III's day for, **38**. 143

German: arrives March 9, **25**. 383; English letters come by, to Italy, **25**. 383; fails to bring mail from London to Italy, **25**. 192; mails brought from England to Florence by, **25**. 205

German prince may stop, **21**. 452

HW awaits, eagerly, from England, **17**. 32

HW colours some things when writing by, lest foreigners should read them, **24**. 493

HW discusses routes of, through France and Germany, **11**. 143

HW does not like to send his predictions through, **24**. 364

HW jokes about, **10**. 282

HW mentions, **10**. 239

HW protests against slowness of transatlantic, **32**. 388, 392

HW's and Hertford's letters unsafe for, **38**. 414

HW's dinner hour conflicts with, in London, **33**. 581

HW seldom uses, in Paris, **40**. 364

HW's letter by, miscarries, **33**. 566

HW's letters forwarded by, when he is out of town, **30.** 179

HW's letters made 'harmless' for, **35.** 212

HW's letters may be read in every post-house in, **24.** 427

HW's *Letter to the Editor of the Miscellanies of Thomas Chatterton* too big for, **16.** 236

HW's *Miscellaneous Antiquities* too heavy for, **42.** 423

HW's new footman puts letter in, by mistake, **25.** 118

HW tells Camden not to reply by, **41.** 305

HW tells Pinkerton to write by, to SH, **16.** 273

HW to put Cole's letters into, **2.** 256, 259

HW would not entrust secrets to, **25.** 185

Hillier requests franks for, **16.** 71

hour of, *see below under* time of

hour of departure of, at Florence, **23.** 515

hour too late for, at Twickenham, **10.** 108

improvement of, by new regulations, **31.** 234

interrupted by capture of packet-boat, **19.** 133

Irish mails shipwrecked on Isle of Man, **10.** 10

irregularity of: **17.** 476, **25.** 567, **33.** 21; aggravated by bad weather, **21.** 141; between England and Ireland, **10.** 3, 9–10; foreign, **32.** 376–7; in France, **17.** 103; in winter, **17.** 213, 286; *see also under* delay in *and* uncertainty of

lack of, at Verona, **34.** 246

lack of privacy of: **3.** 174, 328n, **4.** 3, 10, 73, 107, 143, 151, 152, 246, 256, 264, 274, 334, 370, 395, 489, **5.** 3–4, 18, 38, 42, 44, 72, 98, 113, 174, 244, 247, 261–3, 290, 296, 324, **6.** 113, 169, 266, 372, 396, **7.** 79, 122, 124, 151, 156, 169, 237, **9.** 229, 234, **10.** (?) 155, 161, 197, **12.** 132, **17.** 265, 382–3, 396, 421–2, 453–4, 476, **18.** 362, **22.** 373, 570, **23.** 455, 537, **24.** 364, 427, 493, 507, **25.** 15, 89, 185, 257, **28.** 51, 56, 123, 127, 440, **31.** 144, 145n, **32.** 124, **35.** 168, 212, **37.** 161, **38.** 2, 430, **39.** 90, 189, **40.** 364, **41.** 9, 211; HW hopes, does not prevail in Tuscany, **24.** 38; Leopold opens all letters before delivery, **25.** 412n, 566n

lateness of, **33.** 551

leaves for Munich on 22 Feb., **36.** 232, 233

leaves London on Friday, **23.** 500

leaves Paris Thursday morning, **38.** 532

letter from London reaches Florence in 16 days, **22.** 499

letters copied by employees of, in France, **5.** 131–2, 143–4, 247–8, 261–2, 306–7, 334–5, 343–6, 354–5, 359–61, 376–9, 379, 396–8, 398–9, 414–16, **6.** 24, 31–8

letter sent by express may safely be forwarded by, **41.** 27

letters from Venice and Padua reach Florence on Wednesdays only, **24.** 136

Leyden route retards, **19.** 257

liberty of, now enjoyed by HW, **22.** 309

London letter mailed before 9 P.M. will reach SH next morning, **40.** 134

Lorenzi demands unfranked letters from Genoa, **22.** 347

—— forbids Genoese postmaster to send him unfranked letters, **22.** 362

lottery tickets sent by, **9.** 208

mail packets thrown overboard when ships are taken, **21.** 168, **25.** 339

mails from England and Holland lacking in Italy, **25.** 388

Mann awaits eagerly, from HW, **17.** 32

—— does not believe that HW's letters have been opened by, **23.** 542

—— hurries letters to catch, **24.** 89

—— wishes Sisson's plan to be sent by, **21.** 375, 379

Mantua route of, **18.** 233, **19.** 190

medal too heavy to send by, **24.** 470

miscarries only when nothing to carry, **12.** 17

Montagu has to pay, for HW's letter, **10.** 296

—— hopes HW will not have to pay, for letter, **10.** 288, 296

—— misses, **10.** 149

—— thinks Favre did not send letter to HW by, **10.** 182

—— to complain to Hampden about inefficiency of, **10.** 40

More, Hannah, lives ten miles from, **31.** 304

no fresh news for every day of, **33.** 215

not always safe, **31.** 101

Ostend route followed by, in wartime, **7.** 157, 159, 161–3, 165, 169, 170, 172, 227, 232, 422, 423, 426

overweight packets not charged if sent through secretary of state's office, **28.** 44

packet-boats delayed in carrying, **21.** 464, 465

Palmer's mail-coaches, **33.** 480n

Paris: delayed at New Year's, **5.** 3, 9, 162, 163, 306, **6.** 126, 257, 388; distributed day after arrival, **3.** 61, 157, **4.** 176; hour of collection of, **5.** 88, 343, **7.** 77; hour of delivery of, **3.** 99, 176, 179, **4.** 38, 83, 88, 164, 174, 481, **5.** 11, 18, 101, 125, 156, 162, 430, **6.** 235; hour of departure of, **4.** 38, 94

penny: **1.** 55, 100, 246, 256, **2.** 256, **9.** 282; paper distributed by, **20.** 222; rebus sent to Lovel by, **30.** 42

Pergolesi's *Olimpiade* too big for, **19.** 95

'Pompom' wishes live horse sent by, **6.** 336

prepayment of letters sent by, **31.** 326n

Prevereau blamed for delay in, **18.** 233, 442–3, 448

price of: **1.** 163n, **3.** 86, **4.** 355n, **9.** 2, 347, **10.** 158, 251, 254, 280, 288, 296, **11.** 263, **25.** 608, **33.** 349n, 376n; from Twickenham to Ampthill, 3*d.* for letter, **33.** 348–9; to France, **4.** 355n

print of Camilla Martelli too big for, **25.** 230

Richmond, D. of, cannot write fully by, **41.** 9

schedule of, changed, **33.** 480, 519

scissors not safe to send by, **17.** 98–9

[Post, the, *continued*]

slower in November than in summer, **22**. 265

snow delays, **17**. 207, **42**. 203

speed of: **1**. 229, 230, **3**. 13, 79–80, 237, 258, 336, **4**. 116–17, 226, 269, 270, 281, 312, 383, **5**. 19, 20, 22, 55, **6**. 129, 190, 237, 267, 306, **7**. 196, **11**. 13n; by Ostend compared to that by Calais, **7**. 159, 162, 163, 172, 227; from France to England, **10**. 177, 182; from Ireland to England, **10**. 177

stage-coach supplements, **37**. 511

stopped between Bologna and Florence, **19**. 462

three mails arrive together, in Florence, **24**. 513, **25**. 317, 521

three mails from Italy reported lost, **24**. 468

through Germany to England, **21**. 134

through Holland, interrupted by French, **19**. 146

time of: at Paris, *see above under* Post, the: Paris; at Twickenham, **11**. 18, 89, 159, **12**. 10, 20, 21, 115, **16**. 219, 277, 296, **31**. 234, **32**. 361, **33**. 196, 197, **34**. 8, 95, 112, 121, 169, **39**. 485; between England and Florence, **25**. 313; from London to Florence, **22**. 499, **23**. 541–2; from Paris to Florence, **22**. 352; to Ampthill through London, **33**. 7–8

to be prepaid during war, **7**. 159

to Germany, cannot keep pace with revolutions, **38**. 139

to Jersey, irregular in wartime, **35**. 249

to Milton, carried by Ely postman, **1**. 230, **2**. 35, 62n, 193

Tuesdays and Fridays, departure days for foreign, from London, **24**. 527n

uncertainty of: **11**. 144, 155–6, 157, 159, 166, 344, **28**. 60, **37**. 250; from Adderbury, **10**. 261; from Greatworth, **10**. 194, 226; *see above under* delay in *and* irregularity of

Van Heck to forward, from Leyden, **19**. 145–6

Venice or Mantua, routes of, to Florence, **19**. 190

Walpole, Sir Edward, mentions, **10**. 330

Weymouth tells Mann to send his secrets by, in cipher, **25**. 42

See also Courier; Cover; Express; Frank; Franking privileges; Franks; Letter; Mail; Postage; Post day; Post office; Travel

Post; posts (distances on post roads):

short, from Roye to Paris, **7**. 316

Postage:

double, **1**. 238

French begrudge expense of, **4**. 293n

HW may not think Mann's letter worth, **24**. 463

Mann's expense allowance for, **18**. 516

rates of, **1**. 163n; *see also* Post: price of

Trigge may demand, as Mann's messenger, **24**. 380

Van Heck's account for, at Leyden, **19**. 145n

Post-bag; post-bags:

HW's letters in, cause rejoicing at Ragley, **38**. 190

postman drops, **33**. 21

Post-book; post-books:

obtainable at Calais, **37**. 41

Post-chaise; post-chaises:

Ailesbury, Cts of, hopes, will bring HW to Park Place, **37**. 466

Chute to visit Park Place in, **35**. 69

club members rush out in, to see novelties, **38**. 172

'common open' used by Joseph II, **23**. 103n

Cotes's, to take Wilkes to duel, **35**. 228

covered, HW and Lady Catherine Beauclerk ride in, **10**. 343

Craufurd travels in, **5**. 289, 290

Digby said to be robbed in, **12**. 102, 104

fish conveyed in, **32**. 302n

George II might be seized in, **35**. 221

George III and Q. Charlotte go in, to Portsmouth, **24**. 377n

George III does not envisage breakdown of, **32**. 129

Gloucester, D. of, removed from Verona in, **32**. 363

—— travels in, **24**. 314, **35**. 473

Greville's 'character' of, in his *Maxims*, **37**. 460–1

Gunning, Mrs, drives in, **11**. 201

HW and Chute overturned in, **9**. 96

HW glad he is finished with, **17**. 142

HW goes to Park Place in, **33**. 231

HW invited to come to Park Place in, **37**. 466

HW on way to London in, **38**. 444

HW reluctant to enter, **37**. 49

HW rides in, **10**. 155

HW's: left at SH, **35**. 69; to convey burglar to custody, **9**. 133; will not take him to Florence, **22**. 116

HW's aversion to, **13**. 230, 239

HW to have wheels of, greased after rainy trip, **9**. 118

HW unlike Mrs Nugent not to jump out of, into an assembly, **39**. 167

Hamilton, Ds of, enters, at Yorkshire inn, **20**. 317

Hawke, Capt., killed by, **32**. 381

Hertford overturned in, cutting his face on broken glass, **38**. 387

highwayman attacks, in Piccadilly, **20**. 188

hired, Palliser reaches Admiralty in, **24**. 442

horses of, ridden with saddles, **35**. 142

Mason catches influenza in, **28**. 230

—— to jumble himself in, **28**. 124

Modena, Ds of, travels in, **18**. 227

Modena, Ps of, sees Florence from, **22**. 202

Mordaunt travels in, **30**. 144

North drives with wife in, **33**. 580n

Northumberland, Ds of, rides in, with legs out the window, **34**. 207

Ossory, Lady, has, **33**. 49

Parliament's dissolution causes flurry of, 24. 45

Pembroke nearly destroys, 20. 109

Penn wounded by overturn of, 20. 248

Perrone takes goldfish to Turin in, 35. 226

Pomfret, Cts of, has, in Italy, 19. 390

provincial society helped by improvement in, 9. 350, 10. 348

St Leonard's Hill to be reached by, from SH, 10. 44

Salisbury, E. of, invents, 10. 348

Taaffe carries turtles and pineapples in, 20. 289

trip in, 'one uniform joggle,' 37. 392

visible from SH, 20. 380, 25. 532

Waldegraves start on wedding trip in, 9. 235

warm, HW will be comfortable in, if he goes to Italy, 22. 339–40

Williams, G. J., to read *Life of Lord Herbert* in, 30. 176

York, D. of, goes in, to Marseille, 22. 553

See also Chaise

Post day; post days:

foreign, from London, Tuesday and Friday, 25. 255

in Florence: arrives Wednesdays and Saturdays, 21. 168, 25. 302; from Venice and Padua, 24. 136

Mann dreads, 19. 54, 56

——'s porter repels visitors on, 19. 59

—— writes three days before, 25. 238

Poster; posters:

oil-cloth, to advertise sights, 20. 40

Posterity:

ancestors protected by their, 15. 86, 102, 130, 134

Du Deffand, Mme, indifferent to, 4. 251–2

eighteenth-century England will be lightly regarded by, 24. 266

England will be ridiculed by, for idolizing Dr Samuel Johnson, 25. 638

Fearne's remark about, 21. 61

HW cannot predict opinions of, when he knows so little of actions of his own time, 25. 63–4

HW collects follies of the age to inform, 35. 236

HW imagines himself as, 35. 345

HW proposes discoveries to, 37. 293–4

HW's letters must be limited to events of interest to, 24. 450–1

HW's opinion of, 10. 95, 197

HW's reflections on, 22. 303, 28. 292, 29. 207, 37. 271

HW tells all to, 38. 59

HW to write treatise on future discoveries of, 37. 292–3

newspaper writers have no mercy on, 25. 116

North Briton might deceive, about HW, 38. 176

'peeps over my shoulder,' 33. 54

present age will falsely be considered lively by, 38. 272

younger generation seems to HW to be, 25. 109

See also Futurity

Post-horn; post-horns:

HW dispatches letters with nine, blowing, 33. 156

Post-horse; post-horses. *See under* Horse

Post-horse Act. *See under* Parliament: acts of

Post-house; post-houses:

at Bath, 40. 8

at Canterbury, 40. 3

at Derby, 40. 15

at Pistoia, 22. 222

at Portsmouth, 40. 6

at Shrewsbury, 40. 12

at Twickenham, 12. 102

at York, 11. 47

distance between, in Tuscany, 20. 466n

Florentine, hours of departure from, 23. 515

French, rates and services at, 37. 40–1

HW and Spence regret interruption of mule-counting by stops at, 17. 91

HW mentions, 38. 157

horses at, insufficient, 20. 466n

Leopold and Maria Louisa have servant to announce them at, 23. 220

letters at, are addressed to Ricci in cipher, 23. 517

Mann to have Young Pretender watched at, 17. 13

Modena, Ds of, borrows post-chaise at, 18. 227

Twickenham lacks, 33. 566

Postiglione, Il (ship). See *Il Postiglione*

Postilion, Spanish register ship:

capture of, 19. 81–2

cochineal in cargo of, 19. 82n

Postilion; postilions:

Albemarle bows to, 20. 270

Electress's, separated from coachman by long traces, 19. 369–70

English, wins horse race for Duc de Lauzun, 39. 270

flap their arms from cold, 7. 333

French: Bowman's directions about, 37. 41; use obscenities, 40. 28

HW favoured by, on way to Dover, 39. 253

HW may add, if estate warrants it, 34. 145

HW's letter about victory might be preceded by, blowing horns, 24. 338

Hamilton, James, is, 17. 279n

hats of, decked for victory, 37. 566–7

Hertford's, cause accident, 38. 387

Liechtenstein preceded by, 21. 445

Mann fears, have been frozen, 21. 369

Montagu's, may be sent to meet HW, 10. 83

North's, wounded by highwayman, 24. 47

officer accompanied by, when bearing message to Berlin, 21. 242

pay of, 37. 41

saucy, at Calais and La Recousse, 7. 342

stumbling horse of, may delay mail, 23. 274

to Mrs Elizabeth Montagu, 9. 195

tumble, 35. 278

[Postilion; postilions, *continued*]
Vitelli, Mme, orders, to pass Mme Grifoni's coach, **17.** 37
Werpup's death blamed on, **22.** 306
wheel runs over, **9.** 195
Postillion, English xebec:
Genoese vessels damage, **19.** 235
off Ajaccio, **19.** 207n
Port Mahon visited by, for refitting, **19.** 235
Townshend leaves, off Corsica, **19.** 207
Posting house. *See* Post-house
Postlethwaite, Thomas (1731–98), D. D., master of Trinity College, Cambridge 1789–98:
Lort to give recommendatory letter to, for Porter, **16.** 218
Postman; postmen:
bag dropped by, **33.** 21
floods keep, from SH, **35.** 365
George II's death will be known before arrival of, **35.** 307
'his Majesty's', **33.** 213
Johnston, Lady Cecilia, offers to be, **39.** 420
letter dropped by, on Twickenham Common, **42.** 293
Nicholls offers to be, **39.** 478
Postmark; postmarks:
'Genève,' **32.** 322
HW thinks that Chatterton's letters to him lack, **16.** 220
Lort's friend to look for, on Chatterton's letter, **16.** 222
of Leghorn, on letter, **17.** 47
Postmaster; postmasters:
at Chesterfield, **37.** 566
at Florence, *see* Gazzeri, Giovan Battista; Giusti, Tommaso; Orlandi, Casimirro; Paperini, Giuseppe
at Hounslow, **20.** 109
French, at Genoa, *see* Regny, ——
French and Italian, dispute, **22.** 358
French ones are regulated by post-books, **37.** 41
HW does not wish to be unintelligible to, **25.** 245
HW fears less, than irresponsible young Englishmen, **21.** 374–5
HW implores, not to peek into his mail, **22.** 373
HW may be corresponding with, unawares, **39.** 180
HW's letters harmless enough not to be stopped by, **35.** 212
Mann to get horses from, to attend Court to Pisa and Leghorn, **22.** 417
rupture between, on route from France to Tuscany, **22.** 347
Tuscan underpostmaster furnishes horses for Penthièvre, **20.** 466n
Postmaster general:
at Brussels and Mainz, **37.** 158
Bessborough and Grantham succeed Hyde and Trevor as, **22.** 311

Bessborough, E. of, resigns as, **22.** 97, 471
Fawkener does not become, **19.** 26
—— is, **19.** 456n
Hillsborough and Despenser become, **22.** 473
Sandwich may become, **22.** 569, 571
See also Craggs, James (1657–1721); Eyles, Sir John (d. 1745); Fawkener, Sir Everard (1684–1758); Walpole, Galfridus (1684–1726)
Postmaster general, Tuscan. *See* Suares de la Concha, Baldassare
Post obits:
misery caused by, **20.** 242
Post office; post offices:
Bentley receives position in, **10.** 128
clerks of: alert because of alleged plot, **35.** 231; busy with expresses on Parliament's dissolution, **24.** 45n; can read Conway's unsealed letters, **37.** 568; feared by HW less than travelling Englishmen, **21.** 375; may be the only readers of HW's mail, **35.** 223
Cole's letter never mailed at, **2.** 266
Edgcumbe may succeed Hillsborough in, **39.** 93
Euston's tenant threatened with dismissal from, **18.** 255
Florentine: Leopold opens letters at, **25.** 412n, 566; Richecourt opens letters at, **18.** 362; *see also below under* Post office, Tuscan
foreign: HW cannot write freely when his letters must pass through so many, **24.** 507, **36.** 208; HW does not care to announce England's difficulties to, **23.** 455; HW does not wish to entertain, with bad news, **25.** 89; HW does not wish to test the credulity of, **25.** 15; not likely to be friendly to English letters, **24.** 518–19; will learn nothing new from HW's letters, **25.** 105
French, German, and Tuscan, HW cannot write freely by, **25.** 564
general, Shelvocke secretary to, **20.** 436n
HW invokes goddess of, **35.** 393
HW's correspondence with Conway may be investigated by, **39.** 316
HW's correspondence with Mann unequalled in annals of, **25.** 520
HW's letter returned to him by, **25.** 118
HW's letter to Beauchamp fitter to be read at, than that to Hertford, **38.** 354
HW's numerous letters to Berrys will arouse comment in, **12.** 16
HW writes freely because letter goes by coach not by, **33.** 167
Hardinge told by HW to communicate through, **35.** 555
letters from officers of Rochefort expedition detained by, **37.** 513n
letters must have stayed a week at, **25.** 395
letters often confiscated at, **24.** 124n
letters opened at, **14.** 132
London, **3.** 53
might be set up in balloons in the air, **42.** 176

Paris, central: Colmant re-addresses letters at, **5.** 249; Du Deffand, Mme, capable of seizing Mlle Sanadon's mail at, **5.** 250; letters taken to, **4.** 94, 275; prepayment of letters at, **7.** 159; Wiart goes to, to get letter earlier, **3.** 352, **4.** 465

Pitt, William II, writes to, about Austrian victories, **12.** 177

Tuscan, director of, *see* Rainoldi, G.

Post road; post roads:
good, between Wentworth Castle and Ragley, **38.** 64

Mann, Horace II, unable to travel over, because of bad weather, **25.** 204

Postscript; postscripts:
ladies said to tell their minds in, **32.** 99

'Postscript to the Parish Register of Twickenham,' verses by HW:
HW quotes, **12.** 252

Postscript to the Royal and Noble Authors, by HW:
forty copies printed, making it scarce, **31.** 244

HW criticized for his slight distribution of, **33.** 575

HW sends: to Hannah More, **31.** 243–4; to Lady Ossory, **33.** 552

HW's only recent writing, **33.** 574

Orléans, Duc d', not to be included in, **34.** 7

Pot; pots:
auriculas in, at Ranelagh, **20.** 47

brass, sold in Florence, **17.** 53

for myrtles, **35.** 214

HW buys old broken, from Mrs Kennon's sale, **37.** 439

pewter, used as alm-boxes, **21.** 238

See also Chamber pot

Potato; potatoes:
beaten, with cream, **36.** 130n

boiled, in Ireland, **10.** 2

Cambridge, R. O., collects money for, to feed the poor, **12.** 177

Conway grows, at Park Place, to make whisky, **39.** 551

diamonds may be as plentiful as, **11.** 350

Gloucester, D. of, wishes, in illness, **32.** 373

HW to contribute, to charity, **12.** 180

Pote, Joseph (ca 1703–87), bookseller:
at Eton, **1.** 35n

Catalogus alumnorum compiled by, **42.** 44n

History and Antiquities of Windsor Castle by, **40.** 108n, **43.** 59

Huddesford's aid enlisted by, **1.** 255n

Potemkin, Prince Grigoriĭ Alexandrovich (1739–91):
Catherine II's favourite, **24.** 143n

——'s motives about Minorca misinterpreted by, **25.** 187n

Danube to be crossed by, **23.** 469n

HW hopes, will be driven out of Bulgaria, **11.** 230

Harris negotiates with, for English alliance, **25.** 26n

'Potences, deux':
Braitwitz's, **18.** 524

Potenciani, Giovanni, governor of Rome:
edict by, **24.** 65n

Potency:
Beaufort's, examined by physicians and surgeons, **18.** 185

Potenger. *See* Pottinger

'Potenza':
'potence' and, **43.** 251

Potherat de Corbière, Dom Gaspard-Edmé-Germain, Prior of Scellières:
Troyes, Bp of, corresponds with, **8.** 208

Potier, Étienne-René (1697–1774), Cardinal de Gesvres; Bp of Beauvais:
arrival of, at Conclave, **21.** 207n

Potier, François-Joachim-Bernard (1692–1757), Duc de Gesvres:
expensive burial arranged by, **13.** 163n

profits made by, from keeping a hazard-table, **13.** 165

Young Pretender flouts, as emissary of Louis XV, **20.** 8n

Potier, Louis-Joachim-Paris-René (1733–94), Duc de Gesvres:
Maurepas's social relations with, **7.** 309

Potier, Louis-Léon (1695–1774), Duc de Tresmes:
attends session of parliament of Paris, **8.** 172

said to be promoted, **5.** 179

(?) social relations of, with Comtesse de Brionne, **7.** 295

Potier de Gesvres, François-Bernard (1655–1739), Duc de Tresmes:
funeral of, described by HW, **13.** 163–4

Potier de Gesvres, Léon (1656–1744), cardinal, 1719:
Conclave not attended by, **17.** 21n

Potion; potions:
Young Pretender accuses wife of giving, to him to make him impotent, **25.** 102

Potocki, (?) Comte Ignacy (1750–1809), grand marshal of Lithuania:
arrives from Paris for brief stay, **42.** 162

Buller, Mrs, shown by, a letter from Stanislas II requesting *Anecdotes of Painting*, **42.** 162

HW asked by, for books for Stanislas II, **36.** 281

HW called on by, **42.** 162

HW's *Anecdotes of Painting* delivered by, to Stanislas II, **42.** 163–4

(?) HW's correspondence with, **42.** 163n

'Potophæ.' *See* 'Patapan'

Potosi (Bolivia):
Spain digs for wealth of, **23.** 561–2

whichever party in England had wealth of, would be victorious, **25.** 256

'Pot-Pourri.' *See under* Voltaire

Potpourri; potpourris:
Gray's receipt for, **1.** 67, **43.** 46

HW makes, **1.** 72, 75

Potsdam (Prussia):
Conway tours Sans Souci at, **39.** 537
Frederick II leaves for, **39.** 538
Mitchell confers with Frederick II at, **21.** 2n
Pott, Mr:
SH visited by, **12.** 242
Pott. *See also* Potts
Pottendorf, Count:
Sloane trustee, **20.** 359n
Potter, Hanbury (d. 1800), King's messenger:
Bristol's dispatch brought by, **21.** 548n, 557
Richmond's dispatches sent by, **22.** 405n
Spain left by, in disguise, **21.** 557n
Potter, John (?1674–1747), Bp of Oxford
1715–37; Abp of Canterbury, 1737–47:
Archæologia Græca by, **30.** 289n
George II reprimands, for supporting P. of
Wales for chancellorship of Cambridge,
20. 10n
—— said to have been promised by, that
prayers would be said for him, **19.** 149
——'s consent to daughter's marriage read by,
37. 61n
Gibson supplanted by, as candidate for archbishopric, **19.** 503n
HW identifies, **30.** 289n, 304n
learning of, **30.** 289
Middleton fails to convince, of his orthodoxy,
15. 293
——'s candidacy opposed by, **15.** 306n
Oxford loyal address sent by, **30.** 98
regent, **18.** 209n
son of, **19.** 449, **22.** 184
subscription of, for raising soldiers in Surrey,
19. 149n
Thuanus quoted by, to Sir Robert Walpole,
17. 301
Potter, Paul (1625–54), painter:
painting by, of cows, owned by Thiers, **5.**
148n, **7.** 373
Potter, Rev. Robert (1721–1804), poet:
*Inquiry into Some Passages in Dr Johnson's
Lives of the Poets* by, defends Gray against
Johnson, **29.** 308
Stanley's translation of Pindar supervised by,
29. 8
translation of Æschylus by, pleases HW, **28.**
347–8
Potter, Susanna Robinson (d. 1783), m. (1750)
Sir John Hussey Delaval, cr. (1761) Bt,
(1783) Bn Delaval:
Milbank, home of, **36.** 84
Potter, Thomas (?1718–59), politician; wit;
M.P.:
Augusta, Ps of Wales, has, as secretary, **19.**
449n
birth date of, corrected, **43.** 171
Callington election contested by, **19.** 414n
Cholmondeley succeeded by, as joint vice-
treasurer of Ireland, **21.** 109
Cresset succeeds, as secretary to Augusta, Ps
of Wales, **20.** 247

Darlington succeeded by, as joint paymaster,
21. 25
Dupplin and, **9.** 211
Essay on Woman mostly written by, **22.** 184,
38. 230
Frederick, P. of Wales, recruits, as promising
Opposition leader, **19.** 449
HW to have followed speech of, with second-
ing speech on Buckingham Assizes Bills,
19. 449n
health of, bad constitution, **20.** 32
Opposition aided by, **20.** 32
——'s assembly addressed by, at St Alban's
Tavern, **20.** 50
Parliamentary Address opposed by, **20.** 510n
Parliamentary speeches by: **19.** 449n, **37.** 414,
415; against Assizes Bill, **13.** 20, **19.** 449n;
against Pelham over Buckingham assizes,
19. 470; on Dresden treaty, **42.** 496
Rochefort inquiry pamphlets ascribed to, **37.**
523n
son of Abp of Canterbury, **22.** 184n
Warburton, Mrs, said to have affair with,
22. 184n
Potter, William, King's messenger:
Madrid dispatches brought by, **23.** 246n, 250n
Potter's Field, Tooley St, Southwark:
warehouses in, burn, **25.** 577n
Pottery:
dishes of, sent by Lady Ailesbury to Mme du
Deffand, **6.** 177, 181, 183, 186
Du Deffand, Mme, has, English, **8.** 13
See also China; Crockery; Porcelain
Pottinger, Richard (1724–94), undersecretary
of state:
Gray suspects, of writing Colman's and
Lloyd's *Two Odes*, **28.** 193, 198
(?) Holdernesse, Cts of, entertains, **43.** 304
Pottle; pottles:
of hay, **43.** 66
Potts, Cuthbert, jr; surgeon:
(?) HW tells Ann Bransom to show SH to,
43. 164
(?) Ps Amelia's embalming attended by, **33.**
535n
(?) SH ticket not used by, **12.** 239
Potts, Mrs Cuthbert, jr. *See* Thorpe, Ethelinda
Margaret
Potts, Samuel:
footpads attack, **35.** 365
Radnor House, Twickenham, occupied by,
42. 480
Potts. *See also* Pott
Potvin, John (fl. 1684), upholsterer:
Nell Gwyn employs, **1.** 350
Pouch; pouches:
Conway busy with, **37.** 358
leather, countrymen carry money in, **18.** 148
pandours carry, **37.** 142
Pougens, Marie-Charles-Joseph de (1755–1833),
writer; natural son of Prince de Conti:
SH visited by, **12.** 231

Pougens, Mme Marie-Charles-Joseph de. *See* Sayer, Frances Julia

Pouget, Mlle, sister of the jeweller:
Wiart seeks engraving from, 6. 346

Pouget, Jean-Henri-Prosper (d. 1769), jeweller:
Wiart seeks engraving from heirs of, 6. 346

Pougues (France):
visitors to: Berrys, 11. 126, 130; Boufflers, Comtesse de, 3. 59, 100, 303, 308–9, 319, 334, 4. 106, 110; Conti, 3. 303, 308–9, 311, 319, 4. 106, 253, 5. 225, 256; La Marche, Comtesse de, 3. 303; Pont-de-Veyle, 4. 253, 5. 225, 256

Pouilly, Mme la Baronne de, at Reims:
possible reference to, 13. 178

Pouilly. *See also* Lévesque de Pouilly; Poully

Pouldu Bay (France):
English squadron lands at, 19. 319n

'Poule au pot, la':
verses on, 6. 64, 93

Poulenbourgh, Corn.:
Masters mentions, 1. 24, 43. 44

Poulet. *See* Paulet; Poulett; Powlett

Poulett, Cts. *See* Butt, Mary (1732–1819); Pocock, Sophia (d. 1811)

Poulett, Hon. Anne (1711–85), M.P.:
(?) dances at Robinson's ball, 37. 115
(?) Florence visited by, 20. 387

Poulett, Hon. Catherine, m. James Johnston:
(?) marriage of, 34. 260

Poulett, John (ca 1668–1743), 4th Bn Poulett; cr. (1706) E. Poulett:
daughter of, 9. 264n
death of, 18. 245

Poulett, John (1708–64), 2d E. Poulett, 1743; M.P.:
Bedchamber resigned by, 20. 469–70
brother's breath criticized by, 30. 72
death of, 38. 463
Essex's places sought by, 43. 272
Fox and Lady Yarmouth get regrets from, for Parliamentary motion, 35. 224
house of, in York Buildings, 35. 224n
Kildare, Cts of, wishes to oust, from Bedchamber because he stinks and is poxed, 20. 470n
Mastership of the Horse sought by, 20. 183n
Opposition activity by, at Bridgwater, 35. 225n
papers advertised as lost by, 35. 224
Parliamentary motion by, against George II's Hanoverian trip, 35. 223–4
Rochford's appointment as Groom of the Stole resented by, 35. 223n
Sibylline Leaves by, printed, 35. 224
'turned poet,' 35. 224

Poulett, Hon. Peregrine (1708–52), M.P.:
brother criticizes breath of, 30. 72
(?) dances at Robinson's ball, 37. 115

Poulett, Lady Rebecca (1716–65):
Northumberland, Cts of, pushed by, 9. 264

Poulett, Hon. Vere (1710–88), 3d E. Poulett, 1764; M.P.:
(?) dances at Robinson's ball, 37. 115
Dobson's self-portrait owned by, 1. 171
(?) Florence visited by, 20. 387
Twickenham resident, 42. 481
wife of, 12. 75n

Poulett. *See also* Powlett

Poulett Lodge, Twickenham, Cts Poulett's house:
Heath Lane Lodge next to, 43. 363
Osbaldeston, Mrs, finds, too small, 12. 74

Poullain de St-Foix, Germain-François (1698–1776), writer:
Essais historiques sur Paris by: 1. 134, 137, 138, 43. 49, 107; HW imitates, 11. 93
Frenchman in book by, 7. 360
Histoire de l'ordre du Saint-Esprit by: Du Deffand, Mme, reads, 6. 189; HW orders, 6. 17, 45, 43. 97, 196; superficial, 15. 111
Lettre au sujet de l'homme au masque de fer by, 4. 114, 116, 135, 11. 347
social relations of, with Mme Geoffrin, 7. 309

'Poullayon, M. de.':
Du Deffand, Mme, mentions, 4. 89

Poully, Jacques:
trial of, 3. 35

Poulterer; poulterers:
French, English 'dancing and trading with,' 37. 56, 59
Irish peerage includes, 21. 24

Poultice; poultices:
for gout, 3. 125, 10. 118
prescribed: for Mme de Luxembourg, 7. 209; for Mme du Deffand, 6. 219, 221

Poultney. *See* Pulteney

Poultry *or* Poultry Compter, London:
HW contributes to sick prisoners as advertised from, 42. 454
HW contributes towards poor people as advertised from, 42. 455
Hall, James, lawyer of, 15. 337, 30. 368, 369, 377
Tilly, attorney in, 33. 67n

Poultry:
bantam: Bentley to receive, by Capt. Lys, 35. 182; Edwards observes, 9. 270; HW gives, to Anne Seymour Conway, 38. 405; HW might rescue, in ark, 35. 316; HW offers, to Conway, 37. 344, 345; HW raises, from Montagu's cocks, 9. 77; HW rescues, from SH flood, 35. 228; hen has crowed, 32. 76; Montagu feeds, 10. 111; to be sent by HW to Montagu, 9. 46
French, 'insipid,' 35. 485n
HW receives, from Montagu, 9. 29, 77
HW's, to be described to Conway, 37. 291
HW sends compliments to, 35. 341
HW to send, to Montagu, 9. 25
HW wishes more hens, from Montagu, 9. 51
See also Chicken; Cock; Duck; Fowl; Goose; Hen

Poultry house:
at Park Place, **39.** 350
Pouncy, Benjamin Thomas (d. 1799), engraver:
print by, of abbey of Bec, **2.** 159
Pound; pounds (currency):
Mann wants price in, instead of guineas, **21.** 303
Poupardon d'Amanzy, Marie-Louise-Anne-Constance, m. 1 Jean Boissière; m. 2 Paul-Charles-Marie, Marquis de Loménie:
Du Deffand, Mme, paid interest by, **7.** 456
——'s annuities from, **8.** 43
social relations of, in Paris, **4.** 84, 448, **6.** 222, **7.** 288, 290, 303, 316, 351, 450
successful at loto, **7.** 458
sups at Montmorency, **4.** 84
Toulouse, Abp of, has, as mistress, **4.** 448, **7.** 375
Pourblay, Jacqueline:
account of, by Mme de Meinières, **3.** 351
(*see also* Guichard, Octavie: *Triomphe de l'amitié, Le*)
health of, **3.** 366
installation of, **7.** 321
La Borde gives money to, **8.** 187
social relations of, with Mme du Deffand, **7.** 318
Pourcheresse d'Estrabonne, Claude-François:
(?) attends session of parliament of Paris, **8.** 171
Pourquoi sais-tu plaire:
French song, **38.** 100
Pourteiron de Puigautier, Jean-Guillaume:
legal representative of Mme du Deffand's brothers, at the taking of her inventory after her death, **8.** 11, 46–7
Poussai (France):
abbess of, **9.** 119n, **42.** 90
Hamilton, Richard, dies at, **42.** 90n
See also Gramont, Marie-Élisabeth de
Poussin (originally Dughet), Gaspard (1615–75), painter:
landscapes by: at Burghley House, **10.** 345; at Osterley Park, **32.** 126; HW bequeaths, to Ds of Gloucester, **30.** 354; HW may remember, **21.** 231; Mann buys, for Hoare, **21.** 231, 479; Mann leaves, to HW, **25.** 664–5, 668, **30.** 354; Mann may get, for Hoare, **21.** 208–9; Mann, Horace II, takes, from bad frames, **25.** 668; sold at Furnese's auction, **21.** 172; to go to England on same ship with Mann's body, **25.** 668
Whithed collects paintings by, **20.** 142
Poussin, Nicolas (1594–1665), painter:
Bard, The, should be illustrated by, **35.** 252
bust of wife of, **32.** 282
drawings by Lady Diana Beauclerk are worthy of, **28.** 244
Elector Palatine's paintings by, **39.** 537
Furnese has pictures by, **21.** 172n
landscapes of Greece by, **11.** 128n
Mariette shows drawings by, **7.** 279
Monaco, P. of, has painting by, **7.** 355

painting by, of 'Christ and the Samaritan Woman,' **35.** 149
painting portrays, **21.** 208–9
paintings by, at Colebrooke's sale, **23.** 569n
'Seven Sacraments' by, bought at Rome by Reynolds for D. of Rutland, **33.** 538–9
West imitates, in historical painting, **23.** 210–11
Williams buys painting by, **23.** 466
'Winter, or the Flood' by, at the Luxembourg, **39.** 202
Poussin, Mme Nicolas. *See* Dughet, Anne-Marie
Poutier de Sone, Gabrielle-Antoinette de, m. (1734) François-Nicolas, Marquis de Rose-Dammartin:
(?) social relations of, with Duchesse de la Vallière, **7.** 344
Pover, Diego, Lt:
captured at Velletri, **18.** 492
Poverty:
at Dublin, **37.** 35
at Minorca, **37.** 313
lack of new buildings is sign of, **33.** 29
'parade and, the land divide,' **7.** 357, **35.** 112
shown by houses to be let, **15.** 156
verses to, attributed to C. J. Fox, **32.** 382
Povey, Charles (ca 1652–1743):
Meditations of a Divine Soul by, has story from Luther, **28.** 363n
Powder:
Beaufort, Ds of, now wears, in her hair, **24.** 54
canonici and abbés forbidden to wear, **21.** 224
Coventry, Cts of, cannot use, in France, **20.** 338
Du Barry, Comtesse, does not wear, **10.** 292
—— flings, in Louis XV's face, **23.** 85
Fitzjames wears, in hair, **39.** 9
Fitzpatrick wears little, in hair, **35.** 363
French actors' hair to have, in *Hamlet*, **35.** 121
French footmen always wear, **35.** 112
French opera singers omit, if they represent widows, witches, or distressed ladies, **18.** 496
grey, **35.** 339
Hare Naylor would have used, in hair, had he known his father was to remarry, **18.** 64
Lennox, Lady George, does not wear, **31.** 124n
Pius VI forbids priests to wear, in hair, **24.** 107
red: used by Mrs Siddons, **33.** 359; used for wounds, **17.** 94
Siddons, Mrs, omits, from hair, **33.** 359n
Stanhope does not let son use, in hair, because wheat is expensive, **39.** 183–4
Vere's shoulders covered with, **30.** 270
wig covered with, **23.** 258
See also under Hair-dressing
Powder-mill; powder-mills (for gunpowder):
at Epsom, explode, **35.** 100
at Hounslow, explode, **5.** 172, 173, **17.** 278n, **23.** 365, **32.** 75, 213, **34.** 226, **39.** 152–3
at Moulsey, explode, **17.** 278n

Berrys' dog to be treated at, for mange, **12**. 163
earthquake ascribed to explosion of, **20**. 131
Northumberland, D. of, gets Parliamentary act for erection of, **23**. 365–6
—— pretends, will be corn mills, **23**. 365–6
Powell, Anne (d. 1760), m. 1 —— Wilkins; m. 2 (1747) Rev. Conyers Middleton:
Cole's account of, **15**. 309–10
——'s informant, **1**. 364
Gordon, Mrs, has, as companion, **20**. 167
Gray describes, favourably, **14**. 31
Middleton marries, **15**. 293, 309
——'s creditors threaten, with seizure of his papers, **20**. 216
Radnor gives annuity to, **15**. 312
skilled in music, **15**. 293, 310
Williams, Sir C. H. told by, of Middleton's being ashamed of dedication, **15**. 304
Powell, John, of Boughrood, Radnorshire:
Middleton marries daughter of, **15**. 310
Powell, John (d. 1783):
Burke restores, to Pay Office, **25**. 407–8
Fox, C. J., sells house to, **12**. 125n, **33**. 437n
Pay Office employs, as Bn Holland's tool, **25**. 407
suicide of, after second dismissal from Pay Office, **25**. 407–8
Powell, Robert (d. 1772), convict:
hanged at Tyburn, **32**. 73
Powell, Rev. Thomas (1608–60), D.D., 1660; royalist divine:
Humane Industry by, misleads Lort about Montaigne, **16**. 159
Powell, William (1735–69), actor:
Garrick may be eclipsed by, **22**. 176
Ladbroke's former clerk, **22**. 176
Mann will not mention, to Garrick, **22**. 180
Powell, William Samuel (1717–75), Master of St John's College, Cambridge:
Masters is denied permission by, to publish Baker's history of St John's College, **2**. 231
Power:
evil effects of, **2**. 88, 89
Power of attorney. *See* Attorney, power of
Powerscourt, Vct. *See* Wingfield, Edward (1729–64)
Powerscourt House, Wicklow, Ireland:
Halifax to visit, **10**. 12
Montagu to visit, **9**. 391, **10**. 12
Powis, Bns. *See* Somerset, Elizabeth
Powis, Cts of. *See* Herbert, Barbara (1735–86); Herbert, Lady Henrietta Antonia (1758–1830); Somerset, Elizabeth (d. 1691)
Powis, E. of. *See* Herbert, George Edward Henry Arthur (1755–1801); Herbert, Henry Arthur (ca 1703–72)
Powis, Marchioness of. *See* Somerset, Elizabeth
Powis, M. of. *See* Herbert, William (ca 1629–96); Herbert, William (ca 1698–1748)
'Powis, Lady Mary.' *See* Brudenell, Lady Mary (b. ca 1717); Herbert, Lady Mary (d. 1775)
Powis. *See also* Powys

Powis Castle:
Powis, Cts of, keeps open house at, **38**. 186
Powis House, Knightsbridge, London:
Masserano entertains HW, Bedfords, and Marlborough at, **38**. 399–400
Yarmouth, Cts of, formerly had, **32**. 106n
Powle, George (fl. 1764–71):
mezzotints after portraits by, of Perrot and Lady Pakington, **43**. 384
prints by, **10**. 54n, **15**. 97n
Powlett, Lady Annabella. *See* Bennet, Lady Annabella
Powlett, Annabella (d. 1761), m. (1753) Rev. Richard Smyth:
elopement of, **9**. 154
Powlett, Lady Anne. *See* Powlett, Lady Annabella
Powlett, Charles (1685–1754), 3d D. of Bolton, 1722:
Cabinet Council's move to oust Carteret not aided by, **18**. 535–6
Carteret, Bns (Cts Granville) escorted by, **18**. 501, 537
Chute, Anthony, friend of, **14**. 93n
Chute, John, to get port wine from, in payment of loan, **35**. 86
colonel of the Blues, **20**. 207
Granville's friend, **20**. 207
Irish preferment promised to, **18**. 535–6
Isle of Wight to be commanded by, supposedly in lieu of Beefeaters, **17**. 457
lord lieutenancy for, **18**. 9n
Mastership of the Horse applied for by, **20**. 183n
regent, **18**. 209n
regiment of, **19**. 128n
sister-in-law of, **20**. 231n
wife of, **9**. 272n
Powlett, Charles (ca 1718–65), 5th D. of Bolton, 1759; M.P.:
HW mentions, **9**. 278
red ribbon vacated by, may make room for Mann, **22**. 312
Parliamentary activity of, on Regency Bill, **38**. 542
Stuart's duel with, **9**. 281
suicide of, **22**. 312
unmarried, **10**. 29
Powlett, Charles, illegitimate son of D. of Bolton:
mother leaves fortune away from, **21**. 365
Powlett, Sir Charles Armand (ca 1684–1751), K. B., 1749; M.P.:
Conway succeeds, as dragoon commander, **20**. 297n
installed as K. B., **20**. 71n
Powlett, Harry (1691–1759), 4th D. of Bolton, 1754:
relative of, **14**. 93n
Powlett, Harry (1720–94), 6th D. of Bolton, 1765; naval officer:
'Admiral Sternpost' and 'Captain Whiffle' supposed to be, **18**. 301n

[Powlett, Harry (1720–94), *continued*]
ball by, for D. and Ds of Gloucester, to be attended by HW, 25. 22
ball given by, 7. 212n
George III's remonstrance from, for Keppel trial, 24. 432n, 33. 82n
Grenville attacked by, in Parliamentary debate, 38. 500
house of, visible from Park Place, 39. 550
Keppel, Mrs, entertains, at Isleworth, 33. 481
Mann disobeyed by, 18. (?) 287–8, 301
mission of, to Civita Vecchia, 18. 301
Oxford, ship of, 18. 301n
valour of, questionable, 38. 500
Waldegrave sisters visit, in Hampshire, 31. 200

Powlett, Henrietta (d. 1753), m. (1741) Robert Colebrooke:
Robinson entertains, 17. 185

Powlett, Horatio Armand:
mother leaves fortune away from, 21. 365

Powlett, Lady Nassau. *See* Tufton, Lady Isabella

Powlett, Lord Nassau (1698–1741):
wife of, 20. 231n

Powlett, Percy:
mother leaves fortune away from, 21. 365

Powlett. *See also* Paulet; Poulett

Powlett family:
madness in, 22. 312

Pownall, Commander Philemon; naval Capt., 1771:
Sawyer's prize money shared by, 22. 45
——'s sister weds, 22. 45

Pownall, Mrs Philemon. *See* Majendie, ——

Pownall, Thomas (1722–1805), politician and antiquary; gov. of Massachusetts and South Carolina; M.P.:
'accounts of, for everything immediately,' 1. 384
Administration of the Colonies by, 1. 293n
biographical information about, corrected, 43. 308
Dunning's motion supported by, 25. 45n
HW bored by dissertation of, 29. 129–30
HW converses with, 29. 243
HW refuses to discuss Ds of Gloucester with, 23. 396n
HW's correspondence with, 42. 76–82, 84
HW thanks: for correcting pamphlet on Sir Robert Walpole, 42. 84; for pamphlet on Sir Robert Walpole, 42. 77–8, 84
HW visited by, 32. 94–5, 164
interested in freemasons, 1. 293, 295n, 298, 300
Ledwich's dissertation on Druids addressed to, 33. 478n
'my Phoenician-Irish antiquarian friend,' 32. 94
On the Character and Principles of Sir Robert Walpole, received by HW from, 42. 76–82, 84
(?) stepson accompanied by, in calling on HW, 35. 498
SH visited by, 12. 225

view of, on creation, 32. 94–5
wife of, 6. 409n

Pownall, Mrs Thomas. *See* Churchill, Harriet

Powney, Peniston Portlock (?1743–94), M.P.:
Court candidate, 29. 80n
election of, 25. 86n
Keppel defeated by, at Windsor, 33. 225n
name of, corrected, 43. 353

Powys, Elizabeth (1736–1826), m. (1760) Thomas Townshend, cr. (1783) Bn, and (1789) Vct Sydney:
becomes lady of the Bedchamber, 11. 367n
Williams, Sophia, lives with, 31. 333n

Powys, Lady Mary. *See* Brudenell, Lady Mary

Powys, Rev. Thomas (1736–1809):
(?) charade of, 33. 446
Powys's prologue altered by, 32. 343n
verses written by, in cottage at Park Place, 39. 533–5

Powys, Thomas (1743–1800), cr. (1797) Bn Lilford; M.P.:
Adam and Dundas attacked by, 35. 620
Association, The, opposed by, 25. 401n
(?) charade by, 33. 446
Foote, Mrs, summons, to reading of Edward Louisa Mann's will, 24. 159
Fox-North coalition denounced by, 25. 369n
Fox-Pitt coalition urged by, 25. 490n
Mann's 'half-nephew,' 25. 474
Mann, Horace II, brother-in-law of, 25. 475n
—— may be made imprudent by, 24. 429
M. P. for Northamptonshire, 25. 475n
Pitt, William II, forfeits good will of, in reconciliation attempt, 25. 475n
political career open to, 25. 474
Shelburne's offer of secretaryship of war refused by, 25. 474n
speeches of, acrimonious, 24. 429

Powys, Mrs Thomas. *See* Mann, Eleanor (1747–1823)

Pox:
Chute unwittingly discusses, with Mme Sarrazin, 17. 498
Dorchester, Cts of, tells Dr Radcliff to look for, 39. 54–5
Florentine, mentioned in Mann's letters, 35. 35
French: Cornwallis, Sir William, praises, 14. 179; proclamation concerning, 15. 120
Montagu fears, 10. 142
occurrences of, 9. 252, 17. 480, 20. 470n, 23. 278, 37. 78, 81

Poxwell, Dorset:
Place, rector of, 15. 292n

'Po-Yang,' HW's goldfish pond:
goldfish taken from, for Mrs Clive, 9. 134
HW almost falls into, 35. 308
'natural gravel pit where there is a spring,' 40. 85
See also under Strawberry Hill

Poyanne, Marquis de. *See* Baylens, Charles-Léonard-Bernard de

Poymont, Josef von (d. 1743), Graf von Payers-
berg:
Spaniards capture, 18. 153-4
wounded at Campo Santo, 18. 164
Poynings, Barony of:
Somerset, Ds of, inherited, 20. 11n
Poynings's Act. See under Parliament: acts of
Poyntz, Charles (1735-1809), D. D.:
Cumberland, D. of, has, educated abroad,
20. 208
Poyntz, Louisa (d. 1762):
death of, 38. 167
Poyntz, Margaret Georgiana (1737-1814), m.
(1755) Hon. John Spencer, cr. (1761) Bn,
and (1765) E. Spencer:
Amelia, Ps, entertains, 32. 307
Bath visited by, 31. 130-1, 35. 319
Bologna visited by, 22. 173
Bussy, Marquise de, friend of, 5. 351
Calais visited by, 6. 231
captured by the French, 7. 177
character of, 5. 280
Coke, Lady Mary, concerned for death of
child of, 31. 141
Craufurd's correspondence with, 5. 362
—— visits, 6. 132, 137
daughter of, 35. 357
Devonshire's deterioration reported by, 38.
447
drawing-room of, 32. 178
Du Deffand, Mme, mentions, 7. 111
——'s opinion of, 5. 377, 406
electioneering of, 33. 225
entertainment by, 39. 322
expected from Paris, 32. 392
faro-punter, 39. 377n
Fontainebleau to be visited by, 6. 484
—— visited by, 6. 488, 490, 38. 448, 450
George III's coronation attended by, 9. 387
'goddess of wisdom,' 35. 357
Greville, Mrs, friend of, 5. 362
HW admires appearance of, at coronation,
9. 387
HW does not know, 5. 369
HW ridicules 'mystery' of, about son's match,
33. 253-4
HW's opinion of, 5. 377
HW to receive, at breakfast, 33. 21
Howe, Mrs, and Rachel Lloyd attend, at
Althorp, 39. 273
Isle-Adam to be visited by, 5. 403
Lucans entertain, 33. 253-4
Mann gives assembly for, 22. 180
Montpellier visited by, 5. 280
Naples and Rome visited by, 22. 180n
'not the worst figure at the coronation,' 38.
127
Paris visited by, 5. 280, 351, 6. 482
portrait of, 33. 265
retires to St Albans on death of husband, 33.
428
Roissy to be visited by, 5. 367

social relations of, in Paris, 5. 352, 362, 403,
6. 218, 219, 221, 483, 488
son offers houses to, 33. 428n
(?) son's match disapproved by, 25. 104
Spa benefits, 22. 173
—— to be visited by, 5. 351, 352, 362
—— visited by, 6. 488
success of, 5. 352, 369
Williams, Sophia, lives with, 31. 333n
York, D. of, sups with, and gives her presents,
22. 228
Poyntz, Stephen (1685-1750), D. of Cumberland's treasurer and former 'governor':
brother and wife ruin, 20. 208
character of, 20. 208
Cumberland, William, D. of, aids family of,
20. 208
—— had, as 'governor,' 19. 242n, 20. 207-8,
22. 163n
——'s treasurer, 19. 242n
—— visits, 30. 27
HW's correspondence with, 40. 58-9
house of, in Burlington St, 22. 70n
Midgham, Berks, seat of, 20. 208n
minister to Sweden, 20. 208n
Primate of Scotland's baggage discovered by,
19. 242
Townshend's sons tutored by, 20. 208n, 40.
44n
Walpole, Sir Robert, sends, with plea to D.
of Cumberland, 37. 188n
Williams, Sir C. H., writes ode to, 30. 319
Poyntz, Mrs Stephen. See Mordaunt, Anna
Maria
Poyntz, William (d. 1748), receiver-general of
Excise:
brother ruined by, 20. 208
devout, 20. 208
Poyntz, William (ca 1734-1809), son of Stephen
Poyntz:
Cumberland, D. of, has, educated abroad,
20. 208
Pozsony, parliament of (in Hungary):
nobility's freedom from taxation established
by, 21. 176n
Pozzo. See Dal Pozzo
Pozzobonelli, Giuseppe, (b. 1696), cardinal,
1743:
Benedict XIV makes, cardinal, 18. 302n
Pozzolini, Pietro, Mann's servant:
arrival of, in England, reported to Mann by
HW, 25. 344
detained in England before starting back to
Italy, 25. 350, 351
Mann's annuity to, 25. 667n
—— sends packets to England by, 25. 207,
325, 329, 334
'Pozzolo, Marquis de':
Charles, K. of Naples, enters Rome incognito
as, 18. 519n
Pozzuolo (Italy):
Neapolitan Jesuits sent to, 22. 565n

Prades, —— de:
Fenouilhet, Lady, mother-in-law of, **5**. 398
Prades, Mme de. *See* Edgcumbe, Miss
Prado, Abraham (d. 1782):
death of, **33**. 347
HW receives grapes from, **32**. 207–8
HW's enthusiasm for, **2**. 373
Twickenham resident, **42**. 486
villa of, sold, **29**. 292
Prado, Mrs Abraham. *See* Salvador, (?) Esther
Prado, at Madrid:
Cumberland, Richard, at, **29**. 146
Pradoe, Abram. *See* Prado, Abraham
Prado family:
HW's friends, **10**. 106n
Prætorian Guard:
constitution could be overthrown by, **23**. 304
HW compares Marseillais to, **15**. 236
Pragmatic Sanction:
Jadot attempts to draw, **30**. 9
Prague:
Austrian battle with Bavarian-French army expected at, **17**. 194
Austrians unlikely to capture, **37**. 127
battle of, England hears of, **21**. 91–2
Beauvau said to have escaped from, **18**. 68–9
Belle-Isle escapes from, **18**. 32n
—— ill at, **18**. 108
—— offers to surrender, **17**. 489n
Braitwitz alludes to capture of, **17**. 259
Broglie blockaded by, **18**. 61n
Brown advocates fighting Prussians before they reach, **21**. 95n
capture of: by Austrians, reported, **17**. 466, 472, 481; by Bavarians and French, **17**. 194n; by French, **17**. 221, 226; by Prussians, **18**. 511; Craon, Princesse de, anxious for, **18**. 1–2; England hears no news of, **18**. 32; English fear, will not take place, **18**. 47; expected, **17**. 472, **18**. 58
castle at, Titian's 'Ecce homo,' placed at, **16**. 154
Charles, P., approaches, **17**. 464–5
—— forced to conciliate townspeople of, **18**. 512
coronation at: of Joseph II as K. of the Romans, **22**. 324; of Maria Theresa as Q. of Bohemia, **18**. 240, 241–2
Czaslau near, **17**. 433
Daun's army relieves, **21**. 116
English army not to attack, **18**. 202
escape of Frenchman from, reported in English newspapers, **18**. 68–9
Francis I or P. Charles may capture, **17**. 472, **18**. 58
Francis I's visit to, causes dissension, **18**. 2
—— to destroy French army at, **17**. 481
Frederick II captures, **18**. 511
—— fails to take, **21**. 106–7, **35**. 282
—— menaces, **18**. 499, **21**. 95, 102, **22**. 63
——'s victory at, **9**. 206
—— traps P. Charles at, **21**. 95n
French-Bavarian army driven back to, **17**. 205

futile attacks on, fashionable, **18**. 202–3
HW jokes about Francis I's attempts to capture, **30**. 34–5
HW might get bricks from, **35**. 282
Joseph II crowned at, as K. of the Romans, **22**. 324
light engagements at Geng and Kuttenberg to prevent Daun from reaching, **21**. 95n
Maria Theresa orders a blockade before, **18**. 47n
——'s coronation at, as Q. of Bohemia, **18**. 240, 241–2
news of capture of, premature, **17**. 488
Prussians evacuate, **18**. 543
siege of: changed to blockade, **18**. 61; HW and Sir Robert Walpole laugh at raising of, **18**. 68; raised, **18**. 58, **21**. 109, 112; Te Deums sung for raising of, **21**. 112, 114
Vienna conceals disaster at, **21**. 242
visitors to: Conway and Scott, **39**. 537, 538; Craon, Princesse de, **22**. 324
Praitenstein, ——, Capt. (d. 1743):
killed at Campo Santo, **18**. 164
Prantner, ——, Capt. (d. 1743):
killed at Campo Santo, **18**. 164
Praslin, Comte de. *See* Choiseul, Antoine-César de
Praslin, Comtesse de. *See* O'Brien de Thomond, Charlotte-Antoinette-Marie-Septimanie
Praslin, Duc de. *See* Choiseul, Antoine-César de (1756–1808); Choiseul, César-Gabriel de (1712–85); Choiseul, Renaud-César-Louis de (1735–91)
Praslin, Duchesse de. *See* Champagne-la-Suze, Anne-Marie de (1713–84); Durfort de Lorges, Guyonne-Marguerite-Philippine de (1739–1806); O'Brien de Thomond, Charlotte-Antoinette-Marie-Septimanie (1759–1808)
Praslin, 'Marquise' de. *See* O'Brien de Thomond, Charlotte-Antoinette-Marie-Septimanie
Praslin (France):
Praslin exiled to, **41**. 198
Sanadon, Mlle, gives up visit to, **5**. 249–50
visitors to: Bauffremont, **7**. 426; Beaune, **7**. 461; Sanadon, Mlle, **5**. 376, 380, 382, **6**. 78, 80, 81, 84, 87, 356, 358, 359, **7**. 64, 66, 68, 219, 426, 461
Praslin, Hôtel de, at Paris:
HW describes, **7**. 353
view from Grand Cabinet of, **7**. 353
visitors to: Du Deffand, Mme, **7**. 432; HW, **7**. 353
'Praslinage':
Sanadon, Mlle, liked by, **6**. 356
'Prasline':
'airs à la,' **6**. 290, 361
'Praslin-Thomond, Marquise de.' *See* O'Brien de Thomond, Charlotte-Antoinette-Marie-Septimanie
Prat, Mrs. *See* Brookes, Henrietta (ca 1676–1769)
Prat. *See also* Pratt

Prati della Masone, near Bologna (Italy):
Spaniards encamped near, **17.** 424
Prati della Sala (Italy):
Montemar encamps at, **17.** 427
Prato, Leonard de (fl. 1485), Kt of Jerusalem:
Richard III's letter to, **1.** 156
'Prato' (unidentified Etonian):
West sups with, **13.** 173
Prato (Italy):
Bocchineri, Mme, relegated to, by Regency,
20. 447
Braitwitz to visit, **18.** 134
Del Monte's militia to assemble at, **18.** 85
English fleet could not have conquered, **19.**
215
letters to, from Spanish officers, **17.** 238
Medici commissary at, **18.** 170
Tuscan troops to go to, **18.** 98, 100
Pratolino (Italy):
carved figure by Giovanni Bologna at, **35.** 42
HW visits, **17.** 31
Leopold and Maria Louisa at, **22.** 337, 350
Leopold to visit, **22.** 334
—— transfers statues from, to the Uffizi, **25.**
531n
Mann to take visitors to, **17.** 484
Mozzi not allowed to spend night at, **24.** 23
Orford, Cts of, allowed by Leopold to use
apartment in, in hot season, **24.** 23
Pratt, Miss:
illness of, **41.** 392
Pratt, Anna Maria (d. 1806), m. (1739)
Thomas Barrett Lennard, 17th Bn Dacre of
the South, 1755:
Bayham Abbey recommended by, **35.** 136
brother of, **24.** 103
Chute not visited by, because of Court at-
tendance, **35.** 89
—— responsible for Mann's attentions to, **20.**
173
daughter of, dies, **20.** 92
Davis, Mrs, calls 'Barrett's folks,' **20.** 174
dressing-room of, **40.** 199
Florentine amusements missed by, **20.** 92
Giberne's prospects not to be told to, **20.** 91
Goldsworthy, Mrs, will tire, **20.** 93
HW announces visit from, to Chute, **35.** 90
HW asks Lincoln for ticket for, **30.** 178
HW congratulates, on nephew's marriage,
41. 359–60
HW does not know, **20.** 100
HW entertains, at dinner at SH, **24.** 103
HW known by, through Montagu, **20.** 78
HW pleased by Mann's liking for, **20.** 96
HW sees Mann's partiality for, **20.** 204
HW sends compliments to, **40.** 200
HW sends excuses to Camden by, **41.** 392
HW shops with, in Paris, **7.** 327
HW's relations with, **17.** 1n
HW thanks: **40.** 197; for hospitality at Bel-
hus, **42.** 72
HW to entertain, at SH, **9.** 231
HW to receive compliments of, **35.** 591

Hardinge announces marriage plans to, **35.**
591
—— apologizes to, **35.** 581
—— impresses, with wife's royal lineage, **35.**
610
—— owes to, his friendship with HW, **35.** 620
house taken by, in Florence, **20.** 75
husband may not permit, to live in same
house with Mann, **20.** 194
husband's bequest to, repaid by her care for
his children, **36.** 236
lodgings of, in Paris near HW's, **10.** 290
Mann admits truth of HW's remarks about,
20. 180
—— asks, to live at his house, **20.** 159, 165
—— coolly treated by, **20.** 173
—— declines to meet, at Montopoli, **20.** 194
—— defends, from HW's charge of prudery,
20. 105
—— gets house for, in Florence, **20.** 75
—— gives garden assembly for, **20.** 174, 191
—— likes, for Chute's sake, **20.** 84
—— may invite, to Fiesole, **20.** 194
—— not invited by, to Pisa baths, **20.** 194
——'s admiration for, **20.** 94
—— said to be in love with, **20.** 165n
——'s attentions to, **20.** 94
—— scolds HW for disparaging, **20.** 105
——'s devotion to, noticed by Mme Antinori,
20. 105
—— sees, daily, **20.** 159
——'s hospitality to, praised by HW, **20.** 87
——'s life after departure of, **20.** 98
—— teaches Italian to, **20.** 91–2
—— to accompany, to Pisa baths, **20.** 84, 85,
86
—— to give conversazione for, **20.** 75
Mann, Galfridus, urged by, to come to Italy,
20. 564
Montagu sends compliments to, **10.** 296
mother-in-law of, dies, **9.** 170
Naples visited by, **20.** 92, 105
Niccolini entertains, at dinner, **20.** 174
Paris visited by, **10.** 290, **35.** 121
Pisa visited by, **20.** 91–2
portrait of, at the Vyne, **35.** 639
sister mourned by, **20.** 92
social relations of, in Paris, **7.** 326–8, 330
spaniel bitch of, said to have miscarried, **22.**
546
Sunday opera shunned by, **20.** 86
Tunbridge left suddenly by, for Paris, **10.** 290
Pratt, Caroline (d. 1805), m. Herbert, Bn de
Munster:
(?) Mann teaches Italian to, **20.** 91–2
(?) Pisa baths visited by, **20.** 91
Pratt, Sir Charles (1714–91), Kt, 1761; cr.
(1765) Bn and (1786) E. Camden; M.P.;
lord chancellor, 1766:
American war foreseen by, **41.** 302
anti-Papist, **29.** 63
Bath visited by, **10.** 229, **31.** 130, **35.** 319,
39. 76

[Pratt, Sir Charles, *continued*]

Chatham, Cts of, corresponds with, about Hayes, **36.** 49n

chief justice of Common Pleas, **9.** 413

chief justiceship of, corrected, **43.** 274

Chute's nephew gets preferment from, at HW's request, **41.** 182

Dacre, Bns, to make HW's excuses to, **41.** 392

daughter of, mentioned in newspapers, **33.** 320

Declaratory Bill opposed by, **41.** 9

dismissal of: **15.** 130n; imprudent, **23.** 174

Dunning's friend, **23.** 175

Élie de Beaumont visits, **38.** 461

English constitution upheld by, **41.** 183

epigram attributed to, **29.** 88n

expulsion of, weakens Court party in Parliament, **23.** 182

finances and pension of, **23.** 174n

former lord chancellor, **24.** 103, **25.** 440n

Fox, C. J., promises, to find post for Thomas Walpole, jr, **42.** 73n

——'s India Bill opposed by, as giving patronage to Whigs, **36.** 218n

general warrants condemned by, **41.** 91n

George III insists on keeping, as chancellor, **22.** 538

—— sees, **25.** 679n

Great Seal obtained by, **22.** 442, 443

Guines's ball attended by, **32.** 117

HW advised by, about security of Shorter inheritance, **40.** 79

HW begs Conway to ask Grafton not to dismiss, **39.** 121

HW laments retirement of, **41.** 183–4

HW prefers, as lord chancellor, **41.** 86

HW's correspondence with, **40.** 79, 125–6, 182–4, 302–5

HW's letter of advice displeases, **41.** 306n

HW's old acquaintance with, to be revived, **41.** 184

HW tells, that no new prime minister should accept while policy remains unchanged, **41.** 303–5

HW thanked by, for *Historic Doubts*, **41.** 125–6

HW told by, of Pitt's correspondence with Hon. Thomas Walpole, **36.** 46

HW urges, to consider reprisals against Lord North, **29.** 202n

habeas corpus extension attacked by, **21.** 205

habeas corpus revision prepared by, **21.** 182n, **41.** 182n

Hardinge, nephew of, **32.** 307

——'s essay on libel approved by, **35.** 551

—— will not seek aid from, in entering Parliament, **35.** 618

Hardwicke thinks, inexperienced in constitutional and Parliamentary measures, **21.** 205n

health of, very ill, **22.** 169n

Hillsborough's letter criticized by, as not expressing the Cabinet's opinion, **41.** 315n

House of Lords does not consult, on Habeas Corpus Bill, **21.** 205n

—— shunned by, because outvoted by Court peers, **35.** 588

Inquiry into the Doctrine partly by, **22.** 275n

Kentish Town property of, let for building houses, **11.** 287

London Common Council votes freedom of city to, with portrait to be placed in Guildhall, **38.** 333

lord chancellor, **3.** 104, **30.** 228

Lyttelton abuses, in printed speech, **28.** 203

Mansfield blamed by, for Boston, Quebec, and Restraining Bills, **41.** 304n

—— roughly handled by, in House of Lords, **22.** 520, **23.** 256n, **41.** 10

——'s prosecution dropped by, **23.** 282

——'s speech cowed by sight of, **22.** 464

Mason ridicules, **28.** 437

ministry may dismiss, **23.** 168

ministry might include, **24.** 447n

motto of, part of Magna Carta, **10.** 187

nephew must be a satisfaction to, **41.** 360

nephew removed by, from Trinity College, **14.** 135

Northington and Yorke reportedly displeased by Pitt's summons to, **30.** 227

Northington's co-negotiator in resignation, **22.** 431n

opinion of, sought in affairs of Cts of Orford and her son, **25.** 125, 216, 230, 440

Opposition favourable to, **35.** 618

—— prefers, to Charles Yorke, in privilege dispute, **38.** 285

—— reproached by, **12.** 257

Paoli presented to, **23.** 150n

Parliamentary motion by, on Quebec Bill, **41.** 299–300

peerage offered to, **30.** 194

Pitt (Chatham) devises Habeas Corpus Bill with, **21.** 205n

—— joined by, in attacking George III's Parliamentary address, **41.** 183n

—— may confer with, at Bath, **39.** 95

—— names, for lord chancellor, **22.** 161

—— prefers, to Charles Yorke, for lord chancellor, **38.** 285

——'s remark to, about his peerage, **30.** 197

—— supported by: in attempt to withdraw troops from Boston, **32.** 228; in debate over Wilkes, **23.** 209n

—— upheld by, **39.** 246

—— would give essential post to, **28.** 377

point laboured by, against the Court, in case of Middlesex election, **23.** 167

political failure of, **23.** 216

president of the Council, **25.** 262, **29.** 207

refuses to believe Habeas Corpus Bill, **28.** 283n

remains in place as lord chancellor, **23.** 65

remarks by, on Wilkes's contest with Wood, **41.** 91n

removal of, as lord chancellor, **4.** 311

resignation of, as lord president, rumoured, **39**. 503n

retired, and too old to think merely as a lawyer, **25**. 125

rift of, with Mansfield, Hardwicke, Newcastle, and H. Fox, **21**. 205

rioters respect, **33**. 175n

Sackville believed by, to be entitled to court martial, **21**. 366n

Shelburne administration may include, **25**. 260n

sister of, **12**. 166n, **24**. 103

son of, **25**. 620, **29**. 271

son sways politics of, **36**. 221

Walpole, Hon. Thomas, hears from, and regrets his political stand, **36**. 218–19, 221

Wilkes freed by, **38**. 200–1

——'s arrest warrant considered illegal by, **38**. 197

——'s outlawry discussed by, **23**. 7n

Wilmot succeeds, as chief justice of Common Pleas, **22**. 443

Yorke, Charles, opposes opinion of, on privilege, **38**. 241

—— refuses to serve under, **22**. 443n, **30**. 234

Pratt, Frances (d. 1749):

sister mourns, **20**. 92

Pratt, Frances (ca 1751–1833), m. (1775) Robert Stewart, cr. (1789) Bn Londonderry, (1795) Vct Castlereagh, (1796) E. and (1816) M. of Londonderry:

abduction of, **33**. 320

HW suggests temporary insanity of, **33**. 323

Pratt, Jane (d. 1807), m. (1738) Nicholas Hardinge:

Bayham Abbey recommended by, **35**. 136

HW mentions, **37**. *418*

husband of, **14**. 135n

son must be a satisfaction to, **41**. 360

son of, **12**. 166n

Pratt, Sir John (1657–1725), Kt; lord chief justice:

daughter of, **20**. 87n

Pratt, John (d. 1797):

Gothic house built by, at Bayham Abbey, **35**. 136

Pratt, Mrs John. *See* Brookes, Henrietta

Pratt, Hon. John Jeffreys (1759–1840), styled Vct Bayham 1786–94; 2d E. Camden, 1794; cr. (1812) M. Camden:

aunt retires to Grove Hill near seat of, **35**. 595n

father's politics swayed by, **36**. 221

French attempt on Ireland reported by, **34**. 228n

Grafton's message conveyed by, to Lord Euston, **33**. 457

lord lieutenant of Ireland, **12**. 166

marriage of, **25**. 620, **33**. 506

reversion to, of teller's place, **23**. 174n

Selwyn's witticism on, **29**. 271

wife of, **7**. 13n, **12**. 152n

Pratt, Mrs John Jeffreys. *See* Molesworth, Frances

Pratt, Mary:

List of a Few Cures Performed by Mr and Mrs De Loutherbourg, A, by, **16**. 227n

Pratt, Robert (d. 1775) of Coscomb:

pamphlet by, **14**. 137n

Pratt, Samuel Jackson (1749–1814), actor and hack writer; 'Courtney Melmoth':

Fair Circassian, The, by: **2**. 322, 323–4, **43**. 76; HW comments on, **2**. 323–4; print ridiculing, **2**. 322

HW's correspondence with, **7**. 389

(?) Mason abused by, **28**. 308

Pratt, William, HW's printer 1761–4:

Bathoe's account shows payment to, **40**. 290

disappears because of debts, **30**. *171–2*

HW asked by, for three guineas, **40**. 289

HW hires, **15**. 76n

(?) HW mentions, **10**. 102

HW's correspondence with, **40**. 249, 289

HW's trouble from, **15**. 98

imperfect SH Lucan copies completed by, **40**. 149n

Pratt, Mrs William, wife of the printer:

Bathoe's account shows payment to, **40**. 290

drunken, and responsible for her husband's extravagance, **30**. 172

Prault, Laurent-François or François-Laurent (d. 1780), bookseller in Paris:

(?) Drumgold recommends, to HW as agent at Paris, **40**. 302

(?) HW calls on, **7**. 298

(?) London to be visited by, with Drumgold's letter to HW, **40**. 302

Prault, Marcel, publisher in Paris:

(?) Drumgold recommends, to HW as agent in Paris, **40**. 302

(?) HW calls on, **7**. 298

(?) London to be visited by, with Drumgold's letter to HW, **40**. 302

Prawn; prawns:

eyes and tails of, **21**. 191, **37**. 526

Praxiteles (fl. 5th and 4th cent. B.C.):

mentioned in two inscriptions for sculpture, **33**. 564

Prayer; prayers:

clergyman prefers, to be said by light of tallow candles instead of farthing ones, **17**. 85

contrite expressions customary in, **16**. 207

evening, **9**. 49

family: at R. O. Cambridge's, **12**. 177; Montagu to be awkward at, **10**. 297

Ferrers's, at execution, **21**. 401

for George II, **19**. 149

for Richecourt, **21**. 79

for royal family, George III excludes all but his mother from, **21**. 449

for use of Trinity Hospital, Greenwich, **16**. 91

for Young Pretender at Roman churches, **19**. 171n

HW attends, at House of Commons, to reserve a place, **38**. 323

[Prayer; prayers, *continued*]
HW's reflections on, **23.** 145
inept, for lady on point of marriage, **17.** 142, **30.** 21
in time of war and tumults, **28.** 472, **29.** 40
Mason suggests proper form of, after Bunker Hill, **28.** 215
new form of, for capture of Louisbourg colours, **37.** 567
Northumberland, Cts of, has book of, **42.** 379
ordered, for earthquake relief, **17.** 284
Pennicott not to go to Pavilions to read, **36.** 261
Thomas, Bp, reads, to George II, **20.** 348
Townshend, Vcts, resorts to, **35.** 196
Wettenhall, Mrs, accustomed to, **9.** 231
York, Cardinal, delays expedition with, **19.** 509
Prayer book; prayer books:
René I's, **42.** 93
Stafford has *Portier des Chartreux* bound like, **17.** 273–4
See also *Book of Christian Prayers*; *Book of Common Prayer*; Burgh, Elizabeth: *Lady Eliz. Tirwitt's Morning and Evening Praiers*; Parr, Catherine: *Prayers or Medytacions*
Prayers and Meditations. See under Johnson, Dr Samuel
Prayers or Medytacions. See under Parr, Catherine
Preacher; preachers:
Charles II's witticism about, **22.** 57, **24.** 52
See also Clergyman
Preaching:
HW's reflections on, **31.** 114
Precedence:
ambassadorial dispute over, at George III's birthday ball, **23.** 125–8, 137–8
dispute over, at Sandwich's ball, **20.** 121–2, 144
Mann's ideas about, **20.** 144
Précieuses ridicules, Les. See under Molière
Precipitate. *See* Powder, red
Précis du procès du Comte de Morangiès. See under Voltaire
Précis du siècle de Louis XV. See under Voltaire
Prédiction. See under Voltaire
Prediction; predictions:
HW tells Mann not to trust his, **24.** 379
unforeseen events invalidate, **25.** 369
unreliability of, HW's reflections on, **24.** 256
Prédiction tirée d'un ancien manuscrit. See under Borde, Charles
'Pre-existence.' *See under* Evans, Abel
Preface to an Intended Answer to all Objections, A. See under Middleton, Conyers
Preface to Shakespeare. See under Johnson, Dr Samuel
Preferment:
Death follows after, **23.** 313
HW's reflections on, **9.** 77–8

Prefetti, Via de', at Rome:
Palazzo di Firenze in, **17.** 9n
Preile. *See* Harenc de Presle
Preising. *See* Preysing
Prejudice; prejudices:
Conway's reflections on, **37.** 546
HW's, strong, **34.** 103
origins of, **33.** 579–80
world not easily cured of, to embrace truth, **38.** 152
Préjugé à la mode, Le. See under Nivelle de la Chaussée, Pierre-Claude
Premier mémoire contre le comte de Guines. See under Tort de la Sonde, Barthélemy
Prendergast, Sir Thomas (d. 1760), 2d Bt; M.P.:
Dublin rioters drag, through streets, **9.** 266
Prenner, Giorgio Gasparo de (1721–66), engraver:
Illustri fatti Farnesiani engraved by, **25.** 403
Prentice, Thomas:
Charlemont writes to, **42.** 311n
Preobazhenskiĭ (Preobasinski) Guards:
Catherine II appeals to, **35.** 315
—— may prefer, to husband, **38.** 164
—— proclaimed by, **22.** 57–8, 61n
constitution could be overthrown by, **23.** 204
HW jokes about Pitt commanding, **10.** 39–40
Passeck, Capt-Lt in, **22.** 64n
Preparation for Death, The:
Dauphin jokes about, **31.** 77
French book of devotion, **31.** 77n
See also under Hélyot, Pierre; Martel, Gabriel
Prerogative:
decay of, on continent, a counter-security to England, **34.** 69
emphasized at Oxford, **33.** 483
HW accuses Mason of supporting, **29.** 351
HW mentions, **28.** 417
HW's reflections on, **28.** 411, **29.** 353
Hume's preference for, **16.** 266
Mansfield's concern for, **28.** 227
of free will, must be curtailed by new French constitution, **34.** 67
Parliamentary reform might strengthen, **29.** 18
Parliamentary vacillation about, **25.** 66
royal: *Droit de Roi* concerned with, **38.** 333; ministers wish to decrease power of, **10.** 154; Montagu fears, **10.** 152, 154; not enforced by Louis XVI, **11.** 28; political significance of, diminishes, **10.** 152–3; Tories foster, **24.** 492
shock given to, is a counter-security to liberty, **34.** 102
Stuarts bestow, **33.** 204
Tories adhere to, **29.** 22, 63
tyranny leads to destruction of, **28.** 441
Prerogative Proclamation:
American intercourse forbidden by, **41.** 314
Presbourg; Presburg. *See* Pressburg

Presbyterian; Presbyterians:
alleged Sabbatarianism of, 31. 436
Barrington was, 33. 469–70
Birmingham and Manchester hotbeds of, 34. 182
Burke attacks, 34. 116
Charles I demands homage of, 23. 100
Cole and HW differ about, 2. 229
Cole dislikes, 2. 82, 86
'conflagrations' by, feared, 34. 80
Dashwood, Lady, is, 19. 224
destruction by, in Civil War, 32. 75
HW jokes about, 19. 247
HW on, 15. 109
Kilmarnock is, 19. 283
London has dullness of, 19. 189
meeting-house of, said to be destroyed by Roman Catholics, 25. 56
Melcombe calls, 'Presbytyrants,' 31. 361, 34. 116
northern Irish, favour Roman Catholic emancipation, 25. 529n
pretended self-denials of, 31. 435
Roman Catholics oppose, 25. 64
Scottish: forswear the Pope, 24. 475; Gordon leads, against Roman Catholics, 25. 11; Trail said to be, 38. 347n
Secker bred as, 23. 40n, 30. 304n
Presbyterian Church:
Boswell thinks, endangered, 33. 462n
Charles II lectured by, 23. 386
Secker and Parker start as members of, 20. 188
Presbyterianism:
HW on, 2. 99, 100
Presbyterian meeting-house:
Peterhouse resembles, 13. 80
'Presbyterian money':
newspapers said to be bribed by, 15. 223
'Presbyterian parson':
'Cousin America' elopes with, 32. 245
Prescot, Mr:
imprisoned in France, 11. 84–5, 88
Prescot, Rev. Charles (1745–1820):
prints his father's books, 2. 23
Prescot, Kenrick (1702–79), Master of St Catharine's College, Cambridge:
Cambridge Address presented by, 30. 98n
Cole's account of, 1. 299, 2. 22–3
HW asks Cole to thank, 1. 301, 302
HW does not recollect, 2. 21
HW hears no more of, 2. 26
Letters Concerning Homer the Sleeper in Horace by, 1. 299, 302, 2. 21, 43. 58, 64
mentally disordered, 1. 299, 2. 22–3
Mildenhall, a Poem, by, 43. 64
wishes to send classical discourses to HW, 2. 21
Prescot, Mrs Kenrick. See Appleyard, Mary
Prescot, Mary (1746–76), m. Thomas Preston:
marriage and death of, 2. 23

Prescot, Susanna (1748–76), m. Anthony Fountayne Eyre:
death of, 2. 23
Prescot. See also Prescott
Prescott, —— (fl. 1775), English gardener:
garden 'begotten' on Comtesse de Boufflers by, 28. 222
Prescott, —— (ca 1781–1806) of East India Co.:
birth of, 33. 424
Prescott, George William, 1st Bt:
Theobalds replaced by, with new house, 42. 131n
Prescott, Sir Henry (1783–1874), Adm.:
parents of, 33. 424
Prescott, Isaac (1737–1830), naval officer ('Capt. Prescott'):
wife swears peace against, for brutality, 33. 424–5
Prescott, Mrs Isaac. See Walter, Jane
Prescott. See also Prescot
Presence Chamber, at Dublin:
Halifax attended in, by Irish House of Commons, 10. 19
Presentation, Convent of the, in Paris:
Cholmondeley, Henrietta, may go to, 4. 226
fire in, 4. 53–4
Presentations:
HW's correspondent busy with, 42. 364
Present Crisis with Respect to America Considered, The:
Parliament orders, to be burnt, 28. 179–80, 182
Preserves:
HW sends: to Beauvau, 6. 247, 259; to Beauvau, Princesse de, 6. 368; to Mirepoix, Mme de, 6. 247, 259
Lucan, Bns, sends, to Mme du Deffand, 6. 395, 400
Presidency, the:
Chesterfield's witticism on, 20. 214
'Président, Le'; 'President, the.' See Hénault, Charles-Jean-François
Président; Présidents, French:
Louis XV compensates, for dog shot by Charolais, 20. 340
sister argues with, about names of dinner courses, 22. 163
Président à mortier. See under Parliament of Paris
President of Board of Trade. See under Board of Trade
President of the Council ('lord president'):
Bathurst succeeds Gower as, 24. 534
Bedford, D. of, becomes, 22. 130, 167
Camden becomes, 25. 262
Carteret (Granville) is, 20. 202n, 207, 258–9, 22. 569
Chesterfield declines to be, 20. 207
Dorset resigns as, 20. 202
Gower expected to resign as, 24. 526
—— is, 24. 497, 25. 460n

[President of the Council, *continued*]
—— may become, after Northington and Grenville, **22.** 569, 571
HW suggests Yorke as, **41.** 86
Hardwicke may become, **20.** 202
—— might consent to be, **21.** 92–3
Harrington is, **17.** 333
—— may become, **19.** 327
Henley may be succeeded as, by Talbot, **41.** 73
—— now is, **22.** 500
——'s bargain for becoming, **30.** 233n
—— succeeds Winchilsea as, **22.** 443
—— to become, **22.** 439
Newcastle, D. of, declines to be, **30.** 185n
—— offers to shift to, **20.** 201n
Pulteney, E. of Bath, becomes, **18.** 556
Stormont becomes, **25.** 391
vacancy for, **20.** 202
Weymouth may succeed Gower as, **24.** 526n
See also Carteret, John (1690–1763); Compton, Spencer (? 1674–1743); Henley, Robert (ca 1708–72); Leveson Gower, Granville (1721–1803); Pulteney, William (1684–1764); Russell, John (1710–71); Sackville, Lionel Cranfield (1688–1765); Stanhope, William (ca 1683–1756); Yorke, Philip (1690–1764)

Presidii, the (Italy):
embarkations from, **19.** 55
Montemar may leave garrison at, **18.** 27
Spaniards and Neapolitans near, **18.** 546
Spaniards may retire to, **18.** 325
Spanish expedition said to have reached, **17.** 192
Spanish troops in, ill-equipped, **17.** 261–2
Spanish troops may go towards, **19.** 410

Presle, Bn de. *See* Hœgger, Anton

Presle, Baronne de. *See* Desmares, Christine-Antoinette-Charlotte

Presle, M. de. *See* Harenc de Presle

Présomption punie, La:
Frederick II said to have written, **18.** 337

Press; presses (furniture):
effigies of French kings in, **39.** 203
in Paris dépôt des archives, with wired doors and crimson curtains, **39.** 15

Press; presses (for printing):
Allan's, private, **41.** 351n

Press, the:
freedom of: **28.** 112, 125, 127, 135, 218, **29.** 18; anonymous publications should be barred from, **23.** 274; English defend, **5.** 92–3; HW's love of, **3.** 232; Hertford deplores abuse of, **38.** 439–40; Mann thinks, is abused in England, **23.** 189; Opposition abuses, after previously trying to suppress it, **22.** 315; Whigs uphold and Jacobites abuse, **16.** 30
imprimatur forced upon, **16.** 68
licentiousness of, **39.** 120
Mansfield violently opposes, **38.** 433

Pressburg ('Presbourg'), Austria:
Conway and Scott visit, **39.** 538
gentry of, read (?) Szabó, **39.** 182
Maria Theresa and Berrue visit, **17.** 205
Maria Theresa and Francis I said to be retiring to, **17.** 143

'Pressburg, Court of':
Montemar's name for Francis I, **17.** 261, 280

Press gang; press gangs:
English papers give account of, **23.** 239
HW mistakes parade for, **32.** 331
HW protests against, **32.** 332
highwaymen and footpads swept off the road by, **11.** 74
number of reprobates not thinned by, **25.** 317
officer of, impersonated by Rigby, **30.** 331n

'Press Speaks, The,' by HW:
French translations of, probably not printed, **43.** 129 ꞁ
HW writes, for French visitors, **10.** 71, 73, 74

Press warrant; press warrants:
England issues, to increase navy, **24.** 252
——'s, to overawe France, **39.** 288–9

Prestage (d. 1767) and Hobbs, auctioneers, of Savile Row:
auction by, of Mrs Dunch's effects, **9.** 412
Furnese's pictures sold by, **21.** 172n
Pelham's plate sold by, **35.** 220n
Pesters's furniture sold by, **37.** 465

Preston, Vct. *See* Graham, Richard

Preston, Mr:
SH visited by, **12.** 250

Preston, Sir Charles (ca 1735–1800), 5th Bt, 1779; M.P.; Maj.:
said to be a good commander, **32.** 287
St John's surrendered by, **24.** 157

Preston, Col. George (d. 1748), lt-gov. of Edinburgh Castle:
Edinburgh threatened with fire by, unless rebels supply Edinburgh Castle, **19.** 126

Preston, John:
Hamilton defeats, in Navan election, **37.** 422n

Preston, Patrick (ca 1732–76), army officer:
mentioned by Adam Smith, **32.** 287

Preston, Mrs Thomas. *See* Prescot, Mary

Preston, William, jr:
business at Leghorn relinquished by, **20.** 499
Germany to be wedding-place and Holland the winter residence of, **20.** 499
Pitt, Elizabeth, accompanies, and may become his wife, **20.** 499

Preston, Rev. William:
chargé d'affaires at Naples, **23.** 342n

Preston, William (1753–1807), writer:
Heroic Epistle from Donna Pinna y Ruiz and *Heroic Answer* by, satirize Twiss's *Travels*, **41.** 434n
poems by, dedicated to Charlemont, who gave copy to HW, **41.** 433

Preston, Lancs:
battle of, **30.** 304
Durand sends express to Ligonier at, **19.** 166

few Highlanders consented to go with expedition to, **19**. 107

Jacobite uprising of 1715 reaches, **14**. 244, **37**. 213

Norton's mother lives in hovel at, **38**. 454

rebels expected at, in 1745, **19**. 173

rebels pursued by Oglethorpe at, **19**. 186n

rebels retreat through, **19**. 185n, **40**. 55n

Prestongrange, Lord. *See* Grant, William (1701–64)

Prestonpans, Scotland:
battlefield of, **37**. 217
battle of, Young Pretender defeats Cope at, **14**. 87n, **19**. 116–17, 198
Cope's army at, **19**. 102n
Culloden battle not to be named for, **19**. 247
Cunninghame's execution interrupted by, **20**. 316n
English dragoons flee at, **19**. 117, 203
near Edinburgh, **19**. 116n
rebel army at, **19**. 108n

Prestre de Château-Giron. *See* Le Prestre de Château-Giron

Prétendant, Le. *See* Charles Edward (Stuart); James Francis Edward (Stuart)

Pretender, the Old. *See* James Francis Edward (Stuart)

Pretender, the Young. *See* Charles Edward (Stuart)

Pretorian Palace:
at Cortona, **20**. 423

Prevereau, Daniel (d. 1746), first clerk in D. of Newcastle's office:
HW's and Mann's letters to go through, **17**. 98, 280, 421–2, (?) 425
Mann receives newspapers through, **17**. 421–2
——'s orders to send letters through Holland neglected by, **18**. 418
—— writes to, about mail, **18**. 448
Mann, Galfridus, to complain to, about mail, **18**. 448
packet to be forwarded by, to Mann, **18**. 411
postal packets irregularly sent by officials of, **18**. 233

Préville. *See* Dubus, Pierre-Louis

Préville, Mlle *or* Mme. *See* Drouin, Madeleine-Michelle-Angélique

Prévost *or* Prevost, Augustine (1723–86), Maj.-Gen.:
Briar Creek victory reported by, **24**. 464n
brother makes fortune of, **23**. 526n
news from, suppressed, **33**. 150
victory of, **33**. 155

Prévost *or* Prevost, Jacques *or* James (1725–75), styled McKay; Maj.-Gen., 1762:
Cumberland, D. and Ds of, accompanied by, **23**. 501n, 505n
Cumberland, D. of, left by, to visit Swiss family, **23**. 553–4
English authorities probably disapprove of, **23**. 554
Mann to be informed by, of D. of Cumberland's requirements, **23**. 525–6

Prévost, James Mark (Marcus) (d. 1781), army officer:
Briar Creek victory of, **24**. 464n, **39**. 346

Prévost de Traversay, Jean-François (d. 1776):
death of, **6**. 403

Prévost d'Exiles, Antoine-François (1697–1763):
Clarissa translated by, **5**. 196n, 204
Histoire de Marguerite d'Anjou by, La Harpe's *Comte de Warwik* based on, **38**. 277
Hume's *History* translated by, **5**. 350n
Manuel lexique by, owned by Mme du Deffand, **8**. 25
Middleton's life of Cicero well translated by, **6**. 332
Philosophe anglais, ou histoire de M. Cleveland, Le, by, **13**. 196

Prévôt, le, in Paris:
HW summons, **7**. 266

Prévôt des marchands, Le. See Monsieur le prévôt des marchands

Prévôté de l'hôtel, lieutenant de la:
attends meeting of the parliament of Paris, **8**. 171

Preysing, Johann Carl Joseph (ca 1689–1771), Graf von; Bavarian Maj.-Gen.:
captured by Austrians, **18**. 234

Prezel. *See* Lacombe de Prezel

'Priapus.' *See* Knight, Richard Payne: *Worship of Priapus*; *see also under* Phalli

Priapus:
votive, might be an antique, **35**. 61

'Price':
Mann mistakes Giles's name for, **24**. 260, 266, 271

Price, ——:
house of, visible from Park Place, **39**. 550

Price, Mr:
hypothetical claim of, to Welsh throne, **33**. 454

Price, Mr, London lawyer:
Cony consults, about Houghton pictures, **26**. 55

Price, Mr:
SH visited by, **12**. 225

Price, Cromwell:
Conway mentions, **37**. 332

Price, Goditha:
Gramont's memoirs mention, **41**. 242
maid of honour to Mary of Modena, and mistress to James II, **41**. 242n

Price, Dr Hugh (?1495–1574), founder of Jesus College, Oxford:
HW's note on, at Jesus College, **9**. 289n

Price, John, smuggler, 'Miss Marjoram':
HW jokes about, **9**. 110
outlawed, **9**. 105

Price, Margaret (d. 1778), m. 1 (1750) Sir Jacob Garrard Downing, Bt; m. 2 (1768) George Bowyer:
husband leaves all to, **38**. 322

Price, (?Richard) (d. 1759), Lt:
killed, **21**. 351

Price, Rev. Richard (1723–91), D.D.; LL.D.; moralist; economist:
barbarity enjoyed by, 11. 299
Bastille Day celebrated by, at Crown and Anchor, 35. 399n
'Bonnerian fury' of, 31. 343
Britain's Happiness, and its Full Possession of Civil and Religious Liberty by, reprinted, 11. 315
Burke's *Reflections* should drive, to suicide, 42. 303
——'s reply to, 11. 146
Discourse on the Love of Our Country by: answers Burke, 11. 151; quoted by Birmingham rioters, 11. 314
dying, 11. 239
England's population said by, to decline, 43. 143
English countryside belies, 11. 98
Essay on the Population of England by, 15. 156n
French Revolution admired by, 11. 89n, 31. 343, 361
Goodricke's reply to, 28. 368
HW denounces, 31. 343, 361
Macaulay, Mrs, and, 11. 301
Mason does not wish to be, 28. 369
National Assembly toasted by, before Revolution Society, 11. 135
Observations on Civil Liberty by, said to be owned by Bristol incendiary, 24. 274
revolutionary enthusiasm of, 34. 80, 98–9
revolution in England probably intended by, 31. 361
Price, Uvedale (1747–1829), cr. (1828) Bt:
acts in play at Holland House, 9. 335
Barrington, uncle of, 9. 335
(?) HW sends tea by, 5. 317
Price, William (d. 1765), glass-painter:
chapel window by, in bishop's house at Gloucester, 35. 153
Vyne ante-chapel windows to be painted by, 35. 639
windows by, 1. 201
work of, 1. 21
Price; prices:
admittance to Tower menagerie, 38. 203
advowson, 36. 53
Allectus medal, gold, 17. 378
altar doors, 2. 30n
Anecdotes of Painting: 10. 66, 146, 15. 98, 158, 33. 573n, 34. 35n, 36. 238; 281; reprint of, 29. 252, 253; Vols I–II, 22. 10n
antiquities collected by Hamilton, 32. 70
apartment furnishings, 39. 105
apartment rental: at Pisa, 23. 55; for Coronation, 21. 536
arbor vitæ, Chinese, 9. 176
arbutus, 9. 176
armchairs, 4. 435
armour, 1. 243n, 5. 115n, 185, 233, 7. 412

art collections, 22. 107, 115, 25. 93–4; *see also under* Drawing; Painting; Portrait; Print
art export licence, at Rome, 26. 4
artillery, 18. 457
bacon, 22. 460n
ball, at Florence, 20. 276
balloon admission, 25. 528, 528n
bank construction, 23. 210
Bath order installation fees, 23. 411
bead-work, 9. 274
bed and chairs, 5. 233
bed at Portsmouth, during George III's visit, 32. 128
Bentley's *Wishes*, 9. 373
binding, 1. 35
board, at Cambridge, 13. 59
book publication, 20. 31
books, 1. 45, 2. 28n, 191, 207, 217, 246, 282, 283n, 284, 319, 332n, 6. 306, 10. 180, 15. 203, 28. 86–7, 37. 422
boutonnière of roses, 23. 210
bread: 21. 520, 22. 450, 455, 24. 102n; at Dresden, 9. 268
bridge tolls, 33. 188
brothel, 24. 413
building, 2. 58n
burgundy wine, 21. 491
burial expense, 42. 297
bust; busts: at Rome, 26. 4, 7; of Antinous, 35. 217; of Homer, 35. 217; of Vespasian, 43. 262
butter, 35. 320
buttons, 22. 481
Caius's monument, 14. 112
cameo, 26. 5
Candide translations, 10. 349, 350
candles, in Paris, 31. 80
canonization, 19. 171
canvas and silk, 32. 53
cap, 31. 400
Capell's volumes on Shakespeare, 35. 599
casing art objects, 26. 4
Castle of Otranto, Bodoni edn of, 15. 213
cedars of Lebanon, 9. 176
chair; chairs: 1. 90n, 4. 435, 5. 233, 9. 384, 32. 242n, 38. 206
chair frames, 21. 536–7
chaise rental, in France, 37. 40
champagne, 20. 26on
chariot, 9. 196, 197, 17. 53–4
Chatsworth alterations, 9. 296
Chaucer in black-letter, 29. 163
cheese, 22. 460n
cherries, 34. 8
china: 1. 108, 115, 117, 2. 20, 20. 155, 37. 348; antique, 2. 152–3; Chelsea, 22. 122; Portland vase, 33. 485, 39. 442; Raphael's vases, 10. 345
christening celebration, 33. 59n
clam shells, 37. 439n
Claremont purchase, 32. 71n

coal, **25**. 274, **29**. 245
cocchiata at Florence, **22**. 158
coffee set, French, **32**. 270
coke, **39**. 552
Cole's estate, **1**. 167n
——'s journey to Paris, **1**. 97
concert in London, **25**. 646
Cook's *Voyages*, **33**. 436
copying miniatures, at Dublin, **10**. 12, 16
cord, **20**. 375n, **31**. 339
corn, at Leghorn, **22**. 206n
Coronation celebrations may raise, **9**. 357
country house rental, **38**. 26
courier's fee, **17**. 114n
court plaster, **4**. 68
cracked jar, **20**. 155
criminals' capture or murder, **20**. 446
cross at Ampthill, **1**. 338n
cushion, **31**. 400
custom house export duty, at Rome, **26**. 5
cypresses, **9**. 178
damask, **21**. 447
dancing lessons, **33**. 268n
Delft vase, **2**. 20
Delineator, The, **28**. 335, **39**. 293
dentistry, **20**. 291–2
deserters: **18**. 243, **19**. 23; Sardinian, **17**. 500
desk, **5**. 176
diamond; diamonds: **18**. 353n; buttons, **22**. 481; earrings, **25**. 148
dinners, **17**. 506
dolls, **3**. 377
Donaldson's edn of English translation of *Candide*, **10**. 350
drawing; drawings: Gabburri's collection of, **18**. 338; Guibert's, **30**. 251
Du Deffand (Mme)'s budget, **4**. 386–7
eagle, marble, **19**. 66, 121–2
Ealing Grove's sale, **31**. 239n
earrings, **25**. 148
ebony chairs, **38**. 206
election dinner, **43**. 366
election expense, **20**. 435–6
electrical instruments, **20**. 331
embassy entrance expenses, **21**. 508
emeralds, **18**. 353n
engravers': exceed those of former great painters, **25**. 532; exorbitant, **35**. 429; for plates, **15**. 112
entrance fine for Twickenham house, **10**. 247
exhibition entrance fee, **23**. 211
export duty, **26**. 5
export licence, **26**. 4
fan; fans, **3**. 308, **5**. 20, 23, 172n, **23**. 294–5, 302, **31**. 400
fête champêtre, **24**. 14
Florence oil, in London, **17**. 240
food: at Rome, **13**. 208; in France, **24**. 106; Le Grand d'Aussy discusses, **30**. 279
Fox's copy of Gibbon's *Decline and Fall*, **35**. 615
Francis I's armour, **1**. 243n
French, high, **31**. 134

French horn player's concert, **33**. 471
Fumagalli's travelling allowance, **18**. 96
funeral, at Rome, **21**. 391
furniture, at Castle Ashby, **10**. 337
Garter knighthood, **20**. 109n
gates, iron, **1**. 184n
'George' (jewel), **14**. 75
gesse figures, **19**. 47–8
glazier's daily pay, **20**. 396
gloves, **31**. 400
goldfish, **35**. 206
Gough's *Sepulchral Monuments*, **15**. 334–5
Graham, Dr, for scientific show, **33**. 217
grain from abroad, for Florence, **25**. 314
granite blocks, and polishing, **35**. 208, 231
gratuity of Prince Sulkowsky, **33**. 280
Gray's *Poems*, **14**. 65
green glass compotes and bowl, **6**. 140
Guirlande de Julie, **42**. 93
Gunnersbury House, **33**. 535n
HW does not understand, **23**. 122
HW's Berkeley Sq. house, **36**. 166n
HW's black Gothic chairs, **35**. 181n
HW's bust of Vespasian, **13**. 233
HW's expenses at Paris, **7**. 399–401, 405–8, 410–14
HW's land near Eriswell, **34**. 145
HW's unique medallion, **13**. 233
Hamilton's *Campi Phlegræi*, **35**. 427n
Hamilton's *Collection of Engravings*, **35**. 442n
(?) handkerchiefs, **31**. 400
Haymarket theatre tickets, **39**. 381
head, carved, of Henry III, **16**. 192–3
Heathcote's *Sylva*, **33**. 513
Herbert Lodge, **39**. 263
Hermaphrodite, **17**. 213
high, on Continent, **11**. 158
honey water, **6**. 19
horse; horses: at Florence, **21**. 179; demanded by Lady Walpole, **15**. 327; race-horse, **23**. 497, **32**. 133
horses's rates, at French post-houses, **37**. 40
hospital expenses, **42**. 298
hotels, **11**. 143n
hothouse, **32**. 216n
Houghton collection, **24**. 427, 434, 440–1, 502, **25**. 316
house, **1**. 170, 357n, **6**. 250, **9**. 330, **11**. 284, **28**. 405–6, **33**. 183, **36**. 166n
house construction, **20**. 217
house rental: **32**. 370, 371; at Turin, **21**. 175; in Paris, **38**. 361; in St James's Sq., **25**. 455
Hoyland's *Poems*, **29**. 367
Illustri fatti Farnesiani, **25**. 465
Indiaman, **25**. 134–5
intaglio: **17**. 213n, **19**. 476, 483, 489, **20**. 159; of Apollo, **21**. 457n; of gladiator, **17**. 212, **21**. 151
ivory carving, **26**. 7
jar, **20**. 155
jewel, **14**. 75, **19**. 73, 74, 372, 398, **30**. 50
jewel rental, **21**. 536

[Price; prices, *continued*]
jointure, 33. 205
lace, 9. 358
lace ruffles, 39. 264
land, per acre, 19. 468n
lantern cord, 20. 375n
Lavater's *Physiognomische Fragmente*, 31. 280
lettres de cachet, 28. 227
lignum vitae, 9. 176
linen, 9. 274, 17. 53
livery, footman's, 9. 248
lodgings: at Sluys, 38. 10, 11; in London, 23. 287; in Portsmouth, 32. 128n; in St James's St, 20. 168n
lodgings and servants, at Florence, 23. 397n
(?) Lorenzo's ring, bought by HW, 15. 279
lottery ticket, 5. 157n, 30. 251, 33. 255, 34. 142
Luton Hoo estate, 22. 172n
Lyttelton does not distinguish, from customs duties, 37. 445
MS copy of Van der Doort's catalogue of Charles I's collection, 43. 226–7
manuscript volumes, Lethieullier-Frederick, 1. 13n, 2. 238, 239
marble, antique, 13. 213
marble pavement, 35. 389
Mariette's collection, 32. 282
Mason's ode to Pitt, 29. 251
masquerade tickets, 19. 483
medals, 17. 378, 21. 201–2, 203, 26. 5, 7, 38. 567
medallions, 13. 233, 39. 254
Mereworth's construction, 35. 143
mezzotints, 25. 211
mince pie, 35. 175n
miniatures, *see under* Painting
missal: illuminated, 2. 197n; by Raphael, 20. 470n
Montagu monument at Horton, 10. 333
mosaics, 5. 176
motto collections, 33. 213n
muff, 10. 146
Museum Florentinum, 18. 330n
newspapers in the Argonne, 38. 495
notary public, at Rome, 26. 5
oaks, cut down for timber, 9. 299, 35. 271–2
Oatlands's purchase, 36. 252
oil, 17. 240
opera singer's fee, 18. 281
operas popular when made equal with plays in, 20. 410
opera tickets, 23. 458
orange flowers, 18. 230
orange jelly's ingredients, 4. 63
organ, 20. 331, 35. 211n
ormolu teakettle, 23. 211–12
packet delivery, 17. 262n
painting; paintings: 1. 32n, 170, 305, 2. 57, 9. 365, 20. 142, 21. 172–3, 200, 208–9, 478–9, 23. 466, 569–70, 26. 7, 8, 35. 428, 37. 460; at Lady's Yonge's auction, 10. 123, 124; by Albano, 26. 7; by Canaletto, copies of, 23. 298–9; by Correggio, 18. 355n, 26. 7 (copy), 32. 70; by Cortona, 26. 7; by Domenichino, 17. 226–7, 241, 35. 17; by Franciabigio and Ubertini, 19. 392n; by Guibert, for HW, 30. 251; by Guido Reni (copy of the 'pallione'), 18. 334; by Hogarth, 32. 114n; by Imperiali, 26. 7; by Jamesone, 40. 265, 266, 267, 285; by Le Moine, 31. 80; by Liotard, 20. 324–5, 362, 37. 355; by Maratti, 26. 7; by Müntz, 9. 194, 259; by Occhiali, 26. 8; by Pannini, 26. 7; by Ramsay, of Bns Hervey, 32. 242n; by Raphael, 18. 239; by Reynolds, of Ladies Waldegrave, 35. 532; by Titian, of Caesars, 16. 155; by Van Dyck, 30. 149, 32. 289; by West, 23. 210–11; by Westall, 12. 193; by Zoffany, 24. 540; copies, 16. 97, 18. 334, 23. 298–9, 26. 7, 35. 481; landscape by Claude, 32. 102; landscape by Viviani, 26. 7; miniature, 1. 358n, 2. 43n, 41. 263, 269; miniature, by Cooper, of Cromwell, 33. 539n; miniature, by Maratti, 18. 162; miniature by Petitot, of James II, 9. 412; miniature, by Zincke, 18. 347n; of Drayton, 29. 163; of Mme d'Olonne, 6. 245; of Mme de la Vallière, 32. 102; of marriage of Henry VII, 20. 390n; of SH library ceiling, 35. 79–80; 'views,' 17. 81; water-colours and red chalk drawings, 22. 108n; *see also under names of artists*
Palazzo Madama, 20. 264
pamphlets, 11. 170, 31. 376
Pantheon, in London: construction, 23. 210, 298; entrance fee, 25. 543
paper, 9. 2
Park Place, 12. 176n
Parliament, seat in, 22. 584n
passage across Channel, 11. 116n
passport, in Florence, 21. 482
pencil, 31. 400
petition to House of Commons, 11. 194
pheasants: 34. 64, 69; Chinese, 23. 210
physician's visit, 17. 55n
picture-cleaning, 41. 213
pin-money for wife, 33. 206
Pinkerton's *Vitæ*, 42. 278
pistols, 17. 207
Portland vase, 33. 485n, 39. 442
postage, 9. 2, 347, 10. 158, 251, 254, 280, 288, 296, 11. 263, 25. 608, 33. 349n, 376n
princedom in Holy Roman Empire, 24. 370
print; prints: 1. 60n, 160, 172, 175, 193, 195, 197, 210, 287n, 291, 338, 354, 2. 175, 277n, 308, 10. 301, 28. 86–7, 35. 300; collection of, 41. 219; commission for collecting, 1. 193, 197; English satiric, 25. 496; in England, 23. 465; 25. 496; Irish, 10. 30; mezzotint, 25. 211; of Croyland Abbey, 16. 194; of Gray's portrait, 14. 65; of Hogarth's portrait of Lovat, 19. 391n; *see also under Mezzotint*
prostitutes, 24. 234, 413
quack physician's fee, 23. 251
quarry rental, 35. 191

race horse, **23**. 497, **32**. 133
Ranelagh admission, **17**. 401, 434
Ranelagh shares, **20**. 46n
Raphael's china vases, **10**. 345
Remarks on the Speech of M. Dupont, **31**. 382
rent: half-year, of Little Strawberry Hill, **42**. 306; of French country house, **41**. 11; of glasses, **32**. 115; of house in St James's Sq., **25**. 455; of jewels, **21**. 536
rents, **1**. 218, **9**. 44, **10**. 247, 252, **21**. 176, 536, **23**. 55, **25**. 455, **32**. 370, 371, **35**. 191, **38**. 26, 361
repairs: to coach, **11**. 365n; to HW's house, **14**. 189; to Villa Salviati, **21**. 310, 373
ribbon, ladies', **18**. 281
Rider's English translation of *Candide*, **10**. 349
ridotto al fresco at Vauxhall, **10**. 279
ring, **15**. 279, **19**. 372, 398
roses, **23**. 210
ruffles, lace, **39**. 264
running footman's livery, **9**. 248
St Leonard's Hill, **32**. 132n
scaffold for Coronation, **21**. 536
seals by Costanzi, **26**. 8
secretary of state's office charges, for letters of recommendation, **35**. 440
sheep and wool, reduced, **42**. 393
shells, **37**. 439n
ship, **18**. 521, **20**. 102n, **25**. 204n
shipping: **26**. 4, 5; relative, by land or by water, **11**. 31n
shoes, embroidered, **39**. 264
silk, **32**. 53, **33**. 218
silk hangings, **21**. 468
silver plate, **10**. 286, **18**. 472
snuff-box; snuff-boxes, **4**. 50, **6**. 325, 329, **11**. 214, **31**. 77n, **39**. 234
sofa, **4**. 435
Spaniards' heads, at Algiers, **24**. 122n
stained glass, **1**. 21, 145n, 147
state coach, **22**. 104
statue; statues: **21**. 480; by Francavilla, **22**. 583; model of, **18**. 179; of Laocoön, copy of, **22**. 67n; of 'Livia,' **18**. 177, **26**. 5
stone, artificial, **41**. 227–9
Stosch's library, **21**. 284
Stosch's map collection, **21**. 186–7, 192
straw, **23**. 323
SH Press editions, **29**. 253, **32**. 45, 45n, **33**. 573, **42**. 20
stuffed birds, **23**. 210
subscription to Almack's, **38**. 511n
suits, **6**. 243, 252, 258
sword; swords: **5**. 114; gold, set in brilliants, **22**. 62n
table; tables: ancient mosaic, **26**. 7; granite, **26**. 7; oriental alabaster, **26**. 7; porphyry, **26**. 7; scagliola, **18**. 87, 106
tapestry, **1**. 22
tea-kettle, **5**. 212, **23**. 212
theatre admission: **9**. 70, **20**. 410n; in Florence, **20**. 357, **23**. 458

tickets, lottery, *see* Lottery tickets
tickets to subscription ball, **38**. 291
titles, **9**. 36, 51
tortoise-shell box, **6**. 181
Tortola lands, **24**. 264–5
tourte de cerises, **20**. 260n
transportation: **5**. 233, 257; between London and Cambridge, **1**. 225n, 263n, 281
travel: **11**. 144; in France, **7**. 398–9, 405, 407–8, 409, 410, 412, **37**. 40–1, **39**. 8
trousers, **5**. 233
upkeep of kitchen garden and menagerie at Osterley, **34**. 238, 239
urns, **26**. 8
Van Dyck's, **41**. 465n
varnishing of pictures, **33**. 55
vases: **2**. 20, **26**. 7, **33**. 485, **39**. 442; Etruscan, **23**. 211; Portland, **33**. 485, **39**. 442; Raphael's, **10**. 345
ventletrap, **21**. 173
Viviani's, for Herculaneum volume, **21**. 299
voiturins, **11**. 134, 158
Vyne, the: **9**. 330; alterations to, **35**. 232
Waldegrave auction, **10**. 108
wallpaper, **39**. 49
Wanstead house and garden, **35**. 238
war, waging of, **33**. 295
war increases, **35**. 219
watch; watches: **20**. 57, **21**. 295–6, **34**. 165; at Paris, **39**. 116, **42**. 298
watch-seals, **21**. 296
water-raising machine: **21**. 419; model of, **21**. 407; yearly repairs for, at Marly, **21**. 354n
Westminster Abbey burial space, **38**. 111
Westminster Abbey houses and seats for Coronation, **21**. 536n
Westminster Hall admission, **42**. 222
wheat and butter, **35**. 320
wig, **17**. 506, **25**. 609n
window, rose, **10**. 11
window-renting, to view pageant, **38**. 133
window repairs, in Florence, **20**. 25
wine, **23**. 302
wood and candles for La Borde's house, **31**. 80
Zoffany's, for inclusion in group portrait, **24**. 540n
See also Inventory, of Mme du Deffand's effects; Painting; Rent; Royalty; royalties (financial); Travel: expenses of; Wages and salaries

Prick-song:
All Souls chaplain to teach, **35**. 388
Pridden, J., bookseller:
prosecuted, **23**. 29
Pridden, Sally (1690–1724), *alias* Sally Salisbury; courtesan:
death of, in Newgate Prison, **19**. 389n
Finch stabbed by, **19**. 389
Pride, Col. Thomas (d. 1658):
'purge' of, **15**. 129n

Pride:
  arrogance is a declaration of, 25. 636
  HW considers, a less heinous sin, 25. 655
  HW determined to preserve, 23. 528
  HW's, 33. 574, 584
  HW's reflections on, 2. 188, 33. 95
  HW's reflections on national, as similar to
    that of family, 25. 133
  HW's reverence for, 33. 95
  of family, nursed by self-pride, 7. 364
Prideaux, George (d. 1784):
  HW discusses Italy and Stosch with, 17. 378,
    404
  Mann quotes, 17. 491
Prideaux, Humphrey (1648–1724), orientalist;
    Dean of Norwich 1702–24:
  grandson of, 17. 378n
Prideaux, Humphrey (d. 1793), of Prideaux
    Place, Cornwall:
  HW discusses Italy and Stosch with, 17. 378,
    404
  Mann forwards letters of, to Rome, 17. 491
  son of, 17. 491
Prideaux, Col. John (1718–59):
  Amherst sends, to capture Ft Niagara, 21.
    301n
  army camp at Newport visited by, 37. 503
Prideaux, Mrs John. See Rolt, Elizabeth
Prideaux, John Basset. See Basset, John Pri-
    deaux
Prie, Marquise de. See Berthelot de Pleneuf,
    Agnès
Prie, Louis de (1734–82), Marquis and Comte
    de Prie de Bourbon-Lairey:
  entertains at Bois Prévu, 7. 293
  Lyttelton, Bns, absorbed in, 39. 167
  social relations of, 7. 293, 298
  wife of, 6. 129n
Prie. See also Priero
Prie de Bourbon-Lairey, Comte and Marquis
    de. See Prie, Louis de
Prie-dieu; pre-dieux:
  Chute to get relics for, 35. 62
  in Magdalen House chapel, 9. 273
  in stained glass, at the Vyne, 35. 641
'Prière':
  quoted, 4. 216
  wrongly ascribed to Chevalier de Boufflers, 4.
    216, 218
Prières des quarante heures:
  said for Marie Leszczyńska, 30. 219
Priero, Marchese di. See Turinetti, Ercole
    (1717–81); Turinetti, Giovanni Antonio
    (1687–1757)
Priest; priests:
  (?) Charles I reprieves, but Parliament wants
    him hanged, 42. 235
  despotism supported by, 23. 376
  French, emigrate to England, 15. 224
  French persecution of, 35. 446
  HW calls Conway a, 38. 59
  HW satirizes, 24. 71
  HW's aversion to, 33. 230

Irish: girl escorted by, on voyage to Calais,
    17. 142; iricism by, 30. 20; medicine studied
    by, 17. 142
  massacre of, at Paris, 15. 219, 237
  may be laid aside, in new era, 25. 237
  philosophers hate, while courting adulation,
    35. 117
  religious fashions invented by, 25. 541
  wicked, blinded by looking at unveiled Ma-
    donna dell' Impruneta, 30. 4
  See also Clergy
  See also under Church of England; Church
    of Scotland; Roman Catholic Church
Priest Dissected, The. See under Anstey, Chris-
    topher
Priestley, Joseph (1733–1804), LL.D.; theolo-
    gian; scientist:
  alleged boast by, about followers in Birming-
    ham, 11. 318
  American visit of, pleases HW. 31. 386
  Bewley, friend of, 16. 121n, 43. 351
  Birmingham rioters pursue, 11. 317
  'Birmingham warehouse' of, 42. 304
  Bryant's answer to, 2. 212
  Calvin compared to, 31. 385
  Condorcet friend of, 39. 487
  —— the correspondent of, 34. 125
  Disquisitions Relating to Matter and Spirit
    by, 28. 407n
  France's happiness not proved by, 11. 336
  French Revolution approved by, 31. 361
  HW calls, 'execrable wretch,' 15. 236
  HW denounces, 31. 361, 385–6
  HW's comment on, 11. 350, 15. 236
  house of, burnt, 11. 313n, 315, 31. 385, 34.
    116–17
  Knight compared to, 29. 339
  materiality of soul believed by, 28. 407
  More, Hannah, has seen, only once, 31. 329
  —— reported by newspapers to have married,
    31. 328–9, 332–3
  —— 'reprobates' religious views of, 31. 329
  National Assembly includes, by election, 31.
    386
  'Presbyterian conflagrations' would be raised
    by, in England, 34. 80
  revolutionary proposals of, unsuccessful in
    England, 11. 322, 345
  revolution in England probably intended by,
    31. 361
  Russell's correspondence with, 42. 374n
  Shelburne's librarian, 31. 329n
  son of, 42. 374
Priestley, Mrs Joseph. See Wilkinson, Mary
Priestley, William (b. between 1769 and 1773;
    d. before 1835):
  Paris visited by, 42. 374
Prieto, Tomás Francisco (1716–82); medallist;
    inspector-general of the Spanish mint:
  seals and medals well cut by, 16. 170
Prigionero superbo, Il. See under Pergolesi,
    Giovanni Battista

Primadizzi ('Primaticio'), Francesco (1504–70), painter:
Chesterfield buys landscape by, **32.** 103n
Primate of Ireland. *See* Stone, George
Primate of Lorraine. *See* Beauvau, François-Vincent-Marc de
Primaticio. *See* Primadizzi
Primavera, Jacopo:
medallion by, of Mary, Q. of Scots, **42.** 321n
Prime, Samuel (ca 1750–1813), of Whitton:
SH visited by, **12.** 224, 249
Prime minister; prime ministers:
Chute would not be, **35.** 32
HW says the age is not favourable to, **10.** 109
HW speculates about abolition of, **33.** 392
See also under Treasury, first lord of
Prime sergeant, Irish:
Hutchinson becomes, **38.** 147
See also under Hutchinson, John Hely
Primrose, Vcts. *See* Drélincourt, Anne (d. 1775)
Primrose, Gilbert (?1580–1641), D.D.:
print of, **40.** 236
Primrose; primroses:
Temple, Cts, mentions, in verses, **10.** 114
Prince, Le (surname). *See* Le Prince
'Prince, Le': *See* Beauvau, Charles-Just de, Prince de Beauvau; Bourbon, Louis-François de, Prince de Conti
Prince, Daniel (d. 1796), printer and bookseller at Oxford:
subscriptions to be received by, for Croyland view, **16.** 194
Prince, Mrs Mary:
paintings by, **9.** 114n
Prince, English ship:
in Mediterranean, in Osborne's squadron, **21.** 135n
Prince; princes:
English: abundance of, **11.** 62–3, 322; HW glad, are not all present to be painted by Miss Foldsone, **11.** 145; HW's opinion of, **30.** 217; insignificance of, **30.** 217; Selwyn overly tender towards, **30.** 217
fame earned by, with buckets of blood, **24.** 367
faults of, make virtuous princes the more admirable, **41.** 29
Galluzzi's history reveals, in horrid light, **25.** 202
German, enjoy hunting, **25.** 364
gradations of entertainment of, in England, France, and Italy, **25.** 587, 589
HW prefers churchmen's artful conquests to forcible ones of, **25.** 596
HW's reflections on, **15.** 109, **24.** 140
HW to judge, at their burials and not at their coronations, **24.** 310
have thorns in their ermine, **36.** 245
health and prisons of, both close to their graves, **38.** 526
Mann's reflections on responsibilities of, **25.** 314

ministers hoodwink, to increase their own power, **24.** 140
premiums for assassination of, voted in France, **31.** 373
proper education for, **25.** 282, **31.** 282–3
young, in Tuscany, Mann's letter from Gustav III described by, **25.** 499
See also Crown; King; Monarch; Royalty
Prince Charles, English ship:
Hazard renamed, after capture by rebels, **19.** 239n
Prince de Conty, Le, French frigate:
L'Heureux accompanied by, **19.** 317n
Prince Ferdinand, Prussian privateer:
Tuscan vessel seized by, **21.** 330, 349
Prince Frederic, packet-boat:
capture of, **7.** 160n, **21.** 168
name of, corrected, **43.** 105
Prince Frederick, privateer:
Spanish ship captured by, **19.** 92n
Prince George, English ship:
capture of, **24.** 504
catastrophe of, **21.** 206
French privateer captures, off Marseille, **21.** 414
India ship captured by, **21.** 524
Invincible engaged by, only at last minute, **20.** 38n
operates as a privateer, **21.** 524
plies between London and Leghorn, **21.** 414
Prince George, Keppel's ship:
George III and Q. Charlotte to dine on, **24.** 377n
'Prince héréditaire, Le.' *See* Karl Wilhelm Ferdinand
'Prince Noir, Le.' *See* Edward (1330–76), the Black Prince
Prince of Orange, packet-boat:
capture of, **21.** 451, **24.** 302
Prince of Piedmont, English victualling ship:
loss of, (?) **24.** 236, **32.** 319n
Prince of the Blood; Princes of the Blood, French:
Aiguillon tries to reconcile, to spite Maupeou, **23.** 399
'bourgeois of Rue St-Denis,' **5.** 296
Christian VII and, sup with Louis XV, **4.** 154
Christian VII's visit may make trouble with, **4.** 138
Condé explains his desertion from, **5.** 301–2
Du Barry, Mme, may make valets of, **5.** 214
Fitzjames's arrest causes meeting of, attended by Louis XV, **38.** 302
foreign ministers separated from, by etiquette, **38.** 245
French Court excludes, **5.** 62, 70, 77, **23.** 298
guests of, at country seats, **5.** 277
Gustav III treated with scant courtesy by, **5.** 36
HW has not seen, **31.** 72
Hertford knows, only by sight, **38.** 221
Joseph II's social relations with, **6.** 435
libel against Necker sent to, **7.** 225

[Prince of the Blood, *continued*]
lit de justice of 13 April 1771 not attended by, **5**. 61, 70n
Louis XV forbids attendance of, at parliamentary discussion of d'Aiguillon, **4**. 429–30
—— may be reconciled with, **5**. 214
—— not endangered by opposition of, **23**. 320
—— rebukes, and tells them to ignore parliament of Rouen, **23**. 270n
Maximilian coolly treated by, **6**. 163
may be exiled for asking for recall of parliament, **5**. 47
Montmorency visited by, **5**. 304
Portuguese bastards might be promoted to, **21**. 475n
prevented from volunteering, **18**. 62
protest by, against Louis XV's edicts: **5**. 69, 296; *Examen* of, **5**. 71–2
Richelieu-St Vincent trial attended by, **6**. 292
Richmond, D. of, to call on, **6**. 456
rights of, **5**. 58
verses on: Du Deffand, Mme, sends, to Chanteloup, **5**. 336; HW disparages, **5**. 335
Voltaire's *Irène* attended by, **7**. 30
wives not exiled with, **5**. 71, 77
Prince of Wales, English ship:
French capture, **21**. 414–15
Princesa, Spanish ship:
captured, **25**. 16n
Prince's metal:
Rupert, P., inventor of, **9**. 372
'Princes of the Blood':
HW's term for Dukes of Grafton and Richmond, **30**. 92
Princess; princesses, English:
Albany, Cts of, has no conversation with, **11**. 271
Blenheim, Nuneham, and Castle Howard to be visited by, **36**. 246n
Cumberland, Lady Albinia, appointed lady of Bedchamber to, **12**. 196
Elgin, Lady, reports on breakfast of, at SH, **12**. 160
Foldsone, Anne, paints, **11**. 145, 183
Lysons, Samuel, to send patterns of Roman mosaics to, **12**. 198
SH visited by, **12**. 248
William IV's birthday dinner not attended by, **12**. 151
Princess; Princesses, French:
remarkable only for using excessive rouge, **13**. 165
share profits of gaming tables, **13**. 165
Princess, German, Narrative of. *See under* Moders, Mary
Princess Amelia, English ship:
involved in Mediterranean war, **18**. 393
Princess dowager (of Wales). *See* Augusta (1719–72)
'Princesse, la.' *See* Rohan-Chabot, Marie-Sylvie de, Princesse de Beauvau
Princesse de Babylone, La. See under Voltaire

Princesse de Clèves, La. See under Pioche de la Vergne, Marie-Madeleine, Mme de la Fayette
Princesse gouvernante (Dutch). *See* Anne (1709–59)
'Princesse Palatine, La.' *See* Élisabeth-Charlotte, Duchesse d'Orléans
Princess Louisa, English ship:
in Mediterranean, in Osborne's squadron, **21**. 135n
Michael receives news from lieutenant of, **19**. 410
Noel, Capt., commands, **20**. 536n
Watson, captain of, **19**. 410
Princess of Parma, The. See under Cumberland, Richard
Princess royal (of England). *See* Anne (1709–59); Charlotte Augusta Matilda (1766–1828)
Princess Royal, English ship:
Byron's flagship, sights d'Estaing, **24**. 394n
—— writes from, off St Lucia, **24**. 481n
Prince's St, London:
Montagu writes from, **43**. 137
Princeton, New Jersey:
battle of, **6**. 415n, 417n, **28**. 287n
Prince William, English war ship:
escapes to Ireland, **25**. 152
Prince William Sound:
natives at, **11**. 75n
'Prince, you command in vain,' verses by HW:
quoted, **12**. 261
Principles:
HW jokes about sentiments being, to G. W. Hervey and himself what, are to others, **30**. 86
Principles of Government. See under Nares, Robert
Pringle, Lt:
Quebec dispatches brought by, on *Lizard*, **32**. 287n
Pringle, Henry, army officer:
Amherst to be informed by, of Murray's conduct, **25**. 200
hostage for transport vessels, in attack on Minorca, **25**. 309
Mann cites authority of, in representing need for aid to Minorca, **25**. 199
Minorca said by, to depend on imports by ships, **25**. 198n
presence of, needed for trial of Draper's complaint against Murray, **25**. 309
St Philip's Castle to carry, to Minorca, **25**. 199
Pringle, Sir John (1707–82), cr. (1766) Bt; physician:
Académie des Sciences fails to elect, **7**. 12
Cocchi wishes medical description by, of Galfridus Mann's case, **20**. 544, 554, **21**. 36
Coke, Lady Mary, inquires of, about HW, **31**. 129
Cumberland, D. of, discusses Galfridus Mann's illness with, **20**. 529
—— has, as his physician, **20**. 525, 529
HW attended by, **1**. 119n

HW interviews, about Galfridus Mann, **20.** 554

HW ordered by, to go to Bath, **31.** 125n

HW's gout wrongly diagnosed by, **22.** 454, 459

HW's physician, **31.** 128

HW to send news from, to Mann, **20.** 559

Mann, Galfridus, consults, **20.** 523, 525, 529, 540, 543, 544, 551, 554, 559, **21.** 36

(?) *Observations on the Diseases of the Army* by, sent by Conway to Cocchi, **20.** 544

Orford, Cts of, wishes, to examine her son, **23.** 488

patient of, commits suicide, **14.** 159

social relations of, in Paris, with Franklin, HW, and Mme Geoffrin, **7.** 319, 320

Prinknash ('Prinknage') Park, Glos:

HW buys cradle at, **12.** 155

HW recommends, to Berrys, **12.** 154–5

HW sends S. Lysons to, **15.** 201

HW visits, **1.** 342–3, 346

stained glass at, **43.** 60

Prinsep, John (1716–69), of Eton and Balliol:

disappointment of, **13.** 109

Gray calls, 'Quid,' **13.** 143

Print; prints (engravings):

'Abelard and Eloisa,' **43.** 298

additional, for *Anecdotes of Painting*, **41.** 99

after Harding's drawings: not supervised by him, **16.** 324; poorly engraved, **16.** 323–4

Agincourt's: for history of art, sent to HW, **42.** 64; of Aristotle medal, **42.** 64; of Duc de Chartres, etc., **42.** 64–5

—— sends, to Woollett, **42.** 102

—— sends proofs of, to HW, **42.** 104

'Agriculture and the Arts,' **42.** 154n

Albani's collection of, sold to George III, **22.** 107, 115

Ames a collector of, **1.** 55n

Anecdotes of Painting, 3d edn, lacks, **42.** 20

at Little Strawberry Hill, **42.** 307

at SH, **20.** 380

Berry, Robert and Agnes, look at, at SH, **12.** 194

books of, on fêtes and scenery, **32.** 74

Bramston's 'Scotch Tast in Vista's' illustrated by, **43.** 245

Brand's, sold, **38.** 340n

Bull buys, at Talman sale, and offers them to HW, **42.** 458

(?) —— collects, **43.** 382

—— sends, to HW, **42.** 413

by the following engravers: Alexander, John, **40.** 261n; Allegrini, **25.** 226, 230; Antoniazzo, after Raphael, **23.** 423; Bannerman, Alexander, **14.** 188, 190, **15.** 96n, 133n, **42.** 279n, **43.** 188; Bartoli, **41.** 268; Bartolozzi, after Bunbury, **33.** 401; Bartolozzi, after Copley, **34.** 210; Bartolozzi, of Mary, Q. of Scots, **42.** 322n; Basire, James, **2.** 8n, 129n, 277n, **16.** 73–5, 78, 211, **42.** 21n, 199n, 313n, **43.** 184; Bawtree, **35.** 406n; Bickham, George, **1.** 176, 188; Bowles, Carrington,

33. 571n, **35.** 346, **43.** 298; Breteuil, **11.** 54n; Bretherton, **14.** 188, **35.** 628n; Brune, P. de, **1.** 182n; Bunbury, **32.** 304, **33.** 401, 572, 33. 401n, **34.** 4n, **42.** 318, **43.** 350; Burché, J., **15.** 250; Caldwell, **42.** 56n; Carter, Charles, **1.** 260, 265, 267, **43.** 57; Chambers, **15.** 96n, **31.** 78n; Clouwet, **1.** 182n; Coffin, **41.** 102n; Cook, Thomas, **42.** 313n; Cole, James, **1.** 142n; Cooper, R., **1.** 183n; Cross, **16.** 65, 67; Daullé, **23.** 422n; Dean, **33.** 201n; Delaram, **1.** 62n, **16.** 64; Dickinson, William, **2.** 54, **33.** 572n, **41.** 429n; Dolle, **16.** 66; Droeshout, **1.** 132, 181n; Dürer, **23.** 432; Dürer, compared to Hollar's, **40.** 254; Elder, William, **16.** 67; Ellis, **1.** 363; Englefield, **16.** 345; Evelyn, of his travels, **16.** 59–63; Faber, **1.** 52n, 144, 150n, **15.** 303, **18.** 482, **35.** 346n, **40.** 287, **42.** 249n; Faithorne, **1.** 61, 179–81, **35.** 346n, **42.** 126, **43.** 383; Fillian, **16.** 66; Gammon, **40.** 323n; Gaultier, Léonard, **16.** 64; Gerini, **18.** 477; Gillray, **33.** 540n, 571n; Giomignani, F., **2.** 150n; Glover, G., **16.** 65; Godfrey, R. B., of SH, **2.** 211n, 249n; Gravelot, of 'The Motion,' **18.** 21; Greatbach, **8.** 216; Green, Valentine, **43.** 384; Grignion, after Bentley, in SH Lucan, **35.** 644; Grignion, after Bentley, in SH *Six Poems* by Gray, **14.** 59n, **20.** 368n; Grignion, after Wale, in SH books, **15.** 112n; Grignion for *Anecdotes of Painting*, **1.** 305, **14.** 68n, **15.** 96n; Grignion, of HW's marble eagle, **20.** 485, **31.** 263, **35.** 252; Grignion, of Henry V, **1.** 305n; Grignion, of Rivers's presentation of Caxton to Edward IV, **40.** 119n; Grignion, of White's Club's arms, **40.** 120n; Grignion, of Woolaston's portrait of Britton, **40.** 310; Gulston, Elizabeth, **43.** 57; Haistwell, **42.** 53–4; Harding, G. P., **8.** 216; Haughton, Matthew, **15.** 281–2, 284; Henshaw, **1.** 291, 294n, 296, 298, 301, 314–16, 321, 361, 363, **28.** 59, 60; Herlochs, of Waterhouse, **16.** 67; Hogarth, **16.** 173, 187, 198; Hogarth, at SH, **42.** 175n; Hogarth, copied by Ireland and Sandby, **15.** 338, **42.** 175n; Hogarth, copied by Livesay at HW's, **42.** 153, 154; Hogarth, emblematic, **42.** 154; Holbein, of Erasmus, **16.** 160; Holbein, woodcuts for More's *Utopia*, **16.** 160; Hollar, **40.** 199, 254; Hollar, of 'Dance of Death,' **16.** 156–7; Hollar, of Duchess of Exeter, **2.** 365–6; Hollar, of Dugdale, **15.** 250; Hollar, of Lady Digby, **1.** 182n; Hollar, of Lady Shirley, **1.** 183n; Hollar, of Lord and Lady Arundel, **16.** 153; Hollar, of Richmond Palace, **16.** 74, 78; Hollar, of sea scenes, **16.** 68; Hollar, of Titian's 'Ecce homo,' **16.** 153; Hondius, of painter's heads, **16.** 59; Houbraken, **1.** 207; Jackson, **20.** 380–1; King, Daniel, **1.** 175; King, George, **1.** 182n; Lachon, R., **1.** 365; Lambourn, P. S., **1.** 197, 360n; Lasne, **31.** 78n; Loggan, **1.** 181n; Lombart, after Van Dyck, **35.** 174n; Lom-

[Print; prints, *continued*]

bart, of Cts of Carlisle, 41. 443; MacArdell (*see under* MacArdell, James); Major, Thomas, of plan for Cambridge music-room, 1. 188; Marshall, William, 1. 182n, 16. 66, 42. 140; Mason, Rev. William, of Gray, 1. 235, 291, 294n, 296, 361; Müller, 15. 96n; Nanteuil, 40. 320; Nutting, Joseph, 1. 181n, 16. 67; Orde, Thomas, 1. 188, 207; Pariset, 42. 22n; Pass, 1. 173, 2. 44, 16. 67, 42. 458; Patch, after Andrea del Sarto, 23. 275; Patch, after Fra Bartolommeo, 23. 275, 362, 371, 465, 468–9; Patch, after Giotto, 23. 465; Patch, after Masaccio, 23. 267, 276–7, 287–8, 315–16, 422, 465, 468–9, 25. 280; Patch, after Michelangelo, 23. 276; Patch, of Florentine baptistery, 23. 429–30, 435; Patch, of Sir John Hawkwood, 23. 428; Patch, received by HW, 23. 459; Patch, satirizing Sterne, 23. 5, 27, 33, 37; Payne, 16. 65; Picart, 15. 281n; Pompadour, Mme de, 7. 201; Pozzi, 21. 561n; Prenner, 25. 403; Raphael, 23. 432; Rawlins, Thomas, 16. 66; Reading, 15. 196n; Restrick, 16. 66; Richardson, 40. 310; Riddell, George, 1. 364; Ridley, 41. 394n; Ross, James, 43. 385; Ryland, 41. 389–91; Sadeler, 35. 149, 209; Savage, 1. 181; Schencker, 16. 323; Sharp, W., 2. 167n; Sharpe, Christopher, 1. 207, 216, 296, 360, 362; Sherwin, J. K., 2. 191, 203; Sherwin, W., 16. 66; Simon, John, 2. 354; Smith, Anker, 42. 269n; Smith, John, 1. 183, 15. 102–3; Smith, J. R., 33. 201n; Solly, 16. 66, 67; Spooner, 21. 554n; Stent, 1. 149, 16. 64; Stephens, 23. 427, 429, 435; Sullivan, after Hogarth, 16. 173; Sunderland, E. of, 41. 145; Switzer, 43. 382–3; Tomkins, W., 33. 490n; Tomthwaite, 33. 377n; Townshend, George, 4th Vct, caricatures, 21. 77–8, 90; Tyson, 1. 142, 144, 150, 189, 190, 196–7, 261, 363n, 364, 2. 76, 77, 302; Van den Berghe, 16. 323, 324; Van den Hove, 1. 181, 183, 16. 65; Van de Pass, 1. 182n; Vanderbank, 1. 171, 181, 182n, 16. 67; Van der Gucht, 1. 72n, 35. 628n; Van der Leeuw, 16. 67; Van Voerst, 16. 64, 166; Vertue, for Birch's *Heads*, 1. 207; Vertue, historical, 2. 8n, 11, 16. 166; Vertue, of Bess of Hardwick, 42. 313–14; Vertue of Henry VII and Henry VIII, 2. 323; Vertue, of Lady Jane Grey, 32. 353n; Vertue, of London map, 2. 8n; Vertue, of Lydgate and Chaucer, 16. 134; Vertue, of Mary, Q. of Scots, 42. 320–2; Vertue, of Middleton, 15. 303; Vertue, of Sir Robert Walpole, 42. 249n; Vertue, of Warham, 1. 81; Vertue, reprinted by Society of Antiquaries, 2. 8n, 11, 16. 166; Walker, 15. 97n, 41. 394n; Watson, 1. 281; Watts, 16. 194; White, George, 42. 249n; White, Robert, 1. 355, 16. 365; Williams, R., 1. 182n

Cardigan invents frames for, 20. 381

catalogue of, amuses HW, 12. 58
Cholmondeley, Mrs, seeks, for HW, 36. 57
Chute collects, 18. 284, 35. 31
Cipriani's, 43. 369
Cole and HW exchange, 1. 184, 188–9, 216, 222, 319, 321, 353–4, 357, 361–5, 2. 17, 19
Cole offers to HW, 1. 159
—— offers to index HW's, 1. 29
——'s collection of, 1. 63
collectors cut, from HW's *Anecdotes of Painting*, 33. 573
collectors of, 1. 151
coloured by East Indians, 28. 57, 60, 61, 63
colouring of, 31. 368
commission for collecting, 1. 193, 197
Conway hangs, in Park Place dressing-room, 37. 350
——'s portrait to be copied in, 37. 234
cost of, 10. 301
cut to pieces, and used for japan, 33. 523
Dalrymple wishes to revive publication of, 15. 96
Don Quixote illustrated with, 33. 547
Dormer, Sir Charles Cottrell, sells father's collection of, 1. 60, 15. 92
Du Deffand, Mme, owns, 8. 20
English, of criminals, 20. 199
Fenn sends, to HW, of Sir William Hamilton, 42. 97
Florentine, sent by Mozzi to Duane, 25. 568
for book illustration, use models from Strand or Drury Lane, 42. 271
'for children of Somebody and Nobody,' 34. 194
for Ducarel's *Anglo-Norman Antiquities*, desired by HW, 41. 80
for HW's *Description of Strawberry Hill*: 42. 39; HW dissatisfied with, 25. 531–2
for HW's *Fugitive Pieces*, 37. 551–2
for *Iconographia Scotica*, 16. 323, 324
frames for, 20. 381
French clumsy imitations of English, 34. 85
French received by Harcourt, 29. 274–5
from English portraits: HW has collected, for over 30 years, 23. 211; vogue for, 23. 211
from portraits, now popular, 16. 321
frontispiece by Coleraine to his translation of Loredano, 16. 371
Gonzaga sends, to Grantham, 25. 473
Gough to have made, from HW's monumental drawings, 42. 59–60
Granger asks HW to aid him in cataloguing, 28. 121
—— collects, 1. 56n, 40. 313n
—— includes some, of doubtful attribution, 41. 218
——'s catalogue of, see Granger, James: *Biographical History of England*
—— sells, to Gulston, 41. 219
——'s list of, 40. 322–3
HW ashamed of, in his books, 15. 96
HW asks Montagu to procure, 10. 301

HW attends auction of, **7**. 302

HW binds volume of, by noble authors, **28**. 195, 200

HW buys, at Rome, **37**. 57

HW clips and pastes, **39**. 120

HW collects: **17**. 4n; of persons mentioned in Mme de Sévigné's letters, **25**. 433–4

HW exchanges, with Ratcliffe, **40**. 235–7

HW gives, to Cole, **2**. 19, **43**. 64

HW glad to see, of Sir Henry Lee, **42**. 199

HW has, made from his portrait of Humphrey, D. of Gloucester, **42**. 246

HW knows Marigny's paintings from seeing, **39**. 15

HW lent book of, by Bns Talbot, **42**. 471

HW mentions, **2**. 475

HW passes time with, **24**. 91

HW pastes, **38**. 59, **39**. 120

HW provides in will for completion of his sets of, **30**. 373–4

HW purchases: **5**. 75; at Rome, **37**. 57; on Quai de la Ferraille, **30**. 217

HW receives: from E. of Hardwicke, **40**. 364; from White, **42**. 19

HW returns to Lady Ossory, **34**. 85, 140

HW's: **1**. 56n, 60, 150, 157, **2**. 140, **20**. 380, **28**. 47, **42**. 388; added to, by Cole, **1**. 184, 188–9, 216, 222, 353–4, 357, 361–5; after Guido Reni, **21**. 533n, **30**. 217; collection of, designed for Eton College, **1**. 281n; collection of, prints lacking in, **1**. 179–83, 189; HW arranges, **32**. 304; in exchequer trunk in Berkeley Sq., **30**. 373–4; of arms of the two clubs at Arthur's, **40**. 121; to his *Description of Strawberry Hill*, **33**. 575–6

HW sees, in Bibliothèque du Roi, **39**. 236

HW's fondness for, **10**. 303

HW's letter about, **15**. 100–1

HW's list of, **43**. 79

HW thanks Ireland for, **42**. 120

HW thanks Nichols for, **42**. 21, 33

HW thanks Pennant for, **42**. 279

HW to employ a collector to get, **1**. 164

HW to seek, for Mariette, **41**. 13

HW to send, to Mann through Galfridus Mann, **21**. 90

HW unfavourable towards sets of, for authors, **33**. 547

HW wishes: from Nash's Worcestershire history, **42**. 17, 19; of Cardinal York, **21**. 467, 487; of his 'Ceres' from Knight, **42**. 193–4; of Jephson and Malone, **42**. 409; of Shrewsbury's portrait, **42**. 313; of Young Pretender, **23**. 422

half-penny, **35**. 300

Harcourt sends, to HW. **35**. 455

high price of, in England, **23**. 466

Hillier has, as samples, for HW, **40**. 290

——'s list of, **16**. 65–7

Illustri fatti Farnesiani contains, **25**. 403

in Barrett's *History*: called 'paltry' by HW, **16**. 227; called spurious, **31**. 326

in *Birth of Mankind*, **40**. 306n

in Bull's extra-illustrated copy of *Royal and Noble Authors*, **31**. 298

in Clubbe's *Physiognomy*, **16**. 173

in Combe's *Thames*, **15**. 319, 322

in E. of Pembroke's *Numismata antiqua*, **16**. 209

in edns of *Mémoires . . . de Grammont*, **16**. 323

in exchequer trunk in HW's Berkeley Sq. house, to be sent to SH, **30**. 373–4

in Gough's *Sepulchral Monuments*, **34**. 227, **42**. 59–60

in Lens's *Le Costume*, **16**. 188

in Middleton's *Monumenta*, **15**. 15

in Park Place cottage, **39**. 550

in *Pitture antiche di Ercolano*, **21**. 379

in Puttenham's *Arte*, **16**. 366

in Spence's *Polymetis*, **15**. 20

in SH Lucan, **35**. 644

in Strutt's *Regal and Ecclesiastical Antiquities*, **16**. 187

in Swinburne's *Travels*, **16**. 180

in *Thomæ Gemini Lysiensis compendiosa totius Anatomes delineatio*, **40**. 306n

in Wood's *Ruins of Palmyra*, **35**. 160

Irish: HW instructs Montagu about packing of, **9**. 413; HW returns list of, to Montagu, **9**. 407; HW's opinion of, **10**. 34; Montagu sends list of, to HW from Dublin, **9**. 404, 409; Montagu to collect, in Ireland for HW, **9**. 398, 400–1, 408, **10**. 16; Osborn, Hon. Mrs, sends, to HW, **10**. 34; Osborn, Hon. Mrs, to forward, to HW, **10**. 30, 32

Jamisone sends, to HW, **40**. 261, 263

King, Dr, gives, to HW for Selwyn, **30**. 283

list of, in Ewin's book, **1**. 183

list of, printed at SH, **1**. 195

'Long Minuet, The,' after Bunbury, **34**. 572

Lort's collection of, **16**. 153, 160, 173

Louvre, of Louis XIV's victories and palaces, **36**. 280–1

Mann sends, to HW, **18**. 201; **21**. 495

Mariette's collection of: **32**. 265–6; sold, **35**. 428

Marigny's paintings familiar to HW from having been reproduced in, **39**. 15

Mason sends, to HW, **28**. 26

modern licentiousness in regard to, **16**. 68

Mount Stuart's collection of, **15**. 161

Nash sends, to HW, **43**. 384

obscene: from China, **21**. 202; Stosch's, **21**. 189, 202

of individuals: Addy, W., **40**. 236; Alfred, K., **1**. 172; Allegranti, the, by Bartolozzi, **33**. 322n; Ancaster, Ds of, **39**. 550; Anne, Ps of Orange, **40**. 237; Anne (Nevill) (1456–85), **1**. 133; Aquilar, **43**. 306; Archer, John, **40**. 236; Aristotle, **42**. 64; Arland, **14**. 190n; Armine, Lady, **1**. 181; Armstrong, by Savage, **1**. 181; Arundel, Lord and Lady, by Hollar, **16**. 153; Arundel, 12th E. of, **1**. 190; Atkins, W. **40**. 237; Aurelius, Abraham, by Van Voerst, **16**. 64;

[Print; prints, *continued*]

Backwell, Edward, **10**. 301, 303; Bacon, Francis, **4**. 241, 266; Bailey, Nath., **40**. 237; Baker, by John Simon, **2**. 354; Baliol, John and Dervigilde, **40**. 236; Barefoot, John, **40**. 322; Bargrave, James, **1**. 142; Barker, Robert, **1**. 362; Barnardiston, **1**. 188; Basset, John Prideaux, **40**. 287; Bassompierre, by Lasne, **31**. 78n; Bauderon, **16**. 66; Beauclerk, Elizabeth and Mary, **29**. 71; Beaufort, Mary, Ds of, **1**. 181; Becket, Isaac, **1**. 74; Bedford, Ds of, **11**. 220; Bell, Francis, **1**. 183, 216; Berkeley, George, 1st E., **1**. 181; Bess of Hardwick, by Vertue, **42**. 313–14; Blair, Hugh, **42**. 56; Bluck, **40**. 236; Boehme, by Solly, **16**. 66; Boirombe, Brian, **40**. 236; Boleyn, Catherine, **1**. 181, 188, 189; Bolton, Rev. Robert, **16**. 65; Bolton, Samuel, **40**. 236; Boswell, **25**. 641; Bothmar, **40**. 236; Bouillon, 2d or 3d D. of, by Nanteuil, **15**. 100; Bowes, by Gillray, **33**. 540n; Bowyer, William, **42**. 21n; Breteuil, Bn de, **11**. 54n; Bridgeman, Sir Orlando, **1**. 61, 63; Bright, Edward, **40**. 236; Bristol, John, 1st E. of, **1**. 208; Britton, Thomas, by Grignion after Woolaston, **40**. 310; Brodrick, Thomas, **40**. 236; Broglie, Duc de, **11**. 54n; Brouncker, by Hollar, **1**. 181; Brown, Moses, **40**. 236; Bryan of Bury, Count, **1**. 188; Buckingham, Edward, D. of, **1**. 207n; Bugg, Fr., **40**. 236; Bulkeley, Mrs Henry, **1**. 181; Bulwar, J., **40**. 236; Burghley, Lord, **1**. 180, **40**. 237; Burnet, Mrs, **40**. 237; Burroughes, Rev. Jeremiah, **16**. 65; Burton, Rev. Henry, **16**. 65; Burton, William, **16**. 64; Bury, Comtesse de, **6**. 344–7, 368, **41**. 350; Bute, 3d E. of, **28**. 45n; Butler, Jacob, **1**. 189; Buxton, Jedediah, **1**. 216; Cadière, Catherine, **16**. 173; Calonne, **11**. 54n; Calthorpe, James, **1**. 32–3; Cameron, Dr, **40**. 236; Canynges, Sir William, by Englefield, **16**. 345; Cappello, Bianca, by Pozzi after Gherardini, **21**. 561n; Carew, Sir Nicholas, **28**. 456, 459, 463; Carlisle, Lucy, Cts of, **41**. 442–3; Catherine II, **23**. 242–3; Catherine of Braganza, Q., **41**. 414n; Caxton, **1**. 140; Chamillard, Guy, **15**. 100; Charles I, **16**. 166, **17**. 358, **35**. 346, **40**. 236; Charles I's children, **40**. 236; Charles II, **1**. 180, **16**. 74n; (?) Charles of Lorraine, P., **16**. 195–6; Charlotte, Q., **1**. 188–9, **21**. 554; Chaucer, **14**. 108–9, **16**. 134; Chevreuse, Duchesse de, **1**. 183; Chichester, Arthur, Bn, **1**. 181; Choiseul, Duc de, **41**. 284; Christ and the angels by Faithorne, **40**. 236; Chudleigh, Elizabeth, Ds of Kingston, **21**. 487; Cibizen, F. K., **40**. 236; Clark, J., **40**. 237; Clarke, Rev. Samuel, **16**. 67; Cleveland, Ds of, by Schencker, **16**. 323; Clifford, George, 3d E. of Cumberland, **1**. 353, 357, 360; Clive, Mrs, **2**. 330; Cockain, **40**. 237; Cockburn, W., **40**. 236; Coelson,

Lancelot, **40**. 236; Cole, Abdiah, **40**. 237; Coligni brothers, **1**. 173; Cooper, Mrs Elizabeth, by Faithorne, **1**. 179, 180n; Cornwall, Sir John, by Hollar, **2**. 365–6; Cosin, Bp John, **16**. 66; Cowley, **16**. 67; Cowper, John, **2**. 302, 307–9; Crawford, Charles, **1**. 354, 363; Crisp, Rev. Dr Tobias, **16**. 67; Cromwell, Oliver, **1**. 195, 360n, 362; Cumberland, George, 3d E. of, **1**. 355, 357, 360; Cumberland, Margaret, Cts of, **2**. 323; Cuningham, William, **1**. 173; Cutts, John, Bn, **9**. 187; Cuzzoni, **41**. 452; Dalton, Michael, **1**. 193, 196, 362–3; Dartmouth, Bn, by Vanderbank, **1**. 181, 182n; Dee, Dr John, **34**. 131n; Delorme, Marion, **9**. 118n; Dering, Sir Edward, **16**. 65; Desmond, Cts of, **1**. 329, 332, 339; Devonshire, Georgiana, Ds of, **28**. 386, 419; Digby, Lady, by Hollar, **1**. 181, **2**. 43, **42**. 16; Digby, Lady, from bust, **2**. 43; Dilworth, T., **40**. 237; Drake, James, **40**. 236; Du Deffand, Mme, **8**. 215–17; Dugdale, by Hollar, **15**. 220; Dunstan, St, **40**. 237; Dunton, J., **40**. 237; Edward V, **33**. 210; Elizabeth (1466–1503) of York, Q., **2**. 323; Elizabeth (1533–1603), Q., **1**. 180, **9**. 101, **16**. 366, **40**. 237, **42**. 461–2, **43**. 189; Elizabeth (Plantagenet) (d. 1425), **2**. 365–6; Erasmus, by Holbein, **16**. 160; Erskine, Maj., **40**. 236; Etough, Rev. Henry, **1**. 193, 193n, 196; Eugene, P., **40**. 237; Euston, Cts of, by Faber, **18**. 482; Evans, Henry, **40**. 237; Evely, Mr, by Sharpe, **1**. 216; Ewin, Dr, **1**. 362; Exeter, Cts of, **1**. 149–50, 154, 179, **43**. 53; Exeter, Ds of, by Hollar, **2**. 365–6; Farinelli, **41**. 452; Fauconberg, Cts, **1**. 181; Fitzpatrick, Lady Anne, by Smith, **33**. 201n; Fitzpatrick, Lady Gertrude, by Dean, **33**. 201n; Fitzroy, Lady Caroline, **37**. 228; Flamsteed, John, **2**. 352; Flatman, Thomas, by Walker, **15**. 97n; Foley, Lady Harriet, **42**. 49n; Fontenelle, **31**. 197; Ford, Ann, **43**. 124; Fortescue, Sir John, by Bretherton and Van der Gucht, **35**. 628n; Francis I, **16**. 181; Frederick II of Prussia, **40**. 237; Fryer, John, **40**. 237; Gentileschi, Artemisia, **40**. 231; George III, **21**. 554, **33**. 159, **39**. 550; Gerard of Brandon, Bns, **1**. 181; Gerbier, Sir Balthazar, **1**. 23, 25; Gethin, Lady, **7**. 358; Gibson, Anne, by Walker, **15**. 97n; Gibson, Richard, by Walker, **15**. 97n; Giles, Henry, **40**. 231; (?) Gilmour, Sir Charles, **10**. 7; Girard, Jean-Baptiste, **16**. 173; Glanvill, Rev. Joseph, **1**. 179; Gloucester, Humphrey, D. of, **1**. 181–2, **16**. 187, **42**. 246; Glynne, Sir John, **2**. 77; Godfrey, Ambrose, **45**. 237; Gondomar, **2**. 44, **40**. 236; Goodwin, Rev. John, by Glover, **16**. 65; Gordon, Lord George, **33**. 588n; Gouge, William, **1**. 179; (?) Gower, Granville *or* John, E., **10**. 224; (?) Graham, James, M. of Montrose, **40**. 237; (?) Graham, Hon. James, of Arith,

40. 237; Gramont, Comte de, 31. 78n; Gramont, Comtesse de, 15. 97n; Granville, Sir Bevil, 1. 179; Gray, Thomas, 1. 235, 291, 294n, 296, 298, 361, 15. 20, 52, 56, 60, 61, 28. 59, 60, (?) 140-1; Grey, Lady Jane, by Vertue, 32. 353n; Grignan, Comte de, 9. 21-2; Gulston, Joseph, 43. 57; Gunning, Elizabeth (1769-1823), 11. 220; Gunning, Mary, Cts of Coventry, 39. 550; HW, 15. 196n, 21. 407-8, 446, 25. 10, 31. 263, (?) 265, 41. 348-9; Hall, Jacob, 1. 182, 195; Hallifax, Samuel, Bp of Gloucester, 1. 362; Hardwick, Elizabeth, 42. 313n; Harison, Maj.-Gen., 40. 236; Harrington, Caroline, Cts of, 37. 228; Harrington, Katherine, Lady, by Faithorne, 1. 179; Hatton, Edward, 40. 236; Haveus, Theodore, 2. 76, 77; Hawkwood, Sir John, by Patch, 23. 428; Haywood, Sir John, 16. 67; Heidegger, 41. 452; Henrietta Anne, Duchesse d'Orléans, 1. 30; Henrietta Maria, Q., 1. 179, (?) 365, 16. 166; Henry VII, by Vertue, 2. 323; Henry VIII, 2. 323, 16. 181; Henry Benedict, Cardinal York, 21. 467, 487, 495; Henry Frederick, P. of Wales, 1. 173n, 16. 365; Herbert, Edward, Lord Herbert of Chirbury, 1. 71-2, 75, 10. 133n, 15. 97n, 112n, 42. 43; Hervey, Bns, 31. 417; Heydon, John, 40. 236; Hopkins, Mrs Allen, 1. 363; Hopkins, J., 40. 236; Hoskins, 1. 179; Hotham, Sir John, 1. 182; Houblon, Sir John, 40. 236; Hudson, Jeffery, 28. 28n; Humphrey, D. of Gloucester, 1. 181-2, 16. 187, 42. 246; Hunsdon, Bns, 9. 101; Huntingdon, Cts of, by Bowles, 35. 346; Huntingdon, Theophilus, E. of, 1. 182; Hutton, Matthew, Abp of Canterbury, 1. 52, 53, 61; Ibbot, 42. 22n; Isabella Clara Eugenia, 7. 269; James I, 1. 173, 16. 365; James II, 40. 237; James IV of Scotland, 42. 12n; James V of Scotland, 16. 323; James, Thomas, 15. 281-2, 284; Jamesone, George, 15. 75n; Jamesone family, 40. 261, 263; Jane (Beaufort), Q. of Scotland, 40. 236; Jenkins, Sir Lionel, 1. 72, 74; Jenyns, Soame, 2. 53-4, 56, 57, 58; Johnson, Dr Samuel, 25. 641; Jonson, Ben, 1. 170; Joyeuse, Duc de, 30. 217; Kenrick, John, 40. 237; Kent, Elizabeth, Cts of, 1. 39, 182, 188, 190, 40. 236; (?) Kider, Mr and Mrs, 10. 7; Kingston, Elizabeth, Ds of, 9. 338, 21. 487; Knox, Capt. Robert, 2. 134, 140; La Fosse, by Walker, 15. 97n; Lagden, Mrs, 1. 363, 2. 307; Lambert, 42. 279n; Langham, Lady, 1. 179, 188; Langley, Batty, 40. 237; Langton, by Bickham, 1. 176; Law, John, 15. 180, 42. 387; Lee, Sir Henry, 42. 199n; Leicester, 4th E. of, 10. 128; Lely, Sir Peter, 41. 98; Lennard, Samson, 40. 236; Lennox and Richmond, Ds of, 1. 173, 182, 40. 236; Lilly, W., 40. 236; Lloyd, Rev. John, 2. 167; Locke, John, 29. 19; Lord

Justices, 40. 237; Lorne, Lord, 10. 7; Loubenx de Verdala, 1. 257; Louis XVI, 41. 284; Louisa, 'Maid of the Haystack,' by W. Tomkins, 33. 490n; Louisa Hollandina, 1. 182; 'Louse, Mother,' 40. 322; Lovat, Lord, by Hogarth, 19. 391n; Løvendal, 19. 395-6; Luxembourg, Duc and Duchesse de, 11. 54n; Lydgate, by Vertue, 16. 134; Macclesfield, E. and Cts of, 1. 181, 40. 236; Maclaine, 20. 184, 188; Magdalen, after Guido Reni, 21. 532-3; Malden, Henry, 1. 188; Margaret (Tudor), Q. of Scotland, 15. 123n; Marguerite-Louise, Grand Ds of Tuscany, 25. 434, 444, 473; Marie-Antoinette, 41. 284; Martelli, Camilla, by Allegrini, 25. 226, 230; Mary of Guise, Q. of Scotland, 16. 323, 324; Mary, Q. of Scots, 1. 189, 42. 322n; Mason, Rev. William, 1. 260, 265, 267, 28. 39, 47, 59, 60, 94, 43. 57, 298; Matthew, by James Gammon, 40. 323n; Mayerne, Sir Theodore Turquet de, by Elder, 16. 67; Mayn, Cuthbert, 40. 237; Middleton, Mrs, by Van den Berghe, 16. 324; Middleton, Rev. Conyers, 15. 25, 303, 313; Milton, John, 16. 66, 29. 19, 40. 310n; Molé, Édouard, 15. 100; Monsey, Messenger, 1. 364; Montagu, Mrs, 43. 298; Montaigne, Bp George, 1. 149; Monticelli, 41. 452; Moore, Francis, 40. 237; More, Helen ('Gertrude'), 1. 289, 313, 360, 365; Morell, 43. 184; Morison, Robert, M.D., 40. 237; Mudge, Thomas, 1. 282; Necker, 34. 85; Newcastle, Margaret (Lucas), Ds of, 1. 182, 7. 269, 14. 145-7; Newcastle, William Cavendish, D. of, and family, 1. 182; Newcome, Mrs John, 1. 280, 281, 282, 284, 284n, 285; Newport, E. of, 1. 181; Nicol, Mrs Margaret, 40. 237; Nigel, Th., 40. 237; Northumberland, John Dudley, D. of, 1. 181, 190; Old Pretender, 25. 448; Orange, Ps Dowager of, 40. 237; Ormond, 1st D. of, 9. 118n; Ormond, 2d D. of, 1. 179; Ormond, 5th E. of, 14. 73; Orrery, Lord, 40. 236; Osborne, Lord, with sisters, 40. 236; O'Toole, 1. 62; Overbury, Sir Thomas, 16. 64n; Owen, Sir John, 2. 43; Oxenden, Henry, 40. 236; Pakington, Lady, 43. 384; Parker, G., 40. 236; Parker, Bp Matthew, 1. 193, 196; Parr, Q. Catherine, 2. 163n, 43. 385; Parsons, W., 40. 236; Paston, Lady, 1. 179; Payen, Pierre, 15. 100; Penderel, Richard, by Lambourn, 1. 197n; Pennant, 2. 191, 203, 41. 394; Percy, Thomas (1560-1605), 1. 182; Perkins, 40. 237; Perrot, Sir John, 1. 182, 43. 384; Philippoleos, Abp, 43. 64; Piozzi, Mrs, 25. 641; Pitt, William, E. of Chatham, 30. 125, 34. 210, 35. 262; Playford, J., 40. 236; Polignac, Duc de, 4. 410n; Polignac, Duc and Duchesse de, 11. 54n; Poole, Dr, 40. 237; Pope, Alexander, 15. 189; Porter, Endymion, 42. 126; Primrose, Gilbert, 40. 236; Purkis, by George Riddell, 1. 361, 364; Pym,

[Print; prints, *continued*]

John, 16. 65; Quarles, John, 40. 236; Ramesey, William, 40. 236; Ratcliffe, Charles, 40. 236; Raymond, Sir Robert, 40. 237; Reade, Sir W., 40. 237; Rembrandt's mother, 42. 12; Rich, Jeremy, 40. 236; Richard III, 1. 133, 40. 217, 236; Richardson, Jonathan, sr, by Bretherton, 14. 188; Richelieu, by Van den Berghe, 16. 323; Richmond, Margaret Beaufort, Ds of, 40. 236; Richmond, Mary Bruce, Ds of, 6. 359–60 (*see also* Lennox and Richmond, Ds of); Robert II of Scotland, 40. 237; 'Robin Gray,' 33. 401; Robinson, James, 40. 237; Rochester, E. of, 40. 237; Rogers, Charles, mezzotint by Ryland, 41. 389–91; Rooke, Mary (Luttrell), 1. 179, 180n; Roper, Lady Henrietta, 1. 365; Roscoe, by Picart, 15. 281n, 42. 440; Ross, Alexander, 40. 323; Rous, 1. 147; Rupert, Prince, 9. 118n; Rustat, Tobias, 1. 182; Saltonstall, Capt., 40. 237; Savoyard girl, 9. 94; Saxe, Maréchal de, 19. 395–6; Scheuchzer, 16. 67; Scudder, Rev. Henry, 16. 66; Seaforth *or* Seafield, Cts of, 40. 236; Seddon, John, 40. 237; Selden, John, 16. 65; Seymour, Jane, Q., 2. 323; Shaftesbury, 1st E. of, 1. 180; Shakespeare by Droeshout, 1. 132; Shakespeare, by Marshall, 42. 140; Sheldon, Gilbert, 1. 180; 'Sherley, Lady Elizabeth,' 1. 182; Shirley, Teresia, Lady, by Hollar, 1. 182; Shore, Jane, 1. 142, 144, 150, 150n; Shower, Sir Bartholomew, 40. 237; Shrewsbury, E. and Cts of, 42. 16; Siddons, Mrs, by Tomthwaite, 33. 377n; Sidney, Algernon, 29. 19; Sidney, Lady Dorothy, 10. 128; Sixtus V, 1. 257; Sleidan, Johann, 1. 179; Solander, 43. 337; Somerset, J., E. of, 40. 236; Somerset, Robert, E. of, 1. 208; Sophia, Electress of Hanover, 40. 237; Southampton, Elizabeth, Cts of, 1. 182; Speiss, Mr, 1. 363; Stanhope, Lady Harriet, 32. 49n; Stanley, Hon. Thomas, 1. 362; Stapleton, T., 40. 237; Stephens, by Hoare after Dance, 23. 423; Sterne, Rev. Laurence, 23. 5, 27, 33, 37; Stirling, William Alexander, E. of, 1. 182; Stock, Rev. Richard, 16. 66; Strype, John, 2. 352; Stuart, Lady Arabella, 15. 160–1, 42. 313n; Suckling, Sir John, 16. 66; Suffolk, Ds of, 42. 16n; Sully, Duc de, 4. 254; Taintarier, D., 40. 237; Taylor, Brook, 42. 388; Taylor, George, 40. 236; Temple, Lady Elinor, 40. 236; Tenison, by Vanderbank, 1. 171; Terne, Christopher, 40. 236; Thomson, Dr George, 16. 66; Thornhill, Sir James, 14. 190; Thurloe, 1. 208; 'topsy-turvy Major' and his wife, 31. 272; Townshend, Vcts, 18. 482; Trevor, Bp Richard, 2. 27, 28, 29, 41. 350; Tuer, Herbert, 1. 74, 127, 127–8, 129; Turenne, Maréchal de, 4. 254, 6. 339, 16. 323; Turner, Robert, 40. 236, 237; Tyrconnel, D. of, 1. 182; Vane, Sir Henry, by R. Cooper, 1. 183; Venner, Tobias, 1. 179, 40. 237; Vere of Tilbury, Bns, 1. 183; Viner, Sir Robert, 1. 179; Waldby, Abp, 2. 107n; Waldegrave, 4th E., 42. 413; Wales, Augusta, Ps of, 21. 487; Walker, Dr Richard, by Lambourn, 1. 222–3, 227; Walker, W., 40. 236; Waller, by Vanderbank, 16. 67; Walpole, Sir Robert, 41. 234, 42. 249; Walsingham, Sir Francis, 1. 180, 32. 46–7, 40. 237; Warburton, J., 40. 236; Warwick, Edward Rich, 6th E. of, 1 183; Waterhouse, 16. 67; Weever, John, 16. 64; Wellers, Mr, 1. 179; Wentworth, Darcy, 40. 236; Wharton, Sir George, 1. 179; William I, 15. 123; William of Hatfield, 1. 275; Willis, Browne, 2. 285, 287, 295, 303; Wilson, Benjamin, 16. 167; Winchester, 1st M. of, 1. 213, 216; Wissing, William, 15. 97; Wither, George, 40. 237; Woolley, Mrs Hannah, 1. 179, 188, 190; Wotton, Sir Henry, by Lombart, 1. 173, 173n, 16. 66; Wyatt, Sir Thomas, 1. 183, 189, 261; Wydevill, Anthony, E. Rivers, 1. 140; Wynn *or* Wynne, Sir John, by W. Sharp, 2. 167n, 170n; York, Ernest, D. of, 40. 236; York, Henry Benedict, Cardinal, 21. 467, 487, 495; Young, Dr (?) Edward, 40. 236; Young Pretender, 23. 422; Young Pretender and wife, 23. 427, 429

(?) of painters' heads, 4. 475

of portraits, now popular, 16. 321

of subjects (other than individuals): Alhambra, the, 2. 149, 150, 151–2; Aranjuez, 16. 170; Bec, abbey of, 2. 159; Bell Tavern, 15. 142n; Billingford's tomb, 1. 188; Bristol Castle, 16. 221, 223; Cambridge music room, 1. 188; Capoccio shrine, 35. 406n; *Champ de drap d'or, Le*, 1. 299, 2. 277, 16. 181; Charles I's sufferings, 17. 358; Chatterton's monument, 16. 350–1, 360; Copt Hall, 42. 72; country seats, 42. 17; criminals, 20. 199; Cromwell's funeral, 42. 127; Croyland Abbey, to be engraved by Watts, 16. 194; 'Dance of Death,' 16. 143–4; 'Death of . . . Chatham,' by Bartolozzi after Copley, 34. 210; destruction of Spanish floating batteries at Gibraltar, 25. 582n; Edward III's tomb, 2. 49; Florentine baptistery, 23. 429–30, 435; goitres, 33. 571n; HW's eagle, 20. 485, 489, 21. 461, 470, 31. 263, 35. 352; HW's medal of Antony and Octavia, 42. 262; Henry VIII's embarkation, from copy by S. H. Grimm, 2. 277, 16. 181; Houghton, 18. 36, 60, 35. 44–5; Jamesone's painting, 40. 261, 263; Knight of the Bath, 23. 155; 'Long Minuet, The,' after Bunbury, 33. 572; Louis XIV's victories and palaces, 36. 280–1; Maschere, 22. 202; Medici family, 20. 414, 21. 533, 538, 561, 25. 230, 245, 434; 'Monstrous Craws,' by Gillray, 33. 571n; Moorish buildings in Swinburne's *Travels through Spain*, 16. 180; 'Motion, The,' 18. 21; Newcastle household, 1. 182; Old Pretender's mar-

riage, **25.** 448; Otranto castle, **35.** 436; (?) painters' heads, **4.** 475; Paraclete, **42.** 53n; 'Patriot Exalted,' **34.** 140n; Poggio a Caiano, **22.** 222; Raphael cartoon, **35.** 38; Richmond Hill, **41.** 429n; 'Robin Gray,' by Bartolozzi after Bunbury, **33.** 401; Rome, views of, received by Edward, D. of York, **22.** 229, 232–3; St Paul's Cross, **16.** 167; SH, do not do it justice, **25.** 531–2; 'topsyturvy Major and his inverted wife,' **31.** 372; Vallombrosa, **20.** 317, 320, 329; whale's back, **35.** 151; William of Hatfield's tomb, **1.** 275n; wives of the Medici, **25.** 230

Orange, Princes of, have collection of, **43.** 382

Oxford, E. of, collects, from books' frontispieces, **17.** 357–8

Pennant offers, to HW from *Tour in Wales*, **42.** 38

—— sends, to HW, **41.** 394–5, **42.** 16

Percy may give, of Wyatt and Surrey, **41.** 320

Pompadour, Mme de, engraves, **21.** 201

prices of, **1.** 60n, 172, 175, 193, 195, 197, 210, 286, 287n, 291, 354, **2.** 277n, 308, **10.** 301, **25.** 496

rolls of, in HW's Exchequer chest, **23.** 285

Roscoe sends, to HW, made by Haughton, **15.** 281–2, 284

royal, HW to procure, for Selwyn, **30.** 264

Sandrart ascribes, to Holbein, **16.** 146

satiric: 'Abelard and Eloisa,' **43.** 298; are gross, **38.** 187; are numerous, **33.** 400–1; 'Coalition Dissected, The,' **35.** 381; in Florence, of three abbés' mutual admiration, **22.** 531; 'Motion, The,' **18.** 21, **37.** 96; of Boswell, **25.** 641; of Elizabeth Chudleigh, **21.** 487; of HW and Mrs Clive, **2.** 330; of Johnson, **25.** 641; of Necker, **34.** 85n; of Piozzi, Mrs, **25.** 641; of Pratt's *Fair Circassian*, **2.** 322; of Sterne and Death, **23.** 5, 27, 33, 37; of Wales, Augusta, Ps of, **21.** 487; of Westminster election, **25.** 496; on Coalition, **33.** 401, **35.** 381; on Fox-North coalition, **36.** 209; on Lady Caroline Fitzroy, **37.** 228; 'Patriot Exalted, The,' **34.** 140n; plentiful, **38.** 180; 'Political Wedding, The,' **34.** 241; price of, **25.** 496; 'Razor's Levee,' **33.** 400–1; 'Repeal, The,' **22.** 400; sent by HW to Strafford, **35.** 280; 'Simpling Macaroni,' **43.** 337; Townshend, Etheldreda, Vcts, writes messages on the backs of, **37.** 473; Townshend, George, 4th Vct, designs, **21.** 77–8, 90, **37.** 473–4

Scottish, sent to HW by Colquhoun, **42.** 431–3, 436

Shakespeare illustrated with, **33.** 546–7

spurious, in Barrett's *History and Antiquities of . . . Bristol*, **31.** 326

Stosch's, obscene, **21.** 189, 202

Talbot, Lady, lends book of, to HW, which Roberts later lends to Granger, **42.** 471n

to Waller's works, **23.** 248

two-penny, at Dover inn, **18.** 315

'upside down,' **31.** 272n

Venetian, by Jackson, **20.** 380–1

(?) Waddes's, auctioned, **38.** 371n

wood: Carpi, Antonio da, said to have invented, **16.** 96; in chiaroscuro, Harding struck by, at Hillier's house, **16.** 96

York, Miss, sends, to HW, **42.** 237

See also Aquatinta; Engraver; Engraving; Etching; Gilpin, William: *Essay on Prints*; Mezzotint; Print-seller; Print-shop

Printer; printers:

authors to receive overtures from, **35.** 410

cancelled sheets of, consigned to trunkmakers, **42.** 368

English, absorbed in politics, **23.** 157

Francklin was, of the *Craftsman*, **20.** 374, **35.** 237

French officers threaten, for considering publication of a paper on Louis XV, **23.** 230–1

George III's proclamation for arrest of, **23.** 280

HW's, *see* Farmer, Thomas; Kirgate, Thomas; Lister, James; Pratt, William; Robinson, William; Williams, Benjamin; Yardley, Edward

HW's opinion of, dishonest, **31.** 309–10

HW's troubles with, **15.** 55–6, 59, 76, 98, **35.** 303

House of Lords takes up, for illegally printing Weymouth's letter, **23.** 77

Lord Mayor releases, **23.** 280

of the *Champion*, may be prosecuted by Sir Robert Walpole for mentioning his natural daughter, **18.** 33

of Tory newspaper, **18.** 33

old, Ratcliffe collects works of, **40.** 236

wages of, **40.** 164

wages paid to, by HW and in London, **15.** 58

Printing:

apparatus for, all made by Baskerville himself, **40.** 276

Baskerville to send specimens of, to European courts, **40.** 275

HW's interest in, **35.** 98–9

on birch-bark, **15.** 58

on vellum, **15.** 213

origin of, in England, **15.** 295

preserves authors as if they were Egyptian mummies, **16.** 259–60

rolling press for, **40.** 306

tongues of Europe will not perish, since invention of, **39.** 411

Printing-house, HW's, *see* Strawberry Hill: printing-house at; *see also* Strawberry Hill Press

Printing-presses:

Baskerville prepares, **40.** 276

Print-seller; print-sellers:

monopolistic practices of, **28.** 87

see also Cornell, Thomas; Mariette, Jean; Mariette, Pierre; Stephens, William; Yardley, E.

Print-shop; print-shops:

(?) Gower's print to be bought at, **10.** 224

[Print-shop; print-shops, *continued*]
satiric prints of Boswell, Johnson, and Mrs Piozzi to be bought at, **25.** 641

Prior, Matthew (1664–1721), poet:
Alma by: HW quotes, **11.** 185, **28.** 140, **32.** 95; HW thinks, better than his *Solomon*, but less suitable for Mrs Yearsley, **31** 221; 'King Poltis' in, **33.** 32

Baker not supported by, **2.** 87–8, 90, 91, 96, 98, 341, 343–4, 361

'Chloe' of, **32.** 32

'cup of life' attributed to, **37.** 124

Dahl's portrait of, shown to HW by Harcourt, **35.** 536

'Daphne and Chloe' by, is read by HW to Miss Seton, **11.** 121

Dorset, D. of, said to be brother of, **20.** 62–3

——'s father the benefactor of, **20.** 63n

ease imparted by, to English language, **41.** 297

elegance of, **2.** 52

'Epitaph' by, Sauntering Jack in, **32.** 245

examined by Committee of Secrecy, **13.** 186

Extempore Invitation by, quoted by HW, **42.** 150

Female Phaeton by, **5.** 193n

HW considers, one of his favourites, **2.** 90

HW quotes, **1.** 178, 184

HW thought of quoting, **32.** 374

HW took words of, to Park Place, **33.** 52–3

Henry and Emma by: copied by Cts of Pomfret's daughter, **14.** 248; Hardinge to imitate 'Henry' in, **35.** 596; Warton thinks, spoils original ballad, **29.** 118

interest in, survives to next age, **28.** 280

Jacobites send, to persuade Dorset to give up Dover Castle, **20.** 62–3

Jersey, friend of, **2.** 341n

Johnson, Dr Samuel, dislikes, **11.** 277, **29.** 111

Knole's associations with, **33.** 223

'Ladle, The,' by: paraphrased by Chute, **35.** 56; quoted by Conway, **37.** 198

lines by, on Giordano's picture of Seneca, **15.** 205

'Mercury and Cupid' by, quoted by HW, **18.** 204

Miscellaneous Works of, West makes extracts from, **13.** 186–8, 194

'Ode Inscribed to the Memory of the Honourable Col. George Villiers, An,' quoted by HW, **30.** 92

Oxford, E. of, aids, **2.** 341

Paris sojourn of, as plenipotentiary, **20.** 62n

poems of, called witty and genteel, **11.** 121

Poems of, published by subscription, **2.** 341, 343

Poems on Several Occasions by, **29.** 118n

portrait, column, and flower picture by, at Welbeck, **35.** 271

Queensberry, Ds of, celebrated by, in poem, **19.** 195n

—— friend of, **9.** 61n

—— was goddess in days of, **23.** 299

rhymes of, compared to Cowley's, **11.** 353n

Scots wish to replace, by Ossian, **29.** 105, 135

Solomon by: HW paraphrases, **30.** 302; HW quotes, **33.** 52–3; HW thinks, inferior to his *Alma*, **31.** 221; translated by Duchesse d'Aiguillon, **3.** 190–1

'Turtle and the Sparrow' by: HW quotes, **11.** 98n; HW reads, to Miss Seton, **11.** 121

Yearsley, Mrs, unacquainted with works of, **31.** 218

Prior, Robert (b. ca 1694):
Westminster verses edited by, **13.** 132n

Prior; priors:
(?) Craon, Princesse de, in love with, **17.** 17

social relations of, with Mme Geoffrin, **7.** 316

Prior Park, Bath, Allen's (later Warburton's) seat:
Allen of, **9.** 394n

description of, **43.** 134

HW and Chute to avoid, **10.** 228

Warburton occupies, **10.** 228

Priory, The, Warwickshire:
Wise, Mr, the occupant of, **32.** 353–4, **35.** 77

Priory; priories:
alien, history of, **2.** 166, 173, 175, 177, 182

'Priory of St Hubert's':
Lady Suffolk's Gothic barn called, **35.** 644

'Priscilla Plaw':
Hertford, Cts of, thinks, clever, **39.** 263

lines on, **32.** 247, 251

Prison; prisons:
alms-boxes at, **21.** 238

Caffarelli enjoys, **19.** 438

footman committed to, for getting bastard, **25.** 355

French, overcrowded, **11.** 233

Gordon rioters demolish, and release inmates, **25.** 61, **35.** 354

Hanoverian soldier delivered from, **21.** 12

keepers of, interrogated by Privy Council after Gordon riots, **39.** 349–50

Moravian baron released from, to win money at picquet, **35.** 258

of princes, close to their graves, **38.** 527

ostler taken to, at Worcester, **35.** 150

releases from, increase crimes, **35.** 355

Spanish, condemned men from, to be used in storming St Philip's, **25.** 180

Prisoner; prisoners:
American, Shelburne said to contribute to, **33.** 6

Austrian, Frederick II interrogates, **21.** 258

cartel for exchange of, **19.** 187, 202, 205

chains and tapers of, **9.** 192

Cumberland, D. of, takes, **19.** 273–4

Curzay's magnanimity to, **20.** 206

England and France to exchange, by cartel at Sluys, **37.** 584, **38.** 1, 5, 7, 10, 11

English: Aiguillon's courtesy to, **21.** 251, 255; French conceal, **21.** 368; French treat, cruelly, **21.** 21; French treat, well, **21.** 251; from Minorca, may be sent by the French to Gibraltar, **20.** 581; from Minorca, sent to Spain, **25.** 430; from Oswego and Quebec,

21. 18; in Scotland, released, **19.** 204–5; released by French, are 'ragamuffins,' **37.** 208; *Triton* brings, from France, **37.** 502n; with French captors, pass through French post, **37.** 207–8
English captain brings, to Leghorn, **18.** 354
exchange of: in Irish fashion, **21.** 504; suggested, **19.** 187, 202
French: **39.** 360, 366n; at Knowle, **21.** 367n; Bedford and Grenville dispute over, **38.** 433n; Derwentwater treated as, **19.** 180; England's claims against France for maintenance of, **38.** 423, 447; English magnanimity to, **21.** 367–8; Frederick II hears complaints from, **21.** 180; HW subscribes for benefit of, **42.** 453; House of Commons settles compensation for, **38.** 495–6; in Hungary, may rebel, **18.** 446; not sent back from England, **37.** 279–80; Pitt's witticism on, **38.** 112; ransom for, in exchange for Dauberval, **38.** 460; taken at Cleves, **38.** 77; taken at Jersey, land in England, **39.** 360; taken at Minorca, **25.** 207; taken on Jersey, **25.** 115; Wesley's subscription for, **21.** 367n
Irish, Conway occupied with, **37.** 426
parole of, **19.** 204–5
sick, HW contributes towards, **42.** 454
Spain releases Minorca's garrison after taking them as, **25.** 430
Spanish: at Rivalta, **19.** 262n; Gibraltar garrison may get the itch from, **25.** 59
Wright treats, gently, **21.** 21
Prisoners' Petition. *See under* Gordon, Lord George
Pritchard, ——, (d. 1763), treasurer of Drury Lane Theatre:
HW invites, to dinner, **9.** 70, 73
Kingston play to be attended by, **10.** 70
Pritchard, (?) Mr:
SH visitor sent by, **12.** 234
Pritchard, Miss
SH visited by, **12.** 229
Pritchard, Mrs William. *See* Vaughan, Hannah
Priuli, Antonio (d. 1623), doge of Venice, 1618:
James I served by, **15.** 79–80
Priuli, Michele (d. 1603), Bp of Vicenza:
Shirley's letter about, **15.** 79–80
Private Corrrespondence of Dr Francis Atterbury, Bishop of Rochester. See under Atterbury, Francis
Privateer; privateers:
American: English and Scottish coasts infested with, **24.** 315–16; Grimaldi has prizes restored to, **24.** 263n; HW comments on, **28.** 323; plunders Selkirk's house, and attacks Whitehaven, **24.** 377–8
Anson pays, to resist French invasion, **21.** 306n
at St-Malo, **35.** 228
captured on way to Scotland or lost on Dutch coast, **19.** 173
Conway may have been taken by, to St-Sebastian, **37.** 119
crew of, imprisoned, **24.** 302

Duke and *Prince Frederick*, capture Spanish ships, **19.** 92n
Dunmore captures cannon of, **24.** 157
Dutch war delights, **25.** 108
England better than France at war of, **24.** 448
——'s only success is with, **24.** 472
English: capture French transports, **19.** 230; capture Martinique ships, **19.** 487n; capture supply ships for Brest fleet, **19.** 230; contraband articles to be distinguished by, **21.** 285–6; in Mediterranean, seek Dutch merchant ships, **25.** 120; Lorenzi accuses Mann of justifying, **21.** 356; not numerous in Mediterranean, **25.** 112; to capture unescorted vessels, **21.** 269
English fleet burns, off France, **37.** 527
English packet-boat carried by, to Dunkirk, **24.** 302
Fame, owned by Wright, **19.** 383n
fortune-seekers may well turn into, **24.** 465
France promises distinction to outfitters of, **37.** 437
French: at Corsica, intimidate Leghorn's shipping, **24.** 437; at Corsica, ruin Leghorn's trade, **24.** 476–7; between Corsica and Leghorn, **20.** 577; capture English merchant ships, **19.** 229, **21.** 69, 264; dominate Mediterranean, **21.** 20; English merchant ships pass by Corsica to escape, **22.** 157; French consul at Leghorn warns, when vessels leave, **24.** 476–7; French Court encourages, **24.** 398; HW hopes Berrys not carried off by, **12.** 116, 122, 132, 133; impertinence of, **12.** 89; Jardine and family captured by, **12.** 62; Mediterranean will soon swarm with, **24.** 397–8; off Corsica, blockade Leghorn, **24.** 437, 508–9; prevent Leghorn's commerce, **21.** 115; swarm on Dutch coast to intercept George II's jewels, **21.** 465; triumph in Mediterranean, **24.** 466
French snow is, **19.** 173n
from Jersey, prey on French, **24.** 472
from Minorca, oppose French privateers in Mediterranean, **24.** 466
galleon captured with aid of, **37.** 246
HW's letters might be intercepted by, **24.** 507
Hazard, the, travels with soldiers and volunteers, **19.** 240n
Hunter, Elizabeth, brought back by, only to be released by her father, **22.** 24
Hunter, T. O., obligated to, **22.** 16
ladies captured by, but released unharmed, **30.** 270
Mann's courier liable to be captured by, **25.** 218
Morice sends valuables back to Ostend on sighting, **25.** 89
Murray's, take Levant ships bound for Marseille, **24.** 437
Ossory, Lady, may have share in, **33.** 268
Pembroke and Elizabeth Hunter brought back by, **22.** 16, 24

[Privateer; privateers, *continued*]
Prince George operates as, **21.** 524
prizes taken by, **19.** 441
Prussia borrows, from England, **21.** 335
Prussian, *see* Prince Ferdinand
Rullecourt said to be acting as, **25.** 127
Russia tells England to curb, **25.** 39
St-Malo harbours, **37.** 354
Soleil, prisoners from, **19.** 180n
Spanish: **17.** 153; capture Russian ship, **25.** 39n; Jardine and family recaptured by, from French, **12.** 70
Sturt subjected to quarantine because he travelled in, from Minorca to Leghorn, **25.** 42
Tuscany almost ready to fight England because of rage at, **21.** 335
vessels for relief of St Philip's watched by, **25.** 205

Privateering:
Londoners uphold, **21.** 549

Privernum. *See* Piperno

Privet:
ink made from, **35.** 204

Privilege:
house-painters arrested on breach of, **38.** 502
Parliamentary breach of, **38.** 292

Privileged place, in London:
Theodore lured from, and arrested by creditors, **20.** 164

Privy; privies:
at backs of London gardens, have pert porticoes, **35.** 153
Orléans, Duc d', said to pass fat in, **32.** 264

Privy Council:
Bath, E. of, a member of, though not an office-holder, **20.** 80n
books of: HW swears on, **32.** 120; marriage of D. and Ds of Gloucester entered in, **32.** 118, **36.** 92n
Bristol's recall from Spain prevented by, **38.** 120
Bute's illness should be registered by, **32.** 119
Cabinet Council almost as large as, **21.** 489
Cameron examined by, at the Cockpit, **20.** 373n
causes heard by, in afternoon only, **22.** 443
Charles I's, signs proclamation, **9.** 224
clerk of, *see* Fawkener, William Augustus
committee of, in charge of George II's funeral, **21.** 444n
disputes in, over trial of Oxford vice-chancellor, **20.** 18
Dutch ship restored by, **21.** 285, 287–8
Elliot appointed to, **39.** 504n
embargo on wheat recommended by, **35.** 320n
Éon's affair to be considered by, **38.** 356
export of wheat and flour forbidden by, **22.** 455
factions in, over tax on Irish absentee landlords, **35.** 348
Florentine regency attentive to resolutions of, about Dutch prizes, **21.** 287

George II welcomed by members of, **18.** 340–1
George III sees, **21.** 443
——'s household may be chosen by, **20.** 570
——'s marriage discussed by, **21.** 513
—— summons, to announce marriage intentions, **9.** 376, **38.** 95
Grenville said to be head of, **20.** 216
Halifax warns, of Irish money bills, **43.** 126
Hardwicke asks Newcastle to put Anson in, **20.** 135n
Hertford attends, on authenticating marriages of Dukes of Gloucester and Cumberland, **39.** 170
—— attends prison-keepers' interrogations by, **39.** 349–50
Ireland summons new parliaments for money bills sent over by, **23.** 156n
Johnston-Lyttelton feud in Minorca laid before, **38.** 311
Lee a member of, **17.** 242n
lord president of, *see* President of the Council
Mansfield to succeed Fitzwilliam as president of, **12.** 117
marriage contract of Ps Mary signed by, **37.** 61
Massachusetts assembly's act rejected by, **22.** 520
Massachusetts Bay acts to be considered by, **22.** 507n
meets at Queen's house during Gordon riots, **33.** 188
Montagu, D. of, member of, **20.** 79n
Parliamentary address to remove Sir Robert Walpole from, **37.** 89
report to, of condemned criminals, **11.** 298
Santiago attack to be decided by, **17.** 175
ticket privileges of, **20.** 48n
Wade's answer to Drummond approved by, **19.** 202

Privy Council, Irish:
Stone, Abp, prevents heads of bills from being sent by, to England, **21.** 474n

Privy Council, Scottish. *See under* Scotland

Privy Councillor; Privy Councillors:
Anson, Hyndford, and Robinson become, **20.** 135
Gloucester's child's birth to be witnessed by, **5.** 265
Harley becomes, **23.** 32

Privy Gardens, Westminster:
Bunbury's house in, **4.** 207n
Cardigans' house in, **38.** 357
Judge Advocate General's office in, **21.** 155n
Lennox's house in, **11.** 203n
Montagu, D. of, dies in, **20.** 79n
—— has house in, **24.** 431n, **29.** 68n
Pembroke dies in, **20.** 109n
Portland, Ds of, has museum in her house at, **41.** 165n
Richmond, Ds of, entertains at, **38.** 400n
Richmond, D. of, has house in, **4.** 313n
——'s fireworks at, **9.** 80–2
Williams's house in, **18.** 450n

Privy Purse:
Augusta, Ps of Wales's, Anne Pitt was, **23.** 451n, 558n
George II buys watch from, **20.** 57
Graham, keeper of, to James II, **18.** 193n
to Edward, D. of York, **37.** 479
Privy Seal:
appointments to, rumoured, **10.** 60
Bedford, D. of, begs, to frame because of family connection, **30.** 177
Bristol, E. of, receives, **23.** 65, **32.** 37
—— transferred from, **23.** 173
Cholmondeley receives, **18.** 356
Gower may resign, **18.** 159
—— obtains, **9.** 180
—— prevented by gout from taking, **17.** 478
—— resigns, **20.** 417
—— retains, **9.** 115
—— rumoured to obtain, **22.** 130
—— succeeds Hervey in, **17.** 492, **18.** 70, 89
Grafton and Weymouth may fight for, **23.** 310
Grafton obtains, **23.** 314
HW does not know destination of, **23.** 62
HW is not, **32.** 37
HW to write inscription for, **30.** 177
Hardwicke might accept, **21.** 92–3
Hervey takes, to Ickworth, **17.** 457
Newcastle proposes Temple for, **21.** 86n
Pitt to take, **22.** 442
Pulteney's aspirations for, **18.** 70, 89
——'s intrigues to get refusal of, **18.** 231
Rutland has promise of, **20.** 417–18
Scottish, is again Stuart Mackenzie's post, **22.** 444, 453
Temple has, **9.** 281
—— resigns, **9.** 260, **21.** 345–6
See also Lord Privy Seal
Privy Seal Office:
register book in, **14.** 160
Prize; prizes (for art):
Proctor wins, in drawing, painting, and sculpture, **25.** 577
Prize Bill. *See under* Parliament: acts of
Prize-fighting:
Mathews's taste for, ridiculed by HW, **18.** 79
suppression of, **15.** 70
Prize money:
English seaman eager for, **23.** 242
Prize ship; prize ships:
capture of, **19.** 239n, 383n, 441n
Cocceji's article on seizure of, **21.** 281
court of appeal for, **21.** 287n
Dutch: Florentine regency heeds Privy Council's resolutions about, **21.** 287; taken by English navy, **25.** 134
English captains at Leghorn share, with Townshend, **19.** 277
English captains prefer, to artillery, **19.** 100
English proclamation on seizure of, **21.** 281
English ships capture: **24.** 420; from Martinique, **19.** 487n
Evening Post mentions, **19.** 441
fleet brings in, before storm, **30.** 112

France insists on restitution of, **20.** 541
French: England captures many of, **24.** 472; English ships take, to Genoa, Port Mahon, and Leghorn, **18.** 438
Grenville captures, **19.** 403n
Jersey advertises sale of, **24.** 472
Leopard's, **19.** 245–6
Mann hopes for capture of, at Piombino, **19.** 236
Mathews prefers capture of, to aiding Austrian army, **18.** 452–3
naval procedure about, **17.** 8n
Newcastle brings, to Leghorn, **18.** 448
privateers capture, **19.** 230n, 441
proclamation regarding, **19.** 488n
regulations for English ships taking, **20.** 54
richness of, England's only consolation for war, **24.** 422
St Stephen knights to win, from Turks, **22.** 259
value of, from Martinique, **19.** 487n
Venetian, English ship takes, to Port Mahon, **19.** 81
Walpole, Sir Robert opposes giving, entirely to captors, **21.** 415
—— would have regulated taking of, **20.** 54
Wright's, at Porto Ferrajo, **21.** 69
Probabilités de la vie humaine. See under Demoivre, Abraham
Probart, Joseph, mayor of Orford:
election of, **39.** 265
'Probus':
letter-writers' nom-de-plume, **42.** 505
Proby, Charles (1725–99), naval officer:
Gibraltar visited by, **23.** 261
Mann to convey Weymouth's instructions to, **23.** 244n
son of, receives Jermy's bequest, **25.** 206
Terrible commanded by, **19.** 235n
Proby, Henry:
Twickenham resident, **42.** 482
Proby, John (1720–72), cr. (1752) Bn Carysfort:
Admiralty post for, **21.** 73
change planned for, **38.** 370
Proby-Jermy, Henry Francis (b. ca 1769):
Jermy leaves fortune to, **25.** 206
Probyn, Henry (d. 1780), wholesale silk mercer:
death of, **31.** 199
Probyn, Mrs (?) Henry, of Twickenham:
SH visited by, **12.** 221
SH visitors sent by, **12.** 236
Procaccia (carrier):
Bocchineri, Signora, has affair with, **20.** 447
books sent by, **17.** 64
fanali to be carried by, **17.** 77
fee to, **26.** 4
melon seeds sent by, **17.** 34
model of statue to go by, **18.** 200
Penny to send pictures by, **17.** 241
Regency banishes, to Porto Ferraro, **20.** 447
Procès:
Mme du Deffand refers to HW's reproaches as, **4.** 34, **43.** 86

Procession; processions:
at George II's funeral, 9. 321–2
at George III's coronation, 38. 121–3, 126
ennobled Florentines rank as nobles only in, until third generation, 24. 227
fails to stop rain, 20. 220n
for destruction of Polish dissidents, 22. 577
for Frederick II's birthday, 21. 171
Italian peasants make, for rain, 36. 143
religious, at Florence: for Wachtendonck's recovery, 17. 105; in honour of Madonna dell'Impruneta, 30. 4; two or three a day, at Minorca, 37. 311
Procession and Ceremonies . . . of the . . . Order of the Bath:
(?) Pomfret, Cts of, sends, to Niccolini, 18. 126–7
Proclamation; proclamations:
for Young Pretender's capture: Bath and Richmond do not sign, 30. 92; Grafton hesitates to sign, 30. 92; issued, 30. 91
Proclus (ca 410–85), neo-Platonic philosopher:
'almost unintelligible commentator on Plato,' 34. 83
Taylor's translation of, 34. 83
Proconsulo, Via del, at Florence:
Palazzo del Podestà in, 17. 137n
Proconsuls, Roman:
pensioned by tributary sovereigns, 25. 118
Procopius (d. ca 565), historian:
Gibbon cites, 29. 114–15
Proctor, Catherine (1746–91), m. (1765) Thomas Howard, 3d E. of Effingham:
riding ability of, 28. 208–9
Proctor, John (?1521–84), divine and historian:
history of Wyatt's rebellion by, 42. 445, 447
Proctor, Thomas (1753–94), painter and sculptor:
HW praises, 25. 577
prizes gained by, in drawing, painting, and sculpture, 25. 577
Proctor, Sir William Beauchamp (1722–73), cr. (1745) Bt; K. B., 1761; M.P.:
coaches of supporters of, attacked, 23. 461n
coach of, torn to pieces by mob, 23. 6
election of, 19. 425n
K. B. predicted for, 20. 136
may be prosecuted for hiring mob at Brentford, 23. 79
Middlesex candidate, 23. 6, 30n, 73n
mob of, wrecks Middlesex elections, 23. 78
Proctor; proctors:
at Cambridge, take different sides in chancellor's election, 38. 362
Hervey seeks, for divorce, 39. 105
Proculus, St (d. ca 1393):
epitaph of, at Bologna, 13. 192
Procuratore di San Marco:
election of, at Venice, 17. 75, 77
large sleeve worn by, 17. 75n
Venice to send, to England, to congratulate George III, 21. 508–9
See also Grimani, Pietro

Procureur, of Rennes:
threatened with hanging, 39. 35–6
Procureur-général:
La Chalotais offered reversion of place of, 23. 207
Prodromo. See under Baiardi, Ottavio Antonio
Profanity:
Hertford, E. of, avoids, 32. 94
'Professeur, le.' *See* Sigorgne, Pierre
Profession de foi des théistes, La. See under Voltaire
Professions, learned:
HW's abhorrence of, 33. 230
Professor; professors:
Genevese, makes witticism on Mountrath, 20. 103
of anatomy, Cocchi's salary as, 21. 194
Professorship:
value of Gray's, at Cambridge, 1. 228n
Profits:
from literary productions: HW reflects on, 28. 23–4; Mason reflects on, 28. 21–3
Progenie, F.:
(?) view by, of Vesuvius, 24. 515n
Progress of Civil Society, The. See under Knight, Richard Payne
'Progress of Liberty.' *See under* Cambridge, Richard Owen
Progress of Poesy, The. See under Gray, Thomas
Project, The. See under Tickell, Richard
Projecte conteyning the State . . . of the University of Cambridge, A. See under Lort, Michael
Project for the Advancement of Religion. See under Swift, Jonathan
Projector; projectors:
Argyll 'puddles away' days among, 37. 150
little regarded in England, 19. 460
ruined, while others profit by their inventions, 35. 399
Prole, (?) Capt. Henry (d. 1763), Mrs Bosville's lover:
art collection of, 18. 251n
Bosville tells his wife to follow, 18. 286
Bosville, Mrs, has, as paramour, 35. 41
—— to join, 18. 309
(?) Bosvilles accompanied by, 18. 251
Mann induces, to leave Florence, 18. 286
—— invites, with Mrs Bosville, 35. 41
Mathews may dismiss, 18. 309
Prologue; prologues:
by Lord Holland, 34. 138
difficulty of writing, 33. 553
fragment of, sent to HW by Lady Ossory, 34. 19
Garrick's: 35. 568; to *She Stoops to Conquer*, 32. 109
none, at Richmond House theatricals, 34. 1
Ossory, Lady, sends, to HW, 34. 19–20
to Bentley's *Wishes*, 35. 645
See also under Fitzpatrick, Richard
Prologue to the Satires. See under Pope, Alexander

Promesse del cielo, opera:
Charlotte, Q., sees, **38**. 123, 136
Prometheus. See under Æschylus
Prometheus:
painting of, at Kimbolton, **10**. 76, 78
Denbigh, Cts of, resembles, **35**. 372
Promontorio, Nicolas:
Vie de St-Louis by, (?) owned by Mme du Deffand, **8**. 34
Promotion:
in (?) army, proclaimed in Paris, **7**. 445
Prompter:
Holdernesse entertains, **18**. 130–1
Proof; proofs:
of prints, Gough to give, to HW, **42**. 60
Proof-sheets:
HW wishes to revise character of H. Fox in, if published, **30**. 131
Propagation:
HW's reflections on, **24**. 493
Proper Reply to a Late Scurrilous Libel, Entitled Sedition and Defamation Displayed. See under Pulteney, William (1684–1764), Earl of Bath
Propertius, Sextus Aurelius (1st cent. B.C.), poet:
grace of, **16**. 270
West's imitation of, sent to HW. **13**. 174, **14**. 16, 237–8
Property:
alarmed by French Revolution, **15**. 231
communal in Sparta, **15**. 227
security of: Condorcet's constitution mentions, **31**. 385; unwholesome doctrine in India, **31**. 284
See also Association for Preserving Liberty and Property
Prophecy:
folly of, HW's reflections on, **22**. 572, **33**. 160
from Ezekiel, about English-French, **35**. 218
'Prophet,' (?) E. of Orford's horse:
'Augur,' foal of, **32**. 133n
Prophet; prophets:
HW a gazetteer, with no attempt to be, **23**. 86
HW as, **33**. 160, 284, 290, 430
not honoured in own country, **33**. 160, 430
religious, made predictions after the events, not before, **25**. 37
Proportion; proportions:
divine origin of, **42**. 274
Propylæum, Athens:
Osterley portico resembles, **32**. 126
Prose:
alliterative, worse than alliterative verse, **31**. 350
HW on Home's, **32**. 107
HW on Johnson's, **33**. 287
Proserpine. See under Quinault, Philippe
Proserpine, English ship:
Toulon squadron observed by, **24**. 394n
Proserpine:
Berkeley, Lady, compared with, **30**. 326
HW's name for Ds of Cumberland, **32**. 130

mother of, **34**. 101
Orpheus and, **11**. 148
Storer should be vice-chamberlain to, **33**. 273
Prosody:
HW's comments on, **28**. 139, 143–4
Prospect House, near Broadstairs, Kent:
Berry, Mary, makes a sketch of, **12**. 128
Berrys visit, **12**. 103, 128, 133
HW calls, 'Mount Ararat,' **12**. 121
HW receives Mary Berry's letter from, **12**. 104
Lee not as gay as, **12**. 137
winds at, **12**. 116, 119, 122
See also Broadstairs
Prosperity:
danger of, to nations, HW's reflections on, **24**. 278
'Prospero, Lady' ('Mrs'):
affected accent of, **31**. 291–2
HW ridicules, **31**. 291
More, Hannah, criticizes, **31**. 274
nests in HW's garden, **31**. 274
Prostitute; prostitutes:
business methods of, **30**. 57
costume of, during salivation, **30**. 264
Englishwoman's costume makes her resemble, **30**. 264
HW jokes about, **30**. 40
Rigby would prefer HW's 'The Beauties' to celebrate, **30**. 100–1
See also Whore
Prostitution:
HW's reflections on causes of, **31**. 283
Protecting duties:
Irish mob insults Irish House of Commons for not passing, **25**. 491
Protection, Bill of. *See under* Parliament: acts of
Protector, the. *See* Cromwell, Oliver (1599–1658); Cromwell, Richard (1626–1712); Seymour, Edward (ca 1500–52)
Protector; protectors:
of glass, for candles, **17**. 59
Protestant; Protestants:
Albany, Cts of, probably is not, **23**. 402
cabals of, **20**. 542
Charles II thought too little to be, **16**. 34
Clarendon swings between Catholicism and, **25**. 224
converge on London to burn it, **35**. 355
divines of, join plot against Bower, **20**. 531
English: author of verses on Rollin's death is, **30**. 24; Rome's changed attitude towards, pleases HW, **22**. 177
Florentine lady rejects marriage proposal because her children would be, **23**. 449
foreign: for military service in America, **20**. 531n; may be settled on forfeited Scottish estates, **20**. 310; Pennsylvania regiments to get officers from, **37**. 436, 444
French: **25**. 518n; Dutens is, **25**. 625n; in Ireland, Hertford's compliments from, **39**. 26; Malesherbes protects, **7**. 375; persecution of, on revocation of Edict of Nantes,

[Protestant; Protestants, *continued*]
29. 296; ready to join a French pretender,
19. 309–10; rights of, 33. 582n; St-Sauveur
is, 36. 180; *see also* Huguenot
French invade Ireland in area most domi-
nated by, 21. 381
Fuentes unlikely to become, 21. 428
Gage turned, 30. 291n
Gordon rioters do more damage to, than to
Roman Catholics, 25. 61
Hungarian, Frederick II writes about, to Bp
of Breslau, 20. 269
Irish, form volunteer companies, 28. 469
Irish area controlled by, is short of ammunition, 21. 373
Irish proprietors among, should resist reforms, 35. 382
Irish Volunteers mostly are, 35. 379n
Necker given post in spite of being, 24. 254–5,
25. 21, 159, 39. 478
—— ineligible as comptroller from being,
24. 255n
Norfolk dukedom's heir converted to become,
23. 485
Polish, 22. 574n
prejudices of, not preferred by HW to Catholic practices, 18. 79
reverses may invigorate, 19. 118
ridicule by, of Catholic customs deplored by
Mann, 18. 59
Roman Catholic fasting in Italy upset by,
25. 21
sacrament revered but not worshipped by, 28.
154
Spain allows English to exercise religion free
from Inquisition, 20. 170n
Tuscan priests induce, to escape from parents
and change religion, 22. 249
Young Pretender said to become, 20. 333, 22.
324–5, 368, 23. 402–3
——'s wife probably is not, 23. 402
Protestant Association:
Canadian savages the only fit allies of, 35. 354
Gordon riots disavowed by, 33. 191
Gordon riots fomented by, 29. 52, 57
members of, attack Gordon rioters, 33. 192
petition of, carried to Parliament by Lord
George Gordon and his followers, 25. 52–3
Protestantism:
French, meaningless now that Roman Ca-
tholicism has been abolished, 39. 478
Gordon, Lord George, sets fire to London in
defence of, 25. 131
HW's, 35. 153
interest of, in Germany, 35. 192
Mathews's, ridiculed by HW, 18. 79
Paul V compromises on excommunication of
Venice for fear of, 20. 198n
senility of, 25. 48
'spirit of toleration' animates, 35. 587
writings found with Catherine (? Parr)'s
prayers are tinged with, 16. 207

Protester, The, weekly periodical:
Ralph publishes, 18. 464n
Proteus:
Cumberland's play mentions, 2. 150
gout compared with, 24. 67, 33. 285
HW compares himself to, 23. 537
Ossory, Lady, is, in petticoats, 32. 209
Prothée, English ship:
French and Spanish fleets seen by, 25. 182n
Prothée, French ship:
Sartine writes letter on loss of, 7. 446
Protogenes (d. 200 B.C.), painter:
Apelles criticizes, 34. 243
Pliny describes work of, 28. 300
'Provençal, Le'. *See* Barthélemy, Jean-Jacques
Provençal language:
Richard I's poem in, 21. 156–7, 186
Ste-Palaye interprets, 21. 186
Provençal poetry:
Gray unable to satisfy HW concerning, 14.
132–3
Nivernais translates, 40. 303
Richard I writes, 40. 115, 303
Provençal poets:
Coke, Lady Mary, to learn about, 31. 144
Crescimbeni's book on, 21. 156n
Provence, Comte de. *See* Louis XVIII
Provence, Comtesse de. *See* Marie-Joséphine-
Louise (1753–1810)
Provence, Count of. *See* Berenger, Raymond
Provence:
accent of, 4. 244
advances in, 19. 352
Austrians about to invade, 19. 333
—— blame their defeat in, upon the English,
19. 423
Barthélemy from, 41. 193
Botta responsible for failure of expedition
to, 19. 364
Brown to invade, 19. 323
Charles Emmanuel III's attack on, facilitated
by Savona's capture, 19. 352
—— to coordinate invasion of, 19. 323n
Crescimbeni's book on poets of, 21. 157
Du Deffand, Mme, mentions, 4. 285
embargo on coast of, 18. 360
expedition withdrawn from, 19. 363, 364
French army quiet in, 19. 374
French have no troops in, 21. 223
French preparations in, vigorous, 20. 540–1
French troops assemble in, for Minorcan at-
tack, 20. 528n
French troops in, 19. 334
French troops said to be withdrawn from,
19. 405
French troops withdrawn from Spanish army
in, 19. 8
game laws abolished in, 34. 64n
Genoa tries to exclude provisions from coast
of, 19. 344
Gloucester, D. and Ds of, plan to winter in,
33. 419

Grignan, Comtesse de, visited, 30. 207
HW foresees failure of expedition to, 19. 369
Mann hopes that Austria will invade, 19. 306
Pitt, Anne, visits, 24. 194
provisions from Leghorn for expedition to, 19. 352
Sicard ill-uses shipmasters of, 20. 319n
trade in, interrupted, 21. 123
troops from, said to be shifted to Flanders, 19. 405
visitors to: Boufflers, Comtesse de, 6. 367, 441; Pitt, Anne, 24. 194; Pomme, 5. 183; York, D. of, 7. 365
Provence, Hôtel de, in Paris:
in Rue de Condé, 37. 41
Provence, Hôtel de, in Turin:
Berrys find, full, 11. 143n
Proverb; proverbs:
about cost of gold, 23. 152-3
acted, 4. 12, 272, 277, 278, 6. 493, 7. 331
HW quotes, 31. 227
Irish, about Gunnings' luck, 20. 358
Italian, quoted by Mann, 22. 112-13
Latin, quoted by HW. 23. 208
Mme de Maintenon's, acted by St-Cyr pensioners, 10. 294
More, Hannah, quotes, 31. 289, 319-20
of HW's youth, now inverted, 33. 115
of rats and ship, 33. 115
of younger brother, 13. 109
on Jack Pudding, 33. 197
'scanty kin which have neither whore nor thief,' 15. 30
Proverbs, book of. See Ray, John: Collection of English Proverbs
Providence, American sloop:
Glasgow's battle with, 24. 216
Providence, English register ship:
Defiance captures, 17. 176n
Providence (Rhode Island):
not yet taken, 28. 282
Providence, divine:
arraigned because French wickedness triumphs, 31. 395
chance is the secret agent in, 32. 344
English depend on, in war, 33. 116
HW's opinion of, 33. 337
HW's reflections on, 31. 397
HW urges Hannah More to write sermon vindicating, 31. 395, 397
Providence. See also Provvidenza
Provinces, the United. See Holland
Provincial society:
HW's reflections on, at King's Lynn, 9. 350
post-chaises improve, 9. 350, 10. 348
Provok'd Husband. See under Cibber, Colley; Vanbrugh, Sir John
Provok'd Wife. See under Vanbrugh, Sir John
Provost (surname). See Prévost
Provost, Lord. See Lord provost
Provvidenza, Russian war ship:
at Leghorn, 23. 192

Prowse, Thomas (1707-67), M.P.:
birth date of, corrected, 43. 125, 244
HW calls, 'a leading Tory,' 17. 385n
named in Secret Committee lists, 17. 385
Parliamentary debate by, on amendment to the Address, 26. 23
Pelham favoured by, 20. 32
Speaker's position offered to, 38. 136n
speakership of House of Commons refused by, 9. 398
Tories led by, 20. 32
Proxy:
HW consults Cts of Holdernesse about Mann's duties as, 24. 209
HW urged to name, for himself, in House of Lords, 31. 363
Mann asks about his duties as, at baptism, 24. 199
——'s, for Bath installation, see under Bath, Order of the: installation of
——'s function as, prominently mentioned in gazettes, 24. 238
—— thanks HW for instructions about, 24. 219
Proyart, Liévain-Bonaventure (1743-1808):
Vie de M. d'Orléans de la Motte by, 34. 16n
Vie du Dauphin by, unknown to HW, 33. 416
'Prudence, Dame':
HW becomes acquainted with, late in life, 33. 328
'Prudence, Lady Dowager.' See Augusta, Ps of Wales
Prudence:
Du Deffand, Mme, compliments HW on his remarks on, 3. 164
—— has no further use for, 3. 161-2
HW considers, out of fashion in England, 24. 433
HW on, 3. 153
HW thinks, should be attribute of youth, 10. 269, 270
'Prudence and Parts.' See under Williams, Sir Charles Hanbury: 'Epistle to the Right Hon. Henry Fox'
Prudente, La, English ship:
prizes captured by Capt. Waldegrave in, 33. 272n
Waldegrave commands, 33. 210n
Prudery:
examples of, 17. 495-6, 20. 125, 144, 21. 292
Pope's verses on, see under Pope, Alexander: Answer to Mrs Howe
Prudhoe Castle, Northumberland:
Somerset, D. of, owned, but did not occupy it, 20. 10n
Prujean, (?) Anne (d. before 1774), m. (before 1725) Francis Prujean:
biographical information on, 43. 124-5
Lumley entertains, 9. 367
Pitt, Elizabeth, quarrels with, about religion, 20. 499

Prujean, (?) Francis (d. 1780) of Sutton Gate, Hornchurch, Essex:
Pitt, Elizabeth, receives letter from, **20.** 499
Warren, a friend of, **20.** 499
Prulé. *See* Bonvoust de Prulay
Prunello; prunellos:
Dodd, Mrs, packs, closely, **37.** 21
Prunis, Abbé:
Montaigne's *Journal de voyage* discovered by, **24.** 16n
'Prussia':
in cantata, **35.** 106
'Prussia, K. of':
HW's letter to Rousseau under the name of, *see under* Rousseau, Jean-Jacques
letter under name of, to Colombini, **5.** 427
Prussia, K. of. *See* Frederick II (1712–86); Frederick William I (1688–1740); Frederick William II (1744–97)
Prussia, Ps of. *See* Frederica Charlotte Ulrica Catherina
Prussia, Q. of. *See* Frederica (1751–1805); Sophia Dorothea (1687–1757)
Prussia:
alliance of, with Russia against Poland, **34.** 153
ambassadors from and to, *see under* Ambassador
army of: ammunition discarded by, **18.** 543; Apraxin defeats, at Gross Jägersdorf, **21.** 159n; at Königsberg, prepares against Russians, **21.** 72; Austrians defeat, in Moravia, **17.** 372; Charles, P., intercepts retreat of, **21.** 109; defeated on the Rhine, **21.** 456; defeated at Cosel, **19.** 62n; Derenthal, officer in, **21.** 366n; deserters in, **18.** 547; Dresden to be retained by, **21.** 355; Dutch said to be joined by, **37.** 154; four armies of, **21.** 271n; Grant, officer in, **21.** 153n; Richelieu compelled by, to fight in winter, **21.** 176; Russian battle with, expected in Saxony, **21.** 72; Russians defeat, at Palzig, **38.** 23–4; Russians defeated by, at Zorndorf, **37.** 562, 566; Saxe-Weissenfels opposes, **19.** 61–2; *see also* troops of
army of observation contains Saxon troops in service of, **21.** 73n
Austria and France might combine with, for Dutch partition, **39.** 429
Austria and Russia may be joined by, against Turkey, **25.** 359, 436
Austria compared with, as England's ally, **42.** 496
Austrian-Dutch war may be joined by, **25.** 544
Austria's war with, *see* War, Austrian-Prussian
Belgian convention signed by, **39.** 484n
Cameron supposedly commissioned from, **20.** 384
Catherine II's ambition condemned by England and, **11.** 233

(?) Charles Albert allied with, at France's instigation, to attack Hanover, **18.** 396
Conway visits: to see its army, **24.** 38, 39. 175n, 178; with David Scott, **39.** 537
courier from, **21.** 452
Cours de l'Europe satirizes, **17.** 177
Court of, Williams recalled at wish of, **38.** 393
Danish conspiracy may be instigated by, **23.** 426
defeats of: at Kunersdorf, **30.** 156–7; at Palzig, **30.** 156
Du Deffand, Mme, acquainted with visitors from, **6.** 395
East Friesland claimed by, **18.** 449–50
Elizabeth of Russia drinks destruction to, **21.** 255
England may seek aid from, against Holland, **33.** 337n
—— may substitute, for Austria, as ally, **19.** 238
—— prefers Aranjuez treaty as balance against France and, **20.** 294n
—— promised aid by, **20.** 523
—— resists claims of, on Danzig, **23.** 466n
——'s alliance with: **38.** 1–2; celebrated, **35.** 106; uncertain, **20.** 571
——'s convention with, **19.** 95n
—— should be more allied with, **42.** 495
—— signs Treaty of Westminster with, **37.** 428, 429
——'s joint declaration with, **21.** 355n
——'s reply to, **20.** 362
——'s sole ally, **21.** 84
——'s subsidy to: attacked by Grenville, **22.** 31n; to be opposed by Bunbury, **22.** 8
——'s subsidy treaty with, **21.** 180n, **38.** 7–8
English aid asked by, against Catherine II, **11.** 226–7
English capture ships of, **20.** 348
English diplomatic relations with, **30.** 69, 322
English feel, is almost part of England, **21.** 171
English privateers borrowed by, **21.** 335
English relations with, **19.** 448
English treaty with, alarms French sympathizers, **20.** 528
envoys from and to, *see under* Envoy
Florentines do not favour, **21.** 9
France may aid Turkey against, **25.** 360
—— severs diplomatic relations with, **20.** 589n
—— should protect Holland in concert with, **39.** 429
—— tells Austria and Russia to make peace with, **21.** 497–8
Francis I forbids payment of notes and bonds seized by, in Franconia, **21.** 304n
——'s election to Empire lacked consent of, **42.** 494
Frankfurt and Nuremberg to be punished for recruiting for, **21.** 28–9
Frederick II's death may end power of, **39.** 429

French naval funds diverted to, **20.** 51

French subsidy to, **42.** 495

generals of, beheaded when they misbehave, **37.** 520n

George II demands investigation of claims of, **20.** 348n

—— does not negotiate peace with, **18.** 4–5

——'s negotiations with, demanded by Pulteney for examination, **17.** 250

Gloucester, D. of, might serve in army in, **33.** 32, 35–6, 38

Guelderland occupied by troops of, **39.** 459n

HW calls, transient power, **39.** 429

HW doubts power of, as ally, **11.** 233–4

HW expects partition of France by, **12.** 4

HW expects to see Cts of Coventry as queen of, **38.** 7

HW jokes about Pyrrhus as king of, **38.** 90

HW would be glad to see revolution in, **32.** 184

Hanover may be attacked by, **17.** 202, 208, 316, **20.** 501, **23.** 401

Holland might be divided by, **25.** 539

Hungarian insurgents annihilate regiments of, **19.** 62

Joseph II does not start war with, **24.** 367

—— may fight with, **24.** 364–5

Kunersdorf falsely reported to be victory for, **21.** 331

Legge mismanages affair of, **20.** 39

manifesto of: Mansfield's answer to, **21.** 286; stops payment on Silesian loan, **20.** 348

Mann hopes that peace has been made with, **19.** 95

—— should make peace with, **35.** 32

Maria Theresa demands recompense from, for herself and Frederick Augustus II, **21.** 360n

—— said to have made peace with, **17.** 134

——'s peace with, **19.** 194

—— threatened with war by, unless she consents to Poland's partition, **23.** 439

memorial of, answered by Mansfield, **20.** 362, 365

messenger from, reaches London, **37.** 521

Michel recalled by, **38.** 393

—— secretary of legation of, in London, **20.** 348n

military action expected in, **21.** 71–2

ministers from and to, *see under* Minister

must be contemptuous of western European warfare, **25.** 201

Muzell (Stosch) a baron of, **21.** 380

Newcastle, D. of, delivers refutation of claims of, to Michel, **20.** 348n

officer of, **17.** 206

Peter III likes, **21.** 144n, **22.** 7

Prague evacuated by, **18.** 543

princes of the Empire want Austrian power offset by, **24.** 450

princess of, may wed D. of Cumberland, **18.** 62

privateer of, **21.** 330, 349; see also *Prince Ferdinand*

rescript of, **42.** 497

Russia forbidden by, to aid England, **25.** 39

Russian army again marching towards, **21.** 172

Russian impostor may be sponsored by, **23.** 546–7

Russia refuses to mediate between Austria, Saxony, and, **21.** 53n

——'s campaign against, **21.** 72

—— to send troops against, **21.** 176

Saltykov's action in taking back oath of allegiance for, is disavowed, **22.** 75–6

Saxony and Silesia occupied by, **21.** 271n

Stanley ordered to stop in, **3.** 251n

Stosch from, **17.** 164n

Swedish campaign against, in concert with France, **21.** 119n

Swedish interference with, **23.** 439

troops of: at Memel, prepare against Russians, **21.** 72; Brown advocates battle with, before they reach Prague, **21.** 95n; Königgratz pillaged by, **21.** 229n; money to be voted for, **21.** 261n; *see also* army of

Viennese Court organizes Europe to destroy, **21.** 15

'victory' of, denied by Austrians, **37.** 555–6

Williams, Sir C. H., threatens Russia with attack from, **21.** 53n

Young Pretender to be rescued by, **19.** 311

Prussian; Prussians:

SH visited by, **12.** 246

Prussian cantata. See Cocchi, Signor: *Tempio della gloria*

Pry, Mrs:

SH visited by, **12.** 242

Prydden. *See* Pridden

Prynne, William (1600–69), pamphleteer:

Canterburies Doome, by, **43.** 39

hair-dressing denounced by, **35.** 248–9

Hidden Works of Darkness by, **1.** 11

Laud and, **2.** 12

London mobs reminiscent of, **23.** 19

revolutionary principles of, **11.** 330

'P's, the three':

Irvine, Vcts, toasts, **9.** 207

Psalm; psalms:

at Magdalen House chapel, **9.** 274

Baskerville prints, **40.** 275

Granger makes wrong selection of, **41.** 186–7

HW will never be translator of, **10.** 305

King James version of, **16.** 366

quotations from, *see under* Bible

Psalmanazar, George (b. ca 1679–84, d. 1763) literary impostor:

Chatterton compared with, **16.** 131, **28.** 282

language invented by, **16.** 131

Psalter:

Duane's, illuminated with king's picture, **40.** 247

with Clovis's illuminations, bought by HW at Ds of Portland's sale, **39.** 442, **42.** 165n

Psaltery:
Montagu may strike up, **10**. 223
Pseudo-Dionysius (5th or 6th cent.):
angels classified by, **4**. 421n
Psyche. *See* Cupid and Psyche
Ptisan:
Walpole, Bns (Cts of Orford) takes, to Riche-court, **18**. 66–7
Ptolemy I Sotor (?367–283 B.C.), K. of Egypt 323–283 B.C.:
Euclid discusses geometry with, **31**. 273
Ptolemy (Claudius Ptolomæus) (fl. 127–141 *or* 151), astronomer and geographer:
geography of, **20**. 501
Public, the:
HW's reflections on, **15**. 106
interested only in what is before its eyes, **25**. 331
Public Advertiser:
account in, of Devonshire House robbery, **16**. 204
(?) advertisement in, **34**. 6
announcement in, about *Candide*, **10**. 349, 350
anti-Sejanus letters in, **32**. 20n
Bathurst satirized in, **32**. 61n
Burgoyne parodied and Arnold derided in, **32**. 399n
Chambers attacked in, for panegyric on Somerset House, **17**. 188
collection of public characters in, **28**. 489
Conway, subject of poetic tribute in, by 'Causidicus,' **43**. 290
Cumberland's *Anecdotes* reviewed in, **43**. 76
——'s *Widow of Delphi* described in, **29**. 11–12
'Description of the New Buildings at Somerset House' in, **16**. 187
Draper's pacification plans for America in, **39**. 221
extracts in, from Milles's 'Preliminary Dissertation' to Chatterton's poems, **16**. 238
Gloucester, D. of, guessed by, to be making a political trip, **25**. 164n
Gordon, Lord George, attacks Marie-Antoinette in, **39**. 451n
Grattan's 'Character of Chatham' in, **32**. 177–8
HW reads in, of Horace Mann II's speech, **24**. 450
HW refers Mason to, **29**. 232
HW's advertisement in: of *Mysterious Mother*, **39**. 372; (?) regarding enlarged edition of *Royal and Noble Authors*, **41**. 220–1
HW's contributions to, **13**. 42, **42**. 498–506
HW sends anonymous advertisement to, **42**. 455–6
HW sends list to, of number of copies printed of SH Press publications, **43**. 78–9, 358
HW's letters to, **42**. 498–506
HW's news not as fresh as, **36**. 56
HW's news will not appear in, **33**. 10
HW's undrained field at SH described in, **25**. 146
HW's verses to Conway to be sent to, by Bedford, **40**. 118
Henderson's visit to HW at SH joked about in, **41**. 427n, 455n
Jenkinson's death falsely announced in, **10**. 316
Joseph II's letter to Pius VI in, **33**. 390
Keppel's court martial covered by, **24**. 438n
(?) Luttrell's letter in, **32**. 120n
Mason's letter not printed in, **28**. 260
Milles's edn of Chatterton's poems in extracts in, **43**. 74
Mysterious Mother scene printed in, **33**. 429, **35**. 378–9
Norton attacked in, **23**. 555
—— resents letter in, **32**. 188n
opera news in, describes costume and hair-powdering, **35**. 363
publisher of, *see* Woodfall, Henry Sampson
'Royal Reflections' in, perhaps written by Fitzpatrick, **29**. 32, 50
Scott's attacks on Bute in, **22**. 410n
——'s diatribes in, signed 'Anti-Sejanus,' **22**. 323n
Townsend's election as lord mayor blamed by, on Oliver, **23**. 441n
verses in, on Chesterfield's visit to HW at SH, **43**. 338
widow and orphans advertise plight in, **41**. 384n
Publication:
by numbers, **2**. 78
by subscription, **1**. 155
hazards of, **1**. 151
with contributors to plates, **1**. 160
Public crier. *See* Bellman
Public Devonshire Canal:
bill for, defeated, **34**. 184n
Public house; public houses:
Cholmondeley's regiment not allowed by, to pay, **18**. 408
country magistrates refuse to billet foreign troops in, **21**. 13
English, in Florence, Young Pretender asks permission to use, **24**. 137
Mann looks for Lady William Campbell in, **25**. 272
See also Inn; Tavern
Public Ledger:
HW abused in, for praising the Scots, **38**. 208
Publicola, Antonio, Principe di Santa Croce:
conversazione by, includes D. and Ds of Gloucester, and D. of Saxe-Teschen, **24**. 190n
Publicola, Scipio (d. 1747), Principe di Santa Croce; Charles VI's ambassador extraordinary to the Conclave of 1740:
cantata and ball given by, **17**. 20
Craon, Princesse de, met by, **17**. 3
Craon receives toison d'or from, **17**. 11n, 20
Gages seizes letters of, **18**. 359n

Imperial Court asked by, to let him join Albani faction at Conclave, **37**. 70
Public places:
  HW dislikes, **18**. 231
Public Record Office:
  Conway papers deposited in, **15**. 73n
Public taste:
  HW's low opinion of, **28**. 45–6, 371
Public Virtue:
  (?) Dodsley sends, to HW, **40**. 78
Pucci, Marchesa. *See* Valvasone, Maria Cristina di
Pucci, Signora. *See* Degli Albizzi, Caterina (d. 1750); Valvasone, Maria Cristina di (d. 1747)
Pucci, Domenico (1718–83), Tuscan agent in London:
  anxious to return to Florence, **21**. 180–1
  Botta botches credentials of, **21**. 197
  Francis I orders Botta to accredit, as minister to England, **21**. 180
  letter of, from London to Florence, mentions no Vienna orders, **21**. 116
  Lottinger appointed as successor to, **22**. 215, 345
  Tuscan government notified by, of D. of York's intended visit, **22**. 154n
  uncle succeeded by, **21**. 108n
Pucci, Lorenzo Orazio (1694–1764), senator, 1736:
  (?) Harpur in love with, **37**. 323
  (?) house of, at Pontedera, **22**. 220n
  (?) wife of, **18**. 122
Pucci, Luisa Ninfa (d. 1743), m. (1720) Francesco Gaetano Guicciardini:
  death of, **18**. 138
Pucci, Marchese Orazio Roberto (1730–1802):
  (?) Acciaioli, Signora, the 'flame' of, **20**. 284, **37**. 324, **43**. 270
Pucci, Vincenzo (ca 1675–1757), Tuscan agent in England 1713–57:
  Carteret's retirement predicted by, **18**. 557
  case of Leghorn suicide to be pressed by, at English Court, **20**. 14
  Culloden news announced by, in Florence, **19**. 257
  death of, **21**. 111, 175
  French declaration of war against England sent by, to Florence, **18**. 442
  George II's Hanover trip discussed by, **18**. 213
  ——'s sending for Sir Robert Walpole reported by, **18**. 553
  HW avoids, **17**. *186*
  HW's dealings with, over Riccardi's gems, **19**. 74, 331, 392, 398, 411, 420
  house of, in Grosvenor St, **21**. 111n
  letters of, Lorenzi probably told by, of Mann's baronetcy, **20**. 467
  London papers announce recall of, **21**. 108
  Mann embarrassed by, **18**. 342
  —— encloses letter to, **17**. 307
  —— to answer ill-worded remonstrance by, **18**. 325

Migliorucci, Conte Jacopo, in service of, **20**. 266n
  nephew of, says he is ill, **21**. 116
  recall of, implied by his name joined to Colloredo's in foreign gazettes, **21**. 113–14
  resident in London for 50 years, **21**. 108n
  Riccardi's correspondence with, about game, **19**. 372, 411
  Tornaquinci hears from, of English earthquake, **20**. 143
Pucelle, La. See under Chapelain, Jean; Voltaire
Pucelle d'Orléans, La. See under Voltaire
Puchot, Roland (d. 1755), Comte des Alleurs; French ambassador at Constantinople:
  daughter of, **11**. 88n
  marriage of, **4**. 58n
  marriage of daughter of, **4**. 58–9
  wife of, **3**. 354n
Puchot des Alleurs, Amélie-Constance (ca 1750–1825), m. (1768) Louis-Édouard, Comte de Boufflers (later separated):
  afraid of highwaymen on Hounslow Heath, **11**. 329
  Arles to be visited by, **6**. 349, 355
  Auteuil occupied by, **6**. 67, 469, 472, **7**. 162, 176, 347
  Chanteloup visited by, **6**. 441, 453, **8**. 202
  Craufurd's opinion of, **6**. 485
  Du Deffand, Mme, gives account of, **4**. 58, 106
  ——'s opinion of, **7**. 219
  ——'s relations with, **7**. 102
  family and circumstances of, **4**. 58–9
  Garrick, Mrs, entertains, at dinner, **11**. 329
  HW escorts, through Bushey Park, **11**. 329
  HW has seen, **39**. 323
  HW makes conquest of, **32**. 259
  HW meets, at Ds of Queensberry's, **34**. 121
  HW's dinner for, **11**. 104, 108
  HW visits, **34**. 80, 109
  harp played by, **6**. 363, 469, **11**. 76n, 124, 148, 285, 341
  health of, **5**. 417, 425, 426
  husband takes leave of, in letter from France, **11**. 88
  invited to parties at Richmond, **11**. 148
  Isle-Adam visited by, **6**. 324
  La Tuilerie visited by, **7**. 345
  marriage of, **4**. 58–9, 168, 171
  Moranville brought by, from Richmond to see SH. **39**. 473
  mother-in-law resides with, **3**. 15
  musical talents of, **39**. 223
  Normandy to be visited by, **6**. 462
  Paris visited by, **6**. 453, 467, 493
  Plombières to be visited by, **7**. 53
  Pomme attends, **6**. 349, 355
  Provence visited by, **6**. 367, 441
  Queensberry House visited by, **11**. 341
  Richmond Green house taken by, **11**. 221, **34**. 68, 76
  sings, **6**. 469
  social relations of, in Paris, *see index entries ante* **8**. 480

[Puchot des Alleurs, Amélie, *continued*]
  Spa to be visited by, **7.** 235
  SH visited by, **12.** 236, 237
  teakettle desired by, **6.** 9, 13, 33, 36, 39, 42
  Temple to be occupied by, **6.** 472
  'Trognon, le,' **5.** 69
Puchot des Alleurs, Marie-Sophie (d. 1786), m.
  (1728) Louis-Auguste Sonning:
  marriage of niece of, **4.** 58–9
Puckeridge, Herts:
  road to, **40.** 197
Pudden, Tom:
  dog of, **37.** 26–7
'Pudding, Jack':
  Beaumarchais is, **33.** 537
  proverb on, **33.** 197, **43.** 353
Pudding; puddings:
  black, eaten by Ds of Kingston, **28.** 225
  Devonshires eat, **37.** 341
  English farmers' diet consists of beef and,
    31. 66
  for plain diet, **32.** 191n
  Goldsworthy, Charles, to eat, **17.** 351
  Mann lives upon, **17.** 57
  Mathews's taste for, ridiculed by HW. **18.** 79
  Porter's apprentices have, for Sunday dinner,
    16. 217
  Selwyn eats, **37.** 94
  tansy, **32.** 57, **35.** 125
  See also Bread pudding; Plum pudding
Puddletown. *See* Piddletown
Puebla, Graf von. *See* Portugal, Anton von
Puerperal fever. *See under* Fever
Puerto Cabella:
  Knowles's attack upon, fails, **18.** 279n
Puerto Rico. *See* Porto Rico
Pufendorf, Samuel (1632–94), Freiherr von;
  German jurist and authority on national and
  international law:
  cited in 'The Peach in Brandy,' **32.** 63
  Mann 'laying in such bales of,' **21.** 286
  Turks will be taught to read, **23.** 88
'Puffendorf' (unidentified Etonian):
  West has supper with, **13.** 173–4
  witticism by, **3.** 174
Puff-paste:
  HW scoffs at the French for serving, **13.** 164
'Pug':
  Cambridge beauty, **37.** 27
'Pug.' *See also* Lombard, Marie-Magdelaine,
  Bns Walpole of Wolterton
Pug; pugs (monkeys):
  crucifix tied around neck of, **18.** 59
  dog attacks, **37.** 26–7
  Ds of Argyll's pet, **9.** 367
  HW probably uglier than, **24.** 433
  Indian temple enshrines, **24.** 433
  Talmond, Princesse de, has picture of, **10.** 208
Pugachev ('Pugatscheff'), Emel'ian Ivanovich
  (ca 1742–75), impostor:
  birth date of, corrected, **43.** 284
  Catherine II defeats, **24.** 3

may have contributed to Russo-Turkish peace,
  24. 35
Peter III impersonated by, **23.** 547, **32.** 184
Puget, Hilarion-Paul-François-Bienvenu de
  (1754–1828), Marquis de Barbantane:
  Pisa visited by, **23.** 480
Puget, Joseph-Pierre-Balthazar-Hilaire de
  (1725–ca 1800), Marquis de Barbantane;
  French envoy to Tuscany 1766–84:
  Boufflers, Comtesse de, much connected with,
    22. 434
  Choiseul's disgrace shocks, **23.** 261
  Craon, Princesse de, complains to, **22.** 537
  English victories give Mann right to hold up
    his head to, **24.** 545, **25.** 17, 92
  family of, all at Pisa baths, **23.** 480
  French capture of Jersey wrongly reported
    by, **25.** 127
  French defeat excused by, **25.** 127–8
  French weekly courier takes letters for, **23.** 14
  HW glad to be able to dispel the visitors of,
    25. 73
  La Fayette's alleged letter exhibited by, in
    Florence, **25.** 70
  Leopold ordered by, not to admit English
    ships to Leghorn, **28.** 460–1
  Mann announces English victories to, **25.**
    24, 70–1
  —— argues with, **23.** 278
  —— asked by, for English *Mémoire justifi-
    catif,* **24.** 531
  —— assured by: that Jesuits caused French
    food riots, **24.** 118; that Louis XV will not
    take Mme du Barry, **23.** 90
  —— entertains, at dinner, **22.** 482
  —— forbears to send letters through, to HW,
    23. 317–18
  —— hears from, about Duclos's rage over
    Montesquieu's letters, **22.** 531
  —— hopes to have a chance to tease, **25.** 9
  —— often talks with, but does not exchange
    visits, **24.** 531
  —— on good terms with, **23.** 261
  —— saucily treated by, but avenged by Court
    and town, **25.** 9
  —— sends compliments to, **23.** 141
  —— shown parliament of Paris's anti-Jesuit
    resolutions by, **22.** 519
  ——'s letter from, about *La Belle Perle,* **24.**
    394–5
  —— told by: of way to forward letter to HW,
    22. 557; that wife corresponds with Hume,
    22. 562–3
  monarchical leanings of, **23.** 278
  ombre played by, at Court, **25.** 51n
  plenipotentiary, **23.** 293
  Rosenberg alone called on by, on coming to
    Florence, **22.** 481
  secretary and valet of, *see* Billerey
  snuff-box to have been sent to Mann by,
    probably forgotten, **25.** 206
  social relations of, in Paris, **7.** 308, 309

Tavistock recommends, to Mann, 22. 482
Thurn's letter from, by courier, about Toulon fleet, 24. 394–5
title of, corrected, 43. 280–1
to be French minister at Florence, 22. 445–6
Tuscan titles not acknowledged by, 22. 481
valet-de-chambre of, 28. 461n
wife of: 7. 102n; can forward letters to Hume, 22. 557
Young Pretender persuades, to ask for use of English public house at Florence, 24. 136–7
—— tells, how Mann spoiled his scheme, 25. 526
Puget de Barbantane, Charlotte-Gabrielle-Élisabeth-Aglaé de (ca 1755– ca 1795), m. (1770) Philippe-Antoine de Hunolstein, Comte de Hunolstein:
affairs of, with Chartres, La Fayette, and Jones, 35. 255n
pas de deux at Versailles ball danced by, 32. 255
Puget de Barbantane, Henriette de, m. (1775) Jacques-Anne-Joseph le Prestre, Marquis de Vauban:
breaks arm, 7. 139
La Tuilerie visited by, 7. 345
Pisa visited by, 23. 480
social relations of, in Paris, 7. 345, 351
Pughe, ——, sheriff of London:
Gordon riots mishandled by, 23. 200n
Pugi, ——:
Craon, Princesse de, entertains, 17. 413–14
Pugilists, Grecian:
fighting ladies at the theatre compared to, 11. 9
Pugna Porcorum per P. Porcium Poetam. See under Placentius, Johannes Leo
Puigautier. *See* Pourteiron de Puigautier
Puiguyon. *See* Granges de Puiguyon
Puiset, Hugh de (?1125–95), Bp of Durham; E. of Northumberland:
titles of, 2. 182
Puisieulx, Vicomte ('Marquis') de. *See* Brulart, Louis-Philogène
Puisieulx, Vicomtesse de. *See* Le Tellier de Louvois de Rebenac, Charlotte-Félicité
Pujol, ——, French envoy to Genoa:
France sends, to conciliate Genoa on Corsica, 20. 573n
Pullet; pullets:
at Wentworth Castle, 38. 72
Pulley; pulleys:
Caroline's petticoat has, to pull it up, 38. 110
Pullicat, India:
French Resident at, *see* Raymond, ——
Pulpit:
eagle formed as, 35. 119
in mourning, at Easton Maudit, 10. 339
Pulse:
Albemarle's, felt by his mother, 20. 460
Cocchi's, irregular, 21. 152

Pulteney, Anna Maria (1727–42):
buried in Hatton vault, Westminster Abbey, 10. 68
dances at Robinson's ball, 37. 115
death of, 17. 363, 366
window broken by, unrepaired for four years, 30. 89
Pulteney, Anne (1663–1746), m. 1 (1694) Charles Fitzroy, 1st D. of Cleveland; m. 2 (1733) Philip Southcote:
grandson of, 22. 560n
husband of, 2. 275n
second marriage of, 34. 258
son escapes from, to get birds' nests, 32. 329
Townshend, Lady, jokes about husband's relations with, 30. 11
Pulteney, Frances (1725–82), m. (1760) William Johnstone (later Sir William Pulteney):
pregnant, fat, and not young, 22. 561
Pulteney's bequest to, 3. 365n, 22. 560
Pulteney, Harry (1686–1767), Gen.; M.P.:
death and bequests of, 3. 365, 22. 560–1
HW hopes Conway will not resemble, 10. 252
regiment of: at Culloden, 37. 240; at Perth, 37. 249n
Sackville's court martial avoided by, 21. 366n
wealth of, 10. 252
Pulteney, Henrietta Laura (1766–1808), cr. (1792) Bns and (1803) Cts of Bath, s.j., m. (1794) Sir James Murray Pulteney, Bt:
immune to fortune-hunters, 11. 238
Marble Hill, Twickenham, occupied by, 42. 483
marriage of, 11. 238n
Pulteney's estate may go to, 22. 561
Pulteney, William (1684–1764), cr. (1742) E. of Bath; M.P.:
address against use of Hanover troops discussed in, 18. 158–9
address to George II proposed by, in Parliament, 17. 375–6
Allen, Lady, connected with, 35. 94n
Argyll retorts to, about Scottish taxes, 20. 310–11
—— scolds, 17. 335
army increases supported by, in Parliament, 17. 410
(?) at Chesterfield's assembly, 37. 327
avarice of, 30. 89–90
ballad by Chesterfield and, 31. 415n
ballads satirize, 18. 18–20, 22–4, 49, 71–5, 83, 90–1, 99
Bath visited by, 18. 24, 89
Bathurst's quarrel with, 20. 38
Bolingbroke told anecdote by, 7. 354
Bootle's connection with, 17. 234n, 18. 72
Boyle resembles, in losing power by accepting earldom, 37. 462
bribery practised by, though he talks against corruption, 17. 355
Bristow and Lady Hervey praise SH to, 35. 236

[Pulteney, William (1684–1764), *continued*]
Bristow, friend of, **35.** 236n

brother of, **3.** 365n, **10.** 252n

Brown, Sir Robert, compared with, **10.** 68

Cabinet Council's move to oust Carteret not helped by, **18.** 535–6

'Caleb' nickname of, **18.** 20

Carteret disowns connections with, **20.** 259

—— said to tell George II to grant demands of, **18.** 83

——'s friend, **19.** 167

chancellor of the Exchequer, **19.** 211

chancellorship of Exchequer predicted for, by Gage, **17.** 296

change in ministry must meet approval of, **18.** 147

children of, all dead, **38.** 365

Chudleigh, Elizabeth, befriended by, **35.** 81n

Churchill's promise held by, about Hedon election, **17.** 220–1

—— talks with, **17.** 331

Chute dreams of, **35.** 55

(?) —— has no tenderness for, **35.** 15

Clandestine Marriages Act 'invented' by, **9.** 147, **37.** 361

Cleveland, Ds of, said to be aunt of, **22.** 560n

Colman recommended by, to brother, for Bradford estate, **22.** 560

——'s *Jealous Wife* dedicated to, **16.** 43n

'Congratulatory Letter' to, by (?) Sir C. H. Williams, **30.** 315, **35.** 50

Cope, Sir John, subject of verses by, **14.** 87

Craftsman never written by, **20.** 374

——'s alleged contributor, **13.** 119n

creditor of, points to him in church during sermon on avarice, **19.** 53, 59

Cumberland, D. of, may be injured by, **19.** 347

Cuper's Gardens visited by, **9.** 35

Danvers's witticism on, **17.** 232

daughter of: buried in Hatton Vault, **10.** 68; dies, **17.** 363, 366; keeps him from Parliament by her illness, **17.** 363

deserted, **18.** 89

disinterestedness of, doubtful, considering his greedy followers, **18.** 72

dodges responsibilities of opposing rebels, **19.** 167

Doneraile held by, to voting promise, **17.** 251

Douglas an intimate friend of, **20.** 533

—— lives near London house of, **20.** 533n

earldom may be postponed by, to stay in House of Commons, **17.** 484–5

earldom of Bath granted to, **17.** 467, **37.** 453

epigram by, **30.** 24

epigram on riding accident of, **17.** 437

Epistle from Lord Lovel to Lord Chesterfield by, **37.** 82

faction of, **18.** 550–1

Finch, Lady Isabella, replies to joke by, about giving her a crown, **38.** 359

Fog's and *Mist's* weekly journals influenced by, **18.** 23n

followers of: **18.** 72n; desert to Carteret,

Sandys, and Wilmington, **18.** 74; HW satirizes, **30.** 305

'Fountain' meeting attended by, **17.** 335

—— meeting avoided by, **17.** 436

—— speeches of, satirized, **18.** 91

Frederick, P. of Wales captured by, from Carteret, **19.** 229

—— gains support of, **20.** 3n

—— may deal with, secretly, **20.** 30

—— persuaded by: to make a new Opposition, **19.** 229; to write to George II, **17.** 337, 367

French praise, **22.** 343

Furnese a friend of, **21.** 172n

—— made secretary to Treasury by, **18.** 72, **30.** 305n

Garter may be requested by, **18.** 245

George II denies having offered Privy Seal to, **18.** 231

—— insists on resignation of, from House of Commons before granting places to his followers, **17.** 494

—— instigated by, to refuse Pitt, **19.** 209, 211

—— receives, **20.** 80

——'s appointment of Edgcumbe displeases, **18.** 9

——'s back stairs descended by, **37.** 221

——'s negotiations with Maria Theresa, France, Prussia, and Holland demanded by, for discussion, **17.** 250

——'s reply to, admired by Mann, **18.** 42

—— told by, that House of Commons will not permit new ministry, **19.** 212

—— vainly asked by, for Hill's dismissal, **18.** 24–5

George III asks, to dine with Karl Wilhelm Ferdinand, **38.** 287n

George, P. of Wales (George IV), shoots, with play arrows, **38.** 365

government places dispensed by, **17.** 492–4

Gower joins, at Bath, **18.** 89

—— may be succeeded by, as lord privy seal, **18.** 96

Granville, Cts, entertains, **18.** 527

Gybbon appointed by, **18.** 72

HW and Lady Hervey taken by, to dine with Lady Allen, **35.** 94

HW calls: C. H. Williams's 'friend,' **30.** 92; 'mean exploded miser,' **25.** 8

HW entertained by, **9.** 253

HW expects more from paper by, than from Chesterfield's, **20.** 374

HW gives copy of Hentzner's *Journey* to, **40.** 121

HW learns cost of Rochefort expedition from, **30.** 140

HW mentions, **37.** 418

HW mentions Francklin to, **35.** 94

HW ridicules disinterestedness of, **9.** 394, **18.** 72

HW's allusion to, **35.** 33

HW satirizes, **13.** 14, **18.** 357–8

HW's opinion of, **17.** 220n

HW to dine with, **35.** 111

HW would never pride himself on being richer than, **21.** 57

Hanover troops debate not joined by, **18.** 356

Harrington's refusal to coalesce with, offends George II, **19.** 326n

health of, out of danger though thought to be dying, **38.** 406

Hedon a borough of, **17.** 243n, **19.** 342

—— election concerns, **17.** 220, 355

——'s loss, causes, to rave, **19.** 371

Hervey attacked by, in *A Proper Reply*, **17.** 275n

—— friendly with, at Bath, **18.** 89

—— lives with, **17.** 275

——'s duel with, **29.** 131, **30.** 313, **31.** 416

Hervey, Bns, friendly with, **31.** 416

high bailiff's censure carried by, **17.** 251

Hill opposes, at Hedon, **18.** 24–5

hobbles up back stairs for political purposes, **38.** 365

Hooke governs, **20.** 533

Hooper's flattery of, rewarded with place, **17.** 384n, **30.** 305n

house of, in Arlington St, **13.** 12n, **18.** 231

house of, in Piccadilly: **18.** 231n; broken glass in staircase window of, unrepaired for four years, **30.** 89; Douglas lives near, **20.** 533n; HW's friend lives next door to, **30.** 89; maid's room over staircase in, has no shutters, window- or bed-curtains, **30.** 89–90

House of Lords appeases, by passing Place Bill, **17.** 431

Hussey encouraged by, to attack Sir C. H. Williams, **30.** 312

impartiality professed by, **17.** 454

increase of taxes and stocks attributed to, **18.** 91

Indemnity Bill dispute fomented by, **17.** 429

legatee of many estates, **22.** 277

Leicester's servants receive paltry gratuity from, at Holkham, **19.** 443

Letter to Two Great Men ascribed to: **9.** 270, **16.** 39n; Pembroke, Cts of, discusses, **9.** 270; Piozzi, Mrs, comments on, **9.** 270n

Limerick aided by, **18.** 72n

—— follower of, **30.** 304n

list demanded by, of opposing Hedon electors, **19.** 342

London tavern might satirize, **38.** 137

lord president, **18.** 556

Lovat's trial arouses activity of, **19.** 347

Mann asks about 'disgusts' of, **17.** 455, 476

Marlborough, Ds of, describes intrigue of, to get refusal of Privy Seal, **18.** 231

Marriage Bill invented by, **9.** 147, **37.** 361

ministry of, **9.** 116n

money contributed by, for raising regiment, **21.** 311

money for Maria Theresa's aid proposed by, **17.** 390

name of, stricken from Council Book, **10.** 46n, **22.** 96

neglected by everybody, **9.** 26

Newcastle, D. of, entertains, at Claremont, **17.** 503, **18.** 20

——'s letters from, show anti-government views, **18.** 89n

——'s speech to the Regency parodied by, in a ballad, **19.** 106

new ministry wrecked by association with, **19.** 212

Newport's estate said to have been seized by, **9.** 148

——'s trustee, **9.** 148n

Newton, Bp, aided by, in promise of London see, **38.** 364–5

Newton's life mentions, **2.** 321

odes on, frequent in newspapers, **18.** 90

old age of, degrading, **9.** 348

Onslow's finger commands, **30.** 301

Opposition headed by, **15.** 152n

Orford's coachman drives, home from New Park, **17.** 503, **18.** 22

Orford, Cts of, may intercede with, for Mann, **19.** 310

pamphlet inspired by, **16.** 39n

paper on Newmarket contributed by, to *The World*, **20.** 374

Paris visited by, **20.** 155, **22.** 343n

Parliamentary bill proposed by, on returning officers and regulating elections, **17.** 484

Parliamentary disputes quelled by, **17.** 355

Parliamentary motion by, for examination of foreign negotiations, **17.** 250

Parliamentary speech by, against Sir Robert Walpole, **37.** 91

party betrayed by, **17.** 329n

patent of Bath earldom trampled by, on entering House of Lords, **17.** 485n

Patriot days of, **20.** 257

Patriots abuse, **20.** 31

—— led by, in Parliament, **17.** 231

Pearce made dean of Winchester by, **18.** 319

—— recommended by, to Newcastle, for bishopric of Peterborough, **43.** 251

peerage of, unpopular like Bns Chatham's, **38.** 131

Pelhams offended, **20.** 3n

Pitt as venal as, **21.** 541

pocket of, picked, **9.** 35

Politics on Both Sides, The, by, **16.** 39n

pretends to join Tories and Whigs, **18.** 49–50

privy councillor though not office-holder, **20.** 80n

Privy Seal aspirations of, **18.** 70, 89, 231

—— may be refused by, **18.** 159

proclamation offering reward for Young Pretender's capture not signed by, **30.** 92

Proper Reply to a Late Scurrilous Libel, A, by, **16.** 39n, **43.** 242

refuses to be lord chancellor, **18.** 72

Regency Bill defended by, **20.** 257

regent, **18.** 209

'rhapsody' of, *see* Douglas, John: *Letter Addressed to Two Great Men, A*

[Pulteney, William (1684–1764), *continued*]
Richecourt astonished at conduct of, 18. 10
riding accident of, 17. 437
Rushout's valet sent by, to Hanau, 18. 299
Rushout to be representative of, 17. 333
Sackvilles not to vote for, 17. 221
Sandys's advancement by, satirized, 18. 91
Scrope examined by, 17. 458
Secret Committee motion not introduced by, 17. 375
—— proposed by, 17. 297–8
son of: bequests by, scornfully ignored, 22. 146; buried in Hatton vault, 10. 68; dies, 22. 121
son persuaded by, to change sides on plate tax, 37. 446n
son's extravagance deplored by, to Fanshawe, 10. 68
son's farewell letter to, 9. 148
son's marriage broken off by, 9. 147–8
Spa to be visited by, 20. 80
Stafford formerly the creature of, 20. 9
SH described by, in verses, 9. 168–9, 189, 28. 442, 35. 236–7
tavern sign to show Pitt and, embracing, 38. 137
Townshend, Vcts, ridicules, 18. 277
—— said to be wooed by, 38. 365
Treasury and Exchequer posts given to, 19. 211
Treasury appointees of, called 'dishclouts,' 18. 350
Treasury aspirations of, 18. 265
Treasury post coveted but not accepted by, 19. 212
Treasury post not thought appropriate for, 18. 277
Treasury post refused by, 17. 258n, 18. 72
Treasury post requested by, through Rushout's valet, 18. 299
triumph of, over Sir Robert Walpole, satirized, 18. 91
Tunbridge Wells visited by, 30. 92
Tyrawley's comment on, 18. 104
'unresolved,' 18. 327–8
unsealed letters mailed by, 37. 568
Utrecht, Peace of, described by, 7. 354
Vane, 'creature' of, and owes office to him, 30. 303n
—— receives position through, 18. 72
—— 'toad-eater' to, 17. 487
Vernon's correspondence with, 19. 459–60
verses attributed to, 37. 82
virtue vaunted by, 25. 8
Walpole, Bns (Cts of Orford), turns against 18. 99
Walpole, Sir Robert, answers speech of, 17. 231–2
—— attacked by, 16. 39, 37. 91
—— attacks, 17. 297
—— enemy of, 2. 126, 9. 348
—— excluded, 25. 605

—— induces George II to give peerage to, 17. 485n, 34. 148
—— jokes about, 18. 25
—— might have been executed by, 20. 65
—— not openly demanded by, for impeachment, 17. 328–9, 336
wealth of, has no heir, 22. 121
Westminster petition presented by, 17. 232–3
whist played by, at Richmond Green, 20. 63–4
Whitefield's preaching heard by, 9. 74
White's Club member, 20. 63
wife of: 9. 35n, 20. 496; buried in Hatton vault, 10. 68; said to receive bribes for posts he hands out, 18. 72–3
Williams, Sir C. H. compares Peg Woffington to, 30. 52n
—— fond of anecdotes concerning, 30. 89
—— satirizes, 18. 22n, 319–21, 30. 314–15, 319
'Will' the nickname of, 22. 277
Winchilsea called on by, 19. 53
Winnington gives altered verses by C. H. Williams to, who shows them to Frederick, P. of Wales, 30. 317
witticisms by: on retention of Fox (but not Pitt) in ministry, 35. 199; on Wall's motto, 35. 94; to Chesterfield on being lean and deaf, 37. 474
World contributions by, 20. 374, 395n, 400n
Pulteney, (before 1767, Johnstone), Sir William (1729–1805), 5th Bt, 1794; M.P.:
daughter of, 11. 238n
HW hopes, will protect Mrs Alison, 33. 446
India House orator, 22. 561
London reached by, from Paris, with naval news, 25. 336n
Pulteney, Frances, risks all by marrying, 22. 560
Pulteney, William (ca 1731–63), styled Vct Pulteney; M.P.:
(?) at Chesterfield's assembly, 37. 327
buried in Hatton vault, Westminster Abbey, 10. 68
Chudleigh, Elizabeth, hears Vcts Townshend's stories about herself from, 9. 148
death of, at Madrid on return from Portugal, 22. 121
Douglas, John, tutor to, 20. 533n
father deplores extravagance of, to Fanshawe, 10. 68
father persuades, to change sides on plate tax, 37. 446n
father said to have broken off marriage of, 9. 147–8
father scorns bequests of, to cousins, 22. 146
father's only child after death of sister, 17. 366
father to spend winter in Paris for benefit of, 20. 155n
fits discussed by, at Vcts Townshend's, 35. 80–1
Florence visited by, 20. 174

HW told by, about Bower's persecutors, **20.** 533

Hamilton and guests discuss, at Bushey Park, **9.** 380

Jacobite antiquary recommended to, in Rome, **20.** 174

Leicester's servants receive paltry gratuity from, at Holkham, **19.** 443

mother said to have broken off marriage of, **9.** 148

Nicoll, Frances, engaged to, **9.** 148

political parties shunned by, **20.** 174

regiment may be raised by, for Col. Craufurd, **21.** 311

regiment of, looks like knave of clubs, **38.** 40

runs away to France, **9.** 147–8

Townshend, Vcts, hates, for repeating her stories, **9.** 148

—— incites, to desert his parents, **9.** 148

—— quoted by, about D. of Kingston and Miss Chudleigh, **35.** 81

Pulteney, Mrs William. *See* Gumley, Anna Maria (ca 1694–1758); Pulteney, Frances (1725–82)

Pulteney family:

Granville, Cts, entertains, **18.** 527

Hooke governs, **20.** 533

parsimony of, **19.** 443

Pulteney St, London:

fire in, **40.** 270n

Pultney. *See* Pulteney

Pump; pumps:

at Pisa baths, Gustav III exercises broken arm on, **25.** 442

garden channel watered from, **35.** 126

Sisson designs machine for, **21.** 348, 354, 359–60, 375–6, 384, 390, 407, 414, 430, 432–3

Pumps (footwear):

'double-channeled,' **35.** 209

Pun; puns:

assisted by ambiguities in Hebrew and Chinese, **33.** 26

bad: in Éon's book, **38.** 356; uncommon in French books, **38.** 356

Churchill translates, from jest-books, **18.** 131, 307

HW's, in French, on 'Bienassise,' **5.** 398

HW's, in Latin, about Pygmalion, **39.** 460

HW's on: 'Air,' **33.** 73; 'fair,' **32.** 354; Gooderes, **11.** 124; 'Man-n,' **24.** 144; Minifie, **11.** 123; Miss Pope, **33.** 407; nephews-in-law, **11.** 119; ratifications, **32.** 403; riding of Yorkshire, **12.** 74; water-colour, **11.** 125

HW's 'Saxon' on Witenagemot, **39.** 207, 219

Jenyns makes, on Campbells, **11.** 181

on Cotton, **34.** 260

on Eurydice, **17.** 171–2

on Fordyce, **23.** 418

on Lady Sandys, **19.** 28

on Milan, **20.** 159

on Radclyffe, **19.** 380

Townshend's, on 'mermaid,' **21.** 66

Whithed's, on Spain and Young Pretender, **19.** 97

Winnington's, on Horatio Walpole (1678–1757), **19.** 28

Young addicted to, **41.** 7

Puna (India):

Bombay governor seeks to install new governor at, **24.** 509

Punch (beverage):

arrack, **40.** 9

at Cambridge banquet, **20.** 83

bawds prepare, with aphrodisiacs, **30.** 309

English visitors at Tuscan courts always get a bowl of, **22.** 430

George I and Sir Robert Walpole consume, at New Park, **20.** 455

Leopold's comptroller serves, to Cowper and Tylney, **22.** 379

Londoners to drink, to celebrate Cherbourg's capture, **21.** 227

Montagu serves, **10.** 144

Pyrrhus reluctant to enjoy, **38.** 90

Punch (the puppet):

Beaumarchais might as well moralize as, **33.** 537

North, Lord, and, **33.** 328

Punch bowl:

Choiseul gives, to Mme du Deffand, **4.** 7, 7–8

Du Deffand, Mme, leaves, to Beauvau, **8.** 7, 26

Pomfret's dream about, **17.** 35n

Pupille, La. See under Fagan, Christophe-Barthélemy

Pupilli:

Del Benino, put under, by wife, **17.** 122

Puppet; puppets:

young people resemble, HW thinks, **39.** 296

Puppet-show; puppet-shows:

at Southwark Fair, **32.** 108n

Berry, Mary, not eager for, **11.** 254

Boyle Farm will become, **42.** 197

Foote's 'Handsome Housemaid or Piety in Pattens,' **32.** 97

HW and Mme du Deffand to see, in Paris, **35.** 121

HW compares Court to, **9.** 311

HW compares Coronation to, **38.** 127

HW has less curiosity about ministers than about, **32.** 238

HW's name for London sights, **34.** 3

in Corso de' Tintori, at Florence, **17.** 202

last trumpet would be ascribed to, by London clubmen, **20.** 131

new, at Drury Lane, **38.** 211

of imposition, Dr Graham's called, **33.** 217

Patagonian, Mann calls promenade of ladies, **25.** 174

piece written for, by Mme du Deffand's protégé, **35.** 121

'puppet-show Parnassus' at Batheaston, **32.** 221

Richmond regatta compared to, **32.** 318

[Puppet-show; puppet-shows, *continued*]
Russel's, **19.** 28
vogue for, in France, **20.** 483
Puppy; puppies:
George II's term for D. of Newcastle, **18.** 535
Montagu jokes about, **10.** 189
St Leger called 'romping greyhound puppy,' by HW, **20.** 64
Purbeck, Vcts. *See* Burgh, Lady Margaret de (d. 1698)
Purblindness:
occurrence of, **21.** 443
Purcell, Mrs:
Louisa, Ps, provided by, with wedding clothes, **18.** 278n
Purcell, Henry (ca 1658–95), composer; organist:
Clive, Mrs, to sing songs of, to Montagu, **9.** 375
Dioclesian has music by, **18.** 565n
'God Save the King,' by, **16.** 296n
King Arthur by, described by Gray, **13.** 96–8
mad songs of, sung by Gamon, **33.** 42
Montagu likes, **9.** 375
music by, for Dryden's *King Arthur*, **31.** 152
Purchas, John (fl. 1780), brewer; alderman:
presents petition, **2.** 207
Purchas, Samuel (ca 1575–1626):
Purchas his Pilgrimes by, prints De La Warr's *Relation*, **16.** 140
Purchis, Mr, of Richmond:
SH visited by, **12.** 237
Purea. *See* Tevahine
Purgatory:
Riccardi has masses said for souls in, **21.** 435
Purge; purges:
Wettenhall, Mrs, addicted to, **9.** 231
Purging:
instances of, **19.** 250, **20.** 175, **36.** 126
Puritan; Puritans:
bowing at name of Jesus opposed by, **17.** 3n
Court idolatry of, **2.** 96, 99
Puritanism:
HW accuses Hannah More of, **31.** 260–1
Purkis, Rev. William (d. 1791):
Cole's account of, **1.** 361–2
print of, **1.** 361
Purnell, John (ca 1708–64), warden of New College 1740–64; vice-chancellor of Oxford 1747–50:
may be tried for treason, **20.** 6
Privy Council disputes over trial of, **20.** 18
Purple fever:
Goldsmith dies of, **28.** 144
Purry, Mr, Lisbon merchant:
cash of, saved in Lisbon earthquake, **20.** 520n
Purry, Mellish, and De Visme:
firm of, **11.** 160n
Purse, James:
pardoned, **25.** 67n
Purse; purses:
Chute dreams, is around Venus's neck, **35.** 55
endowing, out of fashion at weddings, **11.** 255
extra, with bad money for robbers, **33.** 296
Gloucester, D. of, robbed of, **35.** 505
gold-wrought, Sir Nathan Wright's, **10.** 332
in Digby portrait, **10.** 333
Maclaine's lodgings contain, **20.** 169
orange-coloured, presented to Williams, **38.** 512
Ossory, Lady, gives, to HW, **33.** 157, 271, 434
—— tells HW to watch, in good company, **33.** 407
pope gives, to man who pretended knowing art of making gold, **33.** 157
regulation of, in ecclesiastical costume, **41.** 223
travellers carry two, one for robbers, **33.** 296n
velvet, blue, in wagon brought by Henrietta Hotham to Cts Temple, **10.** 116
Purser, John (d. 1771), printer:
Old England printed by, **13.** 18
Purser, ship's:
Prole is, **35.** 41
Pursuivant; pursuivants:
HW is, to Harcourt family, **35.** 486, 491
Worcester, M. of, had, instead of a herald, **40.** 179
Pursuivant-at-arms. *See* Lodge, Edmund
Pusey, Hugh de. *See* Puiset, Hugh de
Pushkin. *See* Musin Pushkin
Push-pin:
HW might play at, **29.** 135
'Puss':
Ds of Argyll's pet, **9.** 367
Putello:
Ulysses acted by, in opera, **19.** 355
voice lost by, at Naples, **19.** 355
Putnam, Maj.-Gen. Israel (1718–90), American Revolutionary officer:
Cornwallis defeated by, **32.** 367n
Gage might be executed in place of, **28.** 219
Howe and Clinton now equalled by, **41.** 401
Long Island defeat of, **24.** 249
Putney, near London:
Aylesford, Cts of, gives ball at, **33.** 283
bowling-green at, Maclaine and officer quarrel at, **20.** 168–9
Craven, Bns, builds cottage near, **41.** 404n
Edwin, Lady Charlotte, has house near, **31.** 193n
Faringtons pass by, **15.** 317
Grosley places SH at, **28.** 269
Hertford dies at Lady Lincoln's house at, **39.** 509n
Lincoln, Lady, has house at, **11.** 323, **12.** 158, **36.** 245, **39.** 509n
Lorenzi visits Mirepoix at, **20.** 87
Lysons, Daniel, from, **12.** 144n, 207
miniatures stolen from house at, **39.** 416
Mirepoix family moves to, **20.** 87n
Vanneck's villa at, **28.** 406n
Wood's tombstone at, **41.** 245–9, 254–5, 307–8, 317–18
Putney Common:
Lincoln, Cts of, has house on, **36.** 245
Pigou lives on, **12.** 36n

Putney Lane:
Herbert Lodge in, **39**. 285
Putrid fever. *See under* Fever
Putrid sore throat:
epidemic of, in London, **28**. 354
Puttenham, George (d. 1590):
Arte of English Poesie, The, by: Elizabeth, Q., complimented in, **16**. 366; Elizabeth's sonnet in, **16**. 365; HW has, **40**. 175; Vaux's sonnet in, **16**. 366
Puy, Le. *See* Le Puy
Puy-de-Dôme, France:
Bancal des Issards from, **12**. 1n
Puyguilhem, Comte de. *See* Chapt de Rastignac, Pierre-Louis
Puyguilhem, Comtesse de. *See* Du Lau d'Allemans, Suzanne-Anne
Puyguions. *See* Puyguilhem
Puyol, Signor:
Courcy receives order from, **20**. 353n
Puységur, Abbé de. *See* Chastenet, Jean-Auguste de
Puységur, Comte de. *See* Chastenet, Louis-Pierre de
Puységur, Marquis de. *See* Chastenet, Jacques-François-Maxime de
Puységur, Vicomte de. *See* Chastenet, Barthélemi-Athanase-Hercule de
Puzin de la Martinière, Françoise-Albine, m. —— Benoist:
Élisabeth by, owned by Mme du Deffand, **8**. 33
Puzzuolo (Italy):
Mann, Lady Lucy, not benefited by air of, **24**. 203
—— was to have been taken to, to breathe sulphur, **24**. 190
Pye, Elizabeth, m. (1744) Sir Willoughby Aston, 5th Bt:
social relations of, in Paris, **7**. 271
Pye, Henry (1709–66), of Faringdon, Berks:
death of, **7**. 397
Pye, Mrs Robert Hampden. *See* Mendez, Jael
Pye, Adm. Sir Thomas (ca 1713–85), commander-in-chief at Portsmouth:
Sandwich notified by, of fleet at Portsmouth, **23**. 475n
Pygmalion, mythological king:
Galatea's statue by, **35**. 343–4
HW's Latin poem about, **39**. 460
well-sounding name for Oberon, **39**. 461
Pygmalion. See under Rousseau, Jean-Jacques
Pylades:
Count Rice called, **33**. 72
HW and Mann compared to Orestes and, **22**. 274, **23**. 309, **24**. 283, **25**. 5, 9, 312, 615
HW refers to Churchill, the poet, as, **38**. 234
HW's name for Pitt, **35**. 76
Pyle, Rev. Edmund (1702–76):
letter of, mentions HW, **13**. 27n
tells of Townshend-Orme elopement, **9**. 188n
Pym, John (1584–1643), Parliamentary statesman; M.P.:
burgess for Tavistock, **16**. 65

HW identifies, **30**. 304n
HW wrathful at, as cause of melting down royal 'baubles,' **32**. 324
perished before his cause succeeded, **23**. 200
portrait of, in Onslow's library, **30**. 304n
print of, **16**. 65
Pym, Priscilla (1724–71), m. (1742) Robert Marsham, 2d Bn Romney:
HW has seen, in her 'moods,' **25**. 424
(?) HW mentions, **14**. 120
Pyne. *See* Pine
Pynsent, Lady. *See* Jennings, Mary
Pynsent, Eleanor *or* Leonora Ann (d. 1763):
father's alleged incest with, **38**. 493n
(?) 'femme de cinquante ans,' **3**. 64
Pynsent, Sir William (ca 1679–1765), 2d Bt, 1719; M.P.:
biographical information about, corrected, **43**. 279, 320, 347
Conway to have been in will of, if Pitt did not survive, **38**. 501, 506
generosity of, unequalled outside England, **22**. 280–1
housekeeper of, keeps will, **22**. 276–7
North expects bequest from, **38**. 493
old Whig baronet, **22**. 284
Pitt (Chatham) 'adopted' by, **30**. 217
—— and, confused by HW, **32**. 18
——'s bequest from, **1**. 112n, **22**. 276–7, 284, **38**. 493
—— sells most of estate of, **39**. 95
Somersetshire scandals about incest by, **38**. 493
Utrecht treaty opposed by, **22**. 277, 284
Pynsent. *See also* Burton Pynsent
Pynson, Richard (d. 1530):
Chaucer edition published by, **29**. 163n
Pyramid; pyramids:
at Mereworth, is grotto and greenhouse, **35**. 143
Egyptian: HW's reflections on, **33**. 286, **34**. 206; people wished to last forever in, **12**. 208; travellers to, **11**. 358
on monument at Peterborough, **10**. 347
'Pyrenees, our':
HW's term for English Channel, **25**. 590
Pyrenees, the:
Juliac, Mme de, lives in, **10**. 156
Pyrgo:
royal mansion at, **28**. 318n
Pyrmont:
Conway and Scott visit, **39**. 537
Conway to have visited, **21**. 549
Pyrrha:
present generation might have been tossed aside by, **33**. 456
Pyrrhonisme de l'histoire, Le. See under Voltaire
Pyrrhus (ca 318–272 B.C.), K. of Epirus:
HW paraphrases conversation of, with Cineas. from Plutarch, **31**. 160–1
HW quotes, **35**. 299
'victories' of, **17**. 233

[Pyrrhus, *continued*]
world conquest must precede pleasures of, **38.** 90

Pythagoras (582–ca 507 B.C.), Greek philospher:
belief of, in transmigration of souls, **32.** 80–1
bluestockings not of the school of, **33.** 446
called 'Peter Gower,' **1.** 256, 263, **39.** 158
diet of, **18.** 567
HW compares himself to, **12.** 33, **25.** 559
HW more of a philosopher than, **37.** 259
HW quotes, **9.** 40
life compared by, to Olympic games, **14.** 12
Montagu mentions, **10.** 211
—— not silent enough for, **37.** 258
travelled to Egypt, **33.** 399
voyages of, **31.** 160

'Pythagoras's School':
Merton College owns, **43.** 57

Pyttes, Nicholas (fl. 1470), vicar of St Mary Redcliff, Bristol:
sepulchre presented to, **16.** 133n

Pyx box:
Carmey's, offered to HW, **40.** 259

Q

Quack; quacks:
Craufurd employs, **32.** 267, 271
HW considers Le Fevre to be, **23.** 251
HW prefers, to doctors, **21.** 378
HW's comparison of Rousseau with, **41.** 15
HW's reflections on, **15.** 270
Mann averse to, **21.** 386
testimonials to, in newspapers, **21.** 132
Thompson called, **19.** 249
See also Rock, Dr Richard; Ward, Joshua
See also under Physician

Quack drops:
Orford takes, **36.** 332, 333

Quack oculist. *See under* Oculist

Quack remedies:
plaster for cancers, **20.** 291

Quadri, Giovanni Lodovico:
sun tables of, **17.** 32n

Quadrille (dance):
at 11 P.M., **32.** 205
costumes for, **32.** 96, 101–2, 110–12
danced: at Duc de Guines's ball, **32.** 96, 101–2, 109n, 110–12, 117; at French Court, **6.** 148
of the seasons, at Lord Stanley's ball, **32.** 115–16

Quadrille (game):
ballad on, **32.** 96
Conway to steal HW from his games of, **37.** 301
discussed at Reims, **13.** 178
Florentine society's chief diversion, **20.** 115
HW pities Mme Sarrazin's craving for, **18.** 148
Mann gets up party of, for Stanley, **22.** 326
matadors in, **28.** 479
matrons addicted to, **37.** 126

médiateur: Craon plays, incessantly, **18.** 101; played, **18.** 122, 329; Sarrazin, Mme, forces Mann, Chute, and Whithed to play, **18.** 132, 148; Sarrazin, Mme, languishes for, **18.** 329
played: **9.** 331, 369, 375, **10.** 94, **17.** 483; at Lady Blandford's **31.** 180, 181, **32.** 295n; at SH assembly, **33.** 61n; for half-crowns, **31.** 180, **32.** 295n
Sarrazin, Mme, will not be able to afford, **18.** 361–2
'vole' term used in, **17.** 188n

Quadruple Alliance:
HW's, at Eton, *see under* Eton College
HW's name for authors of *Florence Miscellany*, **25.** 635
Holland obliged by, to supply troops if Protestant succession is threatened in England, **21.** 298n
Old Pretender's claims rejected by terms of, **19.** 481–2

Quai; quais. *See under* Paris; *see also under* Quay

Quail:
at Sandywell, **37.** 107
Old Pretender's sons pretend to shoot, **17.** 13

Quaker; Quakers:
Barnard, Anna, is, **33.** 568
book by two, confined at Malta, **1.** 251–2, 253
Christianity exhibited in actions of, **31.** 351
costume of, 'frightful,' **31.** 350
Dashkov, Ps, and, **39.** 132
doffs hat to Karl Wilhelm Ferdinand at Chelmsford, **22.** 197
Du Deffand, Mme, mentions, **4.** 301
Élie de Beaumont visits, **38.** 461
hats of, broad-brimmed, **31.** 351
Irish, Hertford's compliments from, **39.** 26
meeting of, loo party resembles, **39.** 208
More, Hannah, admires, **31.** 350–1
—— jokes about HW's turning, **31.** 351
of Philadelphia, **28.** 284
old, Fordyce's request for loan refused by, **23.** 418
Orange, P. of, addressed by, at Bath, with their hats on, **24.** 53n
Penn an adherent of, **20.** 20
Porteus as good as, **31.** 351
Provence, Comte de, and Comte d'Artois entertain, with his hat on, **24.** 53, **32.** 212
shipowner, tells his captain to shed no blood, **21.** 264
slave girl rescued and protected by, **31.** 350
worship of, conducted in silence, **31.** 350

Quaker Bill. *See under* Parliament: acts of

Quakerism:
HW has, in his composition, **25.** 40
Penn, William, converted to, **20.** 20n

Quaker meeting:
Dashkov, Ps, attends, **23.** 249

Qualification Bill. *See under* Parliament: acts of

Quality St. *See under* Leith

Quand Biron voulut danser:
quadrille dancers will dance to, **32**. 102
Quand Moïse fit défense:
verses to air of, **7**. 214
Quane, Mrs Richard. *See* Roach, Deodata
Quantz, Johann Joachim (1697–1773):
Frederick II studies the flute under, **14**. 26n
Quarantine:
Admiralty excuses *Pembroke* from, **18**. 282
at Leghorn, lasts 25 days, **25**. 42
cardinals' congregation lifts, **18**. 287n
Cellini's chest performs, **23**. 421
Conway 12 days in, in Italy, **37**. 318
couriers perform, **18**. 297
Ecclesiastical State's, in reprisal for Tuscany's, **18**. 256n
English, for Mediterranean vessels, **18**. 276n
Florentine courier would have to perform, before reaching Genoa, **18**. 375, 376
for plague-stricken crew, **17**. 105
George III's proclamation about, **33**. 409n
HW's cows to perform, in Conway's rosary field, **37**. 345
HW's difficulties with, over Domenichino painting, **18**. 291
HW's pictures listed in orders for, **18**. 282n
HW's present to Mann has to go through, **18**. 406
iris roots detained in, **23**. 362
Lanfranco picture cannot come from Rome because of, **18**. 297
length of, 40 days, **18**. 275
letters from Rome delayed because of, **18**. 282
letters received by sea at Leghorn subject to, **24**. 461
Mann not to bother with shipments during, **18**. 318
—— protests against, for the *Oxford*, **18**. 309n
Mathews complains of difficulties of, **18**. 279, 300
Mediterranean vessels perform, at Standgate Creek, **18**. 276n
Montagu, Lady Mary Wortley, should be in, for dirt, **21**. 540
O'Hara, Gen., undergoes, **11**. 201
on Venetian borders, **18**. 122
Pembroke, the, to perform, **18**. 275, 282
Rome sets up, against the plague, **18**. 263n
ship from England performs, at Leghorn, **22**. 108–9
ships from Sicily perform, before Gravesend, **18**. 276n
travellers from Syria perform, **35**. 521
Tuscan: creates only confusion and taxes, **18**. 295; for persons, merchandise, and vessels, from papal states, **18**. 256n; regulations for English ships, **18**. 284n
Tuscan regency admits English warships under, **18**. 309n
See also under Measles; Smallpox
Quaratesi, Giovanni Francesco (1696–1761), senator, 1736:

annuity to be paid to, as Electress's executor, **18**. 168–9
Quarendon, Vct. *See* Lee, George Henry
Quarendon:
Lee, Sir Henry, buried at, **42**. 199n
Quaresima:
beginning of, **17**. 316
Quarles, Francis (1592–1644), poet:
Charles I said to have pensioned, **41**. 191
Divine Fancies by, **13**. 92
Emblems by, **13**. 187
HW's opinion of, **1**. 379
Milton temporarily less popular than, **9**. 215
Quarles, John:
print of, **40**. 236
Quarrel; quarrels:
HW's reflections on, **10**. 140, 205
Quarry; quarries:
all west Yorkshire is, **35**. 270
for granite, Bentley proposes renting, **35**. 191
in Yorkshire for Gothic builders, **35**. 266
Vanbrugh 'dealt in,' **24**. 93
Quartan fever. *See under* Fever
Quartering (of government places):
Parliament might complain about, **24**. 276–7
Quartering Bill. *See under* Parliament: acts of
Quarterings, armorial:
arms of princely families always have, **41**. 431
HW collects, at SH, **20**. 372
HW hopes Anne Seymour Conway does not return from Germany with, **38**. 155
mansions of old families should be powdered with, **41**. 361
Quarterly Review:
Gifford edits, **12**. 62n
Quartermaster; quartermasters:
Wade captures, on way to Carlisle, **19**. 167
Quartermaster-General:
Cuninghame becomes, **37**. 582
Quarter sessions:
Byron's murder of Chaworth worthy to be tried in, **22**. 284
Waldegraves busy with, **36**. 240
Quatre Facardins, Les. *See under* Hamilton, Anthony
Quatre-fils, Rue du:
Soubise, Hôtel de, near, **7**. 283n
Quatre Nations. *See* Collège des Quatre Nations
Quay. *See* Du Quesne
Quay; quays:
Rotterdam's, **37**. 134
See also Quai
Que. *See* Kew
Quebec:
Acland, Lady Christian, visits, **32**. 402
American campaigns depend on capture of, **21**. 335
Amherst covets coal mines of, **23**. 49
Bussy refuses to illuminate house for success at, **38**. 97
campaign at, said to be a ruse to divert Russians from Frederick II, **21**. 335–6
capture of, **21**. 337, **28**. 411, **38**. 37

[Quebec, *continued*]

capture of, expected, **21.** 301, 327, **24.** 157, 161, 175, 194, 205, 347

Carleton must retire to, **24.** 263

—— repulses Americans at, **24.** 215

—— sends news from, **24.** 339–40

Drummond, Colin, of, **11.** 135n

Edward Augustus asks to be sent to, **38.** 1

England would not exchange Carrickfergus for, **21.** 371

English army in, estimated, **24.** 347n

English fleet for, mostly captured, **36.** 177n

expedition to, **21.** 266–7, **38.** 1

fate of, dubious, **41.** 314

French Court receives news of loss of, **21.** 357

French may recapture, **21.** 416, **38.** 56–7

French victory at, alleged, **21.** 342–3, 344, **22.** 21–2

garrison of, slender, **24.** 347

HW expects, to fall, **32.** 400

HW knows no details of capture of, **35.** 297

HW prepares Mann for probable English defeat at, **21.** 335–6

Haldimand governor of, **28.** 332

Jesuits return from Montreal to college at, **22.** 233n

Johnston, gov. of, **9.** 28n

Lévis defeats English but does not retake, **21.** 357n

Lorenzi stresses possible recapture of, **21.** 421

Mann hopes for onslaught upon, **21.** 270

—— pleased by French disappointment at, **21.** 426

—— reminds Botta of false rumours about, **22.** 89

——'s joy over capture of, **21.** 342

Montgomery's attack on, said to have failed, **24.** 185

New England forces may attack, **24.** 342

provisions at, too scanty for English prisoners, **21.** 18

Richmond's motions for civil regulation of, **41.** 84n

rumours of loss of, **28.** 227

saved, **21.** 419, **32.** 286

scalps from, **31.** 22

siege of, raised, **15.** 71, **38.** 60

surrenders to Townshend, **22.** 16

Syrène arrives at Brest from, **21.** 230n

Townshend, George, has no more contributed to loss of, than to its capture, **38.** 57

—— shares in capture of, **40.** 168

—— takes command at, **9.** 253n

Vaudreuil hopes to regain, **21.** 357–8, 421

well victualled and defended, **21.** 336

Wolfe might be attacked for plan of taking, **38.** 69

—— recommended to Amherst by officers at Louisbourg to command expedition to, **21.** 267n

Wolfe's and Saunders's force against, **21.** 306n

Wolfe's landing near, reported, **21.** 327n

——'s situation at, comparable to Conway's at Rochefort, **38.** 38–9

Quebec, English frigate:

news brought by, **25.** 254n

Quebec Bill; Quebec Government Bill. *See under* Parliament: acts of

Queen, The, English ship:

Prescott commands, **33.** 424n

Queen; queens:

'contending,' quotation about, **33.** 166

HW's reflections on, **31.** 246

Queen Anne St, Cavendish Sq.:

Goodenough lives near Malone in, **33.** 308n

Paine lives in, **32.** 343n

Queen Anne St. *See also* Little Queen Anne St

Queen Anne St East:

Malone's address, **42.** 138

Queen Anne St West, Cavendish Sq.:

Fitzherbert lived in, **32.** 73n

Queen Anne's War:

joke in, about Peterborough hunting in Spain for his army, **18.** 180, **24.** 482

See also under War: English-French

Queenborough:

Rawlinson, M.P. for, **1.** 161, **43.** 54

Queenborough Castle:

constables of, **35.** 141–2

'Queen Eleanor's Confession,' ballad of:

Keith quotes, about interview with George II, **42.** 414

'Queen Elizabeth's Giant Porter.' *See under* Zuccari, Federico

Queenhithe:

in ballad of Eleanor of Castile, **9.** 256, **32.** 348

Queen's Arms, St Paul's churchyard:

Paoli's birthday celebrated in, **23.** 31n

Queensberry, Ds of. *See* Hyde, Lady Catherine (ca 1701–77); Montagu, Elizabeth (1743–1827)

Queensberry, D. of. *See* Douglas, Charles (1698–1778); Douglas, William (1725–1810); Scott, Henry (1746–1812)

Queensberry, Marchioness of. *See* Scott, Lady Caroline

Queensberry, M. of. *See* Douglas, Sir Charles (1777–1831)

Queensberry family:

affectations of, **30.** 100

Fox, Lady Caroline, bred in 'kingdom' of, **30.** 100

Queensberry House, Burlington Gardens, London:

play by Lady Craven acted at, **29.** 235n

Queensberry House, Richmond, Surrey; D. of Queensberry's seat:

Charles I lived on site of, **11.** 152

Cornbury pictures at, **11.** 152

entertainments at, **11.** 152

guests at: Boufflers, Comtesse Amélie de, **11.** 341; Castelcicala, P. and Ps of, **11.** 341; Du Barry, Mme, **11.** 341; Fitzherbert, Mrs, **11.** 152; Frederick, P. of Wales, **19.** 468n; Hamilton, Sir William, **11.** 340; Hart, Emma,

11. 340; Wales, P. of (George IV), 11. 152
HW and Selwyn visit, 33. 541–2
HW visits, 11. 152, 340–1
owners of, 33. 541n
Queensborough; Queensbury. *See* Queensberry
Queen's College, Cambridge:
Crawford expelled from, 1. 363
flood of 1762 spoils beer in, 2. 369
Queen's College, Oxford:
portrait of Q. Elizabeth at, 10. 42
statue at, 13. 99
Queen's County, Ireland:
HW to follow Lady Ossory to, 32. 159
Queen's Head, Gray's Inn Lane, London:
Cambridge fly puts up at, 1. 359, 366, 2. 41, 57, 62, 95, 202, 235, 295
Cole puts up at, 1. 306, 308
Essex at, 2. 81, 83
Queen's House. *See* Buckingham House
'Queen's Library,' Green Park:
York, D. of, pulls down, 20. 48n
Queen Sq., Westminster:
locusts in, 39. 418
St George's Church in, 40. 84n
Queen's St, Mayfair, London:
Middleton, Mrs, takes house in, 15. 314
Montagu to stay in, 10. 253
Porteus, Mrs, dies in, 11. 33n
See also Great Queen Street
Queen's Theatre, Haymarket. *See* Haymarket: King's Theatre in
Queen's ware:
dessert service of, 25. 667n
Quélart, Du. *See* Du Quélart
Quélen de Stuer de Caussade, Antoine-Paul-Jacques de (1706–72), Duc de la Vauguyon:
Adélaïde, Mme, repulses, for suggesting that she receive Mme du Barry, 23. 87
announces to Mesdames the coming presentation of Mme du Barry, 4. 191, 192, 196
attends session of parliament of Paris, 8. 172
Choiseul's dismissal from Swiss Guards said to have been sought by, 5. 167
Dauphin's governor, 23. 87
death of, 5. *179*
Du Barry, Mme, aided by, 23. 87
health of, 5. 35
Jesuits' friend, 23. 87, 94
Marie-Josèphe will be regretted by, 3. 257
Richelieu tells, to notify Marie-Adélaïde of Mme du Barry's presentation, 23. 85n
Rochford, Cts of, suspected of complicity with, 4. 199, 203
Quélen de Stuer de Caussade, Paul-François de (1746–1828), Marquis (later Duc) de St-Maigrin; Duc de la Vauguyon, 1772; governor of the 'enfants de France':
Dauphin's entrées given and withdrawn by, 4. 444
French minister for foreign department, 39. 467n
HW mentions, 6. 64n
Louis XVI gives grandes entrées to, 6. 52

marriage of, 3. 219n
said to be appointed French ambassador to Naples, 6. 87
verses on, 6. 68
wife of, 3. 219n
Quentin, ——, stationer:
Du Deffand, Mme, has receipt from, 8. 42
Quenton. *See* China: Kwangtung
Quercetanus. *See* Duchesne, Joseph
Quercioli, Signora:
in burletta company, 22. 474n
Queries. See Constitutional Queries
Queries Addressed to Every Englishman's Own Feeling, by HW:
(?) Bristol, 2d E. of, sends, to *London Chronicle,* 43. 171–2
London Chronicle prints, 21. 65n
Querini, Angelo Maria (1680–1755), cardinal, 1727:
Benedict XIV and Ricci at odds with, 20. 464
—— resents single-handed negotiating by, 20. 190n
Berlin Catholic church receives ornaments from, 20. 329
death of, 20. 463–4
everything written by and to, printed at Brescia, 20. 329n
HW's Mark Antony medal formerly owned by, 42. 262n
letters published by, at Brescia and Rome, 20. 190n
Porcia exposed by, 17. 22n
sent from Venice to Rome to aid Capello, 20. 190n
Venice tells, to suppress writings about quarrel with Benedict XIV, 20. 190
Voltaire's epistle to, 20. 329
Querini, Tommaso, Procuratore di San Marco; Venetian ambassador extraordinary to England:
Hammersmith house taken by, 22. 76n
Venice sends, to England, 21. 508–9
Querlon. *See* Meusnier de Querlon
Quero, American ship:
Lexington news reaches England by, 24. 109-10
Querouaille. *See* Penancoët de Kéroualle
Querqueville Fort, near Cherbourg:
English attack on, 37. 558
Querzoli, Anna, m. Filippo Laschi; singer:
burletta sung by, 20. 4n
Quesne. *See* Du Quesne
Question de droit publique. Plaidoyer pour Messire Gawen Hamilton:
HW has not seen, 33. 364
Question d'identité d'individu et de suppression d'état du Comte de Solar. See under Élie de Beaumont, Jean-Baptiste-Jacques
Questions sur l'encyclopédie. See under Voltaire
Question Stated, The. See under Hervey, John
Queue; queues:
Conway can tell which general's is longest, 37. 143

Quiberon (France):
  English expedition to, 19. 327
Quiberon Bay:
  battle of, 21. 350-2, 356-7, 358
  English expedition 'discovers,' 37. 536
  Hawke enjoys himself in, 21. 355
  ——'s victory in, 9. 268
  Picquet de la Motte driven back to, 24. 361n
  Sinclair fails at, 19. 456n
  Vannes in, 21. 350n
Quiberon peninsula:
  English plunder, 19. 319n
  Lestock lands on, 19. 319n
  Sombreuil captured on, 12. 152n
'Quickly, Dame':
  Shelburne, Cts of, compared with, 32. 154
Quickset hedges. See under Hedge
Quicksilver. See Mercury
Quid sit Senersis. See under Elizabeth (1533–1603), Q.
Quien de la Neuville, Le. See Le Quien de la Neuville
Quieras, valley of:
  French to invade Piedmont by, 19. 417
Quieta non movere:
  Walpole, Sir Robert, has, as maxim, 20. 409, 22. 111, 23. 289, 304, 359, 25. 434, 506, 529, 541, 603, 28. 416, 459, 33. 389
Quiete, Conservatorio delle, at Florence:
  Electress not to visit, 17. 428
  —— visits, 17. 65, 83
  history of, 17. 65n
Quieting Bill. See under Parliament: acts of
Quieting draughts:
  HW takes, for gout, 32. 340
Quietism:
  HW on, 5. 12
Quietist; Quietists:
  Molinos's followers called, 21. 48n
Quill; quills:
  crow, Vcts Townshend carries 200 to Brompton lodgings, 30. 70
  from black crows, sent by HW to Vcts Townshend, 40. 48
  goose, see Goose quill
Quilt:
  HW throws, from bed, 24. 442
Quimbeau, Mlle:
  Gray's anecdote of, 13. 156
Quimperle:
  convents near, plundered by English, 19. 319n
Quin, ——:
  Mann presents, to Leopold, 23. 527n
Quin, Lady Frances Muriel. See Fox Strangways, Lady Frances Muriel
Quin, James (1693–1766), actor:
  Barry vainly urges, to play ghost in Hamlet, 20. 209
  Bath visited by, 10. 150, 187
  Conway quotes, 37. 311–12
  death of, 7. 397
  excellent as Falstaff, 33. 87, 547, 38. 524

  Garrick inferior to, as 'Sir John Brute' and 'Macbeth,' 38. 525
  Gray considers Barry better than, 14. 7
  'Henry VIII' acted by, 43. 257
  Kemble superior to, as 'Maskwell,' 11. 64
  Mitchell sups with, 20. 209
  Montagu mentions, 10. 151
  plays acted by, 19. 342
  praised by inebriate, 13. 64
  Warburton debates with, 10. 150
  witticisms by: 11. 45; about apostles, 10. 150; about women, 10. 187; on Charles I's execution, 10. 150, 29. 34; to Mitchell about cabin-boys doing nothing, 20. 209–10
Quinault, Jeanne-Françoise (1700–83), actress:
  niece of, receives bequest, 5. 211
Quinault, Olympe:
  Duclos leaves bequest to, 5. 211
Quinault, Philippe (1635–88), dramatist:
  Alceste by, 3. 119
  Armide by, 3. 119, 7. 304
  Atys by, 3. 119, 6. 242, 7. 105, 41. 282
  Du Deffand, Mme, admires, 5. 392, 7. 15
  —— mentions, 5. 43
  HW does not value operas of, 3. 58, 133, 346, 363, 4. 1, 51
  Isis by, 3. 119
  Marmontel revises operas of, for Piccinni's music, 6. 413, 444
  Persée by: given to celebrate Dauphin's marriage, 4. 407, 409; quoted by Mme du Deffand, 3. 88
  Phaéton by, 6. 366
  poetry of, overestimated by the French, 28. 276
  Proserpine by, 4. 302
  Roland by, Marmontel's version of, to Piccinni's music, 6. 445, 7. 9
  Thésée by: Du Deffand, Mme, praises, 3. 119; Du Deffand, Mme, quotes, 4. 296; HW sees, 7. 285; Mondonville's version of, 3. 208–9; Richelieu quotes, 4. 251; Voltaire quotes, 6. 243
  (?) Voltaire defends, against Marmontel, 7. 22–3
Quincey, Seigneur de. See Mesmay, Jean-Antoine-Marie de
Quinette, Nicolas-Marie (1762–1821), Baron de Rochemont:
  named commissioner, 12. 1n
Quinine:
  Du Deffand, Mme, mentions, 4. 13
  for malaria, 5. 352, 358
Quinquina:
  Du Deffand, Mme, and guests play, 7. 264
Quinsy:
  Gray fears, 13. 114
  HW has, 13. 10, 17. 51–2, 54–5, 66, 21. 369, 37. 100, 42. 204, 43. 169
  occurrence of, 10. 103
Quintettos:
  played after dinner, 33. 541n

Quintin, Duc de. *See* Durfort-Civrac, Jean-Laurent de

Quinton, Duchesse de. *See* Durfort de Lorges, Adélaïde-Philippine de

Quintuple Alliance:
Parliamentary reform sought by, **25**. 401

Quintus Erennius:
bust of, destroyed in Uffizi fire, **22**. 68n

Quinze:
Craufurd plays, **3**. 36
gambling at, at White's, **38**. 469
Gloucester, D. of, plays, with Cholmondeley, as his favourite game, **23**. 356
loo being replaced by, **31**. 151
Northumberland and Marlborough play, at Duc de Guines's ball, **32**. 100
played, **9**. 369, **10**. 297, **32**. 187, 345
played by men at Stanhope's, **19**. 485

Quinze-table:
lady's attitudes at, **34**. 6

Quinze-Vingt; Quinze-Vingts:
'aspirant' to, **42**. 408
Du Deffand, Mme, calls herself a, **5**. 433, **6**. 121
Hénault's *Abrégé* treats, **20**. 107
Philippe IV orders, to wear fleur-de-lis, **20**. 107n

Quinze-Vingts, Hospice des:
Louis, St, founds, for the blind, **20**. 107n
Voltaire's *Petite digression* on, **3**. 113

Quipus ('quipos'):
Fitzpatrick, Lady Anne, sends, to HW, **33**. 258
HW amused by, **33**. 263
HW requests, on ode, **33**. 260
HW returns, **33**. 261
HW wishes to know author of, **33**. 263, 266
Peruvian, discussed, **33**. 258, 261–2

Quirinal, Rome:
Benedict XIV receives Charles III in coffee-house at, **18**. 533
Innocent XII furnishes, **25**. 525n

Quirini. *See* Querini

Quistello (Italy):
Broglie loses breeches at, **17**. 465

Quito (Ecuador):
'King of Peru' crowned at, **22**. 426

Quit-rent:
monthly, HW's term for his letters to Mann, **25**. 530
peppercorn for, **32**. 302

Quiver; quivers:
at SH, **20**. 381, **31**. 26
Chinese, **31**. 26

'Quivering dame':
HW lodges with, at Windsor, **9**. 44, 45

'Quixote, Don':
costume of, at masquerade, **17**. 339
Du Deffand, Mme, compares HW to, **4**. 304, 306, 309
England 'out-Quixotes,' **39**. 368
HW compares Pitt to, **37**. 550
Herbert of Chirbury compared with, **30**. 176
See also under Cervantes, Miguel de

'Quixote, Don William.' *See* Pitt, William (1708–78), E. of Chatham

Quixotism:
HW condemns, **16**. 132

Quon. *See* Quane

Quorn, Leics:
Meynell of, **6**. 455n, **9**. 240n, **28**. 391n, **29**. 306n

Quota; quotas:
Colloredo demands, from George II, **21**. 18
England should demand, of Austria against France, **21**. 28

Quoties, Domine ?:
Leneve, Isabella, to explain, **37**. 112

'Quu of Habiculeo.' *See* Montagu, Charles (1661–1715), E. of Halifax

'Quus':
HW's name for Montagu family, **9**. 45

Quy Hall, Cambs:
Cole visits, **2**. 151n
Wards of, **2**. 139n

R

R——, Lord:
retains title without followers, **35**. 352

R., J. *See* Richardson, Joseph

R., N. *See* Roettiers, Robert

Rabbins:
HW's mock sermon mentions, **31**. 424

Rabbit; rabbits:
Fox tames, at Cheltenham, **33**. 526
German princes hunt, **25**. 364

Rabbit burrows:
Irish houses resemble, **37**. 336

'Rabbits':
Finch's confusion about, **9**. 308

Rabbit-warren:
Radnor's, **35**. 174

'Rabbit-woman.' *See* Tofts, Mary

Rabelais, François (ca 1494–1553), writer:
bishops have not heard of, **15**. 67
fais ce que voudras the motto of, **25**. 22
Gargantua by: HW quotes, **11**. 234; newspapers would inspire histories as fabulous as, **24**. 412
HW likes, better as he grows older, **10**. 184
Lyttelton's *Dialogues of the Dead* mention, **21**. 408
Pantagruel by: HW alludes to, **17**. 339; Lyttelton prefers dissertation on Hippocrates to, **21**. 408; 'Papefigues' in, mentioned by Mme du Deffand, **4**. 28, **7**. 176

Rabutin, Roger de (1618–93), Comte de Bussy:
compliment to Louis XIV appears in letters of, **43**. 331
daughter of, said to have been his mistress, **5**. 188
Du Deffand, Mme, gives opinion of, **5**. 187, **6**. 27
Histoire amoureuse des Gaules, by, **5**. 185, **20**. 150n, **43**. 331
illness the occupation of, **5**. 190

[Rabutin, Roger de, *continued*]
lady's cosmetics satirized by, **20.** 150

Lettres of: Du Deffand, Mme, enjoys, **5.** 180–1, 185, 187, 189, 203–4, **6.** 223; HW dislikes, **5.** 185, 201, 204

Mémoires of, **4.** 135, **5.** 185, 189, 190

Scudéry, Mme de, corresponds with, **3.** 387–8, **5.** 187

—— persecutes, **5.** 201

Sévigné, Mme de, called avaricious by, **35.** 198

—— not intentionally imitated by, **5.** 188

'singe de Mme de Sévigné,' **5.** 185

style of writing of, compared to HW's, **5.** 180–1

Rabutin-Chantal, Marie de (1626–96), m. (1644) Henri, Marquis de Sévigné:

Auray visited by, **7.** 87

Bourbon visited by, **3.** 330n

Brinvilliers, Marquise de, poisonings of, discussed by, **30.** 218

Bussy calls, avaricious though she was merely poor, **35.** 198

——'s correspondence with, **5.** 181, 185, **6.** 223

—— the monkey of, **5.** 185

Carnavalet, Hôtel de, occupied by, **7.** 305n, **31.** 50–1

Coke, Lady Mary, leaves anecdotes of, **31.** 143

compliment to Louis XIV appears in Bussy's letters, not in those of, **43.** 331

Conway cannot have letter-writing skill of, **37.** 243

could not have written a letter of grief if her daughter had died first, **32.** 172

cousin of, **4.** 62n, 139n

Craon, Princesse de, would tell Sade to read letters of, to her, **20.** 387

daughter left by, at Paris, to save money in Brittany to pay debts, **35.** 198

daughter receives pearl necklace from, **18.** 291

daughter's letter after death of, **32.** 171–2

Delville called 'Sévigniade' after, **10.** 11

—— reminds Montagu of, **9.** 390–1

Du Deffand, Mme, admires, **3.** 273, **4.** 32, 408, **5.** 202, **7.** 27, 83

—— cites, **3.** 26, 87, 100, 196, 249, 281, 387, **4.** 56, 249

—— compared with, **10.** 89

—— defends herself by comparison with, **3.** 127, 144, **5.** 262

—— does not resemble, **3.** 273, **4.** 408, **5.** 63, 168, 175, 202, **6.** 27, 135, 197, 228, 272, 286, 319, 462–3, 491, 500, **7.** 27, 83, 205

—— tells story about, **7.** 288

Du Plessis, Mlle, rebuked by, **35.** 193

ebony cabinet of: **43.** 104; Du Deffand, Mme, stores, **7.** 82; HW to have, repaired, **33.** 151; Selwyn receives, **7.** 80, **33.** 150–1

(?) Ennery has medallion of, **7.** 325

Filles de Ste-Marie convent visited by, **30.** 207

Fouquet's trial described by, **41.** 259

French neglect of, **31.** 51

French used by, 'genuine,' **33.** 496

frost interrupts HW's researches on, **14.** 157

Gourville's *Mémoires* praised by, **4.** 44n

Gramont, Comtesse de, is 'grande femme' of, **7.** 357

granddaughter of, **3.** 255n

Gray alludes to, **14.** 12

—— inquires about HW's curiosity concerning, **14.** 148

great-granddaughter of, **30.** 263, **41.** 109

Grignan a 'favourite scene of,' **35.** 600

HW admires letters of, **5.** 104n, **17.** 1n, **20.** 90

HW and Hardinge agree in passion for, **35.** 649

HW and Bns Hervey devoted to, **31.** 7

HW calls: 'Notre Dame des Rochers,' **35.** 198, 231; 'our friend,' **30.** 207

HW denies quoting, ludicrously, **31.** 74

HW doubts reports of discovery of new letters of, **31.** 277

HW flees from modern despots to, **35.** 602, 604

HW had suspected, of exaggerating pomp of Grignan, **30.** 267

HW has two letters of, **34.** 81–2

HW mentions, **4.** 55, **9.** 313

HW owns editions of, **43.** 88

HW owns portraits of, **41.** 258

HW paraphrases saying of, about Louis XIV, **39.** 12–13, 213–14

HW praises, **16.** 273

HW quotes, **18.** 291, **28.** 385, **30.** 208, **32.** 152, 165, **33.** 473, **35.** 94

HW said by Mme Necker to resemble, **39.** 292

HW says Ave Marias to, when passing Hôtel de Carnavalet, **30.** 206

HW's collection of letters of, **20.** 382, 387

HW's enthusiasm for, **3.** 51, 71, 77, 88, 144, **4.** 18, 24, 141, **31.** 50–1

HW's favourite, **35.** 584, **37.** 243

HW's fondness for letters of, **28.** 216–17

HW's letters not to be compared to those of, **20.** 90

HW's letters would be appreciated by, **9.** 275

HW's picture of house of, **28.** 196

HW's 'saint,' **31.** 74

HW thinks he is visiting convent of, **7.** 285

HW thinks of, at Bushey Park, **9.** 380

HW to hide under petticoats of, **35.** 604

HW to send edition of, to Lady Ossory, **32.** 169

HW wishes, were alive to write of poisoning of Lauraguais's horse, **30.** 218

HW would believe nonsense by, to be inspired, **31.** 74–5

interested in everything, **3.** 273, **4.** 408, **5.** 63, **6.** 27, 272, 319, 462, 491, **7.** 83, 205

Kildare, Cts of, devoted to, **35.** 23

La Fayette, Comtesse de, friend of, **19.** 5n

(?) La Harpe ignores maternal affection of, **19.** 420

'leaf-gold' spread by: over all her acquaintance, **35.** 466, 601; over places and people, **35.** 601

letter of: *larmoyante*, **34**. 81–2, 85; of 2 March 1689 sent to HW by Grave, **4**. 63, 69, 72, 301, 307, **41**. 143–4, 259; to Mme de Grignan 12 Sept. 1679, sent to HW by Duchesse de Choiseul, **3**. 402, 405, **4**. 1, 2–3, 6, 24, 72, **41**. 109; to M. de la Grange, reported found, **34**. 81, **35**. 393

letters awaited by, on bridge at Livry, **10**. 212

letters of: activity reflected in, **4**. 46; Du Deffand, Mme, and HW prefer, to those of Bussy, **5**. 181, 185, 187; Du Deffand, Mme, prefers HW's letters to her to, **3**. 27; Girard, Mlles, have, **4**. 74, 144, **5**. 301, 307, **22**. 139, **41**. 143–4, 259; (?) Girard, Marquis de, has, copied, **5**. 307; HW collects portrait prints of all people mentioned in, **25**. 433–4; HW knows, by heart, **32**. 222; Hénault compares Mme du Deffand's letters to, **8**. 53; please Mme du Deffand with domestic details, **4**. 255; sought by Grave, **4**. 35, 63, 72, 74, 144, **8**. 139–40; to La Grange, reported found, **34**. 81, **35**. 393; to Pomponne about Fouquet trial, **3**. 187–8, 190, 193, 200, 212, 387, **4**. 24, **5**. 380, 420, **41**. 259; (vol. ix) of, **6**. 286

letters, newly discovered, of: **4**. 74n; advertised, **35**. 188; HW gets two volumes of, **35**. 189–90; HW quotes, **35**. 193; HW sends, to Bentley, **35**. 197, 214; reveal illnesses and financial trouble, **35**. 198; supposedly discovered, **35**. 393, 466

letter under name of, from Mme du Deffand to HW: **3**. 51, **31**. 119, 121; copy of, by HW, **3**. 86; Du Deffand, Mme, disclaims knowledge of, **3**. 70–1; Du Deffand, Mme, disparages, **5**. 399; Du Deffand, Mme, expects criticism of, **3**. 77, 83, 86; finding of, by HW, **3**. 70n, 72, 86; HW attributes, to Duchesse de Choiseul, **3**. 73n, 79, 82, 83, 85, 120, 143; HW fears talk because of, **3**. 134, 143; HW in doubt over authorship of, **3**. 71, 73–5, 80–4; HW praises, **5**. 397, **8**. 59, 213; HW prints, **5**. 397; Jonzac, Mme de, transcribes, **3**. 51, 73; Luxembourg, Mme de, not to see, **3**. 77; method of delivering, **3**. 73–4; praised, **3**. 81, 83

Lettres by: discussion of, **31**. 215; HW alludes to personages in, **31**. 74–5

Lettres de Mme de Sévigné à . . . Pomponne, **43**. 84

Lettres nouvelles ou nouvellement recouvrées by: **35**. 466, **43**. 99; Du Deffand, Mme, gives opinion of, **5**. 419; Du Deffand, Mme, receives, **43**. 95; HW's opinion of, **5**. 423; La Harpe to edit, **5**. 373, 419; Stormont knows all about, **5**. 376; to be printed, **5**. 301n, 330, 350, 373, 380, 395, 405, 408, 413, 419

Livry, former home of, described by HW, **10**. 211–12

—— often visited by, **7**. 311n

Maintenon, Mme de, almost rivals, in letter-writing, **35**. 276

Mann enjoys HW's letters as much as her daughter's were enjoyed by, **20**. 83–4

—— quotes, **20**. 84

Marseilles academy assigns, as topic, **32**. 269

Mason is unable to relish letters of, **28**. 215–16

medallion of, at Livry, **10**. 212

Montagu, Lady Mary Wortley, compared to, as letter-writer, **20**. 282

Moulceau's correspondence with, **5**. 423–4

Ninon de l'Enclos's remark about son of, **37**. 531

Pinkerton prefers Lady Mary Wortley Montagu to, **16**. 265–6

portraits of: **3**. 50n, 51, 70, 73; formerly Mme de Simiane's, copied for HW, **35**. 198; Hervey, Bns, gives, to HW, **31**. 7n; Petitot's, **3**. 73n, **7**. 313

Recueil de lettres choisies, pour servir de suite aux lettres de Mme de Sévigné à Mme de Grignon sa fille, **20**. 275, **43**. 99

Recueil de lettres de diverses personnes amies de ('le huitième volume'): corrected information about, **43**. 88; Du Deffand, Mme, enjoys, **4**. 139, 144; HW finds, mediocre, **4**. 141, 144

remark by, about Louis XIV, applied by HW to Queen of France, **31**. 52, **43**. 331

retreats to convent, **10**. 167n

(?) St-Jean, Mme, gives HW 'tattered scrap' associated with, for Selwyn, **30**. 219

Scarron compared to, **5**. 390

Selwyn's interest in, **3**. 405

—— visits death-chamber of, at Grignan, **7**. 80

'siège,' pun by, **7**. 288

snuff-box with miniature of, given by Mme du Deffand to HW: **3**. 51, 70, 73, 81, 86; Choiseul, Mme de, credited by HW with gift of, **3**. 79; Choiseul, Mme de, forwards, **3**. 73–4; delivery of, **3**. 73–4; finding of, by HW, **3**. 70n, 72, 86; Jonzac, Mme de, prepares, **3**. 73

son-in-law of, **9**. 21n

son's letters rival those of, **35**. 602

Soubise, Princesse de, is 'bonne femme' of, **7**. 357

spends her wit in small change, **5**. 202

(?) SH's patron saint, **10**. 187

style of: Du Deffand, Mme, admires, **3**. 127, 144, 273, **5**. 47, 181, **6**. 197, 223, 319, **7**. 87; HW's style compared with, **4**. 236, 317; *Mercure de France* praises, **7**. 96, 99, 106, 111, 113

tomb of, at Grignan, desecrated, **34**. 86n

uncle built pavilion for, at Livry, **10**. 212

value of letters of, **12**. 22

witticism by, on Princesse de Tarente's not being dressed in mourning, **35**. 193

Rabutin de Bussy, Louise-Françoise de (1646–1716), m. 1 (1675) Gilbert-Allyre de Longeac, Marquis de Coligny; m. 2 (1681) Henri-François de la Rivière:

father of, said to be her lover, **5**. 188

Raby, Louise (ca 1755–72), m. (1770) Charles-Antoine-Étienne, Marquis de Choiseul:
Du Deffand, Mme, gives opinion of, 5. 110
social relations of, with Duchesse d'Aiguillon, 5. 110
Raby:
Wentworth takes title of, enraging Vane, 17. 333n
Raby Castle, Durham:
Vane family's paintings at, 42. 126n
Raccolta di alcune delle più belle vedute d'Italia. See under Stephens, Peter
Raccolta di lettere sulla pittura, scultura, ed archittetura. See under Bottari, Giovanni Gaetano
Raccolta di poesie. See under Crudeli, Tommaso
Raccoon; raccoons:
HW prefers, to hussars, 37. 182
Race; races:
at Barnet, 28. 42
at Derby, 21. 427, 38. 63
at Florence, on St John's Day, 17. 78–9, 454, 35. 28
at Hampton Court, 32. 137
at Hereford, 12. 80
at Huntingdon, 21. 427
at Leghorn, for Tuscan Court, 22. 418, 423
at Lewes, 19. 495, 20. 289
at Newmarket, *see under* Newmarket
at Port Mahon, 37. 311
at Stafford, 21. 427
at Warwick, 21. 427, 38. 16, 18, 64
at York: 23. 48, 25. 373, 28. 333, 429, 459, 34. 64n, 35. 329, 37. 562; attended by D. of York, 11. 59n; attended by George IV, 11. 50, 59n; Berrys leave in middle of, 11. 62; HW mentions, 11. 58; HW pleased at Berrys' not attending, 11. 50
English newspapers concerned about, 22. 174
geese versus turkeys, 21. 7
HW will not attend, at Windsor, 19. 298
held in September, 11. 333
Londoners flock to, 35. 323
macaronies run, in Kensington Gardens, 23. 491
Mann, Horace II, regards Florentine trip as lightly as trip to, 25. 373
Montfort places bets at, 20. 74
music eclipsed by, 23. 571
Orford, E. of, has involvement with, which devolves upon HW, 28. 92, 94
Roman, 17. 79n
Waldegraves busy with, 36. 240
Welsh, attended by Williams, 18. 305
See also Boat race; Chariot race; Horse race, *and under* Newmarket
Race horse. *See under* Horse
Rachel (biblical):
Leah and, 11. 6, 12. 108
Racine, Jean (1639–99), dramatist:
'Agrippine' rôle in *Britannicus* acted by Mlle Clairon, 7. 316

Alexander the Great a translation from, played by Mary Robinson, 33. 354n
Andromaque by: acted at Choisy, 5. 322; Du Deffand, Mme, praises, 5. 391; Du Deffand, Mme, quotes, 6. 372; HW sees, 7. 265
Athalie by: Du Deffand, Mme, knows, by heart, 7. 203; Du Deffand, Mme, mentions, 3. 302; Du Deffand, Mme, praises, 5. 391; Du Deffand, Mme, quotes, 3. 175, 177, 6. 137; HW likes, 5. 393; HW prefers, to Corneille, 6. 44; HW sees, 7. 324; HW to reread, 5. 389; Racine places, in Jewish temple, 40. 154; rhymed, 40. 156; St-Cyr pensioners sing choruses of, 10. 294
Bajazet by: 3. 224n; Belle-Isle's letter reminds HW of passage in, 21. 321; Du Deffand, Mme, sees, 3. 294
Bérénice by: is story of Louis XIV and Ds of Orléans, 41. 155; Voltaire and HW differ over lines from, 4. 119–20, 129, 41. 154; Voltaire's views on, 4. 120
Britannicus by: Clairon, Mlle, acts in, 3. 341; Du Deffand, Mme, mentions, 4. 342; Gray quotes, 14. 11; HW praises, 41. 296; HW prefers, to Corneille, 6. 44; HW prefers, to *Iphigénie*, 29. 111; HW sees, 7. 277; HW to reread, 5. 389
Colisée to supersede, 39. 145
Corneille compared with, 41. 296
—— equalled and Euripides excelled by, 41. 155
Du Deffand, Mme, attributes verses to, 5. 221
—— paraphrases, 4. 77
—— praises style of, 5. 391
—— quotes, as Corneille, 4. 87
—— reads, 7. 178, 180, 187
epigram mentions, 33. 111
Épigrammes by, cited by Mme du Deffand, 7. 166
Esther: Du Deffand, Mme, knows, by heart, 7. 203; Du Deffand, Mme, quotes, 3. 356, 6. 287
French abandon, 31. 43
HW compares: with Corneille, Shakespeare, Voltaire, 6. 44; with Shakespeare, 9. 356n
HW imitates, in couplet, 32. 269
HW praises *Britannicus* and *Phèdre* of, 41. 296
HW prefers Shakespeare to, 6. 44, 8. 142, 144
Iphigénie en Aulide by: Du Deffand, Mme, reads, 7. 178; Du Rollet revises, 6. 39; HW dislikes, 5. 389, 6. 44; HW does not share Voltaire's admiration of, 29. 111; rhymed, 41. 156; Voltaire likes, 5. 389
King John has a scene superior to those of, 29. 370
La Harpe criticizes, 6. 409
Le Sueur's paintings have purity of, 35. 126
Le Tourneur prefers Shakespeare to, 28. 279
—— sacrifices, to Shakespeare, 24. 267n
letters of, please Mme du Deffand because of domestic details, 4. 255

Merchant of Venice could mostly have been written by, **34.** 2

Mithridate by: HW dislikes, **5.** 389, **6.** 44; Maurepas quotes from, on Cornwallis's surrender, **25.** 211

model of purity and taste, **16.** 257

pertness of modern French authors would misbecome, **33.** 543

Phèdre by: Clairon, Mlle, acts in, **3.** 341, **4.** 30, 132; Du Deffand, Mme, paraphrases, **4.** 279; Du Deffand, Mme, quotes, **43.** 87; Dumesnil acts in, **31.** 60; finest French tragedy, **29.** 111; HW fails to see, **7.** 265; HW praises, **41.** 296; HW prefers, to Corneille, **6.** 44; HW sees, **7.** 275; HW to reread, **5.** 389; HW's *Mysterious Mother* compared with, **42.** 352

Plaideurs, Les, by, quoted by Mme du Deffand, **4.** 184, **6.** 94

plays of, have grace of a swan, **16.** 271

Shakespeare's best scenes better than correct elegance of, **41.** 294

Voltaire defends, **4.** 129, **6.** 142–3

Rackstrow, (?) Benjamin (d. 1772): old man by, in coloured plaster, **38.** 198–9 waxworks of, **22.** 135

Racot-Grandval, François-Charles (1710–84), called Grandval; actor: HW calls, 'fat and old,' **10.** 181 HW fails to recognize, **10.** 175, 181 HW sees, in comedies, **7.** 263

Radcliffe, Dr: Moore's chaplain, **16.** 286n

Radcliffe, Dr John (1650–1714), physician: Dorchester, Cts of, tells, to look for pox, **39.** 34–5 fellowship established by, **19.** 191n Oxford library given by, satirized, **38.** 30 Pope's life saved by, **9.** 116n

Radcliffe, Thomas (ca 1525–83), 3d E. of Sussex, 1557: (?) bust of, **33.** 351 New Hall rebuilt by, **9.** 92n wife and arms of, **33.** 350

Radcliffe Camera, at Oxford: King's speech at opening of, **20.** 50 public act at Oxford for opening of, **20.** 71n

Radclyf, Robert: Henry VI's keeper, **14.** 180n

Radclyffe, Charles (1693–1746), titular 5th E. of Derwentwater: captured on board the *Soleil,* **19.** 173 execution of: **9.** 283, **14.** 12–13; expected, **19.** 341 HW sees, at Tower, **9.** 46 Mann wants, executed, **19.** 353 Old Bailey trial proving his condemnation in 1715 will send, to Tyburn, **19.** 180–1 Tower of London reached by, after narrow escape from mob, **19.** 180 wife of, **14.** 4n

Radclyffe, James (1689–1716), 3d E. of Derwentwater: brother of, **19.** 173, 341 prisoner, first to be taken to Transport Office, **19.** 299n Voltaire's false story of execution of, **35.** 284

Radclyffe, James Bartholomew (1725–86), styled Vct Kynnaird 1725–55; 3d E. of Newburgh, 1755: captured on board the *Soleil,* **19.** 173 Dettingen battle preferred by, to English mob, **19.** 180 London mob nearly tears, to pieces, **19.** 180 release of, **19.** 241 Richmond entertains, as a relative, **19.** 241 to be treated as a French prisoner, **19.** 180 York, Cardinal, thought to be, **19.** 177, 180, 241

Radclyffe, John (d. 1731), styled Vct Radclyffe; titular 4th E. of Derwentwater, 1716: father said to have brought, to execution scaffold, **35.** 284

Radclyffe family: Lovat's pun on name of, **19.** 380

Raddon Court, Devon: Tuckfield of, **43.** 182

Rade des Basques: Conway in ship at, **37.** 506, 507

Radick, Capt.: Venetian vessel of, takes engineers to Minorca, **24.** 477n

Radicofani (Italy): HW borrows pen from governor of, **37.** 67 HW describes wretched inn at, **13.** 205 HW disparages, **13.** 230 HW writes from, **13.** 205, **37.** 66 Orford, Cts of, carried to, in Pius VI's litter, **24.** 317 Young Pretender at, **18.** 388

Radier. *See* Dreux de Radier

Radishes: white, served as hors d'œuvre, **19.** 357

Radix, ——: attends session of parliament of Paris, **8.** 173

Radix de Ste-Foix, Marie-Geneviève (b. 1729), m. 1 —— Boudret; m. 2 (1760) Nicolas-Augustin de Malbec de Montjoc, Marquis de Briges: Luxembourg, Mme de, to visit, **6.** 470 social relations of, with Mme Geoffrin, **7.** 317 stables of, **6.** 470

Radix de Ste-Foy, Claude-Pierre-Maximilien (b. ca 1735), French diplomatist: (?) Éon prints letters by, **22.** 217–18

Radnor, E. of. *See* Bouverie, William (1725–76); Pleydell Bouverie, Jacob (1750–1828); Robartes, Charles Bodvile (1660–1723); Robartes, John (1686–1757)

Radnor House, Twickenham; Basset's seat: bow window of, demolished, **32.** 75 Buller, Mrs, visits, **11.** 333 haymaking at, **11.** 351

[Radnor House, *continued*]
Hindley sells, **11.** 333n, **33.** 105, 180, 183
island belonging to, **11.** 351n
Murrays live at, **12.** 58n
Potts lives in, after Hindley, **35.** 365
Radnor leaves, to Hindley who sells it, **11.** 333n
residents of, **42.** 480
Webb buys, **33.** 183
Radnorshire, Wales:
Middleton, Mrs, born in, **15.** 310
Radonvilliers. *See* Lysarde de Radonvilliers
Radstock, Bn. *See* Waldegrave, Granville George (1786–1857); Waldegrave, Hon. William (1753–1825)
Radstock, Bns. *See* Van Lennep, Cornelia Jacoba
Radway Grange, Warwickshire:
Miller of, **9.** 156n
Radziwill, Ps. *See* Lubomirska, Marja
Radziwill, Prince Karol Stanislaw:
divorce of, **4.** 93n
Radziwill, Michael Kazimierz:
great general of Lithuania, **20.** 44n
Lascari governs family of, **20.** 44n
Radziwill, Teofila Konstancia (1738–80), m. (1764) Count Ignacy Morawski:
Young Pretender might wed, **20.** 35, 44
Rae, Mr, of Duke St, St James's:
SH visited by, **12.** 235
Rae, Mrs Margaret:
Hoare's monument to, in Worcester Cathedral, **20.** 86n
Rafaele, Palazzo, Rome:
Wyseman lived near gates of, **17.** 15n
Raffaello Sanzio (Raphael) (1483–1520); painter:
Agincourt's study of church paintings ends with, **42.** 104
angels painted by: **11.** 338; Mann has copy of, by Messini, **20.** 145
Barry includes, in allegorical painting, **29.** 301
Bartolommeo's paintings once regarded by HW as equal to those of, **23.** 465
—— the 'parent' of, **23.** 267
Carmontelle better at resemblances than, **4.** 27
cartoons by: **35.** 37–8; at Boughton House, **10.** 341; in England, **16.** 147, 157; note on, **16.** 168n; tapestry from, at Madrid, **16.** 169; tapestry from, said to be at Burghley House, **16.** 159; Waddilove asks about, **16.** 168–9
Cellini's chest said to be copied from design by, **23.** 432
——'s chest worthy of, **23.** 425
Chambers influenced by, **16.** 188n
china of, **10.** 345
Chute now indifferent to, **35.** 58
copy of painting by, **21.** 200
Coypel inferior to, **3.** 228
death of, at Venice, **16.** 147
'Death of the Blessed Virgin' by, at Burghley House, **10.** 346
designs by, for houses in Florence, **11.** 154

'Doctors' equals any paintings in Italy but those of, **23.** 570
English painters still do not approach, **28.** 195–6
'Ezekiel's Vision' by, at Boughton House, **10.** 341
Faenza ware said to be designed by, **25.** 591n
Félibien and Du Fresnoy praise, **30.** 325
female beauty inspired, **30.** 325
Gaven tries to sell alleged painting by, in Poland, **35.** 37n
HW has not yet seen the paintings by, at Rome, **13.** 170
HW is, in his 'portrait' of D. of Richmond, **4.** 304
HW thinks, inadequate to illustrate Shakespeare, **15.** 206
'Holy Family' by, at Boughton House, **10.** 341
'Last Supper' by, **2.** 169
Le Sueur's 'Vie de St-Bruno' surpasses, **35.** 126
Mabuse's painting perhaps influenced by, **15.** 96n
'Madonna della Sedia ['Seggiola']' by, copied by Strange, **21.** 448n, 470
Mann thinks Flemish painters inferior to, **20.** 398
'Marriage of Cupid and Psyche' and 'Cupid's Accusation' by, are other names for Council and Supper of the Gods, **43.** 270
Masaccio influenced, **11.** 154
——'s designs the precursors of, **23.** 266–7, **26.** 45
missal illuminated by, **20.** 470n
painting attributed to, **5.** 178n
paintings by: at Marigny's, **39.** 15; at Oxford, **33.** 55; at the Escorial, **16.** 180n; at the Vatican, damaged by 'veiling,' **20.** 328n; Beaufort may buy, **18.** 273; Gaven's price for, **18.** 273; in Cybo collection, **18.** 235, **35.** 37–8; Mann to get copies of, **20.** 328–9, 490, **21.** 88; Mariette's collection of, **32.** 266; neglected at Versailles, **35.** 344; of Christ and the Doctors, Charles Emmanuel III would have bought, from D. of Massa for Marlborough, **18.** 235–6; Parker buys, from Cybo collection, **18.** 239; Portland, Ds of, buys, **21.** 200n; 'School of Athens' copied by Mengs, **20.** 490, **21.** 88; Walpole, Sir Robert, refuses to buy, without seeing it, **18.** 254; Walpole, Sir Robert, wants further information about, **18.** 250
portrait of, **2.** 238n
portrait wrongly attributed to, **7.** 373n
Raimondi's print after, **23.** 432
'St John' by, at Palais Royal, **7.** 287
'St Luke Painting the Virgin' by, **43.** 275
'School of Athens' by, **20.** 490, **21.** 88, **35.** 37
(?) self-portrait by, copied by Strange, **21.** 470
Thornhill called the English counterpart of, **40.** 382
'Transfiguration' by, **28.** 473
Vatican loggias painted by, **23.** 298
vellum copies of works of, **22.** 233n

Raffle; raffles:
  at Bath, **10.** 187
  of china, won by Mme Pucci, **17.** 159
  See also Lottery
Raffle-picture:
  HW sees, at Wolterton, **18.** 47
Raffron du Trouillet, Nicolas (1723–1801), tutor;
    Revolutionary official:
  Boufflers accompanied by, at Florence, **22.** 474
Raftor, ——, m. —— Mestivyer; Mrs Clive's
    sister; (?) 'Mrs Metheglin':
  HW entertains, at SH, **36.** 54
  (?) HW invites, to dinner, **9.** 70
  HW leaves Harcourt's invitation (to Mrs
    Clive) in care of, **35.** 509
  HW mentions, **37.** (?) 397
  HW sits with, **35.** 306
  health of, better, **35.** 505
  (?) Kingston play to be attended by, **9.** 70
  living in 1785, **35.** 505n
  low water in Thames explained by, **33.** 57
  (?) 'Mrs Metheglin,' **43.** 114
  rambles, **35.** 533
Raftor, Catherine (1711–85), m. (1732) George
    Clive; 'Kitty Clive'; actress:
  appearance of: 'red face,' **10.** 97, 224, 245, 261,
    32. 360, **35.** 95, 100, 186, 306; 'sun rising
    out of the ocean,' **39.** 133; Townshend,
    Vcts, jokes about, **32.** 360, **35.** 186
  Ashton's sermons admired by, **9.** 72–3
  as 'Mrs Cadwallader' in Foote's *Author*, **33.** 87
  barns torn down by, to improve views, **37.** 348
  basket of shell flowers prized by, **42.** 307
  benefit performance for, **9.** 342
  biographical information on, corrected, **43.**
    147
  brother of, **4.** 475n, **9.** 264n, **28.** 47n
  cards absorb, **35.** 456, 463, 464, 522, 524
  cards still green for, **36.** 54
  Christmas banquet of, **10.** 240
  Cibber, Mrs, resented by, **18.** 124n
  comment by, on HW's fondness for Mme du
    Deffand and. Cts of Suffolk, **3.** 75
  cottage of, **9.** 191n
  cottage to be improved by, **40.** 61
  country gentlewoman's rôle preferred by, to
    popular ones in theatre, **40.** 61
  'cruises' about, despite prevalent robberies,
    35. 522
  currant jelly eaten by, **10.** 241
  death of, **31.** 237–8, 298
  epilogue to *Mysterious Mother* written for,
    18. 260
  famous Twickenham resident, **35.** 234
  fire in June at house of, **39.** 417
  footman of, testifies at Capt. Prescott's trial,
    33. 424–5
  Garrick blamed by, for bad road, **35.** 468
  —— equalled by, in low comedy, **38.** 524
  ——'s jealousy of, **33.** 88
  gone for the winter, **35.** 186
  HW and Montagu to play cards with, **10.** 184
  HW and two parsons visit, **33.** 7

HW buys cup and saucer for, **7.** 409, 410, 414
HW calls, 'Bonny Dame Cadwallader,' **41.** 365
HW calls on: **40.** 60–2; at Cliveden, **35.** 468
HW, Conway, Cts of Ailesbury, and Mary
  Rich call on, **35.** 275
HW cultivates Garrick in order to aid, **35.**
  242
HW does not bring, to Park Place, **38.** 13
HW entertains: at dinner at SH, **35.** 454n; at
  SH, **36.** 54
HW gives goldfish to, **9.** 134
HW gives Little Strawberry Hill ('Cliveden')
  to, **15.** 317, 320, **16.** 345
HW has, at Bedford's house, for coronation,
  38. 123
HW invites, to dinner, **9.** 70, 72, **41.** 365–6
HW jokingly proposes to limit his printing
  to the benefit tickets of, **9.** 231
(?) HW may be invited to visit, after gout,
  39. 238
HW mentions, **8.** 162, **29.** 349, **37.** 337
HW misses, when she is at Franks's, **35.** 509
HW not to relinquish, **9.** 306
HW planting around house of, **35.** 185
HW plays cards with: **31.** 237; at Cliveden,
  35. 95–6
HW pleased by success of, in *Clandestine
  Marriage*, **10.** 205
HW receives dinner invitation from, **31.** 127
HW said to keep, as mistress, **16.** 345
HW's ball attended by, **28.** 446
HW's 'comédienne,' **3.** 75, 77, 80, 105, 107,
  115, 262, 298, **4.** 222, 238, 333, 465
HW's correspondence with, **7.** 376–80, 389,
  393, 395, **9.** 344–5, **31.** 127, **40.** 61–2
HW's 'Epilogue' written for, on her leaving
  the stage, **4.** 222, 233, 238, **13.** 44, **31.** 141
HW's epitaph for, **2.** 374–5
HW sits with, and sees drunken lady's quar-
  rel, **35.** 306
HW's opinion of, **9.** 270
HW's servants warned by, of approach of
  housebreakers, **31.** 298
HW's supper with Mrs Abington may make,
  jealous, **39.** 323
HW sups with, **35.** 239
HW's verses for, **2.** 374–5
HW to be subject of complaint by, as nuis-
  ance, **10.** 2
HW to convey venison to, **10.** 240
HW to eat venison with, at Cliveden, **35.** 533
HW to frank Montagu's letter to, **10.** 235
HW to notify, of arrival of venison, **10.** 238
HW to play cards with, despite dislike of hot
  rooms, **35.** 524
HW to send Montagu's letter to, **10.** 239
HW visits SH meadows with, every evening,
  38. 94
Harcourt gives venison to, **35.** 533
——'s correspondence with, **35.** 531
——'s invitation to, **35.** 509
—— to receive respects of, **35.** 468

[Raftor, Catherine, *continued*]

Harcourts may hear from, when card contests are over, **35**. 464

health of: declining but temporarily better, **35**. 366; illness, **33**. 334, 346; jaundice, **29**. 271, **39**. 300; recovered, **35**. 522, 524; weak and out of order, **35**. 509

High Life Below Stairs acted by, **31**. 14n

house of: an infirmary, **33**. 346; at Twickenham, **2**. 273; broken into, **39**. 420; *see also under* Little Strawberry Hill ('Cliveden')

Jews advised by, to change religion, **10**. 106

Jordan, Mrs, almost equals, **34**. 52n

Kingston play to be attended by, **9**. 70

Le Texier has talent of, **39**. 273

Little Strawberry Hill ('Cliveden') occupied by, **4**. 465, **11**. 263, **30**. 363

Lloyd's Evening Post prints denial by, that she is to act at Covent Garden, **35**. 468

manservant of, **10**. 238

Marlow visited by, for cards, **35**. 463

memory of, decaying before her death, **31**. 237

Montagu asks HW to get theatre box from, for Lucy Rice, **9**. 342, 344–5

—— hopes to drink madeira with, **10**. 281

—— praises, in *Clandestine Marriage*, **10**. 203

——'s appearance to be scorned by, **10**. 196

——'s bulbs desired by, **10**. 235

——'s correspondence with, **10**. 239

——'s departure disappoints, **9**. 375

—— sends compliments to, **10**. 97, 226, 261, 281

—— to give venison to, **10**. 236, 240

—— welcome at house of, **9**. 191

Muscovita mimicked by, in *Miss Lucy in Town*, **17**. 435

nervous, **10**. 245

Nunehams may get letter from, **35**. 464

Passion Week spent by, at Little Strawberry Hill, **9**. 344

Pope, Jane, visits, **28**. 318, **33**. 407, **35**. 533–4

print of, **2**. 330

Purcell to have been sung by, **9**. 375

quadrille to have been played by, **9**. 375

Radnor's bequest to, **35**. 100

retirement of, from stage: **10**. 281, **35**. 582; predicted, **10**. 258

robbed in her own lane, **39**. 300

rôles of, at Drury Lane, **40**. 61n

shaken by explosion of powder-mills, **32**. 75

Shelburne, Cts of, not to be feared by, **10**. 217

sings: for Cherokees at Macclesfield's, **10**. 36; in Handel's *Samson*, **18**. 180n

sister's remark to, on low water in Thames, **33**. 57

site of cottage of, **29**. 272n

social relations of, with: Balfour, Mrs, **3**. 299; Cholmondeley, Robert, **3**. 298–9; Cholmondeley, Mrs Robert, **3**. 298–9, **9**. 269; Griffith, Mrs, **3**. 299; HW, **3**. 298–9, **9**. 269; Hobart, Mrs, **33**. 428n; Macclesfield, **10**. 36; Murphy, **9**. 269; West, Hon. Henrietta Cecilia, **9**. 269

tax gatherer taxes windows of, **35**. 468

theatre audience harangued by, after they pelted her, **30**. 26

Twickenham resident, **42**. 480, 484

venison eaten by, **10**. 241

voice of, inadequate, **18**. 180

vole dreaded by, **35**. 456

vole won by, **35**. 464

witticism by, about HW's decrepit old ladies, **10**. 216

Woffington, 'Peg,' and, **17**. 176n

World praised by, to HW, **9**. 154

Raftor, James (d. 1790), brother of Mrs Clive:

anecdote told by, **29**. 313

coward but has humour, **35**. 525

dances 'th'eclipse in hays,' **41**. 366

dancing master instructs, about dancing the hays in the *Rehearsal*, **35**. 468

fire 'hugged' by, **39**. 417

Garrick tells, of being reconciled with HW, **28**. 47

HW buys snuff-boxes for, **7**. 410

HW entertains, at SH, **43**. 141

HW flattered by, **35**. 244–5

HW hears story of Mrs Mestivyer from, **33**. 57

HW houses, at SH, **31**. 238n

HW invites, to dinner at SH, **41**. 366

HW mentions, **4**. 475

HW might make, his esquire, **35**. 525

HW receives Cibber's snuff-box from, **42**. 158

HW receives Mrs Pitt's proposals through, **9**. 264

HW's ball attended by, **28**. 447

HW's correspondence with, **42**. 158

HW sends for, after Mrs Clive's death, **31**. 238

HW sits with, **35**. 306

housebreakers frighten, **39**. 420

lives at Twickenham, **2**. 373

Prado, Mrs, entertains, until sister's burial, **31**. 238

raconteur, **39**. 251

sister's death afflicts, **31**. 238

SH visited by, **2**. 373, **12**. 225, **15**. 200n

SH visitors sent by, **12**. 228, 232 *bis*

tired of solitude, **39**. 133

Twickenham resident, **42**. 480

(?) Vaughan, Mrs, talks to, about Mrs Mawhood's marriage, **39**. 251

walking enjoyed by, and street lamps yearned for, **39**. 133

'Ragged regiment.' *See under* Westminster Abbey

Ragóba *or* Ragunath Rao. *See* Raghunáthráv Bájiráv

Raghunáthráv Bájiráv, Pandit Pradhán (fl. 1772–9), 6th Peshwa of Poona:

English to place, in Poona, **24**. 509n

Ragley, Warwickshire, E. of Hertford's seat:

Ailesbury, Cts of, to visit, **38**. 67, 70

Beauchamp and Henry Seymour-Conway to visit, **38**. 80

Birmingham rioters threaten, **11.** 317
Brown, Lancelot, improves the landscaping at, **9.** 223
ceiling at, newly painted, **38.** 80
Coke, Lady Mary, persists in reaching, at night, **37.** 563, 564–5
Conway may visit, **37.** 551, 552, 556
—— to be recorded by parson at, **37.** 234
—— to visit, **38.** 64, 67, 70
Conway, Hon. Jane, may visit, **37.** 23
date of, **43.** 117
Gibbs's renovations of Hooke's work at, **43.** 120–1
Graftons to visit, **38.** 18, 19, 62–3, 64, 67, 69–70
—— visit, **9.** 293–4
great rooms at, might be adorned by jars and beakers, **39.** 47
HW and Hertford to visit, **35.** 329
HW discovers Conway papers at, **9.** 120, 223–4, 226, **16.** 17
HW identifies paintings at. **9.** 223, 225
HW impatient for chest of old papers at, **37.** 563
HW may visit, **40.** 2, 7
HW missed Selwyn's letter at, **30.** 150
HW plans to visit Hertford at, **20.** 443n, **43.** 272
HW's comments on, **34.** 16
HW's opinion on ceilings at, wanted, **38.** 62–3
HW's visit to, postponed, **30.** 155
HW to visit: **20.** 265, **21.** 128, 226, **37.** 551, 552, 556, **38.** 16, 17, 18, 19, 25, **39.** 107, 251–2; with Conway, **21.** 226, 228; with Ds of Grafton, **21.** 427; with Graftons, **38.** 62–3, 64, 67, 69–70
HW unable to visit, **37.** 402
HW visits, **9.** 117–18, 120, 223, 243, 292–4, **10.** 264, **16.** 9n, **35.** 103, 406
Hertford, Cts of, finds, wetter than ever, **39.** 262
—— goes to, **31.** 27
—— to ride at, **38.** 122
Hertford, E. of, has 12 children at, **38.** 166
—— if a bachelor would retire to, **38.** 387
—— to visit, on way from Ireland to London, **38.** 115, 119
—— writes from, **37.** 402–3
Hertfords at: **39.** 131–2; with children, **38.** 80
—— to stay at, **39.** 74
'in great beauty,' but wet, **39.** 262
landscape effects at: Brown improves, **9.** 223; meadows and river view opened, **38.** 80
loo at, **9.** 243, 293
lumber room at, **9.** 223, 225
post comes daily to, **38.** 81
Powises to visit, **38.** 191
Seymour-Conways at, **10.** 300n
Van Helmont resident at, **9.** 223n
visitors to: Barry, **39.** 85; Burgoyne, **39.** 118; Coke, Lady Mary, **37.** 561; Conway, **35.**

406; Croft, **39.** 85; Graftons, **9.** 293; Lloyd, Rachel, **39.** 130; Lyttelton, Bn, **35.** 103; Miller, Sanderson, **35.** 103; Richards, **39.** 85; Sarsfield, **39.** 85; Varey, **38.** 70; Vernons, **39.** 131
Ragman's Castle, Twickenham:
Beauclerk, Lady Diana, calls at, **35.** 631
escapes damage in storm, **12.** 175
Fox Lane, Lady Bridget, at, **32.** 124
Hardinge lives at, **11.** 53n, **12.** 74n, **32.** 124n
—— not yet fully settled at, **35.** 625
—— would gladly exchange, for SH, **35.** 633
—— writes from, **35.** 624, 626, 630, 633
Lichfield fails to buy, **35.** 234
occupants of, **42.** 483
Pritchard, Mrs, buys, **35.** 234
road to SH from, unsafe, **35.** 633
rowboat race from, to Lady Dudley's, **11.** 86
Waldegrave, Cts, at, **43.** 185
'Ragotte, La.' *See* Fairfax, Mary (1638–1704), Ds of Buckingham
Ragoût; ragoûts:
French will be unable to get pepper for, **21.** 523
Ragouzinsky, Sava, Count:
Magnan secretary to, **18.** 548n
Rag-picking:
English lady's, **31.** 28
Raguenet, François (ca 1660–1722):
Dalrymple cites, **15.** 31n
Raguenet, Jean-Baptiste (*or* –Nicolas) (ca 1750–75); painter:
HW buys views by, **7.** 304, 404
HW's picture by, of Hôtel de Carnavalet, **4.** 30, 31, **7.** 304n, 404, **28.** 196n
Raigecourt-Gournay, Joseph, Marquis de:
(?) house of, at Gournay, **7.** 316
Raikes, Mr:
SH visited by, **12.** 237
Rail; rails:
in Methodist chapel, **35.** 119
Railings, on London streets:
illumination of, **9.** 246
Rails Head, Isleworth. *See under* Isleworth
Railton, Mr, distiller of Hampton:
SH visited by, **12.** 225, 230
Raimond:
story of priest and, **4.** 57–8
Raimondi, Marcantonio (1480–between 1527 and 1534), engraver:
dates of, corrected, **43.** 284
prints and drawings by, **38.** 371n
Raphael's 'Judgment of Paris' engraved by, **23.** 432
'Rainbow, St':
HW's housekeeper prays to, **33.** 402
Rainbow; rainbows:
HW jokes about symbolism of, **31.** 119
Raincy (France), D. of Orléans's seat:
Paris robbed of good company by, **6.** 100
visitors to: Beauvau, **7.** 440; Beauvau, Princesse de, **5.** 269; Cambis, Vicomtesse de, **6.** 232; Gramont, Duchesse de, **6.** 29; Luxem-

[Raincy (France), *continued*]
bourg, Mme de, **5.** 431, **6.** 224, 228, **7.** 425, 428, 459; Mirepoix, Mme de, **6.** 224, 228; Montesson, Marquise de, **5.** 369

Rainer Joseph (1783–1853), Archduke:
living, **25.** 549
mother expects birth of, at Pisa, **25.** 425

Rainford. *See* Rainsford

Rainham:
Churchill the poet's father vicar of, **7.** 374

Rainham, Norfolk. *See* Raynham

Rainoldi, G., director of Tuscan post office:
Mann writes to, about post horses for D. of Cumberland, **25.** 644n

Rainsford, Mrs:
SH ticket not used by, **12.** 235n

Rainsford, Charles (1728–1809), Maj.-Gen., 1777; Gen., 1795; M.P.:
biographical information about, corrected, **43.** 353
companies of, captured, **29.** 77, **33.** 216
deposition by, about D. of Gloucester's marriage, **39.** 170
Dick's letter from, about D. of Gloucester's marriage, **23.** 437
Gloucester, D. of, accompanied by, to Florence, **23.** 353
—— declares marriage to, at Florence, **23.** 484
governor of Chester and of Cliff Fort, Tynemouth, **25.** 271n
Jennings's letter to: **36.** 144; about D. of Gloucester, forces George III's letter, **36.** 144n
letter from Mann to HW carried by, **25.** 271
Mann consulted by, regarding aid to St Philip's, **25.** 233
—— gets express from, about D. of Gloucester's lodging, **23.** 333
—— tells, to consult Italian physicians about D. of Gloucester, **23.** 393
—— told by, of Charlton's despair over D. of Gloucester, **23.** 335
Minorcan mission of, unsuccessful, **25.** 271
regiment of, **25.** 34n

Raisins:
lady carries, in pocket, **37.** 22

Raisonable, English ship:
American destination of, **39.** 197n

Raisonnable, La, French ship:
Montbazon capt. of, when captured by the *Dorsetshire*, **37.** 545n

Raith, Fifeshire:
Ferguson of, **11.** 111n

Rajadhi Rajasingha, K. of Ceylon 1781–98:
England may bully, **25.** 277

Rajah; rajahs:
sons of, in India, called 'rajah-pouts,' **25.** 609n

Rake, Hants:
Gregory arrested at, **13.** 87n

Rake; rakes:
HW is, **32.** 114
old, at Bath, **10.** 141
reformed, makes good husband, **35.** 441

'Rake's Progress, The.' *See under* Hogarth, William

Rákóczy, Prince of Transylvania. *See* Ferencz II

Ralegh, Lady. *See* Throckmorton, Elizabeth

Ralegh, Mrs:
family portraits to be sold by, **33.** 272n

Ralegh ['Raleigh'], Sir Walter (? 1552–1618), Kt:
Anne of Denmark's letter concerning, **15.** 74
colonies planted by, in America, **33.** 349
cordial of, *see* Confectio Raleana
expedition of, to West Indies, **14.** 107
Fair Quaker of Deal does not mention, **28.** 120
Gray thanks HW for anecdote of, **14.** 115
Hardinge quotes, **35.** 634
History of the World by: mentions Cts of Desmond, **40.** 111, 112; Ross's continuation of, **40.** 323
'Lye, The,' by, **1.** 92
portrait of, **33.** 272

Raleigh. *See* Ralegh

Rall, Johann Gottlieb (*after* 1717–76), Hessian colonel:
Hessians' defeat blamed on, **23.** 285

Ralph (fl. 11th cent.), Count of Ivry:
daughter of, **1.** 387

Ralph, James (ca 1705–62), writer:
British Champion edited by, **18.** 32n
Critical History of the Administration of Sir Robert Walpole by, owned by HW, **1.** 60
Fall of the Earl of Essex by, **41.** 293n
Groans of Germany ascribed to, **17.** 187n
Of the Use and Abuse of Parliaments by, **18.** 464, **43.** 254
Protestor published by, **18.** 464n
Remembrancer by: attacks D. of Cumberland and Hawley, **20.** 73; prepared in case George III is not K. G., **20.** 73
satirized in Pope's *Dunciad*, **13.** 22n
Thirlby said by, to have written *Letter to the Tories*, **43.** 170

'Ralpho,' character in Samuel Butler's *Hudibras*:
Boswell called, **11.** 272

Ram, Andrew:
Leigh defeated by, in Wexford election, **37.** 422n

Ramazzini, Bernardino (1633–1714):
De contagiosa epidemia, quæ in Patavino agro, et tota fere Veneta ditione in boves irrepsit by, **19.** 174n

Rambler, The. See under Johnson, Samuel

Rambouillet, Mlle de. *See* Angennes, Julie-Lucine d'

Rambouillet (France):
visitors to: Forcalquier, Comtesse de, **4.** 207; Louis XV, **3.** 292

Rambouillet, forest of:
St-Hubert between forest of St-Léger and, **3.** 292

Rambouillet, Hôtel de, Paris:
'précieuse' coterie of, **4.** 56

Rameau, Jean-Philippe (1683–1764), composer:
Castor et Pollux by, 6. 439, 443
Fêtes d'Hymen, Les, by, 7. 298
Surprises de l'amour, Les, by, 5. 322
Ramesey. See Ramsay
Ramillie (wig):
'Alexander' wears, in play, 13. 67
Ramillies, battle of:
English deterioration since, 9. 17
Marlborough's victory at, 29. 147
Ramillies, English ship:
Byng aboard, in Gibraltar Bay, 20. 560n
—— calls council of war aboard, 20. 566n
Conway approves of Rochefort attack in conference aboard, 21. 143n
Domingo-men captured by, 24. 464n
midshipmen from, 21. 3n
(?) sunk in storm, 25. 326
Ramillon, ——, Mme du Deffand's cook:
cooks well, 7. 119
(?) Du Deffand, Mme, in a passion with, 39. 269
furniture in chamber of, 8. 13–14
wages of, 8. 46
Rampart; ramparts, of Paris:
Mirepoix, Mme de, takes house on, 6. 11
Stanley, Hans, lives on, 37. 308
Stormont's house abuts on, 6. 282
visited by Churchills, HW, and Mme du Deffand, 7. 336
Ramsay, ——:
Florence visited by, 18. 479
Ramsay, Chevalier:
anecdote by, about Lord Peterborough, 24. 113n
Ramsay, Mr:
SH visited by, 12. 237
Ramsay, Allan (1686–1758), poet:
Evergreen, The, by: Hardyknute published in, 14. 106n, 15. 65n; poem attributed to James V in, 15. 28
Investigator, The, essays in, 15. 47n
son of, 25. 517n, 540n
Ramsay, Allan (1713–84), painter; writer:
absent from London, 31. 9
Arno Miscellany has poems by, 25. 517n, 26. 46
—— sent by, from Florence, for HW, 25. 517n, 633
bad poet and great scribbler, 25. 540
Basset's portrait by, 40. 287
(?) Burgoyne's portrait by, 3. 243n
death of: at Dover on return to England, 25. 517n, 522; on way to meet daughter and son-in-law, 25. 522
French painters inferior to, 39. 32
HW praises writings of, 15. 47
HW's correspondence with, 40. 150, 370
HW sends box by, 7. 404
HW sends letters by, 7. 376
HW's letter to be carried by, 31. 59
HW's nieces' pictures to be finished by, 40. 370

HW's portrait by, for Bns Hervey, 31. 9
HW's social relations with, in Paris, 31. 59
HW surprised that Arno Miscellany should be joined by, 25. 540
Hervey, Bns, friend of, 31. 416
—— provides letters of introduction for, in Paris, 31. 59
Italy visited by, for health, 25. 517n, 522
Mann promised by, that copies of Arno Miscellany will be sent to England, 25. 523
painter and author, 31. 416
political essays and other things written by, 25. 540n
portrait by, of Ds of Gloucester, 30. 370
prints from George III's portrait by, 21. 554n
Reynolds rivalled by, in popularity, 15. 47, 43. 194
riddle by Mme du Deffand baffles, 31. 83
sister to distribute Arno Miscellany for, 25. 523, 26. 46
social relations of, in Paris, 7. 266, 267, 268, 344, 31. 59
well known by pen and pencil, 25. 522
women better painted by, than by Reynolds, 15. 47
Ramsay, Mrs Allan. See Lindsay, Margaret
Ramsay, Amelia (1755–1813), m. (1779) Gen. Sir Archibald Campbell, K.C.B., 1785:
father dies on way to meet, 25. 522
HW called on by, at Paris, 7. 344, 43. 106
HW compares, with Ariel, 31. 59
Paris visited by, 31. 59
returns from Jamaica, 25. 522–3
Ramsay, Catherine (before 1725–after 1798), Allan Ramsay jr's sister:
Arno Miscellany distributed by, 25. 523, 26. 46
Ramsay, Charlotte (1720–1804), m. (1747) Alexander Lennox; poet; actress:
HW disparages acting of, at Richmond, 9. 74
Richmond theatre the 'seminary' of, 9. 74
Ramsay, George (d. 1787), 8th E. of Dalhousie, 1764:
Church of Scotland's general assembly addressed by, 39. 325n
Ramsay, Sir James (ca 1589–1638):
Dalrymple publishes life of, 15. 181n
Ramsay, James (1733–89), abolitionist:
Essay on the Treatment and Conversion of African Slaves, An, by, 31. 328n
(?) mechanical sugar cultivation thought practical by, 31. 328
Ramsay, Michael (fl. 1727–64), Lord Eglintoun's tutor:
Eglintoun derives Jacobite sympathies from, 19. 112–13
Ramsay, William:
print of, 40. 236
Ramsay Abbey. See Ramsey Abbey
Ramsden, Elizabeth (d. 1831), m. (1771) William Weddell:
Mason expects visit from husband and, 29. 259

Ramsden, Sir John (1699–1769), 3d Bt; M.P.:
daughter of, 29. 259n
Lowther's candidate at Appleby, 20. 435n
named in Secret Committee lists, 17. 384

Ramsden, Margaret (d. 1786), m. (1774) Thomas Reynolds Moreton, 2d Bn Ducie, 1770:
SH visited by, 12. 221

Ramses III (d. ? 1167 B.C.):
sepulchre of, 28. 249n

Ramsey Abbey, Hunts:
bequest of Mrs Titus, 12. 257

Ramsgate, Kent:
Calais camp's flag visible from, 12. 122
HW not at, 2. 237
Master of Pembroke at, 2. 234, 237
Rymer practises at, 12. 109n
storm between Broadstairs and, wrecks vessels, 12. 128
visitors to: Anderson, Mrs, 11. 89; Berrys, 12. 112–13; Clifden, Lord and Lady, 12. 156; Dodd, 40. 4; Marlborough, Ds of, 12. 156; Rutland, Ds of, 12. 113; Whaley, 40. 4

Rams' heads:
on eagle's pedestal, 19. 122

Ramus, William (d. 1792), page to George III:
connection of, with Windsor election, 33. 225–6

Ranby, John (1703–73), principal sergeant-surgeon to George II:
Cumberland, D. of, has, change sweaty waistcoat and cap during operation, 38. 456
—— has knee opened by, 38. 456
—— treated by, with bark, 18. 268n
(?) HW mentions, 20. 375
HW would dislike being operated on by, 38. 462
letter of, about French officers wounded at Dettingen, 18. 260
Method of Treating Gunshot Wounds by, 18. 260n
Narrative of the Last Illness of . . . the Earl of Orford by: 19. 17n; illustrates stones removed, 18. 538n
Walpole, Sir Robert, E. of Orford, attended by, 13. 15n, 18. 538, 26. 12
Williams, Sir C. H., asked by, to reassure Dr Brown, 9. 220
wounded French prisoners cared for by, 18. 260n

Rancé. See Le Bouthillier de Rancé

Rancher de la Ferrière, Rosalie-Marguerite-Marie-Thérèse de (1761–1841), m. 1 (1784) Alexandre-Roger-François du Pouget, Marquis de Nadaillac; m. 2 (1798) Jean-François de Pérusse, Baron (later Duc) des Cars:
SH visited by, 12. 244

Rand, Brock (ca 1696–1753), antiquary:
Cole's life of, 2. 226n

Randal, Thomas, Eton College postman:
(?) HW forced to end letter hastily because of, 40. 1

Randall, John (1715–99), professor of music at Cambridge:
Gray's ode set to music by, 1. 168n

Randolph, Rev. Francis (1752–1831):
Caroline, Ps of Wales, entrusts letter to, 12. 185n

Randolph (or Randoll), John, D.D.; Q. Joan's confessor:
Joan of Navarre plots Henry V's death with, 42. 218n
said to be slain by chaplain of the Tower, 42. 220n

Randolph, Thomas (1523–90), agent of Q. Elizabeth:
Robertson's reference to, discussed by HW, 15. 42

Randolph, Rev. Thomas (1701–83):
Gibbon replies to, 33. 84

Randon de Boisset, Paul (1708–86), art collector:
sale of effects of, 6. 377

Ranelagh, E. of, and Vct. See Jones, Richard

Ranelagh, London pleasure garden:
admission price to, 17. 401, 434
Barry seems to depict crowd coming out of, 29. 300
Boodles Club celebrates George III's recovery by ball at, 39. 465n
Carteret, Bns, said to countenance, too much, 18. 501
Chesterfield's obsession for, 37. 164
Christian VII to give masquerade at, 23. 58
closed, 19. 308
coaches from, 32. 53
Colisée imitates, 24. 242n, 39. 145
completion of, 17. 401
concert of music scheduled at, 20. 135n
Conway said to be drunk at, 6. 350
cost of construction of, 17. 434
crowded, 9. 57
crowd goes to, after regatta, 32. 237
Cumberland, D. of, sups at, 20. 57n
Del Campo's ball at, for Q. Charlotte, 39. 465n
Edgcumbe inquires about 'Kitten's' visits to, 30. 66
Edward, D. of York, gives parties at, 38. 94
entertainments at, 39. 322
fashionable hour at, is after the music stops, 24. 310, 25. 317
fireworks and rockets at, for Birthday, 38. 87–8
French princes will not drive to, 33. 399
full, 18. 8
full of foreign dukes, 35. 342
George II enjoys masquerades at, 17. 487, 495
—— sups at, 20. 57n
George III said not to go to, 38. 132–3
German proprietor of, has influence with Cts of Yarmouth, 20. 46–7
'great pigeon-house at,' 32. 48–9
HW breakfasts at, 17. 401
HW frequents, nightly, 37. 164

HW has other consolations than, **28**. 397

HW not to attend ridotto al fresco at, **10**. 280

HW prefers Vauxhall to, **17**. 434

HW seems to get his politics from ladies at, **37**. 166

HW's regret at leaving, **30**. 73

HW to attend masquerade at, **17**. 487

Harrington, Cts of, follows Christian VII to, **35**. 327n

Henley to discuss, **30**. 56

inclement weather must curtail diversions at, **20**. 69

jubilee-masquerade at, **20**. 46, 57

Lacy and Rietti sell 36 shares in, at £1,000 apiece, **20**. 46n

masquerades at: **17**. 487, 495, **19**. 414, **24**. 103; for Christian VII, **35**. 407

new winter, in Oxford Road, *see* Pantheon

opening of, **17**. 434

Ossory, Lady, surrounded by 'tourbillon' of, **33**. 130

Pantheon imitates, **23**. 210

pattern of events at, **38**. 273

Pelham, Frances, clashes with March and Selwyn at, **32**. 6n

Revolution Society not permitted to hold jubilee at, **11**. 313

ridotto al fresco to be held at, **10**. 279

ridottos at, **17**. 434

(?) sky-rockets at, **10**. 156

subscription ball at, **18**. 464

Vauxhall eclipsed by, **37**. 164

Venetian masquerade imitated at, **20**. 46

visitors to: Amelia, Ps, **9**. 57; Augusta, Ps of Wales, **17**. 434, **20**. 57n, **30**. 57; Bathurst, **30**. 63; Bernstorff, **10**. 265; Boufflers, Comtesse de, **10**. 70; Boyle, **30**. 87; Burdett, **20**. 21; Campbell, Frederick, **30**. 87; Carterets, **18**. 464; Carteret, Bns (Lady Sophia Fermor), **18**. 483; Castle-Durrow, **20**. 21; Cathcart, **9**. 42–3; Charlotte, Q., **38**. 128; Cholmondeley, E. of, **9**. 35; Christian VII, **10**. 265, **23**. 41; Conway, Hon. Anne Seymour, **30**. 87; Cumberland, D. of, **9**. 42, **17**. 434, **30**. 57; Edward, D. of York, **9**. 207; Egremont, E. and Cts Dowager of, **25**. 68; Essex, Cts of, **9**. 207; Fermor, Lady Charlotte, **17**. 495; Fermor, Lady Sophia, **17**. 495, **18**. 464, 483, **30**. 47, 63; Finch, Lady Isabella, **17**. 495; Fitzroy, Lady Caroline, **9**. 28, **30**. 87; Frederick, P. of Wales, **17**. 434, **19**. 414, **20**. 57n, 30. 57, 94; George II, **17**. 487, 495, **19**. 414; George III, **38**. 128; George IV, **33**. 399n; Gloucester, D. of, **33**. 189; Gloucester, D. and Ds of, and family, **25**. 68; Gordon, Ds of, **11**. 273; HW, **9**. 57, **17**. 434, 495, **18**. 8, 464, **19**. 414, **30**. 71; Handasyds, **30**. 57; Hertford, Cts of, **39**. 114; (?) Hervey, Thomas, **30**. 57; Hesse, Landgrave of, **9**. 27; Holck, **10**. 265; Johnston, James, **9**. 28; (?) Keppel, Anna Maria, **33**. 189; Kildare, **30**. 87; Lincoln, E. of, **18**. 483, **30**. 47; Pitt, Anne, **32**. 48–9; Pomfret, Cts of, **17**. 495, **18**. 464; Pomfret, E. of, **18**. 464; Stanley, **30**. 71; Stuart, Lady Caroline, **32**. 48–9; Tabuerniga, **18**. 483, **30**. 47; Villiers, Lord, **32**. 48–9; Waldegrave sisters, **25**. 68, **33**. 189; Walpole, Sir Robert, **18**. 8

'worn out,' **37**. 533

Ranelagh House, Chelsea, London:

Carmey lives near, **40**. 259

Hesse, P. of, entertained at, by P. and Ps of Wales, **19**. 265n

Ranélagh Walk, Chelsea:

Watts lives opposite, **16**. 194

'Ranger.' *See under* Hoadly, Benjamin: *Suspicious Husband*

Ranger of the Parks:

Pomfret becomes, **20**. 225–6

Rangerships:

Orford's, to be taken from him, **25**. 266

Rangership of St James's and Hyde Parks:

Ashburnham resigns, **30**. 167

Fox offers, to Orford through HW, **30**. 167–8

value of, **30**. 167n

Rangoni, Bonifaccio Giuseppe (1714–81), Marchese:

Francis III's art sale conducted by, **19**, 314n

Rangoni, Francesco Giovanni Maria (b. 1713), Marchese:

offers himself as cicisbeo, **17**. 46

Paganini, Rosa, and Giuditta pursue, **17**. 45

Rangoni, Lodovico (d. 1762), Marchese:

HW hears news from, **17**. 43

Rangoni, Vittoria, m. Federico Rossi, Conte di S. Secondo:

(?) husband's quarrels with, **17**. 123

Ranieri (? 1118–61), patron saint of Pisa:

festival of, **18**. 455

Rantwick, Bernard (fl. 1577), engraver:

(?) engraving by, **16**. 66

Rantzau, Shack Carl (1717–89), Rigsgreve:

Christian VII closely guarded by, **23**. 386

Danish queen dowager joins, against Struensee, **23**. 374n

dismissed with pension, **23**. 426

'Rantzau.' *See* Vorontsov, ——

Ranuccio II (1630–94), D. of Parma:

money owed by, to depositors of Farnese banks at Rome, **17**. 205n

Ranusi, Prince:

SH visited by, **12**. 222

'Raoul,' Cts of Stafford's cat:

HW jokes about, **31**. 7

Raoul de Courcy:

verses to air of, **6**. 4, **7**. 98

Rape of the Lock, The. See under Pope, Alexander

'Rape of the Sabines':

in Florentine loggia, **22**. 123–4

Raper, (?) Matthew (d. ? 1778):

diamond crochette carried by, from Turin to Lady Mary Wortley Montagu at Genoa, **17**. 138

dines often at Houghton, **17**. 138

[Raper, (?) Matthew, *continued*]
Florence visited by, bringing Jackson's letter to Mann, **17**. 138

Rape seed:
birds to feed on, **35**. 154

Raphael. *See* Raffaello Sanzio

Raphael, Flora:
Agnes Berry and Juliana Dilkes visit, **12**. 175

Raphael ware:
HW's collection of, **25**. 591

Raphoe, Bp of. *See* Barnard, Dr William (1697–1768); Hawkins, James (ca 1724–1807); Oswald, Dr John (d. 1780)

Raphoe, Dean of. *See* Thompson, Anthony (d. 1756)

Rapin, Paul de. *See* Rapin-Thoyras, Paul de

Rapin, René (1621–87), priest:
letters of, **5**. 181

Rapin-Thoyras, Paul de (1661–1725), sieur de Thoyras; historian:
HW finds mention by, of Henry V suspecting his stepmother, **42**. 218, 219
Histoire d'Angleterre by: **9**. 67, 68; Conway reads, **37**. 1; (?) Du Deffand, Mme, owns, **8**. 34; Du Deffand, Mme reads, **3**. 338; Jeffreys and Kirke called tigers by, **20**. 194n; Jeffreys called butcher in, **20**. 194–5; Mann has copy of, **20**. 195; Pomfret, Cts of, objects to, **20**. 194–5; Richard III's picture in, **41**. 131

Rappee (snuff):
French may drink, **38**. 215

Rappresentazione dell' anima dannata, La:
HW describes performance of, at Turin, **13**. 191

Rash:
HW has, with fever, **14**. 85, **40**. 343
occurrences of, **38**. 429, 444–5

Rasomoufski; Rasumofsky; Rasumowsky. *See* Razumovskiĭ

Raspberry; raspberries:
and cream, HW made ill by, **15**. 327
HW made ill by, **12**. 194
Mason recommends wine after, **28**. 418

'Raspberry Plain':
Walpole, Sir Edward, to call his house, in imitation of HW's 'Strawberry Hill,' **36**. 201

Raspe, Rudolf Erich (1737–94), author; mineralogist:
arrested for debt, **29**. 19
Baron Munchausen's Narrative of His Marvellous Travels by, **15**. 145n, **29**. 5n, **41**. 439n
Critical Essay on Oil Painting by: **41**. 439, **42**. 66; HW asks Cadell to deliver copies of, to Raspe, **41**. 439; HW corrects press for, **29**. 91; HW pays for publication of, **15**. 145–6, **29**. 6, 19, 101; HW sends, to Mason, **29**. 136, 137, 143; Mason wants copy of, **29**. 94, 133
Nivernais's *Jardins modernes* given to, **12**. 259

researches of, into origin of oil painting, **29**. 5–6
writes in English, **29**. 6

Rasselas. See under Johnson, Samuel

Rastal; Rastel. *See* Rastell

Rastell, John (ca 1475–1536), printer; lawyer; writer:
Chronicle by, **1**. 306n, **15**. 243n
Pastyme of People, The, by: **43**. 59; account of death of princes in, differs from More's, **15**. *176–7*; discovery in, **1**. 306n
printer, and brother-in-law to Sir Thomas More, **15**. 177

Rastell, William (ca 1508–65), printer:
prints More's books, **15**. 177n

Rastignac, Comtesse de. *See* Hautefort, Angélique-Rosalie de

Rat, Le. *See* Le Rat

Rat; rats:
HW said to have stumbled over, **34**. 200–1
jerboa resembles, **9**. 142
Latimers lacks, **37**. 300
Lovat puns on Williamson's complaints about, **19**. 380
manuscripts gnawed by, **35**. 104
proverb on, and sinking ships, **33**. 115
pun on, **32**. 403
Temple, Cts, mentions, in verses, **10**. 114
Tories' epithet for Hanoverians, **35**. 604

Ratcliffe, Charles:
print of, **40**. 236

Ratcliffe, John (d. 1776), book collector:
HW exchanges prints with, **40**. 235–7
HW has *Anecdotes* bound to give to, **40**. 236
HW's correspondence with, **40**. 235–7

Ratcliffe or Radcliffe, Sir Richard (d. 1485), Kt, 1471:
keeps Tyrell down, **14**. 183n
Richard III accompanied by, at Oxford, **41**. 141

Ratcliffe. *See also* Radcliffe; Radclyf; Radclyffe

Ratcliffe, St Mary. *See* Bristol: church of St Mary Redcliff

Ratcliffe Library. *See* Radcliffe Camera

Rathbone Place, London:
Farington, Joseph, lives in, **12**. 187
Mann, Edward Louisa, has property at, **24**. 159n
Watson of, **11**. 180n, **33**. 513n
Woollett lives in, **42**. 63n

Rathnally, Meath:
Carter of, **11**. 95n

Ratisbon or Regensburg (Germany):
Bologna to be equivalent of, **21**. 494n
Bulkeley minister to, **5**. 134
England's seizure of Dutch contraband might be disapproved by, **25**. 4
Francis I seeks votes at, after contemptuous treatment there, **21**. 90
Frederick II's troops approach, **21**. 102
HW as grave about SH as he could be about statecraft at, **20**. 396

Imperial Diet at: **20.** 90; Austria forbids, to aid Frederick II, **21.** 28n; currency of the Empire and reform of imperial chamber to be discussed by, **20.** 90n; HW to be as merry as if at, **12.** 142; imperial subjects absolved of oath to Frederick II by, **21.** 102n; Maria Theresa protests to, against Frederick II's Bavarian claim, **24.** 403; mémoire about, **21.** 102; publishes ban on Frederick II, **20.** 589n; Plotho, Bn, delivers Frederick II's *Pro-Memoria* to, **21.** 102n; Walpole, Thomas jr, must conform to usages of, **36.** 229

Mainz, Elector of, delivers imperial decrees to, **21.** 28n

peace seldom enforced by conferences at, **25.** 39

Richecourt may be minister to, **19.** 49

'Raton,' Selwyn's dog:
HW jokes about French comic opera 'Raton et Rosette' to be written about 'Rosette' and, **30.** 254–5
HW sends compliments to, **30.** 242
Selwyn's fondness for, **30.** 265

Raton et Rosette, French comic opera:
HW jokes about, **30.** 254–5

'Ratonissa':
HW sends compliments to, **30.** 242

Rat poison. *See* Poison: rat; Ratsbane

Ratsbane:
Louis XV's mistresses not to poison each other with, **35.** 173

Ratta, Mgr:
Clement XIII summons, to advisory congregation, **21.** 308n

Ratta, Casa. *See under* Bologna

Ratta family, of Bologna:
Domenichino's 'Sibyl' owned by, **35.** 19n

Raucour (Raucourt; Raucoux). *See* Roucourt

Raucourt, Mlle; Raucoux, Mlle. *See* Saucerotte, Françoise-Marie-Antoinette-Joseph

Rauzzini, ——, composer:
Omaggio, L', opera by, **39.** 382

Rauzzini, ——, singer:
'first man' in *Armida*, falls ill, **32.** 216n

Ravaillac, François (1578–1610), Henri IV's assassin:
bankrupt man may imitate, **39.** 151
forgotten, **12.** 117
Louis XV threatened with successors to, **20.** 287, 387–8
renewal of age of, **21.** 48

Ravanne. *See* Eynard de Ravanne

Ravant, Miss:
Montagu, Lady Barbara, friend and neighbour of, **10.** 234

Ravelin; ravelins:
More, Mr, talks about, **37.** 71

Raven, English sloop:
French ships pursued by, **37.** 246

Raven; ravens:
caw for breakfast, **33.** 459
English compared to, **21.** 204

Ravenel, Marquise de. *See* Rothe, Marguerite-Josèphe de

Ravenna (Italy):
Chute and Whithed to visit, **19.** 48

Ravensworth, Bn. *See* Liddell, Sir Henry

Ravensworth, Bns. *See* Delmé, Anne

Ravensworth Castle, Durham, Bn Ravensworth's seat:
Grafton, Ds of, to visit father at, **38.** 176

Ravioli:
Chute eats, **17.** 218

Ravoie. *See* Neyret de Ravoye

Ravvivati, Teatro dei. *See under* Pisa

Rawdon, Bns. *See* Hastings, Lady Elizabeth (1731–1808)

Rawdon, Lady Anne (1753–1813), m. (1788) Thomas Brudenell Bruce, cr. (1776) E. of Ailesbury, n.c.:
Albany, Cts of, to be presented by, at Court, **11.** 270
candidate for vacancy in Q. Charlotte's Bedchamber, **11.** 367
Marcus Flaminius read by, **34.** 168n

Rawdon, Sir John (1720–93), cr. (1750) Bn Rawdon, (1762) E. of Moira:
assassination by Jacobites feared by, **17.** 400n
daughter of, **11.** 270n
death of, **12.** 72
expenses at Wallingford election revealed by, to Secret Committee, **17.** 400
kicked downstairs for not drinking Old Pretender's health, **20.** 136
Mann remembers follies of, **20.** 135–6
Montagu, Lady Mary Wortley, accuses, of buying title and pictures for the same reason, **20.** 135n
—— meets, in Venice, **17.** 400n
Naylor resembles, **20.** 136
peerage given to, **20.** 135–6

Rawdon, John Theophilus (1757–1808), M.P.:
mother's letter to, in *Archæologia*, **33.** 474

Rawdon Hastings (before 1790, Rawdon), Francis (1754–1826), styled Lord Rawdon 1762–83; cr. (1783) Bn Rawdon; 2d E. of Moira, 1793; cr. (1817) M. of Hastings, army officer:
abortive expeditions of, against French, **12.** 3n, 66–7, 71, 72, 77, 84, 88, 89, 90, 156
Angoulême, Duc d', visits, at Donington Castle, **12.** 156
Bouillés, Conway, George IV, and Abbés de St-Albin and St-Farre entertained by, **34.** 175–6
Coigny, Comte de, to set out with expedition of, **12.** 79
estates of, inherited from father, **12.** 72
Greene ready to attack, **39.** 383n
Macbride predicts failure of expedition of, **12.** 90
Richmond's quarrel with, **39.** 388
York, Frederick, D. of, seconded by, in duel, **39.** 466

Rawlings. *See* Rawlins

Rawlins *or* Rawlings, Robert, page to Edward, D. of York:
(?) illness of, **22.** 225n
Rawlins, Thomas (fl. 1641), engraver:
engraving by, **16.** 66
Rawlins, Thomas (ca 1620–70), minter:
medal by, of Charles I, **16.** 50
Rawlinson, Arthur (d. 1749), High Constable of Westminster 1737–42:
testimony against, concerning Westminster election, **17.** 246
Rawlinson, Henry (1743–86), M.P.:
House of Commons informed by, of Hood's success at St Kitts, **25.** 253n
Rawlinson, Richard (1690–1755), collector; topographer; non-juring Bp of London, 1728:
HW saw, at book and print sales, **42.** 239
HW's civility to, **1.** 161, 165, 166
History and Antiquities of Glastonbury by, **43.** 43
library of, sold at auction, **42.** 239
New Method of Studying History, A, by, cited, **1.** 257, 258–9
Oxford inherits antiquities of, **42.** 239
St John's College, Oxford, inherits heart of, **42.** 239n
Rawlinson, Susanna (b. before 1744, d. 1816), m. (1765) George Wombwell, cr. (1778) Bt:
SH visited by, **12.** 240
Rawlinson, Sir Thomas (d. 1769), alderman:
death of, leaves vacancy, **32.** 40
son of, **1.** 161n
Rawlinson, Sir Walter (1735–1805), Kt, 1774; M.P.; banker; alderman:
Ewin's letter to, enclosed by Lort, **16.** 201
HW's civility to, **1.** 161, 165, 166
M. P. Queenborough, **43.** 54
Rawstone, Mr:
SH visited by, **12.** 238
Ray, Mr (1):
SH visited by, **12.** 232
Ray, Mr (2):
SH visited by, **12.** 244
Ray, John (1627–1705), naturalist:
Collection of English Proverbs, A, by, sent by HW to Bentley, **35.** 192, 198
Ray, Martha (ca 1745–79), Lord Sandwich's mistress:
children of, **33.** 101
Hackman murders, **2.** 155–6, **7.** 131, **24.** 459, 477, **33.** 98–101
——'s supposed correspondence with, **2.** 204–6, 208
Sandwich's mistress, **7.** 131
Ray, clan of. *See* Reay
Raye, Bn:
Mann escorted by, **23.** 60n
Rayleigh, Bns. *See* Fitzgerald, Lady Charlotte Mary Gertrude
Raymond IV (d. 1105), Comte de Toulouse, 1088:
Richard de Tarascon partisan of, **21.** 169n
Raymond, Bns. *See* Blundell, Hon. Mary

Raymond, ——, French Resident at Pullicat:
Lally's letter to, **21.** 516n
Raymond, Mr, Lisbon merchant:
cash of, saved in Lisbon earthquake, **20.** 520n
Raymond, Amy (ca 1700–89), m. (1723) Peter Burrell:
grandchildren's brilliant marriages witnessed by, **24.** 499
Raymond, Sir Robert (1673–1733), cr. (1731) Bn Raymond; M.P.:
HW inserts, in *Royal and Noble Authors,* **16.** 13
lord chief justice, **17.** 438n
Raymond, Robert (ca 1717–56), 2d Bn Raymond, 1732:
epitaph by, on Indemnity Bill, **17.** 438, 455
father of, **17.** 438n
girl beats, **18.** 322
Halifax answered by, **17.** 230, 263
Stosch receives offer from, for Meleager, **17.** 264
Vaneschi cheats, at Lucca, **17.** 216
wife of, **10.** 14n
Wright's murder seen by, at Florence, **37.** 34n
Raymond, Sophia (d. 1802), m. 1 (1773) Sir William Burrell, 2d Bt, 1788; m. 2 (1797) Rev. William Clay:
SH visited by, **12.** 236
Raynal, Guillaume-Thomas-François (1713–96), abbé; writer:
Anecdotes historiques by, quoted by HW, **34.** 65
Anecdotes littéraires by, **35.** 226
École militaire by, owned by Mme du Deffand, **8.** 34
England visited by, **15.** 136
HW offends, at Holbach's dinner, **39.** 212
Histoire philosophique et politique . . . des Européens dans les deux Indes by: **39.** 167–8, **43.** 93; censored, **5.** 308; Du Deffand, Mme, comments on, **5.** 210–11; HW praises, **15.** 136, **39.** 212; HW's opinion of, **5.** 308
'most tiresome creature in the world,' **39.** 212
St-Ouen visited by, **6.** 229
social relations of, in Paris, **7.** 267, 279, 289, 299, 302
talkative at SH, **32.** 357
Raynald, Thomas:
Birth of Mankind published by, **40.** 306n
Rayner, Lady. *See* Beaumont, Mary
Rayneval. *See* Gérard de Rayneval
Raynham Hall, Norfolk, Vct Townshend's seat:
HW and Rigby visit, **30.** 81
HW jokes about Vcts Townshend's visiting, instead of apothecary's, to reduce, **30.** 83
HW sends Orford's horses to, for Townshend's inspection, **41.** 261
housekeeper at, HW shows house to, **30.** 81
Kneller's portrait of Sir Robert Walpole at, **41.** 234
Leicester's son not to imitate marriage of heir of, **19.** 27

Townshend, 3d Vct, dies at, **38**. 346
—— lives at, **9**. 32n
—— of, **9**. 68n
Townshend, 4th Vct, writes from, **42**. 332
Townshend, Mary, at, **40**. 47
Townshends invite E. of Orford to recuperate at, **42**. 334, 336
Razor; razors:
Selwyn procures, for Aulan, **7**. 131
Siries, Louis, makes for Sultan of Turkey, **19**. 437
'Razor's Levee . . . ,' satirical print:
HW describes, **33**. 401
Razoumovsky. *See* Razumovskiĭ
Razumovskiĭ, Andrei Kirillovich (1752–1836), Fürst Rasumofsky:
(?) Shuvalov accompanied by, at Florence, **22**. 564–5
Razumovskiĭ, Kirill Grigor'evich (1728–1808), Grand Hetman of Little Russia:
(?) *Britannicus* fails to move, **7**. 277
exiled and pensioned by mistress, **22**. 456
forced into conspiracy against Peter III, **22**. 456
HW refuses Shuvalov's invitation to meet, **22**. 456
(?) in power, **22**. 59
Mann saw, in Florence, **22**. 460
(?) son of, **22**. 564–5
Ré. *See* Rhé
Read, ——, Brig.-Gen.:
regiment of, **17**. 300n
Read, Miss (d. after 1801), dau. of Henry Read; m. —— Villebois:
SH visited by, **12**. 222
Read, Catherine (1723–78), portrait painter:
birth date of, **43**. 375
Cathcart told by, of Lady Susan Fox Strangways's affair, **38**. 367
Read, Charlotte (d. 1803), m. (1791) Sir Nelson Rycroft, 2d Bt, 1786:
SH visited by, **12**. 241
Read *or* Reade, George (d. 1756), army officer:
death of, falsely reported, **37**. 356
Read, Henry (d. after 1801), of Crow-wood, Wilts:
SH visited by, **12**. 222
Read, Mrs Henry (d. 1801):
SH ticket not used by, **12**. 235n
SH visited by, **12**. 222
Read, John, sea-captain:
Sea Horse commanded by, **17**. 8n
Read, Nicholas, sculptor:
Ds of Northumberland's monument in Westminster Abbey executed by, **41**. 411n
Read, William, justice of the peace in Massachusetts:
affidavit to, **24**. 112
Read. *See also* Reade; Reed; Reid
Reade, Maj.:
Howe sends, with news, **24**. 248n
Reade, Henry (d. 1762), comptroller of the tax office; Lord Lincoln's steward and tutor:

HW often told, of desire to visit Lincoln, **30**. 174
HW's correspondence with: about Lincoln's ancestress, **40**. 174; about Theodore of Corsica's signed document, **40**. 191–2
HW to see, **40**. 174
Reade, Love (d. 1745), m. (1719) Thomas Winnington:
death of, **37**. 202
'strange,' but well treated by husband, **37**. 202
Reade, Sir W.:
print of, **40**. 237
Reade, William:
HW's note about, at Merton College Library, **9**. 289n
Reade. *See also* Read; Reed, Reid
Reader, Mr, of Bedford St, London:
SH visited by, **12**. 249
Reader, William (fl. 1680), painter:
print from portrait by, **1**. 149
Reader; readers:
foolish, are suited by foolish writers, **35**. 462
Mme du Deffand's, are Pétry and 4 lackeys, **7**. 235, 238
Reading, Burnet (fl. 1780–1820):
print of HW by, **15**. 196n
Reading, Jack of. *See* Jack of Reading
Reading, Berks:
Berrys visit Lovedays near, **11**. 137
Caversham Hill near, **11**. 129n
corruption in borough of, **22**. 584n
Craven's house, near, **11**. 361
military review near, **37**. 382
Pitt visits, **22**. 490, 572
St Mary's at, Nares holds living of, **15**. 218n
tradesmen at, oppose Lord Charles Spencer, **9**. 320
visible from Whiteknights, **35**. 71
Reading:
HW finds, great resource at Houghton, **30**. 34
HW's: **4**. 478–9, **7**. 202; is just for his own amusement, **25**. 584
HW's advice for Mme du Deffand's, **5**. 355–6
Mme du Deffand's, **4**. 426, 447, 478, 482, 488, 489, 491, 492, **5**. 6, 47, 51, 67–9, 72, 180, 184, 190, 308, 350, 383, 432, **6**. 22, 162, 203, 247–8, 253, 259, 286, 288–9, 298, 316, 324, 332, 347–8, 396, 416, 429–30, 447, 452, 469–70, 474, **7**. 67, 70, 72, 107, 133, 178, 181, 191, 202, 216, 235, 237–8
——'s preferences in, **4**. 406, 426, 482, **5**. 16–17, 51, 77–8, **6**. 74, 247–8
See also Criticism, literary; Library
Reading Abbey:
stones brought from, **10**. 104n
Reading-desk; reading-desks:
in mourning, at Easton Maudit church, **10**. 339
Reading-glass; reading-glasses:
HW's grandfather began psalm with, **37**. 181
Reading Mercury and Oxford Gazette, The:
Craven's death reported by, **11**. 361

Real, Spanish ship:
in Spanish fleet, 17. 286
Reale accademia Ercolanese di archæologia:
Antiquities of Herculaneum by, *see* Pitture
antiche di Ercolano Herculanensium vol-
uminum quæ supersunt, 31. 278n
Real Felipe, Spanish ship:
alleged destruction of, 18. 404
*Real galleria di Firenze accresciuta, La. See
under* Lanzi, Luigi Antonio
Reality:
HW speculates on nature of, 25. 133
Re alla caccia, Il, opera:
performed, 23. 171
'Real Love Story, A,' by HW:
HW reads MS of, to Mary Hamilton and
Hannah More, 31. 229
Réamur. *See* Ferchault de Réamur
Reaping:
at Arras, 7. 315
HW avoids, 18. 8
Reason:
Conway's reflections on, 37. 198
Du Deffand, Mme, on, 5. 9, 325
—— on taste and, 4. 268
HW calls: charter obtained only by blood-
shed, 25. 237; 'inadequate judge,' 39. 429
HW no great friend to, 37. 198
HW's reflections on, 11. 22, 12. 89, 32. 78–
83, 345, 33. 447, 545
More, Hannah, questions supposed triumph
of, in 18th century, 31. 280
Réaux. *See* Taboureau de Réaux
Reay, clan of:
Coke, Lady Mary, regrets inability to lead,
38. 17
Rebecca (biblical):
stained glass depicts, 9. 385n
Rebecca. *See also* Child, Rebecca
Rebel, François (1701–75), administrator-gen.
of Opéra 1772–4:
Bishop told to present himself to, 6. 55
director of Opéra, 6. 28, 51
Rebel; rebels, English. *See* Jacobite; Jacobites
Rebellion, great. *See* Civil war, English
Rebellion of 1745:
ministry unsettled and king disregarded in,
35. 216
Walpole, Sir Robert, foresaw, 24. 356
See also Jacobite; Jacobites
'Rebel lords':
execution of: eyewitness accounts of, 19. 298n,
299n; HW describes, 19. 298–302; HW to
stay in town for, 9. 44; Mann comments on,
19. 311
trials of: arouse Mann's sympathies, 19. 303;
described by HW, 9. 38–9, 279, 19. 280–7;
expected, 9. 37, 19. 271–2, 273; Florence
awaits news of, 19. 293, 298; Mann comments on, 19. 311
'Rebel pie':
Townshend, Vcts, fears she will have to eat,
19. 302, 23. 21

Rebours, Le. *See* Le Rebours
Rebout, Marie-Thérèse (1728–1805), m. Joseph-
Marie Vien; painter:
(?) social relations of, with HW, 7. 308
Rebow, Isaac Martin (1731–81), M.P.:
Colchester election successfully contested by,
35. 208n
Rebus; rebuses (architectural):
Gothic, at Beverley, 34. 224
in Islip Chapel at Westminster Abbey, 35. 132
Rebus; rebuses (puzzles):
Conway sends, to HW, 37. 346
HW returns, to Lady Ossory, 32. 230
on Ds of Manchester, Lovel, and Chesterfield,
30. 42
Recanati (Italy):
Austrians seize hospital at, 18. 419
Receipt to Make a Lord:
HW quotes, from *Common Sense,* 17. 469–70
Mann dislikes, 17. 491
Receiver-general; receivers-general, English:
customs receipts go to, 41. 327
Receiver-general; receivers-general, French:
edict suppresses, 7. 449
Receiver of Rents:
Cromarty was, 19. 284
Reception:
Leopold to give, 22. 362
See also Appartement; Drawing-Room
Recherches de la France. See under Pasquier,
Étienne
*Recherches philosophiques sur les Grecs. See
under* Pauw, Cornelius de
Recherches sur les théâtres de France. See under
Godart de Beauchamps, Pierre-François
*Recherches sur l'origine . . . des arts de la Grèce.
See under* Hugues, Pierre-François
Recipe; recipes:
HW's, for 'cheeses,' 9. 168
HW's, 'humorous,' 9. 138–40
Réconciliation normande. See under Dufresny,
Charles Rivière
Recousse, La. See La Recousse
*Recreatio mentis et oculi in observatione ani-
malium testaceorum. See under* Buonanni,
Filippo
Recruiting Officer, The. See under Farquhar,
George
'Recruiting Serjeant, The,' satiric print:
Mann receives, 21. 9
Townshend publishes, 21. 77
'Recueil de lettres,' Mme du Deffand's:
bequeathed to HW, 3. 4n, 4. 225
Du Deffand, Mme, letters to and from, copied
in, 7. 237–8
fears of printing of, 4. 224–5, 232
Greville, Mrs, alarmed about, 4. 224–5
*Recueil de lettres choisies, pour servir de suite
aux lettres de Mme de Sévigné à Mme de
Grignan, sa fille. See under* Rabutin-Chantal,
Marie de, Mme de Sévigné

Recueil de lettres de diverses personnes amies de Mme de Sévigné. See under Rabutin-Chantal, Marie de, Mme de Sévigné

Recueil de lettres militaires. See Griffet, Henri: *Recueil de lettres pour servir . . .*

Recueil de lettres pour servir d'éclaircissement à l'histoire militaire du règne de Louis XIV. See under Griffet, Henri

Recueil des histoires de Troyes. See under Le Fèvre

Recueil d'estampes d'après les plus beaux tableaux. See under Crozat, Joseph-Antoine; Mariette, Pierre-Jean

Recueil des voyages au Nord. See under Bernard, Jean-Frédéric

Recueil d'opéras:
Mme du Deffand owns, 8. 33

Reculver, Kent:
foundation of church of, 2. 160–1

Reda, Mary (b. ca 1725, fl. 1773), m. —— Vemberght; milliner; 'Madame Rheda':
Grosvenor's relations with, 32. 120

'Red Book' (Royal Calendar):
Exodus must precede Genesis in, 33. 395, 396
incidents of, below HW's notice, 33. 385
newspapers could have prevented errors by consulting, 22. 325

Redbridge, near Southampton:
Bunbury, Lady Sarah, and Gordon elope to, 43. 89

'Redcoats' (English troops):
England's dispute should not be settled by, 25. 5

Reddish, Samuel (1735–85), actor:
pitiful and whining, in *Braganza*, 28. 177
print for benefit of, 39. 550
wife of, 10. 40n

Reddish, Mrs Samuel. *See* Hart, Polly

Reddish. *See also* Redish

Rede (Reed), Richard (d. 1550), salter; alderman of Farringdon Without, London:
Henry VIII punishes, 11. 278

Redenhall-with-Harleston:
Oldershaw rector of, 2. 281n

Redesdale, Bn. *See* Mitford, Sir John (1748–1830)

Redford. *See* Retford

Redgrave, Suffolk:
Holt of, 9. 332n

Redi, Francesco (1626–98):
(?) *Annotazioni* by, 40. 116

Redish, Mrs (d. 1762), cousin of Etheldreda, Vcts Townshend:
death of, 38. 167

Redish. *See also* Reddish

Red Lion Court, Fleet St, London:
Nichols, printer in, 2. 295
Purser in, 13. 18n

Red Lion Inn:
at Newmarket, 18. 315

Red Lion Inn, Bagshot:
Tilbury landlord of, 30. 246n

Red Lion Sq., London:
Suckling's address at New North St in, 24. 209

Red Lion St, Holborn:
'Cole-Hole' theatre in, 14. 15n
Pye, Mrs, of, 1. 367n

Redlynch, Somerset, Ilchester's seat:
HW and Bateman to visit, 40. 249
HW to visit, 10. 34
HW visits, 1. 14n, 9. 369n, 40. 251–2

Redmond, Jean de (ca 1709–78), Lt–Gen.; Chevalier:
Aiguillon, Duc d', fond of, 3. 295
Aiguillon, Duchesse d', friend of, 3. 186, 295
Craufurd's correspondence with, 3. 39, 170, 5. 374n
Du Deffand, Mme, buys gift for HW from, 3. 129
—— hears from, of HW, 4. 252, 255
——'s opinion of, 4. 300
—— wishes to see, 4. 253
'fool,' 7. 340
HW''s *Account of the Giants* translated by, 3. 188, 190, 193, 212n, 43. 84
HW's preface to *Historic Doubts* translated by, 4. 38, 42, 43
HW told by: of Young Pretender's alleged conversion, 23. 402; to punish Suard, 7. 340–1
Irish officer in French service, 23. 402
London visited by, 4. 252
Rueil visited by, 7. 320
social relations of, in Paris, *see index entries ante* 8. 484
Young Pretender's bust owned by, 7. 279

Redrice, near Andover, Hants:
Holland dies at, 32. 219n

Redriff ('Redriffe'); Rotherhithe:
house at, destroyed in Gordon riots, 33. 192

Red Sea:
Egyptians in, compared with French in English Channel, 39. 342
Jacobins to be driven into, 11. 325
of claret, 12. 206, 39. 310
spirits laid in, 11. 230, 31. 319

Réduction de Paris, La. See under Farmain de Rozoi, Barnabé

Reebkomp (after ca 1791, Montgomery), Augustus Retnuh (1762–97):
mother declines to give up, 10. 52
Piozzi, Mrs, comments on, 10. 14n

Reed, Isaac (1742–1807), scholar; antiquary:
Baker's *Biographia Dramatica* revised by, 43. 202
Biographical Anecdotes of Willam Hogarth by George Steevens and, 41. 448
disbelieves in Ireland's MSS, 15. 321
HW's correspondence with, 41. 280–1
HW sends Shakespearian questions to, 15. 197–8

[Reed, Isaac, *continued*]
HW's quarrel with Gray explained by, **17.** 50n
HW's receipt of information from, for *Royal and Noble Authors*, **41.** 280
HW to see, in Arlington St, **41.** 281
Ritson attacks, **2.** 335n
See also under Baker, David Erskine
Reed, Joseph, president of Pennsylvania supreme executive council:
congressional committee to act with, **25.** 135n
Reed, Lancelot:
Clement, Jane, returns to Sir Edward Walpole's, on plea from, **36.** 320–1
Reed. *See also* Read; Reade; Reid
Reeds:
Catherine whispers to, at SH pond, **35.** 227
Reels, Scotch:
Berry, Mary, dances, with Lord Galloway and daughter, **12.** 113
Rees, Abraham (1743–1825):
Jenyns's book reviewed by, **28.** 269n
Rees, in Cleves:
Gray mentions, **14.** 127
Reeve, Lady. *See* Foote, Arabella
Reeve, Mr:
SH visited by, **12.** 234
Reeve, Bartlett, watchman at SH:
HW's bequest to, **30.** 362
(?) mentioned in list of visitors to SH, **12.** 246
Reeve, Clara (1729–1807), novelist:
Champion of Virtue, The, original title of *Old English Baron* by, **28.** 381n
Old English Baron, The, by: criticism in, of *Castle of Otranto*, **2.** 107–8, 110; HW's opinion of, **2.** 110; reduces *Castle of Otranto* to reason and probability, **28.** 381–2, **41.** 410
Reeve, Sir Thomas (d. 1777), Kt:
drawings of, 'indifferent,' **10.** 106
HW invites, to Twickenham, **10.** 106
HW offered use of copies by, of Dr Mead's portraits, **10.** 105, **40.** 231
HW's correspondence with, **10.** *105*, **40.** 230–1, **43.** 130
HW's opinion of, **10.** 106
HW visits, briefly, **10.** 106
home of, near Maidenhead, **10.** 105
marriage of, connects Reeve family with Dr Mead, **40.** 231n
Mead, Dr, intimate with, **40.** 231
Walpole, Sir Edward, known by, at Windsor, **40.** 230
Reeve, William:
Black Castle built by, **10.** 232n
Reeve. *See also* Reeves
Reeves, Mrs, of Twickenham:
HW buys land of, **23.** 128n
Reeves, William:
arrested, **33.** 179n
Reeves. *See also* Reeve

Refectory:
at Battle Abbey, **35.** 140
at Newstead Abbey, **9.** 299
Reflections:
HW's reflections on, **9.** 228
Reflections concerning Innate Moral Principles. *See under* St John, Henry, Vct Bolingbroke
Reflections on the Different Ideas of . . . Cruelty. See under Bentley, Richard (1708–82)
Reflections on the Letter to Dr Waterland:
not by Waterland, **43.** 212
Reflections on the Revolution in France. See under Burke, Edmund
Reflections on the Variations, etc. *See under* Middleton, Conyers
Reflections upon the Present State of Affairs. *See under* Hume Campbell, Hugh, E. of Marchmont
Réflexions posthumes sur le grand procès de Jean-Jacques avec David ('lettre posthume'):
Aiguillon, Duchesse d', sends, to Bns Hervey, **3.** 222
Du Deffand, Mme, sends, to HW, **3.** 207, 212, 222, 224, 231
Réflexions sur la poésie et la peinture:
Du Deffand, Mme, owns, **8.** 32
Reform:
fashionable in France, **39.** 270
in religion, **35.** 155
Reformation, The:
bloodshed caused by, **33.** 487, **34.** 51, 102, 111
Butler's couplet on, emended by HW, **42.** 241
England has had Shrove-tide carnival since, **13.** 201
HW dislikes 'fractions' of, **42.** 221
HW's love of abbeys does not alienate him from, **35.** 146
HW's mock sermon mentions, **31.** 426
HW's reflections on, **34.** 51, 101–2
Mysterious Mother laid at beginning of, **39.** 103
papers sent to Spain and Portugal during, **15.** 187
Robertson's *Charles V* will give account of, **15.** 46
sects during, increasingly rigorous, **31.** 435
Reformation of Learning:
Gray starts poem on, **43.** 191
Reformed Commonwealth of Bees, The. See under Hartlib, Samuel
Reformer; reformers:
feelings lacked by, **35.** 398
HW's reflections on, **15.** 131, 237
things brought back by, to natural course, **35.** 474
"Refrigeratory':
Conway's, **39.** 551
Regal and Ecclesiastical Antiquities, The. See under Strutt, Joseph
Regale Accademia Ercolanese:
founding of, **13.** 224n

Regalo:
bringers of, receive money from Modenese princess, 17. 64–5
Regan, Morice (fl. 1171):
'History of Ireland,' Totness's translation of, 16. 13
Regan, Patrice, Ensign:
captured at Velletri, 18. 492
Regatta; regattas:
England transplants, 24. 112
'foolish,' on the Thames, 24. 112, 32. 237, 318
HW attends, at Richmond, 32. 317–18
Venice to give, for D. of York, 22. 241
Regeb:
month of, 30. 36
Regency, Council of, in Tuscany:
Alberti discloses letter of, about Mann's future promotion, 22. 317–18, 346
Algerian war contemplated by, 22. 259
Antinori, Chevalier, member of, 20. 124, 350
—— the sole functioning member of, now that Richecourt and Tornaquinci are incapacitated, 21. 84–5, 90
Austrian artillery permitted by, to pass through Tuscany, 18. 541
author and publisher of *sonetto* banished by, 19. 499
'battle of the bridge' may be forbidden by, 20. 473
Benedict XIV's disputes over, 20. 305
Bocchineri complains to, of wife's affair with procaccia, 20. 447
Bosville, Mrs, might have been summoned before, 18. 286
Botta does not return visits from members of, 21. 148
——'s circular letter to members of, announcing Peter III's overturn, 22. 63
—— to be head of, 21. 107
Braitwitz avoids, to escape Richecourt's affronts, 18. 66
burletta dispute carried before, 17. 163
Calderini member of, 17. 121n
Carteret never wrote to, 18. 382
Castellar tells, to give up deserters, 17. 349
courier sent by, to Francis I, about Montemar's demands, 17. 281
Craon the head of, 17. 9n, 189n, 23. 142n
—— to present demand to, for Electress's jewels, 17. 242
delegate from, escorts Mann to Elizabeth Christina's requiem, 20. 227
Del Monte, Giambattista, excluded by, from Tuscany, 20. 422
Del Vernaccia appeals to, for wife's release, 18. 121–2
duel opposed by, 20. 363
Dumesnil's complaints disregarded by, 18. 491
each member of, has department, 23. 253
edict of, on Francis I's death, copied by Mann for Conway, 22. 329

English captains wish to 'kiss the hand' of, 18. 92–3, 99–100
English protection not welcomed by, for fear of antagonizing Spain, 18. 37–8
Ferrarini's case discussed by, 18. 10, 31
'Fiscal' asks, to forbid masks, 18. 372
Francis I names two members to, 21. 125
—— orders: to ask Naples to seize Del Monte, 20. 437; to have Te Deum sung, 21. 112; to tell Mann that Tuscany will receive English fleet, 21. 114
——'s correspondence with, about Spanish invasion, 17. 206
——'s letter from, mentions Mann's coming promotion, 22. 317–18, 346
——'s message to Electress alarms, 17. 236–8
——'s orders sought by, about Neapolitan cavalry, 19. 297–8
—— to receive news from, by courier, of Del Monte uprising, 20. 423
Francis III's intentions unknown to, 17. 324
Gavi investigated by, 17. 368
George II's protection of Tuscany known to, 18. 27, 38
Ginori excluded from, 19. 394n
—— may resign from, 18. 135
Goldsworthy says that Tuscan danger is belittled by, 18. 107
Haddock's letter to be communicated to, by Craon, 17. 380
Hervey thanked by, 19. 473
Karl Alexander expected by, to call on them, 20. 376
Langlois supported by, in dispute with officer, 19. 366
Leghorn earthquakes to be assuaged by, 17. 304
Leghorn governor asks, how to receive D. of York, 22. 166
Leghorn governor tells, of Saunders's approach, 21. 507
Leghorn's memorial sent to, 20. 267
Leopold II's arrival to be announced in notice by, 22. 330
Lobkowitz's discard of artillery disliked by, 18. 529
local affairs only, entrusted to, 17. 134
Lorenzi asks, whether to celebrate wedding or funeral, 19. 14
—— urges, to expel English fleet from Leghorn, 21. 274
Lucca punished by, for making a new road, 20. 514–16, 521–2
Madonna dell' Impruneta escorted to Duomo by, 30. 4
Mann announces D. of York's changed plans to, 22. 245
—— asked by: to ask Mathews to guard against plague, 18. 256; to help Goldsworthy's difficulties, 18. 485
—— asks, to restore English brig, 21. 334

[Regency, Council of, *continued*]
—— assured by, of Francis I's intention to preserve Tuscan neutrality, **21.** 176
—— avoids dispute with, **20.** 2
—— battles with, to stop French Levant trade, **21.** 282
—— complains to, of General's civilities to Cardinal York, **22.** 250
—— disputes with, over seizure of English ship carrying Tuscan flag, **21.** 269, 273
—— negotiates with, about English interference with Tuscan trade, **21.** 269
—— persuades, to allow amusements at Leghorn, **19.** 1
—— said to have been ordered to complain to, about Niccolini, **20.** 7
——'s garden party considered by, as sufficient celebration, **19.** 115
—— should have denounced *sonetto's* author to, **19.** 498
——'s involved correspondence with, about capture of prizes, **21.** 288
—— takes Almada to members of, **21.** 436
—— to be asked by, for English aid, **18.** 27
—— urges, to defend Leghorn, **17.** 259
—— writes to, defending Langlois, **19.** 366
Maria Theresa honours members of, **17.** 40
Medici, Filippo, to give a caution to, **18.** 445
meets on Thursdays, **18.** 4, 17
members of: **19.** 394n; appointed, **21.** 107n; leave town on eve of St Charles's Day, **20.** 451
Migazzi notifies, of Dumesnil's escape from Rome, **19.** 493
Modena, Ds of, entertained by, **18.** 228
Modenese princess ill-treated by, **17.** 60
Modenese princess refuses invitation of, **17.** 100
Montemar announces intentions to, **17.** 261
—— answered by, **17.** 281
—— requests passports from, **18.** 46
——'s demands considered by, **17.** 226
Naples presents memorial to, on allodials, **18.** 177
Neapolitan cavalry seeks right of way from, **19.** 297–8
Neapolitan minister to be told by, to have Del Monte seized, **20.** 437
Neri heads, in Botta's absence, **22.** 245n
—— member of, **17.** 136n
Niccolini's letter to be read in, **20.** 24
opera attended by, in coronation rejoicings, **17.** 100
Pandolfini, Ferdinando, becomes secretary to, **17.** 52n, **19.** 501
passports formerly issued by, **21.** 482
Pitt sends French declaration to Mann, for transmission to, **21.** 502–3
Privy Council's resolutions about Dutch prizes considered by, **21.** 287
procaccia banished by, **20.** 447
public dispatch of, mentions Mann's rumoured promotion, **22.** 346

Richecourt blames, **17.** 282
—— converts Craon to his opinion about Leghorn suicide, at meeting of, **20.** 14
—— influences, to curtail Mann's privileges, **20.** 205
—— overbears, **18.** 328
—— president of, **20.** 392
—— seeks to discredit, **17.** 282
—— too ill to attend, **18.** 66
—— vice-president of, **17.** 25n
—— wants, to disavow his enmity to Ginori, **18.** 216
Rinuccini a member of, **17.** 40n, **19.** 251
St–Odile to join, **20.** 305–6
Serristori appointed by, as attendant to Modenese princess, **17.** 64
—— member of, **17.** 40n
Te Deum for Maria Theresa's coronation attended by, **17.** 100
Tornaquinci a member of, **21.** 62
Tuscan general honours Cardinal York without approval of, **22.** 250, 256
Uffizi fire combatted by, **22.** 68
Vernaccini presents Neapolitan memorial to, **18.** 177
Vienna neglects, **21.** 107
Walpole, Bns, subjected to search of her suitcases by order of, **17.** 224, 283
Warren examined by, **17.** 223
Regency, Dutch:
may terminate with William IV's death, **20.** 279
Regency, English:
bill regulating, **20.** 247, 248
Bristow and Frankland not discarded by, **20.** 156–7
Cumberland, D. of, dominates, **20.** 491
—— in, **20.** 483
—— to head, **20.** 125, **35.** 225
disputes about, see Parliament: acts of: Regency Bill
'foolish scene' played with Belle-Isle by, **30.** 91
for George II's Hanover trip, **17.** 114n, **18.** 209, 218
for George II's trip to Flanders, disputed, **18.** 61
formed from Cabinet Council, **37.** 60
Frederick, P. of Wales, not included in, **18.** 218
George II does not want P. of Wales in, **18.** 25
——'s absence occasions, **9.** 18, 57
George III might require, if a minor at George II's death, **9.** 113
——'s death provided for by, **10.** 153, 154
——'s plans for, **2.** 294–8
HW jokes about probable reception of Young Pretender by, **30.** 91
Mann hopes, will not be necessary, **20.** 254
Newcastle's speech to, parodied, **19.** 106
no law for, **22.** 42

Parliament may establish, with Ps of Wales as head, **20.** 239

Pelhams establish Augusta, Ps of Wales, as head of, **20.** 249

reward for capture of Young Pretender offered by, **30.** 91

Sandwich's membership in, ridiculed by Selwyn, **20.** 155

Spanish commerce discussed by, during George II's absence in Hanover, **19.** 504

suspended on George III's recovery, **25.** 682

Young Pretender's departure may not be told at once to, **17.** 114

See also Regent; regents, English

Regency, French:

war council in time of, **6.** 222

Regency, in India:

Clive establishes, in Bengal, for Najam-ud-Dowlah, **22.** 416

Regency, Irish:

Dorset family wants to make Stone sole member of, **20.** 316

George IV to receive, **25.** 681–2

Irish Catholics considered by, too dangerous for army, **18.** 566

members of, have aides-de-camp, **20.** 316

Stone dropped from, at Conway's insistence, **20.** 503n

——'s exclusion from, demanded, **35.** 235, 242, 254

Regency Act; Bill. *See under* Parliament: acts of

Regenfuss, Franz Michael (1712–80):

Choix de coquillages by, (?) received by HW from Hon. Thomas Walpole, **36.** 166, 281

Regensburg, Bp of. *See* Johann Theodor (1703–63); Klemens August (1700–61); Klemens Wenzel (1739–1812)

Regensburg, bishopric of:

Saxony covets, **22.** 119

'Regent, the' (French). *See* Bourbon, Philippe de, Duc d'Orléans

Regent; regents:

English: at their country seats in time of crisis, **19.** 79; come to town to quell invasion, **19.** 90; Mann wonders about reaction of, to term 'His Holiness,' **18.** 301; Newcastle's speech to, parodied by Pulteney, **19.** 106; timidity of, **18.** 282

Ireland chooses, in defiance of Parliament, **25.** 681

timidity of, **18.** 282

Reggio (Italy):

'dirty little place,' **13.** 242

earthquake account mentions, **25.** 376

fair at: HW and Gray visit, **13.** 9, 242, **33.** 530–1; HW sees Cts Simonetti at, **22.** 135, 148; HW's prospective party for, **30.** 14, 16

gambling at, **17.** 46

Gray and HW separate at, **28.** 69

HW and Gray pass through, **13.** 192n

HW, Chute, Whithed, and Hervey to be at, together, **30.** 16

HW prefers Canterbury to, **17.** 142

HW sees Forni and Montecuculi at, **17.** 44

HW's illness at, **13.** 10, 243, **30.** 17, **42.** 204, **43.** 169

HW writes from, **13.** 241–2

Lincoln and Spence find HW ill at, **30.** 17

Mary of Modena's maid of honour at, **17.** 43–4

melon seeds sent to, **17.** 34

physician at, **42.** 204

plague at, **18.** 282, 288, 301–2

post from, to Florence, **17.** 47

Rivalta, villa at, **13.** 242, **17.** 44

secrecy at, **17.** 43

Tesi brings fashion from, **17.** 110

visitors to: Berrys, **11.** 135n, 149n; Chute, **17.** 42n, **30.** 16; Fermor, Lady Sophia, **17.** 46; Gray, **13.** 9, 242, **17.** 42n, 59n, 82, **28.** 69; HW, **13.** 9, 242, **17.** 34, 37, 41–7, 51, 57, 59, 61, **28.** 69, **30.** 14, 16, 17, **33.** 530–1, **42.** 203–4; Hervey, **17.** 45, **30.** 16; Lincoln, **30.** 17; Piedmont officers, **17.** 46; Pucci, Mme, **17.** 46; Spence, **30.** 17; Whithed, **30.** 16

York, D. of, to visit, **22.** 232

Reggio e Branciforte, Don Luigi (d. 1757), Principe di Catena; di Iaci; di Campofiorito, 1696; Duca di Valverde; Spanish diplomatist:

Ferdinand VI's intentions to continue Italian war received by, **19.** 278n

Fleury tells, that the guaranty of Tuscany will be maintained, **17.** 230n

passports granted to, **19.** 383n

wife of, **18.** 315n

Wright captures baggage of, **19.** 383

Young Pretender promised aid by, **19.** 105n

Reggio e Branciforte, Don Michele, Knight of Malta:

Knight of Malta, and capt.-gen. of the galleys of Naples, **18.** 420n

Neapolitan regency headed by, **18.** 420

Reghellini di Scio, Dr Giano (fl. 1764):

(?) Northampton, Cts of, accompanied by, **22.** 142

Regicide; regicides (at Charles I's trial):

Dart writes against, **35.** 146

portraits of, at Cornbury, **20.** 182

Regiment; regiments, English:

Albemarle's, of 3d Troop of Horse Guards, **17.** 411n, **18.** 261n

America to receive, from Ireland, **37.** 434

Amherst resigns, **35.** 329

Ancaster's, **19.** 128n

Anstruther's, 26th Foot, **17.** 300n, **18.** 144n

Armstrong's, 18th Foot, **17.** 300n

Barrell's, **18.** 449n

Beauclerk's, **18.** 449n

Bedford, D. of, raises, **19.** 128

—— to lead, in person, **19.** 160

—— to raise, **19.** 110

being disbanded, **29.** 305

Bermuda, independent company, **19.** 69n

'Black Watch': **19.** 116n; reaches London, **18.** 236n

Bligh's, 20th Foot, **17.** 450n, **19.** 41n, **40.** 55

[Regiment; regiments, *continued*]
Bolton's, **19**. 128n
Burton gets Craufurd's, **38**. 468–9
Bury, colonel of, **20**. 459n
Cadogan's: 2d Troop of Horse Guards, **17**. 353n; 6th Dragoons, **17**. 353n
cavalry, light, swarm, **30**. 158
Cholmondeley raises, **18**. 128
——'s, **17**. 34n, **18**. 408, 449n
Churchill's, acquired by Cobham, **19**. 62
Cobham's, 1st Troop of Horse Grenadier Guards, **17**. 457n
commissioning foreign Protestants for, in Pennsylvania, **37**. 436, 444
Conway awaits, **22**. 559–60
—— busy with, in Scotland, **37**. 249
—— expects, of dragoons, **37**. 324
—— hears of vacancies in, **37**. 234
—— may obtain, in Scotland, **37**. 209, 228
—— might resume, **39**. 31
—— obtains, **19**. 240, **37**. 316n
——'s: assembled at Belturbet, **37**. 336; charming at review, **37**. 285–6; 1st Foot Guards, **18**. 273n; in Ireland, **20**. 316, 372; in Minorca, **20**. 264; said to be taken from him, **38**. 375, 376; taken away, **38**. 380–1, 384–6
——'s candidacy for, mentioned by George II to Pelham, **37**. 226
—— to be provided with, **37**. 209
—— to see, settled, **37**. 336
Cornwallis's, **19**. 177n
——'s promotion to, pressed by HW, **37**. 220
Dalzell's, 38th Foot, **19**. 69n
De la Warr's: **17**. 353; 1st Troop of Horse Guards, **17**. 353n
Derby raises, **19**. 128
disbanded, mutinous spirit of, disappears, **25**. 406
Douglas's: casualties in, at Roucour, **30**. 108; of marines, **18**. 146n
Dunmore's, of Foot Guards, **19**. 41n
English army in America to receive, from Ireland and West Indies, **39**. 247
Englishmen busy raising, **19**. 126, 128, **21**. 363
Fleming's, **18**. 449n
Floyd to rejoin, **24**. 508
for West Indies, debated in Parliament, **20**. 531
Fox, Henry Edward, takes, to America, **24**. 5
Fullar's, of foot, **18**. 146n
Fullarton's, **25**. 34
George II assigns, to Drumlanrig, **19**. 420
—— discusses appointments to, with D. of Cumberland before deciding them, **30**. 111
Gloucester, D. of, might resign, **36**. 85
Gower prevented by gout from leading, **19**. 161
——'s, mutinies, **19**. 209
Graham's: casualties in, at Roucour, **30**. 107–8; foot, **19**. 318n
HW jokes about raising, **9**. 264, **10**. 322, **31**. 14–15, **38**. 40

HW minimizes private raising of, **30**. 98n
Halifax raises, **19**. 128
Harrison's, **19**. 78n
Herbert raises, **19**. 128
Hertford not to resign, **17**. 345
Highland: loses Lt-Col., **37**. 434; mutinies, **18**. 236–7
Honywood's, **18**. 260–1
Houghton's: clothing of, **30**. 111; reviewed by Gen. Churchill at Canterbury, **30**. 20
Howard's, 19th Foot, **19**. 318n
Huske's, 32d Foot, **17**. 451n, 459n
Inns of Court raise, under Willes, **19**. 180n
Irish: Braddock's troops drafted from, **35**. 245; said to have been sent to Scotland, **19**. 170; to be augmented, **37**. 455
Johnson's, of foot, **17**. 459n, **19**. 271n
Kildare offers to raise, **19**. 99, 155
King's, of foot, **19**. 248n
Ligonier's, of foot, **19**. 240n
Loudoun's, of Highlanders, **19**. 102n
Maguire seeks, **37**. 132
Malpas accompanies, to Ireland, **22**. 210, **38**. 345
Malton raises, **19**. 128
Manchester, **19**. 177n, 287n
marching, packet-boat captain consigns Lady Ligonier to, **30**. 255
Marlborough's, 1st battalion, 2d Foot Guards, **17**. 411n
Montagu, D. of, raises, **19**. 128, 154n
——'s, to be headed by Sandwich, **19**. 176
Montagu, Charles, colonel of, with Miller as chaplain, **40**. 90–1
—— obtains, **35**. 265
Mordaunt's, **18**. 449n
Napier's, **37**. 446n
new: Parliamentary debate on renewing, **40**. 50; proposed by Jenkinson, **25**. 34n
newly-raised, Court wins victory over, in Parliament, **25**. 34
New York, independent, **19**. 69n
O'Farrel's, 22d Foot, **17**. 300n
of dragoons, *see under* Dragoons
of horse, to be formed from militia, **17**. 123
of militia, to be raised, **17**. 156, 214, 266, 288
Oglethorpe's, in Georgia, **19**. 69n
Onslow's, 8th Foot, **17**. 451n
ordered to America, **24**. 74
Pagett's, quartered at Canterbury, **40**. 4
Pembroke urged not to resign, **20**. 109
Pennsylvania's Germans and Swiss may form, **20**. 531
Phillips's, 40th Foot, **19**. 69n
Ponsonby's, 37th Foot, **17**. 450n
Price's, **18**. 449n
Pringle's, at Minorca, **25**. 199
privately-raised: Carteret opposes Pelham over, **19**. 158; in Ireland, **38**. 148; Jacobites and Patriots oppose, **19**. 154; motion to continue term of, deferred by Fox, **19**. 209; Parliament discusses, **26**. 31–3; voted by House, **19**. 128n

private raising of, irritates regular army, 19. 153–4

Pulteney may raise, for Craufurd, 21. 311

Read's: coveted by colonels, 37. 356; 9th Foot, 17. 300n

Rhode Island, independent company, 19. 69n

Rich's, 1st Foot Guards, 17. 486n

Royal Horse Guards, 19. 340n

Royal Hunters, 19. 127n

Royal Scots, 19. 138n

Royal Scots Fusiliers (infantry), 19. 395n

Rutland, D. of, raises, 19. 128

Sandwich colonel of, 19. 176

Scottish, destined for India, 25. 362

Scottish Lords to raise, 19. 167

Sempill's Black Watch, the 42d Foot, 18. 236n

South Carolina, independent companies, 19. 69n

Stair may lose, 37. 150

Swiss servants in London to form, 18. 409

Townshend, George, may grow impatient for, 37. 572

—— may raise, 18. 566n

—— mentions, as going abroad, 38. 49

Trelawnay's, 49th Foot, 19. 69n

Tyrrell's, 17th Foot, 17. 300n

Virginian, reduced, 20. 455n

volunteer, raised, 30. 98

Waldegrave gets, from Sackville, 35. 295

Washington defeats two, 28. 287

Wentworth's, 18. 146n

Westmorland may get, 17. 353

Regiment; regiments, Jacobite and foreign:

Berlichingen's, of cuirassiers, 17. 266n

Berwick, commanded by Comte de Fitzjames, 19. 208n

Bulkeley's, formerly Lee's Irish regiment of infantry, 18. 429n

Capponi's: 17. 156, 198, 214, 266, 268; arrives at Prato, 18. 100n

Carignan's, 19. 22n

Charles III raises, 18. 542

Clanranald, 19. 117n

Clerici's, 19. 30

Conway, Anne Seymour, does sketches of, 'of all nations,' 38. 156

Croatian, of cavalry, and infantry, in Lombardy, 17. 266n

Del Monte's, 17. 123, 156, 473–4

Fitzjames's, 19. 208–9

French army officers may be summoned to rejoin, 24. 357

German, in French service, 21. 149

Glencoe, 19. 117n

Glengarry, 19. 117n, 208n

Gondrecourt's Royal Tuscan, 19. 366n

Guerchy goes to France to review, 38. 389

Havor's, of hussars, 17. 154n

Highland clan, 19. 117n

Irish, in French service, 19. 138n

Keppoch, 19. 117n

Lobkowitz to send, to Piedmont, 18. 512

Lorraine, 18. 100n, 19. 457n

Macdonald's, 19. 117n

Miglio's, of cuirassiers, 17. 154n, 266n

Orlov's, of guards, 23. 222

Pallavicini's: of infantry, 17. 154n; reinforces Lobkowitz, 19. 30

Pandolfini's, arrives at Prato, 18. 100n

Piedmont, 21. 382–3

Prussian, annihilated by Hungarian insurgents, 19. 62

Sinzani's, 19. 22n

Swiss, try to reinforce Wesel, 38. 77n

Tuscan: of foot-guards, 18. 100n; of foot, near completion, 17. 266n

Wallis's, of infantry, replaced by Capponi's, of militia, 17. 266n

Walloon Guards, 18. 154

Warasdinian, of infantry, in Lombardy, 17. 266n

Regimentals:

camp-followers wear, scoured, 35. 509

Reginello. See La Reginella

Regio Diritto:

spelling of, corrected, 43. 234

Register Book:

Bourchier's, 41. 123

Register ship: register ships (Spanish):

Banff captures, 17. 377

capture of, 37. 246

definition of, 17. 176n

Edgcumbe captures, 19. 82

English capture, 17. 175, 208

See also Hermione; Postilion

Regius Professors:

nabobs are, in plundering, 35. 368

Regnard, Jean-François (1655–1709), dramatist:

Aristophanes inferior to, 41. 155

Coquette, La, by, seen by Mme du Deffand and HW, 7. 317

Joueur, Le, by, cited by Mme du Deffand, 6. 381

Retour imprévu, Le, by, adapted, 20. 289n

Richelieu quotes, 7. 369

Regnauld de Segrais, Jean (1624–1701), writer:

anecdote of, 15. 187, 188

Regnault, Louise (1698–1788), m. (1719) Gaspard, Marquis de Sabran:

(?) social relations of, with Comtesse de la Marche, 4. 12

Regnault d'Irval, Nicolas-Pierre-Joseph:

(?) attends session of parliament of Paris, 8. 171

(?) minutes of parliament of Paris certified by, 8. 169

Regnier, Antoinette-Marie de (b. 1748), called Mlle de Nangis:

HW entertains, at SH, 10. 127

Vauxhall visited by, 10. 127

Regnier, Claude-Louis-François de (1715–67), Comte de Guerchy; French ambassador to England 1763–7:

Bedford, Ds of, complimented by, on fender at Woburn, 22. 218

[Regnier, Claude-Louis-François de, *continued*]
—— tells, that Abp of Canterbury is *sage-femme*, **38**. 264
Bedford, D. of, entertains, at Woburn, **38**. 276
Boufflers, Comtesse de, talks of Hume and Rousseau with, **3**. 133
Buyrette de Belloy wishes to dedicate play to, **7**. 261
Calais visited by, on way to Dover, **38**. 211
Canada bills' agreement signed by, **31**. 97n
Choiseul, Duc de, asks, to supervise Lauzun, **3**. 242
Choiseul, Duchesse de, sends letter to HW by, **3**. 151, **41**. 42
Choiseul, Vicomte de, is expected by, to create scene, **38**. 535
—— to visit, **38**. 531
Compiègne visited by, **3**. 114, 332
Conway's dismissal reported by, to French Court, **38**. 399
——'s visit from, suggested by Hertford, **38**. 478
—— to entertain HW and, at Park Place, **38**. 461
dances at Court, **38**. 402
death of, **7**. 398, **21**. 551, **31**. 136
Dillon, (?) Frances, entertained by, **38**. 407
Du Châtelet succeeds, **4**. 17n
Du Deffand, Mme, approves of, **3**. 114, 123
—— makes acquaintance of, **3**. 114
—— may not see, for some time, **3**. 329
——'s commissions could be expedited by, **3**. 297
—— sends parcels by, **3**. 136, 160, 268, 271, 280
—— talks of HW with, **3**. 114, 118, 123, 138, 177
—— to be remembered to, **3**. 163–4, 191, 226
England's memorial from, on France's indebtedness, **38**. 423
English popularity of, **36**. 39–40
Éon affair makes, ridiculous, **22**. 273
—— robs, while employed as his secretary, **22**. 191, 217
——'s attack on, **36**. 40
——'s book abuses, **38**. 356, 357, 365–6, 372
——'s procurement of indictment against, **38**. 522–3
expected in London, **22**. 175
first servant of, delivers HW's letters to Hertford, **38**. 571
Fitzjames resembles, **39**. 9
foreign ministers at London unite with, against d'Éon, **38**. 377–8
foreign ministers complain to George III in behalf of, **22**. 227
France returns, to English embassy, **38**. 451
—— visited by, only to review regiment, **38**. 389
Fronsac, Duchesse de, friend of, **3**. 226
George III confers with, after meeting at Seilern's on Éon's case, **38**. 369–70

gone for the summer months, **22**. 248
Goodwood visited by, but Egmont forbids Portsmouth excursion, **38**. 401
Grafton has HW and, to dinner, **38**. 321
Gramont, Mme de, formerly loved by, hates him for opposing her marriage, **22**. 551n
HW and Caraman entertained by, at dinner, **38**. 523–4
HW and Conway told by, of Hertford's trouble with Chaulnes, **38**. 306
HW and Conway to send letters to Hertford through, **38**. 458, 460
HW and Masserano dine with, **38**. 250
HW assured by, of Mme de la Vallière's remembrance, **41**. 41
HW, at house of, restrains congratulations to Lady Elizabeth Keppel, **38**. 400
HW avoids presentation at Court by, **7**. 261
HW concerned at neglect by, **31**. 105
HW does justice to Hertford at house of, **38**. 243
HW does not entrust letter to courier of, **38**. 561, 566
HW entertains, at SH, **10**. 127, 215
HW goes to, to find when letter-bearer leaves, **38**. 296
HW hears story told at house of, **38**. 296
HW kindly treated by, **40**. 386
HW led by, to attribute 'Sévigné' letter to Duchesse de Choiseul, **3**. 120
HW mentions, **3**. 341, 342, **22**. 239
HW occasionally attends assemblies and dinners of, **10**. 139
HW praised by, **38**. 451
HW praises Hertford to, **38**. 243
HW presented by, to Choiseul, **39**. 14
HW's civilities from Mme de Choiseul described by, **41**. 42
HW's correspondence with, **7**. 377, 378, 381, 383, **30**. 214, **31**. 105, 115
HW sends compliments and inquiry by, **30**. 213
HW sends letters by, **7**. 377
HW sends letter to Conway through, **39**. 24
HW sends letter to Hertford through, **38**. 553, 556
HW's esteem for, **38**. 457–8
HW's friendship with, **3**. 337
HW's friends may have injured him with, **31**. 105
HW's presents expedited by, **3**. 92
HW's regard for, **31**. 105
HW taken by: to Dépôt des Archives, **7**. 266, **39**. 15; to see Marigny's house at Versailles, **39**. 15, 201
HW to entertain, at SH, **38**. 402, 403
HW to see, in Paris, **10**. 172
HW urged by, to thank Duchesse de Choiseul for 'Sévigné' letter, **31**. 119
health of, **7**. 316
Hertford, Cts of, and her presentation complimented by, **38**. 246

Hertford, E. of, at Paris proposes Park Place visit to, because of liking for Conway, **38.** 478
—— praised by, **38.** 461
——'s letter from, on failure to meet at Calais, **38.** 211
Hervey, Bns, mystified by neglect of HW by, **31.** 115
—— visits, **31.** 115
Hume discussed by, **7.** 261
Lauraguais's vagaries feared by, **38.** 535
Lillebonne related to, **36.** 39, **38.** 520
Louis XV's compensation offer for French prisoners presented by, **38.** 496n
Marie Leszczyńska tells, that HW avoids her, **39.** 14
Nancy to be visited by, **3.** 332
Nivernais and Praslin disparage, in letters, **22.** 218
not to take charge of Mme du Deffand's purchases, **3.** 328
Pecquigny complains to, **38.** 307
—— sent away by, after arrest, **38.** 322
popular in England, **38.** 234
possible successor to, **3.** 278
Praslin's letter from, about Grenville's reinstatement, **38.** 570-1
—— will hate, on Éon's account, **38.** 356
proposes to visit HW at Bath, **3.** 138, 149, 152
Queensberry, Ds of, declines dinner of, but arrives late with false excuse, **38.** 510
reception of, in France, freezing, **21.** 551
returns to France, **3.** 317
Rochefort, Mme de, expects, **41.** 21
Selwyn sends HW's *Counter Address to the Public* to, **30.** 176
servant of, brings letters to Hertford, **38.** 571
Sévigné snuff-box delivered by, **3.** 73-4, 81, 82
social relations of, in Paris, **3.** 114, 123, 133, 287, **7.** 261, 265, 267, 316
Suffolk, Cts of, spoken of by, **3.** 115
Vauxhall visited by, **10.** 127
Vergy accuses, of hiring him to cut d'Éon's throat, **22.** 262, **38.** 467
Waldegrave, Cts, enthralls, **38.** 402
wife of, **3.** 114n
writes of HW's going to Paris, **3.** 247
Regnier de Guerchy, Victoire-Félicité de (ca 1749-1838), m. (1768) Joseph-Louis-Bernard de Cléron, Comte d'Haussonville:
Du Deffand, Mme, discusses Comtesse de Guerchy's mourning with, **4.** 74-5
——'s opinion of, **7.** 107
——'s relations with, **7.** 102
family amity of, **7.** 107
HW inquires after, **4.** 325
Lauzun, Duchesse de, at odds with, **7.** 107
marriage of, **4.** 63, 68, 72, 75
social relations of, in Paris, **7.** 102, 107, 327, 330, 423, (?) 429
Regnon de la Ranconnière, Ursule-Suzanne-Véronique de (b. 1761), m. (1774) Augustin-Joseph-Alexandre de la Roch-St-André:

social relations of, with Mme du Deffand, **7.** 434, 436, 449, 453, 455
Regny, François (d. 1779), French consul at Genoa 1756-75; directeur de la poste at Genoa ca 1740-51:
biographical information on, corrected, **43.** 236
Lorenzi forbids, to forward unfranked mail to him, **21.** 362
Mann's English correspondence forwarded to, **17.** 103
Regulating Bill. *See under* Parliament: acts of
Regulus, M. Atilius (fl. ca 267 B.C.), Roman officer:
HW compared with, **5.** 432
Lyttelton compared with, **35.** 251
Rehearsal, The. See under Villiers, George (1628-87), D. of Buckingham
Rehearsal:
for Handel's jubilee, **25.** 647
Rehoboam:
old counsellors of, **2.** 55
Reich de Penautier, Pierre-Louis (d. 1711), financier:
Bonzi's 'étoile,' **3.** 64
Reichenbach (Germany):
battle of, **22.** 70
Reichenbach, Convention of:
Belgian provinces restored by, to Leopold II, **39.** 474n
Reid, George (fl. ca 1780-? 1810), magistrate:
interrogated in House of Lords, **33.** 176
Reid, Col. John:
Corbet succeeded by, as Lt-Gov. of Jersey, **25.** 111n
Reid, Robert (d. 1558), Bp of Orkney:
Ferrerio invited by, **15.** 120n
Reid, Thomas (1710-96), D.D.; philosopher:
college of, corrected, **43.** 196
Dalrymple's missing letter concerning, **15.** 101
Inquiry into the Human Mind, An, by, HW receives copy of, **15.** 100
professor at Aberdeen, **40.** 320
Smith, Adam, may be replaced by, at Glasgow, **40.** 321
Reid, W. H.:
Rolliad contributor, **25.** 613n
Reid. *See also* Read; Reade; Reed
Reily, Henry Stevens:
Rutland's answer to, on Dublin petition, **25.** 529n
Reims, Abp of. *See* La Roche-Aymon, Charles-Antoine de
Reims; Rheims (France):
Elliot and Liston may settle at, **38.** 413
Fox writes from, **30.** 235
HW asks about old acquaintances at, **38.** 215
HW sends Montagu's letter to, by foreign post, **10.** 145
HW stays at, **13.** 170n
HW to send books to, for Mme Roland, **10.** 174, 182
Holy Ampulla at, **6.** 199n, **24.** 112-13

[Reims; Rheims, *continued*]

La Malle near, **10.** 193, 196

Louis XVI's consecration at, **6.** 195, 197, 198

Montagu meets Mme Roland at, **10.** 143n

——'s affair with lady at, **37.** 7

Peterborough's witticism when shown Holy Ampulla at, **24.** 112–13

Roland, Mme, lives in, **10.** 143, 246, 251, 302

view of, shown in La Malle plan, **10.** 196

visitors to: Beauchamp, **5.** 388, 394, 395; 401; Choiseul, **6.** 198; Gray, **13.** 8, 166, 174, **14.** 147; HW, **9.** 303, **13.** 8, 166, 170n, 174, **14.** 147, **15.** 6, **37.** 71, **38.** 524; Louis XVI, **6.** 195; Montagu, **9.** 9, 303, **10.** 143n, **37.** 7; More, **37.** 71; Seymour-Conway, Hon. H., **5.** 388, 394, 395, 401

Rein; reins:

Electress's, has long traces, **19.** 370

Reindeer:

sheets made from skins of, **32.** 194

Reiner, D. *See* René I (1409–80)

Reinhold, Henry Theodore (d. 1751), bass singer:

sings in *Atalanta*, **13.** 102n

Reinière. *See* Grimod de la Reynière

Reischach, Baron, Imperial ambassador to Holland:

threat from, over Scheldt navigation, **25.** 538n

Reischach ('Reiscack'), Judas Thaddäus (1696–1782), Freiherr von; Austrian envoy to Holland:

daughter of, **22.** 398

Reischach, Maria Gabriele von (d. 1815), m. 1 (1765) Franz, Graf Thurn-Valsassina; m. 2 (1767) Anton, Graf Thurn-Valsassina:

Albizzi, Mme degli, succeeds, as Maria Louisa's grande maîtresse, **23.** 253

apartment of, **22.** *368*

Grande Maîtresse at Tuscan Court, **22.** 398

left at Vienna, **23.** 253

Leopold and Maria Louisa accompanied by, on travels, **23.** 220

Leopold and Maria Louisa reward, on her retirement, **23.** 253

Mann tells, of approach of spaniel puppies, **23.** 54

marriage of, **22.** 398

menservants forbidden by, to enter Maria Louisa's chamber, **22.** 529

Reissin, Jean, Lt:

captured at Velletri, **18.** 492

'Relais,' dog of Louis XII:

Louis XII said to have written life of, **33.** 386

Relapse, The. See under Vanbrugh, Sir John

Relatio Caroli Alberti Cardinalis Cavalchini. See under Cavalchini, Carlo Alberto

Relation; relations:

Mason's 'chapter' on, **28.** 331

Relation de la maladie du jésuite Berthier. See under Voltaire

Relation de la mort du Chevalier de la Barre. See under Voltaire

Relation de la révolution de Russie. See Rulhière, Claude-Carloman de, *Anecdotes sur la révolution de Russie*

Relation du bannissement des Jésuites de la Chine. See under Voltaire

Relation du Groenland. See under La Peyrère, Isaac de

Relation du lit de justice:

HW converted by, from liberty to despotism, **41.** 344–5

Relation of his Travels into Persia. See under Shirley, Sir Anthony

Relation of . . . Lord De-La-Warre. See under West, Thomas

Relation of the Conference. See under Laud, William

'Relation of the Duke of Buckingham's Entertainment in France':

Beauchamp gets transcript of, from Ashmolean for HW, **38.** 158

Relation of Three Embassies. See under Miège, Guy

Relationum historicarum de rebus Anglicis. See under Pits, John

Relative; relatives:

HW's reflections on, **30.** 59, 72

terms of relationship carefully used by, in addressing each other, **30.** 72

Relativism:

HW speculates on size of sublunary objects, **25.** 133

Relazione dei successi di S.A.R. Carlo Principe di Galles:

Latilla, Cesare, sells, **19.** 158n

Relazione dell' orribile terramoto:

HW receives, **25.** 374n, 375–6, **33.** 396, **43.** 356

Relhan, Anthony (1715–76), M.D.:

unusual temerity of, **32.** 334

Relic; relics, holy:

at Genoa, **37.** 320

at Radicofani, **37.** 67, 734

at St Peter's, Rome, **17.** 4

at Wachtendonck's bedside, **17.** 109–10

Chute to get, for HW, **35.** 62

HW asked by St-Cyr nun about state of, in England, **10.** 294

Madonna, painted in pulverized martyr's bones, **20.** 489

Mann ridicules, **20.** 430

Religieuse, La. See La Harpe, Jean-François de: *Mélanie, ou la religieuse*

Religion:

admirers of French Revolution use, as cover, **31.** 362

cannon not to propagate, **35.** 392

Catherine II and Joseph II lack, **25.** 400

Chute's, **35.** 29, 32

Codrington's bequest to, involves perpetuation of slavery, **35.** 178

Cole on, **2.** 100n, 281–2, 309

—— on disregard of, **2.** 127, 152

controversies over, have died down, **19.** 229

Conway wishes world were of one mind over, **37**. 193

decline of, in France, **35**. 127

disputes about, in Poland, **5**. 111

Du Deffand, Mme, indifferent to, **5**. 361

—— takes name of, in vain, **4**. 116

Egyptian custom, **32**. 43

English nabobs do not use, as excuse for plunder, **25**. 400

enthusiasm without, in France, **34**. 182

epigram about disgrace to, in Ireland, **20**. 316

eras of, 'breathe a browner horror on everything,' **33**. 335

Ferrers's opinions about, **21**. 400–1

Flemings in Brabant fight for, **34**. 103

French discuss, **31**. 49, 65

French have no, **34**. 103

French philosophers destroy, **34**. 192–3, **39**. 22

Gloucester, D. of, comforted by, **34**. 246

great rather than small innovations more effective in, **16**. 264

Greek, **35**. 123

HW a coward on points of, **34**. 160

HW believes a new, will start, **34**. 170

HW indifferent to, **5**. 361

HW on, **1**. 124, 179, **2**. 61, 99–100, 283, 309–10

HW's: **37**. 206; consists of literary enthusiasms, **31**. 7

HW's ideas about, **20**. 81–2

HW's opinions of, **3**. 300, **4**. 220, **9**. 73

HW's philosophy of, **24**. 516

HW's reflections on old women's pretence of, **25**. 584

HW thinks that modes in, are like ladies' fashions, **25**. 541

Hervey, Bns, in danger of losing, **37**. 308

inactivity of, considered by HW to indicate the world's senility, **25**. 48

Indians', **25**. 438

Julius II sacrifices, to ambition or revenge, **37**. 15

Leghorn church attendance, **17**. 260

Mann's reflections on, **20**. 378

massacres committed by, in one age; philosophy in another, **25**. 400

Minorcans enjoy their own, **37**. 311

More, Hannah, discusses, with Mary Berry, **31**. 390

National Convention abolishes, in France, **12**. 120

nature would be shunned if love of, were enjoined by, **35**. 370

Neapolitan credulity about, **18**. 305

outrages are often cloaked by, **35**. 354

Peruvians', **41**. 292

philosophers prefer matter to, **41**. 55

Raynal's *Histoire* against all, **39**. 168

reformations in, revive early impostures, **35**. 155

Rousseau and Voltaire endanger, in Switzerland, **35**. 583

Rousseau attacks, **41**. 53

Spaniards and Portuguese used, as an excuse for plunder, **25**. 400

spirit of Christian, love and peace, **31**. 335

the more the better, **34**. 51, 83

trade, the modern, **31**. 269

Uguccioni might change his, to get English preferment, **18**. 554

undermined by lessening belief in devil, **12**. 86

used as an excuse for war, **22**. 39

Voltaire softens expressions about, in *La Pucelle*, **20**. 548

Waldegrave, Cts, testifies to power of, by her composure, **36**. 271–2

women take to, on losing charms, **20**. 378, **25**. 584

See also Absolution; Altar; Altar-piece; Altar rails; Anabaptism; Anabaptist; Ascension; Ash Wednesday; Augustinians; Baptism; Bartholomew-tide; Beatification; Beguine; Benedictines; Benediction; Bernardines; Bible; Bishop; Canticles; Capuchins; Carmelites; Carmes; Catholicism; Chalice; Chapel; Chaplain; Christian; Christmas; Church; Churching; Churchman; Church of England; Churchwardens; Clergy; Clergyman; Communion; Communion table; Confession; Confessors; Confirmation; Consistory; Convent; Cope; Cordeliers; Court, consistory; Creed; Crucifix; Crucifixion; Crusade; Deist; Dissenter; Divinity; Dominican order; Druid; Easter; Enthusiasm, religious; Epiphany; Excommunication; Exorcism; Extreme unction; Faith; Fast day; Fasting; Fathers of the Church; Feast of tabernacles; Font; Friars; Gallican Church; God; Good Friday; Gospels; Grace; Greek Orthodox Church; Grey Friars; Holy Week; Host, The; Huguenot; Hutchinsonians; Hymn; Incense; Infidel; Inquisition; Jansenism; Jesuit; Jesus; Jew; Lady Day; Lent; Life, future; Lights, religious; Litany; Lutheran; Magnificat; Mass; Mass-house; Meeting-house; Methodism; Methodist; Michaelmas; Miracle; Missal; Mitre; Mohammedan; Molenist; Monastery; Monasticism; Monk; Moravian; Mosque; Mottoes; Natural religion; Nonjuror; Nun; Nunnery; Papacy; Parson; Passion Week; Pharisee; Prayer; Prayer Book; Presbyterian; Prie-dieu; Priest; Procession; Profanity; Protestant; Psalm; Psalter; Pulpit; Quaker; Reading-desk; Reformation; Relics, holy; Religious disabilities; Religious orders; Reliquaire; Requiem; Roman Catholic Church; Rosary; Rosicrucians; Sacrament; Sacrilege; Sacristy; Sermon; Shrove Tuesday; Society for the Propagation of the Gospel; Socinian; *Stabat mater*; Subdeacon; Superstition; Swedenborg; Te Deum; Templar; Ten Commandments; Tenebræ; Theologian;

[Religion, *continued*]
Theology; Thirty-nine árticles; Tithes; Transubstantiation; Trent, Council of; Trinity, doctrine of the; Unigenitus; Universalist; Vespers; Vestment; Viaticum; Witchcraft

Religious disabilities:
English, 4. 424
French, 4. 297, 418, 423, 424, 428, 6. 454

Religious orders:
at Florence, Madonna dell' Impruneta escorted by, to Duomo, 30. 4

Reliquaire; reliquaires:
HW sees, at St-Cyr, 10. 294

Reliques of Ancient English Poetry. See under Percy, Thomas

Relongue de la Louptière, Jean-Charles de (1727–84):
(?) verses by, on Voltaire and L'Attaignant, 7. 31

Remains of Christian Antiquity. See under Dalrymple, David

Remarks of a Persian Traveller. See under Magnan, ——

Remarks on a Late Scurrilous Postscript:
pamphlet in miracles' controversy, 15. 297

Remarks on a Treatise. See under Place, Conyers

Remarks on Dr Middleton's Examination of Bishop Sherlock's Use and Intent of Prophecy:
'by a Protestant divine,' 15. 299

Remarks on Dr Sherlock's First Dissertation:
Middleton's attack on Sherlock provokes, 15. 299

Remarks on Forest Scenery. See under Gilpin, William

Remarks on Johnson's 'Life of Milton.' See under Blackburne, Francis

Remarks on Mr Walpole's Catalogue of Royal and Noble Authors:
authorship of, 14. 258–9
Cartwright said to be author of, 16. 29–30
HW is attacked in, 13. 31–2
Revolution aspersed by, 16. 29–30

Remarks on Several Parts of Italy. See under Addison, Joseph

Remarks on the Appendix of the Editor of Rowley's Poems. See under Fell, John

Remarks on the Controversial Writings of Dr Middleton:
Middleton's attack on Sherlock provokes, 15. 302

Remarks on the Free Inquiry. See under Jackson, John

Remarks on the History of Scotland. See under Dalrymple, Sir David

Remarks on the Letter to Two Great Men:
HW thought to be author of, 16. 39

Remarks on the Life and Writings of Dr Jonathan Swift. See under Boyle, John (1707–62), E. of Cork

Remarks on the Speech of M. Dupont. See under More, Hannah

Remarks on Two Pamphlets Lately Published. See under Middleton, Conyers

Remarks . . . upon the Proposals . . . by Richard Bentley. See under Middleton, Conyers

Remarks upon the Situation of Negroes in Jamaica. See under Beckford, William

Rembrandt van Rijn (1606–69), painter:
Daulby's catalogue of, 15. 283
mother's portrait by, at Windsor Castle: 42. 13, 43. 59; not a favourite of HW's, 15. 284; mistaken for Cts of Desmond, 40. 108, 42. 12–13
Opie's portrait of Mrs Delany is said to resemble style of, 29. 185
paintings by: at Devonshire House, 38. 455n; at Julienne's, 7. 287; at Mereworth, 35. 143; at Praslin's, 7. 353; at P. of Monaco's, 7. 335
print of his mother by, 1. 329
prints and drawings by, 38. 371n
sale of pictures by, 38. 340n

Remembrancer, The:
HW attacks D. of Cumberland in, 20. 73n
HW's contributions to, 13. 22, 20. 73n
printer of, arrested, 20. 73n
See also under Ralph, James

Remenham *or* Remnam's, Old Windsor, Berks; Ds of Kent's seat:
HW calls, 'charming place,' 30. 115
Kent, Ds of, bequeaths, to mother and then to daughter, 30. 115

Remi, Joseph-Honoré (1738–82), abbé:
Éloge historique de Michel de L'Hospital by, 6. 471, 473, 474, 476

Remiencourt, Marquis de. *See* Boufflers, Louis-François de (1714–51); Boufflers, Stanislas-Jean de (1737–1815)

Remiencourt, Marquise de. *See* Beauvau, Marie-Françoise-Catherine de

Reminiscence:
pleasures of, to the young, 9. 2

Reminiscences Written . . . in 1788 for the Amusement of Miss Mary and Miss Agnes Berry, by HW:
HW allows D. Lysons to copy some of, 15. 337
HW bequeaths MS of, to Berrys, 15. 337
HW reads to Mr Batt, 11. 309, 311
HW refers to, 11. 5

Remiremont, Abbess of. *See* Lorraine, Anne-Charlotte de (1755–86); Marie-Christine (1735–82)

Remiremont (France):
Christine, Ps, at 3. 40

Rémond de St-Mard, Toussaint (1682–1757):
Montagu, Lady Mary Wortley, has, as lover, 20. 281–2
—— tries to cheat, 20. 281–2

Remonstrance; remonstrances:
HW learns to make and answer, 35. 337

Remonville, M. de. *See* Bourbon-Remonville, Marquis de

Remove; removes (food). *See under* Dinner

'Remy, Mme' (character in *Paysan parvenu*):
Du Deffand, Mme, mentions, 5. 160
Rémy, Pierre:
catalogue by, of Julienne collection, 22. 523n
Rena, 'Contessa':
'Contessa' not used by, in Italy, 23. 119
dog of, HW sends regards to *touffe ébourifée* of, 30. 208
Englishmen and valets knew, in Florence, 21. 162
Florence 'sends,' to England, 21. 156
Florentine wine merchant's wife and Pembroke's and March's former mistress, 23. 106n
HW asks about, 'antique as she is,' 21. 156
HW asks Mann to befriend, 23. 106–7
HW invites, to SH, 30. 166
HW's correspondence with, 40. 280
HW's social relations with, in Paris, 7. 312
HW thanks, for inquiries about Lady Waldegrave, 40. 280
HW to call on, in Paris, 30. 220
HW visited by, at SH, 23. 107, 38. 175
Machault and Marigny lovers of, 21. 162
Mann calls on, at Pisa, 23. 119
—— to entertain, at dinner at Florence, 23. 119, 124
Pollard relieved by, of large sums, 21. 162
Selwyn gives rose to, 32. 6n
title assumed by, in travels, 21. 162
Tuscan Court must exclude, 23. 119
Renadæus. *See* Renou, Jean de
Renai, Via de', at Florence:
Casa Vitelli may be in, 20. 398n
Renaissance:
Agincourt's project on artistic history of, 42. 102
authors of, less impertinent than modern ones, 33. 537
Rendu, ——, notary:
Mme du Deffand's lease signed before, 8. 41
René I (1409–80), Duc de Bar, 1419; de Lorraine, 1431; d'Anjou, 1435; Comte de Provence, 1435; titular K. of Sicily 1435–80; K. of Naples (effective) 1438–42:
age of, in 1444, 14. 76
at daughter's proxy marriage, 14. 71
biographical information about, corrected, 43. 183, 219, 335, 361, 369
Doumenil has portrait of, 7. 313
family of, 31. 143, 438
Gray corrects Stow's reference to, 14. 71
—— mentions, 14. 69
HW's 'character' of, 31. 438–9
HW wants to write life of, 36. 216–17, 218
'Hours' of, in La Vallière sale: coveted by HW, 36. 216–17; sold to Louis XVI, 42. 93
mistress taken by, from coffin, for her portrait to be painted, 31. 143n
portraits and paintings by, 31. 143
Powell's *Humane Industry* misled Lort about, 16. 159

self-portrait mistakenly said to have been presented by, to François II, 16. 143, 156
virtues of, 31. 438–9
wife of, 14. 69n, 35. 163
Renel, Marquis de. *See* Clermont, Jean-Baptiste-Charles-François de
Renel, Marquise de. *See* Colbert, Marguerite-Thérèse (1682–1769); Rohan-Chabot, Marie-Sylvie de (1729–1807)
Renelaugh. *See* Ranelagh
'Renfrew, Count':
Young Pretender's pseudonym, 23. 225–6
Renfrewshire:
election for, 41. 279n
Reni. *See* Guido Reni
Rennes, Bp of. *See* Desnos, Henri-Louis-René
Rennes (Brittany):
Breton parliament to meet at St-Brieuc instead of, 3. 370
Chaulnes commanded at, 31. 74
Couronnement d'un roi acted at, 6. 153
disturbance at, 11. 43n
joy at, on restoration of parliament, 7. 326
La Chalotais accused of telling Pitt that, is nearer to London than Paris, 39. 33
obelisk erected in church at, 7. 326
procureurs of: 39. 35–6; forced to plead, 7. 285
Rennes, parliament of:
affairs of: HW knows little of, 30. 206; HW uninterested in, 31. 74; much agitated in Paris, 30. 206
avocats refuse to plead before, after it is altered, 39. 56
Choiseul compromises with, 14. 149
—— restores, in spite of d'Aiguillon, 23. 134
exiled, 7. 273
Hertford will not discuss, except with Conway, 38. 506
La Chalotais procureur-général of, 11. 43, 23. 206n
Louis XV's replies to, 38. 521, 522
members of, called 'ifs,' 5. 164
mentioned, 3. 109n, 118, 370, 4. 442n, 449n, 10. 202n
parliament of Paris defends, 10. 202
parliament of Paris's remonstrance about dissolution of, 7. 280, 39. 33
recalled, 4. 259, 7. 326
suppressed, 5. 106
Rennommée, French packet boat:
troops arrive at Plymouth in, 21. 18n
Reno, the, river:
Montemar passes, 17. 427
Renou, Jean de (fl. 1600), physician:
Dispensatorium by, 14. 126
Renoux, ——, saddler:
Mme du Deffand's contract with, 8. 42
Rent; rents:
Berrys' house at Teddington, 11. 56, 58, 61
——' house in London, 11. 149, 160, 162
Choiseul's, 7. 144

[Rent; rents, *continued*]

Du Deffand, Mme, pays, **4**. 386

Dudley, Lady, house of, **11**. 30–1

Du Val, Dr, parsonage of, **12**. 75

Forbes not to pay, until house is repaired, **31**. 287

Keppel, Mrs, house of, at Isleworth, **11**. 320–1

Paris: in Rue Bergère, **5**. 140; in Rue de Bourbon, **5**. 435; in Rue Neuve St-Augustin, **6**. 282

Twickenham houses, **10**. 247, 252

unfashionable to worry about collecting, **35**. 370

See also under Price; prices

Renunciation Bill. *See under* Parliament: acts of

Renzi, Bernardina, of Valentano:

Clement XIV's death prophesied by, **24**. 41

Repas:

HW gives, **10**. 126

Mann must give, **22**. 355

Repeater; repeating watch. *See under* Watch

Repertorium sculptile-typicum. See Orlandi, Antonio: *Abcedario pittorico*

Repertory of the Endowments of Vicarages. See under Ducarel, Andrew Coltee

Repinder, Victor:

Pierson son of, **35**. 428n

Réplique pour le Comte de Guines. See under Bonnières, Adrien-Louis de

Reply to Dr Middleton's Examination, A:

Middleton's attack on Sherlock provokes, **15**. 300

Reply to the Counter-Address. See under Guthrie, William

Reply to the Defence of the Letter to Dr Waterland. See under Pearce, Zachary

Reply to the Letter to Dr Waterland. See under Pearce, Zachary

Reply to the Observations of the Rev. Dr Milles, A, by HW:

Cole and HW mention, **1**. 206, 212, 213–14, 219, 292, **2**. 6, 229

Gray's copy of, **28**. 19, 24–5

Mason dislikes, **28**. 246

Milles answered by, **43**. 55, 55–6

Repnin, Prince Nikolaï Vasil'evich (1734–1801), Russian army officer and diplomatist:

Kücük Kainardje treaty signed by, **24**. 40

newspapers announce mission of, to England to make peace, **24**. 487

Réponse au mémoire de . . . Morellet. See under Necker, Jacques

Réponse de Marmontel à Voltaire. See under Marmontel Jean-François

Réponse de M. de la Harpe. See under La Harpe, Jean-François de

Réponse de M. le Prince de Ligne à une lettre de Voltaire. See under Ligne, Charles-Joseph de

Réponse d'un solitaire de la Trappe. See La Harpe, Jean-François de: *Camaldule, La*

Reprisal, American frigate:

Franklin sails in, **32**. 336–7

Repton, Humphry (1752–1818), landscape gardener:

HW calls, 'coxcomb,' **15**. 318

SH visited by, **12**. 243

Republic:

Genoa slavish as, **37**. 319

Republican; republicans:

HW has been called, but denies being, **33**. 342

HW neither royalist nor, **34**. 173

Mahon is 'furious, of Geneva,' **25**. 32

Walpole, Sir Robert, opposed by, **37**. 90

Repulin Bacha, Turkish ship:

Russians captured, **23**. 228, 235

Repulse, English ship:

sinks with all on board, **32**. 367

Requeleyne, Hilaire-Bernard de (1659–1721), Baron de Longepierre; translator of Greek classics:

Rousseau's verses against, quoted by Mme du Deffand, **4**. 448, **5**. 422

Requiem; requiems:

annual, for Francis I at Florence, **25**. 600

for Elizabeth Christina, **20**. 227

Rescription; rescriptions:

Du Deffand, Mme, receives payment on, **7**. 424

—— sells, **7**. 434

—— sells half of, **7**. 433

suspension of payments on, **4**. 373

Rescrit de S. M. le Roi de Prusse. See under Frederick II

Research:

HW's remarks on, **29**. 88, 97

Resentment:

HW's reflections on, **30**. 151

Reservoir; reservoirs:

Chelsea Company's, has water for fire-fighting, **17**. 496n

Resident; residents (diplomatic agents):

Fane's salary as, **18**. 17n

French, at Pullicat, India, *see* Raymond, ——

from England to Holland, *see* Dayrolles, Solomon (1709–86)

from England to Tuscany, *see* Colman, Francis (d. 1733); Fane, Charles (d. 1766); Mann, Sir Horatio (1706–86)

from England to Venice, *see* Murray, John (d. 1775); Strange, John (1732–99); Wright, Sir James (d. 1803)

from Genoa to England, *see* Zuccato, Giovanni Girolamo

from Poland to Tuscany, *see* Agdollo, Gregorio

from Poland to Venice, *see* Agdollo, Gregorio

from Tuscany to England, *see* Pucci, Domenico (1718–83); Pucci, Vincenzo (ca 1675–1757); Salvetti Antelminelli, Giovanni (b. ca 1634)

from Venice to England: Almodóvar claims
to be, 24. 413; *see also* Pizzoni, ——; Sode-
rini, (?) Giulio Maria
Mann's salary as, 18. 516
minister plenipotentiary the next rank above
that of, 22. 356
Prussian, at Hamburg, *see* Hecht, J. G. von
See also Ambassador; Envoy; Minister
Resolution, English ship:
lost at Quiberon Bay, 21. 351
Manners, commander of, 2. 207n, 29. 310n
*Resolutions and Decisions of Divers Practical
Cases of Conscience. See under* Hall, Joseph
Resta, Natale, composer:
burlettas composed by, 20. 4n
Reste, Ann (d. 1781), m. Joseph Bentham:
HW condoles with, on husband's death, 2. 90
HW's compliments to, 1. 183, 196
HW visits, 1. *178*
Reste, George:
Dodd and Whaley travel with, 40. 3n
heiress of, 1. 178n
Shepheard's 'governor,' 40. 3n
Restoration:
of pictures, bad at Palais Royal, 39. 202
Restraining Bill. See under Parliament: acts of
Restrick. *See* Rantwick; Van Riswick
'Resurrection':
subject of Jervais's window in St George's
Chapel, Windsor, 11. 363
Resurrexit:
on Henri IV's statue, a compliment to Louis
XVI, 24. 19, 36
Retaliation. See under Goldsmith, Oliver
Rétaux de Villette, ——:
sentenced for 'Diamond Necklace' affair, 25.
653n
Retes. *See* Martínez de la Vega y Retes
Retford, East, Notts:
White, M.P. for, 29. 354
Retirement:
HW's reflections on pleasures of, 23. 315
hard to achieve, 28. 284
Mann's aversion to, 24. 166
Retiring-chamber:
for Q. Charlotte behind altar at Coronation,
38. 122
Retour imprévu, Le. See under Regnard, Jean-
François
Returning officer (election official):
HW might mistake candidate for, 37. 271
Retz, Cardinal de. *See* Gondi de Retz, Jean-
François-Paul de
Retz, Duchesse de. *See* Clermont-Dampierre,
Claude-Catherine de
Réunion (Île de Bourbon):
force to be sent against, 9. 304n
French retain, 21. 523
visitors to: Sourches, Vicomte de, 7. 445;
Sourches, Vicomtesse de, 7. 442
Reuss zu Ebersdorf, Heinrich XXVIII (1726–
97), Graf:
Moravian, 20. 359

name of, corrected, 43. 271
Sloane Museum trustee, 20. 359
Zinzendorf's assistant at Herrnhut, 20. 359n
Réveillez-vous, belle endormie:
verses to air of: 6. 194 Boufflers's, 4. 361, 6.
3; La Harpe's, 7. 2; Mme du Deffand's,
5. 298
Revelation, Book of. *See under* Bible
Reveley, Willey (1760–99), painter and archi-
tect:
HW given drawing by, of castle at Otranto,
35. 435–6
SH visited by, 12. 232n
Worsley accompanied by, on travels, 35. 435n,
42. 177n
Revely, William, of Newby Wisk, Yorks:
Northumberland, E. of, grandson of, 20. 125n
Revenge, American privateer:
merchantmen captured by, 24. 229n
Revenge, English ship:
French ships defeated by, 21. 192–3
Gracieuse captured by, 7. 7n
involved in war, 21. 192–3
men from, lose arms, 18. 189
St Isidore pursued by, 18. 189
Theodore of Corsica and exiles return to Cor-
sica on, 18. 151n
Theodore of Corsica brought to Leghorn by,
18. 145n
Revenge, The. See under Young, Edward
Revenue:
Waller studies, 30. 291n
Revenue officer; revenue officers:
disenfranchisement of, proposed in Parlia-
ment, 25. 38
Gates's father was, 25. 92n
Revesby Abbey, Lincs:
Banks of, 1. 329n, 11. 2n
Revest. *See* Du Revest
Revett, Mrs John. *See* Russell, Frances
Revett. *See also* Rivett
Reviczky, ——, Imperial ambassador to Eng-
land:
Ferdinand accompanied by, 33. 530n
Review; reviews (military):
at Metz, 39. 178
Conway at, near Hanau, 37. 141
English royal family like, 17. 410
general, at Nistelrode, pleases D. of Cum-
berland, 37. 285–6
George II enjoys, 17. 450–1, 18. 84
HW has never seen, 1. 110
HW never attends, 32. 195, 35. 365
HW passes by, on Hounslow Heath, 39. 418
near Reading, Conway's horse kicks D. of
Cumberland at, 37. 382
Reviewer; reviewers, literary:
Cole's opinion of, 1. 370
Gray's opinion of, 1. 369
HW's opinion of, 1. 368–9
Review of the Late Motion:
publication of, advertised in *Common Sense*,
17. 83

Review of the Memoirs. See under Richards, William
Review of the Whole Political Conduct, A:
Faction Detected answered by, **18.** 319n
Revilla, Marqués, Spanish minister to Parma:
Charles III recalls, from Parma, **23.** 446
Dresden visited by, **22.** 303
Llano leaves Parma with, **23.** 445n
Parma formerly the post of, **22.** 330
return of, to Parma, **23.** 518
Spanish minister to Tuscany, **22.** 330
Revolution; revolutions:
bad men promote, to good effect, **34.** 101
Cibber 'meets,' **19.** 92
HW expects, with new impostures replacing old, **25.** 237
HW regards, as one of the many passing scenes, in which he is little concerned, **25.** 387
HW's reflections on, **15.** 237, **34.** 159, **42.** 250–2
HW thinks, justified in the case of oppression, **39.** 395
promoters of, seldom stay in charge of it, **35.** 399
Revolution, American. *See under* America, English colonies in; America, United States of; War: American-English
Revolution, English, of 1688; 'Glorious Revolution':
anecdotes forged against supporters of, **28.** 192
Bedford, 1st D. of, in, **34.** 128
bishops a disgrace to, **35.** 587
bloodshed scanty in, **16.** 376
centennial of 1588, **34.** 31
English constitution should follow system of, **35.** 355
HW praises, **34.** 159
HW's opinion of, **31.** 324
HW's principles go back to, **29.** 351, **41.** 78–9
Hardinge calls 'second Magna Charta,' **35.** 614
Jacobite parson would hate, **34.** 20
modern bishops would not have brought about, **35.** 569
Remarks on Mr Walpole's Catalogue asperses, **17.** 29–30
Scottish celebrations, **16.** 296
Somers humours Tories to avoid wrecking, **35.** 613–14
Tories call, a unique case, **39.** 395
Revolution, French. *See* French Revolution
'Revolution, Glorious.' *See* Revolution, English, of 1688
Revolutionist; revolutionists, English:
Bastille Day jubilee celebrated by, **11.** 347
Birmingham riots against, **11.** 314–15, 317
French horrors should be tasted by, **12.** 170
Howe, Mrs, repulses, **12.** 90
instruments of, seized, **12.** 119
mentioned, **11.** 345, **12.** 142

Paine's pamphlet, bribes, and handbills distributed by, **11.** 318
suspected of instigating plot against George III, **12.** 119
See also Bastille Day; Crown and Anchor Tavern; Revolution Society
Révolutions d'Angleterre:
HW's letters compose, in imitation of Vertot, **22.** 158
Révolutions de Portugal. See under Vertot, René Aubert de
Revolution Society:
aristocratic members leave, **11.** 131
Bastille Day jubilee celebrated by, **11.** 313–14
Birmingham meeting-houses of, destroyed, **11.** 314–15
congratulations sent by, on Bastille's fall, **34.** 98n
decline of, **11.** 146
English peace threatened by, **11.** 260
Price's toast in, **11.** 135
unsuccessful in changing English government, **11.** 322
Revolutions of England. See under Dorléans, Pierre-Joseph
Révolutions romaines. See under Vertot, René Aubert de
Rey, M. de:
sentiments of, towards Mme de Staal, diminish, **3.** 105n
Rey, Jacob. *See* King, John (ca 1753–1823)
Reynardière; Reynière. *See* Grimod de la Reynière
Reynold, Susanna (d. 1805), m. (1749) Robert Harland, 1st Bt:
Lauzun spends time with, **5.** 378n
Reynolds, ——, lawyer:
Wilkes retires to house of, at South Barrow, Kent, **23.** 205n
Reynolds, Edward (1599–1676), D.D.; Bp of Norwich:
funeral sermon by, **1.** 180n
Reynolds, Francis (d. 1773), M.P.:
Lowther's legacy to, **9.** 184
Reynolds, H. R.:
George III's health reported by, **34.** 43n
Reynolds, John:
imprisoned for election corruption, **22.** 584
Reynolds, Sir Joshua (1723–92), Kt, 1769; painter:
Ampthill visited by, **33.** 571
Baccelli painted by, **29.** 78n
Barnard's verses to, on Dr Johnson, **32.** 288n
Beauclerk, Lady Diana, praised by, for bistre drawings, **35.** 426
'Bedford family' painted by, **32.** 316, 337, 354
beggar-man a model for, **28.** 196
Bolingbroke instructs, about Vcts Bolingbroke's portrait, **10.** 52–3
Boswell breakfasts with, **33.** 486n
Bruce, Lord, caricatured by, at Rome, **20.** 331n

Brussels to be visited by, to see Joseph II's pictures, **33.** 486

Burney calls on, **42.** 330n

—— considers Lock a successor to, **11.** 111n

Carlisle's tribute to, **42.** 278

Catherine II commissions, to paint 'Infant Hercules,' **33.** 539, 571, **36.** 237

Charlotte, Q., advised by, to buy Zoffany's 'Tribuna,' **24.** 540n

Cherokee chiefs sit to, **10.** 36n

Colman's portrait by, unworthy to be with those of other sitters, **42.** 400–1

colours of: as impermanent as crayons, **24.** 93; fade, **10.** 79, **33.** 466, 572; impermanent, **28.** 250

Cooper's miniature of Cromwell bought by, **33.** 539

Cumberland, D. of, painted by, **40.** 284

'Death of Beaufort' by, not worth exhibiting, **15.** 206

Delineator, the, owned by, **39.** 293

—— sanctioned by, **29.** 372

Dufresnoy's *Art of Painting* annotated by, **35.** 361n

ear-trumpet of, **33.** 365

Eccardt occupies house of, **9.** 371n

England's best painter, **23.** 267

English school of painting founded by, **42.** 278

excels in hair-dressing, **41.** 390

fails in attempt to present Dr Johnson to HW, **11.** 276, **15.** 333, **43.** 148

Farrer, friend of, **15.** 162n

Fawkener, Henrietta and Mrs Crewe painted by, **11.** 163n

Felton's *Imperfect Hints* dedicated to, **34.** 10n

Fitzpatrick, Lady Anne and Lady Gertrude, painted by, **33.** 201n

Flanders visited by, **29.** 154, 156, 172

Franks, Ann, sits to, **13.** 36n

French painters inferior to, **39.** 32

Goldsmith presented by, to HW, at Royal Academy, **11.** 276, **43.** 148

HW comments on paintings by, **29.** 138

HW considers, a great painter, **24.** 93

HW glad not to compete with, at Portland sale, **39.** 442

HW introduced by, to Goldsmith, but rejects Dr Johnson, **43.** 148

HW solicited by, for subscription to Johnson's monument, **11.** 276

HW's portrait by: **1.** 64n; HW sends prints of, to Mann, **21.** 407–8; Mann impatient for, **21.** 414; Mann receives and frames, **21.** 446; print after, **1.** 69n; shows print of eagle, **19.** 66n

HW's portrait of 'Henry VII' criticized by, **33.** 466

HW's prospectus for the Delineator to be corrected by, **29.** 372

HW suggests biblical subject to, **29.** 104

HW suggests subject to, for picture commissioned by Catherine II, **31.** 243

HW to show miniatures and Masaccio's heads to, **23.** 267

HW wishes Lord Ossory to employ, **32.** 181

hands drawn badly by, **29.** 285

'Hercules' for Catherine II: not shown to HW, **33.** 539; HW sees, **33.** 571

Hogarth disparages taste of, **9.** 365

Hôtel de Thiers in Paris visited by, **7.** 338, **43.** 107

house of, in Leicester Fields, **33.** 538n

Jervais's window after, **2.** 170, **29.** 301, **33.** 417–18, **39.** 435

Johnson's life of Pope lent to HW by, **29.** 130

'Knight of the Brush,' **33.** 538

Long family's Van Dyck said by, to be a copy, **35.** 594

Marchi, assistant to, **15.** 325n

Mason's *Art of Painting* annotated by, **29.** 91, 99, 104, 113, 117, 132–3, 156, 172, 195, 204, 284

mezzotint after, **29.** 224n

Montagu hints at high prices charged by, **10.** 286

More, Hannah, calls choice by, of Hercules as picture for Catherine II 'nonsensical,' **31.** 243

'Nativity' designed by, for New College Chapel window at Oxford: **2.** 170, **29.** 301, **33.** 417–18, **39.** 435, **43.** 70; depicts him as shepherd, **33.** 417n

Newport St residence of, **10.** 158n

Nivernais's *Jardins modernes* given to, **12.** 259

Nuneham visited by, with two nieces, **33.** 54

offers to buy painting from E. of Orford, **2.** 170n

Ossory's correspondence with, about alleged Titian copy, **33.** 538n

Ossory, Lady, makes tambour waistcoat for, **32.** 220n

—— sends Fitzpatrick's prologue to, **34.** 106n

paralytic stroke suffered by, **29.** 296, **33.** 373

Piozzis possess paintings by, **11.** 106n

portraits by, of: Bolingbroke, Vcts, **10.** 52; Cavendish, Lord Richard, **43.** 308; Cumberland, D. of, **10.** 79; Edgcumbe, **9.** 186n, 417, **43.** 126–7; HW, **1.** 64n, 69n, **3.** 36on, **9.** 186n, **15.** 196n, **19.** 66n, **21.** 407–8, 414, 446; Huntingdon, **9.** 158n; Jenyns, **2.** 54, 58; Keppel, Lady Elizabeth, **9.** 417, **43.** 127; Malone, **42.** 409n; Mansfield, **9.** 158n; Parsons, Nancy, **43.** 375; Paterson, **32.** 153n; Rogers, **41.** 389–91; Selwyn, **9.** 186n, 417, **43.** 126–7; Stormont, **9.** 158n; Townsends, **32.** 153n; Waldegrave sisters, **29.** 45–6, 138, 285, **35.** 532; Williams, G. J., **9.** 186n, 417, **43.** 126–7

Poussins for D. of Rutland in possession of, **33.** 538–9

Prior's portrait not attributed by, to Dahl, **35.** 536

[Reynolds, Sir Joshua, *continued*]
promised to beg print for HW, 1. 150
Ramsay rivals, in popularity, 15. 47, 43. 194
Robinson's portrait by, his best, 28. 196
sale of pictures of, 42. 414
satirized, 16. 186n
sees no more excellence in Jupiter Serapis than in Julio Clovio, 39. 442
seldom succeeds in painting women, 15. 47
Shakespeare to be illustrated by, 33. 547n
Shipley friend of, 11. 269n
'Sibyl' at Palazzo Ratta at Bologna seen by, 35. 19n
Siddons, Mrs, pleases, by unpowdered hair, 33. 359n
—— seen by, in *King Lear*, 34. 2n
social relations of, with: Mariette, 7. 338; Montagu, Mrs, 31. 258; Ord, Mrs, 31. 213; Vesey, Mrs, 33. 466
Stanhope, Lady, sits to, 9. 260n
Storer's 'Delineator' delights, 28. 329
style of: defended in his *Discourses*, 29. 284–5; superior to Johnson's, 29. 132
'Tiresias, Blind,' painted by, 33. 571–2
'Ugolino and his Sons' by, 28. 35n
Reynolds, Richard (fl. 1773–91), butler of Caius College:
Cole receives print from, 1. 365
picture of Elizabeth of York owned by, 2. 8, 320
Reynolds, William (ca 1699–1784), page:
(?) Wales, P. of, attended by, 20. 232
'Reynolds,' (? Montagu's cat):
HW's cat resembles, 9. 25
Reynolds, English ship:
capture of, 24. 229n
Reynolds Moreton, Hon. Augustus John Francis (1777–1854), army officer:
father's estate reserved for, 11. 176
Reynolds Moreton, Francis (1739–1808), 3d Bn Ducie, 1785:
Child, Mrs, to marry, 11. 176
father of, 9. 184n
financial agreement of, with Mrs Child, 11. 176
Reynolds Moreton, Thomas (1733–85), 2d Bn Ducie, 1770:
father of, 9. 184n
SH visited by, 12. 221
Reynolds Moreton, Thomas (1776–1840), 4th Bn Ducie, 1808; cr. (1837) E. of Ducie:
father's estate reserved for, 11. 176
'Rezzonica, Signora':
Pasquin might allude to, 21. 491
Rezzonico, Cardinal. See Clement XIII
Rezzonico, Monsignore:
Rosenberg keeps, waiting, 23. 104n
Rezzonico, Principe, senator of Rome:
Ferdinand, Archduke, accompanied by, 33. 530n
Rezzonico, Abbondio (1742–1810), senator:
(?) Aubeterre suggests that Bourbon ministers treat with, 23. 36n

Roman populace threatens, 22. 229
senator of Rome, 22. 331n
state visitors welcomed by, 23. 23
uncle starved by, 22. 380
Rezzonico, Carlo (1693–1769). See Clement XIII
Rezzonico, Carlo (1724–99), cardinal, 1758:
Clement XIII suggests that Bourbon ministers treat with, 23. 36n
—— summons, to advisory congregation, 21. 308n
French and Spanish declarations to, about Young Pretender, 22. 399
pro-Jesuit cardinals led by, 23. 89n
Roman populace threatens, 22. 229
uncle starved by, 22. 380
Rezzonico, Carlo Gastone della Torre di (1742–96), Neapolitan poet:
SH visited by, 12. 229
Rezzonico, Giovanni Battista (1740–83), cardinal, 1770:
Roman populace threatens, 22. 229
state visitors welcomed by, 23. 23
uncle starved by, 22. 380
Rezzonico, Luigi (1726–ca 86), Gonfaloniere:
Roman populace threatens, 22. 229
uncle starved by, 22. 380
Rhadamanthe:
Du Deffand, Mme, compares Choiseul to, 8. 122
Rhadamiste et Zénobie. See under Crébillon, Prosper Jolyot de
Rhadel, ——, merchant:
HW sends letters by, 7. 377
Rhé (*or* Ré), île de:
Aulan, Bailli d', governs, 3. 366
French forces on, 35. 218
Rheda, Mme. See Reda, Mary
Rheims. See Reims
Rhein, Suzanne-Dorothée (ca 1741–1800), dancer:
mistress of Le Normand d'Etiolles, 20. 340n
Rhett, Sarah (1722–1808), m. (1743) Thomas Frankland, 5th Bt, 1768:
London house of, broken into, 33. 334–5
Rheumatic fever. See under Fever
Rheumatism:
Berry, Mary, may have, 12. 182
cold weather causes, 25. 493–4
Conway suffers from, 29. 96
gout and, 28. 462
gout expels, 11. 313
Gray may have, 14. 85
HW prefers gout to, 25. 497
HW's, may be caused by damps at SH, 22. 450, 456
HW thinks he may have, 22. 450
Hervey, Bns, thinks, worse than gout, 31. 155
in arm, 25. 432
inflammatory, 19. 249
in head, 24. 457, 458, 479
in hip, 28. 462
in loins, 22. 15

Laurenti diagnoses Old Pretender's illness as sciatica or, **20.** 442n

Mann prefers, to gout, **25.** 500

——'s, believed to be gout in head, **24.** 479

mentioned, **31.** 13

Montagu jokes about, **10.** 275

occurrences of: **3.** 269, 316, **6.** 432, **7.** 202, **9.** 370, **10.** 195, 232, 263, 275, **11.** 174, 177, 178, 183, 193, 311, 312, 319, 334, 336, **12.** 26, 203, **16.** 180, **18.** 401, 520, **19.** 234, 249, **21.** 359, 369, 443, **22.** 15, 413, **23.** 59, 462, **24.** 457, 458, 467, **25.** 115, 166, 494, 497, 500, 570, **28.** 462, **29.** 96, **31.** 115, 117, 190, 197, 201, 204–5, 210, 279, 359, **33.** 62, 120, 129, 270, 272, 278, 281, 282, 322, 409, 412, 419, 428, **34.** 105, 106, 125–6, 209, **35.** 321, 376, 531, 585, **36.** 234–5, **37.** 256, 266, **39.** 167, 316, 340, 341, 362, 363, 365, **42.** 75

part of English summer, **11.** 290

treatment for: bleeding, **19.** 250; bootikins, **24.** 463; hare skins, **18.** 520

Rhine, river:

    Austrians drive French beyond, **12.** 192

    Broglie retires towards, **18.** 99

    Charles, P., might cross, **18.** 297, 311, 457

    ——'s crossing of: **18.** 466, 478, 505, **37.** 158–9, 175; Carteret considers, a reprieve, **30.** 60; fruitless, **18.** 481, **30.** 60; invasion threat from Dunkirk averted by, **30.** 53; vainly attempted, **37.** 146

    Clermont about to cross, **21.** 193

    Coke, Lady Mary, would have helped Louis XIV to cross, **31.** 21

    Contades on, at Cologne, **37.** 555

    Conway and Scott ferry across, **39.** 537, 539

    Conway goes down, admiring scenery, **37.** 150

    English army crosses, **18.** 209, **43.** 250

    English army may cross, **18.** 290, 293

    English army on, and due to cross it, **37.** 143–4

    English victory over French unprecedented when on other side of, **18.** 218

    Ferdinand, P., crosses, **21.** 211

    —— may abandon, **37.** 554–5

    French army on the, estimated, **21.** 271

    French cross, **37.** 136

    French retreat to, **38.** 23

    French said to have crossed, **17.** 121

    French should not have been allowed to cross, **21.** 264

    French to keep P. Charles from crossing, **37.** 144

    French troops withdrawn to, from Provence, **19.** 8

    in quotation from Pope's *Essay on Man*, **33.** 25

    Louis XIV crosses, **6.** 292

    Mann hopes that Conway will drive French across, **21.** 493

    pontoon bridges over, **21.** 228n

    Prussian defeat on, **21.** 456

    revolution spreads along, **11.** 61

Swiss and Palatine troops object to crossing, into Germany, **21.** 94n

Young Pretender may make campaign towards, **18.** 434

Rhinoceros:

    appearances of, in Rome, **20.** 128n

    Dürer's woodcut from sketch of, **20.** 128n

    Italian head-dress imitates, **20.** 147–8

    medal of, struck off, **20.** 128

    Montvandermeer brings: from Asia, **20.** 127n; to Rome and Florence, **20.** 127

    shields made from hides of, **20.** 381

Rhode Island:

    Americans quit, **24.** 419

    American troops are mobilized in, **28.** 206

    English capture of, **24.** 273

    English forces in, **19.** 69n

    Estaing may attack, **24.** 410, 416

    —— reaches, **7.** 75n

    French said to have evacuated, **33.** 306

    Howe makes progress in conquering, **24.** 281

    Howe brothers said to have reached, **32.** 303n

    Rodney finds, too strongly fortified, **25.** 99

Rhodes, ——:

    Wright's murder reported by, at Florence, **37.** 33n, 34n

Rhodes, Mr:

    SH visited by, **12.** 245

Rhodes, island of:

    Du Deffand, Mme, likes Vertot's account of siege of, **5.** 17

Rhodes; Rhodez. *See also* Rodez

'Rhodope':

    HW's name for Norton's mother, **38.** 454

Rhominagrobis. *See* Rominagrobis

Rhone, river:

    HW hopes that Forbes will sail up, **35.** 289

    Royalists cross, **12.** 40n

    Saône's conflux with, **35.** 260

    Thames and, compared, **33.** 355, **35.** 264

'Rhubarb, Miss':

    HW's name for physician's daughter, **23.** 93

Rhubarb (medicinal):

    Arras, Bp of, takes, **5.** 254

    Lyttelton takes, **24.** 537

Rhyme:

    English language barren of, **15.** 261

    HW comments on, **33.** 204

    Voltaire's observations on, **41.** 156

Rhymer. *See* Rymer

Rhys ap Gruffydd (d. 1197), P. of South Wales:

    HW's ancestor, **13.** 81n

Rialto. *See under* Venice

Rians, Marquise de. *See* Valbelle, Marguerite-Delphine de

Riazan and Murom, Bp of. *See* Sechenov, Daniil Andreievich

Rib; ribs:

    HW's, not broken by fall, **31.** 305

Ribband. *See* Ribbon

Ribbon; ribbons:

    black: **32.** 237n; chaplain wears, across forehead, **24.** 539

[Ribbon; ribbons, *continued*]
blue: footmen's gallery in Drury Lane strung with, **20**. 231; HW wears, during Gordon riots, **33**. 186; in 'The Turnstile,' **21**. 93
blue, of Garter order: Bedford, D. of, wears. **10**. 235; Dorset's, **40**. 386; Hertford's, fingered by Louis XV, **38**. 261; Hertford wears, under coat, **38**. 261; on HW's watch, **40**. 64n; would not be becoming to HW, **38**. 42; *see also under* Garter, Order of
blue, of the Danish Order of the Elephant, worn in England by Christian VII and Bernstorff, **4**. 128
bunches of, on Englishmen's nosegays, **30**. 211
Carteret, Bns, wears, **18**. 501
Catherine, St, causes miracles by, **20**. 430
colours of, **9**. 241n
Fitzjames wears, **39**. 9
French embroidered, cockades of, **22**. 423
George II distributes, **20**. 311
green, of Thistle order, *see* Thistle, Order of the
grosgrain, Hertford, Cts of, wants HW to bring, from Paris, **39**. 268
HW quotes Cibber on, referring to SH visitors, **38**. 208
horses bedecked with, **21**. 399
in postilions' hats, for Zorndorf victory, **37**. 566–7
Johnston, Lady Cecilia, sends, from Paris to Cts of Ailesbury, **39**. 24
Kilmarnock, Cts of, wants, **37**. 218
ladies', cost of, **18**. 281
Millers' Roman vase dressed with, **39**. 241
of orders of knighthood: Bute and Newcastle have, **35**. 93; mad foreigner wears, in Paris, **24**. 361, **25**. 572; Mann should get, for peacemaking, **35**. 32
rainbow, around Patapan's neck, **18**. 317
red, decorating white dress, **12**. 179
red, of Bath order, *see* Bath, Order of the
washed, worn by humbler Florentine ladies, **25**. 175
watered light blue, Order of St Patrick to wear, **25**. 365
yellow: of retired naval captains might be given to HW's gardener on retirement, **35**. 480; worn by knights of Nova Scotia order, **32**. 279
Ribera, José de (1590–1652), called Lo Spagnoletto, painter:
Modenese artists inferior to, **25**. 247
painting of Duns Scotus attributed to, **15**. 141n
Ribot, Ambroise (d. 1787), intendant of Chanteloup:
ill, **5**. 403
said to be dying, **6**. 97
Ribston, Yorks:
Goodricke of, **28**. 368n
Ricard de Bregançon, Mary-Anne-Pauline de, m. (1759) François-Raymond-Joseph-Her-

mengilde-Amalric de Narbonne-Pelet-Alais-Melguel-Bermond, Vicomte de Narbonne:
(?) buys doll's trousseau for Choiseul's niece, **4**. 299
daughter of, **7**. 215
lacks common sense, **4**. 83–4
(?) Lesrocs attended by, **7**. 321
Rochford, Cts of, friend of, **3**. 333
sister-in-law of, **3**. 351
social relations of, in Paris, *see index entries ante* **8**. 486
Ricardos, Antonio (1727–94), general:
French republicans defeated by, **12**. 40
HW compares, to hero of Mrs Behn's comedy, **12**. 40
Ricasoli, Baronessa. *See* Corsi, Teresa
Ricasoli, Barone Bindaccio:
festa given by, **17**. 136
Ricasoli, Via de':
Cocomero, Via del, becomes, **17**. 56n
Riccardi, Marchesa. *See* Gerini, Maria Maddalena (1717–75)
Riccardi, Signora. *See* Strozzi, Teresa (1747–1816)
Riccardi, —— (ca 1732–52), son of Vincenzo Riccardi:
death of, **20**. 336, 340
Riccardi, Bernardino (1708–86), Marchese di:
(?) father quarrels with, **17**. 147
Frescobaldi, Mme, dismisses, **17**. 136
(?) Grafton, Ds of, to receive letter from, enclosed by Mann, **22**. 108
Grifoni, Mme, replaces Mme Frescobaldi in affections of, **19**. 358
(?) house of, at Pontedera, **22**. 220n
Mann discusses *Demetrio* with, **17**. 120
Ricasolis entertain, **17**. 136
Riccardi, Cosimo:
ball forbidden by, **17**. 122
Carteret wedding shocks, by its simplicity, **18**. 445–6
curiosity of, about weddings and pregnancies, **22**. 8
father's gallery spoiled by candles with rock-crystal lustres provided by, **22**. 157–8
financial arrangements of, with estranged relatives, **17**. 147
(?) George II's accession attended by, **19**. 506n
gossip loved by, **18**. 358n
granddaughter of, **19**. 350
granddaughter of, to be entertained, **17**. 122
granddaughter's death said to afflict, **18**. 405
health of, apoplectic fit, **20**. 192
Lami librarian to, **21**. 476, **22**. 13
Mann constantly asked by, about Adolf Fredrik's marrying Ps Amelia, **18**. 304
—— plagued by inquiries from, **18**. 289
son-in-law's death expected by, **18**. 289
sons and daughter told by, about recent fit, **20**. 192

souls in purgatory reproached by, for not giving him good weather for garden party in return for masses, **17**. 499, **21**. 435

Riccardi, Francesco (1648–1719), Tuscan ambassador to Rome:
(?) Giordani paints gallery for, **22**. 157

Riccardi, Giulia Maria (1737–70), m. (1759) Marchese Lorenzo Niccolini:
approaching marriage of, **21**. 343

Riccardi, Giuseppe Luigi (1744–98):
ball given by, for Archduke and Archduchess from Milan, **25**. 50–1
(?) wedding dinner for, **22**. 458

Riccardi, Laura (1699–1777), m. (1718) Marchese Antonio Corsi:
daughter instructed by, about marriage, **17**. 150
daughter's present from, on birth of heir, **18**. 121
father tells, of recent fit, **20**. 192
husband of, **17**. *137*n

Riccardi, Vincenzo Maria (1704–52), Marchese:
Antinori, Mme, entertains, at villa, **19**. 411
Carlisle and Duncannon interested in buying gems of, **19**. 361, 372, 382, 387, 398
death of, **20**. 336, 340
England formerly the diplomatic post of, **19**. 506, **21**. 464
father quarrels with, **17**. 147
father tells, of recent fit, **20**. 192
festa to be given by, for niece, **17**. 122
Galli, Contessa, mourns, **20**. 336
HW asked by, to send gems to Tempi, **19**. 259
HW decides to keep rings of, **19**. 398
HW has no time to deal with, **19**. 104
HW loses catalogue of gems sent by, **19**. 73
HW receives letter from, asking him to sell gems, **19**. 28–9, 73
HW refuses to forward gems of, to Lisbon, **19**. 273
HW's correspondence with, **19**. 28–9, 73–4, 331
HW's message makes, inquisitive about his gems, **19**. 408
HW tells, through Mann, that he cannot sell his gems for him, **19**. 73–4
HW to receive letter from, **19**. 94
HW would like to buy rings from, **19**. 331–2
Lorenzi entertained by, **17**. 147
Mann awaits HW's instructions before seeing, **19**. 392
—— concludes deal with, for rings for HW, **19**. 411
—— confers with, on sale of gems, **19**. 372–3
—— disputes with, at opera, over 'Onslow' impersonator, **19**. 505, 506
—— not invited by, **17**. 147, 164
—— pays, for HW's rings, **19**. 433
—— plagued by inquiries from, **18**. 289
—— tells HW's instructions to, **19**. 94
—— to pay, for HW's rings, **19**. 420, 427, 435
Pucci's correspondence with, about sale of gems, **19**. 372

Tempi receives list from, of gems to be sold in Portugal, **19**. 349
(?) Vestris mistress to, **43**. 265
Whithed attends festino of, **17**. 146

Riccardi family:
debts of, **20**. 336
Mann does not want, at great assemblies, **18**. 284
wedding in, is Lorenzi's greatest treat, **20**. 92

Riccardo of England. *See* Richard (1209–72), D. of Cornwall

Riccasoli. *See* Ricasoli

Ricci, Francesco (1679–1755), cardinal, 1743; commissary; gov. of Rome 1741–3:
Benedict XIV makes, cardinal, **18**. 302n
death of, **20**. 464
denies having Pontano arrested, **18**. 56
receives Pontano's sequestered papers, **18**. 56
sent to Civita Vecchia to adjudge *Sea Horse's* capture, **17**. 8

Ricci, Lorenzo (1703–75), general of the Jesuits:
Billard to be protected by, **5**. 190
Clement XIII said to have been urged by, to repel Jesuit refugees, **22**. 527
——'s retort to complaints of, **21**. 230
Clement XIV receives, coldly, **23**. 135
——'s orders annulled by counter-briefs of, **23**. 517
——'s orders to, **23**. 494n
death of, **24**. 147
dismissal of, to be decreed, **23**. 473
Frederick II appealed to by, **5**. 302–3
imprisoned and examined daily, **23**. 513
Jesuits' revenues should be used by, to support refugees, **22**. 527
—— suffer from inflexibility of, **22**. 535
rôle of, in *La Passion des Jésuites*, **5**. 315
(?) York, D. of, asked by, for aid for American Jesuits, **22**. 233

Ricci, Roberto de:
Gray mentions, **14**. 68n

Ricci, Salvatore:
Furnese has pictures by, **21**. 172n

Ricci, Sebastiano (1659–1734), painter:
Smith has paintings by, **18**. 465

Ricci family:
Bonaventuri murdered by, at Francesco I's instigation, **20**. 414

Ricciarelli, Daniele (1509–66), called 'Daniele da Volterra'; painter:
altar-piece by, in King's College Chapel, **2**. 251–2, 253, 255

Ricciarelli, (?) Giuseppe, opera singer:
Ailesbury, Cts of, to entertain, **37**. 396
Mingotti's quarrel with, **35**. 256–7
Vaneschi disputes with, **20**. 557
Venetian operatic career of, **20**. 557n

Riccio. *See* Rizzio

Riccio rapito, Il. See under Bonducci, Andrea

Riccoboni, Mme Antonio Francesco. *See* Laboras de Mézières, Marie-Jeanne

Rice, ——:
Richecourt, Cts, has, as lover, **20**. 90
Rice, ——, of Spittle Sq., Bishopsgate St:
HW mentions, **20**. 397
Rice, Lady Cecil. *See* Talbot, Lady Cecil
Rice, Edward, of Newton, Glamorganshire:
genealogy of, **10**. 352
wife of, **9**. 12n
Rice, Mrs Edward. *See* Trevor, Lucy
Rice, George (? 1724–79), M.P.:
becomes lord of Trade, **21**. 489
Cadoxton estate shared by, **41**. 117, 127
dates of, corrected, **43**. 277, 352
Furnese, Selina, dismisses, **9**. 85
genealogy of, **10**. 352, **41**. 117–19, 130
grandmother's legacy to, **9**. 134
marriage of: **25**. 86n; expected, **9**. 85, 190
son of, **10**. 179, **36**. 174
Stanley, Hans, leaves estate in Wales to, **33**. 162
SH visited by, **9**. 134
Vauxhall visited by, **9**. 85
Rice (after 1793 de Cardonnel; after 1817, Rice), George Talbot (1765–1852), 3d Bn Dinevor; M.P.:
birth of, **10**. 179
peerage to revert to, **36**. 174
Rice, Griffith (1667–1729), of New Park:
descent of, **41**. 118, 130
Rice, Mrs Griffith. *See* Hoby, Catherine
Rice, James Louis (ca 1730–1801), Count of the Holy Roman Empire:
Damer, Mrs, meets, at Spa, **33**. 71n
Du Barry killed by, in duel at Bath, **33**. 71–2
Rice, Lucy (ca 1726–1818):
Boscawen, Mrs George, to write to, **9**. 12
coachman of, **9**. 49
genealogy of, **10**. 352
(?) HW mentions, **37**. 425
HW obtains theatre box for, **9**. 346
HW sends compliments to, **9**. 12
health of, cold, **9**. 49
Montagu asks HW for theatre box for, **9**. 342, 344–5
—— to be visited by, **9**. 174
Talbot's promotion may give influence to, in theatre, **9**. 345
Rice (food):
'deity' of, **40**. 17
England sends barrels of, to Portugal, **20**. 512n
Raynal discusses, **39**. 168
Rice, cream of:
for Mme du Deffand, in illness, **7**. 247
Rice family:
HW entertains, at SH, **9**. 105, 134, 161
Hampton Court (?) residence of, **9**. 134
Montagu to be visited by, at Greatworth, **9**. 291
Rich, Bns. *See* Cavendish, Anne (ca 1621–38)
Rich, Lady. *See* Griffith, Elizabeth (ca 1692–1773)

Rich, Misses:
SH visited by, **12**. 241
Rich, Mr, of Mortimer St:
robbed, **12**. 102n
Rich, Lady Anne (d. 1642), m. (1626) Edward Montagu, styled Vct Mandeville; cr. (1626) Bn Kimbolton; 2d E. of Manchester, 1642:
portrait of, at Kimbolton, **10**. 78
Rich, Charles (1616–73), 4th E. of Warwick:
wife of, **16**. 138
Rich, Charlotte (ca 1726–1818), m. (1759) John Beard:
marriage of, **9**. 265
Rich, Christopher (d. 1714):
satire on, **13**. 132n
Rich, Edward (1673–1701), 6th E. of Warwick:
print of, **1**. 183
Rich, Edward Henry (1698–1721), 7th E. of Warwick:
Addison's death, witnessed by, **9**. 236
Warner, Betty, seduced by, **18**. 540
Rich, Elizabeth (ca 1716–95), m. (1749) Sir George Lyttelton, 5th Bt, 1751; cr. (1756) Bn Lyttelton:
Ailesbury, Cts of, and Conway exhaust, with walking, **39**. 158–9
—— asked by HW to tell, of his invitation to her with Churchill and Cadogans, **39**. 300
—— intimate with, **38**. 14n
—— to be visited by, at Park Place, **38**. 35, 37
—— to entertain, **37**. 396
—— visited by, at Park Place, **38**. 165, **39**. 300
Chalfont visited by, **9**. 284
Churchills were to be met by, **38**. 165
Conway expected by, to come over for opening of Parliament, **39**. 222
——'s sow deemed by, to be pregnant, **37**. 349
Du Châtelet, Mme, liked by, **32**. 40n
(?) Durant's and Tenducci's affairs with, **38**. 14n
engagement of, announced, **9**. 84–5
forest thinned by, **42**. 200
Garrick and, to breakfast at SH, **38**. 61
Garrick entertains, **38**. 61
HW admires readiness of, in capping verses, **42**. 119
HW admires singing of, **17**. 166
HW asked by, in letter, if Conway should not attend Parliament, **39**. 222
HW asks Mann to get music for, **17**. 166
HW compliments, by writing in husband's style, **38**. 163
HW entertains, at SH, **10**. 156, **38**. 102
HW invited by, to Hagley, **42**. 467
HW invites, to see new SH gallery, **38**. 207
HW may give Bentley's ormer shells to, for grotto, **35**. 175
HW's correspondence with, **7**. 376, 377, 379, **38**. 167, **42**. 117–19, 199–201, 466–7
HW sends compliments to, **40**. 104
HW sends parcel to, by Cole, **1**. 101

HW's 'heroic epistle' to, hoping to see her in Portugal St, **39.** 430

HW should bring shells to, in Hill St, **40.** 81–2

HW's house found cold by, **39.** 167

HW to be met by, in Portugal St, **42.** 118

HW to be visited by, at SH, **10.** 260, **35.** 85, 165

HW visited by, at SH, **10.** 133, **31.** 142, **32.** 124

HW would like to see, at Park Place, **39.** 138

health of: cramps and rheumatism, **39.** 167; ill, **40.** 104; pretty well, **41.** 106; Johnston, Lady Cecilia, reports, to be good, **42.** 200

husband's separation from, arranged, **38.** 14–15

Johnston, Lady Cecilia, sends parcel to, **7.** 404

looks well, at Coronation, **38.** 126

Mysterious Mother reading to be heard by, **10.** 260

never hears anything that happens, **39.** 222

news of, behindhand, **39.** 320

Nivernais's *Jardins modernes* given to, **12.** 260

opera box not taken by, **37.** 477

pen of, always wants mending, **42.** 466

Piozzi, Mrs, comments upon, **9.** 265n

Prie absorbs, **39.** 167

Ripley Cottage the address of, **42.** 117, 118, 199

sister of, **10.** 260n

Stowe visit brings memories of, to HW, **10.** 314

Rich, Henry (1590–1649), 1st E. Holland:

buried in Kensington Church, **20.** 182

Henrietta Maria loved by, **19.** 397

Holland House owned by, **19.** 397

motto of, interpreted by HW, **19.** 397, 411

portrait of, at Cornbury, **20.** 182

title of, corrected, **43.** 262, 268

Rich, Jeremy:

print of, **40.** 236

Rich, John (1691or2–1761), pantomimist; manager of Covent Garden Theatre; 'harlequin':

Bentley's *Wishes* rejected by, **9.** 372, **35.** 644–5

biographical information on, **43.** 262

daughter of, **9.** 265

finer coronation than real one to be shown by, **38.** 133

Fleetwood's negotiations with, **13.** 143

footman applies to, to become actor, **37.** 141

Gray has surfeit of, **13.** 113

Horton, Mrs, and Miss Norsa intimate with, **19.** 419

manager of Covent Garden, **9.** 48n, **43.** 113

metamorphoses by, **11.** 20n, **12.** 110

Norsa, Hannah, lives at house of, **9.** 109n, **19.** 419

pantomimes by, **29.** 4n, **33.** 361

Sandwich succeeds, **10.** 111n

Theobald's *Orpheus and Eurydice* produced by, at Covent Garden, **37.** 51, **43.** 146

Rich, Mary (d. 1769):

Ailesbury, Cts of, to entertain, **37.** 396

—— visited by, at Park Place, **37.** 505

Buchan, Cts of, asks, about HW, **35.** 119

Clive, Mrs, visited by, **35.** 275–6

(?) Conway calls, 'little Mary,' comparing her to jerboa, **37.** 468

HW, Conway, and Countesses of Ailesbury and of Coventry invited by, **37.** 351

HW falls with, when trying to cross stile, **35.** 275–6

HW taken by, to dine with Millers at Batheaston, **35.** 98

HW to be visited by, at SH, **10.** 260, **35.** 98, 283, **37.** 492

HW to see, at Bath, **39.** 76

HW visited by, at SH, **35.** 275–6

health of: better, **37.** 510; cold, **37.** 505

Italian letter written by, for Cts of Ailesbury, **37.** 476

Mysterious Mother reading to be heard by, **10.** 260

tall hat dwarfs, **35.** 144

Rich, Sir Richard (? 1496–1567), 1st Bn Rich; lord chancellor:

resigns seals, **1.** 220

Rich, Robert, army officer:

Sackville's court martial avoided by, **21.** 366n

Rich, Robert (1587–1658), 2d E. of Warwick:

portrait of, by 'Mytens,' at Kimbolton, **10.** 76, 78

son of, **39.** 139n

Van Dyck's portrait of, **15.** 95

Rich, Robert (1611–59), styled Lord Rich 1619–41; 3d E. of Warwick, 1658:

wife of, **39.** 139n

Rich, Sir Robert (ca 1620–75), styled Lord Kensington 1624–49; 2d E. Holland, 1649:

Kensington burial-place of, **20.** 182n

Rich, Sir Robert (1685–1768), 4th Bt, 1706:

Augusta, Ps, mistakes, for Sir Robert Walpole, at Leicester House, **18.** 219

(?) Bath visited by, **39.** 76

Conway would benefit from death of, **10.** 252

daughter of, **10.** 260n, **17.** *166*n

death of: **4.** 22n; rumoured, **38.** 574

Dutch hat available to, **38.** 11

Flanders visited by, **17.** 486

HW tries to rent house of, **9.** 40

(?) incoherent, **39.** 76

Keppel, Bp, clashes with, at St James's, **38.** 294–5

son of, **19.** 248

son's quarrel to be adjusted by, **17.** 486

Rich, Sir Robert (1717–85), 5th Bt, 1768:

father to settle quarrel of, **17.** 486

(?) HW informed by, of Lytteltons' separation, **38.** 14–15

regiment of, **17.** 486n

Vane's quarrel with, **17.** 486

wounded at Culloden, **19.** 248, **37.** 241

Rich, Mrs Robert. *See* Knyvett, Catherine

'Richard, Beau' (or 'the Beau'). See Richards, Fitzherbert
Richard I (1157–99), K. of England 1189–99; 'Cœur-de-Lion':
Barking Church, where his heart was buried, founded by, 1. 322–3
Chatterton's poem about, 16. 104, 123, 125, 174, 349
——'s poems said to be of time of, 16. 124, 126, 128
crusades of, in tapestry, 40. 213
crusading exploits of, unlikely to be still famous in Edward IV's time, 16. 343
Gaillard's account of, 5. 68
HW's account of, 2. 134n
HW seeks poems by, 21. 156–7
HW thanks Mann for investigation about, 21. 178
HW wants another copy of poem by, 21. 178
Mann will seek poems of, 21. 162
poem by: HW thanks Mann for second copy of, 21. 189; in San Lorenzo library, Mann to send copy of, to HW, 21. 169
Provençal poem by: 40. 303; copied by young Cocchi, 21. 186
Richard II might be mistaken for, as author, 16. 11
Spence investigates poems allegedly by, 40. 115–17
Richard II (1367–1400), K. of England 1377–99:
alleged Grand Justiciary of, 20. 64–5
Anne of Bohemia wife of, 7. 359
authorship might be attributed to, by mistake, 16. 11
Beaufort declared by, to be legitimate, 2. 31n
Cobham's allegiance to, 16. 4
conspirator against, 1. 344
death of, at Pontefract, 35. 269
effigy of, in Westminster Abbey, 12. 105
England's capture not known to, when he visited Ireland, 37. 441
grants title of Lord Mayor of York, 28. 362n
Gray's Odes mention, 40. 103
horse of, used by Bolingbroke, 41. 373
HW's dream about portrait of, 43. 47
Ireland, D. of, favourite of, 9. 67
marriage of, 2. 195n
master-cook of, writes MS, 2. 223
master-cooks of, 43. 71
painting of, 12. 111n
statue of, 1. 276, 342n
Thomas, D. of Gloucester, meditated supplanting, 15. 172
tomb of second wife of, 7. 308
Totness's translations of accounts of, 16. 13
wives of, 42. 139
Richard II. See under Shakespeare, William
Richard III (1452–85), K. of England 1483–5; cr. (1461) D. of Gloucester:
absurdities imputed to, not credible, 15. 173, 176, 183
appearance of: 2. 153, 155, 161; according to Cts of Desmond, 40. 108–9; according to

Manchester's roll, 41. 134, 225
arm of, could not be withered, since he fought Brandon, 41. 112
Astle's discoveries concerning, 2. 2
attainder acts against followers of, 41. 92
attainder of D. of Clarence might have been forged by, 41. 323
Barret admires painting of, 41. 132
biographers of, usually fall in love with him, 32. 340
birth of, 1. 320, 321
bolsters worn by clergy supposedly to ape deformity of, 41. 221–3, 224–5
Buck's and Carte's histories vindicate, 35. 607, 610
Cambridge University's relations with, 1. 138, 144, 147, 43. 50–2
(?) cap and robe of state worn by, in miniature of Caxton's presentation to Edward IV, 41. 112n
Carlisle ridicules HW's idea of vindicating, 30. 252
Catherine II's crimes may make HW believe Lancastrian histories about, 22. 253
character of, will seem better at Day of Judgment, 32. 146
Coke, Lady Mary, not convinced of innocence of, 31. 138
Comines charges, with Henry VI's murder, 14. 181
—— mentions, 35. 608
—— saw, at Ds of Burgundy's court, 41. 112–13
Cornwallis, Sir William, praises, 14. 179
coronation of, 41. 123
'coronation roll' of, 3. 287, 14. 182, 15. 115, 117
cruelty of, to Edward IV's family, 15. 175, 177
Cumberland, D. of, compared with, by verses, 30. 126
death of, 2. 364
Desmond, Cts of, describes, as well-made, 35. 607, 40. 108
—— said to have danced with, 40. 108, 109, 41. 112
Du Deffand, Mme, reads about, in Shakespeare's play, 4. 171
Edward IV's family not ill-treated by, 15. 177
engravings of, 40. 217
État de la maison des Ducs de Bourgogne may give HW information about, 6. 76
evidence of indulgence of, to nephews and nieces, 15. 221–2
father of, 16. 239n
Gloucester visited by, from London, 41. 140, 141
Gray thinks that Henry VI was murdered by, 14. 162–3
HW calls, 'only king I have defended,' 33. 383
HW cannot wholly exonerate, but thinks him innocent of many alleged crimes, 41. 354
HW is convinced, did not murder Henry VI, 14. 169

HW is plagued with questions about, **15.** 243

HW later publishes *Historic Doubts* on, **22.** 253n

HW not prejudiced in favour of, but only against his historians, **15.** 176

HW quotes, from Shakespeare, **32.** 160

HW receives letters on, **32.** 281

HW's defence of, mentioned by Mason, **28.** 436

HW's favourable picture of, questioned by Gray, **14.** 164–5

HW's *Historic Doubts* on, *see Historic Doubts on the Life and Reign of King Richard III*

HW should not abandon, to Hardinge's attack, **35.** 611

HW shows Henry VII to have been a greater devil than, **14.** 166, 169

HW's interest in, **1.** 227, **3.** 287, 288, 291, 292, 295, 302, 309, 338, 391, **4.** 19, 171

HW's opinion of, **42.** 8

HW's palliation of crimes of, partly accepted by Henry, **15.** 183, 242

HW's partiality for, **41.** 156–7

HW's print of, **1.** 133

HW's queries concerning, **2.** 3

HW's rehabilitation of, praised: by Granger, **41.** 133–4; by Hardinge, **35.** 562

HW's vindication of, to be told to Young Pretender, **25.** 104

HW to write verses against, **17.** 234

HW would, if he were judged insane, disappoint ghost of, **12.** 95

Hardinge, like HW, sceptical about, **35.** 598

Henry's account of, transcribed for HW, **15.** 168–9, 170

——'s opinion of, discussed by HW, **15.** 242–3

Historic Doubts to confute Lancastrian aspersions on, **41.** 111–12

Howard, John, created D. of Norfolk by, **33.** 505

Hume's and Rapin's accounts of, read by Mme du Deffand, **3.** 338

inscription concerning, **41.** 134–5

intrigues of reign of, **15.** 175

Lambeth Palace MS depicts, **41.** 112

letters of: **2.** 108n; cited, **1.** 156; Gray comments on, **14.** 159–60

Manchester's pedigree has drawing of, **41.** 134–5, 144, 225

More's account of, **35.** 609–10

mother allegedly accused by, of whoredom, **41.** 115

mother-in-law not maltreated by, **35.** 607–8

murders attributed to, **15.** 171

not unpopular when D. of Gloucester, **15.** 171

oath of, not to murder his nieces, **15.** 184

order by, about Jane Shore's marriage, **16.** 171

Osborne on, quoted, **1.** 154

paradox on, **42.** 302

portrait of son of, **1.** 133

portraits of: **15.** 123–4, 250; in D. of Manchester's MS roll of Earls of Warwick, **1.** 133, **14.** 173, 177–8, **35.** 607, **41.** 134–5, 144, 225; in Kentish family's possession, **41.** 131–2; on Lodge's roll, **42.** 285

priests hated by, **41.** 115

print of, **40.** 236

Ratcliffe accompanies, at Oxford, **41.** 141

reign of: red roses probably not worn in, **16.** 232; 'Rowley' predicts woe in, **16.** 239

reputed stone coffin of, **2.** 243

Richard, D. of York's death believed by, **43.** 200

Rising to the Crowne, The, and *Licia* attributed to, **40.** 297, 300–1

Robinson resembles, **21.** 120

Rous praises, **1.** 133, **15.** 124n

——'s pedigree roll depicts, **35.** 607, **41.** 134–5, 144, 225

'Rowley' predicts woe in reign of, **16.** 239

statue of, **1.** 342n

Vertue's drawing of, **41.** 132

Warwick would also have been killed if nephews were really murdered by, **41.** 113

Waynflete's reception for, at Magdalen College, described by Wood, **41.** 139–41

Windsor mayor's letter from, **41.** 121–2

Wortley, knight of the body to, **35.** 269

writers on, make him a fool rather than a knave, **28.** 239

York choir screen does not include, **28.** 100, 106, 254, 259, 260

See also under *Historic Doubts on the Life and Reign of King Richard III;* Shakespeare, William: *Richard III*

Richard III. See under Shakespeare, William

Richard III, HW's. *See Historic Doubts on the Life and Reign of King Richard III*

'Richard, Duke':
painted-glass portrait of, **1.** 30, 32

Richard (1209–72) (Plantagenet), E. of Cornwall:
Sanchia, wife of, **40.** 298

Richard I (935–96), D. of Normandy:
second wife of, **1.** 387

Richard, D. of Beorn, son of William I:
tomb of, at Winchester, **35.** 250

Richard (Plantagenet) (ca 1375–1415), of Coningsburgh, cr. (1414) E. of Cambridge:
family of, **42.** 139

HW corrects error about, **42.** 21–2

stepmother of, **42.** 139

Richard (Plantagenet) (1411–60), 3d D. of York:
Clay, John, treasurer of Household of, **14.** 73n

family of, **42.** 21–2, 138–9

HW attributes 'old inn' at Fotheringhay to, **10.** 91

in Margaret of Anjou's escort, **14.** 72, 74

lived at Sandal Castle and died at Battle of Wakefield, **35.** 270

Margaret, daughter of, **14.** 163n

register of births of children of, **1.** 319–21

Richard III resembles, **40.** 110

royal pretensions of, **16.** 233

[Richard (Plantagenet) (1411–60), *continued*]
son builds bridge chapel in memory of, **35.**
270
sons of, **16.** 239
tomb of, at Fotheringhay, **10.** 91, (?) 344
wife of, **1.** 319n
Richard (Plantagenet) (1473–83), cr. (1474) D.
of York:
aunt acknowledges Warbeck as, **41.** 114
death of, believed by Richard III and Lord
Howard, invalidates Warbeck's claims, **43.**
200
Guidickins said to have called, 'poor little
fellow,' **10.** 255
HW's theory about: **11.** 347; praised by
Granger, **41.** 133
Henry VII must eliminate, to get throne,
41. 114
marriage of, **2.** 364, **16.** 4, **33.** 504–5
Norfolk, Ds of, to have married, **42.** 422
Richard III's murder of, doubted by HW,
3. 287, **4.** 4, **15.** 177, 184, **33.** 504–5, **41.** 113
room of, in Tower of London, jokingly de-
sired by HW, **17.** 233–4
Warbeck, Perkin, said to be, **35.** 607
Richard, ——:
attends session of parliament of Paris, **8.** 173
Richard, ——, Tuscan financier:
dismissal of, **20.** 327
Richard, ——, Tuscan official under Antinori:
Francis I's dispatch communicated by, to
Mann, **21.** 114n
Richard, ——, Lady Caroline Petersham's foot-
man:
Stanley thrashes, for insolently barring the-
atre box, **37.** 432–3, 443
Richard, François-Marie (1712–89), Baron de
Haute-Sierck; physician:
Choiseul, Duc de, attended by, **4.** 133
Choiseul, Duchesse de, lacks confidence in,
4. 133
Richard, Abbé Jérôme:
Description historique et critique de l'Italie
by: HW reads, **25.** 97; heavy but not bad,
29. 89
Richard Cœur-de-Lion. See under Burgoyne,
John; MacNally, Leonard; Sedaine, Michel-
Jean
Richard de Tarascon, Provençal poet:
partisan of Raymond VI, Comte de Toulouse,
21. 169n
poem by, **21.** 169–70
Richards, Miss:
performs in Savile Row theatre, **11.** 101n
Richards, Fitzherbert (? b. ca 1729), Irish M.P.;
'Richard the Beau':
at Sudbourne, choosing Orford mayor, **39.**
265
HW asked by, to have black (?) velour suit
made for him by Delage at Paris, **39.** 50–1
HW visited by, **30.** 238
Hertford on shooting party with, **39.** 48
(?) —— visited by, at Ragley, **39.** 85

Italian lady assaulted by, in coach at Paris
coming from Conti's, **38.** *507*
Jamaica left by, to go to Suffolk with Hertford, **39.** 261
(?) social relations of, in Paris, **7.** 261, 262,
263, **30.** 238
teeth may be cleaned by, without catching
cold, **39.** 261
Richards, George (d. 1746), M.P.:
death of, **19.** 342n
Richards, Mrs John. *See* Moysey, Mary
Richards, William, of Lynn:
Review of the Memoirs by, **33.** 468
Richardson, ——, engraver:
Cole confuses, with Dickinson, **2.** 54
Richardson, ——, commissary:
in Batchelor's Walk, Dublin, **37.** 333
Richardson, Mrs, housekeeper to Berry family:
mentioned, **11.** 347, **12.** 31–2, 89, 120, 134, 135
Richardson, Francis, adjutant of the Guards:
Sayre denounced by, **6.** 230n, **24.** 138, **28.** 227n
Richardson, Jonathan (1665–1745), painter:
Catherine Howard's miniature bought by,
from Arundelian collection, **40.** 366n
drawing by, of Pope's mother, **29.** 278
HW leaves, to last volume of *Anecdotes*, **40.**
310
HW pleased by engraving of head of, **14.** 188
HW to mention etchings by, **40.** 310
Mary Tudor's portrait owned by, **40.** 365
Milton subject of remark by, **28.** 234
poetry by, shows his piety, **15.** 144
Walpole, Sir Robert, painted by, **41.** 234,
42. 249
Richardson, Jonathan (1694–1771), portrait-
painter:
printer recommended by, **15.** 57
Venus de' Medici described by, **35.** 54
Richardson, Joseph (d. 1763), bookseller:
Dodsley to send *Anecdotes of Painting* to, for
Zouch, **16.** 45
Richardson, Joseph (d. 1766), clerk in the sec-
retary of state's office:
Mann's dispatches acknowledged by, **18.** 290
Richardson, Joseph (1755–1803), writer:
Jekyll a Political Eclogue attributed to:
praised by HW, **15.** 202; reprinted in
Rolliad, **11.** 34n
Rolliad contributor, **15.** 202, **25.** 613n
verses wrongly ascribed to, **11.** 34n
Richardson, Mary (d. 1782), m. Walter Sero-
cold:
death of, **2.** 303n
Richardson, Rev. Robert (1732–81), prebendary
of Lincoln Cathedral:
sends for his father's MSS, **2.** 69–70
(?) Sympson sends compliments to, **40.** 235
Richardson, Samuel (1689–1761), novelist:
Clarissa and *Sir Charles Grandison* admired
in France, but not by HW, **31.** 43
Clarissa by: Du Deffand, Mme, bored by, **5.**
196, 204; Du Deffand, Mme, mentions, **5.**
392; Du Deffand, Mme, owns, **8.** 32; HW

alludes to letters in, **28**. 139; HW dislikes, **22**. 271

Diderot's *Éloge* of, **6**. 247

Du Deffand, Mme, defends, **5**. 392

—— pleased by domestic details in novels of, **4**. 255

——pleased by nuances in, **5**. 391

—— reads novel in style of, **6**. 316

——'s fondness for characters of, **4**. 32–3, 109

dull, but French imitate the English in liking, **40**. 385

epistolary novels made insupportable by, **40**. 379–80

HW ridicules, in Paris, **30**. 208

HW's opinion of, **10**. 172, 176

Holbach and guests dispute about, **7**. 267

novels of: dull, **22**. 555; French adopt, **22**. 555

Pamela by: Fielding's *Shamela* parodies, **15**. 276; Goldoni's play adapted from, **22**. 473n; HW may echo, **38**. 196n; popularity of, **40**. 29

popularity of: in France, **10**. 172, 176; in Paris, **30**. 208

printer, not bookseller, **22**. 271n

Sherlock's enthusiasm for, **2**. 302

Sir Charles Grandison by: **1**. 236; Du Deffand, Mme, mentions hero of, **4**. 109, 320, **5**. 392, **6**. 14, **7**. 200; Du Deffand, Mme, owns, **5**. 392n, **8**. 33n; HW dislikes, **22**. 271; HW refers to Charles Montagu as, **1**. 236; HW sends last volume of, to Bentley, **35**. 168; Johnston surpassed only by, **40**. 245; Mirepoix, Mme de, mentions characters in, **41**. 230; two more volumes of, published, **35**. 160

Young told 'Marcella' story by, **34**. 37n

Richardson, William, printseller in the Strand: SH visited by, **12**. 233

Richardson, William (1698–1775), D.D.; vice-chancellor of Cambridge; antiquary:

Bouquet asked by, to revise verses, **13**. 147

Cornwallis appeals to, **13**. 155n

——'s fellowship the subject of consultation by, **13**. 155

Godwin's *Catalogue* continued by, **1**. 18n

——'s edition has preface by, **2**. 354

King presented with collection of verses by, **13**. 145n

Lyttelton's correspondence with, **40**. 233

MSS of, **2**. 53, 56n, 65n, 69–70

Sympson's letter about inscription at Lincoln sent by, to Lyttelton, **40**. 233–5

'Richard the Beau.' *See* Richards, Fitzherbert

Richauts de Tarascon. *See* Richard de Tarascon

Richauts de Verberil. *See* Rigaut de Barbezieu

Richbell, Anne, m. Samuel Strode:

(?) Mann meets Mrs Morehead at house of, **43**. 264

'Richcourt, Lady.' *See* Rolle, Margaret

Riche, Le. *See* Le Riche

Richecourt, Comte de. *See* Nay, Charles de (d. 1789); Nay, Emmanuel-François-Joseph-Ig-

nace de (1694–1759); Nay, Louis-Hyacinthe de (d. 1752)

Richecourt, Comtesse:

England visited by, **20**. 90

Florence visited by, **20**. 365

HW describes, **20**. 90

itinerary of, to England, **20**. 45

Mann entertains, **20**. 365

Piedmontese, **20**. 90n

Rice lover of, **20**. 90

stays worn by, in England, **20**. 365

Turin returned to by, after husband's death, **20**. 45n

Richecourt, seigneury of:

Nay, Charles-Ignace de, has, made into a barony, **20**. 197n

Richelieu, Cardinal. *See* Du Plessis, Armand-Jean

Richelieu, Duc de. *See* Vignerot du Plessis, Louis-François-Armand (1696–1788); Vignerot du Plessis-Richelieu, Armand-Emmanuel-Sophie-Septimanie (1766–1822); Vignerot du Plessis-Richelieu, Louis-Antoine-Sophie (1736–91)

Richelieu, Duchesse de. *See* Lavaulx de Sommerecourt, Jeanne-Catherine-Josèphe de

Richelieu, Maréchal (Maréchal-Duc) de. *See* Vignerot du Plessis, Louis-François-Armand

'Richelieu, M. de':

Mann mistakes, for Prince de Guise, **19**. 426

Richelieu ('Richlieu'), France:

Choiseul, Duchesse de, visits, **6**. 461

Colebrooke, Robert, 'exiled' to, by father, **30**. 115

visit of Choiseuls to, enrages Duc de Richelieu, **6**. 463

Richelieu, Hôtel de, in Paris:

Ennery lives near, **6**. 135

HW visits, **7**. 265, **31**. 87

Richelieu, Rue de, in Paris:

Bibliothèque du Roi in, **7**. 311n

Choiseul, Hôtel de, in, **5**. 93n

Mars, Hôtel de, in, **4**. 465n

Richelieu quarter, in Paris:

Voltaire buys house in, **7**. 39

Richelle (Flanders):

Conway encamped at, **37**. 277–80

Richelt. *See* Richelle

Richenberg, Bohemia:

battle of, **21**. 88

Riches:

HW's reflections on corrupting power of, **31**. 254, 282–3

HW's reflections on futility of, **25**. 583

See also Money; Wealth

Richie, Robert, English consul at Venice ca 1776–ca 1790:

Mann seldom gets news from, about D. of Gloucester, **24**. 329

Richlieu. *See* Richelieu

Richmond, Cts of. *See* Beaufort, Margaret

Richmond, Ds of (unidentified):

print of, **40**. 236

Richmond, Ds of. *See* Bruce, Lady Mary (1740–96); Brudenell, Anne (d. 1722); Cadogan, Lady Sarah (1706–51); Howard, Frances (ca 1573–1639); Stewart, Frances Theresa (d. 1702)

Richmond, D. of. *See* Lennox, Charles (1672–1723); Lennox, Charles (1701–50); Lennox, Charles (1735–1806); Lennox, Charles (1764–1819); Lennox, Charles (1791–1860)

Richmond, E. of. *See* Henry VII; Tudor, Edmund (1430–56)

Richmond, Mrs ——, Cts of Orford's attendant at Florence:

English alone spoken by, 19. 97

English alone understood well by, 19. 97

English washerwoman refuses proposals of, 19. 46

furniture moved by, 19. 252, 290

HW prefers Richecourt to, as spy on Bns Walpole (Cts of Orford), 18. 31

house retained by, against law, 19. 238

leaves Florence, for England, 19. 304

Mann might have hired, to spy on Cts of Orford, 18. 14

Orford, Cts of, does not tell, whether to renew lease on Florentine house or go to England, 19. 101

—— escorted only part way by, to Bologna, 19. 49

—— expected by, 19. 252

—— orders, to return to England, 19. 290

—— to be accompanied by: 19. 46; only to Bologna, 19. 49

—— writes to, about son, 19. 192

Richecourt advises, to quit house, 19. 238

Richecourt and Cts of Orford leave, to renew lease on Florentine house, 19. 97, 101

Richecourt calls on, constantly, 19. 97, 101

—— may get letters from, 19. 290

—— may keep, in old palace, 19. 101

—— often sees, 19. 80

——'s coach waits at door of, 19. 97, 101

——'s friendship with, prevents her eviction from house in Florence, 19. 192

—— visited by: at Careggi, 19. 97, 101; in his coach, 19. 75, 101

things taken by, to Lappeggi, 19. 238

Richmond, Surrey:

actors at, 9. 70, 74

agreeable society at, 11. 148

Alcock, comptroller of works at, 1. 147–8

(?) archdeacon of, 43. 342

Augusta, Ps of Wales, visits George III at, 23. 345

Baker, Dr, physician at, 20. 523

Beauclerk, Lady Diana, visited at, by HW and Lady Jersey, 35. 506

bells at, are heard at SH, 28. 460

Blackburne rector of, 29. 18–19n

boat-race at: 11. 337, 341–2; HW's MS notes about, 43. 150

Boufflers, Comtesse de, at, 11. 76n, 36. 276

Boufflers, Mmes de, bring Moranville from, to see SH, 39. 473

bridge at, 43. 130–1

Bunbury writes from, 42. 316

Castle Inn at, *see under* Castle Inn

Cholmondeley builds new room at, 9. 35

——'s houses at, 43. 238

Cholmondeley House at, 35. 357

Clarence, D. of (William IV), has house at, 34. 68

—— popular at, 34. 71–2

Clarke, Anna Maria, leaves, 31. 277

Clough, Miss, acts at, 9. 74

Colman quarrels with City over barge facilities at, 33. 207

Crewe, Lady, has Lady Margaret Compton's house at, 35. 390

Croft calls on Edward Louisa Mann at, 23. 379, 383

Darells live in, 34. 59

deserted, 15. 268–9, 28. 406

Devonshire Cottage at, 42. 451n

Dickensons at, 31. 275, 277

embankment at, quarrel over, 29. 69–70

ferry for foot-passengers between Isleworth and, 34. 195

Fitzwilliam, Gen, dies at, 11. 48

—— to be at, 42. 52

floods between HW and, 24. 47

foreign ministers at, 11. 354

French émigrés at: 12. 27, 58, 65, 66, 169, 15. 318, 31. 386, 34. 183, 185; flock thither though it is most expensive place in England, 34. 186; tell of flight and capture of Louis XVI and family, 34. 113–14

George II gives Waldegrave messages at, for P. and Ps of Wales, 20. 562n

gossip at, 11. 29, 61, 104, 121, 283, 289, 12. 25, 33. 523, 567

Greenwich Park superior to, 35. 234

HW at, 11. 39, 92, 109, 124, 155, 247, 300, 323, 325, 329, 358, 370, 12. 103, 133, 134, 138, 13. 157, 161

HW calls on Colman at, 41. 383

HW calls on Edward Louisa Mann at, 24. 36

HW fears going to, to see French émigrés, 34. 165

HW hears news at, 32. 376

HW lives more at, after death of Ds of Montrose, 31. 286

HW mentions, 11. 74, 86, 152, 163, 176, 12. 31, 35–6, 56, 65, 35. 65

HW misinformed at, 36. 187

HW much with French émigrés at, 34. 114

HW pleased at Selwyn's decision to live at, 30. 279

HW's acquaintance at, dispersed, 31. 287

HW sees natives of, 34. 207

HW sends servant to Fermor at, 42. 277

HW's illness at, 34. 200

HW takes Galfridus Mann to, 20. 63

HW to visit, 15. 233, 17. 358

HW visits Lady Diana Beauclerk at, 33. 195

HW visits Lady Fitzwilliam at, **33**. 277

HW visits the Birons and Boufflers at, **34**. 109

Ham House near, **10**. 307

highwaymen in, rob before dusk, **33**. 353

highway robbery near, **34**. 143

inhabitants of, to come to SH to see Gallery, **10**. 281

Jordan, Mrs, cancels performance at, **12**. 142, 151

little news at, **33**. 567

Lysons, S., and Farington go to SH by way of, **15**. 327

Lyttelton entertains HW at, **10**. 108

maid from, wants to see Ds of Montrose in coronation robes, **21**. 535

Mann, Edward Louisa, at, **23**. 379, 383, (?) 506, **24**. 36

—— has property at, **24**. 159n

—— ill at, **23**. 340

—— too ill to be moved to, **24**. 165

Mann, Galfridus, ill at, **20**. 520, 522, **21**. 27

—— persuaded by friends at, to take tar-water, **21**. 30

—— still at, **20**. 549

—— visited at, by Edward Louisa Mann and lawyer, **21**. 33

March ill at, **32**. 139

New Park: Amelia, Ps, closes, to public, **9**. 135, **20**. 322; Amelia, Ps, did not expect reversion of, **20**. 29; Amelia, Ps, succeeds 2d E. of Orford as Ranger of, **20**. 29n, 125, 233, 322; Amelia, Ps, visits, **18**. 449; Caroline, Q., given ground at, by Bird, **20**. 322–3; Court at, **10**. 131; Croydon assizes bring bill against keepers of, **20**. 322n; Faringtons pass through, **15**. 317; George I orders Sir Robert Walpole to have New Lodge in, finished, **20**. 455; George I shoots and dines at, with Sir Robert Walpole, **20**. 455; George II often visits lodge at, **21**. 121n; HW forgets his comment on, **34**. 191; HW's terrace overlooks, **19**. 414, **20**. 16; HW takes Rinuccini to, **19**. 308; HW to go to, **18**. 136; HW would deplore cutting wood in, **34**. 191; Hamgate and East Sheen gates to, **20**. 323n; innkeeper at gate of, **17**. 503; keepership of, surrendered to Bute by Ps Amelia, **20**. 29n; Kingston assizes allow pedestrians into, **20**. 323n; Mann, Mrs Galfridus, robbed in, **25**. 343–4; ministers' servants disappear at inn at gate of, **17**. 503; Newcastle procures venison from, **17**. 506; Orford, Cts of, takes villa in, **19**. 309; Orford, 2d E. of, brings pictures from, for sale, **20**. 261n; Orford, 2d E. of, Ranger of, **15**. 327, **17**. 164n; Orford (3d E. of)'s moose-deer may be kept at, by Dr Hunter, **41**. 265; 'Patapan' to go to, **18**. 136; rangership of, reverts to Ps Amelia, **20**. 125; (?) stolen box abandoned in, **35**. 315; stone lodge at, designed by Pembroke, finished by Ps Amelia, **20**. 455n; Thatched House in, **13**. 157; tickets

not granted for, at breeding time, **20**. 323; tickets required for admission to, **28**. 433; view of, from Sir E. Walpole's villa, **34**. 195; visitors to inn at gate of, **17**. 503, **18**. 20; Walpole, Hon. George, visits, in holidays, **18**. 70; Walpole, Horatio (1678–1757) puts horses to graze in, **18**. 70; Walpole, Sir Robert, at, **18**. 136; Walpole, Sir Robert, builds lodge at, **17**. 164n; Walpole, Sir Robert, catches cold at, while fishing, **18**. 164n, 449; Walpole, Sir Robert, hunts in, on Saturdays, **17**. 247; Walpole, Sir Robert, ill at, **13**. 161n; Walpole, Sir Robert, regarded as ranger of, **20**. 455, **41**. 234n; Walpole, Sir Robert, returns from, **18**. 430; Walpole, Sir Robert, spent his own money at, **42**. 81; Walpole, Sir Robert, stores pictures at, **18**. 249; West's verses about Thatched House in, **13**. 157

Northesk visits Ds of Montrose at, **35**. 373

pantomime at, for Edwin's benefit, **35**. 399

Pelham and Dupplin confer at, **20**. 411n

physician, old, at, **2**. 292

play at, **34**. 143

popularity of, **34**. 62

Pownall writes from, **42**. 76

'quality' of, visit SH, **31**. 392

Queensberry, D. of, entertains French exiles at, **34**. 121

—— gives party at, for D. of Clarence (William IV), **31**. 347

——'s palace, visited by HW and Selwyn, **33**. 541–2

Ramsay, Charlotte, acts at, **9**. 74

regatta at, **6**. 200, **32**. 317–18

residents and visitors at: Bouverie, Mrs, **34**. 62; Bunburys, **34**. 62; Cardigan, Cts of, **31**. 2; Clarence, D. of, **11**. 63; Clifford, Lady, **33**. 528; Crewe, Miss and Mrs, **31**. 287; Derby, Cts of, **11**. 309–10; Douglas, Lady Frances, **31**. 287; Fitzwilliam, Lord, **11**. 296; Ford, Mrs, **11**. 368; Franks, **2**. 393n; Howe, Hon. Juliana, **11**. 112n; Jeffreys, Mrs, **12**. 100; Keppel, Mrs, **31**. 287; Mann, Mary, **17**. 359; Mendips, **12**. 141; Montagu, D. of, **11**. 105; Mount Edgcumbes, **11**. 317; Onslow, Bn and Bns, **31**. 288; Onslow, Lady, **12**. 103; Queensberry, D. of, **11**. 248, 340; Rogers, Charles, **41**. 402n; Sayer, Miss, **35**. 393; Selwyn, George, **30**. 282, **31**. 287, **42**. 451n; Seton, Barbara Cecilia, **11**. 116, 124, 129; Sheridans, **34**. 62; Valletorts, **12**. 134, 138; Walpole, Lady Mary, **17**. 330, 359; Walpole, Sir Robert, **17**. 164, 330, 333, 335, 358; Whelers, **12**. 100; Wray, Mrs, **12**. 100; *see also* **12**. 221–52 *passim*

Robinson's letter mentions, **21**. 121

Selwyn addressed at, **30**. 282

—— leaves books at, for HW, **30**. 279

—— prefers, to Gloucestershire, **30**. 279

—— returns to, **33**. 533, **34**. 13, 28

'Star and Garter, at, **15**. 317

[Richmond, Surrey, *continued*]
storm at, **12.** 161
SH faces towards, **25.** 532
Suffolk, Cts of, resigns, to Q. Caroline, **42.** 488
tale from, in absence of London news, **34.** 201
Thames difficult to cross at, **23.** 47, 73
theatre at, attended by Argyll, Ds of, Barry, Campbell, Lady Elizabeth, Garrick and HW. **9.** 74
Townshend, Vcts, to return to her house at, **40.** 100
view of: from Sir E. Walpole's villa, **34.** 195; from SH, **2.** 368–9, 373
Vorontsov's house at, to be let to Mme de Boufflers, **34.** 68
West sees HW at, **13.** 157
'weird sisters' of, **35.** 391
young lady of, copies drawing, **34.** 8
See also Richmond Bridge; Richmond Green; Richmond Hill
Richmond, Yorks:
(?) archdeacon of, **43.** 342
Wade's cavalry stop at, **37.** 214
Richmond, English ship:
Grasse captures, **33.** 306n
Richmond, House of:
threatened extinction of, **11.** 203
Richmond and Lennox, Ds of. *See* Howard, Frances (ca 1573–1639); Stewart, Frances Teresa (d. 1702)
Richmond Bridge, Surrey:
Cambridges' house near, **11.** 31n, 304, **12.** 159
meadows above, **11.** 337n
Richmond Gardens, London:
Caroline's grotto in, **14.** 39n
George III at, **29.** 304
HW takes Rinuccini to, **19.** 308
Hermitage in, **29.** 34n, 296n
sea might be let into, **28.** 94
See also Privy Garden
Richmond Green, Surrey:
French émigrés at, **11.** 221–2, 247, 285, 325, 342
Montfort gets parsons to play cricket at, **20.** 74
residents at: Biron, Duchesse de, **11.** 221; Boufflers, Comtesse de, **11.** 221; Cambis, Vicomtesse de, **11.** 221; Dundases, **11.** 116n; Fitzwilliam, Gen., **11.** 49n; Roncherolles, Marquise de, **11.** 221
Richmond Palace backs on, **16.** 75
Theatre Royal at, **34.** 51–2
visitors to: Bath, E. of, **20.** 63, 64; Lonsdale, **20.** 63; whist-players from White's Club, **20.** 63
Richmond Hill, Surrey:
appearance of, varies, **12.** 253
Beauclerk, Lady Diana, buys house at foot of, next to D. of Montagu's, **42.** 490
balloon seems to land on, **39.** 419
Bunbury's drawing of, **41.** 429, **42.** 318
Darell of, **12.** 175n
drought at, **10.** 38

Fiesole higher than, **25.** 532
Gilpin prefers northern scenery to, **11.** 358, **34.** 92
Grafton, Ds of, has small house on, **38.** 435
HW mounts, **12.** 164
Ham House near, **10.** 307
Hobart house on, **11.** 63n, 71n, **34.** 68n
insignificance of, in astronomical sense, **33.** 361
Montagu compares Mt Merrion to, **9.** 400
—— to ride at, **10.** 184
new lodge at, by Pembroke, **32.** 141n
ruined castle should adorn, **40.** 252
SH's prospect bounded by, **20.** 16, 380, **37.** 269
taste and leisure 'reside' on, **13.** 118
Thames has not overflowed, **32.** 214
William IV (D. of Clarence) takes Hobart's house on, **34.** 68n
Richmond House, London:
amateur theatricals at, **33.** 585, 586, 588, **34.** 1, 5
Campbell, Caroline, plays harp at, **34.** 34n
Cavendish, Lord John, sups at, **33.** 344
Conway's *False Appearances* performed at, **31.** 263–4
HW and the Conways sup at, **11.** 126
HW dines at, **29.** 145, **31.** 35
HW learns political news at, **30.** 183
HW sees *Way to Keep Him* at, **39.** 448
HW sups with Richmond at, **39.** 329
HW visits, to see regatta, **32.** 237
masquerade and fireworks at, **22.** 148, **43.** 278
masquerade at: **33.** 17; ticket for, **40.** 284
Murphy's *Way to Keep Him* performed at, **33.** 563, **39.** 448, 546
private theatre in, **35.** 391n
secretary of, sets fire to Conway's house, **33.** 584
theatre at, will probably continue, **33.** 564
'Richmondians'; 'Richmondists.' *See* Émigré, French
Richmond Lodge, West Sheen:
George III at, **35.** 326
Richmond Palace, Surrey:
HW has drawing of, **40.** 254–5
HW visualizes, **33.** 542
Hollar's print of, Hillier did not know, was in *Surrey*, **16.** 78
rebels said to have destroyed, **16.** 75
Vertue's drawing of, **16.** 73
vote on, **11.** 152n
Richmond Park. *See* Richmond: New Park
Richter, Ferdinand (b. 1693), painter:
'one-eyed German,' **23.** 28
portrait by, of Mme Grifoni, **11.** 154, **17.** 44, **23.** 28
Richter, John Augustus (fl. 1772–1809), scagliola artist:
chimney-piece executed by, for HW, **2.** 370n
HW bargains with, for chimney-piece ornaments, **35.** 407
mosaic shrine re-erected by, in SH chapel, **35.** 406n

Richter and Bartoli:
scagliola firm in Newport St, 35. 407n
Ricimer (d. 472), ruler of Rome 456–72:
Gibbon's treatment of, 29. 98
Ricimero, opera:
party after, 33. 250
Vestris acclaimed in, 33. 254–5
See also under Galuppi, Baldassare
Rickaby, Thomas (ca 1753–1802), printer:
Nash's *Hudibras* printed by, 43. 390n
proof sheet not collected by, from HW, 43. 390
Rickets:
(?) Joseph II's, 11. 67, 42. 252
Rickmansworth, Herts:
Moor Park at, 9. 285n
Ricouart, Antoine de (ca 1713–82), Comte d'Hérouville de Claye:
HW unacquainted with, 39. 211
made director of troops, 5. 41, 23. 283
Richmonds' social relations with, 7. 294
Ricovere de Recuperis, Alexander, LL.D.; minister of archives at Florence:
Lady Orford's will signed by, 43. 288
Riddel. *See* Riddell
Riddell, George (1752–74), etcher:
print by, of Purkis, 1. 364
Riddell, Sir John Buchanan (1768–1819), 9th Bt, 1784:
questioned about Miss Gunning's visit to Syon Hill, 11. 217
Riddell, Roxburghshire:
Riddell of, 11. 217n
Riddle; riddles:
attributed to Sir Isaac Newton, 32. 137, 144
'Exodus before Genesis' appears as, 33. 396
guessing of, 5. 91
HW's, imitated from French, 28. 364, 367
Ossory, Lady, sends, to HW. 34. 99
Selwyn's, 28. 102–3, 107, 108
'Riddles, House of.' *See* Park Place, Berks
Rider, Cardanus:
British Merlin (almanack) by, 30. 34
Rider, William (1723–85), writer:
Candide translated by, 10. 349
Donaldson's edition of *Candide* translation shows dependence on, 10. 350
scholar of Jesus College, Oxford, 10. 349
Voltaire sends corrected copy of *Candide* to, 10. 349
Rider's *Almanack. See* Rider, Cardanus: *British Merlin*
Ridge, Elizabeth (1746–1808), m. 1 (1766) William Flower, 2d Vct Ashbrook; m. 2 (1790) Rev. John Jones:
marriage of, 10. 210
Ridge, Mrs Humphrey. *See* Bentley, Elizabeth
Ridge, Thomas, waterman:
daughter of, 10. 210
Ridgefield, Connecticut:
British destroy American magazine at, 24. 309n

Ridgeway, Lady Frances (ca 1702–72), m. 1 (1717) Sir Thomas Pitt, cr. (1719) Bn, (1726) E. of Londonderry; m. 2 (1732) Robert Graham:
fever defined by, in sister's illness, 9. 238
husband quotes, 39. 3
Ridgeway, Lady Lucy (d. 1732), m. (1716) Arthur Chichester, 4th E. of Donegall:
sister defines fever at death-bed of, 9. 238
Ridgway, James:
Rolliad printed for, 11. 34n
Ridicule:
HW recommends, as weapon against French, 15. 232, 239
Riding:
academy at Turin teaches, 19. 407n
Astley establishes amphitheatre for, in Southwark, 25. 451n
Conway and Cts of Ailesbury engaged in, at Park Place, 37. 548
Conway's pastime at Sandywell, 37. 105
HW finds, necessary for his health, 30. 80, 81
Leopold's only amusement, 22. 353–4
Mann's, 20. 143, 191, 21. 58
Mann, Galfridus, accustomed to, 20. 549, 554
—— uses, to cure cold, 20. 520
Mann, Horace II, fond of, 24. 170
Riding-clothes:
Amelia, Ps, wears, to chapel, 37. 341
Riding-coat. *See under* Coat
Riding-dress; riding-dresses:
Greenwich, Lady, wears, at HW's ball, 28. 447
sightseers wear, 9. 348
Riding habit:
English, worn by Contessa Delci, 18. 85
Howe, Mrs, portrayed in, 40. 283
white, worn by Cts of Orford, 23. 512n
Riding-hood; riding-hoods:
HW sees, at Boulogne, 7. 259
Howe, Sophia, wears, 34. 256
Riding-house:
at Grove House, 33. 274n
Riding-officer; riding-officers:
Foote, surveyor-general of, for coast of Kent, 18. 354n
Riding parties:
Mann's, shared by Pelham and Milbanke, 20. 172
Riding-school:
Hyde's bequest to Oxford for, 38. 30
Parisian, HW's symbol for artificiality, 42. 214
Riding-stable:
at Welbeck, converted into stable, 35. 271
Ridley, Glocester (1702–74), D.D.; poet;
Gray dismisses poems of, 14. 37
Ridley, Sir Matthew White:
Boswell sketches, 33. 462n
Ridley, Nicholas (? 1500–55), Bp of Rochester; Bp of London:
Grimald chaplain to, 1. 250n
letter of, 1. 273n
opinion of, of William Thomas, 1. 273

Ridley, W.:
Pennant's portrait by Gainsborough engraved by, 41. 394n
Ridlington, Norfolk:
HW's will mentions, 30. 344
living of, 42. 441
Ridolfi, Giuseppe (1694–1756), Marchese; impresario:
Andromache staged by, 18. 128
Bagnolesi's costume for *Iphigenia* pleases, 18. 134
impresario of opera, 17. 239, 284
Mann attends ball given by, 18. 60
—— entertains, 17. *104*
—— mistakenly given Richecourt's theatre box by, 17. 394
Richecourt dislikes, 18. 139
Ridolfi, Palazzo, at Florence:
HW saw fanali at, 17. 59
Pomfret, Cts of, takes, 37. 68–9
Ridotto; ridottos:
Arthur postpones, because of earthquake, 20. 135
at Haymarket, 9. 27
at Ranelagh: 17. 434; al fresco, 10. 279–80
at Reggio, 13. 242
at Vauxhall, al fresco, 10. 279
deserted, after earthquake, 20. 135
English fondness for, on eve of war, 20. 469
HW to attend, 17. 378
Hesse, Landgrave of, attends, 9. 30
Hesse, P. of, to attend, at Haymarket, 19. 265n
officers give, for Friedrich Wilhelm of Hesse, 19. 265
preferable to masquerades, 37. 9
Shaw, Elizabeth, said to have flirted at, with Stuart Mackenzie, 19. 27
Riel, Pierre de (1752–1821), Marquis de Beurnonville:
National Assembly appoints, to arrest Dumouriez, 12. 1–2
Rienzi, Cola di (1314–14), demagogue:
Wilkes's success would astonish, 24. 536
—— the counterpart of, 23. 8
Rieti, Bp of. *See* Clarelli, (?) Girolamo
Rietti, ——, proprietor of Ranelagh:
Ranelagh shares sold by, 20. 46n
Rifler, Capt., Lobkowitz's adjutant:
Lobkowitz sends, to Mann, 18. 519
Riforma d'Italia, La:
Voltaire criticizes, 8. 152
Riga:
Anne of Mecklenburg dies at, 17. 256n
Russian troops approach, 21. 72
Rigadoon:
older generation could talk of, 23. 351
Rigaud, Hyacinthe (1659–1743), painter:
portraits by, 2. 341n, 15. 180n, 32. 102, 42. 387n
Rigaud, Jean-François (1742–1810):
Waldegrave's portrait by, 42. 413n

Rigaud, Joseph-Hyacinthe-François de Paule de (1740–1817), Comte de Vaudreuil:
(?) dances at ball in honour of Dauphin's marriage, 4. *410*
(?) sings, 7. 296
(?) social relations of, in Paris, 7. 291, 296, 303, 317, 320–1
Rigaud, Louis-Philippe de (ca 1691–1763), called Comte de Vaudreuil:
Young Pretender arrested by, 20. 9
Rigaud, Louis-Philippe de (1724–1802), Marquis de Vaudreuil; naval officer:
Elliot's ship engaged with, 25. 220
fleet of, to be observed by Hood off Boston, 25. 351n
Rigaud, Pierre-François de (1704–78), Marquis de Vaudreuil-Cavagnal; governor of Canada:
alleged victory of, at Quebec, 21. 344
Indians join, near Montreal, 21. 357n
Quebec's recapture predicted by, 21. 357
—— to be recaptured by, according to French reports, 21. 421
Rigaud de Vaudreuil, Marie-Josèphe (1743–81), m. (1765) Charles-Armand-Fidèle de Durfort, Comte de Duras:
social relations of, with Gräfin von Bentheim, 7. 312
Rigaut, ——, Paris publisher, near Palais de Justice:
pamphlets about Richelieu and Mme de St-Vincent sold by, 30. 263n
Rigaut de Barbezieu (fl. 1175–1215), Provençal poet:
poem by, 21. 169–70
Rigby, Mrs. *See* Perry, Anne
Rigby, Anne (ca 1717–91):
(?) HW compares, with Sappho, 30. 119
(?) verses by: HW jokes about, 30. 118–19; HW sends, to Sir C. H. Williams, 30. 118
Rigby, Christopher (d. 1783), commissioner for taxes:
Cole friend of, 10. 335
painting by Van Risquet includes, 10. 334–5
Rigby, Richard (d. 1730), factor to the South Sea Co.:
Mistley Hall built by, 9. 15n
son of, 30. 330n
Rigby, Richard (1722–88), politician; M.P.:
administration might have been wrecked by, to satisfy Opposition, 24. 447
Allen insults, at opera, but is carried off, 38. 247
American war instigated but no longer supported by, 29. 171n, 187
any post will be accepted by, 22. 569
'arbitrary Stuart principles' in speech by, aimed at Bute, 38. 501
(?) at Chesterfield's assembly, 37. 326
Barré the dread of, 38. 508
Bath robes will make, pink and blooming enough to arouse Vcts Townshend, 30. 82
Bathurst accompanied by, 9. 84
Beauclerk, Topham, confused with, 31. 68

Bedford, D. of, and E. Gower will dominate, **41.** 71

Bedford, D. of, desires place for, **30.** 232

—— hurried by, into partiality to Kildare for Fox's sake, **21.** 154n

——'s correspondence with, **37.** 422n

—— seeks place for, **22.** 463n

——'s influence to be sold by, **9.** 228

——'s insolence to George III boasted of by, **30.** 186

——'s resentment at marquisates may please, **38.** 392–3

——'s retirement opposed by, **30.** 189

Bedfords entertain, **9.** 232

Bedford House visited by, **20.** 135

Bland put to bed by, **30.** 84

Bute supposedly attacked by, **38.** 501

Cannons visited by, with HW, **30.** 60–2

Cassiobury Park visited by, with HW, **30.** 62

Castle Rising represented by, in Parliament, **30.** 87–8, 330n, **36.** 14n

clergyman beaten by, **30.** 93, 330

Conway abused by, **41.** 82

——'s resignation discussed by, **22.** 578n

Cornwallis accosts, at opera, and later apologizes, **38.** 247

cricket match attended by, **30.** 106

Cumberland answered by, **7.** 369

custom-house officers tricked by, **30.** 331

'Drawcansir' for administration, **29.** 86

Edgcumbe and Lady Bland would be defeated with little ceremony at whist by, **30.** 54

Edgcumbe mentions, **30.** 79

employment demanded for, **30.** 236n

faction led by, **29.** 177n

faction of, blames Opposition's intemperance, **24.** 534n

Fielding, Henry, visited by, **9.** 84

fight of, in inn at Epsom, **30.** 331

Fox, Henry, hurt by ridicule of, **30.** 248

—— hurt by unkindness of, **30.** 191

—— quotes, **7.** 369, **43.** 108

——'s best friend until rift, **30.** 100n

——'s correspondence with, **21.** 190n

—— sends messages to, **30.** 102, 103

—— sent regards by, **30.** 106

——'s rift with, **41.** 68n

—— thinks HW's pleasure in defeat of, deadened by gout, **30.** 202

Frederick, P. of Wales, appoints Trevanion instead of, **30.** 332n

—— fails to assist, at Sudbury, despite promise, **30.** 331n

George III forced to accept ministry of, **7.** 369

——'s and Q. Charlotte's anger could drive, from court, **30.** 190

George IV (P. of Wales) consults, about marriage, **33.** 411

German war opposed by, in debate on foreign estimates, **21.** 553n

Gower characterized by, **30.** 230

—— reported by, to be out of office, **33.** 131

Grafton puts, in Pay Office, **23.** 186n

——'s meeting attended by, **7.** 367

Grenville, George, dependent on, **38.** 508

—— hears dissatisfaction of, with Chatham's ministerial plans, **41.** 71n

—— seen by, **22.** 472n, 538n, 543n

—— supported by, in Parliamentary debate, **38.** 499

Grenville, James, disputes with, over attack on Temple, **38.** 242–3

HW advises, in landscaping, **9.** 88

HW compares: with Abbé de la Rivière, **9.** 228; with Masaniello, **9.** 263

HW designs Chinese drawing-room for, in Essex, **20.** 166

HW dines with, **9.** 93

HW goes with, to Essex, **34.** 22

HW jokes about, **30.** 80, 87

HW laughed at by, **35.** 244

HW likes, 'more and more,' **30.** 51

HW mentions, **10.** 242, **18.** 374

HW no longer abuses, **30.** 176

HW organizes counter-petition in defence of Sudbury election of, **30.** 331n

HW predicts defeat for, in Sudbury election, **9.** 51

HW's candidate for Castle Rising, **43.** 111

HW's correspondence with, **37.** 310

HW's friendship with: **30.** 51n; cools, **9.** 257n

HW's health drunk be by, **9.** 93

HW's leisure treated by, as sacred, **30.** 106

HW's letter from the King of the Mohocks to, **30.** 330–2

HW's negotiations with brother for election of, at Castle Rising, **37.** 194n

HW's portrait by Robinson given to, **30.** 95

HW's portrait by Robinson ill-described by, **30.** 92

HW's reliability as political reporter discussed by, **20.** 503n

HW's shyness in Portsmouth dock-yards witnessed by, **30.** 103

HW's skill in heraldry joked about by, **9.** 93

HW's 'The Beauties' sent to Fox at insistence of, **30.** 100

HW suggests, should be drawn as Autumn, **30.** 93

HW urged by, to celebrate different set of 'ladies' in 'The Beauties,' **30.** 100–1

HW visited by, at Houghton, **30.** 80

HW visits, **9.** 14–15, 59–67, **14.** 85n, **19.** 60n, 494, **20.** 163n, 166n, **34.** 22, **35.** 242, **37.** 302

HW visits Portsmouth and Mt Edgcumbe with, **19.** 92n

HW writes from country-seat of, **14.** 5n

Handasyds visited by, **30.** 57

health of, **9.** 396

Hertford's letter may be taken by, to HW, **38.** 448

Hertfords courted by, in Dublin, **39.** 38

Holland, Bn, quotes, about George III and new ministry, **7.** 369, **43.** 108

[Rigby, Richard, *continued*]
House of Commons adjourns on motion by, **38.** 308
Irish journey of, criticized as attempt to get law place, **38.** 242
Irish Master of the Rolls, **9.** 266, **33.** 411, **38.** 242
Karl Wilhelm Ferdinand stays at house of, **22.** 196n
Lennox, Lady Emily, admired by, **30.** 100
London traversed by, en route from Woburn to Chelmsford, **30.** 222
lord mayor blamed by, for riots, **38.** 258
lord of Trade, **9.** 181, **20.** 517
Mason's *Heroic Epistle* mentions, **28.** 75n
Mistley Hall built by, **9.** 15n
Mistley the seat of, **20.** 490
Montagu invited by, to Mistley, **9.** 88
—— to receive compliments of, **9.** 62, 88
Montagu, Charles, favoured by, **9.** 257
—— recommended to, by Halifax, **9.** 208
Moor Park visited by, with HW, **30.** 62
Mt Edgcumbe may be visited by, with HW, **30.** 92
Müntz not promoted by, **9.** 259
Murray, Fanny, insisted on by, as possible character in HW's 'The Beauties,' **30.** 101
Navy treasurership rumoured for, **22.** 37n
negotiations expected from, **38.** 328
Newcastle House meeting attended by, **22.** 541n
North's removal plotted by, **24.** 533n
—— summons, to Parliamentary inquiry, **24.** 474n
Norton accused by, **28.** 309n
Nugent introduces, to Frederick, P. of Wales, **30.** 331n
Opposition's lost opportunities known to, **38.** 355
Orford, 2d E. of, to make, M.P., **30.** 87
Orford, 3d E. of, and George III bet against, **21.** 531
Oxford opposes Castle Rising candidacy of, **36.** 16n
Oxford proctor defied by, **30.** 330
Oxford University insulted by, and protests against his election, **30.** 87
parents of, **30.** 330n
Paris traversed by, to south of France with Andrews, **38.** 427, 434
Paris trip of, shows he no longer rules D. of Bedford, **38.** 434
Paris visited by, **38.** 190
Parliamentary activity of, on Regency Bill, **38.** 551
Parliamentary career of, **30.** 87–8, 330n, 331n
Parliamentary motion by, on Stamp Act, **22.** 382n
Parliamentary speeches by: **10.** 4n; on resuming committee on state of nation, **33.** 432n; on Sudbury petitions, **30.** 331n
Parliamentary vote by, on privately-raised regiments, **26.** 19

Parsons, Anne, mistress of, **34.** 241–2
patent of, in Irish post, questioned, **10.** 108
paymaster, succeeding Cooke and Thomas Townshend (1733–1800), **39.** 99–100
petition suggested by, **22.** 495n
Pitt's speech makes, fear for his vice-treasurership, **38.** 320
Pitt-Temple faction may dismiss, from secretaryship of Ireland, **9.** 233
politeness of, at Vcts Townshend's cured by laughing at him, **30.** 54
Portsmouth to be visited by, with HW, **30.** 92
prefers 'beautiful' to be 'common,' **30.** 102
press-gang officer impersonated by, **30.** 331n
pride and insolence of, **38.** 247
Raynham visited by, **30.** 81
Reynolds's 'St George' owned by, **32.** 337n
ridicule of, more severe on George III than on Fox, **30.** 248
Rockingham and Grafton betrayed by, **33.** 95n
Rockingham and Grenville factions combined by, **22.** 504n
Rockingham's conversation with, at White's, **22.** 495n
Sackville's deputy rangership of Phoenix Park mistakenly said to be given to, **21.** 328n
sails, **9.** 15
St James's Palace guard fires on, **30.** 330n
Sandwich not defended by, **38.** 499
Selwyn and Fortescue taken to Mistley by, **30.** 51
Selwyn's probable expulsion from Oxford reported by, **30.** 85
—— to dine with, **30.** 280
—— visited by C. H. Williams and, at Oxford, **30.** 330n
sent to France to satisfy D. of Bedford, **22.** 92n
speeches by, in Irish Parliament, **9.** 411
Spencers and Gower join, in approaching Grafton to make Conway commander-in-chief, **24.** 526n
SH Blue Bedchamber will convince, that HW can design without Bentley's aid, **35.** 174
Stanhope, Sir William, to be visited by, **9.** 72
Sudbury election campaign of, **30.** 331
Temple attacked by, in Parliament over Wilkes, **38.** 242, 247
—— receives overtures from, **7.** 367
—— seen by, at Stowe, **22.** 538n
——'s offers from ministry reported by, **30.** 187
testimony by, at Powell's inquest, **25.** 407n
Thurlow's inclusion in Exchequer reform bill pressed by, in Commons, **33.** 406n
to vouch for rapid composition of 'The Beauties,' **30.** 105
Townshend, Vcts, visited by, **30.** 54
vacancy in office of, as Irish Master of the Rolls, **10.** 9

Vernon accused by, of cowardice, **30.** 331

—— accuses, of carrying Sudbury election by violence, **30.** 331n

vice-treasurership of Ireland to go to, **3.** 407n

vice-treasurership slipping away from, **38.** 320

watchman's earthquake warning feigned by, **20.** 135

whist played by, **30.** 54

Williams, Sir C. H., accompanied by, to Wales, **30.** 330n

—— corresponds with, **30.** 64, 85

—— to be attended by, at Bath installation, **30.** 82

—— to be informed by, about Mrs Woffington, **30.** 52

—— visited by, in Wales, **30.** 88n

Wilton to be visited by, with HW, **30.** 92

wishes to come into place, but will not desert Grenville, so leaves town in bad humour, **43.** 322

wit and spirit of, **30.** 332

witticisms by: on Cts of Coventry's toast at Woburn dinner, **37.** 430, 442; on youthful army volunteers, **38.** 34

Woburn visited by, **41.** 71n

Woffington, Peg, accompanied by, in Williams's absence, **30.** 52n

would do anything to save his place, **38.** 534

Wyndham visited by, in Somerset, **30.** 51n

Rigby family:

HW's 'surprise' at poetry from, **30.** 118

intemperance of, **30.** 118–19

Rigge, Mr:

HW's parcel for Charlemont consigned to, **42.** 157n

Riggs, Anna (1741–81), m. (1765) John Miller (from 1780, Riggs Miller), cr. (1778) Bt:

'academy' of, at Batheaston, **24.** 197

Batheaston Vase and poetical circle of, **6.** 137

Conway escapes visiting, **39.** 317

Du Deffand, Mme, dislikes, **5.** 205

——'s social relations with, **5.** 189, 197, **6.** 402

HW entertained by, **10.** 233

HW used to know, at Bath, **24.** 197

Italy visited by, **24.** 197

Letters from Italy by, mentions Mann, **24.** 197, 203–4

Mann remembers little about, **24.** 204

Montagu, Lady Barbara, friend and neighbour of, **10.** 234

name of, corrected, **43.** 135

'Parnassus at Bath' of, **32.** 196, 221, 225, **39.** 240–1

Poetical Amusements at a Villa near Bath by: dull, **32.** 224; HW has, **32.** 221–2; noble authors in, **32.** 225

Rich, Mary, takes HW to dine with, at Batheaston, **39.** 240–1

vase of, **29.** 196n

verses by, **39.** 241–2

Riggs, Mrs Edward. *See* Pigott, Margaret

Riggs Miller, Lady. *See* Riggs, Anna

Riggs Miller, Sir John. *See* Miller, Sir John

Riggs Miller, Sir John Edward Augustus (1770–1825), 2d Bt:

parents leave, with grandmother in France, **24.** 197

Riggs Miller. *See also* Miller

Righelini. *See* Reghellini

Right of search:

English obstinacy in denying, to Spain, **19.** 255

Spanish practice of stopping and searching couriers, **18.** 359n

Rights of Man. See under Paine, Thomas

'Rights of Men':

become injustice and ruin, **34.** 120

declaration of, 'a dissolution of all society,' **34.** 99

in France, increase prisoners, **34.** 109

Rights of the Clergy. See Johnson, John: *Clergyman's Vademecum*

Rights of the Protestant Dissenters. See under Barrington, John

Rights of Women. See under Wollstonecraft, Mary: *Vindication of the Rights of Women, A*

Rihm, Suzanne-Dorothée (ca 1741–1810), dancer:

Etiolles forbidden to keep, **20.** 340

Riley, 'Capt.':

horses for fox-hunting under, **37.** 181

Riley, John (1646–91), painter:

Cartwright's portrait by, at Knole, **35.** 134n

Chiffinch's portrait perhaps by, **35.** 228

Lyttelton's portrait by, **35.** 147n

portraits by, **35.** 73, 147

Riley, William (d. 1750):

condemned at Old Bailey for murder, **20.** 199n

Rimes. See under Pinkerton, John

Rimini, Bp of. *See* Pasarella, Jacopo (d. 1495)

Rimini (Italy):

Austrians at, **18.** 335

La Cattolica near, **18.** 58

Lobkowitz at, **18.** 330, 331, 339

Modena, D. and Ds of, visit, **18.** 222

Montemar may fortify himself at, **18.** 2

—— removes headquarters from, **17.** 408n

——'s headquarters, **17.** 379

Pironi imprisoned at, **18.** 253, 257

Spaniards abandon, **18.** 16, 331

—— at, **18.** 13

—— expected to settle at, **18.** 199

—— quiet at, **17.** 379

Spanish army at, diminished by desertion, **18.** 216

Spanish artillery sent towards, **19.** 35–6

Spanish barks may escape to, **18.** 288

Spanish forces at, increase, **18.** 243

Rinaldi, Signora. *See* Arnaldi, Teresa Maria

Rinaldi, Margherita (1712–90), m. (1731) Duca Alamanno Salviati:

Craons entertain, **17.** 217–18

Rinaldi, Odorico (1595–1671):
Baronius's *Annales ecclesiastici* indexed by, **18.** 391n
Rinaldi Generotti, Francesco Maria (1715–84), Balì di Cortona:
ball given by, at villa, **18.** 84–5
Pitti's duel with, prevented, **17.** 111–12
Rinaldo III (Rinaldo d'Este) (1655–1737), D. of Modena:
daughters of, could not gain his consent to wed, **13.** 242–3, **17.** 55n
death of, **20.** 393n
England visited by son of, to seek George II's aid against Charles VI, **40.** 18n
whimsical and proud, **13.** 242
Rinaldo (d'Este) (b. and d. 1753), P. of Modena:
death of, **20.** 393n
'Rinaldo' (hero of Tasso's *Gerusalemme liberata*):
Conway resembles, **9.** 102
Richelieu compared to, **23.** 329
sword of, **10.** 346
See also under Ariosto, Ludovico: *Orlando Furioso*; Tasso, Torquato: *Gerusalemme liberata*
Rinaldo. See under Handel, George Frideric; Sacchini, Antonio
Rinaldo di Capua (b. ca 1715), composer:
Gray collects compositions of, **13.** 233n
Rinfreschi:
consumption of, at Mann's cocchiata, **18.** 1
Ring; rings:
antique, in Middleton's collection, **15.** 16
Armagh, Abp of, wears Cts of Northumberland's stone in, **10.** 132
bed, **35.** 247
cameo, **19.** 332
Catherine Parr's hand lacks, **42.** 113
Cholmondeley, Mrs, gives, to Mme du Deffand who gives it to HW, **4.** 487
Cosway wants letters on, explained, **42.** 187
diamond: **31.** 158; Electress leaves, to P. Ottojano de' Medici, **18.** 173; Gatti receives, for inoculation, **24.** 330n; given by Maria Theresa to Forrester's officer, **18.** 107; Mirepoix, Mme de, has, **20.** 107; mourning, **21.** 52; presented by Charles I to Jamesone, **40.** 264; thieves overlook, **35.** 315
Du Deffand, Mme, gives, to Duchesse de Choiseul, **4.** 175
Electress leaves, to Old Pretender, **18.** 171
'emerald' given by Lady Mary Wortley Montagu to Barnard, **21.** 473
enamel, Q. Elizabeth's, at Burghley House, **10.** 345
eye set in, **35.** 503n
fancy, **31.** 158
Francis I said to have given, to Falmouth, **10.** 1
Frederick William II's, **35.** 386
gold, English soldier cuts, from old woman's finger, in France, **21.** 221

HW bequeaths money for, **30.** 354, 375
HW mistakes cameo for, **25.** 88, 89
HW's, probably once Lorenzo de' Medici's, **15.** 279, 280
HW will choose any additional, **19.** 420
HW would like to buy, from Riccardi, **19.** 331–2
Hamerani receives, from Old Pretender, **17.** 18n
heart-diamond, given by Cts of Suffolk to Henrietta Hotham, **10.** 113–114
highwaymen take, **33.** 445n
(?) Louis XV gives, to Falmouth, **10.** 1n
Mann receives legacies for, left by Jermy and Cts of Orford, **25.** 206
mourning: for 3d E. of Orford, **42.** 338n; HW and Sir Edward Walpole to receive, from E. of Orford, **25.** 124; left to HW by Cts of Suffolk, **31.** 131n; Ligonier leaves, to Lady Mary Coke, **31.** 8n; Orford, E. of, has probably forgotten to send, to Mann, **25.** 206; out of fashion among people of rank, **25.** 124; sent to Robert Child, **32.** 361; small legacy the equivalent of, **38.** 453
of bed-curtain, Hamilton uses, as wedding ring, **20.** 303
pope's, **21.** 52
Riccardi does not want to sell, to HW, **19.** 372–3
—— offers, at high prices, to HW, **19.** 372–3
——'s: HW decides to take, **19.** 398; Mann and Riccardi settle for, **19.** 411; Mann to pay for, for HW, **19.** 420, 427, 433, 435; Riccardi accepts HW's offer for, **19.** 411
Richard III wears, in portrait, **41.** 131
Richmond, Ds of, leaves, to HW, **34.** 222
ruby, received by (?) Cts of Rochford from (?) Lord Thanet, **35.** 215
Strozzi, Principessa, loses, **19.** 349–50
Turner's, taken by rioters, **33.** 186n
wedding ring: (?) Burlington, Cts of, convey's hint with, **9.** 79–80; Hamilton uses bed-curtain ring for, **20.** 303
See also Cameo; Intaglio
Ring box. *See under* Box
Rinking, George:
Newcastle's letter from, about Sir C. H. Williams, **43.** 274
Rinuccini, Marchesa. *See* Aldobrandini, Maria Camilla (1718–83); Guicciardini, Vittoria (1697–1753)
Rinuccini, Marchese Alessandro (1685–1758):
death of, at Naples, **20.** 336
Rinuccini, Marchese Carlo (1679–1748):
Albani's arrangements with, over Electress's rights to church lands, **18.** 169
Albizzi cousin to, **17.** 481–2
(?) Capello, Signora, formerly loved by, **20.** 174–5
council formed by, **17.** 178
death and will of, **19.** 461–2
dictatorship given to, **19.** 245

Du Châtelet to turn Leghorn keys over to, 17. 199
Electress leaves annuity and silver framed glasses to, 18. 169
envoy in England, 19. 308n
festa di cuoco to be given by, 17. 137
Giovanni Gastone de' Medici's prime minister, 19. 308n
hangings of brocatelle at house of: HW dislikes, 21. 497, 501; HW remembers, 21. 471; Mann sends pattern of, to HW, 21. 481
legacies of, 19. 461–2
Lorraine Guards sent to Leghorn on demand of, 17. 198n
Mann hears from, of Sir Robert Walpole's supposed trip to Italy, 17. 426
—— hears news from, of Fane, 17. 135
—— hears rumour from, of English-French war, 18. 44
——'s neighbour, 17. 137, 481
—— talks politics to, in Florence, 19. 308
—— talks with, 17. 108
—— thanked by, for HW's attentions to his son, 19. 322, 349
—— to be entertained by, 17. 137
—— told by, of French-Spanish rifts, 18. 416
Mathews's treaty discussed by, 18. 455
(?) 'my cautious neighbour,' 17. 490
Panciatichi discusses Albizzi's fistula with, in Mann's presence, 17. 481–2
piles feared by, 17. 112
Pisa visited by, 19. 245
Regency member, 17. 40n, 19. 251
(?) Richecourt may avenge attestations of, against him, 17. 490
——'s disgrace attributed by, to Sir Robert Walpole, 17. 108
——'s opposition to Mann discussed by, with Braitwitz and Tornaquinci, 18. 10
secretary of war, 17. 199n
son of, 19. 251n
three-coloured brocatelle the whim of, 21. 468
(?) Wachtendonck has meeting with, 17. 95n
Rinuccini, Carlo Maria Giuseppe (1742–90):
birth and baptism of, 17. 473
plays acted by, 20. 336
Rinuccini, Mme 'Flora.' *See* Aldobrandini, Maria Camilla
Rinuccini, Folco (1719–60); Marchese:
charities of, at father's death, 19. 461
departure of, 19. 348
Electress leaves annuity and china to, 18. *169*
England hated by, 19. 329, 339
—— visited by, 35. 65
father not regretted by, 19. 461
Francis I's gentleman of the Bedchamber, 19. 251
greatest man in Florence, 20. 356
HW's dinner declined by, 19. 331
HW takes, sight-seeing in London, 19. 308
HW tells Mann not to apologize for introduction for, 19. 331

income of, 20. 336
lodgings of, in Pall Mall, 19. 307n
Madonna di Loreto to be visited by, in hopes of begetting a son, 30. 15
Mann explains to HW his recommendation for, 19. 321
—— hopes to disprove accusations of low birth from, 20. 24
—— recommends, to HW, 19. 251
——'s correspondence with, 19. 322
——'s family disparaged by, 35. 65
Naples visited by, 20. 8
Niccolini entertains, at dinner, 20. 174–5
——'s affair discussed by, in letter, 20. 7–8
plays acted by children of, 20. 336
return of, to Florence, expected, 19. 339
uncle of, dies in Naples, 20. 336
wife thanks Mann for HW's attentions to, 19. 349
Rinuccini, Mme Folco. *See* Aldobrandini, Maria Camilla (1718–83)
Rinuccini, Giovanni (1743–1801):
governor of Rome in 1789, 20. 336n
plays acted by, 20. 336
Rinuccini, Maria Teresa (d. before 1765), m. (1711) Francesco Gioacchino Buondelmonti:
brother's legacy to, 19. 461
Rinuccini, Maria Virginia (d. 1751), m. (1706) Barone Cerbone del Nero:
brother's legacy to, 19. 461
Rinuccini family:
HW hopes that 'Onslow' affair discredited the supposed English knowledge of, 19. 510
Mann avoids house of, 21. 468
Serristori chief follower of, 17. 473
Rinuccini, Palazzo, at Florence:
in Via Santo Spirito, 17. 137n
Mann's neighbour, 17. 137n, 24. 72n
Rio de la Plata, Viceroy of. *See* Ceballos Cortes y Calderón, Gen. Pedro
Rio Grande de San Pedro, Brazil:
Portuguese attack on Spanish settlement at, 24. 223–4
Portuguese governor of, 24. 224n
Spanish governor of, 24. 223n
Riot; riots:
at Bath, 2. 224
at Boston, 23. 39
at Dublin, 39. 421
at Edinburgh over Catholic toleration, 24. 438–9
at Oxford, 20. 50
at Paris, 20. 170, 24. 101–2
at Paris and Versailles, 6. 184, 187, 321
English, frighten Mann, 23. 15
HW's reflections on, 23. 21–2
in England, over price of bread, 22. 455
in France, over corn, 24. 105–6
in French provinces, 6. 185
in London: 7. 112, 10. 272–4, 22. 187–8, 200, 23. 25, 98–9, 290–2; against French actors, 20. 99–100; against French dancers, 35. 260–1; at Cheapside, on burning of *North*

[Riot; riots, *continued*]
Briton, 1. 52n, 38. 256–7; at Keppel's acquittal, 24. 438; at theatres, 38. 193; at time of Keppel's banquet, 24. 449; by coalheavers, 23. 33–4, 39; by glaziers and tallowchandlers, 23. 200; in George I's time, 35. 147; London distracted by, 39. 99; Mann pleased by punishment of ringleaders of, 23. 49; Mann shudders at, 23. 25–6, 49, 110–11, 147; newspapers print insolence from, 23. 305; over Westminster election, 25. 489; reported by Leyden gazette, 23. 110; *see also* Gordon Riots

Luttrell's instatement may cause, 10. 277
Montagu knows nothing about, 10. 274
Neapolitan, 22. 206
Parliamentary committees on, 23. 291–2, 297
Parliamentary Opposition might be aided by, 39. 301–2

Riot Act. *See under* Parliament: acts of

Riou, Lt Edward (ca 1758–1801):
Guardian commanded by, 11. 92n

Rioult de Douilly, Agnès (1681–1758), m. Jean-Étienne Berthelot de Pleneuf:
family of, 6. 423

Rioult de Douilly, Claire-Cécile-Thérèse- Pauline (1706–87), m. (1725) Étienne-Louis-Antoine Guignot, Marquis de Monconseil:
appearance of, 6. 424
Chesterfield's correspondence with, 6. 423, 28. 290
daughter of, 4. 298n
family of, 3. 123, 6. 323, 423
HW agrees with Conway's account of, 39. 214
HW had known, 28. 290
Mirepoix, Mme de, at odds with, 3. 152
mother of, kept gaming-house, 28. 290
poor reputation of, 3. 123
retired to country, 20. 354n
Richmond wants HW to ask, to rent Ennery's house, 41. 10–11
social relations of, in Paris, *see index entries ante* 8. 487

Rioult de Douilly, Marie (1712–84), m. François-Francillon, Marquis de Polignac:
French Court banishes, 20. 354
lady of honour to Duchesses d'Orléans and de Chartres, 20. 354n
Maillebois loved by, 6. 323
of Palais Royal, 3. 123, 194
relatives of, 3. 123, 6. 323
social relations of, with Mme du Deffand, 5. 194, 6. 323

Rioult de Douilly, Nicolas-Marie-Séraphin (1706–66), Marquis de Curzay:
Antibes to be the prison of, 20. 354
arrest of, 20. 353–4
French commandant in Corsica, 3. 123, 20. 206
French restrictions announced by, displeasing to Corsican district chiefs, 20. 353n

Genoese commissary's enmity to, causes arrest, 20. 353n
Lorenzi hears from, about Genoese compliance, 20. 277
magnanimity of, to returning prisoner, 20. 206
sisters of, 3. 123

Rioult de Douilly, Séraphin (d. 1738), Marquis de Curzay:
family of, 6. 423

Ripalta:
Austrians capture Spaniards at, 19. 262

Ripault Desormeaux, Joseph-Louis (1724–93), historian:
Histoire de la maison de Bourbon by, 6. 17, 21, 189, 306, 308, 310, 43. 96
Histoire de la maison de Montmorenci by, 3. 69
Histoire de Louis de Bourbon, Prince de Condé by, 3. 69

Ripert, Jean-Pierre-François de (1711–73), Marquis de Monclar; diplomatist:
anecdote of pension of, 4. 285
HW's acquaintance with, 4. 285
social relations of, with Duc and Duchesse de Choiseul, 7. 330, 331

Ripley:
cottage at, is Lady Lyttelton's address, 42. 117, 118, 199
Lyttelton, Lady, thins forest at, 42. 200

Ripon, Yorks:
Chambers of, 28. 450n
Gent's history of, 15. 266

Ripon Cathedral, Yorks:
James I's statue removed to, from York, 28. 100n
Waddilove, Dean of, 16. 168n

Rippa, Piedmont:
Ferrerio born at, 15. 120n

Ripperda, Jean-Guillaume (1690–1737), Baron de:
HW asks if Wilkes imitates, by becoming Moslem, 22. 290

Ripplington, East Meon, Hants:
Dickins of, 13. 6n

Rippon, English man of war:
Botetourt sails on, to Virginia, 35. 329n

Riquet, Jean-Gabriel-Amable-Alexandre de, seigneur de Bonrepos; (?) Caraman the elder:
(?) social relations of, with Comte and Comtesse de Maurepas, 7. 291

Riquet, Victor-Maurice de (1727–1807), Comte de Caraman:
agreeable, informed, intelligent, 38. 527
Cambis, Vicomtesse de, visits, 7. 73
command given to, 7. 147
Conway and Anne Pitt entertain, 38. 527
daughters of, married, 6. 189, 413, 431
Du Deffand, Mme, defends, to Choiseul, 3. 369
—— likes, 6. 28, 49
——'s correspondence with, 7. 158, 425, 426, 428, 430, 432, 433, 459

——'s neighbour, **7.** 213
——'s opinion of, **6.** 431
—— to inform, of HW's kindness to Sourches, **7.** 221
English learnt by, **38.** 520
family amity of, **6.** 86, 210, 431, **7.** 73
glass door at house of, **7.** 417
Gothic spirit of SH pleases, **31.** 36
Guerchy entertains, with HW. **38.** 523
HW asked by, about Pitt, **38.** 527
HW attends ball given by, **32.** 260, **34.** 7–8
HW entertains, at SH, **10.** 156
HW pleases, by aiding Sourches, **7.** 223
HW receives invitation from, from Roissy, **39.** 16
HW's correspondence with, **7.** (?) 217
HW sends compliments to, **3.** 26, **6.** 419
HW sends medals to, **6.** 247, 259
HW's *Gramont* given to, **5.** 306
HW's letter about Sourches shown to, **7.** 217
Hertford's letter may be taken to England by, **38.** 520, 523–4
La Vallière, Duchesse de, puts Mme du Deffand in the good graces of, **3.** 369
locks ordered by, from Hon. T. Walpole, **7.** 233, **36.** 168
Mirepoix, Mme de, aunt by marriage to, **10.** 156
(?) —— on bad terms with, **6.** 270
—— to have her house built by, **5.** 209, 219
parade arranged by, at Roissy, **5.** 269
Paris to be visited by, **5.** 120
—— visited by, **5.** 426, **6.** 380, **7.** 436
Roissy country-seat of, **3.** 369, **5.** 312
—— occupied by, **4.** 243, 256, **5.** 225, 231, 260, 269, 404, **6.** 72, **7.** 44, 179
—— to be occupied by, **5.** 350, 353, **6.** 33, 49, 272, 281
—— to have been occupied by, **7.** 150
Selwyn's correspondence with, **7.** 217
social relations of, in Paris, *see index entries ante* **8.** 488
Sourches's only merit is his connection with, **7.** 218
SH visited by, **12.** 229
Toulouse visited by, **6.** 373
Vic recommended by, **6.** 30
Vic, Mme, recommended by, **6.** 28, 30, 32
visitors to, at Roissy, *see* Roissy: visitors to
Walpole, Hon. Thomas, to bring locks to, **36.** 168
wife of: pregnant, **39.** 16; related to Mme de Mirepoix, **10.** 156, **38.** 520
Riquet de Caraman, Cécile-Agathe-Adélaïde de (1768–1847), m. (1786) Armand-Jean-Étienne du Mesniel, Comte de Somméry:
ball attended by, **7.** 334, 346
family amity of, **6.** 86, 210, **7.** 73
Riquet de Caraman, Émilie-Rose-Marguerite de (1767–1847), m. (1786) Charles-François Reinier, Comte de Baschi-St-Estève:
ball attended by, **7.** 334, 346
family amity of, **6.** 86, 210, **7.** 73

Riquet de Caraman, François-Joseph-Philippe de (1771–1842), Prince de Chimay:
birth of, **5.** 142
family amity of, **6.** 86, 210, 73
Riquet de Caraman, Gabrielle-Françoise-Marie-Victoire de (1755–1841), m. 1 (1775) Gabriel-Marie-Joseph-Henri, Comte de la Fare; m. 2 (ca 1796) François-Joseph-Alexis Joly:
ball attended by, **7.** 334, 346
Caraman's daughter, **7.** 346
Court presentation of, **6.** 198
daughter born to, **7.** 425
family amity of, **6.** 86, 210, **7.** 73
marriage of, **6.** 189, 196–8
Roissy to be home of, **6.** 196
social relations of, in Paris, **6.** 414, **7.** 334, 346, 430
Riquet de Caraman, Jean-Louis de (1713–83), Abbé de Caraman:
Caraman's social relations with, **7.** 346
Roissy visited by, **7.** 346
Riquet de Caraman, Marie-Anne-Antoinette de (1757–1846), m. (1777) Jean-Louis du Bouchet, Vicomte (later Comte) de Sourches:
ball attended by, **7.** 334, 346
Du Deffand, Mme, gives opinion of, **7.** 213
family amity of, **6.** 86, 210, **7.** 73
husband of, **7.** 213
Île de Bourbon visited by, **7.** 442
marriage of, **6.** *413*, 419
social relations of, in Paris, **6.** 414, **7.** 427, 430
Riquet de Caraman, Maurice-Gabriel-Joseph de (1765–1835), Comte de Caraman:
ball attended by, **7.** 334, 346
birth of, imminent, **39.** 16
family amity of, **6.** 86, 210, **7.** 73
Riquet de Caraman, Pauline-Victoire de (1764–1834), m. (1781) Jean-Louis de Rigaud, Vicomte de Vaudreuil:
ball attended by, **7.** 334, 346
family amity of, **6.** 86, 210, **7.** 73
Riquet de Caraman, Victor-Louis-Charles de (1762–1835), Duc de Caraman:
ball attended by, **7.** 334, 346
family amity of, **6.** 86, 210, **7.** 73
Riquetti, André-Boniface-Louis (1754–92), Vicomte de Mirabeau:
arrest of, **39.** 473–4
Riquetti, Honoré-Gabriel (1749–91), Comte de Mirabeau:
abilities of, almost as great as his villainies, **34.** 109
Catherine II is, in petticoats, **34.** 146
consecrated by the French, **12.** 117
death of, **11.** 238, **34.** 109
Dumouriez deserts, **11.** 1n
French Revolution's only example that 'times produce men,' **34.** 186
greatness not to be expected from, **39.** 468
HW calls, 'villain,' **33.** 111
HW prefers Burke to, **34.** 104
HW wishes, dissected by Burke, **11.** 277

[Riquetti, Honoré-Gabriel, *continued*]
Histoire secrète de la cour de Berlin by: Baron von Nagell has copy of first volume of, **34.** 44; burnt at Paris, **34.** 44
Lettres de cachet et des prisons d'État, Des, by, shocks HW, **33.** 444
Louis XVI to be tool of, **34.** 73
Pétion rises from ashes of, **34.** 154
rapid wealth of, **33.** 109
villain, but once promised to be a great man, **39.** 488
villainous, but only eminent man in the Revolution, **33.** 159
Washington compared with, **33.** 111
Riquetti, Victor de (1715–89), Marquis de Mirabeau:
mistress of, **6.** 23n
pursued by detective, **5.** 365n
social relations of, in Paris, **7.** 266, 269, 277, 280, 290, 297–8, 301, 306, 308, 310, 323, 348
Risby, Suffolk:
Platel, rector of, **10.** 331n
Rise and Progress of the Scandinavian Poetry, The. See under Jerningham, Edward
Rising, Castle. *See* Castle Rising
'Rising in the North, The,' ballad:
(?) HW quotes, **38.** 226
Rising to the Crowne, The. See under Richard III
Riske, Van *or* Risquet. *See* Van Risquet
Rissoles:
as hors-d'œuvre, **19.** 356n
Riswick, Deric van (fl. 1650–3); engraver:
'Restrick' may be, **16.** 66n
Ritberg, ——:
social relations of, with Prie, **7.** 293
Ritson, Joseph (1752–1803), antiquary:
disbelieves in Ireland MSS, **15.** 321
Observations on . . . the History of English Poetry, **2.** 335, 337
Riva, Maria da (b. ca 1703), nun:
Benedict XIV permits transfer of, to Ferrara convent, **18.** 86
Froullay debauches, **18.** 86
Spanish colonel married by, **18.** 86
Rival, Jean (1728–1804), called Aufresne; Swiss actor:
Parisian success of, **38.** 574
Rivalité de France et d'Angleterre. See Gaillard, Gabriel-Henri: *Histoire de la rivalité de la France et de l'Angleterre*
Rival Queens, The. See under Lee, Nathaniel
Rivalta, palace of the Dukes of Modena:
HW sups at, **17.** 44
Ormea visits, **17.** 424
Rivarola, Col. *or* Count (?) Domenico (d. before 1754):
Bastia captured by, **19.** 162
circular letter of, to Corsicans, **19.** 162–3
Corsican revolt not procured by, **19.** 157
Corsicans will not permit, to hoist Sardinian flag, **19.** 171
English fleet awaited by, **19.** 162

French and Genoese force, to retreat, **19.** 437
Giafori affronted by faction of, **19.** 206n
letter of, about capture of Bastia, **19.** 162
Mann's letter to, delivered by Vanbrugh on the *Antelope,* **19.** 276n
nephew of, **19.** 276n
Townshend not assisted by, **19.** 157
—— to land, on Corsica, **19.** 162–3
Rive, La. *See* Mauduit de la Rive
River; rivers:
artificial: **35.** 521; at Horton, **10.** 334; at Wentworth Castle, **35.** 267
Onslow's, at Ember Court, stopped for a mill except on Sundays, **30.** 292n
Rivera. *See* Balbis-Simeone di Rivera
Rivers, Bn. *See* Pitt, George (1721–1803); Pitt, George (1751–1828)
Rivers, Bns. *See* Atkins, Penelope (d. 1795)
Rivers, Cts. *See* FitzLewis, Mary (ca 1465–after 1483); Parker, Catherine (fl. ca 1630)
Rivers or Ryvers, E. of. *See* Wydevill, Anthony (ca 1440–83); Wydevill, Richard (d. 1469)
Rivers, Mrs, actress:
acts at Savile Row Theatre, **11.** 101n
Riversdale, Bn. *See* Tonson, William
Rivertown, castle of, Co. Meath:
Wood born at, **41.** 248
Rivett, Thomas (ca 1713–63), M.P.:
Stanhope defeated, in Derby election, **20.** 19
Riviera, Domenico (1671–1752), cardinal, 1733:
Giuseppe talks to, about Young Pretender, at Petroni's assembly, **19.** 85
HW to help Chute confute, **19.** 176
Old Pretender confers with, **19.** 85
—— secured promotion of, **19.** 176n
Riviera, the:
English bombardment of, might cause insurrection, **19.** 121
Riviera di Levante:
Maria Theresa plans offensive against, **19.** 478
Riviera di Ponente:
Austria expects Charles Emmanuel III to defend, **19.** 478
Charles Emmanuel III's troops at, **19.** 344
Genoa tries to exclude provisions from coast of, **19.** 344
Townshend to send ships to, **19.** 292
Rivière, Abbé de la. *See* Barbier, Louis
Rivière, Mme de la. *See* Rabutin de Bussy, Louise-Françoise de
Rivière. *See also* La Rivière
Rivington, Charles (1754–1831), printer:
Percy's correspondence with, **42.** 423n
wife of, dies, **24.** 101
Rivington, Mrs Charles. *See* Mann, Sarah (d. 1775)
Rivington, Francis and Charles, printers and booksellers:
British Critic published by, **15.** 238n
Rizzio *or* Riccio, David (ca 1533–66), secretary to Mary Q. of Scots:
conspirator against, **15.** 33n
intrigue of, with Mary, Q. of Scots, **15.** 42

Metastasio compared with, **20.** 163–4
picture said to be, **42.** 75
Ruthven's 'Discourse' on murder of, **15.** 34
Struensee shares fate of, **23.** 409
supposed old age of, **16.** 293n
Roach, Miss:
  Othello said to be acted by, **20.** 230n
Roach, Mrs, of Twickenham:
  SH visited by, **12.** 249
Roach, Deodata (ca 1731–59), m. (ca 1743)
    Richard Quane:
  'Desdemona' played by, **20.** 230n
  Louis XV notices, **9.** 189
  Versailles visited by, **9.** 189
Road; roads:
  aerial traffic may make, useless, **39.** 425
  at Syon House, made for ball, **35.** 331
  bad: at Greatworth, **35.** 70; in front of Mrs
    Clive's, **35.** 468; in Kent, **35.** 137, 142, 144;
    in Northamptonshire, **9.** 201, **10.** 214, 220;
    in Sussex, **9.** 96; near Stowe, **9.** 155
  'bad black,' in West Yorkshire, **35.** 270
  clay in Northamptonshire, **9.** 243, **10.** 214
  dusty, near SH, **9.** 82, 243
  English: highwaymen infest, **24.** 47; rain
    makes impassable, **20.** 506, 522–3
  execrable in Yorkshire, **35.** 278
  Francis I permits Lucca to build, **20.** 514
  Francis III makes, from Avenza to Modena,
    17. 323, **37.** 320
  French: lined with maimed trees, **39.** 251;
    more secure, **31.** 360; Séguier proposes that
    soldiers, not peasants, should work on, **41.**
    346, 347
  German, impassable from snow, **24.** 278n
  good, in Oxfordshire, **10.** 258
  Great Road good till Stamford, **35.** 266
  HW favoured by, on way to Dover, **39.** 253
  in Kent, need sober drivers, **35.** 144
  in Yorkshire, 'mended' with large stones, **35.**
    269
  Italian, spoiled by rain, **24.** 145
  Java's, praised by Byron, **22.** 421n
  modern improvement in, **33.** 526
  new, through Paddington, proposed, **37.** 452–3
  October unsuitable for travel on, **9.** 164
  present age prefers riding on streets to riding
    on, **25.** 317
  provincial society helped by improvement in,
    9. 350
  relative cost of travel on, in England and in
    France, **37.** 41
  rough, from Paris to Calais, **32.** 269
  Scottish, bad, **38.** 92
  to Puckeridge, **40.** 197
  to Ragley, execrable, **37.** 564–5
  wagons cut up, **10.** 348
  walnut trees planted along French, stripped
    for firing, **39.** 9
  See also Post road; Turnpike road
Road Bill. *See* Parliament: acts of: Paddington
  Road Bill
Roan. *See* Rouen

Roast; roasts:
  'dish of,' eaten by Devonshires, **37.** 341
  Jonzac provides, in quantities, **6.** 8
'Roast Beef':
  ballad from Fielding's *Grub-Street Opera*,
    18. 180n
  singers of, **18.** 180
'Roast Beef of Old England.' *See under* Hogarth, William
Robartes, Charles Bodvile (1660–1723), 2d E.
    of Radnor, 1685:
  sister of, **34.** 258
Robartes, Lady Essex (d. 1727), E. of Radnor's
    sister:
  niece of, **34.** 258
Robartes, John (1686–1757), 4th E. of Radnor:
  attack upon, **9.** 190–1
  birth date of, corrected, **43.** 113
  Chinese summer-house of, **20.** 382
  Clive, Mrs, gets legacy from, **35.** 100
  flood at Twickenham property of, **35.** 228
  garden of ('Mabland'): houses in, **9.** 53, **20.**
    382; obelisk removed from rabbit-warren
    in, **35.** 174; statues in, **35.** 175; view of,
    hangs at the Vyne, **35.** 639
  house of (Radnor House), **2.** 368, **11.** 333n,
    21. 1n
  Mann, Galfridus, seen by, **21.** 1
  Mann brothers entertained by, at dinner, **20.**
    456
  Mann's friend, **21.** 1n
  Middleton receives annuity from, **15.** 293
  —— takes nephew of, as pupil, **15.** 18, 293,
    312
  Middleton, Mrs, receives annuity from, **15.**
    312
  trees planted by, to ruin prospects, **37.** 348
Robartes, John (ca 1724–46), nephew of Lord
    Radnor:
  Bristol wells visited by, **15.** 309
  Cole's unflattering account of, **15.** 312
  Middleton takes, as pupil, **15.** 18, 293
Robartes. *See also* Robarts; Roberts
Robarts, Maj. (later Lt-Col.), Samuel Wilder:
  (?) SH ticket not used by, **12.** 228
Robarts. *See also* Robartes; Roberts
Robber; robbers:
  George II offers £100 reward for apprehension
    of, **20.** 111n
  numerous, in England, **25.** 497
  See also Footpad; Highwayman
Robbery; robberies:
  art of, now carried to perfection, **37.** 422
  at SH, HW's precautions against, **15.** 284
  by Gregory, **13.** 87
  continues in England, **20.** 199
  English, terrify Mann, **20.** 127
  fear of, because of release of Newgate crim-
    inals, **29.** 59
  HW and Lady Browne suffer, near Twicken-
    ham Park, **29.** 160, **33.** 295–6
  HW expects, **32.** 74–5
  HW knows only of, **29.** 273

[Robbery; robberies, *continued*]
  HW suffers: by highwaymen, **13**. 23. **14**. 42;
    in Hyde Park, **20**. 99, 101, 106, 112; in
    Paris, **7**. 266–9, **39**. 17, 25
  Ilchester loses silver plate from, **32**. 77
  in New Park, of Mrs Mann, **25**. 343–4
  in Sparta, authorized, **15**. 227
  John the Painter commits, **28**. 284
  Little Cassiobury attacked in, **32**. 77
  of Conway's house, **14**. 183–4
  of Frankland's house, **33**. 334–5
  of Harrington's house, **38**. 259
  of Judge Perryn, **33**. 30
  prevalence of, **35**. 355, 365, 378, 521, **39**.
    420, 422
  Twickenham afflicted by, **32**. 213, **33**. 347
'Robbing Peter to pay Paul':
  dispute over Pitt's interment recalls, **24**. 382
Robe; robes:
  Armenian, worn by Rousseau, **35**. 117
  Bath knight's, will make Rigby and Sir C. H.
    Williams pink and blooming, **30**. 82
  Bristol, E. of, sighs for, **22**. 549
  chief justice's, worn by Sir Edward Montagu
    in portrait at Boughton House, **10**. 341
  Dumesnil's, as bishop, held up by his secre-
    tary, **19**. 493
  earl's: given to Hunsdon by Q. Elizabeth on
    his death-bed, **25**. 166; worn by Northamp-
    ton in portrait, **10**. 336
  for Coronation, **38**. 100
  HW receives requests for making his, as a
    peer, **31**. 363
  judge's, worn by judge on monument at
    Easton Maudit, **10**. 339
  legal, lawn sleeves opposed to, **35**. 603
  loose, customary in reigns of Henry VI and
    Edward IV, **16**. 232
  not worn in English costumes, **17**. 170
  of Edward I, **15**. 149
  of Garter order, **41**. 234
  ordered for Edward V, **15**. 117
  Parliamentary, worn by E. of Kent in por-
    trait, **10**. 338
  peers': at Coronation, **9**. 388, **38**. 100; at
    Ferrers's trial, **9**. 280–1; should be used for
    their portraits, **42**. 157
  Richard III's, purple, fur-lined, **41**. 132
  Vaillant wears as sheriff at Ferrers's execu-
    tion, **21**. 400
  velvet, red, and ermine, worn by Ds of
    Buckingham, **17**. 253–4
  viscount's, worn by Manchester, **10**. 335
  white and silver, worn by Q. Charlotte's
    bridesmaids, **21**. 530
Robeck. *See* De Robeck
Robecque, Princesse de. *See* La Rochefoucauld,
  Émilie-Alexandrine de
Robe de chambre. *See* Dressing-gown
Roberspierre. *See* Robespierre
Robert I (Bruce) (d. 1329), K. of Scotland:
  Jamesone's portrait of, **40**. 264

mésalliances of descendants of, **38**. 476
Robert II (1316–90), K. of Scotland, 1370:
  print of, **40**. 237
Robert III (ca 1340–1406), K. of Scotland
  1390–1406:
  Cromarty's vindication of, **15**. 29
Robert (ca 1054–1134), D. of Normandy:
  (?) Montfaucon represents, **40**. 213
  wooden figure of, in Gloucester Cathedral,
    35. 154
Robert (d. 1147), E. of Gloucester:
  (?) art supposedly encouraged by, **16**. 104
Robert (d. 1313) de Winchelsea, Abp of Can-
  terbury, 1295:
  enthronement of, **16**. 46–7
Robert (fl. ca 1265) of Gloucester; chronicler:
  (?) art said to be encouraged by, **16**. 104
  wretched versifier, **16**. 352
Robert (fl. 1080), mason:
  Cole calls, to HW's attention, **2**. 278–80, 282
  Paris quoted on, **2**. 278–9
  portrait of, **2**. 279
Robert, Mme. *See* Guynement de Keralio,
  Louise-Félicité
Robert, ——, Lt:
  captured at Velletri, **18**. 491
Robert, Achille-Joseph (d. ? 1790), Marquis de
  Lignerac:
  enemy of the Capuchins, **3**. 201
  Maurepas's social relations with, **7**. 298
  wife of, **3**. 201n
Robert, Georges (d. 1777):
  (?) attends session of parliament of Paris,
    8. 173
Robert, Nicolas:
  'Guirlande de Julie' has miniatures by, **42**. 93
Robert brothers, aeronauts:
  balloons launched by, **25**. 450n
  Chartres a passenger in balloon of, **25**. 517n
  English Channel to be crossed by, in balloon,
    25. 517n
Roberti, ——, architect:
  Cowdray staircase built by, **11**. 105
Robert Manners. See under Merry, Robert
Robert of Brunne. *See* Mannyng
Roberto Manners. See under Pignotti, Lorenzo
Roberts, Mrs Ann (ca 1764–1857):
  Sardinian Chapel's plate saved by, **33**. 178n
Roberts, Edward, of Pell Office Exchequer:
  (?) Gloucester, Ds of, repays Tomkyns
    through, **36**. 72n
  letter by D. of Gloucester copied by, **36**. 306
'Roberts, James.' *See* Payba, Abraham
Roberts, J[? ames, d. ca 1754], publisher:
  Court Poems published by, **19**. 449n
  pamphlets published by, **18**. 319n
Roberts, James (fl. 1775–1800), portrait-painter:
  HW has water-colour copy by, of Opie's
    portrait of Hannah More, **31**. 279
Roberts, Jane (d. 1778), m. (1752) George
  Beauclerk, 3d D. of St Albans, 1751:
  homely, **32**. 2

Roberts, John (ca 1711–72), M.P.; secretary to Henry Pelham:
Newcastle sends, to Rockingham, **30.** 196n
Pelham the 'guardian angel' of, **35.** 165
Roberts, Mary (d. 1780):
hanged for rioting, **33.** 214n
Roberts, Ned. *See* Roberts, Edward
Roberts, Rev. Thomas (d. 1740):
(?) breaks leg, **10.** 311n
(?) tutor to Lord Castlecomer, **11.** 56
Roberts (after 1750 Roberts Coke), Wenman (ca 1717–76), M.P.:
biographical information about, corrected, **43.** 120, 352
marriage of, **9.** 209
Roberts, William, hosier and hatter:
Gray lodges with, **14.** 184n
Roberts, Rev. William Hayward (1734–91), D.D.:
(?) Granger's correspondence with, **42.** 471n
interested in living of Burnham, **1.** 334
Roberts, Wilson Aylesbury (fl. 1760–80), of Bewdley, Worcs; Lyttelton's literary executor:
Lyttelton's character defended by, **29.** 3
Roberts. *See also* Robartes; Robarts
Robertsbridge (Rotherbridge), Sussex:
Silver Hill near, **9.** 141n
Robertson, Rev. A., of Christ Church, Oxford:
endorsement by, **43.** 208
Robertson, Archibald:
Topographical Survey by, **43.** 69
Robertson, George, master of the *Dolphin*:
Discovery of Tahiti, The, by, **32.** 128n
Robertson, Capt. George (d. 1791), R.N.:
(?) widow of, **12.** 166n
Robertson, Isabella, m. (1775) David Dundas:
SH visited by, **12.** 231, 247
Robertson, Walter, merchant at King's Lynn:
(?) HW to visit, **15.** 21
Robertson, Dr William (d. 1791), surgeon:
(?) widow of, **12.** 106n
Robertson, William (1721–93), D.D.; historian:
Abercorn, Lord, and, **33.** 478
Chatham's 'character' attributed to, **32.** 177, 179
Colman's portrait unworthy to be with that of, **41.** 400
Dalrymple consulted by, about subject of next history, **15.** 30
—— urged by, to continue history, **15.** 140n
George III unlikely to make, historiographer royal, **32.** 178
Gibbon compared with, **34.** 131–2
Goodall accuses, of ignorance about Mary, Q. of Scots, **15.** 28
HW buys López de Gómara's MS for, **15.** 67–8
HW expects, to be more accurate than Hume, **15.** 75
HW one of the first admirers of, **15.** 210
HW praises writing of, **1.** 152
HW recommends history of Sweden to, as a subject, **15.** 56–7

HW's conversation with, **15.** 125, **28.** 381, 382, 385, 386–90
HW's correspondence with, **15.** 39–46, 48–52, 124–6, 135–7, 209–12
Historical Disquisition Concerning the Knowledge which the Ancients Had of India, An: **43.** 149; HW admires, **28.** 390n; HW comments on, **15.** 210–12; HW criticizes, **34.** 131–2; HW discusses, **11.** 294–5
History of America, The, by: Du Deffand, Mme, reads, **7.** 65, 67; HW comments on, **32.** 358; HW looks forward to, **15.** 125; HW thanks Robertson for, **15.** 136; HW thinks, inferior to *History of Scotland*, **28.** 314, 390; philosophizing of, weak, **32.** 358, 364; translated by Pillori, **28.** 171n; 'tritical' applied to, by Lady Ossory, **32.** 364
History of Scotland, The, by: Appendix to, **15.** 62; Dalrymple gives Robertson materials for, **15.** 29n; Du Deffand, Mme, reads, as *Histoire d'Écosse*, **3.** 64; feudalism clarified in, **15.** 43; Gibbon's *Roman Empire* not so deep as, **28.** 243; HW praises, **15.** 32, 125; HW's praise of, gratifies Robertson, **15.** 39; HW's remarks on, **15.** 42–5; HW thanks Robertson for, **15.** 40; HW to make further corrections in, **15.** 51; not yet published, **15.** 28n; penetration and shrewdness in, **28.** 314; publication of, approaching, **15.** 28n, 39; Robertson asks HW to correct, **15.** 40; Robertson's best writing, **34.** 131, 215; universal application of, **15.** 46
History of the Reign of the Emperor Charles V by: begun, **15.** 59; Du Deffand, Mme, reads, **5.** 47, 51; Du Deffand, Mme, sends, to Voltaire, **4.** 357; Gibbon's *Roman Empire* far superior to, **28.** 243; HW alludes to, in epilogue, **13.** 44; HW objects to subject of, **15.** 32n; HW praises, **15.** 124–6; HW praises introduction to, **34.** 215; inferior to *History of Scotland*, **28.** 314, 390; Robertson receives £3000 for, **1.** 152
Hume's relations with, **15.** 103
impartiality of, praised by HW, **15.** 40–1, 42
Mary, Q. of Scots excused by, **15.** 62
moderate Whig, **28.** 387
modesty of, deceives HW, **15.** 48–9
opposes charter for Society of Antiquaries of Scotland, **15.** 179n
recent history cannot be whitewashed by, **28.** 403
style of, praised by HW, **15.** 32, 40, 42, 48–9, 51
subjects recommended to, by HW, **15.** 50–1
supplement to Hume's *History* planned by, **28.** 386
wishes to send works to Voltaire, **4.** 343
works of, except two, are imperfect and inadequate, **34.** 215
Robertson, Mrs William. *See* Seton, Mary

Robertson of Strowan:
　Argyll, D. of, favours, though Jacobite, **20.**
　　310n
Robertspierre. *See* Robespierre
Robertstown, co. Meath:
　Carter of, **11.** 95n
Robes, Keeper of the. *See* Burney, Frances
　(1752–1840); Hagedorn, 'Mrs' (fl. 1761–86)
Robespierre ('Roberspierre;' 'Robertspierre'),
　Maximilien-François-Marie-Isidore de (1758–
　94), politician:
　atrocious monster but his crimes are over-
　　estimated, **34.** 203
　barbarity of, **12.** 162
　Barère not defended by, **12.** 86
　execution of, **12.** 115, **31.** 397, **34.** 203–4
　HW calls: 'Beelzebub,' **12.** 86; murderer, **15.**
　　236
　HW has no feeling for, **34.** 174
　not disinterested, **34.** 202
　reign of terror of, **12.** 126n
Robin, John:
　election return of, accepted, **17.** 247n
　mayor of Bossiney, **17.** 233n
Robin; robins:
　Cotton, Mrs, believes dead daughter to be
　　reincarnated as, **34.** 16, **35.** 154
　HW jokes about, **17.** 234
　HW sees, in December, **32.** 66
'Robin Gray.' *See under* Bunbury, Henry Wil-
　liam
Robin Hood:
　HW compares Montagu to, **10.** 191, 193
　HW 'to wrap myself in my,' **28.** 218
　Montagu compares himself to, as deputy
　　ranger, **10.** 188
'Robin Hood, Duchess.' *See* Chudleigh, Eliza-
　beth
Robin Hood Society:
　Élie de Beaumont visits, **38.** 461
　Foote ridicules, **35.** 200n
Robin Red-Breast's Answer, The:
　in book of ballads, **32.** 200n
'Robins, Tom':
　HW's name for Sir Thomas Robinson, **40.** 88
Robins family:
　Matson owned by, **35.** 152n
Robinson, Lady. *See* Booth, Sarah; Howard,
　Lady Elizabeth (d. 1739)
Robinson, ——:
　Eliott's and Murray's dispatches to, **25.** 136n
Robinson, ——, naval Capt.:
　Worcester commanded by, **24.** 392n
　Guadaloupe commanded by, **33.** 306n
Robinson, ——, naval Capt.:
　Mann not readily obeyed by, **18.** 507
'Robinson, Mrs.' *See* Morris, Sarah
Robinson, Mrs:
　Naples visited by, **21.** 550
Robinson, Anastasia (d. 1755), m. (1722 *or*
　1735) Charles Mordaunt, 3d E. of Peter-
　borough:

Bevois Mount associated with Pope and, **33.**
　42–3
Robinson, Anne (d. 1744), m. (1715) Richard
　Fitzpatrick, cr. (1715) Bn Gowran; Lord Os-
　sory's grandmother:
　death of a contemporary of, **33.** 125
　(?) portrait of, at Ampthill, **32.** 51n
Robinson, Anne (d. 1824), m. William Pirner:
　Robinson's correspondence left to husband
　　and, **28.** 297
Robinson, Lady Camilla Elizabeth. *See* Bennet,
　Lady Camilla Elizabeth
Robinson, Elizabeth (1720–1800), m. (1742)
　Edward Montagu; bluestocking:
　Académie française attended by, **6.** 354, 358
　academies of, HW calls, 'coptic,' **32.** 231
　Alison, Mrs, lacks pretensions and affecta-
　　tions of, **34.** 70
　—— mistreated by, **33.** 446
　Apologie de Shakespeare by, **6.** 486, 488, **8.**
　　204
　'Aspasia,' **34.** 70
　bluestockings led by, **29.** 287
　Boswell's ill-treatment of, **11.** 275
　Boulton encouraged by, **23.** 212n
　brother of Mrs Carter gives account of Bath
　　riot to, **43.** 71
　Burke's eloquence praised by, **8.** 203
　Burney, Fanny, more accomplished than, **33.**
　　498
　Chaillot residence of, **6.** 357
　Conway's verses to, with garden-swords to be
　　used as scythes, **39.** 499–500
　Dialogues of the Dead by, **8.** 204
　Dryden preferred by, to Pope, **31.** 213
　——'s *Fables* praised by, **31.** 221n
　Du Deffand, Mme, receives censers from, **7.**
　　24, **8.** 203–4
　——'s correspondence with, **6.** 494, **7.** 24, **8.**
　　203–4
　——'s opinion of, **6.** 345, 349–50, 366
　—— to receive censers from, **6.** 486
　—— to send parcels by, **6.** 362
　*Essay on the Writings and Genius of Shake-
　　spear, An*, by (*Apologie de Shakespeare*):
　　6. 486, 488, **8.** 204, **11.** 275n, **28.** 203n; Mrs
　　Piozzi condemns Boswell's account of Dr
　　Johnson's disparagement of, **25** 634, 640
　fate of Mason's *Occasional Discourse* to be
　　decided by, **29.** 361
　'feather dressing-room' of, **29.** 287, 291
　friend of, **11.** 108n, **12.** 58n
　Garrick, Mrs, visited by, at Hampton Court,
　　42. 83
　George III and Q. Charlotte attend break-
　　fast of, **11.** 290–1
　'Goddess of Wisdom' in Barry's painting, **29.**
　　296, 297, 300
　Grecian wit of, **31.** 321
　HW admires new house of, **29.** 184
　HW advises Mason to seek hand of, **28.** 203–4
　HW and Hannah More to dine with, **42.** 205

HW called on at SH by Mrs Garrick and, **42.** 83

HW calls, 'Ashtaroth,' **29.** 116, 121, 126

HW dictates Mme du Deffand's treatment of, **7.** 29

HW invites, to breakfast at SH, **42.** 83

HW meets, on a visit, **33.** 266

HW's correspondence with, **42.** 83, 468

HW's gout prevents his attending Sunday party of, **42.** 468

HW supposes, will act in *Sappho,* **28.** 342

HW's wit praised by, **8.** 203

HW visits, to hear Le Texier read Molière, **33.** 383

Harcourt eulogized by, **28.** 330

Harcourts lend *Mysterious Mother* to, **35.** 493n

— praised by, **35.** 495

Hermes and, **33.** 269

house of, in Portman Sq., has garden planned by Harcourt, **35.** 495n

Johnson offends, by despising Lyttelton, **29.** 97, 104, 113, 115–16, 126, 309

Lyttelton's *Henry II* translated by, into Greek, **32.** 30

(?) ——'s intrigue with, **9.** 255, 258

Mason and, satirized in print, **43.** 298

Montagu House of, opens new rooms, **11.** 290

More, Hannah, includes, in *Bas bleu,* **31.** 212n

—— to visit, in Berkshire, **31.** 281

—— visited by, at Cowslip Green, **31.** 321

—— visits, at Sandleford Priory, **31.** 321

mother of, **15.** 292n

'muse' of, **28.** 300

niece of, **31.** 321

Nivernais's *Jardins modernes* given to, **12.** 259

Ossory, Lady, amused by, **33.** 269

Pignotti's poem to, on Shakespeare, **24.** 536

postilion of, gossips, **9.** 255

Potter patronized by, **28.** 347n

quickness of, **31.** 83

'quite hermetically sealed,' **33.** 266

riddle sent by Mme du Deffand baffles, **31.** 83

Rousseau probably admired by, **35.** 117

social relations of, in England, with: Blagden, Dr, **31.** 258; Garrick, Mrs, **31.** 228; HW, **31.** 258; Jerningham, **31.** 258; More, Hannah, **31.** 228, 258; Ord, Mrs, **31.** 213; Pepys, W. W., **31.** 243; Reynolds, Sir Joshua, **31.** 258; Vesey, Mrs, **31.** 215

social relations of, in Paris, **6.** 337, 357

statue seen by, at Oxford, **9.** 122n

Voltaire's attack on Shakespeare at Académie française heard by Suard and, **24.** 267

wealth of, **33.** 446

witticism reported by, on Newcastle's neglect from his clergy, **22.** 37n

Yearsley, Ann, accuses Hannah More of de-luding, **31.** 253

—— admired by, **31.** 222n

—— aided by, as trustee of funds, **33.** 537n

—— befriended by, **33.** 463n

—— sponsored by, **31.** 218n

Robinson, Hon. Frederick (1746–92):
Mme du Deffand's social relations with, **5.** 87

Robinson, George:
farces acted by, at Ampthill, **33.** 552n

Robinson, Sir George (ca 1730–1815), 5th Bt; M.P.:
Beaulieu, Cts of, asked by, for ranger's post, **10.** 188

Cardigan, E. of, promises Rockingham Forest post to, **10.** 200

Montagu thinks, is ready to resign pretensions, **10.** 200

Northamptonshire residence of, **10.** 188

Robinson, George (1737–1801), bookseller:
(?) HW quoted by, for list of unengraved portraits, **16.** 234–5

Pinkerton's *Letters of Literature* published by, **33.** 476

Robinson, Jacob (fl. 1737–58):
Voltaire's *Micromégas* published by, **14.** 62n

Robinson, James:
print of, **40.** 237

Robinson, James, bookseller:
Pinkerton's *Letters of Literature* published by, **33.** 476

Robinson, Sir John (1625–80), cr. (1660) Kt and Bt:
Ossory's ancestor, **32.** 310

will of, mentions Laud's book, **32.** 310

Wright's portrait of, **32.** 51n

Robinson, John (1650–1723), Bp of London, 1714:
wife of, **30.** 61n

Robinson, John (1715–45), painter:
HW dissatisfied with his portrait by, as making him look too young, **30.** 92

HW's portrait by, sent to Mistley, **30.** 95

Williams, Sir C. H., to have copy of HW's portrait by, **30.** 93, 95

Robinson, Capt. John:
Suffolk friends of, oppose Rigby at Sudbury, **30.** 331n

Robinson, John (1727–1802), M.P.; joint secretary to the Treasury:
Bedford to supply, with prices paid in Exchequer work, **41.** 358–9

death of, rumoured, **39.** 225

HW complies with request of, for Exchequer data, **42.** 32–3

(?) HW mentions, **4.** 423

HW's correspondence with, **41.** 325–9, 358–9

house of, at Syon Hill, **41.** 325

North asks, to ask HW for prices paid for articles procured in Exchequer, **41.** 358–9

survey by, for general election of 1780, **25.** 95n

Wyke manor bought by, **41.** 325n

Robinson, John (1753–1813), bookseller:
Pinkerton's *Letters of Literature* published by, 33. 476
Robinson, Mrs John. *See* Charlton, Emma
Robinson, Luke (d. 1773), M.P.:
Chute, Francis, allied with, in disputing Hedon seat with Pulteney, 17. 234n
—— colleague of, 19. 371
Hedon election disputed by, 17. 234n
—— election granted to, 19. 371
—— election won by, 19. 342
—— seat lost by, 17. 220n, 234n, 355
lawyer, 17. 234n
Walpole, Sir Robert, object of sacrifices of, 19. 371
Robinson, M., naval officer:
Worcester commanded by, 39. 307n
'Robinson, Mary'; 'Perdita.' *See* Darby, Mary
Robinson, Palmes [? Palmer (d. 1790)]:
Pomfret said by, never to get as far as Hyde Park for duels, 25. 96
Robinson, 'Perdita.' *See* Darby, Mary
Robinson, Richard (ca 1708–94), cr. (1777) Bn Rokeby; Bp of Killala, 1752, of Leighlin and Ferns, 1759; of Kildare, 1761; Abp of Armagh, 1765:
biographical information about, corrected, 43. 125
Northumberland induces appointment of, as Abp, 22. 276
publication of brother's correspondence to be prevented by, 28. 297–8
Reynolds's portrait of, his best, 28 196
to entertain HW and Burke, 9. 396
Yearsley, Ann, admired by, 31. 222n
—— befriended by, 33. 463n
Robinson, Rev. Robert (1735–90), Baptist divine:
Cole called on by, with message from Kippis, 2. 71–2
Plan of Lectures on the Principles of Nonconformity, A, by, 2. 127
Prior anecdote communicated to, 2. 87n, 91, 341
Robinson, Sarah (1723–95), m. (1751) George Lewis Scott; novelist:
Life of Theodore Agrippa d'Aubigné, 'good only in a religious sense,' 28. 35
Montagu, Lady Barbara, lives with, 10. 166n
Robinson, Sir Septimus (1710–65), Kt, 1761; gentleman usher of the Black Rod:
death of, 7. 396
(?) HW mentions, 38. 388
Sandwich wants Wilkes to be arrested by, 38. 293–4
Waldegrave, Cts of, sends letter to, 38. 388n
Robinson, Sir Thomas (1695–1770), 2d Bt, 1736; K.B., 1742; cr. (1761) Bn Grantham; diplomatist; M.P.:
ambassador at Vienna and Madrid, and secretary of state, 25. 296n
Chatham, object of protest by, 22. 471n
death of, leaves K.B. vacancy, 23. 240

English minister at Vienna, 17. 497n, 20. 417n, 25. 296n
Fox, Henry, and Pitt attack, 20. 453
Fox, Henry, replaces, 9. 179n
Frederick II's camp again visited by, 17. 134
——'s demands on Austria presented by, 17. 76n
Gonzaga, Cardinal, sends prints to, 25. 473
Gower succeeds, in Great Wardrobe, 21. 452n
Great Wardrobe may be left by, 9. 320, 323
Great Wardrobe to be resumed by, 20. 502, 35. 253
Halifax's acceptance depends on Seals being taken by, 39. 412n
Hanover gets courier from, 18. 234
health of, scurvy, 23. 240
Keith minister to Vienna during absence of, 20. 16n
lord of Trade, 20. 17
Maclaine robs, 20. 168
Madrid embassy considered for, 22. 463n
Maria Theresa persuaded by, to give up all Silesia to Frederick II, 18. 107–8
Master of the Great Wardrobe, 20. 417n
Newcastle favours, for secretary of state, 20. 202n, 30. 185
—— induces George II to discard, as secretary of state, 40. 88
—— suggests, as postmaster general, 30. 185n
nominee for secretaryship, 20. 202
North to succeed, as secretary of state, 25. 372n
Parliamentary Address debated by, 37. 415
Parliamentary debate by, on Scotch Bill, 20. 32, 33
Parliamentary seat created for, 20. 17
Parliamentary speech of: compared to storm, 37. 470; on Dresden treaty, 43. 496
peace efforts of: believed to be fruitless, 17. 121; ill-rewarded, 20. 17; unsuccessful, 17. 121
peerage granted to, 9. 344, 21. 490
pension of, 20. 502
Plummer replaced by, as lord of Trade, 20. 17n
postmaster, 22. 311
red ribbon awarded to, for procuring peace with Prussia, 17. 496–7
return of, to Frederick II's camp, 17. 134
secretary of state, 17. 497n, 20. 417
secretaryship of state may go to, 9. 210, 21. 92, 35. 169
son of, 21. 436
Spanish armaments reported by, 24. 98n
Stanhope persuaded by, to 'improve' Pope's garden, 25. 177
Suares recommended by, for preferment, 18. 455
Vienna visited by, 20. 202
Robinson, Sir Thomas (? 1702–77), cr. (1731) Bt, of Rokeby; M.P.; 'long Sir Thomas':
Augusta, Ps of Wales, given breakfast by, at Whitehall, 35. 179

ball given by: **37**. 55, 113–15; for D. of Richmond's daughter, **17**. 174, 183–5; for second time, **17**. 221–2; Walpole, Sir Robert, does not attend, **17**. 185
Barbados post taken by, **17**. 301, **24**. 282n
—— would not lure friends of, **37**. 126
becomes privy councillor, **20**. 135
birth date of, corrected, **43**. 118, 238, 324
Castle Howard façade of, **30**. 257
—— interiors of, noble, **30**. 257
Cornabé's letter to, **43**. 256
correspondence of, not to be published, **28**. 297–8
death of, **24**. 282
gateway designed by, **9**. 310n
HW may imitate those who shun, **35**. 579
HW told by, of Exchequer House's improvement, **37**. 454
Hotham Thompson jokes about assembly of, **9**. 132
Lincoln, E. of, wants house of, **17**. 301
Mann delighted by ball of, **17**. 208
—— remembers, **24**. 282
marriage of, **34**. 259
second wife of, **24**. 282n
social relations of, in London, **17**. 174, 183–5, 221–2, **37**. 55, 113–15
spurned with other toad-eaters, **35**. 579
Suffolk, Cts of (younger), said to be loved by, **9**. 140
wife to be survived by, **9**. 140
Robinson, Thomas (1738–86), 2d Bn Grantham, 1770:
ambassador at Vienna and Madrid, and secretary of state, **25**. 296n
ambassadorship of, corrected, **43**. 352
ambassador to Spain, **16**. 180n, **33**. 118, 140
appointment of: as ambassador to Spain, **31**. 153; as first lord of Trade, **33**. 242
becomes secretary of state, **25**. 296
death of, **33**. 520
Du Deffand, Mme, to entertain, **5**. 87
Etruscan vases said by, to have been discovered, **21**. 561
Floridablanca notifies, that Almodóvar leaves Madrid, **24**. 366n
HW likes, **33**. 422
HW sees, **33**. 140
HW's opinion of *Walpoliana* to be softened for, **33**. 422
Hardwicke, father-in-law of, **33**. 422
Maddison, undersecretary to, **42**. 73n
Mann enjoys meeting, at Florence, **21**. 436
—— receives letter of congratulation from, **25**. 344
——'s dispatches to: **25**. 326; delivered by Cardini in Cleveland Row, **42**. 36
——'s old acquaintance, **25**. 296
—— wants to know opinion of, about Mediterranean affairs, **24**. 437, 453
marriage of, **33**. 202
Ossory, Lady, will see, **33**. 118

painter at Florence misinforms, about Etruscan vases, **22**. 6
resigns as vice-chamberlain, **31**. 153
stays in Spain despite war declaration, **24**. 487
Waddilove, chaplain to, **16**. 168n
Robinson, Mrs Thomas. *See* Darby, Mary
Robinson, William (ca 1720–75), architect; secretary to Board of Works:
death of, **7**. 398
(?) HW buys 'Marriage of Henry VI' from, **35**. 250
HW mentions, **20**. 375
SH enlarged by, **19**. 486n, **30**. 114n
Robinson, William, HW's printer at SH 1757–9:
dismissed for impertinence, **15**. 55
Fugitive Pieces printed by, **15**. 60
Garrick comments on appearance of, **21**. 120
guests see Press operated by, **9**. 215–16
HW finds letter by, **21**. 120–1
HW keeps, at SH, **21**. 120
(?) HW mentions, **21**. 160
Irishman, **16**. 27
leaves, **16**. 27, 33n, **35**. 303n
Mann enjoys letter of, **21**. 125
SH Press delayed by, **16**. 33
'went away,' **35**. 303n
Robinson, William, deputy to House of Burgesses in Virginia:
(?) capture of, rumoured, **24**. 157
Robinson Crusoe. See under Defoe, Daniel
Robinson Crusoe; or Harlequin Friday. See under Sheridan, Richard Brinsley
Robinson family:
HW will identify portraits of, at Ampthill, **32**. 51
Robin's Wood Hill:
Matson on, **35**. 152, **43**. 60
Selwyn wants Llanthony gateway for, **35**. 155
spelling and location of, corrected, **43**. 155
Robsart, Amy (ca 1532–60), m. (1549) Robert Dudley, cr. (1564) E. of Leicester:
aunt of, **12**. 267n
Wood's account of Leicester and, **38**. 158
Robsart, Sir John (1390–1450), K.G.:
HW confuses Sir Terry Robsart with, **12**. 267, **20**. 381n
Robsart, Sir Lewis (d. 1430), K.G.:
Burgundy, Ds of, gives present to, **12**. 267
HW's erroneous note on, **12**. 267
Robsart, Lucy (d. 1560), m. Edward Walpole of Houghton:
HW descended from, **12**. 267
Robsart, Sir Terry (d. 1496):
HW's ancestor, **12**. 267, **20**. 381n
K.G., **20**. 381n
SH trophies supposedly belonged to, **20**. 381
Robson, James (1733–1806), bookseller:
catalogue of, **1**. 175
(?) HW quoted by, for list of unengraved portraits, **16**. 234–5
HW receives Lady Craven's *Journey through the Crimea* from, **34**. 36

[Robson, James, *continued*]
Mason's pamphlet sold by, **16.** 210
Winterton buys books from, **40.** 326
Robuste, French war ship:
in Vilaine River, **21.** 351
Rocca d'Arazzo, Conte di. *See* Cacherano d'Osasco, Giuseppe Ottaviano
Roccella (Italy):
earthquake account mentions, **25.** 376
Roccettini (monastic order):
convent of, at Pisa, suppressed, **23.** 504
Rochalart, ——, French naval officer:
fleet of, returns to Toulon and Brest, **17.** 46n
Rochambaut; Rochambeau; Rochambeure, Comte de. *See* Vimeur, Jean-Baptiste-Donatien de
Rochauard, ——, chief French engineer at Fontenoy:
Lloyd noticed by, **23.** 422n
Roche, Anne, m. Charles Sackville, 6th E. of Dorset:
'player,' **35.** 134
Roche Abbey, Yorks:
HW visits, **1.** 275, 278
Roche-Aymon, La. *See* La Roche-Aymon
Rochechouart, Comtesse de. *See* Barberie de Courteilles, Marie-Mélanie-Henriette de
Rochechouart, Marquise de. *See* Faulcon de Ris, Charlotte-Françoise
Rochechouart, Vicomte de. *See* Rochechouart, Pierre-Paul-Étienne de (1723–99); Rochechouart-Pontville, Louis-François-Marie-Honorine de (ca 1733–79)
Rochechouart, Alice-Elfrède-Victurnienne de (1800–87), m. (1823) Paul, Duc de Noailles:
birth of, in England, **34.** 181n
Rochechouart, Diane-Adélaïde de (d. 1794), m. (1751) Louis-Marie-Florent, Comte (Duc, 1777) du Châtelet; 'notre ambassadrice':
after-dinner balls given by, **5.** 322
arrested in Paris, **12.** 28
Bourbonne visited by, **4.** 468–9, **7.** 177
Chanteloup left by, **5.** 246
—— visited by, **5.** 84, 86, 241, 245, **6.** 450
Coke, Lady Mary, dislikes, but Ladies Holdernesse and Lyttelton (and Mrs Damer) do not, **32.** 40n
—— rudely treated by, **23.** 127n
Craufurd tried to visit, **32.** 263
Du Deffand, Mme, awaits news from, **5.** 88
—— does not know, **4.** 173, 177
—— leaves overtures to, **5.** 13
(?) —— mentions, **4.** 409
—— notified by, of courier, **4.** 43
—— receives nothing through, **5.** 88
——'s opinion of, **4.** 173, 177, 246
—— talks with HW about, **4.** 456–7
—— to be notified of departing couriers by order of, **4.** 94
England left by, **4.** 256, 420, **35.** 333
—— to be visited by for autumn, **22.** 586
Eszterházy lodges with, **6.** 30
Fontainebleau not to be visited by, **8.** 178

Gramont, Comtesse de, close friend of, **4.** 441
HW admires, **23.** 127–8
HW discusses Mme du Barry's presentation with, **4.** 194
HW entertains, at SH, **4.** 176–7, 236n, **10.** 278–9
HW hears of Mme du Barry from, **23.** 85n
HW inquired about by, **4.** 456
HW lent book by, **4.** 213
HW likes, **4.** 378, **32.** 40
(?) HW mentions, **3.** 342
HW quarrels with Lady Mary Coke about, **31.** 141
health of: **8.** 177; bad, **12.** 28
indifference of, **31.** 152
Joseph II converses with, about Mme du Deffand, **6.** 450
Lauraguais, Duchesse de, friend of, **4.** 321
L'Isle brings messages to Mme du Deffand from, **5.** 13
—— in England with, **32.** 169, 173
—— friend of, **4.** 322
London left by, **4.** 256
—— not yet visited by, **32.** 39
Luxembourg, Mme de, converses with, **6.** 450
Orléans visited by, **5.** 239
return of, to England: **31.** 144; implies peace, **23.** 156n
returns to France, **4.** 419n
sister of, **5.** 84, **7.** 124
social relations of, in Paris, *see index entries ante* **8.** 490
stage box at Drury Lane assigned to, for *Jubilee*, **41.** 181
uncertain of husband's tenure, **4.** 250
Rochechouart, Françoise-Athénaïs de (1641–1707), m. (1663) Henri-Louis de Pardaillan de Gondrin; Marquise de Montespan; Louis XIV's mistress:
arms of, on Mme du Deffand's chimney, **7.** 289, **39.** 233–4
children of, legitimated, **7.** 276
Communauté de St Joseph founded by, **3.** 12n, **7.** 289, **8.** 56n
death of, **4.** 445
Du Deffand, Mme, occupies apartment formerly built for, **8.** 3, 56n, **39.** 233–4
English bishops would court modern counterpart of, **35.** 587
(?) Ennery has medallion of, **7.** 325
Harcourt, Lady, will be as jealous as, **23.** 498
La Vallière, Duchesse de, converses with, **6.** 378
Louis XIV governed by, **31.** 13
Necker mentions, **8.** 213
Rochechouart, Jean-François-Joseph de (1708–77), cardinal, 1761:
Choiseul sends message to Luynes through, excluding Cavalchini, **21.** 215n
Florence to be visited by, **22.** 28
French ambassador to Rome, **21.** 207n, 215n, **22.** 28n

Louis XV sends message to Conclave through, **21**. 207n

Rochechouart, Jean-Louis-Roger (1717–76), Marquis de:
(?) Coke, Lady Mary, taken by, to René's portrait at Avignon, **31**. 143n
made member of Ordre du St-Esprit, **6**. 199

Rochechouart, Pierre-Paul-Étienne (1723–99), Vicomte de:
court-martialed, **7**. 179, 431

Rochechouart, Zéphirine-Félicité de (1733–76), m. (1755) Jacques-François, Marquis de Damas d'Antigny:
Bourbonne visited by, **8**. 177
confinement of, **5**. 84
Du Deffand, Mme, does not know, **4**. *173*, 177
—— inquires after, **6**. 30
——'s opinion of, **4**. 173, 177
HW entertains, at SH, **4**. 176–7, **10**. 278–9
social relations of, in Paris, *see index entries ante* **8**. 490
son of, **7**. 124

Rochechouart-Pontville, Louis-François-Marie-Honorine de (ca 1733–79), Vicomte de Rochechouart:
(?) Du Deffand, Mme, does not know, **4**. 71
(?) Selwyn taken by, **4**. 71

Roche de Kerandraon. *See* La Roche de Kerandraon

Rochefort, Comtesse de. *See* Brancas, Marie-Thérèse de

Rochefort, Prince de Rohan-. *See* Rohan, Charles-Louis-Gaspard de

Rochefort (France):
Brest fleet may have gone to, **39**. 313
Bubb Dodington's account of English attempt upon, **39**. 413
Clerk ('Clarke') prompted attack on, **37**. 474n
—— spies upon fortifications of, **7**. 357
—— trusted by governor of, **7**. 357
Conway and Mordaunt apprehensive about expedition to, **21**. 118n
Conway approves attack on, at conference on board the *Ramillies*, **21**. 143n
—— blamed for fruitless expedition to, **9**. 217–18
—— considered by George II too young to lead expedition to, **21**. 118n
—— should conquer English politics before attacking, **38**. 75
English expedition against: **9**. 217–18, **21**. 117n, 118n, 119, 134–5, 137, 143, 153, **30**. 138–43, **35**. 285, **37**. 540, 545; Conway blamed by Guthrie for failure of, **38**. 438; Conway confirmed in doubts about, **37**. 506–9, 515; Conway doubts success of, **37**. 495–6; Conway might have won title if successful in, **38**. 135; Conway's advocacy of limited attacks may not appear in inquiry on, **37**. 515–16; Conway's conduct preferred to Mordaunt's in, **37**. 517; Con-

way's part in, **37**. 535; cost millions, **35**. 286; George II summons Conway and Mordaunt for, **37**. 493n; HW mentions, **37**. 513; Klosterzeven convention tied to, **37**. 518–19; land officers only may be blamed for, **37**. 513; letters from, detained, **37**. 513–14; ministers might divert, to Stade, **37**. 501n; pamphlets on, **37**. 523n; report on, shocks many, **37**. 520–1; to divert French from George II's allies in Germany, **21**. 117n; transports awaited for, by army at Newport, **37**. 495, 499, 501
English fleet not headed for, **37**. 531
English objective in France should be as important as, **21**. 223
France equips men of war at, **20**. 535n
French fleet preparing to leave, **18**. 360
French Mediterranean fleet moved to, **19**. 78
French ships arrive at, **7**. 446
French ships from, captured by English, **19**. 411
George II joins Mordaunt to Conway for attempt on, **21**. 118n
Guay's squadron reaches, **20**. 498n
inquiry into English attack upon: **21**. 145, 154–5, 158, 160–1, 163, 164–5; to be held in Privy Garden, **21**. 155n; Wolfe a witness at, **21**. 267n
militia might be used to attack, **37**. 572–3
Montbazon at, during English attempt, **37**. 545
newspapers report capture of, **30**. 144
Pitt endorses Frederick II's idea of expedition to, **21**. 117n
—— sends no cannon against, **21**. 213
—— suggests attack on, **21**. 213n
Wolfe's situation at Quebec comparable to Conway's at, **38**. 38–9
—— witness against Mordaunt and Conway in inquiry about, **21**. 267n

Rochefoucauld, La. *See* La Rochefoucauld

Roche-Guyon, La. *See* La Roche-Guyon

Rochelle. *See* La Rochelle

Rochemaure. *See* La Rochemaure

Rocheouart. *See* Rochechouart

Rochers, Les, Mme de Sévigné's seat, near Vitré, Brittany:
HW would not give unlimited commission even for views of, **35**. 197
Montagu compares Delville with, **9**. 390–1
'Notre Dame des Rochers,' **35**. 198, 231
Peyre, Mme, lives at, **30**. 213, **41**. 258
Selwyn has ground plan of, **41**. 258

Roches-Baritaud, Comtesse des. *See* Mouchard, Marie-Anne-Françoise

Rochester, Bp of. *See* Alcock, John (1430–1500); Atterbury, Francis (1662–1732); Dampier, Thomas (1748–1812); Fisher, John (1469–1535); Horsley, Samuel (1733–1806); Pearce, Zachary (1690–1774); Russell, John (d. 1494); Sprat, Thomas (1635–1713); Thomas, John (1712–93); Wilcocks, Joseph (1673–1756)

Rochester, Cts of. *See* Malet, Elizabeth (d. 1681)

Rochester, E. of:
Anson might get title of, **35**. 170
See also Hyde, Laurence (1642–1711); Wilmot, John (1647–80)

Rochester, Kent:
cathedral at, sculptures of Henry I and Matilda in, **40**. 213, 221
Chute and HW visit, **35**. 144
Dampier, dean of, **29**. 241n
Foote prebendary of, **11**. 81n
HW sends letters by postilion of, **7**. 379
HW visits, **7**. 258, 353
HW writes from, **35**. 144
innkeeper at, **7**. 258
Markham, dean of, **28**. 64n
Newcome, dean of, **1**. 280n, **2**. 16n
Page condemned at assizes at, for robbery, **21**. 184n
Pearce not to be succeeded by Newton as Bp of, **38**. 364
—— tries to resign see of, **38**. 364
riots at, by sailors from Vernon's fleet, **30**. 29
(?) St Catherine's Hospital at, **7**. 258
Thorpe's researches on history of, **40**. 213
Vernon's head unpopular at, **35**. 11

Rochester, English ship:
captured ships brought by, into Leghorn, **19**. 55n
in danger, **21**. 350
Mogg, Thomas, captain of, 18, 404n
Neapolitan troops to be blockaded by, **18**. 453
(?) oats transported by, **18**. 453

Rochette de la Morlière, Jacques (1719–85):
Angola by, **35**. 588

Rochford, Cts of. *See* Young, Lucy (ca 1723–73)

Rochford, E. of. *See* Nassau de (*or* Van) Zuylestein, William Henry (1649–1708); Nassau de Zuylestein, William Henry (1717–81)

Rochford, Vct. *See* Boleyn, George (d. 1536)

Rochford, Dr:
'dormitory' of, at Walpole St Peter, **40**. 225

Rochford, Mrs. *See* Cromwell, Miss; Goddard, Miss

Rochford. *See also* Rochefort; Rochfort

Rochfort, Arthur (1711–? 72), Irish M.P.:
biographical information about, corrected, **43**. 249
sister-in-law's intrigue with, **18**. 220

Rochfort, Lady Jane (1737–1828), m. 1 (1754) Brinsley Butler, 2d E. of Lanesborough; m. 2 (ca 1785) John King:
Hamilton's affair with, **38**. 250–1
King, John, takes, to Leghorn, **25**. 601
refuses Leghorn merchants' offer of separation from King, **25**. 601

Rochfort, Mrs John Staunton. *See* Mann, Harriet

Rochfort, Robert (1708–74), cr. (1738) Bn and (1751) Vct Belfield, (1756) E. of Belvidere; Irish M.P.:

wife's intrigue with brother of, **18**. 220
'Kitten's' relations with, **30**. 90

Rochfort. *See also* Rochefort; Rochford

Rochfoucault. *See* La Rochefoucauld

Rochon de Chabannes, Marc-Antoine Jacques (1730–1800):
Heureusement by, **7**. 274

Rochouart. *See* Rochechouart

Rochow, Hans Friedrich von; Prussian army officer:
Berlin garrison under, **21**. 441n

Roch-St-André, Mme de la. *See* Regnon de la Ranconnière, Ursule-Suzanne-Véronique de

Rock, Dr Richard (fl. 1731–69), quack doctor:
Pitt compared with, **21**. 547
testimonials from patients of, **21**. 132

Rock crystal:
lustres of, **22**. 157
vase of: sent by Mann to HW, **25**. 65, 165, 169, **26**. 56; sold from Tribune at Uffizi gallery, **25**. 65

Rocke, Mrs Mary, housekeeper to Gen. Fitzwilliam:
Fitzwilliam leaves fortune to, **11**. 49, **34**. 59

Rocker; rockers:
HW procures, for Cts of Hertford to give to P. of Wales (George IV), **38**. 168

Rocket; rockets:
at D. of Richmond's fireworks, **20**. 56
at peace celebration, **20**. 47
for Rodney, disturb HW, **25**. 281
for Valenciennes surrender, **34**. 186
HW to send, to Cts of Ailesbury from Viry's fireworks, **39**. 256
See also Skyrocket

Rockingham, Cts of. *See* Furnese, Katherine (d. 1766)

Rockingham, E. of. *See* Watson, Lewis (ca 1714–45); Watson, Thomas (ca 1715–46)

Rockingham, Marchioness of. *See* Bright, Mary (d. 1804); Finch, Lady Mary (d. 1761)

Rockingham, M. of. *See* Watson Wentworth, Charles (1730–82); Watson Wentworth, Thomas (1693–1750)

Rockingham:
earldom of, extinct, **19**. 244

Rockingham Club:
at York, **28**. 362

Rockingham faction. *See under* Watson Wentworth, Charles, M. of Rockingham

Rockingham family:
credit lost by, in its own counties, **25**. 488

Rockingham Forest:
Cardigan's lodge near, **10**. 200
deputy ranger has little power over, **10**. 214
Glass reports to Montagu about, **10**. 213–14
HW calls, 'Sherwood,' **10**. 191
HW hopes Montagu will not live in, **10**. 216
HW would rather have Montagu in, than at Greatworth, **10**. 191
Halifax wishes to shoot game in, **10**. 209

Harcourt's house near, offered to Montagu, **10.** 199

keeper of: Glass's letter to, **10.** 238, 241; HW to send letter and warrant to, **10.** 238, 240–1

Montagu, D. of, warden of, **20.** 79n

Montagu, George, leaves London to attend to affairs of, **10.** 213

—— may be deputy ranger of, **10.** 188, 191, 192, 194, 199

——'s trip to, postponed, **10.** 215, 217

—— to look at, **10.** 214

Robinson, Sir George, wishes to be deputy ranger of, **10.** 188

Rockingham Hall, Hagley, Worcs:

Miller builds, **35.** 149

Rocksavage, E. of. *See* Cholmondeley, George Horatio (1792–1870)

Rockwell, Mary, m. (1760) John Greenway: SH visited by, **12.** 223, 232, 235, 237, 240, 244, 247

Rocour (Rocourt; Roucoux). *See* Roucour

Rocque, La. *See* La Rocque de Varengeville; Rocca d'Arazzo

Rod; rods:

black, *see* Gentleman Usher of the Black Rod

fishing, not used by HW, at SH, **9.** 155

white, of lord chamberlain, **22.** 103n

See also Staff

Rodborough, Glos:

Agnes Berry visits, **15.** 251

Roddam, Robert (1719–1808):

convoy commanded by, **19.** 485n

Rode, La. *See* Sénezergues de la Rode

Roden, E. of. *See* Jocelyn, Robert

Roderic (O'Connor) (ca 1116–98), K. of Ireland:

turned harp into harpsichord, **32.** 92

Rodet, Marie-Thérèse (1699–1777), m. (1713) François Geoffrin; keeper of salon; 'Princesse Geoffrinska':

admits there is nothing to talk of, in Paris, **31.** 93

Alembert's eulogy of, **6.** 498

arrives in Paris, **31.** 45

Boucher's collection visited by, **7.** 394

Burke meets *philosophes* at salon of, **32.** 103n

Catherine II gives furs to, **41.** 7

costume of, informal, **31.** 59n

daughter excludes *philosophes* from bedside of, **6.** 363, 367

daughter of, **7.** 295n

death of, **6.** 484

diplomatic appointment may be given to, **31.** 102

dinners of, for literati in Paris, **32.** 31

Du Deffand, Mme, does not emulate, **7.** 9

—— meets, **6.** 141–2

—— not on good terms with, **39.** 190

——'s opinion of, **3.** 178, 209

——'s verses on, finished by HW, **6.** 495, 497

—— thought to hate, **4.** 87

Egmont, Mme d', praised by, to Stanislas II, **3.** 42n

enemies of, **31.** 102

England not to be visited by, **30.** 210–11, **31.** 101

esteemed in London, **4.** 65

'exceedingly sensible,' **32.** 23

Foley to deliver letter and parcel to, **31.** 86

Gazette d'Utrecht comments on, **3.** 373

Guasco protected by, from her friends' resentment, **22.** 575

—— punished by, for indiscretion, **22.** 529

HW at salon of, jokes about Rousseau, **39.** 42–3

HW called 'le nouveau Richelieu' by, **31.** 58, 74

HW describes, admiringly, **14.** 150

HW discussed in letters of, **31.** 82

HW gives Gramont's memoirs to, **41.** 238–9

HW hears wise observation by, about England, **22.** 343

HW meets Berthelots at house of, **4.** 284n

HW mentions, **3.** 342, **6.** 97

HW might hint to, that there is corn at Genoa and Leghorn, **24.** 106

HW praises, **31.** 51, 59, 96

HW receives snuff-box for Cts of Albemarle from, **31.** 113

HW's attentions from, **31.** 91

HW's 'confessor and director,' **31.** 59

HW's correspondence with, **7.** 381, **41.** 238–9

HW's figure admired by, **31.** 82

HW's letter to Rousseau first mentioned at house of, **7.** 295

HW's opinion of, **30.** 205

HW's proposed epic about civil war in salon of, **4.** 214–15, 217

HW to execute Selwyn's commission for, **30.** 210

HW to give seal to, **7.** 415

HW to send Gramont's memoirs to, **7.** 416

HW visited by, in Paris, **32.** 23

HW well treated by, in Paris, **22.** 524

health of, **6.** 296, 308, 354–5, 359, 363, 367

Hervey, Bns, admires, **3.** 239, 335

—— corresponds with, **31.** 45, 82, 86

—— fond of, **22.** 524

—— friend of, **31.** 42, 416

—— gives HW letter of introduction to, **31.** 42

—— receives knotting-bags from, **31.** 73, 76–7, 86

—— transcribes letters from, for HW, **31.** 82

—— writes 'character' of, **31.** 59n

Holland, Bns, corresponds with, **31.** 82

Joseph II asked by, to call on her, **6.** 448

La Vallière, Duchesse de, approaches Mariette's heirs through, **6.** 102

Montesquieu's letters to Guasco about, **3.** 335

——'s letters will hurt, **22.** 523–4

Montmorency visited by, **4.** 87

Morellet's eulogy of, **6.** 496, 497

not visible on Sundays, **31.** 45

not young and handsome, **32.** 31

[Rodet, Marie-Thérèse, *continued*]
Orford, Cts of, and Cavaliere Mozzi call on, in Paris, 23. 141–2
Poland to be visited by, 31. 101–2
'Queen-Mother' of Poland, 4. 214
St-Honoré, Rue, residence of, 4. 214
St-Roch, church of, attended by, 6. 296
Selwyn given permission by, for copy of her portrait, 30. 213
—— to ask, for Guibert's address, 30. 251
social life of, busy, 4. 94
social relations of, in Paris, *see index entries ante* 8. 491 and 31. 507
Stanislas II invites, 31. 102
—— rescued by, from debtors' prison, 3. 109n
—— writes to, 3. 268n
success of, 3. 178
successor to Mme de Tencin, 28. 291
Thomas's eulogy of, 6. 494, 497
Voltaire mentions, 6. 357
will of, 6. 484
work-bags from, 1. 101n
Rodet, Pierre (d. 1706):
'valet de garde-robe,' 14. 150n
Rodez, Bp of. *See* Champion de Cicé, Jérôme-Marie (1735–1810); Colbert de Seignelay, François (1736–1815)
Rodi, Abp of. *See* Dugnani, Antonio
Rodington, Shropshire:
Alison, rector of, 42. 264n
Rodmarton, Glos:
Lysons, D., rector of, 15. 200n
Lysons, S., rector of, 15. 269n
Rodney, Lady. *See* Clies, Henrietta
Rodney, Sir George Brydges (1719–92), Adm., 1778; cr. (1764) Bt and (1782) Bn Rodney:
Admiralty recalls, 25. 278, 282
biographical information about, corrected, 43. 265
Boyle Walsingham said to have joined, 25. 74n, 79
Burdett cheats, 20. 20–1
Burke moves for inquiry into St Eustatius conduct of, 25. 218n, 36. 199n
Clevland's letter from, in *London Gazette*, 21. 309
Common Council gives banquet for, 25. 343
convoy of, captured by French, 25. 159
Dutch colonies capitulate to, 25. 145n
Dutch settlements 'stifled' by, 25. 150
English reputation retrieved by, at sea, 25. 32
fleet of: 29. 46n, 250; coming from Martinique meets French squadron, 22. 32; probably exceeded by French and Spanish ones, 25. 73; Walsingham said to have joined, 25. 74n
French fleet eludes, 25. 311
French fleet in West Indies engaged by, 29. 46, 48
French invasion from Le Havre to be watched for by, 21. 300n
Guichen's battle with, 25. 52n
HW knows nothing about, 33. 295, 297

HW's windows broken because of triumph of, 33. 374
Havre-de-Grâce burnt by, 21. 305
Havre governor summoned by, to deliver all flat-bottomed boats, 21. 310
Hood to have replaced, in Parliament, 25. 284
house of, in Hertford St, 33. 374n
in port, 25. 221
Joseph II's army reported by, to be on march, 33. 495
London Gazette news of, 21. 309, 29. 137
London illuminated for, 25. 280
Lord Mayor and aldermen refuse to give banquet for, 25. 343
loss of English fleets from East and West Indies will depress, 25. 83
Mann hopes, will not let laurels wither, 25. 291
Martinique news awaited from, 22. 7n
——'s conquest due to, 21. 21
Mason wants to hear more about, 29. 51
messenger-sloop of, 25. 17
Mordaunt's red ribbon is expected to go to, 29. 87
no news from, 25. 291, 318
parades through London with window-breaking rabble, 25. 343
peerage for, 29. 251
Pitt nominated by Westminster to replace, 25. 278
prints of victories of, 25. 582n
recall of: embarrasses ministry, 29. 251; regretted by Mann despite probable reinstatement, 25. 282
reputed father of Miss Ashe, 9. 106n
Rhode Island too impregnable for, 25. 99
runs blockade of Gibraltar, 29. 151n
St Eustatius captured by, 25. 139, 29. 122n, 36. 192n
—— plundered by, 25. 194n, 278
Spa visited by, 33. 495
Spanish squadron destroyed by, 2. 192–3, 194
Tobago's capture reported by, 25. 172n
'vain fool,' 33. 374
victory of: 7. 205n, 212n; at Cape St Vincent, over Lángara, 25. 16, 17, 21, 24; at the Saintes, over French, 25. 277–8, 281; should give England an advantage in peace treaty, 25. 352
West Indies supposed to be destination of, 25. 24, 99
Wraxall's *Short Review* makes, a hero, 33. 558n
Rodogune. See under Corneille, Pierre
Rodriguez, P. F. Antonio Giuseppe:
(?) Almada's secretary, 21. 430, 476
Rodt, Franz Conrad von (1706–75), cardinal, 1756:
cardinals await, 21. 215
Roe, Mr:
SH visited by, 12. 234
Roe, J., bookseller:
Mysterious Mother advertised by, 33. 579n

Roe, Sir John:
verses credited to, 9. 258n
Roe, Rev. Stephen (d. 1764), ordinary of New-
gate Prison:
(?) Cock Lane ghost 'patronized' by, 10. 5–6
indifference of, to heroes, 10. 113
writes for monthly half-crown, 10. 113
Roe, Sir Thomas (ca 1581–1644), diplomatist;
M.P.:
letters of, 9. 224, 15. 93
Roebuck, English war ship:
Haddock returns in, to England, 17. 361n
peace commissioners return in, 33. 80n
Roebuck, English fire ship:
at Port Mahon, 17. 285
'Roe G':
(?) Lort's memorandum, 16. 216
Roehampton, Surrey:
Bessborough's house at, 36. 42
Clarence, D. of (William IV), takes house at,
11. 70, 34. 68
Fordyce of, 12. 154n
HW hopes Montagu will move to, 10. 184, 187
Montagu may take house at, 10. 182, 187
——'s house at, to be shrine of St Genevieve,
10. 187
SH near, 10. 187
Roel, Glos, George Montagu's seat:
HW jokes about Bentley's schemes for, 43. 118
Montagu decorates, 9. 213
—— leaves, 9. 146
—— occupies, 9. 361n, 10. 16n, 285
(?) —— rides around premises of, 10. 261
—— to occupy, 9. 56, 87, 10. 126
Montagu, Christopher, leaves, to George
Montagu, 10. 352
Walcot House near, 9. 245
Roermond (Holland):
Ferdinand, P., stationed at, 37. 555
Roestraten, Pieter van (1627–1700), painter:
still life by, 30. 370
Roet, Katharine (1350–1403), m. 1 Sir Hugh
Swynford; m. 2 (1396) John of Gaunt, D. of
Lancaster:
John of Gaunt marries, 2. 31n, 15. 172n
Montagu compares Dorothy Clement to, 9.
302
son of, 2. 39n
Roettiers, Norbert (ca 1665–1727), medallist:
HW to include, in *Anecdotes of Painting*, 16.
157
medal by, of Charles I, 16. 150
medals by, 40. 239
Rofey. *See* Roffey
Roffeni, Signora. *See* Paleotti, Adelaide
Roffey, Mr:
SH visited by, 12. 224, 228, 233, 249
visitors sent by, to SH, 11. 25n
Roffey, William (1713–85):
'rout' given by, at Kingston, 35. 468
Roger, ——, Guines's secretary:
(?) Du Deffand, Mme, to send furniture by,
5. 139, 148

Guines's mémoire against, 30. 264n
reprimanded, 8. 200
*Rogeri Aschami epistolarum librī quatuor. See
under* Ascham, Roger
Rogeri Hovedani Annalium. See under Hove-
den, Roger of
Rogers, Mr, peruke-maker:
fire in house of, 17. 496n
Rogers, Mr and Mrs:
SH visited by, 12. 232
Rogers, Mrs (1) and Mrs (2):
SH visited by, 12. 222
Rogers, Charles (1711–84), art collector:
*Collection of Prints in Imitation of Drawings,
A*, by, presented to HW, 41. 377
Custom House address of, 41. 389
Dante's *Inferno* translated by, and dedicated
to Sir Edward Walpole, 35. 384n, 42. 9n
HW asks for (and receives) another copy of
print of, 41. 389–91
HW called on by: 41. 389–90; with gift, 41.
389
HW's correspondence with, 41. 377, 389–92,
402, 42. 9
HW thanks, for Dante translation, 42. 9
Rogers, Mrs John. *See* Mann, Eleanor
Rogers, Jonathan (1677–1742), attorney; hus-
band of Gray's aunt:
dog-lover, but gout bars him from hunting,
13. 105–6
equestrian tastes of, 13. 114n
wife of, 14. 32n
Rogers, Mrs Jonathan. *See* Antrobus, Anne
Rogers, Samuel (1763–1855), poet:
(?) disbelieves in Ireland's MSS, 15. 321
Rogers, William, grocer:
(?) Petersham, Lady Caroline, serves fruit
from shop of, 9. 109
Roguish Miller, The:
in 'Cheap Repository Tracts,' 31. 396n
Rohampton. *See* Roehampton
Rohan, Bailli de:
Mann invited by, to Leghorn celebration, 22.
557
—— visited by, 22. 557
Rohan, Cardinal de. *See* Rohan, Armand-Gaston-Maximilien de (1674–1749); Rohan-
Guéménée, Louis-René-Édouard de (1734–
1803)
Rohan, Duc de. *See* Rohan-Chabot, Louis-Antoine-Auguste de (1733–1807); Rohan-Chabot,
Louis-Marie-Bretagne-Dominique de (1710–
1801)
Rohan, Mlle de. *See* Rohan-Guéménée, Charlotte-Victoire-Josèphe-Henriette de
Rohan, Princesse de. *See* Rohan-Guéménée, Charlotte-Victoire-Josèphe-Henriette de (1761–
71); Rohan-Guéménée, Marie-Louise-Jose-
phine de (1765–1839)
Rohan, Anne de (1604–85), m. (1616) Louis de
Rohan, Prince de Guéménée:
(?) husband's witticism on Jewish visitor to,
33. 367

Rohan, Anne de (1648–1709). *See* Rohan-Chabot, Anne-Julie de

Rohan, Armand-Gaston-Maximilien de (1674–1749), cardinal, 1712; Bp of Strasbourg:
château of, occupied by hussars, 18. 293
Corsini's party supported by, 17. 21n
HW sees, 13. 209n
pope to be chosen from faction of, 17. 20–1
Rome to be visited by, for Conclave, 37. 47

Rohan, Prince Camille de. *See* Rohan, Eugène-Hercule-Camille de

Rohan, Charles de (1693–1766), Prince de Rohan-Montauban:
death of: 39. 57

Rohan, Charles de (1715–87), Prince de Soubise; Maréchal de France, 1758:
Austrians under Hildburghausen join, to recover Saxony, 21. 137n
ball said to be attended by, on eve of battle, 22. 47n
bankers aided by, 4. 376
Beauvau at odds with, 4. 447
Bernis disputes with Mme de Pompadour about, 21. 263n
Broglie's approach awaited by, 38. 95n
———'s forces blame defeat on, 21. 519
Brunswick threatened by, 21. 226n
Cagliostro said to have cured, 33. 507n
Castries, friend of, 4. 341
Condé's reconciliation with Louis XV negotiated by, 5. 296
Contades to be joined by, 21. 227n
Conway commands advance guard opposing, 38. 84n
defeat of: 9. 379, 21. 153, 515; would vindicate Broglie, 22. 50–1
detained until Contades defeats P. Ferdinand, 21. 254
England may be invaded by, 35. 90
English fleet thought by, too weak to fight, 21. 358n
English troops must join Isenburg to oppose, 37. 555
entrée, Dauphin's, given to, 4. 444
entrenches himself instead of attacking, 38. 101
epigram on, 21. 178
Estrées and Broglie compared with, 22. 47
Ferdinand, P., and Conway defeat, at Kirch Denckern, 38. 105
Ferdinand, P., defeats, 9. 379, 22. 46n
——— may be overcome by army of, 21. 229
——— must be dislodged by, or retreat will be necessary, 22. 50
fête given by, 4. 159, 7. 457
Frederick II allows P. Henry to permit Hanover's invasion by, 21. 227n
——— defeats, at Rossbach, 21. 153
——— had expected to outwit, 21. 136–7
French and German army in Thuringia commanded by, 21. 137n

German warfare of, 5. 303–4
Granby's army cannonaded by that of, 22. 86
HW dreads name of, 35. 308
HW grateful to, for Kirch Denckern defeat, 38. 112
HW jokes about, 9. 378
HW mentions, 21. 168
Hanover invaded by, after defeating Hessians, 21. 226–7
——— may be taken by, 21. 226n, 251, 30. 146
Hesse-Cassel invaded by, 21. 226n, 229
Isenburg and Oberg defeated by, 21. 251
Isenburg defeated by, 37. 554
Isenburg observes, at Göttingen and pursues him to the Eder, 21. 254n
Karl Wilhelm Ferdinand expected to fight, 9. 377
Louis XV asks, to dismiss Mme de Pompadour after Damiens's attempt, 21. 56n
Lutterberg victory of, 40. 144
Maillebois favoured by, 6. 323
Mazarin, Duchesse de, learns news from, 5. 161
mistress of, 4. 256, 23. 322
newspaper mentions, 4. 64n
Richelieu must aid, 21. 158
——'s army an aid to tactics of, 21. 146
St-Ouen château of, 3. 122
social relations of, in Paris, 3. 13, 4. 288, 6. 156
verses on, 5. 303–4, 9 254

Rohan, Charles-Louis-Gaspard de (1765–1843), Prince de Rohan-Rochefort:
engagement and marriage of, 7. 456

Rohan, Eugène-Hercule-Camille de (1737–after 1791), called P. Camille de Rohan-Rochefort:
Leopold invited by, to supper and illumination at Leghorn, 22. 556
Pinto de Fonseca sends, with galleys, to Leopold II, 22. 556

Rohan, François de (1631–1712), Prince de Soubise:
slippers lent by, 7. 357
wife of, 7. 283n

Rohan, Henri-Louis-Marie de (1745–1808), styled Prince de Guémenée:
biographical information about, corrected, 43. 103, 355
flees France because of swindling, 25. 604
Florence lately visited by, 25. 313
Rohan, Cardinal, related to, 42. 148–9
uncle's friendship with Charlotte Stuart described by, 25. 513

Rohan, Henri-Louis-Mériadec de (1745–1802), Prince de Guémenée:
bankruptcy of, 33. 366, 367
Lauzun's bargain with, 7. 32–3
'Madame' dances with, 7. 343n

Rohan, Jules-Hercule-Mériadec de (1726–1800), Prince de Guémenée:
bankruptcy of, 33. 471n

biographical information about, corrected, 43. 357

horn-players in service of, 33. 471n

Rohan, Louis de (1598–1667), Prince de Guéménée:
(?) witticism by, on wife's Jewish caller, 33. 367

Rohan, Louis-Armand-Constantin (1731–94), Chevalier de; Prince de Montbazon:
Townshend told by, at Stanley's, of Rochefort's defence, 37. 545

Rohan, Louis-René-Édouard (1734–1803). See Rohan-Guéménée, Louis-René-Édouard

Rohan, Marie de (1600–79), m. 1 (1617) Duc de Luynes; m. 2 (1622) Claude de Lorraine, Duc de Chevreuse:
daughter of, 42. 236
poem on swimming by, across Thames, 42. 235, 238
print of, 1. 183
swims across Thames, 15. 265–6

Rohan-Chabot, Duchesse de. See Crussol, Émilie de (1732–91); La Rochefoucauld, Élisabeth-Louise de (1740–86)

Rohan-Chabot, Alexandrine-Charlotte-Sophie de (1763–1839), m. 1 (1780) Louis-Alexandre, Duc de la Rochefoucauld; m. 2 (1810) Boniface-Louis-André, Comte de Castellane:
husband of, murdered before her eyes, 15. 220
marriage of, 7. 447
social relations of, with Mme du Deffand, 7. 447

Rohan-Chabot, Anne-Julie de (1648–1709), m. (1663) François de Rohan, Prince de Soubise:
emerald earrings of, a signal to Louis XIV that husband is away, 43. 106
husband's slippers borrowed by, to visit Louis XIV, 7. 357
(?) portrait of, 7. 283
Sévigné, Mme de, calls, 'bonne femme,' 7. 357

Rohan-Chabot, Guy-Auguste de (1683–1760), Comte de Chabot:
marriage of, 18. 429–30
widow of, 3. 38n, 301n, 10. 172n

Rohan-Chabot, Louis-Antoine-Auguste de (1733–1807), Comte and (1775) Duc de Chabot; Duc de Rohan, 1791:
Chanteloup visited by, 5. 95
Châtillon visited by, 7. 331
Du Deffand, Mme, has, at her chaise longue, 39. 271
Granby and Conway to cut off the army corps of, 21. 549n
recalled by relative's death, 5. 95
sister of, 22. 341–2n
social relations of, in Paris, see index entries ante 8. 492
wife of, 4. 318n

Rohan-Chabot, Louis-Marie-Bretagne-Dominique de (1710–1801), Duc de Rohan:
attends meeting of parliament of Paris, 8. 172

brother of, 3. 301n
protests illegal parliament, 5. 61
social relations of, with Lady Mary Chabot, 7. 272
wife of, 4. 265n

Rohan-Chabot, Marie-Charles-Rosalie de (1740–1813), Vicomte de Chabot, later Comte de Jarnac:
Du Deffand, Mme, to send parcels by, 6. 496, 498
HW's attentions to, 6. 452
model for letter to Orléans sent to, 8. 183
social relations of, in Paris, 4. 196, 6. 268, 7. 303
SH visited by, 12. 247, 249
wife's migraine keeps, from SH dinner, 32. 357

Rohan-Chabot, Marie-Sylvie de (1729–1807), m. 1 (1749) Jean-Baptiste-Louis de Clermont d'Amboise, Marquis de Renel; m. 2 (1764) Charles-Just de Beauvau, Prince de Beauvau:
Aiguillon, Duchesse d', shocks, by countenancing Mme du Barry, 5. 116
always arrives late, 3. 75
Bayeux to be visited by, 7. 68
Beauvau endangered by imprudence of, 5. 47–8, 118, 138, 169
——'s relations with, 3. 47, 245, 6. 417
(?) Besenval occupies theatre box of, 7. 344
Broglie avoided by, 5. 363, 374
——'s camp visited by, 7. 72
Caraccciolo's friendship with: 5. 232, 311, 381; cools, 6. 288
Chanteloup to be visited by, 5. 1, 32, 256, 380, 432, 6. 212, 214
—— visited by, 4. 464, 469, 5. 37, 48, 264, 338, 6. 3, 8
Choiseul, Duc and Duchesse de, visited in exile by, 5. 30, 32, 48 (see also entries above)
Choiseul, Duc de, braves Mme du Barry to please, 23. 264
——— influenced by, 4. 372, 421
——'s violence against Mme du Barry incited by, 23. 144
Choiseul, Duchesse de, could do without, 4. 446, 5. 338
Choiseuls to be visited by, at Chanteloup, 41. 197
Cholmondeley, Mrs, avoids, 4. 461
——— liked by, 4. 279–80
Compiègne visited by, 3. 319
Conway and Cts of Ailesbury see, in Paris, 39. 218
Craufurd's relations with, 6. 487–8, 490
desire of, for popularity, 3. 47
dominating, 3. 245, 4. 421, 6. 417
Du Barry, Comtesse, hated by, 5. 63, 116
——— wagered on by, 4. 196, 203–4
Du Deffand, Mme, considers going to, for news, 4. 458
——— cordially treated by, 41. 4

[Rohan-Chabot, Marie-Sylvie de, *continued*]
—— has, at her chaise longue, 39. 271
——'s correspondence with, 3. 127, 356, 4. 195, 5. 90, 238–9, 7. 458
——'s opinion of, 3. 59, 173, 182n, 225, 245, 4. 109, 256, 421, 446, 5. 48, 50, 63, 118, 148–9, 6. 308
——'s quarrel with Mme de Forcalquier known to, 4. 391
——'s relations with, 3. 368, 369, 4. 195, 196, 256, 491, 5. 353, 6. 261, 7. 102
——'s youthfulness complimented by, 5. 204
—— wagers with, over Mme du Barry, 4. 196, 203–4
'Éve,' 5. 138–9
Fontainebleau visited by, 5. 120, 123, 137, 6. 221, 224, 232, 368
Formont adored by, 3. 29
Gibbon's opinion of, 8. 90
gold pigeon sent by, to Mme de Gramont at Pentecost, 5. 284n
Gramont, Mme de, friend of, 41. 192–3
—— visited by, at Chanteloup, 4. 464, 469
HW admired by, 3. 29, 368
HW occupies theatre box of, 7. 344
HW prefers society of, to convent life, 6. 44
HW's dispute with Craufurd remembered by, 7. 36
HW's extraordinary conversation with, 7. 341
HW's gift to, of: Gramont's memoirs, 5. 304; pineapple preserves, 6. 368, 7. 417; salt-cellars, 3. 83n, 118, 136, 7. 416
HW thanked by: 6. 452; for pineapple confections, 41. 331
HW to receive barley sugar from, 6. 368
HW to receive book from, 7. 28, 31, 36, 37
HW to send green plums to, 7. 417
HW to thank, 7. 32, 39
health of, 4. 195, 253, 5. 49, 6. 8, 11, 15–16, 7. 186, 444
Hénin's marriage displeases, 3. 123, 127
hostess in absence of Duchesse de Gramont, 4. 195
husband of, 3. 107n, 4. 193n
in mourning for mother-in-law, 4. 193, 195
kingdom upset by, 5. 63
La Marck, Comtesse de, exchanges houses with, 6. 397
Languedoc visited by, 4. 341
La Tuilerie visited by, 7. 345
leaves Paris, 7. 449
Le Boulingrin exchanged by, for Le Val, 6. 397
Le Val occupied by, 7. 176, 186, 239, 429, 446
Lorraine trip of, postponed, 4. 253
—— visited by, 5. 296, 403
Louis XV defied by, 39. 143
Luxembourg, Mme de, hates, and is hated by her, 3. 173, 182n
Marly visited by, 4. 447
marriage of, 22. 342n
midnight Mass to be attended by, 5. 159

Mirepoix, Mme de, avoided by, 5. 363
—— hates and is hated by, 3. 173, 182n, 323, 4. 256n, 298, 5. 105, 269, 353, 6. 27, 261, 23. 144, 28. 290
—— reconciled with, 6. 59, 60
Misanthrope, Le, acted by, 7. 351
Montpellier visited by, 3. 186, 4. 310
(?) Mun occupies theatre box of, 7. 344
Orléans, Duc d', visited by, 5. 269
Paris to be visited by, 3. 225, 4. 17, 341, 5. 412, 6. 232, 234, 358, 363, 467, 470
—— visited by, 3. 225, 237, 240, 354, 6. 11, 365, 472, 493
Poix, Princesse de, visits, at Marly, 4. 447
Pont-de-Veyle given message by, for Mme du Deffand, 4. 195
'portrait' of, by Duchesse de Chabot, 22. 89–91
Raincy visited by, 5. 269
Roissy to be visited by, 6. 209
St-Lambert's patron, 4. 216–17
Ségur, Comtesse de, occupies theatre box of, 7. 344
self-laudatory anecdotes told by, 5. 323
Sévigné letters discussed by, 5. 301
social relations of, in Paris, *see index entries ante* 8. 493
tea ordered by, from Hon. T. Walpole, 7. 233, 234
to leave Paris, 6. 270, 272, 281, 419
Tronchin, physician to, 3. 114
(?) Usson, Comtesse d', occupies theatre box of, 7. 344
Valentinois, Comtesse de, avoided by, 5. 363
Versailles visited by, 4. 404, 5. 210, 225
Villers-Cotterêts visited by, 3. 114, 123
Walpole, Hon. Thomas, to bring locks to, from England, 36. 168, 169
York, D. of, has misunderstanding about, 3. 333
Rohan family:
portraits of early members of, 7. 283
should not suffer for Cardinal de Rohan's folly, 25. 654
Rohan-Guéménée, Charlotte-Louise de (1722–86), m. (1737) Vittorio Filippo Ferrero di Biella, Principe di Masserano:
at home but twice a week, 31. 57
attachment of, to Seilern, 32. 20
Castille's social relations with, 6. 438
Coke, Lady Mary, has social relations with, 31. 133
HW's social relations with, 7. 343, 347, 353, 414, 31. 133
HW's sympathy for, 32. 20
husband guesses, to be oldest guest at Anne Pitt's ball, 38. 476
Powis House visited by, with son, 38. 399n
Rohan-Guéménée, Charlotte-Victoire-Josèphe-Henriette (1761–71), Princesse de:
(?) ball in honour of Dauphin's marriage attended by, 4. 409, 410

Rohan-Guéménée, Ferdinand-Maximilien-Mé-
riadec de (1738–1813), Abp of Bordeaux
1770–81, of Cambrai 1781–1801:
Stuart, Charlotte, often visits, 25. 513
Rohan-Guéménée, Louis-René-Édouard (1734–
1803), Cardinal-Prince de; Bp coadjutor of
Strasbourg; French ambassador to Austria;
'Cardinal de Guéménée':
abandoned by bishops and clergy, 33. 508
Braschi Onesti carries cardinal's hat to, 24.
470n
conversation about, 25. 639, 31. 242
England entertained by stories of Cagliostro
and, 36. 236
Florence visited by, 24. 113n
grand aumônier, 6. 404, 410, 7. 50
HW not acquainted with, 42. 148
implicated in Diamond Necklace affair, 33.
494, 496–7
imprisoned in Bastille for forging Marie-Antoinette's signature to get diamonds, 25. 603
insufficiently punished, 25. 654
Joseph II confers with, perhaps about Corsica, 24. 108n
—— will be pleased to hear of imprisonment
of, 42. 148
made cardinal, 7. 50
name of, corrected, 43. 357
Pius VI and cardinals censure, for preferring
French tribunal to that of a consistory, 25.
658
procès of, against Mme de la Motte, 11. 4n
recent ambassador to Vienna, 6. 157n
released after Diamond Necklace affair, 25.
653n
social relations of, in Paris, 5. 83, 6. 156–7,
7. 284, 294, 299, 301
spoken of, for ambassador to Vienna, 5. 83
very gallant, 25. 603
Rohan-Guéménée, Marie-Louise-Joséphine de
(1765–1839), m. (1780) Charles-Louis-Gaspard de Rohan, Prince de Rohan-Rochefort:
engagement and marriage of, 7. 456
Rohan-Montauban, Louise-Julie-Constance de
(1734–1815), m. (1748) Charles-Louis de Lorraine, Comte de Brionne:
beauty of: 14. 156, 31. 47–8; Conway should
see remains of, 39. 215
bust of, 7. 294
Castries and Choiseul reconciled by, 4. 341
Castries, friend of, 4. 341
Chanteloup to be visited by, 5. 231, 234, 7.
150
—— visited by, 5. 238, 243, 245, 363, 8. 207
Choiseul, Duc and Duchesse de, visited by,
in exile, 5. 45, 59, 169; see also entries above
Choiseul, Duc de, friend of, 4. 341, 372
—— to visit, 6. 439, 473
compensation given by, to injured priest, 7.
447
Coventry, Cts of, eclipsed by, 20. 337–8
Damas, Comtesse de, cousin of, 7. 126

Du Deffand, Mme, gives opinion of, 5. 243
entrées, grandes, given to, 4. 330
grandmother of, 37. 353
HW describes, 32. 26–7
HW hopes to meet, 31. 95
HW receives invitation from, 39. 42
health of, 31. 95
Limours, seat of, 6. 439, 473
social relations of, in Paris, 6. 62, 7. 295, 299,
301
son of, marries, 7. 92
tall, 4. 25
York, D. of, makes joke about, 7. 365
Rohan-Rochefort, Prince de. See Rohan,
Charles-Louis-Gaspard de
Rohan-Rochefort, Princesse de. See Rohan-
Guéménée, Marie-Louise-Joséphine de
Rohan-Soubise, Marie-Louise-Geneviève de
(1720–1803), m. (1736) Gaston-Jean-Bap-
tiste-Charles de Lorraine, Comte de Marsan:
Choiseul's dismissal from Swiss Guards said
to have been sought by, 5. 167
Jesuits might be restored by, 32. 266
La Borde's gifts from, 31. 80
Louis XVIII's governess, 32. 266
Marie-Josèphe will be regretted by, 3. 257
retired without pension, 32. 268
social relations of, in Paris, 7. 266, 350
'Roi de Garbe.' See under La Fontaine, Jean de
'Roi de la fève' (Twelfth Night king):
Mme du Deffand and guests draw for, 7. 293
'Roi d'Yvetot':
Nassau-Siegen called, by HW, 24. 472
Roi et le fermier, Le. See under Sedaine, Michel-
Jean
Roi fainéant; rois fainéants:
HW is, 32. 217
pensions of, 7. 354
Roi Pepin, Le. See 'Le Roi Pepin'
Roissy, Anne-Josèphe-Michelle de (ca 1754–
75), m. (1767) Ange-Augustin-Gabriel de
Franquetot, Comte de Coigny:
affairs of, 6. 22
Chanteloup to be visited by, 6. 22
Choiseul, Duchesse de, loves, 6. 22
Roissy (France), country seat of Comte and
Comtesse de Caraman:
ball at, attended by HW and Mme du Deffand, 32. 260
Caraman, Comte de, occupies, 3. 4n, 4. 243,
256, 5. 260, 269, 404, 6. 72, 210, 7. 44, 179
—— to have occupied, 7. 150
—— to occupy, 5. 225, 231, 350, 6. 33, 49,
272, 281
Caraman, Comtesse de, occupies, 3. 4n, 4. 243,
256, 5. 260, 269, 370, 404, 413, 6. 56, 72,
210, 237, 7. 44, 179, 334, 346, 426, 453, 454,
460
—— to have occupied, 7. 150
—— to occupy, 3. 225, 231, 233, 350, 6. 33,
49, 272, 281
Du Deffand, Mme, mentions, 5. 85

[Roissy (France), *continued*]

plays acted by Caraman family at, **5.** 269

supper at, **34.** 77–8

visitors to: Beauvau, Princesse de, **6.** 210; Boisgelin, Comtesse de, **6.** 84, 86, 209, **7.** 455; Boufflers, Comtesse de, **6.** 86; Cambis, Vicomtesse de, **6.** 211, 212, 462, 474, 482, 484, 485, **7.** 65, 68, 75, 150, 176, 334; Caraman, Abbé de, **7.** 346; Churchills, **7.** 334; Crewe, Mrs, **5.** 367; Du Deffand, Mme, **4.** 83, **5.** 81, 269, 370, 413, 413–14, **6.** 56, 72, 80, 81, 83, 84, 86, 198, 209, 210, 212, 214, 215, 217, 273, **7.** 54, 66, 334, 346; Gérente, Abbé de, **7.** 346; Gibbon, **6.** 485; Greville, Mrs, **5.** 367; HW, **5.** 82, **7.** 334, 346; La Fare, Comte and Comtesse de, **6.** 196; La Salle, **7.** 346; La Vallière, Duchesse de, **7.** 426; Mirepoix, Bp of, **7.** 346; Mirepoix, Mme de, **6.** 56, 81, 84, 86, **7.** 66, 454, 460; St-Antoine, Abbess of, **7.** 346; Shuvalov, **6.** 72; Shuvalov, Comte and Comtesse André, **7.** 54; Spencer, E., Cts, and Lady Georgiana, **5.** 367

Rokeby, Bn. *See* Montagu, Matthew (1762–1831); Robinson, Richard (ca 1708–94)

Rokeby, Lady. *See* Darcy, Dorothy

Rokeby, Yorks:

Robinson of, **9.** 132n, 310n, **24.** 282n

Roland. See under Piccinni, Niccolò; Quinault, Philippe

Roland, —— (d. 1752), son of Conte Lorenzi: death of, **20.** 306

Roland, ——, tailor:

Du Deffand, Mme, has receipt from, **8.** 41

Roland, Mme, wine-dealer of Reims:

correspondent of, in Paris, **10.** 246

Dessain knows, **10.** 183

English literary tastes of, gratified by HW, Montagu, and others, **10.** 170, 172, 174, 177, 180, 182, 183, 187, 188, 197, 200, 251

friends of, learn English to read HW's books, **10.** 251

HW's agency in Montagu's correspondence with, **10.** 143, 145, 183, 193, 207, 208, 226, 246, 248, 250, 261, 263

HW's attempts to meet, in Paris, **10.** 201–2, 205, 207, 211

HW's books requested and received by, **7.** 416, **10.** 197, 200, 226, 251

HW's correspondence with, **7.** 386

HW's friendship with Montagu forgotten by, **10.** 198

HW's social relations with, **7.** 311

HW to miss youthful bloom of, **10.** 202

HW to receive compliments of, **10.** 302

Montagu, George, angry with, for neglect of HW, **10.** 210

—— appreciates HW's kindness to, **10.** 206

—— hopes that HW will see, **10.** 200

——'s correspondence with, **10.** *143*, 193–4, 207, 226, 246, 248, 251, 261, 263, 302

—— sends letter from, to HW, **10.** 226

—— sent by, plan of La Malle, **10.** 193, 196

—— to give silver casket to, through HW, **10.** 246–8, 250, 251

Paris may dazzle, **10.** 207–8, 210

—— to be visited by, **10.** 188, 200

Scottish books only have been read by, **10.** 182

toilette of, **10.** 246

Versailles visited by, **10.** 211

wine for Grosvenor from, **10.** 143

Roland, Francesco Orlando (1754–1823): birth of, **20.** 437

Roland, Jacques (d. 1784), Chevalier de Lorenzi:

Beauclerk asks about, **41.** 310

blunders, **41.** 7

boastfulness of, **20.** 584

brother has not heard from, **22.** 369

brother's correspondence with, **20.** 98, **22.** 362

brother's dismissal a great surprise to, **22.** 362

brother told by: of false rumour of promotion, **22.** 356; of HW's civilities, **20.** 92

Chute told by, of plan to land at Bristol, **20.** 114

costume of, a frock in the morning, **20.** 285

England praised by, **20.** 285

—— to be visited by, with Mirepoix, **20.** 67, 68

English events will be described by, in letters, **20.** 100

Florence seldom visited by, **20.** 68

Florence visited by, **22.** 557

(?) HW accompanied by, at Paris, **1.** 105

HW entertains, at SH, **1.** 105n, **20.** 89

HW has not met, **20.** 67, 68

HW met, in Florence, **20.** 87

HW's civilities to, pleasing, **20.** 92, 98

HW's letters should not be entrusted to, **22.** 362

HW's letter to Mann enclosed by, to brother, **22.** 358

HW to entertain, at SH, **20.** 87

HW told by: about dispute between French and Italian postmasters, **22.** 358; that letters should be franked to Genoa, **22.** 347

health of, gout, **22.** 557

iricisms of, **20.** 106–7, 117

long in French service, **20.** 67, 68

Louis XV thought by, not to be separated from Mme de Pompadour, **20.** 542

Mann asked by, to give HW his compliments, **22.** 557

—— called on by, in Florence, **20.** 584

—— meets, at Stormont's, **20.** 285

Mirepoix visited by, at Putney, **20.** 87

Mirepoix, Mme de, hears absurd comments by, on sapphire and Lincoln's gesse, **20.** 106–7

Mirepoix family amused by absurdities of, **20.** 106

Paris visited by, **20.** 542

Schutz mistaken by, for Chute, **20.** 89–90

social relations of, in Paris, *see index entries ante* **8.** 494

venison compared by, to beef, **20.** 89

Yarmouth, Cts of, and Lady Middlesex subjects of inquiry by, **20.** 96–7

Roland, Mme Jean-Marie. *See* Phlipon, Manon-Jeanne

Roland, Luigi *or* Louis (d. 1766), Conte Lorenzi; French minister to Tuscany:

Agdollo advised by, **17.** 149

allowance to, for ball, **20.** 276

Amelot's correspondence with, **18.** 415

ball to be given by, for D. of Burgundy's birth, **20.** 276

ball would have been given by, if Dauphiness had had a son, **20.** 191–2

Bavarian-French alliance may embroil, **17.** 119

Botta and Vienna Court reprimand, for embroiling them about Leghorn, **21.** 475

Botta called on by, with book on Klosterzeven convention, **21.** 235

—— criticizes, for attentions to Wilkes, **22.** 282

—— exasperated by complaints of, **21.** 275n

—— may be informed by, of English secret expedition, **21.** 446

——'s circular letter to, on Peter III's overthrow, **22.** 63

bread given by, to Florentine poor, **19.** 14

brother astonished at dismissal of, **22.** 362

brother has not written to, **22.** 369

brother of, 1. 105n, **22.** 347n

brother of, to go to England, **20.** 67, 68

brother's correspondence with, **20.** 98, **22.** 362

brother sends HW's letter through, to Mann, **22.** 358

brother tells false rumour to, of increased rank and salary, **22.** 356

Cartagena victory contradicted by news of, from Barcelona, **21.** 193

Chauvelin tells, of Curzay's arrest, **20.** 354

Chavigny assures, that Louisbourg will be saved, **21.** 234–5

Choiseul may be ashamed of his treatment of, **22.** 371

—— notifies that he must yield post to a Frenchman, **22.** 346, 351

Chute's dispute with, over yellow and green colours for his chariot, **21.** 501

—— to receive compliments of, **20.** 89

clothes of, in bad taste though said to come from Paris, **21.** 501

Craon, Princesse de, takes, through Corso in phaeton, **17.** 83

crime of degraded army officers guessed by, **21.** 383

Curzay's correspondence with, **20.** 277

daughter's illness was to have been described by, to La Condamine, **22.** 153

Dauphin's marriage celebrated by, with Te Deum instead of ball, **19.** 14

——'s wedding to be celebrated by, **18.** 559

death of, **22.** 430

Dettingen slain estimated by, **18.** 269

dispatches of, discuss the whole state of Europe, **21.** 475

Elizabeth Christina's requiem avoided by, out of jealousy of Mann's rank, **20.** 227

English damage to French flat-bottomed boats denied by, **21.** 309

English victory announced by, **21.** 356

Éon's book desired by, **22.** 230

Feroni, Mme, entertains, **17.** 317

Fleury sent cedrati by, **17.** 317

Florentine baptisms and weddings the greatest events for, **20.** 92

Florentine by birth, but employed by France, **18.** 466

Florentine Regency asked by, whether he should celebrate Dauphin's wedding or mourn for Madame Royale, **19.** 14

France orders, to protest to Tuscany against hospitality to English ships, **21.** 36n

——'s treatment of, considered ungrateful by Maria Louisa, **22.** 430

Francis I's demand for Electress's jewels told to, **17.** 238

franking of mail at Genoa demanded by, **22.** 347

French Court corresponds heavily with, **21.** 356

French Court may order, into mourning, **18.** 175

French letters tell, that Dunkirk will not be demolished, **22.** 118

Frenchman of higher rank to replace, at Florence, **39.** 24

Frenchmen presented by, to Mann at assembly, **20.** 489

French minister at Florence, though a Florentine, **21.** 362n

'great abbé at Rome' corresponds with, **17.** 206–7

Grotius tortured by, to draw up remonstrances, **21.** 274–5

HW grieved by Mann's enmity with, **21.** 362

HW liked by, **17.** 326

HW refuses to be introduced by, to La Condamine, **22.** 149, 151

HW sorry for, **22.** 440

HW's regard for, **20.** 87

HW thanked by, for civilities to brother, **20.** 92, 98

HW to receive compliments of, **22.** 369

Havana's capture not expected by, **22.** 88–9

health of, weak constitution and lame leg, **20.** 192

house of, too small for festino, **18.** 559

La Condamine's letter from, forwarded by Mann, **22.** 149

Lally said by, to be Irish, **21.** 523

lame, **17.** 119, 206, 326, **20.** 192, **21.** 274

letters from Paris encourage, **22.** 370–1

low credentials of, exclude him from chambellan's ante-chamber, **22.** 346

Maillebois informs, of Young Pretender's landing, **19.** 87

[Roland, Luigi *or* Louis, *continued*]
——'s correspondence with, 19. 334
manifesto will probably be sent by, on capture of English brig, 21. 334
Mann accused by, of justifying English privateers, 21. 356
—— called on by, 22. 369
—— does not talk to, 18. 484–5
—— hears from: about travelling time from Paris, 22. 352; that Spaniards may take Lombardy and exchange it for Tuscany, 17. 206
—— hears of Richecourt from, 17. 98
—— hears story from, of French abbé's irregular baptism, 17. 62
—— hears Viennese gossip from, 17. 325–6
—— not allowed to enter house of, 20. 584
—— not supposed to speak to, except at accidental meetings, 18. 559
——'s 'civil whisper' with, 18. 466
——'s conferences with Botta invented by, 21. 356
—— sends letter through, 17. 422
——'s friendship with: cooled by political disputes, 18. 438; will be interrupted by war, 20. 485
——'s regard for, 20. 67
——'s trick on Niccolini pleases, 18. 372
—— told by, of baronetcy and of Hertford's embassy, 20. 467
—— warned by, against Richecourt, 18. 362
—— whispers with, about Toussaint's intrigues, 20. 98
—— will not tell, of brother's iricisms, 20. 117
marriage of, to take place, 20. 191–2
matrimonial prospects of, amuse HW, 20. 197
ministerial gazette of, announces d'Éon's new book, 22. 272
Modena, Ds of, meets, at dinner, 18. 228
mourning for Electress prescribed to, by French Court, 18. 206
'my little lame brother,' 22. 118
never out of Tuscany, 20. 96
Newfoundland's capture the boast of, 22. 69
Orford, Cts of, clears out Florentine house for, 19. 385
—— hoped by, to pay him rent, 19. 238
—— permitted by, to retain house, 19. 238
passport for France may be granted through, to Thomas Pitt, 21. 524
pension of: disappointing, 22. 351, 356, 360; may be raised, 22. 370–1; vaguely promised, 22. 346
permission asked by, to attend meeting of kings at Lyon, 21. 283
Praslin tells, of dismissal, 22. 356
Pucci probably writes to, of Mann's baronetcy, 20. 467
Quebec's possible recapture stressed by, 21. 421
recalled from Florence, 39. 23–4

Regency urged by, to expel English fleet from Leghorn, 21. 274
Riccardi entertains, 17. 147
Richecourt's dispute with, over citizenship of French at Leghorn, 20. 266–7
—— shown by, Maillebois's letter to him, 19. 86–7
—— tries to console, for child's death, 20. 306
St-Aignan gives presents to, 17. 95–6
secretary of, replaced, 17. 157
son of: born, 20. 437; dies, 20. 306
successor of, may have new title, 22. 346, 355–6
Te Deum given by, for Dauphin's wedding, 19. 14
Tencin's correspondence with, 17. 62, (?) 206–7
wax torches in three windows of, 19. 14
Wilkes brings letters of recommendation to, from Paris, 22. 282
will be *ministre de famille* at Leopold's wedding, 22. 319
Roland. *See also* Rolland
[?Roland de] Lorenzi, Luisa Elisabetta, m. Senatore Conte Cavalieri Balì Federigo Barbolani: smallpox attack of, after inoculation, 22. 153
Role; Roles. *See* Rolle
Rolfe, Edmund, sr:
Walpole, Sir Robert, has, as election agent, 17. 166n
Rolfe, Edmund, jr (1738–1817); of Heacham, Norfolk:
executor to 3d E. of Orford, 42. 344
Mackreth's correspondence with, 42. 344n
Roll, MS:
Lodge discovers, with portrait of Richard III, 42. 285
Rous's, *see under* Rous
Roll; rolls, hot:
English supposed by Maréchale de Villars to like, 22. 105, 113
for breakfast, 30. 132n
HW serves, at SH party, 10. 69
poultry to get, due to embargo, 35. 320
Rolla, Nicolò:
uprising in Genoa led by, 19. 343n
Rolland de Challerange, Jean-François (d. 1786):
(?) attends session of parliament of Paris, 8. 171–3
Rolland de Juvigny, Charles:
(?) attends session of parliament of Paris, 8. 171–3
Rolle, Lady Arabella. *See* Clinton, Lady Arabella
Rolle, Rev. Edward (ca 1705–91), divine and poet:
'ethic epistles' by, 34. 35n
Gray dismisses poems by, 14. 37
Rolle, Henry (1708–50), cr. (1748) Bn Rolle; M.P.:
peerage granted to, 19. 419

Rolle, John, of Shipwick:

Rolle, Samuel, leaves reversion of estates to, **20.** 424n

Rolle, John (? 1714–70). *See* Rolle Walter, John

Rolle, John (1756–1842), M.P.; cr (1796) Bn Rolle:

Burke asked by, about Powell and Bembridge, **25.** 408n

Parliamentary motion by, censuring Pigot, **25.** 278n

titular hero of *Rolliad*, **15.** *202*

Rolle, Margaret (1709–81), m. 1 (1724) Robert Walpole, cr. (1723) Bn Walpole; 2d E. of Orford, 1745; m. 2 (1751) Hon. Sewallis Shirley; Bns Clinton, s.j., 1760:

abbé-secretary of, gets maid with child, **19.** 224, 238

absence of, will not help son, **32.** 123

academy of savants to be collected by, **20.** 476

affairs closely tended by, **20.** 433

affairs of, Sharpe reports to Mozzi about, **25.** 144

agent of, insists on sale of E. of Orford's horses, **32.** 134

Aix visited by, **23.** 155, 161

Aix youths preferred by, to Neapolitans, **35.** 410

Albani answers letter of, announcing her trip to England, **19.** 51

allowance of: may be doubled, **19.** 210; rumoured to be increased, **18.** 122; to be demanded, **19.** 104

altered since fall from horse, **18.** 364

amorousness of: **9.** 144; HW jokes about, **18.** 306

ancestry of, **25.** 501n

Andreasi discusses Newton and Voltaire with, **18.** 555

appearance of, **15.** 324–5, **19.** 224, **23.** 230, **24.** 255, 312, 318, 374

appears only at Richecourt's house, **18.** 122

Ashburton borough assigned by, to HW's care, **23.** 548

Atri, Duchesse d', talks with, **25.** 130

attendants forbidden by, to write to Mann, **24.** 467

attentive to small expenses, **25.** 129

Banks, Margaret, thanked by, with card, after conversation at opera, **19.** 230

(?) Barbarigo's affair with, **17.** 196

Berkeley Sq. house taken by, **19.** 42n

(?) Berry, Mary, misidentifies, **12.** 205n

Blair's talk with, **19.** 99, 119

Borghese, Principessa, friend of, **17.** 12n

boroughs lost by, from not trusting HW, **24.** 308

boroughs of, should have been more completely entrusted to her agents, **24.** 67

Buondelmonti receives letter from, from The Hague, **19.** 101

—— talks sentiments with, **13.** 231

burial of, **2.** 260, **25.** 114, 195

Busoni invests money for, in French funds, **25.** 113

bust of, done by sculptor for Mozzi, **25.** 504

Caffarelli's affair with, **17.** 448

Calais twice visited by, but she returns to Paris, **23.** 141, 155, 218, **25.** 641

Callington borough brought into Walpole family by, **9.** 51n, **13.** 11n

Callington borough promised by, to Sir William Hamilton, **23.** 548, 557, **24.** 52

Callington borough subject of correspondence by, with HW, **23.** 545–6, 547, 548

Callington borough under influence of, **19.** 414n, **41.** 376

Camden's opinion sought in affairs of, **25.** 230, 440

Carder, Mrs, brought by, from England, **25.** 151, 169

—— poorly recompensed by, in will, **25.** 122

Carteret expected by, to vex Sir Robert Walpole, **17.** 461

——'s conversation with, **17.** 441

——'s coolness puts off English journey of, **18.** 4

—— tells Theodore of Corsica about application of, **18.** 194

'case' of, containing claims on son, probably drawn up by Sharpe, **25.** 162

cases of, searched by order of Regency council, **17.** 224–5, 283

chambermaid of, **19.** 224, 238

character and appearance of, **15.** 324–5

Chesterfield receives letter from, **19.** 60–1

—— ridicules mistakes in letter of, to him, **19.** 70

—— unable and unwilling to aid, **17.** 409

—— would never satisfy, **20.** 439

(?) Chute fears that his lawyer may be seen by, **35.** 24–5

claim of, on money arising from sale of Pall Mall house, **25.** 162–3

Clinton an ancestor of, **25.** 298n

Clinton, Bns, in her own right, **25.** 195

Clinton barony improperly represented on proposed monument to, **25.** 226–7

Clinton barony inherited by, **1.** 342, **18.** 126, 143n, **21.** 385, **25.** 151, 157

Clinton barony may be secured by, through Chesterfield, **17.** 360–1, 367, 389–90, 406

Clinton portrait brought by, from England, **25.** 240

coachman robs, **19.** 88

coach ordered by, to be made, **19.** 59

Cocchi contradicts, about HW, **17.** 448

—— rebuked by, for not congratulating her on Sir Robert Walpole's retirement, **17.** 371

——'s defence of Sir Robert Walpole may offend, **18.** 133

Compagni and Libri approached by, for credit in England, **17.** 422, 461

complexion blistered by, in Richecourt's absence, **19.** 31

[Rolle, Margaret, *continued*]

Conti, Abbate, to rent apartment to, 17. 217

cook of, 18. 4

Cork, Cts of, to dine with, 20. 480

country house in England to be visited by, after trip to Wanstead House, 23. 120

courier accompanies, 19. 48

Court of Chancery would not entrust son to, unless she lived in England, 23. 481, 510

Cox, courier to, 18. 516

——'s difficulties with, do not surprise HW, 18. 505–6

—— sent by HW with papers for, 18. 486

Craon invites, only on most public occasions, 17. 462

Craon family stories exhumed by, 17. 327

Craon tells Mann that Francis I would expel, from Florence if Sir Robert Walpole wished it, 17. 326

Crew detained by, 18. 272

Cumberland, D. of, angers, by German campaign, 21. 96

Dashwood forces wife to consort with, 19. 224

death certificate of, 43. 287, 288

death of, at Pisa: 2. 257, 25. 113–14, 120–1, 195, 29. 106; benefits her son, 25. 125–6; may restore her son's fortunes, 36. 99; might have prevented sale of Houghton collection, 25. 108, 121; perhaps reported by courier, 25. 121; premature report of, justified by event, 25. 129; rumoured in England, 25. 119, 120–1; wished by Mann and Chute, 17. 432

Declaration of, accompanying will: 43. 288; shows 'extensive intention' in favour of Mozzi, 25. 169

deeds may have been left by, with elder Sharpe, 25. 160

Del Monte's affair with, 17. 448

Denbigh, Cts of, to be visited by, 19. 61

Devonshire estates of, subject of inquiries, 25. 414

Devonshire estate visited by, 25. 224

(?) Diharce writes to, that she will soon see him in Italy, 20. 421

dined out shortly before her death, 25. 129

donation to poor of the parish refused by, when making her will, 43. 289

dress of, English, 19. 111

education of, poor, 25. 121

effects of, at Florence and Naples, 25. 113, 114

elbow broken by, in fall from horse, 18. 314

Electress's funeral attended by, 18. 173

England can spare, 35. 418

—— disgusts, 19. 210

—— reached by, 19. 104

——'s revenues may satisfy spite of, 19. 118–19

—— to be visited by: 17. 167, 422, 426, 441, 19. 54, 60, 23. 2, 218; for two months, 24. 2, 121; in spring, 20. 342, 23. 152, 155, 161; to settle her affairs, 23. 113

—— visited by, with kisses and embraces, 23. 224

English agents' letters disregarded by, 25. 129

English journey repugnant to, 23. 464, 468, 472, 481, 486, 488, 493

English might forget son's alienation from, 25. 396

English news dispensed by, 17. 406

English politics meddled in by, 19. 224

English relations with Tuscany might be guided by, through Chesterfield, 17. 387

English reputation at Florence lowered by, 18. 309

English servants not brought by, to England, 19. 61

English trip of, may be put off, 17. 460–1

English visit of: deferred, 23. 135, 141, 155, 218, 25. 641; would be unwise, 19. 38–9

English winters dreaded by, 23. 155

entourage of, for English trip, 19. 49, 50

epitaph for, at Leghorn, to be in English, 25. 195

Essex discussed by, 18. 114

estate and jointure retained by, 20. 439

estate of: cannot be settled in Florence, 25. 128; son intends to give, to the Rolles, 25. 148, 156

estate said to have been bought by, 24. 187

estate to be reclaimed by, 17. 406, 424

exercises much, 24. 488

expects congratulations on father-in-law's retirement, 17. 371

father's estates entailed on, 20. 424n

festine attended by, to meet Richecourt, 18. 439

Fiesole to be visited by: in autumn and winter, 24. 322, 330; to see remodelled house, 24. 305

Fiesole villa (Villa Medici) of: bought, 23. 190, 463, 468; improved, 24. 190, 260; leased and then bought, 24. 190; snow confines her at, 24. 347; used for autumn and winter, 24. 322

finances of: improved (?) by Sturgis's death, 18. 217; mistaken notions concerning, 25. 130

fines on renewal of leases were paid to, instead of to son, 25. 335

Florence may not be revisited by, 19. 263, 20. 342

—— not now to be visited by, 20. 97

—— reached by, 17. 283, 24. 19, 317

—— to be left by, 19. 46

—— to be revisited by, 17. 264, 19. 59, 252, 394, 20. 392–3, 421, 476, 23. 113, 24. 9, 12

—— visited by: 23. 120, 37. 78; because of sale of her Fiesole villa, 23. 463

Florentine and Leghorn gossip about HW and, 17. 146

Florentine and Lorraine people told by, that she would return after recovering English estates, 19. 75

Florentine banker sees account of, 25. 113
Florentine half-house bought by, 24. 260
Florentine house of, Richecourt's Italian secretary lives in, 17. 224
Florentine house sought by, 23. 468
Florentine and 'Pannonian' abbés too much influenced by, 18. 557
Florentines hear from, of her intention to return, 19. 144
—— might hear London gossip from, 19. 502
forsaken by the world, 19. 502
Fortescue, William, related to, 18. 236n
fortune of, 2. 171
frailties not disguised by, 25. 122
France and Italy to be visited by, 20. 439
Franceschi's house near Pitti Palace taken by, 18. 391
France to be visited by, 23. 2
Francis I's courier escorts, 19. 50
furniture of: Gavi to have, 19. 290; listed by Mozzi, 25. 169; may be removed from Naples, 24. 467; moved to country, 19. 252; stored in Richecourt's apartment, 19. 385
Geoffrin, Mme, called on by, in Paris, 23. 141
George II barely speaks to, at Court, 19. 111
—— did not regard with any special favour in Hanover, 19. 11
—— graciously receives, in Hanover, 19. 72, 80
—— said to have been applied to by, through Hanover, 18. 194
—— 's disavowal of civility to, 19. 144
Givrecourt, Comtesse de, may supplant, in Richecourt's affections, 19. 452, 457
Gloucester, D. and Ds of, graciously receive, at Rome, 24. 164, 170, 222
Gloucester, D. of, not liked by, when he was at Florence, 24. 175
Goldsworthy, Mrs, told by, of Haddock's rumoured recall, 17. 361
Gray's Odes sent to, by post, 21. 163
HW 'amused' by, with words, 24. 311
HW amused by expectations of, on Sir Robert Walpole's death, 19. 53
HW and Sir Edward Walpole not paid their legacies after death of, 25. 315–16
HW and Sir Edward Walpole want, to look after her son, 23. 471, 476, 481, 485
HW approves of Mann's being on good terms with, 20. 490
HW became referee in dispute about estate of, only to save her honour from public courts, 25. 445
HW calls: mad, 18. 140; 'Omphale,' 20. 439
HW confirms prophecy of, about his getting Tesi a dog, 18. 350–1
HW curious about audience of, with D. of Gloucester, 24. 175
HW discusses son's boroughs with, 35. 416
HW disparaged by, 17. 448
HW does not understand politics of, 20. 510

HW explains claim of, to Clinton barony, 18. 143–4
HW fears showing prejudice against, 25. 216
HW had not met, for at least 16 years, 23. 231
HW has money paid to banker of, 23. 498
HW ill-used by, over her son's affairs, 36. 96
HW knows little of, 19. 362
HW meets: at Lady Pomfret's, 18. 364; at Florence, 19. 111; at Vcts Townshend's, twice, 19. 111; when she calls on Hollands at Holland House, 23. 229–30, 231–2
HW must have written authorization from, 23. 496, 501, 505, 510, 523
HW not concerned in business affairs of, 25. 125
HW pities son for behaviour of, 20. 439
HW pleased that Mann did not force, to discuss her son, 24. 320
HW prefers Richecourt to Mrs Richmond as spy upon, 18. 31
HW reassures Mann about, 17. 439–40
HW said to dislike Richecourt's affair with, 17. 97–8
HW's attitude towards, 23. 121, 551, 24. 316, 25. 124, 195, 445
HW scorns claim of, to jointure arrears, 23. 519
HW's correspondence with, over son, 23. 470, 472, 476, 478, 485–8, 492, 496, 505, 509–10, 512, 514–17, 519, 523, 525, 529, 531–2, 534, 537, 541, 544, 545, 548, 551, 552, 557–60, 563, 24. 52, 57, 58, 61, 66, 70, 91–2, 105, 292, 32. 121, 35. 416, 417, 36. 91, 94, 98, 99, 104, 112, 332, 333
HW's lack of confidence from, will be regretted by her, 24. 316–17
HW's motives should not be mistrusted by, 24. 91–2
HW's opinion of, 30. 93
HW's 'wife' will not run to Italy after lovers and books like, 37. 333–4
HW tells, that he will never again manage her son's affairs, 24. 53
HW tells Sharpe to tell, of her son's latest insanity, 24. 292
HW to tell schemes of, to her husband, 17. 389–90
HW to write to her husband about, 30. 95
HW wants Mann to urge, to come to England, 23. 467, 471, 472, 476–8, 481–2, 488–9
HW wants to keep her son on good terms with, 23. 557, 24. 17
HW will probably be relieved of correspondence with, 24. 57–8
HW wished by, to resume managing her son's affairs, 13. 49, 24. 305
HW writes to, through Mann, to ask favour for Boone, 24. 82, 105, 292
habits of, procrastinatory, 23. 545
Haddock's return wished by, 17. 423
Hague, The, to be first step of, on way to England, 19. 49
—— visited by, 19. 75, 101

[Rolle, Margaret, *continued*]

Hamilton, Sir William, deals with, about Callington borough, **23.** 548, 557, **24.** 52, **35.** 417

—— forwards letters by, **23.** 558, **35.** 416

Hanover left by, **19.** 92

—— receives, well, **19.** 69–70

—— visit of, suspected by Mann to be a scheme concealed by Richecourt, **19.** 97

health of: amazingly recovered, due to Fiesole air, **24.** 346–7; asthma, **20.** 433, **23.** 83, 230, **24.** 244, **25.** 112; bled, **25.** 102, 112; bled by having foot lanced, **24.** 79; blisters applied to, **25.** 113; cold, **23.** 512; convulsed and cannot swallow water, **25.** 102; cough, **24.** 467; elbow 'put out,' **18.** 314; emaciated, **25.** 112; emaciated and weak, **24.** 312, 318; erysipelas, **24.** 244, 255, **25.** 112; face frequently red, **24.** 255; fall from horse, **18.** 314, 364; fever, **24.** 312; foot injury, **23.** 464, **24.** 79; HW hears, is bad, **23.** 505, 512; HW learns nothing about, **23.** 230; habitual disorder, described by Mann, **25.** 112; heart palpitations, **25.** 102; humour in the ears, **24.** 83; in bad state, **24.** 467; indisposed, due to air of Florence, **24.** 79; inflammation in the face, **24.** 83; pale and haggard, **18.** 153; past recovery, **25.** 113; perfect, **23.** 525; quite rosy, **24.** 374; recovered, **24.** 251, 322; recovered except for cough, **24.** 487–8; relapses of usual disorder, **25.** 107; rides every morning, **23.** 512; suffocation relieved by bleeding, **25.** 112; teeth missing, **23.** 230; thighs rubbed, **18.** 153; very ill, **24.** 316; vomits, **18.** 153; well but much decayed, **24.** 330

Herrenhausen visited daily by, **19.** 80

Hesse, Ps of, receives, favourably, **19.** 80

Hesse-Cassel visited by, **19.** 70

Hoare custodian of money of, in London, **25.** 113, 114, 123, 130, 131, 143, 157, 160, 217, 335, 426

Hobart ousted by, **19.** 290

——'s friendship with, **19.** 252

Holland, Bns, called on by, **23.** 229–30

Holland visited by, **19.** 252

Houghton mortgaged to, **23.** 510

household of, starts arriving in Florence, **24.** 312

housekeeping of, **18.** 4

house next to Mozzi's to be recombined with it by, **24.** 330

house of: at Naples, **23.** 2, **35.** 410; at New Park, Richmond, **19.** 309; at Stanhoe, **18.** 249; at Venice, **19.** 50; in Florence, **17.** 224; in Florence, half-house, **24.** 260; in Florence, leased from Lorenzi, **19.** 61, 75, 238, 385; in Florence, 'little,' **17.** 71; in Florence, next to Mozzi, **24.** 322, 330; in Florence, two, **23.** 2; in London, **19.** 309, **25.** 162–3; in Via dell' Orto, Florence, **43.** 284; outside Florence, near Richecourt's, reoccupied by her, **20.** 479–80; Palazzo Franceschi, **18.**

391; recommended by Rucellai, **17.** 107; Villa Medici, *see under* Medici, Villa; Villa Salviati, **21.** 310

houses and horses at Naples to be kept for, **35.** 410

houses stripped of furniture and plate by, **25.** 144

house taken by, at Padua, **17.** 235

house to be changed by, **18.** 217

husband disliked by, **9.** 78

husband expected by, to write to her, **19.** 37

husband fees lawyers in preparation for visit from, **19.** 61

husband gives allowance to, **19.** 88, 224

husband gives in to, too much, **19.** 219

husband has substitute for, **18.** 249

husband may be forced by, to give back her estate to her, **19.** 49

husband said to have written to, **19.** 47, 49

husband's allowance to, reduced, **19.** 88

husband's death would not frighten, **20.** 233

husband separated from, **36.** 295

husband settles affairs with, **19.** 348

husband's harsh letter cherished by, **19.** 50

husband should lock up, **19.** 192

husband's intercourse with, restricted after son's birth, **19.** 203

husband's separation and negotiations with, **19.** 111, 202, 290, **20.** 547–8, 568–9

husband wants proof of infidelity of, with Richecourt, **19.** 200

husband will lose property to, if he divorces her, **19.** 88

improved, except in appearance, **23.** 230, 237

income of, insufficient for life in England, **19.** 348

intrigues of, **17.** 326

invited to Pitti Palace gala, **25.** 50n

Italy not to be revisited by, **19.** 290

—— to be revisited by, **23.** 113, 141, 224

itinerary of, from Florence to England, **23.** 2, 120

Jermy, Mrs, should be imitated by, **18.** 311

Jervas's portrait of, at SH, **23.** 512n

jewels of: bought with money she brought to the Walpoles, **42.** 82; carried abroad, **25.** 144, 158; claimed to be at her disposal, **19.** 162; diamond earrings not permitted by Sir Robert Walpole to be carried abroad, **25.** 148; few given her by husband, **25.** 148; given to Richecourt's daughter, **20.** 499, 505, **25.** 144; husband receives demand from her for, after he takes them, **25.** 162; husband retains most of, when she goes abroad, **25.** 472; mother's diamonds, **25.** 148; Niccolini gets, **17.** 95, 134–5, 217; son's right to, **25.** 169; Tylney buys, **25.** 144

jewels taken from, by husband, demanded by her, **25.** 162

jointure of; arrears in, not mentioned, **25.** 144; arrears of interest on, computed, **25.** 440, 445, 456; deficiencies should be made good, **25.** 172; deficiency being examined

by Orford and Lucas, **25**. 176; deficiency estimated, **25**. 412; deficient according to 'case' drawn by Sharpe, **25**. 162; farm to be rented for, **24**. 308; HW not allowed to raise, **25**. 140; in arrears, **23**. 512; should be sacrificed to son instead of demanding arrears, **20**. 486

laudanum or liquor may be taken by, **17**. 89–90

lawyers may be consulted by, **24**. 91

learned ladies considered ridiculous by, **20**. 584

'learned luminary' visiting Rome, **13**. 227

leases not signed by, until her allowance is on its way, **18**. 39

leases received by, **18**. 39, 272

leases signed by, **17**. 115

leases to be received by, **17**. 108, 115

Leghorn correspondence of, to see if her allowance is paid, **18**. 39, 272

Leghorn merchants tell lies to, **17**. 462

legs soaked by, in hot water, **18**. 153

Leheup's remark about his not calling on, **19**. 111–12

Leicester not to let his son marry an heiress like, **19**. 27

letters of, intercepted by her husband, **20**. 247–8

letters of credit on Augsburg taken by, **19**. 49

letters to: Mann sends HW copies of, **25**. 171; to be sent in Richecourt's care, **17**. 34n

Lichfield, E. of, connected with, **18**. 210

——'s earldom will please, **18**. 188

London cannot be endured by, even for one night, **23**. 492

London house of, rented, **19**. 309

London to be visited by, **23**. 120

Lorenzi hopes for rent from, **19**. 238

—— permits, to retain house, **19**. 238

—— to inhabit house of, after Hobart's departure, **19**. 385

Lorraine faction knows plans of, **19**. 75

(?) Louis XV's amours known to, when in France, **20**. 542

Lucas and Sharpe seek agreement on estate of, **25**. 150

Lyon visited by, **23**. 152

Mackreth said to have lent money to, **24**. 53

Maffei praises, **17**. 150

maître d'hôtel of, see Waters, Charles

'Makenzie' (? Stuart Mackenzie) accompanies, at The Hague, **19**. 101n

Mann approves of George II's disavowal of civilities to, **19**. 144

—— asked by, to get satisfaction for her affronts, **17**. 283

—— asks HW about calling on, **19**. 232

—— blamed for not inviting, to cocchiata, **18**. 4

—— called on by, **17**. 317

—— calls on, at villa near Florence, **23**. 492

—— conceals contents of HW's letter from, **24**. 19

—— confers with, about HW and her son, **23**. 501, 503, 515–17, **24**. 17, 57, 61

—— congratulates, on becoming unmarried, **20**. 548

—— described by, to HW, **23**. 231–2

—— discusses, with Richecourt, **18**. 11

—— discusses son's situation with, **23**. 468

—— disliked by: **19**. 119, 139; for preventing Crudeli from translating 'Pope's' satire, **17**. 491

—— does not want, back in Florence, **19**. 172, 232, 305, 323, **20**. 335

—— entertains, at dinner, **20**. 480

—— expects English stay of, to end soon, **19**. 219

—— forwards letter to, **19**. 51, **23**. 531

—— hopes that husband is not worried by, **19**. 132

—— hopes that husband will not divorce, **19**. 80

—— ignorant of estates and marriage settlements of, **25**. 129

—— informs, of son's relapse but she does not discuss it, **24**. 318

—— inherits legacy from, **25**. 124, 206

—— inquires about, **19**. 59

—— may be summoned by, to bury Sturgis, **18**. 198

—— mentions election to, **24**. 59

—— might have hired Mrs Richmond to spy upon, **18**. 14

—— need not fear malice of, **18**. 382

—— never mentions her son to, **24**. 23, 353

—— not to complain about son to, **24**. 47

—— not to prod, into writing to HW, **24**. 91–2

—— not to read HW's letter to, **23**. 499

—— not to tell, that her son has broken with HW, **24**. 17

—— pities, **20**. 444

—— pleased by Carteret's conduct to, **17**. 460

—— pleased by Sir Robert Walpole's opinion of, **18**. 4

—— praised by, at Hanover, **19**. 99

—— reassured about, **18**. 196

—— represented by, as hostile to Maria Theresa, **18**. 476

——'s cold greetings to, **18**. 364

——'s conversation with Rucellai 'impeached' by, **17**. 30

——'s correspondence with, over HW and her son's situation, **23**. 472, 476, 478, 486, 531–2, 534, 541, 544, 545, 552, 558–9, **24**. 305

—— sees: frequently, **24**. 330; often, in bed, **24**. 318

——'s letters about departure of, may be retarded, **19**. 64

——'s letters from, conceal her poor health, **24**. 467

——'s letters possibly detained until after departure of, **19**. 75

——'s motives for being on good terms with, **20**. 487

[Rolle, Margaret, *continued*]
—— suspected by, of tampering with her mail, **19.** 172
—— suspects, of tampering with his letters, **17.** 361, 422
——'s veracity questioned by, **17.** 406
—— tells, of her son's recovery, **24.** 376
—— thinks, is moving, **17.** 95
—— to deliver in person HW's letter to, **24.** 52
—— to notify, of son's recovery, **24.** 368
—— urges HW to send, to Venice, **19.** 369
—— will no longer try to bow to, **18.** 173
—— will not mention son, since she never asks about him, **24.** 353
Mann, Galfridus, to convey news of, to HW, **19.** 54
—— writes to Mann about, **19.** 200
marriage date of, corrected, **43.** 95
marriage of: **25.** 121; arranged by Sir Robert Walpole, **25.** 156–7; settlements for, **17.** 406n, **19.** 37n, **25.** 129–30, 440n, **36.** 295, 296
marriage (second) of, **9.** 113
Mary of Hesse's children fondled by, **19.** 70
Maynard, Vcts, shunned by, at Naples, **24.** 451
men solicited by, **15.** 325
metaphysics discussed by, **18.** 555
Milan visited by, **23.** 135
Molo di Gaeta visited by, **24.** 312, 317
money taken away by, from country seats, **25.** 496
Montagu, Lady Mary Wortley, laughs at, **37.** 78
monument for, in Leghorn cemetery, commissioned by son: **33.** 300; arms and design for, **25.** 206, 219, 226–7, 239–40, 345, 350, 436; HW says, will be ugly but not costly, **25.** 226; inscription to be in Italian, **25.** 219; payment for, **25.** 427, 436; son may forget, **25.** 213; to be superintended by Mann, **25.** 195–6
mother accused by, of 'selling' her to Sir Robert Walpole, **20.** 439
mother and stepfather of, **17.** 486
mother gives allowance to, **19.** 224
mother, husband, and son all wounded by misconduct of, **19.** 38–9
mother leaves nothing to, **20.** 418
mother of, **14.** 50n
mother offers house to, **19.** 104
mother receives coolly, **19.** 139
mother's diamonds went to, **25.** 148
mother told by: of approaching visit, **19.** 60; that Orford is best and HW the worst of family, **19.** 139
mourning for father-in-law may be worn by, **19.** 37, 42, 47, 49, 53
Mozzi accompanies: at Holland House, **23.** 229–30; at Naples, **23.** 155; to England, **23.** 113n; to Paris, **23.** 141–2, 155
—— cannot be given a bed by, while at Pratolino, **23.** 23

—— chosen by, for his beauty, **25.** 130
—— desired by Sharpe to make list of belongings of, **25.** 151
—— enriches himself from, **23.** 158
—— expects effects of, from Naples, **25.** 160
—— finds it easier to be a gallant to, than to marry a young wife, **25.** 571
—— leaves, because of his family affairs, **24.** 145
—— may abandon, unless she leaves Naples, **24.** 305
—— may forsake, if she stays away from Florence, **23.** 559
—— might be unpopular in England for getting inheritance from, away from her son, **25.** 396, 404
—— nearly discarded by, for lack of sexual prowess, **21.** 70
——'s bequest from, contested by her son, **36.** 202
——'s claims against landed estate of, requested by Sharpe, **25.** 168
—— sends Orford a list of family things taken by, to Italy, **25.** 156
—— sends to England list and valuation of plate and jewels of, **25.** 163
—— sent by, to Mann, **23.** 464
——'s family abuse, for obstructing his marriage, **25.** 130
—— to send HW list of possible demands of, on son, **25.** 158
—— turns back, at Calais, to keep her from meeting son, **23.** 158
—— wants release from son of, for acting as her executor, **25.** 466, 498
—— will probably inherit Italian property of, **25.** 113
Naples left by, **23.** 512, **24.** 220, 312, 317, 479
—— may be visited by, **20.** 476, **23.** 2, **24.** 82
—— may be summer residence of, **23.** 559
—— not to be visited by: **20.** 505; till following winter, **24.** 83
—— to be left by, for Florence, because of disappointment over a house, **24.** 9
—— to be visited by: **20.** 499, **21.** 550, **23.** 155, 525, 529, 531, **24.** 57, 70, 164, 251; probably to get her furniture away, **23.** 464, 468, 472
—— visit deferred by, because of Mozzi's absence, **24.** 145
—— visited by, **23.** 537, 559, **24.** 260
—— visit of: for last time, **24.** 467; given up, **25.** 107; impossible, **24.** 70; in autumn, prevented by illness, **25.** 112
Neapolitan estate might be the one bought by, **24.** 187
Neapolitan friends of, press her to stay there, **24.** 305
Neapolitan houses of, **23.** 2
Neapolitan journeys may be too much for, **24.** 244, 322
nerves of, unshaken by son's calamities, **24.** 293

never travels in hot weather, **24**. 467

new affluence of, will make her more impudent on her return to Florence, **19**. 238

New Park house taken by, **19**. 309

news sent by, through Niccoli, **19**. 290

Newton studied by, **20**. 555

Niccoli accompanies, to England, **19**. 42, 46, 50, 54, 290, **20**. 335

—— ordered by, to send her clothes, **17**. 223–4

—— receives furniture from, **17**. 107

Niccolini knows little about, **19**. 398

—— may see, in London, **19**. 353, 362

—— predicts return of, to Florence, **19**. 394

—— to get jewels of, for debt payment, **17**. 95

—— to sell jewels of, **17**. 134–5, 217

Nice or Naples may be winter resort of, **23**. 2

nobody would expect anything from, **14**. 50

nothing can be said about, if she says nothing about son, **24**. 327

offers to take bootikins to Mann, **23**. 231

Old Pretender's boys fussed over by, **19**. 70

opera attended by, in London, with Lady Dashwood, **19**. 224

opera supported by, in Florence, **18**. 555

Orange, Ps of, to be visited by, **19**. 49

Orford family deeds supposed to have been taken by, to Italy, **25**. 160

Orford family said to have given nothing to, **25**. 130

Oxenden lover of, **19**. 5, **33**. 222

Padua visited by, **17**. 217, 224, 235

paintings inherited from, by Mozzi, **25**. 524

Palazzo Vecchio visited by, **17**. 283

papers of, from Naples, received by Mozzi, **25**. 162

Paris visited by, **20**. 335, **23**. 120, 141–2, 230

Parliament's dissolution blamed by, for mismanagement of her boroughs, **24**. 57, 67

passes her time between Florence and Fiesole, **24**. 488

physician from Florence attends, at Molo di Gaeta, **24**. 312

Pisa baths may be visited by, **23**. 83, **25**. 107

Pisa baths visited by, **24**. 105

Pisa visited by, **25**. 112–13

plate and jewels of, right of disposal claimed, **25**. 163

plate carried by, to Italy, **25**. 144, 169

Platonic love does not satisfy, **13**. 233–4

Podestà of Verona's son has affair with, **17**. 196

politics and 'metaphidgets' of, **20**. 504

Pomfret, Cts of, entertains, **18**. 364

—— friend and fellow-pedant of, **14**. 248

—— receives letter from, **19**. 61

—— takes, to Court after Cts of Yarmouth refuses to do so, **19**. 111

Pratolino apartment occupied by, with Leopold's consent in hot season, **24**. 23

pregnancy of, suspected, **18**. 153

pretensions of, to learning, **25**. 122

property of, may not escape English lawyers, **25**. 131

prudence of, **20**. 481

public and private calamities do not disturb tranquillity of, **24**. 488

Pulteney might be influenced by, **19**. 310

—— opposed by, **18**. 99

quack oculist patronized by, **18**. 272

Radicofani visited by, in Pius VI's litter, **24**. 317

rent arrears due at death of, **25**. 511–12

rents of estates of, collected by son, **25**. 144

Richecourt accompanied by, at Padua, **17**. 217, 224, 235, 419n

—— admired by, **17**. 360, 367

——assists, in journey, **19**. 54

—— attended by, in illness with home-made ptisan, **18**. 66–7

—— avenges quarrels of, **18**. 10

—— constantly hears from, **19**. 97

—— discusses with his son the marriage of, **20**. 255

—— does not discuss, with Mann, **19**. 54

—— encourages, to visit England, **17**. 426

—— entertained by, on Thursdays, **18**. 4

—— forbids, to interrupt his devotions, **19**. 31

—— gives attendants to, **19**. 49–50

—— had expected to marry, **20**. 255, 268

—— has chariot made for, **17**. 53–4

—— incited by, to oust Mann, **18**. 362

—— influenced by: **18**. 140; against England, **18**. 329

—— jokes about, **20**. 444

—— lends money to, **17**. 461

—— loses, **20**. 272

—— may be tempted by wealth of, **20**. 439

—— may follow, to Venice, **19**. 47

—— may have entrusted, with Hanoverian negotiation, **19**. 70

—— might dress, as a man to answer his duel challenge, **17**. 468

—— might encourage, to seek bank credit, **17**. 422–3

—— not to be accompanied by, to country, **18**. 314

—— not to be followed by, to Vienna, **17**. 89, 95

—— not to be married by, **20**. 239

—— not to rely on, **17**. 409

—— persuades, to sign papers, **18**. 487

—— prejudiced by, against Mann, **19**. 452

—— probably does not hear from, **20**. 143

—— receives letter from, from Hanover, **19**. 80

—— recovers from influence of, **20**. 68

——'s access to, by door into palace corridor, **18**. 391

——'s affair with: **17**. 90, 409n; said by Rinuccini to have displeased Sir Robert Walpole, **17**. 108

—— said to be preparing apartment for, in his country house, **19**. 80

[Rolle, Margaret, *continued*]
—— said to have received letters from, from England, 19. 64
——'s daughter dines with, 20. 480
——'s daughter receives gifts from, 20. 499, 505, 25. 144
——'s 'deary,' 18. 12
——'s departure impels, to leave Florence, 17. 107
——'s departure probably foreseen by, 19. 49
——'s disgrace attributed by, to Wachtendonck, 17. 107
——'s fears soothed by, 18. 520
——'s house near that of, 20. 480
——'s lodgings to be prepared by, 18. 309
——'s misbehaviour incited by, 20. 313
——'s opinion of, rises after gift of jewels, 20. 505
——'s return from Vienna will be awaited by, 19. 144
——'s rudeness to, 17. 34, 53
——'s son brought up by, 20. 90
——'s success encourages, 18. 122
—— supposedly father of two daughters by, 25. 122, 130
——'s villa to be visited by, 17. 34n
—— to join, at Verona for return to Florence, 17. 107
—— to repeat Mann's conversation to, 18. 12
—— unlikely to be troubled by, 20. 480
—— visited by, 18. 364
—— will not be pleased by return of, 20. 476
—— would not have been left by, had he shown more prowess, 20. 395
Richmond, Mrs, escorts, only part way to Bologna, 19. 50
—— expects, 19. 252
—— hears from, about meeting with son, 19. 192
—— not told by, whether to go to England or to renew lease on Florentine house, 19. 101
—— ordered by, to return to England, 19. 290
—— replaces, in Richecourt's coach, 19. 75, 101
—— to accompany: 19. 46; only to Bologna and then await her return to Florence, 19. 49–50
—— to vacate Florentine house of, 19. 192, 238
—— wonders whether to renew lease on Florentine house, 19. 97
rides horseback, 18. 314, 364, 23. 512
Rolle family to receive estate of, 25. 148
Rome visited by, 13. 227, 23. 478, 492, 24. 164, 170, 222, 304, 317, 318
Rucellai's affair with, 17. (?) 30n, 54
——'s defence of, silenced, 17. 448
—— second in affections of, 17. 71
—— supervises making of bed of, 17. 107
Salimbeni aided by, in road accident, 17. 116
Salo visited by, 17. 196, 217
Salviati villa may be taken by, 21. 310

satire by Crudeli liked by, 17. 424, 491, 18. 11
scandal exhausted by, 19. 229
scandals concerning, would be revived if will is contested, 25. 124
scientific folly of, worse than religious folly, 20. 555
Scott, Lady Isabella, receives letter from, 19. 61
Scully's renting of Florentine house at Mann's expense for Walpole family asserted by, 18. 14
servant dismissed by, under suspicion of being Mann's spy, 18. 14
servants of, unaware of postal hours, 23. 515
Sharpe corresponds with, about her son, 23. 464, 472, 476, 477, 486, 491–3, 496, 501, 503, 509, 514, 516, 525, 537, 548, 24. 47, 57, 304, 305, 317, 318, 35. 417
—— disappointed at not getting legacy from, 25. 320, 328
—— handles English affairs of, 25. 160
—— has confidence of, 23. 477
—— may be consulted by, 24. 91
—— mistakenly trusted by, 25. 172
—— no longer entitled to salary paid him by, 25. 496
—— offered a borough by, for his nephew, 24. 52
—— should produce counter-demands in favour of, 25. 333
——'s letters probably never opened by, 24. 318
——'s letter to, forwarded by Mann, 24. 304
——'s salary from, 25. 492
—— thinks: should have left son funds in England, 25. 157; should not have left so much to Mozzi, 25. 162
—— threatens, because of failure to send him order for money, 25. 129
—— to give consent of, for HW to run Orford's affairs, 36. 93
—— wants English funds of, divided by Mozzi with E. of Orford, 25. 155, 157, 160, 217, 335, 426
—— wants HW to aid in letting jointure farm of, 24. 308
—— was lawyer of, 25. 320
—— will tell, of her son's neglect of boroughs, 24. 47
Shirley, Hon. Sewallis, discarded by, 20. 438–9, 476, 479
—— disparaged by, 20. 476, 479, 481, 487
—— engages affections of, 19. 309, 20. 143
—— given separate maintenance by, 20. 547, 568
—— loves, for several years, 20. 239n
—— may eclipse Richecourt in the favour of, 19. 385
—— might yet make, pregnant, 20. 250, 254–5
—— probably accompanies, 20. 143
——'s death leaves free, to wed a third time, 22. 366
—— sends dunning letters to, 20. 479
—— slave to jealousy of, 20. 433

——'s marriage with, **20**. 239, 255

——'s name omitted from monument of, **25**. 227

——'s separation from, **20**. 444

—— to marry, **20**. 239, 250

Shirley arms worn by, but not to be used on her monument, **25**. 240

Smollett's *Adventures of Peregrine Pickle* includes Lady Vane's mention of, **17**. 459n

snow confines, at Fiesole, **24**. 347

snow turns back, at Siena, from trip to Naples, **24**. 70

snuff-box with cipher of, supposed to have been sent to Mann by Barbantane, **25**. 206

son apparently the object of concern by, **20**. 479, 481, 486

son approves of disposition by, in favour of Mozzi, **25**. 168, 181

son avoids, **23**. 224

son cannot well be disinherited by, **20**. 433

son collects rents on estates of, **25**. 144

son does not pay uncles' fortunes after death of, **25**. 316

son expresses regard for memory of, **25**. 168

son given power over her boroughs by, **24**. 46

son inherits barony of Clinton from, **25**. 165

son inherits estate and jointure of, **25**. 125, **30**. 169n

son left by, to care of HW and Sir Edward Walpole, **23**. 464, 491, 492, 496, 514, **32**. 118, 133

son liked by, though she robs him, **20**. 247

son may be taken by, to Italy, **20**. 247

son may meet, in England, **23**. 121

son might join, in running boroughs, **35**. 417

son neglected by, **5**. 360

son neglects, in her lifetime but is to honour her with monument, **25**. 195

son never inspired tenderness in, **24**. 376

son never the subject of inquiries by, **24**. 322, 347, 374

son not to be rescued by, from scoundrels, **23**. 58

son not to repay Mackreth until death of, **24**. 53

son pretends that Mackreth borrowed money from, **24**. 53n

son resembles, **17**. 450

son respects Ferrers's relationship to, **9**. 279

son's affairs avoided by, **41**. 266

son's character disparaged by, **9**. 78

son's claims against estate of, **25**. 143, 158, 412, **33**. 274, 372

son's condition may not be known to, **24**. 330

son's correspondence with, **23**. 559, 560, 563, **24**. 541–2

son's dismissal of HW will offend, **24**. 4

son sees, **19**. 192, **23**. 230

son's estate ruined by, **25**. 239

son should not give portrait of, to Mozzi, **25**. 501

son's ingratitude to her and HW condemned by, **24**. 57

son's letter to, praises HW, **36**. 202

son's letter to be brought by, to Mann to be deciphered, **24**. 541–2

son slights, **20**. 482

son's neglect of, did not exceed hers for him, **25**. 195

son's paternity doubted by HW, **25**. 132, **33**. 222n

son's recovery feared by, to be transitory, **24**. 376

son too far away to be aided by, **23**. 460

son welcomes delay in settling affairs of, **25**. 247

Spry, Commodore, to take, in ship from Naples to Marseille, **23**. 2

Stephan accompanies, to England, **19**. 46, 50

steward of, Lucas pretends to have found paper of, **25**. 440

'Stitara' the signature of, **20**. 248

Sturgis bores, **18**. 198

—— goes abroad with, **17**. 71n

—— housed by, **17**. 70–1

—— incited by, to tell lies at coffee-houses, **17**. 406, 462

—— or her health may have caused foreign sojourn of, **43**. 236

——'s affair with, **17**. (?) 90, 461, **43**. 179

——'s clothes found in effects of, **17**. 224

——'s death affects, **18**. 199

—— sent by, to Leghorn, **17**. 95

sums in French funds said to be deposited by, in Mozzi's name, **15**. 113

taxes disliked by, **20**. 504–5

Tesi told by, that HW will forget to send her a dog, **18**. 334

testamentary powers not claimed by, over landed estates in England, **25**. 121

Theodore of Corsica's account of, confirms his connection with Carteret, **18**. 210

tomb of, *see* monument for

Toussaint said to be courted by, through Richecourt, **18**. 210, 363

Townshend, Vcts, chief companion of, **19**. 119

—— corresponds with, **17**. 101n

—— protects, **19**. 111

—— receives letter from, **19**. 60

tragedies preferred by, to operas, **18**. 128

Turin to be visited by, **23**. 120

Tuscany unlikely to be again the residence of, **23**. 2

Tylney buys jewels from, **25**. 144

——'s house in Florence occupied by, in winter, **23**. 468

Uguccioni gets recommendation from, for Guise and Valtravers, **20**. 393

—— may be asked by, to get her a house, **20**. 393

——'s affair with, **17**. 448, **43**. 271

—— says that house has been taken by, in Florence, **19**. 61, 75

'universally lamented' according to son's epitaph for, **25**. 195

[Rolle, Margaret, *continued*]

unpopular during English visit, **19.** 111

Vane, Vcts, emulates adventures of, **17.** 459

Venetian costume and conversation of, **17.** 317

Venetian visit of, **17.** 71n, 107, 115, 125, 134

Venice may become residence of, **19.** 47, 50

veracity of, defective, **19.** 140

Verona visited by, **17.** 107, 134, 150

Vienna may be visited by, **17.** 125, **19.** 48

villa of, at Fiesole, *see* Medici, Villa

Villa Salviati may be taken by, **21.** 310

vivacity of, uncommon for one of her age, **23.** 512

Wachtendonck disparaged by, **17.** 107

Walpole, Hon. Robert, seen by, in Paris, **23.** 141

Walpole, Sir Robert, disparaged by, **17.** 387, 406, 423, 448

—— expected by: to be beheaded, **17.** 444; to flee to Florence, **17.** 450n, **18.** 14

—— indifferent to actions of, **17.** 326

—— knows infidelities of, **17.** 425

—— pleases, by his disgrace, **17.** 360, 367, 393–4

—— rents jewels for, for George II's coronation, **21.** 536

—— said to enrich, by his death, **19.** 37

—— said to have 'bought,' **20.** 439

—— should not by his death encourage, to go to England, **19.** 38, 46, 49

Walpole family jewels the responsibility of, **25.** 144

Walpole family now mentioned by, with regard, **20.** 479, 481, 486

Walpole family pictures not valued by, enough to take them to Italy, **25.** 227

Walpole family receives only £20,000 from, spent on her jewels, **42.** 82

Walpole name to be abandoned by, **17.** 367, 406, 423–4, **18.** 126

Walter related to, **20.** 393

Wasner instigated by Richecourt to plead for, **18.** 194

whist played by, **19.** 111

Wilkes seen by, at Naples, **22.** 292n

Williams, Sir C. H., offers to mention, in his satires, **30.** 93

will of: **2.** 257, **43.** 287, 288, 289, 290; caveat against, **25.** 124, 126, 137, 143, 167, 195, 493, 504, 509; codicil not valid in England, **25.** 121; contest concerns what she had no right to dispose of, **25.** 144; correction to, **43.** 274; deposited at Florentine archivio in 1773, **25.** 114; droll and illiterate, **25.** 121–2; Florentine lawyers allowed, to be valid, **25.** 137; HW condemns Lucas for advising E. of Orford to contest, **25.** 315, 510; in her writing-box, **25.** 114; intention of testator evident in, **25.** 137; Mann consults lawyer about, **25.** 120; Mann sends copy of, to HW, **25.** 114; Mozzi desires only what is justly his by, **25.** 162; Mozzi entitled to make additional claims under. **25.** 168–9;

Mozzi to deposit, in archivio, **25.** 114; Mozzi to inherit everything by, **19.** 114; probate received by HW, **25.** 123; 'proof' of, **43.** 288–9; sent to son, **25.** 121, 136; servants neglected in, **25.** 122; Sharpe disapproves of, **25.** 134–5, 162; son and alleged daughters not named in, **25.** 122; son may remove caveat against, **25.** 493; son not to contest, **25.** 124, 172; son's business with Mozzi to be settled by probate of, **25.** 167; son should not have contested, **25.** 217; son's name omitted from, **25.** 120; tenants withhold rent until caveat is withdrawn from, **25.** 493; to be proved in England, **25.** 167; trumpery understanding shown in, **25.** 140; validity of, doubted, **25.** 123

Wood hears plans and complaints of, **20.** 476

Wray at Exeter receives letter from, **19.** 284

—— cousin to, **19.** 238

—— lived with, at Florence, **19.** 238

—— lodged with, in London, **19.** 284

writing-box of, brought to Mann by Mozzi, **25.** 114

(?) Yorke's opinion on case of, **25.** 162, 186

Young Pretender said to be friend of, **19.** 70, 310

Zincke's portrait of; on snuff-box for her husband, **25.** 501; son to do with, as he pleases, **25.** 504

Rolle, Samuel (1646–1719), of Heanton Satchville; M.P.:

daughter left estates by, with remainder to her son and John Rolle of Shipwick, **20.** 424n

daughter of, **13.** 227n

death of, **20.** 418n

wife of, **14.** 50n, **20.** 418n

Rolle, Mrs Samuel. *See* Roy, Frances; Tuckfield, Margaret (d. 1754)

Rolle family:

arms of, to be on Cts of Orford's monument, **25.** 240

Clinton title may come to, **18.** 143n; *see also under* Clinton, barony of

estate of, inherited by E. of Orford with power to cut off entail, **25.** 164n

estate of Cts of Orford to revert to, **25.** 148, 156

insanity in, **23.** 495

Orford, E. of, to sell old estate of, **25.** 148

Rolleston, John (fl. 1667), D. of Newcastle's secretary:

HW has not heard story of, **40.** 176

(?) Newcastle, Ds of, dictates to, at night, **16.** 367–8

Rollet, Bailli du. *See* Gand-Leblanc, Marie-François-Louis

Rolle Walter, John (? 1714–79), M.P.:

Mann told by, of Cts of Orford's plans, **20.** 393

Rolli, Paolo Antonio (1687–1767), poet:

Arsaces by, **13.** 142n

biographical information about, corrected,
    43. 239
Bolingbroke's protégé, lives in England, **17**.
    191n
excessive charges by, **17**. 191
lines by, on Pope's death, **18**. 468, 485
lyrics for *Alexander in Persia* adapted by, **17**.
    184n
operas composed and translations made by,
    18. 468n
Penelope by, **17**. 256
Rolliad, The:
    group of poets compose, **25**. 612
    HW praises, **15**. 202
    Wraxall's *Short Review* courts authors of, **33**.
        558n
Rollin, ——:
    attends session of parliament of Paris, **8**. 173
Rollin, Charles (1661–1741), historian:
    Histoire ancienne and *Histoire romaine* by,
        (?) owned by Mme du Deffand, **8**. 35
    Histoire ancienne by: **41**. 152; called well-
        written, by Hume, **15**. 49n
    verses on death of, attributed to Spence by
        HW, **30**. 24
Rolling press:
    introduction of, **40**. 306
Rollo, Andrew (1703–65), 5th Bn Rollo, 1758:
    Dominica captured by, **21**. 516n
'Rolls, Capt.':
    HW signs himself as, **30**. 19, 28
Rolls Chapel, clerk of. *See* Rooke, Henry
Rolls, Master of. *See* Master of the Rolls
Roll-ups (stockings):
    out of fashion, **28**. 208
Rolt, Elizabeth, m. Col. John Prideaux:
    army camp at Newport visited by, **37**. 503
Rolt, Henry:
    (?) Argyll wants cornetcy for, **37**. 31
Rolt, Richard (? 1725–70):
    Crawford's life written by, **20**. 110n
Rolt. *See also* Bayntun Rolt
Roma, ——, artist:
    from Greek isles, **35**. 642
    Vyne chapel painted by, **35**. 186n, 642
Romagna, Priore di. *See* Ximenes d'Aragona,
    Ferdinando
Romagna, the (Italy):
    epidemic in, **21**. 359
    Leopold tours Tuscany in direction of, **24**. 343
    Neapolitans to retire from, **18**. 43
    taxes at, **18**. 344
'Romain, le.' *See* Phélypeaux, Jean-Frédéric
Romain, Mme Nicolas. *See* Gaillard, Geneviève
Romain, Pierre-Ange (ca 1761–85), attorney,
    aeronaut:
    death of, **25**. 590, **33**. 467
Roman; Romans, ancient:
    Æneas not the ancestor of, **41**. 177
    Americans imitate, **32**. 248
    artistic skill of, **16**. 101–2
    Barthélemy compares French bridges to those
        of, **8**. 201
effeminate because they went into winter
    quarters, **25**. 105
English magnanimity to prisoners should
    shame, **21**. 367
fashion of, to wish to die, **33**. 121
Greeks imitated by, with grace, **16**. 270
HW bored by, **4**. 479
HW calls London rabble, **25**. 343
HW lacks obliviousness of, to personal mat-
    ters, **33**. 163
havocked world for glory, **25**. 142
ignorant of riches in India, **11**. 295
Israel's conquest by, may resemble France's
    by England, **33**. 24, 167
Jews fight Pharisees instead of, **33**. 24
language of, superseded, **33**. 240
Louis XVI's death surpasses any of, **34**. 179
Mesdames de France unlikely to succeed
    Brennus as conquerors of, **11**. 222
only once suffered a second army to be taken,
    25. 210
sometimes had sense, **25**. 337
titles acquired by, from their conquests, **33**.
    421
virtues admired by, **32**. 266, 347
writings of, except Horace's, lack wit and
    humour, **16**. 272
'Romana, the.' *See* Romani, Angela
Roman antiquities:
    Cole uninterested in, **2**. 208
    HW uninterested in, **1**. 212, 368, **2**. 116, 204
    Lysons, Samuel, digs up, near Cirencester,
        12. 59
Roman cabinet:
    HW's, at SH, **23**. 285
Roman Catholic; Roman Catholics:
    'bigots,' **2**. 226
    decrease of, reported by Bp Porteus, **29**. 125
    Derry, Bp of, advocates removing test from,
        28. 469
    English clergy pray for, **28**. 443
    Gage bred as, **30**. 291n
    Glamorgan to enlist, for Charles I, **40**. 138
    HW asks if Louisa is, **31**. 207
    Irish, **12**. 120
    Jerningham, Charles, mentioned as being, **11**.
        175
    Joseph II's rescript on suppression of, **29**. 181
    purgatory, witticism concerning, **12**. 265
    relief of, in Britain, from restrictions: bishops
        approve, **29**. 66; HW and Mason oppose,
        29. 315, 318; Markham advocates, **28**. 312;
        Savile's bill for, **2**. 66n, 79n, 82, 83–4,
        197n; Savile's motion in House of Commons
        to remove, **28**. 395, 398
    Shrewsbury pays for ferrying, to his chapel
        across river, **34**. 195
    Terrick's persecution of, **30**. 209, **31**. 94
    See also under Gordon Riots; Roman Catholic
        Church
Roman Catholic Church:
    altar-pieces not bought by members of, **33**.
        487

[Roman Catholic Church, *continued*]

Anglican bishop pleads for toleration of, while Joseph II suppresses convents, **25.** 439

Anglican bishop to urge Pius VI to give autonomy to Irish bishops of, **24.** 430

Anglican divines as absurd as those of, **20.** 186

Argenson deems Louis XV's devotion to, necessary for monarchy, **21.** 48

Arundell and Booth, adherents of, **21.** 339

Aspinwall writes against, **21.** 46n

attacks on, resented by English clergy, **15.** 9

Bath chapel of, **25.** 63n

Bedingfield the most bigoted member of, in Norfolk, **20.** 532

Benedict XIV tells princes of, not to disturb *anno santo,* **20.** 98

Benedictines want to eat no more fish than is customary in, **39.** 2

Berlin church of, receives ornaments from Querini, **20.** 325

bishop; bishops of: appointed for Corsica, *see* Crescenzi de Angelis, Cesare; Clement XIV to bestow mitres on, **24.** 39; French, are required by parliament of Paris to live at their sees, **38.** 339; French, call on Cts of Hertford, **38.** 245

Bower deserts from, and writes against it, **20.** 157

——'s alleged conversion to, **20.** 532–4

Brandenburg-Bayreuth, Margrave of, to build church for members of, **20.** 479n

Browne, Lady, belongs to, **39.** 187

Brownlow, Lady Betty, joins, **18.** 117

Burke and Lord George Gordon debate over, **39.** 325

canonization by, not undertaken hastily, **28.** 152

cardinal of, abandoned by bishops and clergy, **33.** 508

cardinals of, *see under* Cardinal

cattle murrain attributed to poisoning of pools by, **19.** 174

chapel of: at Sardinian embassy in Lincoln's Inn Fields, **21.** 46n; at Standon, **40.** 198; at Twickenham, **30.** 209; in London, **10.** 216; in London, demolished in Gordon riots, **25.** 54–5, 56, **33.** 196; in London, Pitt, Elizabeth, frequents, **21.** 46

chapels and schools of, attacked, **25.** 56n

Charles II's conversion to, ignored by Clarendon, **16.** 33

—— thought too much to be really of, **16.** 34

Choiseul annihilates power of, **23.** 130

Chute would sacrifice to, to get Raphael painting, **35.** 37

Clarendon swung between Protestantism and, **25.** 224

Clement XIII cannot persuade princes of, to crusade against Polish dissidents, **22.** 574

—— orders women to cover their faces in, **21.** 292

——'s death may keep France and Portugal in, **22.** 331

—— would sacrifice, to his brief, **23.** 16

Clement XIV's murder may become the destruction of, **24.** 51

clergy of: Anglican clergy as absurd as, **20.** 186; benediction *in articulo mortis* almost never given by, when recovery seems possible, **22.** 14; continue in sick-room after death of patient, **21.** 391; Cosimo III impoverished his subjects to enrich, **25.** 223–4; Duke of Burgundy called a pretender by, **20.** 287; epigram by, on Richecourt, **20.** 268, 272; finesse and jealousy of, traditional, **24.** 497; gendarmes preserved by from mob, **17.** 79; Henry Benedict (Stuart) joins, **18.** 499–500, 501; high headdresses condemned by, **25.** 183; interpret earthquake as a judgment, **20.** 150; Irish, **17.** 142, **19.** 12; licentiousness of, to be curbed, **20.** 458; Louis XV may fall into hands of, **38.** 350; Louis XV's relations with, **20.** 199, 206, 294, **23.** 399; Louise, Princesse, at centre of intrigues of, **23.** 398; mentioned in HW's 'Peach in Brandy,' **32.** 62; Maupeou cultivates, **23.** 398; Mazzei's prank offends, **21.** 495; Pius VI forbids, to powder hair, **24.** 107; Protestant girls induced by, to forsake parents and change religion, **22.** 249–50; riots incited by, **24.** 102; Wachtendonck's death-bed dominated by, **17.** 109–10

Cocchi's treatise on matrimony banned by, **22.** 204

Cole's attachment to, **1.** 105, **2.** 48, 79, 82, 229, 309, **32.** 53, **43.** 48

'consumptive,' **1.** 124

Crawford's French servant has rites of, before going to save his master, **20.** 110

Dalhousie's speech to Church of Scotland's assembly, opposing, **39.** 325n

declining, **25.** 541, 603

Derry, Bp of, and, *see below under* Hervey, Bp

Diharce an adherent of, **20.** 421n

donations and decretals formerly forged by, **25.** 603

Duane an adherent of, **25.** 216

duellers excommunicated by, **20.** 364

Edinburgh riots against, **24.** 439, **33.** 91

Elizabeth, Q., excommunicated by, **22.** 177, 390

Ellis's bill against, in Parliament, **25.** 66n, 67n

end will be obtained by, in time, **24.** 106–7

England's lenity to members of, may make it renounce Young Pretender, **22.** 369, 386

English adherents of, persecuted by Bp of London, **22.** 394–5, **30.** 209, **31.** 94

English bishops establish, in Canada, **35.** 587

English bishops favour toleration of, **25.** 66

English legislation for, shows vacillation, **25.** 66–7

Englishman at Florence offers to join, **35.** 52

English members of: circulate story about the Young Pretender's not being in Scot-

land, in person, 19. 172, 198–9; publish mournful letters about Jesuits, 23. 524; send contributions to Young Pretender, 19. 176

English newspaper squib warns English butchers against fasting practices of, 19. 129

Eyre adheres to, 33. 84n

Fitzherbert, Mrs, a member of, 25. 628

Florentine bishops of, accused by Benedict XIV of fearing Vienna, 20. 305n

Florentine jurisdizione defends Francis I against encroachments of, 19. 491

Florentine members of, told by confessors: to hate the English, 19. 196–7; to pray for the Young Pretender's success, 19. 112

French, Cole inquires about, 1. 122

French abolition of, makes Protestantism meaningless, 39. 478

French clergy of: at odds with Louis XV, 20. 199, 287, 294; refuse sacraments to those opposing Unigenitus bull, 20. 337n; squabble with parliament of Paris, 35. 173

French clergy's persecution may provoke papal domination by, 34. 103

French lower clergy of, prefer hardship to perjury, 34. 181

French *philosophes* avow war against, 39. 22

French priests of, should be sent to Ireland to warn people against Dissenters, 34. 166

Friday fasting of, 17. 254, 19. 129

Friedrich II of Hesse converted to, 24. 274–5, 35. 192

Gage a former member of, 17. 255

Gage, Lady, belongs to, 34. 260

Garrick married in chapel of, 20. 74

Giberne's love affair with Italian girl stopped by, 20. 128–9

girl of, escorted by Irish priest to England, 17. 142

Glamorgan to enlist foreign members of, for Charles I, 40. 138n

Gordon, Lord George, leads Scottish Presbyterians against, 25. 11

—— persecutes, 2. 223–6, 25. 131; *see also* Gordon Riots

——'s followers to demonstrate against, 34. 173

Gordon family formerly belonged to, 25. 11

Gordon rioters plunder more Protestants than members of, 25. 61

Gower, Lord, offends, by absence from Council, 33. 131

HW averse to tolerating, because it is an intolerant church, 25. 541

HW calls: 'Madame of Babylon,' 24. 255; 'Old Mother Babylon,' 22. 420; 'Whore of Babylon,' 23. 81

HW despises, for abandoning Young Pretender when his family sacrificed all for her sake, 24. 255

HW fears restoration of, 33. 9

HW jokes about chalice denied to laity by, 9. 375, 10. 3

HW jokes about possible uprising by, in Ireland, 10. 15

HW must censure More's devotion to, without censuring it, 41. 290

HW prefers, to Catherine II and Joseph II, 34. 19

HW reproduces chapel of, 21. 306, 22. 136

HW's second assembly to be attended by members of, 10. 107

HW's opinion of, 1. 124, 241, 2. 100, 229

Henry VIII and, 1. 81–2

Hervey, Bp, heads Irish resistance by, 25. 529n

—— may expect to be admitted into, 25. 454

—— proposes relief for, 33. 127

—— seeks autonomy for Irish bishops of, 24. 430

—— urges admittance of, to seats in Parliament, 25. 438n

—— urges enfranchisement of, in Ireland, 25. 439, 529

—— wants regiments raised from, in Ireland, to subdue America, 25. 454n

Holman belonged to, 35. 77

Hooke a convert to, 20. 533

House of Commons to consider emancipation for members of, 33. 178

Howard family's relations with, 23. 485

Howe, Lady, converted to, because it is more entertaining, 20. 378, 416, 24. 107–8

ingratitude of, to benefactors, 24. 4

in Italian earthquakes, priests of, seek to rescue Hosts from churches before rescuing people, 33. 415

intercourse with heretics disapproved by, 20. 128–9

Ireland better protected by conciliation than by toleration of, 33. 153

Irish adherents of: civilized by landlords despite resistance, 26. 32; considered too dangerous for English army, 18. 566; forbidden to carry swords, 20. 289; France might get secret agents from, 20. 491; landowners fear to enfranchise, 25. 529, 541; might have to supply rebel army in Wales, 19. 160; more dangerous to England than a Spanish grandee, 20. 171; said to stop supplies to Young Pretender because he renounced church, 23. 402; should be warned by plight of French priests, 15. 224; should not vote for Irish parliament, 25. 529; would dislike repeal of Catholic Relief Act, 39. 350

Irish and Scottish members of, said to encourage French invasion, 18. 415

Irish bishops of, might be put on footing of Gallican church, 24. 430

Irish emancipation for, 34. 166

Irish members of, said to be aroused by North ministry, 41. 312–13

Irish Parliament concerned with, 37. 426–7, 428

Irish priests of: 17. 142, 19. 116, 21. 202; interpret for English naval captains, 19. 12

[Roman Catholic Church, *continued*]

Irish reform should not be entrusted to members of, **35.** 379

Irish reform would benefit, **35.** 382

Irish Volunteers thought by HW to consist mostly of members of, **35.** 379

Italian members of: permitted by Pius VI to eat meat in Lent because of fish shortage, **25.** 17, 21; usually include Madonna in Trinity, **23.** 459

Jansen's propositions condemned by, **32.** 80

Jesuits the janizaries of, **23.** 214

—— to be under control of bishops of, **23.** 473

jewels stolen out of, by soldier, **25.** 499

Jortin's zeal against, **2.** 353

Joseph II may press claims against, for its usurpations from the Medici, **25.** 595

—— will find Rohan's crime an excuse for punishing, **42.** 148

—— will not squander lands of, on courtiers, **25.** 544

jubilee observances by, **20.** 82–3

Julius III strikes medal on restoration of, in England, by Mary I, **21.** 189n

Lancashire members of, threaten loyal citizens, **19.** 172

legend of, perhaps in pictures owned by Fenn, **42.** 191–2

Leghorn privileges prohibit English children under 13 from joining, **22.** 249n

Lenten fasting of, upset by Protestant Necker and Protestant English fishmongers, **25.** 21

London members of, expected to rise up, **19.** 138, 171–2

Louis XV diverted by Mme de Pompadour to keep him from, **37.** 340

——'s quarrel with, **20.** 199, 287, 294

Louis XVI may become a champion of, in Poland, **24.** 11

Luther would not have attacked, if he could see bloodshed resulting, **34.** 161

Maguire deserts, **17.** 420

Mann delighted at exposure of villainy of, **20.** 542

Markham, Abp, may aid chapels of, **33.** 98

Marsan, Comtesse de, might restore, in France, **32.** 266

Mary, Q. of Scots, revered by, **15.** 27–8

Mathews's crew disturbs ceremonies of, on Italian island, and hangs crucifix on monkey's neck, **18.** 59, 79n

medal for St Bartholomew massacre suppressed by, **21.** 201

members of, hope for Young Pretender's success, **19.** 131

Methodists, modern, not opposed to, **25.** 11

Middleton attacks, **15.** 308–9

——'s *Letter from Rome* discusses, **30.** 56

Miserere of, to be sung in London, **18.** 211

misfortunes of, **22.** 324–5

More, Hannah, dislikes, **31.** 329

Necker resists, **25.** 21

—— will shock, by holding office in France while a Protestant, **24.** 254–5

Norfolk, Ds of, as member of, cannot be Ps Louisa's mourner, **34.** 240

—— fears that rebellion may injure, **19.** 176

Norfolk dukedom's heir, though a member of, dresses as a cardinal at masquerade, **23.** 194

Norfolk, Dukes of, debarred from acting as Earls Marshal while adhering to, **21.** 535n

Norfolk House to have services of, in HW's newspaper parody, **9.** 128–9

North administration restores toleration of, **39.** 322

northern Irish Presbyterians favour emancipation of, **25.** 529n

Nugent a former member of, **17.** 255, 431

O'Brien's membership in, bars him from employment, **38.** 379

opera to start in London despite prejudice against, **19.** 177n

papers dispersed among members of, **16.** 172

Parisians are ashamed to defend, **14.** 149

passion play as Lenten devotion in, **23.** 459

Pitt, Elizabeth, converted to, **20.** 416, 507n

Pius VI probably pleased that Joseph II attacks Holland instead of property of, **25.** 544

Polish adherents of, invited to turn Mohammedan, **23.** 81

political interference of, in England, enrages Mann, **18.** 428

Powis a member of, **19.** 467

Presbyterian meeting-house said to be destroyed by, **25.** 56

Presbyterians oppose, **25.** 64

priests of: interest of, to be patriots, **39.** 456; Lancastrians upheld, but Richard III hated them, **41.** 115; Limerick, Vct, proposes law to license secular, in Ireland, **37.** 426–7; murdered in Paris, **34.** 163, 165

proof of miracles in, **30.** 299

Protestant prejudices not preferred to practices of, by HW, **18.** 79

Protestant ridicule of customs of, deplored by Mann, **18.** 59

Quebec Act permits tithes to be collected by, in Canada, **24.** 161n

—— restores, in Canada, **41.** 312

——'s toleration of, opposed by London, **39.** 175n

relics of, **15.** 280

religion of, forces its members to hate Turkey and England, **18.** 428

repeal of relief bill for, will not stop disorders, **39.** 350

riots against, **7.** 112–13; *see also* Gordon Riots

Rohan's disgrace will not prop, **25.** 603

said to be waning in England, **25.** 66

St-Germain possibly trained for, **26.** 20

St John wants to unite, with Church of England, **19.** 358

saints of, restrain folly, **32.** 334

Scotland not to tolerate, **24**. 439
Scottish bishop of, would not use same dialect as Somersetshire monk, **16**. 351–2
Scottish colonization barred to members of, **26**. 33
Selwyn drinks out of chalice belonging to, at tavern, **30**. 89
senility of, **25**. 48
services of, imitated in Vyne chapel, **35**. 185
Shrewsbury's chapel for, at Isleworth, **30**. 209n
Stafford, Cts of, forsakes, **38**. 42
SH Cabinet modelled upon chapel of, **21**. 306, **22**. 136
SH Chapel ready for restoration of, **32**. 197
suppression of, in Ireland, planned, **34**. 166n
suppression of Lombard convents disgorges wealth of, **25**. 594
Taaffe forsakes, to fight duel, **20**. 289
Test Act against, may be removed, **33**. 127
Thorold renounces, to get inheritance, **22**. 380
toleration would be forgone by, to avoid state control, **24**. 431n
tradition the authority of, **16**. 75
treaties made by, with intention of breaking them, **22**. 574
Trinity Hospital statutes tinged by doctrines of, **16**. 90
Turenne's conversion to, **24**. 255
Turkey regarded by, as Christianity's bulwark against Russia, **23**. 140
Tuscan clergy of, to have their licentiousness curbed by nuncio's edicts, **20**. 458
Tuscan friars of, forbidden to go out alone, **20**. 458
vipers of, have more than metaphoric poison, **25**. 245
Wall an adherent of, **21**. 347n
Walpole family branch adhering to, **1**. 128
wealth formerly bequeathed to, **25**. 514
Winnington jokes about, to Stafford, **18**. 283
women take to, in old age for entertainment, **20**. 378, 416, **24**. 107–8
Young Pretender receives remittances from gentlemen of, **19**. 176n
—— reverts to, **21**. 392n
—— said to have joined Polish members of, **23**. 337
—— said to have renounced, **20**. 333, **22**. 324, 368, 379–80, **23**. 402
——'s alleged renunciation of, a false rumour, **22**. 379–80
See also Cardinal; Clergy; Gordon Riots; Priest
Roman Catholic Relief Bill. *See under* Parliament: acts of
Romance, The. See Poinsinet, Antoine-Alexandre-Henri: *Tom Jones*
Romance; romances:
ancient, imitated in *Castle of Otranto*, **40**. 377
Conway longs to read, on the Rhine, **37**. 150
HW's fondness for, **37**. 126, 150, 189, 203

HW should write, **37**. 263
HW to read, on his return to SH, **24**. 117
'history that is not believed,' **15**. 173
knights cured by young ladies in, **42**. 468
metaphysical poems have not imagination of, **37**. 261
old, beast of the Gévaudan belongs in, **38**. 525
Romancier homme d'affaires, Le:
HW to write comedy about himself called, **5**. 398
Roman comique. See under Scarron, Paul
Roman correspondences:
HW offered, by Montagu, **9**. 144
Roman costume. *See under* Costume
Romanelli, Giovanni Francesco (1617–63), painter:
ceiling by, at Bibliothèque du Roi, **7**. 311
Roman Empire:
British Empire compared with, **22**. 513, **23**. 32
contending factions in, called greens and blues, **39**. 496
See also Gibbon, Edward: *Decline and Fall*
Roman faïence:
HW buys, **7**. 402
Roman Garmon Spinosa de los Monteros, Josèphe-Athanase, m. Louis Balbe-Berton, Marquis de Crillon:
Mme du Deffand's social relations with, **7**. 426, 427, 433
Roman Gate, in Florence (Porta Romana):
Pace outside of, **17**. 342
Spaniards to pass, **17**. 342
Roman History. See under Hooke, Nathaniel
Roman history:
HW forgets, **29**. 84
Romani, Angela, opera singer:
(?) Albergotti jealous of applause for, **17**. 162
Parma, dowager Ds of, patroness of, **17**. 162n
Roman medals. *See under* Medal
Roman mosaic. *See under* Mosaic
Romano, Giulio. *See* Pippi, Giulio
Roman pavements:
in Gloucestershire, copied for oil-cloths, **34**. 222–3, 225
Roman political parties. *See under* Political parties
Roman Portraits. See under Jephson, Robert
Romans, Bibliothèque des. See Bibliothèque des romans
Romans, Mlle de. *See* Couppier, Anne
Romans, King of the:
England solicits Frederick Augustus's vote for Joseph II as, **30**. 320
Francis II may become, **25**. 613n, 661
Joseph II's election and coronation as, **22**. 324
——'s election as: expected, **20**. 294; Frederick Augustus II promises to vote for, **20**. 186n, 187n; may be chosen, **42**. 496; Newcastle negotiates with Richecourt's brother over,

[Romans, King of the, *continued*]
    20. 178n; Newcastle presses Frederick II
    and Elector of Cologne to stop blocking,
    20. 394n

Roman Sacrifice, The. See under Shirley, William (fl. 1739–80)

Roman sailor:
    Corinthian statues belittled by, **19.** 264

'Roman Slave Plucking the Thorn out of his Foot':
    painting of, at Deane House, **40.** 4

Romantic, the:
    HW's fondness for, **1.** 55

Roman urn. *See under* Urn

Roman writers:
    English poets imitate in treatment of summer, **10.** 262

Romanzov; Romanzow. *See* Rumiantsev

Rome, governor of. *See* Archinto, Alberigo;
    Buondelmonti, Filippo Manente; Potenciani,
    Giovanni; Rinuccini, Giovanni

Rome, ancient:
    adulation of literati in, **41.** 63
    amphitheatre of, near Dorchester, **37.** 491
    authors of, inferior to Shakespeare, **41.** 294
    army camp of, near Dorchester, **37.** 491
    Brutus and, **18.** 19
    Cæsar and Brutus at, **41.** 305
    Caligula's horse becomes consul of, **35.** 375
    camp sites of, inferior to letters as historical
    evidence, **42.** 100
    capitol at: **13.** 209; HW writes humourous
    inscription for altar in, **10.** 23
    Carthaginian author would be proud to be
    translated at, by Scipio, **42.** 129
    Cicero the orator of, **35.** 262
    coins of, **15.** 16, **34.** 10n, **35.** 477n, **42.** 239n
    consuls and tribunes of, Livy wrote history
    of, well, **30.** 221
    consuls of: not imitated by Onslow, **35.** 286;
    receive Gauls in Forum, **20.** 469, **33.** 327
    Conway's bridge at Park Place will be ascribed to, **39.** 460
    copper dish of, **17.** 364
    Corinthian statues belittled by sailors of, **19.** 264
    dedication of Julian curia at, **20.** 128n
    defeats of, were not reflected in stock exchange, **21.** 558
    destroyed by public vices, **15.** 128
    Dorchester's army camp and amphitheatre
    founded by, **37.** 491
    duels not customary in senate of, **25.** 31
    eagles of, **22.** 404, **23.** 32, **38.** 137
    eighteenth-century England will be revered
    like, **38.** 187–8
    England compared with, **23.** 212, **38.** 187–8
    —— excels, in eloquence and extravagance,
    23. 400
    ——'s empire compared with that of, **10.** 221,
    33. 158
    English victories surpass those of, **35.** 294

epitaphs of, to be imitated for Wood's tombstone, **41.** 247
fathers of families rewarded in, despite devastation of other lands, **24.** 393
Forum Boarium in, **14.** 20
Forum of: consuls receive Gauls in, **20.** 469;
    33. 327; pasquinades in style of, **17.** 351;
    Trajan's, **26.** 7
Gellius gives interesting details about, **15.** 246
HW admires five emperors of, **33.** 479
HW jokes about House of Commons as, **31.** 22
HW proud of England as first nation on
    earth, like, **38.** 513
HW's coins and medals of, **35.** 477n
HW's 'Gothic Vatican' of, **33.** 529
HW's simile concerning, **15.** 257
HW studies history of, **9.** 3–4
Hardinge deplores lowering of heroes of, **35.** 561
Henley bridge keystones worthy of, **35.** 386
hippopotamus and rhinoceros make first appearances in, **20.** 128n
historians of, inspire modern wars, **38.** 121
history of, before Republic's fall, compared
    to modern England, **25.** 118
Knight's *Marcus Flaminius* shows knowledge
    of, **34.** 167
legions of, flee from Scotland, **16.** 374
Lincoln's antiquities from time of, **40.** 233
Livy wrote history of, well, **30.** 221
lore of, **34.** 244
'lower empire' of, **16.** 210
manners of people of, contained little nature,
    15. 65
matrons of, addicted to mysteries, **20.** 41
medals of, **16.** 204, **23.** 383, **35.** 477n, **42.** 111,
    239n; *see also under* Medal
Middleton a 'citizen' of, **15.** 14
——'s antiquities illustrate customs of, **15.** 15–16
——'s treatise on senate of, **15.** 296
naumachia of, **37.** 297
Nugent's verses mention fall of, **31.** 269
politics in, **35.** 215
Pontine marshes not drained by, **24.** 344
power and skill of people of, **15.** 202
probably stared at its own downfall, **24.** 228
proconsuls of, pensioned by tributary sovereigns, **25.** 118
racing in, imitated in Florence, **17.** 79n
relics of, found in England, **15.** 179, 202
religion of, **14.** 19
Renaissance Latin would be unintelligible to
    all but scavengers of, **33.** 537
senate of: appears to barbarian ambassadors
    like an assembly of kings, **23.** 562, **32.** 171;
    Whaley's epigram mentions, **40.** 23
senator of, would not have matched daughter
    to a king, **18.** 221, **22.** 499, **24.** 186
sensualists' refinements at, **39.** 3
ship's prow of, **37.** 320
statuary from, at Wilton, **40.** 8

swimming and running the usual exercises of youth at, **37**. 8

Trajan's, **26**. 7

tribune of, **38**. 120

Virgil's probable intelligibility to social groups of, **16**. 269

virtue was in fashion in, **32**. 266

writers of, rivalled by Robertson, **15**. 46–7

See also under Gibbon, Edward: *Decline and Fall*; Middleton, Conyers: *A Treatise on the Roman Senate*; ibidem, *De medicorum . . . conditione* and *Dissertationis . . . defensio*

Rome, modern:

Accademia di San Luca at, **13**. 26n

Acciaiolis leave, **19**. 407

accounts from: of Acciaioli's expulsion, **21**. 476; of D. and Ds of Gloucester, favourable, **24**. 181; printed at, of rebels' success in Scotland, **19**. 158

Acquaviva omnipotent at, **18**. 55

—— sends recruits from, to Spanish army, **18**. 542

Admiralty appointments to, please, **17**. 355

agents to and from, *see under* Agent

Agincourt's valet the doyen of guides to, **42**. 64–5

Agincourt to be addressed at, **42**. 104

—— writes from, **42**. 63, 101

air of, determined by D. of Gloucester to be favourable to his health, **24**. 130

Albani introduces Chute and Whithed to society in, **19**. 59

—— 's circular letter to foreign ministers at, **22**. 76

—— 's villa surpasses all sights of, **22**. 229

Albany, Cts of, called a prisoner at, by HW, **25**. 115

—— discourages Gustav III at, **25**. 475

—— protected at, by brother-in-law, **25**. 108n

—— to occupy convent at, **25**. 106

Alfieri expelled from, **33**. 438–9

Almada's absence from, required by Clement XIII's advisers, **21**. 425

—— 's house in, **21**. 426

'almost reduced to her own bawdy-house,' **23**. 81

altar, sepulchral, may be sought at, **20**. 325

ambassadors from and to, *see under* ambassador

annona at, short of grain, **22**. 453n

anno santo to draw visitors to, **20**. 43

antiques not to be exported from, **18**. 161

antiquities restored at, **21**. 344

aqueducts of, **13**. 208

architecture of, *see under* Architecture: Roman

armies near, **18**. 531–4

Ashburnham shuns, for fear of imprisonment, **19**. 454

assemblies at, attended by D. of Gloucester, **24**. 163

Atrisco's approach terrifies, **18**. 444

Aubeterre learns little at, **23**. 158

Augustus, P., to visit, **35**. 443

Austrian party at, **19**. 114

Balhaldies and Bandini leave, **18**. 380

balls postponed at, till after Easter, **23**. 95

Barberini collection in, being sold, **13**. 214

Barberini palace at, **21**. 533

Basquiat, former secretary of Swedish delegation at, **23**. 439

Batoni's portrait of D. of York to come from, **22**. 255

Bavarian representative at, calls on Old Pretender, **17**. 445

Bayreuth, Margrave and Margravine of, not to change religion at, **20**. 479

Benedict XIV closes borders of, **18**. 270

—— furbishes up churches and theatres at, **20**. 98

—— might prevent eagle from leaving, **19**. 149

—— 's death reported at Basel from, **21**. 44n

—— suggests Young Pretender leave Avignon for, **20**. 22n

—— to return to, and hold congregation of cardinals, **19**. 416

Bernis, Cardinal de, lives at Palazzo Carolis on the Corso at, **25**. 675n

—— minister to, **3**. 405n

—— publishes at, mistaken news of French victory, **25**. 127

Billard to visit, **5**. 190

Boccapadugli Gardens at, **3**. 405n

book on Portuguese conspiracy printed in, **21**. 275

Borghese villa at, Silenus and Bacchus at, imitated by Guido, **32**. 169n

Bottari at, **23**. 469

Bourbon ministers at: begin to press Clement XIV to dissolve Jesuits, **23**. 214; treat Almada with contempt, **23**. 221

Bouverie, Clephane, Fuller and Trapp to visit, **17**. 154

Braitwitz's retirement will displease, because hard-working people are scarce, **19**. 3

Brand to visit, **20**. 434, 456

Breton designs bas relief at, for Wolfe's tomb, **21**. 436

Bridgwater to visit, **20**. 451

(?) Bruce, Miss, pupil of Alexander Cozens at, **20**. 145n

bust of Vespasian considered the fourth or fifth at, **22**. 523

Bute to return to, **20**. 96

caballing expected at, over papal election, **21**. 197

Campagna near, bad air in, **13**. 221

Capello's departure from, **20**. 173, 176, 177

cardinals at, protect different countries, **33**. 245

cardinals at, *see also under* Cardinal

Carlisle, Cts of, to stay at, 'for the air,' **23**. 447

carnival dull at, **24**. 280

[Rome, modern, *continued*]

Castel Sant'Angelo, Coscia imprisoned in, **13.** 216

Castellum Aquæ Martiæ at, **13.** 207

catacombs and churches of, searched by Agincourt, **42.** 104

Catherine II sends minister to, **25.** 389

Charles of Naples (Charles III of Spain) enters, incognito, **18.** 519n

—— marches to, **18.** 525

——'s edict brought to, **23.** 10

—— to make pilgrimage to, **18.** 519

—— to visit, for *anno santo*, **20.** 43

Chartres, Duchesse de, visits, for 5 days, **24.** 222

Cholmondeley's portrait to be painted at, **23.** 349, 357, 371

—— to visit, **25.** 324

churches at, *see below, under* Del Anima; Gésu; St Apollinare; St Ignazio; St-Isidore; St Thomas's; San Carlo ai Catinari; San Giovanni (Lateran); San Giovanni e Paolo (convent); Santa Bibiana; Santa Maria del Anima; Santa Maria in Cosmedin; Santa Maria Maggiore; Santi Apostoli

Chute and Whithed may visit, **35.** 46, 52

Chute asserts at, that Young Pretender is not really in Scotland, **19.** 198

—— occupies HW's old lodging at, **35.** 58

—— should get dispensation from, **35.** 39

——'s indifference to, **35.** 58

—— to spread reports in, about English zeal, **19.** 128

—— writes from, **35.** 57, 60

Clark avoids, **19.** 454

Clement XIII puts, into a bustle, **21.** 230

—— regulates printing of Portuguese *Sentença* at, **21.** 275n

——'s quarrel with Genoa forgotten at, **21.** 422

Clement XIV invites D. of Gloucester to, **23.** 343, 348

——'s death at: not discussed, **24.** 50; shocks people, **24.** 49; the only recent crime, **24.** 154

——'s nephew a fiddler at, **23.** 117

—— well received on return to, **23.** 526

Coke, Lady Mary, may have trouble at, **23.** 547

—— should visit Young Pretender's court at, **23.** 550

Coliseum at: Borghese's explanation of, **13.** 210; HW will not describe to West, **13.** 209–10; modelled after Solomon's temple, **13.** 218

Conclaves at. *See under* Conclave

Conecte burnt at, **9.** 78

confusion at, **23.** 35–6

convent at, Wortley Montagu's daughter said to be in, **22.** 113

conversazioni at, bad, **37.** 57

Conway should get recommendation for, from HW and E. of Orford, **37.** 312

—— to visit, **20.** 293, 295–6

Cope's defeat predicted at, **19.** 142

corn shortage at, **22.** 223, 224n, 229, 446

Corsi prevented from going to, **18.** 121

corso at, **13.** 209, **17.** 3, **19.** 358

courier from: **18.** 477, **20.** 42; awaited by Mann, **19.** 501; Paris courier outruns, **22.** 405, 407; seeks Young Pretender, **22.** 383, 387; to Florence, prevented by floods, **19.** 131

courier from Naples to stop at, **21.** 463

couriers from: forbidden, **18.** 525; to Vienna, **19.** 158

couriers sent to, about Dumesnil's arrest, **19.** 493

courier to: from France, **19.** 150, 218, 253, 257, **24.** 10; from Milan, **18.** 515; spreads reports of Young Pretender's successes, **19.** 197

courier to Old Pretender walks about streets of, **19.** 89

Cours de l'Europe, Les, satirizes, **17.** 177

Court of: Acciaioli's expulsion from Lisbon published by, **21.** 476; Choiseul tells Aubeterre to treat, with a high hand, **22.** 384; claims Monte Santa Maria, **20.** 428; dislikes Leopold's letter, **22.** 378; England obliges, by lenity to Roman Catholics, **22.** 369; Francis III disgusted by, **23.** 45; Galluzzi's history unfavourable to, **25.** 87n; George III acknowledged by, **22.** 389–90; may placate England by refusing to acknowledge Young Pretender, **22.** 369; Neapolitan Court differs with, over cardinals' costume, **23.** 18; opposed to Richecourt, **20.** 334; shocked by narrative about Fiore case, **22.** 328; tries to destroy Gregory XIII medal, **21.** 201

Cowpers to visit, **24.** 251

Craon, Princesse de, dislikes fleeing to, **17.** 178

Crescimbeni's blunder about Richard I's letter at, **21.** 178

crimes no longer characteristic of, **22.** 254, **24.** 154

Cumberland, D. and Ds of, may be ill-received at, **23.** 502

Cumberland, D. of, and D. of Gloucester did not make good impressions at, **24.** 123

Damer, Mrs, to visit, **25.** 213

Damer's and Gascoigne's fray with coachman at, **22.** 286, 300n

dangerous in summer, **38.** 531

Dashwood's hatred of George II exposed in letters from, **17.** 417

decrees from, must be passed by parliament of Paris, **5.** 213–14

degradation of, **25.** 589

Del Anima church at, **23.** 36

Dick, Sir John and Lady, to spend winter at, **24.** 240, 251

documents preserved at, **15.** 186

Doria said to have sent peace news to, **17.** 134

Du Deffand, Mme, mentions, 6. 325
Dumesnil escapes from, 19. 493
Dunbar about to leave, 19. 378
—— may have left, 19. 143
—— slanders Chute and Whithed to, 19. 136
eagle found at, 19. 66, 79, 121–2, 197, 420
edict to be published by, for Del Montes' arrest or death, 20. 446
Electress's money at, to be used to finish chapel, 18. 113
——'s will deposited at, 18. 168
enamellers of, 21. 313
England's enemies at, distort news, 19. 158, 217, 362
—— will allow, to starve, 22. 462
English at: arrive at Florence, 23. 296, 24. 214, 25. 672; attentive to D. and Ds of Gloucester, 24. 190; believe in Young Pretender's success, 19. 191; crowd from Florence, 24. 131; painted by Maratti, 42. 159n; play faro, 17. 29; see design for Wolfe's tomb, 21. 436
English College at: 21. 339n; medallion found at, 42. 64
English crowd to, for jubilee, 20. 82–3, 98
English-French war expected at, 17. 24
English Jacobites at: call on Dunbar, 19. 136; court Old Pretender's sons when forbidden to see himself, 19. 112, 136; make junkets after Falkirk news, 19. 218; might molest Chute and Whithed, 19. 113; more confident than those in England, 19. 139
English news echoed from, to Florence, 18. 368–9, 19. 217
English Parliament may be like the sole senator of, 33. 221
English visit, for Holy Week, 22. 492, 25. 672
Esquiline, the, at, 13. 207n
Evelyn's journey from, to Naples, 16. 61, 63
experience of, in maintaining dignity in difficult circumstances, 22. 236
falling into decay, 13. 208, 213–14
famine threatens, 22. 446, 448
faro suppressed at, 17. 29
fishermen of, to be lured to Leghorn, 20. 217
floods in, 20. 77, 23. 378
Florentine intercourse with, cut off, 18. 525
Florentine society surpasses that of, 22. 528n
foreign ministers at: dispatch couriers to their courts, 23. 16; report Pius VI's illness to their courts, 24. 468
Forum at, 41. 6
fountains the only water supply of, 24. 179
France has little influence at, 21. 220
French again dictating to, 34. 217
French couriers to and from, 20. 42, 147, 23. 10, 14, 16
French depredations at, expected, 12. 195
French people's expulsion from, demanded by mob, 12. 77
funeral price at, 21. 391
Gages's plans reported from, 19. 556

Galluzzi's history may be suppressed at, 25. 59, 80
——'s history not controverted in, 25. 238
—— treats Court of, unfavourably, 25. 80, 87n
Gascoigne and Hon. George Damer have drunken fray with coachman at, 22. 286
gates of: 13. 208; see also Flaminian Gate; Porta Angelica; Porta del Popolo; Porta Maggiore; Porta Pia; Porta San Giovanni; Porta San Lorenzo
Genoese quarrel with Clement XIII causes commotion in, 21. 394
George II's illness rumoured at, 19. 377
George III indebted to, for hospitality to D. of Cumberland, 23. 566
——'s art purchases at, 22. 115
German cardinals not at, 23. 95
Germans, French, Spaniards, English, Poles, and Italians not to bring riches to, for jubilee, 20. 83n
Gésu, S. Ignazio and St Apollinare the only Jesuit churches in, left open, 23. 507n
girandole de, la, 4. 402
Girifalco, Duchessa di, retires to, 35. 434
Giustiniani's palace at, 23. 287
glory of, family pride on a large scale, 25. 133
Gloucester, D. and Ds of, leave, for the summer, 24. 290
—— may visit, 24. 298, 312, 25. 618, 624
—— not pleased with all the great ladies at, 24. 247
—— pleased with, 24. 186
—— probably already on way to, 24. 144
—— to have 'babe of Brunswick' born at, 32. 249
—— to return to, 34. 246
—— to spend winter at, 24. 82
—— urged by HW not to go to, 24. 125
Gloucester, Ds of, writes from, 36. 326, 327
Gloucester, D. of, able to set out for, 24. 141
—— and Young Pretender can live only in, 36. 114n
Gloucester, D. of, approaches, though he seemed averse to revisiting it, 24. 129
—— has more faith than most people in air of, 24. 84
—— house kept for, at, 24. 312
—— in no condition to go to, 23. 370
—— insults, 23. 556
—— may be unable to set out to, 24. 140
—— may deter Ds of Kingston from visiting, 24. 220
—— may not be well received at, 24. 123
—— may visit, 23. 384, 24. 117, 130
—— plumper in England than at, 24. 332
—— prevented by physicians from going to, 23. 357
—— to spend winter at, 24. 117, 36. 309
—— writes from, 24. 291, 36. 306
Gloucester, P. William and Ps Sophia of, painted at, 42. 71n
gossip of, 17. 24

[Rome, modern, *continued*]

Gothic remains probably non-existent at, **20.** 372

government of, in state of confusion, **25.** 588

governor of: inhabits Palazzo Madama, **20.** 264n; *see also* Buondelmonti, Filippo (1671–1741); Caprara, Cornelio (1703–65); Piccolomini, Eneo Silvio (1709–68); Ricci, Francesco (1679–1755); Rinuccini, Giovanni; Spinelli, Ferdinando Maria (1728–95)

Gower jokingly said to await dispensation from, **17.** 499

Grafton, Ds of, to visit, **21.** 554

Graftons take other road to, **21.** 565

Gray's alcaic odes written at, **43.** 191

'great abbé' at, *see* Guérin de Tencin, Pierre

great ladies of: are proud and saucy, **24.** 123; ignore Ds of Kingston, **24.** 95; offended by D. of Gloucester's postponed reception, **24.** 164

Guido Reni's 'Aurora' in Casino Rospiglione at, **20.** 328n

HW asks Mann for gossip in, about Murray and Stone, **20.** 360

HW calls: 'Babylon,' **23.** 212; 'Catholic dunghill,' **22.** 237; 'Madame of Babylon,' **24.** 255; 'Old Mother Babylon,' **22.** 420

HW commissions statue to be made at, **13.** 26, **17.** 212, **18.** 161–2, 177–9

HW compares English conquests to those of, **10.** 22

HW expects Lady Mary Coke to have trouble at, **23.** 547

HW imagines medieval news bulletins from, **35.** 322

HW imagines pope's poisoning at, **35.** 222

HW inquires whether Lincoln likes, **30.** 5

HW pleased by changed attitude of, to English Protestants, **22.** 177

HW prefers art of Bologna to that of, **15.** 332

HW prophesied dullness of, to Lincoln, **30.** 6

HW saw Poussin's 'Seven Sacraments' in, **33.** 538

HW's departure from, **40.** 30

HW's eagle restored at, **11.** 293

HW's fondness for, mentioned by Whaley, **40.** 49

HW's *jeu d'esprit* on, **14.** 239

HW's lodging at, **35.** 58

HW studies history of, **9.** 3–4

HW sure Lincoln likes, because Lady Sophia Fermor is there, **30.** 14

HW's views of, *see under* Locatelli

HW wants altar from, to use as pedestal, **21.** 461

Hamilton, Gavin, settled at, **41.** 444

Hamilton, Sir William, buys Cignani painting at, **21.** 208

health office at, quarantines against plague, **18.** 263n

Henry Benedict (later Cardinal York) said to leave, **17.** 13, **18.** 436, **19.** 98–9

——'s return to, **19.** 415n

Hervey, Bp, informed from, that Church would forgo toleration to avoid state control, **24.** 431n

—— sends speech to agent at, **25.** 443, 459n

history of, made into romance for lack of heroes, **37.** 261

Hobart writes from, **40.** 57

holy days cancelled at, **22.** 17

hospital at, receives surgical instruments from D. of Gloucester, **24.** 129; *see also* Portuguese Hospital at; Santo Spirito Hospital at

house in, falls, **22.** 17

hurricane at, **20.** 69–70, 77

ignorance at, **11.** 295

Illustri fatti Farnesiani may be scarce at, **25.** 403

'inexhaustible,' **17.** 22

inoculation not used in, **22.** 150

Irish priest at, does medal, **21.** 202

Jacobite antiquarian at, **20.** 174

Jacobites at: call Falkirk a victory, **19.** 214; depress Mann, **19.** 182

Jenkins, Thomas, art agent in, **20.** 174n

Jerusalem's recovery dubious at downfall of, **23.** 195

Jesuit refugees too numerous for, **22.** 516

Jesuits' College at, Jesuits' correspondence about Gunpowder Plot said to be found at, **23.** 517–18, 532, 539n, **25.** 458

Jesuits escape to, from Corsica, **22.** 546n

—— flock to, **24.** 43

——' silver weighed at, **23.** 512–13

——' suppression planned at, **23.** 135

—— to be expelled from, **23.** 473

——' vast wealth at, **22.** 527

——' war at, uninteresting to HW, **21.** 491

João V may visit, **20.** 43

José Manoel may precipitate revolt by withdrawing subjects from, **21.** 430

Joseph II acclaimed at, as 'king,' **23.** 103

—— and Maria Josefa to visit, **21.** 556

jubilee year's pilgrims to, estimated at three million, **20.** 43n

Karl Friedrich's reception at, amuses England, **20.** 155

Kingston, Ds of, invests money at, **6.** 311

—— leaves jewels and furniture at, **24.** 83–4, 123, 162n, 203, 298, 404, 409

—— may not visit, while D. and Ds of Gloucester are there, **24.** 220

lady from, *see* Savelli, Barbara

Laocoön duplicate at, **22.** 71

La Rochefoucauld's arrival at, **35.** 59

Lascari to visit, ostensibly for jubilee, **20.** 44n

Leicester to obtain statues from, **20.** 104

Leopold opposes dictates of, **25.** 81

—— suppresses Pisa abbey without consulting, **23.** 504

Leslie's history published at, **15.** 120

letters from: about Old Pretender's health, **21.** 392, 406; delayed because of quarantine, **18.** 282; expected at Florence, **19.** 13; from St Thomas Aquinas's, Piazza Navona, **19.**

227–8; lost, **19.** 143; say that Spanish progress is arrested, **19.** 8–9; tell of Benedict XIV's stand about Monte Santa Maria, **20.** 428; to Goldsworthy, **19.** 226

letters to: from France and Germany, ask about Clement XIV's health, **24.** 43–4; from Paris, about Young Pretender, **19.** 451

Lobkowitz and Maria Theresa acclaimed at, **18.** 446–7

—— sends stores and old women to, for safety, **18.** 447

London compared with, **24.** 228

Louis XV avoids break with, **23.** 518

lower classes at, disarmed for fear of bread riots, **22.** 229

Lucan, Bn or Bns, gets sarcophagus at, **24.** 462

Macdonald ill at, **3.** 110

malaria prevalent at, **37.** 66

Mann afraid to ask at, about Gloucester family, **24.** 181

—— alarmed by reports from, of Young Pretender's Scottish invasion, **19.** 130–1

—— awaits Benedict XIV's medals from, **21.** 231

—— buys *Illustri fatti Farnesiani* at, **25.** 412, 417

—— denies having visited, **20.** 473

—— forwards letter received from, **17.** 3

—— gets altar at, for HW. **20.** 365

—— gets news from: of Scottish emissaries, **17.** 145; of Young Pretender's departure, **17.** 113

—— has not heard from, about pedestal for Vespasian bust, **21.** 482

—— hears from: about Lanfranco, **18.** 296–7; of Clement XIII's reception of Young Pretender, **22.** 517

—— hears nothing from, about Lanfranco picture, **18.** 290

—— may have to wait at, **17.** 196

—— misled by reports from, **17.** 118

—— not to spread news at, of Edinburgh troubles, **19.** 129

—— offers to send Young Pretender's acquaintances at, to England to identify him, **19.** 141

—— plans Sir Robert Walpole's visit to, **18.** 211–13

—— prevented Young Pretender's coronation at, **23.** 329

—— receives account through, of Russo-Turkish naval battle, **23.** 226–7

—— rumoured to be visiting, **20.** 470

——'s abbé at, **17.** 3, 113, 114, 145, **18.** 466, 485, **19.** 140

——'s art advisers at, are Chambers and Vierpyl, **20.** 391–2

—— sends sketch of eagle's pedestal to, **20.** 333

——'s friends at, warn him about Young Pretender, **19.** 368

——'s information about Young Pretender all comes from, **19.** 86

——'s letters limited to area of Florence and, **25.** 464

——'s 'neighbour' at, *see* James Francis Edward

——'s spy at, an abbé, **17.** 13, **19.** 40

—— tells architect to get Gothic ornaments at, **20.** 368–9

—— tells Horace Mann II to pay respects to D. and Ds of Gloucester at, **24.** 163

—— to get copies of paintings at, **20.** 328–9

—— to inquire at, about mould of 'Livia' statue, **22.** 98

—— to recommend Pars at, **24.** 135, 144

—— to send English propaganda to, **18.** 259, 427, **19.** 205, 298, **22.** 386–7

—— tries to engage Antonio Bracci as agent in, to observe Old Pretender, **20.** 221n

—— unable to go to, to investigate rumours, **17.** 116

—— would like to send Irish epigram to, **20.** 318

—— writes to: about Lanfranco, **18.** 275; about pedestal, **21.** 470; for antique sepulchral urn, **20.** 333; for medals of Benedict XIV, **21.** 215; for prints of Young Pretender and wife, **23.** 427, 429

Mann, Horace II, and Lady Lucy to go to, **24.** 118, 129, 131, 140, 145, 146, 181

—— urge Mann to accompany them to, **24.** 129

many at, think Pius VI will pay visit to Joseph II, **25.** 239

map of, requested from Mann by D. of Cumberland, **20.** 459

Maria Amalia to visit, **18.** 435, 438, **20.** 43

Maria Carolina, Leopold, and Maria Louisa not to enter, **23.** 2, 17

Maria Carolina's subjects at, pay homage to her at Marino, **23.** 23

——'s visit to, forbidden but will be forgiven, **23.** 26

Maria Josefa to visit, **22.** 556

Maria Theresa acclaimed at, **18.** 447

——'s affairs at, no longer managed by Albani, **19.** 475

——'s representative at, tells Mann of Young Pretender's flight, **18.** 373

Mathews's protest forwarded to, **18.** 301

medal of Henry IX struck at, **11.** 270

medals at, **16.** 204

medals procured from estate of deceased collector at, **18.** 478

medals sent from, to Mann, **18.** 45

medals sent to, from England, **17.** 229

Mengs to visit, **16.** 170

Minerva Medici, so-called temple at, described by HW, **13.** 207–8

ministers from and to Holy See at, *see under* Minister

mob at: Austrian in sympathies, **17.** 114; bread thrown by, into Clement XIII's coach, **22.** 446; celebrates Francis I's election, **19.** 113

[Rome, modern, *continued*]

Modenese rulers may take refuge in, **17.** 489

Moniño's friends during stay at, inform Mann of his character, **24.** 478

Monti's account of Young Pretender's departure from, **18.** 418–19

Moretti a merchant at, **20.** 46

mosaic craftsmen at, **28.** 301

mosaic shrine from, sent to HW, **1.** 244, **2.** 370, **35.** 409

Mount Palatine at, compared to Sion House, **38.** 429

Murray's promotion may be rumoured from, to Mann, **18.** 118

Naples and Tuscany might be shut off from, **18.** 270

narrative burnt at, by hangman, **22.** 328

Neapolitan Court may flee to, **17.** 501, **18.** 3, 13

—— quarrels with, over cardinals' costume, **23.** 18

Neapolitan troops reach Porta del Popolo at, **19.** 144

Necker's appointment in France may cause comment in, **24.** 255

nobility of: attentive to D. and Ds of Gloucester, **24.** 190; entertain Joseph II and Leopold, **23.** 108–9; lead dismal lives, **13.** 208–9; prepare festivals for Leopold, **23.** 95; said to be jealous of Young Pretender, **22.** 394; to give tragedy at Frascati, **21.** 481; York, Cardinal, despised by, **25.** 397

Nugent's verses mention fall of, **31.** 269

nuncios from, *see under* Nuncio

O'Brien leaves, **20.** 45

Old Pretender acknowledged at, by representatives of George II's allies, **18.** 428

—— at, receives English news from Goddard, **17.** 368

—— joined at, by Cardinal York, **20.** 354

—— languishes forgotten at, **22.** 106

—— lives at, **5.** 218n

—— may leave, **19.** 94, 96, 99, 135, 141–2

——'s burial eagerly awaited at, so that theatres may reopen, **22.** 385

——'s condition reported from, **21.** 391, **22.** 379

——'s Court, troublesome and expensive to, **22.** 369

——'s faction at, **19.** 400

——'s funeral still expected at, **21.** 412

——'s furniture brought from, to Florence, by son, **25.** 525

——'s Herrenhausen, **20.** 341

——'s high spirits reported from, **17.** 306

——'s property in, left to Cardinal York, **22.** 387

——'s underling and Bandini leave, for Tuscany, **18.** 379–80

—— thought by, to be last English king to cure King's Evil, **21.** 392

old princesses of, offended by Clement XIII's exclusion of them, **23.** 431

old saying about pope of, **23.** 128

old senators of, keep Adonis wigs with their robes for days of ceremony, **24.** 32

opera at, reportedly fine, **30.** 5

Orford, Cts of, ill at, **24.** 317–18

—— to visit, **23.** 478, **24.** 222, 304

Ormond sends courier to, **19.** 85

owl replaces eagle at, **6.** 426

palaces of, *see* Asti, Palazzo; Barberini Palace; Bolognetti, Palazzo; Cancelleria, Palazzo della; Carolis, Palazzo; Farnese, Palazzo; Firenze, Palazzo di; Madama, Palazzo; Massimo, Villa; Negroni, Villa; Pamfili Palace; Santi Apostoli, palace of; Teodoli Palace

Palatine Hill at, painting found at, **37.** 67

Palazzo Madama at, **20.** 264

Paris letters in, quoted about new attempt by Young Pretender, **19.** 451

Parker antiquarian at, **17.** 82n

—— a Roman Catholic refugee at, **17.** 81n

parliament of Paris defends Parma against, **23.** 4

Parliament's disapprobation of peace treaty attributed by, to Young Pretender, **20.** 27

Pars dies at, **26.** 48

—— to study in, **24.** 144

pasquinade in style of, **17.** 351

pasquinades in, on imperial election, **17.** 351

Passionei invites Niccolini to, **21.** 127

Patch studied under Vernet in, **23.** 275

pedestal to have been sent from, **21.** 521

Philip, Don, may stay near, **18.** 389

physician from, attends Cts of Orford, **24.** 312

physicians should not prescribe air of, **23.** 451

Piazza d'Espagna at, *see* Spagna, Piazza di

Piccolomini to obtain act of oblivion so that Damer and Gascoigne may return to, **22.** 287

Pitt, Anne, nurses French female servant at, **24.** 344, 353

Pius VI and Cardinal York invite Cts of Albany to convent at, **25.** 106

Pius VI may not be applauded at, on return from Vienna, **25.** 283

——'s illness concealed at, **24.** 467–8

——'s *possesso* draws crowds to, **24.** 131, 136, 145

——'s unpopularity at, **25.** 383, 587–8

——'s visit to Vienna disapproved at, **25.** 250

pleasures of, to be found in no other city, **13.** 221

Poelenburg goes to, **7.** 355n

Ponte Milvio, seen by HW, **13.** 206

Pontine drainage expensive to, **25.** 383, 588

pope to be chosen at, **32.** 209

Porta Angelica at: road to, **18.** 532; Spaniards fear to seize, **18.** 533

Porta del Popolo at: Lobkowitz's army passes near, **18.** 531; Neapolitan troops at, **19.**

144; road to, **18**. 532; Young Pretender's escape by, **18**. 388
Porta Maggiore at, **13**. 207n
Porta San Giovanni at: Lobkowitz's army passes near, **18**. 531; Young Pretender escapes through, **18**. 387, 388
Portugal's quarrel with, over Jesuits, **21**. 423–6, 475–7
Portuguese banker at, *see* Rosa, Lopez
Portuguese Hospital at, **21**. 423
Portuguese Jesuits not to be permitted to go to, **21**. 340n
Portuguese representatives threaten to leave, **21**. 423, 425–6
post from, brings Ds of Gloucester's letter to Mann, **24**. 250
Poussin's 'Seven Sacraments' at, **33**. 538
—— 's sketches from, **7**. 279
poverty of: caused by Cardinal Corsini, **13**. 208; encourages banditti, **13**. 221
Prideaux's letters forwarded to, by Mann, **18**. 491
Priero to leave, after arrival of Viennese couriers, **19**. 158
princes and princesses of, act at Frascati, **20**. 481
prints of, given to D. of York, **22**. 229, 232–3
Protestant cemetery in, first monument in, **22**. 306n
Prussian resident at, *see* Ciofani, Matthäus
Querini, Cardinal, publishes letters at, **20**. 190n
—— sent from Venice to, to assist Capello, **20**. 190n
Raphael painting praised at, **35**. 37
rebels' executions have no effect at, **19**. 311
reports fabricated at, **19**. 155–6
Reynolds buys Poussins at, for D. of Rutland, **33**. 538
rhinoceros goes to jubilee at, **20**. 127
Richard I's poem not at, **21**. 169, 178
Richecourt's persecution from, **20**. 334
—— 's subservience to, **20**. 448
Rienzi a demagogue of, **23**. 8n
Rinuccini, Giovanni, governor of, **20**. 336n
Rospigliosi Palace at, has Guido Reni's 'Aurora,' **30**. 327n
rumour from, of Austrian-Prussian peace, **17**. 134
Sabbatini dies at, **9**. 81n
Sacchetti collection in, being sold, **13**. 214
St-Aignan enters, **17**. 12
sainthood delayed by cabals at, **23**. 124
St Peter's at: French cardinal unimpressed by, **13**. 209; 'from, to St Paul's,' **13**. 195; relics displayed in, **13**. 210
St Peter's Day to be celebrated at, **18**. 462
San Carlo ai Catinari, church of, Domenichino painting in, **14**. 20
San Giovanni in Laterano, church of, **13**. 207
Santa Bibiana, church of, **13**. 207n
Santa Croce entertains people of, **17**. 20

Santa Maria dell' Anima, church of, **23**. 36
Santa Maria Maggiore, church of: **1**. 244n, **13**. 207; shrine from, **43**. 284
Santi Apostoli, church of, **19**. 191, 196, **21**. 392
Santo Spirito Hospital in, **24**. 129
satires at, about Conclave, **21**. 217
seal cut at, **19**. 9
searchers prevent antiquities from leaving, **18**. 161–2
Secret Committee's defeat disheartens Jacobites at, **17**. 388
sede vacante at, compared to English change of administration, **25**. 377–8
senate, *see under* Senate
senator of, Rezzonico becomes, **22**. 331n
sepulchral altar bought in, **20**. 365
Shirley enlists supporters of James I in, **15**. 80
shrine at, bought by HW, **1**. 244, **2**. 370, **35**. 409
silver scarce at, **17**. 4
Skrine's letter from important personage in, **22**. 447
snow cuts off, from Florence, **25**. 470
'soil of Neros and Borgias,' **24**. 154
Spain lowers revenue of, by buying nomination to benefices, **21**. 349
—— said by, to be about to aid Young Pretender, **19**. 335
Spaniards and Neapolitans near, **18**. 546
Spaniards chase people back to, **18**. 532
Spanish army reported from, to be advancing, **19**. 15
Spanish cardinals arrive at, **23**. 113
Spanish success alarms, **18**. 460
Stephens's prints not to be found at, **23**. 429
Stoppani sends Falkirk news to, by courier, **19**. 214
Stormont to visit, **20**. 296
Stosch carries medals from, **17**. 416
—— driven from, **17**. 164n
—— manages English secret service in, **21**. 149–50
—— 's agent at, dies, **18**. 380–1
Strange copies pictures at, **22**. 108
—— looks in vain for art purchases at, **22**. 115
Strozzi, Principessa, loses museum articles from cabinet in, **19**. 350
Stuart family must resent D. of York's welcome at, **22**. 237
tapestry from Raphael's cartoons now at, **16**. 169
Templum Solis Aureliani at, **13**. 213
Tencin visits Old Pretender at, **17**. 481
Teodoli Palace at: **24**. 181n; Gloucester, D. of, writes from, **36**. 115
Tissot advises Cts of Carlisle to fix at, **23**. 447
Titchfield does not see, **21**. 543, 550–1
Trasteverini at, *see under* Trasteverini
travellers visit, in Holy Week, **35**. 440
travelling fellowship to, **2**. 83

[Rome, modern, *continued*]

troops said to advance towards, from Naples, **17**. 110

Tuscan agreement with, **20**. 420

Tuscany not yet severely treated by, **20**. 458

—— stops intercourse with, for fear of plague, **18**. 270

Veers sets out for, **19**. 506, 510n

Venice's quarrel with, **20**. 173, 189–91, **21**. 219–20, 230, **23**. 56

Vernon's victory depreciated at, **17**. 7

Verskovics returns to, **19**. 420–1

Via Appia at, **13**. 230

Via Cassia and Via Flaminia at, HW disappointed in, **13**. 206

Via Curva at, **13**. 207n

Viale Principessa Margherita at, **13**. 207n

Via Manzoni at, **13**. 207n

'views' of, *see under* Locatelli, Andrea

Villa Ludovisi at, mask of Bacchus in, **13**. 208

Villa Negroni ('Villa Montalta') at, Chute sees Fabius's image at, **35**. 62

Villa Patrizzi at, HW to attend assembly at, **13**. 217

visitors to: Anhalt-Dessau, Princes of, **22**. 418n; Ansbach, P. of, **20**. 370n; Astley, Lady, **25**. 480; Astley, Sir Jacob Henry, **25**. 480; Astley, John, **20**. 310n; Auvergne, Cardinal d', **37**. 47; Baden-Durlach, Margrave, **20**. 148n, 155n; Bagot, **22**. 142; Beauchamp, **38**. 531; Beauvau, **17**. 16, 22–3; Bouverie, **19**. 191, 196, 400; Brand, **20**. 471; Brandenburg-Bayreuth, Margravine of, **20**. 477n; Bruce, Lord, **20**. 331n; Bulstrode, **17**. 11, (?) 14; Burgoyne, Lady Charlotte, **3**. 243n; Bute, **23**. 83, 91; Byres, **42**. 101; Cameron, Jeanie, **22**. 453; Carlisle, Cts of, **23**. 447; Carpenter, Lady Almeria, **25**. 674; Chambers, Sir William, **20**. 368n, 392n; Charlemont, **37**. 324; Charles of Naples (Charles III of Spain), **18**. 533; Chute, **19**. 48–210, **35**. 57–63; Clephane, **17**. 317; Cologne, Elector of, **20**. 508; Conway, **20**. 285n, 297, 299, 304, **37**. 322–5, 327; Cowper, **24**. 94, 251; Cowper, Lady, **24**. 94, 251; Craon, Prince de, **17**. 9, 11, 16, 20, 21; Craon, Princesse de, **17**. 3, 9, 10, 16, 28, **19**. 358; Cumberland, D. and Ds of, **23**. 559, 564, 565–6; Damer, Mrs (Anne Seymour Conway), **25**. 645, 646, 650; Damer, Hon. George, **22**. 286, 300n; Damer, Hon. John, **22**. 300n; Damer, Joseph and Lady Caroline, **20**. 225n; Deskford, **17**. 7, 9; Dumesnil, **19**. 491–3; Englebert, **17**. 13, 15, 17, 19; Eszterházys, **20**. 350n; Exeter, E. of, **15**. 204; Fox family, **22**. 492n; Francis III of Modena, **18**. 532; Friedrich II of Hesse-Cassel, **24**. 274–5, **28**. 284; Gages, **18**. 532; Gascoigne, **22**. 286, **24**. 451n; German baron, **20**. 546; Giles, **24**. 243; Gloucester, D. and Ds of, **24**. 82, 129, 130, 144, 163–4, 170–1, 174–5, 181, 184, 186, 190, 201, 214, 222, 247–8, 252, 291, **25**. 618, 624, 674; Glouces-

ter, D. of, **23**. 140, 141, 357, 370, 384, 396–7, 405, 566, **24**. 129, 290; Gloucester, Ds of, **31**. 187; Grafton, Ds of, **22**. 12, 17, 22; Grafton, D. of, **22**. 12, 20; Gray, **13**. 9, 205–21, **43**. 191; Gustav III, **25**. 475; HW, **13**. 9, 205–21, **15**. 12, 13, 151, **17**. 2–31, **26**. 3–8, **28**. 155, **37**. 46, 49, 56–8, 59, 66, 72; Hamilton, Lady, **23**. 448, **24**. 337; Hamilton, Gavin, **21**. 208n; Hamilton, Sir William, **23**. 2n, 448, **24**. 337, **35**. 434; Harte, Walter, **20**. 174n; Hartington, **17**. 7–8, 16, 23, **37**. 56–7; Hervey, Bn, **25**. 651; Hervey, Bp, **24**. 430, **25**. 651; Hessenstein, **22**. 291n; Hillsborough, **22**. 429; Hoare, Prince, **20**. 86n; Hobart, **19**. 421; Holland, Bn, **22**. 467; Holland, Bns, **22**. 467, 503n; Holt, **19**. 191, 196, 400; Jablonowska, Ps, **23**. 319; Jenkins, Thomas, **20**. 174n; Jones, Thomas, **24**. 134n; Joseph II, **23**. 103, 109, **25**. 468; Karl Wilhelm Ferdinand, **22**. 458; Kent, Mr and Mrs, **21**. 521n; Kilmorey, Vcts, **21**. 406; Kingston, Ds of, **23**. 559, 564, 566–7, **24**. 79, 83–4, 123, 162n, 203, 398, 404, 409; Leopold, **23**. 23, 91, 95, 103, 108–9; Lincoln, elder E. of, **17**. 31, 41, **30**. 5; Lincoln, younger E. of, **24**. 252; Liotard, **20**. 362n; Lockhart, **20**. 78; Lorraine, Primate of, **17**. 12, 17, 22; Lucans, **24**. 462; Lyttelton, Sir Richard, **22**. 12; Macdonald, Sir James, **22**. 447; Macgregor, **18**. 379–80; Mann, Horace II, **24**. 140, 163, 181, **25**. 673–5; Mann, James II, **25**. 581, 586, 592; Mann, Lady Lucy, **24**. 140, 181; Maria Carolina of Naples, **23**. 23; Maria Louisa of Tuscany, **23**. 23; Maximilian, Archduke, **24**. 123; Mengs, **20**. 331; Middleton, **15**. 19; Milles, Miss, **25**. 480; Monro, **19**. 191, 196, 400; Montagu, Lady Mary Wortley, **17**. 92, **30**. 8; Montemar, **17**. 281; Morice, **25**. 435; Murray, Lady Augusta, **35**. 442n; Newdigate, **24**. 144; Nightingale family, **20**. 278; Northampton, Cts of, **22**. 142; Northington, **25**. 652; Orford, Cts of, **23**. 492, **24**. 164, 170–1, 175, 222, 312; Östergötland, D. of, **24**. 240n; Pars, **24**. 134n, **26**. 48; Patch, Thomas, **21**. 209n, **23**. 390; Paul I of Russia, **25**. 250; Phelps, **19**. 191, 196; Pitt, Anne, **24**. 105, 337–8, 344, 353, 374, **31**. 187; Pitt, George, **30**. 7; Pitt, Mrs George, **23**. 447; Pitt, Thomas, **21**. 543, 545; Pomfret, E. and Cts of, **17**. 35, **30**. 15; Pope, **17**. 68; Reynolds, Sir Joshua, **20**. 331n, **33**. 538; Righellini, **22**. 142; Rochechouart, **22**. 28; Rochford, E. and Cts of, **20**. 370n, 376n; Rohan, Cardinal de, **37**. 47; Rohan-Rochefort, Prince Camille de, **22**. 556n; Rosenberg, **23**. 91n; Roxburghe, **21**. 550; St-Aignan, **17**. 12, 81; St John, **22**. 231; St John, Vcts, **20**. 23; St-Odile, **20**. 305; Saxe-Teschen, D. and Ds of, **24**. 190n; Scott, Arthur, **18**. 461; Shrewsbury, E. of, **17**. 4; Skrine, Mrs, **22**. 398; Smyth, **17**. 10, 14, 15, 16, 23, 25; Spencer, E. and Cts, **22**. 180n;

Stanhope, Philip, **20.** 174n; Stanhope, Sir William, **20.** 472n; Stanley, **22.** 327; Stephens, **23.** 427–8; Stormont, **20.** 285n, 298, **23.** 2, **37.** 324; Strange, **21.** 470, **22.** 108, 115; Strathmore, **21.** 543, 564; Stuart, Charlotte, **26.** 47; Swinburne, **24.** 451n; Swymmer, Mr and Mrs, **20.** 376n; Taylor, **20.** 458, 461; Thorpe, Rev. John, **23.** 533n; Thun, **17.** 282; Thurn, **23.** 91n; Trigge, **24.** 380; Trumbull, **19.** 232; Tylney, **24.** 251, **37.** 324–5; Vance, Abbé de, **17.** 63; Vierpyl, Simon, **20.** 392n; Walker, **42.** 384; Walkinshaw, Clementina, **26.** 47, **33.** 442; Walpole, Horatio (1723–1809), **19.** 232, 238–9; Werpup, **22.** 306; Whithed, **19.** 48–210, **35.** 57–63; Wilkes, **22.** 290, 292; Wilson, Richard, **20.** 174n; Wilton, **20.** 368n, 391n, 392n; Wortley Montagu, **22.** 72n, 76–7; Wyseman, **17.** 15, 18, **21.** 23, 380n; York, D. of, **22.** 171, 177, 180, 204, 223, 224, 226–34, 257n, 325, 384

Walkinshaws had lived in, **33.** 442
Wallmoden summons servants from, **22.** 357
—— to return by way of, **22.** 362
Walpole, Sir Robert, might visit, **18.** 202, 211–13
Walpole family not likely to be a good recommendation to, **20.** 461
Warsaw's courier to, **22.** 119
washerwoman at, **17.** 461
William Frederick, P., of Gloucester, christened at, **24.** 181
—–'s birth at, **24.** 178
Wilton does statue at, **20.** 397
Wolfe's monument designed at, by Breton, **21.** 421–2, 428
world will see, no more, **35.** 127
York, Cardinal, called at: 'Cardinal di Orco,' **19.** 428; *Sua Eminenza Reale*, **24.** 480
—— carries brother through, in coach, **22.** 392
—— does not tell father about D. of York's visit to, **22.** 256, 257
—— expected to return to, **17.** 18
—— leaves, with Abbé Lercari, **20.** 332n
—— may leave, **19.** 96
—— receives courier at, with news of brother's illness, **25.** 394, 467
—— retires to convent of S. Giovanni e S. Paolo at, **20.** 332n
—— returns to, **18.** 354
—— will not return to, except on independent footing, **20.** 332
Young Pretender brings bride to, **23.** 406
—— brings companions to, from France, **23.** 351
—— called P. of Wales at, **22.** 389, 406
—— can exist decently only at, **22.** 394
—— drinks and quarrels at, **23.** 351
—— driven from, by Clement XIII's non-recognition, **24.** 244
—— leaves, **5.** 111, **18.** 373–81, 384–9, 419, 421–2, **19.** 98, **23.** 242

—— less dangerous at Avignon than at, **20.** 27
—— loses crown for, **11.** 271
—— may leave, **17.** 13, 14, 113, 116, 159, **18.** 101, 373, **22.** 393
—— may visit, to make public confession of faith, **20.** 333
—— moves furniture from, **24.** 245n
—— no more a king at, than in London, **22.** 399
—— pursued to, by Clementina Walkinshaw, **26.** 47
—— ridiculed on his return to, **23.** 343
—— said by, to be still in Scotland, **19.** 311
—–'s alleged conversion not known at, **22.** 336
—–'s alleged success celebrated at, **19.** 257
—–'s apartment at, prepared by Jews, **22.** 379
—–'s attendants return to, from Siena, **23.** 318–19
—–'s aversion to, **20.** 15
—–'s Bavarian alliance rumoured from, **18.** 396
—–'s cause seems more favourable at, than in Scotland, **19.** 140
—— sends 'Lockat' to, **20.** 27
—–'s French trip may be financed by, **18.** 101
—–'s house at, shorn of English arms, **22.** 408
—–'s illness announced to his wife and brother at, **25.** 394
—–'s ingratitude from, despised by HW, **24.** 255
—–'s marriage negotiations discussed at, **20.** 35
—–'s negotiations about returning to, **22.** 368, 384–90
—–'s plans announced to, **19.** 509
—–'s recognition at, as king, prevented, **22.** 374, 383–5, 388–9, 405–6, 408, **24.** 244
—–'s return to, expected, **17.** 18
—–'s second expedition rumoured at, **19.** 330, 335
—–'s Spanish negotiations discussed in, **19.** 97, 140, 330, 335
—–'s speeches repeated at, **19.** 170
—–'s staff leave, to join him, **18.** 433–4
—–'s success proclaimed at, **19.** 140–1, 257
—–'s treatment by, does not interest HW, **22.** 397, 405–6
—–'s 'valet' arrives at, **19.** 312
—–'s whereabouts announced to, from Paris, **19.** 399
—— to be induced by, to leave Avignon, **20.** 22
—— to make, his family residence, **25.** 627
—— wants permission to return to, **22.** 368, 374
Zoffany to go to, **23.** 430
Romeo and Juliet. See under Shakespeare, William
Romes, ——:
house of, in Saragossa, sacked, **8.** 120
'Rominagrobis.' *See under* La Fontaine, Jean de

Romney, Bn. *See* Marsham, Hon. Charles (1744–1811); Marsham, Robert (1717–93)

Romney, Bns. *See* Pym, Priscilla (1724–71); Shovell, Elizabeth (1692–1750); Wyndham, Lady Frances (1755–95)

Romney, E. of. *See* Marsham, Hon. Charles (1744–1811); Sidney, Hon. Henry (ca 1641–1704)

Romney, George (1734–1802), painter:
Cumberland dedicates *Odes* to, 28. 252
Foldsone, Anne, pupil of, 11. 133n
Hotham, Miss, painted by, 10. 93n
Watson's print after, 7. 127n

Romney, English ship:
Grenville commands, 18. 26, 27
Johnstone commands, at Lisbon station, 24. 465n
Mathews sends, to Leghorn, with letters to Mann, 18. 26, 37

Romney:
Dodd and Whaley visit, 40. 5

Romney family:
Mann, Horace II, decides to leave Parliament because of treatment by, 25. 465

'Romney Marsh Farmer':
letter from, 25. 290n

Romp, The. See under Bickerstaffe, Isaac; Lloyd, T. A.

Romulo ed il Tarquino. See under Malvezzi, Virgilio

Romulus, legendary founder of Rome:
Nassau-Siegen, P. of, imitates, 24. 472
wolf the wet-nurse of, 39. 14
younger generation knows, better than George II, 23. 350

Romulus and Tarquin. See under Carey, Henry

Roncée, Comtesse de. *See* Hurault de Vibraye, Adélaïde-Julie-Sophie

Roncherolles, Marquise de. *See* Amelot de Chaillou, Marie-Louise

Roncherolles, Anne-Michelle-Dorothée de (1752–1844), m. (1772) Ignace de Montboissier-Beaufort, Vicomte (later Comte) de Canillac:
marriage of, 5. 225
named to accompany Mme Élisabeth, 32. 258

Roncherolles, Antoine-Gaspard-Dorothée-Michel (1755–1812), Comte de:
(?) SH visited by, 12. 235

Roncherolles (France):
Maupeou retires to, 28. 221n

Ronchetti, Elisabetta, opera singer:
(?) performs in Florence, 18. 462

Ronciglione (Italy):
Damer and Gascoigne at, 22. 286
Farnese allodial pawned to Pope, 17. 204
Leopold, Maria Carolina, and Maria Louisa to visit, 23. 17
Naples and Spain may seize, 23. 10, 24, 36, 45, 413
Parma may gain, 23. 24
Rosa of, 17. 8n
Spaniards and Neapolitans at, 18. 527

Spaniards may take winter quarters at, 17. 204

Rondé, Mme:
social relations of, in Paris, *see index entries ante* 8. 495
Ussé leaves andirons, shovel, and tongs to, 5. 276

Rondeau (platform):
architect adds, to Pitti Palace for military parades, 22. 291

Rondinelli, Via de', at Florence:
Giambologna's 'Hercules' at corner of, 22. 124n

Ronquillo, Don Pedro (1630–91), Spanish ambassador to England 1680–91:
unburied, 22. 216, 230

Rooke, Lady. *See* Luttrell, Mary

Rooke, George, master of Christ's College, Cambridge:
Bentley's mock heroics to, 35. 643

Rooke, Giles (?) (ca 1701–90), East India Co. director:
withdraws at East India Co. election, 38. 378n

Rooke, Henry (d. 1775), clerk of the Rolls Chapel:
Edmondson aided by, in research, 41. 92
(?) Middleton employs, to carry charters, 15. 1–3

Rooker, Michael (1743–1801), artist:
drawing by, of Waltham Cross, 2. 240

Rook's Nest, Surrey:
Boone of, 10. 7n

Roome, Edward (d. 1729):
Blast Upon Blast or Dean Jonathan's Parody by: Chute has already seen, 18. 60; Fielding said to have written, 18. 34; HW transcribes, 18. 34–6

Roope, Mr, of Charterhouse:
SH visited by, 12. 236

Rooper, Philippa Elizabeth Dorothy (d. 1831), m. (1778) Richard Malone, Bn Sunderlin:
Malone (and sisters), Boswell, and Courtenay accompany, to SH, Hampton Court, Bushey Park, and Pope's grotto, 42. 143n
SH visited by, 12. 223n, 42. 143n

Roos, Bn. *See* Manners, Charles (1754–87)

Roos, Bns. *See* Boyle, Charlotte (1769–1851)

Roos, Philipp Peter (ca 1655–1706), called Rosa di Tivoli:
Hôtel de Bouillon has paintings by, 7. 317

Roos, Sir Richard (fl. 1438–46):
(?) in Margaret of Anjou's escort, 13. 73

Roos. *See also* Ros

Roots:
HW thanks Bentley for, 35. 258
hermits eat, 10. 277
Hume Campbell lives on, 20. 5
See also Iris roots

Roots for the teeth:
HW desires, 6. 358, 359, 362, 367
Hertford, Cts of, wants HW to bring, from Paris, 39. 267–8

Rope; ropes:
at Cock Lane séance, to dry clothes, **10.** 6
Ferrers's executioners fight over, **21.** 403
lady in Pope's elegy uses, to hang herself, **42.** 123
Violante descends St Martin's steeple by, **25.** 450

Rope-dancer; rope-dancers:
monkey dressed as, **33.** 515n

Rope-dancing:
Astley established amphitheatre for, at Southwark, **25.** 451n
at Southwark Fair, **32.** 108n
HW jokes about, at Cock Lane séance, **10.** 6
spectators pained by watching, **35.** 350

Ropehouse:
at Portsmouth, ablaze, **21.** 420n

Ropemaker's Alley, Moorfields:
chapel in, **25.** 56n

Roper, Hon. Charles (d. 1754):
genealogy of, **10.** 352

Roper, Hon. Mrs Charles. *See* Trevor, Gertrude

Roper, Gertrude (1750–1819), m. (1771) Thomas Brand; Bns Dacre, s.j., 1794:
death of, reported, **33.** 95
marriage of, **1.** 198n

Roper, Lady Henrietta:
print inscribed to, **1.** 365

Roper, Thomas (d. 1598):
painting owned by, **16.** 48n

Roper, Trevor Charles (1745–94), 18th Bn Dacre, 1786:
HW to recommend, to Conway, **41.** 185

Roper, Mrs William. *See* More, Margaret

Roque, La. *See* La Roque de Varengeville; Rocca d'Arazzo

Roquefeuil, Aimard-Joseph (d. 1782), Adm.:
English Channel to be cleared by, for invasion from French ports, **18.** 383n
Isle of Wight expects, with 17 ships, **18.** 398n
mission of, to support Saxe's invasion of England, **18.** 375n
Young Pretender with Brest fleet commanded by, **18.** 375n

Roquefeuille, Jeanne-Thérèse de (d. 1725), m. (1704) Ferdinand, Marquis de Lunati-Visconti:
Leopold makes advances to, **20.** 351
mistress of P. Charles of Lorraine, **20.** 351n

Roquefort, Comtesse de. *See* Le Tonnelier de Breteuil, Louise-Gabrielle-Rosalie

Roquefort. *See also* Bausset de Roquefort

Roquette, Gabriel de (1623–1707), Bp of Autun 1667–1707:
Sévigné, Mme de, praises, **5.** 181

Roquette, Rue de la, Paris:
faïence factories in, **7.** 337n
play given in, **6.** 147

Ros, Bn. *See* Cecil, William (1590–1618)

Ros *or* Roos, Bns. *See* Boyle, Charlotte (1769–1831); Manners, Lady Katherine (d. 1649)

Ros, William de (d. 1414), 6th Bn Ros:
Henry IV's lord treasurer, **42.** 139
peerage of, corrected, **14.** 73, **43.** 183

Rosa, Lopez (fl. 1740), Portuguese banker at Rome:
ship belonging to, captured by English, **17.** 8, 15–16

Rosa, Salvator (1615–73), painter:
Alpine scenery reminiscent of, **13.** 181
Bannister's acting compared to painting of, **12.** 78
Bard, The, should be illustrated by, **35.** 252
Barry places Mortimer above, **29.** 301
Beauclerk, Lady Diana, equals, **24.** 524
——'s landscapes as bold as those of, **28.** 244
—— superior to, **32.** 289
HW prefers, to modern artists, **25.** 247
HW's satirical character sketch in style of, **29.** 342
Macbeth might be illustrated by, **23.** 547
paintings by: at Julienne's, **7.** 286; at Osterley Park, **32.** 126
Rhine views reminiscent of, **37.** 150

Rosach. *See* Rossbach

Rosa di Tivoli. *See* Roos, Philipp Peter

Rosaio, Via del. *See* Colonna, Via della

Rosalba. *See* Carriera, Rosalba

Rosales, Chevalier:
Ferdinand, Archduke, accompanied by, **33.** 530n

Rosambo. *See* Le Pelletier de Rosambo

Rosamond. See under Addison, Joseph; Arne, Thomas Augustine

'Rosamond, Fair.' *See* Clifford, Rosamond

Rosamond's Pond. *See under* St James's Park

Rosamouski. *See* Razumovskiĭ

Rosario, El, Spanish galleon:
in Spanish fleet, **17.** 286

Rosarno (Italy):
earthquake damages, **25.** 376

Rosary:
Almada and secretary say, **21.** 430

Rosati, Rosato (1560–1622):
church of S. Carlo ai Catinari designed by, **14.** 20n

Rosciad. See under Churchill, Charles (d. 1764)

'Roscius.' *See* Garrick, David

Roscoe, Margaret, m. Daniel Daulby:
marriage of, **15.** 283n

Roscoe, William (1753–1831), of Liverpool; HW's correspondent; historian:
candour and modesty of, **15.** 262, 264
Farington praises countenance of, in HW's miniature, **15.** 328
General View of the African Slave Trade by, **15.** 282n
HW's correspondence with, **15.** 258–86, **42.** 439–40
HW's praise for writings of, to be communicated by Edwards, **42.** 399–400
HW thanks: for book, **15.** 259; for print, **42.** 440

[Roscoe, William, *continued*]

Life and Pontificate of Leo X, The, by, **15.** 286n

Life of Lorenzo de' Medici by: **34.** 215, **42.** 440, 446–7; engravings from HW's medals to be inserted in, **15.** 286; Grecian simplicity of style of, **15.** 260; HW reassures Roscoe as to reviews of, **15.** 277; HW receives first copy of, **15.** 263; HW's criticism of, **34.** 215–16; HW thanks Edwards for letting Mary Berry show him part of, **15.** 249; HW thanks Roscoe for, **15.** 259, 260; impartial, modest and equal, **15.** 328; praised by Noble, **42.** 448; published, **15.** 53n; Roscoe asks HW to correct second volume of, **15.** 276–7; Roscoe sends HW copy of first volume of, **15.** 258; second edn of, **15.** 280; second volume of, sent to HW, **15.** 273–6; supplemented by Noble's book, **42.** 446

miniature of, requested by HW, **15.** 279, 281, 283–4, 328

Mount Pleasant by: good lines in, **15.** 284; Roscoe apologizes for sending to HW, **15.** 282; slave trade denounced in, **15.** 282

ode by, on institution of society in Liverpool, **15.** 282

poetry by, praised by HW, **15.** 261–2, 284, 328

wife of, **15.** 280n

Wrongs of Africa, The, by, **15.** 282n

Roscoe, Mrs William. *See* Griffies, Jane

Roscoff, Brittany:

Young Pretender lands at, **19.** 319n

Roscommon, E. of. *See* Dillon, James (ca 1605–49); Dillon, Wentworth (ca 1637–85)

Rose, La. *See* La Rose

Rose, Mr:

SH ticket not used by, **12.** 250

Rose, George (1744–1818), secretary to the Treasury:

HW's correspondence with, **42.** 29–30, 31–3, 34

Shelburne tells, to explain to HW the Exchequer inquiry, **42.** 31

Treasury tells, to ask HW for stationery accounts, **42.** 29–30, 34

Rose, John (1619–77), gardener to Charles II:

Ashmole mentions, **12.** 258

charity school founded by, **42.** 45

Charles II's gardener, **14.** 120n

English Vineyard Vindicated, The, by, has preface by Evelyn, **2.** 200n

HW's portrait of, **29.** 45, **43.** 70, 166

picture of, **2.** 200, 239, **15.** 191n

Rose, Susan Penelope (ca 1652–1700):

painting by, **15.** 192n

Rose, Toussaint (1611–1701), Marquis de Coye:

Alembert's eulogy of, **7.** 68

Rose; roses:

and pomegranate, on font owned by Catherine of Aragon, **32.** 323–4

Atabalipa's 'bed' of, **12.** 120

at SH: **9.** 149, 190, **10.** 127, **11.** 25, 29, 296, **39.** 3; *treillage* of, **29.** 310, **39.** 316

Austrian, at SH, **9.** 134

boutonnière of, costs half a guinea, **23.** 210

bud, buds of: sent in letter to HW, **33.** 92; would gladly sit by a fire, **39.** 415

Byrom, John, mentions, in verses, **12.** 35

chaplet of, **33.** 286

Chudleigh, Elizabeth, wears, **10.** 245

daisies are weeds compared to, **42.** 273

damask, at Nuneham, **35.** 461

essence of, scarce, **18.** 214

French inns would be penance for having smelled, **35.** 123

from Damascus, **21.** 113

HW mentions, **10.** 202, **11.** 80

HW needs rain for, **39.** 497, 499

HW plants, against *treillage* at SH, **39.** 316

HW regrets missing, at Marble Hill, **31.** 37

HW's: drowned, **32.** 302; HW to enjoy, **42.** 245; ruined by rain, **39.** 176

HW's, and lilies (complexion), **32.** 21, **33.** 324

in ceiling design, **31.** 106

laurier, **32.** 254

man in Fenn's unidentified portrait carries, **16.** 232

More, Hannah, mentions, **31.** 295

of India, to be Mann's title, **24.** 454

of Paphos, **32.** 219

Ossory, Lady, to come to London with the, **33.** 130

Provence, box shaped like, **12.** 111

red, in miniature of Henry VII, **43.** 43

Rosette's bier decked with, **35.** 464

season for, is over, **10.** 93

symbol of Houses of York and Lancaster, **16.** 232, 233, 234

vest, HW's, painted with, **32.** 219

white: HW lacks, for Pretender's birthday, **35.** 228; Jacobite emblem, **33.** 238; Jacobites use, because of Yorkist associations, **33.** 334n; not blooming on June 10, **33.** 334

worm-eaten in Florence in 1742, **18.** 214

yellow, **10.** 223

Rose Castle:

HW tells Lyttelton to move from, to richer diocesan seat, **40.** 288

Lyttelton said to dislike, **40.** 271–2

Rosedale, near Richmond, Mrs Boscawen's cottage; formerly Thomson's:

Boscawen, Mrs, buys, **11.** 34n, **32.** 335n

HW jokes about James Thomson at, **31.** 348

More, Hannah, invited to visit, **31.** 347–9

Rose-Dammartin, Marquise de. *See* Poutier de Sone, Gabrielle-Antoinette de

Rose-Dammartin, François-Nicolas, Marquis de (elder *or* younger):

(?) social relations of, with Duchesse de la Vallière, **5.** 362

Rose et Colas. See under Sedaine, Michel-Jean

Rosehaugh:

Mackenzie of, **28.** 164n

Rosemary:

HW content with sprig of, **34.** 231

smoke of, used to subdue bees, **40.** 256

used in tincture for eyes, 18. 365n

Rosemary Lane, London:

HW hopes never to belong to Beefsteak Club in, 35. 539

'Rosemary's green':

HW quotes, 12. 36

Rosenberg-Orsini, Franz Xaver Wolf (1723–96), Graf (Fürst, 1790); Tuscan war and finance minister 1766–71:

Barbantane calls on, 22. 481

Botta to be replaced by, as major-domo and first minister, 22. 447–8, 453–4

convents ordered by, to send plate to the mint, 22. 476n

Craon, Princesse de, driven by, from Petraia, 23. 296

dinner to be given by, 23. 64

effects of, to be sold to pay debts, 23. 294

employments abandoned by, 23. 253

English visit of, results in love of liberty of the press, 22. 530

Florence left by, 23. 294

Florentines hope, will become Grand Chamberlain, 22. 400

Guasco favoured by, 22. 530–1

Joseph II and Maria Theresa refuse to pay large debts of, 23. 220, 294

Joseph II's relations with Leopold to be settled by, on visit to Florence from Vienna, 22. 393–4

Karl Wilhelm Ferdinand welcomed by, 22. 457n, 458n

Leopold accompanied by: 23. 253; to Rome, 23. 91n

—— decides with, about festivities, 22. 559

——'s exposure to smallpox feared by, 22. 559

—— should not be encouraged by, to hate Florence, 23. 94–5

—— tells, of print satirizing three abbés' mutual admiration, 22. 531

Mann and Dicks to dine with, 23. 59

Mann jokes with, about publications of Guasco, Niccolini and Cerati, 22. 530–1

—— told by, of Leopold's congratulations on Bath ribbon, 23. 9

Maria Theresa orders, to restore order in Parma, 23. 411n, 412n

—— paid debts of, in Denmark and Spain but not in Tuscany, 23. 294

Montesquieu's letters printed in Tuscany by favour of, 22. 530

opera regulated by, 22. 559

Pisa palace to be inspected by, 23. 253

resignation of, 23. 220

(?) Richmond's invitation to, 19. 308n

Vienna visited by, to get his debts paid, 23. 220

wants to become a foreign minister, 23. 220

Wilczek's house formerly occupied by, 23. 333n

'Rosencrans.' See under Shakespeare, William: Hamlet

Rosen-Kleinroop, Sophie de (1764–1828), m. 1 (1779) Charles-Louis-Victor, Prince de Broglie; m. 2 Marc-René-Marie de Voyer, Marquis d'Argenson:

marriage of, 7. 109

Rosen Ropp, Comtesse de. See Harville-Trainel, Marie-Antoinette-Louise-Esprit de

Roses (France):

Cornish, Capt., looks for Mathews at, 18. 415

French convoy takes refuge in bay of, 19. 367n

Roses, manor in Norfolk:

HW's will mentions, 30. 368

Roses, Wars of the. See under War

Roses Hill [? Hall] House, manor in Norfolk:

HW's will mentions, 30. 368

Rose Tavern, Fleet St, London:

Cole sends servant to, 2. 62

painting at, 1. 382–3, 384, 2. 1–2, 4–5, 7, 7–8

Rose Tavern, Russell St, Covent Garden, London:

audience and dramatists familiar with, 33. 553, 564

'Rosette,' Selwyn's. See Fagnani, Maria Emily

'Rosette,' Duchesse de Choiseul's dog:

wants no puppies, 5. 245

'Rosette' (d. 1773), HW's dog:

Cole and HW accompanied by, to Ely, 1. 178

daughter to receive blessings of, 35. 124

death of, 5. 393, 413, 415, 417, 6. 13, 30

Du Deffand, Mme, alludes to, 3. 372, 4. 6, 156, 5. 171, 350

—— fears for, 5. 46

—— inquires after, 4. 281, 293, 456, 5. 56, 139, 200, 235, 347, 395, 401

—— resigns, to HW, 3. 340

—— sends compliments to, 3. 334, 354, 4. 296, 394, 5. 184

—— to have pastry for, 4. 259

—— to renew acquaintance with, 5. 82

—— would like puppy of, 4. 394, 405

dying, 32. 137, 139, 160

French fleas and bugs attend, 35. 123

HW accompanied by, to Calais, 10. 283

HW bird's-nesting with, 32. 66

HW distressed over, 4. 222

HW jokes about French comic opera named after Raton and, 30. 254–5

HW recovers, 5. 128

HW's account of, amuses Mme du Deffand, 3. 329

HW saved by, from chimney fire, 23. 200–1

HW's devotion to, 3. 365, 4. 152, 363, 6. 67, 84, 110, 206, 334, 430, 7. 171, 10. 312

HW's epitaph on, 35. 464, 43. 364

HW takes: calling, 3. 299; for walks in Paris gardens, 35. 121

health of: better, 35. 463; paralytic bowel complaint, 35. 460; recovers, 5. 387; rheumatism, 5. 53, 56

housekeeper at Castle Howard gives basin of water to, 30. 258

Jonzac, Mme de, inquires after, 4. 233

not to imitate Maroquine, 4. 296

['Rosette,' HW's dog, *continued*]
sleeps in chair at Adderbury, **10.** 312
Stowe to be visited by, **10.** 312
taken ill at Nuneham, **35.** 460, 464
tanned black, **23.** 200
'Tonton' buried near, **34.** 45
—— the successor of, **29.** 145
(?) 'vachette,' **4.** 233, 255
whelps, **4.** 146, 152
See also Dog: HW to bring, to Mme du Deffand
Rosetti (garment):
scarlet, resembling English wrappers, **42.** 236
Rose water:
baptism with, **17.** 62–3
Rosewood (kingwood):
cabinet of, at SH for medals and miniatures, **9.** 83, **18.** 277, **34.** 208n, **42.** 111n, 262n
Rosicrucians:
Darwin, Erasmus, uses doctrine of, **42.** 269
Rosier. *See* Pilâtre de Rosier, Jean-François
Rosières, seigneur de. *See* Terray, Pierre
Rosina. *See* Paganini, Rosa
Roslin, Alexandre (1718–93), painter:
Swedish princes painted by, **7.** 339
Roslin, Mme Alexandre. *See* Giloust, Marie-Suzanne
Rosnay, Comte de. *See* L'Hôpital, François de
Rosny, Baron de. *See* Béthune, Maximilien de
Rospigliosi, Giuseppe (1755–1833), Principe:
SH visited by wife and, **12.** 230, **15.** *198*
Ross, Bn. *See* Cecil, William (1590–1618), 17th Bn Ros
Ross, Bp of. *See* Leslie, John (1527–96); Wetenhall, Edward (1636–1713)
Ross, E. of. *See* Gore, Sir Ralph (1725–1802)
Ross, Lady. *See* Fitzgerald, Lady Mary Rebecca
Ross, ——:
Sharpe explains Callington election prospects to, **35.** 417
Ross, Capt., Cornwallis's aide-de-camp:
news brought by, **25.** 92n
Ross, Rev. Alexander (1591–1654), chaplain to Charles I:
print of, from his continuation of Raleigh's *History*, **40.** 323
Ross, Hon. Charles (1721–45), M.P.; army officer:
HW mentions, **18.** 374
killed at Fontenoy, **18.** 244n, **19.** 43, **36.** 11, **37.** 192
story told by, in Parliament, **18.** 355
votes against his party, **17.** 244
Walpole, Sir Robert, saves, from going to West Indies, **17.** 244
Ross, David (1728–90), actor:
Murray, Fanny, marries, **22.** 184n
wife of, **9.** 80n
Ross, Mrs David. *See* Murray, Fanny
Ross, George:
Balmerinoch's solicitor, at trial of rebel lords, **19.** 283n

Ross, George (1681–1754), 13th Lord Ross of Halkhead; commissioner of customs:
son of, **17.** 244n
Ross, James (1745–1821):
print by, of Q. Catherine Parr's corpse, **43.** 385
Ross, John, naval officer:
Shrewsbury commanded by, **39.** 307
Ross, John (1719–92), Bp of Exeter 1778–92:
information from, on Baker, **2.** 344
Ross, Mrs John. *See* Foote, Catherine
Ross, Sir John Lockhart (1721–90), 6th Bt, 1778; naval officer:
England supposed to be destination of, **25.** 24–5
Ross, Mary (d. 1767), m. (1710) John Murray, 1st D. of Atholl:
(?) West hears Ethiopian musician belonging to, **13.** 173–4
Ross. *See also* Ros; Rosse
Rossbach (Germany):
battle of, **21.** 153, 158, 180
Rossdhu, on Lake Lomond, Scotland:
Colquhoun's seat, **42.** 322n
Rosse, Vct. *See* Parsons, Richard (ca 1656–1703)
Rosse, Vcts. *See* Hamilton, Elizabeth (d. 1724)
Rosset, André-Hercule de (1715–88), Duc de Fleury:
(?) Aiguillon said to have support of, **4.** 197
attends session of parliament of Paris, **8.** 172
Chartres, Bp of, brother of, **6.** 52
first gentleman of the Bedchamber, **4.** 191n
Gazette d'Utrecht maligns, **25.** 557n
graver than his predecessor as Bedchamber lord, discouraging amusements, **38.** 451
Hertford to ask, to let Dauberval rejoin London opera, **38.** 460, 477
protests illegal parliament, **5.** 61
Richelieu differs with, in actors' quarrel, **38.** 538n
Rosset, André-Hercule-Alexandre de (1750–82), Marquis de Fleury:
(?) HW entertains, at SH, **10.** 70–1
Rosset, Jean-André-Hercule de (1726–81), called Chevalier or Commandeur de Fleury:
(?) Aiguillon said to have support of, **4.** 197
(?) HW to accompany, in London, **22.** 135
Rosset de Ceilhes de Fleury, Henri-Marie-Bernardin de (1718–81), Abp of Tours 1751–74, of Cambrai 1775–81:
(?) Aiguillon said to have support of, **4.** 197
appointed Abp of Cambrai, **6.** 98
Rosset de Fleury, Pons-François de (1727–74), Bailli de Fleury:
(?) Aiguillon said to have support of, **4.** 197
brother of, **38.** 451
HW saw, in England, **38.** 451
Holdernesse compared to, **3.** 77
social relations of, in Paris, *see index entries ante* **8.** 496
verses from fête given by, **3.** 76, 78

Rosset de Rocozel de Fleury, Pierre-Augustin-Bernardin de (1717–80), Bp of Chartres, 1746:
(?) Aiguillon said to have support of, 4. 197
death of, 7. 199, 441
Fleury, Duc de, brother of, 6. 52
HW and companions admitted to St-Cyr by order from, 7. 330, 10. 292, 34. 82
HW to preserve St-Cyr admittance order of, at SH, 10. 292
Marie-Antoinette's grand aumonier, 6. 52

Rosset de Rocozel de Pérignan, André-Hercule-Marie-Louis de (b. 1770, d. before 1814), Marquis and (1788) Duc de Fleury:
absconds from Paris, 12. 79
coachmaker demands £500 from, 12. 79
HW visits, in London, 12. 3
(?) wife glad to be rid of, 12. 30
wife of, 11. 181n, 12. 79n

Rosseter, James (d. 1773):
elected alderman on Tory interest, 32. 40n

Rossi, ——:
governor of the fortress of Seravalle, 19. 78n

Rossi, Mlle (d. 1799), dancer:
Damer, Mrs, does bust of son of, 12. 272, 273

Rossi, Signora. See Rangoni, Vittoria

Rossi, Bianca Colonna. See Colonna, Bianca

Rossi, Federico, Conte di S. Secondo:
(?) wife's quarrels with, 17. 123

Rossi, Giuseppe de, Papal physician 1774–98:
Pius VI's illness considered by, to be serious, 24. 461

Rossi, Venturi (d. 1766):
negotiations for buying Francis III's art collection conducted by, 19. 314n

Rossignol d'Anneville, ——, French agent in Russia:
Sabatier de Cabre replaces, 23. 127n

Rossington, Yorks:
Jackson rector of, 15. 297

Rosslyn, Cts of. See Courtenay, Hon. Charlotte

Rosslyn, E. of. See Wedderburn, Alexander

Rossmore, Bn. See Cunninghame, Robert

Rosso, Domenico, Abp of Palermo:
aid for plague victims requested by, 18. 262n

Rostaing, house of:
tombs of, 7. 282

Rostatt, Treaty of:
Treaty of Utrecht followed by, 35. 276n

Rota, Papal court:
Lepri, Marchesa, granted verdict by, against Pius VI, 25. 587
Thun-Hohenstein auditor of, 17. 201n

Rotari, Pietro (1707–62), painter:
Catherine II's portrait by, 23. 242

Rotenkreuz. See Feronce von Rotenkreuz, Jean-Baptiste

Roth:
regiment or battalion of, 18. 164

Rothe, Comtesse de. See Lavaulx de Sommerecourt, Jeanne-Catherine-Josèphe de

Rothe, Antoine-Edmond-Joseph (1765–1842), Comte de:
mother of, 7. 204

Rothe, Antoinette-Catherine-Josèphe de (b. 1766), m. (1785) Abel-Alexis-François le Conte de Nonant, Marquis de Pierrecourt:
mother of, 7. 204

Rothe, Edmond-Joseph de (b. 1768):
mother of, 7. 204

Rothe, Louise (or Lucie)-Thérèse de (1750–82), m. (1769) Col. Arthur Dillon:
dances at ball in honour of Dauphin's marriage, 4. 410
social relations of, with Comtesse Jules de Polignac, 7. 453

Rothe, Madeleine-Josèphe de (1769–1847), m. (1792) Louis-Alexandre-Marie Martin de Boislecomte:
mother of, 7. 204

Rothe, Marguerite-Josèphe de (1767–1852), m. (1786) Louis-Ernest Prondre, Marquis de Ravenel:
mother of, 7. 204

Rothelin, Marquis of:
consummates marriage by proxy, 9. 99n

Rotherbridge or Robertsbridge, Sussex:
Chute and HW visit, 35. 137

Rotherfield, Sussex:
Tatton rector of, 2. 304n

Rotherham, Thomas (1423–1500), Abp of York:
Bourchier's commission to, as Edward IV's executor, 41. 124
HW finds fault with, 14. 166n
Henry does not explain conduct of, 15. 173
in custody, 1. 138
Richard III complained to, of wife's barrenness, 14. 179

Rotherham, Yorks:
Aston near, 28. 165, 198
Byron raises recruits at, 28. 472
HW's letters sent by, 28. 147, 29. 29
Holmes near, 28. 208n
post to and from, 28. 353n

Rotherhithe:
East Lane in, is Ratcliffe's address, 40. 235
See also Redriff

Rothes, Cts of. See Leslie, Jane Elizabeth

Rothes, E. of. See Leslie, John (ca 1600–41)

Roti; Rotier. See Roettiers

Rotonda, Villa, at Vicenza:
Mereworth resembles, 35. 143

Rotterdam:
Ailesbury, Cts of, stays at, but Cts of Ancram leaves, 37. 283
Conway visits, 37. 134, 281
Cumberland, D. of, at, 37. 281
Pichegru's army occupies, 12. 121n

Rottofredo, battle of. See Rottofreno; Tidone

Rottofreno:
battle of, 19. 291, 302

Rottschutz, Lt-Col. Baron von:
Torgau casualties estimated by, 21. 453n
Vienna mission of, 21. 456n
Rotuli parliamentorum:
'Attainder of George Duke of Clarence' in,
15. 176n, 41. 324n
Rotunda, at Rome:
closed because of floods, 23. 378
Roualle, ——:
attends session of parliament of Paris, 8. 173
Rouault de Gamaches, Constance-Simonne-
Flore-Gabrielle (1725–81), m. 1 (1746)
Charles-Yves le Vicomte, Comte du Rumain;
m. 2 (ca 1771) Jacques-Gilbert, Marquis de
Fraignes:
Du Deffand, Mme, may depend on, for com-
pany, 3. 385
(?) ——'s social relations with, 3. 345
Roubiliac, Louis-François (? 1705–62), sculptor:
Charles I's bust by, placed at Matson by
Selwyn, 30. 121n
design and model by, for Wolfe's monument,
21. 428n
Hough's tomb by, 35. 151n
intaglio of Sir Robert Walpole said to be
copied from cast by, 16. 69
Newton's statue by, 2. 330
Rouble; roubles:
value of, 18. 495n
Roucour (Roucourt; Roucoux), Battle of:
account of, 19. 318, 30. 107–9
casualties at, 30. 107–8
HW requests details of, from H. Fox, 30. 107
Montagu, Charles, falsely reported killed at,
30. 106, 107–8
Roucy, Charlotte de. *See* La Rochefoucauld,
Charlotte de Roye de Roucy de
Roue. *See* Larue
Rouelle, ——, apothecary:
Du Deffand, Mme, has receipt from, 8. 41
Rouen, Abp of. *See* La Rochefoucauld, Domi-
nique de (1713–1800); Luxembourg St Pol,
Louis de (d. 1443)
Rouen, Intendant of. *See* Thiroux de Crosne,
Louis
Rouen:
Alincourt on road to, 41. 309
balloon flight from, 25. 527n
disturbance at, 11. 43n
Du Deffand, Mme, receives bill of exchange
from, 7. 442, 459
——'s annuities from city of, 4. 387, 7. 39
Du Hallier of, 3. 115n
Formont's residence, 3. 144
HW hopes for letter from Mary Berry at,
11. 113
HW's packages go by way of, 6. 411, 7. 405
Hue de Miromesnil, former first president of,
6. 88, 32. 205
Lormier of, 8. 32n
(?) Louis XV sends courier to, for presidents,
39. 55

Margaret of Anjou consigned to English attendants at, 14. 72
merchant at, to forward Comtesse d'Egmont's
parcel to Bns Hervey, 38. 279
Robinson, Mrs Elizabeth, sends censers by
way of, 6. 486, 8. 204
scarcity of money in, 11. 122n, 164–5
Rouen, Parliament of:
Harcourt forces, to register edicts, 38. 299–
300
Louis XV asked by, for taxing powers in
return for giving him revenue, 38. 299–300
—— petitioned by, for taxing powers in return for more revenue, 38. 299
—— tells Princes of the Blood to ignore, 23.
270n
premier président of, *see* Hue de Miromesnil,
Armand-Thomas
to be abolished, 5. 106
Rouette, ——:
noels played by, 7. 317
social relations of, with Marquis and Marquise de Brancas, 7. 317
Roué vertueux, Le. See under Coqueley de
Chaussepierre, Charles-Georges
Rouge:
Amelia, Ps, compliments Duchesse de Mirepoix on leaving off, 20. 89
Amiens, Bp of, advises lady about, 34. 17
Archer, Bns, addicted to, 33. 500n
Bolingbroke applies, to ladies for Corona-
tion, 9. 388
cost of, 18. 281
Coventry wipes, from wife's face, 20. 338
Coventry, Cts of, cannot use, in France, 20.
338
Du Barry, Mme, does not wear, 10. 292
Englishwoman does not wear, 30. 264
expense of, to Mesdames de France, 20. 500
fashionable at Paris, 18. 220
French princesses might have to give up,
37. 535
French use, extravagantly, 32. 13
Grafton, Ds of, does not use, 22. 80
HW jokes about French fondness for, 31. 90
HW mentions, 10. 133
HW smeared with, 32. 253
HW suggests adorning sculptures of Niobe's
family with, 25. 178
HW would not put, on St Ethelburgh's statue,
21. 471
Hewet, Mrs, wears, 24. 204
Maria Theresa does not permit ladies to wear,
in mourning period, 22. 354
middle-class ladies shun, 43. 221
Parisians use, extravagantly, 13. 165
Pompadour, Mme de, may abandon, 20. 530
Starhemberg, Fürstin von, wears too much
of, 38. 220
worn by young members of Parliament, 28.
87

Rougham, Norfolk:
  Burwell family's seat, 1. 374, 377
  Davers buys, 1. 377
  HW jokes about, 18. 238
Rouillé, Mme:
  social relations of, with Duc and Duchesse de
    Choiseul, 7. 330
Rouillé, Marie-Catherine de, m. (1749) Anne-
François d'Harcourt, Marquis de Beuvron:
  social relations of, in Paris, 4. 241, 7. 301
  Thiard and Ps of Monaco try to unlock secre-
    tary of, 3. 61–2
Rouillé (or de Roville), Guillaume (1515–89),
French printer:
  Prima pars Promptuarii iconum printed by,
    42. 219n
Rouillé du Coudray, Antoine-Louis (ca 1689–
1761) Comte de Jouy, minister of marine
1749–57:
  Fox's mémoire from, a partial war declara-
    tion, 20. 524, 526
  French reply to English peace conditions
    given by, to Knyphausen, 20. 541n
  Louis XV gives marine secretaryship to, 14.
    153n
Rouillé du Coudray, Marie-Eugénie, m. (1777),
Michel-Félix-Victor de Choiseul-Beaupré,
Comte d'Aillecourt:
  son born to, 7. 438
Rouillius. See Rouillé
Rouleau:
  coat of arms depicts, 9. 186
Roulers. See Rousselaere
Roundhouse:
  at St Margaret's church, 21. 536
  HW prefers confinement at, to supping with
    his grandmother, 19. 27–8
  women suffocated in, 17. 503–5
Round Robin:
  sent by Lady Ossory to HW and signed by
    him as 'Orford,' 34. 136
Rouph de Varicour, Reine-Philibert (1757–
1822), m. (1777) Charles, Marquis de Vil-
lette:
  Du Deffand, Mme, gives opinion of, 7. 20
  Ferney visited by, 7. 12
  Voltaire accompanied by, to Paris, 7. 17
Rouquet, Jean-André (1701–58), Swiss minia-
ture-painter:
  État des arts en Angleterre, L', by, refutes
    Leblanc, 40. 239
Roure, Du. See Du Roure
Rous, George:
  Thoughts on Government by, 11. 169n
Rous, John (? 1411–91) antiquary):
  Historia regum Angliæ by, 1. 147
  pedigree roll of Earls of Warwick by: 1. 133,
    147, 2. 2n, 14. 177, 182, 15. 124, 243n, 35.
    606–8, 43. 49, 188, 196; Astle helps HW
    decipher, 2. 2n; portraits in, of Richard
    III and Q. Anne, 15. 124, 41. 134, 225, 42.
    285

print of, 1. 147
  Richard III flattered by, in pedigree roll,
    15. 185
Rous, Sir John (1750–1827), 6th Bt; M.P.:
  Parliamentary motion by, against North ad-
    ministration rejected, 25. 256n, 258n, 29.
    197n
Rous, Thomas (d. 1771):
  (?) East India Co.'s new proposals submitted
    by, 22. 508n
  (?) House of Commons told by, not to print
    East India Co.'s papers, 22. 496n
  Sulivan's enemy, made chairman by East
    India Co., 38. 378
Rousham, Oxon, Cottrell Dormer's seat:
  Cottrell Dormer of, 1. 60n, 9. 274n
  HW visits, 9. 285, 290
  Kent's landscaping at, 9. 290
  library at: admired by HW, 9. 290; to be
    made into dining-room, 10. 86
  Mason visits, 28. 45
  portico for green-house at, 38. 198
  room at, 10. 86n
Rousseau, Jean-Baptiste (1671–1741), poet:
  Du Deffand, Mme, quotes, 4. 112, 448, 5. 422
  Épitres by, quoted by Mme du Deffand, 4. 355
  Longepierre attacked by, in verses, 4. 448,
    454, 5. 422
  Voltaire writes too much about, 35. 284
Rousseau, Jean-Jacques (1712–78), philosopher:
  answer by, to HW's letter, 22. 434
  Armenian costume of, 3. 96, 35. 117
  Arnaud resembles, 6. 366
  Boswell distressed by HW's treatment of, 14.
    170–1
  Boufflers, Comtesse de, avoided by, 4. 434
  —— does not discuss, with HW, 41. 32
  —— favours, 3. 133, 172
  —— may abandon, 3. 91, 109
  —— receives letter from, 3. 15, 132, 188, 202
  —— speaks of, 3. 26, 281
  —— spreads tale of follies of, 3. 301
  —— the protectress of, 22. 434
  —— thinks, crazy, 3. 172
  —— writes to Trouillet about, 22. 475
  Burke's invective against, 11. 277
  celebrity achieved by, through absurdity
    rather than sense, 33. 492–3
  children abandoned by, 31. 383
  Choiseul, Duchesse de, asked to protect, 3.
    296
  —— detests, 3. 102
  Cole's opinion of, 1. 104–5, 112n
  Confessions by: 7. 48, 51, 64, 68, 28. 426–7;
    a lesson against keeping journals, 33. 494;
    HW disgusted by, 33. 39, 475
  Conti, Prince de, aids, 3. 310
  —— avoided by, 4. 434
  —— discusses with HW his letter to, 7. 295
  —— never mentions, 3. 301
  —— protects, in Paris, 31. 89

[Rousseau, Jean-Jacques, *continued*]

Contrat social, Le, by, followed by Girardin, **16.** 191n

Conway's correspondence with, **10.** 235

Davenport's quarrel with, **3.** 296, 300–1

—— visited by, at Wootton, **3.** 15, 95, 96, 296

death of, **7.** 57, **16.** 191, **28.** 412

Devin du village by, **4.** 89, **7.** 260, **31.** 45–6

Dictionnaire de musique by, consulted by HW on Harcourt's advice, **35.** 514

Du Deffand, Mme, cites, **3.** 128

—— compares Fox with, **4.** 322

—— did not admire, **28.** 420

—— jokes about novels of, **4.** 212

—— said to have corrected HW's letter to, **7.** 294–5

——'s poor opinion of, **3.** 91, 108, 298, 300–1, **6.** 414

——'s 'portrait' by, **8.** 53–4

Émile, ou de l'éducation by: **43.** 186; deserved to be burnt, **14.** 138; Girardin raises children according to, **16.** 191n; HW reads, at Park Place, **38.** 181; used for education of Veillard's son, **7.** 287

England may be visited by, **4.** 173

——'s reception of, **1.** 105–6, 109, **3.** 96–7

—— to be visited by, **31.** 89, 92

—— visited by, **1.** 104–6, **14.** 156, **15.** 108n, **35.** 116

French do not try to find children of, **31.** 383

—— fuss over ashes of, **31.** 383

French parliament proscribes, **3.** 310, 314

'friend' of, **36.** 169

Fulham to be residence of, **31.** 94

Geneva disturbed by, **31.** 89

Genlis, Mme de, the 'hen' of, **33.** 475–6

Girardin and, **29.** 282

government and religion attacked by, **41.** 53

HW attacks, **39.** 44

HW borrows volumes of, from Selwyn, **30.** 282

HW calls, hypocrite and impostor, **10.** 184

HW copies work of, for Mme du Deffand, **4.** 173

HW deemed French language unsuitable for verse and eloquence until he read, **42.** 231

HW does not answer Mme du Deffand's questions about, **4.** 440

HW helps, **10.** 243

HW hopes, will quarrel with Bp Terrick, **31.** 94

HW jokes about contentiousness of, **31.** 94

HW jokes about sending one of Thomas Hervey's letters to, **30.** 223

HW quarrels with Conti over, **39.** 231

HW quotes, about foretelling cities' fates, **23.** 400, **24.** 62

HW ridicules, **35.** 116–17

HW seeks pension for, **3.** 250, 257, 259–60, 322

HW's letter to, in name of Frederick II of Prussia: **1.** 104, 105, 109, 110–11, 112n, 113, **3.** 95n, 179, 232n, **4.** 96, **7.** 290, **13.** 41,

14. 156, 157, **30.** 210, 212, 223, 238, 239, **31.** 99–101, (?) 111, **35.** 117, **39.** 43, 179, **41.** 14–15, 24–6, 32, 44, 47, 49, 53, 54, 56; *Année littéraire* has article on, **3.** 21–2; believed by d'Alembert, **28.** 420; Boufflers, Comtesse de, discusses, **3.** 172, 174, **7.** 294; Choiseul admires, **4.** 183; Conti and Comtesse de Boufflers angry about, **22.** 434; Conti discusses, with HW, **7.** 295; Du Deffand, Mme, wishes copy of, **7.** 19; Frederick II indifferent to, **8.** 117; HW remorseful over, **3.** 298, 314; imitation of, **5.** 427–8; Ligne tries to equal, **4.** 434; Luxembourg, Mme de, dislikes, **7.** 294–5; Nivernais thought to have corrected, **3.** 174; Pont-de-Veyle defends Mme du Deffand from charge of having corrected, **7.** 294; Rousseau attributes, to d'Alembert, **3.** 97, **41.** 53, 54, 56; Talmond, Princesse de, likes, **8.** 58

HW's opinion of, **1.** 109, **8.** 55, **31.** 92

HW's quarrel with, **31.** 215

HW's suppressed letter to, under name of 'Émile': **3.** 4, 6, 9, 10, 11, 13, 27, 30–1, 50, 59; text of, **8.** 117–18

HW wishes to help, **3.** 95, 308

HW writes account of affair of, **13.** 42

HW writes to Mme du Deffand about, **7.** 382

hated by the devout, **8.** 58

Holland rumoured to be the refuge of, **7.** 48

Hume accompanies, to England, **1.** 104–6, **31.** 92

—— asked by Comtesse de Boufflers to aid, **3.** 172

——, HW, and d'Alembert accused by, of conspiring against him, **30.** 223

Hume gets letter of grievances from, **30.** 223

——'s quarrel with: **3.** 89–90, 91, 94–8, 100, 108–9, 112, 117, 131–3, 207, 211, 256, **10.** 241, **22.** 434, 465, 475, **30.** 238, **43.** 82, 83, 84; *Exposé succinct* concerning, **3.** 128, 131, 158, 160, 161, 163, 170, 171, 179, 180; *Justification de Jean-Jacques Rousseau* in, **3.** 183, 190; *Réflexions posthumes* on, **3.** 207, 212, 222, 224, 231

—— to settle, in England, **39.** 34n

Julie, ou la nouvelle Héloïse by: **3.** 96, **4.** 56, 92, **7.** 78, 417, **32.** 27; Borde's *Prédiction* analyzes, **3.** 93, 110; Girardin designs gardens after, **16.** 191n; Gray comments on, **14.** 118; Gray's condemnation of, **28.** 186; HW almost re-enacts, **35.** 308; HW criticizes character in, **31.** 43; translated by Kenrick, **28.** 216n; Voltaire said to ridicule, **21.** 514; Voltaire summarizes, **15.** 239

leaves England, **3.** 296, 300n

letters of: from Wootton, **1.** 112n, 113; to editor of *St James's Chronicle*, **3.** 9, 22, 26; to Hume, shows madness, **28.** 428

letters of defiance circulated by, all over Europe, **41.** 44, 51, 60

letters to: called *Le Docteur Pansophe*, **3.** 178–9, 190; in name of Voltaire, **1.** 113–14

Lettres écrites de la montagne by, **14.** 138, **31.** 89n

Ligne offers asylum to, **4.** 434

Luxembourg, Mme de, a protectress of, **3.** 91, 133

Mason inquires about cause of death of, **28.** 418

——'s compassion excited by, **28.** 428

ministers help, **10.** 243

Montagu pities, **10.** 243

music copied by, **4.** 434

not discussed, **3.** 253

not in Paris, **3.** 314, 317

odes of: HW quotes, in 'Lettre d'Émile,' **43.** 109; unsuccessful, **28.** 276

paradoxes, affectations, and eloquence of, **28.** 420, 427

Paris visited by, **3.** 310, **4.** 434, **31.** 89

pensions of, **3.** 24, 57, 91, 94–5, 98, 250, 257, 259–60, 267, 281, 320, 322, **4.** 434, **10.** 242

persecution mania of, **29.** 48

prints of tomb and apotheosis of, **29.** 274–5

Pygmalion, Le, by: acted by Le Texier, **32.** 342; Le Texier fails to produce, **39.** 381; Mason's translation of, **28.** 183, 184

St James's Chronicle prints allegory on, **3.** 37

singularities of, **31.** 92

spectacle, like those of Nicolet, **4.** 434

Swiss government and religion endangered by, **35.** 583

talents misused by, **34.** 220

Wilkes received by, but is later complained about, to Hume, **35.** 117

writes more sense and nonsense than anyone, **38.** 181

Rousseau juge de Jean-Jacques:

eloquent but frenzied, **29.** 48–9

Roussel, Louis-Nicolas:

(?) attends session of parliament of Paris, **8.** 171

Rousselaere *or* Roulers:

English battle corps may be stationed at, **37.** 130

Roussi, Lady Charlotte de. See La Rochefoucauld, Charlotte de Roye de Roucy de

Roussillon (France):

Philip, Don, at, **17.** 362n

Spanish army in, **12.** 40n

troops rumoured to be sent to, **7.** 151

Rout; routs:

Mann gives, for Vorontsovs, **22.** 193

—— has, during Lent, **23.** 458

Roffey gives, at Kingston, **35.** 468

Rouvigny. See Ruvigny

Rouvroy, Louis de (1675–1775), Duc de St-Simon:

Mémoires of: at Chanteloup, **5.** 6, 57; Bibliothèque du Roi said to possess, **5.** 88; Choiseul, Duc de, lends, to Mme du Deffand, **4.** 478; Choiseul, Duc de, said not to possess, **5.** 88; Choiseul, Duchesse de, will

lend, to HW, **5.** 74, 78, 81, 86; Du Deffand, Mme, comments on, **4.** 489, **5.** 6; Du Deffand, Mme, mentions, **5.** 109, 110, 283; Du Deffand, Mme, not to receive, **5.** 88; Du Deffand, Mme, seeks, for HW, **5.** 57n, 34. 29–30; Du Deffand, Mme, would like HW to read, **4.** 480–1, 482, 489, **5.** 6, 51, 63, 72, 78, 85; HW curious about, **4.** 489; HW doubts arrival of, **34.** 64–5; HW mentions Mme du Deffand's pleasure in, **5.** 12; HW to read, **5.** 81, 82; locked up in Paris, **34.** 29–30; parts of, in *Galerie de l'ancienne cour,* probably from Choiseul's copy, **34.** 54–5; published but not yet in England, **34.** 29; Voltaire's anecdotes in, **34.** 29

Regent's favourite, **34.** 29

would stare, at fall of Bourbons, **34.** 55

Rouvroy de St-Simon, Blanche-Marie-Élisabeth de (b. 1737), m. (ca 1762) Balthazar-Henri de Rouvroy, Comte de St-Simon-Sandricourt:

(?) social relations of, in Paris, **7.** 297, 302

Rouvroy de St-Simon, Marie-Christine-Chrétienne de (1728–74), m. (1749) Charles-Maurice Goyon-de-Matignon de Grimaldi, Comte de Valentinois:

Cambis, Vicomtesse de, former friend of, **6.** 71

Craufurd may not be approved by, **41.** 8

death of, **6.** 71

(?) Du Barry, Comtesse, has same title as, **7.** 372

Du Deffand, Mme, and Mme de Forcalquier rescued by, **3.** 56

Du Deffand, Mme, gives opinion of, **4.** 121

—— suggests, as author of 'Sévigné' letter, **3.** 71

English hated by, **3.** 4n

entertains dancers at Mirepoix ball, **3.** 217

Fontainebleau not visited by, **4.** 298

Gramont, Duchesse de, wishes to avoid, **5.** 363

health of, **4.** 104, 106, 108, 119, 121, 298

Holdernesse preferred by, **41.** 8

Louis XV accompanied by, **4.** 256n

Passy, home of, **6.** 71

Provence, Comtesse de, attended by, **4.** 442, **5.** 30

social relations of, in Paris, *see index entries ante* **8.** 498

Thiard, friend of, **6.** 71

will of, **6.** 71–2

Roux, Augustin (1726–76), chemist:

Lauraguais assisted by, **7.** 262

—— quarrels with, **7.** 262

social relations of, with Holbach, **7.** 262, 272, 299

Rovere, Giuliano della. See Julius II

Roverisi, Conte:

San Remo deputy, **19.** 123

Rovezzano, Benedetto da (1474–1552), sculptor:

Gray sends name of, to HW, **14.** 117

Rovezzano (Italy):

Bracci's villa near, **20.** 221n

Roviglia. See Revilla

Roville. See Rouillé

Rowan, Jane, m. Gawen Hamilton:
house of, in Marlborough St, 33. 364n
Rowe, Mrs. *See* Singer, Elizabeth
Rowe, Milward (ca 1716–92), chief clerk of the Treasury:
cloth transactions of, irregular, 41. 206
Rowe, Nicholas (1674–1718), dramatist:
Ambitious Stepmother, The, by, 7. 261, 13. 67
ballad by, on Mrs Strawbridge, 9. 169n, 35. 237
Bentley's remark about, 13. 39n
'Colin's Complaint' by: HW compares himself with Colin in, 11. 16; HW quotes, 11. 16; written on Sir Conyers Darcy, 14. 243
Fair Penitent, The, by: 13. 194; acted at Winterslow House, 32. 176n; Berry, Mary, quotes, 12. 122; first four acts of, good, 41. 297; HW quotes, 23. 181, 33. 424n; lines from, set at SH Press, 9. 216; 'Lothario' in, poorly acted by Garrick, 38. 524; York, D. of, Delavals, and Lady Stanhope act in, 22. 521; York, D. of, plays 'Lothario' in, 10. 237
Gray prefers half-line of Racine to all of, 14. 11
Hervey, Bns, praised in verses by, 31. 418, 33. 37
Jane Shore by: acted at Holland House, 9. 335–6; best English play after Shakespeare, 41. 296; Garrick as 'Lord Hastings' in, 33. 87, 38. 525; HW calls, a perfect tragedy, 41. 374; HW paraphrases, 35. 269; HW wants, 36. 2; Pritchard, Mrs, in, 32. 145–6; Siddons, Mrs, in, 11. 237
Lucan translated by, 33. 257
prefaces by, to Shakespeare, 24. 267n
Shakespeare edition by: 9. 120n; HW's notes to, 42. 137n, 138–9
Tamerlane by: acted in November, 13. 16n; 'Bajazet' in, 23. 224, 40. 10; Dodd acts in, at Eton, 40. 11n; HW's Epilogue to, 9. 48, 13. 16, 22, 19. 333, 350–1, 28. 183n
Rowell, John (d. 1756):
stained glass by, at Hartlebury Castle, 35. 149
Rowing contest:
badge to be prize for, 9. 239
Rowlandson, Thomas (1756–1827), caricaturist:
Tours of Dr Syntax illustrated by, 28. 303n
'Rowley.' *See under* Chatterton, Thomas
Rowley, Lady. *See* Burton, Sarah
Rowley, Mr:
SH visited by, 12. 225
Rowley, John (fl. 1764), linen-draper:
parcel for Cole to be left with, 1. 68
Rowley, Sir Joshua (1734–90), cr. (1786) Bt; naval officer:
convoying ships of, survive Jamaica hurricane, 39. 352–3
daughter of, 11. 139n
expected at Martinique, 24. 456
father leaves little to, 22. 578
fleet of, damaged, 33. 245
nothing heard of, 25. 105–6

Rowley, Sir Joshua Ricketts (ca 1790–1857), 3d Bt, 1832:
heir of family, 22. 578
Rowley, Philadelphia (ca 1763–1855), m. (1788) Charles Cotton, 5th Bt, 1795:
(?) at Park Place, 11. 132
'Rowley, Thomas,' Chatterton's fictitious monk:
alleged letters and papers of, 16. 101–5, 107–12, 223
Chatterton did not write under name of, after leaving Bristol, 16. 224
controversy over, 16. 239–40, 243, 360
Milles asserts authenticity of poems of, 16. 349
miracles supposedly worked by, 42. 382
Paston letters probably contain no mention of, 16. 237
verses on, in *Morning Chronicle,* 16. 351
will be abandoned after Glynn is gone, 16. 228
See also under Chatterton, Thomas
Rowley, Sir William (ca 1690–1768), K.B., 1753; naval officer:
Admiralty includes, 20. 259, 21. 25, 73
Ambrose to be sent to England by, under arrest, 19. 55
Birtles told by, to leave Genoa when it aids Spanish army, 19. 65
Cadiz supposedly watched by, 19. 81
Cartagena squadron followed by, to Cadiz, 19. 12n
Charles Emmanuel III asks, to pacify Genoa, 18. 509
—— blames Corsican rebellion on instigation of, 19. 276
Cooper imitates conduct of, 19. 81
Court, M. de, attacked by, 18. 414
Craon, Princesse de, receives beer from, 19. 9
death of, makes vacancy in Bath order, 22. 578
D'Ormea's agreement with, 19. 10
Dutchman meets, near Alicante, 18. 525
English captains to be scolded by, for disobeying Mann, 18. 507
Finale, scene of failure by, 19. 120
fleet at Genoa awaits orders from, 19. 76
fleet of: largely unfit for service, 19. 10; to be diminished though continuing to awe Genoa and protect Tuscany, 19. 12
Forbes ordered by, to join Medley, 19. 192n
Gardiner introduced by, to Mann, 18. 507, 543–4
Genoa said to have bribed, 19. 120
—— threatened by, 19. 12
Genoese assure, that they mobilize in self-defence, 18. 546–7, 554
Genoese coast to be patrolled by, with whole fleet, 19. 37
Gorsegno approves of Mann's telling, of English captain's disloyalty, 19. 146–7, 150
great-grandson the chief heir of, 22. 578
leave of, to return home, brought in ship from Port Mahon, 19. 132

lieutenant of, to carry Mann's letter to HW, **19.** 146

Mann has not heard from, **19.** 120, 132

—— has seal made for, **19.** 9

—— may send eagle with, to England, **19.** 122

—— receives gifts from, **19.** 9

——'s conference with, at Leghorn, **18.** 503, 506–7, **19.** 9

——'s correspondence with, **19.** 29, 147, 150

——'s good relations with, **18.** 506–7, **19.** 9, **22.** 581

—— tells, of English officer's suspected disloyalty, **19.** 146–7, 150

Medley may succeed, **19.** 132, 146

men of war sent by, to England, **19.** 110, **43.** 258

Money brings dispatches to, **19.** 12

oxen for the fleet of, to be at Leghorn, **18.** 503n

Port Mahon may be left by, **18.** 555

—— visited by, on way to England, **19.** 146

San Remo destroyed by, **19.** 120, 132

seal lost by, **19.** 9

Spanish preparations for Genoese invasion reported to, **19.** 555

Theodore of Corsica cannot get passage to, **19.** 132

Townshend told by, to conquer Corsica, **19.** 146

Walpole, Sir Robert, resembles, **18.** 506

Walpole family esteemed by, **18.** 507, 544

will of, **22.** 578, 581

wounded, **18.** 415

Rowley, Sir William (1761–1832), 2d Bt; M.P.:

grandfather leaves little to, **22.** 578

'Rowley poems.' *See under* Chatterton, Thomas

Rowson, Susanna:

Critical Review criticizes novels of, **31.** 274n

'Rowwaggon':

auctioneer's word, **38.** 87

Roxana (d. 311 B.C.), wife of Alexander the Great:

Conway might attend Cts of Coventry as, **38.** 75

HW's early passion was not, **11.** 362

Roxana. See under Lampugnani, Giovanni Battista

'Roxana, strolling':

HW's term for Bns Craven, **25.** 633

'Roxane' (character in Racine's *Bajazet*):

Clairon, Mlle, plays, **3.** 224, 231

Roxburghe, D. of. *See* Ker, John (ca 1680–1741); Ker, John (1740–1804); Ker, Robert (ca 1709–55)

Roxburghe, E. of. *See* Ker, John (ca 1680–1741)

Roy, Le. *See* Le Roy; Leroy

Roy, Frances, m. Samuel Rolle:

Piddletown manor transmitted by, to Rolle family, **25.** 148n

Royal academy (riding school). *See under* Foubert, Henry de

Royal Academy of Art:

annual dinners of, **28.** 264, 385

Baretti publishes *Guide* to, **29.** 139

Barry professor of painting to, **29.** 292n

Berrys to attend exhibition of, **12.** 187

Buller, Mrs, as unresponsive as members of, **11.** 183

Bunbury exhibits in, **41.** 429

Carter, Charles, studies drawing at, **28.** 369

Chambers becomes treasurer of, **28.** 451n

—— is seen at, **29.** 47

design schools of, moved to Somerset House, **35.** 344n

exhibitions at: **2.** 120, 240, **23.** 210–11, **24.** 92–3, **28.** 195–6, **29.** 33–4, 45n, 137–8, 296; Farington invites Berrys, Mrs Damer, and HW to, **15.** 322–3; Farington's landscape in, **15.** 322; HW and Ossory dine at, **32.** 291n; HW dines at, **24.** 92–3; HW, Goldsmith, Reynolds, and Dr Johnson attend dinner at, **16.** 129–30, **43.** 148; HW hears about Chatterton from Goldsmith at, **2.** 205; HW identifies those present at, **16.** 349; HW meets Goldsmith at, **11.** 276, **43.** 148; Harding's paintings shown at, **16.** 95; in Christie's rooms in Pall Mall, **32.** 289n, 291n; Lawrence's portrait of Farington in, **15.** 322; Lysons, S., exhibits at, **42.** 439n; Westall's pictures in, **12.** 192

foundation of, **1.** 211n

Hunter, Dr William, gives lecture to, at Somerset House, **43.** 307

members of, unfit to illustrate Shakespeare, **33.** 547, 549

models of Henley bridge keystones and kittens exhibited at, by Mrs Damer, **25.** 576

new rooms of, at Somerset House, opened, **29.** 33

Opie professor to, **29.** 184n

Pars exhibits at, **35.** 424n

portrait of Lord Richard Cavendish exhibited at, **29.** 138n

Sandby, professor of architecture to, **1.** 208n

Shirreff a student at schools of, **15.** 116n

Somerset House will be made by, into a fine ruin, **2.** 246

Wale, professor to, **15.** 112n

Walpole, Hon. Thomas, attends dinner by, **24.** 92n

Zoffany's 'Tribune' exhibited at, **23.** 519n

Royal Academy of Music:

opera at the Haymarket sponsored by, **25.** 558n

Royal and Ecclesiastical Antiquities of England. See under Strutt, Joseph

Royal and Noble Authors, by HW. See *Catalogue of the Royal and Noble Authors of England, A*

Royal Anne, English ship:

unfit for Rochefort expedition, **37.** 495n

Royal blood:

princes of, *see* Princes of the Blood Royal

Richmond, D. of, agreeable because of, **30.** 62

Royal Botanical Society, Florence:

Gualtieri a fellow of, **18.** 88

Royal Charlotte, English ship:
   Emeralde accompanied by, 39. 362n
Royal connoisseurs:
   Mann's reflections on, 20. 398
Royal Constantinople, Turkish ship:
   (?) destroyed, 23. 227
Royal Exchange, London:
   Guards engage Gordon rioters at, to defend
      the Bank, 33. 187–8, 190
   HW drives beyond, to see illuminations, 33.
      93
   North Briton burnt at, 1. 52n
   paper posted at: 9. 320; Piozzi, Mrs, com-
      ments upon, 9. 320n
   Pope's Head Alley opposite, 16. 70
   rioting near, 29. 56n
   seditious papers posted in, 38. 173n
   Sweeting's Alley in, 21. 293n
   Young Pretender's declaration burnt at, 19.
      161
   See also Change Alley
Royal family, English:
   Augusta, Ps of Wales, brings 'evil' into, 25.
      406, 412n
   Flanders not to be destination of, 18. 32
   interest with, not to be counted on, 15. 334
   lawyers to guard, at St James's Palace in
      George II's absence, 19. 180
   military reviews loved by, 17. 410
   mourning deferred by, till after Birthday,
      35. 189
   privacy and economy of, at Richmond, 38.
      434–5
   rebel lords' trial not attended by, 19. 280
   red-eyed, 17. 410
   Richmond the chief (temporary) home of,
      with Bute and few servants, 38. 418
   stupid questions asked by, of visitors, 18. 148
   surgeons used to attend, when they went
      hunting, 35. 107
Royal family, French:
   army practice at Compiègne seen by, 38. 410
   HW presented to, at Versailles, 7. 266, 10.
      291–2, 22. 289n, 31. 52, 56, 35. 112–13,
      39. 13–14
   knowledge of, needed for conversation in
      Paris, 38. 238
Royal Fusiliers:
   Bertie's, to be landed at Minorca, 35. 92n
Royal Gardens (English):
   Hervey surveyor of, 17. 244n
Royal Genealogies. See under Anderson, James
Royal George, English ship:
   Boscawen in, 21. 120n
   Clives arrive in, 21. 429n
   loss of: 33. 354, 358; learned in Florence, 25.
      323
   Ross goes to Plymouth with, 25. 25n
Royal Horse Guards ('the Blues'):
   Argyll restored to, 17. 345
   colonelcy of: Conway succeeds Granby in, 4.
      478, 23. 246; Granby may have, 9. 115;
      Granby retains, 23. 175; Honywood may

have, 20. 203; Johnston has, 34. 260; 'most
   agreeable post in the army,' 23. 246; Rich-
   mond succeeded by Ligonier in, 20. 202n;
   rumoured to go to Bolton, 20. 207
Conway may get commission in, 37. 24, 31
—— reviews, 35. 365
Ferdinand, P., may be joined by, 21. 227
Fontenoy distinction of, 36. 13
George II's funeral attended by, 9. 321–2
George III and Conway review, 11. 258, 32.
   124
Germany the destination of, 9. 221
Granby commands, 21. 227n
HW sees, fording flooded lane, 9. 195
HW would prefer that Conway visit, first,
   39. 385
Newcastle, D. of, told by bishop he should
   have led, at Minden, 39. 105
Onslow calls out, to defend him from rioters,
   35. 286
Sackville, Lord George, disgraced at Minden
   for not bringing up, 24. 187n
—— 'leads up,' in Parliamentary attack, 38.
   309
Royal Hotel, Pall Mall:
   Chartres and wife at, 33. 399n
   Grasse at, 33. 351n
'Royal hunter':
   Mann's term for Ferdinand, 24. 505
Royal Incorporated Society of Artists:
   exhibit of, 23. 210–11
Royal Irish Academy:
   Walker active in, 42. 305n
Royalist; royalists, English:
   HW neither republican nor, 34. 173
   portraits of, at Cornbury, 20. 182
   Strafford the only one esteemed by HW, 35.
      268
   See also Cavalier
Royalist; royalists, French:
   Loire, withdrawal to, by, 12. 84
   Louis XVII's restoration falsely reported by,
      12. 118, 119
   Vendée, La, in, 12. 51, 53, 66, 71, 84, 89
Royal Kalendar:
   incidents in, beneath HW's notice, 33. 385
Royal Library:
   HW jokes about, 31. 247
   in St James's Park, 33. 319
Royal Louis, Le, French ship:
   Kempenfelt encounters, 25. 221n, 33. 315n
Royal Marriage Act (*or* Bill). *See under* Parlia-
   ment: acts of
'Royal Martyr.' *See* Charles I, of England
Royal Mews, London:
   joke about, 10. 116
Royal Military Academy, Chelsea:
   balloon ascent from, 39. 424n
   Conway as master-general of Ordnance would
      be governor of, 39. 123–4
Royal Naval Hospital:
   (?) Hertford reports no vacancy in, 39. 352

Royal Oak, English ship:
expected at Port Mahon, **17**. 285
Howe to be joined by, **24**. 411
involved in war, **19**. 25
Williams commands, **19**. 25n
Royal Philip (ship). See *Real Felipe*
Royal Regiment of Hunters:
at Durham under Oglethorpe, **19**. 127n
Royal Scots (regiment):
Drummond arrives in Scotland with, **19**. 138n
Fuller commands battalions of, **19**. 395n
Zeeland to be relieved by, **19**. 395n
Royal Slave, The. See under Cartwright, William
Royal Society of Arts. *See* Society for the Encouragement of Arts, Manufactures, and Commerce
Royal Society of London:
Albani recommends Fantoni to, **22**. 527
Boščović's California trip approved by, **22**. 527
Clarke's letter to, on Patagonians, **22**. 421n
Dick forwards Fantoni's credentials to, **22**. 527
dissertation on *arbor vitæ* presented to, as joke, **24**. 290
Élie de Beaumont visits, **38**. 461
experiment on gun barrels by, **18**. 232n
fish exhibited to, **1**. 282
French members of, come to study longitude, **22**. 146n
HW a Fellow of, **13**. 28, **14**. 22
HW a member of, but attends no meetings, **15**. 155, **24**. 284
HW compares French invasion to expeditions by, **19**. 327
HW's 'Most Noble She-Witch' mentions, **26**. 9
Hamilton's paper for, on volcanoes, **26**. 46, **35**. 409–10
Henshaw, secretary of, **16**. 61n
Hillsborough to recommend Fantoni to, **22**. 527
Karl Wilhelm Ferdinand made a member of, **22**. 199
Macclesfield, president of, **20**. 557n
Montagu, D. of, 'brother' of, **20**. 79n
Morton and Northumberland contend for presidency of, **38**. 463
Nichols printer to, **29**. 182
Oxford, E. of, receives gifts from, **17**. 357
Philosophical Transactions by: **1**. 282; HW will search, for Brouncker, **16**. 12; Wren's method of etching said to be in, **16**. 35
Pringle, president of, **7**. 12n
sailor's repair of wooden leg reported to, **24**. 283–4, 290
Walpole, Horatio (1678–1757) writes appendix to Whytt's *Essay* read before, and printed in its *Transactions*, **19**. 510n
West, treasurer to, **20**. 371n
Wilkins first secretary to, **15**. 168n
Wortley Montagu elected to, **25**. 226

Royal Sovereign, English ship:
unfit for Rochefort expedition, **37**. 495n
Royal Terrace, Adelphi, London:
'Temple of Health' on, **29**. 109n
Royalty:
French *philosophes* aim at destruction of, **37**. 22
HW jokes about abundance of, **9**. 330
HW regards, as actors on a stage, **25**. 552, 624
HW's attitude towards, **34**. 23
HW's reflections on, **31**. 177
HW's taste for, **37**. 257
HW thought, never haggled about blood when experiments are in question, **39**. 419
'inward voice' inspires, **33**. 390
See also Crown; King; Monarch; Prince; Queen; Royal Family
Royalty; royalties (financial):
Baskerville's, to Cambridge University and Stationers Co., **40**. 275
Royal Wills. See Collection of All the Wills
Roy de Vacquières. *See* Du Roy de Vacquières
Roydon, Suffolk:
Frere of, **16**. 244n, 246n, **42**. 97n
Roye, Mme de:
social relations of, with Duchesse d'Anville, **7**. 311
Roye, Charlotte de. *See* La Rochefoucauld, Charlotte de Roye de Roucy de
Roye, Henrietta de la Rochefoucauld de. *See* La Rochefoucauld, Henrietta de
Roye (France):
church at, 'Saxon,' **7**. 315
Soleil d'Or (inn) at, **7**. 343
visitors to: Craufurd, **5**. 289–90, 294; HW, **3**. 343n, **7**. 315, 343
Roye family:
from Roye, **7**. 315
Royer, ——:
attends session of parliament of Paris, **8**. 173
Royer de Surbois, Jean-François, secretary to the procureur-général:
imprisoned in the Bastille, **6**. 112
Royou-Pennanrun, Annetic (ca 1748–1814), m. (1766) Élie-Catherine Fréron:
Année littéraire to be edited by, **6**. 284
Royston, Vct. *See* Yorke, Philip (1720–90)
Royston, Vcts. *See* Campbell, Jemima
Royston, Herts:
letters postmarked at, **13**. 72n
market at, **1**. 239
Roze. *See* Rose
Rozel de Beaumanoir. *See* Du Rozel de Beaumanoir
Rozier. *See* Pilâtre de Rosier, Jean-François
Rozoi. *See* Farmain de Rozoi
Ruabon, Denbighshire:
Middleton of, **16**. 324n
Rua Formosa, Lisbon:
house in, **11**. 160n
Rubbio; rubbia:
each contains 3 sacks, **22**. 453n
Rubens, Mme. *See* Fourment, Helena

Rubens, Jan (d. 1587):
Leicester's anecdote about, **41**. 270
Rubens, Peter Paul (1577–1640), painter:
Astley not to be compared to, **20**. 341
Buckingham's portrait allegedly by, **34**. 239
cabinet painted by, at Burghley House: **10**. 345; revealed by HW to E. of Exeter, **10**. 91; HW sees copies of, at King's Lynn, **9**. 350
ceiling by, at Osterley Park, **32**. 126
Charles I helped by, in purchase of Raphael cartoons, **16**. 147n, 168n
Cipriani's paintings to replace those of, at Houghton, **25**. 316
Cumberland's life of, **2**. 326
—— spells name of, in Spanish form, **29**. 232
Damer, Mrs, gives opinion of, **11**. 266
'delineator' should enable Reynolds and West to excel, **28**. 329
Eccardt's painting of Churchills modelled on painting by, at Blenheim, **35**. 174n
Elector Palatine's paintings by, **39**. 537
'Escurial' by, recommended by HW, **15**. 321
Furnese has pictures by, **21**. 172n
Guise consults Richardson about, **17**. 485n
HW buys print of house of, **7**. 402
HW sees copies of, at King's Lynn, **9**. 350
HW's figure of child by, **5**. 65, **7**. 335
heads by, in Palazzo Pitti, copied by Maria Hadfield, **25**. 646n
Hogarth emulates, **9**. 365
Jamesone and Van Dyck study under, at Antwerp, **40**. 263
Jamesone imitates, in painting himself with hat on, **40**. 264
Julienne has landscape by, **7**. 286
—— has sketches by, **7**. 287
Leicester's anecdotes about father of, **41**. 270
Lens's copies of, **2**. 222n
Marie de Médicis painted by, **7**. 335
master of chiaroscuro, **33**. 466
Monaco, P. of, has design and painting by, **7**. 335
—— has painting of little girl by, **7**. 335
Montagu, D. of, has landscape by, **7**. 346
Orford, E. of, complained of having too many pictures by, **25**. 418
paintings by: **10**. 78n, **16**. 67n; at Blackheath, **33**. 137; at Devonshire House, **38**. 455n; at Oxford, **33**. 55; in the Luxembourg, **32**. 181; of Prometheus at Kimbolton, **10**. 76, 78; said to be in Scotland, **16**. 51; to be sold by auction at Brussels, **33**. 487
plates attributed to, **2**. 152–3, 155–8
Presle has landscape by, **7**. 346
prints and drawings by, **38**. 371n
probable figure of, **40**. 226
'Prometheus' by, with eagle by Snyders, **43**. 129
'Tribute Money' by, at Burghley House, **10**. 346
Van Dyck imitates, **16**. 149
——'s sketch attributed to, **9**. 222–3

Veen, Otto van, the master of, **42**. 248
Wade sells cartoon by, to Sir Robert Walpole, **9**. 56
West asks for list of works of, in England, **42**. 312
wives of, **35**. 206
Rubicon (river in Italy):
'Airgonauts' have passed, **33**. 458
in quotation from Pope's *Essay on Man*, **33**. 25
Mansfield's allusion to crossing, **28**. 415, 459, **29**. 60, 187
'Rubiconians':
applied to zealous loyalists, **33**. 389
Rubinelli, Giovanni Battista (1753–1829), opera singer:
HW has heard at London opera house, **25**. 646
HW hears, at Westminster Abbey in Handel's jubilee rehearsal, **25**. 648
one song sung by, at Mrs Cosway's concert, **25**. 646
Sheridan does not pay, **31**. 343
voice of, more distinct in Handel jubilee than at opera, **25**. 648
Ruby, English ship:
Frogmore, captain of, **19**. 33n
survives Jamaica hurricane, **39**. 353n
Ruby, French ship:
captured off Cape Finisterre, **19**. 410
Ruby; rubies:
ballast, mentioned by HW, **40**. 226
Clive may not again return with, **22**. 243
Elizabeth, Q., head of, carved on, at Burghley House, **10**. 345
England will get, from Ceylon conquest, **25**. 277
in Tudor portraits, perhaps taken from convents, **33**. 487
oriental, **30**. 297
palace studded with, **31**. 293
Poland pawns, to John Sobieski to be redeemed in a century, **25**. 525
ring with, *see under* Ring
Rumbold carries off, from Mogul's golden throne, **25**. 545
unhurt by heat, in experiment, **7**. 372, **31**. 158
York, Cardinal, does not trust brother with, **25**. 525
Rucellai, Senator Giulio (1702–78), head of the Segretaria della Giurisdizione at Florence:
Cocchi receives warning from, to stop defending Sir Robert Walpole in Bns Walpole's presence, **18**. 133
Dumesnil accuses, of heresy, **19**. 491
—— seeks to remove, as auditor of the Giurisdizione, **19**. 490–1
Francis I orders Dumesnil to apologize to, **19**. 491
HW to show snuff-box to, **17**. 30
house recommended by, to Bns Walpole, **17**. 107
Ligniville, Comtesse de, denounces works of, **20**. 118

Mann abandoned by, **17.** 71, 460, **18.** 133, 148
—— silences defence of Bns Walpole by, **17.** 448

Misantropo by, **20.** 118

Suares, Bp, persecuted by, **17.** 40, 63

Tamburro notturno translated by, from Addison's *Drummer*, **20.** 118, 151

Walpole, Bns, favours, **17.** 54, 71, 448
—— has bed made by direction of, **17.** 107
—— said to have affair with, **17.** 30n

Rudd, Mrs Valentine. *See* Young, Margaret Caroline

Rudder, Samuel (d. 1801), printer:
New History of Gloucestershire, A, by: **2.** 178, 179, 182, 204, **43.** 70; Atkyns continued by, **42.** 115; Catherine Parr's death and funeral described in, **42.** 114, 115

Ruddier. *See* Rudyerd

Ruden, Mr:
SH visited by, **12.** 250

Rudeness:
HW's reflections on, **39.** 242

Rudge, Margaret, m. Sir William Stanhope: daughter of, **11.** 41n

Rudge Hall, Salop:
Boycott of, **11.** 194–5n

Rudhall, John (fl. 1768–94), apprentice:
said by Croft to have aided Chatterton in preparing parchments, **29.** 182n

Rudhall. *See also* Rudder

Rudman, Fanny. *See* Murray, Fanny

Rudolph II (1552–1612), Holy Roman Emperor 1576–1612:
Arundel created by, a Count of the Holy Roman Empire, **1.** 5n

Rudyerd, Sir Benjamin (1572–1658), Kt, 1618; M.P.:
Pembroke's poems answered by, **41.** 443

Rueil (France), Aiguillon's seat:
Aiguillon, Duc d', occupies, **5.** 40
Aiguillon, Duchesse d', dies at, **5.** 256, 258
—— has house at, **4.** 143n
—— occupies, **3.** 9, 19, 65, 99, 118, 319, **4.** 61, 124, 245, 267, 430, **5.** 40, 73, 107, 122, 225, 231, **7.** 320, 329, 335, 337
—— seeks verses for, **7.** 363
Aiguillon, Duchesse d' (younger), occupies, **5.** 40, **6.** 48
Bois Prévu near, **7.** 293
Du Barry, Comtesse, sent to, by Louis XV, **6.** 48, 51
—— retires to, **24.** 2
Du Deffand, Mme, mentions, **4.** 115, **5.** 85
HW and Cts of Rochford dine with Duchesse d'Aiguillon at, **31.** 136
HW and Mme du Deffand go to, **4.** 62n, **6.** 145n
HW's verses for, **7.** 363
Nivernais and Mme de Rochefort regret missing party at, **41.** 214
visitors to: Agen, Bp of, **7.** 335; Bauffremont, **4.** 443, **7.** 337; Bédée, Mlle de, **4.** 443; Boucault, Mme, **4.** 130, **7.** 320; Boufflers, Comte

and Comtesse de, **4.** 130; Boufflers, Marquise de, **7.** 337; Broglie, Comte and Comtesse de, **7.** 335; Bulkeley, **7.** 337; Caswall, **7.** 320; Chabrillan, **7.** 320, 329, 335; Cholmondeley, Mrs, **4.** 242, 245, 443, **7.** 329; Cholmondeley, Henrietta Maria, **4.** 443; Churchills, **7.** 335; Creutz, **5.** 40; Crussol, Marquise de, **4.** 443, **7.** 329; Du Barry, Mlle, **6.** 48; Du Barry, Vicomtesse, **6.** 48; Du Deffand, **3.** 19, **4.** 130, 240, 242, 245, 266, 270, 443, **5.** 40, 73, 78, 80, **7.** 320, 329, 335, 337; Forcalquier, Comtesse de, **4.** 130; Gustav III, **5.** 40; HW, **3.** 337, **4.** 61, 266, 270, 299n, **5.** 82, 87, **7.** 320, 329, 335, 337; Hessenstein, **5.** 40; Irwin, **4.** 130; Karl, Prince, **5.** 40; Maurepas, **5.** 40; Mirepoix, Mme de, **7.** 335; Pont-de-Veyle, **4.** 130; Redmond, **7.** 320; Richelieu, **5.** 40, **7.** 335; Rochford, Cts of, **7.** 320; Scheffer, **5.** 40; Walpole, Hon. Robert, **4.** 245

Rues de Paris. See Essais historiques sur Paris

Ruff; ruffs:
Chute dreams of a chaise-percée seat used as, **35.** 55
man in portrait wears, **30.** 371
Montagu would be as unintelligible to children as if he wore, **10.** 259
St-Cyr pensioners wear, **10.** 293
SH's, old, **10.** 133

Ruffec (France), Broglie's seat:
Broglie, Comte de, comes from, **6.** 71n
—— exiled to, **5.** 402, **23.** 521
—— occupies, **7.** 177, 450, 451
—— to occupy, **5.** 225, 256, **6.** 74, 358
Broglie, Comtesse de, occupies, **5.** 225, 256, **6.** 211
Du Deffand, Mme, gives opinion of, **6.** 74
position of, **5.** 402
visitors to: Jonzac, Marquise de, **6.** 211; Macartney, **7.** 177

'Ruffham, Ds of':
HW's nom-de-plume, **18.** 238

Ruffham. *See also* Rougham

Ruffhead, Owen (1723–69), writer:
Considerations on the present Dangerous Crisis by, Montagu reads about, **10.** 75
Contest written by, **9.** 203n, **21.** 38n
HW's *Royal and Noble Authors* reviewed by, **35.** 107n
life of Pope by, **29.** 278
(?) review of Clarendon's *Life* by, **16.** 34

Ruffle; ruffles:
canonici and abbés forbidden to wear, **21.** 224
deep, **24.** 192n
French, seized by customs, **38.** 415n
grief will vent itself in muslin, **31.** 88
HW sends, to Lady Lucy Clinton from Lincoln, **30.** 22
HW should bring, from Paris, **37.** 105
Hotham, Lady Gertrude, sets fire to, **24.** 90
lace, Montagu wishes, from England, **10.** 1, 9, 10
lady catches on fire from, **22.** 403

[Ruffle; ruffles, *continued*]
men's lace, Hertford, Cts of, wants, from Paris, **39.** 264, 267
Pitt, Mrs, mends, before attending ball, **23.** 456
Saxon, HW asks E. of Lincoln to bring him, from Paris, **30.** 25

Ruffo, Antonio (1687–1753), cardinal, 1743:
Benedict XIV makes, cardinal, **18.** 302n

Ruffo, Fabrizio (1763–1832), Principe di Castelcicala; Neapolitan ambassador to England:
dances at Queensberry House, **11.** 341
HW to send letter in packet of, **35.** *447*

Ruffo, Tommaso (1663–1753), cardinal, 1706:
Benedict XIV consults, about Young Pretender, **20.** 22
—— ridicules complaints of, at Castel Gandolfo, **19.** 415–16
Conclave faction headed by, **13.** 220n
election of, to Papacy, rumoured, **17.** 9, 16
Louis XV wants French candidate elected by, **17.** 21
Old Pretender wants Cardinal York to succeed, **20.** 589
York, Cardinal, tries to take place next to, **19.** 415

Rufford, Lancs:
Hesketh of, **11.** 235n

Rug, coat. *See* Coat: horseman's

Ruhnken, *or* Ruhnkenius, David (1723–98), professor at University of Leyden:
Homeric poem to be published by, **16.** 179

Ruins:
Gothic, should be painted by Bentley, **35.** 208
of Netley Abbey, **35.** 251
Saxon, at Kirkstall, **35.** 270

Ruins of Balbec; *Ruins of Palmyra. See under* Wood, Robert

Ruins of Rome. See under Dyer, John

Rule; rules:
Du Deffand, Mme, on, **4.** 135, 167
Rule a Wife and Have a Wife. See under Fletcher, John (1579–1625)

Rulhière, Claude-Carloman de (1735–91), poet:
Anecdotes sur la révolution de Russie by, **4.** 319
Conway hears MS account by, of Catherine II's coup, **39.** 243
Discours sur les disputes by, **4.** *313*, 319, 322, 324
epigram by, on Mme du Deffand, **5.** 338n

Rullecourt, Baron de. *See* Macquart, Philippe-Charles-Félix

Rum:
American, destroyed, **24.** 309n
Atkinson's, cheap, **33.** 269
for punch, at Cambridge banquet, **20.** 83
Indian convert prefers, to Sacrament, **17.** 477
Medley's body embalmed in, **19.** 434n
old, HW uses, to cure his eyes, **21.** 168

Rumain, Comtesse du. *See* Rouault de Gamaches, Constance-Simonne-Flore-Gabrielle

Rumain de Coëtanfao. *See* Le Vicomte du Rumain de Coëtanfao

Rumbold, Lady; Rumbold, Mrs Thomas. *See* Law, Joanna (d. 1823)

Rumbold, Sir Thomas (1736–91), cr. (1779) Bt; M.P.; gov. of Madras 1777–80:
anecdote of christening of son of, **29.** 35
Arthur perhaps related to, **25.** 141n
Clive's riches nearly equalled by, **39.** 369–70
Dundas prosecutes, for corruption at Madras, **25.** 400
former waiter at White's, **11.** 295n, **25.** 141, 400, **29.** 122
General Barker's cargo partly owned by, **25.** 135n
(?) HW calls, 'Thomas Kouli Kan,' **25.** 545
HW mentions, **25.** 272
Haidar 'Alī thinks he has as much right as, to Indian diamonds, **25.** 141
Hardinge employed in defence of, **35.** 623–4
House of Commons to investigate, **25.** 277
Ireland reached by, on East India fleet, **25.** 119
Macartney expects recall of, **33.** 219n
Mason's couplet on, **29.** 246
may have robbed Indies of climate as well as diamonds, **33.** 410–11
may have to disgorge million acquired as nabob, **25.** 274
Mogul's crown jewels carried off by, **25.** 545
Parliamentary investigation of, **25.** 277, **29.** 299, **39.** 369–70
plundering by, **31.** 219
tours Italy for son's health, **25.** 651
trial of, discloses tyranny of East India Co., **25.** 400
verses on, **29.** 88
wealth of, **25.** 119

Rumbold, William Richard (1760–86), Capt.; M.P.:
health not recovered by, at Naples, so he must return to England, **25.** 651

Rumiantsev (later Rumiantsev-Zadunaĭskiĭ), Petr Alexandrovich (1725–96), Russian general:
army of: Catherine II orders return of, **22.** 59n; destined against Denmark but takes oath in favour of Catherine II, **22.** 53n; not to cross Danube, **23.** 310n; seizes Azov, **23.** 116n
Danube crossed by, to attack Grand Vizir at Schuma, **24.** 29
—— may be crossed by, with army, **24.** 479
—— said to have been crossed by, after defeat, **24.** 504
—— to be crossed by, **23.** 469n, 479n
Grand Vizir concludes treaty with, **24.** 33n
——'s retreat cut off by, **24.** 33
name of corrected, **43.** 282
Obreskov to be conveyed to headquarters of, **23.** 309n
Russian army commanded by, **23.** 146n, *202*

Rumney, English ship:
at Port Mahon, **17**. 285n
Rumours, false:
HW's reflections on, **33**. 91
'Rump days':
Walpole, Lady, coins phrase of, **35**. 86
Runaway (of horses and carriage):
Cole's, **2**. 180–1, 183–4
Runciman, Alexander (1736–85), painter:
Buchan's account of, in *The Bee*, **15**. 189
Runcton Holme, Norfolk:
Jenkin, rector of, **15**. 300
Rundle, Thomas (ca 1688–1743), Bp of Derry, 1735:
Venn prevents, from becoming Bp of Gloucester, **15**. 296
'Runic savage':
activities of, uninteresting to modern readers, **10**. 255
Running:
Roman youths' usual exercise, **37**. 8
Running footman. *See under* Servant
Runnington, Mrs, in Vcts Townshend's household; (?) 'Dorcas':
HW to be informed by, **40**. 166
Runnymede, Surrey, scene of Magna Carta signing:
inscription for, **37**. 99
Ruota. *See* Rota
Rupee; rupees (currency in India):
lacks of, Alexander the Great did not carry off, **25**. 545
Rumbold's sacks of, to be squeezed by House of Commons, **25**. 277
Rupert (1619–82), Prince; Count Palatine of Rhine; D. of Bavaria:
inventions of, **9**. 372
portrait of, **30**. 370
print by, **1**. 175
print of, **9**. 118n
Watts, William, chaplain to, **42**. 42n
Rupert, English ship:
at Port Mahon, **17**. 285n
involved in war, **19**. 25
Rupini, ——:
witness at Mrs Cornelys's trial, **23**. 272n
Rupture; ruptures:
occurrences of, **17**. 276n, **20**. 109, **37**. 256
Rural life:
HW's reflections on appeal of, to those too old to be active in it, **10**. 298
Ruramonde. *See* Roermond
Ruremond. *See* Rémond
Rusca, Cavaliere Carlo Francesco (1696–1769), painter:
(?) portrait by, of Lady Mary Wortley Montagu, **35**. 271
Rush, Dublin County:
Echlin, surveyor of customs at, **41**. 398
Rush; rushes:
bed of, at Park Place, for fish, **37**. 381

Rushout, Sir John (1685–1775), 4th Bt, 1711; M.P.:
birth date of, corrected, **43**. 243
Bubb Dodington replaces, as treasurer of the Navy, **18**. 551, **30**. 292n
Carteret's party to be led by, in House of Commons, **19**. 212
'dishclout,' **18**. 350
HW calls, 'fool,' **30**. 164
HW jokingly proposes, for D. of Cumberland's groom, **39**. 78
HW ridicules, **13**. 14n
lord of the Treasury, **17**. 332–3
mannerisms of, **30**. 291
ministerial repair attempted by, **37**. 485
named in Secret Committee lists, **17**. 385
Norton, who once prosecuted him, clashes with, in Parliamentary debate, **38**. 242
oldest member of House of Commons, **39**. 78
Onslow pension urged by, **30**. 164
——'s impartiality praised by, **30**. 292n
Parliamentary debate by, on privately-raised regiments, **26**. 17
Pulteney's follower, **17**. 333, **18**. 72n
——'s second, in duel with Hervey, **17**. 332n
Scrope defended by, **17**. 467
Secret Committee not attended by, **17**. 401
Speaker's position rumoured for, **38**. 136
'tough old knight,' **38**. 485
treasurer of the Navy's post to go to, **18**. 350, 356
valet of, sent to Hanau by Pulteney, **18**. 299
Walpole, Sir Robert, opposed by, **17**. 332n
Williams, Sir C. H., satirizes, **18**. 320
Wilmington and Compton outvoted by, **18**. 50n
Ruspanti:
Medici, Giovanni Gastone de', employs, **17**. 273n
Suares, Bp and Mme, and Uguccioni are, **17**. 273n
Suares, Bp, secret member of, **18**. 40n
'Ruspantism':
Lorraine, Primate of, addicted to, **17**. 273
Ruspi (sequins), Florentine coins:
Ruspanti paid with, **17**. 273n
value of, **17**. 273n
Rusponi (zecchini gigliati), Florentine coins:
value of, **20**. 334
Russborough, Bn. *See* Leeson, Joseph (1711–83)
'Russel':
letter-writer's nom-de-plume, **42**. 505
Russel, —— (d. ca 1745):
puppet-show by, burlesques Italian operas, **19**. 28
Russel, Mr:
SH visited by, **12**. 226, (?) 237
Russel, Mrs:
forty years needed by, to see all of SH, **33**. 523
SH visited by, **12**. 226

'Russel, Jack':
HW's name for D. of Bedford, **40.** 88
Russel, (?) John (1745–1806), painter:
Huntingdon, Cts of, painted by, **35.** 346n
Russel, Mrs Richard. *See* Smith, Hannah Catherine Maria
Russel, Theodore (1614–89), Flemish painter in England:
copies of Van Dyck made by, **15.** 205
Russel. *See also* Russell
Russel MS:
HW cites, about Cts of Desmond, **40.** 112
Russell, Bns. *See* Cooke, Elizabeth (1528–1609); Wriothesley, Lady Rachel (ca 1637–1723)
Russell, Mr, Lady Suffolk's butler:
HW mentions in fictitious letter, **31.** 432
Russell, Lady Anne (d. 1604), m. (1565) Ambrose Dudley, 1st E. of Warwick, n.c.:
portrait of, at Appleby Castle, **10.** 185
Russell, Anne (d. 1639), m. (1600) Henry Somerset, 5th E. of Worcester, cr. (1643) M. of Worcester:
monument of, in Bisham Church, **9.** 101
Russell, Lady Caroline (1743–1811), m. (1762) George Spencer, 3d [4th] D. of Marlborough, 1758:
at Mrs Boyle Walsingham's ball, **42.** 222n
Beauclerk, Lady Diana, visited by, **11.** 81–2
brother and Lady Elizabeth Keppel shut up together by, **38.** 400, 403
Buckingham House ball attended by, **38.** 290
Charlotte, Q., has, as bridesmaid, **21.** 529, **38.** 117
comments on Ds of Leinster's marriage, **32.** 206
court ball attended by, **9.** 406, **38.** 143
Craven, Bns, sends play to, **34.** 27n
dictates charity to Lord Clifden, **34.** 167
Gunning, Miss, and, **11.** 108, 123–4, 185–6, 217, 229
Gunning, Mrs, fails to find, at Blenheim, **11.** 201
HW calls, 'the old bittern,' **12.** 156
HW entertains, at SH breakfast, **35.** 225, **39.** 418
HW mentions, **9.** 402, 403, **10.** 7
HW's invitation from, **32.** 264
HW's lassitude at house of: **5.** 65; Du Deffand, Mme, alarmed by, **5.** 75n
HW visited by, **11.** 82
Hamilton's emblematic portrait of mother and, **41.** 444
handsome, **21.** 530
husband inseparable from, **39.** 3
letter of, on Lord Blandford's marriage, **11.** 366
loo played by, **38.** 341n
Marlborough to wed, despite dislike of her mother, **22.** 73
marriage of, **38.** 170
marriages of children of, **11.** 108, 198, 349, 352
Masserano entertains, at supper, **38.** 399n

miscarriage of, at time of brother's accident, **22.** 498
mother corrected by, about son's marriage, **39.** 479
mother not invited to visit, at Blenheim, **38.** 177
mother's rouge makes her resemble, **9.** 388n
plate of print of Ds of Devonshire said to be owned by, **28.** 419
Ramsgate visited by, **12.** 156
song with unseemly stanza sung by, **37.** 565
SH to be visited by, **33.** 11
SH visited by, **12.** 221
Russell, David (fl. 1774–5), printer at York:
Scottish, **28.** 157
text of memoir of Gray to be settled by, **28.** 163
Russell, Edward (d. ? 1572), styled Lord Russell:
biographical information about, corrected, **43.** 117
family of, **9.** 124–5
Otway's *Orphan* said to be based on, **34.** 126
portrait of, **9.** 124, **34.** 126
Russell, Edward (1652–1727), cr. (1697) E. of Orford:
great-niece of, **17.** 333
title of, **13.** 11n
Russell, Lady Elizabeth (d. 1605), m. (1583) William Bourchier, 3d E. of Bath:
portrait of, at Appleby, Castle, **10.** 185
Russell, Elizabeth (1575–1600):
legend about death of, **33.** 288
Russell, Lady Elizabeth (d. 1784), m. (1726) William Capell, 3d E. of Essex:
chatters, **38.** 343
Euston's rudeness enrages, **18.** 273
HW and Ladies Suffolk and Yarmouth play whist at party of, **33.** 313
Russell, Mrs Frances, Bedchamber woman to Ps Amelia:
footpads rob, on way to Kensington, **35.** 189n
Russell, Frances (1699–1775), m. John Revett:
Frederick, P. of Wales, gets retort from, **33.** 443–4
Russell, Francis (1527–85), 2d E. of Bedford, 1555; M.P.:
buried at Chenies, **37.** 298n
daughter of, **1.** 38n, **2.** 323n
sons of: **9.** 124; furnish subject of Otway's *Orphan*, **34.** 126
Russell, Francis (d. 1585), styled Lord Russell 1584–5:
family of, **9.** 124–5
Otway's *Orphan* said to be based on, **9.** 124n, **34.** 126
peerage of, corrected, **43.** 117
portrait of, **9.** 124, **34.** 126
Russell, Francis (1593–1641), 4th E. of Bedford, 1627:
commissioned to drain fens, **1.** 132
Covent Garden church built by, **34.** 122
son of, **9.** 124n

Russell, Francis (1739–67), styled M. of Tavistock; M.P.:
accident to, falling from horse, 3. 270, 274,
   277, 22. 497, 30. 243
Ampthill Park visited by, 10. 170
Barbantane recommended by, to Mann, 22.
   482
Bedford coalition supported by, 41. 70
Boufflers, Comtesse de, concerned about accident and death of, 3. 271, 278, 281, 4. 132
Canterbury visited by, on way to Paris, 22.
   78n
Conolly entertains, 9. 234
Conti entertains, at supper, 38. 359–60
Craufurd to visit, 3. 122
death of: 10. 235n, 22. 506, 34. 248; expected,
   22. 497; father goes to India House soon
   after, 22. 507; father mourns, 4. 132; Os-
   sory mourns, 34. 248
father's offer of support for Grafton trans-
   mitted through, 30. 232
Grafton transmits Admiralty offer to Gower
   through, 22. 449n
HW amused by Hertford's account of Paris
   journey of, 38. 380
HW cannot understand statement by, about
   Pitt's abuse of Neville, 38. 368–9
HW entertains, at SH breakfast, 35. 225
HW sends letters by, 7. 381
HW's social relations with, in Paris, 7. 312
Hertford called on by, 38. 360
Houghton Park House occupied by, 32. 44n
Keppel, Lady Elizabeth, to wed, 22. 243, 38.
   396, 399
Mann encloses letter to, 22. 482
—— praised in letters of, 22. 2
—— presents, to Botta, 21. 564
—— told by, of Bunbury's 'chicken' oratory,
   22. 19
marriage of, to be decided on his return to
   England, 38. 380
Montagu, Lady Elizabeth, said to be marry-
   ing, 38. 358
Opposition favoured by, 38. 433
Ossory a cousin of, 31. 62
—— mourns, 34. 248
——'s manner resembles, 31. 62, 40. 386
Paris visited by, 38. 358, 359
Pecquigny's fight with Virrette avoided by,
   38. 307
sister contrives marriage of, 38. 400, 403
son of, 11. 131n
trepanned, 22. 497
wife of, 4. 132n, 9. 235n
Woburn Abbey visited by, for wedding, 38.
   401
Russell, Francis (1765–1802), 5th D. of Bedford, 1771:
Bedford populace cheers, 34. 209–10
Burke's Letter to a Noble Lord may enrage,
   34. 215
Fitzwilliam attacked by, 34. 214n
genealogy of, 34. 123

grandmother's expulsion perhaps planned by,
   33. 521–2
grandmother to accompany, abroad, 33. 208
HW needs no thanks for catalogue of pic-
   tures of, 34. 123
HW's account of pictures at Woburn Abbey
   pleases, 34. 130–1
HW's correspondence with, 42. 340–1
HW's notes on pictures of, see Notes to the
   Portraits at Woburn Abbey
HW's Notes please, 42. 340
HW thanks, for Cts of Devonshire's picture,
   42. 340
HW tries to forestall visit from, 34. 111–12
HW wishes to borrow picture from, for
   Lysons, 34. 130–1
Holland, Henry, directs alterations for, 34.
   188n
Houghton Park House demolished by, 34.
   183n
infant at time of father's death, 22. 498
King's Birthday guests eclipsed by clothes of,
   11. 284
minority of, will accumulate wealth, 23. 274
O'Reilly friend of, 11. 95n
Palmer ordered by, to have all houses made
   ready, 33. 521–2
petition by, to House of Lords against Seditious Meetings and Treasonable Practices
   Bills, 34. 209n
portrait of, 32. 337
Reynolds depicts, as St George, 32. 316n, 337n
servant of, 25. 534n
(?) verses by, 34. 131
will be eclipsed by Margrave and Margravine
   of Ansbach, 34. 133
Russell, John (d. 1494), Bp of Lincoln:
Bourchier's commission to, as Edward IV's
   executor, 41. 124
chancellor to Richard III, 14. 160
Richard III's letter to, 1. 156, 2. 108n
third continuation of Croyland Chronicle
   perhaps by, 14. 162n, 15. 170n
Russell, John (ca 1485–1555), cr. (1539) Bn
Russell, and (1550) E. of Bedford:
buried at Chenies, 37. 298n
Russell, Hon. John (1620–81):
Gramont's memoirs praise skill of, in dancing,
   9. 124
Russell, John (d. 1744), Capt.:
wounded, 18. 415
Russell, John (1710–71), 4th D. of Bedford;
'little Æolus':
Admiralty post of, 18. 550, 37. 200
agrees with rest of Cabinet Council, 22. 295
Albemarle, Cts of, informed by, at Ds of
   Richmond's, of daughter's engagement,
   38. 400
allowance to, for journey to Paris, 38. 269n,
   284
Amelia, Ps, congratulates wife of, on his
   becoming a grandfather, 38. 397
—— entertained by, 9. 324, 363, 369

[Russell, John (1710–71), *continued*]
—— influenced by, **38.** 567
American colonies would be conquered by, **22.** 401
appearance of: at Coronation, **9.** 388; flowers in hair, **10.** 94
appointment of: as ambassador to France, **30.** 166; as lord privy seal, **9.** 406
Argyll accused by, of favouring Jacobites, **20.** 310
—— 's bill attacked by, in House of Lords, **20.** 310–11
(?) at Chesterfield's assembly, **37.** 325
ball given by, **37.** 54
Bath to be visited by, **10.** 229, **35.** 320, **39.** 76
—— visited by, **35.** 120
Bath-Woburn journey made by, without coming to London, **38.** 460
bishops' appointments and Henley's peerage made without approval by, **38.** 392
blue ribbon worn by, **10.** 235
Bolingbroke's and Oxford's fate will be that of, **38.** 513
Boufflers, Comtesse de, accompanied by, **32.** 14n
Brand connected with, **20.** 435
—— entertained by, **9.** 233
Bridgen's vote justifies charges by, against London heads for not suppressing riot, **38.** 263
brother of, **34.** 259
Bunbury's motion attacks, **22.** 8n
Bute affronted by opposition of, to Regency Bill, **22.** 299–300
Bute and Ps of Wales ignored by, **38.** 534
Bute and Ps of Wales may be overcome by, **38.** 561
Bute angers, by seeking reversion of Ampthill Manor, **38.** 433–4
—— broke promise to, **30.** 185
—— called 'bitter enemy' by, **30.** 185
—— courted by, **38.** 354–5
—— joins Grenville and, in wanting troops sent to America, **22.** 401
—— may be conciliated by faction of, **9.** 341
—— opposed by, **38.** 186
—— 's choice for lord privy seal, **21.** 541n
—— 's offer to, of Council presidency, rejected, **22.** 130n
Cabinet Council avoided by, **38.** 433
Cambridgeshire election and, **1.** 200
Cape Breton's abandonment opposed by, **19.** 255
Carmichael's appointment to Armagh archbishopric sought by, **22.** 276
Carrickfergus's loss might be attributed to, **21.** 371
Carteret, Robert, wakens, after cropping horses' ears during visit, **18.** 501
cavalry and infantry ordered by, against Dublin rioters, **21.** 382n
Chenies owned by, **35.** 145
Chinese house wanted by, at Woburn, **35.** 177

Choiseul's peace negotiations with, **22.** 81n
Choiseul, Duchesse de, writes to, **4.** 49
circle of, HW's favourite topic of abuse, **30.** 176
Clandestine Marriages Act opposed by, **9.** 147, **37.** 362
Clanricarde challenges, and blames Irish troubles on him, **38.** 79n
—— 's letter to, in *London Chronicle*, **38.** 79
Cobhamite dismissal wished by, **19.** 188–9
Conway and Hertford to visit, at Woburn, **37.** 63
Conway goes from opera to tavern with, **37.** 54
—— opposed by, as leader of House of Commons, **22.** 542, 570
—— 's administration to be endured by, despite former opposition, **22.** 571
—— 's intention of resigning unknown to, **41.** 85
Conways aided by, **3.** 255
Council presidency offered to, **22.** 130
Court attended by, **9.** 89
Craufurd to visit, **3.** 122
Cumberland, D. of, entertained by, **9.** 232, 363
—— might secure Navy through Sandwich and, **20.** 222n
—— supports, **20.** 113, 120, 201, 207, 224
—— supports Sandwich and, against Newcastle, **20.** 113n
—— visits, at Woburn, **20.** 89
daughter-in-law accompanied by, to opera at time of her husband's accident, **22.** 498
daughter of, **9.** 406n, **11.** 81n, **21.** 529–30, **22.** 73n, 498n
death of: **23.** 262; leaves Lord North in full security, **31.** 151
Delaval could be influenced by, **28.** 1
Denbigh and Pomfret attack, in House of Lords, **38.** 529
Devonshire lord lieutenancy sought by, **40.** 67–8
dismissals of anti-Court officers blamed on, **38.** 264
dismissed as lord president, **22.** 310
dissatisfaction of, augurs political revolution, **38.** 440
Dublin Castle left by, for Woburn Abbey, **21.** 199n
Dublin University's chancellor, **39.** 107
Durand informs, of Louis XV's order to arrest Young Pretender, **20.** 35n
Dutch deputies and young Dutchman entertained by, **9.** 232
Egmont defended by, in barring Guerchy from Portsmouth, **38.** 401–2
Egremont's appointment may displease, **38.** 134
Elliot, John, receives circular letter of, **21.** 376n
engaged to elect D. of Newcastle, **9.** 72n

England's victories over France sacrificed by, **22.** 401

Essex election lost because of speech of, **38.** 263

Exeter mob attacks, **23.** 139

faction of: Anson deserts, **20.** 135; attachments of, few, **20.** 201; Bedford forbids opposition by members of, **30.** 236; Bute and Holland oppose, on Poor Bill, **38.** 528–9; Bute-Pitt negotiations worry, **38.** 405; care nothing about England's disgraces, **39.** 101; Conway not to be involved with, **23.** 179n; divisions in, **30.** 240; does not resign, **19.** 27; Du Deffand, Mme, inquires about, **3.** 178, 407; East India inquiry shunned by, **41.** 65; fall of, may not take place, **20.** 230; Fox enlists, **20.** 502; Fox opposed by, at Gower's instigation, **41.** 67n; Fox's opinion of, **30.** 230; Fox to bring, to Court, **35.** 89; Frederick, P. of Wales, may league with, **20.** 230; George III's wish to patch up administration seconded by, **25.** 379; Gower head of, **25.** 261n; Gower's plea to Hertford may be overture from, **38.** 460; Grafton, former enemy to, embraces them, **39.** 101; Grafton impelled to, by Rigby, **34.** 242; Grafton ministry makes overtures to, through Rockingham, **22.** 538; Grafton's separation would be encouraged by, **38.** 436; Grenville, George, deserted by, **22.** 462, 463, 566, **30.** 240; Grenville, George, not forsaken by, **22.** 533; Grenville, George, Northington, and secretaries of state adhere to, **38.** 534; Grenville, George, rejoined by, **10.** 236; Grenville, George, the tool of, **38.** 283; Grenville, George, will dampen the rage of, **22.** 549; HW doubts that Temple dupes, about Gower, **30.** 233; HW frequents, **20.** 207; HW's dislike of, makes him abet Conway's opposition, **39.** 530; Hertford said to be disliked by, **38.** 283; House of Commons deserted by, **22.** 464; House of Commons' opening debate attended by, **30.** 236; London mob conjured up by, **23.** 549; Mastership of the Horse to Queen desired by, **30.** 186–7; Mistley conference of, upset by Irish news and Bridgwater, **24.** 526n; money and liquor divert, from public business, **39.** 101; Newcastle, D. of, at odds with, **20.** 201; Newcastle, D. of, to unite, with Rockingham faction, **22.** 533, 565–6; not accommodated in ministry, **22.** 449; (?) offers by, to fill vacancies in ministry, **30.** 228; Opposition supported only by, **22.** 382; Parliamentary members of, **37.** 416; Pitt and Newcastle oppose, **20.** 222; Pitt bargains with, **10.** 236; Pitt begins negotiations with, at Bath, **22.** 472; Pitt detaches himself from, **20.** 138; Pitt's defeat strengthens, **20.** 223; Pitt, Elizabeth, once intimate wiith, **20.** 416; Poor Bill's being dropped is a blow to,

38. 536; quarrels with Rockingham faction, **22.** 565–6; receives offices, **3.** 407; reign of, probably over, **38.** 501; Rockingham faction may force Pitt into alliance with, **30.** 232; Rockingham faction meets, at Newcastle House, **22.** 541–2; Rockingham faction would decline ministry unless joined by, **41.** 85; Rockingham negotiates with, at Woburn, **22.** 538; Rockingham to be reconciled with, by D. of Newcastle, **22.** 549; Rockingham wants to unite with, **22.** 504n, 505n; Shelburne opposed by, **22.** 571; Shelburne's removal demanded by, **23.** 61; Stormont's appointment as secretary of state delayed by, **24.** 525n; Tavistock's death weakens, **22.** 498; too shameless to be hypocrites, **22.** 570; trifles to be conferred upon, **22.** 572; Weymouth wanted by, to be Irish lord lieutenant, **38.** 545, 557; will be more difficult if Conway resigns, **41.** 73; worn out in House of Commons, pert in House of Lords, **41.** 10

Fane protégé of, **17.** 247

—— told by, that he cannot go to Spain, **20.** 203

Fielding appointed by, as justice of the peace, **9.** 84n

Fitzwilliam sent by, to drive the French from Carrickfergus, **21.** 373

Forrester, lawyer of, **38.** 550

'Fountain' meeting attended by, **17.** 336

Fox, Henry, and, oppose Northampton and Halifax on Turnpike Bill, **20.** 112n

Fox, Henry, attached to, **20.** 224

—— joins with, **13.** 26n

——'s offer to, of privy seal, rejected, **35.** 89n

Francis III of Modena entertained by, **20.** 56–7

French popularity of, **38.** 184

French visit of, to last a year, **38.** 176

friends of: forbidden to oppose Pitt, **30.** 236; may keep places if he retires, **30.** 186; places desired for, **30.** 232; *see also under* faction of

Garter may be conferred upon, **17.** 497

George II attended by, at St James's Palace, **17.** 338

—— dislikes, because of his attachment to Sandwich, **20.** 235n

—— makes, K.G., **9.** 89n, **20.** 72

——'s Cambridge orders must be justified by, **9.** 72

——'s circle entertained by, **9.** 324

—— wants, to resign, as secretary of state, **20.** 207n, 235n

George III accused of breaking promise to, **30.** 185

—— and D. of Cumberland unite in hating, **22.** 364

George III arrogantly treated by, **22.** 309

—— entertained by, **9.** 232

—— forced to accept ministry of, **7.** 369, **22.** 302

[Russell, John (1710–71), *continued*]
—— inquires of, about Leinster's promised dukedom, 30. 348
—— offended by, 30. 201
—— probably influenced by, to exclude Ps of Wales from regency, 22. 298
—— receives ultimatum from other ministers and, 22. 307
——'s conversation with, about excluding Bute, 30. 185n
——'s Coronation attended by, 9. 388
——'s dislike of, shown by hasty Garter chapter, 22. 572n
——'s memo calls, 'arrogant,' 22. 307n
——'s need for, allegedly keeps him at Streatham, 38. 423
—— to get resignation of, 38. 558
German war opposed by, in House of Commons, 22. 7
Gower breaks with, 20. 258
—— informs, of Chatham's plans for new ministry, 41. 70n
—— to be visited by, at Trentham, 38. 423, 433
Grafton, Ds of, entertained by, 9. 369
Grafton, D. of, disputes with, over turnpike road, 20. 549
—— offered allegiance of faction by, 22. 569
—— receives offer of support from, 30. 232
—— supports construction of Marylebone Road against, 20. 120n
Gray asks HW to approach, concerning Pembroke election, 14. 89, 91
Grenville, George, confers with, 22. 569, 41. 72
—— differs with, over French prisoners, 38. 433n
—— opposes coalition with, but wife and others approve, 41. 70
—— reportedly promised Temple to force retirement of, 30. 186
——'s interview with, attempting to prevent his union with Pitt, 30. 236
——'s union with, probably no longer popular at Bedford House, 30. 236
Grenville faction's agent, at Newcastle House, 22. 541
Grenville ministry doomed by dissatisfaction of, 38. 440
Grenville ministry said by, not to resign, 30. 181–2
Guerchy and Pecquigny entertained by, at Woburn, 38. 276, 295
HW calls, 'honest man,' 20. 203
HW compares, to Gaston d'Orléans, 9. 228
HW converses with, about Mme de Choiseul, 41. 17
HW describes, 22. 69–70
HW entertained by, 9. 233, 363, 369
HW entertains, at SH breakfast, 35. 225
HW may propose union of (? D. of Newcastle) with, 40. 344n
HW mentions, 20. 292, 37. 418, 488

HW's correspondence with, 37. (?) 465, 40. 65–6, 67–8, 71–2, 90–1
HW sends notes on debates on Dresden treaty to, 20. 299n, 300n
HW's recommendations would not influence, 9. 210, 215
HW's request to, for army chaplain's leave, 9. 210, 215, 40. 90–1, 43. 120
HW sups with, at Masserano's, 38. 399–400
HW to acquire stained glass from, 9. 102
HW to reconcile, to Waldegrave wedding, 9. 232
HW urges, to print grandmother's letters, 20. 283, 28. 85n
HW will avenge his worry over Conway upon, 38. 380
HW would like anecdotes of French embassy of, 38. 314
Hague, The, may be visited by, on way to negotiate at Paris, 38. 170
Halifax entertained by, 9. 363
—— Grenville, and Sandwich dine with, 22. 298n
Halifax may succeed: in Irish post, 21. 485; in plantations post, 20. 259
—— recommended by, as first lord of Trade, 20. 121n
(?) Hardwicke entertained by, 9. 363
health of: 4. 336, 348; Bath visit required by, 38. 433n; boils on the head, 22. 498; cataracts to be couched, 22. 567; gout, 21. 198–9, 22. 498; illness, 36. 58; loses speech and limbs, 23. 262; nearly blind, 22. 498, 23. 262; operation, 41. 110, 137; wounded by weavers, 22. 301
(?) Henley entertained by, 9. 363
Hertford asks former servants of, about precedents, 38. 279
—— loves, 39. 19
—— offers Paris furniture to, 38. 170
Holdernesse to succeed, as secretary of state, 20. 259
Hôtel de Grimbergh the Paris residence of, 38. 304n
Houghton Park House of, used by Tavistock and then by Ossory, 32. 44n
house and family of, narrowly escape weavers' riot, 22. 301
House of Lords attended by, 19. 336, 338, 20. 300, 22. 7, 366, 463–4, 507
Hussey entertained by, 9. 232
impatient for grandson, 38. 401, 403
income of, 35. 178
India House visited by, to vote, 22. 507
Ireland mismanaged by, 21. 154, 371, 376–7
—— to be visited by, 9. 331
Irish disturbances to be quelled by, 9. 331
Irish lord lieutenancy of, successful but unpopular, 38. 184
Irish pensions promised to, for sister and followers, 21. 485n
Irish popularity of, grows after gout confines him, 21. 199

Irish post of: arranged, **21.** 31; relinquished, **21.** 484–5

Junius letter about, **7.** 367

Karl Wilhelm Ferdinand compliments, for making peace, **38.** 291

——'s naturalization moved by, in House of Lords, **38.** 289

Kildare had letter from, promising dukedom, **30.** 248

——'s faction joined by, to please Fox, **21.** 154

Kinsale notified by, of invasion, **21.** 376

Kingston, D. of, mistaken for, **23.** 99

Knight of the Garter, **9.** 89, **10.** 29, 235

Legge appeals to, for protection, **17.** 493n

—— courts, **19.** 458

letters against, **42.** 505

'little Duke,' **38.** 186

London leaders attacked by, for allowing riot in Wilkes's favour, **22.** 188

London seldom visited by, showing that George III can easily do without him, **38.** 423

——'s lord mayor, common council, and charter attacked by, **38.** 257, 262–3

lord lieutenancy of Ireland to go to, at Fox's instigation to spite Pitt, **21.** 31

lord lieutenant of Ireland, **9.** 208

lord privy seal, **38.** 132n, 142

Louis XV compelled by, to surrender America, **38.** 188

Lovel calls, 'Muley,' **17.** 497

Lowther rich enough to hire, **37.** 459

Lyttelton's overture to, reported to Pitt, **35.** 194

Mann asked by, to aid Megliorucci Nevill, **20.** 265–6

—— corresponds with, about India, **20.** 97–8, 101–2, **22.** 547–8

——'s correspondence with, **19.** 474, **20.** 265–6

Mansfield likes to mortify, **38.** 258

Mar, Cts of, and her daughter borrow house from, **20.** 281

Marlborough asked by, to summon brother to Blenheim, **38.** 327

Marriage Bill opposed by, **9.** 147

Massachusetts act opposed by motion of, **22.** 507

Mastership of the Horse may go to, **20.** 235

—— would have gone to, if he had got the reversion for Sandwich, **20.** 217n

military books studied by, at Blandford, **21.** 373–4

(?) militia estimated by, **37.** 472

Mirepoix, Mme de, gives precedence to, at Sandwich's ball, **20.** 122

Montagu, Charles, recommended by, to Halifax, **9.** 208

Morices opposed by, at Launceston election, **20.** 113

Newcastle, D. of, about to clash with, over Turnpike Bill, **20.** 112

—— cannot oust, because of D. of Cumberland's and Ps Amelia's protection, **20.** 201n

—— embraces, **20.** 201

—— entertained by, **9.** 232–3, 363

—— induces George III to discard, as secretary of state, **40.** 88

—— negotiates with Granville to strengthen himself against, **20.** 72n

—— presses for removal of, **20.** 235n

——'s aversion to, may provoke resignation, **21.** 201n

——'s breach with, **20.** 38, 222

—— sends commands through, **9.** 71

—— sends express to, at Woburn about rumoured dissolution of Parliament, **30.** 246

—— shows to, Rockingham faction's anti-Grenville paper, **22.** 566n

Newcastle House meeting attended by, **22.** 541–2

Newry to be visited by, to join army, **21.** 373

Niccolini's banishment discussed at office of, **20.** 3

niece of, **20.** 226n

Nivernais to meet, at Dover, **22.** 55, 70

North's militia bill defeated by, in House of Lords, **24.** 497n

Northumberland, D. of, insulted by, **38.** 563

offers to resign, **38.** 558

office not desired by, for himself, **30.** 232

opposes inclusion of Ps of Wales in Regency Bill, **10.** 152n

Opposition member, **22.** 381n

——'s defeat will enhance reputation of, **22.** 172

Osborn, Sir George, attacks, politically, **10.** 235

Palmer sent on to Honiton by, **23.** 139n

Paris arrival of, coincides with Te Deum for French victory, **22.** 90

Paris embassy of: arranged, **22.** 69–70; followed by daughter's marriage, **22.** 73; for peace negotiations, **31.** 30; successful and popular, **38.** 184

Paris journey of, hissed, **38.** 176

Paris mission of, may be his wish, or result from friends' intrigues, **38.** 166

Paris visited by, 'in a fury' to make peace, **38.** 172

Parliamentary activity of, on Regency Bill, **38.** 542–4, 550–2

Parliamentary Address supported by, in House of Lords, **37.** 416

Parliamentary moderation of, in House of Lords debate, **30.** 236

Parliamentary motion against Stone voted by, **20.** 366n

Parliamentary motion by, to stop war in Germany, **38.** 154

Parliamentary speeches by: on Dresden treaty, **40.** 72n; shows temper, **22.** 463–4

Parliamentary voting by, with minority on Poor Bill, **38.** 529

Parliament asked by, to investigate charges about toasts to Old Pretender, **20.** 366

[Russell, John (1710–71), *continued*]

Parliament's adjournment opposed by, 30. 181n

Patriots formerly included, 20. 72

peace delegate to France, 22. 55, 69–70, 73, 86, 90, 92–3, 31. 30

peace efforts of, earnest, 38. 178

Pelham, Henry, aids, in defending privately-raised regiments, 19. 154

—— and Pitt enrage, over Navy Bill, 20. 38

Pelham's plan to make, Master of the Horse, 20. 235n

Pelham coterie entertained by, 9. 232

Pelhams support, 20. 120

Pitt (Chatham) close to, at Bath, 41. 41

—— may get overtures from, 38. 434

—— opposed to adherents of, 22. 308

—— rejects demands of, 22. 472

——'s Bath negotiation with, 30. 236

——'s connection with, wished by wife and brother-in-law, 41. 72

——'s demands from, few but considerable, 30. 236

—— sends Gower to Woburn with overtures to, 22. 472

——'s meeting with, proposed, 7. 279

——'s return no longer wanted by, since Pitt ignores him, 22. 167

—— to be punished by, 20. 38

play by company of, could not be memorized by Shirley, 19. 309, 20. 395

plays acted by, at Woburn, 19. 309n

politicians of, say that he will soon recover from son's death, 22. 506

Poor Bill supported by, 38. 529

populace hostile to, 30. 187

presidency of the Council held by, 10. 60, 161

presidency of the Council to go to, 22. 130, 167

privately-raised regiments defended by, 19. 154

property of, 9. 102

Protestor, The, supported by, 13. 22n

Prussian subsidy opposed by, 22. 32n

Purnell's trial urged by, 20. 18

rebellion asserted by, to have occurred, 10. 273

rebel lords' right to counsel supported by, 19. 287

Regency Bill opposed by friends of, in House of Commons, 22. 299

regent, 10. 153

regiment led by, in person, 19. 160–1

regiment raised by, 19. 110, 128, 30. 98

'Repeal, The,' caricatures, 22. 400

resignation of, 20. 249n, 258

resigns Admiralty post, 19. 463–4

riches of, surpassed, 9. 185

Rigby boasts of insolence of, to George III, 30. 185–6

—— cannot dissuade, from accepting Chatham's terms, 41. 71n

—— entertained by, 9. 232

—— hurries, into partiality to Kildare for sake of Fox, 21. 154n

(?) —— may be pleased by anger of, 38. 393

—— opposes retirement of, 30. 189

—— political manager for, 9. 14n

——'s correspondence with, 37. 422n

——'s dominance over, probably ended, 38. 434

—— secretary to, 9. 208, 14. 5n

—— sells influence of, 9. 228

—— sent to France to satisfy, 22. 92n

——'s rôle with, 41. 71–2

road through Paddington resisted by, 37. 452, 457n

Robinson opposed by, for archbishopric, 22. 276n

Rochford chosen by, as envoy to Turin, 20. 58n

Rockingham differs with, over Conway, 22. 542n

rumoured marquisates disliked by, though perhaps pleasing to (?) Rigby, 38. 392–3

Russell, Lord, called 'very silly fellow' by, 28. 85

—— imitated by, 9. 316

——'s unreasonableness inherited by, 9. 316

'St George' (lesser George) worn by, in button-hole, 10. 235

Sandwich abandons, 20. 305

—— and, most unpopular people in England, 20. 202n

Sandwich 'espoused' by, 20. 113

—— governs, through his wife, 20. 120

—— lieutenant-colonel to, 19. 176

—— may succeed, as secretary of state, 20. 217, 235

——'s protector, 20. 144

satiric verses on, made at Bath, 38. 462

Scottish peers insulted by letter of, asking them to vote for Turnpike Bill, 20. 124

secretary of state, 9. 115, 200, 341, 19. 463

Selwyn calls, 'mamamouchi,' 39. 107

—— entertained by, 9. 233

Shelburne defeats, 7. 367

short-sighted, 37. 453

sister of, 19. 189n

son mourned by, 4. 132

son of, 4. 132n, 9. 234n, 11. 131n, 22. 2n

speaks like Pitt, 20. 310

Stair's discussion of Patinson at George II's levee, corrected by, to George II, 19. 165

Stanley affected by dismissal of, 22. 326

—— to follow, 22. 92–3

—— writes to Duchesse de Choiseul about, 3. 243

Stone's overtures rejected by, 21. 154

supporters of, 'Bedford-Hussars,' 32. 10

tavern visited by, after opera, 37. 54

teeth and nails of, scanty, 22. 541

Temple may be connected with, 22. 308

—— offered his place by, 30. 187

—— rejects overtures from, 7. 367

——'s proposal answered by, 21. 547

Thurot does not await army of, **21.** 376
Tories said to declare for, **30.** 186n
Treaty of Paris signed by, **22.** 118n
treaty with Saxony opposed by, in Parliament, **20.** 300
Trentham, brother-in-law to, **20.** 113n
Turnpike Bill of, **20.** 112, 120
tutor of, supported by Sandwich for Eton fellowship, **20.** 121
'untoward knight errant' at Coronation, **38.** 126
Vernon visits, at Woburn, **20.** 301
Violette, Eva, entertained by, **9.** 28
Waldegrave preferred to Conway by, **38.** 84n
Waldegrave, Cts, boasts of insolence of, to George III, **30.** 185–6
Walpole, Sir Robert, 'cut' by, in House of Lords, **17.** 338
—— opposed by, **17.** 247n
wealth of: **3.** 101; brings him little happiness, **23.** 274
weavers attack, **38.** 558, 559n
weavers' relief opposed by, in House of Lords, **22.** 301
West and East Indies may be taken by fondness of, for global war, **37.** 249
Westminster election paid for by, **20.** 112–13
wife fears delaying supper of, **9.** 232
wife influences, **9.** 210
wife of, **9.** 32n, **11.** 121n, **28.** 231n
wife opposes retirement of, **30.** 189
wife summoned to Paris by, **38.** 178
Wilkes entertained by, at Paris, **38.** 274
——'s treatment at Paris by Hertford based on precedents from, **38.** 279, 290
Williams, Sir C. H., recommends Bentley's design to, **35.** 177
Winchilsea succeeds, as lord president, **22.** 310
windbound at Yarmouth, **9.** 32, 34
Woburn Abbey monopolizes, to neglect of George II and business, **20.** 201n
—— reached by, from Bath, without going through London, **38.** 460
—— to be visited by, **10.** 170
—— visited by, **38.** 565
—— would never be relinquished by, **19.** 255
wrangling by, over *Essay on Woman* in House of Lords, **38.** 229, 230n
Yarmouth, Lady, advises George II to make, Master of the Horse if he would resign as secretary of state, **20.** 183n
Yonge attacked by, **17.** 336
York, Edward, D. of, allies, with Bute and Grenville, **22.** 402
—— entertained by, **9.** 232, 363
Yorke family oppose, on Marriage Bill, **38.** 318
Russell, John (1745–1806), painter:
(?) Huntingdon, Cts of, painted by, **35.** 346n
Russell, Lord John (1766–1839), 6th D. of Bedford, 1802; M.P.:
Byng, Georgiana Elizabeth, to marry, **31.** 238

Gunnings occupy London house of, **11.** 204–5
infant at time of father's death, **22.** 498
Reynolds depicts, in St George picture, **32.** 316n, 337n
SH visited by, **12.** 243
Russell, Lady John. *See* Byng, Georgiana Elizabeth
Russell, Lady Margaret (1560–1616), m. (1577) George Clifford, 3d E. of Cumberland:
epitaph by, **1.** 38–39
family of, **9.** 124–5
HW's comment on, **2.** 323
HW to present portrait of, to Russell family, **9.** 124–5
marriage of, **43.** 76
new to HW, **1.** 41
portrait of, at Appleby Castle, **10.** 185
print of, **2.** 323, **42.** 16n
Russell, Lady Rachel (ca 1637–1732). *See* Wriothesley, Lady Rachel (ca 1637–1732)
Russell, Lady Rachel (d. 1777), m. 1 (1722) Scroop Egerton, 4th E. of Bridgwater; cr. (1720) D. of Bridgwater; m. 2 (1745) Sir Richard Lyttelton:
children of, **19.** 189
daughter of, **20.** 226n
daughter's caprices mentioned by, to son-in-law, **37.** 339, 340
HW praises, **21.** 505–6
health of, gout, **22.** 247
Irish pension for, **21.** 485n
Lyttelton marries, **19.** 189, **20.** 33n
Naples visited by, **21.** 550
Paris visited by, **22.** 155
Pitt, Thomas, leaves, at Leghorn, **21.** 501
Temple, Cts, entertains, at Stowe, **22.** 247
Russell, Theodore:
Devonshire, Cts of, painted by, **42.** 341n
Russell, William (1616–1700), 5th E. of Bedford, 1641; cr. (1694) D. of Bedford:
Burke quotes remark of, to James II, **28.** 373
concerned with both Civil War, and Revolution, **34.** 128
confused with 2d D. of Bedford, **34.** 122
portrait of, **34.** 128
son of, **2.** 359n
Stratford's tragedy includes, **29.** 224
tomb of, in Chenies church, **9.** 102
Russell, William (1639–83), styled Lord Russell:
Bedford, 4th D. of, acts as if heir to, **9.** 316
—— calls, 'very silly fellow,' **28.** 85
Burke quotes Bedford's remark to James II about, **28.** 373
HW's 'hero,' **2.** 60, 66–7
HW urges Mason to revenge, against Dalrymple, **28.** 67
levee of, in Newgate Prison, **23.** 82
Macpherson and Dalrymple unsympathetic to, **2.** 66n
martyrdom of, discussed in Lady Rachel Russell's *Letters*, **28.** 85
Murray attended, at scaffold, **16.** 50
patriot, **29.** 262

[Russell, William (1639–83), *continued*]
Scots traduce, 29. 105, 135
Stratford's tragedy on, 29. 223–5
Tillotson's letter to, 2. 359
title of, 43. 66
wife of, 20. 282–3, 28. 84n, 85n
Russell, Lord William (1767–1840), M.P.:
birth of, expected, 22. 498
farces acted by, at Ampthill, 33. 552n
Jerseys to stay at house of, in Pall Mall, 12. 150
Keppel, Mrs, entertains, at Isleworth, 33. 481–2
Ossory, Lady, may be in charge of, 32. 181n
(?) Priestley's correspondence with, 42. 374n
resigns from Revolution Society, 11. 131
Reynolds depicts, in St George picture, 32. 316n, 337n
Russell, Lady William. *See* Villiers, Lady Charlotte
Russell, Wriothesley (1680–1711), 2d D. of Bedford, 1700:
confused with 1st D. of Bedford, 34. 122
Russell, Wriothesley (1708–32), 3d D. of Bedford, 1711:
gambling of, exceeded by Bland's, 35. 208
Pope hints at Janssen's cheating, at White's, 18. 124n
widow of, remarries, 34. 259
Russell family:
Boufflers, Mme de, friend of, 3. 271n
credit lost by, in their own counties, 25. 488
crest of, 1. 38n
Gower, Cts, mourned by, because opera attendance prevented by her death, 9. 342
portraits of, at Woburn Abbey, 9. 123–4
tombs of, at Chenies, 9. 102
Russell St, Bloomsbury, London:
Garrick marries in chapel in, 20. 74n
Russell St, Covent Garden, London:
Rose Tavern in, 33. 553n
Tom's Coffee-House in, 17. 296n
Russia, Emperor (Czar) of. *See* Ivan VI (1740–64); Paul I (1754–1801); Peter I (the Great) (1672–1725); Peter III (1728–62)
Russia, Empress of. *See* Anne (1693–1740); Catherine I (ca 1683–1727); Catherine II (1729–96); Elizabeth (1709–62); Maria Sofia (1759–1828)
Russia, Grand Duke of. *See* Paul I
Russia:
admiralty of, *see* Admiralty
allies of, insist on conclusion of Turkish war, 24. 33
ambassadors from and to, *see under* Ambassador
American alliance with, rumoured, 33. 332
armament against, 11. 263n
'armed neutrality' of, 25. 160, 29. 29
army of: again marching towards Prussia, 21. 172; Apraxin's, defeats Prussians at Gross-Jägersdorf in Courland, 21. 144n; Austrian savagery restrained by, 21. 444; Azov seized

by, 23. 116; barbarity of, 11. 207; Bender the theatre of, 23. 155, 160, 245; Berlin may be sacked by, 21. 441; Berlin not captured by, 21. 332; Choiseul impels Turks against, 23. 134, 143; covey of partridges resembles, 21. 237; Danube crossed by, 23. 478–9; Danube must not be crossed by, 23. 310; Frederick II aided by, 22. 59, 62–3; Frederick II defeats, at Zorndorf, 37. 562–3; Frederick II drives, into Pomerania and Poland, 21. 246–7; Frederick II opposed by, 21. 72, 229, 236, 237, 244, 246–7, 258, 317, 319, 327, 331, 419; gives and accepts no quarter, 21. 255; halted by lack of men, money, and supplies, 21. 78; horses, cattle, and camels captured by, 23. 160; inactive on the Danube, 23. 331; Moldavia the theatre of, 23. 148, 154–5; Oder may be crossed by, 21. 308; Prussians allegedly defeat at Palzig, 35. 293; Prussians defeated by at Palzig, 38. 23–4; Prussian troops at Memel prepare against, 21. 72; retires to Poland, 37. 556; retreats, 21. 144; Riga approached by, 21. 72; Rumiantsev commands, 23. 202; Silistria invaded by, 23. 479; Silistrian side of Danube might be taken by, 24. 29; take oaths on their sabres, 21. 255; Turkish Grand Signor will probably be given a good account by, 23. 91; Turks defeated by, 23. 146; Wedell said to have defeated, 21. 315; Wrangel defeated by, 17. 155n
Austria and Prussia may join, against Turks, 25. 359, 436
Austria denies alliance with, 21. 2n
Austrian subsidy for, 21. 53n
Austria urges, to continue war, 21. 360n
bankrupt, 21. 502
Buckingham's failure in embassy to, 22. 205, 212
campaigns of: against Turkey, 35. 392; cruel, 35. 306
Catherine II cannot civilize, in one reign, 25. 389
—— 'imperial vulture' of, 33. 452
—— may lend troops from, to England for American war, 24. 127
——'s seizure of throne of, 10. 38, 35. 314–15
—— tells Frederick II to return troops of, 22. 59
—— tries to codify laws of, 34. 153
—— wants Jesuits reestablished in, 25. 389–90
celebration in: for heir's birth, 20. 457–8; for Turkish defeat, 23. 249
Chinese dispute with, 23. 116, 24. 333
Chinese emperor writes to people of, 32. 390
Choiseul's fall liked by, 23. 259
—— will be hurt by successes of, 23. 151, 154
Cholmondeley, E. of, declines embassy to, 33. 336
Chute speculates about future czar of, 35. 54
claimants to throne of, 34. 3

Constantinople's capture delayed by, 23. 323

Court of: Baskerville sends specimen to, 40. 275; Orlov's dispatches to, 23. 235

Cracow incendiary removed by, 22. 574

Craon's comment on news from, 17. 20

crime now shifts to, 22. 253–4

Damer, Mrs, works of, sent to, 12. 272

Denmark's war with, see War: Danish-Russian

Dick honoured by, 24. 96

discoveries in, 2. 191

Du Deffand, Mme, acquainted with visitors from, 6. 56, 268, 395

eagle of, turns vulture, 24. 55

England and Holland expect military aid from, 37. 283

England and Holland promised troops and subsidy from, 19. 466n

England expected to aid, 4. 203

—— hopes for reinforcements from, 19. 466, 20. 501, 21. 54, 24. 127, 132, 138, 324, 37. 179, 41. 316–17

—— insults, 28. 455

—— may cede Georgia to, 24. 132, 138

—— receives rescripts from, 25. 39, 118

—— rejects friendliness of, 39. 355

——'s alliance with, promoted by Lloyd, 23. 422n

—— should not enhance the maritime power of, 24. 132

—— should not subsidize, 42. 495

——'s mediation offer with Austria, Saxony, and Prussia rejected by, 21. 53

——'s negotiations with, 18. 495n

——'s only friend, but Turkey and internal troubles may preoccupy her, 39. 304

——'s relations with, 11. 186, 336

——'s subsidy treaty with: 30. 322, 35. 253, 255, 262, 37. 405n, 407n, 409, 413–14, 416, 38. 488; disapproved, 35. 88, 91; unpopular, 35. 91

—— threatened by, 29. 96, 101, 102

—— to be reconciled with, 25. 267

English and Prussian peace negotiations with, 11. 272n

English-Dutch peace may be mediated by, 25. 188n

English sculptor at Florence makes chimneypieces for, 25. 93

English simpletons visit, 23. 195

English weather like that of, 35. 171

envoys from and to, see under Envoy

European powers may not let England cede maritime post to, 24. 138

fleet of: agent for, see Rutherfurd, Robert; at Lemnos to starve Constantinople, 23. 245; at Port Mahon and Leghorn, 23. 191–2; coming to Mediterranean, 25. 59–61; Constantinople may be attacked by, but Louis XVI and Charles III are said to tell Ferdinand of Naples to keep it out of his ports, 25. 616n; Constantinople unlikely to be captured by, 23. 169; Danish officers

leave, 23. 326; Dardanelles threatened by, 23. 161, 245, 331; direct passage to England from Leghorn must be made by, 24. 114; disasters to, in Mediterranean, 23. 202; Dolgorukov discusses arrangements for, 23. 160–1; England left by, 33. 220; England prevents French fleet from attacking, 23. 474, 478; expected at Leghorn, 25. 160, 415; expected in Mediterranean, 25. 59–60; France may attack, 5. 348; France to aid, 23. 161; French merchant ships intercepted by, 23. 307; frigate of, injured, 23. 192; frigates of, reach Leghorn from Paros, 23. 326; gets provisions from Leghorn, 23. 172; Greek Islands the destination of, 23. 306; Greig to command, 25. 60; HW ridicules, as troop of schoolboys, 23. 187; in Ægean, 23. 212; in Downs, 7. 367, 33. 212, 220; in western European waters, 36. 56; Leghorn expenditure for, 23. 222, 24. 95, 114; Leghorn to be visited by, 25. 84; Malta may be station of, 23. 189; may appear at Leghorn or Caligari, 23. 148; may pass Dardanelles but army must not pass the Danube, 23. 310; near Plymouth, 33. 214; off Chios, 23. 232–3; on Yorkshire coast, 23. 146; Orlov appoints English agent for, 23. 161; Orlov commands, 23. 234–5; Orlov finds, in gulf of Napoli di Romania, 23. 226; partly at Port Mahon, 23. 162, 172, 185, 189, 192; Peter III's ghost should hail, at Constantinople, 23. 195; reaches coast of Morea, 23. 204–5; repaired at Leghorn or wintered at Paros, 23. 307; said to be attacking Negropont castle, 23. 331; said to have returned to North Sea, 25. 79; sails from Cronstadt, 23. 222; sails from England to Mediterranean, 23. 151, 159; slowness of, 23. 157, 185, 187, 224, 331; Spain may intercept, 25. 415; stalks in English Channel, 25. 77; still at Leghorn, 23. 308; supposedly in Mediterranean, 23. 187; Swedes defeat, 39. 462n; to return to St Petersburg, 24. 84; Turkey might be frightened by, into peace, 23. 192; Turkey thinks England should have stopped, in English Channel, 23. 479; Turkey to be attacked by, 23. 148; Turkish fleet destroyed by, 23. 226–8, 232–3, 234–5, 236, 239; Turkish fleet said to have been burnt by, at Lemnos, 23. 319, 330

France eager for war against, 5. 344n

—— incited Turkey against, 23. 307

—— may aid Turkey against, 25. 360

—— said to plot insurrection in, 18. 495n

—— tries to embroil, with Turks, 33. 14

Franco-Prussian peace negotiations denied by, 21. 159

Frederick II may have provoked rebellion in, 23. 556

—— receives assurances from, 18. 512

—— removed by, from French alliance, 20. 524

[Russia, *continued*]

——'s alleged alliance with, **24**. 389

——'s losses to, bring peace overtures, **21**. 360n

—— tries to deceive, about Mustafā Aġa's mission, **30**. 321

French illusions will be shattered by, **24**. 498

George II makes treaty with, to keep Frederick II in awe, **20**. 524n

German campaigns of, ridiculous, **21**. 312

German couriers to, **21**. 369

Germany drains money from, **9**. 268

Greeks do not aid, **23**. 222, 226

—— said to aid, **23**. 204

—— to get arms from, **23**. 202

—— will be sacrificed by, to Turkish vengeance, **23**. 212

HW gives goldfish to Chernyshev for, **40**. 85

HW threatens to write by way of, **11**. 161

HW would be afraid to be in, **22**. 65

Houghton pictures will be burnt at first insurrection in, **24**. 441

impostor claims throne of, **23**. 547, 556

instability of, feared in Florence, **25**. 156

Kingston, Ds of, might send courier from, to husband, **24**. 333

La Chétardie said to have been dismissed by, **17**. 20, **18**. 466

Leeds's negotiations with, **11**. 251n

Lloyd in, arranging Anglo-Russian alliance, **23**. 422n

—— in military service in, **23**. 421n

long-boat of, sinks at Leghorn, **25**. 493

Mackenzie served in, **37**. 236n

Mann refuses honours from, **24**. 96, **25**. 84

Maria Theresa's alliance with, **22**. 564

—— threatened with war by, unless she consents to Polish partition, **23**. 439

Mediterranean area does not trade with, **25**. 61, 84

Memel captured by, **21**. 72n

minister of, released from Seven Towers, **23**. 308–9

ministers from and to, *see under* Minister

Minorca said to be ceded by, **25**. 187

Morea abandoned by, **23**. 226

must be contemptuous of western warfare, **25**. 201

news from, comes through Holland, **17**. 255–6

officer; officers of: **23**. 233, 444, **25**. 2, 84; takes Turkish ornament, **40**. 89n

old gentleman seeks 'best intelligence' from, **42**. 503

order of St Catherine of, *see under* St Catherine

Orléans, Duc d', may marry princess of, **18**. 564

Paris as cold as, **31**. 93

peace delegates of, at Paris, **21**. 498

peace negotiations for war of American Revolution may be aided by, **24**. 523

peace with, expected, **29**. 118

Peter I teaches, to read, **22**. 71

Peter III possesses, **10**. 39

—— resigns all conquests by, **38**. 154

Pitt (Chatham) congratulates Alt on defeat of, **21**. 316

—— desires alliance with, opposed by Frederick II, **30**. 233n

Pitti palace heated as if in, **22**. 291

plague in, **18**. 271n

Poissonnier visits, **3**. 334

Poland crushed by, **34**. 153, 156

—— invaded by, **15**. 225

Poles may pray for success of rebellion in, **23**. 556

Polish incendiaries removed by, **22**. 574

Polish king may be dethroned and constitution destroyed by, **36**. 281

Prussia forbids, to aid England, **25**. 39

Pugachev's rebellion in, pleases HW, **32**. 184

Quebec campaign might be said to be a stratagem to divert, from Frederick II, **21**. 336

revolution in: against Ivan VI, **17**. 255, 264; against Peter III, **10**. 38, **22**. 52–4, 56–62, 64–6, 68, 71, 74–6, **35**. 314–15

Reynolds's 'Hercules' for, **33**. 539

Rome regards Turkey as Christianity's bulwark against, **23**. 140

Rutherfurd and Dick the agents and commissaries of, at Leghorn, **23**. 222, **24**. 114, 453

ship-of-war of, ordered by Catherine II to take Ds of Kingston's treasure to Calais, but sails too soon from Leghorn, **24**. 404, 409–10

ships of, at Copenhagen, **33**. 207

Shuvalov has lived out of, since Czarina Elizabeth's death, **38**. 516

soldiers of, engaged by England to defend Hanover in case of Franco-Prussian alliance, **30**. 322

sovereigns often changed by, **35**. 314

Spanish privateers capture ship of, **25**. 39n

Stanley dislikes going to, **30**. 233

—— made ambassador to, **3**. 251n

—— to have post in, **22**. 444

Stormont reveals war plans of, **23**. 438–9

successes of: cannot be concealed, **23**. 154; not followed up, **23**. 331

Sweden agrees with, about King of the Romans, **42**. 496

Sweden's war with, **39**. 462–3; *see also* War: Russian-Swedish

Swedish interference by, **23**. 439

Te Deums sung in, for Zorndorf 'victory,' **21**. 246

theatre head from, has translated *Hamlet*, **22**. 426

topic of conversation in Florence, **23**. 503

troops of: commanded by Keith, **18**. 495n; George II hires, 'to recover the Ohio,' **37**. 407; treaty for bringing, into Louis XV's pay, **21**. 176n

Turkey's grumbling against, more audible in England than in Italy, **25.** 436

——'s negotiations with, **23.** 224, 441, 469–70, **24.** 40

——s threat to, **21.** 247

——'s war with, **4.** 188, 203, **5.** 344, **6.** 397, **7.** 162, **11.** 161n, 186n, **28.** 382, **33.** 14n, **39.** 175–6; *see also under* War, Russian-Turkish

—— unlikely to cede Holy Land to, **23.** 194

Turkish dismemberment may be plotted by, with Austria, **25.** 399

Turkish invasion by, disliked by France, **23.** 204–5

Turkish military chest captured by, **23.** 479

Tuscany's connection with, **25.** 128

Versailles treaty to be acceded to by, **21.** 53n

vice-chancellor of, *see* Vorontsov

victories of: at Kunersdorf, **30.** 156–7; at Paltzig, **30.** 156; not readily believed by HW, **23.** 231

Vorontsov afraid of revolutions in, **22.** 202–3, 205

—— the 'soul' of ministry of, **21.** 247

war extends from: to Alsace, **35.** 290; to Senegal, **21.** 290

Whitworth's *Account* of, published by HW, **13.** 29

Williams, Sir C. H., allows precedence to, in signing subsidy treaty, **30.** 322

—— leaves, **21.** 183

—— said to have died in, **33.** 78

—— threatens, with Prussian attack, **21.** 53n

—— to ascertain military intentions of, **20.** 187n

Zoffany may return to, **24.** 92

See also Siberia; Tartary; *and under names of sovereigns*

Russian; Russians:

at Pisa; rejoice over end of Turkish war, **24.** 84; spend lavishly, **24.** 95

England may hire, for American war, **24.** 127, 132, 138, 324

English in Paris treated like, **31.** 107

HW calls, 'Vandals of the North,' **25.** 146

HW's verses mention, **31.** 96

kingdoms overrun in a few weeks by, **25.** 146

ladies, must be entertained by Mann in Florence, **25.** 340–1

Leghorn will regret loss of lavish expenditures by, **24.** 95

Mann calls, 'horse-eaters,' **21.** 446

—— considered the protector of, at Florence, **25.** 84

—— entertains, at dinner, **23.** 161

social customs recorded by, **40.** 210

SH visited by, **12.** 236

Russian language:

Kingston, Ds of, said to be learning, **23.** 559

Latin as useless as, when addressing kings, **22.** 84

Magnan has knowledge of dialects of, **18.** 548n

musical when sung, **42.** 230

Regent has his son study, **19.** 564

Rustat, Tobias, (? 1606–94), Yeoman of Robes: print of, **1.** 182

Ruth (biblical):

HW compares Chute to, **17.** 209, **35.** 14

Rutherford. *See* Rutherforth; Rutherfurd

Rutherforth, Thomas (1712–71), D.D.; regius professor of divinity, Cambridge:

Defence of the Bishop of London's Discourses, A, by, **15.** 300

Rutherforth. *See also* Rutherfurd

Rutherfurd, John (ca 1748–1834), M.P.:

laird of Scottish family, **24.** 453

Rutherfurd, Robert (1719–94), cr. (ca 1775) Bn (Russian):

Catherine II makes, baron, and gives him jewelled box with her portrait, **24.** 453

HW often meets, at Gloucester House and hears Mann's praises, **24.** 445, 453

Leghorn the home of, during business career and service as Russian commissary, **24.** 453

Mann presents, at Tuscan Court, **24.** 251n

Mann visited by, **24.** 289

Order of St Anne of Holstein rejected by, **24.** 453

Orlov closes his accounts with, **24.** 114

Russian agent at Leghorn, **23.** 161, 222

Rutherfurd. *See also* Rutherforth

Ruthven, Alexander (ca 1580–1600), master of Ruthven, and Ruthven, John (1577–1600), 3d E. of Gowrie:

supposed conspiracy by, against James VI, **15.** 29, 47, 165, 166–7

Ruthven, Patrick (ca 1520–66), 3d Lord Ruthven:

authenticity of 'Discourse' by, concerning Rizzio's murder, doubted by HW, **15.** 34–5

HW's account of, sent to Dalrymple, **15.** 34–5

Mackenzie's account of, doubted by HW, **15.** 33–4

sagacity of, contradicted by Mackenzie, **15.** 35

Ruthven, Scotland:

Mulloy defends barracks at, **19.** 105n

Rutland, Ds of. *See* Howard, Lady Elizabeth (1780–1825); Noel, Katherine (1657–1733); Sherard, Lucy (ca 1685–1751); Somerset, Lady Mary Isabella (1756–1831)

Rutland, D. of. *See* Manners, Charles (1754–87); Manners, John (1696–1779)

Rutland, E. of. *See* Edmund (Plantagenet) (1443–60); Manners, Francis (1578–1632)

Rutland Lodge, Petersham, Ds of Rutland's house:

(?) Brooke takes, **9.** 135

Rutlandshire:

HW jokes about John Paul Jones landing in, **33.** 135

Mann, Horace II, in, **25.** 222

Wright's *History* of, **1.** 132, 141

'Rutlandshire Invasion, The':

fancied title of farce, **33.** 135

Rutledge, Edward (1749–1800), member of Continental Congress:
Howe receives, 24. 270
Rutowsky, ——:
Leopold, P. of Anhalt, defeats, at Kesseldorf, 19. 189n
Rutt, John (d. ?1731):
nephew inherits from, 42. 418
Twickenham manor bought by: 12. 257n; (?) from trustees of forfeited estates, 42. 417–18
Ruvigny, Rachel de (1603–40), Cts of Southampton:
Cole's correction about, 1. 21
Rwiski; Rwski. See Rzewuski
Ryan, Lacy:
Hamlet's ghost played by, at Covent Garden, 20. 209n
Rycroft, Lady. See Read, Charlotte
Rycroft, Sir Nelson (1761–1827), 2d Bt, 1786:
SH visited by, 12. 241
Rydal Mount, Westmorland:
Daulby of, 15. 283n
Ryder, ——, silk merchant in Coventry St:
Rudd, Mrs, arrested at suit of, 24. 153n
Ryder, Sir Dudley (1691–1756), Kt, 1740; attorney-general; lord chief justice; M.P.:
attorney-general at Lovat's trial, 19. 380
Clandestine Marriages Act supported by, 37. 362, 365
death of, on eve of getting peerage, 20. 556, 557
Fox opposes, on Clandestine Marriages Act, 37. 363
Gower's conversation with, about Purnell's trial, 20. 18
King's Bench Court refuses, permission to see statutes of Oxford University, 20. 18n
Lee succeeded by, as lord chief justice, 20. 453n
lord chief justice, 19. 380n
Mathews's friend, 19. 33n
Murray excels, 19. 380
—— succeeds, as attorney-general, 20. 453n
Onslow opposes, on Clandestine Marriages Act, 37. 365
Parliamentary speech by, 17. 297
promotion of, to lord chancellor, suggested, 20. 202
Selwyn consults, on expulsion from Oxford, 30. 93n
Seymour, Sir Edward, confirmed by, in Somerset title, 20. 139
Ryder, Hon. Dudley (1762–1847), 2d Bn Harrowby, 1803; cr. (1809) E. of Harrowby:
declines invitation to ball at Windsor, 11. 329
Ryder, Nathaniel (1735–1803), cr. (1776) Bn Harrowby:
Conway and wife visited by, at Park Place, 39. 419n
peerage rumoured for, 38. 159n
peerage to go to, 20. 557

SH visited by, 12. 230
Ryder. See also Rider
Ryder St, London:
Walpole, Sir Edward, leaves house in, to Margaret, Jane, and Anne Clement, 36. 156n, 317n
Rye, Sussex:
Beckley near, 9. 326
decay of, 40. 6
Dodd and Whaley visit, 40. 6
Rye, English ship:
African conquest by, 21. 212
Rye House Plot:
Capell involved in, 29. 224n
Grey, Ford, engaged in, 16. 141
Howard implicated in, 29. 223n
Russell executed for, 2. 60n, 9. 316n
Sidney executed for, 2. 60n
Ryland, Mr:
SH visited by, 12. 228
Ryland, William Wynne (1732–83):
engraving by, 6. 360n
mezzotint by, of Charles Rogers, 41. 389–91
Rymer, James (d. ca 1841), surgeon:
(?) HW's comment on, 12. 109
Rymer, Thomas (1641–1713), writer and archæologist:
first part of Ralph's Of the Use and Abuse of Parliaments written by, 43. 254
Fœdera by: Conway buys, 37. 422; Gray quotes from, 14. 75–6; Gray refers to, 14. 79, 80; HW mentions, 14. 182; Innocent VIII's bull on Henry VII's marriage in, 42. 207n; 'jejune scraps' of, on Richard III, 15. 171; reports Edward I's corpse being given a new cere-cloth yearly, 24. 4
Rysbrack, John Michael (1694–1770), sculptor:
birth date of, corrected, 43. 256
busts by: of Pope, 15. 189n; of Sir Robert Walpole, 15. 69n, 16. 300n
'Ganymede' and statue model mended by, 19. 63
'Ganymede' statue to be mended by, 18. 561
George I's statue by, 13. 120n
HW's addition to monumental inscription awaited by, 40. 80
HW's correspondence with, 40. 80
Newton's monument by, 35. 151n
pedestal for Lady Walpole's monument in Westminster Abbey carved by, 13. 26, 17. 212n
Stowe busts attributed to, 35. 75n, 76n
Ryvers, Bn and E. See Rivers
Ryves, Elizabeth (1750–97), writer:
dedicates Whiggish ode to Mason, who gives her five guineas, 29. 40
HW returns poems to, without seeing or helping her, 41. 329
HW's correspondence with, 41. 329
Rzewuski, Count Adam Wawrzyniec (d. 1825):
(?) social relations of, with Mme Geoffrin, 7. 327, 329

S

S——, Lord:
Fitzroy, Lady, and, at Wanstead, **35**. 238

Saarbrück (Germany):
skirmish at, **12**. 26n

Saarlouis (Germany):
Conway, Lord George, brings news of surrender at, **12**. 73
skirmish at, **12**. 26n

Sabatier de Cabre, Honoré-Auguste (1737–1802), French chargé d'affaires in Russia:
appointment of, **23**. 127

Sabatier de Castres, Antoine (1742–1817), abbé:
Condorcet's letter to, **6**. 82
Tableau philosophique de l'esprit de Voltaire by, **5**. 79–80
Trois siècles de notre littérature by, **5**. 313–14, 320, 322, 325, 335, **43**. 95

Sabatin, Mme. *See* Cusack, Marie-Madeleine-Joséphine de

Sabatina:
on Saturday nights in Florence, **17**. 97

Sabbatarianism:
HW criticizes, **31**. 261
HW jokes about Hannah More's, **31**. 260–1, 271, 300, 348, 359, 363, 365, 393–4, 396, 399
HW's reflections on, **31**. 363, 365, 399, 434–7

Sabbath. *See* Sunday

Sabbatini, Giuliano (1685–1767), Bp of Modena; secretary of state:
HW flattered by, **20**. 57
(?) HW questioned by, **9**. 81
(?) Richmond's fireworks attended by, **9**. 81

Sabina:
gold medal of, bought by HW, **26**. 7

'Sabine, La.' *See* Marie-Antoinette

Sabine, Mrs William. *See* Malyn, Elizabeth

'Sabine' (painting):
Mann to bequeath, to Sir Robert Walpole, **18**. 93

'Sabine farm':
Conway's, *see* Park Place
Pitt's, **21**. 518

Sabinus, Flavius (A.D. ca 8–69):
HW mentions Gibbon's treatment of, **29**. 98

Sables:
double, gown trimmed with, **10**. 198
Montagu, Lady Mary Wortley, wears, **22**. 17

Sablon, Plaine de, near Paris:
HW sees horse race at, **7**. 304

Sabot; sabots:
floor-sweepers at Versailles wear, **35**. 112

Sabran, Comtesse de. *See* Coste de Champeron, Marie-Antoinette-Élisabeth; Foix, Madeleine-Louise-Charlotte de (ca 1693–1768; Jean de Manville, Françoise-Éléonore de (1750–1827)

Sabran, Marquise de. *See* Regnault, Louise

Sabran, Louis-Hector-Honoré-Maxime de (1739–1811)), Bp of Nancy, 1774, of Laon, 1778:
Marie-Antoinette's premier aumônier, **6**. 52, **7**. 199

social relations of, with Mme du Deffand, **7**. 437, 453

Sabre; sabres:
Acquaviva's guard armed with, **19**. 113
Conway's, 'drenched in blood,' **37**. 522
English sailor boards Spanish ship with, **24**. 543
grenadiers draw, **34**. 96
horse-guard officers carry, at George II's funeral, **9**. 322
Indian, owned by HW, **31**. 26
Russians take oaths upon, **21**. 255

Sabridgeworth. *See* Sawbridgeworth

Sacchetti family, of Rome:
Albano and Cortona pictures bought from, by HW, **26**. 7

Sacchi, Andrea (1599–1661), painter:
drawings by Lady Diana Beauclerk have simplicity of, **28**. 244
Furnese has pictures by, **21**. 172n
painting by: desired by Sir Robert Walpole, **21**. 173; Spencer buys, at Furnese's auction, **21**. 172

Sacchini, Antonio (1734–86), composer:
Armida by, **11**. 202n, **23**. 547n, **35**. 350n, **39**. 211
Cidde, Il, by: Bottarelli alters, **32**. 92n; new opera, **32**. 89
Finto passo per amore, Il, by, performed by Lord Cowper's troupe, **23**. 325
Lucio Vero by, **23**. 547n, 570n, **35**. 468n, 468–9
Motezuma by, **24**. 89
Nitetti and *Perseo* by, **23**. 570n
Rinaldo by, **25**. 134
Tamerlane by, thought to reflect on royal family, **39**. 169

Sacchis, Giovanni de'. *See* Pordenone

Sacco, Gioseffo Pompeo, prime minister of Parma 1772–3:
Llano replaced by, **23**. 445
—— replaces, **23**. 518n

'Sacharissa.' *See* Sidney, Lady Dorothy

Sachée. *See* Sack

Sachet; sachets:
Du Deffand, Mme, sends, to HW, **4**. 461

Sacheverell, Rev. Henry (ca 1674–1724), D.D.:
Gunnings more famous than, **20**. 312
King, Dr William, supported, **32**. 311
life of, paralleled by modern occurrences, **22**. 186
times of, serious, **15**. 130
trial of, is Norfolk's latest news, **40**. 47
Walpole, Sir Robert, opposes, **22**. 26
Wilkes and d'Éon compared with, **22**. 263
Wilkes as dead as, **23**. 360

Sachsen-Gotha. *See* Saxe-Gotha

Sachsen-Hildburghausen, Wilhelm von:
fought at Rossbach, **21**. 194n

Sachsen-Hildburghausen. *See also* Saxe-Hildburghausen

Sachsen-Weissenfels, D. of. *See* Johann Adolf II

Sack; sacks (garment):
   black: of silk, **24**. 192n; to be discarded by
      Mme Vitelli, **18**. 334
   Conway and Lady Ailesbury may find daugh-
      ter in, **37**. 334, 335
   Conway borrows, for masquerade, **37**. 2, 5
   green, **37**. 289
   green velvet, worn by Q. Caroline, **13**. 142
   'Nousvoullone' expected to wear, at Tuscan
      Court, **22**. 357
Sack (beverage):
   butt of, **10**. 116
Sackbut (instrument):
   HW mentions, **10**. 223
Sackcloth:
   HW asks if Vatican is hung with, **25**. 237
Sackcloth and ashes:
   English clothes should be made of, **37**. 437
Sackville, Lady. See Leveson Gower, Hon.
   Frances
Sackville, Vct. See Sackville, Lord George
Sackville, Anne (d. 1595), m. (ca 1558) Gregory
   Fiennes, Lord Dacre of the South:
   Desmond, Cts of, said to have talked to, of
      Richard III, **40**. 108
   Emanuel Hospital founded by husband and,
      15. 223n
Sackville, Lady Caroline (1718–75), m. (1742)
   Joseph Damer, cr. (1753) Bn Milton, (1792)
   E. of Dorchester:
   death of, **24**. 98
   (?) Germain, Lady Elizabeth, entertains, at
      dinner, **38**. 358
   HW does not repeat Mann's compliments to,
      22. 301
   HW jokes about dancing with, **31**. 140
   HW, Lady George Sackville, and, joke about
      Lady Hertford's alleged death, **38**. 494
   HW meets, at Ds of Argyll's, **38**. 358
   HW mentions, **20**. 292
   HW not to tell, about son's escapade, **22**. 287,
      300
   HW's opinion of, **20**. 179
   Italians avoided by, because they play whist
      games, **20**. 175
   Macclesfield's body seen by, **38**. 358–9
   Mann's invitation refused by, **20**. 175
   —— thanked by, for civilities to son, **22**. 284,
      286
   —— told by, about Elizabeth Pitt, **20**. 416
Sackville, Charles (1638–1706), 6th E. of Dorset,
   1677; cr. (1675) E. of Middlesex:
   ballad by, **21**. 57
   Charles II conveys Burford House to, in
      trust for Nell Gwyn, **1**. 350n
   Knole's associations with, **33**. 223
   player said to have married, **35**. 134
   poem of, needs no special mention, **16**. 18
   poet, **35**. 134
   poet, and Prior's patron and benefactor, **20**.
      63n
   Pompée partly translated by, **16**. 6
   Pope's epitaph on, **32**. 145

Prior's praise of, applied by HW to Fanny
   Burney, **42**. 150
wife of, **10**. 1n
Sackville, Charles (1711–69), styled E. of Middlesex; 2d D. of Dorset, 1765; M.P.:
   ambassador's post rumoured for, **18**. 289, 346,
      365
   appearance of, altered, **37**. 116
   at 'fray' in Florence, **37**. 34
   brother carries, into opposition, **38**. 311
   Constitutional Queries attributed to, **20**. 235,
      245
   constitution and estate worn out by, **23**. 83
   Copt Hall sold to, **9**. 93n
   cricket prowess of, **40**. 6
   death of, **23**. 82–3
   Dilettanti Society led by, **18**. 211
   father made unhappy by, **21**. 321
   father may stop opera subsidies of, **18**. 225–6
   father scolded about, by George II, **17**. 221
   Florence left by, for England, **20**. 416n
   Frederick, P. of Wales, adds, to his party,
      20. 3n
   ——'s Master of the Horse, **20**. 235n
   —— to have, as Master of the Horse, **19**. 370
   (?) freemason lodge in Florence founded by,
      19. 364n
   George II discards, **20**. 245
   —— objects to, as Master of the Horse, **20**. 245
   HW has no interest with, **18**. 210
   Haymarket burlettas managed by, **20**. 4n
   Hume Campbell, counsel for, **20**. 5
   Kent lieutenancy may go to, **22**. 375
   Knight of the Garter, **10**. 29
   Knole's trees sacrificed by, **23**. 83
   Mann's old acquaintance, **20**. 235, **23**. 82
   —— told by, about Elizabeth Pitt, **20**. 416
   marriage of, **18**. 481, 501, 523, 527, **43**. 255
   mistress might have been married by, **23**. 83
   Monticelli sues, for salary, **20**. 4–5
   Morley, agent of, **17**. 400n
   Muscovita mistress to, **17**. 191
   —— retained at opera to please, **17**. 358
   Nardi mistress of, **19**. 293
   opera deficits due to mismanagement by, **18**.
      210–11, 225–6, 293–4
   opera director, **16**. 280n, **17**. 191
   opera house contributes, to politics, **18**. 365
   opera intrigues of, **19**. 293–4
   opera performers unpaid by, **19**. 294, 370
   operas sponsored by, **19**. 342
   opera to be administered by, as chief under-
      taker, **30**. 5
   Parliamentary membership of, corrected, **43**.
      240
   royal children and P. of Wales entertained
      by, at masked ball, **19**. 398
   seldom sober in Italy, **18**. 211
   Sergison opposes, in Sussex by-election, **30**. 20
   Stuart, Lady Jane, may wed, **38**. 406
   Treasury post of, **18**. 365, **19**. 370, 419
   Vaneschi cheats: at Lucca, **17**. 216; in Eng-
      land, **18**. 198

—— dominates, **17.** 191

—— the poet of, **17.** 200

—— under protection of, **17.** 141n

verses by: **20.** 235; on Sir Henry Bellenden, **9.** 359

Violette's dancing belittled by, **19.** 294n

weeps over wife's miscarriage, **19.** 447

Weymouth takes house of, in Arlington St, **10.** 271

wife of, **9.** 28n, **18.** 481n, **19.** 62n

wife's fortune may be used by, for operas, **18.** 501

Wright tries to stop, from playing cards with Fotheringham, **37.** 33n

Sackville, Charles (d. 1795):

Dorset's reputed son, **23.** 83n

Sackville, Edward (1590–1652), 4th E. of Dorset, 1624; K.B., 1616; K.G., 1625; M.P.:

Knole's associations with, **33.** 223

Sackville, Elizabeth (b. 1762), m. (1781) Henry Arthur Herbert:

family of, **33.** 307

wedding of, **33.** 307

Sackville, Lady George. *See* Sambrooke, Diana (d. 1778)

Sackville (later Sackville Germain), Lord George (1716–85), cr. (1782) Vct Sackville; M.P.:

abuse against, equals that against Byng, **30.** 158

American unconditional surrender expected by, **24.** 193n

Anecdotes of Painting does not discuss, **9.** 326

anxiety over military campaign of, **21.** 316

arrested, **21.** 374

Barré may succeed, as Irish vice-treasurer, **22.** 365n

Barrington succeeded by, as secretary at war, **9.** 211, **21.** 104

biographical information about, corrected, **43.** 240, 296

Bligh's command of army in Germany displeases, **37.** 545n

——'s regiment obtained by, **37.** 220n

Boston threatened by, like Alva, **39.** 239

Botta cannot understand how rank was retained by, after court martial, **21.** 411

Boyle affronts, **20.** 316

brother and 4 others carried into opposition by, **38.** 311

Byng compared with, **21.** 320–1

calls Washington 'dictator,' **6.** 424n

Carleton's appointment opposed by, **25.** 241n

Carmarthen attacked by, in House of Lords, **29.** 184

Charlotte's birthday not to be attended by, **25.** 236

Chatham administration not to include, **10.** 222

Cinque Ports offered to, **28.** 145

conduct reportedly explained by, in letter to D. of Richmond, **30.** 158

Conway goes from opera to tavern with, **37.** 54

——'s attack on Grenville administration continued by, in debate over Wilkes, **38.** 309

——'s relations with, **38.** 23

—— speech praised by, **41.** 317n

—— would be preferred by, as one of his judges, **21.** 366–7

courage of, **32.** 277

Court attendance denied to, **21.** 403

court martial of, **9.** 275, 276, 278–9, **13.** 35, **21.** 328, 366–7, 374, 377, 384–5, 387, 403

court martial requested by, **35.** 295

Court party defended by, in Parliament, **6.** 146

Court revisited by, **43.** 123

cowardice imputed to, **29.** 87, 135

Cumberland, D. of, sends, to Saxe, about Maestricht siege, **19.** 481

Cuninghame placed by, **37.** 582

Dartmouth succeeded by: as lord of Trade, **32.** 276n; as secretary of state for American province, **24.** 142

death of, **25.** 506

deputy ranger of Phoenix Park, near Dublin, **21.** 328n

discontented with other ministers, **32.** 320

disgraced at Minden battle, **21.** 320n, **24.** 187

Dorset (1st D.)'s son, **9.** 130n

Dorset (3d D.)'s affair with Cts of Derby may affect future of, **31.** 194

Dundas forces resignation on, **33.** 327n

Dutch ships' searching advocated by, **33.** 156n

East Grinstead's representative, **24.** 187

Ellis succeeds, as secretary of state, **25.** 241

English are brutal to, **35.** 306

English forces in Germany commanded by, **21.** 254n

English invasion of France led by, **21.** 204

English mob wants to tear, to pieces, **21.** 320

expeditions to France refused by, **37.** 549

fame of, **32.** 276

father disappointed by, **21.** 321

father scolded by George II about, **17.** 221

Ferdinand, P., and, **32.** 277

—— differs with, over Minden battle, **30.** 157–8

—— reflects on misconduct of, **38.** 22–3

first 'tome' of, remembered because of failure of second one, **25.** 237

Fisher gets post in office of, **42.** 225

followers of, join Parliamentary minority, **38.** 311

Fox, C. J., abuses, **6.** 500n

—— debates with, in Parliament, **24.** 341

—— opposes, in House of Commons, **32.** 401

—— wants to bring, to a second trial, **24.** 341n

French-Spanish naval juncture reported by, **24.** 496n

French war preparations belittled by, **24.** 262n

George II asked by, to recall him from command, **21.** 316n

[Sackville, Lord George, *continued*]

—— does not accept, as secretary at war, **21.** 109

—— does not speak to, at Kensington hand-kissing, **37.** 545–6

—— permits, to relinquish command in Germany, **21.** 320n

——'s letter from, reportedly presented by father, **30.** 157

—— tells Lady Yarmouth he intends to deal with, as with Byng, **21.** 320n

George III influenced by, to write to D. of Gloucester, **36.** 136n

—— insists on retention of, in ministry, despite unpopularity, **39.** 348n

—— not influenced by, **9.** 321

—— said to be friend of, **21.** 320n

——'s Court no longer countenances, **21.** 403

—— should have sword of state carried by, at thanksgiving, **38.** 200

—— thinks, should not be tried without being heard, **21.** 387n

Georgia loyal to, **32.** 346

Germain, Lady Elizabeth, leaves estates to, **4.** 324n, **17.** 221n

Germain name assumed by, on inheriting Lady Elizabeth Germain's estates, **23.** 256n

Gloucester, Ds of, asks Jebb and Adair to write to, **36.** 130

goes to the country, **21.** 403

government post may be sought by, through Grenville not Bute, **38.** 498n

Granby given ordnance post of, **21.** 328n

—— prevented by, from advancing at Minden, **21.** 315n

——'s rift with, **38.** 20

Grenville, George, ministry of, dissatisfies, **38.** 286

Grenville, James, succeeds, as vice-treasurer of Ireland, **22.** 443

HW asks what has been done for, by father's death, **40.** 386

HW buys pamphlets on, **38.** 35

HW calls, 'Duke of Alva,' **6.** 146

HW compares, with Alexander and Queen Eleanor, **32.** 348

HW disclaims *Letter from the Late E[arl] of Harrington* as offensive to, **40.** 98–9

HW distrusts, **37.** 583

HW identifies, **16.** 346

HW makes unsuccessful ministerial proposals to, **21.** 98n

HW proposes, as secretary at war, **21.** 98n, **37.** 487n

HW proposes ministerial scheme to, **37.** 487n

HW's correspondence with, **40.** 98–9

HW sends *Trial* of, to Mann, **21.** 407

HW would protect, from Duc de Broglie, **33.** 25

Hervey, Bp, compliments, on plan for American subjugation, **25.** 454n

Holdernesse and Ligonier inform, about court martial, **21.** 328

Holdernesse attaches himself to, **32.** 320

holiday of, **33.** 49

house of: at Stoneland Lodge, Sussex, **25.** 606n; in Pall Mall, **24.** 255n; stoned, **28.** 450n

House of Commons left by, in protest, **23.** 289n

—— told by, when secretary of state, that America must yield unlimited submission, **24.** 282n

Howe on bad terms with, **37.** 545

—— said to object to, **24.** 439

——'s dispatches given by, to George III, **24.** 306n

income of, reduced, **21.** 328

Ireland upset by, when secretary to his father, **25.** 606

Jebb's letter from, **36.** 135

Johnstone's duel with, after abuse in House of Commons, **23.** 256

Junius papers attributed to, **36.** 52

lawyers examine case of, **38.** 35

Leicester House favours, **21.** 387n

letters of, to P. Ferdinand, Fitzroy, Holdernesse, and Granby, **21.** 321n

London opposes, **9.** 320–1

Lord George Sackville's Vindication of Himself, in a Letter to Col. Fitzroy by, **38.** 32

Luttrell's quarrel with, **24.** 383, **28.** 401–2

Marlborough's command really under, **21.** 198

Mason does not expect, to be converted to Christianity, **28.** 256

member of Dorset's party, **20.** 402n

merchants ask, about dubious news, **32.** 396n

Minden conduct of: forgotten, **28.** 235–6; orders disobeyed, **38.** 20–3

mob angry at escape of, **9.** 283

Montagu pleased at acquittal of, **9.** 281

name of, stricken from Council Book, **10.** 46n, **22.** 96

news about, awaited in Florence, **21.** 406

North, Lord, notifies dismissal of, **33.** 327

Norton opposed as Speaker by, **43.** 282

office of, as colonial secretary, not to be filled up, **25.** 237

Oxford Loungers discuss, over custards and syllabubs, **38.** 46

pamphlets about, **9.** 247, **38.** 35

Parliamentary inquiry opened by, **24.** 474n

Parliamentary motion by, for using peers' sons to carry bills to House of Lords, **23.** 256n

Parliamentary speeches by: **28.** 488n; good, **38.** 325; on seizure of Wilkes's papers, **22.** 208; proposes Hanoverian and noblemen's regiments, **37.** 452

Parliament not attended by, **21.** 345

patch box would contain all the laurels of, **37.** 536

patent place (in Ireland) of, **21.** 328

peace commissioners' manifesto laid by, before House of Commons, **24.** 426n

(?) peerage for, rumoured, **14**. 121

peerage to be given to, **25**. 237, 241, **29**. 176–8

Pitt (E. of Chatham) said to have spoken to George II in behalf of, **21**. 320n

—'s speech supported by, **38**. 319

place expected by, if Townshend gets one, **38**. 498

Pratt and Yorke rule, to be entitled to court martial, **21**. 366n

quarrels of, with Burgoyne and Howes over American war, **24**. 424n

refuses to avow confiscation of French property in St Eustatius, **29**. 124–5

regimental appointment of, **37**. 234n

removal of, planned, **24**. 439n

report on battle of Minden sent by, **21**. 314n

request of, to return to England, granted, **30**. 158

resignation of: **29**. 176–8, **33**. 325, 326, 327; as minister of colonies, expected, **25**. 236, 237; imminent, **25**. 240; neither voluntary nor a disgrace but the result of disagreement with colleagues, **25**. 240–1; suggested, **24**. 447n

resigns army command, **38**. 22

retirement of, welcomed by everybody, **25**. 238

retires to Knole, **33**. 6

Rochefort inquiry conducted by, **21**. 155

Rockingham ministry favoured by, **39**. 40

Royal Marriage Act criticized by, **36**. 144

Sandwich the principal enemy of, **25**. 238

scandalous career of, **20**. 315

Second Letter to, published, **38**. 31–2

secretary of state, **28**. 235–6, **32**. 273

secretaryship at war not to go to, **21**. 109

secret expedition planned by, for George II, **21**. 205n

Short Address . . . to the Public by, **38**. 32

Smith, Capt., aide-de-camp to, **21**. 211, 320n, **32**. 52n, **38**. 21n

spirited behaviour of, during trial, **21**. 387

spirits of, raised by 'fine season,' **32**. 309

Stone, Abp, friend of, **20**. 315

— will not be helped by disgrace of, **38**. 28

'summoned in haste from Ireland,' **35**. 162

tavern visited by, after opera, **37**. 54

Temple tells, he will not join Bedford-Grenville ministry, **30**. 186

— thought by, to hint Pitt's willingness to accept peerage, **30**. 188

Townshend, Hon. Charles, concerts trimming plan with, **38**. 502

— resents appointment of, **21**. 104

Townshend, Thomas, proposed by, for Speaker, **23**. 180

turned out of his posts, **35**. 295

Tyrawley abuses, **30**. 158

—'s censure moved by, in House of Commons, **30**. 158n

unpopular, **24**. 383

viscountcy requested by, to be superior to Wedderburn, **32**. 401n

Waldegrave received regiment of, **21**. 328n

Walpole, Sir Edward, asks, for bill to pay D. of Gloucester's debts, **36**. 130n, 306n, 307n

— writes to, in D. of Gloucester's behalf, **36**. 306–9, 327

West Indies merchants protest to, against Sandwich, **36**. 199n

West Indies merchants remonstrated to, **29**. 125n

wife of, dies, **33**. 6

Wilkes's gross witticisms on, **38**. 232

—'s witticism on American rôle and German failure of, **24**. 187

windows of, broken by mob, **24**. 442

wounded at Fontenoy, **36**. 12, 37, 192

Yorktown surrender blamed by, on navy, **25**. 241n

Sackville, John Frederick (1745–99), 3d D. of Dorset, 1769:

Ampthill visited by, **32**. 145

appearance of, big and dark, **39**. 108

at Chewton wedding, **29**. 245n

Baccelli permitted by, to dance in Paris, wearing Garter insignia, **31**. 268

Broglie described by, **11**. 27n

Christian VII jealous of, **39**. 108–9

courier arrives in London from, **11**. 35–6, **39**. 467

courier of (Lanyun), not allowed to leave Paris, **11**. 40

Derby, Cts of, to wed, after her divorce, **24**. 435

Du Deffand, Mme, has not seen, **4**. 306

— inquires about, **4**. 296

— not called on by, **6**. 395

Gordon's scandal about, in *Morning Post*, **33**. 117n

HW advises Lady Ossory to keep, at Ampthill, **32**. 178

HW calls, 'Grace of Courts,' **32**. 145

HW criticizes appointment of, **36**. 215

(?) HW sends letters by, **7**. 380, **39**. 58

(?) HW sends red snuff-box by, **7**. 404

HW's packet from Lady Ossory delivered by, **32**. 175

HW's verses mention, **32**. 373, 374

inefficient as English ambassador in France, **25**. 486–7

(?) Irvine, Lady, haggles with, **33**. 182

— woos, **33**. 182n

marriage of, rumoured, **36**. 240

messenger from, with French news, **43**. 140

Motezuma dedicated to, **24**. 90n

Parsons, Anne, mistress of, **5**. 132, **23**. 344n, **24**. 435n, **43**. 375

Shelburne's witticism about, **25**. 487

wife of, **11**. 206n

Yeomen of the Guard headed by, as captain, in succession to Vct Falmouth, **25**. 241

Sackville, Lady John Philip. *See* Leveson Gower, Hon. Frances (1720–88), also called Lady Sackville

Sackville, Lord John Philip (1713–65), M.P.:
cricket introduced by, at SH, **37.** 270
cricket prowess of, **40.** 6n
dances at Robinson's ball, **37.** 115
death of, **7.** 397
father scolded by George II about, **17.** 221
tavern visited by, after opera, **37.** 54
Sackville, Lionel Cranfield (1688–1765), 7th E.
of Dorset, cr. (1720) D. of Dorset:
again to be lord steward, **20.** 470
Allen, Bns, connected with, **35.** 94n
Argyll, Ds of, entertained by, **9.** 368
ball at Haymarket attended by, **37.** 50
Beauclerk, Lord Vere, owes appointment to,
17. 356
Berkeley's influence upon, **17.** 221
Boyle differs with, on George II's prerogative
over Irish treasury, **20.** 402n
—— removed by, at George II's command,
20. 425n
——'s opposition to, in Irish parliament, **20.**
316, 402
——'s strife with, in Ireland, **9.** 130–1
Cinque Ports and Dover posts lost by, **20.** 63
Cinque Ports to remain in custody of, **21.** 109
Cinque Ports wardenship of, corrected, **43.**
266
daughter imitates, **20.** 179
daughter-in-law of, **19.** 62n
daughter of, **24.** 98n
death of, **7.** 397, **22.** 361, **40.** 386
Devonshire succeeds, as lord steward, **18.** 550
dismissions not executed by, in Ireland, **20.**
410
Dublin left by, without being mobbed, **37.**
376
George II asked by, not to subscribe to opera,
18. 226
—— has Holdernesse write to Lord Newport
that he expects support for, **20.** 440n
—— scolds, about his sons, **17.** 221
George III carried by, **9.** 89
Gower succeeds, as Master of the Horse, **21.**
104
HW mentions, **9.** 211
HW proposes, for Treasury, **21.** 98n
HW proposes ministry under, **37.** 487n
Harrington replaced by, in Ireland, **20.** 202
—— succeeded by, as lord president, **18.** 550
Hartington succeeds, in Irish post, **20.** 469
health of, poor, **21.** 489
Holdernesse to inherit Cinque Ports post of,
21. 489
impatient to escape from Ireland, **31.** 5
Ireland about to be left by, **37.** 375–6
—— or lord presidency to be offered to, **19.**
327
Irish disturbances during viceroyalty of, **35.**
158n
Irish fail to send address to George II
through, **9.** 130–1
Irish lord lieutenancy seized by, **20.** 207

Irish lord lieutenant, with son as secretary,
25. 606
Irish opposition to, because of son's scandal,
20. 315
Jacobites try, through Prior, to persuade,
to give up Dover Castle, **20.** 62–3
Kent lieutenancy held by, **22.** 361
Kildare presents manifesto to George II, protesting against administration of, in Ireland, **20.** 440n
Knole's associations with, **33.** 224
lord presidency vacated by, **20.** 202
members of party of, in Ireland, **20.** 402n
Middlesex's opera-subsidizing may be stopped
by, **18.** 226
Ormonde, D. of, replaces, as governor of
Dover and warden of Cinque Ports, **20.** 63n
pension offered to, **21.** 104, 109
Prior probably brother of, **20.** 63
regent, **18.** 209n
son of, **4.** 324n, **19.** 293n
son's disgrace distresses, **30.** 158
son's letter to George II reportedly presented
by, **30.** 157
sons of, make him unhappy, **21.** 321
spaniel of, **9.** 368
Stone asks, to promote Cuninghame, **20.** 316n
Vere entertained by, **9.** 368
warden of the Cinque Ports, **21.** 104n
will of, **31.** 71
Williams, Sir C. H. satirizes, in 'Peter and
My Lord Quidam,' **30.** 317
Sackville, Mary (1746–78), m. (1767) Sackville
Tufton, 8th E. of Thanet, 1753:
death of, **33.** 58–9
Sackville, Richard (1589–1624), 3d E. of Dorset, 1609:
(?) Knole's associations with, **33.** 223
portraits of: at Appleby Castle, **10.** 185; at
Castle Ashby, **10.** 336
wife of, **9.** 125n, **15.** 82n
Sackville, Richard (1622–77), 5th E. of Dorset;
M.P.:
(?) portrait of, **10.** 336
Sackville, Robert (d. 1609), 2d E. of Dorset,
1608:
widow of, **15.** 83
Sackville, Thomas (1536–1608), cr. (1567) Lord
Buckhurst, (1604) E. of Dorset:
Gorboduc by Norton and, **35.** 134n
induction to *A Mirrour for Magistrates* attributed to, by Puttenham, **16.** 367
Knole's associations with, **33.** 223
Teddington built by, **11.** 30n
Sackville family:
arms of, quartered with those of Compton
family, **10.** 336
ballads and epigrams against, **20.** 316
blood of, 'worst,' **19.** 442
Devonshire, D. of, appeased, by concessions,
to his son's opposition to, in Ireland, **37.**
409
Hedon election concerns, **17.** 221

influence of, vast, **20.** 316
Middlesex's opera transactions may ruin, **18.** 226
——'s wedding not announced by, **18.** 527
pedigree of, **15.** 83
Sackville St, London:
Damer, Mrs, has house in, **11.** 8, 237–8n, **12.** 69, 85, **33.** 564
Darell, Robert, of, **34.** 59n
fire near, **9.** 362
Winchilsea, E. of, lives in, **19.** 52n
Sacombe Park, Herts:
Caswall of, **2.** 1, **9.** 319n
Sacontalá. See under Jones, Sir William
Sacque. *See* Sack
Sacrament; sacraments:
Balmerinoch takes, before execution, **19.** 301
Bell's treatise on, **29.** 125, 134
Clement XIII receives, **22.** 331
Corsican rebels receive, from Clement XIII's bishop, **21.** 394
Electress takes, on deathbed, **18.** 160, 173
English troops bicker over, with Flemish friars, **18.** 30
exposed in churches for Wachtendonck's recovery, **17.** 105
exposure of, in Roman churches, **21.** 392
French army said to take, before attacking English, **37.** 137
Germain, Lady Elizabeth, persuades husband to take, on deathbed, **33.** 278n
Hoadly's treatise on, **15.** 292
Indian convert prefers rum to, **17.** 477
Louis XV kneels before, at Pont Neuf, **39.** 55
—— receives, **18.** 503
Protestants revere, but do not worship them, **28.** 154
Selwyn profanes, **30.** 89, 93
Spanish officers take, **17.** 427
Vane, Vcts, 'comforted' by, **17.** 210, 240
See also Host
Sacra Rota Romana. *See* Rota
Sacre de Louis XV, Le. See under Danchet, Antoine
Sacrilege:
HW's reflections on: **15.** 149; on execution at Venice, **17.** 85
Johnson, Dr Samuel, defines, **35.** 497
Sacristy:
Pius VI builds, at St Peter's, **24.** 344, **25.** 383–4
Sacy, Père:
Pompadour, Mme de, takes, as confessor, **20.** 530n
Saddle; saddles:
Chute and HW borrow, to ride post-horses, **35.** 142
Conway busy with, **37.** 358
HW uses, for blankets, **18.** 315
refugees from fire take, to Sir Robert Walpole's house, **17.** 496
Saddle cloths:
Wren's, sold, **40.** 348
Saddlers' Company, London:
Frederick, P. of Wales belongs to, **17.** 451n

Sadducees. *See under* Bible
Sade, Donatien-Alphonse-François (1740–1814), Comte (known as 'Marquis') de:
encounter of, with Rose Keller, **4.** 56–7, 58, 85
imprisonment and sentence of, **43.** 87–8
Sade, Jacques-François-Paul-Aldonce de (1705–78), abbé:
conduct of nephew of, **4.** 56–7
Mémoires pour la vie de François Pétrarque by: **32.** 95n, **43.** 87; HW recommends, to Lady Mary Coke, **31.** 143; HW recommends, to Joseph Warton, **40.** 377; sent to HW, **4.** 22n, 24, 28, 33, 37n, 46, 56
Sade, Jean-Baptiste-François-Joseph (1701–67), Comte de:
capture of, **19.** 18
Sade, Richard-Jean-Louis, Chevalier de:
brother of, captured by Austrians, **19.** 18
clothes pawned by, **18.** 62, 318
Craon borrows from, **18.** 38–9, 62
—— plays quadrille with, **18.** 329
—— told by, that his cold house caused Mann's illness, **18.** 110
Craon, Princesse de, entertains, **17.** 413
—— tells, to negotiate about etiquette with Modenese princess, **17.** 60
—— would tell, to read Mme de Sévigné's letters to her, **20.** 387
Craons dissuaded by, from Leghorn trip, **18.** 38
debts of, in Florence, **17.** *46*
HW asks about, **17.** 402, **18.** 318, **19.** 18
Mann entertains, at dinner, **18.** 17
—— serves chocolate to, **17.** 413
—— talks with, at opera, **17.** 283
—— tells, to distinguish between France and England, **19.** 80
Modena, Ds of, asks HW about, **17.** 46
—— supplies, **18.** 39
Orléans, Duchesse d', said by, to hate her daughter, **18.** 386
verses of, **17.** 46n
Sadeler, Jan (1550–1600):
prints by, depict hermits, **10.** 276–7, **35.** 149, 209
Sadler, James (1753–1828), aeronaut:
balloon ascent by, as Windham's pilot, **25.** 579
Fitzpatrick starts to make balloon ascent with, **33.** 469n
missing, but is found, **25.** 590, 591
not heard of, **33.** 467
Sadler's Wells:
Abingdon lowers House of Lords to level of, **35.** 381
booths at, resemble magic lantern, **39.** 266
dancers at Haymarket performance worthy of, **35.** 106
Fox, C. J., and 'Perdita' frequent, **35.** 523n
frequented even when disaster threatens England, **33.** 196
pantomimes at, **34.** 71n

Saffron:
  Hotham, Henrietta, has face and neck spotted with, **10**. 115
Saffron Walden, Essex:
  burials in church at, **33**. 387
  Cole corrects HW about, **1**. 8
  letters postmarked at, **13**. 72n, **43**. 183
  portrait in, **1**. 175
  Shortgrove near, **10**. 30n
  Tyson's shop at, **1**. 175n
Sage, Le. *See* Le Sage
Sage; sages, Venetian:
  long sleeves worn by, **17**. 75n
Sage (herb):
  HW uses, for eyes, **18**. 365
Sagunto:
  regiment of, **18**. 489
Saham Toney, Norfolk:
  Storer of, **28**. 329n, **29**. 372, **41**. 366
Sahuguet, Marc-René (1753–94), Abbé d'Espagnac:
  Éloge de Nicolas Catinat by: **32**. 258; (?) HW to bring, to Conway, **39**. 260
Sahuguet d'Espagnac, Léonard de (d. 1781):
  (?) attends session of parliament of Paris, **8**. 171, 172
Said. *See* Sayde
Said Effendi, Turkish ambassador to France:
  English naval supremacy observed by, **18**. 15
Sail-boat:
  in Richmond Palace print, **16**. 73, 79
Sailing:
  Orford, 3d E. of, takes up, **24**. 38
Sailly, Félicité de (1716–living 1805), m. (1767) François-Louis le Tellier, Marquis de Souvré:
  grandes entrées granted to, **4**. 339
Sailor; sailors:
  Admiralty stops, from leaving Portsmouth to join weavers' mob, **38**. 560
  America recruits, **24**. 81
  at Dover, predict winds, **37**. 158
  at Villafranca, reports victory, **17**. 471
  characteristic dialect of, **16**. 256
  Conway praised by, **30**. 143
  drunken, Augustus incompatible with, **41**. 154
  English: Admiralty stops, from leaving Portsmouth to join weavers' mob, **38**. 560; Anson's leadership not envied by, **21**. 223; coal-heavers feud with, in London, **23**. 30, 33; Conway's arm almost rebroken by, **25**. 115; crucifix hung by, on monkey's neck, **18**. 59, 79n; Edgcumbe leaves, to strengthen St Philip's garrison, **20**. 559; England enlists, **24**. 81; enlist to capture prizes, **23**. 242; Fermor might have to eat with, unless given money, **19**. 148; generosity of, with captured Spanish booty, **24**. 543; gentlemen disguised as, **17**. 211; Gray, Sir James, must be preceded by, to Spain, **21**. 560; Green aided by, **23**. 39; HW wishes something could be done for, **38**. 205; Hood employs, against Fox in Westminster elec-

tion, **25**. 489; impressment of, indicates war, **24**. 262; Ireland contributes, **25**. 285; Lisbon people blamed by, for ingratitude, **17**. 456; Mann disgusted with rudeness of, **19**. 275; Mann opposes enlistment of, in Tuscan navy, **20**. 472; Mann receives, and sends to Leghorn, **17**. 158; mends broken leg, **24**. 283–4, 290; merchant fleets provide navy with, **33**. 24; merchant ships prevented by, from sailing, **23**. 21; Nova Scotia lands granted to, **20**. 40n; often tamper with wine shipments, **21**. 304; old, Boscawen gets letter from, about Port Mahon's capture, **21**. 52; Parliament petitioned by, **23**. 21; Parliament to vote, for American war, **24**. 127; received from West Indian and Mediterranean fleets, **24**. 392; reduction of, proposed, **38**. 496; riot at Rochester by, from Vernon's fleet, **30**. 29; secret mobilization of, authorized, **23**. 156; shipping embargo to get, for navy, **37**. 446; tosses sword to unarmed opponent, **24**. 543; Wilkes's mob driven off by, **23**. 21
  English, Danish, French, and Swedish, on Prussian privateer, **21**. 349
  French: France loses, in war with England, **25**. 7; French navy lacks, **21**. 264; from Languedoc for Toulon fleet, **18**. 396; obtained from Corsica, **23**. 47, 478
  galley, **17**. 471
  Jesuits disguised as, **22**. 545
  Leghorn hopes to convert fishermen into, **20**. 217
  Papal, fear enslavement by Turkish pirates, **17**. 16
  Roman, belittle Corinthian statues, **19**. 264
  Slavonian, seize *Great Duchess of Tuscany* and turn pirates, **25**. 479–80
Sainsbury, John (d. 1792), steward to E. of Salisbury:
  Rutt's bequest to, **42**. 418
Sainsbury, Thomas (d. 1795), alderman and sheriff of London:
  brother of, **42**. 418
Saint; saints:
  ancient British, in Harleian MSS, **40**. 216
  Benedict XIV's canonization of, **19**. 171n
  Browne, Lady, screams to, in ferry-boat accident, **39**. 187
  corpse of, on board Spanish fleet at Algiers, **24**. 122
  HW compares Mme de Sévigné's relics with those of, **33**. 151
  HW jokes about, going to heaven for gratitude, **37**. 431
  HW's in stained-glass windows at SH: long, **20**. 372; lose heads in explosion, **39**. 152
  HW's reflections on, **31**. 67
  Maximilian wishes to become, **25**. 468
  price for making, **19**. 171
  Sobieski, Ps, aspires to be, **21**. 424, **25**. 106
St-Aignan, Duc de. *See* Beauvilliers, Charles-Paul-François de (1745–1828); Beauvilliers,

François-Honorat de (1610–87); Beauvilliers *or* Beauvillier, Paul-Hippolyte de (1684–1776)

St-Aignan, Duchesse de. *See* Geré-de-Rancé, Françoise (ca 1642–1728); Turgot, Hélène-Françoise-Étiennette (1729–84)

St Alban, Vct. *See* Bacon, Sir Francis

St Alban, Mme de (d. before 1812), 4th E. of Cholmondeley's mistress:
arrested and examined on leaving Paris, 11. 87–8
daughters of, 11. 245
HW jokes about, 11. 109–10
HW's 'pinchbeck niece,' 11. 87
pregnancy of, 11. 109

St Alban, Hugh de (fl. 1350), painter:
sergeant-painter to Edward III, 1. 153–4

St Albans, Ds of. *See* Ponsonby, Lady Catherine (1742–89); Roberts, Jane (d. 1778); Vere, Lady Diana de (d. 1742)

St Albans, D. of. *See* Beauclerk, Aubrey (1740–1802); Beauclerk, Aubrey (1765–1815); Beauclerk, Charles (1670–1726); Beauclerk, Charles (1696–1751); Beauclerk, George (1730–86); Beauclerk, Lord William (1766–1825)

St Albans, E. of. *See* Jermyn, Henry (ca 1604–84)

St Albans, Vct. *See* Bacon, Sir Francis

St Albans, Herts:
abbey church (later cathedral) of: architect of, 2. 278–9; Humphrey, D. of Gloucester, buried in, 2. 31, 37; sacrist of, was Walter de Colchester, 42. 42
book of, in Benet College Library, 2. 279
franks to be addressed to Hillier at, 16. 71
HW's copyist can stay at, not at Gorhambury, 40. 193
hostess of inn at, 32. 369
Juliana Berners's *Boke* of, 34. 146
road through, 1. 38
road to, narrow in winter, 32. 290
St Michael's Church at, 1. 18–19
Smith's estate near, 1. 166n
Spencer, Lady, electioneers at, 33. 225
—— retires to, 33. 428
West, M.P. for, 20. 371n
White Hart Inn at, 19. 391n, 23. 165n

St Alban's Court, Nonington:
HW visits, 29. 78n

St Alban's St, London:
apothecary in, 34. 130

St Alban's Tavern, near Pall Mall, London:
Board, the, moves to, from Bedford Head, 20. 50n, 43. 249
county deputies meet in, 29. 16n
Jacobite club meets at, 25. 12n
Jacobites meet at, with P. of Wales's party, 20. 50
militia discussed at meeting in, 38. 146n
new opposition forms in, 21. 552–3
Parliamentary gathering at, 25. 477n
Townshend, Charles attends assemblies at, 21. 553

young men at, have street littered with straw, 23. 323

St-Albin, Louis-Philippe (1761–after 1826), Abbé de, natural son of the Duc d'Orléans:
dines at Lord Rawdon's, 34. 175–6

St-Aldegonde, ——, 'Lieutenant de Roy' at Ostend:
Conway bows to, 38. 3

St-Aldegonde. *See also* Ste-Aldegonde

St Alexander, Order of:
Orlov appears in robes of, 28. 477

St-Amand-les-Eaux (France):
Duchesse de Lauzun and Princesse de Poix at, 6. 214
(?) Lanti's French benefice, 43. 275

St Andero (Spain):
Jardine consul at, 12. 62n

St-André, Maréchale de. *See* Lustrac, Marguerite de

St-André. *See also* La Roche-de-St-André

St Andrea, near Marciana (Italy):
barks pursued into, by Osborne, 18. 28

St-André-des-Arts, church of, at Paris:
HW visits, 7. 282

St-André-des-Arts, Rue, in Paris:
Plumard de Dangeul lives in, 6. 260n, 7. 417

St Andrew, Order of:
cross of: given to La Chétardie, 18. 495n; Young Pretender wears, 23. 225
Orlov wears, 24. 143n

St Andrew le Mot:
manor of, 16. 47n

St Andrews, Abp of. *See* Beaton, David (1494–1546)

St Andrews, Bp of. *See* Turgot (d. 1115)

St Andrew's, Holborn, London:
Barton, rector of, 20. 155

St Andrews, Scotland:
Morvo directs mason work at, 42. 69n

St Andrew's Day:
Young Pretender celebrates, in drunkenness, 25. 100

St Andrew's Sq. *See under* Edinburgh

St Andrews University, Scotland:
Watson, professor at, 15. 136n, 32. 339

St Angelo in Vado (Italy):
Clement XIV from, 23. 117

St Anne of Holstein, Order of:
Catherine II distributes: in son's name, 24. 84; to Sir John Dick, 24. 84–5, 96
Dick assumes, when no longer degraded by being consul, 24. 96, 114, 239
Orlov delivers, to Dick, 24. 84, 96
Rutherfurd rejects, though Dick accepted it, 24. 453

St Anne's, Soho, London:
Dagge, Henry, of parish of, 21. 32n
Dean St near, 21. 131n
HW erects monument at, to K. Theodore of Corsica, 3. 183n, 13. 28, 21. 140, 148
rector of, *see* Squire, Samuel (1713–66)

St Anne's, Westminster:
Richardson, rector of, 2. 69n

St Anselm and St Cecilia, church of:
Sardinian chapel becomes, 25. 55n
St Antholin's, London:
Venn, rector of, 15. 295n
St Anthony's Fire (erysipelas):
Mme du Deffand unacquainted with name of, 3. 297
See also Erysipelas
St Antoine, Abbess of. See Beauvau, Gabrielle-Charlotte de
St-Antoine, château de, at Paris:
Young Pretender stays at, 19. 509n
St-Antoine, convent of, at Paris:
Mirepoix, Mme de, does not lodge at, 7. 3
St-Antoine, Rue du Faubourg de. See Faubourg de St-Antoine, Rue du
St-Antoine de St-André, Agathe-Louise (d. 1774), m. (1773) Louis-René-Mans de la Tour de Charce:
birth of, 35. 173
St Antonio. See San Antonio
'St Antonio Abate.' See Parma: convent at
St-Apolline, Rue, at Paris. See Ste-Apolline
St Apostoli. See Santi Apostoli
St Asaph, Bp of. See Bagot, Lewis (1740–1802); Drummond, Robert Hay (1711–76): Halli-fax, Samuel (1733–90); Hare, Francis (1671–1740); Horsley, Samuel (1733–1806); Mad-dox, Isaac (1697–1759); Shipley, Jonathan (1714–88); Tanner, Thomas (1674–1735)
St Asaph, Dean of. See Shipley, W. D.
St Asaph, Vct. See Ashburnham, George
St Asaph, Vcts. See Thynne, Lady Sophia
St Aubin. See Ducrest de St-Aubin; see also St Aubyn
St Aubyn ('St Aubin'), Sir John (?1702–44), 3d Bt; M.P.:
birth date of, corrected, 43. 244
Cornish by-election after death of, 30. 78n
named in Secret Committee lists, 17. 385
Parliamentary motion seconded by, 13. 12n
Secret Committee seconded by, 17. 364, 375
St Aubyn, Sir John (1758–1839), 5th Bt, 1772:
SH visited by, 12. 221
St-Augustin, Rue neuve de, at Paris:
Deux-Ponts, Hôtel de, in, 7. 34n
Gesvres, Hôtel de (Hôtel de Tresmes) in, 13. 165n
Tresmes lives in, 13. 163n
St Augustine, Florida:
Spain cedes, to England, 22. 95n
St Augustine's Abbey, Canterbury:
HW and Berrys admire gate of, 12. 105
view of ruins of, from cathedral window, 12. 109
St Austin's Abbey. See St Augustine's Abbey
St Austin's Church, Bristol. See under Bristol
St Barnabas's, Venice. See San Barnaba
'St Bartelemi, the.' See St Bartholomew's Day
St Bartholomew's Day, massacre of:
account of, supposedly found in lodgings of Bristol incendiary, 24. 274
Charles IX's effigy looks suitable for, 39. 203

cruelty of, 34. 57
French Revolutionists repeat, 11. 78, 86, 91, 15. 218–19, 31. 343, 371, 34. 158, 161, 42. 373, 376
HW compares Fête de la Fédération with, 31. 343
medal made by Gregory XIII to commemo-rate, 21. 189n
St Bartholomew's Hospital, London:
Henley, governor of, 38. 275
St Benet Fink, church in London:
Clarke clergyman of, 16. 67n
St Bennet's Hill:
ecclesiastical courts at, 17. 453n
St-Benoît, Rue, in Paris:
HW lives in, 7. 263
St-Bernard, Quai, in Paris:
Jardin des Plantes in, 7. 310n
St Bernard Pass, in the Alps:
Charles Emmanuel III retreats through, into Piedmont, 18. 142n
St Botolph's, Aldgate, London:
Freeman, curate of, 16. 166n
St Botolph's Bishopsgate, London:
Ashton, rector of, 20. 164n
——'s sermon preached at, published, 14. 236
St-Brieuc, Bp of. See Barreau de Girac, François
St-Brieuc, Brittany:
Breton parliament to meet at, 3. 370
St-Brisson, Comte de. See Séguier, Nicolas-Maximilien
St-Brisson, Comtesse de. See Huguet de Sémon-ville, Élisabeth-Catherine
St-Brisson, Marquis de. See Séguier, Sidoine-Charles-François
St-Calès:
Benedictine abbey of, 4. 16n
St Caroline, ship:
artillery brought by, to Italian coast, from Barcelona, 17. 286
St-Cas. See St-Cast
St-Cast, bay on French coast:
battle of: Aiguillon's supper for English pris-oners after, 21. 251; Armytage killed at, 9. 264n; English defeated at, 9. 225–6, 37. 569–71, 573–4; York, D. of, alludes to, 7. 366
English embark at, 21. 243
failure at, prompts new expedition, 37. 582
French flotilla said to have returned to, 39. 320
St Castaldo, Italy:
Lobkowitz stationed near, 19. 30
St Catherine of Russia, Order of:
declined by Maria Louisa, 25. 128
Peter III said to have bestowed, on Vorontsov lady who tried to resign it to Catherine II, 22. 58–9, 65
St Catherine's Hall, Cambridge:
Etough attends, 10. 343
'St Cecilia, Cardinal of':
HW imagines poisoning of a pope by, 35. 222

St-Chamans, Marquise de. *See* Malézieu, Louise-Françoise-Charlotte de

St-Chamans, Armand de (b. 1754), styled (1778) Marquis de St-Chamans:
  (?) Hampton Court visited by, **33**. 409
  (?) SH visited by, **25**. 423, **33**. 408–9

St-Chamans, Auguste-Gabriel-Louis de (b. 1761), Vicomte de St-Chamans:
  (?) Hampton Court visited by, **33**. 409
  (?) SH visited by, **25**. 423, **33**. 408–9

St-Chamans, Joseph-Louis (b. 1747), Vicomte de:
  (?) social relations of, with Comtesse de Rochefort, **7**. 270, 323

St Charles's Day. *See under* Borromeo, Carlo, St

St-Christophe, Marquis de. *See* Ténay, Chevalier Marc-Jean de

St Christopher (St Kitts), West Indies:
  Blake of, **1**. 240n
  British merchants at, **29**. 124n
  Hood relieves, from French threat, **25**. 253n
  hurricane at, **25**. 105
  lost, like Minorca, **25**. 263
  Mann, Edward, has interests at, **24**. 168n
  Molineux dies at, **2**. 207n
  Pym of, **14**. 120n
  reported to have been rescued by Hood, **25**. 254, 257

'St-Chrysostome, Mlle.' *See* Sanadon, Mlle

St Clair, Mrs. *See* Dalrymple, Janet (1698–1766)

St Clair, Sir John:
  detachment under Braddock commanded by, **20**. 495n

St Clair. *See also* St Clere; Sinclair

St Clement's Church, London:
  chop-house behind, **29**. 181
  cutler behind, **31**. 84
  HW thinks, has round portico, **35**. 144

St Clere family:
  figures of knights of, **2**. 175

St Cloud, Duc de. *See* Beaumont du Repaire, Christophe de

St-Cloud (France):
  balloon ascent at, **25**. 517n
  cascades of, **11**. 120
  Coventry forsakes fête at, for Worcester music festival, **20**. 338
  HW prevented by gout from going to, **10**. 180
  Louis XVI's journey to, **11**. 259
  visitors to: Buckner, **7**. 314; Cholmondeley, Mrs, **4**. 466; HW, **7**. 314; Lauzun, Duchesse de, **6**. 441; Lennox, Lord and Lady George, **7**. 314; Luxembourg, Mme de, **6**. 182, 441

St Clouet. *See* Chloé

St Contest. *See* Barberie de St-Contest

St Crispino. *See* Crespino

St Croce. *See* Santa Croce

St Croix, West Indies:
  La Fortuna bound for, from Cadiz, **21**. 269n

St-Croix-de-la-Bretonnerie, Rue, in Paris:
  'Toilette de Psyche' in, **13**. 164n

St-Cyr (France):
  Athalie choruses sung at, **10**. 294

chapel at, HW and friends attend vespers at, **10**. 293

garden at, pensioners play games at, **10**. 294

HW describes, **10**. 292–4

HW fears French reformation may destroy, **10**. 167

HW sits in Mme de Maintenon's seat in chapel at, and obtains her letter, **34**. 82

minuets and country dances danced at, **10**. 294

Montagu would like to visit, **10**. 299

proverbs by Mme de Maintenon acted at, **10**. 294

superior of, *see* Du Han de Crèvecœur, Marguerite-Suzanne

(?) view of, in Ferdinand's portrait of Mme de Maintenon, **10**. 294

visitors to: Ailesbury, Cts of, **6**. 133, 144; Cholmondeley, Mrs, **10**. 292–4, **34**. 82; Conway, **6**. 133, 144; Damer, Mrs, **6**. 133, 144; Grave, **10**. 292–4, **34**. 82; HW, **6**. 144–5, **7**. 330, **10**. 292–4, **34**. 82; Hart, Mrs, **10**. 292–4, **34**. 82

St David's, Bp of. *See* Bull, George (1734–1810); Burgess, Thomas (1756–1837); Horsley, Samuel (1733–1806); Lowth, Robert (1710–87); Moss, Charles (1711–1802); Smalbroke, Richard (1672–1749); Squire, Samuel (1713–66); Stuart, Hon. William (1755–1822); Trevor, Richard (1707–71); Watson, Thomas (1637–1717); Willes, Edward (d. 1773); Yorke, Hon. James (1730–1808)

St David's Cathedral, Wales:
  Powell, canon of, **16**. 159
  Tudor's body transferred to, **42**. 20

St-Denis (France):
  better seen on excursion from Paris than en route, **37**. 42
  Carmelite convent at, **4**. 399
  Chartres, Duc de, and Duc d'Orléans refuse to visit, **6**. 77
  Coke, Lady Mary, enters Louis XIV's vault at, **24**. 14
  Conway to get, from Mme du Deffand, admission to effigies of kings at, **39**. 203
  Grand Prior of, *see* Chrestien, Dom Jacques-Nicolas
  HW at, **7**. 260, 274
  HW's expenses at, **7**. 399
  HW to visit, **39**. 9
  Louis XV and Maupeou visit Ps Louise's cell at, **23**. 321
  Louis XV's solemn requiem at, **32**. 201n
  —— to be buried at, **6**. 51
  Mariette gives HW a letter for admittance to, **40**. 389
  monuments at, **13**. 163
  St Denis's journey to, **3**. 305
  St-Ouen between Paris and, **5**. 388n
  soldiers of, see Bourdeaux, ——; Humain, ——

  Turenne buried at, with kings of France, **17**. 153n

St-Denis, Plaine de:
Louis XV hunts on, 3. 122n
St-Denis, Rue de, in Paris:
convent in, with only two friars, 34. 193
princes become bourgeois of, 5. 296
St Dionis, Backchurch, London:
Tatton rector of, 2. 304n
St-Dizier, France:
HW and Gray spend night at, 13. 180n
St Domingo, Spanish register ship:
capture of, 24. 543
St-Domingue. See Santo Domingo
St-Dominique, Rue, in Paris:
Broglie, Hôtel de, in, 5. 140n
Conti, Hôtel de, in, 4. 351n, 6. 250n
Grimbergh, Hôtel de, in, 38. 304n
Luynes, Hôtel de, in, 4. 353n, 6. 330n
Mme du Deffand's convent in, 8. 3–5, 9, 11,
56n; see also St Joseph, convent of
Mirepoix, Hôtel de, in, 31. 49n
Rue Bergère distant from, 5. 99
St Dunstan's Church, London:
Wren may not have designed, 40. 348
'Sainte, la petite.' See Lallemant de Betz, Marie-
Françoise
Ste-Aldegonde-Noircarmes, Comtesse de. See
Du Hamel de St-Rémy, Marie-Charlotte- Fé-
licité-Amélie
Ste-Ampoulle, la:
Peterborough's witticism on seeing, at Reims,
24. 112–13
Ste-Anne, French ship:
capture of, 21. 524
Ste-Anne, Rue, in Paris:
Tresmes lives near, 13. 163n
Ste-Anne Butte St-Roch, Rue, in Paris:
Lutton in, 6. 27n
Ste-Apolline, Rue, in Paris:
Alexandre Alexander in, 13. 184n, 239
Selwin's address, 37. 99, 105
Ste-Assise (St-Port), France, Marquise de Mon-
tesson's country house:
Montesson, Marquise de, buys, 5. 386
—— occupies, 6. 102, 163, 211, 329, 330, 7.
124, 183
Paris emptied of good company by, 6. 367
visitors to: Choiseul, 7. 452; Gramont, Duch-
esse de, 7. 452; Lauzun, Duchesse de, 6.
329; Luxembourg, Mme de, 6. 102, 236,
329, 330, 363, 365, 368, 371, 491, 7. 47, 432,
433; Mirepoix, Mme de, 6. 102, 211, 236,
237, 368, 491; Orléans, Duc d', 6. 163, 7.
124; Toulouse, Abp of, 7. 452; see also
under Béraud de la Haie de Riou
Ste-Aulaire, Marquis de:
Mme du Deffand's MSS owned by, 36. 312
See also Beaupoil, François-Joseph de
Ste-Baume, convent of, in Provence:
Coke, Lady Mary, should visit, 31. 143
Ste-Catherine, Rue, in Paris:
Carnavalet, Hôtel de, in, 31. 50n
Ste-Chapelle, Paris:

Champrond, Abbé de, treasurer of, 4. 228n,
7. 225n
Du Deffand, Mme, would like to send to HW
the windows of, 5. 172
HW pleased with, 1. 103
HW visits, 7. 276
Louis XV goes to parliament of Paris from,
8. 172
portraits in ante-chapel of, 39. 203
Ste-Croix (France):
bridge near, 37. 159
Ste-Croix de la Bretonnerie:
order of, reduced, 39. 147n
St Edmundsbury. See Bury St Edmunds
Ste-Foix; Ste-Foy. See Radix
Ste-Geneviève, Abbey of, in Paris:
HW visits, 7. 305, 337, 348
Orléans, Duc d', passed last years at, 7. 305
Ste-Geneviève, church of, at Paris:
HW has not seen portail of, 32. 260
new front of, 35. 429
Voltaire buried at, 34. 117
Ste-Hermine, Henri-René-Louis (1743–87), Vi-
comte de; Marquis de Vervant:
Condé gives reversion of captaincy of the
guard to, 7. 441
St Elmo, castle (Italy):
Perroni released from, 18. 253n
Ste-Marguerite (Lérins), îles de:
France offers to Malta, 20. 406
French bombard, and capture it, 19. 406
Ste-Marguerite, Rue, in Paris:
Delage, tailor in, 39. 51
Ste-Marie, Dames de:
Stuart, Charlotte, prefers Abp of Bordeaux's
society to that of, 25. 513
Ste-Marie, Filles de. See Filles de Ste-Marie
Ste-Maure, Mme de. See Guérin, Marie de;
Sauvage, Victoire-Françoise de; see also St-
Maur, Mme
Ste-Ovide, Foire. See Foire Ste-Ovide
Ste-Palaye. See La Curne de Ste-Palaye
Ste-Pélagie:
prison, 3. 219
Saintes, Bp of. See La Rochefoucauld-Bayers,
Pierre-Louis de
St-Esprit, French ship:
Hood captures, 29. 250n
Jersey fights, possibly sinking it, 19. 82
St-Esprit, Hôtel du, in Paris:
HW lives at, 7. 263
HW's expenses at, 7. 399
proprietors of, see Menard, ——; Menard,
Mme
St-Esprit, Ordre du:
Beauvau receives, for storming Ft St Philip,
20. 579n
blue ribbon worn by, 4. 452n
ceremony of, at Versailles, 6. 127, 314, 441
'cordon bleu' of: 4. 452, 6. 2; Grimaldi re-
ceived, at Paris, 21. 560; mad foreigner
forbidden to wear, at Paris, 24. 361, 25.
572; Maupeou receives, 23. 259; received

by Bulkeley, **18**. 429n; sought by Vandières, **20**. 228
costumes of: Charlemont asks about representations of, in drawings, **42**. 156; imitated, **6**. 144, 152
Frenchman talks to Dane about, **35**. 241
HW to see installation ceremony of, **13**. 168
hall of, *see under* Grands Augustins, Convent of
investments in, **6**. 401, 403, **8**. 6, 37, 44, 46
portraits of knights of, at Grands Augustins, **7**. 276, **31**. 78, **42**. 155, 157
Poullain de St-Foix's history of, **15**. 111
promotion in, expected, **5**. 179, **6**. 2
reception of knights of, depicted, **7**. 276
St Estevan, galleon:
in Spanish fleet, **17**. 286
St-Eustache, church of, at Paris:
curé of, *see* Secousse, Jean-François-Robert
HW visits, **7**. 279
suicide in, **5**. 205
St Eustatia, Russian ship. See *Evstafïĭ*
St Eustatius, governor of. *See* Graef, Johannes de
St Eustatius, West Indies:
capture of, celebrated by firing guns, **36**. 192
Dutch not to be comforted for loss of, **25**. 152
Dutch ships from, **33**. 272n
England does not regard French goods at, as Dutch property, **21**. 268n
English fleet from, captured, **25**. 152, 159, **36**. 198–9
French property in, confiscated, **29**. 124–5
French 'purchase' of, from Cockburn, **25**. 235–6
French retake, **29**. 191
illumination for Rodney's capture of, **29**. 121
La Fortuna bound for, from Cadiz, **21**. 269n
merchandise taken by British at, said to be equalled by that taken by Spanish at Minorca, **25**. 189
Parliamentary inquiry into, **36**. 199
Rodney conquers, **25**. 139, 141, **29**. 121
—— plunders, **25**. 194n, 278
ships from: consigned to Leghorn, **21**. 269n; detained, **21**. 288n
St-Évremond. *See* Marguetel de St-Denis de St-Évremond
St-Fargeau, Comte de. *See* Le Pelletier, Michel-Étienne
St-Farre, Louis-Étienne (1759–1825), Abbé de, natural son of the Duc d'Orléans:
brother's plan to murder, **34**. 175–6
Coigny, Mme de, ridicules, for indecent story at George IV's, **34**. 155n
dines at Lord Rawdon's, **34**. 175–6
St Firenzo. *See* San Fiorenzo
St-Florent:
Lauzun goes to, **4**. 135n
St-Florentin, Comte de. *See* Phélypeaux, Louis (1705–77)
St-Foix, Philippe-Auguste de (d. 1779), Chevalier d'Arc:

Lettres d'Osman by, owned by Mme du Deffand, **8**. 35
St-Foix. *See also* Poullain de St-Foix
St-Fond. *See* Faujas de St-Fond
St François de Paule, order of. *See* Minimes
St-Gelais, Armande de (d. 1709), m. Charles, Duc de Créqui:
Richmond quarrels with, **7**. 357
St George, Bns. *See* Dominick, Elizabeth
St-George, Chevalier de. *See* James Francis Edward (Stuart), the Old Pretender
St George, Hon. Emilia Olivia (d. 1798), m. (1775) William Robert Fitzgerald, 2d D. of Leinster:
daughter born to, **6**. 421
St George, George (d. after 1769), army officer:
uncle not to prefer, **37**. 570
St George (formerly Usher), St George (ca 1715–75), 1st Bn St George:
Cole gives HW's letters to be delivered by, **32**. 21
conveys packet of HW's letters for Cole, **1**. 100
'St George' ('lesser George' of the Order of the Garter):
Bedford, D. of, wears, in button-hole, **10**. 235
St George, English ship:
Byng's trial on, in Portsmouth harbour, **21**. 39n
St George, Wright's privateer:
built at Leghorn, **21**. 21n
sequestered at Leghorn after fight off Monte Nero, **21**. 20n
St George, Fort. *See* Fort St George
'St George and the Dragon':
HW does not believe, **32**. 354, **33**. 580
Reynolds's picture of, **32**. 316, 337, 354
story of, **30**. 69
St-Georges, ——, French admiral:
Anson defeats squadron led by, **19**. 402n
St-Georges, Charles-Olivier de (1743–1828), Marquis de Vérac:
appointed French minister to Denmark, **6**. 90
St-Georges, Claude-Josèphe-Marie de (1742–75), m. (1764) Abel-Claude-Marthe-Marie-Cécile, Comte de Champrond; Marquis de Vichy:
Du Deffand, Mme, has social relations with, **6**. 188, 283
Paris visited by, **4**. 464–5, **6**. 188, 283
Wiart takes, walking, **6**. 283
St George's Chapel, Mayfair, London:
Ashe, Elizabeth, marries Wortley Montagu in, **20**. 289n
Hamilton marries Elizabeth Gunning in, **20**. 303
Keith the founder of, **20**. 241n
marriages at, **9**. 76n
sermon at, on Frederick, P. of Wales, **20**. 241, 243–4
Tracy and Susannah Owens married at, **9**. 76
St George's Chapel, Windsor Castle. *See under* Windsor Castle

St George's Church, Hanover Sq., London:
Coventry marries Maria Gunning in, **20.** 303n
Dodd offers bribe to Lord Chancellor for liv-
ing of, **32.** 185
parish of: Berkeley Sq. in, **30.** 355; Grosvenor
St in, **30.** 358
St George's Church, Queen Sq., London:
Swinburn active in vestry of, **40.** 84n
St George's Day:
Mann told not to wait for, before presenting
his memorial to Senate, **20.** 198
St George's Dragoons:
Smith, John, sergeant in, **19.** 274n
St George's Fields, London:
foot guards in, **23.** 12n
Gordon rioters assemble in, **25.** 53, **33.** 173
Gordon rioters attacked in, by Protestant
Association, **29.** 57, **33.** 192
guards fire on mob in, **23.** 20, 77, 98
Keppel family drive through, after Gordon
riots, **33.** 191
pantomimes in, **34.** 71n
St George's Hospital, London:
(?) Hertford reports no vacancy in, **39.** 352
Hunter, John, dies in, **12.** 38
——'s associates at, **15.** 244n
victim of fire lies in, **40.** 270n
Westminster Abbey concerts benefit, **25.**
647n
St George St, London:
Bute, Cts of, rents house in, for Lady Mary
Wortley Montagu, **22.** 3n
St-Germain, Chevalier de. *See* Foucault de St-
Germain-Beaupré, Armand-Louis-Joseph
St-Germain, ——, commandant at Daka:
Arabs waylay, **24.** 510n
St-Germain, Count (d. 1784), adventurer:
description of, after his arrest and release,
19. 181–2
Frederick, P. of Wales, curious about, **19.** 182
Giovanni Gastone de' Medici said to have
reared, **19.** 181n
HW's accounts of, **26.** 20–1
Rousseau resembles, **35.** 116
St-Germain, Claude-Louis (1707–78), Comte de,
French minister of war:
army under, to go to the lower Rhine, **21.**
438n
Blaye office not sought by, **6.** 251
Boufflers recommended by, **6.** 305–6
Du Deffand, Mme, describes, **6.** 226, 227
health of, **6.** 277
Louis XVI sees, **6.** 228, 295
Maillebois protected by, **6.** 322
Malesherbes said to favour, **6.** 227
Marie-Antoinette questions, about chevaux-
légers, **6.** 251
Maurepas confers with, **6.** 228
—— deferred to by, **6.** 251, 300
Mémoires of, **7.** 166, 172, 183
minister of war, **6.** 226
ordinances of, sought by Mme du Deffand
for Conway, **6.** 278, 331

pension of, **6.** 226
popularity of: **6.** 228, 230, 254, 277; diminishes, **6.** 272, 277, 365
projects of, ruined, **7.** 225
reforms of, **6.** 251, 254, 261, **7.** 226
resignation of, expected, **6.** 326, 365
retires, **6.** 479, 483
Rhine crossed by, at Wesel, **21.** 193n
war parley attended by, **6.** 459
St-Germain, Abbey of:
Bourbon, Abbé de, may obtain, **6.** 410
La Roche-Aymon controls, **6.** 404
prisoners in, **11.** 233n
St-Germain, Boulevard de:
St-Nicolas-du-Chardonnet near, **7.** 274
St-Germain, faubourg, in Paris:
Dal Pozzo, Mme, takes house in, **17.** 80n
HW 'rises' in, **14.** 156
Petit Hôtel d'Entragues in, **37.** 41
'Sévigné, Mme de,' urges HW to live in, **3.** 51
St-Germain, Foire. *See* Foire St-Germain
St-Germain, forest of:
Le Val in, **7.** 235
St-Germain-des-Prés, church of, in Paris:
antiques and rarities in, **42.** 287
Benedictines at: **22.** 325n; wish to discard
habits and rules, **39.** 2
HW recommends convent and collections at,
39. 204
HW visits, **7.** 290
St-Germain-en-Laye (France):
Artois obtains new château at, **6.** 397
Berrys go from, to Paris, **11.** 122n
Bulstrode died at, **17.** 11n
Charles II's letter from, **15.** 104
Court of: compared to Hampton Court, **33.**
42; HW assumes that Mme St-Jean was con-
nected with, **30.** 213
Hamilton dies at, **41.** 470
Fitzjames family at, **38.** 214
French nobleman exiled to, **23.** 298
Hoegger at, **6.** 424
Jacobites to move to England from, **9.** 24
Jerningham, Lady, at, **41.** 470
La Marck, Comtesse de, questions the Irish
at, **8.** 192
—— resident at, **5.** 337, **7.** 431
Le Boullingrin belongs to new château at, **6.**
397
Le Val near, **6.** 232, 397n, **7.** 176, 186, 239
Louis XIV's apartment at, near his sister-in-
law's, **4.** 120n, **41.** 155
Louis XV's accident near, **4.** 195–6
Magnan, Marquise de, from, **18.** 548
Marlborough implicated in schemes of, **20.**
322
Noailles may be exiled to, **5.** 63
pun on, **26.** 20, 21
Ward, Mrs, said to have died at, **5.** 332
St-Germain l'Auxerrois, church of, in Paris:
HW visits, **7.** 277
St-Germain l'Auxerrois, Rue:
Fort l'Évêque in, **6.** 134n, **19.** 450n

St Germano. *See* San Germano

St Germans, E. of. *See* Eliot, Hon. John

St-Gervais, Comte de:
SH visited by, 12. 222

St-Gervais, church of, in Paris:
HW visits, 7. 285

St Giles-in-the-Fields, church of, in London:
'Broad St Gyles's,' 2. 199
Gally, rector of, 28. 352n
St Giles's Pound near, 31. 302n

St Giles's Church (?Cripplegate), London:
Hardinge lives near, 35. 601
Piozzi, Mrs, writes as if she had never been out of parish of, 42. 244
Selwyn finds Moore and his whore buried in vault of, 20. 181

St Giles's Pound, London:
pen for stray animals, 31. 302n
Piozzi, Mrs, apparently educated in, 31. 302

St-Gilles, Mme de. *See* Coardi di Carpanetto, Caterina Maria Teresa

St-Giniez, near Marseille:
Simiane, Mme de, lives at, 34. 85, 43. 359

St Giorgio (Italy):
earthquake account mentions, 25. 376

St Giorgio Gate, at Florence:
Spaniards pass out by, 17. 342

St Giovanni. *See* John the Baptist, St; St John's Day; San Giovanni

St Giuliano (Italy):
Philip, Don, captures, 19. 84

St Gregory's Church, London:
Inigo Jones accused of demolishing part of, to make room for St Paul's, 40. 207n

St Hedwig's, Berlin:
built with contributions from Roman Catholics, 20. 329n

St Helena (island):
Bazett of, 11. 238n
woman of, thinks London must be deserted when fleet has sailed, 7. 364, 11. 249, 25. 110

St Helens, Bn. *See* Fitzherbert, Alleyne

St Helens, Isle of Wight:
Feilding arrives at, 29. 2n
Howe reported as returned to, 29. 266
Norris returns to, 13. 226n

St Hélier, Jersey:
Bentley designs town-house at, 35. 241
capture and recapture of, 39. 358, 359
'Druid' temple found at, 11. 75n

St-Hérem, Marquis de. *See* Montmorin, Jean-Baptiste-François de

St Hermandad, brotherhood:
pilgrims protected by, from robber knights on Spanish roads, 12. 40n
Ricardos should be officer of, 12. 40

Sainthill, Edward (d. 1782), of Bradninch, Devon:
Florence visited by, with Cholwick as his 'ass,' 35. 30
Mann to take, to Pratolino, 17. 484
Newcastle recommends, to Mann, 17. 483

'St-Honoré, Messieurs de la rue de.' *See* Parliament of Paris

St-Honoré, church of, in Paris:
HW visits, 7. 280

St-Honoré, Paris faubourg:
Mirepoix, Mme de, may rent house beyond, 7. 5

St-Honoré, Rue. *See* Faubourg St-Honoré, Rue du

Sainthood:
HW's reflections on, 31. 401

St-Hubert (France):
Du Deffand, Mme, mentions, 3. 337, 4. 257
Louis XV holds council at, 8. 169–70
visitors to: Choiseul, 8. 122; Choiseul, Duchesse de, 4. 137; Louis XV, 3. 292, 4. 238, 242–3, 430, 5. 84, 421, 8. 169–70; Louis XVI, 6. 110; Mirepoix, Mme de, 5. 421

St Hubert, Order of, of Bavaria:
Cowper gets George III's permission to accept, from Karl Theodor, 25. 470
—— to be installed in, 25. 568
HW ridicules Cowper for accepting, 25. 572, 646

St Hubert's Day:
Conway presented to Louis XVI on, 39. 205

St-Hyacinthe. *See* Cordonnier, Hyacinthe

St Iago. *See* Santiago

St Isidore, Irish church in Rome:
prayers at, for Young Pretender, 19. 171n

St Isidore. See San Isidoro (or Isidro)

'St Islée.' *See* Chantilly

St Ives, Hunts:
Ashton visits, 13. 116

'St Jack.' *See* St John

St-Jacques, Capuchin convent of, at Paris:
superior of, found with throat cut, 3. 50

St-Jacques, Rue du Faubourg. *See* Faubourg St-Jacques, Rue du

St James, Court of. *See* Court, English

St James's Chapel. *See* St James's Palace: Chapel Royal at

St James's Chronicle:
allegory on Rousseau from, read by Mme de Jonzac to Mme du Deffand, 3. 37
anti-Sejanus letters reprinted in, 32. 20n
Deyverdun's squibs in, on Hume-Rousseau quarrel, 40. 166n
'Friend to Rousseau's' letter in, not by Boswell, 43. 188
(?) HW does not read political letters in, 31. 74
(?) HW forced to believe, in Paris, 31. 68
HW's letter to Mayor of King's Lynn printed in, 13. 42, 44, 22. 531n
Llangollen ladies described in, 34. 94n
Rousseau's letter to editor of, 3. 9n, 22, 26
Walpole, Sir Edward, verses by, in, 43. 45

St James's Church, Piccadilly, London:
Cole used to walk from, to Bishopsgate St, 2. 198n
HW's parish, 19. 167n
Huntingtowers married at, 9. 301, 21. 439n

[St James's Church, *continued*]
Kidgell expects to become rector of, **14.** 130n
King St in parish of, **3.** 333n
Secker retains rectory of, until he becomes dean of St Paul's, **20.** 133n
——'s sermon in, **20.** 133n
—— to preach at, about earthquakes, **20.** 155
St James's Coffee-house, London:
Du Deffand, Mme, mentions, **3.** 229, 235
waiter at, says he could thrash Nivernais, **22.** 84
Worsley, Lady, gallantries of, aired in, **25.** 228
St James's Evening Post:
HW does not subscribe to, **32.** 84
HW parodies, **9.** 125–30
(?) HW's piece called 'Jocasta' sent to, **32.** 84
St James's House, London:
Gray, watchmaker at, **40.** 64n
St James's Magazine:
Bentley's epistle on decay of poetry printed in, **35.** 645
——'s *Epistle to Lord Melcombe* printed in, **10.** 57
——'s poem on Bendal Martyn's sonatas printed in, **35.** 645
St James's Market, London:
Fitzwilliam wedding postponement disappoints, **30.** 49–50
HW imagines Lord North in, **33.** 327–8
HW jokes about executions in, by French, **9.** 418
HW mentions, **9.** 365, **10.** 112
HW will not sit in, to await French invaders, **20.** 469
herbwomen in, **33.** 131
St James's Palace, London:
Albany, Cts of, presented at, **11.** 270
Anne of Denmark's canopies outnumber chairs of, **32.** 325
'arrant fear' at, **28.** 374
Augusta, Ps of Wales, does not occupy, **9.** 313
ball at: attended by George II and grandsons, **35.** 189n; for George II's birthday, **18.** 95n; for Karl Wilhelm Ferdinand's wedding and Q. Charlotte's birthday, **22.** 197, 199
Berwick introduced at, to George III, **38.** 406n
Brunswick, P. and Ps of, to lodge at, **32.** 16–17
Burdett meets Castle-Durrow at, **20.** 20
Burney, Fanny, addressed at, **42.** 293
—— wishes to see James Colomb at, **42.** 290
Bute does not relinquish keys of, to Pitt, **22.** 130
Caroline, Ps, spends years shut up in chambers at, **21.** 165n
Caroline of Brunswick, Ps of Wales, bows to public at, **12.** 139
Caswell, captain on guard at, **9.** 319
Chapel Royal at: choristers of, **35.** 209, **38.** 87; Coke, Lady Mary, attends, **31.** 297;

George II hears Denne's sermon at, **20.** 46n; George III advised to have thanksgiving in, **38.** 199–200; George III at, to hear Bp of Rochester, **38.** 526; Handel's Te Deum at, **35.** 39n; Kingston, Ds of, screams in, **24.** 150, **39.** 272; Markham preaches in, **29.** 129, 159; marriage contract of Ps Mary signed in, **37.** 61n; Mason reads prayers in, **29.** 349
Charlotte, Q., arrives at, **21.** 528, **38.** 116
——'s first impression of, **32.** 3
Chatham's crutch might draw circle around, **28.** 370
Christian VII at, **10.** 264, **23.** 41–2, 48, **35.** 326, **39.** 105
Coke, Lady Mary, attends Court at, **31.** 140
Court display at, **33.** 582
crowd near, as colliers pay tribute to George III, **32.** 185
Cumberland, D. and Ds of, denied attendance at, **32.** 65
Dashwood, Catherine, at, as Q. Charlotte's duenna, **21.** 531
Drawing-Room at: for Q. Charlotte, **38.** 115n; Hammond spreads news at, **33.** 199n
foreigners think that riot may endanger, **22.** 200
Fox, C. J., writes from, **42.** 73
Franklin should kick English to, **32.** 404
French mail robbed within call of guard of, **25.** 619
Garter chapter at, **22.** 227n
Garter king-of-arms reads war declaration at, **20.** 556n
gate of, HW does not know if Chatham is summoned to guard or to storm, **39.** 115
George II arrives at, from abroad, **18.** 340
—— keeps, mostly locked up, **20.** 88
—— returns to, **20.** 3n
——'s birthday celebrated at, in mourning, **20.** 280n
——'s oldest daughters live at, **34.** 260
——'s messages from, to Parliament, **35.** 216
George III and brothers to live at, **20.** 239
George III besieged at, by mob, **23.** 98
—— excludes D. of Cumberland's followers from, **23.** 358
——'s levee at, after illness, **38.** 526
—— to move to, **21.** 443
Gray, Sir James, seized by fit at levee at, **23.** 455n
great apartment at, enlarged for Q. Charlotte, **9.** 377
Grenville faction must divide spoils before storming, **22.** 489
Grenville's friends point to, **23.** 263
guards at: **23.** 12n; fire on Rigby and friends after assault, **30.** 330n
HW avoids, after niece's marriage to D. of Gloucester, **39.** 161
HW born near, **13.** 3
HW calls visit to, his 'greatest earthly joy,' **35.** 456

HW did not see James IV's portrait at, **16.** 322

HW dislikes, **35.** 227

HW ignorant of events at, **29.** 288, **37.** 122

HW jokes about Bentleys and Müntz at, **9.** 345

HW lives near, **17.** 279

HW prefers, to Norfolk, **18.** 218

HW summons guard from, to fire, **9.** 363

HW to call at, **9.** 305

HW to send his servant to Fanny Burney at, **42.** 296

HW will not accompany Rockingham ministry to, **35.** 317

HW will perhaps be seen at, **28.** 48

Harcourt at, to get mission to bring Q. Charlotte, **21.** 517n

—— should be tied and shipped to, **32.** 160

Henry VIII's ointment made at, **2.** 332

Hertford hints that HW might be employed at, **38.** 171

—— not surprised by news from, **38.** 574

'Indian idol' must not be abused at, **35.** 603

Jacobites entertained at, **21.** 409

Karl Wilhelm Ferdinand greets English soldier on way to, **22.** 197

—— not sorry to leave, **38.** 292

—— slights concert at, **38.** 287–8

Kensington pictures moved to, **9.** 377

Keppel attends levee at, **24.** 445n

ladies of the Bedchamber at, in hostile groups, **32.** 19

lawyers to guard royal family at, in George II's absence, **19.** 180

Leicester House no longer at odds with, **20.** 549

'little, tottering, ruined,' **33.** 360

London Common Council's affront to, **21.** 77

lord of the Bedchamber at, gets news of George III's health, **34.** 43

Mabuse's 'Adam and Eve' at, **15.** 96

Mann jokes about sending the Pope to, **22.** 390

—— wishes Francis III's pictures were at, **19.** 314

—— wishes the Genoese doge and senate to visit, **19.** 76

Mary, Q. of Scots' portrait at, **42.** 320

Mason mentions, **28.** 55

——'s appearance at, would provoke anonymous letters in bad verse, **29.** 364

merchants to present address at, **23.** 98–9

ministers in control of, **22.** 302

mob have not replaced George III by Pitt in, **21.** 541

Münchhausen heads German chancery in, **20.** 212n

Newcastle's return to, improper, **30.** 196

news of Carolina uprising pleases, **33.** 155

Northumberland, D. of, kisses hands at, **34.** 210

officers of, absent from Q. Charlotte's birthday ball, **39.** 374

Old Coachman, The, mentions, **18.** 22

Old Pretender born at, **17.** 450n

Orford, Cts of, may be lodged at, **19.** 72

paintings from Arnaldi collection would be worthy of, **21.** 479

Patriots used to think of Albano when dismissed from, **22.** 257

portrait of P. Henry at, **34.** 189

posterity will be indifferent to revolutions in, **22.** 303

princes at, **33.** 582

princesses spend summer at, **18.** 218

Queen's caudle in Drawing-Room at, **32.** 19, 29

Rich and Bp Keppel clash at, **38.** 294–5

Richecourt prefers Santi Apostoli to, **19.** 441

royal family not yet to move from Kensington to, **20.** 89n

Secker seeks preferment from, **20.** 187

secretary of state's office for southern department moved to, **22.** 176n

Shakespear, carpenter at, **16.** 197n

sombre, **9.** 324

'Stainberg' entertains at house near, **18.** 97n

Stratford's tragedy includes, **29.** 223

Suffolk, E. of, tries to force wife from, **31.** 420

Temple insolent at, **10.** 168

Thatched House Tavern near, **23.** 200

tyranny of, hinted at, **35.** 603

visitors throng to, **9.** 325

visitors to: Augusta, Ps of Wales, **18.** 343; Bedford, D. of, **17.** 338; Brunswick, P. and Ps of, **22.** 342; Frederick, P. of Wales, **18.** 340–1; Halifax, **17.** 338; Jacobites, **9.** 321; Lichfield, E. of, **9.** 321; Stanley, **9.** 319

Walpole, Sir Edward, would not visit, even if daughter were queen, **36.** 66

Walpole, Sir Robert, comes down from, for opening of Parliament, **24.** 361

—— does not go to, **17.** 403

Wotton carries memorial from, to Venice, **20.** 198

Young Pretender has not reached, **19.** 125

—— to meet brother at, **35.** 61

—— vows not to change linen till he lies at, **30.** 94

See also under Court, English

St James's Park, London:

'beaux flutter along,' **13.** 66

Buckingham House in, **29.** 205n

Charlotte, Q., and George, P. of Wales at opposite ends of, **11.** 227

Charlotte's arrival brings crowds to, **35.** 312

Chatham could be persuaded to walk through, **28.** 350–1

deputy rangership of: **36.** 157–8; corrected, **43.** 348, 367

Downing St house of Sir Robert Walpole looks out upon, **17.** 478

Duck Island in: **20.** 226; under Churchill as Ranger, **37.** 75n

encampment at, **33.** 207, 214

[St James's Park, *continued*]
Éon talks to people in, 22. 239
Estaing's defeat hailed in, 24. 545
fashionable ladies walk in, 34. 262
fire strews, with half-burnt grain, 11. 213
foot guards in, 23. 12n
Frederick, P. of Wales, and D. of Cumberland appear before mob in, 19. 288
Frederick, P. of Wales, sits under wall of, 20. 131
gates of, shut against mob, 23. 98
Godfrey, Mrs, seen in chair in, by HW, 25. 571
Gower walks in, 33. 131
guns in: announce victory, 33. 314; fired for Q. Charlotte's arrival, 35. 314n; for St Eustatius's capture, 36. 192; for Torgau victory, 21. 452n; never cool, 38. 105; ready to proclaim George IV's birth, 22. 52n
Hardinge, through HW and Orford, seeks ticket to ride in, 35. 549, 550, 557
Hervey, Bns, permitted to cross, 38. 75
Huntingdon may succeed Ashburnham as ranger of, 22. 113n
ladies mobbed in, 9. 94, 239–40
Le Nôtre, designer of, 28. 30n
Mathews wears tricolour cockade in, 18. 522
mob pursues Waldegrave to, 20. 156
Orford, 3d E. of, to be removed as ranger of, 25. 266
Pelham walks in, just before death, 20. 413
Pitt, Mrs George, mobbed in, 9. 94
rangership of: Orford, E. of, has, 43. 366, 374; vacated by Ashburnham and offered to Orford, 36. 37
Rosamond's Pond in, fit for suicides, 37. 189
Royal Library in, 33. 319
Sandwich crosses, 29. 123n
(?) Selwyn, John jr, meets Lord Conway in, 40. 27
sentinel in, accosted by mad parson, 17. 197
Shirley resigns deputy rangership of, to Lord William Gordon, 41. 378–80
tattered refugees in, 35. 123
tickets not made out for, till George III has one, 41. 350
Tracy and Susannah Owens meet in, 9. 75
Tracy chases girls in, 9. 74
trees in, uprooted by hurricane, 24. 431n
troops in, 29. 75
Wharton arrested in, 42. 10n
See also under Mall, the
St James's Place, London:
Damers live in, 20. 225n
Delany, Mrs, lives in, 33. 394n
Hervey, Bns, lives in, 1. 325n, 31. 104, 416, 33. 149n, 150n
house in, formerly Bns Hervey's, given to Col. Hervey, 33. 149
Rawdon's house in, 34. 175n
Smyth, John, of, 32. 351n
Stormont's house in, 6. 172n

Waldegrave, Lady Elizabeth, lives in, 34. 110n
St James's Square, London:
Amherst, Lady, lives in, 11. 230n
Clarendon's house in, 37. 28n
crowd in, to see Macclesfield lie in state, 38. 358
Germain, Lady Betty, lives in, 31. 81, 32. 38n
Gordon, Ds of, in, 11. 273n
Hardwicke's house in, 33. 202n, 400n, 41. 240, 241, 285
Hervey, Bp, rents house in, at high rate, 25. 455
illuminations in, 33. 93
James St at, 42. 492
Lee, Sir George, dies in, 21. 261n
Lincoln's house in, prepared for him, 17. 210n
Macclesfield's house in, 22. 211n
Norfolk, Ds of, opens new house in, 37. 438n
Pitt's house in, to be let, 38. 136n
—— writes from, 40. 170, 191
Ravensworth, Lady, dies in, 34. 198
—— has house in, 33. 435n
statue of William III to be erected in, 13. 85n
Strafford's house in, 35. 286n
Verelst lives in, 28. 63, 322, 333
Vere's house in, 25. 191n
Walpole, Sir Robert, moves into, 28. 470n
Wilmington dies at his house in, 18. 265n
Wynn's house in, 32. 371n
St James's St, London:
Almack's (later Brooks's) moves to, 28. 104n, 32. 67n
Arlington St near, 13. 3n
Carlisle's house in, 33. 237n
Charlotte's whereabouts unknown in, 35. 311
club opened in, 24. 186
Cocoa Tree Club in, 18. 186n, 43. 249
Comyns, Mrs, in, 9. 19
Conway wants snug cheap house near, 37. 184
fire in Bury St near, 35. 210
Fox's goods in, seized by creditors, 39. 376
Frankland's house in Bond St near, 33. 334
George II hates mob in, 21. 63
Gunnings lodge in, 11. 205, 307, 346
Harrington's house in, to be sold, 33. 97
Herries, banker in, 11. 250n
Herries, Lady, lives in, 11. 211n
Hobart, Mrs, invited guests from, 11. 290
Howe might parade his captives in, 12. 75
Ligne takes house in, 3. 333n
Lincoln's house in, 17. 300n
Maclaine lodges in, 20. 168
nabobs and American chiefs fill, 21. 518
Ossory, Lord, will bring news from, 34. 138
Pickerings in, 5. 331n
Richecourt takes P. Sherbatov's house in, 20. 90n
robbery near, 33. 334
Russell, Lord John, lives in, 11. 205n
'St Apollo's Street,' 11. 295

Savoir Vivre Club in, **32.** 205n
Sherwin's studio in, **29.** 185n
Smyrna Coffee-House in, **29.** 159n
Thatched House in, **32.** 103n, **33.** 30n
White's Chocolate House in, **13.** 75n
White's (Arthur's) Club in, **20.** 168, **25.** 483n, **35.** 209, **42.** 380
St January, Order of:
governor of Messina a knight of, **18.** 262n
St-Jean, ——, Mme du Deffand's attendant:
Du Deffand, Mme, dictates afternoon letters to, in Wiart's absence, **7.** 81
—— shares lottery ticket with, **7.** 422, 455
——'s legacy to, **8.** 6
(?) ——'s reader, **7.** 238
furniture in bedroom of, **8.** 17
(?) letters in handwriting of, **7.** 127–8, 232–3
wages of, **8.** 46
St-Jean, Mme:
HW assumes, to be Jacobite, **30.** 213
HW executes commission for Selwyn to, **30.** 210, 213, 217, 219
Selwyn's hints concerning, unflattering, **30.** 217
St-Jean, Gabrielle-Angélique Anquetin de la Chapelle de:
age of, **30.** 213
Marivaux lived with, **30.** 213
Selwyn's Mme St-Jean probably not the same as, **30.** 213
senility and garrulity of, **30.** 213
St-Jean. *See also* St John, 'old'
St-Jean-en-Grève, church of, in Paris:
HW visits, **7.** 285
St John, Vct. *See* St John, Sir Henry (1652–1742); St John, John (ca 1695–1748)
St John, Vcts. *See* Clarke, Hester (1723–52)
St John, Hon. Mr:
farces acted by, at Ampthill, **33.** 552n
St John, Mr and Mrs:
Foley knows, but says they are not the people Selwyn is looking for, **30.** 213
St John, 'old':
(?) Craons accompanied by, **17.** 414
HW and Princesse de Craon play faro with, **21.** 533
Mann receives offer from, to preside over cooks at coronation celebration, **21.** 533
suppers prepared by, for HW at Craon's, **21.** 33
St John, Anne (1614–96), m. (ca 1644) Henry Wilmot, 1st E. of Rochester:
brother of, **28.** 240n
Rochester's mother, **9.** 411n
St John, Anne (d. ca 1742), m. (before 1728) Giuseppe Grisoni:
brother says that he hears from, from heaven, **19.** 84
St John, Hon. Charlotte (b. 1762):
birth of, **38.** 143
St John, Edith:
Henry VII's aunt, **2.** 364n

St John, Hon. Elizabeth Barbara (d. 1833), m. (1795) Henry Vaughan, M.D., cr. (1809) Bt:
SH visited by, **12.** 251
St John, Hon. Elizabeth Louisa (ca 1744–1820), m. (1760) Sir William Bagot, 6th Bt; cr. (1780) Bn Bagot:
Guilford's illness delays wedding of, **9.** 293
(?) Montagu to be visited by, at Greatworth, **9.** 291
St John, Frederick (1734–87), 2d Vct Bolingbroke, 1751; 'Bully':
approaching marriage of, **30.** 137
Bedchamber position for, **22.** 569n
Bedford, Ds of, rouged by, for Coronation, **9.** 388
brother of, **4.** 73n, **22.** 553n
'Bully' nickname of, **30.** 252
confined in madhouse, **25.** 11
Coventry, Cts of, admired by, **9.** 185, 280
—— in love with, **35.** 163, 283
—— ostensibly mourned by, **9.** 307
death of, **39.** 334
divorce of, **11.** 82n, **22.** 567, **29.** 354n
favour of, at Bedford House, **31.** 71
Ferrers's trial attended by, **9.** 280
George III's coronation attended by, **9.** 388
Guilford, Cts of, fears that Cts of Coventry may marry, **9.** 203
HW jokes about previous attachments of, **30.** 137
HW mentions, **9.** 402
HW's anxiety about, **30.** 267
HW serves tea to, at SH, after Hampton Court visit, **39.** 104
HW sorry that Beauclerk is not in as much danger as, **30.** 269
health of: **33.** 107, 110; brain affected, **30.** 269
Hervey consults, about possible divorce, **39.** 105
madness does not terminate Bedchamber appointment of, **36.** 187
Mann to entertain, at dinner, **20.** 387
Newmarket visited by, **9.** 307
posturings of, **32.** 13
races, at Huntingdon, **10.** 92n
resignation of, expected, **30.** 196
Reynolds instructed by, about wife's portrait, **10.** 52–3
St John's portrait owned by, **42.** 126
Selwyn 'advises,' to seek rehabilitation by HW, **30.** 252
—— regrets absence of, from dinner party, **30.** 252
separation of, from wife, rumoured, **14.** 141
son of, **11.** 190n, **15.** 320n
Spencer, Lady Diana, to wed, disappointing Cts of Coventry **37.** 499
wife of, **5.** 392n, **9.** 377n, **15.** 270n, **16.** 280n, **22.** 148n, **24.** 524n, **28.** 244n, **42.** 490n
wife rouged by, for Coronation, **9.** 388
wife's acknowledgment of adultery will please, **30.** 250

[St John, Frederick (1734–87), *continued*]
wife's portrait supervised by, **10.** 52–3
Williams, Sir C. H., at Chelsea house of, **33.** 78n

St John, Hon. Frederick (1765–1844), army officer:
death of wife of, **11.** 190

St John, Hon. Mrs Frederick. *See* Craven, Arabella

St John, George Richard (1761–1824), 3d Vct Bolingbroke, 1787:
elopes with his half-sister, **34.** 56
illegitimate children of, **43.** 213
sister travels with, **15.** 320

St John, Hon. Henrietta (1699–1756), m. (1727) Robert Knight, cr. (1745) Bn Luxborough and (1763) E. of Catherlough:
(?) affair of, **17.** 126
Berry, Mary, inquires about, **11.** 64
corresponds with contemporary poets, **11.** 65
Dalton's affair with, **32.** 243–4, 283
gossip about, **11.** 65–6
Gray's *Elegy* not sufficiently admired by, **28.** 233
illegitimate daughter of, **32.** 244n
Letters of: **43.** 298; artfully concluded, **32.** 285; HW expects to be diverted by, **32.** 243; to Shenstone, disparaged by HW, **17.** 126n, **28.** 233

St John, Sir Henry (1652–1742), 4th Bt; cr. (1716) Vct St John:
(?) auction of effects of, **17.** 477
Custom House place of, bought from Ds of Kendal for his son, **20.** 18
daughter of, **11.** 65n

St John, Henry (1678–1751), cr. (1712) Vct Bolingbroke:
Aix-la-Chapelle to be visited by, **18.** 304
amusing, though vitriolic, **42.** 499
'apostle of the Stuarts,' **28.** 72
Bath, E. of, tells anecdote of, **7.** 354
British isles 'sold' by, to France, **18.** 247
Burke imitates, **9.** 380, **43.** 125
Bute's principles drawn from, **28.** 416
character of detestable, **25.** 7
Chesterfield discusses, **6.** 38
—— visits, **17.** 133n
Chetwynd agent to, **17.** 356
——'s friend, **10.** 117, **18.** 191, **22.** 544n
Cork's intimacy with, **20.** 452
Cornbury's letter from, **20.** 59
correspondence between Swift, Arbuthnot, Pope, and, published, **30.** 24
Craftsman, The, prints contributions by, **13.** 119n
Craftsmen written by, against Moses and St Paul, **20.** 454
Dissertation upon Parties, A, by, **20.** 59
dying, **20.** 291
Essays by, introduced by letter to Pope, **37.** 354
false prophet, **32.** 393

Familiar Epistle to the Most Impudent Man Living by: bound by HW in volume of tracts, **20.** 65n; replies to Warburton, **20.** 62n
faults of, **20.** 66
Ferrers thinks that religious notions should not have been published by, **21.** 401
forgotten, **19.** 460
Fraigneau lived with, **20.** 452
French Court receives secrets from, **18.** 247n
French negotiations of, shameful, **29.** 65
friend of, gives information to HW, **4.** 10
George I gives memorial of, to Sir Robert Walpole, **20.** 455
—— would have replaced Sir Robert Walpole by, **20.** 452, 455
George III's tutors governed by, after Bolingbroke's own death, **20.** 323
Grenville and D. of Bedford will be discredited like, **38.** 513
Groans of Germany may be attributed to, **37.** 112
HW asks, if Wilkes resembles, in courting Old Pretender, **22.** 290
HW calls: 'arch-fiend,' **25.** 6; 'rascal,' **25.** 7
HW interested in letters of, **17.** 1n
HW not to emulate, in making plans for next reign, **32.** 303, 306
HW's grandfather would have treated clerk of, with contempt if he assumed airs, **29.** 232
HW talks to Mildmay about, **10.** 150n
half-sister of, **11.** 65n
health of: cancer, **20.** 291; ill, **20.** 225
Heberden advised by, to burn Middleton's discourse on prayer, **15.** 303
impeachment of, **13.** 186n, 240
Jenkinson stigmatizes, **28.** 72
letters of: HW interested in, **17.** 1n; HW reads, **37.** 360; much commended, **30.** 25
Letters on the Spirit of Patriotism, on the Idea of a Patriot King, and on the State of Parties at the Accession of King George the First by: **35.** 613; Dartmouth comments on, **20.** 208; HW discusses, **20.** 59–62; Mallet writes preface to, **20.** 61n; Mann hopes to read, **20.** 76; Pope prints, and alters it, **20.** 59n, 61; Spence ridicules profit-making as motive of, **20.** 62n; Walpole, Horatio (1678–1757) to answer, **20.** 62
Letters on the Study and Use of History by, Mme du Deffand seeks HW's opinion of, **6.** 167
Letter to Sir William Wyndham by, **6.** 167, **20.** 452
Lyttelton a friend of, **20.** 61
——'s letters from, **20.** 59–60
—— tells, not to publish reflections against Sir Robert Walpole, **20.** 59
Mallet receives letter from, as a bribe, **20.** 62
Mann discusses, with E. of Cork, **20.** 452, 454
—— hopes to get anecdotes about, from E. of Cork, **20.** 452

Mansfield and Stone 'begotten' by, **28.** 72
Marlborough overborne by cabal of, **25.** 605
(?) Mason alludes to, **35.** 527
Mémoires secrets by, owned by Mme du Deffand, **8.** 35n
metaphysical writings of, ruin his reputation in England, **20.** 454–5
Middleton's discourse burnt by, **14.** 55n
Mirepoix, Mme de, invites, with HW, to dinner, **20.** 225
(?) *Miscellaneous State Papers* praises, **35.** 603
nephew of, **12.** 29n
Newcastle, D. of, may imitate, **22.** 442
Pitt, Anne, recommended by, to Frederick, P. of Wales, **31.** 1n
Pitt's respect for, declines, **20.** 59
Pope an idolator of, **25.** 6
—— often entertains, at Twickenham, **42.** 488, 490
—— persuades, to pay for printing book, **20.** 65–6
—— praises, **35.** 466
—— ranks, with Locke and Malebranche, **29.** 169
——'s friends attack, in pamphlets, **20.** 65
——'s satires hurt by influence of, **28.** 440
Pope, Swift, and, flatter one another, **35.** 568
Prior, subject of letter by, **2.** 344
Reflections Concerning Innate Moral Principles attributed to, **40.** 143
return of, unlucky, **17.** 134
Rolli, protégé of, **17.** 191n
Scott, Murray, and Cresset disciples of, **20.** 323n
Scott recommended by, as George III's under-preceptor, **20.** 203, 344
silver tubes used by, to ventilate bed, **20.** 203
sister of, **32.** 244
'Some Reflections on the Present State of the Nation' by, **37.** 354
Stone, Cresset, and Scott 'creatures' of, **20.** 343n
subordinates of, not as guilty as himself, **25.** 7–8
Suffolk, Cts of, relations of, with, **31.** 420
Swift begs, to punish pamphleteers, **14.** 183n
—— insolent to, **7.** 354
——'s letters from, **25.** 6–7
—— urged by, to burn history of Anne's reign, **21.** 184
Tencin, Mme de, steals dispatches of, **18.** 247n
Twickenham manor owned by, **12.** 257
Vernon introduced by, to Duchesse du Maine, **17.** 126
Villettes, Marquise de, second wife of, **7.** 354
Walpole, Sir Robert, annihilated the falsely boasted abilities of, **25.** 7
—— attacked by, in *The Craftsman*, **18.** 20n
—— excluded, **25.** 605
—— forgave, **16.** 20
——'s enemy, **2.** 126

—— treated ungratefully by, **20.** 452
Warburton, but not other bishops, to answer, **35.** 167
wife of: **9.** 21n, **28.** 403n; dies, **20.** 136
Windham's letter from, **37.** 354
works of, published, **35.** 167
St John, Hon. Henry (1738–1818), M.P.; D. of York's groom of the Bedchamber:
accompanies D. of York's body to England, **22.** 554
biographical information about, corrected, **43.** 87, 279
brother and, 'abominable' in Cts of Coventry's affair, **35.** 283
Du Deffand, Mme, aided by, in sending parcel, **4.** 77
—— discreet in conversations with, **4.** 82
—— receives parcels through, **4.** 73
——'s social relations with, **4.** 73
expresses about D. of York's illness must have been sent by, **22.** 556
ill at Rome, **22.** 231
Mann assured by, that D. of York remembers his request for Bath ribbon, **22.** 390
—— informed by: about D. of York, **22.** 244n, 245n; that D. of York will tour Germany and Italy, **22.** 408
—— praises, **22.** 223
——'s letter from, thanking him for attentions to D. of York, **22.** 230
wife may accompany, to America, **32.** 251
York, D. of, accompanied by, on Tuscan tour, **22.** 213, 220
—— considers, favourite servant, **7.** 366
—— dictates letter to, **7.** 366
—— has, as groom of the Bedchamber, **22.** 553n
——'s body attended by, **7.** 366
—— sends message by, to Mann, **22.** 417
—— taken by, to Monaco, **22.** 553
—— tells, to write regrets to Hertfords, **38.** 440
—— wishes to recommend, to George III, in dictated letter, **22.** 553
St John, Mrs Henry. *See* Bladen, Barbara
St John, Hon. Holles (d. 1738):
sister of, **32.** 244
St John, Johanna (d. ca 1704), m. (ca 1651) Sir Walter St John:
Bentley's witticism on, **28.** 239–40
Rochester's letters burnt by, **28.** 239–40
St John, John (ca 1695–1748), 2d Vct St John:
death of, **20.** 15, 18
father buys Custom House place for, **20.** 18
son of, **12.** 29n, **28.** 403n
widow mourns, **20.** 23
St John, Hon. John (? 1746–93), M.P.; writer:
biographical information about, corrected, **43.** 151, 354
contract of, for furnishing coaches, **33.** 268–9
death of, **12.** 29
St John, Lady Mary. *See* Ker, Lady Mary

St John, Sir Oliver (d. 1437):
descendants of, 9. 411n
St John, Oliver (d. 1582), 1st Bn St John of
Bletso:
Bentley's ancestor, 9. 411n
house of, in London, 1. 194
St John, Oliver (ca 1598–1673), chief justice:
Bolingbroke had portrait of, 42. 126
family of, 9. 411n, 28. 239n
St John, Oliver (ca 1691–1749), F. R. S.:
Carducci refuses to pay, 19. 84
confessor of, receives Latin letters, 18. 205
converted to Roman Catholicism, 17. 283n
estate of, made over to relative in return for
allowance, 17. 283n
George II cursed by, 19. 191
Great News to the Listening Jews by, 17. 292
Grisoni brother-in-law of, 17. 283n
Horton's correspondence with, about convert-
ing the Leghorn Jews, 17. 292
madman in religion, 17. 283
Mann harassed by, 18. 205
—— refuses money offered by, 17. 292
—— refuses pier glasses offered by, 17. 283,
292
—— saves library of, 17. 283, 292
——'s letter from, about Carducci and tes-
ticles, 19. 84
—— urged by, to unite churches of England
and Rome, 19. 358
Old Pretender's connections with, 17. 283n
poetry by, 17. 292
sister communicates to, from heaven, 19. 84
Trevor, Robert, relative of, 17. 283n
St John, Robert William (1791–1851), consul-
general at Algiers:
birth of, 11. 190
St John, St Andrew (1759–1817), 14th Bn St
John, 1805; M.P.:
Bedfordshire elects, 33. 226n
Fox, C. J., friend of, 33. 226n
St John. *See also* St-Jean
St John, gates of. *See* Baptistery, at Florence:
gates of
St John family:
Bentley related to Rochester through, 9. 411
St John of Jerusalem, Knights of (Knights of
Malta):
Albergotti, Girolamo, is, 17. 111n
Beauvau, Chevalier de, is, 18. 298n
books concerning, 1. 248–53, 257–9
Broglie's children ineligible for, from wife's
low birth, 33. 393
cardinal honoured by presence of, in his ante-
chamber, 21. 380
Cole thanked for notes on, 1. 265
Conti, Grand Prior of, 3. 15n
France offers Îles de Ste-Marguerite to, 20.
406
Grand Master of, *see* Pinto de Fonseca,
Manuel
HW jokingly compares requirements of, to
those for Norfolk House parties, 9. 331

knighthood in, purchasable, 40. 18
Naples disputes with, 20. 405–6
Novillars is, 10. 11
sovereignty over Malta claimed by, derived
from Charles V, 20. 405n
tombs of, have cross-legged effigies, 35. 146
wills of, invalid without permission of the
Order, 17. 110
See also under Malta, *and under* Vertot,
René-Aubert de
St John's, near Montreal, Canada:
Americans capture, 32. 284n
English force in, 24. 347n
Montgomery said to have captured, 24. 157,
161
St John's Church, Bristol. *See under* Bristol
St John's Church, Paddington, London:
Fitzgerald buried at, 11. 266n
St John's College, Cambridge:
Baker's expulsion from fellowship at, 2. 98,
341, 343, 344, 346–7
——'s MS history of, *see* Baker, Thomas:
'History of the College of St John the
Evangelist'
——'s residence in, 2. 344
Brooke, fellow of, 15. 299
Cole procures information from, 2. 174
divided in election, 2. 167
elms of, damaged, 2. 136
Exeter attends, 10. 344, 345
fellow-commoner of, defends Sherlock, 15. 302
Hoccleve's portrait of Chaucer not in, 14. 108
Holbein painting found in lodge of, 14. 148
inscription in books given by Baker to, 2. 351
Jenkin, late fellow of, 15. 300
—— master of, 10. 346
library of, Baker's notes in volume in, 2. 344
lodge of, 2. 235
MS register of, 2. 69, 250
Nichols's articles on, 2. 182
portraits of Lady Margaret Beaufort at, 14.
114
Prior's fellowship at, 2. 341
Rutherforth, fellow of, 15. 300
students of, worthy men, 13. 58
treasures of, 15. 19
St John's College, Oxford. *See under* Oxford
University
St John's Day, Florentine festival:
celebrations on, 17. 78–80, 454, 456, 463,
35. 28
drawing of, sent to HW, 18. 81
eve of, Mann writes on, 18. 462
Florentine senators avoid, 18. 251
Gerini to return on, 17. 68
HW's plans for, 17. 29
Leopold to visit Florence on, 22. 427
Mann takes Mrs Bosville to, 18. 251
—— writes on, 17. 69, 453
operas on, 17. 79–80, 449, 454, 463, 18. 435,
439, 445
races held on: 17. 79, 454, 456, 18. 251, 462;
at Port Mahon, 37. 311

Richecourt's orders about celebration of, **19**. 8

See also under John the Baptist, St; San Giovanni

St Joseph, Spanish register ship:

capture of, **24**. 543

St Joseph, church of, at Paris:

Choiseul-Beaupré, Comte Hippolyte de, married in, **21**. 450

St Joseph, Convent of, in Paris; Mme du Deffand's home:

Angosse, Marquis and Marquise d', live at, **7**. 131, 139–40

buildings demolished on right-hand side of court of, **6**. 72, 207

buildings erected on right-hand side of court of: **6**. 176, 207; filled, **6**. 348, 431

chapel of: **7**. 289; Mme du Deffand's tribune opening into, **5**. 54, 73, 159n, **6**. 180; HW's bootikins to hang in, **6**. 124

'chez l'époux de Marie,' **4**. 291

Cholmondeley, H. F., to return to, **4**. 400

Cholmondeley girls at, **4**. 217, 220, 223, 225

company at, **4**. 294, **41**. 42

description of, **8**. 3–4, 56

Du Barry, Vicomtesse, to live at, **7**. 184, 434

Du Deffand, Mme, has 'petit cabinet bleu' in, **7**. 314, **41**. 34

—— lives at, **5**. 159n, **8**. 56n, **30**. 220, **34**. 82, **41**. 348

—— moves to, **8**. 53

—— rents apartment at, for Marquis and Marquise d'Aulan, **7**. 84–5, 94, 122, 126

——'s apartment at: **3**. 12n, 55, 104, **4**. 88, 217, 221, **8**. 3–4, 5, 8; blue cabinet in, **7**. 314, **41**. 34; lease of, **8**. 41; plan of, **6**. 180

——'s 'compatriots' of, **4**. 275

——'s horses return to, after accident, **3**. 55

——'s tribune opening into chapel of, **5**. 54, 73, 159n, **6**. 180

fire-escape facilities of, **6**. 180

fire in Mme du Deffand's apartment at, **6**. 176, 180

Fontainebleau draws visitors away from, **36**. 54

gateman at, **3**. 55, **7**. 412

Grave lives at: **3**. 210; in apartment above Mme du Deffand's, **34**. 82

HW addresses Hon. Thomas Walpole at Mme du Deffand's at, **36**. 173, 175

HW addresses Mrs Cholmondeley at, **36**. 54

HW describes, **8**. 56

HW hears midnight mass at, **7**. 289, **39**. 233

HW mentions, **3**. 113

HW's lackey returns from, **39**. 271–2

HW wishes again to see company at, **41**. 42

La Galissonnière, Mme de, rents apartment in, **3**. 19

lodging at, offered by Mme du Deffand to: Greville, Mrs, **5**. 323, 330, 351, 358; HW, **3**. 108, 113, 115, 119–20, **4**. 376, 391, 395, **30**. 220; Taaffe, **5**. 231, 242, **8**. 3

lodging at, to be sublet, **5**. 330, 358, 369–70

Maulévrier's apartment at, at Mme du Deffand's disposal, **4**. 351, 376, 391

nuns of, aroused by Mme du Deffand's rage at cook, **39**. 269

occupants of, attend ball, **4**. 415

Orléans, Bp of, lodges Mlle Guimard in, **23**. 324–5

privies of, emptied, **4**. 37–8

St-Chamans, Mme de, lives at, **7**. 139, 184

society in, **7**. 51

stables of, demolished, **6**. 5

Talmond, Princesse de, lives at, **20**. 44n

'Tonton' despotic at, **39**. 370

vacant apartment in, **3**. 12, 19

Wiart remains temporarily at, after Mme du Deffand's death, **7**. 250, 253

Young Pretender's chief hiding-place for 3 years, **20**. 44n

St Julian's, Monmouthshire:

Herbert of, **14**. 126n, **40**. 356n, 358

St-Julien, Comtesse de. *See* Laage, Marie-Anne de

St-Julien, Mme de. *See* La Tour, Anne-Madeleine-Louise-Charlotte-Auguste de

St-Just (France):

suitable for overnight stay, **37**. 40

St Kilda:

Grange confines wife on, **14**. 244n

St Kitt's. *See* St Christopher

St-Lambert, Jean-François (1716–1803), Marquis de:

Beauvau, Prince and Princesse de, patrons of, **4**. 216–17

Clément's attack upon, **5**. 195

Du Deffand, Mme, mentions, **4**. 217

——'s opinion of, **4**. 216

Fables orientales by: **43**. 89; HW comments on, **4**. 214

Foljambe not to be recommended to, **28**. 50

HW attends theatre with, **7**. 303

Saisons, Les, by: **35**. 233; Du Châtelet, Mme, lends, to HW, **4**. 213; Du Deffand, Mme, cites, **7**. 31, 74, 94, 170, 190; Du Deffand, Mme, comments on, **4**. 205, 209, 216; Du Deffand, Mme, sends, to HW, **4**. 205, 207, 212, **36**. 49; 'four fans spun out into a Georgic,' **39**. 233; HW comments on, **4**. 213–14; person 'slept against,' **39**. 233

Sarah, Th . . . by, **39**. 21

social relations of, in Paris, **6**. 268, 303, 381, **7**. 304, 318, 329, 431

verses by: for Mme du Deffand's gift to Mme de Luxembourg, **7**. (?) 2, 97; (?) sung by 'Pompom' at Mme du Deffand's, **7**. 2

St-Landri, church in Paris:

HW visits, **7**. 277

St Laurance, English schooner:

Plymouth reached by, from Boston, **39**. 238

St Laurence, church at Florence. *See* San Lorenzo

St-Laurent, Mme de:

Mme du Deffand's social relations with, **7**. 323

St-Laurent, Jean-Baptiste (d. 1782), Chevalier de:
(?) Mme du Deffand's opinion of, 3. 369
(?) social relations of, in Paris, 4. 279, 7. 272, 316, 320, 322, 323, 332
St-Laurent (France):
French forces at, 19. 336
St Lawrence, Gulf of (Canada):
Perrier de Salvert thought to be bound for, 20. 538n
St Lawrence River:
Amherst proceeds down, 9. 308n
English fleet said to be destroyed in, 21. 344
English ships must quit, in winter, 21. 357
France claims entire watershed of, 20. 468n
—— tries to keep fishing rights to, 21. 526n
St-Lazare, Chevaliers de:
promotion of, 7. 423
St-Lazare. See also St-Nazaire
St Lazaro. See San Lazaro
St Leger, Anthony (d. 1786), army officer:
(?) HW mentions, 7. 142
St Leger, Arthur Mohun (1718–50), 3d Vct Doneraile, 1734; M.P.:
comptroller to Frederick, P. of Wales, 19. 388
Frederick, P. of Wales's lord of the Bedchamber, 17. 251n
Kildare's proposals for raising regiments read by, 19. 155
Lyttelton plagued by, in Parliamentary committee, 19. 388
Parliamentary speeches by: hinting at impeachment, 17. 354; on privately-raised regiments, 26. 14
Pulteney holds, to promise about Westminster election voting, 17. 251
St Leger, Barry Matthew (b. 1733):
(?) dinner given by, 20. 260
(?) sharper ducked by, 20. 260
St Leger, Henry (ca 1722–43):
death of, 40. 43
St Leger, Jane (1719–41), m. (1739) John Dodd:
death date of, corrected, 43. 313, 359
HW praises, 30. 27
St Leger, Sir John (d. 1743), Kt, 1701:
(?) son of, 20. 260
St Leger, (?) John (1726–69):
Craon's letter to Mme de Mirepoix recommends, 20. 55–6, 64, 77
'romping greyhound puppy,' 20. 64
St Leger, John Hayes (1756–1800), army officer:
(?) arrest of, for riot, 25. 565
(?) HW mentions, 7. 142
St-Léger, forest of:
St-Hubert near, 3. 292n
St Leger family:
HW and Lady Ossory remember, 34. 170
St Leonard's Hill, Clewer, Bucks:
HW has not seen, 10. 44
HW wishes Montagu would buy, 10. 44

Montagu visits, admires, and might buy, 10. 42
St Leonard's Hill, Windsor Forest, Berks:
Gloucester, D. and Ds of, at, 5. 346, 32. 132
Gloucester, Ds of, lodged at, 4. 9n
—— writes from, 36. 66, 82, 88, 323
Gloucester Lodge the new name for, 36. 88
St Loe, Lady. See Hardwick, Elizabeth
St Loe, Sir William (d. 1564 or 1565):
wife inherits property of, 9. 298, 40. 182
St Lorenzo. See San Lorenzo
St-Louis, Île de, at Paris:
Hôtel de Lambert on, 7. 337
St Louis, Ordre de:
Croix de: Beauvau wins, 18. 216; Louis XV said to have given, to Brown, 19. 217; Montagu compares Bedford's ornament to, 10. 235; Pilâtre de Rosier said to have carried, 25. 590
elections to, 6. 412
grand cordon rouge of, worn by Grands-Croix and commandeurs, 20. 27n
St-Louis-du-Louvre, church of, in Paris:
Fleury's tomb in, 39. 203
HW visits, 7. 280
Richelieu's statue in, 4. 471
St-Louis-Couture, Jesuits' church in Paris:
Condé's tomb at, 39. 203
St-Louis-en-l'isle, Rue, in Paris:
Hôtel de Lambert in, 7. 337n
St Lucia (West Indies):
attack on, 24. 424n
English capture, 7. 117n, 135, 24. 447, 449, 454, 33. 94
epidemic at, attacks English forces, 24. 475
Estaing does not capture, 7. 117
——'s failure to save, ridiculed in Paris, 24. 450
France agrees to peace terms except about, 22. 55n
peace negotiations include, 21. 526n
St Luke's Hospital, London:
Battie physician to, 13. 6n, 123n
St-Lunaire Bay, France:
English land at, 21. 243
St-Magloire, seminary of, in Paris:
Orvilliers retires to, 7. 176n
St-Maigrin, Marquis (later Duc) de. See Quélen de Stuer de Caussade, Paul-François de
St-Maigrin, Marquise (later Duchesse) de. See Pons, Antoinette-Rosalie de
St-Maime, Comte de. See Félix d'Ollières, Jean-Baptiste-Louis-Philippe de
St-Malo, Bp of. See La Bastie, Jean-Joseph Fougasse d'Entrechaux de
St-Malo (Brittany):
bread at, described, 12. 77
cannon lacking for, 37. 538
Caraman's letters from, to Mme du Deffand, 7. 158, 425, 426, 428, 430, 432, 433, 459
commission at, relinquished by Louis XV, 7. 303

Conway investigates, 39. 343
Duke of Cumberland captured and taken to, 21. 75n
England threatened from, 24. 502
English attempt upon: ridiculed by Downe, 37. 545; satirized by HW, 35. 287–9
English burn vessels at, 21. 212–13
English expedition against: 21. 210–11, 212, 218, 223, 228, 243, 245, 37. 533–4, 569–70, 39. 526; brings sickness back with it, 37. 550
English failure at, 37. 535–7
French embarkation prepared at, 28. 457n, 39. 336
French said to be preparing Jersey attack at, 39. 349n
Marlborough abandons teaspoons in retreat from, 21. 221
Moira's expedition supposed to sail to, 12. 71
Montbarey visits, 7. 422
Paris fireworks to celebrate victory at, 21. 246
Pitt never intended to capture, 21. 213
prisoners transferred from Dinant to, 12. 77
quatrain on English attack on, 21. 244
St-Cast near, 7. 366n
secret expedition diverted from, to Cancale on Breton coast, 21. 205n
unpaving of, for defence, 37. 502
Walpole, Edward performs bravely at, 21. 240
St-Marc:
Œuvres by, owned by Mme du Deffand, 8. 33
St-Marc, Rue, in Paris:
Hôtel de Luxembourg on, 3. 22n
St-Marcel, Comtesse de. *See* Albon, Julie-Claude-Hilaire-Françoise d'
St Marco. *See* San Marco
St Margaret's Church, Westminster:
crucifix removed from window of, 10. 339–40
east window of, 43. 115
painted windows of, 2. 186n
roundhouse at, scaffold from, to church, rented for Coronation, 21. 536
window in, defended by Wilson, 41. 142
St Mark's, Venice:
library of: Chute has seen, 18. 63; Houghton gallery's ceiling copied from, 18. 63
St Mark's. *See also* San Marco
St-Marsault. *See* Green de St-Marsault
St-Marseill. *See* San Marcello
St-Martin, Marquise de. *See* Beauvau, Élisabeth-Charlotte de
St-Martin, Rue, in Paris:
St-Merry church in, 7. 282n
St Martino. *See* San Martino
St Martin's, Abbot of. *See* Montagu, Walter (ca 1603–77)
St Martin's Day:
Mann writes on, 17. 178
St Martin's-in-the-Fields, church in London:
Amelia, Ps, takes sacrament at, as ranger of Hampton Court, 20. 29n
HW indifferent to identity of churchwarden of, 33. 319

parish of: Ashe, Elizabeth, of, 20. 289n; Christian of, 16. 181n; said to include overseas areas, 23. 551, 25. 357–8, 642, 33. 302, 382; Yonge promotes troop-raising by, 26. 15
Rose's monument in, 42. 45n
Thorold abjures Roman Catholicism in, 22. 380
vicar of, *see* Pearce, Zachariah (1690–1774)
Violante's descent from steeple of, 25. 450
Young Pretender's alleged conversion in, 22. 324, 368, 380
St Martin's Lane, London:
Dixwell, J., bookseller in, 22. 216n
Faden lives in, 16. 194
Gordon riots thought to set fire to, 29. 56, 33. 187
Hamilton's studio in, 32. 140n
Palmer, glazier in, 20. 396n
Strange probably lives in, 24. 24
St Martin's Roundhouse, London:
women confined in, by drunken constables, 17. 504
St Martin's St, London:
residents in: Burney, 16. 121n, 42. 171; Hyde, 29. 58n
St Martin's Summer:
Florentines prolong villeggiatura till, 20. 451
war revives with, 37. 178
St Mary Abchurch, church in London:
Williams requests rectorship of, 1. 224
St Mary Axe, church in London:
Hindustan may be peopled by colony from parish of, 23. 551
St Mary Isle, Kirkcudbright; Lord Selkirk's seat:
John Paul Jones plunders, 24. 377
St Mary-le-Bow, church in London:
Minorca said to be in parish of, 23. 551n
monument to Q. Elizabeth in, 2. 202n
St Mary-le-Strand, church in London:
round portico of, 35. 144
Young Pretender's alleged conversion in, 22. 324n
St Mary Redcliff, church at Bristol. *See under* Bristol
St Mary's, Cambridge:
Gray attends, 13. 67
St Mary's, Oxford. *See under* Oxford
St Mary's, Warwick. *See under* Warwick
St Mary's, Whitechapel, London (St Mary Matfelon):
Welton, rector of, has Fellowes depict White Kennett as Judas, in altarpiece, 13. 86n
St Mary Steyning, London:
rector of, 11. 141n
St Matthew's Church, Friday Street, London:
Burton, incumbent at, 16. 65
Lort, rector of, 1. 281n, 16. 137n
St-Maur, Mme de. *See* La Marche, Anne-Françoise de; La Marche, Marguerite de; La Marche, Marie-Anne de; *see also* Ste-Maure, Mme de

St-Maur (France):
Nivernais to visit Mme de Rochefort at, **41.** 19–20, 21
Rochefort, Mme de, writes from, **41.** 21
St-Mauris, Alexandre-Marie-Léonor de (1732–96), Prince de Montbarey:
department of stables granted to, **7.** 453
dispatch council joined by, **6.** 359
health of, **7.** 124
leaves Paris, **7.** 422
made member of Ordre du St-Esprit, **7.** 14
Marie-Antoinette has Du Châtelet replace, as war secretary, **33.** 264n
St-Germain's associate, **6.** 277
St-Malo visited by, **7.** 422
social relations of, with Duchesse de Choiseul, **7.** 330
war parley attended by, **6.** 459
St-Mauris, Claude-Anne-François de (1701–81), Chevalier de Montbarey:
HW's correspondence with Voltaire approved by, **4.** 117–18
retort of, **4.** 134
social relations of, in Paris, **4.** 117–18, **7.** 332, 334
St-Mauris, Marie-Françoise-Maximiliane de (1761–1838), Princesse de Montbarey, m. (1779) Heinrich Karl Ludwig, P. of Nassau-Saarbrücken:
marriage of, **7.** 180–1
(?) marriage of, rumoured, **6.** 499
St-Merry, church of, in Paris:
HW visits, **7.** 282
St-Mesme. *See* L'Hôpital-St-Mesme
St Michael ('Mitchell'), Cornwall:
election at, **29.** 30n
HW's quarrel with E. of Orford over disputed election at, **30.** 168–9
St Michael's, Mile End, London:
Lort rector of, **16.** 137n
St Michael's, Wood St, London:
rector of, **11.** 141n
St Michael's Alley, London:
Gray's house in, **13.** 95n
St-Michel, Ordre de:
Pilâtre de Rosier expected, **25.** 590
St-Nazaire (France):
Young Pretender embarks at, **19.** 86
St-Nectaire, Henri de (1600–81), Maréchal de la Ferté:
jealousy of, **7.** 275–6
wife of, **3.** 169n
St-Nectaire. *See also* Senneterre
St-Nicaise, Rue, in Paris:
'Magasin, Le,' probably in, **3.** 201n
St-Nicolas-du-Chardonnet, church in Paris:
Du Deffand, Mme, baptized in, **8.** 44
HW visits, **7.** 274
St Ninian's, near Stirling, Scotland:
rebels' magazine in church at, **19.** 208n
St-Odile, Barone di. *See* Poirot, Domenico Matteo

St-Omer, Bp of. *See* Chastenet, Jean-Auguste de (1740–1815); Conzié, Joachim-François-Mamert de (1736–95); Conzié, Louis-François-Marc-Hilaire de (1732–1804)
St-Omer (France):
actors send messenger to D. and Ds of Cumberland at, **23.** 520
Cumberland, D. of, insulted at, by players from Calais, **32.** 151
director of coaches at, **5.** 160n
Gastaldi lives at, **20.** 275n
Jesuit college at, **28.** 322
MSS burnt at, **15.** 103n
Thicknesse's abuse on inn window at, **7.** 315
visitors to: Conway, **39.** 536; Craufurd, **5.** 294; Cumberland, D. and Ds of, **23.** 520, **32.** 151; HW, **7.** 315, 342; Scott, David, **39.** 536
Saintonge:
regiment of, assigned, **7.** 212
St-Osyth, Essex, E. of Rochford's seat:
HW to visit ruined abbey at, **9.** 88
Rochford dies at, **25.** 191n
St-Ouen (Paris suburb):
HW to sup at, with Mme Necker, **32.** 259
Necker's home at, **5.** 388, **6.** 51, 191, 216, 318, **7.** 346, 348
visitors to: (?) Albaret, **6.** 229, **7.** 348; Beaune, **6.** 357; Du Deffand, Mme, **5.** 388, **6.** 51, 81, 82, 191, 216, 224, 229, 320, 342, 357; Le Texier, **6.** 82; Luxembourg, Mme de, **6.** 224, 229; Marchais, Baronne de, **6.** 82; Marmontel, **6.** 229; Mirepoix, Bp of, **7.** 348; Mirepoix, Mme de, **3.** 122–3, 127; Raynal, **6.** 229; Strogonov, M. and Mme, **6.** 229
St-Ouen (France), château of Prince de Soubise:
account of, **3.** 122n
Louis XV at, **3.** 122
St-Palais. *See* La Curne de Ste-Palaye
St Patrick, Order of:
Charlemont told by HW to have portraits done of members of, **42.** 155–7
George III institutes, **25.** 365
St Patrick's Cathedral, Dublin. *See under* Dublin
St Paul (formerly Paul), Horace (1729–1812), Col.; secretary of English embassy at Paris:
Channel crossing of, stormy, **6.** 280
Craufurd instructed by, as to how to send tea, **5.** 305, 307
Dalton killed by, in duel, **9.** 113
departure of, imminent, **6.** 262, 263, 266
Du Deffand, Mme, may appeal to, for Lady Fenouilhet, **5.** 371
—— never sees, **6.** 178
—— receives news from, **6.** 41, 198, 392
——'s commissions will be executed by, **6.** 248
—— seeks information from, **6.** 262
—— sends letter through, **5.** 326, **6.** 190, 313
—— sends parcels through, **5.** 326, 420, **6.** 23, 26, 179, 182, 185, 197, 308, 411, **7.** 10

——'s opinion of, **5.** 363, **6.** 18, 310
—— to have sent letter by, **6.** 271, 272, 276
—— to send letter by, **6.** 266
—— to send parcels through, **5.** 320, 411, **6.** 401, 418
HW and, **43.** 100
HW receives Olonne portrait from, **6.** 280
HW secures place at Versailles through, **7.** 343n
HW sends goods through, **5.** 317
HW sends letter by, **5.** 308, 332, **6.** 297
HW to meet Lady Mary Coke at house of, **31.** 182
HW to receive Olonne portrait through, **6.** 251, 254, 255, 260, 262, 263, 266, 267, 269, 271
HW to send letter by, **6.** 291, 295
health of, **6.** 231
marriage of, **6.** 18, **43.** 96
minister plenipotentiary to France, **6.** 301
Orford's condition reported to, **5.** 403
Paris to be visited by, **6.** 291, 292
—— visited by, **6.** 297
Rochford instructs, to observe Aranda's conduct, **24.** 101n
social relations of, in Paris, *see index entries ante* **8.** 504
Stormont asks, to tell Mme du Deffand of his engagement, **6.** 308
Versailles visited by, **7.** 343
St Paul, Sir Horace (1775–1840), Bt:
birth of, **6.** 18n, **43.** 96
St Paul, Mrs Horace. *See* Weston, Anne
St Paul. *See also* Noizet de St-Paul
St Paul, English sloop:
American news arrives on, **39.** 225, 226
St-Paul, church of, at Paris:
curé of, *see* Gueret, N. P.
Du Deffand, Mme, married at, **8.** 30
HW visits, **7.** 310
St-Paul, Rue de, in Paris:
church of St-Paul in, **7.** 310n
St Paul's Cathedral, London:
aviators might break necks trying to fly from, **37.** 551
Bayly minor canon of, **15.** 301
Bourchier's 'Constitutions' issued at, **41.** 222
Cavallini's alleged work at, **42.** 67
Chatham, E. of, may be buried in, **2.** 80, 82, **24.** 382
Church, Thomas, prebendary of, **15.** 298
Cornwallis, dean of, **13.** 184n
'Dance of Death' carved in chapel of, **16.** 47
'Dance of Death' painted in cloister of, **16.** 143–4
deanery of: **29.** 188, 192; Secker covets, **20.** 133n, 187; Thurlow asks North for, for Bp Thurlow, **39.** 388
Donne's monument in, **1.** 7n
door-case of, imitated in SH library, **35.** 164
Dugdale's history of, *see under* Dugdale, Sir William
'Duke Humphrey's Walk' in, **43.** 128

Elizabeth, Q., goes to, after Armada triumph, **12.** 33
Englishmen who never visited, go to see St Peter's at Rome, **23.** 213
festival at, **25.** 71n
Franklin said to have machine that could destroy, **28.** 287
from St Peter's to, **13.** 195
George II does not visit, on peace proclamation, **20.** 46
HW enters St Peter's with as little emotion as at, **13.** 199
HW imagines, in ruins, **28.** 393
height of, **12.** 56
Johnson's monument in, **11.** 277n
Jones, Inigo, accused of demolishing part of St Gregory's Church to make room for, **40.** 207n
Lort, prebendary of, **2.** 253n
Louisbourg standards carried to, **21.** 237, 238, **37.** 567
Mason would like to preach before George III in, **28.** 215
Newton, dean of, **2.** 304n
North Briton advises George III not to go to, **38.** 199–200
Northesk takes daughter to, **35.** 373
nudity of, **2.** 80, 82
(old), picture of procession to, **2.** 216, 217
'Patapan' should face bishop's throne in, **35.** 41
Somerset tears down chapels of, to build Somerset House, **16.** 47
Stowe stairs as high as, **39.** 127
Strong, Edward and Thomas, master masons of, **40.** 350n
Taylor, prebendary of, **14.** 115n
Te Deum at: George III would go to, **32.** 389; Scipio less attractive at, than playing leap-frog, **33.** 552
thanksgiving at, for Dettingen victory, **35.** 39, 41
Thornhill's decoration of dome in, **41.** 76
traveller may view ruins of, **24.** 62
Wren's genius shown by, **40.** 347
——'s visits to, **40.** 350, 354
St Paul's Church, Covent Garden, London:
Murray persuades mob to break windows in vestry of, **20.** 225n
O'Brien marries Lady Susan Fox Strangways at, **22.** 219, **38.** 367
St Paul's Churchyard, London:
Queen's Arms in, **23.** 31n
St Paul's Cross, London:
HW imagines sermon at, **38.** 103
Lort's papers about, are mere memoranda, **16.** 169
prints of, given by Lort to HW, **16.** 167
St Paul's School, London:
Colet founded, **16.** 84
St Pelegrino (Italy):
Spaniards approach Lucca across mountains of, **19.** 35

St Pelten. *See* Sankt Pölten

St Peter. *See* Peter, St

St Peter's, at Rome:
a subject for letters, **37.** 49
Benedict XIV opens 'holy gate' of, to begin jubilee, **20.** 105n
canons of, to have apartments in new sacristy, **24.** 344
chapter of, Clement XIV's body to be consigned to, **24.** 43
English, who never visited St Paul's, go to see, **23.** 213
French cardinal unimpressed by, **13.** 209
Frescobaldi, canon of, **21.** 224n
HW and Princesse de Craon visit, to see relics, **17.** 4
jubilee at Rome ends with closing the gates of, **20.** 220n
Leopold, Maria Carolina, and Maria Louisa visit, **23.** 23
mausoleum in, for Ps Sobieska, **21.** 391
Old Pretender's burial to be in, **21.** 391, 392, **22.** 385
Pius VI builds costly new sacristy at, **24.** 344, **25.** 383–4
—— might send, to England, for preservation from French atheists, **12.** 56
popes abandon, in summer, for Monte Cavallo, **24.** 344
relics displayed at, **13.** 210, **17.** 4
to be illuminated for D. of Cumberland, **23.** 564
to St Paul's from, **13.** 195

St Petersburg (Leningrad), Russia:
Anne, Czarina, dies at, **13.** 236n
Artois, Comte d', said to be in, **11.** 355
Austria sends courier to, to persuade Russia to continue war, **21.** 360n
Buckinghamshire accepts post at, **22.** 54
Catherine II's celebration at, over naval battle with Turks, **23.** 249
——'s crimes at, **22.** 65, 74, **23.** 195, **24.** 154
Coke, Lady Mary, might set out for, **35.** 314
convention for Polish partition signed at, **23.** 419n
Craven, Bns, writes from, **42.** 176
Czarina Elizabeth's burial at, should help England, **22.** 1
'devil' rules at, **22.** 570
East India Co.'s tyranny as bad as that of, **25.** 400
England to dictate to, **11.** 227
Éon carries treaties from, **22.** 217
Fawkener leaves, **11.** 324n
Frederick II not at, **37.** 573
from Cape of Good Hope to, French are defeated, **21.** 352
giants have gone to, **32.** 174
HW expects amusing news from, under Catherine II, **10.** 39
Hamlet acted in, in Russian translation, **22.** 426
Hobart, George, embassy secretary at, **23.** 3n

Houghton pictures arrive at, **25.** 2
Houghton pictures might be burnt in Hermitage at, **34.** 88
inundation at, **24.** 332
Jesuits should start revolution in, **22.** 514
Joseph II and Maria Theresa send Lobkowitz to, **23.** 310
Keith ambassador to, **9.** 45n
La Trémoïlle, Duchesse de, dies at, **12.** 3n
messenger from, to Orlov, **23.** 160, **24.** 33, 40
Munnich hopes to rejoin his family at, **22.** 11
Mustafa III might be sent captive to, **31.** 152
Natter dies at, **16.** 299n
no *poissardes* at, **34.** 146
Orlov, Alexei, returns to, **24.** 114
—— tells about revolution at, **23.** 185
Orlov, Grigoriï supplanted at, **23.** 441
peace expected by, **23.** 438
Peter III's ghost should be heard in, **23.** 195
Peterhoff near, **22.** 57
Pole's portrait in, **5.** 178n
report from, in Bologna gazette, **21.** 247
royal academy of, Sloane's museum offered to, **20.** 358
Russian fleet returns to, **24.** 84
Stanley on his way to, **3.** 251n
Te Deum sung in, **21.** 246n
Turkish ambassador's state entry into, **37.** 104n
visitors to: Algarotti, **37.** 64; Artois, **7.** 139n; Baltimore, **37.** 64; Craven, Bns, **25.** 632, 654; Joseph II, **25.** 72; Kingston, Ds of, **25.** 632; Lobkowitz, **23.** 310; Shuvalov, **6.** 492, **7.** 72, **8.** 205–6
Voltaire receives order from, **9.** 327
Vorontsovs' reasons for leaving, **22.** 173
Williams, Sir C. H., disliked at, **21.** 53n
—— leaves, **9.** 219n, **21.** 183n

St Peter's Day:
HW's plans for, **17.** 29
opera arrangements on, **17.** 81
Roman celebrations for, **18.** 462

St Peter's keys:
candidates for, **37.** 77

St Philippe. *See* San Felipe

St Philip's Castle, Port Mahon, Minorca:
affairs at, proceeding favourably, **25.** 219
Boyd passes from, **21.** 3
Byng does not reinforce, **25.** 562, 566–7
cannon from Barcelona to attack, **25.** 229
communication between England and, through Florence, **25.** 192
Crillon hopes to starve, but dares not assault it, **25.** 249–50
—— offers Murray a bribe to let him take, **25.** 207–8, 213n
defended as long as possible, **25.** 269
Edgcumbe leaves sailors to strengthen garrison of, **25.** 559
enemy preparations for attack upon, **25.** 233–4
France and Spain complain to Leopold about supplies to, **25.** 250

French about to attack, **20**. 552

French and Spaniards to storm, using prisoners, **25**. 180

frigates and privateers watch attempts to relieve, **25**. 205

garrison at, worn out by fatigue and sickness, **25**. 269

Mann grants commissions to foreign officers going to, **25**. 249

—— sends to Hillsborough accounts of expenditures for aid to, **25**. 204–5

——'s labours for relief of, rewarded, **25**. 246

——'s ships reach, **25**. 219

——'s zeal and prudence in aiding defence of, approved by George III, **25**. 229

Murray and Draper to defend, **25**. 190

only a powerful fleet can aid, **25**. 234

Rainsford consults Mann about aid for, **25**. 233

siege of, in 1756: **37**. 470–1; becomes a blockade, **20**. 570, 582; French did not foresee difficulty of, **20**. 567; surrender terminates, **20**. 571–6, 578, 581–2

siege of, in 1781–2; expected to last long, **25**. 229; may be retarded if Mann's vessels arrive, **25**. 249; successful sally by garrison of, reported from Spain, **25**. 205, 207; supplies sent to, from Leghorn, **25**. 249–50

surprise prevented cattle being driven into, **25**. 190, 198–9

See also Minorca; Port Mahon

St Philip's Castle, English brig:

captain of, brings news from Minorca, **25**. 196

Mann sends, to Minorca, **25**. 199, 204, 219, 249

Murray's dispatches come on, **25**. 207

Parker, Lt John, commands, **25**. 198n

Pringle and officers sail in, to Minorca, **25**. 199

'small scuttling vessel,' **25**. 205

St Phillip's. *See* St Philip's

St-Pierre, Duchesse de. *See* Colbert, Marguerite-Thérèse

'St-Pierre, Patrimoine de.' *See* Patrimoine

St-Pierre, Martinique:

La Touche should have surrendered, with Martinique, **22**. 29–30

St-Pierre, near Newfoundland:

England cedes, to France, **32**. 19n

St-Pierre, port of, near Sardinia:

Oiseau escapes to, **21**. 292

St-Pierre, Rue, in Paris:

Lauzun's house in, **7**. 6n

St-Pierre d'Arena:

Townshend and Villettes visit Austrian camp at, **19**. 312

St-Pol. *See* Noizet de St-Pol

St-Pol-de-Léon, Bp of. *See* Andigné de la Chaise, Joseph-François (d. 1806); La Marche, Jean-François de (1729–1806)

St-Port. *See* Ste-Assise

St-Prie, Mme de:

social relations of, with Princesse de Beauvau, **7**. 307

St-Prie, Mme de. *See also* St-Priest, Vicomtesse de

St-Priest, Chevalier de. *See* Guignard, François-Emmanuel de

St-Priest, Comte de. *See* Guignard, François-Emmanuel de

St-Priest, Comtesse de. *See* Ludolf, Constance-Guillelmine de

St-Priest, Vicomtesse de. *See* Barral de Montferrat, Louise-Jacqueline-Sophie de

St-Quentin (France):

Conway and his party see, **6**. 159

Conway and his party to visit, **6**. 156, 159

St Quintin, English merchant ship:

captain of, *see* Barker, John

HW sends Giberne and box on, to Mann, **17**. 279, 302, 324, 325, 407

voyage of, **17**. 302, 394, 419

St Ranieri's Day:

Pisa to celebrate, **18**. 455

St Remo. *See* San Remo

St-Rémy de Valois, Jeanne de (1756–91), m. (1780) Marc-Antoine-Nicolas, Comte de Lamotte:

'convict,' **33**. 568

HW knows nothing of, **34**. 37

Mémoires justificatifs by, Mrs Damer's copy of, recovered by HW for Mary Berry, **11**. 4–5

name of, corrected, **43**. 139

Rohan, Cardinal, suspected of giving diamond necklace to, **25**. 603

sentenced, **25**. 653n

St-Roch, church of, in Paris:

HW likes 'scenery' of, when sun shines, **39**. 202

in Rue St-Honoré, **13**. 163n

Tresmes's funeral at, **13**. 163

visitors to: HW, **7**. 263, 308, 317; Lennox, Lady George, **7**. 308; Nicolson, **7**. 308

St-Roch, Rue, in Paris:

Despueches in, **13**. 184n

St-Rock. *See* San Roque

St-Ruf, Order of:

France reduces, **39**. 147n

St-Sacrement, Lac du. *See* Lake George

St-Saire, Comte de. *See* Boulainvilliers, Henri de

St-Sauveur, Abbess of. *See* Suarez d'Aulan, Anne-Gabrielle-Françoise de

St-Sauveur, Chevalier (later Comte) de. *See* Grégoire, Hyacinthe-Philémon de

St-Sauveur, Marquise de. *See* Goulet de Rugy, Madeleine-Suzanne de

St-Sauveur, Rue, in Paris:

Panchaud, banker in, **39**. 245

St-Sébastien (Spain):

captured prizes taken to, **37**. 119

Jesuit convoy from, **22**. 532n

La Fayette stopped at, **6**. 435

St Sepulchre's Church, London:
Moore of, **10**. 5n
St-Servan, Brittany:
Marlborough burns ships at, **21**. 212n
St-Séverin d'Aragon, Alphonse-Marie-Louis (1705–57), Comte de:
Aix preliminary treaties signed by, **19**. 476n
Sandwich's instructions from Newcastle known to, **19**. 482n
—— told by, that Aix treaty preliminaries can be signed, **19**. 482
—— to make representations to, about Young Pretender's stay at Fribourg, **19**. 509n
St Severins. *See* San Severino
St-Simon, Duc de. *See* Rouvroy, Louis de
St-Simon, Maximilien-Henri (1720–99), Marquis de Sandricourt, also called Marquis de St-Simon:
arrives from Paris, **35**. 238
Bentley's designs for Gray's odes please, **35**. 238–9
English understood by, **35**. 238
HW asked by, to revise translation of Swift, **35**. 241
HW pleases, as owner of 'Selima,' **35**. 238–9
HW's correspondence with, **40**. 82–3
(?) Petersham, Lady Caroline, accompanied by, to theatre, **37**. 433
title of, corrected, **43**. 373
translation by, of Swift's *Tale of a Tub* sent to HW, **40**. 82–3
St-Simon-Sandricourt, Comtesse de. *See* Rouvroy de St-Simon, Blanche-Marie-Élisabeth de
St Sophia, Constantinople. *See under* Constantinople
Sts-Pères, Rue des, in Paris:
L'Hôpital de la Charité in, **3**. 330n
St Stefano. *See* Porto San Stefano; *see also* San Stefano, Order of
St Stephen, Order of. *See* San Stefano, Order of
St Stephen of Hungary, Order of:
Maria Louisa receives, from Joseph II, **25**. 128
St Stephen's Chapel, Westminster (Houses of Parliament):
Gloucester, Ds of, tried in, **14**. 75n
HW calls 'hot-house,' **10**. 263
House of Commons formerly was, **30**. 291n
Jenyns rejoices at entering, no more, **2**. 219
more rejoicing in, over one turncoat than over 99 just men, **25**. 23
Parliamentary drama to be enacted in, **25**. 10
play to be acted in, **9**. 129
session in, quiet, **9**. 229
to be pointed out, in schoolboys' lessons, **23**. 400
See also under Parliament: House of Commons
St Stephen's Green, Dublin:
Montagu compares, with Lincoln's Inn Fields, **9**. 386
—— reaches, **9**. 385
Montagu, Charles, leases house at, **9**. 357

St-Sulpice, church of, in Paris:
curé of, *see* Faydit de Tersac, Jean-Joseph
Du Deffand, Mme, buried in, **7**. 252
HW visits, **7**. 274
La Fare wedding in, **6**. 196
Mailly-Rubempré, Comtesse de, attends, **7**. 364, **10**. 295
Voltaire refused burial in, **7**. 48
St-Sulpice, seminary of:
Boufflers, Chevalier de, studies at, **4**. 296n
St Teresa's Day:
opera on, **25**. 558–9
See also Maria Theresa: name-day of
St-Thierry, Abbey of:
view of, shown in La Malle plan, **10**. 196
St-Thomas-du-Louvre, Rue, in Paris:
St-Louis-de-Louvre church in, **4**. 471n
St Thomas's, English church at Rome:
prayers at, for Young Pretender, **19**. 171n
St Thomas's Hospital, London:
plague said to be at, **21**. 427
St Thomas's Priory. *See* Priory of St Thomas
St Thomas the Martyr, Augustinian priory:
Maer Manor belonged to, **42**. 145n
St-Tropez (France):
Spanish galleys destroyed near, **17**. 471, 481
St-Val (Sainval), Mlle. *See* Alziary de Roquefort, Marie-Pauline
St Vedast's Church, Foster Lane, London:
Maddox, rector of, **18**. 246n
St Victor, church of:
Haistwell's etching of, **42**. 53n
St Vincent, E. and Vct of. *See* Jervis, Capt. Sir John (1735–1823)
St-Vincent, Présidente de. *See* Villeneuve, Julie de
St Vincent, island in the West Indies:
affair of, debated in House of Commons, **32**. 99, 100
Burke's stake in, **28**. 142, **39**. 239
Burke, William, said to be involved against Caribs of, **32**. 103n
England's troubles with Caribs in, **23**. 455, 462, **24**. 503
Estaing takes over, **7**. 173n
French conquer, **7**. 173n, **24**. 503, **29**. 473n
North's victory in Parliament over, **23**. 462
secured, **24**. 447
St Vincent. *See also* Cape St Vincent
St Vitale. *See* San Vitale
St-Vrain, château de (also called Chanteloupe):
Du Barry, Mme, buys, **24**. 99n
St Woolsten's [? St Wolstans]:
Harcourt family at, **5**. 74n
Saisons, Les. See under St-Lambert, Jean-François, Marquis de
'Saisons, Les' (verses):
quoted, **4**. 216
wrongly ascribed to Chevalier de Boufflers, **4**. 216, 218
Saisseval, Marquise de. *See* Beauvoir de Grimoard du Roure, Louise-Sophie de

Saisseval, Claude-Louis-Joseph (1754–1825), Marquis de:
marriage of, **7**. 453

Saiz, Angelica:
actress in burlettas in London, **43**. 265

'Sakuntalā.' *See under* Jones, Sir William: *Sacontalá*

'Sal, poor':
Townshend's epigram on, **43**. 185

Salad:
entremets of, **19**. 357n
gallon bowl of, West dines on, **13**. 174
HW scoffs at French for serving, **13**. 164
'killing' of, **35**. 65

Saladin (Salah-al-Din-Yusuf ibn-Ayyub) (ca 1138–93), Sultan of Egypt and Syria:
maxim of, on growing old, **32**. 321, **33**. 477

'Salamalec':
Du Deffand, Mme, explains meaning of, **4**. 448

Salamander; salamanders:
antiquary preferable to. **35**. 415
Conway becomes, on hot Minorca, **37**. 312

Salamander nymph. *See under* Nymph

Salary; salaries. *See under* Wages and Salaries

Salas, Marchese di. *See* Guzmann, José Joaquín

Salburg, (?) Franz Ludwig, Graf von:
Hofkriegsrat member, **21**. 96n

Salcey Forest:
Montagu ranger of, **2**. 211n
——'s lodge in, **29**. 84n, **43**. 137

Saldanha, Francisco de (1723–76), cardinal, 1756; patriarch 1759–76:
Benedict XIV appoints, visitor and reformer of the Jesuits in Portugal, **21**. 217n
Portugal to be preserved by, for the Church, **22**. 331
Pombal related to, **21**. 217n

Sale; sales. *See* Auction

Salem, Mass.:
sloop brings news from, **28**. 206n

Sale of Authors, The. See under Campbell, Archibald (ca 1726–80)

Salerno:
mosaic from church at, **35**. 408–9

Sales, Comte de, Charles Emmanuel III's illegitimate uncle:
Lanze, Cardinal de, son of, **21**. 207
Mann receives paper sent by, from Bologna, **19**. 226
niece recommended by, to Mann, **19**. 499

Sales, St Francis de. *See* Francis de Sales, St

Salesiane nuns. *See* Filles de la Visitation de Ste-Marie

Saletti, Lorenzo, castrato singer:
Farinelli unsuccessfully imitated by, **30**. 14

Saliceti, Natale (d. 1789), papal physician:
Clement XIV's autopsy by, **24**. 42–3
Pius VI's illness considered by, to be serious, **24**. 461

Saliciennes. *See* Filles de la Visitation de Ste-Marie

Salic law:
HW opposed to, **33**. 454–5

Salignac, François-Louis de (1722–67), Chevalier, later Marquis, de la Mothe-Fénelon:
captured at Dettingen, **18**. 260

Salignac, Gabriel-Jacques de (1688–1746), Marquis de la Mothe-Fénelon:
act of neutrality offered by, for Catholic Low Countries, **18**. 124n
at Aix-la-Chapelle, **18**. 304n
Dunkirk's neutrality to be preserved by Dutch proposal of, **18**. 61n
son of, **18**. 260

Salignac de la Mothe-Fénelon, François de, (1651–1715), Abp of Cambrai:
Alembert's eulogy of, **7**. 68
Bossuet to mortify, **28**. 221
Du Deffand, Mme, gives opinion of, **6**. 435
Saurin defends, against Voltaire, **4**. 180
Télémaque by: **3**. 209; HW imitates, **32**. 58

Salimbene collection:
Mann buys Guercino painting from, **20**. 263n

Salimbeni, Felice (ca 1712–51), singer:
Feroni, Mme, wishes to hear, **17**. 81
Mann entertains, **17**. 104
—— expects to prefer, to Egizziello, **17**. 454
opera ill-adapted to voice of, **17**. 79
shoulder of, well-set, and teeth fast, **17**. 132
sings in Mann's garden, **17**. 240
Suares, Mme, brings, to Mann, **17**. 101
Suares girls sing with, **17**. 101
Tedeschino imitates, **17**. 284
Venetian airs sung by, to Mann, **17**. 101, 240
Walpole, Bns, aids, after road accident, **17**. 116

Salimbeni. *See also* Bartolini Salimbeni

Saline draughts:
HW takes, for fever, **11**. 316

Salins, Conte de. *See* Lamesan, Gaetano Carlo

Salins, Contessa de. *See* Kalnoki, Maria Caterina

Salis, Jérôme de (ca 1708–94), Count of the Holy Roman Empire; Reichsgraf von Salis-Soglio, 1748:
Fane's news to be told by, **18**. 269
minister at Coire, **18**. 215

Salis, Rodolphe-Antoine-Hubert (1732–1807), Baron de:
Choiseul consulted by, on troops, **5**. 32

Salisbury, Bp of. *See* Audley, Edmund (d. 1524); Ayscough, William (d. 1450); Barrington, Hon. Shute (1734–1826); Burgess, Thomas (1756–1837); Burnet, Gilbert (1643–1715); Douglas, John (1721–1807); Drummond, Robert Hay (1711–76); Earle, John (ca 1601–65); Gilbert, John (1693–1761); Hoadly, Benjamin (1676–1761); Hume, John (ca 1706–82); Sherlock, Thomas (1678–1761); Thomas, John (1691–1766); Thomas, John (1696–1781); Townson, Robert (1575–1621); Ward, Seth (1617–89)

Salisbury, Cts of. *See* Chaucer, Alice (d. 1475); Grandison, Katharine de (d. 1349); Hill, Mary Amelia (1750–1835); Joan (1331–85)

[Salisbury, Cts of, *continued*]
of Kent; Keet, Elizabeth (ca 1721–76); Margaret (Plantagenet) (ca 1474–1541); Montagu, Lady Alice de (ca 1406–62); Tufton, Lady Anne (1693–1757)

Salisbury, Cts of:
figure misidentified as, **42**. 247

Salisbury, E. of. *See* Cecil, James (1713–80); Cecil, James (1748–1823); Cecil, James Brownlow William (1791–1868); Cecil, Robert (1563–1612); Montagu, John de (ca 1350–1400); Montagu, Thomas de (d. 1428); Nevill, Sir Richard (1400–60)

Salisbury, Earls of:
arms of, **2**. 29
martial prowess of Montagu earls, **9**. 394
tombs of, at Bisham Abbey, **9**. 100–1

Salisbury, Marchioness of. *See* Hill, Lady Mary Amelia

Salisbury, M. of. *See* Cecil, James (1748–1823); Cecil, James Brownlow William (1791–1868)

Salisbury, Jean de. *See* John of Salisbury

Salisbury, Sally. *See* Pridden, Sally

Salisbury, Rev. William (1707–96):
letter by, in *Gentleman's Magazine*, on Arundel marbles, **16**. 182–3

Salisbury, Wiltshire:
bishopric of, vacant, **33**. 340
Burke's testimony to jury at, **25**. 117n
camp at, **28**. 448n
cathedral of, *see* Salisbury Cathedral
chancellor of, *see* Talbot, William
coach to, robbed by Maclaine, **40**. 65n
Dodd and Whaley visit, **40**. 8
Douglas, Bp, lives at, **16**. 317n
Easton's address is market-place at, **40**. 8
French princes do not frequent the equivalent of, **40**. 387
HW familiar with neighbourhood of, **10**. 280–1
HW visits, **42**. 165
Hale near, **10**. 280
Harris of, **28**. 131n, **32**. 183
Hume to be bishop of, **22**. 324n
Idmerstown near, **40**. 305
ill-built save for cathedral spire, **40**. 8
Jacob, Dr, physician at, **2**. 137
man from, killed in London accident, **19**. 386
manufactures of, **40**. 8
Muzell (Stosch) at, **21**. 433, 440, 459
'Philo-Gray' of, **28**. 209
races at, **13**. 89n
St Edmund's Church at, **1**. 8
Sherfield recorder of, **1**. 8n
Vertue visits, **16**. 156n
William III advised by Lords, probably at, **15**. 148

Salisbury, English ship:
arrives at Portsmouth from Port Mahon, **18**. 325n
at Port Mahon, **17**. 285
Leghorn to be defended by, **18**. 38
Osborn captain of, **18**. 28n

powder and arms delivered by, at Campomoro, **18**. 174n
Theodore of Corsica and exiles return on, to Corsica, **18**. 151n
Townshend sends snuff-box in, to England, **18**. 445

Salisbury Cathedral:
Alison prebendary of, **42**. 264n
Chafy prebendary of, **2**. 304n
Cowslade and HW condemn new choir of, **41**. 420
Dodwell, prebendary of, **15**. 302
Greene, dean of, **1**. 146n, 162n
HW and Gough fear destruction of Beauchamp and Hungerford chapels in, **42**. 259–60
HW belittles new choir of, **41**. 420
HW does not know chapter or subscribers of, **42**. 260
HW visits, **38**. 25
Hungerford chapel in, **16**. 144–5, 156
Jacob, prebendary of, **2**. 137n
Montagu's opinion of, **10**. 284
Ridley, prebendary of, **14**. 37n
Sherfield's glass-breaking was not at, **1**. 8
SH chapel copied from, **41**. 420
subscribers to renovation of, might protest against destruction of chapels, **42**. 260
verger of, *see* Dodsworth, William

Salisbury Court. *See under* Fleet St

Salisbury Plain:
Fleury's tomb big enough for, **39**. 203
may become an airfield, **39**. 425

Salisbury St, the Strand, London:
hosier's opposite to, **32**. 109n

Salivation:
applications of, **19**. 248, **20**. 175, 537, 543
Cumberland, D. of, needs, **19**. 483
prostitute's appearance during, **30**. 264

Salive, Capt.:
SH visited by, **43**. 160

Salkeld, Thomas, Jacobite:
Atterbury accompanied by, to France, **20**. 499n
Cork employs as tutor to sons, **20**. 499n

Sall (Salle), Norfolk:
Addison, Leonard, holds living of, **14**. 90n

Salle, La. *See* La Salle

Sallers de Montlor, Mme. *See* Vaulserre des Adretz, Marie-Olympe de

Salles, Dom des. *See* Des Salles, Dom

Sallier de la Tour, Vittorio Amadeo (1726–1800), Marchese di Cordon; Sardinian envoy to England 1774–84, to France 1788–ca 1792:
brother of Ps Dashkov seized in chapel of, **29**. 60, **33**. 179
Cordon, Abbé, mistaken for, **11**. 87
formerly envoy to England, **11**. 87
Gordon rioters break into house and chapel of, **25**. 55, **29**. 51, **33**. 177–8, 179
mob in France dislikes, **11**. 87
name of, corrected, **43**. 143
Sardinian envoy, **29**. 52n